# Ethical Theory
# and Business

## EIGHTH EDITION

# Ethical Theory and Business

EIGHTH EDITION

Edited by

**Tom L. Beauchamp**
*Georgetown University*

**Norman E. Bowie**
*University of Minnesota*

**Denis G. Arnold**
*University of Tennessee*

Pearson Education International

**Senior Editor:** Dave Repetto
**Editor in Chief:** Dickson Musslewhite
**Editorial Assistant:** Jack Cashman
**Marketing Manager:** Sasha Anderson-Smith
**Senior Managing Editor:** Mary Rottino
**Production Liaison:** Fran Russello
**Senior Operations Supervisor:** Brian Mackey
**Operations Specialist:** Cathleen Petersen
**Cover Design:** Bruce Kenselaar
**Cover Illustration/Photo:** Getty Images, Inc.
**Manager, Cover Visual Research & Permissions:** Karen Sanatar
**Composition/Full-Service Project Management:** Shelley L. Creager/Aptara, Inc.
**Printer/Binder:** RR Donnelley & Sons Company

If you purchased this book within the United States or Canada you should be aware that it has been wrongfully imported without the approval of the Publisher or the Author.

Pearson Education LTD., London
Pearson Education Singapore, Pte. Ltd
Pearson Education, Canada, Ltd
Pearson Education—Japan
Pearson Education Australia PTY, Limited

Pearson Education North Asia Ltd
Pearson Educación de Mexico, S.A. de C.V.
Pearson Education Malaysia, Pte. Ltd
Pearson Education, Upper Saddle River, New Jersey

10 9 8 7 6 5 4 3 2 1

ISBN-13: 978-0-13-208003-3
ISBN-10:    0-13-208003-6

# Contents

## Chapter 4
## DIVERSITY, DISCRIMINATION AND HARASSMENT
## IN THE WORKPLACE   184

## INTRODUCTION   184

## DIVERSITY AND AFFIRMATIVE ACTION

## SEXUAL HARASSMENT

## LEGAL PERSPECTIVES

## CASES

*Chapter 5*
## MARKETING AND THE DISCLOSURE OF INFORMATION   273

## INTRODUCTION   273

## ADVERTISING AND DISCLOSURE

## MARKETING

## LEGAL PERSPECTIVES

*Chapter 6*
**ETHICAL ISSUES IN FINANCE AND ACCOUNTING    352**

**INTRODUCTION    352**

**AUDITING AFTER ENRON**

**FINANCIAL SERVICES**

**LEGAL PERSPECTIVES**

**CASES**

## *Chapter 9*
## ETHICAL ISSUES IN INTERNATIONAL BUSINESS   571

## INTRODUCTION   571

## CASES

*Chapter 10*
## SOCIAL AND ECONOMIC JUSTICE   665

## INTRODUCTION   665

## THEORIES OF SOCIAL JUSTICE

## COMPENSATION

## GLOBAL JUSTICE

## LEGAL PERSPECTIVE

## CASES

# Preface

The seventh edition of *Ethical Theory and Business* was published at a time of international crisis and confusion. The September 11, 2001, terrorist attack imposed large transaction costs on the U.S. economy and on most of the economies of the industrialized world. Globalization was dramatically increasing, but many features of globalization were also under attack. The wisdom of many policies shaped by the International Monetary Fund and the World Bank was also being questioned. Corporate scandals were undermining trust in corporations and in the integrity and fairness of markets. Major corporations tainted by scandal included WorldCom, Enron, and Global Crossing. A record number of companies have since restated their financial results. The accounting firm of Arthur Andersen, for all practical matters, was at the time doomed.

As we now go to press with this eighth edition, the crises created by terrorism, globalization, and corporate misconduct remain central features of our lives. Seemingly unjust levels of executive compensation, the backdating of stock options, global climate change, and justice in the face of runaway global poverty are some of the issues receiving increased attention. Globalization offers many opportunities to reshape the global order but also remains controversial. Of particular concern are the impact of global warming, labor practices in the developing world, and various abuses by truly globalized companies. The United States and many other countries remain highly dependent on foreign sources for oil, and enormous corporate profits at firms such as Exxon/Mobil are being seriously questioned. The eighth edition addresses these crises as well as many old and new issues of business ethics.

The press deadline for the first edition of *Ethical Theory and Business* was exactly 30 years prior to the press deadline of this eighth edition. Many of the students who will use this eighth edition were not born at the time, and many who will teach this edition will not know that, in effect, there was no textbook of business ethics 30 years ago. "Times change" seems an understatement as we, the editors, now look back over the years and editions.

We would, of course, hope that *Ethical Theory and Business* will be around for another 30 years, but we realize that the original two editors, Tom Beauchamp and Norman Bowie, will not be doing this kind of work for another 30. In line with good succession planning, Denis Arnold has been invited by the editors to join as coeditor. Some years back, Denis was a research assistant for Norman and he has assisted in some capacity on each of the three most recent editions of the book. Denis has published extensively on topics in business ethics and teaches the subject at all levels at his university. Tom and Norm are lucky to be able to put this book in such competent hands.

The eighth edition has been substantially revised to take into account many helpful suggestions we received from reviewers. There is a new chapter on ethical issues in finance and accounting. The responsibility of business to the environment now has a separate chapter, and the table of contents has expanded (though the number of pages has not) and includes more case studies. The chapter on information technology has been replaced by a chapter on intellectual property; however, a significant part of this new chapter addresses intellectual property on the World Wide Web. The remainder of that chapter considers the implications that result from the current patent protection given to pharmaceutical drugs. We have highlighted the most extensive changes, but every chapter including the chapter on ethical theory has been revised. This edition also has an expanded international flavor reflecting the importance of globalization. Not only is there a separate chapter on ethical issues in international business, but there are numerous international articles and cases in other chapters.

Special thanks to the Prentice Hall reviewers: David O'Hara, Augustana College, Sioux Falls, ID; K. Praveen Parboteeah, University of Wisconsin–Whitewater, Whitewater, WI; Thomas J. Smedinghoff, Dominican University, River Forest, IL; and Chris Meyers, University of Southern Mississippi, Hattiesburg, MS, who gave us many helpful suggestions, most of which have been incorporated. Tom Beauchamp wishes to express great appreciation to two research assistants: Patrick Connolly and Xiaoqian Helene Shen. Denis Arnold wishes to express appreciation to his research assistants: Tom Harter, Todd Johnson, and Keith Bustos. He would also like to thank the many students and instructors at the University of Tennessee who have made helpful suggestions for improving the text.

Tom L. Beauchamp
*Georgetown University*

Norman E. Bowie
*University of Minnesota*

Denis G. Arnold
*University of Tennessee*

Chapter *1*

# Ethical Theory and Business Practice

## INTRODUCTION

Can business organizations be just? Should the chief obligation of business be to look out for the bottom line, or do businesses also have obligations to other stakeholders such as customers and employees? How far should business go to protect and preserve the environment? Do global business organizations have obligations to protect human rights wherever they do business? These are some of the many questions that permeate discussions of the role of ethics in business.

The essays and cases in this book provide an opportunity to discuss these questions by reading and reflecting on influential arguments that have been made on these subjects. The goal of this first chapter is to provide a foundation in ethical theory sufficient for reading and critically evaluating the material in the ensuing chapters. The first part of this chapter introduces basic and recurring distinctions, definitions, and issues. The second part examines influential and relevant types of normative ethical theory.

## FUNDAMENTAL CONCEPTS AND PROBLEMS

### Morality and Ethical Theory

A distinction between morality and ethical theory is employed in several essays in this volume. *Morality* is concerned with social practices defining right and

---

wrong. These practices—together with other kinds of customs, rules, and mores—are transmitted within cultures and institutions from generation to generation. Similar to political constitutions and natural languages, morality exists prior to the acceptance (or rejection) of its standards by particular individuals. In this respect morality cannot be purely a personal policy or code and is certainly not confined to the rules in professional codes of conduct adopted by corporations and professional associations.

In contrast with *morality*, the terms *ethical theory* and *moral philosophy* point to reflection on the nature and justification of right actions. These words refer to attempts to introduce clarity, substance, and precision of argument into the domain of morality. Although many people go through life with an understanding of morality dictated by their culture, other persons are not satisfied to conform to the morality of society. They want difficult questions answered: Is what our society forbids wrong? Are social values the best values? What is the purpose of morality? Does religion have anything to do with morality? Do the moral rules of society fit together in a unified whole? If there are conflicts and inconsistencies in our practices and beliefs, how should they be resolved? What should people do when facing a moral problem for which society has, as yet, provided no instruction?

Moral philosophers seek to answer such questions and to put moral beliefs and social practices of morality into a unified and defensible shape. Sometimes this task involves challenging traditional moral beliefs by assessing the quality of moral arguments and suggesting modifications in existing beliefs. Morality, we might say, consists of what persons ought to do in order to conform to society's norms of behavior, whereas ethical theory concerns the philosophical reasons for and against aspects of social morality. Usually the latter effort centers on *justification*: philosophers seek to justify a system of standards or some moral point of view on the basis of carefully analyzed and defended concepts and principles such as respect for autonomy, distributive justice, equal treatment, human rights, beneficence, and truthfulness.

Most moral principles are already embedded in public morality, but usually in a vague and underanalyzed form. Justice is a good example. Recurrent topics in the pages of the *Wall Street Journal, Fortune, Business Week,* and other leading business journals often discuss the justice of the present system of corporate and individual taxation as well as the salaries paid to chief executive officers and the offshore outsourcing of jobs from one country to another. However, an extended or detailed analysis of principles of justice is virtually never provided in the media. Such matters are left at an intuitive level, where the correctness of a particular moral point of view is assumed, without argument.

Yet, the failure to provide anything more than a superficial justification, in terms of intuitive principles learned from parents or peers, leaves people unable to defend their principles when challenged. In a society with many diverse views of morality, one can be fairly sure that one's principles will be challenged. A business person who asserts that a particular practice is morally wrong (or right) can expect to be challenged within her organization by colleagues who disagree. She will have little influence within her organization if she cannot also explain *why* she believes that action is wrong (or right). To defend her assertion she must be able to *justify* her position by providing reasoned arguments. The tools of moral philosophy, then, can be of significant value to students of business.

## Morality and Prudence

Many students do not encounter moral philosophy as a topic of study until college or graduate school. Morality, however, is learned by virtually every young child as part of the acculturation process. The first step in this process is learning to distinguish moral rules from rules of prudence (self-interest). This task can be difficult, because the two kinds of rules are taught simultaneously, without being distinguished by the children's teachers. For example, people are constantly reminded in their early years to observe rules such as "Don't touch the hot stove," "Don't cross the street without looking both ways," "Brush your teeth after meals," and "Eat your vegetables." Most of these "oughts" and "ought nots" are instructions in self-interest— that is, rules of prudence, but moral rules are taught at the same time. Parents, teachers, and peers teach that certain things *ought not* to be done because they are "wrong" (morally) and that certain things *ought* to be done because they are "right" (morally): "Don't pull your sister's hair." "Don't take money from your mother's pocketbook." "Share your toys." "Write a thank-you note to Grandma." These moral instructions seek to control actions that affect the interests of other people. As people mature, they learn what society expects of them in terms of taking into account the interests of other people.

One common observation in business is that self-interest and good ethics generally coincide, because it is usually in one's interest to act morally. We continually hear that good ethics is good business. This fact makes evaluating another's conduct difficult and may tend to confuse moral reasoning with prudential reasoning. A simple example of moral and prudential reasoning run together in business is found in the decision of the Marriott Corporation to make a concerted effort to hire persons who had been on welfare. These individuals had often been considered high risk as employees, but changes in the U.S. welfare system forced many welfare recipients to seek work. Marriott was one of the few major companies to take the initiative to hire them in large numbers. Such behavior might be considered an example of moral goodwill and ethical altruism. Although corporate officials at Marriott clearly believed that their decision was ethically sound and promoted the public good, they also believed that their initiative to hire former welfare recipients was good business. J. W. Marriott Jr. said, "We're getting good employees for the long term, but we're also helping these communities. If we don't step up in these inner cities and provide work, they'll never pull out of it. But it makes bottom line sense. If it didn't, we wouldn't do it."[1]

The mixture of moral language with the language of prudence is often harmless. Many people are more concerned about the *actions* businesses take than with their *motivations* to perform those actions. These people will be indifferent as to whether businesses use the language of prudence or the language of morality to justify what they do, as long as they do the right thing. This distinction between motives and actions is very important to philosophers, however, because a business practice that might be prudentially justified also might lack moral merit or might even be morally wrong. History has shown that some actions that were long accepted or at least condoned in the business community were eventually condemned as morally dubious. Examples include pollution of the air and water, forced labor, deceitful marketing, and large political contributions and lobbying directed at people of political influence.

Businesspeople often reflect on the morality of their actions not because it is prudent to do so but because it is right to do so. For example, Elo TouchSystems Inc., a subsidiary of Raychem Corporation that manufactures computer and other monitors, decided to relocate the company from Oak Ridge, Tennessee, to Freemont, California. As a matter of fidelity to its 300 employees, the company attempted to find new jobs for them in the Oak Ridge area by placing advertisements, sponsoring job fairs, and the like. It also offered generous bonuses for those who would relocate to California. In light of the pool of talent known to the company to be available in California, none of this activity in Tennessee seemed in the company's prudential interest. It simply seemed the morally appropriate policy.

It is widely believed that acting morally is in the interest of business, and thus prudence seems to be one strong motive—perhaps the main motive—for acting ethically. However, throughout this text we will repeatedly see that prudence often dictates a different business decision than does morality.

## Morality and Law

Business ethics is currently involved in an entangled, complex, and mutually stimulating relationship with the law in various countries and international agreements such the World Trade Organization's *Agreement on Trade-Related Aspects of Intellectual Property Rights.* Morality and law share concerns over matters of basic social importance and often have in common certain principles, obligations, and criteria of evidence. Law is the public's agency for translating morality into explicit social guidelines and practices and for stipulating punishments for offenses. Several selections in this book mention case law (judge-made law expressed in court decisions), statutory law (federal and state statutes and their accompanying administrative regulations), and international law (treaties and agreements among nations). In these forms law has forced vital issues before the public and is frequently the source of emerging issues in business ethics. Case law, in particular, has established influential precedents that provide material for reflection on both legal and moral questions.

Some have said that corporate concern about business ethics can be reduced or eliminated by turning problems over to the legal department. The operative idea is "Let the lawyers decide; if it's legal, it's moral." Although this tactic would simplify matters, moral evaluation needs to be distinguished from legal evaluation. Despite an intersection between morals and law, the law is not the sole repository of a society's moral standards and values, even when the law is directly concerned with moral problems. A law-abiding person is not necessarily morally sensitive or virtuous, and the fact that something is legally acceptable does not imply that it is morally acceptable. For example, forced labor and slavery have been legal in the United State but are clearly unjust. Currently, the U.S. doctrine of employment at will permits employers to fire employees for unjust reasons and is (within certain limits) legal, yet such firings are often morally unacceptable. Many questions are raised in subsequent chapters about the morality of business actions such as plant relocation, outsourcing, and mergers that cause unemployment, even though such actions are not illegal.

Consider the following examples: It was perfectly legal when Houston financier Charles E. Hurwitz doubled the rate of tree cutting in the nation's largest privately owned virgin redwood forest. He did so to reduce the debt he incurred when his company, the Maxxam Group, borrowed money to complete a hostile takeover of Pacific Lumber Company, which owned the redwoods. Before the takeover, Pacific Lumber had followed a sustainable cutting policy but nonetheless had consistently operated at a profit. Despite the legality of the new clear-cutting policy initiated by the new owner, it has been criticized as immoral.[2] So too, it was legal when in early 2007 CJW Inc. fired its employee 24-year-old Isac Aguero of Racine, Wisconsin, for drinking a Bud Light at a local bar after work. CJW is the local distributor of Miller beer, and Aguero's bosses disliked his supporting the competition. Because Aguero was an "at-will" employee, he had no legal recourse (see Chapter 3).[3]

A related problem involves the belief that a person found guilty under law is therefore morally guilty. Such judgments are not necessarily correct, as they depend on either the intention of the agents or the moral acceptability of the law on which the judgment has been reached. For example, if a chemical company is legally liable for polluting the environment, or a pharmaceutical firm is liable for a drug that has harmed certain patients, it does not follow that any form of moral wrongdoing, culpability, or guilt is associated with the activity.

Asbestos litigation is a well-known example. Because of the strength, durability, and fire resistance of asbestos, it was used in thousands of consumer, automotive, scientific, industrial, and maritime processes and products. Virtually no serious social attention was paid to asbestos in the United States until 1964, when a strong link was established between asbestos dust and disease. As many as 27 million U.S. workers may have been exposed to this fiber, and 100 million people may have been exposed to asbestos in buildings. Manufacturers did not know about these problems of disease until around 1964; but beginning with the 1982 bankruptcy of the Johns-Manville Corporation, many corporations were successfully sued. The problem continues to escalate today, especially owing to cases brought by mesothelioma patients and by persons who worked with asbestos but actually have no asbestos-related illness. Companies such as Georgia-Pacific and Asarco are still battling in court. From 2000 through 2006 there were 43 asbestos-related bankruptcies (compared with 15 for all of the 1990s); over the years of litigation, 8,000 companies have been sued, 70 corporations have been bankrupted, and costs have accumulated to about $70 billion. Although asbestos manufacturers and their customers originally had good intentions and good products, they paid a steep price under the law.[4]

Furthermore, the courts have often been accused—with some justification—of causing moral inequities through court judgments rendered against corporations. Here are some examples:[5] (1) Dow Corning was successfully sued by plaintiffs alleging that personal injuries resulted from Dow's silicone breast implants, leading the company to file bankruptcy. In 2006, after an exhaustive study, the U.S. Food and Drug Administration concluded that there is no evidence that silicone breast implants present health risks. (2) Chevron Oil was successfully sued for mislabeling its cans of paraquat, although the offending label conformed exactly to federal regulations, which permitted no other form of label to be used. (3) Although whooping cough vaccine indisputably reduces the risk of this disease for children who receive the vaccine, almost no manufacturer will produce it for fear of costly suits brought under product liability laws. (4) In the wake of the Enron scandal, the firm of Arthur Andersen was successfully prosecuted by federal prosecutors in Houston for obstruction of justice. The 2002 conviction resulted in the dissolution of the accounting division at Andersen and the termination of 28,000 employees. This decision was overturned by the U.S. Supreme Court in 2005, but by then Arthur Andersen accounting had ceased to exist.[6]

In each instance it is easy to understand why critics have considered various regulations, legislation, and case-law decisions unjustified. Taken together, these considerations lead to the following conclusions: If something is legal, it is not necessarily moral; if something is illegal, it is not necessarily immoral. To discharge one's legal responsibilities is not necessarily to discharge one's moral responsibilities.

### The Rule of Conscience

The slogan "Let your conscience be your guide" has long been, for many, what morality is all about. Yet, despite their admiration for persons of conscience, philosophers have typically judged appeals to conscience as alone insufficient and untrustworthy for ethical judgment. Consciences vary radically from person to person and time to time; moreover, they are often altered by circumstance, religious belief, childhood, and training. One example is found in the action of Stanley Kresge, the son of the founder of S. S. Kresge Company—now known as the K-Mart Corporation—who is a teetotaler for religious reasons. When the company started selling beer and wine, Kresge sold all his stock. His conscience, he said, would not let him make a profit on alcohol. The company, though, dismissed his objection as "his own business" and said that it saw nothing wrong with earning profits on alcohol.[7] As a second example, there are many individuals who believe that business has been conducted in ways that damage the environment. These feelings are particularly strong in the Pacific Northwest, where the lumber industry has allegedly threatened endangered species such as the spotted owl. The consciences of members of Earth First have been so aroused that they have engaged in acts of ecoterrorism such as putting large spikes in trees that can injure loggers who are cutting them. The members of Earth First believe that they are acting as required by conscience. But whether their particular strategies and acts are morally acceptable is doubtful.

The reliability of conscience, in short, is not self-certifying. Moral justification must be based on a source external to individual conscience.

### Approaches to the Study of Morality and Ethical Theory

Morality and ethical theory can be studied and developed by a variety of methods, but three general approaches have dominated the literature. Two of these approaches describe and analyze morality, presumably without taking moral positions. The other approach takes a moral position and appeals to morality or ethical theory to underwrite judgments. These three approaches are (1) descriptive, (2) conceptual, and (3) normative (prescriptive). These categories do not express rigid and always clearly distinguishable approaches. Nonetheless, when understood as broad positions, they can serve as models of inquiry and as valuable distinctions.

Social scientists often refer to the *descriptive approach* as the *scientific study* of ethics. Factual description and explanation of moral behavior and beliefs, as performed by anthropologists, sociologists, and historians, are typical of this approach. Moral attitudes, codes, and beliefs that are described include corporate policies on sexual harassment and codes of ethics in trade associations. Examples of this approach can be found in *Harvard Business Review* articles and *Forbes* magazine polls that report what business executives believe is morally acceptable and unacceptable.

The second approach involves the *conceptual study* of significant terms in ethics. Here, the meanings of terms such as *right, obligation, justice, good, virtue,* and *responsibility* are analyzed. Crucial terms in business ethics such as *liability, deception, corporate intention,* and *stakeholder* can be given this same kind of careful conceptual attention. The proper analysis of the term *morality* (as defined at the beginning of this chapter) and the distinction between the moral and the nonmoral are typical examples of these conceptual problems.

The third approach, *normative* (prescriptive) *ethics*, is a prescriptive study attempting to formulate and defend basic moral norms. Normative moral philosophy aims at determining what *ought* to be done, which needs to be distinguished from what *is*, in fact, practiced. Ideally, an ethical theory provides reasons for adopting a whole system of moral principles or virtues. *Utilitarianism* and *Kantianism* are widely discussed theories, but they are not the only such theories. Utilitarians argue that there is but a single fundamental principle determining right action, which can be roughly stated as follows: "An action is morally right if and only if it produces at least as great a balance of value over disvalue as any available alternative action." Kantians, by contrast, have argued for principles that specify obligations rather than a balance of value. For example, one of Kant's best-known principles of obligation is "Never treat another person merely as a means to your own goals," even if doing so creates a net balance of positive value. Both forms of these theories, together with other dimensions of ethical theory, are examined in the second part of this chapter.

Principles of normative ethics are commonly used to treat specific moral problems such as famine, conflict of interest, improper disclosure of information, environmental pollution, mistreatment of animals, and racial and sexual discrimination. This use of ethical theory is often referred to, somewhat misleadingly, as *applied ethics.* Philosophical treatment of medical ethics, engineering ethics, journalistic ethics, jurisprudence, and business ethics involves distinct areas that employ general ethical principles to attempt to resolve moral problems that commonly arise in the professions.

Substantially the same general ethical principles apply to the problems across professional fields and in areas beyond professional ethics as well. One might appeal to principles of justice, for example, to illuminate and resolve issues of taxation, health care distribution, environmental responsibility, criminal punishment, and racial discrimination. Similarly, principles of veracity (truthfulness) apply to debates about secrecy and deception in international politics, misleading advertisements in business ethics, balanced reporting in journalistic ethics, and disclosure of illness to a patient in medical ethics. Increased clarity about the general conditions under which truth must be told and when it may be withheld would presumably enhance understanding of moral requirements in each of these areas.

The exercise of sound judgment in business practice together with appeals to ethical theory are central in the essays and cases in this volume. Rarely is there a straightforward "application" of principles that mechanically resolves problems. Principles are more commonly *specified,* that is, made more concrete for the context, than applied. Much of the best work in contemporary business ethics involves arguments for how to specify principles to handle particular problems.

### Relativism and Objectivity of Belief

Some writers have contended that moral views simply express the ways in which a culture both limits and accommodates the desires of its people. In the early part of the twentieth century, defenders of relativism used the discoveries of anthropologists in the South Sea Islands, Africa, and South America as evidence of a diversity of moral practices throughout the world. Their empirical discoveries about what is the case led them to the conclusion that moral rightness is contingent on cultural beliefs and that the concepts of rightness and wrongness are meaningless apart from the specific historical and cultural contexts in which they arise. The claim is that patterns of culture can be understood only as unique wholes and that moral beliefs about moral behavior are closely connected in a culture.

*Descriptive* claims about what *is* the case in cultures have often been used by relativists to justify a *normative* position as to what *should* be the case or what *ought* to be believed. That is, some ethical relativists assert that whatever a culture thinks is right or wrong really is right or wrong for the members of that culture. This thesis is normative, because it makes a value judgment; it delineates *which standards or norms correctly determine right and wrong behavior.* Thus, if the Swedish tradition allows abortion, then abortion really is morally permissible in Sweden. If the Irish tradition forbids abortion, then abortion really is wrong in Ireland. If ethical relativism is correct, then there is no criterion independent of one's culture for determining whether a practice really is right or wrong.

Ethical relativism provides a theoretical basis for those who challenge what they consider to be the imposition of Western values on the rest of the world. Specifically, some spokespersons in Asia have criticized what they regard as the attempts of Westerners to impose their values (as the normatively correct values) on Asian societies. For example, it is argued that Asians give more significant value than do Westerners to the welfare of society when it is in conflict with the welfare of the individual. However, it has also been pointed out that because of the range of values embraced by and within Asian nations it is all but impossible to say that there is such an entity as "Asian values." Secular Asian societies such as India, for example, have long traditions of respect for individual rights and embrace values consonant with Western societies. Also, younger generations tend to have significantly different views about the rights of individuals from those of older generations.

Despite the influence of relativism and multiculturalism, there have been many recent attempts by both government agencies and multinational corporations to promulgate international codes of business conduct that surmount relativism (see Chapter 9). In the era of economic globalization, these efforts are increasing rather than diminishing.

Moral philosophers have tended to reject relativism, and it is important to understand why. First, moral philosophers ask, What does the argument from the fact of cultural diversity reveal? When early anthropologists probed beneath surface "moral" disagreements, they often discovered agreement at deeper levels on more basic values. For example, one anthropologist discovered a tribe in which parents, after raising their children and when still in a relatively healthy state, would climb a high tree. Their children would then shake the tree until the parents fell to the ground and died. This cultural practice seems vastly different from Western practices. The anthropologist discovered, however, that the tribe believed that people went into the afterlife in the same bodily state in which they left this life. Their children, who wanted them to enter the afterlife in a healthy state, were no less concerned about their parents than are children in Western cultures. Although cultural disagreement exists concerning the afterlife (a disagreement about what is or is not the case), there is no ultimate *moral* disagreement over the moral principles determining how children should treat their parents.

Despite their many obvious differences of practice and belief, people often do actually agree about what may be called *ultimate moral standards*. For example, both Germany and the United States have laws to protect consumers from the adverse affects of new drugs and to bring drugs to the market as quickly as possible so that lives are saved. Yet, Germany and the United States have different standards for making the trade-off between protecting consumers from side effects and saving lives as soon as possible. This suggests that two cultures may agree about basic principles of morality yet disagree about how to implement those principles in particular situations.

In many "moral controversies" people seem to differ only because they have different *factual* beliefs. For instance, individuals often differ over appropriate actions to protect the environment, not because they have different sets of standards about environmental ethics, but because they hold different factual views about how certain discharges of chemicals and airborne particles will or will not harm the environment. Identical sets of normative standards may be invoked in their arguments about environmental protection, yet different policies and actions may be recommended.

It is therefore important to distinguish *relativism of judgments* from *relativism of standards.* Differing judgments may rely on the same general standards for their justification. Relativism of judgment is so pervasive in human social life that it would be foolish to deny it. People may differ in their judgments regarding whether one policy for keeping hospital information confidential is more acceptable than another, but it does not follow that they have different moral standards of confidentiality. The people may hold the same moral standard(s) on protecting confidentiality but differ over how to implement the standard(s).

However, these observations do not determine whether a relativism of standards provides the most adequate account of morality. If moral conflict did turn out to be a matter of a fundamental conflict of moral *standards,* such conflict could not be removed even if there were perfect agreement about the facts, concepts, and background beliefs of a case. Suppose, then, that disagreement does in fact exist at the deepest level of moral thinking—that is, suppose that two cultures disagree on basic or fundamental norms. It does not follow even from this *relativity of standards* that there is no ultimate norm or set of norms in which everyone *ought* to believe. To see why, consider the following analogy to religious disagreement: From the fact that people have incompatible religious or atheistic beliefs it does not follow that there is no single correct set of religious or atheistic propositions. Nothing more than skepticism seems justified by the facts about religion that are adduced by anthropology. Similarly, nothing more than such skepticism about the moral standards would be justified if fundamental conflicts of *moral standards* were discovered in ethics.

The evident inconsistency of ethical relativism with many of our most cherished moral beliefs is another reason to be doubtful of it. No general theory of ethical relativism is likely to convince us that a belief is acceptable merely because others believe in it strongly enough, although that is exactly the commitment of this theory. At least some moral views seem relatively more enlightened, no matter how great the variability of beliefs. The idea that practices such as slavery, forced labor, sexual exploitation under severe threat, employment discrimination against women, and grossly inequitable salaries cannot be evaluated across cultures by some common standard seems morally unacceptable, not morally enlightened. It is one thing to suggest that such beliefs might be *excused* (and persons found nonculpable), still another to suggest that they are *right.*

When two parties argue about some serious, divisive, and contested moral issue—for example, conflicts of interest in business—people tend to think that some fair and justified judgment may be reached. People seldom infer from the mere fact of a conflict between beliefs that there is no way to judge one view as correct or as better argued or more reasonable than the other. The more absurd the position advanced by one party, the more convinced others become that some views are mistaken, unreasonable, or require supplementation.

### Moral Disagreements

Whether or not ethical relativism is a tenable theory, we must confront the indisputable fact of moral disagreement. In any pluralistic culture many conflicts of value exist. In this volume a number of controversies and dilemmas are examined, including occupational safety when toxic chemicals are present in the workplace, whistleblowing, advertising intended to manipulate people's feelings, preferential hiring policies that use criteria of race and gender, exploitation of labor in sweatshops, and the like. Although disagreements run deep in these controversies, there are ways to resolve them or at least to reduce levels of conflict. Several methods have been employed in the past to deal constructively with moral disagreements, each of which deserves recognition as a method of easing disagreement and conflict.

*Obtaining Objective Information.* Many moral disagreements can be at least partially resolved by obtaining additional factual information on which moral controversies turn. Earlier it was shown how useful such information can be in trying to ascertain whether cultural variations in belief are fundamental. It has often been assumed that moral disputes are by definition produced solely by differences over moral principles or their application and not by a lack of scientific or factual information. This assumption is misleading inasmuch as moral disputes—that is, disputes over what morally ought or ought not to be done—often have nonmoral elements as their main ingredients. For example, debates over the allocation of tax dollars to prevent accidents or disease in the workplace often become bogged down in factual issues of whether particular measures such as the use of protective masks or lower levels of toxic chemicals actually function better to prevent death and disease.

Another example is provided by the dispute between Greenpeace and Royal Dutch Shell. After lengthy investigation, Royal Dutch Shell proposed to sink a loading and storage buoy for oil deep in the North Sea (off the coast of England). Despite evidence that such an operation posed no environmental danger, Greenpeace conducted protests and even used a group of small boats to thwart the attempt. Royal Dutch Shell yielded to its critics, and the buoy was cut up and made into a quay in Norway. Later, however, Greenpeace came to the conclusion that new facts indicated that there had never been any serious environmental danger. Furthermore, it appears that Greenpeace's recommended method of disposing of the buoy caused environmental harm that would have been avoided by sinking it, as Shell had originally planned.

Controversial issues such as the following are laced with issues of both values and facts: how satisfactorily toxic substances are monitored in the workplace; how a start-up company has "appropriated" an established company's trade secrets; what effects access to pornography through the Internet produces; whether an extension of current copyright laws would reduce sharing of copyrighted recordings on the Internet; and how vaccines for medical use should be manufactured, disseminated, and advertised. The arguments used by disagreeing parties may turn on a dispute about liberty, harm, or justice and therefore may be primarily moral; but they may also rest on factual disagreements over, for example, the effects of a product, service, or activity. Information may thus have only a limited bearing on the resolution of some controversies, yet it may have a direct and almost overpowering influence in others.

*Definitional Clarity.* Sometimes, controversies have been settled by reaching conceptual or definitional agreement over the language used by disputing parties. Controversies discussed in Chapter 4 about the morality of affirmative action, preferential treatment, and sexual harassment, for example, are often needlessly complicated because different senses of these expressions are employed, and yet disputing parties may have a great deal invested in their particular definitions. If there is no common point of contention in such cases, parties will be addressing entirely separate issues through their conceptual assumptions. Often, these parties will not have a bona fide moral disagreement but, rather, a purely conceptual one.

Although conceptual agreement provides no guarantee that a dispute will be settled, it will facilitate direct discussion of the outstanding issues. For this reason, many essays in this volume dwell at some length on problems of conceptual clarity.

*Example–Counterexample.* Resolution of moral controversies can also be aided by posing examples and opposed counterexamples, that is, by bringing forward cases or examples that are favorable to one point of view and counterexamples that are in opposition. For instance, a famous case against AT&T involving a dispute over discriminatory hiring and promotion between the company and the Equal Employment Opportunities Commission (EEOC) was handled through the citation of statistics and examples that (allegedly) documented the claims made by each side. AT&T showed that 55 percent of the employees on its payroll were women and that 33 percent of all management positions were held by women. To sharpen its allegation of discriminatory practices in the face of this evidence, the EEOC countered by citing a government study demonstrating that 99 percent of all telephone operators were female, whereas only 1 percent of craft workers were female. Such use of example and counterexample serves to weigh the strength of conflicting considerations.

*Analysis of Arguments and Positions.* Finally, a serviceable method of philosophical inquiry is that of exposing the inadequacies in and unexpected consequences of arguments and positions. A moral argument that leads to conclusions that a proponent is not prepared to defend and did not previously anticipate will have to be changed, and the distance between those who disagree will perhaps be reduced by this process. Inconsistencies not only in reasoning but in organizational schemes or pronouncements can be uncovered. However, in a context of controversy, sharp attacks or critiques are unlikely to eventuate in an agreement unless a climate of reason prevails. A fundamental axiom of successful negotiation is "reason and be open to reason." The axiom holds for moral discussion as well as for any other disagreement.

No contention is made here that moral disagreements can always be resolved or that every reasonable person must accept the same method for approaching disagreement. Many moral problems may not be resolvable by any of the four methods that have been discussed. A single ethical theory or method may never be developed to resolve all disagreements adequately, and the pluralism of cultural beliefs often presents a barrier to the resolution of issues. Given the possibility of continual disagreement, the resolution of cross-cultural conflicts such as those faced by multinational corporations may prove especially elusive. However, if something is to be done about these problems, a resolution seems more likely to occur if the methods outlined in this section are used.

## The Problem of Egoism

Attitudes in business have often been deemed fundamentally egoistic. Executives and corporations are said to act purely from prudence—that is, each business is out to promote solely its own interest in a context of competition. Some people say that the corporation has no other interest, because its goal is to be as economically successful in competition as possible.

The philosophical theory called *egoism* has familiar origins. We have all been confronted with occasions on which we must make a choice between spending money on ourselves or on some worthy charitable enterprise. When one elects to purchase new clothes for oneself rather than contribute to a university scholarship fund for poor students, one is giving priority to self-interest over the interests of others. Egoism generalizes beyond these occasions to all human choices. The egoist contends that all choices either do involve or should involve self-promotion as their sole objective. Thus, a person's or a corporation's goal and perhaps only obligation is self-promotion. No sacrifice or obligation is owed to others.

There are two main varieties of egoism: psychological egoism and ethical egoism. We will discuss each in turn.

*Psychological Egoism.*  Psychological egoism is the view that everyone is always motivated to act in his or her perceived self-interest. This factual theory regarding human motivation offers an *explanation* of human conduct, in contrast with a *justification* of human conduct. It claims that people always do what pleases them or what is in their interest. Popular ways of expressing this viewpoint include the following: "People are at heart selfish, even if they appear to be unselfish;" "People look out for Number One first;" "In the long run, everybody does what he or she wants to do;" and "No matter what a person says, he or she acts for the sake of personal satisfaction."

Psychological egoism presents a serious challenge to normative moral philosophy. If this theory is correct, there is no purely altruistic moral motivation. Yet, normative ethics appears to presuppose that people ought to behave in accordance with the demands of morality, whether or not such behavior promotes their own interests. If people *must act* in their own interest, to ask them to sacrifice for others would be absurd. Accordingly, if psychological egoism is true, the whole enterprise of normative ethics is futile.

Those who accept psychological egoism are convinced that their theory of motivation is correct. Conversely, those who reject the theory do so not only because they see many examples of altruistic behavior in the lives of friends, colleagues, saints, heroes, and public servants, but also because contemporary anthropology, psychology, and biology offer some compelling studies of sacrificial behavior. Even if people are basically selfish, critics of egoism maintain that there are at least some compelling examples of preeminently unselfish actions such as corporations that cut profits to provide public services (see Chapter 2) and employees who "blow the whistle" on unsafe or otherwise improper business practices even though they could lose their jobs and suffer social ostracism (see Chapter 3).

The defender of psychological egoism is not impressed by the exemplary lives of saints and heroes or by social practices of corporate sacrifice. The psychological egoist maintains that all who expend effort to help others, to promote fairness in competition, to promote the general welfare, or to risk their lives for the welfare of others are, underneath it all, acting to promote themselves. By sacrificing for their children, parents seek the satisfaction that comes from their children's development or achievements. By following society's moral and legal codes, people avoid both the police and social ostracism.

Egoists maintain that no matter how self-sacrificing one's behavior may at times seem, the desire behind the action is self-regarding. One is ultimately out for oneself, whether in the long or the short run, and whether one realizes it or not. Egoists view self-promoting actions as perfectly compatible with behavior that others categorize as altruistic. For example, many corporations have adopted "enlightened self-interest" policies through which they respond to community needs and promote worker satisfaction to promote their corporate image and ultimately their earnings. The clever person or corporation can appear to be unselfish, but the action's true character depends on the *motivation* behind the appearance. Honest corporate leaders will, in the view of the egoist, emulate General Electric chairman and CEO Jeffery Immelt, who announced GE's new "ecoimagination" environmental intiative in 2005, saying "we can improve the environment and make money doing it. We see that green is green."[8] According to the egoist, apparently altruistic agents who are less honest than Immelt may simply believe that an unselfish appearance best promotes their long-range interests. From the egoist's point of view, the fact that some (pseudo?) sacrifices may be necessary in the short run does not count against egoism.

Consider the following example. Since the late 1980s the pharmaceutical company Merck has spent hundreds of millions of dollars to help eradicate diseases such as river blindness (onchocerciasis) and elephantiasis (lymphatic filariasis) in the developing world (see Chapter 2). Partly as a result of these activities, Merck enjoys what has been described as a "sterling reputation" as "the most ethical of the major drug companies."[9] However, in 2004 Merck's chairman and CEO, Raymond Gilmartin, was called before the U.S. Senate Finance Committee to testify about his company's problematic arthritis drug Vioxx (rofecoxib) (see Chapter 7). Observers noted that Gilmartin was treated gently—even kindly—by the senators. They attributed the gentle treatment to Merck's past record of ethical leadership. (This treatment contrasted significantly with the harsh criticism executives at companies such as Enron and Tyco received from Congress.) From the perspective of egoists, Merck's efforts at combating diseases in the developing world should be understood entirely as self-interested activity. As evidence of this claim they point to the favorable treatment Merck received by Congress as a direct result of those and other allegedly altruistic activities.

Even if Merck's behavior is best explained as motivated by self-interest, it need not follow that all human behavior can be best explained as motivated by self-interest. The question remains: Is psychological egoism correct? At one level this question can be answered only by empirical data—by looking at the facts. Significantly, there is a large body of evidence both from observations of daily practice and from experiments in psychological laboratories that counts against the universality of egoistic motivation. The evidence from daily practice is not limited to heroic action but includes such mundane practices as voting and leaving tips in restaurants and hotels where a person does not expect to return and has nothing to gain.

It is tempting for the psychological egoist to make the theory *necessarily* true because of the difficulties in proving it to be *empirically* true. When confronted with what look like altruistic acts, egoists may appeal to unconscious motives of self-interest or claim that every act is based on some desire of the person performing the act. For example, the egoist will note that people will feel good after performing allegedly altruistic acts and then claim that it is the desire to feel good that motivated the person in the first place.

The latter explanation seems to be a conceptual or verbal trick: the egoist has changed the meaning of *self-interest*. At first, *self-interest* meant "acting exclusively on behalf of one's own self-serving interest." Now the word has been redefined to mean "acting on any interest one has." In other words, the egoist has conceptualized "interest" to entail motivation by self-interest. If psychological egoists are right, we never intend impartially to help a child, loved one, friend or colleague but only to achieve our own satisfaction. But even if an act brings satisfaction, it does not follow that one was motivated by the goal of satisfaction or intended some form of satisfaction.

***Ethical Egoism.*** Ethical egoism is a theory stating that the supreme principle of conduct is to promote one's well-being above everyone else's. Whereas psychological egoism is a *descriptive,* psychological theory about human motivation, ethical egoism is a *normative* theory about what people ought to do. According to psychological egoism, people always *do* act on the basis of perceived self-interest. According to ethical egoism, people always *ought* to act on the basis of self-interest.

Ethical egoism contrasts sharply with common moral beliefs. Consider the maxim "You're a sucker if you don't put yourself first and others second." This maxim is generally thought morally unacceptable, because morality obligates people to return a lost wallet to an owner and to correct a bank loan officer's errors in their favor. Nevertheless, questions about why people should look out for the interests of others on such occasions have troubled many reflective persons. Some have concluded that acting against one's interest is contrary to reason. These thinkers, who regard conventional morality as tinged with irrational sentiment and indefensible constraints on the individual, are the supporters of ethical egoism. It is not their view that one should always ignore the interests of others but, rather, that one should take account of and act on the interests of others only if it suits one's own interests to do so.

What would society be like if ethical egoism were the conventional, prevailing theory of proper conduct? Some philosophers and political theorists have argued that anarchism and chaos would result unless preventive measures were adopted. A classic statement of this position was made by the philosopher Thomas Hobbes (1588–1679). Imagine a world with limited resources, he said, where persons are approximately equal in their ability to harm one another and where everyone acts exclusively in his or her interest. Hobbes argued that in such a world everyone would be at everyone else's throat, and society would be plagued by anxiety, violence, and constant danger. As Hobbes declared, life would be "solitary, poor, nasty, brutish, and short."[10] However, Hobbes also assumed that human beings are sufficiently rational to recognize their interests. To avoid the war of all against all, he urged his readers to form a powerful government to protect themselves.

Egoists accept Hobbes's view in the following form: Any clever person will realize that she or he has no moral obligations to others besides those obligations she or he voluntarily assumes because it is in one's own interest to agree to abide by them. Each person should accept moral rules and assume specific obligations only when doing so promotes one's self-interest. In agreeing to live under laws of the state that are binding on everyone, one should obey these laws only to protect oneself and to create a situation of communal living that is personally advantageous. One should also back out of an obligation whenever it becomes clear that it is to one's long-range disadvantage to fulfill the obligation. When confronted by a social revolution, the questionable trustworthiness of a colleague, or an incompetent administration at one's place of employment, no one is under an obligation to obey the law, fulfill contracts, or tell the truth. These obligations exist only because one assumes them, and one ought to assume them only as long as doing so promotes one's own interest.

An arrangement whereby everyone acted on more or less fixed rules such as those found in conventional moral and legal systems would produce the most desirable state of affairs for each individual from an egoistic point of view. The reason is that such rules arbitrate conflicts and make social life more agreeable. These rules would include, for example, familiar moral and legal principles of justice that are intended to make everyone's situation more secure and stable.

Only an unduly narrow conception of self-interest, the egoist might argue, leads critics to conclude that the egoist would not willingly observe conventional rules of justice. If society can be structured to resolve personal conflicts through courts and other peaceful means, egoists will view it as in their interest to accept those binding social arrangements, just as they will perceive it as prudent to treat other individuals favorably in personal contexts.

The egoist is not saying that his or her interests are served by promoting the good of others but, rather, is claiming that his or her personal interests are served by observing impartial rules that protect one's interest, irrespective of the outcome for others. Egoists do not care about the welfare of others unless it affects their welfare, and this desire for personal well-being alone motivates acceptance of the conventional rules of morality.

***Egoistic Business Practices and Utilitarian Results.*** A different view from that of Hobbes, and one that has been influential in some parts of the business community, is found in Adam Smith's (1723–1790) economic and moral writings. Smith believed that the public good—especially in the commercial world—evolves out of a suitably restrained clash of competing individual interests. As individuals pursue their self-interest, the interactive process is guided by an "invisible hand," ensuring that the public interest is achieved. Ironically, according to Smith, egoism in commercial transactions leads not to the war of all against all but, rather, to a utilitarian outcome—that is, to the largest number of benefits for the largest number of persons. The free market is, Smith thought, a better method of achieving the public good, however inadvertently, than the highly visible hand of Hobbes's all-powerful sovereign state.

Smith believed that government should be limited in order to protect individual freedom. At the same time, he recognized that concern with freedom and self-interest could get out of control. Hence, he proposed that minimal state regulatory activity is needed to provide and enforce the rules of the competitive game. Smith's picture of a restrained egoistic world has captivated many people interested in the business and economic community.[11] They, like Smith, do not picture themselves as selfish and indifferent to the interests of others, and they recognize that a certain element of cooperation is essential if their interests are to flourish. They recognize that when their interests conflict with the interests of others, they should pursue their interests within the established rules of the competitive game.

Such a restrained egoism is one form of defense of a free-market economy; competition among individual firms advances the utilitarian good of society as a whole. Hence, a popular view of business ethics is captured by the phrase "Ethical egoism leads to utilitarian outcomes." As Smith said, corporations and individuals pursuing their individual interests thereby promote the public good, so long as they abide by the rules that protect the public.

Some people believe that a contemporary example is found in the way world hunger can be alleviated as a result of capitalistic behavior (see Chapter 10). They claim that capitalistic investment and productivity increase jobs, social welfare, social cooperation, wealth in society, and morally responsible behavior. The thesis is that these benefits accrue widely across the society, affecting both poor and wealthy, even if the goal of capitalists is purely their own economic gain.[12]

Critics of this argument note that although global capitalism can generate significant benefits, the ability to generate many of those benefits presumes that certain regulatory controls are in place in the nations in which business is conducted. At the very least, there must be regulation to ensure that there is a free market. Also, developing nations often lack the framework of laws, policing authorities, and judicial review presumed by Smith. In such circumstances, the unrestrained pursuit of self-interest can result in the exploitation of workers, and environmental practices that are harmful to human welfare and increase rather than decrease poverty. For example, a business may take advantage of the fact that a developing nation has no means of occupational safety enforcement and, to save money, may choose not to put in place standards for protecting workers from injury by exposure to toxic chemicals or poorly maintained machinery.

An important and neglected aspect of Smith's defense of capitalism is that it was predicated on his theory of ethics.[13] (Smith held the Chair in Moral Philosophy at the University of Glasgow for over 10 years.) Egoists typically neglect important features of Smith's thinking about ethics and human behavior. Smith did argue that *prudence*, or the careful pursuit of one's self-interest, is a virtue. But he also argued that *benevolence*, or actions directed at the good of others, is an equally important virtue, one that is necessary for social welfare. And he warned against the self-interested partiality in our judgments. A minimal regulatory environment for business was possible without resulting in the anarchy predicted by Hobbes, Smith argued, because of the sympathetic nature of persons and our capacity for benevolence.

# NORMATIVE ETHICAL THEORY

The central question discussed in this section is: What constitutes an acceptable ethical standard for business practice, and by what authority is the standard acceptable? One time-honored answer is that the acceptability of a moral standard is determined by prevailing practices in business or by authoritative, profession-generated documents such as codes. Many businesspersons find this viewpoint congenial and therefore do not see the need for revisions in practices that they find already comfortable and adequate.

Professional standards do play a role in business ethics and will be discussed in later chapters in this book. Ultimately, however, the internal morality of business does not supply a comprehensive framework for the many pressing questions of business ethics. Morality in the world of business evolves in the face of social change and critical philosophical argument; it cannot rely entirely on its own historical traditions. Its standards therefore need to be justified in terms of independent ethical standards such as those of public opinion, law, and philosophical ethics—just as the moral norms of a culture need to be justified by more than an appeal to those norms themselves. The following two parts of this section are devoted to two ethical theories that have been particularly influential in recent moral philosophy: utilitarianism and Kantianism. Some knowledge of these theories is indispensable for reflective study in business ethics, because a sizable part of the field's literature draws on methods and conclusions found in these theories.

## Utilitarian Theories

Utilitarian theories hold that the moral worth of actions or practices is determined by their consequences. An action or practice is right if it leads to the best possible balance of good consequences over bad consequences for all the parties affected. In taking this perspective, utilitarians believe that the purpose or function of ethics is to promote human welfare by minimizing harms and maximizing benefits.

The first developed philosophical writings that made the category of "utility" central in moral philosophy were those of David Hume (1711–1776), Jeremy Bentham

(1748–1832), and John Stuart Mill (1806–1873). Mill's *Utilitarianism* (1863) is still today considered the standard statement of this theory. Mill discusses two foundations or sources of utilitarian thinking: a *normative* foundation in the "principle of utility" and a *psychological* foundation in human nature. He proposes his principle of utility—the "greatest happiness principle"—as the foundation of normative ethical theory. *Actions are right*, Mill says, *in proportion to their tendency to promote happiness or absence of pain, and wrong insofar as they tend to produce pain or displeasure.* According to Mill, pleasure and freedom from pain are alone desirable as ends. All desirable things (which are numerous) are desirable either for the pleasure inherent in them or as means to promote pleasure and prevent pain.

Mill's second foundation derives from his belief that most persons, and perhaps all, have a basic desire for unity and harmony with their fellow human beings. Just as people feel horror at crimes, he says, they have a basic moral sensitivity to the needs of others. Mill sees the purpose of morality as tapping natural human sympathies to benefit others while controlling unsympathetic attitudes that cause harm to others. The principle of utility is conceived as the best means to these basic human goals.

***Essential Features of Utilitarianism.***  Several essential features of utilitarianism are present in the theories of Mill and other utilitarians. First, utilitarianism is committed to the maximization of the good and the minimization of harm and evil. It asserts that society ought always to produce the greatest possible balance of positive value or the minimum balance of disvalue for all persons affected. The means to maximization is efficiency, a goal that persons in business find congenial, because it is highly prized throughout the economic sector. Efficiency is a means to higher profits and lower prices, and the struggle to be maximally profitable seeks to obtain maximum production from limited economic resources. The utilitarian commitment to the principle of optimal productivity through efficiency is, in this regard, an essential part of the traditional business conception of society and a standard part of business practice.

Many businesses, as well as government agencies, have adopted specific tools such as cost-benefit analysis, risk assessment, or management by objectives—all of which are strongly influenced by a utilitarian philosophy. Other businesses do not employ such specific tools but make utililitarian judgments about the benefits and costs of having layoffs, conducting advertising campaigns, hiring lobbyists, paying CEOs, and providing employee benefits. Though unpopular in the short term, many adjustments are often welcomed because they are directed at long-term financial improvement, favorable government regulation, and job security. In this respect business harbors a fundamentally utilitarian conception of the goals of its enterprise. Much the same is true of the goals of public policy in many countries.

A second essential feature of the utilitarian theory is a *theory of the good.* Efficiency itself is simply an instrumental good; that is, it is valuable strictly as a means to something else. Even growth and profit maximization are only means to the end of intrinsic goods. But what is "good" according to the utilitarian? An answer to this question can be formed by considering the New York stock market. Daily results on

Wall Street are not intrinsically good. They are extrinsically good as a means to other ends, such as financial security and happiness. Utilitarians believe that people ought to orient their lives and frame their goals around conditions that are good in themselves without reference to further consequences. Health, friendship, and freedom from pain are among such values.

However, utilitarians disagree concerning what constitutes the complete range of things or states that are good. Bentham and Mill are hedonists. They believe that only pleasure or happiness (synonymous for the purposes of this discussion) can be intrinsically good. Everything besides pleasure is instrumentally good to the end of pleasure. *Hedonistic* utilitarians, then, believe that any act or practice that maximizes pleasure (when compared with any alternative act or practice) is right. Later utilitarian philosophers have argued that other values besides pleasure possess intrinsic worth, for example, friendship, knowledge, courage, health, and beauty. Utilitarians who believe in multiple intrinsic values are referred to as *pluralistic* utilitarians.

In recent philosophy, economics, and psychology, neither the approach of the hedonists nor that of the pluralists has prevailed. Both approaches have seemed relatively unhelpful for purposes of objectively stating and arraying basic goods. Another and competitive theory appeals to individual preferences. From this perspective, the concept of utility is understood not in terms of states of affairs such as happiness or friendship, but in terms of the satisfaction of individual preferences, as determined by a person's behavior. In the language of business, utility is measured by a person's purchases. More generally, utility may be said to be measurable by starting with a person's actual pursuits. To maximize a person's utility is to provide that which he or she has chosen or would choose from among the available alternatives. To maximize the utility of all persons affected by an action or a policy is to maximize the utility of the aggregate group.

Although the *preference* utilitarian approach to value has been viewed by many as superior to its predecessors, it is not trouble free as an ethical theory. A major problem arises over morally unacceptable preferences. For example, an airline pilot may prefer to have a few beers before going to work, or an employment officer may prefer to discriminate against women, yet such preferences are morally intolerable. Utilitarianism based purely on subjective preferences is satisfactory, then, only if a range of acceptable preferences can be formulated. This latter task has proved difficult in theory, and it may be inconsistent with a pure preference approach. Should products such as cigarettes, fireworks, heroin, and automatic rifles be legally prohibited because they cause harm, even though many people would prefer to purchase them? How could a preference utilitarian answer this question?

One possible utilitarian response is to ask whether society is better off as a whole when these preferences are prohibited and when the choices of those desiring them are frustrated. If these products work against the larger objectives of utilitarianism (maximal public welfare) by creating unhappiness and pain, the utilitarian could argue that preferences for these products should not be counted in the calculus of preferences. Preferences that serve to frustrate the preferences of others would then be ruled out by the goal of utilitarianism. But would the resulting theory be one entirely based on preferences and only preferences?

A third essential feature of utilitarianism is its commitment to the measurement and comparison of goods. In a hedonistic theory, people must be able to measure pleasurable and painful states and be able to compare one person's pleasures with another's to decide which is greater. Bentham, for example, worked out a measurement device that he called the *hedonic calculus*. He thought he could add the quantitative units of individual pleasure, subtract the units of individual displeasure, and thereby arrive at a total measure of pleasure (or happiness). By the use of this system it is allegedly possible to determine the act or practice that will provide the greatest happiness to the greatest number of people.

When Bentham's hedonic calculus turned out to be of limited practical value, Mill shifted to a criterion that we would today call a panel of experts (persons of requisite experience). Because Mill believed that some pleasures were better or higher order than others, a device was needed to decide which pleasures were in fact better. The experts were designated to fill that role. Subsequently, this idea of Mill's also turned out to be of limited practical value, and notions like that of *consumer choice* were substitued in some utilitarian theories. Consumer behavior, in this conception, can be empirically observed as prices change in the market. If one assumes that consumers seek to rationally order and maximize their preferences, given a set of prices, an objective measurement of utility is possible.

***Act and Rule Utilitarianism.*** Utilitarian moral philosophers are conventionally divided into two types—act utilitarians and rule utilitarians. An *act utilitarian* argues that in all situations one ought to perform that act that leads to the greatest good for the greatest number. The act utilitarian regards rules such as "You ought to tell the truth in making contracts" and "You ought not to manipulate persons through advertising" as useful guidelines but also as expendable in business and other relationships. An act utilitarian would not hesitate to break a moral rule if breaking it would lead to the greatest good for the greatest number in a particular case. *Rule utilitarians*, however, reserve a more significant place for rules, which they do not regard as expendable on grounds that utility is maximized in a particular circumstance.

There are many applications of both types of utilitarianism in business ethics.[14] Consider the following case in which U.S. business practices and standards run up against the quite different practices of the Italian business community. The case involves the tax problems encountered by an Italian subsidiary of a major U.S. bank. In Italy the practices of corporate taxation typically involve elaborate negotiations among hired company representatives and the Italian tax service, and the tax statement initially submitted by a corporation is regarded as a dramatically understated bid intended only as a starting point for the negotiating process. In the case in question, the U.S. manager of the Italian banking subsidiary decided, against the advice of locally experienced lawyers and tax consultants, to ignore the native Italian practices and file a conventional U.S.-style tax statement (that is, one in which the subsidiary's profits for the year were not dramatically understated). His reasons for this decision included his belief that the local customs violated the moral rule of truth telling.[15]

An act utilitarian might well take exception to this conclusion. Admittedly, to file an Italian-style tax statement would be to violate a moral rule of truth telling; but the act utilitarian would argue that such a rule is only a guideline and can justifiably be violated to produce the greatest good. In the present case, the greatest good would evidently be done by following the local consultants' advice to conform to the Italian practices. Only by following those practices would the appropriate amount of tax be paid. This conclusion is strengthened by the ultimate outcome of the present case: the Italian authorities forced the bank to enter into the customary negotiations, a process in which the original, truthful tax statement was treated as an understated opening bid, and a dramatically excessive tax payment was consequently exacted.

In contrast with the position of act utilitarians, rule utilitarians hold that rules have a central position in morality that cannot be compromised by the demands of particular situations. Compromise threatens the general effectiveness of the rules, the observance of which maximizes social utility. For the rule utilitarian, then, actions are justified by appeal to abstract rules such as "Don't kill," "Don't bribe," and "Don't break promises." These rules, in turn, are justified by an appeal to the principle of utility. The rule utilitarian believes this position can avoid the objections of act utilitarianism, because rules are not subject to change by the demands of individual circumstances. Utilitarian rules are in theory firm and protective of all classes of individuals, just as human rights are rigidly protective of all individuals regardless of social convenience and momentary need.

Act utilitarians have a reply to these criticisms. They argue that there is a third option beyond ignoring rules and strictly obeying them, which is that the rules should be regarded as "rules of thumb" to be obeyed *only sometimes*. In cases in which adhering to the rule of thumb will result in a decline in overall welfare, the rule should be ignored.

*Criticisms of Utilitarianism.*  A major problem for utilitarianism is whether preference units or some other utilitarian value such as happiness can be measured and compared to determine the best action among the alternatives. In deciding whether to open a pristine Alaskan wildlife preserve to oil exploration and drilling, for example, how does one compare the combined value of an increase in the oil supply, jobs, and consumer purchasing power with the value of wildlife preservation and environmental protection? How does a responsible official—at, say, the William and Melinda Gates Foundation—decide how to distribute limited funds allocated for charitable contributions (for example, as this foundation has decided, to international vaccination and children's health programs)? If a corporate social audit (an evaluation of the company's acts of social responsibility) were attempted, how could the auditor measure and compare a corporation's ethical assets and liabilities?

The utilitarian reply is that the alleged problem is either a pseudo-problem or a problem that affects all ethical theories. People make crude, rough-and-ready comparisons of values every day, including those of pleasures and dislikes. For example, workers decide to go as a group to a bar rather than have an office party because they think the bar function will satisfy more members of the group. Utilitarians acknowledge that accurate measurements of others' goods or preferences can seldom be provided because of limited knowledge and time. In everyday affairs such as purchasing supplies, administering business, or making legislative decisions, severely limited knowledge regarding the consequences of one's actions is often all that is available.

Utilitarianism has also been criticized on the grounds that it ignores nonutilitarian factors that are needed to make moral decisions. The most prominent omission cited is a consideration of justice: the action that produces the greatest balance of value for the greatest number of people may bring about unjustified treatment of a minority. Suppose society decides that the public interest is served by denying health insurance to those testing positive for the AIDS virus. Moreover, in the interest of efficiency, suppose insurance companies are allowed to weed out those covered because they have some characteristics that are statistically associated with an enhanced risk of injury or disease—for example, genetic disorders. Suppose such policies would, on balance, serve the public's financial interest by lowering insurance costs. Utilitarianism seems to *require* that public law and insurance companies deny coverage to persons with genetic disorders and to many others at higher risk of disease or injury. If so, would not this denial be unjust to those who are at high risk through no fault of their own?

Utilitarians insist, against such criticisms, that all entailed costs and benefits of an action or practice must be weighed, including, for example, the costs that would occur from modifying a statement of basic rights. In a decision that affects employee and consumer safety, for example, the costs often include protests from labor and consumer groups, public criticism from the press, further alienation of employees from executives, the loss of customers to competitors, and the like. Also, rule utilitarians deny that narrow cost-benefit determinations are acceptable. They argue that general rules of justice (which are themselves justified by broad considerations of utility) ought to constrain particular actions and uses of cost-benefit calculations. Rule utilitarians maintain that the criticisms of utilitarianism previously noted are short-sighted because they focus on injustices that might be caused through a superficial or short-term application of the principle of utility. In a long-range view, utilitarians argue, promoting utility does not eventuate in overall unjust outcomes.

### Kantian Ethics

CNN reported that online shoppers who visited the Internet auction site eBay were surprised to find a "fully functional kidney" for sale by a man giving his home as "Sunrise, Florida." He was proposing to sell one of his two kidneys. The price had been bid up to more than $5.7 million before eBay intervened and terminated the (illegal) auction.[16] Although it was never determined whether this auction was genuine, it is known that kidneys are for sale in some parts of Asia, notably India. One study showed, after locating 305 sellers, that Indians who sold their kidneys actually worsened rather than bettered their financial position as a result of the sale; the study also showed that some men forced their wives to sell a kidney and that many sellers suffered a decline in health status.[17] Irrespective of the consequences of a kidney sale, many people look with moral indignation on the idea of selling a kidney, whether in the United States or in India.[18] They see it as exploitation, rather than opportunity, and they don't care whether it has strong utilitarian benefits for society. What is it about selling a kidney that provokes this sense of moral unfairness, and can a moral theory capture the perceived wrongness?

***Kantian Respect for Persons.*** Many have thought that Immanuel Kant's (1724–1804) ethical theory helps clarify the basis of such moral concern as well as what should be done about it. A follower of Kant could argue that using human organs as commodities is to treat human beings as though they were merely machines or capital, and so to deny people the respect appropriate to their dignity as rational human beings. Kant argued that persons should be treated as ends and never purely as means to the ends of others. That is, failure to respect persons is to treat another as a means in accordance with one's *own* ends, and thus as if they were not independent agents. To exhibit a lack of respect for a person is either to reject the person's considered judgments, to ignore the person's concerns and needs, or to deny the person the liberty to act on those judgments. For example, manipulative advertising that attempts to make sales by interfering with the potential buyer's reflective choice violates the principle of respect for persons. In the case of kidney sales, almost all sellers are in desperate poverty and desperate need. Potentially all organ "donations" will come from the poor while the rich avoid donating their kidneys even to their relatives. In effect, the organ is treated as a commodity and the owner of the organ as merely a means to a purchaser's ends.

In Kantian theories respect for the human being is said to be necessary—not just as an option or at one's discretion—because human beings possess a moral dignity and therefore should not be treated as if they had merely the conditional value possessed by machinery, industrial plants, robots, and capital. This idea of "respect for persons" has sometimes been expressed in corporate contexts as "respect for the individual."

An example in business ethics is found in the practices of Southwest Airlines, which has the reputation of treating its employees and customers with unusual respect. Employees report that they feel free to express themselves as individuals and that they feel a strong loyalty to the airline. Following the terrorist attacks of September 11, 2001, Southwest was the only airline that did not lay off employees or reduce its flight schedule. As a consequence, some employees offered to work overtime, without pay, to save the company money until people resumed flying.[19] The firm prides itself on a relationship with all stakeholders that is a relationship of persons, rather than simply a relationship of economic transactions.

Another example is found at Motorola, where respect for individual persons is one of the "key beliefs" that has served as a foundation for their Code of Conduct for decades. As understood by Motorola, "Constant respect for people means we treat everyone with dignity, as we would like to be treated ourselves. Constant respect applies to every individual we interact with around the world."[20] The Motorola Code of Conduct specifies how this principle should be applied to "Motorolans," customers, business partners, shareholders, competitors, communities, and governments. All employees at Motorola are evaluated, in part, on the extent to which they demonstrate respect for each of these stakeholders.

Some have interpreted Kant to hold categorically that people can never treat other persons as a means to their ends. This interpretation is mistaken. Kant did not categorically prohibit the use of persons as means to the ends of other people. He argued only that people must not treat another *exclusively* as a means to their ends. An example is found in circumstances in which employees are ordered to perform odious tasks. Clearly, they are being treated as a means to an employer's or a supervisor's ends, but the employees are not exclusively used for others' purposes because they are not mere servants or objects. In an economic exchange, suppose that Jones is using Smith to achieve her end, but similarly Smith is using Jones to achieve her end. So long as the exchange is freely entered into without coercion or deception by either party, neither party has used the other merely for her end. Thus even in a hierarchical organization an employer can be the boss without exploiting the employee, so long as the employee freely entered into that relationship. The key to not using others merely as a means is to respect their dignity.

This interpretation suggests that the example of the kidney sale does not necessarily show any disrespect for persons. Kant seems to require only that each individual *will the acceptance* of those principles on which he or she is acting. If a person freely accepts a certain form of action and it is not intrinsically immoral, that person is a free being and has a right to so choose. Selling a kidney might fall into this category. It is conceivable, for example, that if as a condition of the exchange, kidney sellers were guaranteed first-rate medical care for the rest of their lives to help prevent sickness and death from complications related to transplant surgery, purchasing a kidney might be regarded as permissible.[21] However, because kidney sellers are seldom provided with such care, they develop serious medical complications and their life span is often reduced as a result. In this way they are literally regarded as disposable. It is this judgment that informs the assessment some Kantians make today that unregulated kidney sales are immoral.

Respecting others does not merely entail a negative obligation to refrain from treating others as mere objects, it also entails positive obligations to help ensure the development of rational and moral capacities. For example, some Kantians argue today that employers of low-skill workers in the developing world have obligations to ensure that the workers enjoy sufficient free time and the wages to develop their capacities to function as moral agents. Accordingly, workers who are paid more than they would make if they were living on the street, but not enough to live decent human lives, are treated with impermissible disrespect.

Kant's theory finds *motives* for actions to be of the highest importance, in that it expects persons to make the right decisions *for the right reasons*. If persons are honest only because they believe that honesty pays, their "honesty" is cheapened. It seems like no honesty at all, only an action that appears to be honest. For example, when corporate executives announce that the reason they made the morally correct decision was because it was good for their business, this reason seems to have nothing to do with morality. According to Kantian thinking, if a corporation does the right thing only when (and for the reason that) it is profitable or when it will enjoy good publicity, its decision is prudential, not moral.

Consider the following three examples of three people making personal sacrifices for a sick relative. Fred makes the sacrifices only because he fears the social criticism that would result if he failed to do so. He hates doing it and secretly resents being involved. Sam, by contrast, derives no personal satisfaction from taking care of his sick relative. He would rather be doing other things and makes the sacrifice purely from a sense of obligation. Bill, by contrast, is a kindhearted person. He does not view his actions as a sacrifice and is motivated by the satisfaction that comes from helping others. Assume in these three cases that the consequences of all the sacrificial actions are equally good and that the sick relatives are adequately cared for, as each agent intends. The question to consider is which persons are behaving in a morally praiseworthy manner. If utilitarian theory is used, this question may be hard to answer, especially if act utilitarianism is the theory in question, because the good consequences in each case are identical. The Kantian believes, however, that motives—in particular, motives of moral obligation—count substantially in moral evaluation.

It appears that Fred's motives are not moral motives but motives of prudence that spring from fear. Although his actions have good consequences, Fred does not deserve any moral credit for his acts because they are not morally motivated. To recognize the prudential basis of an action does not detract from the goodness of any consequences it may have. Given the purpose or function of the business enterprise, a motive of self-interest may be the most appropriate motive to ensure good consequences. The point, however, is that a business executive derives no special moral credit for acting in the corporate self-interest, even if society is benefited by and satisfied with the action.

If Fred's motive is not moral, what about Bill's and Sam's? Here moral philosophers disagree. Kant maintained that moral action must be motivated by a maxim (rule) of moral obligation. From this perspective, Sam is the only individual whose actions may be appropriately described as moral. Bill deserves no more credit than Fred, because Bill is motivated by the emotions of sympathy and compassion, not by obligation. Bill is naturally kindhearted and has been well socialized by his family, but this motivation merits no moral praise from a Kantian, who believes that actions motivated by self-interest alone or compassion alone cannot be morally praiseworthy. To be deserving of moral praise, a person must act from obligation.

To elaborate this point, Kant insisted that all persons must act for the *sake of* obligation—not merely *in accordance with* obligation. That is, the person's motive for action must involve a recognition of the duty to act. Kant tried to establish the ultimate basis for the validity of rules of obligation in pure reason, not in intuition, conscience, utility, or compassion. Morality provides a rational framework of principles and rules that constrain and guide all people, independent of their personal goals and preferences. He believed that all considerations of utility and self-interest are secondary, because the moral worth of an agent's action depends exclusively on the moral acceptability of the rule according to which the person is acting.

An action has moral worth only if performed by an agent who possesses what Kant called a "good will." A person has a good will only if the motive for action is moral obligation, as determined by a universal rule of obligation. Kant developed this notion into a fundamental moral law: "I ought never to act except in such a way that I can also will that my maxim should become a universal law." Kant called this principle the *categorical imperative*. It is categorical because it admits of no exceptions and is absolutely binding. It is imperative because it gives instruction about how one must act. He gave several examples of imperative moral maxims: "Help others in distress," "Do not commit suicide," and "Work to develop your abilities."

*Universalizability.* Kant's strategy was to show that the acceptance of certain kinds of action is self-defeating, because *universal* participation in such behavior undermines the action. Some of the clearest cases involve persons who make a unique exception for themselves for purely selfish reasons. Suppose a person considers breaking a promise to a coworker that would be inconvenient to keep. According to Kant, the person must first formulate her or his reason as a universal rule. The rule would say, "Everyone should break a promise whenever keeping it is inconvenient." Such a rule is contradictory, Kant held, because if it were consistently recommended that all individuals should break their promises when it was convenient for them to do so, the practice of making promises would be senseless. Given the nature of a promise, a rule allowing people to break promises when it becomes convenient makes the institution of promise-making unintelligible. A rule that allows cheating on an exam similarly negates the purpose of testing.

Kant's belief was that the conduct stipulated in these rules could not be made universal without the emergence of some form of contradiction. If a corporation kites checks to reap a profit in the way E. F. Hutton Brokerage did in a scandal that led to the end of the firm, the corporation makes itself an exception to the system of monetary transfer, thereby cheating the system, which is established by certain rules. This conduct, if carried out by other corporations, violates the rules presupposed by the system, thereby rendering the system inconsistent. Similarly, the Russian economy stalled in recent years because suppliers were not being paid for the goods and services they provided. If such practices were "universalized" (in Kant's sense), suppliers would stop supplying. Russia has also had difficulty in establishing a stock market because the information on the businesses listed has been so inaccurate. If deception were "universal" (that is, widely practiced), investors would not invest, and a stock market would be impossible. Kant's view was that actions involving invasion of privacy, theft, line cutting, cheating, kickbacks, bribes, and the like are contradictory in that they are not consistent with the institutions or practices they presuppose.

*Criticisms of Kantianism.* Despite Kant's contributions to moral philosophy, his theories have been criticized as narrow and inadequate to handle various problems in the moral life. He had little to say regarding moral emotions or sentiments such as sympathy and caring. Some people also think that Kant emphasized universal obligations (obligations common to all people) at the expense of particular obligations (obligations that fall only on those in particular relationships or who occupy certain roles, such as those of a business manager). Whereas the obligation to keep a promise is a universal obligation, the obligation to grade students fairly falls only on teachers responsible for submitting grades.

Many managerial obligations result from special roles played in business. For example, businesspersons tend to treat customers according to the history of their relationship. If a person is a regular customer and the merchandise being sold is in short supply, the regular customer will be given preferential treatment because a relationship of commitment and trust has already been established. Japanese business practice has conventionally extended this notion to relations with suppliers and employees: after a trial period, the regular employee has a job for life at many firms. Also, the bidding system is used less frequently in Japan than in the West. Once a supplier has a history with a firm, the firm is loyal to its supplier, and each trusts the other not to exploit the relationship.

However, particular obligations and special relationships may not be inconsistent with Kantianism, because they may not violate any universal ethical norms. Although Kant wrote little about such particular duties, he would agree that a complete explanation of moral agency in terms of duty requires an account of *both* universal *and* particular duties.

A related aspect of Kant's ethical theory that has been scrutinized by philosophers is his view that moral motivation involves *impartial* principles. Impartial motivation may be distinguished from the motivation that a person might have for treating a second person in a certain way because the first person has a particular interest in the well-being of the second person (a spouse or valued customer, for example). A conventional interpretation of Kant's work suggests that if conflicts arise between one's obligation and one's other motivations—such as friendship, reciprocation, or love—the motive of obligation should always prevail. In arguing against this moral view, critics maintain that persons are entitled to show favoritism to their loved ones. This criticism suggests that Kantianism (and utilitarianism as well) has too broadly cast the requirement of impartiality and does not adequately account for those parts of the moral life involving partial, intimate, and special relationships.

Special relationships with a unique history are often recognized in business. For instance, the Unocal Corporation sharply criticized its principal bank, Security Pacific Corporation, for knowingly making loans of $185 million to a group that intended to use the money to buy shares in Unocal for a hostile takeover. Fred Hartley, chairman and president of Unocal, argued that the banks and investment bankers were "playing both sides of the game." Hartley said that Security Pacific had promised him that it would not finance such takeover attempts three months before doing so and that it had acted under conditions "in which the bank [has] continually received [for the last 40 years] confidential financial, geological, and engineering information from the company."[22] A 40-year history in which the bank stockpiled confidential information should not simply be cast aside for larger goals. Security Pacific had violated a special relationship it had with Unocal.

Nonetheless, impartiality seems at some level an irreplaceable moral concept, and ethical theory should recognize its centrality in many business relationships. For example, in 1991, some U.S. banks were involved in a major scandal because they were caught lending money to bank insiders.[23] Then, as investing became more precarious in the early years of the twenty-first century, several companies were involved in questionable insider loans to corporate executives. For example, at the height of its crisis, WorldCom loaned then-CEO Bernie Ebbers $160 million for his personal "stock purchase/retention." The essence of federal rules governing banks—to the extent explicit rules exist—is that banks can lend money to insiders if and only if insiders are treated exactly as outsiders are treated. Here the rule of impartiality is an essential moral constraint. By contrast, 75 percent of America's 1,500 largest corporations made insider loans strictly on the basis of partiality; most loans were made for stock purchases. This partiality massively backfired in 2000–2003, and many companies had to "forgive" or "pardon" the loans and charge off millions of dollars. Loans at Tyco, Lucent, Mattel, Microsoft, and Webvan became famous cases.[24]

Corporate America continues to suffer from a series of business scandals, many of which end in the criminal prosecution of corporate executives and the dissolution of the company. Violations of the demand for impartiality and fair dealing are virtually always present in these scandals. In a notorious case, the accounting firm of Arthur Andersen had such a close and partial relationship with its client Enron that it could not perform an objective audit of the firm. Enron was treated with a deference, partiality, and favoritism that contrasted sharply with auditing of other firms, who were treated with the conventional impartiality expected of an auditing firm.

As a result of this scandal, problems of undue partiality began to be widely discussed as problems of conflict of interest. In an attempt at restoring public confidence in a fair and impartial system, the U.S. Securities and Exchange Commission (SEC) approved plans for a new oversight system that was itself independent of the accounting industry and therefore more likely to be impartial. However, political lobbyists almost immediately raised questions about the impartiality of the new plans to assure impartiality.

More recently, executives at many U.S. companies have been discovered to be "backdating" their stock options. *Backdating* is the practice of looking back in time for the date on which one's company stock price was at its lowest and granting the purchase on that date. Typically this is done when the stock value is much higher so that the executive can immediately cash in the stock and make a substantial profit. For example, in 2007 the former CEO of Take-Two Interactive Software Inc., the maker of the video game "Grand Theft Auto," pleaded guilty to granting undisclosed, backdated options to himself and others.[25] More than 80 companies have revealed that they are investigating instances of backdating as a result of prompting from regulators and internal audit committees. By allowing insiders the opportunity to make large profits in this way, companies give unfair, partial advantage to corporate executives. Backdating is not, after all, an option for individual investors outside the company. A Kantian might further observe that if everyone were given this option, then stock markets would not be possible.

In concluding this section on Kantian ethics, we point out almost no moral philosopher today finds Kant's system fully satisfactory. His defenders tend to say only that Kant provides the main elements of a sound moral position. By appealing to these elements, some philosophers have attempted to construct a more encompassing theory. They use the Kantian notion of respect for persons, for example, to provide an account of human rights. Controversy persists as to whether Kantian theories are adequate to this task and whether they have been more successful than utilitarian theories.

## Contemporary Challenges to the Dominant Theories

Thus far only utilitarian and Kantian theories have been examined. Both meld a variety of moral considerations into a surprisingly systematized framework, centered around a single major principle. Much is attractive in these theories, and they were the dominant models in ethical theory throughout much of the twentieth century. In fact, they have sometimes been presented as the only types of ethical theory, as if there were no available alternatives from which to choose. However, much recent philosophical writing has focused on defects in these theories and on ways in which the two theories actually affirm a similar conception of the moral life oriented around universal principles and rules.

These critics promote alternatives to the utilitarian and Kantian models. They believe that the contrast between the two types of theory has been overestimated and that they do not merit the attention they have received and the lofty position they have occupied. Three popular replacements for, or perhaps supplements to, Kantian and utilitarian theories are (1) rights theories (which are based on human rights); (2) virtue theories (which are based on character traits); and (3) common morality theories (which are generally obligation-based). These theories are the topics of the next three sections.

Each of these three types of theory has treated some problems well and has supplied insights not found in utilitarian and Kantian theories. Although it may seem as if there is an endless array of disagreements across the theories, these theories are not in all respects competitive, and in some ways they are even complementary. The reader may profitably look for convergent insights in these theories.

## Rights Theories

Terms from moral discourse such as *value, goal,* and *obligation* have thus far in this chapter dominated the discussion. *Principles* and *rules* in Kantian, utilitarian, and common morality theories have been understood as statements of obligation. Yet, many assertions that will be encountered throughout this volume are claims to have rights, and public policy issues often concern rights or attempts to secure rights. Many current controversies in professional ethics, business, and public policy involve the rights to property, work, privacy, a healthy environment, and the like. This section presents theories that give rights a distinctive character in ethical theory and yet allow rights to be connected to the obligations that we have previously examined.

In recent years, public discussions about moral protections for persons vulnerable to abuse, enslavement, or neglect have typically been stated in terms of rights. Many believe that these rights transcend national boundaries and particular governments. For example, we have seen several controversies over exploitative labor conditions in factories (so-called sweatshop conditions) that manufacture products for Nike, Reebok, Abercrombie and Fitch, Target, Gap, J. C. Penney, Liz Claiborne, L.L.Bean, and many other companies. At stake are the human rights of hundreds of thousands of workers around the globe, including rights to appropriate working conditions, a code of conduct for the industry, open-factory inspections, new monitoring systems, reduction of the illiteracy rate among workers, and collective bargaining agreements.[26] In addition, activists have urged that American companies not do business in countries that have a record of extensive violation of human rights. China, Nigeria, and Myanmar have all come under severe criticism. (These issues, and others surrounding violations of human rights in sweatshops, are discussed in Chapter 9.)

Unlike legal rights, human rights are held independently of membership in a state or other social organization. Historically, human rights evolved from the notion of natural rights. As formulated by Locke and others in early modern philosophy, natural rights are claims that individuals have against the state. If the state does not honor these rights, its legitimacy is in question. Natural rights were thought to consist primarily of rights to be free of interference, or liberty rights. Proclamations of rights to life, liberty, property, a speedy trial, and the pursuit of happiness subsequently formed the core of major Western political and legal documents. These rights came to be understood as powerful assertions demanding respect and status.

A number of influential philosophers have maintained that ethical theory or some part of it must be "rights-based."[27] They seek to ground ethical theory in an account of rights that is not reducible to a theory of obligations or virtues. Consider a theory to be discussed in Chapter 10 that takes liberty rights to be basic. One representative of this theory, Robert Nozick, refers to his social philosophy as an "entitlement theory." The appropriateness of that description is apparent from this provocative line with which his book begins: "Individuals have rights, and there are things no person or group may do to them (without violating their rights)." Nozick grounds this right in Kant's arguments regarding respect for persons. Starting from this assumption, Nozick builds a political theory in which government action is justified only if it protects the fundamental rights of its citizens.

This political theory is also an ethical theory. Nozick takes the following moral rule to be basic: all persons have a right to be left free to do as they choose. The moral obligation not to interfere with a person follows from this right. That the obligation *follows* from the right is a clear indication of the priority of rights over obligations; that is, in this theory the obligation is derived from the right, not the other way around.

Many rights-based theories hold that rights form the justifying basis of obligations because they best express the purpose of morality, which is the securing of liberties or other benefits for a right-holder.[28] However, few rights-based theories *deny* the importance of obligations (or duties), which they regard as central to morality. They make this point by holding that there is a correlativity between obligations and rights: "*X* has a right to do or to have *Y*" means that the moral system of rules (or the legal system, if appropriate) imposes an obligation on someone to act or to refrain from acting so that *X* is enabled to do or have *Y*.[29]

These obligations are of two types: *negative obligations* are those that require that we not interfere with the liberty of others (thus securing liberty rights); *positive obligations* require that certain people or institutions provide benefits or services (thus securing benefit rights or welfare rights).[30] Correlatively, a *negative right* is a valid claim to liberty, that is, a right not to be interfered with, and a *positive right* is a valid claim on goods or services. The rights not to be beaten, subjected to unwanted surgery, or sold into slavery are examples of negative or liberty rights. Rights to food, medical care, and insurance are examples of positive or benefit rights.

The right to liberty is here said to be "negative" because no one has to act to honor it. Presumably, all that must be done is to leave people alone. The same is not true regarding positive rights; to honor these rights, someone has to provide something. For example, if a starving person has a human right to well-being, someone has an obligation to provide that person with food. As has often been pointed out, positive rights place an obligation to provide something on others, who can respond that this requirement interferes with their property rights to use their resources for their chosen ends. The distinction between positive and negative rights has often led those who would include various rights to well-being (to food, housing, health care, etc.) on the list of human rights to argue that the obligation to provide for positive rights falls on the political state. This distinction has intuitive appeal to many businesspersons, because they wish to limit both the responsibilities of their firms and the number of rights conflicts they must address. This point has recently become more compelling in light of the rise of theories of justice that address global poverty. Assuming, as the United Nations does, that humans have a fundamental right to have access to basic goods including housing, food, and health care, it can be argued that ensuring these rights to basic goods requires that coercive institutions such as governments, the World Health Organization, and the World Bank be designed to guarantee these rights to everyone.

A conflict involving negative rights is illustrated by the debate surrounding attempts by employers to control the lifestyle of their employees. Some employers will not accept employees who smoke. Some will not permit employees to engage in dangerous activities such as skydiving, auto racing, or mountain climbing. By making these rules, one can argue that employers are violating the liberty rights of the employees as well as the employees' right to privacy. Conversely, the employer can argue that he or she has a right to run the business as he or she sees fit. Thus, both sides invoke negative rights to make a moral case.

Theories of moral rights have not traditionally been a major focus of business ethics, but this situation is changing at present. For example, employees traditionally could be fired for what superiors considered disloyal conduct, and employees have had no right to "blow the whistle" on corporate misconduct. When members of minority groups complain about discriminatory hiring practices that violate their human dignity and self-respect, one plausible interpretation of these complaints is that those who register them believe that their moral rights are being infringed. Current theories of employee, consumer, and stockholder rights all provide frameworks for debates about rights within business ethics.

The language of moral rights is greeted by some with skepticism because of the apparently absurd proliferation of rights and the conflict among diverse claims to rights (especially in recent political debates). For example, some parties claim that a pregnant woman has a right to have an abortion, whereas others claim that fetuses have a right to life that precludes the right to have an abortion. As we shall see throughout this volume, rights language has been extended to include such controversial rights as the right to financial privacy, rights of workers to obtain various forms of information about their employer, the right to work in a pollution-free environment, the right to hold a job, and the right to health care.

Many writers in ethics now agree that a person can legitimately exercise a right to something only if sufficient justification exists—that is, when a right has an overriding status. Rights such as a right to equal economic opportunity, a right to do with one's property as one wishes, and a right to be saved from starvation may have to compete with other rights. The fact that rights theorists have failed to provide a hierarchy for rights claims may indicate that rights, like obligations, are not absolute moral demands but rather ones that can be overridden in particular circumstances by more stringent competing moral claims.

The idea of grounding duties or obligations in correlative rights is attractive to managers of many large global corporations because it provides a transcultural and transnational set of ethical norms that apply in all nations and can be used as the basis for uniform global corporate policies. For example, pharmaceutical companies that conduct research with human subjects in 30 countries would like to be able to apply the same moral rules in all 30 countries. Otherwise, chaos and inconsistency constantly threaten.

Because of this interest in human rights on the part of many global managers, but also because of vocal critics of some global business activities, the United Nations Working Group on the Methods and Activities of Transnational Corporations has produced "Draft Norms on the Responsibilities of Corporations and Other Business Enterprises with Respect to Human Rights." These draft norms articulate a list of rights and specify that corporations are responsible for their fulfilment. Once adapted, adherence to these norms on the part of corporations is to be monitored and verified by the UN (see Chapter 9).

## Virtue Ethics

Our discussion of utilitarian, Kantian, and rights-based theories has looked chiefly at obligations and rights. These theories do not typically emphasize the agents or actors who perform actions, have motives, and follow principles, yet people commonly make judgments about good and evil persons, their traits of character, and their willingness to perform actions. In recent years, several philosophers have proposed that ethics should redirect its preoccupation with principles of obligation, directive rules, and judgments of right and wrong and should look to decision making by persons of good character, that is, virtuous persons.

*Virtue ethics* descends from the classical Hellenistic tradition represented by Plato and Aristotle, in which the cultivation of a virtuous character is viewed as morality's primary function. Aristotle held that virtue is neither a feeling nor an innate capacity but a disposition bred from an innate capacity properly trained and exercised. People acquire virtues much as they do skills such as carpentry, playing a musical instrument, or cooking. They become just by performing just actions and become temperate by performing temperate actions. Virtuous character, says Aristotle, is neither natural nor unnatural; it is cultivated and made a part of the individual, much like a language or tradition.

But an ethics of virtue is more than habitual training. This approach relies even more than does Kant's theory on the importance of having a correct *motivational structure*. A just person, for example, has not only a psychological disposition to act fairly but also a morally appropriate desire to act justly. The person characteristically has a moral concern and reservation about acting in a way that would be unfair. Having only the motive to act in accordance with a rule of obligation (Kant's only demand) is not morally sufficient for virtue. Imagine a person who always performs his or her obligation because it is an obligation but who intensely dislikes having to allow the interests of others to be taken into account. Such a person does not cherish, feel congenial toward, or think fondly of others, and this person respects others only because obligation requires it. This person can, nonetheless, on a theory of moral obligation such as Kant's or Mill's, perform a morally right action, have an ingrained disposition to perform that action, and act with obligation as the foremost motive. The virtue theorist's criticism is that if the desire is not right, a necessary condition of virtue is lacking.

Consider an encounter you might have with a tire salesperson. You tell the salesperson that safety is most important and that you want to be sure to get an all-weather tire. He listens carefully and then sells you exactly what you want, because he has been well trained by his manager to see his primary obligation as that of meeting the customer's needs. Acting in this way has been deeply ingrained in this salesperson by his manager's training. There is no more typical encounter in the world of retail sales than this one. However, suppose now that we go behind the salesperson's behavior to his underlying motives and desires. We find that this man detests his job and hates having to spend time with every customer who comes through the door. He cares not at all about being of service to people or creating a better environment in the office. All he really wants is to watch the television set in the waiting lounge and to pick up his paycheck. Although this man meets his moral obligations, something in his character is morally defective.

When people engage in business or take jobs simply for the profit or wages that will result, they may meet their obligations and yet not be engaged in their work in a morally appropriate manner. However, if persons start a business because they believe in a quality product—a new, healthier yogurt, for example—and deeply desire to sell that product, their character is more in tune with our moral expectations. Entrepreneurs often exhibit this enthusiasm and commitment. For example, Apple Computer employees are genuinely excited about bringing new products to market in the belief that they greatly improve others' quality of life. The practice of business is morally better if it is sustained by persons whose character manifests enthusiasm, truthfulness, justice, compassion, respectfulness, and patience.

Interesting discussions in business ethics now center on the appropriate virtues of managers, employees, and other participants in business activity, as will be seen many times in this book. Among the many virtues that have been discussed are integrity, truthfulness, courage, and compassion. However, some alleged "virtues" of business life have been sharply contested in recent years; and various of these "virtues" of the businessperson have seemed not to be *moral* virtues at all. Competitiveness and toughness are two examples. *Fortune* has long published a list of the toughest bosses. For many years before he was fired as CEO of Sunbeam, Al Dunlap was perennially on the list. He had earned the nickname "Chainsaw Al" for his propensity to fire people and shut down plants even when they were marginally profitable. Dunlap made stock price and profitability the only worthy goals of a business enterprise. In his case business toughness was eventually judged a moral vice. This example suggests that some alleged business virtues may not turn out to be virtues at all.

There is another reason why virtue ethics may be important for business ethics. A morally good person with the right desires or motivations is more likely to understand what should be done, more likely to be motivated to perform required acts, and more likely to form and act on moral ideals than would a morally bad person. A person who is ordinarily trusted is one who has an ingrained motivation and desire to perform right actions and who characteristically cares about morally appropriate responses. A person who simply follows rules of obligation and who otherwise exhibits no special moral character may not be trustworthy. It is not the rule follower but the person disposed by *character* to be generous, caring, compassionate, sympathetic, and fair who should be the one recommended, admired, praised, and held up as a moral model. Many experienced businesspersons say that such trust is the moral cement of the business world.

Furthermore, studies indicate that for employees to take corporate ethics policies seriously, they need to perceive executives both as personally virtuous and as consistent enforcers of ethics policies throughout the organization.[31]

## Common-Morality Theories

Finally, some philosophers defend the view that there is a common morality that all people share by virtue of communal life and that this morality is ultimately the source of all theories of morality. This view is especially influential in contemporary biomedical ethics, an area of applied ethics that shares many topics of concern with business ethics.[32] According to this approach, virtually all people in all cultures grow up with an understanding of the basic demands of morality. Its norms are familiar and unobjectionable to those deeply committed to a moral life. They know not to lie, not to steal, to keep promises, to honor the rights of others, not to kill or cause harm to innocent persons, and the like. The *common morality* is simply the set of norms shared by all persons who are seriously committed to the objectives of morality. This morality is not merely *a* morality that differs from *other* moralities.[33] It is applicable to all persons in all places, and all human conduct is rightly judged by its standards.

The following are examples of *standards of action* (rules of obligation) in the common morality: 1. "Don't kill"; 2. "Don't cause pain or suffering to others" 3. "Prevent evil or harm from occurring" and 4. "Tell the truth." There are also many examples of *moral character traits* (virtues) recognized in the common morality, including (1) nonmalevolence, (2) honesty, (3) integrity, and (4) conscientiousness. These virtues are universally admired traits of character, and a person is regarded as deficient in moral character if he or she lacks such traits.

The thesis that there are universal moral standards is rooted in (1) a theory of the objectives of the social institution of morality and (2) a hypothesis about the sorts of norms that are required to achieve those objectives. Philosophers such as Thomas Hobbes and David Hume pointed out that centuries of experience demonstrate that the human condition tends to deteriorate into misery, confusion, violence, and distrust unless norms such as those listed earlier—the norms of the common morality—are observed. These norms prevent or minimize the threat of social deterioration.

It would be an overstatement to maintain that these norms are necessary for the *survival* of a society (as various philosophers and social scientists have maintained),[34] but it is not too much to claim that these norms are necessary to *ameliorate or counteract the tendency for the quality of people's lives to worsen or for social relationships to disintegrate.*[35] In every well-functioning society norms are in place to prohibit lying, breaking promises, causing bodily harm, stealing, commiting fraud, taking of life, neglecting children, failing to keep contracts, and the like.[36] These norms are what they are, and not some other set of norms, because they have proven that they successfully achieve the objectives of morality. This success in the service of human flourishing accounts for their moral authority, and there is no more basic explanation of or justification for their moral authority. Thus, defenders of common morality maintain that there is no *philosophical* ethical theory that uproots or takes priority over the common morality; indeed, all philosophical theories start out from an understanding of the common morality and build a theory on top of this understanding.

These theories do not assume that every person accepts the norms in the common morality. It would be implausible to maintain that all persons in all societies do in fact accept moral norms. Unanimity is not the issue. Many amoral, immoral, or selectively moral persons do not care about or identify with various demands of the common morality. Some persons are morally weak; others are morally depraved. It would also be implausible to hold that a *customary* set of norms or a *consensus* set of norms in a society qualifies, as such, for inclusion in the *common* morality. The notion that moral justification is ultimately grounded in the customs and consensus agreements of particular groups is a moral travesty. Any given society's customary or consensus position may be a distorted outlook that functions to block awareness of common-morality requirements. Some societies are in the influential grip of leaders who promote religious zealotries or political ideologies that depart profoundly from the common morality.

From the perspective of those who emphasize the common morality, only universally valid norms warrant our making intercultural and cross-cultural judgments about moral depravity, morally misguided beliefs, savage cruelty, and other moral failures. If we did not have recourse to universal norms, we could not make basic distinctions between moral and immoral behavior and therefore could not be positioned to criticize even outrageous human actions, some of which are themselves proclaimed in the name of morality. This takes us to the subject of how *particular* moralities are viewed in common-morality theories.

Many justifiable moral norms are particular to cultures, groups, and even individuals. The common morality contains only general moral standards. Its norms are abstract, universal, and content thin. Particular moralities tend to be the reverse: concrete, nonuniversal, and content rich. These moralities may contain norms that are often comprehensive and detailed. Business ethics, and indeed all professional ethics, are examples of particular moralities. Many examples are found in codes of professional practice, institutional codes of ethics, government regulations, and the like.

Business ethics is fundamentally an attempt to make the moral life specific and practical. The reason why the norms of business ethics in particular cultures often differ from those of another culture is that the abstract starting points in the common morality can be coherently applied in a variety of ways to create norms that take the form of specific guidelines, institutional and public policies, and conflict resolutions. Universal norms are simply not appropriate instruments to determine practice or policy or to resolve conflicts unless they are made sufficiently specific to take account of financial constraints, social efficiency, cultural pluralism, political procedures, uncertainty about risk, and the like.

General moral norms must be *specified* to make them sufficiently concrete so that they can function as practical guidelines in particular contexts. Specification is not a process of producing general norms such as those in the common morality; it assumes that they are already available. Specification reduces the indeterminateness and abstractness of general norms to give them increased action-guiding capacity, without loss of the moral commitments in the original norm(s).[37] For example, the norm that we must "respect the autonomous judgment of competent persons" cannot, unless it is specified, handle complicated problems of whether workers have a right to know about potential dangers in a chemical plant. This will have to be specified in light of the dangers in the plant (or in that type of plant). The process of specification will have to become increasingly concrete as new problems emerge. That is, even already specified rules, guidelines, policies, and codes will almost always have to be specified further to handle new or unanticipated circumstances.

As defenders of the common morality theory see it, this is the way business ethics actually works, and it is through this progressive specification that we retain the common morality and make moral progress by creating new norms. The common morality can be extended as far as we need to extend it to meet practical objectives. There is, of course, always the possibility of developing more than one line of specification when confronting practical problems and moral disagreements. It is to be expected—indeed, it is unavoidable—that different persons and groups will offer conflicting specifications to resolve conflicts or vagueness. In any given problematic or dilemmatic case, several competing specifications may be offered by reasonable and fair-minded parties, all of whom are serious about maintaining fidelity to the common morality.

For example, many international organizations and multinational corporations are currently struggling with the nature of their obligations to protect the privacy of patient, client, and customer records. A striking example is the problem of how to rewrite rules of privacy in the Swiss banking system, which has been undergoing massive changes in its understanding of obligations to supply information to third parties. It is apparent that there are many sincere attempts in Switzerland and elsewhere to address this issue and that obligations of disclosure and privacy will be expressed differently in different institutions. There is no reason to think that only one set of privacy-protection rules is justifiable.

This diversity does not distress defenders of a common-morality theory, because they believe that all that we can ask of moral agents is that they impartially and faithfully specify the norms of the common morality with an eye to overall moral coherence.

Another challenge to common-morality theory comes from those who argue that reasonable people from disparate cultures *disagree* about what constitutes the common morality itself and that there are therefore a variety of different and inconsistent common moralities.[38] This particular criticism is not compelling, however, because it has never been shown and even seems inconceivable that some morally committed cultures do not accept rules against lying, breaking promises, stealing, and the like. This is what would have to be shown to prove that common-morality theories do not hold universally.

However, critics of common-morality theories also point out that although the hypothesis that there is a common morality is testable, common-morality theorists have not provided compelling evidence in support of their claims. In reply to the latter criticism, common-morality theorists tend to acknowledge the point and state that such research is needed, though very difficult to conduct.

## A Prologue to Theories of Justice

The concluding chapter of this book focuses on justice in relation to business. Many rules and principles form the terms of cooperation in society. Society is laced with implicit and explicit arrangements and agreements under which individuals are obligated to cooperate or abstain from interfering with others. Philosophers are interested in the justice of these terms of cooperation. They pose questions such as these: What gives one person or group of people the right to expect cooperation from another person or group of people in some societal interchange (especially an economic one) if the former benefit and the latter do not? Is it just for some citizens to have more property than others? Is it fair for one person to gain an economic advantage over another, if both abide strictly by existing societal rules?

In their attempts to answer such questions, some philosophers believe that diverse human judgments and beliefs about justice can be brought into systematic unity through a general theory of justice. Justice has been analyzed differently, however, in rival and often incompatible theories. Some features of these general normative theories of justice are treated in Chapter 10. Here we need note only that a key distinction between just *procedures* and just *results* exists in the literature on justice.

Ideally, it is preferable to have both, but this is not always possible. For example, a person might achieve a just result in redistributing wealth but might use an unjust procedure to achieve that result, such as undeserved taxation of certain groups. By contrast, just procedures sometimes eventuate in unjust results, as when a fair trial finds an innocent person guilty. Some writers in business ethics are concerned with issues of procedural justice when they discuss such concerns as the use of ombudsmen, grievance procedures, peer review, and arbitration procedures.

Many problems of justice that a cooperative society must handle involve some system or set of procedures that foster, but do not ensure, just outcomes. Once there is agreement on appropriate procedures, the outcome must be accepted as just, even if it produces inequalities that seem unjust by other standards. If procedural justice is the best that can be attained—as, for example, is claimed in the criminal justice system—society should accept the results of its system with a certain amount of humility and perhaps make allowances for inevitable inequalities and even inequities and misfortunes.

In the age of globalization, questions of global justice have been given more attention by political philosophers. The facts that inspire much contemporary work on global justice are well known. Nearly 1 billion people are malnourished and without access to safe drinking water, and 50,000 humans die each day owing to poverty related causes. Additionally, increases in global warming, caused primarily by a long history of disproportionate carbon emissions per capita by industrialized nations, are expected to worsen the situation of the world's poorest people over the next century.

Political philosophers are attempting to work out the obligations of the world's advantaged peoples to the world's poorest peoples. One common view taken by many economists is that rapid economic liberalization in the interest of job creation in the world's poorest nations is the best means of promoting a just global distribution of wealth. In reply, many theorists of global justice argue that rapid economic liberalization by itself may be insufficient or may introduce more problems than it solves. So-called Cosmopolitan theorists argue instead for adherence to careful economic development strategies that adhere to core ethical norms such as basic human rights. More recently, they have also begun to argue for an ethical obligation to reduce carbon emissions to curb climate change. (In addition to Chapter 10, these issues are addressed in Chapters 7, 8, and 9.)

## The Moral Point of View[39]

A student whose first introduction to moral philosophy is this introductory chapter would not be unjustified in feeling a little frustrated at this point. "How," one might ask, "am I supposed to decide which of the normative theories presented thus far— utilitarianism, Kantian ethics, rights theory, virtue ethics, and common-morality theory— is the most appropriate basis for making sound ethical decisions regarding business decisions?" This is a reasonable concern. Our response is threefold. First, moral philosophy is a 2,500-year-old tradition. It is not surprising that there should be a significant body of work that merits careful attention. To ignore or downplay this tradition would impoverish any discussion of the ethical practice of business. Second, not all these theories are incompatible. Although some of these views, most notably the Kantian and utilitarian traditions, seem to stand in opposition to one another, other views are more compatible. For example, Kant recognized and discussed at length the importance of the virtues in the life of moral agents, and common morality theories welcome the idea of universally important virtues. Scholars are now beginning to pay more attention to Kant's writings on virtue as well as to the compatibility of virtue theory with a number of other kinds of theory. So too, many of the most prominent rights theories can be grounded in various theories of obligation, including both Kantian ethics and rule utilitarianism. So we can see that several types of theories—or *elements* of the theories such as justice, nonmalevolence, honesty, or integrity—may be compatible. Different theorists tend to emphasize different ideas, but at least in the case of these views, we can see that a resourceful student of ethics will be able to draw some elements from each view without falling into inconsistency.

The third response is more complicated. All the theories discussed in this chapter share certain elements that could be referred to as the right attitude to take in ethics. This is often referred to as "the moral point of view." When we take the moral point of view, we seek to adjudicate disputes rationally; we take an appropriately impartial stance; we assume that other persons are neither more nor less important than ourselves (so that our own claims will be considered alongside and not above those of others). These components of the moral point of view are respectively concerned with rationality, impartiality, and universalizability.

The moral point of view is *rational* in the sense that it involves the application of reason rather than feeling or mere inclination. This is not to denigrate the great importance of the moral emotions and sentiments (e.g., love, devotion, and compassion), but moral issues also frequently invoke unwarranted emotional responses in individuals. The attempt to justify a moral stance by appeal to reasons that may be publicly considered and evaluated by other persons facilitates a process whereby individuals with distinctly different emotional responses to a moral issue may seek mutual understanding and, perhaps, agreement. In business the fact that one person wields more economic power than another person cannot by itself outweigh the needs for both parties to offer a rational basis for their competing moral perspectives.

The moral point of view is *universal* in the sense that the principles or propositions ascertained therefrom apply to all persons and to all relevantly similar circumstances. Thus, if a moral principle or proposition is valid, no persons are exempt from its strictures. The notion of universalizability has particular relevance in the era of economic globalization. It requires that we regard all persons as equal in dignity and as such that we respect them in our business dealings wherever they may live or work. It is not reasonable to expect highly concrete and practical standards that are universal (e.g., "Don't permit the lobbying of political officials"), but it is hoped that the basic principles on which such concrete rules are erected can be shown to apply to all persons (e.g., "Avoid conflicts of interest").

The moral point of view is *impartial* in the sense that a moral judgment is formed without regard to particular advantaging or disadvantaging properties of persons. Moral judgments are formed behind what John Rawls has called the "veil of ignorance": A judgment should be formed without regard to the particular fortuitous advantages or disadvantages of persons such as special talents or handicaps, because these properties are morally arbitary. The ideal, then, is an unbiased evaluation without regard to a person's race, sex, nationality, and economic circumstances, which cannot be regarded as legitimate bases for treating persons differently from other persons. Impartiality is important in many business contexts, including human resource management, where such considerations may interfere with the fair evaluation, promotion, or dismissal of employees.

This understanding of the moral point of view does not exclude *partiality* as if it were illicit. Favoring the interests of one party over another is justified when there are overriding reasons for ranking the specific interests of one party over another. Such partiality is most likely to occur in contexts of familial, professional, or contractual responsibilities.

This point is of obvious importance to business managers who must discharge distinct moral and legal obligations to their employers. The challenge of the ethical manager is to determine when the interests of his or her employers trump those of other stakeholders, and when the interests of those stakeholders override the interests of his or her employers.

To sum up, a business organization that is solely guided by economic considerations is an amoral or unethical organization. The ethical organization, in contrast, is one in which managers and employees alike recognize the importance of moral considerations in their everyday business activities, as well as in their strategic planning, and act accordingly.

## NOTES

1. Dana Milbank, "Hiring Welfare People, Hotel Chain Finds, Is Tough but Rewarding," *Wall Street Journal* (October 31, 1996), pp. A1–A2.
2. Robert Lindsey, "Ancient Redwood Trees Fall to a Wall Street Takeover," *New York Times* (March 2, 1988).
3. Dustin Block, "He Had a Bud Light; Now He Doesn't Have a Job," *Journal Times* (February 9, 2007).
4. Insurance Information Institute, "Asbestos Liability" (New York, January 15, 2003): www.iii.org/media/hottopics/insurance/asbestos/; and Mark D. Plevin et al. "Where Are They Now, Part 3: A Continuing History of the Companies That Have Sought Bankruptcy Protection Due to Asbestos Claims," *Mealey's Asbestos Bankruptcy Report* 5, no. 4 (November, 2005); updated on February 2, 2007, and available at http://www.crowell.com/pdf/AsbestosChart1.pdf
5. Taken from Peter Huber, "The Press Gets Off Easy in Tort Law," *Wall Street Journal* (July 24, 1985), editorial page.
6. U.S. Supreme Court, *Arthur Andersen LLP v. United States,* No. 04-368; and Charles Lane, "Justices Overturn Andersen Conviction," *Washington Post* (June 01, 2005), p. A1.

7. "Principle Sale," *Wall Street Journal* (May 22, 1985), p. 35.

8. Jeff Immelt, "Global Environmental Challenges." Lecture delivered at George Washington School of Business (Washington, DC, May 9, 2005).

9. Alex Berenson, "For Merck Chief, Credibility at the Capitol," *New York Times* (November 19, 2004), p. C1; and John Simons and David Stipp, "Will Merck Survive Vioxx?" *Fortune* (November 1, 2004), pp. 91–104. See also Roy Vagelos and Louis Galambos, *The Moral Corporation: Merck Experiences* (Cambridge: Cambridge University Press, 2006).

10. Thomas Hobbes, *Leviathan*, pt. 1, chap. 13, par. 9.

11. Smith's economic work focused primarily on businesses such as sole proprietorships and small companies and almost not at all on corporations or what he called "joint stock companies." Although a few joint stock companies existed in his time, he could hardly have imagined the economic dominance and power of modern corporations in the twenty-first century. For this reason, caution is in order when one applies Smith's views to modern economic relations. See Adam Smith, *An Inquiry into the Nature and the Causes of the Wealth of Nations* (Indianapolis, IN: Liberty Fund, 1981). See, especially, vol. 2, bk. 5, chap. 1, pt. 3.

12. This thesis is argued (without reference to philosophical theories of egoism) by Wolfgang Sauer, "Also a Concrete Self-Interest," *United Nations Chronicle* (issue on "Global Sustainable Development: The Corporate Responsibility"), online edition (2002): www.un.org/pubs/chronicle/2002/issue3.

13. Smith's classic work on the subject is *The Theory of Moral Sentiments* (Indianapolis, IN: Liberty Fund, 1982) the sixth and final edition of which appeared in 1790 shortly before his death.

14. For an act-utilitarian example in business ethics, see R. M. Hare, "Commentary on Beauchamp's Manipulative Advertising," *Business and Professional Ethics Journal* 3 (1984): 23–28; for a rule-utilitarian example, see Robert Almeder, "In Defense of Sharks: Moral Issues in Hostile Liquidating Takeovers," *Journal of Business Ethics* 10 (1991): 471–84.

15. Tom L. Beauchamp, ed., *Case Studies in Business, Society, and Ethics*, 5th ed. (Upper Saddle River, NJ: Prentice Hall, 2004), chap. 3.

16. CNN.com (Sept. 3, 1999), "Online Shoppers Bid Millions for Human Kidney."

17. Madhav Goyal et al., "Economic and Health Consequences of Selling a Kidney in India," *Journal of the American Medical Association* 288 (October 2, 2002): 1589–93.

18. For discussion of these issues see Mark J. Cherry, *Kidney for Sale: Human Organs, Transplantation, and the Market* (Washington D.C.: Georgetown University Press, 2005).

19. Mary Schlangenstein, "Workers Chip In to Help Southwest Employees Offer Free Labor," *Seattle Times* (September 26, 2001), p. E1.

20. Motorola, "Code of Business Conduct" (revised September 29, 2004). Available at http://www.motorola.com/content.jsp?globalObjectId=75-107

21. For a defense of a similar view see James S. Taylor, *Stakes and Kidneys: Why Markets in Human Body Parts are Morally Imperative* (Burlington, VT: Ashgate Publishing Co, 2005).

22. See Jennifer Hull, "Unocal Sues Bank," *Wall Street Journal* (March 13, 1985), p. 22; and Charles McCoy, "Mesa Petroleum Alleges Unocal Coerced Banks," *Wall Street Journal* (March 22, 1985), p. 6.

23. See David S. Hilzenrath, "Taking Aim at Insider Bank Deals," *Washington Post* (September 30, 1991), Washington Business sec., p. 1.

24. Ralph King, "Insider Loans: Everyone Was Doing It," Business 2.0: www.business2. com/articles/mag (as posted January 15, 2003).

25. Reuters, "Ex-CEO Pleads Guilty in Backdating Probe," *Los Angeles Times* (February 15, 2007).

26. For a landmark agreement on the island of Saipan (a class action settlement), see *Legal Intelligencer* 227, no. 64 (September 30, 2002), National News Section, p. 4.

27. Ronald Dworkin argues that political morality is rights-based in *Taking Rights Seriously* (London: Duckworth, 1977), p. 171. John Mackie has applied this thesis to *morality generally* in "Can There Be a Right-Based Moral Theory?" *Midwest Studies in Philosophy* 3 (1978): esp. p. 350. Henry Shue has defended this view as it applies to foreign policy and development in *Basic Rights: Subsistence, Affluence, and U.S. Foreign Policy,* 2nd ed. (Princeton: Princeton University Press, 1996). See further Judith Jarvis Thomson, *The Realm of Rights* (Cambridge, MA: Harvard University Press, 1990), 122ff.

28. See further Alan Gewirth, "Why Rights Are Indispensable," *Mind* 95 (1986): 333, and Gewirth's later book, *The Community of Rights* (Chicago: University of Chicago Press, 1996).

29. See David Braybrooke, "The Firm but Untidy Correlativity of Rights and Obligations," *Canadian Journal of Philosophy* 1 (1972): 351–63; and Carl P. Wellman, *Real Rights* (New York: Oxford University Press, 1995).

30. See the treatment of these distinctions in Eric Mack, ed., *Positive and Negative Duties* (New Orleans: Tulane University Press, 1985).

31. Linda Klebe Trevino and Michael E. Brown, "Managing to Be Ethical: Debunking Five Business Ethics Myths," *Academy of Management Executive* 18 (2004): 69–81.

32. See, for example, Tom L. Beauchamp and James F. Childress, *Principles of Biomedical Ethics*, 6th ed. (New York: Oxford University Press, 2008), esp. chap. 10; and Bernard Gert, Charles M. Culver, and Danner K. Clouser, *Bioethics: A Return to Fundamentals* (New York: Oxford University Press, 1997).

33. Although there is only a single, universal common morality, there is more than one theory of the common morality. The common morality is universally shared; it is not a theory of what is universally shared. For examples of diverse theories of the common morality, see Alan Donagan, *The Theory of Morality* (Chicago: University of Chicago Press, 1977); Gert, Culver, and Clouser, *Bioethics: A Return to Fundamentals*; and W. D. Ross, *The Foundations of Ethics* (Oxford: Oxford University Press, 1939).

34. See Sissela Bok, *Common Values* (Columbia: University of Missouri Press, 1995), 13–23, 50–59. She cites a body of influential writers on the subject.

35. Compare the arguments in G. J. Warnock, *The Object of Morality* (London: Methuen, 1971), esp. 15–26; John Mackie, *Ethics: Inventing Right and Wrong* (London: Penguin, 1977), 107ff.

36. Such norms are referred to as "hypernorms" by Thomas Donaldson and Thomas Dunfee. See their *Ties That Bind: A Social Contracts Approach to Business Ethics* (Cambridge, MA: Harvard Business School Press, 1999). Donaldson and Dunfee's social contracts approach to business ethics is influential among social science scholars but less so among philosophers and practitioners.

37. See Henry Richardson, "Specifying Norms as a Way to Resolve Concrete Ethical Problems," *Philosophy and Public Affairs* 19 (1990): 279–310; Richardson, "Specifying, Balancing, and Interpreting Bioethical Principles," *Journal of Medicine and Philosophy* 25 (2000): 285–307.

38. See, for example, Leigh Turner, "Zones of Consensus and Zones of Conflict: Questioning the 'Common Morality' Presumption in Bioethics," *Kennedy Institute of Ethics*

*Journal* 13, no. 3 (2003): 193–218; and Turner, "An Anthropological Exploration of Contemporary Bioethics: The Varieties of Common Sense," *Journal of Medical Ethics* 24 (1998): 127–33; David DeGrazia, "Common Morality, Coherence, and the Principles of Biomedical Ethics, *Kennedy Institute of Ethics Journal* 13 (2003): 219–30; Ronald A. Lindsay, "Slaves, Embryos, and Nonhuman Animals: Moral Status and the Limitations of Common Morality Theory," *Kennedy Institute of Ethics Journal* 15, no. 4 (December 2005): 323–46.

39. Elements of this section are excepted and reprinted with the permission of the publisher from Denis G. Arnold, "Moral Reasoning, Human Rights, and Global Labor Practices," in *Rising Above Sweatshops: Innovative Approaches to Global Labor Challenges* (Westport, CT: Praeger, 2003).

# Chapter 2

# The Purpose of the Corporation

## INTRODUCTION

THIS CHAPTER FOCUSES on corporate social responsibility. The socially responsible corporation is the good corporation. Over 2,000 years ago the Greeks thought they could answer questions about the goodness of things by knowing about the purpose of things. These Greek philosophers provided a functional analysis of good. For example, if one determines what a good racehorse is by knowing the purpose of racehorses (to win races) and the characteristics—for instance, speed, agility, and discipline—horses must have to win races, then a good racehorse is speedy, agile, and disciplined. To adapt the Greeks' method of reasoning, one determines what a good (socially responsible) corporation is by investigating the purpose corporations should serve in society.

## STOCKHOLDER MANAGEMENT VERSUS STAKEHOLDER MANAGEMENT

For many, the view that the purpose of the corporation is to make a profit for stockholders is beyond debate and is accepted as a matter of fact. The classical U.S. view that a corporation's primary and perhaps sole purpose is to maximize profits for stockholders is most often associated with the Nobel Prize–winning economist Milton Friedman. This chapter presents arguments for and against the Friedmanite view that the purpose of a corporation is to maximize stockholder profits.

Friedman has two main arguments for his position. First, stockholders are the *owners* of the corporation, and hence corporate profits *belong* to the stockholders. Managers are agents of the stockholders and have a moral obligation to manage the firm in the interest of the stockholders, that is, to maximize shareholder wealth. If the management of a firm donates some of the firm's income to charitable organizations, it is seen as an illegitimate use of stockholders' money. If individual stockholders wish to donate their dividends to charity, they are free to do so, since the money is theirs. But managers have no right to donate corporate funds to charity. If society decides that private charity is insufficient to meet the needs of the poor, to maintain art museums, and to finance research for curing diseases, it is the responsibility of government to raise the necessary money through taxation. It should not come from managers purportedly acting on behalf of the corporation.

Second, stockholders are entitled to their profits as a result of a contract among the corporate stakeholders. A product or service is the result of the productive efforts of a number of parties—employees, managers, customers, suppliers, the local community, and the stockholders. Each of these stakeholder groups has a contractual relationship with the firm. In return for their services, the managers and employees are paid in the form of wages; the local community is paid in the form of taxes; and suppliers, under the constraints of supply and demand, negotiate the return for their products directly with the firm. Funds remaining after these payments have been made represent profit, and by agreement the profit belongs to the stockholders. The stockholders bear the risk when they supply the capital, and profit is the contractual return they receive for risk taking. Thus each party in the manufacture and sale of a product receives the remuneration it has freely agreed to.

Friedman believes that these voluntary contractual arrangements maximize economic freedom and that economic freedom is a necessary condition for political freedom. Political rights gain efficacy in a capitalist system. For example, private employers are forced by competitive pressures to be concerned primarily with a prospective employee's ability to produce rather than with that person's political views. Opposing voices are heard in books, in the press, or on television so long as there is a profit to be made. Finally, the existence of capitalist markets limits the number of politically based decisions and thus increases freedom. Even democratic decisions coerce the opposing minority. Once society votes on how much to spend for defense or for city streets, the minority must go along. In the market, each consumer can decide how much of a product or service he or she is willing to purchase. Thus Friedman entitled his book defending the classical view of the purpose of the firm *Capitalism and Freedom.*

The classical view that a corporation's primary responsibility is to seek stockholder profit is embodied in the legal opinion *Dodge v. Ford Motor Company* included in this chapter. The Court ruled that the benefits of higher salaries for Ford workers and the benefits of lower auto prices to consumers must not take priority over stockholder interests. According to *Dodge*, the interests of the stockholder are supreme.

Some have criticized Friedman on the grounds that his view justifies anything that will lead to the maximization of profits including acting immorally or illegally if the manager can get away with it. We think that criticism of Friedman is unfair. In his classic article reprinted in this chapter Friedman says:

> In such a society, "there is one and only one social responsibility of business—to use its resources and engage in activities designed to increase its profit so long as it stays within the rules of the game, which is to say, engages in open and free competition without deception or fraud." (1970, p. 126)

Thus, the manager may not do anything to maximize profits. Friedman's arguments presume the existence of a robust democracy in which citizens determine the rules of the game, and businesses do not unduly influence the process by which those rules are determined. Unfortunately, Friedman never fully elaborated on what the rules of the game in a capitalist economy are. And some of his followers have argued for tactics that strike many as unethical. For example, Theodore Levitt has argued in defense of deceptive advertising[1] and in favor of strong industry lobbying to have the government pass laws that are favorable to business and to reject laws that are unfavorable.[2] And Albert Carr has argued that business is like the game of poker and thus, just as in poker, behavior that is unethical in everyday life is justified in business.[3] (Carr does admit that just as in poker there are some moral norms for business.)

Others have criticized Friedman on the grounds that the manager should use employees, customers, and suppliers as mere tools if by doing so he can generate profit. Thus, if wages can be cut to generate profit, they should be cut. Theoretically, that may indeed follow from Friedman's view, and some managers and CEOs even behave that way. But as a practical matter, the manager usually can generate profits only if she treats employees, customers, and suppliers well—thus the expression "close to the customer" and books such as Jeffery Pfeiffer's *Competitive Advantage Through People* and Frederick F. Reichheld's book *The Loyalty Effect.* In 1953, the legal system acknowledged the connection between corporate philanthropy and goodwill. In the case of *A.P. Smith Manufacturing v. Barlow et al.* a charitable contribution to Princeton University was deemed to be a legitimate exercise of management authority. In the appeals case reprinted in this chapter, Judge Jacobs recognized that an act that supports the public welfare can also be in the best interest of the corporation itself. The implication of this discussion is that in terms of behavior there may be no discernible difference between an "enlightened" Friedmanite and a manager who holds to the view that the purpose of the corporation involves more than the maximization of profit. The difference, to put it in a Kantian context, is in the motive. The enlightened Friedmanite treats employees well in order to generate profit. The non-Friedmanite treats employees well because that is one of the things a corporation is supposed to do.

Nearly all business ethicists concur with the general public that one of the purposes of a publicly held firm is to make a profit, and thus making a profit is an obligation of the firm. Although many people also believe that the managers of publicly held corporations are legally required to maximize the profits for stockholders, this is not strictly true. Even in the most traditional interpretation managers have a fiduciary obligation to the corporation, which is then interpreted as a fiduciary obligation to stockholder interests. But during the merger and acquisition craze of the 1980s, several states passed laws permitting the managers to take into account the needs of the other stakeholders. Indiana was one of the first states to do so, and many other states followed. Other countries are even less enamored with the Friedman model. The London Stock Exchange has endorsed the Turnbull Committee report and as a result all companies listed on the London Stock Exchange will have to take into account "environment, reputation, business probity issues" when implementing internal controls.[4]

Although managers may not be obligated to maximize profits, they certainly do have an obligation to avoid conflicts of interest where it appears that they benefit at the expense of the stockholders. Many groups that defend stockholder rights are legitimately concerned with serious issues of corporate governance. Such issues as excessive executive pay, especially when it is not linked to performance, overly generous stock options, and golden parachutes in case of a hostile takeover and even friendly mergers have all legitimately come under scrutiny.

Concerns about these issues reached a pinnacle in 2002 as a wave of corporate scandals including Enron, Arthur Andersen, and WorldCom swept across the United States. Federal legislation and revised industry standards have led to reform in the area of corporate governance, but the success of these reforms remains to be determined. And some issues such as excessive executive compensation need further attention.

Stockholders need to be concerned about more than conflicts of interest. Managers like to keep information secret as well. Even if a case can be made for charitable contributions on the part of corporations, it would seem that stockholders have a right to know which charities receive corporate funds. But corporations have opposed a law that would require disclosing such information to shareholders.[5]

An alternative way to understand the purpose of the corporation is to consider those affected by business decisions, who are referred to as corporate stakeholders. From the stakeholders' perspective, the classical view is problematic in that all emphasis is placed on one stakeholder—the stockholder. The interests of the other stakeholders are unfairly subordinated to the stockholders' interests. Although any person or group affected by corporate decisions is a stakeholder, most stakeholder analysis has focused on a special group of stakeholders: namely, members of groups whose existence was necessary for the firm's survival. Traditionally, six stakeholder groups have been identified: stockholders, employees, customers, managers, suppliers, and the local community. Managers who manage from the stakeholder perspective see their task as harmonizing the legitimate interests of the primary corporate stakeholders. In describing stakeholder management, R. Edward Freeman argues that managers have an ethical responsibility to manage the organization for all stakeholders.

Both in corporate and academic circles, stakeholder terminology has become very fashionable. For example, many corporate codes of conduct are organized around stakeholder principles.

However, many theoretical problems remain. Stakeholder theory is still in its early developmental stage. Much has been said of the obligations of managers to the other corporate stakeholders, but little has been said about the obligations of the other stakeholders, for instance, the community or employees, to the corporation. Do members of a community have an obligation to consider the moral reputation of a company when they make their purchasing decisions? Do employees have an obligation to stay with a company that has invested in their training even if they could get a slightly better salary by moving to another corporation?

Perhaps the most pressing problems for stakeholder theory are to specify in more detail the rights and responsibilities that each stakeholder group has and to suggest how the conflicting rights and responsibilities among the stakeholder groups can be resolved.

## WHICH VIEW IS BETTER?

Is the Friedmanite view that the purpose of the firm is to maximize profits or the stakeholder view that the firm is to be managed in the interests of the various stakeholders more adequate? In his article John Boatright presents additional difficulties for the stakeholder position.

Boatright concedes that the purpose of the firm is to benefit every stakeholder group. However, he argues that management decision making is an inefficient means of protecting the interests of nonshareholder stakeholders and that a system of corporate governance marked by shareholder primacy better serves the interests of all stakeholders. Such a system of governance, he believes, most efficiently maximizes the welfare of all stakeholder groups. As Boatright points out, stockholders have been given special attention because lawmakers have believed it was in the public interest to do so. Despite his generally negative assessment of stakeholder theory, Boatright argues that the theory actually complements the stockholder view in two ways. First, it reminds managers that they have an obligation to correct for such things as market failures and externalities to ensure that markets work as they should to produce benefits for all. Second, stakeholder management can be seen as a guide for the ethical management of the firm rather than as an alternative system of corporate governance.

What is one to conclude with respect to this dispute? It seems that stockholders are in a special relationship with respect to profits, but the relationship is not so special as has been traditionally thought. Moreover, it may not even be in the public interest to retain the traditional idea about the preeminence of the stockholder. Critics have argued that U.S. managers are forced to manage to please Wall Street, which means they are forced to manage for the short term. And these critics have gone on to argue that the focus on the short term has led to inordinate cutbacks in employees and frayed relationships with top managers of corporations and the rank and file. However, if a shift is made to consider long-term profitability, then there is a greater likelihood that in terms of managerial behavior, the stockholder theory and the stakeholder theory will coincide.

The concluding article in this chapter by Wayne Cascio compares the management of Sam's Club, a warehouse retailer that is part of Wal-Mart, and its competitor Costco. Wal-Mart and Sam's Club are famous for low prices that make products affordable for customers who lack ample financial resources. However, Wal-Mart has come under sustained criticism in recent years for allegedly unfair and illegal labor practices such as underpayment of earnings, sexual discrimination against women, the use of illegal alien workers, and transferring the burden of employee health-care costs to taxpayers. Cascio points out that Costco is an aggressive and highly successful competitor to Wal-Mart. Over a 5-year period ending in 2006 Costco's stock rose 55 percent while Wal-Mart's declined 10 percent. At the same time, Costco was taking extraordinarily good care of its employees and customers and had excellent relationships with other stakeholders. Cascio argues that if Costco can be profitable while ensuring that all its stakeholders are treated well, Wal-Mart should be able to do the same.

It can be argued that as a practical matter there may not be a great difference between stockholder governance and stakeholder governance. Even charitable giving and the attempt by corporations to solve social problems can be defended on Friedmanite grounds. In the twin cities of Minneapolis/St. Paul, it is believed that Target maintains a competitive advantage over Wal-Mart because of the former's reputation for charitable activities. What distinguishes a Friedmanite from a stakeholder theorist is the motivation a manager has for considering stakeholder interests. The Friedmanite treats stakeholders well to make a profit, whereas the stakeholder theorist treats stakeholders well because it is the right thing to do. Paradoxically, treating stakeholders well because it is right may end up being more profitable. In 1987 the Dayton Hudson Corporation was able to avoid a hostile takeover by the Hafts because the Minnesota legislature intervened to protect a good corporate citizen.

## NOTES

1. Theodore Levitt, "The Morality (?) of Advertising," *Harvard Business Review* (July–August, 1970): 84–92.
2. Theodore Levitt, "The Dangers of Social Responsibility," *Harvard Business Review* (September–October, 1958): 41–50.
3. Albert Z. Carr, "Is Business Bluffing Ethical?" *Harvard Business Review* (January–February, 1968): 143–53.
4. *Ethical Performance*, 1 (1999).
5. Adam Bryant, "Companies Oppose Idea of Disclosing Charitable Giving," *New York Times* (April 3, 1998).

STOCKHOLDER MANAGEMENT VERSUS STAKEHOLDER MANAGEMENT

# The Social Responsibility of Business Is to Increase Its Profits

*Milton Friedman*

When I hear businessmen speak eloquently about the "social responsibilities of business in a free-enterprise system," I am reminded of the wonderful line about the Frenchman who discovered at the age of 70 that he had been speaking prose all his life. The businessmen believe that they are defending free enterprise when they declaim that business is not concerned "merely" with profit but also with promoting desirable "social" ends; that business has a "social conscience" and takes seriously its responsibilities for providing employment, eliminating discrimination, avoiding pollution and whatever else may be the catchwords of the contemporary crop of reformers. In fact they are—or would be if they or anyone else took them seriously—preaching pure and unadulterated socialism. Businessmen who talk this way are unwitting puppets of the intellectual forces that have been undermining the basis of a free society these past decades.

The discussions of the "social responsibilities of business" are notable for their analytical looseness and lack of rigor. What does it mean to say that "business" has responsibilities? Only people can have responsibilities. A corporation is an artificial person and in this sense may have artificial responsibilities, but "business" as a whole cannot be said to have responsibilities, even in this vague sense. The first step toward clarity in examining the doctrine of the social responsibility of business is to ask precisely what it implies for whom.

Presumably, the individuals who are to be responsible are businessmen, which means individual proprietors or corporate executives. Most of the discussion of social responsibility is directed at corporations, so in what follows I shall mostly neglect the individual proprietors and speak of corporate executives.

In a free-enterprise, private-property system, a corporate executive is an employee of the owners of the business. He has direct responsibility to his employers. That responsibility is to conduct the business in accordance with their desires, which generally will be to make as much money as possible while conforming to the basic rules of the society, both those embodied in law and those embodied in ethical custom. Of course, in some cases his employers may have a different objective. A group of persons might establish a corporation for an eleemosynary purpose—for example, a hospital or a school. The manager of such a corporation will not have money profit as his objective but the rendering of certain services.

In either case, the key point is that, in his capacity as a corporate executive, the manager is the agent of the individuals who own the corporation or establish the eleemosynary institution, and his primary responsibility is to them.

---

From Milton Friedman, "The Social Responsibility of Business Is to Increase Its Profits," *New York Times Magazine*, September 13, 1970. Copyright © 2001 by The New York Times Company. Reprinted by permission.

Needless to say, this does not mean that it is easy to judge how well he is performing his task. But at least the criterion of performance is straightforward, and the persons among whom a voluntary contractual arrangement exists are clearly defined.

Of course, the corporate executive is also a person in his own right. As a person, he may have many other responsibilities that he recognizes or assumes voluntarily—to his family, his conscience, his feelings of charity, his church, his clubs, his city, his country. He may feel impelled by these responsibilities to devote part of his income to causes he regards as worthy, to refuse to work for particular corporations, even to leave his job, for example, to join his country's armed forces. If we wish, we may refer to some of these responsibilities as "social responsibilities." But in these respects he is acting as a principal, not an agent; he is spending his own money or time or energy, not the money of his employers or the time or energy he has contracted to devote to their purposes. If these are "social responsibilities," they are the social responsibilities of individuals, not of business.

What does it mean to say that the corporate executive has a "social responsibility" in his capacity as businessman? If this statement is not pure rhetoric, it must mean that he is to act in some way that is not in the interest of his employers. For example, that he is to refrain from increasing the price of the product in order to contribute to the social objective of preventing inflation, even though a price increase would be in the best interests of the corporation. Or that he is to make expenditures on reducing pollution beyond the amount that is in the best interests of the corporation or that is required by law in order to contribute to the social objective of improving the environment. Or that, at the expense of corporate profits, he is to hire "hardcore" unemployed instead of better qualified available workmen to contribute to the social objective of reducing poverty.

In each of these cases, the corporate executive would be spending someone else's money for a general social interest. Insofar as his actions in accord with his "social responsibility" reduce returns to stockholders, he is spending their money. Insofar as his actions raise the price to customers, he is spending the customers' money. Insofar as his actions lower the wages of some employees, he is spending their money.

The stockholders or the customers or the employees could separately spend their own money on the particular action if they wished to do so. The executive is exercising a distinct "social responsibility," rather than serving as an agent of the stockholders or the customers or the employees, only if he spends the money in a different way than they would have spent it.

But if he does this, he is in effect imposing taxes, on the one hand, and deciding how the tax proceeds shall be spent, on the other.

This process raises political questions on two levels: principle and consequences. On the level of political principle, the imposition of taxes and the expenditure of tax proceeds are governmental functions. We have established elaborate constitutional, parliamentary, and judicial provisions to control these functions, to assure that taxes are imposed so far as possible in accordance with the preferences and desires of the public—after all, "taxation without representation" was one of the battle cries of the American Revolution. We have a system of checks and balances to separate the legislative function of imposing taxes and enacting expenditures from the executive function of collecting taxes and administering expenditure programs and from the judicial function of mediating disputes and interpreting the law.

Here the businessman—self-selected or appointed directly or indirectly by stockholders—is to be simultaneously legislator, executive, and jurist. He is to decide whom to tax by how much and for what purpose, and he is to spend the proceeds—all this guided only by general exhortations from on high to restrain inflation, improve the environment, fight poverty and so on and on.

The whole justification for permitting the corporate executive to be selected by the stockholders is that the executive is an agent serving the interests of his principal. This justification disappears when the corporate executive imposes taxes and spends the proceeds for "social" purposes. He becomes in effect a public employee, a civil servant, even though he remains in name an employee of a private enterprise. On grounds of political principle, it is intolerable that such civil servants—insofar as their actions in the name of social responsibility are real and not just window-dressing—should be selected as they are now. If they are to be civil servants, then they must be elected through a political process. If they are to impose taxes and make expenditures to foster "social" objectives, then political machinery must be set up to make the assessment of taxes and to determine through a political process the objectives to be served.

This is the basic reason why the doctrine of "social responsibility" involves the acceptance of the socialist view that political mechanisms, not market mechanisms, are the appropriate way to determine the allocation of scarce resources to alternative uses.

On the grounds of consequences, can the corporate executive in fact discharge his alleged "social responsibilities?" On the other hand, suppose he could get away with spending the stockholders' or customers' or employees' money. How is he to know how to spend it? He is told that he must contribute to fighting inflation. How is he to know what action of his will contribute to that end? He is presumably an expert in running his company—in producing a product or selling it or financing it. But nothing about his selection makes him an

expert on inflation. Will his holding down the price of his product reduce inflationary pressure? Or, by leaving more spending power in the hands of his customers, simply divert it elsewhere? Or, by forcing him to produce less because of the lower price, will it simply contribute to shortages? Even if he could answer these questions, how much cost is he justified in imposing on his stockholders, customers, and employees for this social purpose? What is his appropriate share and what is the appropriate share of others?

And, whether he wants to or not, can he get away with spending his stockholders', customers' or employees' money? Will not the stockholders fire him? (Either the present ones or those who take over when his actions in the name of social responsibility have reduced the corporation's profits and the price of its stock.) His customers and his employees can desert him for other producers and employers less scrupulous in exercising their social responsibilities.

This facet of "social responsibility" doctrine is brought into sharp relief when the doctrine is used to justify wage restraint by trade unions. The conflict of interest is naked and clear when union officials are asked to subordinate the interest of their members to some more general purpose. If the union officials try to enforce wage restraint, the consequence is likely to be wildcat strikes, rank-and-file revolts, and the emergence of strong competitors for their jobs. We thus have the ironic phenomenon that union leaders—at least in the U.S.—have objected to government interference with the market far more consistently and courageously than have business leaders.

The difficulty of exercising "social responsibility" illustrates, of course, the great virtue of private competitive enterprise—it forces people to be responsible for their own actions and makes it difficult for them to "exploit" other people for either selfish or unselfish purposes. They can do good—but only at their own expense.

Many a reader who has followed the argument this far may be tempted to remonstrate that it is all well and good to speak of government's having the responsibility to impose taxes and determine expenditures for such "social" purposes as controlling pollution or training the hard-core unemployed, but that the problems are too urgent to wait on the slow course of political processes, that the exercise of social responsibility by businessmen is a quicker and surer way to solve pressing current problems.

Aside from the question of fact—I share Adam Smith's skepticism about the benefits that can be expected from "those who affected to trade for the public good"—this argument must be rejected on grounds of principle. What it amounts to is an assertion that those who favor the taxes and expenditures in question have failed to persuade a majority of their fellow citizens to be of like mind and that they are seeking to attain by undemocratic procedures what they cannot attain by democratic procedures. In a free society, it is hard for "evil" people to do "evil," especially since one man's good is another's evil.

I have, for simplicity, concentrated on the special case of the corporate executive, except only for the brief digression on trade unions. But precisely the same argument applies to the newer phenomenon of calling upon stockholders to require corporations to exercise social responsibility (the recent GM crusade for example). In most of these cases, what is in effect involved is some stockholders trying to get other stockholders (or customers or employees) to contribute against their will to "social" causes favored by the activists. Insofar as they succeed, they are again imposing taxes and spending the proceeds.

The situation of the individual proprietor is somewhat different. If he acts to reduce the returns of his enterprise in order to exercise his "social responsibility," he is spending his own money, not someone else's. If he wishes to spend his money on such purposes, that is his right, and I cannot see that there is any objection to his doing so. In the process, he, too, may impose costs on employees and customers. However, because he is far less likely than a large corporation or union to have monopolistic power, any such side effects will tend to be minor.

Of course, in practice, the doctrine of social responsibility is frequently a cloak for actions that are justified on other grounds rather than a reason for those actions.

To illustrate, it may well be in the long-run interest of a corporation that is a major employer in a small community to devote resources to providing amenities to that community or to improving its government. That may make it easier to attract desirable employees, it may reduce the wage bill or lessen losses from pilferage and sabotage or have other worthwhile effects. Or it may be that, given the laws about the deductibility of corporate charitable contributions, the stockholders can contribute more to charities they favor by having the corporation make the gift than by doing it themselves, since they can in that way contribute an amount that would otherwise have been paid as corporate taxes.

In each of these—and many similar—cases, there is a strong temptation to rationalize these actions as an exercise of "social responsibility." In the present climate of opinion, with its widespread aversion to "capitalism," "profits," the "soulless corporation," and so on, this is one way for a corporation to generate goodwill as a by-product of expenditures that are entirely justified in its own self-interest.

It would be inconsistent of me to call on corporate executives to refrain from this hypocritical window-dressing because it harms the foundations of a free society. That would be to call on them to exercise a "social responsibility"! If our institutions, and the attitudes of the public make it in their self-interest to cloak their actions in this way, I cannot summon much indignation to denounce them. At the same time, I can express admiration for those individual proprietors or owners of closely held corporations or stockholders of more broadly held corporations who disdain such tactics as approaching fraud.

Whether blameworthy or not, the use of the cloak of social responsibility, and the nonsense spoken in its name by influential and prestigious businessmen, does clearly harm the foundations of a free society. I have been impressed time and again by the schizophrenic character of many businessmen. They are capable of being extremely farsighted and clear-headed in matters that are internal to their businesses. They are incredibly short-sighted and muddle-headed in matters that are outside their businesses but affect the possible survival of business in general. This short-sightedness is strikingly exemplified in the calls from many businessmen for wage and price guidelines or controls or income policies. There is nothing that could do more in a brief period to destroy a market system and replace it by a centrally controlled system than effective governmental control of prices and wages.

The short-sightedness is also exemplified in speeches by businessmen on social responsibility. This may gain them kudos in the short run. But it helps to strengthen the already too prevalent view that the pursuit of profits is wicked and immoral and must be curbed and controlled by external forces. Once this view is adopted, the external forces that curb the market will not be the social consciences, however highly developed, of the pontificating executives; it will be the iron fist of government bureaucrats. Here, as with price and wage controls, businessmen seem to me to reveal a suicidal impulse.

The political principle that underlies the market mechanism is unanimity. In an ideal free market resting on private property, no individual can coerce any other, all cooperation is voluntary, all parties to such cooperation benefit or they need not participate. There are no values, no "social" responsibilities in any sense other than the shared values and responsibilities of individuals. Society is a collection of individuals and of the various groups they voluntarily form.

The political principle that underlies the political mechanism is conformity. The individual must serve a more general social interest—whether that be determined by a church or a dictator or a majority. The individual may have a vote and say in what is to be done, but if he is overruled, he must conform. It is appropriate for some to require others to contribute to a general social purpose whether they wish to or not.

Unfortunately, unanimity is not always feasible. There are some respects in which conformity appears unavoidable, so I do not see how one can avoid the use of the political mechanism altogether.

But the doctrine of "social responsibility" taken seriously would extend the scope of the political mechanism to every human activity. It does not differ in philosophy from the most explicitly collectivist doctrine. It differs only by professing to believe that collectivist ends can be attained without collectivist means. That is why, in my book *Capitalism and Freedom*, I have called it a "fundamentally subversive doctrine" in a free society, and have said that in such a society, "there is one and only one social responsibility of business—to use its resources and engage in activities designed to increase its profits so long as it stays within the rules of the game, which is to say, engages in open and free competition without deception or fraud."

# Managing for Stakeholders[1]

*R. Edward Freeman*

## INTRODUCTION

The purpose of this essay is to outline an emerging view of business that we shall call "managing for stakeholders".[2] This view has emerged over the past 30 years from a group of scholars in a diverse set of disciplines, from finance to philosophy.[3] The basic idea is that businesses, and the executives who manage them, actually do and should create value for customers, suppliers, employees, communities, and financiers (or shareholders). And, that we need to pay careful attention to how these relationships are managed and how value gets created for these stakeholders. We contrast this idea with the dominant model of business activity, namely, that businesses are to be managed solely for the benefit of shareholders. Any other benefits (or harms) that are created are incidental.[4]

Simple ideas create complex questions, and we proceed as follows. In the next section we examine why the dominant story or model of business that is deeply embedded in our culture is no longer workable. It is resistant to change, not consistent with the law, and for the most part, simply ignores matters of ethics. Each of these flaws is fatal in the business world of the twenty-first century.

We then proceed to define the basic ideas of "managing for stakeholders" and why it solves some of the problems of the dominant model. In particular we pay attention to how using "stakeholder" as a basic unit of analysis makes it more difficult to ignore matters of ethics. We argue that the primary responsibility of the executive is to create as much value for stakeholders as possible, and that no stakeholder interest is viable in isolation of the other stakeholders. We sketch three primary arguments from ethical theory for adopting "managing for stakeholders." We conclude by outlining a fourth "pragmatist argument" that suggests we see managing for stakeholders as a new narrative about business that lets us improve the way we currently create value for each other. Capitalism is on this view a system of social cooperation and collaboration, rather than primarily a system of competition.

## THE DOMINANT STORY: MANAGERIAL CAPITALISM WITH SHAREHOLDERS AT THE CENTER

The modern business corporation has emerged during the twentieth century as one of the most important innovations in human history. Yet the changes that we are now experiencing call for its reinvention. Before we suggest what this revision, "managing for stakeholders" or "stakeholder capitalism," is, first we need to understand how the dominant story came to be told.

Somewhere in the past, organizations were quite simple and "doing business" consisted of buying raw materials from suppliers, converting it to products, and selling it to customers. For the most part owner-entrepreneurs founded such simple businesses and worked at the business along with members of their families. The development of new production processes, such as the assembly line, meant that jobs could be specialized and more work could be accomplished. New technologies and sources of power became readily available. These and other social and political forces combined to require larger amounts of capital, well beyond the scope of most individual owner-manager-employees. Additionally, "workers" or non–family members began to dominate the firm and were the rule rather than the exception.

Ownership of the business became more dispersed as capital was raised from banks, stockholders, and other institutions. Indeed, the management of the firm became separated from the ownership of the firm. And, in order to be successful, the top managers of the business had to simultaneously satisfy the owners, the employees and their unions, suppliers, and customers. This system of organization of businesses along the lines set forth here was known as managerial capitalism or laissez faire capitalism, or more recently, shareholder capitalism.[5]

As businesses grew, managers developed a means of control via the divisionalized firm. Led by Alfred Sloan at General Motors, the divisionalized firm with a central headquarters staff was widely adapted.[6] The dominant model for managerial authority was the military and civil service bureaucracy. By creating rational structures and processes, the orderly progress of business growth could be well-managed.

Thus, managerialism, hierarchy, stability, and predictability all evolved together, in the United States and Europe, to form the most powerful economic system in the history of humanity. The rise of bureaucracy and managerialism was so strong that the economist Joseph Schumpeter predicted that it would wipe out the creative force of capitalism, stifling innovation in its drive for predictability and stability.

During the last 50 years this "Managerial Model" has put "shareholders" at the center of the firm as the most important group for managers to worry about. This mindset has dealt with the increasing complexity of the business world by focusing more intensely on "shareholders" and "creating value for shareholders." It has become common wisdom to "increase shareholder value," and many companies have instituted complex incentive compensation plans aimed at aligning the interests of executives with the interests of shareholders.

These incentive plans are often tied to the price of a company's stock, which is affected by many factors not the least of which is the expectations of Wall Street analysts about earnings per share each quarter. Meeting Wall Street targets and forming a stable and predictable base of quarter over quarter increases in earnings per share has become the standard for measuring company performance. Indeed, all of the recent scandals at Enron, WorldCom, Tyco, and others are in part due to executives trying to increase shareholder value, sometimes in opposition to accounting rules and law. Unfortunately, the world has changed so that the stability and predictability required by the shareholder approach can no longer be assured.

## The Dominant Model Is Resistant to Change

The Managerial View of business with shareholders at the center is inherently resistant to change. It puts shareholders' interests over and above the interests of customers, suppliers, employees, and others, as if these interests must conflict with each other. It understands a business as an essentially hierarchical organization fastened together with authority to act in the shareholders' interests. Executives often speak in the language of hierarchy as "working for shareholders," "shareholders are the boss," and "you have to do what the shareholders want." On this interpretation, change should occur only when the shareholders are unhappy, and as long as executives can produce a series of incrementally better financial results there is no problem. According to this view the only change that counts is change oriented toward shareholder value. If customers are unhappy, if accounting rules have been compromised, if product quality is bad, if environmental disaster looms, even if competitive forces threaten, the only interesting questions are whether and how these forces for change affect shareholder value, measured by the price of the stock every day. Unfortunately in today's world there is just too much uncertainty and complexity to rely on such a single criterion. Business in the twenty-first century is global and multifaceted, and shareholder value may not capture that dynamism. Or, if it does, as the theory suggests it must eventually, it will be too late for executives to do anything about it. The dominant story may work for how things turn out in the long run on Wall Street, but managers have to act with an eye to Main Street as well, to anticipate change to try and take advantage of the dynamism of business.[7]

## THE DOMINANT MODEL IS NOT CONSISTENT WITH THE LAW

In actual fact the clarity of putting shareholders' interests first, above that of customers, suppliers, employees, and communities, flies in the face of the reality the law. The law has evolved to put constraints on the kinds of trade-offs that can be made. In fact the law of corporations gives a less clear answer to the question of in whose interest and for whose benefit the corporation should be governed. The law has evolved over the years to give *de facto* standing to the claims of groups other than stockholders. It has, in effect, required that the claims of customers, suppliers, local communities, and employees be taken into consideration.

For instance, the doctrine of "privity of contract," as articulated in *Winterbottom v. Wright* in 1842, has been eroded by recent developments in product liability law. *Greenman v. Yuba Power* gives the manufacturer strict liability for damage caused by its products, even though the seller has exercised all possible care in the preparation and sale of the product and the consumer has not bought the product from nor entered into any contractual arrangement with the manufacturer. *Caveat emptor* has been replaced, in large part, with *caveat venditor*. The Consumer Product Safety Commission has the power to enact product recalls, essentially leading to an increase in the number of voluntary product recalls by companies seeking to mitigate legal damage awards. Some industries are required to provide information to customers about a product's ingredients, whether or not the customers want and are willing to pay for this information. Thus, companies must take the interests of customers into account, by law.

A similar story can be told about the evolution of the law forcing management to take the interests of employees into account. The National Labor Relations Act gave employees the right to unionize and to bargain in good faith. It set up the National Labor Relations Board to enforce these rights with management. The Equal Pay Act of 1963 and Title VII of the Civil Rights Act of 1964 constrain management from discrimination in hiring practices; these have been followed with the Age Discrimination in Employment Act of 1967, and recent extensions affecting people with disabilities. The emergence of a body of administrative case law arising from labor–management disputes and the historic settling of discrimination claims with large employers have caused the emergence of a body of management practice that is consistent with the legal guarantee of the rights of employees.

The law has also evolved to try and protect the interests of local communities. The Clean Water Act of 1977 and the Clean Air Act of 1990, and various amendments to these classic pieces of legislation, have constrained management from "spoiling the commons." In a historic case, *Marsh v. Alabama,* the Supreme Court ruled that a company-owned town was subject to the provisions of the U.S. Constitution, thereby guaranteeing the rights of local citizens and negating the "property rights" of the firm. Current issues center around protecting local businesses, forcing companies to pay the health care costs of their employees, increases in minimum wages, environmental standards, and the effects of business development on the lives of local community members. These issues fill the local political landscapes, and executives and their companies must take account of them.

Some may argue that the constraints of the law, at least in the U.S., have become increasingly irrelevant in a world where business is global in nature. However, globalization simply makes this argument stronger. The laws that are relevant to business have evolved differently around the world, but they have evolved nonetheless to take into account the interests of groups other than just shareholders. Each state in India has a different set of regulations that affect how a company can do business. In China the law has evolved to give business some property rights but it is far from exclusive. And, in most of the European Union, laws around "civil society" and the role of "employees" are much more complex than even U.S. law.

"Laissez-faire capitalism" is simply a myth. The idea that business is about "maximizing value for stockholders regardless of the consequences to others" is one that has outlived its usefulness. The dominant model simply does not describe how business operates. Another way to see this is that if executives always have to qualify "maximize shareholder value" with exceptions of law, or even good practice, then the dominant story isn't very useful anymore. There are just too many exceptions. The dominant story could be saved by arguing that it describes a normative view about how business should operate, despite how actual businesses have evolved.[8] So, we need to look more closely at some of the conceptual and normative problems that the dominant model raises.

## The Dominant Model Is Not Consistent with Basic Ethics

Previously we have argued that most theories of business rely on separating "business" decisions from "ethical" decisions.[9] This is seen most clearly in the popular joke about "business ethics as an oxymoron." More formally we might suggest that we define:

The Separation Fallacy

It is useful to believe that sentences like "x is a business decision" have no ethical content or any implicit ethical point of view. And, it is useful to believe that sentences like "x is an ethical decision, the best thing to do all things considered" have no content or implicit view about value creation and trade (business).

This fallacy underlies much of the dominant story about business, as well as in other areas in society. There are two implications of rejecting the Separation Fallacy. The first is that almost any business decision has some ethical content. To see that this is true one need only ask whether the following questions make sense for virtually any business decision:

The Open Question Argument

1. If this decision is made for whom is value created and destroyed?
2. Who is harmed and/or benefited by this decision?
3. Whose rights are enabled and whose values are realized by this decision (and whose are not)?
4. What kind of person will I (we) become if we make this decision?

Since these questions are always open for most business decisions, it is reasonable to give up the Separation Fallacy, which would have us believe that these questions aren't relevant for making business decisions, or that they could never be answered. We need a theory about business that builds in answers to the "Open Question Argument" above. One such answer would be "Only value to shareholders counts," but such an answer would have to be enmeshed in the language of ethics as well as business. Milton Friedman, unlike most of his expositors, may actually give such a morally rich answer. He claims that the responsibility of the executive is to make profits subject to law and ethical custom. Depending on how "law and ethical custom" is interpreted, the key difference with the stakeholder approach may well be that we disagree about how the world works. In order to create value we believe that it is better to focus on integrating business and ethics within a complex set of stakeholder relationships rather than treating ethics as a side constraint on making profits. In short we need a theory that has as its basis what we might call:

### The Integration Thesis

Most business decisions, or sentences about business have some ethical content, or implicit ethical view. Most ethical decisions, or sentences about ethics have some business content or implicit view about business.[10]

One of the most pressing challenges facing business scholars is to tell compelling narratives that have the Integration Thesis at its heart. This is essentially the task that a group of scholars, "business ethicists" and "stakeholder theorists," have begun over the last 30 years. We need to go back to the very basics of ethics. Ethics is about the rules, principles, consequences, matters of character, etc., that we use to live together. These ideas give us a set of open questions that we are constantly searching for better ways to answer in reasonable complete ways.[11] One might define "ethics" as a conversation about how we can reason together and solve our differences, recognize where our interests are joined and need development, so that we can all flourish without resorting to coercion and violence. Some may disagree with such a definition, and we do not

intend to privilege definitions, but such a pragmatist approach to ethics entails that we reason and talk together to try and create a better world for all of us.

If our critiques of the dominant model are correct then we need to start over by reconceptualizing the very language that we use to understand how business operates. We want to suggest that something like the following principle is implicit in most reasonably comprehensive views about ethics.

### The Responsibility Principle[12]

Most people, most of the time, want to, actually do, and should accept responsibility for the effects of their actions on others.

Clearly the Responsibility Principle is incompatible with the Separation Fallacy. If business is separated from ethics, there is no question of moral responsibility for business decisions. More clearly still, without something like the Responsibility Principle it is difficult to see how ethics gets off the ground. "Responsibility" may well be a difficult and multifaceted idea. There are surely many different ways to understand it. But, if we are not willing to accept the responsibility for our own actions (as limited as that may be due to complicated issues of causality and the like), then ethics, understood as how we reason together so we can all flourish, is likely an exercise in bad faith.

If we want to give up the separation fallacy and adopt the integration thesis, if the open question argument makes sense, and if something like the responsibility thesis is necessary, then we need a new model for business. And, this new story must be able to explain how value creation at once deals with economics and ethics, and how it takes account of all of the effects of business action on others. Such a model exists, and has been developing over the last 30 years by management researchers and ethics scholars, and there are many businesses who have adopted this "stakeholder framework" for their businesses.

## MANAGING FOR STAKEHOLDERS

The basic idea of "managing for stakeholders" is quite simple. Business can be understood as a set of relationships among groups which have a stake in the activities that make up the business. Business is about how customers, suppliers, employees, financiers (stockholders, bondholders, banks, etc.), communities, and managers interact and create value. To understand a business is to know how these relationships work. And, the executive's or entrepreneur's job is to manage and shape these relationships, hence the title, "managing for stakeholders."

Figure 1 depicts the idea of "managing for stakeholders" in a variation of the classic "wheel and spoke" diagram.[13] However, it is important to note that the stakeholder idea is perfectly general. Corporations are not the

**FIGURE 1**

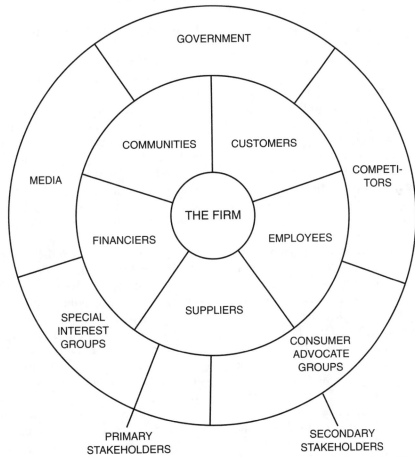

*Source:* R. Edward Freeman, Jeffrey Harrison, and Andrew Wicks, *Managing for Stakeholders* (New Haven: Yale University Press, 2007).

center of the universe, and there are many possible pictures. One might put customers in the center to signal that a company puts customers as the key priority. Another might put employees in the center and link them to customers and shareholders. We prefer the generic diagram because it suggests, pictorially, that "managing for stakeholders" is a theory about management and business; hence, managers and companies are in the center. But, there is no larger metaphysical claim here.

### Stakeholders and Stakes

Owners or financiers (a better term) clearly have a financial stake in the business in the form of stocks, bonds, and so on, and they expect some kind of financial return from them. Of course, the stakes of financiers will differ by type of owner, preferences for money, moral preferences, and so on, as well as by type of firm. The shareholders of Google may well want returns as well as be supportive of Google's articulated purpose of "Do No Evil." To the extent that it makes sense to talk about the financiers "owning the firm," they have a concomitant responsibility for the uses of their property.

Employees have their jobs and usually their livelihood at stake; they often have specialized skills for which there is usually no perfectly elastic market. In return for their labor, they expect security, wages, benefits, and meaningful work. Often, employees are expected to participate in the decision making of the organization, and if the employees are management or senior executives, we see them as shouldering a great deal of responsibility for the conduct of the organization as a whole. And, employees are sometimes financiers as well, since many companies have stock ownership plans, and loyal employees who believe in the future of their companies often voluntarily invest. One way

to think about the employee relationship is in terms of contracts.

Customers and suppliers exchange resources for the products and services of the firm and in return receive the benefits of the products and services. As with financiers and employees, the customer and supplier relationships are enmeshed in ethics. Companies make promises to customers via their advertising, and when products or services don't deliver on these promises, then management has a responsibility to rectify the situation. It is also important to have suppliers who are committed to making a company better. If suppliers find a better, faster, and cheaper way of making critical parts or services, then both supplier and company can win. Of course, some suppliers simply compete on price, but even so, there is a moral element of fairness and transparency to the supplier relationship.

Finally, the local community grants the firm the right to build facilities, and in turn, it benefits from the tax base and economic and social contributions of the firm. Companies have a real impact on communities, and being located in a welcoming community helps a company create value for its other stakeholders. In return for the provision of local services, companies are expected to be good citizens, as is any individual person. It should not expose the community to unreasonable hazards in the form of pollution, toxic waste, etc. It should keep whatever commitments it makes to the community, and operate in a transparent manner as far as possible. Of course, companies don't have perfect knowledge, but when management discovers some danger or runs afoul of new competition, it is expected to inform and work with local communities to mitigate any negative effects, as far as possible.

While any business must consist of financiers, customers, suppliers, employees, and communities, it is possible to think about other stakeholders as well. We can define "stakeholder" in a number of ways. First of all, we could define the term fairly narrowly to capture the idea that any business, large or small, is about creating value for "those groups without whose support, the business would cease to be viable." The inner circle of Figure 1 depicts this view. Almost every business is concerned at some level with relationships among financiers, customers, suppliers, employees, and communities. We might call these groups "primary" or "definitional." However, it should be noted that as a business starts up, sometimes one particular stakeholder is more important than another. In a new business start-up, sometimes there are no suppliers, and paying lots of attention to one or two key customers, as well as to the venture capitalist (financier), is the right approach.

There is also a somewhat broader definition that captures the idea that if a group or individual can affect a business, then the executives must take that group into consideration in thinking about how to create value. Or, a stakeholder is any group or individual that can affect or be affected by the realization of an organization's purpose. At a minimum some groups affect primary stakeholders and we might see these as stakeholders in the outer ring of Figure 1 and call them "secondary" or "instrumental."

There are other definitions that have emerged during the last 30 years, some based on risks and rewards, some based on mutuality of interests. And, the debate over finding the one "true definition" of "stakeholder" is not likely to end. We prefer a more pragmatic approach of being clear of the purpose of using any of the proposed definitions. Business is a fascinating field of study. There are very few principles and definitions that apply to all businesses all over the world. Furthermore, there are many different ways to run a successful business, or if you like, many different flavors of

"managing for stakeholders." We see limited usefulness in trying to define one model of business, either based on the shareholder or stakeholder view, that works for all businesses everywhere. We see much value to be gained in examining how the stakes work in the value creation process, and the role of the executive.

## THE RESPONSIBILITY OF THE EXECUTIVE IN MANAGING FOR STAKEHOLDERS

Executives play a special role in the activity of the business enterprise. On the one hand, they have a stake like every other employee in terms of an actual or implied employment contract. And, that stake is linked to the stakes of financiers, customers, suppliers, communities, and other employees. In addition, executives are expected to look after the health of the overall enterprise, to keep the varied stakes moving in roughly the same direction, and to keep them in balance.[14]

No stakeholder stands alone in the process of value creation. The stakes of each stakeholder group are multifaceted, and inherently connected to each other. How could a bondholder recognize any returns without management's paying attention to the stakes of customers or employees? How could customers get the products and services they need without employees and suppliers? How could employees have a decent place to live without communities? Many thinkers see the dominant problem of "managing for stakeholders" as how to solve the priority problem, or "which stakeholders are more important," or "how do we make trade-offs among stakeholders." We see this as a secondary issue.

First and foremost, we need to see stakeholder interests as joint, as inherently tied together. Seeing stakeholder interests as "joint" rather than "opposed" is difficult. It is not always easy to find a way to accommodate all stakeholder interests. It is easier to trade off one versus another. Why not delay spending on new products for customers in order to keep earnings a bit higher? Why not cut employee medical benefits in order to invest in a new inventory control system?

Managing for stakeholders suggests that executives try to reframe the questions. How can we invest in new products and create higher earnings? How can we be sure our employees are healthy and happy and are able to work creatively so that we can capture the benefits of new information technology such as inventory control systems? In a recent book reflecting on his experience as CEO of Medtronic, Bill George summarized the managing for stakeholders mindset:[15]

> Serving all your stakeholders is the best way to produce long term results and create a growing, prosperous company . . . Let me be very clear about this: there is no conflict between serving all your stakeholders and providing excellent returns for shareholders. In the long term it is impossible to have one without the other. However, serving all these stakeholder groups requires discipline, vision, and committed leadership.

The primary responsibility of the executive is to create as much value as possible for stakeholders.[16] Where stakeholder interests conflict, the executive must find a way to rethink the problems so that these interests can go together, so that even more value can be created for each. If trade-offs have to be made, as often happens in the real world, then the executive must figure out how to make the trade-offs, and immediately begin improving the trade-offs for all sides. **Managing for stakeholders is about creating as much value as possible for stakeholders, without resorting to trade-offs.**

We believe that this task is more easily accomplished when a business has a sense of purpose. Furthermore, there are few limits on the kinds of purpose that can drive a business. Wal-Mart may stand for "everyday low price." Merck can stand for "alleviating human suffering." The point is that if an entrepreneur or an executive can find a purpose that speaks to the hearts and minds of key stakeholders, it is more likely that there will be sustained success.

Purpose is complex and inspirational. The Grameen Bank wants to eliminate poverty. Fannie Mae wants to make housing affordable to every income level in society. Tastings (a local restaurant) wants to bring the taste of really good food and wine to lots of people in the community. And, all of these organizations have to generate profits, or else they cannot pursue their purposes. Capitalism works because we can pursue our purpose with others. When we coalesce around a big idea, or a joint purpose evolves from our day-to-day activities with each other, then great things can happen.

To create value for stakeholders, executives must understand that business is fully situated in the realm of humanity. Businesses are human institutions populated by real live complex human beings. Stakeholders have names and faces and children. They are not mere placeholders for social roles. As such, matters of ethics are routine when one takes a managing for stakeholders approach. Of course this should go without saying, but a part of the dominant story about business is that business people are only in it for their own narrowly defined self-interest. One main assumption of the managerial view with shareholders at the center is that shareholders only care about returns, and therefore their agents, managers, should only care about returns. However, this does not fit either our experiences or our aspirations. In the words of one CEO, "The only assets I manage go up and down the elevators everyday."

Most human beings are complicated. Most of us do what we do because we are self-interested and interested in others. Business works in part because of our urge to create things with others and for others. Working on a team, or creating a new product or delivery mechanism that makes customer's lives better or happier or more pleasurable, all can be contributing factors to why we go to work each day. And, this is not to deny the economic incentive of getting a pay check. The assumption of narrow self-interest is extremely limiting, and can be self-reinforcing—people can begin to act in a narrow self-interested way if they believe that is what is expected of them, as some of the scandals such as Enron, have shown. We need to be open to a more complex psychology—one any parent finds familiar as they have shepherded the growth and development of their children.

## SOME ARGUMENTS FOR MANAGING FOR STAKEHOLDERS

Once you say stakeholders are persons then the ideas of ethics are automatically applicable. However you interpret the idea of "stakeholders," you must pay attention to the effects of your actions on others. And, something like the Responsibility Principle suggests that this is a cornerstone of any adequate ethical theory. There are at least three main arguments for adopting a managing for stakeholders approach. Philosophers will see these as connected to the three main approaches to ethical theory that have developed historically. We shall briefly set forth sketches of these arguments, and then suggest that there is a more powerful fourth argument.[17]

### The Argument from Consequences

A number of theorists have argued that the main reason that the dominant model of managing for shareholders is a good idea is that it leads to the best consequences for all. Typically these arguments invoke Adam Smith's idea of the invisible hand, whereby each business actor pursues her own self-interest and the greatest good of all actually emerges. The problem with this argument is that we now know with modern general equilibrium economics that the argument only works under very specialized conditions that seldom describe the real world. And further, we know that if the economic conditions get very close to those needed to produce the greatest good, there is no guarantee that the greatest good will actually result.

Managing for stakeholders may actually produce better consequences for all stakeholders because it recognizes that stakeholder interests are joint. If one stakeholder pursues its interests at the expense of all the others, then the others will either withdraw their support, or look to create another network of stakeholder value creation. This is not to say that there are not times when one stakeholder will benefit at the expense of others, but if this happens continuously over time, then in a relatively free society, stakeholders will either (1) exit to form a new stakeholder network that satisfies their needs; (2) use the political process to constrain the offending stakeholder; or (3) invent some other form of activity to satisfy their particular needs.[18]

Alternatively, if we think about stakeholders engaged in a series of bargains among themselves, then we would expect that as individual stakeholders recognized their joint interests, and made good decisions based on these interests, better consequences would result than if they each narrowly pursued their individual self-interests.[19]

Now it may be objected that such an approach ignores "social consequences" or "consequences to society" and, hence, that we need a concept of "corporate social responsibility" to mitigate these effects. This objection is a vestigial limb of the dominant model. Since the only effects, on that view, were economic effects, then we need to think about "social consequences" or "corporate social responsibility." However, if stakeholder relationships are understood to be fully embedded in morality, then there is no need for an idea like corporate social responsibility. We can replace it with "corporate stakeholder responsibility," which is a dominant feature of managing for stakeholders.

## The Argument from Rights

The dominant story gives property rights in the corporation exclusively to shareholders, and the natural question arises about the rights of other stakeholders who are affected. One way to understand managing for stakeholders is that it takes this question of rights seriously. If you believe that rights make sense, and further that if one person has a right to X then all persons have a right to X, it is just much easier to think about these issues using a stakeholder approach. For instance, while shareholders may well have property rights, these rights are not absolute, and should not be seen as such. Shareholders may not use their property to abridge the rights of others. For instance, shareholders and their agents, managers, may not use corporate property to violate the right to life of others. One way to understand managing for stakeholders is that it assumes that stakeholders have some rights. Now, it is notoriously difficult to parse the idea of "rights." But, if executives take managing for stakeholders seriously, they will automatically think about what is owed to customers, suppliers, employees, financiers, and communities, in virtue of their stake, and in virtue of their basic humanity.

## The Argument from Character

One of the strongest arguments for managing for stakeholders is that it asks executives and entrepreneurs to consider the question of what kind of company they want to create and build. The answer to this question will be in large part an issue of character. Aspiration matters.

The business virtues of efficiency, fairness, respect, integrity, keeping commitments, and others are all critical in being successful at creating value for stakeholders. These virtues are simply absent when we think only about the dominant model and its sole reliance on a narrow economic logic.

If we frame the central question of management as "how do we create value for shareholders," then the only virtue that emerges is one of loyalty to the interests of shareholders. However if we frame the central question more broadly as "how do we create and sustain the creation of value for stakeholders" or "how do we get stakeholder interests all going in the same direction," then it is easy to see how many of the other virtues are relevant. Taking a stakeholder approach helps people decide how companies can contribute to their well-being and the kinds of lives they want to lead. By making ethics explicit and building it into the basic way we think about business, we avoid a situation of bad faith and self-deception.

## The Pragmatist's Argument

The previous three arguments point out important reasons for adopting a new story about business. Pragmatists want to know how we can live better, how we can create both ourselves and our communities in ways where values such as freedom and solidarity are present in our everyday lives to the maximal extent. While it is sometimes useful to think about consequences, rights, and character in isolation, in reality our lives are richer if we can have a conversation about how to live together better. There is a long tradition of pragmatist ethics dating to philosophers such as William James and John Dewey. More recently philosopher Richard Rorty has expressed the pragmatist ideal:[20]

> pragmatists . . . hope instead that human beings will come to enjoy more money, more free time,

and greater social equality, and also that they will develop more empathy, more ability to put themselves in the shoes of others. We hope that human beings will behave more decently toward one another as their standard of living improves.

By building into the very conceptual framework we use to think about business a concern with freedom, equality, consequences, decency, shared purpose, and paying attention to all of the effects of how we create value for each other, we can make business a human institution, and perhaps remake it in a way that sustains us.

For the pragmatist, business (and capitalism) has evolved as a social practice, an important one that we use to create value and trade with each other. On this view, first and foremost, business is about collaboration. Of course, in a free society, stakeholders are free to form competing networks. But the fuel for capitalism is our desire to create something of value, and to create it for ourselves and others. The spirit of capitalism is the spirit of individual achievement together with the spirit of accomplishing great tasks in collaboration with others. Managing for stakeholders makes this plain so that we can get about the business of creating better selves and better communities.

## NOTES

1. The ideas in this paper have had a long development time. The ideas here have been reworked from: R. Edward Freeman, *Strategic Management: A Stakeholder Approach* (Boston: Pitman, 1984); R. Edward Freeman, "A Stakeholder Theory of the Modern Corporation," in T. Beauchamp and N. Bowie (eds.) *Ethical Theory and Business* (Englewood Cliffs: Prentice Hall, 7th edition, 2005), also in earlier editions coauthored with William Evan; Andrew Wicks, R. Edward Freeman, Patricia Werhane, Kirsten Martin, *Business Ethics: A Managerial Approach* (Englewood Cliffs: Prentice Hall, forthcoming in 2008); and R. Edward Freeman, Jeffrey Harrison, and Andrew Wicks, *Managing for Stakeholders* (New Haven: Yale University Press, 2007).

I am grateful to editors and coauthors for permission to rework these ideas here.

2. It has been called a variety of things: "stakeholder management," "stakeholder capitalism," "a stakeholder theory of the modern corporation," and so on. Our reasons for choosing "managing for stakeholders" will become clearer as we proceed. Many others have worked on these ideas, and should not be held accountable for the rather idiosyncratic view outlined here.

3. For a stylized history of the idea see R. Edward Freeman, "The Development of Stakeholder Theory: An Idiosyncratic Approach" in K. Smith and M. Hitt (eds.), *Great Minds in Management* (Oxford: Oxford University Press, 2005).

4. One doesn't manage "for" these benefits (and harms).

5. The difference between managerial and shareholder capitalism is large. However, the existence of agency theory lets us treat the two identically for our purposes here. Both agree on the view that the modern firm is characterized by the separation of decision making and residual risk bearing. The resulting agency problem is the subject of a vast literature.

6. Alfred Chandler's brilliant book *Strategy and Structure* (Boston: MIT Press, 1970) chronicles the rise of the divisionalized corporation. For a not-so-flattering account of General Motors during the same time period see Peter Drucker's classic work *The Concept of the Corporation* (New York: Transaction Publishers, reprint ed., 1993).

7. Executives can take little comfort in the nostrum that in the long run things work out and the most efficient companies survive. Some market theorists suggest that finance theory acts like "universal acid" cutting through every possible management decision, whether or not, actual managers are aware of it. Perhaps the real difference between the dominant model and the "managing for stakeholders" model proposed here is that they are simply "about" different things. The dominant model is about the strict and narrow economic logic of markets, and the "managing for stakeholders" model is about how human beings create value for each other.

8. Often the flavor of the response of finance theorists sounds like this. The world would be better off if, despite all of the imperfections, executives tried to maximize shareholder value. It is difficult to see how any rational being could accept such a view in the face of the

recent scandals, where it could be argued that the worst offenders were the most ideologically pure, and the result was the actual destruction of shareholder value (see *Breaking the Short Term Cycle,* Charlottesville, VA: Business Roundtable Institute for Corporate Ethics/CFA Center for Financial Market Integrity, 2006). Perhaps we have a version of Aristotle's idea that happiness is not a result of trying to be happy, or Mill's idea that it does not maximize utility to try and maximize utility. Collins and Porras have suggested that even if executives want to maximize shareholder value, they should focus on purpose instead, that trying to maximize shareholder value does not lead to maximum value, see J. Collins and J. Porras, *Built To Last* (New York: Harper Collins, 2002).

9. See R. Edward Freeman, "The Politics of Stakeholder Theory: Some Future Directions," *Business Ethics Quarterly* 4:409–22.

10. The second part of the integration thesis is left for another occasion. Philosophers who read this essay may note the radical departure from standard accounts of political philosophy. Suppose we began the inquiry into political philosophy with the question, How is value creation and trade sustainable over time? and suppose that the traditional beginning question, How is the state justified? was a subsidiary one. We might discover or create some very different answers from the standard accounts of most political theory. See R. Edward Freeman and Robert Phillips, "Stakeholder Theory: A Libertarian Defense," *Business Ethics Quarterly* 12, no. 3 (2002): 331ff.

11. Here we roughly follow the logic of John Rawls in *Political Liberalism* (New York: Columbia University Press, 1995).

12. There are many statements of this principle. Our argument is that whatever the particular conception of responsibility there is some underlying concept that is captured like our willingness or our need to justify our lives to others. Note the answer that the dominant view of business must give to questions about responsibility. "Executives are responsible only for the effects of their actions on shareholders, or only insofar as their actions create or destroy shareholder value."

13. The spirit of this diagram is from R. Phillips, *Stakeholder Theory and Organizational Ethics* (San Francisco: Berret-Koehler Publishers, 2003).

14. In earlier versions of this essay in this volume we suggested that the notion of a fiduciary duty to stockholders be extended to "fiduciary duty to stakeholders." We believe that such a move cannot be defended without doing damage to the notion of "fiduciary." The idea of having a special duty to either one or a few stakeholders is not helpful.

15. Bill George, *Authentic Leadership* (San Francisco: Jossey Bass, 2004).

16. This is at least as clear as the directive given by the dominant model: create as much value as possible for shareholders.

17. Some philosophers have argued that the stakeholder approach is in need of a "normative justification." To the extent that this phrase has any meaning, we take it as a call to connect the logic of managing for stakeholders with more traditional ethical theory. As pragmatists we eschew the "descriptive vs. normative vs. instrumental" distinction that so many business thinkers (and stakeholder theorists) have adopted. Managing for stakeholders is inherently a narrative or story that is at once *descriptive* of how some businesses do act; *aspirational* and *normative* about how they could and should act; *instrumental* in terms of what means lead to what ends; and *managerial* in that it must be coherent on all of these dimensions and actually guide executive action.

18. See S. Venkataraman, "Stakeholder Value Equilibration and the Entrepreneurial Process," *Ethics and Entrepreneurship,* The Ruffin Series, 3 (2002): 45–57; S. R. Velamuri, "Entrepreneurship, Altruism, and the Good Society," *Ethics and Entrepreneurship,* The Ruffin Series 3 (2002): 125–43; and, T. Harting, S. Harmeling, and S. Venkataraman, "Innovative Stakeholder Relations: When "Ethics Pays" (and When it Doesn't)" *Business Ethics Quarterly* 16 (2006): 43–68.

19. Sometimes there are trade-offs and situations that economists would call "prisoner's dilemma" but these are not the paradigmatic cases, or if they are, we seem to solve them routinely, as Russell Hardin has suggested in *Morality Within the Limits of Reason* (Chicago: University of Chicago Press, 1998).

20. E. Mendieta (ed.), *Take Care of Freedom and Truth Will Take Care of Itself: Interviews with Richard Rorty* (Stanford: Stanford University Press, 2006), 68.

# What's Wrong—and What's Right—with Stakeholder Management

*John R. Boatright*

The concept of a stakeholder is one of the more prominent contributions of recent business ethics. Since the introduction of this concept by R. Edward Freemen in *Strategic Management: A Stakeholder Approach* (1984), a concern for the interests of all stakeholder groups has become a widely recognized feature, if not the defining feature, of ethical management.

Although the stakeholder concept has been developed in various ways, it has been expressed most often in the moral prescription that managers, in making decisions, ought to consider the interests of all stakeholders. The list of stakeholders is commonly taken to include employees, customers, suppliers, and the community, as well as shareholders and other investors. This obligation to serve all stakeholder interests, which is often called stakeholder management, is generally contrasted with the standard form of corporate governance, in which shareholder interests are primary. This latter view—which might be called "stockholder management"—is regarded by advocates of stakeholder management as morally unjustified. To focus attention on only one stakeholder, they allege, is to ignore other important groups whose interests a business organization ought to serve.

Advocates of stakeholder management get one point right: the modern for-profit corporation should serve the interests of all stakeholder groups. On this point, however, there is no conflict with the argument for the current system of corporate governance. Where stakeholder management goes wrong is in failing to recognize that a business organization in which managers act in the interest of the shareholders can also be one that, at the same time, benefits all stakeholder groups. This failure is due to a second mistake on the part of those who advocate stakeholder management. It is the simple fallacy of passing from the true premise that corporations ought to serve the interests of every stakeholder group to the false conclusion that this is a task for management. Stakeholder management assumes that management decision making is the main means by which the benefits of corporate wealth creation are distributed among stakeholders, but these benefits can also be obtained by groups interacting with a corporation in other ways, most notably through the market. Insofar as the market is able to provide the desired benefits to the various stakeholder groups, they have no need for management to explicitly consider their interests in making decisions.

At bottom, the dispute between stockholder and stakeholder management revolves around the question of how best to enable each stakeholder group or corporate constituency to benefit from the wealth-creating activity of business. Stakeholder management goes wrong by (1) failing to appreciate the extent to which the prevailing system of corporate governance, marked by shareholder primacy, serves the interests of all stakeholders, and (2) assuming that all stakeholder interests are best served by making this the task of management rather than using other means. Stakeholder management is right, however, to stress the moral requirement that every stakeholder group

---

benefit from corporate activity and to make managers aware of their responsibility to create wealth for the benefit of everyone.

## Two Forms of Stakeholder Management

It is important at the outset to distinguish two forms of stakeholder management. The main point of difference is whether stakeholder management is incompatible with and an alternative to the prevailing form of corporate governance, or whether it is a managerial guide that can be followed within corporations as they are currently legally structured.

First, it is a simple fact that a corporation has stakeholders in the sense of "groups who can affect, or who are affected by, the activities of the firm" (Freeman 1984). And any successful corporation must manage its relations with all stakeholder groups, if for no other reason than to benefit the shareholders. To manage stakeholder relations is not necessarily to serve each group's interest (although this might be the effect), but to consider their interests sufficiently to gain their cooperation. The manager's role is not merely to coordinate the contribution of the various stakeholders, but to inspire them to put forth their best efforts in a joint effort to create valuable products and services. Any firm that neglects its stakeholders or, worse, alienates them is doomed to failure.

Second, managers also have obligations to treat each stakeholder group in accord with accepted ethical standards. These obligations include not only those that are owed to everyone, such as honesty and respect, but also the obligations to abide by agreements or contracts made with a firm. In most countries, basic moral obligations concerning the treatment of employees, customers, and other parties as well as agreements and contracts are codified in laws that constitute the legal framework of business. Treating all stakeholders ethically is a requirement of any form of business

organization, although differences may exist about what ethics requires.

This version of stakeholder management, which is roughly what Donaldson and Preston (1995) call instrumental, does not constitute a system of corporate governance. Another form of stakeholder management, however, goes beyond the necessity of managing stakeholder relations and the obligations that are owed to stakeholder groups to the question of how stakeholder interests ought to be considered. Indeed, most advocates of stakeholder management hold that stakeholder interests should be central to the operation of a corporation in much the same way that shareholder interests dominate in the conventional shareholder-controlled firm. In general, Freeman and his colleagues contend that in making key decisions, managers ought to consider, all interests—those of shareholders and non-shareholders alike—and balance them in some way.

This form of stakeholder management, which corresponds more or less to Donaldson and Preston's normative stakeholder theory, does have implications for corporate governance. More specifically, the prevailing system of corporate governance may be expressed in three related propositions: (1) that shareholders ought to have control; (2) that managers have a fiduciary duty to serve shareholder interests alone; and (3) that the objective of the firm ought to be the maximization of shareholder wealth. The main theses of stakeholder management can then be stated by modifying each of these propositions as follows: (1) all stakeholders have a right to participate in corporate decisions that affect them; (2) managers have a fiduciary duty to serve the interests of all stakeholder groups; and (3) the objective of the firm ought to be the promotion of all interests and not those of shareholders alone.

The issues in these two sets of propositions—who has control or the right to make decisions, who is the beneficiary of management's fiduciary duty, and whose interests ought to be the objective of a firm—are at the heart of corporate governance. Consequently, stockholder management and this form of stakeholder management constitute two competing models of how corporations ought to be governed. Stakeholder management goes wrong when it is developed as an alternative system of corporate governance. As a prescription for corporate governance, stakeholder management not only is inferior to the prevailing system but involves several crucial mistakes. Stakeholder management as a guide for managers, on the other hand, contains much that is helpful to managers and constitutes a valuable corrective to some common misunderstandings of the argument for stockholder management.

## An Economic Approach to Corporate Governance

The prevailing stockholder model of corporate governance is founded on an economic approach that conceives a firm as a nexus of contracts between a legal entity called the firm and its various constituencies, which include employees, customers, suppliers, investors, and other groups. This approach begins with the assumptions that in a market, all individuals with economic assets—such as employees with skills, suppliers with raw materials, customers and investors with money, and so on—would trade with each other in order to obtain a greater return, and that the greatest return will often be obtained by combining individual assets in joint production. That is, individuals will frequently realize a greater economic return by cooperating with others in productive activity than by participating in a market alone.

## The Purpose of a Firm

In a seminal article, "The Theory of the Firm" (Coase 1937), Ronald Coase noted that cooperative productive activity could take place entirely in a market. So, he asked, why do firms exist? The answer lies in the costs that would be incurred by individuals in coordinating joint or cooperative production in a market. The transaction costs of making and enforcing all the contractual agreements that would be required are substantial. These costs could be reduced by creating firms in which hierarchical authority relations replace the market as the means for coordinating joint productive activity. Thus, for Coase, markets and hierarchies constitute two fundamentally different means for conducting productive activity. The former operates by exchange, the latter by direct control.

As individuals contribute their assets to joint production, they will voluntarily form firms because doing so brings a greater return insofar as conducting business in a firm rather than a market reduces costs. That is, the transaction costs of organizing productive activity entirely in a market can be reduced by bringing some of this activity into a hierarchical organization, and this reduction in costs will enable each participant to realize a greater return on the assets that are contributed to joint production. Because of this greater return, individuals with assets would voluntarily agree to contribute their assets to production in a firm.

On this theory, then, the purpose of a firm is to enable individuals with economic assets to realize the full benefits of joint production.[1] Every stakeholder group benefits from production in a firm. Employees, suppliers, and investors gain by the opportunity to contribute their assets—labor, materials, and capital respectively—in a lower-cost form of production that brings a corresponding higher return. Customers benefit by being able to purchase abundant, low-priced goods, and society as a whole is enriched by the wealth creation firms make possible. Although some of these benefits can be obtained in a market, there is an additional gain or return from deploying assets in a hierarchical form of production. It is this additional gain that a firm provides, and realizing this gain constitutes the reason why it is formed.

A firm serves the interests of all participants in much the way a market does. A market is a device that enables everyone to advance their interests by making mutually advantageous trades. Similarly, a firm enables those with assets to engage in joint production and thereby realize a greater gain than they could make alone in a market. Although market outcomes benefit everyone, no one has the task of ensuring these outcomes. So, too, in a firm. Managers, for the most part, are economic actors like employees, customers, and other stakeholders. Their particular role is to provide managerial or decision-making skills. In so doing, they act like other market participants, making agreements and keeping their word, in a cooperative productive activity that benefits everyone.

## The Role of Governance

A firm requires many inputs. Economists classify these as land, labor, and capital, although they also recognize the need for managerial expertise to coordinate these inputs. Traditional stakeholder groups interact with a business organization or firm as input providers—employees providing labor, suppliers providing raw materials, and so on. Each input brings a return such as employees' wages, suppliers' payments, and investors' interest and dividends. It is necessary in a firm for each input provider to secure their return, that is, to employ some means for ensuring that wages are paid, supplier payments are made, and so on. Generally, this security can be obtained by contracts or legal rules that obligate a firm to provide the return due to each corporate constituency.

Governance can be understood as the contractual agreements and legal rules that secure each input provider's claim for the return due on that input provider's contribution to the productive activity of a firm. Accordingly, every asset contributed to joint production will be accompanied by a governance structure of some kind, which may vary depending on the features of the asset provided. That is, the governance structure for securing employees' wages and other benefits may be different from those protecting suppliers, and similarly for other input providers.

When the protection for each group's input can be provided by fully specified contracts or precise legal rules, the governance structure is relatively uncomplicated. Customers, for example, are adequately protected, for the most part, by sales contracts, warranties, and the like. The market also provides some protection. Thus, customers are protected by the opportunity to switch from one seller to another. The greatest problems of governance occur for firm-specific assets, which are assets that cannot easily be removed from production. When assets are firm specific, the providers become "locked in."

For example, employees, who ordinarily assume little risk when they can easily move from one firm to another, are at greater risk when they develop skills that are of value only to their current employer. When their skills are firm specific, a move to another firm usually results in lower pay. Similarly, a supplier who invests in special equipment to manufacture goods used by only one customer is providing a firm-specific asset. In both cases, the input provider becomes "locked in" and thus has a greater need for protection than, say, customers.

Developing governance structures to protect input providers is also more complicated when contracts and legal rules cannot be developed easily due to complexity and uncertainty. Contracts and legal rules provide protection only when the situations likely to be encountered can be anticipated and the ways of proceeding in each situation can be specified. When planning is difficult because of the complexity and uncertainty of the situations that might arise, other means must be found to protect stakeholder interests.

Despite the three problems of lock-in, complexity, and uncertainty, governance structures for the assets of each input provider are relatively easy to provide for each stakeholder group except one, namely shareholders, the providers of equity capital.

**Shareholder Governance**

Although shareholders are commonly called the owners of a corporation, this sense of ownership is different from its ordinary use. Shareholders do not "own" General Motors in the same way that a person owns a car or a house. Rather, shareholders have a certain bundle of rights that includes the right of control and the right to the profits of a firm. To ask why shareholders should have these rights and thus be the owners of a firm makes no sense. The shareholders are, by definition, whatever group has the rights to control and to receive the profits of an enterprise. The more relevant question is why, in most corporations, this group is equity capital providers and not, say, employees or customers or, indeed, all stakeholders.

Part of the answer to this question is also a matter of definition. Equity capital is money provided to a firm in return for a claim on profits—or, more precisely, for a claim on residual revenues, which are the revenues that remain after all debts and other legal obligations are paid. Just as customers buy a company's products, equity capital providers "buy" the future profits of a firm; or, alternatively, in order to raise capital, a company "sells" its future profits to investors. In addition, since future profits are risky, investors not only provide

capital but also assume much of the risk of a firm. The willingness of shareholders to bear this residual risk—which is the risk that results from having a claim on residual revenues rather a fixed claim—benefits all other input providers. As long as a firm is solvent—which is to say that it can pay all its fixed obligations, such as employee wages, supplier's payments, and so on—then the claims of these groups are secure.

The remaining question, then, is why equity capital providers, who in effect "buy" the future profits of a firm and "sell" their risk-bearing services, should also have control and thus the right to have the firm run in their interest. The answer is very simple: control is the most suitable protection for their firm-specific asset. If their return on the asset they provide, namely capital, is the residual earnings or profit of a firm, then this return is very insecure unless they can ensure that the firm is operated for maximum profit. By contrast, the right of control is of little value to other input providers or stakeholder groups because their return is secure as long as a firm is solvent, not maximally profitable. In addition, the return on the firm-specific contribution of other, nonshareholder groups is better protected by other means.

That equity capital provides control is in the best interests of the other stakeholder groups. First, everyone benefits when business organizations are maximally profitable because of the greater wealth creation. If firms were controlled by groups whose interests are served only by firms that are solvent, not maximally profitable, then they would create less wealth. Second, every nonshareholder group benefits when shareholders assume much of the risk of an enterprise because their return is all the more secure. Shareholders are willing to assume this risk—in return for some compensation, of course—because they are better able to diversify their risks among a large number of companies. Employees, by contrast, are very undiversified inasmuch as their fortunes depend wholly upon the employing firm. Third, without the right of control, equity capital providers would require a greater return to compensate for the increased risk to their investment. This in turn would drive up the price of capital, thus increasing the cost of production for everyone.

Firms can be owned by groups other than equity capital providers. Some corporations are employee-owned, and others are owned by customers or suppliers (these are usually called *cooperatives*). Mutual insurance companies are owned by the policy holders. These forms of ownership are not common, however, because of their relative inefficiency. It is only under certain economic conditions that they would be preferred by the corporate constituencies involved.

The bottom line is that equity capital providers are usually (but not always) the shareholders of a firm, the group with control, because control rights are the best means for protecting their particular firm-specific asset. Each group has the opportunity to seek the best protections or safeguards for their own interests, which is to say the return on the firm-specific assets that they provide to a firm. Usually, nonshareholder groups are better served by safeguards other than control, which is left to shareholders. This outcome is not only efficient but also morally justified because it best serves the interests of all stakeholder groups and results from voluntary agreements or contracts made by all the relevant groups.

## Comparing Stockholder and Stakeholder Management

On one point, stockholder and stakeholder management are in agreement: the purpose of the firm is to enable each corporate constituency or stakeholder group to obtain the maximum benefit from their involvement. The economic approach to the firm expresses this purpose in terms of realizing the full benefits of engaging in joint production. Although the advocates of stakeholder management speak in general terms of having each group's interest taken into account and balanced one against the other, they must surely recognize that all benefits result from the wealth-creating economic activity and that stakeholders can receive no more benefits than this activity creates. In short, wealth must be created before it can be distributed.

However, two questions remain. One question is how best to protect or serve each stakeholder group's interests. On the economic approach, what each group is due is a return on the assets that they provide for joint production, and each asset is accompanied by a governance structure that protects this return. The distribution of the benefits or wealth that firms create is largely determined by the market, and the main concern of governance is to ensure that groups receiver what the market allots. There are many means for securing each group's return, one of which is reliance on management's decision-making powers. In the prevailing system of corporate governance, this means is utilized by giving shareholders control, making them the beneficiaries of management's fiduciary duty, and setting shareholder wealth as the objective of the firm. The question, then, is whether the means of relying on management's decision making would also best serve the interest of non-shareholder groups or whether they are better served by other means.

The second question is what are the interests of each group that ought to be protected or served? Stakeholder management advocates might contend that even if the market return due to each group is adequately protected by other means, they are sometimes due more, and that these additional, nonmarket benefits can be best provided by management. This position is a challenge to the use of the market to determine how the benefits of economic activity are to be distributed. Instead of using the market alone to make this determination, stakeholder management would make this a task of management.

### Protecting Stakeholder Interests

The first question is largely an empirical one about how best to protect the interests of each corporate constituency or stakeholder group. One way to answer this question is by conducting a thought experiment. Suppose that stakeholder management were practiced by a great many firms or even all firms in an economy. In such a system of corporate governance, all groups would share control of a firm; managers would have a fiduciary duty to act in the interests of all groups; and the objective of the firm would be to maximize the return to every group. The resulting economy would be a model of stakeholder management.

Now, add one more condition: that each group is free to opt out of such a system of governance and choose other means for protecting their interests. That is, they would have the opportunity to forgo the protection of management acting in their interests and to seek different contracts with a firm or different legal rules for protecting their interests. This could be achieved by allowing new firms to spring up that would offer different employment opportunities for workers, different purchasing opportunities for customers, different investment opportunities for investors, and so on. Governments could also experiment with different legal rules that promise to provide better protection.

Although opinions may different on the system of corporate governance that might emerge from this thought experiment, there is good reason to believe that each group would prefer stockholder management.

First, management decision making is a weaker form of protection than legally enforceable contracts or legal rules. When such contracts and rules are available, they are more likely to be preferred than a reliance on management's fiduciary duty. Shareholders are forced to rely on the protection of a fiduciary duty because of the problems of uncertainty and complexity that prevent them from utilizing fully specified contracts or precise legal rules. Fiduciary duty should be viewed, accordingly, not as a special privilege that shareholders enjoy but as an imperfect substitute when more effective means for protecting a group's interests are not available.

Second, corporate decision making is more efficient and effective when management has a single, clearly defined objective, and shareholder wealth maximization provides not only a workable decision guide but one that, if pursued, increases the total wealth creation of the firm. This, in turn, enables each group to obtain a greater share. That is, each group can get a larger piece of pie if the pie itself is larger. Thus, employees who seek greater job security or expanded benefits—which advocates of stakeholder management would support—are more likely to get these goods if the employing company is prospering. A similar argument can be developed for customers, suppliers, investors, and every other stakeholder group. The benefits of a single objective would be compromised if other groups sought, like shareholders, to protect themselves with claims on management's attention.

If the disagreement between stockholder and stakeholder management is an empirical one about the most effective means for protecting or serving the interests of each stakeholder group, then a definitive resolution is not easy. What the argument for stockholder management shows, however, is that reliance on management decision making, as stakeholder management proposes, is but one means and that many other means are available. Therefore, from the premise that corporate activity should benefit all stakeholder groups, it does not follow that ensuring this outcome is a task for management. It is an outcome that should be achieved by some means, but the alternative of contractual agreements and legal rules, which do not involve management decision making, may secure this end more effectively.

To conclude immediately that it is management's task to ensure that all stakeholders benefit would be to commit a rather elementary mistake in reasoning that might be called the stakeholder fallacy. Just because every stakeholder group ought to benefit from participation in a firm, it does not follow that the task of ensuring this outcome belongs to management—or, indeed, to any persons. This fallacy can be avoided by adding a second premise that gives reasons for believing that management decision making is a better means for protecting all stakeholder interests than the other means that might be employed. The argument for stockholder management gives good reasons for believing that this is not true—that nonshareholder interests are usually better protected or served by various contractual agreements and legal rules rather than a reliance on management decision making. So far, advocates of stakeholder management have not presented a compelling case to the contrary.

### Securing Fairness for Stakeholders

The second question about the interests that ought to be protected or served assumes that some stakeholders are due more than a secure return on the assets that they contribute to joint production. Stakeholder management advocates might contend that the prevailing system unduly favors one group, shareholders, and that more of the wealth created by firms ought to flow to other groups, such as employees, customers, and the community, even if this introduces some inefficiency and hence less wealth creation. In other words, stockholder management may be efficient, critics complain, but it is not fair. This is a charge to take seriously, and it is recognized in economics as the familiar equity–efficiency trade-off.

Without question, there are many ways in which stakeholders could be treated unfairly, and such unfair treatment might increase efficiency or it might merely benefit one stakeholder group at the expense of another. It is morally required that any economic system ensure basic fairness and, where necessary, make a morally defensible trade-off between fairness (or equity) and efficiency. Indeed, the law already contains extensive legal protection for stakeholders with regard to fairness and other ethical concerns. As previously noted, managers have an obligation to treat all stakeholders in accord with accepted ethical standards, which include considerations of fairness. A case can be made for stakeholder management, then, only if these ethical and legal obligations are inadequate to ensure the fair treatment of all stakeholders. Just as corporations should protect and serve the interests of all stakeholders, they should also treat all stakeholders fairly. The question, as before, is how best to do this. Is this a task for management or should it be handled in some other way?

Three points should be observed. One is that there is no reason to believe that contractual agreements and legal rules are any less adequate to ensure fairness than they are to secure each group's rightful return. Just as reliance on management's decision making to protect each group's return on its assets is generally inferior to other, more effective means, so, too, is it inferior for ensuring that the wealth created by firms is fairly distributed. In short, there are better ways than stakeholder management to ensure fairness.

Second, a case can be made that ensuring fairness is not a task of management. Aside from the question of efficacy—whether management decision making is an effective means for achieving this—there is a more fundamental question about who or what should determine the distribution of wealth. Broadly speaking, an economy faces two questions: how to produce wealth and how to distribute it. Generally, decisions about production are made in a market where managers, like employees, customers, and other participants, make decisions primarily on the basis of economic considerations. The market also determines how wealth is to be distributed, but the resulting distribution may not be fair or otherwise desirable.[2] When it becomes necessary or advisable to interfere in the operation of a market and alter the distribution of wealth, this task usually falls, and rightly falls, to government. Because the interests involved bear so heavily on people's welfare, decisions about the distribution of wealth that depart from market outcomes should be made, for the most part, through the political process. It is not only unreasonable to expect managers, who have enough responsibility making decisions about how to produce wealth, to handle questions about how it should be distributed, but it is also dangerous in a democracy to allow unelected managers to make such crucial decisions.

Third, it is a mistake to pursue fairness by means of corporate governance. As already noted, governance consists primarily in the contractual agreements and legal rules that protect the assets individuals contribute to production and their return on these assets. Corporate governance—which is the contract that shareholders make with a firm—answers the basic questions of who has control and whose interests should be served by management and made the objective of the firm. Questions about how the wealth created by firms should be distributed are separate from the concerns of governance and are answered by the market and by government. Not only are matters of

distribution not central to corporate governance, but changes in corporate governance are rarely effective in altering the distribution of wealth or in achieving other desirable social goals. As Easterbrook and Fischel (1991, 39) observed, there are many difficult moral and social questions, but "to view . . . [them] as governance matters "is to miss the point."

## Summary

Viewed in terms of an economic approach to the firm, stakeholder management offers managerial decision making as a means for protecting and advancing stakeholder interests. Insofar as it proposes that managers have a fiduciary duty to serve the interests of all stakeholders and that maximizing all stakeholder interests be the objective of the firm, it seeks to extend the means used to safeguard shareholders to benefit all stakeholders. In short, stakeholder management proposes that all stakeholders be treated like shareholders.

The fundamental mistake of stakeholder management is a failure to see that the needs of each stakeholder group, including shareholders, are different and that different means best meet these needs. The protection that shareholders derive from being the beneficiaries of management's fiduciary duty and having their interests be the objective of the firm fit their particular situation as residual claimants with difficult contracting problems, but employees, customers, suppliers, and other investors (such as bondholders, who provide debt rather than equity) are better served by other means, which include contractual agreements and various legal rules. Management decision making is a relatively ineffective means for protecting the interests of non-shareholder stakeholders. In any event, the choice of means for protecting each stakeholder group's interest is mainly an empirical one about what works best in practice, and the evidence tends to support the prevailing stock-holder-centered system of corporate governance.

Finally, insofar as stakeholder management assigns to managers the task of ensuring that the wealth created by a firm is distributed in a fair way that departs from the distribution that results from purely market forces, this task, too, is better done by other means, most notably through the political process. Managers lack both the ability and the legitimacy that are required to fulfill this task, and, in any event, the attempt to address pressing social problems by making changes in corporate governance is ill-conceived. Corporate governance, which is designed to solve specific problems of economic organization, is simply the wrong tool, like using a screwdriver to hammer a nail.

## What's Right with Stakeholder Management

Despite this generally negative appraisal of stakeholder management, it is still an important, constructive development in business ethics. Its positive contributions are obscured to some extent by those who present it as an alternative form of corporate governance and thus create a false choice between stakeholder and stockholder management. Stakeholder management can be understood in a way that complements rather than challenges the prevailing system of corporate governance.

First, stakeholder theory rightly insists that the purpose of a firm is to benefit every corporate constituency or stakeholder group. The prevailing system of corporate governance may obscure this purpose by failing to emphasize that management's fiduciary duty to shareholders and the objective of shareholder wealth maximization are merely means to an end. These benefits result from the agreements that a firm makes with one input

provider, namely, shareholders. However, a firm also makes agreements or contracts with other constituencies, including employees, customers, suppliers, and other investors, all for mutual advantage. When the assets contributed by these parties are firm-specific, they are accompanied by safeguards that constitute forms of governance. The agreements between these groups and a firm create both moral and legal obligations that are every bit as binding as those owed to shareholders. In addition, each stakeholder group, including managers, has an obligation to treat all others in accord with accepted ethical standards.

Although stockholder and stakeholder management are agreed on the purpose of a firm—to conduct economic activity in ways that benefit everyone—there is disagreement on how this is done. In particular, the stakeholder view makes it a task of management to ensure that this outcome occurs, whereas on the economic approach, mutual benefit is a result of the opportunity each group has to make mutually advantageous agreements. That is, a firm works like a market in creating mutual benefit from the opportunity to trade. Just as a market achieves this result without any person directing it, so, too, does a firm—in theory!

In practice, though, some stakeholders fail to benefit as they should from a firm's activity. This may occur for a variety of reasons including management's willful violation of agreements, market failures, and externalities or third-party effects. For example, a company might fail to make expected contributions to a pension plan, sell a product to consumers with undisclosed defects or operate a polluting factory. In general, it is the responsibility of government to prevent or correct for these possibilities, but managers, especially those at the top of a business organization, might also be held to have some responsibility. Stakeholder management asks managers to recognize that a firm should benefit all stakeholders, to be aware when it fails to do so, and to take some responsibility for correcting the problems that lead to this failure. Just as we all have a responsibility to make sure that markets work as they should to produce a benefit for all, so, too, do we all, including managers, have a responsibility for ensuring the proper functioning of firms.

Second, corporate governance is concerned with how business organizations should be legally structured and controlled. The provisions that management has a fiduciary duty to serve shareholder interests and that shareholder wealth maximization should be the objective of the firm dictate how decisions about major investment decisions and overall strategy should be made. They tell us very little about how managers should actually go about their task of managing a firm so as to create wealth for shareholders or anyone else. Everyone can benefit from the productive activity of a firm only if there is a vision for a creating a valuable product or service as well as a strategy for achieving this vision. As Michael Jensen (2002, 245) observes,

> Value maximizing tell the participants in an organization how they will assess their success in achieving a vision or in implementing a strategy. But value maximizing says nothing about how to create a superior vision or strategy. And value maximizing says nothing to employees or managers about how to find or establish initiatives or ventures that create value. It only tells us how we will measure success in the activity.

Freeman and his colleagues (Freeman, Wicks, and Parmar 2004, 364) describe stakeholder management as addressing this matter of what managers and other need to do to create wealth. They write,

> Economic value is created by people who voluntarily come together and cooperate to improve everyone's circumstances. Managers must develop relationships, inspire their stakeholders, and create communities where everyone strives to give their best to deliver the value the firm promises.

The first sentence expresses the fundamental principle that firms exist to benefit all those who take part in them, which is shared with the economic approach. The second sentence is concerned with how managers should actually carry out their role. Left unaddressed, though, is who should have control of a firm and in whose interest a firm should be run. If, as the economic approach holds, the answer is the shareholders, then stakeholder management is not only compatible with stockholder management but an essential complement.

Stakeholder management, then, as a guide for managers rather than a form of corporate governance, provides a valuable corrective to managers who fail to appreciate how shareholder primacy benefits all stakeholders and use it as a reason for disregarding other stakeholders. Such managers commit a mistake of their own by confusing how a corporation should be governed with how it should be managed. There is no reason why managers who act in the interests of shareholders and seek maximum shareholder wealth cannot also run firms that provide the greatest benefit for everyone. Indeed, a manager who fails to benefit every stakeholder group is not achieving the full potential of a firm.

## NOTES

1. The term *purpose* is used here in the sense of the function served by organizing economic activity in firms. Like a market, a firm can be said to have no purpose of its own but to be an organizational form that allows individuals to carry out what purposes or goals they have. Thus, a firm enables workers to earn a wage, customers to obtain goods, and investors to gain a return. In addition, a corporation is generally formed to carry on some economic activity, such as making automobiles, which may also be said to be its purpose. Different groups may participate in a firm, as in a market, for different ends, and they may or may not share

an interest in the activity for which a firm is organized. That is, a person may work for the Ford Motor Company merely to earn a wage and not share the purpose of the firm to make cars.

2. With regard to the criticism that shareholders receive a disproportionate return, it should be noted that their return is the market rate for capital. Thus, the return to shareholders is determined by a market for capital just as wages for workers and prices charged to customers are determined by their respective markets.

## REFERENCES

Boatright, John R. 2002a. Contractors as Stakeholders: Reconciling Stakeholder Theory with the Nexus-of-Contracts Firm. *Journal of Banking and Finance* 26:1837–52.

———. 2002b. Corporate Governance: Justifying the Role of Shareholder. In *Blackwell Guide to Business Ethics,* ed. Norman E. Bowie. Malden, MA: Blackwell.

———. 2004. "Employee Governance and the Ownership of the Firm." *Business Ethics Quarterly* 14:1–21.

Coase, Ronald H. 1937. "The Nature of the Firm." *Economica,* N.S., 3:1–44.

Donaldson, Thomas, and Lee E. Preston. 1995. "The Stakeholder Theory of the Corporation: Concepts, Evidence, and Implications." *Academy of Management Review* 20:65–91.

Easterbrook, Frank H., and Daniel R. Fishel. 1991. *The Economic Structure of Corporate Law.* Cambridge, MA: Harvard University Press.

Freeman, R. Edward. 1984. *Strategic Management: A Stakeholder Approach.* Boston, MA: Pitman.

Freeman, R. Edward, and D. L. Reed. 1983. "Stockholders and Stakeholders: A New Perspective on Corporate Governance." *California Management Review* 25:88–106.

Freeman, R. Edward, Andrew C. Wicks, and Bidhan Parmar. 2004. "Stakeholder Theory and 'The Corporate Objective Revisited.'" *Organization Science* 15:364–69.

Jensen, Michael C. 2002. "Value Maximization, Stakeholder Theory, and the Corporate Objective Function." *Business Ethics Quarterly* 12:235–56.

# Decency Means More than "Always Low Prices": A Comparison of Costco to Wal-Mart's Sam's Club

*Wayne F. Cascio*

To be sure, Wal-Mart wields its awesome power for just one purpose: to bring the lowest possible prices to its customers. Sam Walton, affectionately known as "Mr. Sam" by Wal-Mart associates, embodied a number of admirable values that he instilled in the company he founded: hard work, discipline, modesty, unpretentiousness, and frugality. By all accounts he also wanted his employees to be motivated, inspired, and happy to work for Wal-Mart. At the same time, however, he was driven, tireless, and determined to drive a hard bargain. His brilliance lay in his ability to execute a singularly powerful idea: Sell stuff that people need every day, just a little cheaper than everyone else, sell it at that low price all the time, and customers will flock to you. Wal-Mart's mission is found as a slogan printed on every

From *Academy of Management Perspectives,* August 2006. Reprinted with permission.

Wal-Mart bag: "Always low prices. *Always.*" Wal-Mart's obsessive focus on that single core value created what has become the largest and most powerful company in history.

The company espouses those same core values today, but ironically, their application is quite different from that in the 1960s, the 1970s, even the 1980s. Today, the very characteristics that allowed Wal-Mart to prosper and grow are the source of unrelenting criticism. As Fishman (2006) notes, the company's core values seem to have become inverted, for they now sometimes drive behavior that is not only exploitive but, in some cases, illegal as well. Consider the pressure on store managers to control labor cost. As noted in its 2005 annual report, Wal-Mart is a defendant in numerous class-action lawsuits involving employment-related issues as varied as failure to pay required overtime to hourly employees, challenges to exempt (from overtime) status by assistant store managers, and allegations of gender-based discrimination in pay, promotions, job transfers, training, job assignments, and health-care coverage.

There is another aspect of the Wal-Mart effect that is more troubling, and it concerns how Wal-Mart gets those low prices: low wages for its employees, unrelenting pressure on suppliers, products cheap in quality as well as price, offshoring jobs. "Wal-Mart has the power to squeeze profit-killing concessions from suppliers, many of whom are willing to do almost anything to keep the retailer happy, in part because Wal-Mart now dominates consumer markets so thoroughly that they have no choice . . . Wal-Mart's price pressure can leave so little profit that there is little left for innovation . . . [As a result] decisions made in Bentonville routinely close factories as well as open them" (Fishman 2006, 89).

This paper focuses on a company that is already more than "always low prices." That company is warehouse-retailer Costco—one that may provide an alternative to the Wal-Mart

model by delivering low prices to consumers, but not at the cost of employees' wages or quality of life. In the following sections we will begin by providing some background on the company, including its history, its business model, its ethical principles, core beliefs, and values. Then we will consider some typical Wall Street analysts' assessments of this approach, followed by a systematic comparison of the financial performance of Costco with that of Sam's Club, a warehouse retailer that is part of Wal-Mart.

### Costco, A Brief History

The company's co-founder and chief executive officer, Jim Sinegal, is the son of a coal miner and steelworker. In 1954, as an 18-year-old student at San Diego Community College, a friend asked him to help unload mattresses for a month-old discounter called Fed-Mart. What he thought would be a one-day job turned into a career. He rose to executive vice-president for merchandising, and became a protégé of Fed-Mart's chairman, Sol Price. Mr. Price is credited with inventing the idea of high-volume warehouse stores that sell a limited number of products.

Sol Price sold Fed-Mart to a German retailer in 1975, and was fired soon after. Mr. Sinegal then left and helped Mr. Price start a new warehouse company, Price Club. Its huge success led others to enter the business: Wal-Mart started Sam's Club, Zayre's started BJ's Wholesale Club, and in 1983 a Seattle entrepreneur, Jeffrey Brotman, helped Mr. Sinegal to found Costco Wholesale Corporation. The company began with a single store in Issaquah, Washington, outside of Seattle. At the end of fiscal 2005, as the fourth largest retailer in the United States and the ninth largest in the world, it had a total of 460 warehouses in 37 U.S. states, Puerto Rico, and several additional countries: Canada, Mexico, United Kingdom,

Taiwan, South Korea, and Japan. Costoco and Price Club merged in 1993.

## Ethical Principles, Core Beliefs, and Values

In their most recent letter to shareholders, co-founders Jeff Brotman and Jim Sinegal wrote: "We remain committed to running our company and living conscientiously by our Code of Ethics every day: to obey the law; take care of our members; take care of our employees; respect our suppliers; and reward you, our shareholders" (Costco Wholesale Corp. Annual Report 2005, 5). Note the modern-day heresy in Costco's numbered code of ethics: taking care of customers and employees takes precedence over rewarding shareholders. As we will see below, this has not escaped the critical appraisal of Wall Street analysts.

In contrast to Wal-Mart, which believes, as many other companies do, that shareholders are best served if employers do all they can to hold down costs, including the costs of labor, Costco's approach is decidedly different. In terms of how it treats its workers, Mr. Sinegal says, "It absolutely makes good business sense. Most people agree that we're the lowest-cost provider. Yet we pay the highest wages. So it must mean we get better productivity. It's axiomatic in our business—you get what you pay for" (Shapiro 2004, 5).

Wages at Costco start at $10 an hour, rising to $18.32, excluding *twice*-a-year bonuses of between $2,000 and $3,000 for those at the top wage for more than a year. Its average hourly wage is $17 an hour. Wal-Mart does not share its wage scale, and does not break out separately the pay of its Sam's Club workers, but the average pay of a full-time worker at Wal-Mart is $10.11 an hour. The pay scale of unionized grocery clerks in the Puget Sound area, very good jobs as far as retail goes, provides a further comparison. Those jobs start at $7.73 an hour and top out at $18.

Labor costs at Costco are expensive, accounting for about 70 percent of the company's total cost of operations, and they are more than 40 percent higher than those at Wal-Mart. So how can the company compete based on cost leadership and still pay such high wages? According to co-founder Sinegal: "It's just good business. I mean obviously anyone who is a business person thinks about the importance of people to their operation. You've got to want to get the very best people that you can, and you want to be able to keep them and provide some job security for them. That's not just altruism, it's good business" (Frey 2004, 3).

## Turning Over Inventory Faster Than People

Costco's wages help keep turnover unusually low, 17 percent overall and just 6 percent after the first year. In contrast, turnover at Wal-Mart is 44 percent per year, close to the retail-industry average. "We're trying to turn our inventory faster than our people," says Mr. Sinegal. "Obviously it's not just wages that motivate people. How much they are respected, and whether they feel they can have a career at a company, are also important" (Shapiro 2004, 5).

Toward that end, Costco also has some rules about discipline and promotion. An employee with more than two years of service cannot be fired without the approval of a senior company officer. (It used to be that only one of the cofounders, Sinegal or Brotman, could issue this approval.) The company also requires itself to promote internally for 86 percent of its openings in top positions. "In truth, it turns out to be 98 percent" according to Mr. Sinegal (Shapiro 2004, 5). By comparison, and this is also very high, 76 percent of all store managers at Wal-Mart started their careers in hourly positions.

Costco's chief financial officer, Richard Galanti, speaks the same language. "One of the things Wall Street chided us on is that we're too good to our employees . . . We don't think that's possible." In his office, he keeps a memo from Sol Price, dated August 8, 1967, posted on his bulletin board. It reads: "Although we are all interested in margin, it must never be done at the expense of our philosophy." To Galanti, there is an object lesson in that approach with respect to employee relations: "Costco is not going to make money at the expense of what's right" (Shapiro 2004, 6).

### The View from Wall Street Analysts

How is Costco's treatment of employees received on Wall Street? Not everyone is happy with this business strategy. Some Wall Street analysts argue that Mr. Sinegal is overly generous, not only to Costco's customers, but to its employees as well. They worry that the company's operating expenses could get out of hand. In the opinion of Deutsche Bank Securities, Inc. analyst Bill Dreher, "At Costco, it's better to be an employee or a customer than a shareholder" (Holmes & Zellner 2004, 76). Sanford C. Bernstein & Co. analyst Ian Gordon argued similarly: "Whatever goes to employees comes out of the pockets of shareholders" (Shapiro 2004, 1).

Another Sanford C. Bernstein & Co. analyst, Emme Kozloff, faulted Mr. Sinegal for being too generous to his employees. She noted that when analysts complained that Costco's workers were paying just 4 percent toward their health-care costs, he raised that percentage only to 8 percent, when the retail average is 25 percent. "He has been too benevolent," she said. "He's right that a happy employee is a productive, long-term employee, but he could force employees to pick up a little more of the burden" (Greenhouse 2005, 2). She added, "Their benefits are amazing, but shareholders get frustrated from a stock perspective" (Zimmerman 2004, 3).

Like other companies, public and private, small and large, surging health-care costs forced Costco to move aggressively to control expenses. The increase in Costco employees' contribution to 8 percent was the company's first increase in employee health premiums in eight years. According to CEO Jim Sinegal, the company held off from boosting premiums for as long as it could, and it did not give in until it had lowered its earnings forecast twice (Zimmerman 2004).

Analyst Bill Dreher agrees with Emme Kozloff. "From the perspective of investors, Costco's benefits are overly generous. Public companies need to care for shareholders first. Costco runs its business like it is a private company" (Zimmerman 2004, 1). According to Mr. Dreher, Costco's unusually high wages and benefits contribute to investor concerns that profit margins at Costco aren't as high as they should be.

Analyst Ian Gordon also noted another Costco sin: it treats its customers too well. Its bargain-basement prices are legendary, and, as a result, customers flock to its stores. At about the same time that these analysts were commenting on Costco, the company was planning to add staff at checkouts in order to shorten lines. While business schools often teach that caring for customers is a cardinal rule for business success, Wall Street tended to put a different spin on the company's customer-care initiative, as analyst Gordon noted: "It was spending what could have been shareholders' profit on making a better experience for customers" (Shapiro 2004, 1).

What is Costco's response to this criticism? According to CEO Sinegal: "On Wall Street they're in the business of making money between now and next Thursday. I don't say that with any bitterness, but we can't take that view. We want to build a company that will still be here 50 and 60 years from now" (Greenhouse 2005, 2).

If shareholders mind Mr. Sinegal's philosophy, it is not obvious. Consider a 5-year comparison of the performance of Costco's and Wal-Mart's common stock, as of May 1, 2006. Based on an index value of 100 on May 1, 2001, Costco's stock has risen 55 percent during that time period, while Wal-Mart's has fallen 10 percent. According to Forbes.com, on May 20, 2006, Costco shares traded at 24.8 times expected earnings. At Wal-Mart the multiple was 17.4.

If anything, Costco's approach shows that when it comes to wages and benefits, a cost-leadership strategy need not be a race to the bottom. In the words of CEO Sinegal, "We pay much better than Wal-Mart. That's not altruism, that's good business" (Shields 2005). The contrast is stark and the stakes are high. Which model of competition will predominate in the United States? As we shall see below, Costco's magic lies in its ability to lift productivity, to compete on employee smarts, management savvy, and constant innovation, rather than to skimp on pay and benefits.

## Costco's Merchandise and Pricing Strategy

It starts with the buyers. Companies that do business with Sam's Club and Costco, like Mag Instrument, Inc., the manufacturer of Maglite brand flashlights, notice that the warehouse clubs' buyers have far different approaches to selecting merchandise. Sam's Club buyers tend to think about value—meaning price—while Costco's buyers tend to think about value—meaning quality. John Wyatt, Vice-president of sales at Mag Instrument says, "There's just a different mentality, a safer mentality at Sam's, less cutting-edge. Costco's buyers have full authority to do what they want. They're given freedom to make mistakes" (Coleman-Lochner 2006, 8C).

Costco CFO Richard Galanti linked the company's employees to the company's pop-ularity with customers. "We certainly believe that the quality of our employees is one very important reason—realizing they're ambassadors to the customer—for our success" (Coleman-Lochner 2006, 8C). The fact that Costco rewards workers for treating customers well, through its bonus program, is something you don't see on the shelves, yet it contributes to the stores' popularity. So also does its pricing policy.

To appreciate the pricing policy, consider a single item, men's all-cotton button-down shirts that bear Costco's signature brand name, Kirkland. They sell for $12.99 each. A few years ago they sold for $17.99, a bargain even then. Costco had committed to the manufacturer that it would buy at least 100,000 a year. Two years ago, however, it was selling a million per year. So it negotiated a better price with the manufacturer. As a result, Costco dropped the price it charges customers by $5 a shirt (Shapiro 2004).

Acknowledging the temptation to charge a little more, CEO Sinegal asks, "Who the hell's going to notice if you charge $14.99 instead of $12? Well, we're going to know. It's an attitudinal thing—you always give the customer the best deal" (Shapiro 2004, 9). That is the essence of Costco's pricing strategy: wow consumers with unbelievably low prices so they keep coming in.

In fact, Costco sets a strict cap on its profit margin per item: 14 percent for all goods except Kirkland-brand items, which have a 15 percent cap. Department stores typically mark up items by 30 percent or more. That cap on markup stays the same no matter how great the demand or how limited the supply.

## Relations with Suppliers

Fishman and others have described Wal-Mart's legendary squeeze plays on its suppliers. Costco takes a slightly different, but no less tough, approach toward its suppliers. It simply warns suppliers not to offer other retailers lower prices than Costco gets.

When a frozen-food supplier mistakenly sent Costco an invoice meant for Wal-Mart, Mr. Sinegal discovered that Wal-Mart was getting a better price. Costco has not brought that supplier back. Costco has to be flinty, because the competition is so fierce. Says Mr. Sinegal, "We have to be competitive against the biggest competitor in the world. We cannot afford to be timid" (Greenhouse 2005, 3).

Nor can Costco allow personal relationships to get in the way. As an example, consider what happened when Starbucks did not pass on savings from a drop in coffee-bean prices. Although Mr. Sinegal is a friend of Starbucks Chairman Howard Schultz, Mr. Sinegal warned that he would remove Starbucks coffee from his stores unless it cut its prices. Starbucks relented. According to Tim Rose, Costco's Senior Vice-President for food merchandizing, "Howard said, 'Who do you think you are, the price police?'" Mr. Sinegal replied emphatically that he was.

To sum up the previous two sections, a reasonable conclusion is that Costco offers high-quality merchandise at low prices, and it does not hesitate to lean on its suppliers—all of its suppliers—to ensure that it is getting as good a deal as any other retailer. What it sacrifices in margin it makes up in volume. Such frugality extends to the chief executive officer's pay, but when it comes to Costco employees, generous benefits and accommodation to labor unions set Costco apart from almost any other retailer.

## CEO Pay and Employee Benefits at Costco

For the last three years, CEO Sinegal has received a salary of $350,000, excluding stock options. That is very low for a CEO of a $52 billion-per-year business. By comparison, the typical CEO of a large American company makes more than 430 times the pay of the average worker. In a 2005 interview with *ABC News* Mr. Sinegal said, "I figured that if I was making something like 12 times more than the typical person working on the floor, that was a fair salary." Of course, as a co-founder of the company, Sinegal owns a lot of Costco stock—more than $150 million worth. He's rich, but only on paper (Goldberg & Ritter 2005).

In terms of employee benefits, Costco contributes generously to its workers' 401(k) plans, starting with 3 percent of salary the second year, and rising to 9 percent after 25 years. Its insurance programs absorb most dental expenses. Costco workers pay 8 percent of their health premiums. Full-time workers are eligible for health insurance after three months, and part-timers after six months. The retail-industry average is 23 percent. Eighty-five percent of Costco employees have health-insurance coverage, compared to less than half at Wal-Mart and Target.

Perhaps Chief Financial Officer Richard Galanti best sums up Costco's philosophy of employee relations. "From day one, we've run the company with the philosophy that if we pay better than average, provide a salary people can live on, have a positive environment and good benefits, we'll be able to hire better people, they'll stay longer, and be more efficient" (Zimmerman 2004, 2–3).

In return for all of its largesse, Costco does enjoy low employee turnover, as we mentioned earlier, but it also reaps a less obvious benefit: low inventory shrinkage. Shrinkage is a combination of employee theft, shoplifting, vendor fraud, and administrative error. Of these four components, employee theft is by far the largest contributor. How much does shrinkage cost? A 2002 study by Ernst & Young of 55 of the largest and most successful American retailers operating an average of 1,076 stores with mean revenues of approximately $8.8 billion, revealed that the average loss was

1.7 percent of sales, or roughly $19 million annually. At a national level that amounts to more than $31 billion, costing the average family of four more than $440 a year in higher prices. Costco's inventory shrinkage is the lowest in the industry, well below 0.20 percent of sales for fiscal 2005. That also keeps prices low for consumers.

## Relations with Unions

When 70,000 employees of the nation's three largest grocery chains, Kroger, Safeway, and Albertson's, went on strike in Southern California in 2004, Costco avoided the fray, quietly renegotiating a separate contract with its union employees there. The 3-year deal, which was ratified by more than 90 percent of the workers, included higher wages and increased company contributions to employee pension plans.

In contrast, the strike at the supermarket chains lasted four months before a settlement was reached on February 29, 2004. It resulted in cuts in wages and benefits for new workers, thereby creating a two-tier system in which new workers coming in do not have the same wages and benefits as older workers.

About 13 percent of Costco's employees belong to unions (in California, Maryland, New Jersey, New York, and Virginia), and they work at warehouses that were previously Price Club locations. The relative labor peace is symbolic of the company's relations with its employees. According to Rome Aloise, an international union representative for the Teamsters, Costco is one of the better companies he deals with. "They gave us the best agreement of any retailer in the country." The contract guarantees employees at least 25 hours of work a week, and requires that at least half of a store's employees be full time (Greenhouse 2005).

Wal-Mart takes a different tack. Its official stance, as stated on its Web site, Walmartfacts. com, is as follows:

Our Wal-Mart union stance is simple. There has never been a need for a Wal-Mart union due to the familiar, special relationship between Wal-Mart associates and their managers. Wal-Mart has encouraging and advantageous relationships with both our loyal and happy associates on the floor of each Wal-Mart facility and our wonderful managerial staff. There has yet to be a standard in Wal-Mart union history for a union to be needed.

According to the *Los Angeles Times,* at the first sign of union activity, Wal-Mart managers are supposed to call a hotline, prompting a visit from a special team from Wal-Mart headquarters. Wal-Mart spokesperson Mona Williams told the *Times* that such teams do exist, but that their purpose is merely to help managers respond effectively and legally to union organizing activity. Judges have ruled in cases across the country that Wal-Mart has illegally influenced employees seeking to organize.

A few Wal-Mart employees have succeeded in organizing. A Wal-Mart store in Jonquière, Canada, was certified as a union shop, represented by the United Food & Commercial Workers (UFCW), in August, 2004. Two months later, just as the UFCW and Wal-Mart representatives were preparing to begin mandatory contract negotiations, Wal-Mart Canada issued an ominous press release from its headquarters near Toronto. "The Jonquière store is not meeting its business plan, and the company is concerned about the economic viability of the store." In February, 2005, before a collective-bargaining agreement was reached, Wal-Mart closed the store.

In 2000, 10 butchers at a Wal-Mart Supercenter in Jacksonville, Texas, voted to join a union. Less than a month later, Wal-Mart switched to pre-packaged meats, eliminating jobs for butchers from its stores nationwide.

Having examined business models, pricing strategies, and employment policies at Costco and some of its competitors, it is appropriate to look at their relative financial and operating performance in the marketplace. To do that, we will compare some relevant operating and financial-performance statistics of warehouse retailer Sam's Club, a business unit of Wal-Mart, to those of Costco.

## Costco versus Sam's Club: A Test of High- and Low-Wage Strategies

All data in this section come from the 2005 annual reports of Costco and Wal-Mart, unless otherwise noted. In 2005 Costco employed approximately 67,600 workers at its 338 warehouses in the United States, while Sam's Club employed approximately 110,200 at its 551 U.S. warehouses.[1] In terms of wages alone, a Costco employee earned, on average, $35,360 ($17 per hour). The average Sam's Club employee earned $21,028 ($10.11 per hour).[2] Labor rates at Costco are therefore more than 40 percent higher than those at Sam's Club. One important effect of high-versus-low wages is on employee turnover, and the financial effects of such turnover. These effects are quite different at Costco and Sam's Club.

The fully loaded cost of replacing a worker who leaves (separation, replacement, and training costs), depending on the level of the job, typically varies from 1.5 to 2.5 times the annual salary paid for that job, excluding lost productivity (Cascio 2000). To be extremely conservative, let us assume that the fully loaded cost to replace an hourly employee at Costco or Sam's Club costs only 60 percent of his or her annual salary.

If a Costco employee quits voluntarily, the fully loaded cost to replace him or her is therefore $21,216. If a Sam's Club employee leaves, the cost is $12,617. At first glance it may look like the low-wage strategy at Sam's Club yields greater savings in turnover. But wait. Employee turnover at Costco is 17 percent per year (11,492 employees), excluding seasonal workers. At Sam's Club it is more than 2.5 times

higher, 44 percent a year (48,488 employees). The total annual cost to Costco is therefore $21,216 × 11,492 = $243.81 million, while the total annual cost to Sam's Club is $12,617 × 48,488 = $611.77 million.

Of course the overall costs and numbers of employees who leave at Sam's Club is higher, because it employs more people. If Costco had an annual employee-turnover rate equivalent to that of Sam's Club (44 percent), that is, 29,744 employees who leave, its annual cost would be $631.05 million. Costco's opportunity savings (costs not incurred) therefore are $387.24 million *per year*.[3] Averaged over the total number of employees at each firm, however, the per-employee cost at Sam's Club is still higher, $5,274.41 versus $3,628.11 at Costco. High employee-turnover rates are expensive any way you look at it.

Wages are not the only distinguishing characteristic between the two retailers. At Costco, 85 percent of employees are covered by the company's health-care insurance plan, with the company paying an average of $5,735 per worker. Sam's Club covers 47 percent of its workers, at an average annual outlay of $3,500. Fully 91 percent of Costco's employees are covered by retirement plans, with the company contributing an average of $1,330 per employee, versus 64 percent of employees at Sam's Club, with the company contributing an average of $747 per employee.

In return for all of its generosity, Costco gets one of the most loyal and productive workforces in all of retailing. While Sam's Club's 110,200 employees generated some $37.1 billion in U.S. sales in 2005, Costco did $43.05 billion in U.S. sales with 38 percent fewer employees. As a result, Costco generated $21,805 in U.S. operating profit per hourly employee, compared to $11,615 at Sam's Club.[4]

Costco's productive workforce more than offsets its higher costs. Labor and overhead costs at Costco (selling, general, and administrative expenses, or SG&A) were 9.73 percent of sales in 2005. Wal-Mart does not break out SG&A at Sam's Club, but it is likely higher than at Costco, but lower than Wal-Mart's 17 percent of sales. By comparison, it was 24 percent at Target Stores. Costco's motivated employees also sell more: $886 of sales per square foot, versus only $525 of sales per square foot at Sam's Club, and $461 at BJ's Wholesale Club, its other primary club rival.[5]

These figures illustrate nicely the common fallacy that labor rates equal labor costs. Costco's hourly labor rates are more than 40 percent higher than those at Sam's Club ($17 versus $10.11), but when employee productivity is considered (sales per employee), Costco's labor costs are lower than those at Sam's Club (5.55 percent at Costco versus 6.25 percent at Sam's Club).[6]

## Conclusions

As Holmes and Zellner (2004) noted, "Given Costco's performance, the question for Wall Street shouldn't be why Costco isn't more like Wal-Mart. Rather, why can't Wal-Mart deliver high shareholder returns and high living standards for its workforce?" Says Costco CEO James Sinegal: 'Paying your employees well is not only the right thing to do, but it makes for good business'" (p. 77).

To make its high-wage strategy pay off, however, Costco is constantly looking for ways to increase efficiency, such as by repackaging goods into bulk items to reduce labor, speeding up Costco's just-in-time inventory and distribution system, and boosting sales per square foot. Nor have rivals been able to match Costco's innovative packaging or merchandising mix. For example, Costco was the first wholesale club to offer fresh meat, pharmacies, and photo labs.

Defenders of Wal-Mart's low-wage strategy focus on the undeniable benefits its low prices bring to consumers, but the broader question

is this: Which model of competition will predominate in the United States? While shareholders may do just as well with either strategy over the long run, it is important to note that the cheap-labor model is costly in many ways. It can lead to poverty and related social problems, and transfer costs to other companies and taxpayers, who indirectly pay the healthcare costs of all the workers not insured by their frugal employers.

Fishman described the extent to which Wal-Mart shifts the burden of payments for health care to taxpayers in Georgia and Tennessee. Those are not the only states where this has occurred. According to a study by the Institute for Labor and Employment at the University of California, Berkeley, California, taxpayers subsidized $20.5 million for medical care for Wal-Mart employees in that state alone.

At a broader level, the Democratic Staff of the Committee on Education and the Workforce estimates that one 200-person Wal-Mart store may result in a cost to federal taxpayers of $420,750 per year—about $2,103 per employee. Those additional public costs stem from items such as the following for qualifying Wal-Mart employees and their families: free and reduced lunches, housing assistance, federal tax credits and deductions for low-income families, additional federal healthcare costs of moving into state children's health-insurance programs, and low-income energy assistance.

If a large number of employers adopted the same low-wage strategy, their policies would certainly reduce the wages of U.S. workers, along with their purchasing power and standards of living. Such a low-wage strategy would crimp consumer spending, and constrict economic growth. In that sense, Wal-Mart is a problem, but also an opportunity. Consumer sentiment may provide some encouragement. Thus, in a recent survey, 89 percent of consumers said they would be willing to spend "a little extra" for products that are produced by companies that pay workers good wages and have good working conditions. Only 10 percent of respondents answered "no" to that item, and 1 percent were unsure. Costco's strategy of combining high wages and benefits with innovative ideas and a productive workforce shows that consumers, workers, and shareholders all can benefit from a cost-leadership strategy.

## NOTES

1. These figures were derived under the assumption that each warehouse at Sam's Club and Costco employs an average of 200 workers. In 2005 Costco had 338 warehouses in the United States. In 2005 Sam's Club had 551 U.S. warehouses.

2. The average wage rate for Costco employees was reported in Coleman-Lochner (2006). The average wage rate for Sam's Club employees is based on the average wage rate for Wal-Mart's hourly workers. The company does not identify the pay rate of Sam's Club employees separately. Annual wages are computed by multiplying 2,080 (40 hours per week × 52 weeks) times the average employee's hourly wage in each company.

3. $631.05 million (costs that would be incurred with a 44 percent turnover rate) minus $243.81 million (costs actually incurred with a 17 percent turnover rate) = $387.24 million.

4. Wal-Mart measures the profit of each of its segments, of which Sam's Club is one, as "segment operating income," which is defined as income from continuing operations before net income expense, income taxes, and minority interest (Wal-Mart 2005 annual report, p. 48). Sam's Club's operating income for 2005 was $1.28 billion. At Costco, it was $1.474 billion. When Sam's Club's operating income is divided by the number of employees (110,200) it equals $11,615.25. When Costco's operating income is divided by the number of employees (67,600) it equals $21,804.73.

5. In its 2005 annual report, Costco reported that each of its warehouses averaged $124 million in sales, and that each warehouse averaged 140,000 square feet. Wal-Mart's 2005 annual report showed Sam's Club's total square footage as 70.7 million, with $37.119 billion in sales. Information for BJ's Wholesale Club for 2005 comes from the 5-year financial-information summary presented at following website: http://www.bjsinvestor.com/factsheet.cfm.

6. These figures were computed as follows. Costco generates $636,849 in annual sales per employee, and it pays each employee an average of $35,360 in wages. That is 5.55 percent of the sales generated. Sam's Club generates $336,660 in annual sales per employee, and it pays each employee an average of $21,028 in wages. That is 6.25 percent of the sales generated.

## REFERENCES

Coleman-Lochner, L. 2006. "Costco Service Key to Outpacing Rival Sam's Club." *Denver Post,* March 4: 1C, 8C.

Costco Wholesale Corporation. 2005. *Annual Report, 2005.* Retrieved from www.Costco.com on April 8, 2006.

Democratic Staff of the Committee on Education and the Workforce. 2004. Everyday Low Wages: The Hidden Price We All Pay for Wal-Mart. In *Taking Sides: Clashing Views on Economic Issues*, 12th ed., 2006, ed. F. J. Bonello 162–78. Dubuque, IA: McGraw-Hill/Dushkin.

Ernst & Young. 2003. "Ernst & Young Estimates Retailers Lose $46 Billion Annually to Inventory Shrinkage." Retrieved from www.clear-vu.com/industrynews.cfm?newssel9 on May 21, 2006.

Fishman, C. 2006. *The Wal-Mart Effect.* New York: Penguin.

Fortune 500. 2006. "Fortune 500: America's Largest Corporations." *Fortune* (April 17): F-1–F-20.

Frey, C. 2004. "Costco's Love of Labor: Employees' Well-being Key to Its Success." *Seattle Post-Intelligencer,* March 29. Retrieved from www.seattlepi.nwsource.com on May 1, 2006.

Goldberg, A. B., & Ritter, B. 2005. "Costco CEO Finds Pro-worker Means Profitability." *ABC News,* December 2. Retrieved from http://abcnews.go.com/2020 on April 24, 2006.

Greenhouse, S. 2005. "How Costco Became the Anti-Wal-Mart." *New York Times,* July 17. Retrieved from www.nytimes.com/2005/07/17/business/yourmoney/17costco.html on May 1, 2006.

Holmes, S., & Zellner, W. (2004). "The Costco Way." *Business Week,* (April 12): 76, 77.

Shapiro, N. 2004. "Company for the People." *Seattle Weekly,* December 15. Retrieved from www. seattleweekly.com/generic/show_print.php on May 1, 2006.

Shields, M. 2005. "Treating Workers Justly Pays Off." *CNN.com,* September 5, 2005. Retrieved from http://cnn.worldnews.com on May 1, 2006.

Zimmerman, A. 2004. "Costco's Dilemma: Is Treating Employees Well Unacceptable for a Publicly-Traded Corporation?" *Wall Street Journal,* March 26. Retrieved from www.reclaimdemocracy. org/articles_2004/costco_employee_benefits_ walmart.html on May 1, 2006.

## LEGAL PERSPECTIVES

# Dodge v. Ford Motor Co.

*Michigan Supreme Court*

. . . When plaintiffs made their complaint and demand for further dividends, the Ford Motor Company had concluded its most prosperous year of business. The demand for its cars at the price of the preceding year continued. It could make and could market in the year beginning August 1, 1916, more than 500,000 cars. Sales of parts and repairs would necessarily increase. The cost of materials was likely to advance, and perhaps the price of labor; but it reasonably might have expected a profit for the year of upwards of $60,000,000. . . . Considering only these facts, a refusal to declare and pay further dividends appears to be not an exercise of discretion on the part of the directors, but an arbitrary refusal to do what the circumstances required to be done. These facts and others call upon the directors to justify their action, or failure or refusal to act. In justification, the defendants have offered testimony tending to prove and which does prove, the following facts: It had been the policy of the corporation for a considerable time to annually reduce the selling price of cars, while

keeping up, or improving, their quality. As early as in June, 1915, a general plan for the expansion of the productive capacity of the concern by a practical duplication of its plant had been talked over by the executive officers and directors and agreed upon; not all of the details having been settled, and no formal action of directors having been taken. The erection of a smelter was considered, and engineering and other data in connection therewith secured. In consequence, it was determined not to reduce the selling price of cars for the year beginning August 1, 1915, but to maintain the price to accumulate a large surplus to pay for the proposed expansion of plant and equipment, and perhaps to build a plant for smelting ore. It is hoped, by Mr. Ford, that eventually 1,000,000 cars will be annually produced. The contemplated changes will permit the increased output.

The plan, as affecting the profits of the business for the year beginning August 1, 1916, and thereafter, calls for a reduction in the selling price of the cars. . . . In short, the plan

---

204 Mich. 459, 170 N.W. 668, 3 A.L.R. 413 (1919). Majority opinion by Justice J. Ostrander.

does not call for and is not intended to produce immediately a more profitable business, but a less profitable one; not only less profitable than formerly, but less profitable than it is admitted it might be made. The apparent immediate effect will be to diminish the value of shares and the returns to shareholders.

It is the contention of plaintiffs that the apparent effect of the plan is intended to be the continued and continuing effect of it, and that it is deliberately proposed, not of record and not by official corporate declaration, but nevertheless proposed, to continue the corporation henceforth as a semi-eleemosynary institution and not as a business institution. In support of this contention, they point to the attitude and to the expressions of Mr. Henry Ford. . . .

> My ambition," said Mr. Ford, "is to employ still more men, to spread the benefits of this industrial system to the greatest possible number, to help them build up their lives and their homes. To do this we are putting the greatest share of our profits back in the business.
> With regard to dividends, the company paid sixty per cent, on its capitalization of two million dollars, or $1,200,000, leaving $58,000,000 to reinvest for the growth of the company. This is Mr. Ford's policy at present, and it is understood that the other stockholders cheerfully accede to this plan.

He had made up his mind in the summer of 1916 that no dividends other than the regular dividends should be paid, "for the present."

> "Q. For how long? Had you fixed in your mind any time in the future, when you were going to pay—A. No."
> "Q. That was indefinite in the future? A. That was indefinite; yes, sir."

The record, and especially the testimony of Mr. Ford, convinces that he has to some extent the attitude towards shareholders of one who has dispensed and distributed to them large gains and that they should be content to take what he chooses to give. His testimony creates the impression, also, that he thinks the Ford Motor Company has made too much money, has had too large profits, and that, although large profits might be still earned, a sharing of them with the public, by reducing the price of the output of the company, ought to be undertaken. We have no doubt that certain sentiments, philanthropic and altruistic, creditable to Mr. Ford, had large influence in determining the policy to be pursued by the Ford Motor Company—the policy which has been herein referred to.

It is said by his counsel that—

> Although a manufacturing corporation cannot engage in humanitarian works as its principal business, the fact that it is organized for profit does not prevent the existence of implied powers to carry on with humanitarian motives such charitable works as are incidental to the main business of the corporation. . . .

In discussing this proposition counsel have referred to decisions [citations omitted]. These cases, after all, like all others in which the subject is treated, turn finally upon the point, the question, whether it appears that the directors were not acting for the best interests of the corporation. We do not draw in question, nor do counsel for the plaintiffs do so, the validity of the general proposition stated by counsel nor the soundness of the opinions delivered in the cases cited. The case presented here is not like any of them. The difference between an incidental humanitarian expenditure of corporate funds for the benefit of the employees, like the building of a hospital for their use and the employment of agencies for the betterment of their condition, and a general purpose and plan to benefit mankind at the expense of others, is obvious. There should be no confusion (of which there is evidence) of the duties which Mr. Ford conceives that he and the stockholders owe to the general public and the duties which in law he and his codirectors owe to protesting, minority stockholders. A business corporation is organized and carried on primarily for the profit of the stockholders. The powers of the directors are to be employed for that end. The discretion of directors is to be exercised in the choice of means to attain that end, and does not extend to a change in the end itself, to the reduction of profits, or to the nondistribution of profits among stockholders in order to devote them to other purposes. . . . As we have pointed out, and the proposition does not require argument to sustain it, it is not within the lawful powers of a board of directors to shape and conduct the affairs of a corporation for the merely incidental benefit of shareholders and for the primary purpose of benefiting others, and no one will contend that, if the avowed purpose of the defendant directors was to sacrifice the interests of shareholders, it would not be the duty of the courts to interfere. . . . It is obvious that an annual dividend of 60 per cent, upon $2,000,000, or $1,200,000, is the equivalent of a very small dividend upon $100,000,000, or more.

The decree of the court below fixing and determining the specific amount to be distributed to stockholders is affirmed. . . .

# A. P. Smith Manufacturing Co. v. Barlow

*Supreme Court of New Jersey*

The Chancery Division, in a well-reasoned opinion by Judge Stein, determined that a donation by the plaintiff The A.P. Smith Manufacturing Company to Princeton University was *intra vires*. Because of the public importance of the issues presented, the appeal duly taken to the Appellate Division has been certified directly to this court under Rule 1:5–1(a).

The company was incorporated in 1896 and is engaged in the manufacture and sale of valves, fire hydrants, and special equipment, mainly for water and gas industries. Its plant is located in East Orange and Bloomfield and it has approximately 300 employees. Over the years the company has contributed regularly to the local community chest and on occasions to Upsala College in east Orange and Newark University, now part of Rutgers, the State University. On July 24, 1951, the board of directors adopted a resolution which set forth that it was in the corporation's best interests to join with others in the 1951 Annual Giving to Princeton University, and appropriated the sum of $1,500 to be transferred by the corporation's treasurer to the university as a contribution towards its maintenance. When this action was questioned by stockholders the corporation instituted a declaratory judgment action in the Chancery Division and trial was had in due course.

Mr. Hubert F. O'Brien, the president of the company, testified that he considered the contribution to be a sound investment, that the public expects corporations to aid philanthropic and benevolent institutions, that they obtain good will in the community by so doing, and that their charitable donations create favorable environment for their business operations. In addition, he expressed the thought that in contributing to liberal arts institutions, corporations were furthering their self-interest in assuring the free flow of properly trained personnel for administrative and other corporate employment. Mr. Frank W. Abrams, chairman of the board of the Standard Oil Company

96 A 2d 581 (1953). Opinion by Judge J. Jacobs.

of New Jersey, testified that corporations are expected to acknowledge their public responsibilities in support of the essential elements of our free enterprise system. He indicated that it was not "good business" to disappoint "this reasonable and justified public expectation," nor was it good business for corporations "to take substantial benefits from their membership in the economic community while avoiding the normally accepted obligations of citizenship in the social community." Mr. Irving S. Olds, former chairman of the board of the United States Steel Corporation, pointed out that corporations have a self-interest in the maintenance of liberal education as the bulwark of good government. He stated that "Capitalism and free enterprise owe their survival in no small degree to the existence of our private, independent universities" and that if American business does not aid in their maintenance it is not "properly protecting the long-range interest of its stockholders, its employees, and its customers." Similarly, Dr. Harold W. Dodds, President of Princeton University, suggested that if private institutions of higher learning were replaced by governmental institutions our society would be vastly different and private enterprise in other fields would fade out rather promptly. Further on he stated that "democratic society will not long endure if it does not nourish within itself strong centers of non-governmental fountains of knowledge, opinions of all sorts not governmentally or politically originated. If the time comes when all these centers are absorbed into government, then freedom as we know it, I submit, is at an end." . . .

When the wealth of the nation was primarily in the hands of individuals they discharged their responsibilities as citizens by donating freely for charitable purposes. With the transfer of most of the wealth to corporate hands and the imposition of heavy burdens of individual taxation, they have been unable to keep pace with increased philanthropic needs. They have therefore, with justification, turned to corporations to assume the modern obligations

of good citizenship in the same manner as humans do. Congress and state legislatures have enacted laws which encourage corporate contributions, and much has recently been written to indicate the crying need and adequate legal basis therefor[e]. . . .

During the first world war corporations loaned their personnel and contributed substantial corporate funds in order to insure survival; during the depression of the '30s they made contributions to alleviate the desperate hardships of the millions of unemployed; and during the second world war they again contributed to insure survival. They now recognize that we are faced with other, though nonetheless vicious, threats from abroad which must be withstood without impairing the vigor of our democratic institutions at home and that otherwise victory will be pyrrhic indeed. More and more they have come to recognize that their salvation rests upon sound economic and social environment which in turn rests in no insignificant part upon free and vigorous nongovernmental institutions of learning. It seems to us that just as the conditions prevailing when corporations were originally created required that they serve public as well as private interests, modern conditions require that corporations acknowledge and discharge social as well as private responsibilities as members of the communities within which they operate. Within this broad concept there is no difficulty in sustaining, as incidental to their proper objects and in aid of the public welfare, the power of corporations to contribute corporate funds within reasonable limits in support of academic institutions. But even if we confine ourselves to the terms of the common-law rule in its application to current conditions, such expenditures may likewise readily be justified as being for the benefit of the corporation; indeed, if need be the matter may be viewed strictly in terms of actual survival of the corporation in a free enterprise system. The genius of our common law has been its capacity for growth and its adaptability to the needs of the times.

Generally courts have accomplished the desired result indirectly through the molding of old forms. Occasionally they have done it directly through frank rejection of the old and recognition of the new. But whichever path the common law has taken it has not been found wanting as the proper tool for the advancement of the general good. . . .

In the light of all of the foregoing we have no hesitancy in sustaining the validity of the donation by the plaintiff. There is no suggestion that it was made indiscriminately or to a pet charity of the corporate directors in furtherance of personal rather than corporate ends. On the contrary, it was made to a preeminent institution of higher learning, was modest in amount and well within the limitations imposed by the statutory enactments, and was voluntarily made in the reasonable belief that it would aid the public welfare and advance the interests of the plaintiff as a private corporation and as part of the community in which it operates. We find that it was a lawful exercise of the corporation's implied and incidental powers under common-law principles and that it came within the express authority of the pertinent state legislation. As has been indicated, there is now widespread belief throughout the nation that free and vigorous nongovernmental institutions of learning are vital to our democracy and the system of free enterprise and that withdrawal of corporate authority to make such contributions within reasonable limits would seriously threaten their continuance. Corporations have come to recognize this and with their enlightenment have sought in varying measures, as has the plaintiff by its contribution, to insure and strengthen the society which gives them existence and the means of aiding themselves and their fellow citizens. Clearly then, the appellants, as individual stockholders whose private interests rest entirely upon the well-being of the plaintiff corporation, ought not be permitted to close their eyes to present day realities and thwart the long-visioned corporate action in recognizing and voluntarily discharging its high obligations as a constituent of our modern social structure.

The judgment entered in the Chancery Division is in all respects Affirmed.

# Johnson & Johnson: Our Credo

We believe our first responsibility is to the doctors, nurses and patients, to mothers and fathers and all others who use our products and services.
In meeting their needs everything we do must be of high quality.
We must constantly strive to reduce our costs in order to maintain reasonable prices.
Customers' orders must be serviced promptly and accurately.
Our suppliers and distributors must have an opportunity to make a fair profit.

We are responsible to our employees, the men and women who work with us throughout the world.
Everyone must be considered as an individual.
We must respect their dignity and recognize their merit.
They must have a sense of security in their jobs.
Compensation must be fair and adequate, and working conditions clean, orderly and safe.

We must be mindful of ways to help our employees fulfill their
family responsibilities.
Employees must feel free to make suggestions and complaints.
There must be equal opportunity for employment,
development and advancement for those qualified.
We must provide competent management, and their actions
must be just and ethical.
We are responsible to the communities in which we live and
work and to the world community as well.
We must be good citizens—support good works and charities
and bear our fair share of taxes.
We must encourage civic improvements and better health and
education.
We must maintain in good order the property we are
privileged to use, protecting the environment and natural
resources.
Our final responsibility is to our stockholders.
Business must make a sound profit.
We must experiment with new ideas.
Research must be carried on, innovative programs developed
and mistakes paid for.
New equipment must be purchased, new facilities provided
and new products launched.
Reserves must be created to provide for adverse times.
When we operate according to these principles, the
stockholders should realize a fair return.

Courtesy of Johnson & Johnson.

# CASES

## CASE 1.   *The NYSEG Corporate Responsibility Program*

*We are responsible to the communities in which we live and work and to the world commu-*
*nity as well. We must be good citizens and support good works and charities. . . . We must*
*encourage civic improvements and better health and education.*[1]

Many large corporations operate consumer
responsibility or community responsibility programs, which aim to return something to the
consumer or to the community in which the
company does business. The motivation is at
least twofold: these programs create a positive

This case was prepared by Tom L. Beauchamp and Kelley MacDougall, and revised by John Cuddihy and Jeff Greene.
Not to be duplicated without permission of the holder of the copyright, © 1991, 1996, 2003 by Tom L. Beauchamp. This
case is indebted to Cathy Hughto-Delzer, NYSEG Manager, Consumer Affairs.

image of the company, and they make life much better for various unlucky members of the community. However, these programs are not good for corporate profits. They operate at a net loss and are, in effect, a form of corporate philanthropy.

New York State Electric and Gas Corporation (NYSEG) has created a program to fulfill what its officers consider to be the company's social responsibility to its public, in particular its consumers. When this program started two decades ago, NYSEG was a New York Stock Exchange–traded public utility with approximately 60,000 shareholders. Recently, NYSEG became a subsidiary of the Energy East Corp., a superregional energy services and delivery company with more than 5,800 employees. Energy East Corp. serves 1.4 million electricity customers and 600,000 natural gas customers in the northeastern United States. It is traded on the New York Stock Exchange.

In general, eastern public utilities have not enjoyed strong returns to shareholders in recent years because of relatively mild winters, increased plant costs, and a lower electric market price. However, Energy East has been able to increase earnings per share and dividends per share every year. Operating revenues have also gone up significantly. Energy East has been aggressively attempting to increase profitability by selling power plants and focusing on energy delivery. It has expanded its services rapidly and intends to continue the expansion. NYSEG itself continues to deliver electricity to more than 800,000 customers and natural gas to around 250,000 customers across more than 40 percent of upstate New York.

NYSEG's corporate responsibility program has not, as yet, been altered by the change to Energy East Corporation or by the relatively weak financial returns for utilities in recent years. NYSEG designed the program—and continues it today—to aid customers who are unable to pay their utility bills. The program does more than simply help customers pay their bills. It locates and attempts to remedy the root causes of bill nonpayment, which almost invariably involve financial distress. However, NYSEG attempts to reach beyond financial exigency. It seeks to rescue people in the community who are in unfortunate circumstances because of industrial injury, the ill health of a spouse or child, drug dependency, and the like. The company offers its assistance whether or not it is reasonable to suppose that the assistance provided will restore a paying customer.

To implement this plan, NYSEG has created a system of consumer advocates—primarily social workers trained to deal with customers and their problems. Since the program's 1978 inception, NYSEG has maintained a staff of several consumer representatives. Each of them handles approximately one hundred cases a month, over half of which result in some form of financial assistance. The remaining cases are referred to other organizations for assistance.

The process works as follows: When the company's credit department believes that a special investigation should be made into a customer's situation, the employee refers the case to the consumer advocate. Referrals also sometimes come from human service agencies and from customers directly. Examples of appropriate referrals include unemployed household heads; paying customers who suffer serious injury, lengthy illness, or death of a wage-earner; and low-income senior citizens or those on fixed incomes who cannot deal with rising costs of living. To qualify for assistance, NYSEG requires only that the customers suffer from hardships that they are willing to work to resolve.

Consumer advocates are concerned with preventing the shutoff of service to these customers and to restore them to a condition of financial health. They employ an assortment of resources to put customers back on their feet, including programs offered by the New York State Department of Social Services and the federal Home Energy Assistance Program (HEAP), which awards annual grants of varying amounts to qualified families. In addition, the consumer advocates provide financial counseling and help customers with their medical bills and educational planning. They arrange for assistance from churches and social services, provide food stamps, and help coordinate Veterans Administration benefits.

NYSEG also created a direct financial-grants program called Project Share, which is funded by a foundation created by NYSEG and by direct contributions from NYSEG employees, retirees, and customers. The latter can make charitable donations through their bills. They are asked voluntarily to add one, two, or five extra dollars to their bill each month. This special fuel fund is intended to help customers pay for energy emergencies, repairs to heating equipment, home weatherization, and water heater replacements. Grants of up to $200 are available to households in which someone is over 60 years old, has a disability, or has a serious medical condition—and with insufficient means of paying basic bills. The special fund of money created is overseen by the American Red Cross, which receives applications, determines eligibility, and distributes the collected funds. By 2002, over $4 million has been distributed to more than 20,000 customers since Project Share began in 1982.[2]

The rationale or justification for this corporate responsibility program is rooted in the history of public utilities and rising energy costs in North America. Public utilities originally provided a relatively inexpensive product. NYSEG and the entire industry considered its public responsibility limited to the functions of providing energy at the lowest possible cost and returning dividends to investors. NYSEG did not concern itself with its customers' financial troubles. The customer or the social welfare system handled all problems of unpaid bills, which was considered strictly a matter of business.

However, the skyrocketing energy costs in the 1970s changed customer resources and NYSEG's perspective. The energy crisis caused many long-term customers to encounter difficulty in paying their bills, and the likelihood of power shutoffs increased as a result. NYSEG accepted the responsibility to assist its valued customers by creating the Consumer Advocate system. NYSEG believes that its contribution is especially important now because recent reductions in federal assistance programs have shifted the burden of addressing these problems to the private sector.

The costs of NYSEG's involvement in the program are paid for from company revenues, which in principle (and in fact) entails that returns to shareholders are lowered. However, these costs are regarded by company officers as low. The program has few costs beyond office space and the consumer advocates' salaries and benefits, which total a half-million dollars. All expenses are treated as operating expenses. To augment Project Share's financial support, NYSEG shareholders have voted the program an annual, need-based grant. In the past, these shareholder gifts have ranged from $40,000 to $100,000 annually. NYSEG shareholders also fund related personnel and printing costs. The company itself has also supported Project Share through direct contributions to the Red Cross.

The company views some of the money expended for the corporate responsibility program as recovered funds because of the customers retained and the bills paid through the program. NYSEG officials assume that these charges would, under normal circumstances, have remained unpaid and would eventually have been written off as losses. NYSEG's bad-debt level is 20 percent lower than that of the average U.S.

utility company. The company believes that its corporate responsibility policy is *both* altruistic *and* good business, despite the program's maintenance costs. Though these costs well exceed recovered revenue, the service builds excellent customer relations. In other words, staffing and otherwise paying for these programs is a net financial loss for the company and its shareholders—what many businesses would call a "losing proposition"—but managers and shareholders do not (in public) complain about these unnecessary expenses, and most seem to feel good about the extra services the company provides to its customers.

It is unknown what view Energy East Corp. will ultimately take of this program, which it acquired from prior management at NYSEG. The program could be disbanded, cut back, or enlarged to serve all of Energy East's several utility services.

**Questions**

1. Do you agree that NYSEG's Project Share is both altruistic and good business? Why, or why not? Explain.
2. Would Milton Friedman and R. Edward Freeman believe that Project Share is consistent with NYSEG's fiduciary responsibility to its shareholders? Why, or why not? Explain.
3. Would John Boatright believe that Project Share is consistent with NYSEG's fiduciary responsibility to its shareholders? Why, or why not? Explain.

### NOTES

1. "The Johnson and Johnson Way" (from the Johnson and Johnson Company credo).
2. www.nyseg.com/nysegweb/main.nsf/doc/ share and www.nyseg.com/nysegweb/faqs.nsf/ pwrprtnr (as posted January, 2003).

## CASE 2.   *Outsourcing at Any Cost? Do Corporations Ever Have a Moral Obligation Not to Outsource?*

In 1997, when Galaxywire.net, a successful Internet service provider, was looking for a new central office location, it found a very receptive community in Green Fork, Ill. With the unemployment rate hovering at 16 percent, the city was ready to offer the company a great deal in return for moving there. Galaxywire planned to hire 3,000 in its first year, primarily in customer service, software engineering, and Web design.

City development officials offered a $300,000 low-interest loan for employee training, a 50 percent tax abatement for the first 10 years, and even landed a federal grant to construct a new $2.3 million secondary building for day care and executive suites. With Green Fork only about an hour's drive from Chicago, it seemed this small city of 30,000 with plenty of willing and able workers was the perfect spot for Galaxywire's home office.

The company accepted the offer and at the official announcement ceremony, CEO Dale Horner predicted a bright future. For 35 years, Green Fork's largest employer was Freedman Steel, but the company left town after a lengthy and bitter labor dispute. Since then, locals had

---

This case was prepared by Julian Friedland. Reprinted by permission.

grown distrustful of large corporations. Acknowledging this, Horner made a substantial commitment to the residents: "We plan to stay and be an integral part of the community," he promised. "Our employees are really a family. Across the board, everyone is considered as important as the highest executive. Lots of companies say that, but as I hope you'll come to see, we're rather different from most companies."

Seven years later, Galaxywire was thriving. Not only was the home office extremely productive, the company had expanded considerably, opening dozens of offices across the country. Nevertheless, top management was considering closing the Green Fork office and moving its customer service, software engineering, and Web design units to India. The company stood to save at least $10 million a year by doing so. Customer service employees earning $10–15 an hour in the U.S. earn only $2–4 in India. Similarly, Web designers and software engineers earning $60–70 an hour here earn only $6–8 an hour there.

Furthermore, new research by the Software Engineering Institute (SEI) at Carnegie Mellon University had shown that 85 Indian software companies had received a level 5 Compatibility Maturation Model Rating (CMM) which is the highest rating of engineering excellence. By comparison, only 42 other organizations worldwide had achieved that rating. So management realized that India offered a highly skilled, English-speaking workforce particularly competitive in information technology at a bargain-basement price. And to top it off, the company could deduct the cost of moving from its taxable income as a business expense. As a result, most of Galaxywire's competitors were already outsourcing to Southeast Asia. This trend was making it more difficult for American customer service agents and IT professionals to find work. Many were seeking new careers in non-outsourceable service sectors such as

restaurants, retail sales, tourism, construction, and teaching.

Galaxywire decided to let its employees know immediately of its intention to close the home office before the media could get hold of the story, giving the workers 10 months notice—8 months more than federal law requires for mass layoffs. It also provided severance packages of a month's full pay and extended health insurance coverage for five months. However, none of the top executives based in Green Fork would be laid off. They would move to smaller offices in California and were likely to receive particularly high year-end bonuses as a result of the savings outsourcing would bring.

Upon hearing the news of the closure, the workers and the city tried to find a solution that would have allowed the company to stay and still recoup most of the money it hoped to save by moving. With the unemployment rate still at 10 percent, the town simply could not afford to lose its largest employer. Negotiators proposed a deal that would save the company $7 million in the first year, $8 million the second, and $9 million yearly thereafter. The city extended the tax abatement for another decade, increasing the yearly reduction to 60 percent.

The employees agreed to a 15 percent paycut and a considerable reduction in benefits. But still, the company would not stay. So the workers went back to the drawing board, cutting another 5 percent of their wages, slashing a third of their vacation days and doubling their health insurance premiums. The city increased the tax reduction by another 5 percent. The resulting deal saved the company $10 million in the first year, $11 million the next, and $12 million yearly thereafter. This time, the company took several days to review the offer seriously.

The top executives met the next day to discuss this new offer. They realized that this deal did have a number of advantages:

1. Deciding not to move would increase employee loyalty and make good on the promise they initially made to stay.
2. There was already a highly skilled and dedicated workforce in Green Fork.
3. The workforce in India had not been fully tested. And several companies had already brought their customer service centers back from India, where the agents did not always master American colloquialisms, frustrating many customers, especially those hostile to outsourcing.
4. If they accepted this offer, they might be able to influence other cities where their offices were located to give them similar deals and thus avoid the risk and hassle of moving altogether.
5. If they decided not to move, they might be able to save a good deal on marketing since staying could provide a lucrative advertising angle such as: "Galaxywire.net is working to keep jobs in America."
6. They could still move their executive suites to sunny California.

But there were also some potential negatives to accepting the offer:

1. There might be growing resentment in the community about Galaxywire forcing its employees and the city to bend over backwards, creating a dangerous precedent that could further strip the community of tax support from other businesses and lower the salaries and benefits of employees elsewhere.
2. It seemed unlikely that the employees and city would be prepared to continue making such extensive sacrifices indefinitely. Eventually, the workers might unionize and make things more difficult.

These negatives made one executive suggest rejecting the offer, but make amends for breaking the promise to stay in the community by covering tuition for employee retraining.

Another suggested exploring the possibility of staying in Green Fork, but in order to stem the tide of negative press and morale, to accept the original offer, which seemed to preserve most of the advantages of the second offer but without the disadvantages. The first offer would save them close to as much as the second but also allow them to retain a truly appreciative and non-resentful staff, and even provide the company with a potentially potent advertising campaign that could keep Galaxywire in a leadership position in a competitive market which had suffered negative press over outsourcing.

But by then it was time to go home and think about all the options. What should the board decide?

### Discussion Questions

1. Does Galaxywire.net have a moral duty to keep its promise to stay in Green Fork so long as it can do so profitably? Why or why not? If so, is accepting even the first offer from the city and workers too much to ask?
2. Could entire white-collar professions be lost to lesser-developed countries if the outsourcing trend continues? Would this be fair to Americans?
3. Should the community have focused its attention instead on the state and federal government, asking it to discourage or even ban outsourcing?
4. Should the employees simply take this loss as a valuable opportunity to seek new careers instead of assuming they would be able to keep one career all their lives despite a rapidly changing global economy?

# CASE 3.   *Merck and River Blindness*

Merck & Co., Inc. is one of the world's largest pharmaceutical products and services companies. Headquartered in Whitehouse Station, New Jersey, Merck has over 70,000 employees and sells products and services in approximately 150 countries. Merck had revenues of $47,715,700,000 in 2001, ranked 24th on the 2002 Fortune 500 list of America's largest companies, 62nd on the Global 500 list of the World's Largest Corporations, and 82nd on the Fortune 100 list of the Best Companies to Work For.

In the late 1970s Merck research scientists discovered a potential cure for a severely debilitating human disease known as river blindness (onchocerciasis). The disease is caused by a parasite that enters the body through the bite of black flies that breed on the rivers of Africa and Latin America. The parasite causes severe itching, disfiguring skin infections, and, finally, total and permanent blindness. In order to demonstrate that it was safe and effective, the drug needed to undergo expensive clinical trials. Executives were concerned because they knew that those who would benefit from using it could not afford to pay for the drug, even if it was sold at cost. However, Merck research scientists argued that the drug was far too promising from a medical standpoint to abandon. Executives relented and a seven-year clinical trial proved the drug both efficacious and safe. A single annual dose of Mectizan, the name Merck gave to the drug, kills the parasites inside the body as well as the flies that carry the parasite.

Once Mectizan was approved for human use, Merck executives explored third-party payment options with the World Health Organization, the U.S. Agency for International Development, and the U.S. Department of State without success. Four United States Senators went so far as to introduce legislation to provide U.S. funding for the worldwide distribution of Mectizan. However, their efforts were unsuccessful, no legislation was passed and, and no U.S. government funding was made available. Finally, Merck executives decided to manufacture and distribute the drug for free.

Since 1987, Merck has manufactured and distributed over 700 million tablets of Mectizan at no charge. The company's decision was grounded in its core values:

1. Our business is preserving and improving human life.
2. We are committed to the highest standards of ethics and integrity.
3. We are dedicated to the highest level of scientific excellence and commit our research to improving human and animal health and the quality of life.
4. We expect profits, but only from work that satisfies customer needs and benefits humanity.
5. We recognize that the ability to excel—to most competitively meet society's and customers' needs—depends on the integrity, knowledge, imagination, skill, diversity, and teamwork of employees, and we value these qualities most highly.

This case was prepared by Denis G. Arnold and is based on Erik Eckholm, "River Blindness: Conquering an Ancient Scourge," *The New York Times,* January 8, 1989; David Pilling, "Public Private Health Deal Aims to End Elephantiasis," *The Financial Times* (London), January 21, 2000; Karen Lowry Miller, "The Pill Machine," *Newsweek*, November 19, 2001; "The Merck Mectizan Donation Program," www.merck.com/about/cr/policies_performance/social/mectizan_donation.html (03 October 2002); "The Story of Mectizan," www.merck.com/about/cr/mectizan/ (03 October 2002); "MERCK Annual Report 2001" http://www.anrpt2001.com/index.html (03 October 2002); "About Merck: Mission Statement," www.merck.com/about/mission.html (03 October 2002); "The 2002 Fortune 500," www.fortune.com/lists/F500/index.html (03 October 2002); "The 2002 Global 500," www.fortune.com/lists/G500/index.html (03 October 2002); and "Best Companies to Work For," http://www.fortune.com/lists/bestcompanies/index.html www.fortune.com/lists/F500/index.html (03 October 2002). © Denis G. Arnold 2003, 2008.

George W. Merck, the company's president from 1925 to 1950, summarized these values when he wrote, "medicine is for the people. It is not for the profits. The profits follow, and if we have remembered that, they have never failed to appear. The better we have remembered that, the larger they have been."

Today, the Merck Mectizan Donation Program includes partnerships with numerous nongovernmental organizations, governmental organizations, private foundations, the World Health Organization, The World Bank, UNICEF, and the United Nations Development Program. In 1998, Merck expanded the Mectizan Donation Program to include the prevention of elephantiasis (lymphatic filariasis) in African countries where the disease coexists with river blindness. In total, approximately 30 million people in 32 countries are now treated annually with Mectizan. Merck reports that it has no idea how much the entire program has cost, but estimates that each pill is worth $1.50. The United Nations reports that river blindness may soon be eradicated.

**Questions**

1. Given the fact that Merck is spending corporate resources to manufacture and distribute Mectizan, is the Merck Mectizan Donation Program morally justifiable? Explain.
2. Would Friedman approve of the Merck Mectizan Donation Program? Explain.
3. Should the fact that Merck's values are clearly stated in corporate publications that are widely available to investors make a difference to someone who accepts Friedman's position? Explain.
4. Should the Merck Mectizan Donation Program serve as a model for other pharmaceutical companies who are in a unique position to facilitate the eradication of other diseases in the developing nations? Explain.

# CASE 4. *H. B. Fuller in Honduras: Street Children and Substance Abuse*

Kativo Chemical Industries, a wholly owned foreign subsidiary of H. B. Fuller, sells a solvent-based adhesive (glue) in several countries in Latin America. The brand name of the glue is Resistol. In 1985 it came to H. B. Fuller's attention that large numbers of street children in the Central American country of Honduras were sniffing glue and that Resistol was among the glues being abused. Indeed all these children who sniff glue are being referred to as *Resistoleros*.

Resistol has a number of industrial uses, although one of its primary uses is in small shoe repair shops. The glue has properties that are not possible to attain with a water-based formula. These properties include rapid set, strong adhesion, and water resistance. Resistol is similar to airplane glue.

This case is based on a much longer case with the same name authored by Norman E. Bowie and Stefanie Lenway. The full "H. B. Fuller in Honduras: Street Children and Substance Abuse" was the Case award winner in the Columbia University Graduate School of Business Ethics in Business Program.

Widespread inhalant abuse among street children in Honduras can be attributed to the depth of poverty there. Honduras is one of the poorest countries in Latin America. The unemployment rate is high. Infant and child mortality rates are high, life expectancy for adults is 64 years, and the adult literacy rate is estimated to be about 60 percent. Its exports, bananas and coffee, are commodities that are subject to the vagaries of the weather and the volatility of commodity markets. Government deficits caused in part by mismanagement and corruption have prevented desirable spending on public services.

Migrants to the urban areas typically move first to cuarterias (rows) of connected rooms. The rooms are generally constructed of wood with dirt floors, and they are usually windowless. The average household contains about seven persons who live together in a single room. For those living in rooms facing an alley, the narrow way between buildings serves both as a sewage and waste disposal area and as a courtyard for as many as 150 persons.

That the name of a Fuller product should be identified with a social problem was a matter of great concern to the H. B. Fuller Company. H. B. Fuller was widely known as a socially responsible corporation. Among its achievements were an enlightened employee relations policy that included giving each employee a day off on his or her birthday and, on the 10th anniversary of employment, bonus vacation time and a substantial check so that employees could travel and see the world. H. B. Fuller contributes 5 percent of its pretax profits to charity and continually wins awards for its responsibility to the environment. A portion of its corporate mission statement reads as follows:

> H. B. Fuller Company is committed to its responsibilities, in order of priority, to its customers, employees and shareholders. H. B. Fuller will conduct business legally and ethically, support the activities of its employees in their communities, and be a responsible corporate citizen.

The issue of the abuse of glue by Honduran street children received attention in the Honduran press as early as 1983.

The man on the spot at Kativo was Vice President Humberto Larach (Beto) who headed Kativo's North Adhesives Division. Beto had proved his courage and his business creativity when he was among 105 taken hostage in the Chamber of Commerce building in downtown San Pedro Sula by Honduran guerrillas from the Communist Popular Liberation Front. Despite firefights between the guerrillas and government troops, threats of execution, and being used as a human shield, Beto had convinced two fellow hostages to buy from Kativo rather than from a competitor. Not surprisingly, Beto had a reputation for emphasizing the importance of making the bottom line that was an important part of the Kativo corporate culture.

Initial responses to the problem were handled by officials at Kativo. These responses included requests to the press not to use "Resistolero" as a synonym for a street child glue sniffer and attempts to persuade the Honduran legislature not to require the addition of oil of mustard to its glue. Beto had requested H. B. Fuller's U.S. headquarters to look into the viability of oil of mustard as an additive to the glue. H. B. Fuller's Corporate industrial hygiene staff found evidence that indicated that oil of mustard was a carcinogen and hence was potentially dangerous to employees and consumers. Kativo officials believed that glue sniffing was a social problem and that Kativo was limited in what it could do about the problem. The solution was education.

From 1985 through 1989, officials at H. B. Fuller headquarters in St. Paul, Minnesota, were only dimly aware of the problem. While some of these officials assisted their Kativo subsidiary by providing information on the dangers of oil of mustard, the traditional policy of H. B. Fuller was to give great autonomy to foreign-owned subsidiaries.

However, in late April 1986 Elmer Andersen, H. B. Fuller chairman of the board received a letter from a stockholder who pointedly asked how a company with its enlightened business philosophy could be responsible for selling a product that was causing harm to the children of Honduras. Three years later, on June 7, 1989, Vice President for Corporate Relations Dick Johnson received a call from a stockholder whose daughter was in the Peace Corps in Honduras. The stockholder's question was how can a company like H. B. Fuller claim to have a social conscience and continue to sell Resistol which is "literally burning out the brains" of children in Latin America. Johnson knew that headquarters should become actively involved in addressing the problem. But given the nature of the problem and H. B. Fuller's policy of local responsibility, what should headquarters do?

## Questions

1. To what extent can Honduran street children who obtain an H. B. Fuller product illegitimately be considered stakeholders? If they are stakeholders, how can their interests be represented?
2. What obligations does a company have to solve social problems?
3. Where does the responsibility for solving this problem rest—with the local subsidiary Kativo or with H. B. Fuller headquarters?
4. To what extent should officials at H. B. Fuller headquarters be concerned about potential criticisms that they are meddling in a problem where they don't understand the culture?

## CASE 5.   *From Tension to Cooperative Dialogue: Holcim*

Holcim is one of the world's largest suppliers of cement, as well as aggregates (gravel and sand), concrete and construction-related services. The Holcim Group, which includes Union Cement of the Philippines, has majority and minority interests in more than 70 countries on all continents.

The company has a long history of constructive engagement, particularly with local communities in many countries. A productive way of addressing specific issues that emerge from stakeholders in areas close to its operations is through the community advisory panels (CAP). With a broad cross section of representative voices, CAPs can directly generate substantive input from the community as well as experts in specific technical fields.

Before Holcim invested in Union in 1988, Union's relationship with external stakeholders was based on limited or selective engagement, in some cases characterized by an adversarial relationship with local communities. However, it was recognized that this did not present a supportive environment in which to maintain its license to operate.

In one instance, a flood that devastated the area close to Union's Lugait plant in 1999 became a turning point in community relations for the company. Prior to this people in the local community knew of the company, but they did not know its people. In response to the flood, Union employees volunteered assistance with provisions of food and medicine, infrastructure repair and emotional support for victims, and in so doing opened the door to improved relations.

A community advisory panel was then created, involving company management, unions, local community representatives, non-governmental organizations (NGOs), government agencies and local government units. Membership in this committee is both by invitation from the company and nomination from either local officials or an NGO.

The mandate of this committee is to assess and validate the plants' proposals for community activities, which are identified through local stakeholder engagement processes. Projects are then carried out in collaboration with partner organizations.

For example, the "Women's Livelihood Program" trains women in sewing and production of various handicrafts. The objective is to augment the family income and help provide for family needs. To date membership to the women's livelihood program has increased from less than 50 to more than 200 and a livelihood center was constructed for production and display. This program was established in partnership with the local government, the women's association and the Department of Social Welfare and Services.

Since the formation of the CAP committee at the Lugait plant, the relationship with the community has blossomed. The company now regularly opens its doors to the community every Friday and Saturday so that local officials, NGOs, students and community residents can visit the plant. Similar community groups are also being organized at the other plants of Union.

CAPs are also good for business. Zita Diez, Union's CSR coordinator and Communications Manager highlights that: "At the Lugait plant, security concerns are high due to the presence of rebel groups in the area. But if you are responsible and open to discussion, then your community can actually become your first line to defense. In fact our security guard numbers have not increased but on the contrary they have reduced to about 20 percent over the last 3 years—primarily because we have improved our relationship with the community and we know that they will help 'protect' us."

In addition to helping develop community projects, strong community relations have also helped the company introduce the use of alternative fuels and raw materials (AFR). Union has held specific consultations on the topic of AFR to inform local communities and key people. As a result the company has received overwhelming support. And this is not because the community understands specifically how the AFR works but because—as surveys have shown—they know and trust the company. As a result AFR permits were received quickly.

The shift in community relations for Union Cement has not only positively impacted the community but also the company's employees who now feel and understand that they are part of a bigger community. Engagement with different stakeholder groups has led to increased awareness about environmental responsibility and the overall role the company and its employees can play in the community.

## Questions

1. What would Milton Friedman think of the CAPs? Explain.
2. What would R. Edward Freeman think of the CAPs? Explain.
3. What would John Boatright think of the CAPs? Explain.
4. What do you think of the CAPs? Explain.

## Suggested Supplementary Readings

ARNOLD, DENIS G. 2003. "Libertarian Theories of the Corporation and Global Capitalism." *Journal of Business Ethics* 48 (December): 155–73.

CARSON, THOMAS. 1993. "Friedman's Theory of Corporate Social Responsibility." *Business and Professional Ethics Journal* 12 (Spring): 3–32.

CLARKSON, MAX B. E. 1995. "A Stakeholder Framework for Analyzing and Evaluating Corporate Social Performance." *Academy of Management Review* 20 (January): 92–117.

DONALDSON, THOMAS, and LEE E. PRESTON. 1995. "The Stakeholder Theory of the Corporation: Concepts, Evidence, and Implications." *Academy of Management Review* 20 (January): 65–91.

FORT, TIMOTHY L. 1996. "Business as Mediating Institution." *Business Ethics Quarterly* 6:149–64.

FREEMAN, R. EDWARD. 1984. *Strategic Management: A Stakeholder Approach.* Boston: Pitman.

FREEMAN, R. EDWARD, and DANIEL R. GILBERT, JR. 1998. *Corporate Strategy and the Search for Ethics.* Englewood Cliffs, NJ: Prentice Hall.

FREEMAN, R. EDWARD, JEFFREY HARRISON, and ANDREW WICKS. 2007. *Managing for Stakeholders.* New Haven: Yale University Press.

FRIEDMAN, MILTON. 1962. *Capitalism and Freedom.* Chicago: University of Chicago Press.

GOODPASTER, KENNETH E. 1991. "Business Ethics and Stakeholder Analysis." *Business Ethics Quarterly* 1:53–73.

JENSEN, MICHAEL C. 2002. "Value Maximization, Stakeholder Theory, and the Corporate Objective Function." *Business Ethics Quarterly* 12 (April): 235–56.

JONES, THOMAS M. 1995. "Instrumental Stakeholder Theory: A Synthesis of Ethics and Economics." *Academy of Management Review* 20 (April): 404–37.

JONES, THOMAS M., and ANDREW C. WICKS. 1999, "Convergent Stakeholder Theory." *Academy of Management Review* 24 (April): 191–221. Commentaries by Linda Klebe Trevino and Gary R. Weaver, Dennis Gioia, R. Edward Freeman, and Thomas Donaldson follow in the same volume.

JONES, THOMAS M., ANDREW C. WICKS, and R. EDWARD FREEMAN. 2002. "Stakeholder Theory: The State of the Art." In *Blackwell Guide to Business Ethics*, ed. Norman E. Bowie, 19–37. Malden, MA: Blackwell.

LANGTRY, BRUCE. 1994. "Stakeholders and the Moral Responsibilities of Business." *Business Ethics Quarterly* 4 (October): 431–43.

LEVITT, THEODORE. 1958. "The Dangers of Social Responsibility." *Harvard Business Review* 36 (September–October): 41–50.

MAITLAND, IAN. 1994. "The Morality of the Corporation: An Empirical or Normative Disagreement?" *Business Ethics Quarterly* 4 (October): 445–58.

MARENS, RICHARD, and ANDREW WICKS. 1990. "Getting Real: Stakeholder Theory, Managerial Practice, and the General Irrelevance of Fiduciary Duties Owed to Shareholders." *Business Ethics Quarterly* 9 (April): 273–92.

MINTZBERG, HENRY. 1983. "The Case for Corporate Social Responsibility." *Journal of Business Strategy* 4 (Fall): 3–15.

MITCHELL, RONALD, K. BRADLEY, R. AGLE, and DONNA WOOD. 1997. "Toward a Theory of Stakeholder Identification and Salience: Defining the Principle of Who and What Really Counts." *Academy of Management Review* 22:853–86.

SCHLOSSBERGER, EUGENE. 1994. "A New Model of Business: Dual Investor Theory." *Business Ethics Quarterly* 4 (October): 459–74.

WICKS, ANDREW C., DANIEL R. GILBERT, JR., and R. EDWARD FREEMAN. 1994. "A Feminist Reinterpretation of the Stakeholder Concept." *Business Ethics Quarterly* 4 (October): 475–97.

# Chapter 3

# Ethical Treatment of Employees

## INTRODUCTION

TRADITIONALLY, BUSINESS FIRMS are organized hierarchically, with production line employees at the bottom and the CEO at the top. Also, the interests of the stockholders are given priority over the interests of the other stakeholders. However, much recent literature presents a challenge to these arrangements, especially to underlying classic economic assumptions whereby labor is treated as analogous to land, capital, and machinery, that is, as replaceable and as a means to profit. Employees primarily want to be treated as persons who are genuine partners in the business enterprise. They want decent salaries and job security, as well as appreciation from supervisors, a sense of accomplishment, and fair opportunities to display their talents. Many employees are also interested in participating in planning the future directions of the company, defining the public responsibilities of the corporation, evaluating the role and quality of management, and—most especially—helping to set the tasks assigned to their jobs. These new developments in labor relations are all to the good, but they must be understood in light of a very different tradition whereby an employee is clearly subordinate to the employer, is legally obligated to obey the employer's orders, and has few rights except the right to quit.

### Status and Scope of Employee Rights

In the traditional view, the freedom of the employee to quit, the freedom of the employer to fire, and the right of the employer to order the employee to do his or her bidding define the essence of the employment contract. The legal principle behind the traditional view is called the *employment-at-will principle*. This principle says that in the absence of a specific contract or law, an employer may hire, fire, demote, or promote an employee whenever the employer wishes. Moreover, the employer may act with justification, with inadequate justification, or with no justification at all. In the selection that opens this chapter, Patricia Werhane and Tara Radin consider several arguments for the employment-at-will doctrine and find them wanting.

Over the years this master–servant relationship, which is at the core of the employment-at-will doctrine, has been legally constrained. Once unions were given legal protection, collective bargaining produced contracts that constrained the right of employers to fire at will. Employees who were protected by union contracts usually could be fired only for cause and then only after a lengthy grievance process. During the height of the union movement, the chief protection against an unjust firing was the union-negotiated contract. However, during the 1980s and early 1990s the percentage of the U.S. workforce belonging to unions fell into the teens, and as a result the protection offered by the union-negotiated contract covers millions fewer workers.

Some might argue that the decline in the number of U.S. workers who belong to unions has not significantly increased the number of employees who are at risk of an unjust dismissal. These people argue that a large number of enlightened companies have adopted policies that provide the same type of protection against unjust dismissal as was previously found in union-negotiated contracts. Moreover, where such policies exist they have the force of law. For example, on May 9, 1985, the New Jersey Supreme Court held that Hoffman-LaRoche Inc. was bound by job security assurances that were implied in an employee manual. The manual seemed to pledge that employees could be fired only for just cause and then only if certain procedures were followed. Hoffman-LaRoche argued that although the company manual gave company policy, adherence to it was voluntary and not legally enforceable. The court, however, said employers cannot have it both ways without acting unfairly and, so, illegally. Hoffman-LaRoche had to reinstate an employee who had been fired on grounds that his supervisor had lost confidence in his work.

In response to this and similar rulings, a number of corporations have taken steps to make it more difficult for employees to use company manuals and policy statements to protect their jobs. Some are simply eliminating the manuals and dismantling their grievance procedure apparatus. Sears Roebuck and other employers have their employees sign a form declaring that they can be fired "with or without just cause."

Others point out that during the 1980s and early 1990s, certain grounds for firing employees were made illegal by federal or state law. Antidiscrimination statutes protect workers from being fired because of their race or sex, because they are handicapped, or because of age. Federal law also protects workers from being fired because they resist sexual advances from their bosses or refuse to date them. The protection given employees from this and other forms of sexual harassment is discussed in Chapter 4.

Yet another important development was the evolution of a common-law protection of one's job if an employee disobeys an employer on the grounds that the employer ordered him or her to do something illegal or immoral. The notion that employees should not lose their jobs because they refuse to behave illegally or immorally might seem obvious, but as the two New Jersey cases included in this chapter show, the situation is more complex than it might appear. On some issues there is near-unanimity that a course of action is right or wrong. But on other matters there is considerable difference of opinion. As a practical matter, a large corporation cannot allow employees to refuse to abide by a corporate decision whenever it conflicts with a personal moral position. On the other hand, the public must support employees who refuse to obey an order or accept a decision that threatens the public with serious harm. *Potter v. Village Bank of New Jersey,* and *Warthen v. Toms River Community Memorial Hospital* illustrate how the courts try to balance the public interest and legitimate business concerns on this issue.

Even more important, these laws do not provide sufficient protection for what many employees consider their most important workplace right—the right to a job. From the perspective of most employees, the most important contribution of capitalism is providing work. Job security is often ranked higher than increased pay in terms of what employees most want from employers. The desire for job security is captured in employee demands that workers have a right to a job and that this right deserves protection. The claim that a person has a right to a job has two components. First, workers believe they have a right to a job in the first place. Second, as employees continue to work at a job, they believe they have a right to retain that job. Provision of the right to a job in the first place is usually considered to be the responsibility of government and is not discussed here. However, the notion that employees gain rights to a job that they have been holding is a new idea. In an era in which downsizing has destroyed even the traditional social contract, the idea that a person can come to hold a right to one's job is not widely held.

Indeed, some scholars, especially from the law and economics school, have continued to support the traditional employment-at-will doctrine. For example, Richard A. Epstein has argued, in the article reprinted in this chapter, that employment-at-will is both fair and efficient. Spokespersons from the law and economics school take efficiency concerns very seriously, and Epstein spends considerable time developing some of these concerns.

## Worker Safety, Occupational Risk, and the Right to Know

Critics of business and government have long contended that uninformed workers are routinely, and often knowingly, exposed to dangerous conditions. For example, employers did not tell asbestos workers for many years of the known dangers of contracting asbestosis. Although little is currently understood about the knowledge and comprehension of workers, evidence from at least some industries indicates that ignorance is a causal factor in occupational illness or injury. The simplest solution is to ban hazardous products from use, but to do so would involve shutting down a large segment of industrial manufacturing. Hundreds of products still contain asbestos either because no functional substitute is available or replacement is not cost efficient.

The implications of worker ignorance are chillingly present in the following worker's testimony before an Occupational Safety and Health Administration (OSHA) hearing on the toxic agent DBCP (1,2-dibromo-3-chloropropane):

> We had no warning that DBCP exposure might cause sterility, testicular atrophy, and perhaps cancer. If we had known that these fumes could possibly cause the damage that we have found out it probably does cause, we would have worn equipment to protect ourselves. As it was, we didn't have enough knowledge to give us the proper respect for DBCP.[1]

The regulation of workplace risks has consistently sought to determine an objective level of acceptable risk and then to ban or limit exposure above that level. However, the goal of safety is not the primary justification for disclosures of risk. Individuals need the information upon which the objective standard is based to determine whether the risk it declares acceptable is *acceptable to them.* Here a subjective standard of acceptable risk seems more appropriate than an objective standard established by "experts." Choosing to risk testicular atrophy seems rightly a worker's personal choice, one not fully decidable by health and safety standards established for groups of workers. Even given objective standards, substantial ambiguity prevails when the experts are uncertain about the risks, and dangerous dose levels cannot be established.

Problems also surface about the strategy of information disclosure and the strategy of protective schemes—especially if one or the other is used in isolation. Often, there are no meaningful figures to define the relationship between acceptable risk and the ease with which the risk can be eliminated or controlled. There also may be no consensus about which levels of probability of serious harm, such as death, constitute risks sufficiently high to require that steps be taken to reduce or eliminate the risk or to provide information to those affected.

Both the employer's responsibility to inform employees and the employee's right to refuse hazardous job assignments are the concerns of the essay by Ruth Faden and Tom L. Beauchamp. They support a standard of information disclosure and consider three possible standards for determining the justifiability of a refusal to work or of a safety walkout. In a second essay in this section, John R. Boatright focuses on the worker's right to receive information from employers and the effectiveness of the current system. He also looks at the worker's right to refuse to work and the government's obligation to regulate the workplace. He concentrates on particularly controversial regulatory programs and policies and how they affect the rights to know and refuse. Also included in the legal perspectives section of this chapter is the case of *Automobile Workers v. Johnson Controls, Inc.,* which determined that employers cannot legally adopt "fetal protection policies" that exclude women of childbearing age from a hazardous workplace, because such policies involve illegal sex discrimination. However, the Supreme Court decision was, in some respects, narrow; it left U.S. corporations in a state of uncertainty over an acceptable policy for protecting fetuses from reproductive hazards.

# WHISTLE-BLOWING AND THE DUTY OF LOYALTY

To suggest that the moral problems in employee–employer relationships are all about employee rights would, of course, be one-sided. No less important are employee obligations. Employees have moral obligations to respect the property of the corporation, to abide by employment contracts, and to operate within the bounds of the company's procedural rules. Indeed, it is legally established that an employer has a right to loyalty. This right is captured in the so-called law of agency. For example, Section 387 of the Restatement of Agency (1958) expresses the general principle that "an agent is subject to his principal to act solely for the benefit of the principal in all matters connected with his agency."[2] Specifically, the "agent is also under a duty not to act or speak disloyally," and the agent is to keep confidential any information acquired by him as an employee that might damage the agent or his business.[3]

Early scholarship by philosophers on whistle-blowing focused on the conditions that constitute justified whistle-blowing. That focus was caused in large part by the belief that whistle-blowing breached a duty of loyalty of the employee to the employer. As a result of that analysis, a fairly standard list of conditions was drawn up that needed to be met if whistle-blowing was morally justifiable. In the final articles in this chapter, two authors challenge the standard view in two very different ways. Michael Davis argues that the standard list is incorrect because it does not adequately deal with paradigm cases of justified whistle-blowing. To remedy this situation, he proposes an alternative theory that he calls the *complicity* theory.

Ronald Duska's critique is even more radical. He challenges the assumption that the employee has a duty of loyalty to the employer. He has argued that loyalty can apply only in a relationship that transcends self-interest and must be based on a stable relationship of trust and confidence. The relationship of an employee to the corporation is not that kind of relationship, in his view, because it is a relationship of mutual self-interest. In this form of relationship, the employee does not have an obligation of loyalty to the employer.

If a corporation takes the position advocated by Milton Friedman in Chapter 2, then Duska's argument seems persuasive and indeed Friedman himself would probably accept it. In Friedman's view the only concern of the firm is to manage its assets to obtain profits for the stockholders, and the only concern of the workers is to get the best working conditions they can. Loyalty simply isn't in the picture. But if a broader stakeholder theory like R. Edward Freeman's is adopted, the corporation does have genuine obligations to employees. In a stakeholder-managed firm, the relationship between the employer and the employee is more likely to be characterized as a relationship of trust and confidence that transcends self-interest. If Duska accepted this characterization of the stakeholder account, these firms would be morally entitled to loyalty.

However, the duty of loyalty is not absolute. That an employee should be loyal is a *prima facie* duty. The object of the employee's duty must be deserving if the duty is genuine and overriding rather than prima facie. The virtue of loyalty does not require that the employee accept blindly the boss or corporate cause to which he or she is loyal. Nor does it require that when loyalty to the employer conflicts with other duties—such as protecting the public from harm—the duty to the employer is always overriding. Indeed, when a corporation is engaged in activity that is seriously wrong, employees may have a higher obligation to be disloyal to their employer and blow the whistle.

Well-publicized cases of whistle-blowing bring public acclaim to the whistle-blower but little else. The whistle-blower finds it nearly impossible to get an equivalent job in the same industry and difficult enough to get another job at all. Many corporate executives share the sentiments of the former president of General Motors James M. Roche:

> Some of the enemies of business now encourage an employee to be disloyal to the enterprise. They want to create suspicion and disharmony, and pry into the proprietary interests of the business. However this is labelled—industrial espionage, whistle-blowing, or professional responsibility—it is another tactic for spreading disunity and creating conflict.[4]

Although Roche illegitimately confuses industrial espionage and whistle-blowing, the attitude expressed by his remarks explains why it is so difficult for the whistle-blower to find another job. Roche's point may seem extreme but whistle-blowing does undermine trust and it should not be undertaken lightly. Both the whistle-blower and the corporation have responsibilities toward a wide range of stakeholders. In 2002 *Time* named three whistle-blowers as persons of the year and whistle-blowers received some protection under the Sarbanes-Oxley Act passed by Congress in the summer of 2002. In 1999 the United Kingdom adopted the Public Interest Disclosure Act that provides financial compensation for whistle-blowers who act in the public interest.

In conclusion, many of the moral grounds for employee loyalty have been destroyed. Commentators refer to the collapse of the social contract between a company and its employees. Each day seems to bring another announcement of a corporate downsizing. Yet there are some minimum requirements of loyalty based in law. Even today the most disgruntled employees usually treat others who whistle-blow negatively; for them whistle-blowing seems to violate a moral obligation to loyalty. Thus it is important pragmatically as well as ethically that whistle-blowing be justifiable.

## NOTES

1. Occupational Safety and Health Administration, "Access to Employee Exposure and Medical Records—Final Rules," *Federal Register* (May 23, 1980), p. 35222.
2. Quoted from Phillip I. Blumberg, Corporate Responsibility and the Employee's Duty of Loyalty and Obedience, in *Ethical Theory and Business,* ed. Thomas Beauchamp and Norman E. Bowie (Englewood Cliffs, NJ: Prentice Hall, 1979), 307.
3. Ibid., pp. 308, 307.
4. James M. Roche, "The Competitive System, to Work, to Preserve, and to Protect," *Vital Speeches of the Day* (May 1971), p. 445.

# Employment at Will and Due Process

*Patricia H. Werhane and Tara J. Radin*

In 1980, Howard Smith III was hired by the American Greetings Corporation as a materials handler at the plant in Osceola, Arkansas. He was promoted to forklift driver and held that job until 1989, when he became involved in a dispute with his shift leader. According to Smith, he had a dispute with his shift leader at work. After work he tried to discuss the matter, but according to Smith, the shift leader hit him. The next day Smith was fired.

Smith was an "at-will" employee. He did not belong to, nor was he protected by, any union or union agreement. He did not have any special legal protection, for there was no apparent question of age, gender, race, or handicap discrimination. And he was not alleging any type of problem with worker safety on the job. The American Greetings Employee Handbook stated that "We believe in working and thinking and planning to provide a stable and growing business, to give such service to our customers that we may provide maximum job security for our employees." It did not state that employees could not be fired without due process or reasonable cause. According to the common-law principle of employment at will (EAW), Smith's job at American Greetings could, therefore, legitimately be terminated at any time without cause, by either Smith or his employer, as long as that termination did not violate any law, agreement, or public policy.

Smith challenged his firing in the Arkansas court system as a "tort of outrage." A "tort of outrage" occurs when an employer engages in "extreme or outrageous conduct" or intentionally inflicts terrible emotional stress. If such a tort is found to have occurred, the action, in this case, the dismissal, can be overturned.

Smith's case went to the Supreme Court of Arkansas in 1991. In court the management of American Greetings argued that Smith was fired for provoking management into a fight. The court held that the firing was not in violation of law or a public policy, that the employee handbook did not specify restrictions on at-will terminations, and that the alleged altercation between Smith and his shift leader "did not come close to meeting" criteria for a tort of outrage. Howard Smith lost his case and his job.[1]

The principle of EAW is a common-law doctrine that states that in the absence of law or contract, employers have the right to hire, promote, demote, and fire whomever and whenever they please. In 1887, the principle was stated explicitly in a document by H. G. Wood entitled *Master and Servant*. According to Wood, "a general or indefinite hiring is prima facie a hiring at will."[2] Although the term *master-servant*, a medieval expression, was once used to characterize employment relationships, it has been dropped from most of the recent literature on employment.[3]

In the United States, EAW has been interpreted as the rule that when employees are not specifically covered by union agreement, legal statute, public policy, or contract, employers "may dismiss their employees at will . . . for good cause, for no cause, *or even for causes morally wrong*, without being thereby guilty of legal wrong."[4] At the same time,

---

at-will employees enjoy rights parallel to employer prerogatives, because employees may quit their jobs for any reason whatsoever (or no reason) without having to give any notice to their employers. At-will employees range from part-time contract workers to CEOs, including all those workers and managers in the private sector of the economy not covered by agreements, statutes, or contracts. Today at least 60 percent of all employees in the private sector in the United States are "at-will" employees. These employees have no rights to due process or to appeal employment decisions, and the employer does not have any obligation to give reasons for demotions, transfers, or dismissals. Interestingly, while employees in the *private sector* of the economy tend to be regarded as at-will employees, *public-sector* employees have guaranteed rights, including due process, and are protected from demotion, transfer, or firing without cause.

Due process is a means by which a person can appeal a decision in order to get an explanation of that action and an opportunity to argue against it. Procedural due process is the right to a hearing, trial, grievance procedure, or appeal when a decision is made concerning oneself. Due process is also substantive. It is the demand for rationality and fairness: for good reasons for decisions. EAW has been widely interpreted as allowing employees to be demoted, transferred, or dismissed without due process, that is, without having a hearing and without requirement of good reasons or "cause" for the employment decision. This is not to say that employers do not have reasons, usually good reasons, for their decisions. But there is no moral or legal obligation to state or defend them. EAW thus sidesteps the requirement of procedural and substantive due process in the workplace, but it does not preclude the institution of such procedures or the existence of good reasons for employment decisions.

EAW is still upheld in the state and federal courts of this country, as the Howard Smith case illustrates, although exceptions are made when violations of public policy and law are at issue. According to the *Wall Street Journal*, the court has decided in favor of the employees in 67 percent of the wrongful discharge suits that have taken place during the past three years. These suits were won not on the basis of a rejection of the principle of EAW but, rather, on the basis of breach of contract, lack of just cause for dismissal when a company policy was in place, or violations of public policy. The court has carved out the "public policy" exception so as not to encourage fraudulent or wrongful behavior on the part of employers, such as in cases where employees are asked to break a law or to violate state public policies, and in cases where employees are not allowed to exercise fundamental rights, such as the rights to vote, to serve on a jury, and to collect workers' compensation. For example, in one case, the court reinstated an employee who was fired for reporting theft at his plant on the grounds that criminal conduct requires such reporting.[5]

During the last 10 years, a number of positive trends have become apparent in employment practices and in state and federal court adjudications of employment disputes. Shortages of skilled managers, fear of legal repercussions, and a more genuine interest in employee rights claims and reciprocal obligations have resulted in a more careful spelling out of employment contracts, the development of elaborate grievance procedures, and in general less arbitrariness in employee treatment.[6] While there has not been a universal revolution in thinking about employee rights, an increasing number of companies have qualified their EAW prerogatives with restrictions in firing without cause. Many companies have developed grievance procedures and other means for employee complaint and redress.

Interestingly, substantive due process, the notion that employers should give good reasons for their employment actions, previously dismissed as legal and philosophical nonsense, has also recently developed positive advocates. Some courts have found that it is a breach of contract to fire a long-term employee when there is not sufficient cause—under normal economic conditions even when the contract is only a verbal one. In California, for example, 50 percent of the implied contract cases (and there have been over 200) during the last five years have been decided in favor of the employee, again, without challenging EAW.[7] In light of this recognition of implicit contractual obligations between employees and employers, in some unprecedented court cases *employees* have been held liable for good faith breaches of contract, particularly in cases of quitting without notice in the middle of a project and/or taking technology or other ideas to another job.[8]

These are all positive developments. At the same time, there has been neither an across-the-board institution of due process procedures in all corporations nor any direct challenges to the *principle* (although there have been challenges to the practice) of EAW as a justifiable and legitimate approach to employment practices. Moreover, as a result of mergers, downsizing, and restructuring, hundreds of thousands of employees have been laid off summarily without being able to appeal those decisions.

At-will employees, then, have no rights to demand an appeal to such employment decisions except through the court system. In addition, no form of due process is a requirement preceding any of these actions. Moreover, unless public policy is violated, the law has traditionally protected employers from employee retaliation in such actions. It is true that the scope of what is defined as "public policy" has been enlarged so that at-will dismissals without good reason have been greatly reduced. It is also true that many companies have grievance procedures in place for at-will employees. But such procedures are voluntary, procedural due process is not *required*, and

companies need not give any reasons for their employment decisions.

In what follows we shall present a series of arguments defending the claim that the right to procedural and substantive due process should be extended to all employees in the private sector of the economy. We will defend the claim partly on the basis of human rights. We shall also argue that the public/private distinction that precludes the application of constitutional guarantees in the private sector has sufficiently broken down so that the absence of a due process requirement in the workplace is an anomaly.

## EMPLOYMENT AT WILL

EAW is often justified for one or more of the following reasons:

1. The proprietary rights of employers guarantee that they may employ or dismiss whomever and whenever they wish.
2. EAW defends employee and employer rights equally, in particular the right to freedom of contract, because an employee voluntarily contracts to be hired and can quit at any time.
3. In choosing to take a job, an employee voluntarily commits herself to certain responsibilities and company loyalty, including the knowledge that she is an at-will employee.
4. Extending due process rights in the workplace often interferes with the efficiency and productivity of the business organization.
5. Legislation and/or regulation of employment relationships further undermine an already overregulated economy.

Let us examine each of these arguments in more detail. The principle of EAW is sometimes maintained purely on the basis of proprietary rights of employers and corporations. In dismissing or demoting employees, the employer is not denying rights to *persons*. Rather, the employer is simply excluding that person's *labor* from the organization.

This is not a bad argument. Nevertheless, accepting it necessitates consideration of the proprietary rights of employees as well. To understand what is meant by "proprietary rights of employees" it is useful to consider first what is meant by the term *labor*. *Labor* is sometimes used collectively to refer to the workforce as a whole. It also refers to the activity of working. Other times it refers to the productivity or "fruits" of that activity. Productivity, labor in the third sense, might be thought of as a form of property or at least as something convertible into property, because the productivity of working is what is traded for remuneration in employee–employer work agreements. For example, suppose an advertising agency hires an expert known for her creativity in developing new commercials. This person trades her ideas, the product of her work (thinking), for pay. The ideas are not literally property, but they are tradable items because, when presented on paper or on television, they are sellable by their creator and generate income. But the activity of working (thinking in this case) cannot be sold or transferred.

Caution is necessary, though, in relating productivity to tangible property, because there is an obvious difference between productivity and material property. Productivity requires the past or present activity of working, and thus the presence of the person performing this activity. Person, property, labor, and productivity are all different in this important sense. A person can be distinguished from his possessions, a distinction that allows for the creation of legally fictional persons such as corporations or trusts that can "own" property. Persons cannot, however, be distinguished from their working, and this activity is necessary for creating productivity, a tradable product of one's working.

In dismissing an employee, a well-intentioned employer aims to rid the corporation of the costs of generating that employee's work products. In ordinary employment situations, however, terminating that cost entails terminating that employee. In those cases the justification for the at-will firing is presumably proprietary. But treating an employee "at will" is analogous to considering her a piece of property at the disposal of the employer or corporation. Arbitrary firings treat people as things. When I "fire" a robot, I do not have to give reasons, because a robot is not a rational being. It has no use for reasons. On the other hand, if I fire a person arbitrarily, I am making the assumption that she does not need reasons either. If I have hired people, then, in firing them, I should treat them as such, with respect, throughout the termination process. This does not preclude firing. It merely asks employers to give reasons for their actions, because reasons are appropriate when people are dealing with other people.

This reasoning leads to a second defense and critique of EAW. It is contended that EAW defends employee and employer rights equally. An employer's right to hire and fire at will is balanced by a worker's right to accept or reject employment. The institution of any employee right that restricts at-will hiring and firing would be unfair unless this restriction was balanced by a similar restriction controlling employee job choice in the workplace. Either program would do irreparable damage by preventing both employees and employers from continuing in voluntary employment arrangements. These arrangements are guaranteed by "freedom of contract," the right of persons or organizations to enter into any voluntary agreement with which all parties of the agreement are in accord.[9] Limiting EAW practices or requiring due process would negatively affect freedom of contract. Both are thus clearly coercive, because in either case persons and organizations are forced to accept behavioral restraints that place unnecessary constraints on voluntary employment agreements.[10]

This second line of reasoning defending EAW, like the first, presents some solid arguments. A basic presupposition upon which EAW is grounded is that of protecting equal freedoms of both employees and employers. The purpose of EAW is to provide a guaranteed balance of these freedoms. But arbitrary treatment of employees extends prerogatives to managers that are not equally available to employees, and such treatment may unduly interfere with a fired employee's prospects for future employment if that employee has no avenue for defense or appeal. This is also sometimes true when an employee quits without notice or good reason. Arbitrary treatment of employees *or* employers therefore violates the spirit of EAW—that of protecting the freedoms of both the employees and employers.

The third justification of EAW defends the voluntariness of employment contracts. If these are agreements between moral agents, however, such agreements imply reciprocal obligations between the parties in question for which both are accountable. It is obvious that in an employment contract, people are rewarded for their performance. What is seldom noticed is that if part of the employment contract is an expectation of loyalty, trust, and respect on the part of an employee, the employer must, in return, treat the employee with respect as well. The obligations required by employment agreements, if these are free and noncoercive agreements, must be equally obligatory and mutually restrictive on both parties. Otherwise one party cannot expect— morally expect—loyalty, trust, or respect from the other.

EAW is most often defended on practical grounds. From a utilitarian perspective, hiring and firing at will is deemed necessary in productive organizations to ensure maximum efficiency and productivity, the goals of such organizations. In the absence of EAW, unproductive employees, workers who are no longer needed, and even troublemakers, would be able to keep their jobs. Even if a business *could* rid itself of undesirable employees, the lengthy procedure of due process required by an extension of employee rights would be costly and time-consuming, and would likely prove distracting to other employees. This would likely slow production and, more likely than not, prove harmful to the morale of other employees.

This argument is defended by Ian Maitland, who contends

> [I]f employers were generally to heed business ethicists and institute workplace due process in cases of dismissals and take the increased costs or reduced efficiency out of workers' paychecks—then they would expose themselves to the pirating of their workers by other employers who would give workers what they wanted instead of respecting their rights in the workplace. . . . In short, there is good reason for concluding that the prevalence of EAW does accurately reflect workers' preferences for wages over contractually guaranteed protections against unfair dismissal.[11]

Such an argument assumes (a) that due process increases costs and reduces efficiency, a contention that is not documented by the many corporations that have grievance procedures, and (b) that workers will generally give up some basic rights for other benefits, such as money. The latter is certainly sometimes true, but not always so, particularly when there are questions of unfair dismissals or job security. Maitland also assumes that an employee is on the same level and possesses the same power as her manager, so that an employee can choose her benefit package in which grievance procedures, whistle-blowing protections, or other rights are included. Maitland implies that employers might include in that package of benefits their rights to practice the policy of unfair dismissals in return for increased pay. He also at least implicitly suggests that due process precludes dismissals and layoffs. But this is not true. Procedural due process demands a means of appeal, and substantive due process demands good reasons, both of which are requirements for other managerial decisions and judgments. Neither demands benevolence or lifetime employment, or prevents dismissals. In fact, having good reasons gives an employer a justification for getting rid of poor employees.

In summary, arbitrariness, although not prohibited by EAW, violates the managerial ideal of rationality and consistency. These are independent grounds for not abusing EAW. Even if EAW itself is justifiable, the practice of EAW, when interpreted as condoning arbitrary employment decisions, is not justifiable. Both procedural and substantive due process are consistent with, and a moral requirement of, EAW. The former is part of recognizing obligations implied by freedom of contract, and the latter, substantive due process, conforms with the ideal of managerial rationality that is implied by a consistent application of this common-law principle.

## EMPLOYMENT AT WILL, DUE PROCESS, AND THE PUBLIC/ PRIVATE DISTINCTION

The strongest reasons for allowing abuses of EAW and for not instituting a full set of employee rights in the workplace, at least in the private sector of the economy, have to do with the nature of business in a free society. Businesses are privately owned voluntary organizations of all sizes from small entrepreneurships to large corporations. As such, they are not subject to the restrictions governing public and political institutions. Political procedures such as due process, needed to safeguard the public against the arbitrary exercise of power by the state, do not apply to private organizations. Guaranteeing such rights in the workplace would require restrictive legislation and regulation. Voluntary market arrangements, so vital to free enterprise and guaranteed by freedom of contract, would be sacrificed for the alleged public interest of employee claims.

In the law, courts traditionally have recognized the right of corporations to due process, although they have not required due process for employees in the private sector of the economy. The justification put forward for this is that since corporations are public entities acting in the public interest, they, like people, should be afforded the right to due process.

Due process is also guaranteed for permanent full-time workers in the public sector of the economy, that is, for workers in local, state, and national government positions. The Fifth and Fourteenth Amendments protect liberty and property rights such that any alleged violations or deprivation of those rights may be challenged by some form of due process. According to recent Supreme Court decisions, when a state worker is a permanent employee, he has a property interest in his employment. Because a person's productivity contributes to the place of employment, a public worker is entitled to his job unless there is good reason to question it, such as poor work habits, habitual absences, and the like. Moreover, if a discharge would prevent him from obtaining other employment, which often is the case with state employees who, if fired, cannot find further government employment, that employee has a right to due process before being terminated.[12]

This justification for extending due process protections to public employees is grounded in the public employee's proprietary interest in his job. If that argument makes sense, it is curious that private employees do not have similar rights. The basis for this distinction stems from a tradition in Western thinking that distinguishes between the public and private spheres of life. The public sphere contains that part of a person's life that lies within the bounds of government regulation, whereas the private spheres contains that part of a person's life that lies outside those bounds. The argument is that the portion of a person's life that influences only that person should remain private and outside the purview of law and regulation, while the portion that influences the public welfare should be subject to the authority of the law.

Although interpersonal relationships on any level—personal, family, social, or employee–employer—are protected by statutes and common law, they are not constitutionally protected unless there is a violation of some citizen claim against the state. Because entrepreneurships and corporations are privately owned, and since employees are free to make or break employment contracts of their choice, employee–employer relationships, like family relationships, are treated as "private." In a family, even if there are no due process procedures, the state does not interfere, except when there is obvious harm or abuse. Similarly, employment relationships are considered private relationships contracted between free adults, and so long as no gross violations occur, positive constitutional guarantees such as due process are not enforceable.

The public/private distinction was originally developed to distinguish individuals from the state and to protect individuals and private property from public—i.e., governmental—intrusion. The distinction, however, has been extended to distinguish not merely between the individual or the family and the state but also between universal rights claims and national sovereignty, public and private ownership, free enterprise and public policy, publicly and privately held corporations, and even between public and private employees. Indeed, this distinction plays a role in national and international affairs. Boutros Boutros-Ghali, the head of the United Nations [1991–1996], confronted a dilemma in deciding whether to go into Somalia without an invitation. His initial reaction was to stay out and to respect Somalia's right to "private" national sovereignty. It was only when he decided that Somalia had fallen apart as an independent state that he approved U.N. intervention. His dilemma parallels that of a state, which must decide whether to intervene in a family quarrel, the alleged abuse of a spouse or child, the inoculation of a Christian Scientist, or the blood transfusion for a Seventh-day Adventist.

There are some questions, however, with the justification of the absence of due process with regard to the public/private distinction. Our economic system is allegedly based on private property, but it is unclear where "private" property and ownership end and "public" property and ownership begin. In the workplace, ownership and control is often divided. Corporate assets are held by an ever-changing group of individual and institutional shareholders. It is no longer true that owners exercise any real sense of control over their property and its management. Some do, but many do not. Moreover, such complex property relationships are spelled out and guaranteed by the state. This has prompted at least one thinker to argue that "private property" should be defined as "certain patterns of human interaction underwritten by public power."[13]

This fuzziness about the "privacy" of property becomes exacerbated by the way we use the term *public* in analyzing the status of businesses and in particular corporations. For example, we distinguish between privately owned business corporations and government-owned or -controlled public institutions. Among those companies that are not government owned, we distinguish between regulated "public" utilities whose stock is owned by private individuals and institutions; "publicly held" corporations whose stock is traded publicly, who are governed by special SEC regulations, and whose financial statements are public knowledge; and privately held corporations and entrepreneurships, companies, and smaller businesses that are owned by an individual or group of individuals and not available for public stock purchase.

There are similarities between government-owned public institutions and privately owned organizations. When the air controllers went on strike in the 1980s, Ronald Reagan fired them and declared that, as public employees, they could not strike because it jeopardized the public safety. Nevertheless, both private and public institutions run transportation, control banks, and own property. While the goals of private and public institutions differ in that public institutions are allegedly supposed to place the public good ahead of profitability, the simultaneous call for businesses to become socially responsible and the demand for governmental organizations to become efficient and accountable further question the dichotomy between "public" and "private."

Many business situations reinforce the view that the traditional public/private dichotomy has been eroded, if not entirely, at least in large part. For example, in 1981, General Motors (GM) wanted to expand by building a plant in what is called the "Poletown" area of Detroit. Poletown is an old Detroit Polish neighborhood. The site was favorable because it was near transportation facilities and there was a good supply of labor. To build the plant, however, GM had to displace residents in a nine-block area. The Poletown Neighborhood Council objected, but the Supreme Court of Michigan decided in favor of GM and held that the state could condemn property for private use, with proper compensation to owners, when it was in the public good. What is particularly interesting about this case is that GM is not a government-owned corporation; its primary goal is *profitability*, not the common good. The Supreme Court nevertheless decided that it was in the *public* interest for Detroit to use its authority to allow a company to take over property despite the protesting of the property owners. In this case the public/private distinction was thoroughly scrambled.

The overlap between private enterprise and public interests is such that at least one legal scholar argues that "developments in the twentieth century have significantly undermined the 'privateness' of the modern business corporations, with the result that the traditional bases for distinguishing them from public corporations have largely disappeared."[14] Nevertheless, despite the blurring of the public and private in terms of property rights and the status and functions of corporations, the subject of employee rights appears to remain immune from conflation.

The expansion of employee protections to what we would consider just claims to due process gives to the state and the courts more opportunity to interfere with the private economy and might thus further skew what is seen by some as a precarious but delicate balance between the private economic sector and public policy. We agree. But if the distinction between public and private institutions is no longer clear-cut, and the traditional separation of the public and private spheres is no longer in place, might it not then be better to recognize and extend constitutional guarantees so as to protect all citizens equally? If due process is crucial to political relationships between the individual and the state, why is it not central in relationships between employees and corporations, since at least some of the companies in question are as large and powerful as small nations? Is it not in fact inconsistent with our democratic tradition *not* to mandate such rights?

The philosopher T. M. Scanlon summarizes our institutions about due process. Scanlon says,

> The requirement of due process is one of the conditions of the moral acceptability of those institutions that give some people power to control or intervene in the lives of others.[15]

The institution of due process in the workplace is a moral requirement consistent with rationality and consistency expected in management decision-making. It is not precluded by EAW, and it is compatible with the overlap between the public and private sectors of the economy. Convincing business of the moral necessity of due process, however, is a task yet to be completed.

## NOTES

1. *Howard Smith III v. American Greetings Corporation*, 304 Ark. 596; 804 S.W. 2d 683.

2. H. G. Wood, *A Treatise on the Law of Master and Servant* (Albany, NY: John D. Parsons, Jr., 1877), 134.

3. Until the end of 1980 the *Index of Legal Periodicals* indexed employee–employer relationships under this rubric.

4. Lawrence E. Blades, "Employment at Will versus Individual Freedom: On Limiting the Abusive Exercise of Employer Power," *Columbia Law Review* 67 (1967): 1405, quoted from *Payne v. Western*, 81 Tenn. 507 (1884), and *Hutton v. Watters*, 132 Tenn. 527, S.W. 134 (1915).

5. *Palmateer v. International Harvester Corporation*, 85 Ill. App. 2d 124 (1981).

6. See David Ewing, *Justice on the Job: Resolving Grievances in the Nonunion Workplace* (Boston: Harvard Business School Press, 1989).

7. See R. M. Bastress, "A Synthesis and a Proposal for Reform of the Employment at Will Doctrine," *West Virginia Law Review* 90 (1988): 319–51.

8. See "Employees' Good Faith Duties," *Hastings Law Journal* 39 (198). See also *Hudson v. Moore Business Forms* 609 Supp. 467 (N.D. Cal. 1985).

9. See *Lockner v. New York*, 198 U.S. (1905), and Adina Schwartz, "Autonomy in the Workplace," in *Just Business*, ed. Tom Regan (New York: Random House, 1984) 129–40.

10. Eric Mack, "Natural and Contractual Rights," *Ethics* 87 (1977): 153–59.

11. Ian Maitland, "Rights in the Workplace: A Nozickian Argument," in Lisa Newton and Maureen Ford, eds., *Taking Sides* (Guilford, CT: Dushkin Publishing Group, 1990), 34–35.

12. Richard Wallace, "Union Waiver of Public Employees' Due Process Rights," *Industrial Relations Law Journal* 8 (1986): 583–87.

13. Morris Cohen, "Dialogue on Private Property," *Rutgers Law Review* 9 (1954): 357. See also *Law and the Social Order* (1933) and Robert Hale, "Coercion and Distribution in a Supposedly Non-Coercive State," *Political Science Quarterly* 38 (1923): 470; John Brest, "State Action and Liberal Theory," *University of Pennsylvania Law Review* (1982): 1296–329.

14. Gerald Frug, "The City As a Legal Concept," *Harvard Law Review* 93 (1980): 1129.

15. T. M. Scanlon, "Due Process," in *Nomos XVIII: Due Process*, ed. J. Roland Pennock and John W. Chapman (New York: New York University Press, 1977), 94.

# In Defense of the Contract at Will

*Richard A. Epstein*

The persistent tension between private ordering and government regulation exists in virtually every area known to the law, and in none has that tension been more pronounced than in the law of employer and employee relations. During the last 50 years, the balance of power has shifted heavily in favor of direct public regulation, which has been thought strictly necessary to redress the perceived imbalance between the individual and the firm. In particular the employment relationship has been the subject of at least two major statutory revolutions. The first, which culminated in the passage of the National Labor Relations Act in 1935, set

From Richard A. Epstein, "In Defense of the Contract at Will," *University of Chicago Law Review* 34 (1984). Reprinted by permission of the University of Chicago Law Review.

the basic structure for collective bargaining that persists to the current time. The second, which is embodied in Title VII of the Civil Rights Act of 1964, offers extensive protection to all individuals against discrimination on the basis of race, sex, religion, or national origin. The effect of these two statutes is so pervasive that it is easy to forget that, even after their passage, large portions of the employment relation remain subject to the traditional common-law rules, which when all was said and done set their face in support of freedom of contract and the system of voluntary exchange. One manifestation of that position was the prominent place that the common law, especially as it developed in the nineteenth century, gave to the contract at will. The basic position was set out in an oft-quoted passage from *Payne v. Western & Atlantic Railroad:*

> [M]en must be left, without interference to buy and sell where they please, and to discharge or retain employees at will for good cause or for no cause, or even for bad cause without thereby being guilty of an unlawful act *per se.* It is a right which an employee may exercise in the same way, to the same extent, for the same cause or want of cause as the employer.[1]

In the remainder of this paper, I examine the arguments that can be made for and against the contract at will. I hope to show that it is adopted not because it allows the employer to exploit the employee, but rather because over a very broad range of circumstances it works to the mutual benefit of both parties, where the benefits are measured, as ever, at the time of the contract's formation and not at the time of dispute. To justify this result, I examine the contract in light of the three dominant standards that have emerged as the test of the soundness of any legal doctrine: intrinsic fairness, effects upon utility or wealth, and distributional consequences. I conclude that the first two tests point strongly to the maintenance of the at-will rule, while the third, if it offers any guidance at all, points in the same direction.

## THE FAIRNESS OF THE CONTRACT AT WILL

The first way to argue for the contract at will is to insist upon the importance of freedom of contract as an end in itself. Freedom of contract is an aspect of individual liberty, every bit as much as freedom of speech, or freedom in the selection of marriage partners or in the adoption of religious beliefs or affiliations. Just as it is regarded as prima facie unjust to abridge these liberties, so too is it presumptively unjust to abridge the economic liberties of individuals. The desire to make one's own choices about employment may be as strong as it is with respect to marriage or participation in religious activities, and it is doubtless more pervasive than the desire to participate in political activity. Indeed for most people, their own health and comfort, and that of their families, depend critically upon their ability to earn a living by entering the employment market. If government regulation is inappropriate for personal, religious, or political activities, then what makes it intrinsically desirable for employment relations?

It is one thing to set aside the occasional transaction that reflects only the momentary aberrations of particular parties who are overwhelmed by major personal and social dislocations. It is quite another to announce that a rule to which vast numbers of individuals adhere is so fundamentally corrupt that it does not deserve the minimum respect of the law. With employment contracts we are not dealing with the widow who has sold her inheritance for a song to a man with a thin mustache. Instead we are dealing with the routine stuff of ordinary life; people who are competent enough to marry, vote, and pray are not unable to protect themselves in their day-to-day business transactions.

Courts and legislatures have intervened so often in private contractual relations that it may seem almost quixotic to insist that they bear a heavy burden of justification every time they wish to substitute their own judgment for that of the immediate parties to the transactions. Yet it is hardly likely that remote public bodies have better information about individual preferences than the parties who hold them. This basic principle of autonomy, moreover, is not limited to some areas of individual conduct and wholly inapplicable to others. It covers all these activities as a piece and admits no ad hoc exceptions, but only principled limitations.

This general proposition applies to the particular contract term in question. Any attack on the contract at will in the name of individual freedom is fundamentally misguided. As the Tennessee Supreme Court rightly stressed in *Payne*, the contract at will is sought by both persons.[2] Any limitation upon the freedom to enter into such contracts limits the power of workers as well as employers and must therefore be justified before it can be accepted. In this context the appeal is often to an image of employer coercion. To be sure, freedom of contract is not an absolute in the employment context, any more than it is elsewhere. Thus the principle must be understood against a backdrop that prohibits the use of private contracts to trench upon third-party rights, including uses that interfere with some clear mandate of public policy, as in cases of contracts to commit murder or perjury.

In addition, the principle of freedom of contract also rules out the use of force or fraud in obtaining advantages during contractual negotiations; and it limits taking advantage of the young, the feeble-minded, and the insane. But the recent wrongful discharge cases do not purport to deal with the delicate situations where contracts have been formed by improper means or where individual defects of capacity or will are involved. Fraud is not a frequent occurrence in employment contracts, especially where workers and employers engage in repeat transactions. Nor is there any reason to believe that such contracts are marred by misapprehensions, since employers and employees know the footing on which they have contracted: the phrase "at will" is two words long and has the convenient virtue of meaning just what it says, no more and no less.

An employee who knows that he can quit at will understands what it means to be fired at will, even though he may not like it after the fact. So long as it is accepted that the employer is the full owner of his capital and the employee is the full owner of his labor, the two are free to exchange on whatever terms and conditions they see fit, within the limited constraints just noted. If the arrangement turns out to be disastrous to one side, that is his problem; and once cautioned, he probably will not make the same mistake a second time. More to the point, employers and employees are unlikely to make the same mistake once. It is hardly plausible that contracts at will could be so pervasive in all businesses and at all levels if they did not serve the interests of employees as well as employers. The argument from fairness then is very simple, but not for that reason unpersuasive.

## THE UTILITY OF THE CONTRACT AT WILL

The strong fairness argument in favor of freedom of contract makes short work of the various for-cause and good-faith restrictions upon private contracts. Yet the argument is incomplete in several respects. In particular, it does not explain why the presumption in the case of silence should be in favor of the contract at will. Nor does it give a descriptive account of *why* the contract at will is so commonly found in all trades and professions. Nor does the argument meet on their own terms the concerns voiced most frequently by the critics of the contract at will. Thus, the commonplace belief today (at least outside the actual world of business) is that the contract at will is so unfair and one-sided that it cannot be the outcome of a rational set of bargaining processes any more than, to take the extreme case, a contract for total slavery. While we may not, the criticism continues, be able to observe them, defects in capacity at contract formation nonetheless must be present: the ban upon the contract at will is an effective way to reach abuses that are pervasive but difficult to detect, so that modest government interference only strengthens the operation of market forces.

In order to rebut this charge, it is necessary to do more than insist that individuals as a general matter know how to govern their own lives. It is also necessary to display the structural strengths of the contract at will that explain why rational people would enter into such a contract, if not all the time, then at least most of it. The implicit assumption in this argument is that contracts are typically for the mutual benefit of both parties. Yet it is hard to see what other assumption makes any sense in analyzing institutional arrangements (arguably in contradistinction to idiosyncratic, nonrepetitive transactions). To be sure, there are occasional cases of regret after the fact, especially after an infrequent, but costly, contingency comes to pass. There will be cases in which parties are naive, befuddled, or worse. Yet in framing either a rule of policy or a rule of construction, the focus cannot be on that biased set of cases in which the contract aborts and litigation ensues. Instead, attention must be directed to standard repetitive transactions, where the centralizing tendency powerfully promotes expected mutual gain. It is simply incredible to postulate that either employers or employees, motivated as they are by self-interest, would enter routinely into a transaction that leaves them worse off than they were before, or even worse off than their next best alternative.

From this perspective, then, the task is to explain how and why the at-will contracting arrangement (in sharp contrast to slavery) typically works to the mutual advantage of the parties. Here, as is common in economic matters, it does not matter that the parties themselves often cannot articulate the reasons that render their judgment sound and breathe life into legal arrangements that are fragile in form but durable in practice. The inquiry into mutual benefit in turn requires an examination of the full range of costs and benefits that arise from collaborative ventures. It is just at this point that the nineteenth-century view is superior to the emerging modern conception. The modern view tends to lay heavy emphasis on the need to control employer abuse. Yet, as the passage from *Payne* indicates, the rights under the contract at will are fully bilateral, so that the employee can use the contract as a means to control the firm, just as the firm uses it to control the worker.

The issue for the parties, properly framed, is not how to minimize employer abuse, but rather how to maximize the gain from the relationship, which in part depends upon minimizing the sum of employer and employee abuse. Viewed in this way the private contracting problem is far more complex. How does each party create incentives for the proper behavior of the other? How does each side insure against certain risks? How do both sides minimize the administrative costs of their contracting practices? . . .

*1. Monitoring Behavior.* The shift in the internal structure of the firm from a partnership to an employment relation eliminates neither bilateral opportunism nor the conflicts of interest between employer and employee. Begin for the moment with the fears of the firm, for it is the firm's right to maintain at-will power that is now being called into question. In all too many cases, the firm must contend with the recurrent problem of employee theft and with the related problems of unauthorized use of firm equipment and employee kickback arrangements. . . . [The] proper concerns of the firm are not limited to obvious forms of criminal misconduct. The employee on a fixed wage can, at the margin, capture only a portion of the gain from his labor, and therefore has a tendency to reduce output. The employee who receives a commission equal to half the firm's profit attributable to his labor may work hard, but probably not quite as hard as he would if he received the entire profit from the completed sale, an arrangement that would solve the agency-cost problem only by undoing the firm. . . .

The problem of management then is to identify the forms of social control that are best able to minimize these agency costs. . . . One obvious form of control is the force of law. The state can be brought in to punish cases of embezzlement or fraud. But this mode of control requires extensive cooperation with public officials and may well be frustrated by the need to prove the criminal offense (including mens rea) beyond a reasonable doubt, so that vast amounts of abuse will go unchecked. Private litigation instituted by the firm may well be used in cases of major grievances, either to recover the property that has been misappropriated or to prevent the individual employee from further diverting firm business to his own account. But private litigation, like public prosecution, is too blunt an instrument to counter employee shirking or the minor but persistent use of firm assets for private business. . . .

Internal auditors may help control some forms of abuse, and simple observation by coworkers may well monitor employee activities. (There are some very subtle trade-offs to be considered when the firm decides whether to use partitions or separate offices for its em-

ployees.) Promotions, bonuses, and wages are also critical in shaping the level of employee performance. But the carrot cannot be used to the exclusion of the stick. In order to maintain internal discipline, the firm may have to resort to sanctions against individual employees. It is far easier to use those powers that can be unilaterally exercised: to fire, to demote, to withhold wages, or to reprimand. These devices can visit very powerful losses upon individual employees without the need to resort to legal action, and they permit the firm to monitor employee performance continually in order to identify both strong and weak workers and to compensate them accordingly. The principles here are constant, whether we speak of senior officials or lowly subordinates, and it is for just this reason that the contract at will is found at all levels in private markets. . . .

In addition, within the employment context firing does not require a disruption of firm operations, much less an expensive division of its assets. It is instead a clean break with consequences that are immediately clear to both sides. The lower cost of both firing and quitting, therefore, helps account for the very widespread popularity of employment-at-will contracts. There is no need to resort to any theory of economic domination or inequality of bargaining power to explain at-will contracting, which appears with the same tenacity in relations between economic equals and subordinates and is found in many complex commercial arrangements, including franchise agreements, except where limited by statutes.

Thus far, the analysis generally has focused on the position of the employer. Yet for the contract at will to be adopted ex ante, it must work for the benefit of workers as well. And indeed it does, for the contract at will also contains powerful limitations on employers' abuses of power. To see the importance of the contract at will to the employee, it is useful to distinguish between two cases. In the first, the employer pays a fixed sum of money to the worker and is then free to demand of the employee whatever services he wants for some fixed period of time. In the second case, there is no fixed period of employment. The employer is free to demand whatever he wants of the employee, who in turn is free to withdraw for good reason, bad reason, or no reason at all.

The first arrangement invites abuse by the employer, who can now make enormous demands upon the worker without having to take into account either the worker's disutility during the period of service or the value of the worker's labor at contract termination. A fixed-period contract that leaves the worker's obligations unspecified thereby creates a sharp tension between the parties, since the employer receives all the marginal benefits and the employee bears all the marginal costs.

Matters are very different where the employer makes increased demands under a contract at will. Now the worker can quit whenever the net value of the employment contract turns negative. As with the employer's power to fire or demote, the threat to quit (or at a lower level to come late or leave early) is one that can be exercised without resort to litigation. Furthermore, that threat turns out to be most effective when the employer's opportunistic behavior is the greatest because the situation is one in which the worker has least to lose. To be sure, the worker will not necessarily make a threat whenever the employer insists that the worker accept a less favorable set of contractual terms, for sometimes the changes may be accepted as an uneventful adjustment in the total compensation level attributable to a change in the market price of labor. This point counts, however, only as an additional strength of the contract at will, which allows for small adjustments *in both directions* in ongoing contractual arrangements with a minimum of bother and confusion. . . .

*2. Reputational Losses.* Another reason why employees are often willing to enter into at-will

employment contracts stems from the asymmetry of reputational losses. Any party who cheats may well obtain a bad reputation that will induce others to avoid dealing with him. The size of these losses tends to differ systematically between employers and employees—to the advantage of the employee. Thus in the usual situation there are many workers and a single employer. The disparity in number is apt to be greatest in large industrial concerns, where the at-will contract is commonly, if mistakenly, thought to be most unsatisfactory because of the supposed inequality of bargaining power. The employer who decides to act for bad reason or no reason at all may not face any legal liability under the classical common law rule. But he faces very powerful adverse economic consequences. If coworkers perceive the dismissal as arbitrary, they will take fresh stock of their own prospects, for they can no longer be certain that their faithful performance will ensure their security and advancement. The uncertain prospects created by arbitrary employer behavior is functionally indistinguishable from a reduction in wages unilaterally imposed by the employer. At the margin some workers will look elsewhere, and typically the best workers will have the greatest opportunities. By the same token the large employer has more to gain if he dismisses undesirable employees, for this ordinarily acts as an implicit increase in wages to the other employees, who are no longer burdened with uncooperative or obtuse coworkers.

The existence of both positive and negative reputational effects is thus brought back to bear on the employer. The law may tolerate arbitrary behavior, but private pressures effectively limit its scope. Inferior employers will be at a perpetual competitive disadvantage with enlightened ones and will continue to lose in market share and hence in relative social importance. The lack of legal protection to the employees is therefore in part explained by the increased informal protections that they obtain by working in large concerns.

*3. Risk Diversification and Imperfect Information.* The contract at will also helps workers deal with the problem of risk diversification. . . . Ordinarily, employees cannot work more than one, or perhaps two, jobs at the same time. Thereafter the level of performance falls dramatically, so that diversification brings in its wake a low return on labor. The contract at will is designed in part to offset the concentration of individual investment in a single job by allowing diversification among employers *over time.* The employee is not locked into an unfortunate contract if he finds better opportunities elsewhere or if he detects some weakness in the internal structure of the firm. A similar analysis applies on the employer's side where he is a sole proprietor, though ordinary diversification is possible when ownership of the firm is widely held in publicly traded shares.

The contract at will is also a sensible private adaptation to the problem of imperfect information over time. In sharp contrast to the purchase of standard goods, an inspection of the job before acceptance is far less likely to guarantee its quality thereafter. The future is not clearly known. More important, employees, like employers, *know what they do not know.* They are not faced with a bolt from the blue, with an "unknown unknown." Rather they face a known unknown for which they can plan. The at-will contract is an essential part of that planning because it allows both sides to take a wait-and-see attitude to their relationship so their new and more accurate choices can be made on the strength of improved information. ("You can start Tuesday and we'll see how the job works out" is a highly intelligent response to uncertainty.) To be sure, employment relationships are more personal and hence often stormier than those that exist in financial markets, but that is no warrant for replacing the contract at will with a for-cause contract provision. The proper question is: Will the shift in methods of control work a change for the benefit of both parties, or will it only make a difficult situation worse?

*4. Administrative Costs.* There is one last way in which the contract at will has an enormous advantage over its rivals. It is very cheap to administer. Any effort to use a for-cause rule will in principle allow all, or at least a substantial fraction of, dismissals to generate litigation. Because motive will be a critical element in these cases, the chances that either side will obtain summary judgment will be negligible. Similarly, the broad modern rules of discovery will allow exploration into every aspect of the employment relation. Indeed, a little imagination will allow the plaintiff's lawyer to delve into the general employment policies of the firm, the treatment of similar cases, and a review of the individual file. The employer for his part will be able to examine every aspect of the employee's performance and personal life in order to bolster the case for dismissal. . . .

## DISTRIBUTIONAL CONCERNS

Enough has been said to show that there is no principled reason of fairness or utility to disturb the common law's longstanding presumption in favor of the contract at will. It remains to be asked whether there are some hitherto unmentioned distributional consequences sufficient to throw that conclusion into doubt. . . .

The proposed reforms in the at-will doctrine cannot hope to transfer wealth systematically from rich to poor on the model of comprehensive systems of taxation or welfare benefits. Indeed it is very difficult to identify in advance any deserving group of recipients that stands to gain unambiguously from the universal abrogation of the at-will contract. The proposed rules cover the whole range from senior executives to manual labor. At every wage level, there is presumably some differential in worker's output. Those who tend to slack off seem on balance to be most vulnerable to dismissal under the at-will rule; yet it is very hard to imagine why some special concession should be made in their favor at the expense of their more diligent fellow workers.

The distributional issues, moreover, become further clouded once it is recognized that any individual employee will have interests on both sides of the employment relation. Individual workers participate heavily in pension plans, where the value of the holdings depends in part upon the efficiency of the legal rules that govern the companies in which they own shares. If the regulation of the contract at will diminishes the overall level of wealth, the losses are apt to be spread far and wide, which makes it doubtful that there are any gains to the worst off in society that justify somewhat greater losses to those who are better off. The usual concern with maldistribution gives us situations in which one person has one hundred while each of one hundred has one and asks us to compare that distribution with an even distribution of, say, two per person. But the stark form of the numerical example does not explain how the skewed distribution is tied to the concrete choice between different rules governing employment relations. Set in this concrete context, the choices about the proposed new regulation of the employment contract do not set the one against the many but set the many against each other, all in the context of a shrinking overall pie. The possible gains from redistribution, even on the most favorable of assumptions about the diminishing marginal utility of money, are simply not present.

If this is the case, one puzzle still remains: Who should be in favor of the proposed legislation? One possibility is that support for the change in common law rules rests largely on ideological and political grounds, so that the legislation has the public support of persons who may well be hurt by it in their private

capacities. Another possible explanation could identify the hand of interest-group politics in some subtle form. For example, the lawyers and government officials called upon to administer the new legislation may expect to obtain increased income and power, although this explanation seems insufficient to account for the current pressure. A more uncertain line of inquiry could ask whether labor unions stand to benefit from the creation of a cause of action for wrongful discharge. Unions, after all, have some skill in working with for-cause contracts under the labor statutes that prohibit firing for union activities, and they might be able to promote their own growth by selling their services to the presently nonunionized sector. In addition, the for-cause rule might give employers one less reason to resist unionization, since they would be unable to retain the absolute power to hire and fire in any event. Yet, by the same token, it is possible that workers would be less inclined to pay the costs of union membership if they received some purported benefit by the force of law without unionization. The ultimate weight of these considerations is an empirical question to which no easy answers appear. What is clear, however, is that even if one could show that the shift in the rule either benefits or hurts unions and their members, the answer would not justify the rule, for it would not explain why the legal system should try to skew the balance one way or the other. The bottom line therefore remains unchanged. The case for a legal requirement that renders employment contracts terminable only for cause is as weak after distributional considerations are taken into account as before. . . .

## CONCLUSION

The recent trend toward expanding the legal remedies for wrongful discharge has been greeted with wide approval in judicial, academic, and popular circles. In this paper, I have argued that the modern trend rests in large measure upon a misunderstanding of the contractual processes and the ends served by the contract at will. No system of regulation can hope to match the benefits that the contract at will affords in employment relations. The flexibility afforded by the contract at will permits the ceaseless marginal adjustments that are necessary in any ongoing productive activity conducted, as all activities are, in conditions of technological and business change. The strength of the contract at will should not be judged by the occasional cases in which it is said to produce unfortunate results, but rather by the vast run of cases where it provides a sensible private response to the many and varied problems in labor contracting. All too often the case for a wrongful discharge doctrine rests upon the identification of possible employer abuses, as if they were all that mattered. But the proper goal is to find the set of comprehensive arrangements that will minimize the frequency and severity of abuses by employers and employees alike. Any effort to drive employer abuses to zero can only increase the difficulties inherent in the employment relation. Here, a full analysis of the relevant costs and benefits shows why the constant minor imperfections of the market, far from being a reason to oust private agreements, offer the most powerful reason for respecting them. The doctrine of wrongful discharge is the problem and not the solution. This is one of the many situations in which courts and legislatures should leave well enough alone.

## NOTES

1. *Payne v. Western & Atlantic R.R.*, 81 Tenn. 507, 518–19 (1884), overruled on other grounds; *Hutton v. Watters*, 132 Tenn. 527, 544, 179 S.W. 134, 138 (1915). . . .
2. Ibid.

## OCCUPATIONAL RISK

# The Right to Risk Information and the Right to Refuse Workplace Hazards

*Ruth R. Faden and Tom L. Beauchamp*

Chemicals pose numerous hazards in the American workplace, ranging from health conditions of cancer, lung damage, and irritation to physical hazards such as flammable liquids and corrosive materials. It is widely agreed that workers have a moral and legal right to know about the risks involved in exposure to these chemicals. However, the nature and scope of the right of employees to be informed about health hazards remains indeterminate. It is unclear who must discover and communicate the information, under which conditions it must be communicated, and how to determine that a successful communication has occurred. We focus on several philosophical and policy-oriented problems concerning the right to know and correlative obligations to communicate relevant information. Related rights are also addressed, notably the right to refuse hazardous work.

# I

A government and industry consensus has gradually evolved that workers have a right to know about occupational risks, and correlatively that there is a moral and a legal obligation to communicate relevant information to workers. The National Institute for Occupational Safety and Health (NIOSH) and other U.S. federal agencies informed the U.S. Senate as early as July 1977 that "workers have the right to know whether or not they are exposed to hazardous chemical and physical agents regulated by the Federal Government."[1] The Occupational Safety and Health Administration (OSHA) implemented regulations in 1980 guaranteeing workers access to medical and exposure records,[2] and then developed regulations from 1983 through the early years of the twenty-first century regarding the right to know about hazardous chemicals and requiring right-to-know training programs in many industries. These issues are now widely discussed using the language of OSHA's "Hazard Communication Standard" (HCS) because OSHA's standards of information dissemination have de facto become the standard of practice.[3] States and municipalities have passed additional legislation, and OSHA requires conformity to many of these local rules.[4]

Although some form of right to risk information—that is, the right to know about exposure to workplace hazards—is now well established in law and ethics, no consensus exists about the nature and extent of a producer's, importer's, distributor's, or employer's obligation to communicate such information—or about how employers must implement the standards in their facilities. Considerable ambiguity attends the nature and scope of the right—that is, which protections and actions the right entails, to whom these rights apply, when notification should occur, and under which conditions. OSHA requires that chemical producers, importers, and distributors "evaluate" the hazards of their chemicals, place labels on containers, and provide training programs for exposed employees. However, government agencies, corporations, and workers often do not distinguish between the obligation to communicate currently available information, the obligation to seek new information through searches of the scientific literature, the obligation to generate information through new research, and the like. The "right to know" can be understood as correlative to only one of these obligations—or to all of them. This is a critical ambiguity at the heart of "the right to know."

Further, those who purchase and distribute hazardous products currently meet their legal obligations by passing on risk information about a product; they are not obligated to evaluate the adequacy of the information provided by manufacturers or suppliers. As OSHA states, "the HCS is designed so that employers who simply use chemicals . . . are not required to evaluate the hazards of those chemicals. Hazard determination is the responsibility of the producers and importers."[5] The relevant literature also does not adequately discuss the central question in business ethics: Do corporations owe workers information that exceeds federal and state requirements?

# II

A diverse set of U.S. laws and federal regulations reflects the belief that citizens in general, and workers in particular, have a right to learn about significant risks. These include the Freedom of Information Act, the Federal Insecticide, Fungicide, and Rodenticide Amendments and Regulations, the Federal Food, Drug, and Cosmetic Act, the Consumer Product Safety Act, the Worker Retraining Notification Act, and the Toxic Substances Control Act. Taken together, this body of legislation communicates the message that manufacturers and other businesses have a moral and legal obligation to communicate information needed by individuals to decide about their participation, employment, or enrollment.

Developments in the right to know in the workplace have consistently held to this general trend toward disclosure and have included an expanded notion of corporate responsibility to provide adequate information to workers. These developments could revolutionize corporate workplace practices. Until the 1983 OSHA HCS went into effect in 1986 for the manufacturing sector and in 1988 for the non-manufacturing sector, workers did not receive extensive information (if any) from a great many employers. Not until October 2001 was there a "HazCom" rule governing chemical hazards in the vast territory of sand, gravel, and crushed stone operations; this rule was passed in November 2000 by the Mine Safety and Health Administration (MSHA).[6]

Subsequent to some of these developments, various corporations quickly established model programs. For example, in the early years of this legislation the Monsanto Company created a right-to-know program in which it distributes information on hazardous chemicals to its employees, and both notifies and monitors past and current employees exposed to carcinogenic and toxic chemicals. Hercules Inc. developed videotape training sessions that incorporate frank discussions of workers' anxieties. The tapes depict workplace dangers and on-the-job accidents. Those employees who view the Hercules film are then taught how to read safety data and how to protect themselves.[7]

Job-training programs, safety data sheets, proper labels, and a written program are all HCS-mandated. Employers must establish hazard-communication programs that transmit information to their employees. Updated information may be provided to employees through computers, microfiche, the Internet, CD-ROM, and the like. The training of new employees must occur before they are exposed to hazardous substances, and each time a new hazard is introduced. Each employee must sign a written acknowledgment of training, and OSHA inspectors may interview employers and employees to check on the effectiveness of the training sessions.

The sobering statistics on worker exposure and injury and on dangerous chemicals in the workplace make such corporate programs essential. OSHA has estimated that 3 million work sites in the United States expose 32 million workers to approximately 650,000 hazardous chemicals.[8] Six thousand U.S. workers die from workplace injuries each year, and perhaps as many as 100,000 deaths annually are caused to some degree by workplace exposure and consequent disease. Roughly 1 percent of the labor force is exposed to known carcinogens.[9]

Despite OSHA's HCS regulations and use of inspections by compliance officers, compliance problems persist. OSHA has recorded thousands of HCS violations in the workplace. The agency once described the noncompliance rate as "incredible."[10]

## III

The most developed models of general disclosure obligations and the right to know have long been found in the literature on informed consent, which also treats the topic of informed refusal. Medical professionals have broadly recognized moral and legal obligations to communicate known risks (and benefits) that are associated with a proposed treatment or form of research. No parallel fiduciary obligation has traditionally been recognized in relationships between management and workers. Workmens' compensation laws have governed risks in this environment, but these laws were originally designed for problems of accident in instances of immediately assessable damage. Obligations to warn or to communicate were irrelevant under the "no-fault" conception in workmens' compensation.

However, the importance of information that will decrease occupational risk has been increasingly appreciated in recent years. In particular, knowledge is needed about the serious long-term risks of injury, disease, and death presented by exposure to toxic substances and forms of physical injury. These risks to health carry increased need for information on the basis of which a person may wish to take various actions, including choosing to forego employment completely, to refuse certain work environments within a place of employment, to request improved protective devices, and to request lowered levels of exposure.[11]

Employee–employer relationships, unlike physician–patient relationships, are often confrontational and present to workers a constant danger of undisclosed or underdisclosed risk. This danger and the relative powerlessness of employees justify employer disclosure obligations in all hazardous conditions. By what criteria, then, shall such disclosure obligations be determined?

One plausible argument is the following: Because large employers, unions, and government agencies must deal with multiple employees and complicated causal conditions, no standard should be more demanding than the so-called reasonable-person standard, which remains today the standard in Department of Labor literature. This standard is what a fair and informed member of the relevant community believes is needed. Under this standard, no employer, union, or other party should be held responsible for disclosing information beyond that needed to make an informed choice about the adequacy of safety precautions, industrial hygiene, long-term hazards, and the like, as determined by what the reasonable person in the community would judge to be the worker's need for information.

However, this reasonable-person standard of disclosure is not adequate for all disclosures. In the case of serious hazards, such as those involved in short-term, concentrated doses of radiation, a standard tied to individual persons is more appropriate. When disclosures to individual workers may be expected to have a subjective impact that varies with each individual, the reasonable-person standard should be supplemented by a standard that addresses each worker's personal informational needs.

The best solution to the problem of a general standard is a compromise between a reasonable-person standard and a subjective standard: Whatever a reasonable person would judge material to the decision-making process should be communicated, and in addition any remaining information that is material to an individual worker should be provided through a process of asking whether he or she has any additional or special concerns. This standard avoids a narrow focus on the employer's obligation to communicate information and promotes a worker's understanding and consent. These problems center on the importance of communication, rather than on legal standards of disclosure. The key to effective communication is to invite participation by workers in a dialogue. Asking questions, eliciting concerns, and establishing a climate that encourages questions may be more meaningful than the full corpus of communicated information. Different levels of education, linguistic ability, and sophistication about the issues need to be accommodated.

The majority of the nation's workplaces are presently exempted from OSHA regulations, leaving these workers largely uninformed. Even in workplaces that are covered, former workers often have as much of a need for the information as do presently employed workers. The federal government has the names of hundreds of thousands of former workers whose risk of cancer, heart disease, and lung disease has been increased by exposure to asbestos, polyvinyl chloride, benzene, arsenic, betanaphthalamine, and dozens of other chemicals. Employers have the names of several million such workers.

The U.S. Congress once passed a bill to notify workers at greatest risk,[12] so that checkups and diagnosis of disease can be made before a disease's advanced stage. However, neither industry nor the government has developed a systematic program with teeth. It has often been stated that the expense of notification would be prohibitive, that many workers would be unduly alarmed, and that existing screening and surveillance programs should prove adequate in monitoring and treating disease. Critics rightly charge, however, that existing programs are inadequate and that workers have a right to know strong enough to enable them to investigate potential problems at their initiative.

## IV

Despite the apparent consensus on the desirability of having some form of right to know in the workplace, it has proven difficult to implement this right. Complicated questions arise about the kinds of information to be communicated, by whom, to whom, under what conditions, and with what warrant. Trade secrets have also been a thorn in the side of progress, because companies resist disclosing information about an ingredient or process claimed as a trade secret.[13] They insist that they should not be required to reveal their substances or processes if their competitors might then obtain the information. OSHA therefore regards itself as duty-bound to balance the protection of workers through disclosure against the protection of corporate interests in nondisclosure.[14] In addition, economic and social constraints sometimes inhibit workers from exercising their full range of workplace options. For example, in industries in which ten—or even a hundred—people apply for every available position, bargaining for increased protection is an unlikely event.

We here set aside this sort of problem in order to consider perhaps the most perplexing difficulty about the right to know in the workplace: the right to refuse hazardous work assignments and to have effective mechanisms for workers to reduce the risks they face. Shortly after the HCS went into effect, labor saw that the right to know was often of little practical use unless it was accompanied by a meaningful right to escape and modify hazardous working conditions. Although U.S. law generally makes unsafe working conditions a punishable offense, the United States Occupational Safety and Health Act (OSH Act of 1970[15]) limited rights of refusal to work that presented life-threatening conditions and risks of serious bodily injury. Specifically, the OSH Act grants workers the right to request an OSHA inspection if they believe an OSHA standard has been violated or an imminent danger exists. Under the act, employees also have the right to participate in OSHA inspection tours of the worksite and to consult freely with the compliance officer. Most important, the OSH Act protects employees who request an inspection or otherwise exercise their rights under the OSH Act from discharge or any discriminatory treatment in retaliation for *legitimate* safety and health complaints.[16]

These worker rights under the OSH Act are essential, but they do not assure that all workers have effective mechanisms for initiating inspections of suspected health hazards. The

OSH Act does not cover small businesses (those employing fewer than ten workers) or federal, state, and municipal employees.[17] Questions also remain about OSHA's ability to enforce these provisions of the OSH Act. The agency tends to develop policy on the basis of cost-benefit principles, rather than strict enforcement of the right to know. If workers are to use disclosed information on health hazards effectively, they must have access to an inclusive, workable, and efficient regulatory system. The OSH Act is also written to protect the rights of individuals, not groups (although there are provisions for "authorized employee representatives" such as a union representative chosen by the employee). It has no provisions for collective action by workers and does not mandate workplace health and safety committees, as does legislation in some countries. Workers therefore still need an adequately protected right to refuse unsafe work and a meaningful right to refuse an employer's request that they sign OSHA-mandated forms acknowledging that they have been trained about hazardous chemicals. One cannot easily determine the current extent to which these rights are protected.[18]

OSHA regulations allow workers to walk off the job if there is a genuine danger of death or serious injury, while the LMRA permits refusals only under "abnormally dangerous conditions."[19] Under the LMRA, the nature of the occupation determines the extent of danger justifying refusal, while under OSHA the character of the threat, or so-called imminent danger, determines worker action. Here "imminent danger" is defined in terms of a reasonable expectation of "death or possible serious physical harm" that might occur before normal enforcement procedures could be acted upon.[20]

By contrast, under the NLRA a walkout by two or more workers may be justified for even minimal safety problems, so long as the action can be construed as a "concerted activity" for mutual aid and protection and a no-strike clause does not exist in any collective bargaining agreements. While the NLRA appears to provide the broadest protection to workers, employees refusing to work under the NLRA can lose the right to be reinstated in their positions if permanent replacements can be hired.

The current legal situation concerning the right to refuse hazardous work also fails to resolve other questions, such as whether the right to refuse hazardous work entails an obligation to continue to pay nonworking employees or to award the employees back-pay if the issue is resolved in their favor. On the one hand, workers without union strike benefits or other income protections would be unable to exercise their right to refuse unsafe work due to economic pressures. On the other hand, to permit such workers to draw a paycheck is to legitimize strike with pay, a practice traditionally considered unacceptable by management and by Congress.

The situation does not resolve whether the right to refuse unsafe work should be restricted to cases of obvious, imminent, and serious risks to health or life (the current OSHA and LMRA position) or should be expanded to include lesser risks and uncertain risks—for example, exposure to suspected toxic or carcinogenic substances that, although not immediate threats, may prove more dangerous over time. In order for "the right to know" to allow for meaningful worker action, workers would have to be able to remove themselves from exposure to suspected hazards, as well as obvious or known hazards.

The question of the proper standard for determining whether a safety walkout is justified is connected to this issue. At least three different standards have been applied in the past: (1) a good-faith subjective standard, which requires only that the worker honestly believe that a health hazard exists; (2) a reasonable-person standard, which requires that the belief be reasonable under the circumstances, as well as sincerely held; and (3) an objective standard, which requires evidence—commonly established by expert witnesses—that the threat in fact exists.[21]

No less important is whether the right to refuse hazardous work should be protected only until a formal review of the situation is initiated (at which time the worker must return to the job) or whether the walkout should be permitted until the alleged hazard is at least temporarily removed. Requirements that workers continue to be exposed while OSHA or the NLRB conduct investigations is unacceptable if the magnitude of potential harm is significant. However, compelling employers to remove suspected hazards during the evaluation period may also result in unacceptable economic burdens. This situation is worsened by the fact that workers are often not in a position to act on information about health hazards by seeking alternative employment elsewhere.

We need, then, to delineate the conditions under which workers may be compelled to return to work during an alleged hazard investigation and the conditions that can compel employers to remove alleged hazards.

## V

Legal rights are useless if workers remain ignorant of their options or cannot exercise their rights. Despite recent requirements that employers initiate training programs, it remains doubtful that many workers, particularly nonunion workers, are aware that they have a legally protected right to refuse hazardous work. Even if workers were to learn of such a right, they could probably not weave their way through the maze of legal options unaided.

Programs of information and training in hazards are as important for employers and managers as for workers. Workplace disease and injury are expensive, and they profoundly affect morale. Occupational deaths can be investigated as homicides. Corporate executives have been tried, and in some cases convicted, for murder and manslaughter, on grounds that they negligently caused worker deaths by failing to notify of hazards. An improved system of corporate disclosures of risk and the rights of workers therefore stands to benefit everyone.

## NOTES

1. NIOSH et al., "The Right to Know: Practical Problems and Policy Issues Arising from Exposures to Hazardous Chemical and Physical Agents in the Workplace" (Washington, D.C.: July 1977), pp. 1 and 5; see also Ilise L. Feitshans, "Hazardous Substances in the Workplace: How Much Does the Employee have the Right to Know?" *Detroit Law Review* 3 (1985).

2. Occupational Safety and Health Administration, "Access to Employee Exposure and Medical Records—Final Rules," *Federal Register* (May 23, 1980), 35212–77.

3. Dept. of Labor, OSHA, www.osha.gov (2003); see, in particular, "Laws and Regulations," "OSHA Regulations," 29 CFR 1910.1200.

4. Dept. of Labor, OSHA, www.osha.gov, 29 CFR 1910.1200 App. E, sec. 1.

5. Dept. of Labor, OSHA, www.osha.gov, 29 CFR 1910.1200 App. E.

6. U.S. Dept. of Labor, Mine Safety and Health Administration, 30 CFR, Part 47—Hazard Communication. See also Charlotte S. Garvey, "Mine Operators Face New Hazard Communication Rule," *Primedia Business Magazines and Media*, Washington Letter Section (November 2000), as posted, with copyright, by Lexis-Nexis.

7. Laurie Hays, "New Rules on Workplace Hazards Prompt Intensified On the Job Training Programs," *Wall Street Journal* (July 8, 1986), p. 31; Cathy Trost, "Plans to Alert Workers," *Wall Street Journal* (March 28, 1986), p. 15.

8. U. S. Dept. of Labor, OSHA, www.osha.gov, "Safety/Health Topics," "Hazard Communication" (as posted January 2003).

9. Department of Labor, Bureau of Labor and Statistics: www.bls.gov/iif/oshwc/cfoi/cftb0155.pdf. The 6,000 figure remained remarkably stable from 1996 to 2001, varying only from 5,900 to 6,202 in these years. See earlier 48 CFR 53, 282 (1983); Office of Technology

Assessment, *Preventing Illness and Injury in the Workplace* (Washington: U.S. Government Printing Office, 1985); Sheldon W. Samuels, "The Ethics of Choice in the Struggle against Industrial Disease," *American Journal of Industrial Medicine* 23 (1993): 43–52; and David Rosner and Gerald E. Markowitz, eds. *Dying for Work: Workers' Safety and Health in Twentieth-Century America* (Bloomington: University of Indiana Press, 1987).

10. Current Reports, *O.S.H. Reporter* (March 15, 1989), p. 1747.

11. See the articles by Gregory Bond, Leon Gordis, John Higgenson and Flora Chu, Albert Jonsen, and Paul A. Schulte in *Industrial Epidemiology Forum's Conference on Ethics in Epidemiology*, ed. William E. Fayerweather, John Higgenson, and Tom L. Beauchamp (New York: Pergamon Press, 1991).

12. High Risk Occupational Disease Notification and Prevention Act, HR 1309.

13. An employer is not required to disclose the name or any information about a hazardous chemical that would require disclosure of a bona fide trade secret; but in a medical emergency the company must disclose this information to physicians or nurses as long as confidentiality is assured. Under the HCS, even nonemergency disclosure is required under specified conditions of occupational health necessity.

14. For the current language, which is often vague, see 29 CFR 1910.1200(i) and 1910.1200 App. D (Definition of "Trade Secret") (as posted on January 22, 2003).

15. OSHA was first authorized by the OSH Act of 1970 (29 USC §651 *et seq.*).

16. OSH Act, Section 8. If the health or safety complaint (filed by the employee) is not determined to be legitimate, there are no worker protections.

17. OSHA regulations govern only business with 11 or more employees. They also do not apply to government agencies, self-employed individuals, and family farms.

18. The right to refuse an employer's request to sign a training acknowledgment form is upheld in *Beam Distilling Co. v. Distillery and Allied Workers' International*, 90 Lab. Arb. 740 (1988). See also Ronald Bayer, ed. *The Health and Safety of Workers* (New York: Oxford University Press, 1988); James C. Robinson, *Toil and Toxics: Workplace Struggles and Political Strategies for Occupational Health* (Berkeley: University of California Press, 1991).

19. 29 USC §143 (1976), and 29 CFR §1977.12 (1979).

20. Dept. of Labor, OSHA, www.osha.gov (2003), "Worker's Page," "Imminent Danger."

21. OSHA's current general standard is that "employees do have the right to refuse to do a job if they believe in good faith that they are exposed to an *imminent danger*. 'Good faith' means that even if an imminent danger is not found to exist, the worker had reasonable grounds to believe that it did exist." Dept. of Labor, OSHA, www.osha.gov (2003), "Worker's Page," "Refusing to Work Because Conditions are Dangerous."

# Occupational Health and Safety

*John R. Boatright*

## THE SCOPE OF THE PROBLEM

Many Americans live with the possibility of serious injury and death every working day. For some workers, the threat comes from a major industrial accident, such as the collapse of a mine or a refinery explosion, or from widespread exposure to a hazardous substance, such as asbestos, which is estimated to have caused more than 350,000 cancer

*Ethics and the Conduct of Business* by John R. Boatright. Adapted by permission of Pearson Education Inc., Upper Saddle River, NJ.

deaths since 1940.[1] The greatest toll on the workforce is exacted, however, by little-publicized injuries to individual workers, some of which are gradual, such as hearing loss from constant noise or nerve damage from repetitive motions. Some of the leading causes of death, such as heart disease, cancer, and respiratory conditions, are thought to be job-related, although causal connections are often difficult to make. Even stress on the job is now being recognized as a workplace hazard that is responsible for headaches, back and chest pains, stomach ailments, and a variety of emotional disorders.

### The Distinction between Safety and Health

Although the term *safety* is often used to encompass all workplace hazards, it is useful to make a distinction between *safety* and *health*. Safety hazards generally involve loss of limbs, burns, broken bones, electrical shocks, cuts, sprains, bruises, and impairment of sight or hearing. These injuries are usually the result of sudden and often violent events involving industrial equipment or the physical environment of the workplace. . . .

Health hazards are factors in the workplace that cause illnesses and other conditions that develop over a lifetime of exposure. Many diseases associated with specific occupations have long been known. In 1567, Paracelsus identified pneumoconiosis, or black lung disease, in a book entitled *Miners' Sickness and Other Miners' Diseases*. . . . Mercury poisoning, once common among felt workers, produces tremors, known as "the hatters' shakes," and delusions and hallucinations, which gave rise to the phrase "mad as a hatter."

In the modern workplace, most occupational health problems result from routine exposure to hazardous substances. Among these substances are fine particles, such as asbestos, . . . heavy metals, gases, . . . solvents, . . . and certain classes of chemicals. Pesticides pose a serious threat to agricultural workers, and radiation is an occupational hazard to X-ray technicians and workers in the nuclear industry.

Because occupationally related diseases result from long-term exposure and not from identifiable events on the job, employers have generally not been held liable for them, and they have not, until recently, been recognized in workers' compensation programs. The fact that the onset of many diseases occurs years after the initial exposure—30 or 40 years in the case of asbestos—hides the causal connection. The links are further obscured by a multiplicity of causes. The textile industry, for example, claims that byssinosis among its workers results from their own decision to smoke and not from inhaling cotton dust on the job. Lack of knowledge, especially about cancer, adds to the difficulty of establishing causal connections.

### Regulation of Occupational Health and Safety

Prior to the passage of the Occupational Safety and Health Act (OSH Act) in 1970, government regulation of occupational health and safety was almost entirely the province of the states. Understaffed and underfunded, the agencies charged with protecting workers in most states were not very effective. Only a small percentage of workers in many states were even under the jurisdiction of regulatory agencies; often, powerful economic interests were able to influence their activities. Because the agencies lacked the resources to set standards for exposure to hazardous substances, they relied heavily on private standard-setting organizations and the industries themselves. The emphasis in most states was on education and training, and prosecutions for violations were rare. State regulatory agencies were also concerned almost exclusively with safety rather than with health.

States still play a major role in occupational health and safety through workers' compensation systems, but in 1970, primary responsibility for the regulation of working conditions passed to the federal government. The "general duty clause" of the OSH Act requires employers "to furnish to each of his employees employment and a place of employment which are free from recognized hazards that are causing or are likely to cause death or serious injury."[2] In addition, employers have a specific duty to comply with all the occupational safety and health standards that OSHA is empowered to make. Employees also have a duty, under Section 5(b), to "comply with occupational safety and health standards and all rules, regulations, and orders issued pursuant to this Act which are applicable to his own actions and conduct." OSHA regulates occupational health and safety primarily by issuing standards, which are commonly enforced by workplace inspections. Examples of standards are permissible exposure limits (PELs) for toxic substances and specifications for equipment and facilities, such as guards on saws and the height and strength of railings.

## The Right To a Safe and Healthy Workplace

At first glance, the right of employees to a safe and healthy workplace might seem to be too obvious to need any justification. This right—and the corresponding obligation of employers to provide working conditions free of recognized hazards—appears to follow from a more fundamental right—namely, the right of survival. Patricia H. Werhane writes, for example, "Dangerous working conditions threaten the very existence of employees and cannot be countenanced when they are avoidable."

Without this right, she argues, all other rights lose their significance.[3] Some other writers base a right to a safe and healthy workplace on the Kantian ground that persons ought to be treated as ends rather than as means. Mark MacCarthy has described this view as follows:

> People have rights that protect them from others who would enslave them or otherwise use them for their own purposes. In bringing this idea to bear on the problem of occupational safety, many people have thought that workers have an inalienable right to earn their living free from the ravages of job-caused death, disease, and injury.[4]

Congress, in passing the OSH Act granting the right to all employees of a safe and healthy workplace, was apparently relying on a cost-benefit analysis, balancing the cost to industry with the savings to the economy as a whole. Congress, in other words, appears to have been employing essentially utilitarian reasoning. Regardless of the ethical reasoning used, though, workers have an undeniable right not to be injured or killed on the job.

It is not clear, though, what specific protection workers are entitled to or what specific obligations employers have with respect to occupational health and safety. One position, recognized in common law, is that workers have a right to be protected against harm resulting directly from the actions of employers where the employer is at fault in some way. Consider the case of the owner of a drilling company in Los Angeles who had a 23-year-old worker lowered into a 33-foot-deep, 18-inch-wide hole that was being dug for an elevator shaft. No test was made of the air at the bottom of the hole, and while he was being lowered, the worker began to have difficulty breathing. Rescue workers were hampered by the lack of shoring, and the worker died before he could be pulled to the surface. The owner of the drilling company was convicted of manslaughter, sentenced to 45 days in jail, and ordered to pay $12,000 in compensation to the family of the victim. A prosecutor in the Los Angeles County district attorney's office explained the decision to bring criminal charges with the words, "Our opinion is you can't risk somebody's life to save a few bucks. That's the bottom line."

Few people would hesitate to say that the owner of the company in this case violated an employee's rights by recklessly endangering his life. In most workplace accidents, however, employers can defend themselves against the charge of violating the rights of workers with two arguments. One is that their actions were not the *direct cause* of the death or injury, and the other is that the worker *voluntarily assumed the risk.* These defenses are considered in turn.

### The Concept of a Direct Cause

Two factors enable employers to deny that their actions are a direct cause of an accident in the workplace. One factor is that industrial accidents are typically caused by a combination of factors, frequently including the actions of workers themselves. When there is such a multiplicity of causes, it is difficult to assign responsibility to any one person. The legal treatment of industrial accidents in the United States incorporates this factor by recognizing two common-law defenses for employers: that a workplace accident was caused in part by (1) lack of care on the part of the employee (the doctrine of "contributory negligence") or by (2) the negligence of coworkers (the "fellow-servant rule"). As long as employers are not negligent in meeting minimal obligations, they are not generally held liable for deaths or injuries resulting from industrial accidents.

The second factor is that it is often not practical to reduce the probability of harm any further. It is reasonable to hold an employer responsible for the incidence of cancer in workers who are exposed to high levels of a known carcinogen, especially when the exposure is avoidable. But a small number of cancer deaths can be statistically predicted to result from very low exposure levels to some widely used chemicals. Is it reasonable to hold employers responsible when workers contract cancer from exposure to carcinogens at levels that are considered to pose only a slight risk? The so-called Delaney amendment, for example, forbids the use of any food additive found to cause cancer. Such an absolute prohibition is practicable for food additives, because substitutes are usually readily available. But when union and public-interest groups petitioned OSHA in 1972 to set zero tolerance levels for ten powerful carcinogens, the agency refused on the ground that workers should be protected from carcinogens "to the maximum extent practicable *consistent with continued use.*"[5] The position of OSHA, apparently, was that it is unreasonable to forgo the benefit of useful chemicals when there are no ready substitutes and the probability of cancer can be kept low by strict controls. This is also the position of philosopher Alan Gewirth, who argues that the right of persons not to have cancer inflicted on them is not absolute. He concluded, "Whether the use of or exposure to some substance should be prohibited should depend on the degree to which it poses the risk of cancer. . . . If the risks are very slight . . . and if no substitutes are available, then use of it may be permitted, subject to stringent safeguards."[6] . . .

### The Voluntary Assumption of Risk

A further common-law defense is that employees voluntarily assume the risk inherent in work. Some jobs, such as coal mining, construction, longshoring, and meatpacking, are well known for their high accident rates, and yet some individuals freely choose these lines of work, even when safer employment is available. The risk itself is sometimes part of the allure, but more often the fact that hazardous jobs offer a wage premium in order to compensate for the greater risk leads workers to prefer them to less hazardous, less well-paying jobs. Like people who choose to engage in risky recreational activities, such as mountain climbing, workers in hazardous occupations, according to the argument, knowingly accept the risk in return for benefits that cannot be obtained without it. Injury and even death are part of the price they may have to pay. And except when an employer or a fellow employee is negligent in some way, workers who have chosen to work under dangerous conditions have no one to blame but themselves.

A related argument is that occupational health and safety ought not to be regulated because it interferes with the freedom of individuals to choose the kind of work that they want to perform. Workers who prefer the higher wages of hazardous work ought to be free to accept such employment, and those with a greater aversion to risk ought to be free to choose other kinds of employment or to bargain for more safety, presumably with lower pay. To deny workers this freedom of choice is to treat them as persons incapable of looking after their own welfare. . . .

The argument that employees assume the risk of work can be challenged on several grounds. First, workers need to possess a sufficient amount of information about the hazards involved. They cannot be said to assume the risk of performing dangerous work when they do not know what the risks are. Also, they cannot exercise the right to bargain for safer working conditions without access to the relevant information. Yet, employers have generally been reluctant to notify workers or their bargaining agents of dangerous conditions or to release documents in their possession. Oftentimes, hazards in the workplace are not known by the employer or the employee until after the harm has been done. In order for employers to be relieved of responsibility for injury or death in the workplace, though, it is necessary that employees have adequate information *at the time they make a choice.*

Second, the choice of employees must be truly free. When workers are forced to perform dangerous work for lack of acceptable alternatives, they cannot be said to assume the risk. For many people with few skills and limited mobility in economically depressed areas, the only work available is often in a local slaughterhouse or textile mill, where they run great risks. Whether they are coerced into accepting work of this kind is a controversial question. Individuals are free in one sense to accept or decline whatever employment is available, but the alternatives of unemployment or work at poverty-level wages may be so unacceptable that people lack freedom of choice in any significant sense.

**Risk and Coercion**

In order to determine whether workers assume the risk of employment by their free choice, we need some account of the concept of coercion. A paradigm example is the mugger who says with a gun in hand, "Your money or your life." The "choice" offered by the mugger contains an undesirable set of alternatives that are imposed on the victim by a threat of dire consequences. A standard analysis of coercion that is suggested by this example involves two elements: (1) getting a person to choose an alternative that he or she does not want, and (2) issuing a threat to make the person worse off if he or she does not choose that alternative.

Consider the case of an employer who offers a worker who already holds a satisfactory job higher wages in return for taking on new duties involving a greater amount of risk. The employer's offer is not coercive because there is no threat involved. The worker may welcome the offer, but declining it leaves the worker still in possession of an acceptable position. Is an employer acting like a mugger, however, when the offer of higher pay for more dangerous work is accompanied by the threat of dismissal? Is "Do this hazardous work or be fired!" like or unlike the "choice" offered by the mugger? The question is even more difficult when the only "threat" is not to hire a person. Is it coercive to say, "Accept this dangerous job or stay unemployed!" because the alternative of remaining out of work leaves the person in exactly the same position as before? Remaining unemployed, moreover, is unlike getting fired, in that it is not something that an employer inflicts on a person.

In order to answer these questions, the standard analysis of coercion needs to be supplemented by an account of what it means to issue a threat. A threat involves a stated intention of making a person worse off in some way. To fire a person from a job is usually to make that person worse off, but we would not say that an employer is coercing a worker by threatening dismissal for failure to perform the normal duties of a job. Similarly, we would not say that an employer is making a threat in not hiring a person who refuses to carry out the same normal duties. A person who turns down a job because the office is not provided with air conditioning, for example, is not being made worse off by the employer. So why would we say that a person who chooses to remain unemployed rather than work in a coal mine that lacks adequate ventilation is being coerced?

The answer of some philosophers is that providing employees with air conditioning is not morally required; however, maintaining a safe mine is. Whether a threat is coercive because it would make a person worse off can be determined only if there is some baseline that answers the question, worse off compared with what? Robert Nozick gives an example of an abusive slave owner who offers not to give a slave his daily beating if the slave will perform some disagreeable task the slave owner wants done.[7] Even though the slave might welcome the offer, it is still coercive, because the daily beating involves treating the slave in an immoral manner. For Nozick and others, what is *morally required* is the relevant baseline for determining whether a person would be made worse off by a threatened course of action.

It follows from this analysis that coercion is an inherently ethical concept that can be applied only after determining what is morally required in a given situation. As a result, the argument that the assumption of risk by employees relieves employers of responsibility involves circular reasoning. Employers are freed from responsibility for workplace injuries on the ground that workers assume the risk of employment only if they are not coerced into accepting hazardous work. But whether workers are coerced depends on the right of employees to a safe and healthy workplace—and the obligation of employers to provide it. . . .

## Whirlpool Corporation

The Whirlpool Corporation operates a plant in Marion, Ohio, for the assembly of household appliances.[8] Components for the appliances are carried throughout the plant by an elaborate system of overhead conveyors. To protect workers from the objects that occasionally fall from the conveyors, a huge wire mesh screen was installed approximately 20 feet above the floor. The screen is attached to an angle-iron frame suspended from the ceiling of the building. Maintenance employees at the plant spend several hours every week retrieving fallen objects from the screen. Their job also includes replacing paper that is spread on the screen to catch dripping grease from the conveyors, and occasionally they do maintenance work on the conveyors themselves. Workers are usually able to stand on the frame to perform these tasks, but occasionally it is necessary to step on to the screen.

In 1973, several workers fell partway through the screen, and one worker fell completely through to the floor of the plant below but survived. Afterward, Whirlpool began replacing the screen with heavier wire mesh, but on June 28, 1974, a maintenance employee fell to his death through a portion of the screen that had not been replaced. The company responded by making additional repairs and forbidding employees to stand on the angle-iron frame or step onto the screen. An alternative method for retrieving objects was devised using hooks.

Two maintenance employees at the Marion plant, Virgil Deemer and Thomas Cornwell, were still not satisfied. On July 7, 1974, they met with the maintenance supervisor at the plant to express their concern about the safety of the screen. At a meeting two days later with the plant safety director, they requested the name, address, and telephone number of a representative in the local office of the Occupational Safety and Health Administration. The safety director warned the men that they "had better stop and think about what they were doing," but he gave them the requested information. Deemer called the OSHA representative later that day to discuss the problem.

When Deemer and Cornwell reported for the night shift at 10:45 P.M. the next day, July 10, they were ordered by the foreman to perform routine maintenance duties above an old section of the screen. They refused, claiming that the work was unsafe, whereupon the foreman ordered the two employees to punch out. In addition to losing wages for the six hours they did not work that night, Deemer and Cornwell received written reprimands, which were placed in their personnel files.

## THE RIGHT TO KNOW ABOUT AND REFUSE HAZARDOUS WORK

The Whirlpool case illustrates a cruel dilemma faced by many American workers. If they stay on the job and perform hazardous work, then they risk serious injury and even death. On the other hand, if they refuse to work as directed, then they risk disciplinary action, which can include loss of wages, unfavorable evaluation, demotion, and dismissal. Many people believe that it is unjust for workers to be put into the position of having to choose between safety and their job. Rather, employees ought to be able to refuse orders to perform hazardous work without fear of suffering adverse consequences. Even worse are situations in which workers face hazards of which they are unaware. Kept in the dark about dangers lurking in the workplace, employees have no reason to refuse hazardous work and are unable to take other steps to protect themselves.

### Features of the Right to Know and Refuse

The right to refuse hazardous work is different from a right to a safe and healthy workplace. If it is unsafe to work above the old screen, as Deemer and Cornwell contended, then their right to a safe and healthy workplace was violated. A right to refuse hazardous work, however, is only one of several alternatives that workers have for securing the right to a safe and healthy workplace. Victims of racial or sexual discrimination, for example, also suffer a violation of their rights, but it does not follow that they have a right to disobey orders or to walk off the job in an effort to avoid discrimination. Other means are available for ending discrimination and for receiving compensation for the harm done. The same is true for the right to a safe and healthy workplace.

The right to know is actually an aggregation of several rights. Thomas O. McGarity classifies these rights by the correlative duties that they impose on employers. These are (1) the duty to *reveal* information already possessed; (2) the duty to *communicate* information about hazards through labeling, written communications, and training programs; (3) the duty to *seek out* existing information from the scientific literature and other sources;

and (4) the duty to *produce* new information (for example, through animal testing) relevant to employee health.[9] Advocates of the right of workers to know need to specify which of these particular rights are included in their claim.

Disagreement also arises over questions about what information workers have a right to know and which workers have a right to know it. In particular, does the information that employers have a duty to reveal include information about the past exposure of workers to hazardous substances? Do employers have a duty to notify past as well as present employees? The issue at stake in these questions is a part of the "right to know" controversy commonly called *worker notification.*

The main argument for denying workers a right to refuse hazardous work is that such a right conflicts with the obligation of employees to obey all reasonable directives from an employer. An order for a worker to perform some especially dangerous task may not be reasonable, however. The foreman in the Whirlpool case, for example, was acting contrary to a company rule forbidding workers to step on the screen. Still, a common-law principle is that employees should obey even an improper order and file a grievance afterward, if a grievance procedure is in place, or seek whatever other recourse is available. The rationale for this principle is that employees may be mistaken about whether an order is proper, and chaos would result if employees could stop work until the question is decided. It is better for workers to obey now and correct any violation of their rights later.

The fatal flaw in this argument is that later may be too late. The right to a safe and healthy workplace, unlike the right not to be discriminated against, can effectively provide protection for workers only if violations of the right are prevented in the first place. Debilitating injury and death cannot be corrected later; neither can workers and their families ever be adequately compensated for a loss of this kind.

The right to refuse hazardous work, therefore, is necessary for the existence of the right to a safe and healthy workplace.

## The Justification for Refusing Hazardous Work

A right to a safe and healthy workplace is empty unless workers have a right in some circumstances to refuse hazardous work, but there is a tremendous amount of controversy over what these circumstances are. In the *Whirlpool* case, the Supreme Court cited two factors as relevant for justifying a refusal to work. These are (1) that the employee reasonably believes that the working conditions pose an imminent risk of death or serious injury, and (2) that the employee has reason to believe that the risk cannot be avoided by any less disruptive course of action. Employees have a right to refuse hazardous work, in other words, only as a last resort—when it is not possible to bring unsafe working conditions to the attention of the employer or to request an OSHA inspection. Also, the hazards that employees believe to exist must involve a high degree of risk of serious harm. Refusing to work because of a slight chance of minor injury is less likely to be justified. The fact that a number of workers had already fallen through the screen at the Whirlpool plant, for example, and that one had been killed strengthens the claim that the two employees had a right to refuse their foreman's order to step on to it.

The pivotal question, of course, is the proper standard for a reasonable belief. How much evidence should employees be required to have in order to be justified in refusing to work? Or should the relevant standard be the actual existence of a workplace hazard rather than the belief of employees, no matter how reasonable? A minimal requirement, which has been insisted on by the courts, is that employees act in *good faith.* Generally, acting in good faith means that employees have an honest belief that a hazard exists and that their only intention is to protect themselves from the hazard. The "good faith" requirement serves primarily to exclude refusals based on deliberately false charges of unsafe working conditions or on sabotage by employees. Whether a refusal is in good faith does not depend on the reasonableness or correctness of the employees' beliefs about the hazards in the workplace. Thus, employees who refuse an order to fill a tank with a dangerous chemical in the mistaken but sincere belief that a valve is faulty are acting in good faith, but employees who use the same excuse to conduct a work stoppage for other reasons are not acting in good faith, even if it should turn out that the valve is faulty. . . .

### The Justification of a Right to Know

Unlike the right to refuse hazardous work, the right to know about workplace hazards is not necessary for the right to a safe and healthy workplace. This latter right is fully protected as long as employers succeed in ridding the workplace of significant hazards. Some argue that the right to know is still an effective, if not an absolutely essential, means for securing the right to a safe and healthy workplace. Others maintain, however, that the right to know is not dependent for its justification on the right to a safe and healthy workplace; that is, even employees who are adequately protected by their employers against occupational injury and disease still have a right to be told what substances they are handling, what dangers they pose, what precautions to take, and so on.

*The Argument from Autonomy.* The most common argument for the right to know is one based on autonomy. This argument begins with the premise that autonomous individuals are those who are able to exercise free choice in matters that affect their welfare most deeply. Sometimes this premise is expressed by saying that autonomous individuals are those who are able to *participate* in decision making about these matters. One matter that profoundly affects the welfare of workers is the amount of risk that they assume in the course of earning a living. Autonomy requires, therefore, that workers be free to avoid hazardous work, if they so choose, or have the opportunity to accept greater risks in return for higher pay, if that is their choice. In order to choose freely, however, or to participate in decision making, it is necessary to possess relevant information. In the matter of risk assumption, the relevant information includes knowledge of the hazards present in the workplace. Workers can be autonomous, therefore, only if they have a right to know.

In response, employers maintain that they can protect workers from hazards more effectively than workers can themselves without informing workers of the nature of those hazards. Such a paternalistic concern, even when it is sincere and well founded, is incompatible, however, with a respect for the autonomy of workers. A similar argument is sometimes used to justify paternalism in the doctor–patient relation. For a doctor to conceal information from a patient even in cases where exclusive reliance on the doctor's greater training and experience would result in better medical care is now generally regarded as unjustified. If paternalism is morally unacceptable in the doctor–patient relation, where doctors have an obligation to act in the patient's interest, then it is all the more suspect in the employer–employee relation, where employers have no such obligation.[10]

Although autonomy is a value, it does not follow that employers have an obligation to further it in their dealings with employees. The autonomy of buyers in market transactions is also increased by having more information, but the sellers of a product are not generally required to provide this information except when concealment constitutes fraud. The gain of autonomy for employees must be balanced, moreover, against the not inconsiderable cost to employers of implementing a "right to know" policy in the workplace. In addition to the direct cost of assembling information, attaching warning labels, training workers, and so on, there are also indirect costs. Employees who are aware of the risk they are taking are more likely to demand higher wages or else safer working conditions. They are more likely to avail themselves of workers' compensation benefits and to sue employers over occupational injury and disease. Finally, companies are concerned about the loss of valuable trade secrets that could occur from informing workers about the hazards of certain substances.

*Bargaining Over Information.* An alternative to a right to know policy that respects the autonomy of both parties is to allow bargaining over information. Thomas O. McGarity has described this alternative in the following way:

> Because acquiring information costs money, employees desiring information about workplace risks should be willing to pay the employer (in reduced wages) or someone else to produce or gather the relevant information. A straightforward economic analysis would suggest that employees would be willing to pay for health and safety information up to the point at which the value in wage negotiations of the last piece of information purchased equaled the cost of that additional information.[11]

Although promising in theory, this alternative is not practical. It creates a disincentive for employers, who possess most of the information, to yield any of it without some concession by employees, even when it could be provided at little or no cost. Bargaining is feasible for large unions with expertise in safety matters, but reliance on it would leave members of other unions and nonunionized workers without adequate means of protection. In the absence of a market for information, neither employers nor employees would have a basis for determining the value of information in advance of negotiations. Finally, there are costs associated with using the bargaining process to decide any matter—what economists call "transaction costs"—and these are apt to be quite high in negotiations over safety issues. It is unlikely, therefore, that either autonomy or worker health and safety would be well served by the alternative of bargaining over matters of occupational health and safety.

**Utilitarian Arguments for a Right to Know**

There are two arguments for the right to know as a means to greater worker health and safety. Both are broadly utilitarian in character. One argument is based on the plausible assumption that workers who are aware of hazards in the workplace will be better equipped to protect themselves. Warning labels or rules requiring protective clothing and respirators are more likely to be effective when workers fully appreciate the nature and extent of the risks they are taking. Also, merely revealing information about hazardous substances in the workplace is not apt to be effective without extensive training in the procedures for handling them safely and responding to accidents. Finally, workers who are aware of the consequences of exposure to hazardous substances will also be more likely to spot symptoms of occupational diseases and seek early treatment.

The second utilitarian argument is offered by economists who hold that overall welfare is best achieved by allowing market forces to determine the level of acceptable risk. In a free market, wages are determined in part by the willingness of workers to accept risks in return for wages. Employers can attract a sufficient supply of workers to perform hazardous work either by spending money to make the workplace safer, thereby reducing the risks, or by increasing wages to compensate workers for the greater risks. The choice is determined by the marginal utility of each kind of investment. Thus, an employer will make the workplace safer up to the point that the last dollar spent equals the increase in wages that would otherwise be required to induce workers to accept the risks. At that point, workers indicate their preference for accepting the remaining risks rather than forgoing a loss of wages in return for a safer workplace.

Unlike the autonomy argument, in which workers bargain over risk information, this argument proposes that workers bargain over the trade-off between risks and wages. In order for a free market to determine this trade-off in a way that achieves overall welfare, it is necessary for workers to have a sufficient amount of information about the hazards in the workplace. Thomas O. McGarity has expressed this point as follows:

> A crucial component of the free market model of wage and risk determination is its assumption that workers are fully informed about the risks that they face as they bargain over wages. To the extent that risks are unknown to employees, they will undervalue overall workplace risks in wage negotiations. The result will be lower wages and an inadequate incentive to employers to install health and safety devices. In addition, to the extent that employees can avoid risks by taking action, uninformed employees will fail to do so. Society will then under invest in wages and risk prevention, and overall societal wealth will decline. Moreover, a humane society is not likely to require diseased or injured workers to suffer without proper medical attention. In many cases, society will pick up the tab. . . .[12]

Although these two utilitarian arguments provide strong support for the right to know, they are both open to the objection that there might be more efficient means, such as more extensive OSHA regulation, for securing the goal of worker health and safety. Could the resources devoted to complying with a right-to-know law, for example, be better spent on formulating and enforcing more stringent standards on permissible exposure limits and on developing technologies to achieve these standards? Could the cost of producing, gathering, and disseminating information be better borne by a government agency than by individual employers? These are difficult empirical questions for which conclusive evidence is largely lacking.

## NOTES

1. The estimate is made in W. J. Nicholson, "Failure to Regulate—Asbestos: A Lethal Legacy," U.S. Congress, Committee of Government Operations, 1980.
2. Sec. 5(a) (1).
3. Patricia H. Werhane, *Persons, Rights, and Corporations* (Upper Saddle River, NJ: Prentice Hall, 1985), 132.
4. Mark MacCarthy, "A Review of Some Normative and Conceptual Issues in Occupational Safety and Health," *Environmental Affairs* 9 (1981): 782–83.
5. *Federal Register* 39, no. 20 (29 January 1974): 3758. Emphasis added.
6. Gewirth, "Human Rights and the Prevention of Cancer," in *Human Rights: Essays on Justification and Applications* (Chicago: University of Chicago Press, 1982), 189.
7. Robert Nozick, "Coercion," in *Philosophy, Science and Method*, ed. Sidney Morgenbesser, Patrick Suppes, and Morton White (New York: St. Martin's Press, 1969), 440–72.
8. *Whirlpool Corporation v. Marshall*, 445 U.S. 1 (1980).
9. Thomas O. McGarity, "The New OSHA Rules and the Worker's Right to Know," *Hastings Center Report* 14 (August 1984): 38–39.
10. This point is made in Ruth R. Faden and Tom L. Beauchamp, "The Right to Risk Information and the Right to Refuse Health Hazards in the Workplace," in *Ethical Theory and Business*, 4th ed., ed. Tom L. Beauchamp and Norman E. Bowie (Upper Saddle River, NJ: Prentice Hall, 1993), 205.
11. McGarity, 40.
12. McGarity, 41.

# Some Paradoxes of Whistle-Blowing

*Michael Davis*

## INTRODUCTION

By "paradox" I mean an apparent—and, in this case, real—inconsistency between theory (our Systematic understanding of whistle-blowing) and the facts (what we actually know, or think we know, about whistle-blowing). What concerns me is not a few anomalies, the exceptions that test a rule, but a flood of exceptions that seems to swamp the rule.

This paper has four parts. The first states the standard theory of whistle-blowing. The second argues that the standard theory is paradoxical, that it is inconsistent with what we know about whistle-blowers. The third part sketches what seems to me a less paradoxical theory of whistle-blowing. The fourth tests the new theory against one classic case of whistle-blowing, Roger Boisjoly's testimony before the presidential commission investigating the *Challenger* disaster ("the Rogers Commission"). I use that case because the chief facts are both uncontroversial enough and well known enough to make detailed exposition unnecessary. For the same reason, I also use that case to illustrate various claims about whistle-blowing throughout the paper.

## JUSTIFICATION AND WHISTLE-BLOWING

The standard theory is not about whistle-blowing, as such, but about justified whistle-blowing—and rightly so. Whether this or that

is, or is not, whistle-blowing is a question for lexicographers. For the rest of us, mere moral agents, the question is—when, if ever, is whistle-blowing justified?

We may distinguish three (related) senses in which an act may be "justified." First, an act may be something morality permits. Many acts, for example, eating fruit at lunch, are morally justified in this weak sense. They are (all things considered) morally all right, though some of the alternatives are morally all right too. Second, acts may be morally justified in a stronger sense. Not only is doing them morally all right, but doing anything else instead is morally wrong. These acts are *morally* required. Third, some acts, though only morally justified in the weaker sense, are still required all things considered. That is, they are mandatory because of some non-moral consideration. They are *rationally* (but not morally) required.

I shall be concerned here only with *moral* justification, that is, with what morality permits or requires. I shall have nothing to say about when other considerations, for example, individual prudence or social policy, make (morally permissible) whistle-blowing something reason requires. . . .

Most acts, though permitted or required by morality, need no justification. There is no reason to think them wrong. Their justification is too plain for words. Why then is whistle-blowing so problematic that we need *theories* of its justification? What reason do we have to think whistle-blowing might be morally wrong?

Michael Davis, "Some Paradoxes of Whistleblowing." *Business & Professional Ethics Journal,* 15 (1) (1996). Reprinted by permission.

Whistle-blowing always involves revealing information that would not ordinarily be revealed. But there is nothing morally problematic about that; after all, revealing information not ordinarily revealed is one function of science. Whistle-blowing always involves, in addition, an actual (or at least declared) intention to prevent something bad that would otherwise occur. There is nothing morally problematic in that either. That may well be the chief use of information.

What seems to make whistle-blowing morally problematic is its organizational context. A mere individual cannot blow the whistle (in any interesting sense); only a member of an organization, whether a current or a former member can do so. Indeed, he can blow the whistle only on his own organization (or some part of it). So, for example, a police officer who makes public information about a burglary ring, though a member of an organization, does not blow the whistle on the burglary ring (in any interesting sense). He simply alerts the public. Even if he came by the information working undercover in the ring, his revelation could not be whistle-blowing. While secret agents, spies, and other infiltrators need a moral justification for what they do, the justification they need differs from that which whistle-blowers need. Infiltrators gain their information under false pretenses. They need a justification for that deception. Whistle-blowers generally do not gain their information under false pretenses. . . .

What then is morally problematic about the whistle-blower's organizational context? The whistle-blower cannot blow the whistle using just any information obtained in virtue of membership in the organization. A clerk in Accounts who, happening upon evidence of serious wrongdoing while visiting a friend in Quality Control, is not a whistle-blower just because she passes the information to a friend at the *Tribune*. She is more like a self-appointed spy. She seems to differ from the whistle-blower, or at least from clear cases of the whistle-blower, precisely in her relation to the information in question. To be a whistle-blower is to reveal information with which one is *entrusted*.

But it is more than that. The whistle-blower does not reveal the information to save his own skin (for example, to avoid perjury under oath). He has no excuse for revealing what his organization does not want revealed. Instead, he claims to be doing what he should be doing. If he cannot honestly make that claim—if, that is, he does not have that intention—his revelation is not whistle-blowing (and so, not justified as whistle-blowing), but something analogous, much as pulling a child from the water is not a rescue, even if it saves the child's life, when the "rescuer" merely believes herself to be salvaging old clothes. What makes whistle-blowing morally problematic, if anything does, is this high-minded but unexcused misuse of one's position in a generally law-abiding, morally decent organization, an organization that *prima facie* deserves the whistle-blower's loyalty (as a burglary ring does not).

The whistle-blower must reveal information the organization does not want revealed. But, in any actual organization, "what the organization wants" will be contested, with various individuals or groups asking to be taken as speaking for the organization. Who, for example, did what Thiokol wanted the night before the *Challenger* exploded? In retrospect, it is obvious that the three vice presidents, Lund, Kilminster, and Mason, did not do what Thiokol wanted—or, at least, what it would have wanted. At the time, however, they had authority to speak for the company—the conglomerate Morton-Thiokol headquartered in Chicago—while the protesting engineers, including Boisjoly, did not. Yet, even before the explosion, was it obvious that the three were doing what the company wanted? To be a whistle-blower, one must, I think, at least temporarily lose an argument about what the organization wants. The whistle-blower is disloyal only in a sense—the sense the winners of the internal argument get to dictate. What can justify such disloyalty?

## The Standard Theory

According to the theory now more or less standard,[1] such disloyalty is morally permissible when:

(S1) The organization to which the would-be whistle-blower belongs will, through its product or policy, do serious and considerable harm to the public (whether to users of its product, to innocent bystanders, or to the public at large);

(S2) The would-be whistle-blower has identified that threat of harm, reported it to her immediate superior, making clear both the threat itself and the objection to it, and concluded that the superior will do nothing effective; and

(S3) The would-be whistle-blower has exhausted other internal procedures within the organization (for example, by going up the organizational ladder as far as allowed)—or at least made use of as many internal procedures as the danger to others and her own safety make reasonable.

Whistle-blowing is morally required (according to the standard theory) when, in addition:

(S4) The would-be whistle-blower has (or has accessible) evidence that would convince a reasonable, impartial observer that her view of the threat is correct; and

(S5) The would-be whistle-blower has good reason to believe that revealing the threat will (probably) prevent the harm at reasonable cost (all things considered).

Why is whistle-blowing morally required when these five conditions are met? According to the standard theory, whistle-blowing is morally required, when it is required at all, because "people have a moral obligation to prevent serious harm to others if they can do so with little cost to themselves." In other words, whistle-blowing meeting all five conditions is a form of "minimally decent Samaritanism" (a doing of what morality requires) rather than "good Samaritanism" (going well beyond the moral minimum).[2]

A number of writers have pointed out that the relation between the first three conditions and the full five does not seem to be that between the morally permissible and the morally required.[3] If, for example, the whistle-blower lacks evidence that would convince a reasonable, impartial observer of the threat in question (S4), her whistle-blowing could not prevent harm. Since it could not prevent harm, her whistle-blowing would not be even morally permissible: what could make morally permissible an attempt to help a stranger when the attempt will probably fail and the cost be high both to the would-be Samaritan and to those to whom she owes a competing obligation? The most that can be said for blowing the whistle where only conditions S1–S3 are met seems to be that the whistle-blower has an excuse when (without negligence) she acts on inadequate evidence. So, for many writers, the standard view is that S1–S5 state sufficient conditions for morally *required* whistle-blowing even though S1–S3 do not state sufficient conditions for morally permissible whistle-blowing but (at best) for morally *excusable* whistle-blowing.

The standard theory is not a definition of whistle-blowing or even of justified whistle-blowing. The theory purports to state sufficient conditions, not necessary conditions (a "when" but *not* an "only when"). But these sufficient conditions are supposed to identify the central cases of morally justified whistle-blowing. Since a theory that did only that would be quite useful, we cannot object to the theory merely because it is incomplete in this way. Incomplete only in this way, the theory would be about as useful as theories of practical ethics ever are.

## Three Paradoxes

That's the standard theory—where are the paradoxes? The first paradox I want to call attention to concerns a commonplace of the whistle-blowing literature. Whistle-blowers are not minimally decent Samaritans. If they are Samaritans at all, they are good Samaritans.

They always act at considerable risk to career, and generally, at considerable risk to their financial security and personal relations.[4]

In this respect, as in many others, Roger Boisjoly is typical. Boisjoly blew the whistle on his employer, Thiokol; he volunteered information, in public testimony before the Rogers Commission, that Thiokol did not want him to volunteer. As often happens, both his employer and many who relied on it for employment reacted hostilely. Boisjoly had to say goodbye to the company town, to old friends and neighbors, and to building rockets; he had to start a new career at an age when most people are preparing for retirement.

Since whistle-blowing is generally costly to the whistle-blower in some large way as this, the standard theory's minimally decent Samaritanism provides *no* justification for the central cases of whistle-blowing. That is the first paradox, what me might call "the paradox of burden."

The second paradox concerns the prevention of "harm." On the standard theory, the would-be whistle-blower must seek to prevent "serious and considerable harm" in order for the whistle-blowing to be even morally permissible. There seems to be a good deal of play in the term "harm." The harm in question can be physical (such as death or disease), financial (such as loss of or damage to property), and perhaps even psychological (such as fear or mental illness). But there is a limit to how much the standard theory can stretch "harm." Beyond that limit are "harms" like injustice, deception, and waste. As morally important as injustice, deception, and waste can be, they do not seem to constitute the "serious and considerable harm" that can require someone to become even a minimally decent Samaritan.

Yet, many cases of whistle-blowing, perhaps most, are not about preventing serious and considerable physical, financial, or psychological harm. For example, when Boisjoly spoke up the evening before the *Challenger*

exploded, the lives of seven astronauts sat in the balance. Speaking up then was about preventing serious and considerable physical, financial, and psychological harm—but it was not whistle-blowing. Boisjoly was then serving his employer, not betraying a trust (even on the employer's understanding of that trust); he was calling his superiors' attention to what he thought they should take into account in their decision and not publicly revealing confidential information. The whistle-blowing came after the explosion, in testimony before the Rogers Commission. By then, the seven astronauts were beyond help, the shuttle program was suspended, and any further threat of physical, financial, or psychological harm to the "public" was—after discounting for time—negligible. Boisjoly had little reason to believe his testimony would make a significant difference in the booster's redesign, in safety procedures in the shuttle program, or even in reawakening concern for safety among NASA employees and contractors. The *Challenger's* explosion was much more likely to do that than anything Boisjoly could do. What Boisjoly could do in his testimony, what I think he tried to do, was prevent falsification of the record.[5]

Falsification of the record is, of course, harm in a sense, especially a record as historically important as that which the Rogers Commission was to produce. But falsification is harm only in a sense that almost empties "harm" of its distinctive meaning, leaving it more or less equivalent to "moral wrong." The proponents of the standard theory mean more by "harm" than that. De George, for example, explicitly says that a threat justifying whistle-blowing must be to "life or health."[6] The standard theory is strikingly more narrow in its grounds of justification than many examples of justified whistle-blowing suggest it should be. That is the second paradox, the "paradox of missing harm."

The third paradox is related to the second. Insofar as whistle-blowers are understood as people out to prevent harm, not just to prevent moral wrong, their chances of success are not good. Whistle-blowers generally do not prevent much harm. In this too, Boisjoly is typical. As he has said many times, the situation at Thiokol is now much as it was before the disaster. Insofar as we can identify cause and effect, even now we have little reason to believe that—whatever his actual intention—Boisjoly's testimony actually prevented any harm (beyond the moral harm of falsification). So, if whistle-blowers must have, as the standard theory says (S5), (beyond the moral wrong of falsification) "good reason to believe that revealing the threat will (probably) prevent the harm," then the history of whistle-blowing virtually rules out the moral justification of whistle-blowing. That is certainly paradoxical in a theory purporting to state sufficient conditions for the central cases of justified whistle-blowing. Let us call this "the paradox of failure."

## A Complicity Theory

As I look down the roll of whistle-blowers, I do not see anyone who, like the clerk from Accounts, just happened upon key documents in a cover-up.[7] Few, if any, whistle-blowers are mere third parties like the good Samaritan. They are generally deeply involved in the activity they reveal. This involvement suggests that we might better understand what justifies (most) whistle-blowing if we understand the whistle-blower's obligation to derive from *complicity* in wrongdoing rather than from the ability to prevent harm.

Any complicity theory of justified whistle-blowing has two obvious advantages over the standard theory. One is that (moral) complicity itself presupposes (moral) wrongdoing, not harm. So, a complicity justification automatically avoids the paradox of missing harm, fitting the facts of whistle-blowing better than a theory which, like the standard one, emphasizes prevention of harm.

That is one obvious advantage of a complicity theory. The second advantage is that complicity invokes a more demanding obligation than the ability to prevent harm does. We are morally obliged to avoid doing moral wrongs. When, despite our best efforts, we nonetheless find ourselves engaged in some wrong, we have an obligation to do what we reasonably can to set things right. If, for example, I cause a traffic accident, I have a moral (and legal) obligation to call help, stay at the scene until help arrives, and render first aid (if I know how), even at substantial cost to myself and those to whom I owe my time, and even with little likelihood that anything I do will help much. Just as a complicity theory avoids the paradox of missing harm, it also avoids the paradox of burden.

What about the third paradox, the paradox of failure? I shall come to that, but only after remedying one disadvantage of the complicity theory. That disadvantage is obvious—we do not yet have such a theory, not even a sketch. Here, then, is the place to offer a sketch of such a theory.

*Complicity Theory.* You are morally required to reveal what you know to the public (or to a suitable agent or representative of it) when:

(C1) what you will reveal derives from your work for an organization;
(C2) you are a voluntary member of that organization;
(C3) you believe that the organization, though legitimate, is engaged in serious moral wrongdoing;
(C4) you believe that your work for that organization will contribute (more or less directly) to the wrong if (but *not* only if) you do not publicly reveal what you know;
(C5) you are justified in beliefs C3 and C4; and
(C6) beliefs C3 and C4 are true.

The complicity theory differs from the standard theory in several ways worth pointing out here. The first is that, according to C1, what the whistle-blower reveals must derive from his work for the organization. This condition distinguishes the whistle-blower from the spy (and the clerk in Accounts). The spy seeks out information in order to reveal it; the whistle-blower learns it as a proper part of doing the job the organization has assigned him. The standard theory, in contrast, has nothing to say about how the whistle-blower comes to know of the threat she reveals (S2). For the standard theory, spies are just another kind of whistle-blower.

A second way in which the complicity theory differs from the standard theory is that the complicity theory (C2) explicitly requires the whistle-blower to be a *voluntary* participant in the organization in question. Whistle-blowing is not—according to the complicity theory—an activity in which slaves, prisoners, or other involuntary participants in an organization engage. In this way, the complicity theory makes explicit something implicit in the standard theory. The whistle-blowers of the standard theory are generally "employees." Employees are voluntary participants in the organization employing them.

What explains this difference in explicitness? For the Samaritanism of the standard theory, the voluntariness of employment is extrinsic. What is crucial is the ability to prevent harm. For the complicity theory, however, the voluntariness is crucial. The obligations deriving from complicity seem to vary with the voluntariness of our participation in the wrongdoing. Consider, for example, a teller who helps a gang rob her bank because they have threatened to kill her if she does not; she does not have the same obligation to break off her association with the gang as someone who has freely joined it. The voluntariness of employment means that the would-be whistle-blower's complicity will be more like that of one of the gang than like that of the conscripted teller.

A third way in which the complicity theory differs from the standard theory is that the complicity theory (C3) requires moral wrong, not harm, for justification. The wrong need not be a new event (as a harm must be if it is to be *prevented*). It might, for example, consist in no more than silence about facts necessary to correct a serious injustice.

The complicity theory (C3) does, however, follow the standard theory in requiring that the predicate of whistle-blowing be "serious." Under the complicity theory, minor wrongdoing can no more justify whistle-blowing than can minor harm under the standard theory. While organizational loyalty cannot forbid whistle-blowing, it does forbid "tattling," that is, revealing minor wrongdoing.

A fourth way in which the complicity theory differs from the standard theory, the most important, is that the complicity theory (C4) requires that the whistle-blower believe that her work will have contributed to the wrong in question if she does nothing, but it does *not* require that she believe that her revelation will prevent (or undo) the wrong. The complicity theory does not require any belief about what the whistle-blowing can accomplish (beyond ending complicity in the wrong in question). The whistle-blower reveals what she knows in order to prevent complicity in the wrong, not to prevent the wrong as such. She can prevent complicity (if there is any to prevent) simply by publicly revealing what she knows. The revelation itself breaks the bond of complicity, the secret partnership in wrongdoing, that makes her an accomplice in her organization's wrongdoing. The complicity theory thus avoids the third paradox, the paradox of failure, just as it avoided the other two.

The fifth difference between the complicity theory and the standard theory is closely related to the fourth. Because publicly revealing what one knows breaks the bond of complicity, the complicity theory does not require the whistle-blower to have enough evidence to convince others of the wrong in question. Convincing others, or just being able to convince them, is not, as such, an element in the justification of whistle-blowing.

The complicity theory does, however, require (C5) that the whistle-blower be (epistemically) justified in believing both that his organization is engaged in wrongdoing and that he will contribute to that wrong unless he blows the whistle. Such (epistemic) justification may require substantial physical evidence (as the standard theory says) or just a good sense of how things work. The complicity theory does not share the standard theory's substantial evidential demand (S4).

In one respect, however, the complicity theory clearly requires more of the whistle-blower than the standard theory does. The complicity theory's C6—combined with C5—requires not only that the whistle-blower be *justified* in her beliefs about the organization's wrongdoing and her part in it, but also that she be *right* about them. If she is wrong about either the wrongdoing or her complicity, her revelation will not be justified whistle-blowing. This consequence of C6 is, I think, not as surprising as it may seem. If the would-be whistle-blower is wrong only about her own complicity, her revelation of actual wrongdoing will, being otherwise justified, merely fail to be justified *as whistle-blowing* (much as a failed resuce, though justified as an attempt, cannot be justified as a rescue). If, however, she is wrong about the wrongdoing itself, her situation is more serious. Her belief that wrong is being done, though fully justified on the evidence available to her, cannot justify her disloyalty. All her justified belief can do is *excuse* her disloyalty. Insofar as she acted with good intentions and while exercising reasonable care, she is a victim of bad luck. Such bad luck will leave her with an obligation to apologize, to correct the record (for example, by publicly recanting the charges she publicly made), and otherwise to set things right.

The complicity theory says nothing on at least one matter about which the standard theory says much—going through channels before publicly revealing what one knows. But the two theories do not differ as much as this difference in emphasis suggests. If going through channels would suffice to prevent (or undo) the wrong, then it cannot be true (as C4 and C6 together require) that the would-be whistle-blower's work will contribute to the wrong if she does not publicly reveal what she knows. Where, however, going through channels would *not* prevent (or undo) the wrong, there is no need to go through channels. Condition C4's if-clause will be satisfied. For the complicity theory, going through channels is a way of finding out what the organization will do, not an independent requirement of justification. That, I think, is also how the standard theory understands it.[8]

A last difference between the two theories worth mention here is that the complicity theory is only a theory of morally required whistle-blowing, while the standard theory claims as well to define circumstances when whistle-blowing is morally permissible but not morally required. This difference is another advantage that the complicity theory has over the standard theory. The standard theory, as we saw, has trouble making good on its claim to explain how whistle-blowing can be morally permissible without being morally required.

**Testing the Theory**

Let us now test the theory against Boisjoly's testimony before the Rogers Commission. Recall that under the standard theory any justification of that testimony seemed to fail for at least three reasons: First, Boisjoly could not testify without substantial cost to himself and Thiokol (to whom he owed loyalty). Second, there was no serious and substantial harm his testimony could prevent. And, third, he had little reason to believe that, even if he could identify a serious and considerable harm to prevent, his testimony had a significant chance of preventing it.

Since few doubt that Boisjoly's testimony before the Rogers Commission constitutes justified whistle-blowing, if anything does, we should welcome a theory that—unlike the standard one—justifies that testimony as whistle-blowing. The complicity theory sketched above does that:

(C1) Boisjoly's testimony consisted almost entirely of information derived from his work on booster rockets at Thiokol.

(C2) Boisjoly was a voluntary member of Thiokol.

(C3) Boisjoly believed Thiokol, a legitimate organization, was attempting to mislead its client, the government, about the causes of a deadly accident. Attempting to do that certainly seems a serious moral wrong.

(C4) On the evening before the *Challenger* exploded, Boisjoly gave up objecting to the launch once his superiors, including the three Thiokol vice presidents, had made it clear that they were no longer willing to listen to him. He also had a part in preparing those superiors to testify intelligently before the Rogers Commission concerning the booster's fatal field joint. Boisjoly believed that Thiokol would use his failure to offer his own interpretation of his retreat into silence the night before the launch, and the knowledge that he had imparted to his superiors, to contribute to the attempt to mislead Thiokol's client.

(C5) The evidence justifying beliefs C3 and C4 consisted of comments of various officers of Thiokol, what Boisjoly had seen at Thiokol over the years, and what he learned about the rocket business over a long career. I find this evidence sufficient to justify his belief both that his organization was engaged in wrongdoing and that his work was implicated.

(C6) Here we reach a paradox of *knowledge*. Since belief is knowledge if, but only if, it is *both* justified *and* true, we cannot *show* that we know anything. All we can show is that a belief is now justified and that we have no reason to expect anything to turn up later to prove it false. The evidence now available still justifies Boisjoly's belief both about what Thiokol was attempting and about what would have been his part in the attempt. Since new evidence is

unlikely, his testimony seems to satisfy C6 just as it satisfied the complicity theory's other five conditions.

Since the complicity theory explains why Boisjoly's testimony before the Rogers Commission was morally required whistle-blowing, it has passed its first test, a test the standard theory failed.

## NOTES

I should thank Vivian Weil for several discussions provoking this paper, as well as for commenting on several drafts; members of the Program in Ethics, Science, and Environment, Oregon State University, for raising several hard questions after I read an early version of this paper to them, April 24, 1996; those who asked questions (including my copanelist, Roger Boisjoly) at a session of the annual meeting of the Northwest Section of the American Society of Engineering Educators, Oregon Institute of Technology, Klamath Falls, Oregon, April 26, 1996; attendees at a symposium sponsored by the Centre for Professional Ethics, University of Central Lancashire, Preston, England, November 12, 1996; and the editors of *Business and Professional Ethics Journal*.

1. Throughout this paper, I take the standard theory to be Richard T. De George's version in *Business Ethics*, 3rd. ed. (New York: Macmillan, 1990), 200–214 (amended only insofar as necessary to include nonbusinesses as well as businesses). Why treat De George's theory as standard? There are two reasons: first, it seems the most commonly cited; and second, people offering alternatives generally treat it as the one to be replaced. The only obvious competitor, Norman Bowie's account, is distinguishable from De George's on no point relevant here. See Bowie's *Business Ethics* (Englewood Cliffs, NJ: Prentice Hall, 1982), 143.

2. There is now a significant literature on the responsibilities of the minimally decent Samaritan. See, for example: Peter Singer, "Famine, Affluence, and Morality," *Philosophy and Public Affairs* 7, no. 2 (1972): 229–43; Alan Gewirth, *Reason and Morality* (Chicago: University of Chicago Press, 1978), 217–30; Patricia Smith, "The Duty to Rescue and the Slippery Slope Problem," *Social Theory and Practice* 16, no. 1

(1990): 19–41; John M. Whelan, "Charity and the Duty to Rescue," *Social Theory and Practice* 17, no. 3 (1991): 441–56; and David Copp, "Responsibility for Collective Inaction," *Journal of Social Philosophy* 22, no. 2 (1991): 71–80.

3. See, for example, David Theo Goldberg, "Tuning In to Whistle Blowing," *Business and Professional Ethics Journal* 7, no. 2 (1988): 85–94.

4. For an explanation of why whistle-blowing is inevitably a high risk undertaking, see my "Avoiding the Tragedy of Whistleblowing," *Business and Professional Ethics Journal* 8, no. 4 (1989): 3–19.

5. After I presented this paper in Klamath Falls, Boisjoly told me that though his motive for testifying as he did was (as I surmised) to prevent falsification of the record, part of his reason for wanting to prevent that was that he wanted to do what he could to prevent the managers responsible for the disaster from having any part in redesigning the boosters. This *secondary* motive is, of course, consistent with the complicity theory.

6. De George, p. 210: "The notion of *serious* harm might be expanded to include serious financial harm, and kinds of harm other than death and serious threats to health and body. But as we noted earlier, we shall restrict ourselves here to products and practices that produce or threaten serious harm or danger to life and health."

7. See Myron Peretz Glazer and Penina Migdal Glazer, *The Whistleblowers: Exposing Corruption in Government and Industry* (New York: Basic Books, 1989) for a good list of whistle-blowers (with detailed description of each); for an older list (with descriptions), see Alan F. Westin, *Whistleblowing! Loyalty and Dissent in the Corporation* (New York: McGraw-Hill, 1981).

8. Compare De George, p. 211: "By reporting one's concern to one's immediate superior or other appropriate person, one preserves and observes the regular practices of firms, which on the whole promote their order and efficiency; this fulfills one's obligation of minimizing harm, and *it precludes precipitous whistle blowing.*" (Italics mine.)

# Whistle-Blowing and Employee Loyalty

*Ronald Duska*

There are proponents on both sides of the issue—those who praise whistle-blowers as civic heroes and those who condemn them as "finks." Maxwell Glen and Cody Shearer, who wrote about the whistle-blowers at Three Mile Island say, "Without the *courageous* breed of assorted company insiders known as whistle-blowers—workers who often risk their livelihoods to disclose information about construction and design flaws—the Nuclear Regulatory Commission itself would be nearly as idle as Three Mile Island. . . . That whistle-blowers deserve both gratitude and protection is beyond disagreement."[1]

Still, while Glen and Shearer praise whistle-blowers, others vociferously condemn them. For

example, in a now infamous quote, James Roche, the former president of General Motors said:

> Some critics are now busy eroding another support of free enterprise—the loyalty of a management team, with its unifying values and cooperative work. Some of the enemies of business now encourage an employee to be *disloyal* to the enterprise. They want to create suspicion and disharmony, and pry into the proprietary interests of the business. However this is labeled—industrial espionage, whistle-blowing, or professional responsibility—it is another tactic for spreading disunity and creating conflict.[2]

From Roche's point of view, not only is whistle-blowing not "courageous" and not deserving of "gratitude and protection" as

Reprinted by permission of the author.

Glen and Shearer would have it, it is corrosive and impermissible.

Discussions of whistle-blowing generally revolve around three topics: (1) attempts to define whistle-blowing more precisely, (2) debates about whether and when whistle-blowing is permissible, and (3) debates about whether and when one has an obligation to blow the whistle.

In this paper I want to focus on the second problem, because I find it somewhat disconcerting that there is a problem at all. When I first looked into the ethics of whistle-blowing it seemed to me that whistle-blowing was a good thing, and yet I found in the literature claim after claim that it was in need of defense, that there was something wrong with it, namely that it was an act of disloyalty.

If whistle-blowing is a disloyal act, it deserves disapproval, and ultimately any action of whistle-blowing needs justification. This disturbs me. It is as if the act of a good Samaritan is being condemned as an act of interference, as if the prevention of a suicide needs to be justified.

In his book *Business Ethics*, Norman Bowie claims that "whistle-blowing . . . violate(s) a *prima facie* duty of loyalty to one's employer." According to Bowie, there is a duty of loyalty that prohibits one from reporting his employer or company. Bowie, of course, recognizes that this is only a prima facie duty, that is, one that can be overridden by a higher duty to the public good. Nevertheless, the axiom that whistle-blowing is disloyal is Bowie's starting point.[3]

Bowie is not alone. Sissela Bok sees "whistle-blowing" as an instance of disloyalty:

> The whistle-blower hopes to stop the game; but since he is neither referee nor coach, and since he blows the whistle on his own team, his act is seen as a *violation of loyalty*. In holding his position, he has assumed certain obligations to his colleagues and clients. He may even have subscribed to a loyalty oath or a promise of confidentiality. . . . Loyalty to colleagues and to clients comes to be pitted against loyalty to the public interest, to those who may be injured unless the revelation is made.[4]

Bowie and Bok end up defending whistle-blowing in certain contexts, so I don't necessarily disagree with their conclusions. However, I fail to see how one has an obligation of loyalty to one's company, so I disagree with their perception of the problem and their starting point. I want to argue that one does not have an obligation of loyalty to a company, even a prima facie one, because companies are not the kind of things that are properly objects of loyalty. To make them objects of loyalty gives them a moral status they do not deserve and in raising their status, one lowers the status of the individuals who work for the companies. Thus, the difference in perception is important because those who think employees have an obligation of loyalty to a company fail to take into account a relevant moral difference between persons and corporations.

But why aren't companies the kind of things that can be objects of loyalty? To answer that we have to ask what are proper objects of loyalty. John Ladd states the problem this way, "Granted that loyalty is the wholehearted devotion to an object of some kind, what kind of thing is the object? Is it an abstract entity, such as an idea or a collective being? Or is it a person or group of persons?"[5] Philosophers fall into three camps on the question. On one side are the idealists who hold that loyalty is devotion to something more than persons, to some cause or abstract entity. On the other side are what Ladd calls "social atomists," and these include empiricists and utilitarians, who think that at most one can only be loyal to individuals and that loyalty can ultimately be explained away as some other obligation that holds between two people. Finally, there is a moderate position that holds that although idealists go too far in postulating some superpersonal entity as an object of loyalty, loyalty is still an important and real relation that holds between people, one that cannot be dismissed by reducing it to some other relation.

There does seem to be a view of loyalty that is not extreme. According to Ladd, "'loyalty' is taken to refer to a relationship between persons—for instance, between a lord and his vassal, between a parent and his children, or between friends. Thus the object of loyalty is ordinarily taken to be a person or a group of persons."[6]

But this raises a problem that Ladd glosses over. There is a difference between a person or a group of persons, and aside from instances of loyalty that relate two people such as lord/vassal, parent/child, or friend/friend, there are instances of loyalty relating a person to a group, such as a person to his family, a person to this team, and a person to his country. Families, countries, and teams are presumably groups of persons. They are certainly ordinarily construed as objects of loyalty.

But to what am I loyal in such a group? In being loyal to the group am I being loyal to the whole group or to its members? It is easy to see the object of loyalty in the case of an individual person. It is simply the individual. But to whom am I loyal in a group? To whom am I loyal in a family? Am I loyal to each and every individual or to something larger, and if to something larger, what is it? We are tempted to think of a group as an entity of its own, an individual in its own right, having an identity of its own.

To avoid the problem of individuals existing for the sake of the group, the atomists insist that a group is nothing more than the individuals who comprise it, nothing other than a mental fiction by which we refer to a group of individuals. It is certainly not a reality or entity over and above the sum of its parts, and consequently is not a proper object of loyalty. Under such a position, of course, no loyalty would be owed to a company because a company is a mere mental fiction, since it is a group. One would have obligations to the individual members of the company, but one could never be justified in overriding those obligations for the sake of the "group" taken collectively. A company has no moral status except in terms of the individual members who comprise it. It is not a proper object of loyalty. But the atomists go too far. Some groups, such as a family, do have a reality of their own, whereas groups of people walking down the street do not. From Ladd's point of view the social atomist is wrong because he fails to recognize the kinds of groups that are held together by "the ties that bind." The atomist tries to reduce these groups to simple sets of individuals bound together by some externally imposed criteria. This seems wrong.

There do seem to be groups in which the relationships and interactions create a new force or entity. A group takes on an identity and a reality of its own that is determined by its purpose, and this purpose defines the various relationships and roles set up within the group. There is a division of labor into roles necessary for the fulfillment of the purposes of the group. The membership, then, is not of individuals who are the same but of individuals who have specific relationships to one another determined by the aim of the group. Thus we get specific relationships like parent/child, coach/player, and so on, that don't occur in other groups. It seems then that an atomist account of loyalty that restricts loyalty merely to individuals and does not include loyalty to groups might be inadequate.

But once I have admitted that we can have loyalty to a group, do I not open myself up to criticism from the proponent of loyalty to the company? Might not the proponent of loyalty to business say: "Very well. I agree with you. The atomists are shortsighted. Groups have some sort of reality and they can be proper objects of loyalty. But companies are groups. Therefore companies are proper objects of loyalty."

The point seems well taken, except for the fact that the kinds of relationships that loyalty requires are just the kind that one does not find in business. As Ladd says, "The ties that bind the persons together provide the basis of loyalty." But all sorts of ties bind people together. I am a member of a group of fans if I go to a ball game. I am a member of a group if I merely walk down the street. What binds people together in a business is not sufficient to require loyalty.

A business or corporation does two things in the free enterprise system: It produces a good or service and it makes a profit. The making of a profit, however, is the primary function of a business as a business, for if the production of the good or service is not profitable, the business would be out of business. Thus nonprofitable goods or services are a means to an end. People bound together in a business are bound together not for mutual fulfillment and support, but to divide labor or make a profit. Thus, while we can jokingly refer to a family as a place where "they have to take you in no matter what," we cannot refer to a company in that way. If a worker does not produce in a company or if cheaper laborers are available, the company—in order to fulfill its purpose—should get rid of the worker. A company feels no obligation of loyalty. The saying "You can't buy loyalty" is true. Loyalty depends on ties that demand self-sacrifice with no expectation of reward. Business functions on the basis of enlightened self-interest. I am devoted to a company not because it is like a parent to me; it is not. Attempts of some companies to create "one big happy family" ought to be looked on with suspicion. I am not devoted to it at all, nor should I be. I work for it because it pays me. I am not in a family to get paid, I am in a company to get paid.

The cold hard truth is that the goal of profit is what gives birth to a company and forms that particular group. Money is what ties the group together. But in such a commercialized venture, with such a goal, there is no loyalty, or at least none need be expected. An employer will release an employee and an employee will walk away from an employer when it is profitable for either one to do so.

Not only is loyalty to a corporation not required, it more than likely is misguided. There is nothing as pathetic as the story of the loyal employee who, having given above and beyond the call of duty, is let go in the restructuring of the company. He feels betrayed because he mistakenly viewed the company as an object of his loyalty. Getting rid of such foolish romanticism and coming to grips with this hard but accurate assessment should ultimately benefit everyone.

To think we owe a company or corporation loyalty requires us to think of that company as a person or as a group with a goal of human fulfillment. If we think of it in this way we can be loyal. But this is the wrong way to think. A company is not a person. A company is an instrument, and an instrument with a specific purpose, the making of profit. To treat an instrument as an end in itself, like a person, may not be as bad as treating an end as an instrument, but it does give the instrument a moral status it does not deserve; and by elevating the instrument we lower the end. All things, instruments and ends, become alike.

Remember that Roche refers to the "management team" and Bok sees the name "whistle-blowing" coming from the instance of a referee blowing a whistle in the presence of a foul. What is perceived as bad about whistle-blowing in business from this perspective is that one blows the whistle on one's own team, thereby violating team loyalty. If the company can get its employees to view it as a team they belong to, it is easier to demand loyalty. Then the rules governing teamwork and team loyalty will apply. One reason the appeal to a team and team loyalty works so well in business is that businesses are in competition with one another. Effective motivation turns business practices into a game and instills teamwork.

But businesses differ from teams in very important respects, which makes the analogy between business and a team dangerous. Loyalty to a team is loyalty within the context of sport or a competition. Teamwork and team loyalty require that in the circumscribed activity of the game I cooperate with my fellow players, so that pulling all together, we may win. The object of (most) sports is victory. But winning in sports is a social convention, divorced from the usual goings on of society. Such a winning is most times a harmless, morally neutral diversion.

But the fact that this victory in sports, within the rules enforced by a referee (whistle-blower), is a socially developed convention taking place within a larger social context makes it quite different from competition in business, which, rather than being defined by a context, permeates the whole of society in its influence. Competition leads not only to victory but to losers. One can lose at sport with precious few consequences. The consequences of losing at business are much larger. Further, the losers in business can be those who are not in the game voluntarily (we are all forced to participate) but who are still affected by business decisions. People cannot choose to participate in business. It permeates everyone's lives.

The team model, then, fits very well with the model of the free market system, because there competition is said to be the name of the game. Rival companies compete and their object is to win. To call a foul on one's own teammate is to jeopardize one's chances of winning and is viewed as disloyalty.

But isn't it time to stop viewing corporate machinations as games? These games are not controlled and are not ended after a specific time. The activities of business affect the lives of everyone, not just the game players. The analogy of the corporation to a team and the consequent appeal to team loyalty, although understandable, is seriously misleading, at least in the moral sphere where competition is not the prevailing virtue.

If my analysis is correct, the issue of the permissibility of whistle-blowing is not a real issue since there is no obligation of loyalty to a company. Whistle-blowing is not only permissible but expected when a company is harming society. The issue is not one of disloyalty to the company, but of whether the whistle-blower has an obligation to society if blowing the whistle will bring him retaliation.

## NOTES

1. Maxwell Glen and Cody Shearer, "Going After the Whistle-Blowers," *Philadelphia Inquirer*, (August 2, 1983), Op-Ed, p. 11A.
2. James M. Roche, "The Competitive System, to Work, to Preserve, and to Protect," *Vital Speeches of the Day* (May 1971), p. 445.
3. Norman Bowie, *Business Ethics* (Englewood Cliffs, N.J.: Prentice Hall, 1982), 140–43.
4. Sissela Bok, "Whistleblowing and Professional Responsibilities," *New York University Education Quarterly* 2 (1980): 3.
5. John Ladd, "Loyalty," *Encyclopedia of Philosophy* 5: 97.
6. Ibid.

---

## LEGAL PERSPECTIVES

# *Warthen v. Toms River Community Memorial Hospital*

*Superior Court of New Jersey*

Plaintiff Corrine Warthen appeals from a summary judgment of the Law Division dismissing her action against defendant Toms River Community Memorial Hospital (Hospital). Plaintiff sought to recover damages for her allegedly wrongful discharge in violation

488 A.2d 299 (1985). Opinion by Judge Michels.

of public policy following her refusal to dialyze a terminally ill double amputee patient because of her "moral, medical and philosophical objections" to performing the procedure.

The facts giving rise to this appeal are not in dispute and may be summarized as follows. The Hospital, where plaintiff had been employed for eleven years as a registered nurse, terminated plaintiff from its employment on August 6, 1982. For the three years just prior to her discharge, plaintiff had worked in the Hospital's kidney dialysis unit. It is undisputed that plaintiff was an at-will employee.

Plaintiff alleges that during the summer of 1982 her supervisor periodically assigned her to dialyze a double amputee patient who suffered from a number of maladies. On two occasions plaintiff claims that she had to cease treatment because the patient suffered cardiac arrest and severe internal hemorrhaging during the dialysis procedure. During the first week of 1982 plaintiff again was scheduled to dialyze this patient. She approached her head nurse and informed her that "she had moral, medical, and philosophical objections" to performing this procedure on the patient because the patient was terminally ill and, she contended, the procedure was causing the patient additional complications. At that time the head nurse granted plaintiff's request for reassignment.

On August 6, 1982, the head nurse again assigned plaintiff to dialyze the same patient. Plaintiff once again objected, apparently stating that she thought she had reached agreement with the head nurse not to be assigned to this particular patient. She also requested the opportunity to meet with the treating physician, Dr. DiBello. Dr. DiBello informed plaintiff that the patient's family wished him kept alive through dialysis and that he would not survive without it. However, plaintiff continued to refuse to dialyze the patient, and the head nurse informed her that if she did

not agree to perform the treatment, the Hospital would dismiss her. Plaintiff refused to change her mind, and the Hospital terminated her.

Plaintiff subsequently instituted this action alleging that she was wrongfully discharged by the Hospital without justification and in violation of public policy. The Hospital denied liability to plaintiff and alleged, by way of a separate defense, that plaintiff's termination was appropriate because she had the status of an at-will employee. Following completion of pretrial discovery, the Hospital moved for summary judgement; which the trial court denied because it perceived "that there [was] . . . a question of fact as to whether or not there is a public policy as articulated in the nurses' code of ethics that would permit somebody in the nursing profession to refuse to participate in a course of treatment which is against her principles in good faith." However, upon reconsideration, the trial court granted the motion, concluding that "the nurses' code of ethics is a personal moral judgment and permits the nurse to have a personal moral judgement, but it does not rise to a public policy in the face of the general public policies that patients must be cared for in hospitals and patients must be treated basically by doctors and doctors' orders must be carried out." This appeal followed.

Plaintiff contends that the trial court erred in granting summary judgment because her refusal to dialyze the terminally ill patient was justified as a matter of law by her adherence to the *Code for Nurses*, a code of ethics promulgated by the American Nurses Association, and that determining whether adherence to the *Code* "constitutes a public policy question" is a question of fact which should be resolved by a jury, not by the trial court. We disagree. . . .

Plaintiff relies on the "public policy" exception to the "at-will employment" doctrine to justify her claim that defendant wrongfully discharged her. As has often been stated at common law, "in the absence of an employment contract, employers or employees have been free to terminate the employment relationship with or without cause.". . . Recently, in *Pierce v. Ortho Pharmaceutical Corp., supra,* the Supreme Court recognized a developing exception to the traditional "at-will employment" doctrine, holding that "an employee has a cause of action for wrongful discharge when the discharge is contrary to a clear mandate of public policy.". . .

As a preliminary matter plaintiff contends that identifying the "clear mandate of public policy" constitutes a genuine issue of material fact for the jury rather than, as occurred in the instant case, a threshold question for the trial judge. To support her contention plaintiff cites *Kalman v. Grand Union Co.,* . . . in which we said:

> It is the employee's burden to identify "a specific expression" or "a clear mandate" of public policy which might bar his discharge. [Citation omitted]. What constitutes a qualifying mandate is a fact question. . . .

However, quoting the following explanatory language from *Ortho Pharmaceutical,* we went on to emphasize that "the judiciary must define the cause of action in case-by-case determinations." . . .

In *Ortho Pharmaceutical* plaintiff, a physician and research scientist, was dismissed because of her opposition to continued laboratory research, development and testing of the drug loperamide, which Ortho intended to market for the treatment of diarrhea. The plaintiff was opposed to the drug because it contained saccharin and because she believed that by continuing work on loperamide she would violate her interpretation of the Hippocratic oath. The Court held, *as a matter of law,* that where plaintiff merely contended saccharin was controversial, not dangerous, and the FDA had not yet approved human testing of loperamide, the Hippocratic oath did not contain a clear mandate of public policy preventing the physician from continuing research. Then, not finding any issue of material fact, the Supreme Court remanded the case to the trial court for the entry of summary judgment.

Thus, identifying the mandate of public policy is a question of law, analogous to interpreting a statute or defining a duty in a negligence case. . . . As the Chancery Court said in *Schaffer v. Federal Trust Co.,* . . .

> Public policy has been defined as that principle of law which holds that no person can lawfully do that which has a tendency to be injurious to the public, or against the public good. . . . The term admits of no exact definition. . . . The source of public policy is the statutes enacted by the legislature and in the decisions of the courts; there we find what acts are considered harmful to the public and therefore unlawful.
>
> Public policy is not concerned with minutiae, but with principles. Seldom does a single clause of a statute establish public policy; policy is discovered from study of the whole statute, or even a group of statutes *in pari materia.* . . .

Based on the foregoing, we hold that where a discharged at-will employee asserts wrongful discharge on public policy grounds, the trial court must, as a matter of law, determine whether public policy justified the alleged conduct. Then, assuming the pleadings raise a genuine issue of material fact, it is for the jury to determine the truth of the employee's allegations. Here, therefore, the issue of whether the *Code for Nurses* represented a clear expression of public policy did not present a genuine issue of material fact precluding the entry of summary judgment.

Plaintiff next contends that, as a matter of law, the *Code for Nurses* constitutes an authoritative statement of public policy which justified her conduct and that the trial court therefore improperly granted defendant's motion for summary judgment. In *Ortho Pharmaceutical* the Supreme Court discussed the role of professional codes of ethics as sources of public policy in "at-will employment" cases:

> In certain instances, a professional code of ethics may contain an expression of public policy. However, not all such sources express a clear mandate of public policy. For example, a code of ethics designed to serve only the interests of a profession or an administrative regulation concerned with technical matters probably would not be sufficient. Absent legislation, the judiciary must define the cause of action in case-by-case determinations. An employer's right to discharge an employee at will carries a correlative duty not to discharge an employee who declines to perform an act that would require a violation of a clear mandate of public policy. However, unless an employee at will identifies a specific expression of public policy, he may be discharged with or without cause. . . .

The Court carefully warned against confusing reliance on professional ethics with reliance on personal morals:

> Employees who are professionals owe a special duty to abide not only by federal and state law, but also by the recognized codes of ethics of their professions. That duty may oblige them to decline to perform acts required by their employers. However, an employee should not have the right to prevent his or her employer from pursuing its business because the employee perceives that a particular business decision violates the employee's personal morals, as distinguished from the recognized code of ethics of the employee's profession. . . .
>
> The burden is on the professional to identify "a specific expression" or "a clear mandate" of public policy which might bar his or her dismissal. . . .

Here, plaintiff cites the *Code for Nurses* to justify her refusal to dialyze the terminally ill patient. She refers specifically to the following provisions and interpretive statement:

> THE NURSE PROVIDES SERVICES WITH RESPECT FOR HUMAN DIGNITY AND THE UNIQUENESS OF THE CLIENT UNRESTRICTED BY CONSIDERATIONS OF SOCIAL OR ECONOMIC STATUS, PERSONAL ATTRIBUTES, OR THE NATURE OF HEALTH PROBLEMS.
>
> 1.4 The nature of health problems
>
> The nurse's concern for human dignity and the provision of quality nursing care is not limited by personal attitudes or beliefs. If personally opposed to the delivery of care in a particular case because of the nature of the health problem or the procedures to be used, the nurse is justified in refusing to participate. Such refusal should be made known in advance and in time for other appropriate arrangements to be made for the client's nursing care. If the nurse must knowingly enter such a case under emergency circumstances or enters unknowingly, the obligation to provide the best possible care is observed. The nurse withdraws from this type of situation only when assured that alternative sources of nursing care are available to the client. If a client requests information or counsel in an area that is legally sanctioned but contrary to the nurse's personal beliefs, the nurse may refuse to provide these services but must advise the client of sources where such service is available. [American Nurses Association, *Code for Nurses with Interpretive Statements.* . . .
>
> Plaintiff contends that these provisions constitute a clear mandate of public policy justifying her conduct. . . .

It is our view that as applied to the circumstances of this case the passage cited by plaintiff defines a standard of conduct beneficial only to the individual nurse and not to the public at large. The overall purpose of the language cited by plaintiff is to preserve human dignity; however, it should not be at the expense of the patient's life or contrary to the family's wishes. The record before us shows that the family had requested that dialysis be continued on the patient, and there is nothing to suggest that the patient had, or would have, indicated otherwise. . . .

Recently, in *In re Conroy, supra,* our Supreme Court confirmed this State's basic interest in the preservation of life, . . . and our recognition, embraced in the right to self-determination, that all patients have a fundamental right to expect that medical treatment will not be terminated against their will. . . . This basic policy mandate clearly outweighs any policy favoring the right of a nurse to refuse to participate in treatments which he or she personally believes threatens human dignity. Indeed, the following passage from the *Code for Nurses* echoes the policy cited by *Conroy* and severely constrains the ethical right of nurses to refuse participation in medical procedures:

### 1.4 THE NATURE OF HEALTH PROBLEMS

The nurse's respect for the worth and dignity of the individual human being applies irrespective of the nature of the health problem. It is reflected in the care given the person who is disabled as well as the normal; the patient with the long-term illness as well as the one with the acute illness, or the recovering patient as well as the one who is terminally ill or dying. It extends to all who require the services of the nurse for the promotion of health, the prevention of illness, the restoration of health, and the alleviation of suffering. [American Nurses Association, *Code for Nurses with Interpretive Statements. . . .*

The position asserted by plaintiff serves only the individual and the nurses' profession while leaving the public to wonder when and whether they will receive nursing care. . . . Moreover, as the Hospital argues, "[i]t would be a virtual impossibility to administer a hospital if each nurse or member of the administration staff refused to carry out his or her duties based upon a personal private belief concerning the right to live. . . ."

Concededly, plaintiff had to make a difficult decision. Viewing the facts in a light most beneficial to plaintiff, she had dialyzed the particular patient on several occasions in the past,

and on two of those occasions plaintiff says the patient had suffered cardiac arrest and severe internal hemorrhaging during the dialysis procedure. The first time plaintiff objected to performing the procedure her head nurse agreed to reassign her, and at that time plaintiff apparently believed she had an agreement with the head nurse not to be assigned to this particular patient. She also believed she had fulfilled her ethical obligation by making her refusal to participate in the procedure "known in advance and in time for other appropriate arrangements to be made for the client's nursing care."

Nonetheless, we conclude as a matter of law that even under the circumstances of this case the ethical considerations cited by plaintiff do not rise to the level of a public policy mandate permitting a registered nursing professional to refuse to provide medical treatment to a terminally ill patient, even where that nursing professional gives his or her superiors advance warning. Beyond this, even if we were to make the dubious assumption that the *Code for Nurses* represents a clear expression of public policy, we have no hesitancy in concluding on this record that plaintiff was motivated by her own personal morals, precluding application of the "public policy" exception to the "at-will employment" doctrine. Plaintiff alleged that each time she refused to dialyze the patient she told the head nurse that she had "moral, medical and philosophical objections" to performing the procedure. She makes no assertion that she ever referred to her obligations and entitlements pursuant to her code of ethics. In addition, the very basis for plaintiff's reliance on the *Code for Nurses* is that she was personally opposed to the dialysis procedure. By refusing to perform the procedure she may have eased her own conscience, but she neither benefited the society-at-large, the patient, nor the patient's family.

Accordingly, the judgment under review is affirmed.

# Automobile Workers v. Johnson Controls Inc.

*United States Supreme Court*

In this case we are concerned with an employer's gender-based fetal-protection policy. May an employer exclude a fertile female employee from certain jobs because of its concern for the health of the fetus the woman might conceive?

## I

Respondent Johnson Controls, Inc., manufactures batteries. In the manufacturing process, the element lead is a primary ingredient. Occupational exposure to lead entails health risks, including the risk of harm to any fetus carried by a female employee.

Before the Civil Rights Act of 1964, 78 Stat. 241, became law, Johnson Controls did not employ any woman in a battery-manufacturing job. In June 1977, however, it announced its first official policy concerning its employment of women in lead-exposure work. . . .

Johnson Controls "stopped short of excluding women capable of bearing children from lead exposure," *id.*, at 138, but emphasized that a woman who expected to have a child should not choose a job in which she would have such exposure. The company also required a woman who wished to be considered for employment to sign a statement that she had been advised of the risk of having a child while she was exposed to lead. . . .

Five years later, in 1982, Johnson Controls shifted from a policy of warning to a policy of exclusion. Between 1979 and 1983, eight employees became pregnant while maintaining blood lead levels in excess of 30 micrograms per deciliter. Tr. of Oral Arg. 25, 34. This appeared to be the critical level noted by the Occupational Health and Safety Administration (OSHA) for a worker who was planning to have a family. See 29 CFR §1910.1025 (1989). The company responded by announcing a broad exclusion of women from jobs that exposed them to lead:

> [I]t is [Johnson Controls'] policy that women who are pregnant or who are capable of bearing children will not be placed into jobs involving lead exposure or which could expose them to lead through the exercise of job bidding, bumping, transfer or promotion rights." App. 85–86.

The policy defined "women . . . capable of bearing children" as "[a]ll women except those whose inability to bear children is medically documented." *Id.*, at 81. It further stated that an unacceptable work station was one where, "over the past year," an employee had recorded a blood lead level of more than 30 micrograms per deciliter or the work site had yielded an air sample containing a lead level in excess of 30 micrograms per cubic meter. *Ibid.*

## II

In April 1984, petitioners filed in the United States District Court for the Eastern District of Wisconsin a class action challenging Johnson Controls' fetal-protection policy as sex discrimination that violated Title VII of the Civil Rights Act of 1964, as amended,

---

89 U.S. 1215 (1991). Opinion delivered by Justice Blackmun.

42 U.S.C. §2000e *et seq.* Among the individual plaintiffs were petitioners [such as] Mary Craig, who had chosen to be sterilized in order to avoid losing her job. . . .

## III

The bias in Johnson Controls' policy is obvious. Fertile men, but not fertile women, are given a choice as to whether they wish to risk their reproductive health for a particular job. Section 703(a) of the Civil Rights Act of 1964, 78 Stat. 255, as amended, 42 U.S.C. §2000e-2(a), prohibits sex-based classifications in terms and conditions of employment, in hiring and discharging decisions, and in other employment decisions that adversely affect an employee's status. Respondent's fetal-protection policy explicitly discriminates against women on the basis of their sex. The policy excludes women with childbearing capacity from lead-exposed jobs and so creates a facial classification based on gender. Respondent assumes as much in its brief before this Court. Brief for Respondent 17, n. 24.

Nevertheless, the Court of Appeals assumed, as did the two appellate courts who already had confronted the issue, that sex-specific fetal-protection policies do not involve facial discrimination. . . . The court assumed that because the asserted reason for the sex-based exclusion (protecting women's unconceived offspring) was ostensibly benign, the policy was not sex-based discrimination. That assumption, however, was incorrect.

First, Johnson Controls' policy classifies on the basis of gender and childbearing capacity, rather than fertility alone. Respondent does not seek to protect the unconceived children of all its employees. Despite evidence in the record about the debilitating effect of lead exposure on the male reproductive system, Johnson Controls is concerned only with the harms that may befall the unborn offspring of its

female employees. . . . Johnson Controls' policy is facially discriminatory because it requires only a female employee to produce proof that she is not capable of reproducing.

Our conclusion is bolstered by the Pregnancy Discrimination Act of 1978 (PDA), 92 Stat. 2076, 42 U.S.C. §2000e(k), in which Congress explicitly provided that, for purposes of Title VII, discrimination "on the basis of sex" includes discrimination "because of or on the basis of pregnancy, childbirth, or related medical conditions." "The Pregnancy Discrimination Act has now made clear that, for all Title VII purposes, discrimination based on a woman's pregnancy is, on its face, discrimination because of her sex." *Newport News Shipbuilding & Dry Dock Co. v. EEOC*, 462 U.S. 669, 684 (1983). In its use of the words "capable of bearing children" in the 1982 policy statement as the criterion for exclusion, Johnson Controls explicitly classifies on the basis of potential for pregnancy. Under the PDA, such a classification must be regarded, for Title VII purposes, in the same light as explicit sex discrimination. Respondent has chosen to treat all its female employees as potentially pregnant; that choice evinces discrimination on the basis of sex. . . .

The beneficence of an employer's purpose does not undermine the conclusion that an explicit gender-based policy is sex discrimination under §703(a) and thus may be defended only as a BFOQ [bona fide occupational qualification].

The enforcement policy of the Equal Employment Opportunity Commission accords with this conclusion. On January 24, 1990, the EEOC issued a Policy Guidance in the light of the Seventh Circuit's decision in the present case. . . .

In sum, Johnson Controls' policy "does not pass the simple test of whether the evidence shows 'treatment of a person in a manner which but for that person's sex would be different.'" . . .

## IV

Under §703(e)(1) of Title VII, an employer may discriminate on the basis of "religion, sex, or national origin in those certain instances where religion, sex, or national origin is a bona fide occupational qualification reasonably necessary to the normal operation of that particular business or enterprise." 42 U.S.C. §2000e-2(e)(1). We therefore turn to the question whether Johnson Controls' fetal-protection policy is one of those "certain instances" that come within the BFOQ exception. . . .

The PDA's amendment to Title VII contains a BFOQ standard of its own: Unless pregnancy employees differ from others "in their ability or inability to work," they must be "treated the same" as other employees "for all employment-related purposes." 42 U.S.C. §2000e(k). This language clearly sets forth Congress' remedy for discrimination on the basis of pregnancy and potential pregnancy. Women who are either pregnant or potentially pregnant must be treated like others "similar in their ability . . . to work." *Ibid.* In other words, women as capable of doing their jobs as their male counterparts may not be forced to choose between having a child and having a job. . . .

## V

We have no difficulty concluding that Johnson Controls cannot establish a BFOQ. Fertile women, as far as appears in the record, participate in the manufacture of batteries as efficiently as anyone else. Johnson Controls' professed moral and ethical concerns about the welfare of the next generation do not suffice to establish a BFOQ of female sterility. Decisions about the welfare of future children must be left to the parents who conceive, bear, support, and raise them rather than to the employers who hire those parents. Congress has mandated this choice through Title VII, as amended by the Pregnancy Discrimination Act. Johnson Controls has attempted to exclude women because of their reproductive capacity. Title VII and the PDA simply do not allow a woman's dismissal because of her failure to submit to sterilization.

Nor can concerns about the welfare of the next generation be considered a part of the "essence" of Johnson Controls' business. . . .

Johnson Controls argues that it must exclude all fertile women because it is impossible to tell which women will become pregnant while working with lead. This argument is somewhat academic in light of our conclusion that the company may not exclude fertile women at all; it perhaps is worth noting, however, that Johnson Controls has shown no "factual basis for believing that all or substantially all women would be unable to perform safely and efficiently the duties of the job involved." *Weeks v. Southern Bell Tel. & Tel. Co.*, 408 F. 2d 228, 235 (CA5 1969), quoted with approval in *Dothard*, 433 U.S., at 333. Even on this sparse record, it is apparent that Johnson Controls is concerned about only a small minority of women. Of the eight pregnancies reported among the female employees, it has not been shown that any of the babies have birth defects or other abnormalities. The record does not reveal the birth rate for Johnson Controls' female workers but national statistics show that approximately nine percent of all fertile women become pregnant each year. The birthrate drops to two percent for blue collar workers over age 30. See Becker, 53 U. Chi. L. Rev., at 1233. Johnson Controls' fear of prenatal injury, no matter how sincere, does not begin to show that substantially all of its fertile women employees are incapable of doing their jobs. . . .

It is no more appropriate for the courts than it is for individual employers to decide whether a woman's reproductive role is more important to herself and her family than her economic role. Congress has left this choice to the woman as hers to make.

The judgment of the Court of Appeals is reversed and the case is remanded for further proceedings consistent with this opinion.

# *Potter v. Village Bank of New Jersey*

*Superior Court of New Jersey*

The crucial question raised in this appeal is whether a bank president and chief executive officer who blows the whistle on suspected laundering of Panamanian drug money is protected from retaliatory discharge by the public policy of this State. We answer in the affirmative. We also hold that the retaliatory discharge in this case constituted an intentional tort which exposed defendants to compensatory and punitive damages. We affirm the judgment.

## A

Plaintiff Dale G. Potter became the president and chief executive officer of the Village Bank of New Jersey (Village Bank) on November 15, 1982. His employment was terminated in May or June 1984. On June 13, 1984, plaintiff filed a complaint in the Chancery Division against Village Bank alleging that his job had been wrongfully terminated. Plaintiff sought reinstatement to his position as chief executive officer and president of the bank. . . .

After the matter was transferred to the Law Division, plaintiff filed an amended complaint. . . . In the four-count amended complaint plaintiff sought compensatory and punitive damages based on (1) fraudulent inducement, (2) breach of contract, (3) tortious interference with the employment relationship and (4) wrongful termination.

The case was tried to a jury over a four-day period. . . . At the end of plaintiff's case, the trial judge granted defendants' motion for involuntary dismissal of plaintiff's claims of fraudulent inducement, breach of contract and wrongful interference with the employment

relationship. The only remaining claim was for wrongful discharge. . . .

The claim of wrongful discharge was submitted to the jury as to the remaining defendants, Village Bank and Em Kay. The jury answered the following special interrogatories:

Q1. Did the Defendants wrongfully discharge the plaintiff?
A. Yes.
Q2. Was the plaintiff damaged by such wrongful discharge?
A. Yes.
Q3. What amount of compensatory damages, if any, should the plaintiff be awarded for such wrongful discharge?
A. $50,000.
Q4. What amount of punitive damages, if any, should the plaintiff be awarded for such wrongful discharge?
A. $100,000.

After the trial judge denied defendants' motion for judgment notwithstanding the verdict, final judgment was entered in the sum of $162,575.40, which consisted of $100,000 in punitive damages, $50,000 in compensatory damages plus $12,575.40 in prejudgment interest on the compensatory damages.

Village Bank and Em Kay Holding Corporation have appealed from the entire judgment. Plaintiff has cross-appealed from the involuntary dismissals at the end of plaintiff's evidence.

The pivotal issue presented to the jury was whether plaintiff resigned or was discharged in violation of a clear mandate of public policy. Based on the evidence presented, the jury concluded he was fired contrary to a clear mandate of public policy. The following evidence supports that finding. Em Kay Holding

Corporation (Em Kay) owns 93 percent of the stock of Village Bank. The remaining 7 percent is distributed among other shareholders. Em Kay is owned by the Em Kay Group which has its headquarters in Panama City, Panama. Em Kay Group is owned by Mory Kraselnick and Moises Kroitoro.

Bart and Kraselnick negotiated with plaintiff for employment at Village Bank. In September 1982 when the president of Village Bank suffered a heart attack, plaintiff was offered and accepted a position with the bank as a "holding company consultant." Plaintiff became president and chief executive officer of Village Bank two months later. Between then and January 1983, Kraselnick frequently telephoned plaintiff to request that Village Bank make large loans to companies that did business with Kraselnick and companies owned by Kraselnick. With few exceptions, plaintiff refused these requests.

After a January 21, 1983, meeting Kraselnick told plaintiff: "[I]f I ever ask you to do anything wrong, I'll stand up in front of you." At the time, plaintiff did not understand the meaning of the statement. Over the next couple of months, however, many cash deposits of between $8,000 and $9,300 were made into the accounts of Kraselnick, Bart, Noel Kinkella (office manager of Em Kay Equities whose president was Bart) and several of the companies in the Em Kay Group.

On March 24, 1983, plaintiff learned that Village Bank was advertising his job in the *Wall Street Journal*. When plaintiff confronted Kraselnick about this, he was told "You're not as outspoken and enthusiastic as I want you to be when you meet me." After plaintiff defended his position, the two temporarily reconciled.

On March 31, 1983, Kinkella went to Village Bank with a shopping bag filled with money. She made seven $9,000 deposits to accounts held by Kraselnick, Bart, Kinkella, and four Em Kay–related companies. Plaintiff became suspicious that drug money was being laundered, so he called the New Jersey Commissioner of

Banking and reported the transactions and requested advice. Before plaintiff could meet with the Commissioner, Kinkella deposited another package of about $50,000 in cash. When plaintiff asked Bart about the money, Bart told him that it was for lease payments between two related aeronautical companies in the Em Kay Group. Plaintiff became more suspicious that the large cash deposits were related to laundering of Panamanian drug money. When the Commissioner eventually met with plaintiff, he told plaintiff to maintain anonymity and that a full investigation would be undertaken. The jury was not informed about the details of plaintiff's suspicions.

Audits of the bank were conducted starting around the end of April or the beginning of May 1983, On June 28, 1983, plaintiff advised Village Bank's board of directors of the examination, but not of his meeting with the Commissioner. In July 1983 plaintiff filed currency transaction reports with the Department of the Treasury reporting the cash deposits.

In September 1983 Village Bank's board of directors raised plaintiff's salary from $65,000 to $75,000. Kraselnick also offered plaintiff a $10,000 bonus in cash so he "wouldn't pay income taxes" on it. When plaintiff refused to accept the bonus in cash, the bonus was not paid. In December 1983 the United States Attorney's Office for New Jersey issued subpoenas to the bank for the production of documents "on a list of accounts" related to the Em Kay Group. Plaintiff was also interviewed by representatives from that office.

On January 6, 1984, plaintiff executed his first written employment contract with Village Bank. The term was for one year beginning November 15, 1983. The contract provided for a base salary of $75,000, with a bonus at the discretion of the board of directors.

At some time between July and December 1983, plaintiff told Steven S. Radin, secretary to the Village Bank board of directors, that he "had gone to the Commissioner and reported the [cash] transactions." In January 1984 Radin informed Bart and Kraselnick of what plaintiff had told him. This angered Kraselnick. At the next scheduled board meeting, the directors were informed.

Immediately after the board meeting, Kraselnick asked plaintiff why he went to the Commissioner of Banking. When plaintiff responded "I thought that it was drug money," Kraselnick stated "you're probably right." From that point on, plaintiff contended that he was isolated from running the bank effectively since his subordinates in the bank were ordered not to talk to him. Further, there were several instances where Kraselnick questioned plaintiff's judgment and accused him of doing things incorrectly.

Plaintiff testified that Radin and at least two of Village Bank's directors advised him that he was about to be fired before plaintiff wrote a letter on May 22, 1984. The letter was written to Kraselnick which stated in pertinent part:

> I wanted to be able to communicate directly with you and since my requests for a face to face meeting with you have been rejected, I am using this as my only recourse. At this point in time, I am considering myself "de facto" fired since Allan Bart has told several directors and John Bjerke, among others, that "Potter's gone" and in turn at least one director has communicated the same to several customers who have even discussed it with people in the Bank including myself. Needless to say, the lack of discretion in discussing this situation in this way can only serve to hurt the Bank and the people in it. However, it has been done and the effect of it, in my opinion, has been that I consider myself at this point in time essentially to be terminated only without the prerequisite action of the Board of Directors.

Shortly after the letter was written, plaintiff told members attending a board meeting that the letter was not intended as a letter of resignation. He reiterated this point in a May 31, 1984, letter to Radin.

By letter dated June 1, 1984, Radin notified plaintiff that

> . . . it was the consensus of the Board that the Bank pay you full salary until the termination (November 15, 1984) of your present contract. During that period of time you would have the use of a car, office, and secretarial assistance. Also you would receive all ordinary employee benefits. In consideration of these severance terms the Board requested a general release from you for the Bank, its directors, and officers. The Board gave you until June 1, 1984, to accept or reject this offer. From May 24, 1984, until June 1, 1984, you were placed on leave of absence with pay.

Plaintiff rejected the proposal made by the board. When plaintiff attempted to attend a June 11 board meeting with his attorney, the board asked him to leave the bank. . . .

## B

Subsequent to the trial in this matter Kraselnick, Bart, Bjerke, and Village Bank were indicted by a federal grand jury for the District of New Jersey for allegedly conspiring to defraud the United States and making fraudulent statements in violation of 31 *U.S.C.* § 5311 *et seq.*, 31 *C.F.R.* § 103.22 *et seq.*, and 18 *U.S.C.* §§ 371, 1001 and 1002. The alleged criminal violations are based on their failure to report large cash transactions at Village Bank during the time Potter was president and chief executive officer.

> 31 *U.S.C.* § 5313(a) provides, in pertinent part:
> (a) When a domestic financial institution is involved in a transaction for the . . . receipt . . . of United States coins or currency (or other monetary instruments the Secretary of the Treasury prescribes), in an amount, denomination, or amount and denomination, or under circumstances the Secretary prescribes by regulation, the institution and any other participant in the transaction the Secretary may prescribe shall file a report on the transaction at the time and

in the way the Secretary prescribes. A participant acting for another person shall make the report as the agent or bailee of the person and identify the person for whom the transaction is being made.

Pursuant to this authority, the Secretary of the Treasury promulgated regulations which mandate the reporting of transactions in currency of more than $10,000.

Because the deposits in this case were slightly less than $10,000, plaintiff was not required by the strict wording of the statute and regulations to report the cash transactions. However, there is existing authority holding that a bank officer may not structure a single transaction in currency as multiple transactions to avoid the reporting requirements. A financial institution must aggregate all transactions by one customer in one day.

. . . Potter did much more than "protest [] [the] directors' improprieties" relating to a regulatory scheme. He blew the whistle on suspected criminal conduct involving one or more directors. Hence, Potter's termination relates to the public policy designed to encourage citizens to report suspected criminal violations to the proper authorities in order to ensure proper enforcement of both state and federal penal laws. . . . Nowhere in our society is the need for protection greater than in protecting well-motivated citizens who blow the whistle on suspected white-collar and street-level criminal activities. If "no person can lawfully do that which has a tendency to be injurious to the public or against the public good" because of public policy, *Allen v. Commercial Casualty Insurance Co.*, . . . surely whistle-blowers of suspected criminal violations must be protected from retaliatory discharge. It stands to reason that few people would cooperate with law enforcement officials if the price they must pay is retaliatory discharge from employment. Clearly, that would have a chilling effect on criminal investigations and law enforcement in general.

Additionally, after the plaintiff's employment was terminated, the Legislature enacted the Conscientious Employee Protection Act, . . . effective September 5, 1986. Under the act, an employee who has been terminated because of reporting suspected criminal violations, has the right to file a retaliatory tort claim in addition to other remedies. We read this legislative enactment as a codification of public policy established through judicial decisions. . . .

We hold that the public policy of the State of New Jersey should protect at-will employees— including bank presidents—who in good faith blow the whistle on one or more bank directors suspected of laundering money from illegal activities. . . .

## C

We hold that an at-will employee who has sustained a retaliatory discharge in violation of a clear mandate of public policy is entitled to recover economic and noneconomic losses. Such an employee may recover (1) the amount he or she would have earned from the time of wrongful discharge for a reasonable time until he or she finds new employment, including bonuses and vacation pay, less any unemployment compensation received in the interim, . . . (2) expenses associated with finding new employment and mental anguish or emotional distress damages proximately related to the retaliatory discharge, . . . and (3) the replacement value of fringe benefits such as an automobile and insurance for a reasonable time until new employment is obtained. . . .

The jury awarded $50,000 in compensatory damages. In addition, the jury awarded $100,000 in punitive damages. We are completely satisfied that both the compensatory and punitive damages awarded are supported by sufficient credible evidence and were consonant with the law. . . .

CASES

# CASE 1.  *Off-Duty Smoking*

Rob, the Personnel Manager at the ShopRight Super Store, interviewed two candidates for a floor manager position. The candidates had similar résumés—both had about 10 years of relevant experience, and good references—and both interviewed well. When Rob interviewed Cathy, the second candidate, he noticed that she was a smoker. He could tell by the smell of her clothes and breath, and he noticed a pack of Camel Lights in her purse when she opened it to find a pen. He decided to hire Jen, the first candidate.

Since both candidates were good, Rob had to go with what he called "soft" reasons, the central one of which was that Cathy was a smoker. Rob didn't like smoking—he considered it disgusting, and a sign of weakness of character; anyone with a strong personality would have the determination to quit. In the back of his mind, Rob also felt that he was doing his employer a favor. The company had a good health plan—for the moment. But smokers and other unhealthy people were putting increasing strain on employer-sponsored health insurance plans.

According to the National Workrights Institute, 25 percent of those surveyed would be less likely to hire someone who was a smoker (NWI, p.1). Although employer health expenditures for smokers are indeed higher on average than for nonsmokers, other "modifiable" risk factors such as depression, stress, and obesity actually may cost employers more (Health Enhancement Research Organization).

**Discussion Questions**

1. Was Rob's choice justified? Why or why not?
2. Is it fair for an employer to refuse to hire a smoker? What about an overweight person? (Are there any relevant differences between a smoker and an overweight person?) Be sure to define what you mean by 'fair.'
3. Does the job position being filled—floor manager—make any relevant difference in this case? If not, can you think of a position where smoking would be relevant?
4. Should employers be free not to hire employees whose personal behaviors are considered high risk?
5. Should employers be able to restrict employee's high-risk behavior? Why or why not?

**References**

1. Health Enhancement Research Organization (2005). "Research." Retrieved September 19, 1995, from the Health Enhancement Research Web site: http://www.thehero.org/research.htm
2. National Workrights Institute (2005). "Lifestyle Discrimination: Employer control of legal off duty employee activities." Retrieved August 30, 2005, from the National Working Institute Web site: www.workrights.org

This case was prepared by Jessica Pierce. Reprinted with permission.

## CASE 2.    *Fired for Drinking the Wrong Brand of Beer*

Ross Hopkins, 41, ordered a Budweiser at a Denver bar in May 2003. The waitress mistakenly brought him a Coors. Not wanting to wait, he sipped the Coors. Also at the bar that night was the son-in-law of the majority shareholder of his employer, American Eagle Distribution Company. The next Monday Hopkins was fired. American Eagle is the local distributor of Budweiser, and Hopkins' bosses did not like his supporting the competition. They stated that he failed to avoid a conflict of interest with his responsibilities at American Eagle. Isac Aguero, 24, can empathize with Hopkins, since he was fired from CJW, Inc. for the same reason in 2005. Aguero was a forklift operator at CJW, the local Miller Brewing Co. distributor in Racine, Wisconsin. Aguero was photographed during Racine's annual Mardi Crawl enjoying a Bud Light, and the photo appeared in the "On the Town" section of the local newspaper. His bosses saw the photo and fired him the following Monday. Aguero claims that he was never told not to drink Budweiser and that nothing in the employee handbook said he should avoid certain drinks. His employer would not comment on the circumstances of his dismissal.

### Questions

1. Is it morally permissible for employers to fire at-will employees for legal behavior off duty? Explain.
2. Were American Eagle and CJW justified in terminating Hopkins and Aguero? Explain.
3. Should there be legal protection for workers to prevent them from being fired for legal, off-duty behavior? Explain.

© 2007. This case was prepared by Denis G. Arnold and is based on the Associated Press, "Wrong beer costs man his job," (May 18, 2005) and Dustin Block, "He had a Bud Light; now he doesn't have a job," *Journal Times* (February 11, 2005).

## CASE 3.    *Exposing Workers to Plutonium*

In August 1999 it was learned that several thousand uranium workers in a 750-acre plant in Paducah, Kentucky, had been exposed to plutonium and other radioactive materials. The exposures occurred at the Paducah Gaseous Diffusion Plant, which is owned by the Department of Energy of the U.S. government and is still in operation today. The 1,800 workers in the plant once labored to produce material for bombs from uranium dust. The radioactive contaminants that caused the exposure also spilled into ditches and eventually were carried into wildlife areas and private water wells. Some of the material had been deliberately dumped into landfills and nearby fields. In the last few years the enriched uranium produced at the plant has been sold to commercial nuclear power plants.

This case was prepared by Tom Beauchamp, based in part on reports by J. Warrick in the *Washington Post* (August 8, 1999), p. A1; (August 29, 1999), p. A1; (September 16, 1999), p. A1; (January 29, 2000), p. A8; (April 12, 2000), p. A1; and (October 5, 2000), p. A3.

Many records on plutonium contamination were kept in archives, but workers were never told of potential risks to health. Recent studies indicate that the workers have experienced higher rates of cancers from the ionizing radiation. Because they were never alerted to the risks, workers did not wear sufficient protection while working with the harmful products. Workers were told that there were insignificant amounts of plutonium and were not monitored to determine the actual levels of exposure. High levels of radiation have been discovered in the plant, and more recently, reports indicate that plutonium has been found up to 1 mile from the plant. In several locations half a mile from the plant, tests in the year 2000 revealed that plutonium levels were above 20 times the maximally acceptable limit. Groundwater cleanups have been underway since 1988, when the serious levels of pollution in wells was discovered. Individuals continue not to draw water from personal wells that may be contaminated.

Union Carbide managed the plant for a 32-year period, when most of the pollution occurred. Lockheed Martin and Martin Marietta managed the plant during the 1980s and 1990s. The federal government for decades took the position that the amounts of exposure were too small to amount to a threat to health. However, internal documents show that Martin Marietta was very concerned during this same period about significant environmental damage that had occurred. Workers now maintain that even if their health was not jeopardized, not disclosing levels of pollution and failing to monitor for health problems were serious moral failures.

In September 1999 the Clinton administration announced that it would spend several million dollars to compensate workers harmed by the exposures at the Paducah Gaseous Diffusion Plant. According to the plan, workers may receive a lump sum of $100,000 or may negotiate another compensation package that covers medical costs, lost wages, and job retraining. The Department of Energy announced that it would allot $21.8 million in new spending for environmental cleanup in the region.

**Questions**

1. Should management in the plant make a full disclosure of known risks, even when the risks are believed to be insignificant?
2. Did the government have the responsibility to pay the workers for the risks that they were asked to undertake as well as the health effects that resulted?
3. In failing to make a full disclosure, are the plant owner and managers guilty of a moral violation? What is the moral violation, and is some form of punishment in order?

## CASE 4.  *BP Workers Ill-Trained for Dangers*

When a unit at BP's Texas City refinery unexpectedly shut down during a power outage a few weeks ago, newly hired operators froze in confusion, not knowing how to handle the potentially dangerous situation. "I never saw so many scared faces in my life," said one seasoned operator. "These were brand-new operators. Some of these guys had not been trained, and they did not know what to do," said the operator, who spoke on condition of anonymity out of fear of retribution.

Anne Belli, *Houston Chronicle* ( January 21, 2007). Reprinted with permission.

Indeed, BP's training of its workers—who operate and oversee some of the most dangerous equipment in the country-falls short of providing them with the expertise they need to safely do their jobs, said a panel of experts headed by former Secretary of State James A. Baker III. The safety review panel was formed at the behest of federal investigators looking into the March 2005 blast at the Texas City plant, where 15 people were killed and scores more seriously injured.

BP spokesman Scott Dean confirmed that an outage happened a few days before Christmas but said that all units were brought down and restarted safely and without incident. "Regardless of someone's opinion of how people appeared, they did react, followed procedures, and took action in a professional and safe manner," Dean said. "No one was injured, and there was no significant environmental impact apart from the flaring that was reported and standard practice when you have a power failure."

Nonetheless, in its scathing report, released after a 15-month investigation, the panel lambasted BP's training programs—not only at the Texas City site but also at four other refineries the company operates nationwide—saying that a lack of knowledge among workers, supervisors, and managers was at the root of many safety woes. "The panel believes that the effects of widespread deficiencies in process safety training and education have manifested themselves in a number of ways at BP's U.S. refineries," the report states. BP has acknowledged training shortfalls at Texas City, and the Baker report notes several steps that the company already has taken to beef up its education programs nationwide.

Among the encouraging moves is that a new company vice president in the Safety and Operations Group told panelists that better training for supervisors "is one of the first programs" that would be implemented, the report says. Further, the company has said it has implemented a new "leadership development" program and other enhanced training initiatives at Texas City. "During the past 18 months, BP has made significant progress in imple-

menting a comprehensive program at its Texas City refinery that includes investment in people, plant, and process," Dean said. But the Baker panel's report indicates that the oil giant—whose refineries have the capability of processing roughly 1.3 million barrels of crude a day into gasoline, jet fuel, and other products—has widespread training problems to fix.

According to interviews with workers, newly hired operators sometimes were trained by inexperienced supervisors, the report said. Operators were promoted to supervisor positions without being required to demonstrate that they understood the units they were overseeing. And engineers "routinely indicated that they believed they were not given sufficient training to do their jobs." Outdated manuals were being used, and workers often asked in vain for more mentoring, the report says.

At Texas City, more than one in three hourly operators—or 35 percent—agreed in a survey done by the panel that "the training that I received does not provide me with a clear understanding of the process safety risks at my refinery." There and elsewhere, training too often has meant requiring workers to take self-administered computer courses while mentoring and so-called gun drills designed to simulate emergencies don't happen often enough, the report said. "At most of BP's U.S. refineries the implementation of and overreliance on BP's computer-based training contributes to inadequate process safety training of refinery employees," the panel found. Computer training seemed to be preferred, the panel found, because it provided a quick and easy way to prove compliance with federal training regulations to inspectors. But what on paper was adequate training in reality was not, it added.

The report indicates that Texas City workers agree. "In operations, it can't be like that," said the experienced operator who witnessed the recent power outage. "It has to be hands-on. You have to have face-to-face training. One operator is responsible for thousands of valves, and you can't have a computer explain all of that."

Part of BP's training problems, the panel concluded, stems from a lack of financial backing and workforce. That was especially evident at Texas City, where the training budget plummeted from $2.8 million in 1998 to $1.7 million in 2005, the year of the blast, the report stated. Full-time employees devoted to training also dipped from 28 to 9 in the same period. Even then, some of those training coordinators spent as little as 5 percent of their time actually training, the report said. Steve Erickson, executive director of the Gulf Coast Process Technology Alliance, said BP isn't the only oil company that has reduced training positions in recent years as more training has been done by computer. Erickson, whose alliance advocates the hiring of degreed process technicians, said computer training is a good alternative to classroom training when it comes to "general" instruction. But computers should not take the place of well-qualified people who know the peculiarities of a specific plant's equipment, he said. He said simulators, similar to those used in the aviation industry, are very helpful because they teach workers how to react in emergency situations. Simulation technology had been "horrendously expensive" but has become more affordable in recent years, Erickson said.

Union officials hope to finalize new training agreements with BP at a meeting at the end of this month, said Kim Nibarger, coordinator of the United Steelworkers' Triangle of Prevention Program. He said the union safety trainers have long favored a more hands-on approach to training than the use of computer programs and testing. "We train on the small-group level," he said. "That's the way adults learn."

**Questions**

1. What would Faden and Beauchamp say about BP's worker safety practices? Explain.
2. What would Boatright say about BP's worker safety practices? Explain.
3. How would you characterize BP's attitude toward its workers at the Texas City refinery? Is that attitude ethically acceptable in your judgment? Explain.
4. Does BP's attitude seem more consistent with the stockholder view of the purpose of the corporation or the stakeholder view? Why? Explain.

## Case 5.  *Roger Boisjoly and the* Challenger *Disaster: Disloyal Employee or Courageous Whistle-Blower?*

In the winter of 1985 Morton Thiokol Inc. engineer Roger Boisjoly conducted postflight analysis on the rocket boosters from NASA's STS 51-C Discovery. Morton Thiokol managed the reusable rocket booster program for NASA's space shuttle program, and

© 2007. This case was prepared by Denis G. Arnold for teaching purposes only and is based on the following sources: *Report of the Presidential Commission on the Space Shuttle Challenger Accident*, Washington, DC, June 6, 1986; Roger M. Boisjoly, "Ethical Decisions— Morton Thiokol and the Space Shuttle Challenger Disaster." Online Ethics Center for Engineering, May 15, 2006, National Academy of Engineering. Available at www.onlineethics.org/CMS/profpractice/ppessays/thiokolshuttle.aspx; "Memo from Roger Boisjoly on O-Ring Explosion," Morton Thiokol Inc., July 31, 1985. Online Ethics Center for Engineering August 29, 2006, National Academy of Engineering. Available at http://www.onlineethics.org/CMS/profpractice/exempindex/RB-intro/Erosion.aspx; and Russell P. Boisjoly, Ellen Foster Curtis, and Eugene Mellican, "Roger Boisjoly and the Challenger Disaster: The Ethical Dimensions," *Journal of Business Ethics* 8 (April 1989): 217–30.

Boisjoly was one of their leading rocket experts. The booster rockets were designed to be reusable like the shuttle itself. After each launch the rockets would detach from the shuttle and its external fuel tank and parachute back to Earth, landing in the ocean, where they would be recovered by special ships. Experts at Thiokol would then examine and refurbish the rockets so that they could be used again. On this occasion Boisjoly discovered a problem. The rockets from STS 51-C exhibited signs of failed O-ring seals and what is known as "hot-gas blowby," which occurs when ignited fuel leaks from joints in the rocket assembly. The leaking fuel acts as a blowtorch on either the shuttle itself or on the giant liquid hydrogen fuel tank. Alarmed by these findings, Boisjoly wrote to his boss, R. K. Lund, Vice President of Engineering for Morton Thiokol, and reported that "we stand in jeopardy of losing a flight."[1] A five-member Seal Erosion Task Force was assigned to address the problem. Boisjoly and the other members of the task force concluded that lower launch temperatures greatly affected the reliability of the O-ring seal. Further evidence of hot-gas blowby was detected on STS-61-A *Challenger* in October 1985. This evidence convinced the Seal Erosion Task Force that it was not safe to launch until the O-ring problem was resolved.

On January 28, 1986, STS-51L *Challenger* was scheduled for launch with a predicted temperature of 18°F at the launch pad. This mission would carry a seven-person crew including Christa McAuliffe, a New Hampshire school-teacher, who had been selected from 11,000 applicants to be the first "teacher in space." Thousands of U.S. school children would watch the launch live from their classrooms and school auditoriums. That evening, during his State of the Union address, President Ronald Reagan planned to congratulate McAuliffe and her fellow as-

tronauts. On January 27th Boisjoly and other engineers succeeded in persuading Thiokol management to scrub the launch. This decision angered NASA rocket booster manager Larry Mulloy, who applied pressure on senior managers at Thiokol. Mulloy argued that it was not reasonable for Thiokol to change their judgment about the launch parameters of the rockets they had built for NASA. A Morton Thiokol management team composed in part by Lund; Jerry Mason, Thiokol's Senior Vice President of the 7,000-employee Wasatch Operations in Utah; and Joe Kilminsiter, Vice President of Space Booster Programs, voted to override the judgment of their engineers and gave NASA permission to launch. On January 28th, approximately 73 seconds after launch, hot-gas blowby from failed O-ring seals resulted in a catastrophic explosion and the loss of the *Challenger* and her crew. The prediction of Boisjoly and the Seal Erosion Task Force team had come true.

President Reagan appointed a commission to look into the reasons for the disaster. The Rogers Commission interviewed nearly everyone involved in the decision to allow the *Challenger* to launch, including Roger Boisjoly. During their interviews with the commission, Boisjoly and fellow engineer Arnie Thompson truthfully reported the sequence of events leading to the disaster. In so doing they repeatedly contradicted the testimony of senior Morton Thiokol managers including Kilminister. Because Boisjoly believed senior management was engaged in a cover-up, he provided copies of memos and activity reports to the Rogers Commission that supported his and Thompson's version of the events preceding the *Challenger* launch. Boisjoly justified his actions as follows: "I thought it was unconscionable that Morton Thiokol and NASA wouldn't tell the whole truth so that the program could go forward with proper corrective measures."[2] As a result of the testimony of Boisjoly and Thompson, Morton Thiokol was roundly criticized by Congress, the Roger's Commission, and the press. Senior Morton Thiokol management chastised Boisjoly and Thompson for airing the company's dirty laundry and for being disloyal employees.

When he returned to work at Morton Thiokol Wasatch Operations, Boisjoly found that he was ostracized by management and removed from responsibility for the redesign of the rocket booster. He could not understand why his expertise was not being utilized in the redesign effort. Eventually he discovered that he had been intentionally isolated from NASA on the orders of Edward Garrison, Morton Thiokol's President of Aerospace Operations. Boisjoly felt that his work environment had become hostile toward him. Eventually, the psychological strain became too great, and he took sick leave and eventually resigned from Morton Thiokol.

## NOTES

1. "Memo from Roger Boisjoly on O-Ring Explosion," Morton Thiokol Inc., July 31, 1985. Online Ethics Center for Engineering August 29, 2006, National Academy of Engineering. Available at http://www.onlineethics.org/CMS/profpractice/exempindex/RB-intro/Erosion.aspx.
2. Roger M. Boisjoly, "Post Disaster Treatment" in "Ethical Decisions—Morton Thiokol and the Space Shuttle Challenger Disaster." Online Ethics Center for Engineering 5/15/2006, National Academy of Engineering, p. 1. Available at www.onlineethics.org/CMS/profpractice/ppessays/thiokolshuttle.aspx.

### Questions

1. Do you regard Boisjoly as a disloyal employee or a heroic whistle-blower? Why?
2. Did Morton Thiokol treat Boisjoly fairly? Why, or why not? Explain.
3. What, if anything, ought Morton Thiokol managers have done differently? Explain.

## CASE 6.  *The Reluctant Security Guard*

David Tuff, 24, is a security guard who has been working for the past 17 months for the Blue Mountain Company in Minneapolis, Minnesota. Blue Mountain manages and operates retail shopping malls in several midwestern states. The company has a security services division that trains and supplies mall security guards, including those for the Village Square Mall where Tuff has been employed.

Minnesota state and local laws require that security officers be licensed and approved by the county police department. Security officers are required to obey the police unit's rules. Tuff completed the required training, passed the security guard compulsory examination, and was issued a license. Tuff has consistently carried out his guard duties conscientiously. Previously a four-year military policeman in the U.S. Marine Corps. his commanding officer had praised both his service and his integrity.

Part of his job training at Blue Mountain required that Tuff learn the procedures found in the *Security Officer's Manual*, which uses military regulations as a model. Two sections of this manual are worded as follows:

**Section V, subsection D.**

Should a serious accident or crime, including all felonies, occur on the premises of the licensee,

---

From Anna Pinedo and Tom L. Beauchamp, "The Reluctant Security Guard." *Case Studies in Business, Society and Ethics*, ed. Tom L. Beauchamp (Prentice Hall, Upper Saddle River, NJ. 1998). Reprinted with permission.

it shall be the responsibility of the licensee to notify the appropriate police department immediately. Failure to do so is a violation of the provisions of this manual.

Furthermore, the manual permits the following action if the provisions are violated:

### Section XI—disciplinary and deportment
#### A. General

1. The Private Security Coordinator may reprimand a licensee as hereinafter provided. In cases of suspension or revocation, the licensee shall immediately surrender his identification card and badge to the County Police Department. . . .

#### B. Cause for Disciplinary Action

13. Any violation of any regulation or rule found in this manual is cause for disciplinary action.

The reverse side of a security officer's license bears these statements:

Obey The Rules and Regulations Promulgated By The Superintendent Of Police.
   We will obey all lawful orders and rules and regulations pertaining to security officers promulgated by the superintendent of police of the country or any officer placed by him over me.

Given this language, Tuff believed that his license could be revoked or suspended for *any* failure to report illegal behavior such as drunk driving and selling narcotics. He had sworn to uphold these regulations at the end of his training and had later signed a statement acknowledging that he knew a police officer could ask for his badge if a conflict should arise.

Fourteen months after Tuff joined the company, Blue Mountain issued new rules of procedure outlining certain assigned duties of its security guards. These rules required security officers "to order and escort intoxicated persons, including persons driving under the influence of alcohol, off its parking lots and onto the public roads." The rules did not instruct security officers to either arrest the drivers or to contact or alert the police.

Tuff immediately, and publicly, opposed the company's new policy. Over the ensuing months, he expressed his dissatisfaction to every company officer he could locate. He complained to his immediate superiors, sometimes several times a day, that he was being asked to set a drunk out on the road who might later kill an innocent person. Tuff described to these supervisors imagined scenarios in which a drunk clearly violated the law, and he then asked them what he would be expected to do in these circumstances under the new rules.

His immediate supervisor, Director of Security Manuel Hernandez, told him that if any such situation arose he should contact the supervisor in charge, who would make the decision. Hernandez noted that most drunks do not weave down the road and hit someone. Tuff was not satisfied and used abusive language in denouncing the rules. Hernandez became angry and told Tuff that his complaints irritated his supervisors and that they could tolerate only so much of his behavior. Hernandez also cautioned him that he should worry less about his license and more about his paycheck. Neither man put any complaint in writing. Tuff never received a written warning or reprimand from any company official. Tuff maintained that he considered the policy to be illegal, violative of the rules he had sworn to uphold, and dangerous to the maintenance of his license. Neither his supervisor nor the company manager agreed with his interpretation. They encouraged him to continue his job as usual, but under the new rules.

Tuff then contacted a volunteer organization working to prevent drunk driving. At first he simply sought the organization's interpretation of the law, but later, he voiced a specific complaint about the Blue Mountain policy. His supervisors were approached by some representatives of the volunteer organization, who expressed strong opposition to Blue Mountain's policy for security guards and treatment of drunk drivers.

In the following weeks, Tuff discussed the company policy with several other concerned security guards. He met with security officers Fred Grant and Robert Ladd at a restaurant after work. They discussed the company procedure and its conflict with their licensing requirements and sworn commitments. They considered going to the local newspaper with their grievances against the company policy.

Tuff then contacted a local television news station and a local newspaper. He talked to four reporters about several drunk driving incidents at Blue Mountain parking lots. The reporters pursued Tuff's complaint by talking to company officials about the policy. The reporters proved to their editors' satisfaction that Tuff's complaints to the media were not given in reckless disregard of the truth and were, in fact, entirely truthful.

Hernandez called Tuff into his office to discuss these disclosures to the newspaper. Hernandez asked Tuff to sign a document acknowledging that he had spoken with news reporters concerning Blue Mountain company policies, but he refused to sign. Hernandez reminded him of a company policy prohibiting an employee from talking to the media about company policies. This policy is mentioned on a list of company rules distributed to all employees that states that violation of the rules could result in dismissal or in disciplinary procedures. Tuff knew the company rule but did not consider his revelations a violation, because he had not spoken with the press *on company time.*

Hernandez considered Tuff's interpretation of the rule's scope ridiculous. He consulted with the company's Council of Managers that afternoon. Every manager agreed that Tuff's interpretation of the rule showed a blatant disregard for company policy and that Tuff's excuse was an ad hoc rationalization. They also agreed that Tuff had shown himself to be a complainer and a man of poor judgment, qualities that rendered him unsuitable to be a Blue Mountain se-

curity guard. The discussion of this problem at the meeting took little more than five minutes. Council members instructed Hernandez to give Tuff a few days' leave to reflect on the situation. Hernandez duly reported this conclusion to Tuff, who then departed for his home. The number of days of leave he should take was not specified, but both men agreed in an amicable though tense setting that they would be in touch.

Three days later an article about the company's policies appeared in the local newspaper, along with a picture of Tuff in the mall, about to report for work. This story prompted an editorial that was critical of the company on a local television station. The story relied entirely on data provided by Tuff, some of which had been copied from his nightly shift reports.

The newspaper had also interviewed Sergeant Shriver of the county police department. He corroborated Tuff's interpretation that any failure by a security guard to report those driving while intoxicated or those under the influence of drugs constituted a violation of the security manual and the specific terms of the officer's license. He also confirmed Tuff's statement that police officers routinely inspect security officers' activities and that the police have instructions to look for failures to comply with license requirements.

After the television editorial, Blue Mountain began to receive phone calls at a rate of approximately 15 per hour, with over 90 percent of the callers expressing opposition to the company's policies. Several callers indicated that they would no longer patronize the malls mentioned in the newspaper story.

The Council of Managers immediately reconvened to consider this escalation of the problem. Its members agreed that Tuff had to be fired for his violation of the company rule against disclosures to the news media. The managers considered Tuff's revelations an unforgivable act of disloyalty. They discussed whether the proper and precise reason for Tuff's dismissal was his disclosure of confidential information or his approaching the media. Their decision on this point required a sharpening of a vaguely worded corporate rule; a careful process of interpretation revealed that approaching the media is grounds for dismissal even if no disclosure of confidential information is made.

Five working days later, Tuff was called into the company manager's office and dismissed. The manager informed him that the reason for this dismissal was his discussions with the press, a violation of company policy.

Tuff then issued a public statement. He explained that his complaints against Blue Mountain Company's procedures had stemmed from his concern to protect the public and other security officers. Tuff had discussed the policy with the company's other security guards, who had all expressed some degree of concern over the policy because it forced them to violate their licensing requirements and subjected them to possible license suspension or revocation. Based on these encounters, Tuff believed that he was acting on their behalf as well as on his own.

Tuff also disclosed a legal argument he wanted to pursue: He contended that his admissions to the media and his complaints about company policy were protected activities. The company interfered with, restrained,

and coerced its employees in the exercise of their rights, as protected by the National Labor Relations Act of 1935, by suspending and eventually dismissing Tuff for his disclosures to the press, which violated company policy.

Tuff brought his case to the National Labor Relations Board (NLRB), whose members determined that Blue Mountain was within its legal rights to fire him. The board found that whistle-blowers are legally protected only if they engage in "concerted activity" together with their fellow workers. Because Tuff had acted alone for the most part, he was not protected. However, a NLRB spokesperson said the board made no moral judgment on either the employer's or the employee's conduct. The parties' moral behavior, he said, was not at stake in the NLRB decision.

## Questions

1. Was the security guard right to take the action he did? Would you have taken the same action? Why or why not?
2. Is this a case of an unjust dismissal?
3. Should there be a law to protect employees from losing their jobs for this kind of activity?
4. Think of some creative ways other than dismissal to handle this situation.

## CASE 7.    *A Matter of Principle*

Nancy Smith was hired May 1, 1988, as the associate director of Medical Research at a major pharmaceutical company. The terms of Ms. Smith's employment were not fixed by contract, and as a result she is considered to be an at-will employee. Two years later Ms. Smith

---

This case was prepared by Norman E. Bowie on the basis of the appeal decision in *Pierce v. Ortho Pharmaceutical Corporation*, Superior Court of New Jersey, 1979.

was promoted to Director of Medical Research Therapeutics, a section that studied nonreproductive drugs.

One of the company's research projects involved the development of loperamide—a liquid treatment for acute and chronic diarrhea to be used by infants, children, and older persons who were unable to take solid medication. The formula contained saccharin in an amount that was 44 times higher than that the Food and Drug Administration permitted in 12 ounces of an artificially sweetened soft drink. There are, however, no promulgated standards for the use of saccharin in drugs.

The research project team responsible for the development of loperamide unanimously agreed that because of the high saccharin content, the existing formula loperamide was unsuitable for distribution in the United States (apparently the formula was already being distributed in Europe). The team estimated that the development of an alternative formula would take at least three months.

The pharmaceutical's management pressured the team to proceed with the existing formula, and the research project team finally agreed. Nancy Smith maintained her opposition to the high-saccharin formula and indicated that the Hippocratic oath prevented her from giving the formula to old people and children. Nancy Smith was the only medical person on the team, and the grounds for her

decision was that saccharin was a possible carcinogen. Therefore Nancy Smith was unable to participate in the clinical testing.

Upon learning that she was unwilling to participate in the clinical testing, the management removed her from the project and gave her a demotion. Her demotion was posted, and she was told that management considered her unpromotable. She was charged specifically with being irresponsible, lacking in good judgment, unproductive, and uncooperative with marketing. Nancy Smith had never been criticized by supervisors before. Nancy Smith resigned because she believed she was being punished for refusing to pursue a task she thought unethical.

### Questions

1. Was Nancy Smith terminated, or did she resign voluntarily?
2. Should the pharmaceutical's management have the right to terminate Nancy Smith if she refused to participate in the clinical testing?
3. Under the circumstances of her "resignation," should she have the right to sue for reinstatement to her position as Director of Medical Research Therapeutics?
4. If you were the judge in such a court case, how would you rule and on what grounds?

## Suggested Supplementary Readings

ADLER G. STONEY. 1998. "Ethical Issues in Electronic Performance Monitoring." *Journal of Business Ethics* 17; 729–43.

ALDERMAN, ELLEN, and CAROLINE KENNEDY. 1995. *The Right to Privacy*. New York: Alfred A. Knopf.

ARVEY, RICHARD D., and GARY L. RENZ. 1992. "Fairness in the Selection of Employees." *Journal of Business Ethics* (May): 331–40.

ARNOLD, DENIS G. 2009. "Working Conditions: Safety and Sweatshops." In George Brenkert and Tom Beauchamp, eds., *The Oxford Handbook of*

*Business Ethics.* New York: Oxford University Press.

BAKER, JAMES A., ET AL. 2007. *The Report of the BP U.S. Refineries Independent Safety Review Panel.* (January).

BERITIC, T. 1993. "Workers at High Risk: The Right to Know." *Lancet* 341 (April 10): 933–34.

BOATRIGHT, JOHN. 2000. Occupational Health and Safety. In *Ethics and the Conduct of Business.* Upper Saddle River, NJ: Prentice Hall, pp. 307–35.

BRENKERT, GEORGE. 1981. "Privacy, Polygraphs, and Work." *Business Professional Ethics Journal* 1 (Fall): 19–34.

BRENKERT, GEORGE. 1992. "Freedom, Participation and Corporations: The Issue of Corporate (Economic) Democracy." *Business Ethics Quarterly,* 2 (July): 251–69.

BROCKETT, PATRICK L., and SUSANE E. TANKERSLEY. 1997. "The Genetics Revolution, Economics, Ethics, and Insurance." *Journal of Business Ethics,* 16: 1661–76.

DALTON, DAN R., and MICHAEL B. METZGER. 1993. "Integrity Testing' for Personnel Selection: An Unsparing Perspective." *Journal of Business Ethics* 12 (February): 147–56

DANDEKAR, NATALIE. 1991. "Can Whistleblowing Be FULLY Legitimated?" *Business and Professional Ethics Journal* 10 (Spring): 89–108.

DECEW, JUDITH WAGNER. 1997. *In Pursuit of Privacy.* Ithaca: Cornell University Press.

DE GEORGE, RICHARD. 1984. "The Right to Work: Law and Ideology." *Valparaiso University Law Review* 19 (Fall 1984): 15–35.

DESJARDINS, JOSEPH R., and JOHN J. McCALL. 1985. "A Defense of Employee Rights." *Journal of Business Ethics* 4 (October): 367–76.

ETZIONI, AMITAI. 1999. *The Limits of Privacy.* New York: Basic Books.

EWIN, R. E. 1993. "Corporate Loyalty: Its Objects and Its Grounds." *Journal of Business Ethics* 12 (May): 387–96.

EWING, DAVID W. 1977. *Freedom Inside the Organization: Bringing Civil Liberties to the Workplace.* New York: E. P. Dutton.

EZORSKY, GERTRUDE, ed. 1987. *Moral Rights in the Workplace.* Albany, N.Y.: State University of New York Press.

FIELDER, JOHN H. 1992. "Organizational Loyalty." *Business and Professional Ethics Journal* 11 (Spring): 71–90.

GLAZER, M. P., and P. M. GLAZER. 1989. *The Whistle Blowers: Exposing Corruption in Government and Industry.* New York: Basic Books.

HANSON, KAREN. 1986. "The Demands of Loyalty." *Idealistic Studies* 16 (April): 195–204.

HAUGHEY, JOHN C. 1993. "Does Loyalty in the Workplace Have a Future?" *Journal of Business Ethics* 3 (January): 1–16.

HIRSCHMAN, ALBERT. 1970. *Exit, Voice and Loyalty.* Cambridge, MA: Harvard University Press.

HUBBARD, RUTH, and ELIJAH WALD. 1993. *Exploding the Gene Myth.* Boston: Beacon Press.

KEELEY, MICHAEL, and JILL W. GRAHAM. 1991. "Exit, Voice and Ethics." *Journal of Business Ethics* 10 (May): 349–55.

KOEHN, DARYL. 2001. "Whistleblowing and Trust: Some Lessons from ADM Scandal." *Online Journal of Ethics,* http://www.sthom.edu/cbes

KUPFER, JOSEPH. 1987. "Privacy, Autonomy, and Self-Concept." *American Philosophical Quarterly* 24 (January): 81–89.

LEE, BARBARA A. 1989. "Something Akin to a Property Right: Protections for Job Security." *Business and Professional Ethics Journal* 8 (Fall): 63–81.

LIPPKE, RICHARD L. 1989. "Work, Privacy, and Autonomy." *Public Affairs Quarterly* 3 (April): 41–53.

MAITLAND, IAN. 1989. "Rights in the Workplace: A Nozickian Argument." *Journal of Business Ethics* 8 (December): 951–54.

NEAR, JANEY P., and MARCIA P. MICELI. 1987. "Whistle-Blowers in Organizations: Dissidents or Reformers?" *Research in Organizational Behavior.* 321–68.

NIXON, JUDY L., and JUDY F. WEST. 1989. "The Ethics of Smoking Policies." *Journal of Business Ethics* 8 (December): 409–14.

PETTIT, PHILIP. 1988. "The Paradox of Loyalty." *American Philosophical Quarterly* 25 (April): 163–71.

PFEIFFER, RAYMOND S. 1992. "Owing Loyalty to One's Employer." *Journal of Business Ethics* 11 (July): 535–43.

PHILLIPS, MICHAEL J. 1994. "Should We Let Employees Contract Away. Their Rights against Arbitrary Discharge?" *Journal of Business Ethics* 13 (April): 233–42.

ROSNER, DAVID, and GERALD MARKOWITZ. 1995. "Workers, Industry, and the Control of Information: Silicosis and the Industrial Hygiene

Foundation." *Journal of Public Health Policy* 16: 29–58.

SASS, ROBERT. 1986. "The Worker's Right to Know, Participate, and Refuse Hazardous Work: A Manifesto Right." *Journal of Business Ethics* 5 (April).

WALTERS, VIVIENNE, and MARGARET DENTON. 1990. "Workers' Knowledge of Their Legal Rights and Resistance to Hazardous Work." *Industrial Relations* 45 (Summer).

WERHANE, PATRICIA H., and TARA J. RADIN. 2004. *Employment and Employee Rights.* Malden, MA: Blackwell.

WESTIN, ALAN F., and STEVEN SALISBURY. 1980. *Individual Rights in the Corporation: A Reader on Employee Rights.* New York: Pantheon.

# Chapter 4

# Diversity, Discrimination, and Harassment in the Workplace

## INTRODUCTION

For decades women and various minorities were barred from some of the most desirable institutions and positions in North America. Even when declared unconstitutional, discrimination persisted in many quarters. This discrimination has led to a widespread demand for effective policies that will provide justice for those previously and presently discriminated against. Problems of diversity and affirmative action arose in this context, and sexual harassment policies were soon to follow, with their own set of issues.

### The Goals and Definition of "Affirmative Action"

Several U.S. federal policies and laws have encouraged or required corporations and other institutions to advertise jobs fairly and to promote the hiring and advancement of members of groups formerly discriminated against, most notably women and minority ethnic groups. Target goals and timetables were originally imposed on corporations to ensure more equitable opportunities by counterbalancing apparently intractable prejudice and systemic favoritism. Many policies that were initiated with these lofty ambitions provoked controversy and were criticized on grounds that they established quotas that unjustifiably elevated the opportunities of members of targeted groups, discriminated against equally qualified or even more qualified members of majorities, and perpetuated racial and sexual paternalism. The moral problem of affirmative action is whether the goals of such policies are justified and, if so, under which conditions. At its roots, this problem is moral rather than legal, but the issues have often been played out in a legal setting.

The term *affirmative action* refers to laws, policies, or guidelines that specify positive steps to be taken to hire and promote persons from groups previously and presently discriminated against. Usually, discrimination had been caused by beliefs in the inferiority of or vast difference in those discriminated against. The term *affirmative action* has been used to refer to everything from open advertisement of positions to employment and admission quotas. Laws or guidelines that require mere nondiscrimination in hiring and promotion do not qualify as forms of affirmative action, because they do not aim to increase the numbers of individuals in groups formerly or presently discriminated against. By contrast, corporate planning has often adopted specific employment goals or targeted employment outcomes to eliminate the vestiges of discrimination, and these policies are ones of affirmative action.

The term *preferential treatment* refers to hiring, promotion, or forms of admission that give preference in recruitment and ranking to groups previously and presently affected by discrimination. This preference can be in the form of goals or quotas or in the act of choosing minorities over other candidates with equal credentials; or it can come in more camouflaged forms, such as the policy of a state university to accept every student in the top 10 percent of her or his graduating class (irrespective of school district).

## The Moral Basis of Preferential Policies

Preferential policies are often said to find their moral justification in the principle of compensatory justice, which requires that if an injustice has been committed, just compensation or reparation is owed to the injured person(s). Everyone agrees that if an individual has been injured by past discrimination, he or she should be compensated for the past injustice. That is, *individuals* who have been injured by past discrimination should be made whole for injuries to them. However, controversy has arisen over whether *past* discrimination against *groups* such as women and minorities justifies compensation for *current* group members. Critics of group preferential policies hold that only identifiable discrimination against individuals requires compensation.

Some have doubted that compensation for *past* wrong is the major moral problem about affirmative action. They argue that affirmative action policies (in whatever form) are justified if (and some say only if) necessary to overcome *present* discriminatory effects that could not otherwise be eliminated with reasonable efficiency. Those who support policies of affirmative action point to the intractable, often deeply hurtful, and consequential character of racism and sexism. The history of affirmative action, from their perspective, is a still ongoing history of fulfilling once-failed promises, displacing disillusion, and protecting the most vulnerable members of society against demeaning abuse.

Many disputes in the literature on affirmative action center on whether policies or practices of preferential treatment are (1) just, (2) unjust, or (3) not just but still permissible.

1. Those who claim that certain forms of affirmative action are just, or are required by justice, generally argue that past discrimination warrants present remedies to those previously discriminated against. Proponents note, for example, that African Americans who were victims of past discrimination are still handicapped or discriminated against, whereas the families of past slave owners are still being unduly enriched by inheritance laws. Those who have inherited wealth accumulated by iniquitous practices have no more right to their wealth than the sons of slaves, who have some claim to it as a matter of compensation. In the case of women, the argument is that our culture is structured to foster in women a lack of self-confidence, that it still prejudicially excludes them from much of the domestic and international work forces, and that it treats them as a low-paid auxiliary labor unit. Consequently, only highly independent women can be expected to compete with males on initially fair terms; and even these women may not be able to compete equally in the setting of multinational corporations with operations in many countries.

2. Those who claim that group compensatory measures are unjust argue that no criteria exist for measuring just compensation, that employment discrimination in society is presently minor and controllable, and that, for the most part, those harmed by past discrimination are no longer alive to be compensated. Instead of providing compensation, they argue, strict equality as well as merit hiring and promotion should be enforced while attacking the roots of discrimination. Also, some now successful but once underprivileged minority groups argue that their long struggle for equality is being jeopardized by programs of "favoritism" to African Americans and women.

3. The third view is that some compensatory measures are not just because they violate principles of justice pertaining to equal treatment, but compensatory measures are still justifiable by moral considerations, whether the appeals are to principles of justice other than equality or to some other moral principles. Proponents of this view argue that although affirmative action policies aimed at large groups will inevitably involve some forms of unfairness to individuals, these plans are justified as a means to the end of eradicating an intolerable social situation.

Many supporters of affirmative action do not hold that it is needed, even at the present time, for *all* social institutions. They believe that racial, sexual, and religious discrimination has been so substantially reduced or eliminated in some sectors of society that affirmative action no longer has a purpose or justification in these sectors. However, in other social sectors it is still common to encounter discrimination in favor of a preferred group or discrimination against disliked, distrusted, unattractive, or neglected groups. Thus, supporters argue that programs of affirmative action should be specifically targeted to avoid discrimination against disliked, distrusted, unattractive, or neglected groups.

In the first selection in this chapter, Tom L. Beauchamp discusses the voluntary preferential treatment programs that have been of special interest to senior management. He concludes that these policies can be justified under a variety of circumstances. Beauchamp does not employ arguments that compensation is owed to classes for *past* wrongs; rather, he maintains that policies of affirmative action are permissible to eliminate or alleviate *present* discriminatory practices that affect whole classes of persons (especially practices of minority exclusion). He mentions factual evidence for his claim that invidious discrimination is pervasive in society. Because discrimination now prevails, Beauchamp contends that policies that may eventuate in reverse discrimination are unavoidable in reaching the end of eliminating ongoing discrimination.

In his contribution in this chapter, Scott Arnold argues that most of the controversial affirmative action programs are unjustified. He tries to cut across competing ideologies by using arguments based on management's fiduciary responsibility to its shareholders to act in the firm's best financial interest and the state's responsibilities to its citizens. Arnold presents the striking thesis that "even if the demands of justice require preferential treatment programs, the government is not justified in requiring or encouraging them."

As Arnold points out, there exist quite a variety of arguments in opposition to affirmative action. Arguments that have received widespread attention include the following: (1) Some persons who are not responsible for the past discrimination (for example, qualified young white males) pay the price; preferential treatment is invidiously discriminatory because innocent persons are penalized solely on the basis of their race or sex. (2) Male members of minority groups such as Polish, Irish, Arabic, Chinese, and Italian members of society—who were previously discriminated against—inevitably will bear a heavy and unfair burden of compensating women and other minority groups. (3) Many members of any class selected for preferential treatment have never been unjustly treated and therefore do not deserve preferential policies. (4) Compensation can be provided to individuals who were previously treated unfairly without resorting to reverse discrimination.

## Decisions in the Courts

The U.S. Supreme Court has upheld some affirmative action programs and found others insupportable. The legal problems associated with preferential and discriminatory hiring are moral in nature and turn out to be surprisingly complicated. In two cases featured in this chapter—both expected to be enduring landmark cases—the Supreme Court supported the permissibility of affirmative action, but the cases were decided in very different fashions.

In *Local 28 v. Equal Employment Opportunity Commission*, often called *Sheet Metal Workers*, a minority hiring goal of 29.23 percent had been established by a lower court. The Supreme Court held that specific numerical goals of this sort are justified when dealing with persistent or egregious discrimination; affirmative action plans that are intended to combat a manifest imbalance in traditionally segregated job categories thus can be shown to be justified. The Court found that the history of Local 28 was one of complete "foot-dragging resistance" to the idea of hiring without discrimination in their apprenticeship training programs from minority groups. The Court argued that "affirmative race-conscious relief" may be the only reasonable means to the end of assuring equality of employment opportunities and to eliminate deeply ingrained discriminatory practices and devices that have fostered racially stratified job environments to the disadvantage of minority citizens.

In the second case, *Grutter v. Bollinger,* the Court was faced with a law school admissions question. In a 5–4 decision, the Court found that the University of Michigan law school's affirmative action program was constitutional, reaffirming earlier decisions asserting that a "compelling state interest can justify the use of race in university admissions." Justice Sandra Day O'Connor said in the opinion of the Court that "In order to cultivate a set of leaders with legitimacy in the eyes of the citizenry, it is necessary that the path to leadership be visibly open to talented and qualified individuals of every race and ethnicity." The law school's policy was found to be legally permissible because it makes a separate assessment of the merits of each applicant and uses criteria such as race as only one of "many possible bases for diversity admissions" and also uses many other criteria not centered on the goal of diversity. The law school believes that this incorporation of diverse aspects of an applicant as "pluses" allows for the admission of "critical masses" of minority students, and that this is the only means for doing so while maintaining the school's elite status.

Justice Thomas, in a dissenting opinion also reprinted in this chapter, argued that the law school's admissions policy does violate the constitutional right to equal protection, finding that diversity in the classroom is not a compelling state interest. Justice Thomas rejected the Court's deference to the law school's beliefs that diversity enhances education and that there exist no race-neutral means of ensuring that minorities are meaningfully represented in the student body. [*Note:* In a separate opinion (*Gratz v. Bollinger*), the Court did not allow to stand the University of Michigan's *undergraduate* affirmative action admissions program, which used set numerical formulas that seemed to the Court to be unjustifiable quotas.]

In the *Grutter* case, amicus curiae (friend of the court) briefs were filed by 65 corporations. They argued that diversity and affirmative action policies have been widely judged in the business world to be necessary for appropriate training of corporate managers as well as vital to the encouragement of innovation in the business world. With the increasing diversity of the nation and international focus of contemporary businesses, the corporations believe that educational diversity is essential for the development of future leaders in business. The amicus brief is also reprinted in this chapter. It shows how deeply intertwined affirmative action policies are in the way major corporations are run today.

Some writers have interpreted *Grutter* and a number of recent decisions of the Court as severely restricting affirmative action policies, in effect dismantling aggressive affirmative action plans that use numerical goals. Other readers of these cases, however, find a continuation of the Supreme Court's long line of vigorous defenses of minority rights and the protection of those rights. Arguably, the U.S. Supreme Court has never established *comprehensive* criteria for legally valid affirmative action plans, instead taking problems case by case and engaging in a strategy of balancing the interests of affected parties. Comprehensive criteria will likely await a clearer judgment from society about the moral justifiability of affirmative action and its attendant goals of diversity.

## Diversity

Large corporations generally agree today that workplace diversity is an extremely important objective, and many think that affirmative action is needed to achieve it. In this conception, affirmative action is a means to the end of achieving diversity. The corporate world seems gradually to be coming to the view that the language of "diversity" is less controversial and legally less worrisome than the language of "affirmative action." However, in many companies it is unclear whether this is merely a shift in language or a change of goals, in part because it is unclear what diversity means and how many forms of diversity are to be included—for example, racial, cultural, national, sexual, geographical, and educational.

The meaning and scope of *diversity* have long been in question. Innumerable forms of diversity can be used for admissions, hiring, and promotion—so many forms that no corporation is likely to cover them all. An institution may concentrate on geographical and educational diversity without even considering factors such as race, sex, veteran status, or disadvantage. Thus, even if diversity is a solidly supportable goal, it would seem that the forms of diversity that should be satisfied may shift from institution to institution.

It is sometimes asked what it means to have an "outreach" program to achieve diversity. Clearly, outreach will vary from corporation to corporation, but it is not difficult to find many examples of outreach programs. Here, for example, is one statement in a quite detailed policy of diversity at the McGraw-Hill Company: "We sponsor and recruit prospective employees at national diversity recruiting events such as the National Black MBA Association, the National Society of Hispanic MBAs, and the National Journalist Associations. Our sponsorship includes national print advertising and job fair participation with these associations. We also sponsor various programs that attract and cultivate talented minority students to our Corporation."[1]

Although the language of "quotas" has virtually vanished from corporate policies of diversity, the use of numbers and percentages has not vanished. Here, for example, is a statement in 2007 of one aspect of Texaco's "diversity activities": "To enhance Texaco's workforce diversity, the Comprehensive Plan established hiring and promotion goals for every department in the company. We measure against those goals every year and managers are held accountable for reaching them. Last year, 68 percent of all of our U.S. hires were minorities and women, and 66 percent of all promotions were of minorities and women. During the same period, the overall percentage of women and minorities in executive positions increased from 18 percent to 20 percent."[2]

Use of diversity criteria has both defenders and challengers in moral philosophy. In his article in this chapter, James Sterba attempts to justify affirmative action in terms of its "immediate goal" of diversity, a goal that is itself justified by its educational benefits and its ability to create a more effective workforce. He tries to show how leading legal cases, among other considerations, fit his model. In contrast, George Sher considers whether preferential treatment is needed to increase diversity in the workplace. He maintains that diversity arguments take multiple forms, but that every version involves some appeal to past wrongdoing. (He primarily attacks arguments that are, in this regard, backward looking rather than those focused on present discrimination.) Sher finds it difficult to pin down what sort of past wrongness justifies present preferences. He finds that many half-truths and half-arguments have been involved in attempts to justify preferential treatment. On the whole, he finds arguments from compensatory justice and preferential treatment to be "immensely problematic."

## Impact on Business

Affirmative action programs and target goals of diversity in the workplace have affected U.S. businesses in profound ways. Some of these plans were imposed by government on business, and were therefore called *involuntary* plans. In the typical circumstance, the government announced that it had found a pattern of discrimination, that appropriate diversity was noticeably lacking in a company, and that affirmative action must be enforced. However, a great many plans that survive today have been voluntarily undertaken by corporations. These are now commonly called *voluntary* plans.

As an example of the how involuntary beginnings have evolved into voluntary affirmative action policies consider the history of policies at the Monsanto Chemical Company. In 1971 Monsanto found itself with few black and few female employees. In that same year the Department of Labor announced that diversity was noticeably lacking in the company and that affirmative action must be enforced. In complying with what it had been *ordered* to do, Monsanto decided to adopt its own still higher *voluntary* standards. It tripled the number of minority employees in the next years, aggressively promoted women and African Americans into middle management positions, and eliminated racial hiring patterns in technical and craft positions. Monsanto reported that it achieved these goals without diluting the quality of its employees. The firm has also said that it has no intention of abandoning its affirmative action programs.

Many American businesses have a similar history, but discussion today has little to do with involuntarily imposed plans. The major concern is rather over whether there is adequate justification for voluntary plans.

## Problems of Sexual Harassment

Sexual *discrimination* in the workplace has long been a major issue in business ethics, but sexual *harassment* is a relatively new topic in the literature of this field. No one seriously doubts that true sexual harassment is wrong. However, there has been considerable controversy regarding which forms of behavior constitute sexual harassment and also whether strictly worded sexual harassment policies overly restrict freedom of speech in the workplace.

Establishing a precise definition of *sexual harassment* has proved difficult. At a minimum, sexual harassment is verbal or threatening behavior that is unwelcome and sexual in nature. A range of behaviors from minor aggravations to serious coercion and physical abuse are included within its scope. It was at one time considered essential to sexual harassment that some form of coercive pressure with the goal of a sexual favor be brought on a person in an inferior position by a superior, for example, by supervisors on a person under their authority. However, today harassment is generally recognized as including behavior that creates an environment that is hostile to those negatively affected. Both sexually explicit and sexually suggestive behavior, including forms of speech, can function to make a workplace hostile.

Accordingly, definitions of sexual harassment today must be broad enough to include persistent behavior involving unwelcome sexual remarks, advances, or requests that negatively affect working conditions. The conduct need not involve making a sexual favor a condition of employment or promotion, and it need not be imposed on persons who are in no position to resist the conduct. Even someone who is in a strong position to resist the approach can be sexually harassed. Derogatory gestures, offensive touching, and leering can affect a worker's performance and create a sense that the workplace is inhospitable, irrespective of an employee's ability to resist. The conduct need not be "sexual" in a narrow sense or even sexually motivated. For example, the conduct can be gender specific, involving demeaning remarks about how women underperform in their job assignments.

Sexual harassment is often said to involve *illegal* discrimination, but whether the conduct is legal or illegal has nothing to do with whether it should be classified as sexual harassment. It is also often said that sexual harassment must have an intent, aim, or design, such as to obtain sexual favors or access, to make a work situation hostile or to harass. However, it is doubtful that sexual harassment need involve such a clear intention or design. Much recent discussion of the behaviors at work in sexual harassment notes the gap between men's and women's understandings and interpretations of sexual language, on whether a display of pornography in the workplace is in itself a form of sexual harassment, and the like. Certain forms of language and displays of sexual material might constitute harassment even though there is no specific intent to make a workplace threatening or hostile.

Ideas of causing or allowing a *hostile* working environment have been at the forefront of recent attempts in government, law, and philosophy to define sexual harassment, but it has proved difficult to pin down the meaning of "hostile." What makes for a hostile or intimidating workplace? Do teasing and denigrating remarks count? What is it to denigrate? Which forms of conduct overstep the bounds of being friendly and humorous? Employees in some corporations have complained that corporate policies are written so that asking someone out for a drink after work or expressing sexual humor can be construed as unwelcome conduct that creates a hostile working environment.

In their article in this chapter, Jaimie Leeser and William O'Donohue consider many problems and subtleties in defining "sexual harassment." They evaluate three major definitions that have been proposed, finding something of value in each, but also finding that each definition is missing some important aspect of sexual harassment. They are attentive not only to the *meaning* of "sexual harassment" but also to what makes it *wrong*. The key condition of its wrongness, they argue, is that the harasser treats another as a "mere sex object," thus displaying a lack of respect for the other as a person.

Larry May, in his article in this chapter, is concerned with the concept of sexual harassment but more so with features in the landscape of its moral wrongness, especially its more subtle features. He focuses on its noncoercive dimensions, on the nature of hostile environments, and on how male solidarity excludes women from full participation. He finds that in contemporary society it is too easy for heterosexual male solidarity to be in control of who gets to fully participate in institutions and what is allowed in the way of harassment.

The most widespread form of sexual harassment now seems to be offensive sexual innuendos that generate embarrassment and anger, rather than coercive threats demanding sexual favors or physical abuse. Some studies suggest that sexual harassment has recently become less overt but not less commonplace. Forms of sexual harassment that condition a job or promotion on sexual favors have declined, but unwanted sexual advances such as propositions, offensive posters, degrading comments, kisses and caresses, and improper joking and teasing have increased.

Statistics on the prevalence of sexual harassment are somewhat unreliable, but various studies and surveys suggest that at least 15 percent and perhaps as many as 65 percent of working women encounter some form of sexual harassment, depending on type of job, workforce, location, and the like—and also depending on one's definition of "sexual harassment." Studies also reveal an increase in sexual harassment complaints during the past two decades.

The landmark U.S. Supreme Court case *Meritor Savings Bank v. Vinson* (reprinted in this chapter) was decided in 1986. This case established that a hostile or abusive work environment can result from many activities in the workplace that constitute sexual harassment. This case, which was brought under Title VII of the Civil Rights Act of 1964, has significantly affected discussions and policies of workplace discrimination—especially as it relates to First Amendment issues of free speech.

In *Meritor*, the Supreme Court extended protections against sexual harassment beyond circumstances of asking for sexual favors to any form of offensive remark or sexual conduct that creates a hostile working environment. Before *Meritor*, sexual harassment had often been thought to involve attempted coercion—that is, an attempt to present a threat the person approached could not reasonably resist. In the typical case, a person's job, promotion, or company benefit was conditioned on performing a sexual favor. However, after *Meritor*, it has been widely agreed that many forms of sexual harassment do not involve an irresistible threat and are not coercive.

In the case in this chapter, *Teresa Harris v. Forklift Systems*, a central issue is whether *noncoercive* comments based on employee gender cause an abusive work environment. In this case it was found that gender insults, gender ridicule, and sexual innuendo can constitute sexual harassment when they negatively alter the conditions of a victim's employment and constitute an abusive environment. The Court found that conduct may constitute sexual harassment even if that conduct does not involve a serious disturbance of psychological well-being or an injury. This case reaffirmed the finding in *Meritor* that "an objectively hostile or abusive environment" is enough for sexual harassment.

Efforts by management to eliminate sexual harassment from the corporate workplace appear to have increased since the *Meritor* decision, although there is controversy about how seriously to take the increased interest. Many major corporations now have some form of training and grievance policies. Corporations with sexual harassment policies for all management levels report that unwelcome comments and touching have declined significantly after initiating the policies. One reason for increased corporate interest is that corporations have been held legally liable for the behavior of their supervisors, even when corporate officials above the supervisors were unaware of the behavior.

Weighing an individual's right to "free speech" against an employee's right to a "nonhostile workplace" has been at the center of much recent discussion of sexual harassment. If legal restrictions on harassment in the workplace come into serious conflict with legal protections of free speech, which form of protection should prevail? This can be interpreted as either a moral or a legal question, or both. One view is that sexual harassment restrictions derive from rights of equal employment opportunity (in particular, a woman's right to be on an equal level with men) and that this right trumps freedom of expression in the workplace. A weaker view is to strike a balance between the two—that is, a balance between the captivity women can suffer in the workplace and the free-speech rights of all workers.

However, some have taken a very different view. They argue that there is a constant danger, given the loose terms at work in harassment law, that the law will function to suppress core areas of protected speech, so that all forms of gender-specific or sexual speech will be banned so long as *anyone* in the workplace finds the language objectionable. If this were the prevailing norm, then employers would need to restrict any statement that might be construed as contributing to a hostile environment. A cautious employer might ban all forms of political speech connected to sex or gender as long as one person in the workplace might find it offensive. Would this be a good or a bad outcome?

## NOTES

1. http://www.mcgraw-hill.com/careers/diversity_recruiting_hiring.shtml
2. "Diversity at Texaco," http://www.chevron.com/news/archive/texaco_speech/2000/av_09-20.asp

## DIVERSITY AND AFFIRMATIVE ACTION

# Affirmative Action Goals in Hiring and Promotion

*Tom L. Beauchamp*

Since the 1960s, government and corporate policies that set goals for hiring women and minorities have encountered many forms of criticism. Opponents maintain that these policies establish indefensible quotas and discriminate in reverse against sometimes more qualified white males. Although some policies undoubtedly do violate rules of fair and equal treatment, I will argue that well-constructed policies with specific, targeted goals are morally justified. My objective is to support corporate policies that set such goals. I will also argue that affirmative action goals are congenial to good corporate management, and that the public interest is served by carefully selected preferential policies.

## TWO POLAR POSITIONS

In 1965, President Lyndon Johnson issued an executive order that announced a toughened federal initiative requiring that employers with a history of discrimination in employment supply goals and timetables for the achievement of equal employment opportunity.[1] Since this order, several U.S. government policies and laws have encouraged or required corporations and other institutions to advertise jobs fairly and to promote members of groups formerly discriminated against, most notably women, minority ethnic groups, and the handicapped. ("Minorities" has been used in literature on affirmative action to refer to almost any un-derrepresented group, but primarily those groups delineated by race, ethnicity, or gender.) Implementation of both the letter and the spirit of these federal requirements has often involved employment goals and targeted employment outcomes intended to eliminate the vestiges of discrimination. These goals and policies are the core of affirmative action.

Eventually these goals and policies came into sharp conflict with a competing school of thought. Its proponents denounced preferential policies as themselves discriminatory and argued that all persons are equally entitled to a fair employment opportunity and to constitutional guarantees of equal protection in a color-blind, nonsexist society. They argue that affirmative action is preferential and in being so violates impartial principles of fair treatment and equal opportunity. Civil rights laws, in this approach, should offer protection only to those individuals who have themselves been explicitly victimized by forms of discrimination, not to groups. A nonvictim who is advantaged by preferential treatment (an already advantaged black woman, say) is, in effect, violating the rights of another person (e.g., a white male) to be treated equally. From this perspective, corporate hiring goals, timetables, and especially quotas only work to create new victims of discrimination by introducing "reverse discrimination."

These two schools of thought often do not agree on the core meaning of the term *affirmative action*, which has been defined in both minimal and maximal ways. The original meaning of "affirmative action" was minimalist. It referred to plans to safeguard equal opportunity, to protect against discrimination, to advertise positions openly, and to create scholarship programs to ensure recruitment from specific groups.[2] Few now resist open advertisement and the like, and if this were all that "affirmative action" meant, few would oppose it. However, "affirmative action" has assumed new and expanded meanings. Today it is typically associated with preferential policies that target specific groups, especially women and minority groups, in order to promote the interests of members of those groups and to raise their status because of discrimination that previously diminished their standing. Here "affirmative action" refers to positive steps to rank, admit, hire, or promote persons. Although it is sometimes said that only *government-imposed* policies are ones of affirmative action, voluntary *corporate* and *university* policies should also be so classified.

Although the meaning of "affirmative action" is still contested, I will, for purposes of this article, *stipulate* the meaning as functionally equivalent to the following statement (in 2005) of the IBM Company:

> To provide equal opportunity and affirmative action for applicants and employees, IBM carries out programs on behalf of women, minorities, people with disabilities, special disabled veterans and other veterans covered by the Vietnam Era Veterans Readjustment Act. . . . This includes outreach as well as human resource programs that ensure equity in compensation and opportunity for growth and development.

*Affirmative action* here, as with many American corporations, means that the company extends its commitment beyond mere equal opportunity (a negative condition of nondiscrimination) to proactively recruit, hire, develop and promote qualified women, minorities, people with disabilities, and Vietnam-era veterans (a positive condition requiring organized action).[3] I too will use *affirmative action* to refer to both

equal opportunity provisions and positive steps taken to hire persons from groups previously and presently discriminated against, leaving open what will count as a "positive step" to remove discrimination and also leaving open precisely what "equal opportunity" means.

The two schools of thought identified thus far may not be as far apart morally as they at first appear. If legal enforcement of civil rights law could efficiently and comprehensively identify discriminatory treatment and could protect its victims, both schools would agree on the centrality of the principle of equal opportunity and would agree that the legal-enforcement strategy is preferable. However, there are at least two reasons why this solution will not be accepted, at the present time, by proponents of affirmative action. First, there is an unresolved issue about whether those in contemporary society who have been advantaged by *past* discrimination (for example, wealthy owners of family businesses) deserve their advantages. Second, there is the critical issue of whether *present*, ongoing discrimination can be successfully, comprehensively, and fairly overcome by identifying and prosecuting violators and without resorting to the outreach programs involved in affirmative action. This second issue is the more pivotal one.

In many corporate policies today, the language of "diversity policy" has been either substituted for or merged with "affirmative action policy." For example General Motors now states its commitment to "Diversity Management" as follows:

> We believe that diversity is the collective mixture of similarities and differences. This recognizes that managing diversity includes race and gender as well as the broader aspects of age, education level, family status, language, military status, physical abilities, religion, sexual orientation, union representation, and years of service. . . . We remain committed to Affirmative Action as required by the Federal law. As such, we monitor our programs to determine whether recruitment, hiring and other personnel

practices are operating in a nondiscriminatory manner. This process includes outreach programs designed to identify qualified individuals of any race or gender who are not fully represented in the talent pools from which we select and promote employees. . . . We recognize that it is essential that our work force structure reflects both the marketplace and our customers.[4]

General Motors also states that "workplace diversity is so important that affirmative action is often appropriate to achieve it," thus suggesting that affirmative action is a means to the end of achieving diversity. This is an increasingly common conception in the corporate world, which now seems to prefer the language of "diversity" to that of "affirmative action."[5]

## DATA ON DISCRIMINATION

Discrimination affecting hiring and promotion is, of course, not present everywhere in American society, but it is pervasive and persistent. Although blatant forms of employment discrimination against women and minorities have largely vanished, more nuanced discrimination in admissions, hiring, promotion, and salary level persist. Data indicate that in sizable parts of American society white males continue to receive the highest entry-level salaries when compared with all other social groups and that women with credentials and experience similar to those of men are commonly hired at lower positions or earn lower starting salaries. Data also indicate that women are promoted at half the rate of their male counterparts, with the consequence that the gap between salaries and promotion rates is still growing at an increasing rate; that 70 percent or more of white-collar positions are held by women, although they hold only about 10 percent of management positions; that three out of seven U.S. employees occupy white-collar positions, whereas the ratio is but one of seven

for African Americans; and, finally, that a significant racial gap in unemployment statistics is a consistent pattern in the U.S., with the gap now greatest for college-educated, African American males.[6] At the same time, American secondary schools have steadily returned, since approximately 1988, to patterns of older segregation (now styled "resegregation") that were common prior to 1964.[7]

Additional facts also support the conclusion that racist and sexist biases powerfully influence the marketplace. Here are two examples.

*Mortgage Lending and Housing.* Studies of real estate rentals, housing sales, and home mortgage lending show a disparity in loan rejection rates between white applicants and minority applicants who have comparable bank and credit histories. Wide disparities exist even after statistics are adjusted for economic differences. Minority applicants are over 50 percent more likely to be denied a loan than white applicants of equivalent economic status. Other studies indicate that discrimination in sales of houses is prevalent in the United States. Race appears to be as important as socioeconomic status in failing to secure both houses and loans, and studies also show that the approval rate for African Americans increases in lending institutions with an increase in the proportion of minority employees in that institution.[8]

Discriminatory practices have a long history in the United States, a history moving from blatant forms of discrimination to the more subtle forms that exist today. In today's market, mortgages are far more available to minorities than in the past, but mortgage brokers have learned how to seek out minority and lower-income borrowers and then steer them into higher-cost, less desirable mortgages. The result is two streams of mortgage lending in the United States, each using its own mix of products. The products that target lower-income borrowers, especially African Americans, have both higher interest rates and less favorable terms than those found in the mainstream market serving upper-income levels. Many of the "alternative" mortgages for lower-income persons fall outside the scope of federal regulatory authority established to provide mortgage capital to minorities.[9]

*Jobs.* A similar pattern is found in employment. Various independent studies have shown striking disparities in the employment levels of college-trained African Americans and whites, even in the best markets for African Americans, such as Washington, DC. Studies have found that college-trained African Americans have much more difficulty than their white counterparts in securing employment and that discrimination is the major underlying factor. In some studies, matched pairs of minority and white applicants showing essentially identical credentials applied for jobs, in response to newspaper-advertised positions. Whites and African Americans were matched identically for speech patterns, age, work experience, personal characteristics, and physical build. Investigators found repeated discrimination against African American male applicants—and the higher the position, the higher the level of discrimination. The white men received job offers three times more often than the equally qualified African Americans who interviewed for the same position. The authors of the studies conclude that discrimination against African American men is widespread and entrenched.[10]

Other studies indicate a great array in forms of discrimination and also show that not all employers discriminate in the same ways. The most blatant forms of discrimination and the deepest discrimination appear to occur in small businesses, which hire informally, without objective records, and are the least visible to both applicants and law-enforcement officials. Other patterns that emerge include increased discrimination by employers in suburban areas that primarily serve a white constituency when jobs involve customer contact.[11]

These studies help frame racial discrimination in the United States. Although much is known about patterns of discrimination, much remains to be discovered, in part because of its hidden and subtle character.

## UNINTENTIONAL DISCRIMINATION AND PROBLEMS OF PROOF

Although racism and sexism are commonly conceived as *intentional* forms of favoritism and exclusion, intent to discriminate is not a necessary condition of discrimination. Institutional patterns and networks can unintentionally hold back or exclude persons. Employees are frequently hired through a network that, without design, excludes women or minority groups. For example, hiring may occur through personal connections or by word of mouth, and layoffs may be controlled by a seniority system. It has proved particularly difficult in the more camouflaged areas to shatter patterns of discrimination and reconfigure the environment through affirmative action remedies.[12]

The U.S. Supreme Court has rightly held that persons may be guilty of discriminating against the handicapped when there is no "invidious animus, but rather [a discriminatory effect] of thoughtlessness and indifference—of benign neglect." The Court held that discrimination would be difficult and perhaps impossible to prove or to prevent if *intentional* discrimination alone qualified as discrimination.[13] The Court acknowledged that discrimination is often invisible to those who discriminate as well as invisible to the public.

This, in my judgment, is the main reason why target goals in affirmative action policies are an indispensable government and management tool: they may be the only way to break down patterns of discrimination and bring meaningful diversity to the workplace.

Courts in the United States have on a few occasions either required or endorsed specific numerical targets on grounds that an employer had an intractable history and a bullheaded resistance to change that necessitated strong measures. The Supreme Court has never directly supported quotas using the term "quota"[14] (a term now largely displaced by "target goals" and "diversity objective,") but it has upheld affirmative action programs that contain numerically expressed hiring formulas that are intended to reverse the patterns of both intentional and unintentional discrimination.[15] At the same time, the Supreme Court has suggested that some affirmative action programs using numerical formulas have gone too far.[16] Whether the formulas are excessive depends on the facts in the individual case. The Court has long suggested that judging affirmative action programs requires that we weigh and balance many different interests.

The reasons for using race, sex, and other such properties in corporate affirmative action policies are far distant from the role these properties have historically played in so-called invidious forms of discrimination. Historically, racial discrimination and sexual discrimination spring from feelings of superiority and a sense that other groups deserve a lower social status. Affirmative action entails no such attitude or intent. Its purpose is to restore to persons a status they have been unjustifiably denied, to help them escape stigmatization, and to foster relationships of interconnectedness in society.[17]

Affirmative action in pockets of the most vicious and visceral racism will likely be needed for only another two decades or so, after which it can reasonably be expected that we will have reached appropriate goals of fair opportunity and equal consideration. Once these goals are achieved, policies of affirmative action will no longer be justified and should be abandoned. The goal to be reached at that point is not proportional representation, which has occasionally been used as a basis for fixing target numbers. Rather, the goal is to use affirmative action policies as a means to the end of discrimination. The ultimate goal is simply fair opportunity and equal consideration, not proportional representation. Likewise, diversity policies are a means to a justified end of nondiscrimination; diversity per se is not the target.

Issues about the breadth and depth of discrimination may divide us as a society more than any other issue about the role of diversity and affirmative action policies. Some believe that there is but a narrow slice of surface discrimination in the United States, whereas others believe that discrimination is deeply, and often invisibly, entrenched in society. I have defended the second view and have cited available data to support it, but affirmative action policies undertaken from this perspective must be specifically tailored and made relevant to context to prevent them from assuming a bullheaded insensitivity. Discriminatory attitudes and practices are likely to be deep seated in some institutions, while thin or absent in others. Society is not monolithic in the depth and breadth of discrimination. In some institutions and corporations affirmative action programs are not needed even now; in others only modest good-faith programs are in order; and in still others numerical goals will be necessary to break down discriminatory patterns. Thus, well-developed requirements in affirmative action policies will be context sensitive and will be manifest in a multiplicity of forms. Sometimes, broad advertisement of positions will be adequate; in other cases, minorities will have to be targeted and recruited; in others, managerial training programs may be sufficient; and so forth.

# THE OBJECTIVES OF CORPORATE POLICIES

Many writings about corporate affirmative action programs suggest that *legal* requirements determine the *moral* obligations of corporations. However, this is to confuse ethics with law, and most forward-looking corporations have not been confused about their extralegal moral commitments. In 1995, shortly after the United States Department of Labor gave an award to Proctor & Gamble for its commitment to pursuing equal employment opportunities, Edwin L. Artzt, then chairman of the board and CEO of Proctor & Gamble, said, "Affirmative action has been a positive force in our company. What's more, we have always thought of affirmative action as a starting point. We have never limited our standards for providing opportunities to women and minorities to levels mandated by law. . . . Regardless of what government may do, we believe we have a moral contract with all of the women and minorities in our company—a moral contract to provide equal opportunity for employment, equal opportunity for advancement, and equal opportunity for financial reward."[18] Starting from this perspective, many corporations make positive commitments, in voluntary programs, of hiring and promotions that build significantly on and move well beyond what laws and federal agencies determine to be basic responsibilities.

There are many reasons why corporations should find carefully targeted policies of affirmative action not only morally acceptable but of the highest moral importance and congenial rather than intrusive. The reason just given by Mr. Artzt of a *moral contract*—both with society and with those employed by a company—is one important moral reason, but not the only one. Another moral objective of such a policy is diversity itself (a goal I will here simply assume to be morally worthy). Corporations that fail to seek broadly for diversity will recruit narrowly and will fail to look at the full range of qualified persons in the market. This will be a moral unfairness of narrow recruiting, as well as a failure to act in the best interest of the company. Many corporations have reported that promoting diversity in the workforce by recruiting widely is correlated with higher-quality employees, reductions in the costs of discrimination claims, a lowering of absenteeism, less turnover, and increased customer satisfaction. While the desire to achieve these goals, so stated, comes more from corporate self-interest rather than moral commitment, these reports strongly suggest that the claim made by opponents of affirmative action that corporations lower standards and hire weaker employees under affirmative action plans have turned out not to be supported in fact.[19]

An example is found in the Dell Computer Corporation, which announced in 2003 that, by design, it had substantially increased its diversity recruiting and global diversity. Dell noted that "companies that diversify workforce and supply bases are more successful in gaining access to multicultural markets. Mutually beneficial relationships with minority suppliers open doors for Dell to market its products and services to women and minority customers, provide growth opportunities for our suppliers, and benefit our communities."[20] Dell and many other companies have noted that diversity plans are not merely a moral good, but also are good for business and for the wider society the business serves.

Maintaining a high-quality workforce through outreach programs is also consistent with the management style already implemented in many companies. For example, James R. Houghton, chairman of Corning Glass, expressly established voluntary target goals (some say quotas) to increase the *quality* of employees by increasing the *number* of women and black applicants for positions. Corning began by establishing the following increased-percentage targets for the total employment population to be met between 1988 and 1991: women professionals to increase from 17.4 percent to 23.2 percent, black professionals to increase from 5.1 percent to 7.4 percent, the number of black senior managers to increase from 1 to 5, and the number of women senior managers to increase from 4 to 10. Corning management interpreted these targets as follows: "Those numbers were not commandments set in stone. We won't hire people just to meet a number. It will be tough to meet some of [our targets]." Corning found that it could successfully recruit in accordance with these targets, but also found severe difficulty in maintaining the desired target numbers in the workforce because of an attrition problem. However, the company persisted in the view that in an age in which the percentage of white males in the employment pool is constantly declining, a "total quality company" must vigorously recruit women and minorities using target goals.[21]

If such companies were today to withdraw their carefully developed affirmative action plans, they would violate moral commitments that have been set in place after direct negotiations with and promises made to minority groups, unions, and others. Many corporations report that they have, for moral as well as business reasons, invested heavily in eliminating managerial biases and stereotypes by training managers to hire through outreach programs. These plans also represent corporate investments in their future. Without the pressures introduced by affirmative action policies and attendant management training, managers run the risk of failing to recognize or deal with their own biases and stereotypes. Elimination of voluntary affirmative action programs also can stigmatize a business by signaling to minorities that a return to older patterns of discrimination is permissible.

Affirmative action programs have for years been successful for many corporations in creating and then maintaining an appropriate moral atmosphere. To prematurely abandon these plans seems an attempt to try to fix what is not broken. As the editors of *Business Week* once maintained, "Over the years business and regulators have worked out rules and procedures for affirmative action, including numerical yardsticks for sizing up progress that both sides understand. It has worked and should be left alone."[22] It has worked because of the above-mentioned improved work force, the introduction of a better moral climate in the workplace, and because of a businesslike approach typical of managerial planning: Managers set goals and timetables for almost everything—from profits to salary bonuses. Setting goals and timetables for affirmative action is simply a way of measuring progress that is no different than the way many other goals and timetables are set and assessed.

## CONCLUSION

If the social circumstances of discrimination change in the future, my conclusions in this paper could be substantially modified. I agree with critics of affirmative action that the introduction of programs of preferential treatment on a large scale runs the risk of producing economic advantages to individuals who do not deserve them, protracted court battles, a lowering of admission and work standards, increased racial and minority hostility, and the continued suspicion that well-placed minorities received their positions purely on the basis of preferential and unfair treatment. These reasons constitute a strong case *against* affirmative action policies that set specific goals. However, this powerful case is not sufficient to overcome the still stronger counterarguments in favor of specifically targeted affirmative action policies.

# NOTES

1. Executive Order 11246. C.F.R. 339 (1964–65). This order required all federal contractors to develop affirmative action policies. The U.S. Department of Labor still today explains government policy in terms of the practical implications of this order: "Facts on Executive Order 11246—Affirmative Action," as revised January 4, 2002: www.dol.gov/esa/regs/compliance/ofccp/aa.htm (as posted 2007). The Department of Labor has in the past given awards to businesses for "outstanding affirmative action programs." Awards have been given to The Rouse Company, Union Bank of California, Eli Lilly and Company, United Technologies Corporation, and Pacific Gas and Electric.

2. For historical and definitional issues, see Carl Cohen and James P. Sterba, *Affirmative Action and Racial Preference* (New York: Oxford University Press, 2003), 14, 18–20, 25, 40, 101, 200–201, 253, 279, 296.

3. IBM, "Equal Opportunity," www-03.ibm.com/employment/us/diverse/equal_opportunity.shtml

4. General Motors, "Diversity Management," www.gm.com/.../sustainability/reports/01/social_and_community_info/socialmanagement/diversity_manage.html (January 13, 2007).

5. See www.acca.com/gcadvocate/gm/cover.html and also chronicle.com/indepth/michigan/documents/briefs/respondent/GM.pdf (2007).

6. Patricia Gaynor and Garey Durden, "Measuring the Extent of Earnings Discrimination: An Update," *Applied Economics* 27 (Aug 1995): 669–76; Marjorie L. Baldwin and William G. Johnson, "The Employment Effects of Wage Discrimination against Black Men," *Industrial & Labor Relations Review* 49 (1996): 302–16; Thomas J. Bergman and G. E. Martin, "Tests for Compliance with Phased Plans to Equalize Discriminate Wages," *Journal of Applied Business Research* 11 (1994/1995): 136–43; Andrew Hacker, *Two Nations: Black and White, Separate, Hostile, Unequal* (New York: Scribner, 1992).

7. Gary Orfield, "Schools More Separate: Consequences of a Decade of Resegregation," Harvard University, The Civil Rights Project, 2001. Executive Summary and Full Report available at www.

civilrightsproject.harvard.edu/research/deseg/separate_schools01.php

8. Helen F. Ladd, "Evidence on Discrimination in Mortgage Lending," *Journal of Economic Perspectives* 12 (1998): 41–62; Brent W. Ambrose, William T. Hughes, Jr., and Patrick Simmons, "Policy Issues Concerning Racial and Ethnic Differences in Home Loan Rejection Rates," *Journal of Housing Research* 6 (1995): 115–35; Sunwoong Kim and Gregory D. Squires, "Lender Characteristics and Racial Disparities in Mortgage Lending," *Journal of Housing Research* 6 (1995): 99–113.

9. William C. Apgar and Allegra Calder, "The Dual Mortgage Market: The Persistence of Discrimination in Mortgage Lending," in *The Geography of Opportunity: Race and Housing Choice in Metropolitan America* (Brookings Institution Press, 2005)—also distributed by Harvard University: http://www.jchs.harvard.edu/publications/finance/w05-11.pdf; "Wells Fargo: Report on Racial Disparities in Mortgage Lending," http://www.responsiblewealth.org/shareholder/2006/WF-MortgageLending.html; CNN Money report, http://money.cnn.com/2006/05/31/news/mortgage_study/index.htm, referring to the May 31, 2006, study by Debbie Bocian, et al., "Unfair Lending: The Effect of Race and Ethnicity on the Price of Subprime Mortgages," http://www.responsiblelending.org/pdfs/rr011-Unfair_Lending-0506.pdf; and Stephen L. Ross and John Yinger, *The Color of Credit: Mortgage Discrimination, Research Methodology, and Fair-Lending Enforcement* (Cambridge: MIT Press, 2002).

10. Margery Austin Turner, Michael Fix, and Raymond Struyk, *Opportunities Denied, Opportunities Diminished: Discrimination in Hiring* (Washington, DC: The Urban Institute Press, 1991); and Michael Fix and Raymond Struyk. *Clear and Convincing Evidence* (Washington DC: The Urban Institute Press, 1994). William A. Darity Jr. and Patrick L. Mason, "Evidence on Discrimination in Employment: Codes of Color, Codes of Gender," *Journal of Economic Perspectives* 12 (1998): 63–90.

11. Harry Holzer, "Why Do Small Establishments Hire Fewer Blacks Than Larger Ones?" *Journal of Human Resources* (Fall 1998); Holzer and Keith Ihlanfeldt, "Customer Discrimination and the Employment Outcomes of Minority Workers," *Quarterly Journal of Economics* (Summer 1998); Harry Holzer, "Career Advancement

Prospects and Strategies for Low-Wage Minority Workers," http://www.urban.org/url.cfm?ID=410403 (posted March 1, 2000).

12. See Laura Purdy, "Why Do We Need Affirmative Action?" *Journal of Social Philosophy* 25 (1994): 133–43; Farrell Bloch, *Antidiscrimination Law and Minority Employment: Recruitment Practices and Regulatory Constraints* (Chicago: University of Chicago Press, 1994); Joseph Sartorelli, "Gay Rights and Affirmative Action" in *Gay Ethics*, ed. Timothy F. Murphy (New York: Haworth Press, 1994).

13. *Alexander v. Choate*, 469 U.S. 287, at 295.

14. But the Court came very close in *Local 28 of the Sheet Metal Workers' International Association v. Equal Employment Opportunity Commission*, 106 S.Ct. 3019.

15. *Fullilove v. Klutznick*, 448 U.S. 448 (1980); *United Steelworkers v. Weber*, 443 U.S. 193 (1979); *United States v. Paradise*, 480 U.S. 149 (1987); *Johnson v. Transportation Agency*, 480 U.S. 616 (1987).

16. *Firefighters v. Stotts*, 467 U.S. 561 (1984); *City of Richmond v. J. A. Croson Co.*, 109 S.Ct. 706 (1989); *Adarand Constructors Inc. v. Federico Pena*, 63 LW 4523 (1995); *Wygant v. Jackson Bd. of Education*, 476 U.S. 267 (1986); *Wards Cove Packing v. Atonio*, 490 U.S. 642.

17. See Robert Ladenson, "Ethics in the American Workplace," *Business and Professional Ethics Journal* 14 (1995): 17–31; Thomas E. Hill, Jr., "The Message of Affirmative Action," *Social Philosophy and Policy* 8 (1991): 108–29; Jorge L. Garcia, "The Heart of Racism," *Journal of Social Philosophy* 27 (1996): 5–46.

18. American Council on Education, "Making the Case for Affirmative Action" (Washington, DC, 2007), http://www.acenet.edu/bookstore/descriptions/making_the_case/works/business.cfm

19. John Yinger, *Closed Doors, Opportunities Lost* (New York: Russell Sage Foundation, 1995); Jerry T. Ferguson and Wallace R. Johnston, "Managing Diversity," *Mortgage Banking* 55 (1995): 32–36.

20. http://www.dell.com/us/en/gen/corporate/vision_diversity.htm (2007).

21. Tim Loughran, "Corning Tries to Break the Glass Ceiling," *Business & Society Review* 76 (Winter 1991): 52–55.

22. Editorial, "Don't Scuttle Affirmative Action," *Business Week* (April 5, 1985): 174. Cf. American Council on Education, "Making the Case for Affirmative Action," www.acenet.edu/bookstore/descriptions/making_the_case/works/business.cfm (2007).

# Affirmative Action and the Demands of Justice

*N. Scott Arnold*

This essay is about the moral and political justification of affirmative action programs in the United States. Both legally and politically, many of these programs are under attack, though they remain ubiquitous. The concern of this essay, however, is not with what the law says but with what it should say. The main argument advanced in this essay concludes that most of the controversial affirmative action programs are unjustified. . . .

## AFFIRMATIVE ACTION PROGRAMS

Affirmative action programs exist in a variety of institutional settings. They can be found as

N. Scott Arnold © 1998 *Social Philosophy & Policy* 15, no 2. Reprinted with the permission of Cambridge University Press.

a part of the policies that govern hiring, promotion, and retention (in both the public and private sectors); the awarding of contracts; and admissions to training programs, universities, and professional schools. All such programs can be classified in two broad categories, what can be called "outreach efforts" and "preferential treatment programs." Outreach efforts are intended to broaden the search for the best talent, where "best" is defined by reference to the institution's goals and objectives. One purpose of such programs is to seek to reassure women and minorities that the institution in question does not discriminate on the basis of race, gender, or ethnicity, and that the institution is genuinely concerned to recruit the best talent or award the contract to the most deserving firm. Such programs include advertising in minority-targeted media (e.g., black-owned newspapers), taking extra time and effort to examine the credentials of minority applicants (time and effort that would not be extended to majority applicants with identical records), and setting up or attending special job-fairs or minority-owned business exhibitions to get acquainted with talent that firms and organizations would otherwise not be aware of. Some may complain about these programs on the grounds of unfairness to those not targeted, but such complaints are not widely voiced and are not the subject of the main controversy over affirmative action.

Preferential treatment programs are another matter. These involve taking race, gender, or ethnicity into account as a positive factor in the awarding of contracts, in hiring, or in admissions. It may be a small factor, breaking ties between otherwise equally qualified applicants or contractors, or it may be a rather more important factor, which operates to give preference to the minimally qualified or the less qualified over the more qualified applicants or contractors. Let us consider the various categories of preferential treatment programs in a bit more detail:

*1. Minority set-asides.* Minority set-aside programs require or encourage government agencies or general contractors who do business with the government to set aside a certain percentage of the total dollar value of a contract for minority-owned (or women-owned) businesses. This may involve an inflexible requirement, or there may be financial incentives for general contractors to do this, or there may even be a form of "bid-rigging" by government agencies to ensure that minority firms are awarded the contract.

*2. Preferential hiring.* Hiring policies in the public sector or in the private sector sometimes take race into account as a positive factor in hiring decisions. The operation of preferential hiring programs results in the hiring of members of minorities who would not be hired if race were not a non-negligible factor in the decision. Those doing the hiring may have in mind target percentages that they would like to meet for minority hires ("goals," as they are sometimes called), or they may be operating with relatively hard quotas. The line between goals and quotas is never a clear one, however; few quotas are insensitive to (other) qualifications, and few goals are mere aspirations. What makes something a quota is that those doing the hiring will not seriously consider nonminority candidates for a position or a range of positions for an extended period of time while they search for suitable minority candidates. The mind-set is to find the best qualified minority person for the job. A nonminority candidate would be considered only if no minimally qualified minority candidate could be found at a reasonable search cost.

Quotas are of dubious legality in most settings, since Section 703(j) of Title VII of the 1964 Civil Rights Act states:

> [N]othing contained in this subchapter shall be interpreted to require any employer . . . to grant preferential treatment to any individual or to any group because of the race, color, religion, sex, or national origin of such individual or group

on account of an imbalance which may exist with respect to the total number or percentage of persons of any race, color, religion, sex, or national origin employed by any employer . . . in comparison with the total number of percentage of persons of such race, color, religion, sex, or national origin in any community. . . . [1]

However, in some settings quotas have been upheld.[2] Indeed, the courts have sometimes ordered hiring by the numbers as a remedy in discrimination suits.[3] In any event, the dubious legality of quotas does not prevent them from being used. If a manager is in part evaluated and rewarded on the basis of his contribution to his organization's affirmative action goals, minority status will be an important factor in his hiring decisions. As historian Herman Belz has written, describing preferential treatment programs developed in the private sector:

> Many corporations used an equal employment opportunity measurement system that offered rewards and penalties intended to change the behavior of managers, showing them how to arrive at an "ideal" number of minorities in the work force. . . . [C]ompany executives increasingly included equal employment opportunity performance along with traditional business indicators as a standard in overall evaluation.[4]

An important subcategory of preferential treatment programs in the private sector are what might be called *defensive preferential hiring programs.* Firms that do business with the U.S. government and have more than 50 employees, or contracts with the government worth more than $50,000, are required to submit elaborate affirmative action plans, complete with minority hiring goals and timetables within which those goals are to be achieved. Failure to meet these goals according to the timetables can result in an investigation by the Office of Federal Contract Compliance Programs (OFCCP). This in turn can mean enormous administrative burdens for the firm, lawsuits, and/or the loss of the contract. To avoid these burdens, risks, and

the sheer intrusiveness of the bureaucracy, very often the rational thing for firms to do is to hire by the numbers. This is certainly more efficient than designing and implementing ever more elaborate outreach programs whose prospects for success are uncertain.

Another situation in which defensive preferential hiring programs are used is to avoid what are called "disparate impact lawsuits." Anytime a company with 15 or more employees (whether or not it is a government contractor) has job requirements, uses tests, or has hiring practices that have a negative "disparate impact" on minorities, it is risking a discrimination lawsuit from disappointed job applicants or from public-spirited lawyers who recruit clients to bring these suits. For example, suppose that 12 percent of the relevant population is African American and the use of a test or job qualification results in hiring only 6 percent African Americans. This test or job qualification is said to have a (negative) disparate impact on African Americans and can serve as a basis for a lawsuit. The company can still use the test or qualification, but it faces certain hurdles. It can argue that the definition of the reference population that serves to define the disparate impact should be restricted to those with certain job related qualifications or to those who actually applied for the position, or it can contest the definition of the firm's workforce (e.g., does the workforce include other divisions of the firm located elsewhere?). Perhaps most importantly, the company can argue that the test or qualification that produced the disparate impact is job related and consistent with business necessity. This can defeat a claim of discrimination based on disparate impact. For example, if one is hiring physicians, applicants must be licensed to practice medicine, and if this requirement has a disparate impact on a protected minority population, that would be legally acceptable. Once the business necessity of the challenged practice has been established, it is then open to the plaintiff to argue that there are other selection criteria that would have a less disparate impact which the employer could have used in place of the challenged practice.

The way the law is currently interpreted has had some perverse effects. It is often very difficult or expensive to establish that a test or requirement is in fact a business necessity, at least given the stringent way the courts have interpreted this.[5] Consequently, it is often rational for companies to drop the requirement or practice before it is challenged and hire by the numbers as best they can, so as to ward off a disparate-impact lawsuit. Or they can continue to use the practice that has a disparate impact and bundle it with a more subjective screening device (e.g., an interview) and use the latter to get the numbers to "come out right." Although the government does not mandate these strategies—and indeed specifically prohibits them in Section 703(j), as quoted above—these strategies are clearly encouraged by the way Title VII of the Civil Rights Act has been interpreted to allow hiring practices with disparate impact to serve to get a lawsuit started. . . .

This essay offers a rather different argument against preferential treatment programs. I want to begin by discussing a relatively rare variant of these programs—purely voluntary preferential treatment programs in publicly traded corporations in the private sector. These programs are *not* defensive in nature but are voluntarily instigated by senior management. For example, the Disney Corporation instituted a set-aside program for minority contractors in the planned expansion of its California facilities. There seems to have been no pressure on the firm to do this from any layer of government, but they decided to set aside $450 million for minority contractors out of a total budget of $3 billion.[6] Similarly, a corporation might have a preferential hiring program that is voluntary in the sense that it would remain in place even if the law were changed so that firms did not need to maintain such programs in order to receive government contracts or to avoid lawsuits. Although there may be few such programs

in either hiring or contracting, a discussion of them will prove a useful preliminary to a discussion of the much more common mandated set-asides and defensive preferential hiring programs. More specifically, the next section argues that, subject to some qualifications and exceptions, these voluntary set-asides and hiring programs are wrong; subsequent sections apply the same reasoning to more common types of preferential treatment programs that are mandated or encouraged by the government.

## THE PROBLEM WITH PURELY VOLUNTARY PREFERENTIAL TREATMENT PROGRAMS

The argument to be advanced in this section is a moral one, not a legal one. The law introduces complications that will he addressed shortly, but the main argument of this section concerns the morality of purely voluntary preferential treatment programs in contracting and hiring. The first premise is that management has a fiduciary responsibility to its shareholders to act in the firm's best financial interests, subject to the constraints imposed by the law. There may be exceptions to this general principle, and thus it is a rebutable presumption, but typically when a board of directors hires a chief executive officer (CEO) or a management team, there is a shared understanding that management will act in the firm's best financial interests. This shared understanding is the basis of the fiduciary responsibility (and thus the moral obligation) of the CEO or management team. Possible exceptions to one side, there is an ambiguity in the concept of what constitutes the firm's best financial interests. Is it maximizing profits in the near term? Increasing market share? Maximizing shareholder value? Or some combination of these? Answers to these questions can be variable and indeterminate, though they may be addressed at the time the board hires the CEO or management team. Nevertheless, as agents for the firm's principals (i.e., the stockholders), management's primary goal and responsibility is to advance the financial interests of the firm. However the ambiguity about the firm's best financial interests is resolved, there is the further difficulty of identifying which policies will actually further that goal. Management's moral responsibility to the shareholders does not require perfection in the choice of policies, but it does require that managers act according to their best judgment about what will advance the financial interests of the firm. One thing this implies is that managers are not permitted to further their own conception of justice by instituting programs such as Disney's, at least when they foresee that this is not financially advantageous to the firm. . . .

Now for the exceptions and complications. Note that this argument does not apply to privately held firms owned and managed by one individual. An owner of such a firm might decide on his own to implement a preferential treatment program; if there is any thing morally objectionable about this, it is not because the managers have violated a fiduciary obligation to the owners. Similarly, the owners of a closely held corporation might jointly agree to order management (which might consist of one or more of their number) to institute a preferential treatment program not required or encouraged by law. Finally, there could be cases in which the owners of a privately held company announce, upon making an initial public offering of stock, that the company will pursue such programs as a matter of company policy, even if it is detrimental to the firm's financial interests. Or they could go before the shareholders at the annual shareholders' meeting and announce their intention to pursue preferential policies that are not in the firm's financial interests, detailing their best estimates of the costs and benefits (both financial and otherwise) of

these policies. Under the circumstances, shareholders would have no grounds for complaint. Let us suppose, however, that a firm's management does not do either of these things. Suppose instead that they simply decide, perhaps with the acquiescence of the board of directors, to pursue a social-justice agenda (or an environmental agenda, or a charitable-giving agenda) that foreseeably harms the firm's financial interests. They do not tell the shareholders about it, or if they do, they do so after the fact and mislead them about its costs and benefits. Under such circumstances, they have violated their fiduciary obligations to the shareholders and thus have acted wrongly.

One objection to this argument would be to charge that purely voluntary preferential treatment programs in contracting and hiring really are in a firm's best financial interests. Proponents of affirmative action often claim that a diverse workforce is in the company's best financial interests, and indeed can point to an array of diversity programs that large corporations have instituted and an army of diversity consultants whom companies have hired to run them.

It is difficult to evaluate this objection for the simple reason that it is difficult to determine how many preferential treatment programs in contracting or hiring are truly voluntary in the sense that they would persist in the absence of any legal pressure to maintain them. The proliferation of diversity programs does not prove very much in this context for at least two reasons. First, and most obviously, antidiscrimination law is extremely far-reaching in its coverage. As I noted above, disparate-impact lawsuits can be brought against any firm with more than 15 employees. As for set-asides, an estimated 27 million people work for firms that do business with the federal government. . . . An expensive and elaborate diversity program is part of a well-conceived defensive preferential treatment program for large companies.

Second, diversity programs include much more than preferential programs in hiring and contracting. They often include attempts to achieve a more harmonious and effective workforce by sensitizing workers to cultural and gender differences. They also try to prevent, or at least insulate the company from, other types of lawsuits (e.g., those arising from the Americans with Disabilities Act, sexual harassment lawsuits). For these reasons, the percentage of preferential hiring and contracting programs that would continue to exist in the absence of threats of Title VII litigation or the loss of government contracts is impossible to determine. For the sake of argument, however, let us grant that there could be purely voluntary preferential treatment programs which management reasonably believes are in a firm's best financial interests; the above argument would not apply to such programs, if in fact they do exist. . . .

## NONVOLUNTARY PREFERENTIAL TREATMENT PROGRAMS: THE PEROTIAN ARGUMENT AND THE DEMANDS OF JUSTICE

The argument of Section II does not address the most common types of preferential treatment programs that are currently in force— those which the state mandates or encourages. These include minority set-asides and preferential hiring programs involving government contractors, as well as defensive programs in the private sector that are instituted to avoid disparate-impact lawsuits. When people talk about the affirmative action controversy, these are the programs (along with similar programs in higher education) that they are talking about.

It seems that an argument parallel to the one set out above could be mounted against

these programs as well. Government bureaus are analogous to firms, with citizens occupying a role analogous to that of shareholders. Because former presidential candidate Ross Perot reminds us that in a democracy the citizens own their government, let us call this "the Perotian Argument."[7] Whether or not citizens literally own their government as Perot maintains, it is clear that they have a legitimate expectation that the government will try to get the best mix of quality and price in the goods and services that it buys from the private sector. They also have a legitimate expectation that the government will not gratuitously impose added costs or reduced quality on goods and services exchanged in purely private business dealings. Of course, the legitimacy of these expectations is purely moral, not epistemic. Only the very naive believe that governments generally meet these expectations. Most citizens are well aware that governments very often do not. But they should. By mandating and encouraging preferential treatment programs, however, the government violates citizen's legitimate expectations about how their government will behave.

There are two premises in this argument: that the citizens of a democracy have a legitimate expectation that the government will not act in such a way as to raise the price and/or reduce the quality of goods and services in both the public and private sectors; and that nonvoluntary preferential treatment programs violate this expectation. The first is hard to argue with, at least as a general proposition. It is simply a demand that government act efficiently in procuring goods and services and in affecting the private sector. There are undoubtedly exceptions to this general proposition, and thus it is a rebuttable presumption; indeed, proponents of preferential treatment programs may insist that in this area an exception should be made because of the demands of justice. This claim will be taken up in due course, but for now it is sufficient to note that those who control the government in a democracy do not own the resources they control. They have a fiduciary relationship with the citizenry that closely parallels the relationship between corporate officers and shareholders; this serves as the basis for the legitimate expectations just mentioned. . . .

Proponents of these programs might agree with all this and yet insist that even though these programs do impose real costs, that is simply the price of justice. Justice, John Rawls asserts, is the first virtue of social institutions.[8] If justice requires preferential treatment programs, so be it. This is essentially the same objection raised against the purely voluntary programs considered in the last section. It is now time to give it full consideration. I shall argue that even if the demands of justice require preferential treatment programs, the government is not justified in requiring or encouraging them. In other words, the argument that follows grants, for the sake of discussion, that justice requires preferential treatment programs and yet concludes that these programs are, all things considered, unjustified.

This argument starts with some suggestive parallels with Locke's observations about the problems of a state of nature. Recall that a state of nature is a prepolitical society in which people have various natural rights, including the rights to life, liberty, and property. In addition, they have the right to punish those who violate their other rights. All this gives rise to what Locke calls the "inconveniences of a state of nature." These include the following: Some people cannot enforce their rights. Some people do not correctly apply the natural law, or they tend to be biased when judging in their own cases, or they tend to mispunish, overpunish, etc. They use the demands of justice as a cloak to further their own interests and/or the interests of their friends at the expense of others and at the expense of justice. This worry is a special case of the central worry of Western political philosophy, at least in the liberal tra-

dition: How is government to be limited? Whether or not one believes in Lockean rights, there is no doubt that the state faces a permanent threat—very often realized—of being hijacked to serve private interests. Historically, state power has been used to advance private interests at the expense of the public interest, including the demands of justice, however one understands these concepts. . . .

Two plausible requirements . . . must be met if the power of the state is to be used to further some conception of the demands of (distributive or compensatory) justice:

(i) Proponents of state action must get a political consensus for doing what justice requires. A political consensus does not require unanimity among the people or their elected representatives, but it does require that supporters of government intervention make their case publicly and get an on-the-record vote from the legislature or from the electorate through a referendum. Let us call this the *Public Justification requirement.* . . .

(ii) Proponents of state action must explain how and why their proposal will not permit state power to be systematically abused to further private interests at the expense of those disadvantaged by the policies in question. Very often, proposed legislation will foreseeably but unavoidably help groups and individuals it is not intended to help at the expense of groups and individuals it is not intended to harm; if this is so, that fact has to be made public and a case has to be made that this is a cost worth paying. . . .

## MINORITY SET–ASIDE PROGRAMS

The main question this section and the next will address is whether minority set-aside programs and nonvoluntary preferential hiring programs satisfy the two requirements. Let us begin with the former. Minority set-asides began in 1968 with the Small Business Administration. The SBA served as prime contractor for other governmental agencies, awarding procurement contracts to small businesses. It interpreted its statutory authority to allow it to set aside a certain percentage of its contracts to businesses owned by "socially and economically disadvantaged" individuals, which was further interpreted to apply primarily to "minority business enterprises" (MBEs). The first set-aside program legislated by Congress was included in the 1977 Public Works Employment Act (PWEA).[9] It required each prime contractor to set aside 10 percent of the dollar value of the contract for MBEs, which were explicitly defined as businesses at least 50 percent owned by members of minority groups; or, if the business was a joint stock company, at least 51 percent of the stock had to be owned by minorities. Targeted minorities included African Americans, Hispanics, Asians, Native Americans, Eskimos, and Aleuts. The PWEA contained a provision to suspend the requirement if there were no available minority firms. In subsequent years, state and local governments instituted their own minority set-aside programs modeled on federal programs. Other set-aside programs at the federal level were introduced piecemeal, either by executive order or as part of other legislation.

Do minority set-aside programs meet the Public Justification requirement? Set-aside programs instituted by the executive branch (such as the SBA's program) were not subject to any public debate and discussion in Congress; they were simply imposed by the executive branch, so they clearly do not meet the requirement. The case of set-asides mandated by Congress is not as simple, since set-aside provisions can be found in many pieces of legislation that Congress passed and that the president signed into law. The crucial issue is the legislative history of a given set-aside provision.

The first of these provisions—the one included in the PWEA—is especially important, since it set the precedent; proponents of subsequent programs appealed to it as conferring presumptive validity on their proposals. One would expect that the first modern attempt to introduce race-conscious programs by legislation would occasion considerable congressional debate and discussion, but in fact that did not happen. There were no committee hearings or reports relating to the minority set-aside provision in the PWEA, probably because the provision was offered as a floor amendment in the House of Representatives. It passed on a voice vote and was accorded similar treatment in the Senate. . . .

## PREFERENTIAL TREATMENT IN HIRING

Though minority set-asides are an important form of preferential treatment, preferential hiring programs are more significant. They impact many more people and seem to have provoked more passionate debate. The vast majority of preferential hiring programs are mandated or encouraged by the government and would likely not exist but for that pressure. They fall into three categories: (1) those mandated by the courts in response to successful discrimination suits; (2) defensive preferential hiring programs encouraged by the executive branch for contractors doing business with the federal government; and (3) defensive preferential hiring programs undertaken to ward off disparate-impact lawsuits. Let us consider each of these in turn to see if the Public Justification and Anti-Hijacking requirements were satisfied when these programs were instituted.

*1. Court-ordered preferential hiring programs.* Courts occasionally order hiring (or promotions) by the numbers in response to successful lawsuits brought under Title VII of the 1964 Civil Rights Act. Section 706 of Title VII of the 1964 Civil Rights Act. Section 706 of Title VII gives a court considerable discretion in ordering remedies for discriminatory practices. In response to a finding of discrimination, Section 706(g) (1) says,

> the court may enjoin the respondent from engaging in such unlawful employment practice and may order such affirmative action as may be appropriate which may include but is not limited to reinstatement or hiring of employees, with or without back pay . . . or any other equitable relief that the court deems appropriate.[10]

Though it is doubtful whether "quota relief" is consistent with Section 703(j) of Title VII, the courts have assumed that it is and have on occasion ordered hiring or promotion by the numbers. They have forced employers to hire a certain percentage of minorities against whom no discrimination has been proven or even alleged. Typically, these remedies are imposed on employers who seem particularly racist or sexist in their policies and practices. This remedy fails to satisfy the Public Justification requirement, even if it is legally permissible, since nowhere in the Civil Rights Act is this remedy explicitly mentioned. Congress never debated and sanctioned hiring or promotion by the numbers as a remedy for discrimination, no matter how egregious. The fact, if indeed it is a fact, that Congress somehow left the door open for quota remedies is irrelevant for the purposes of the Public Justification requirement, since this requirement imposes burdens on the legislature. This form of affirmative action is relatively rare, however, in comparison to the next two types to be considered, so perhaps we should not make too much of this failure.

*2. Preferential hiring under various executive orders.* In 1965, President Lyndon Johnson issued Executive Order 11246, which created the Office of Federal Contract Compliance (later renamed the Office of Federal Contract Compliance Programs) and led to the establishment of defensive preferential hiring programs by government contractors. Later,

President Richard Nixon extended preferential hiring requirements to cover the civil service in Executive Order 11478. The story of the development of this policy has been told elsewhere. The "goals and timetables" approach to hiring was inaugurated under these executive orders, which remain in effect to this day. The OFCCP has considerable power over firms doing business with the government. Many such firms do business exclusively (or nearly exclusively) with the government and can ill-afford to walk away from government contracts. Though firms are nominally prohibited from hiring by the numbers, they must submit an affirmative action plan, complete with goals and timetables. The failure of so-called good-faith efforts to yield the right hiring numbers can bring the OFCCP down on a contractor with a vengeance. This office has much more power than the EEOC, since it can deny contracts without a court finding that a company has been guilty of discrimination. OFCCP officials can simply refuse to certify a company as able to bid on contracts. Although this sanction has seldom been applied, the threat of it is usually sufficient to get compliance. . . .

*3. Other defensive preferential hiring programs.* Defensive preferential hiring programs among firms not doing business with the federal government came into existence in response to judicial interpretation of Title VII of the 1964 Civil Rights Act. In *Griggs v. Duke Power* (1971)[11] and subsequent cases, the Supreme Court ruled that hiring practices and policies having a disparate impact on minorities were prima facie suspect and could be grounds for a Title VII lawsuit. Moreover, the EEOC has made it clear that it will not bring disparate-impact lawsuits against employers who abide by what is called "the 80 percent rule."[12] This rule states that if the percentage of women or minorities a firm hires is at least 80 percent of their percentage in the relevant populations, the firm will not ordinarily be subject to an investigation and a disparate-impact lawsuit. Rational firms have responded to these pressures by instituting preferential hiring programs to reach safe harbor from such lawsuits. In 1989, the Supreme Court pulled back from the standards imposed by *Griggs* and its progeny in *Ward's Cove Packing Co. v. Antonio.*[13] It lessened the pressure on businesses to engage in preferential hiring by redistributing the burden of proof in disparate-impact cases. In response to the Court's ruling in *Ward's Cove,* Congress reimposed the *Griggs* standards in the Civil Rights Act of 1991. Were the Public Justification and Anti-Hijacking requirements satisfied for preferential hiring programs anywhere in this series of events? Let us begin with the original legislation: Title VII of the 1964 Civil Rights Act.

If one purpose of Title VII was to foster preferential hiring programs, proponents of the law would have had to make clear that employment practices that have a disparate impact on minorities create a rebuttable presumption of discrimination. Under this construal of Title VII, the intended beneficiaries would be the women and minorities who successfully sued, as well as those who would be hired to avoid such suits, and presumably other women and minorities who might indirectly benefit from preferential hirings and promotions. The intended victims would be the owners of the businesses who, for whatever reason, used employment practices (or hired managers who used such practices) that created a disparate impact. Others in the firm, such as other managers who would have to struggle with affirmative action regulations and other employees who would be negatively affected in a variety of ways, might also count as intended victims of the policy, though that depends on how the argument is framed. The argument would have to be made that the benefits of the law, as so interpreted, outweigh the costs.

What about the unintended beneficiaries and victims? The Anti-Hijacking requirement stipulates that they have to be identified as well. The main unintended victims are, of course, the nonminority candidates who otherwise would have gotten the jobs. Academic defenders of preferential hiring are quick to point out that their being excluded is not a result of stereotyping and does not stigmatize them in the way ordinary racial discrimination would. Moreover, if there were ways to solve the underlying social problems without hurting these people, defenders of preferential hiring programs would probably embrace them. All this makes the victim status of disappointed majority job candidates unintended, however foreseeable their plight is. However, they are still adversely affected, and whatever the demands of justice, the lack of stigmatization is cold comfort to someone who did not get a job or promotion because of his or her race or gender. The unintended beneficiaries of preferential hiring programs are a little harder to identify. Clearly, government bureaucrats and lawyers in the equal employment opportunity/affirmative action industry count as foreseen though unintended beneficiaries. In addition, the private sector has its affirmative action officers, "diversity consultants," and others who profit from attempts to eliminate (perceived) social injustice.

The above identifies the intended and unintended beneficiaries and victims of preferential hiring programs, an identification essential to satisfying the Public Justification and Anti-Hijacking requirements. The main problem for defenders of preferential hiring programs is that legislators supporting Title VII never made this case. . . .

## NOTES

1. 42 U.S.C. 2000e-2(j).
2. Kaiser Aluminum had a training program that used racial preferences for blacks over whites, which was upheld by the Supreme Court in *United Steelworkers of America v. Weber,* 443 U.S. 193 (1979).

3. See, e.g., *Morrow v. Crisler*, 491 F.2d 1053 (1974), and *NAACP v. Allen*, 493 F.2d 614 (1974).

4. Herman Belz, *Equality Transformed* (New Brunswick, NJ: Transaction Publishers, 1991), 105. See also Theodore V. Purcell, S.J., et al., "What Are the Social Responsibilities for Psychologists in Industry? A Symposium." *Personnel Psychology* 27 (Autumn 1974): 436.

5. See Richard Epstein, *Forbidden Grounds: The Case against Employment Discrimination Laws* (Cambridge, MA: Harvard University Press, 1992), 212–22.

6. Chris Woodyard, "Disney to Boost Minority Builders," *Los Angels Times* (June 16, 1992), p. D2. Subsequently, the planned expansion was significantly scaled back.

7. Or is it the taxpayers who own the government? Not all citizens are taxpayers and not all taxpayers are citizens, though the two groups substantially overlap. Since I do not wish to claim that anyone literally owns the government, this complication need not be pursued. All that is claimed in what follows is that citizens or taxpayers have a principal-agent relationship with their government analogous to shareholders' relationship to management, at least when it comes to the government's dealings in the economy.

8. John Rawls, *A Theory of Justice* (Cambridge, MA: The Belknap Press of Harvard University Press, 1971), 3.

9. Information in this and subsequent paragraphs on the set-aside provision in the PWEA comes from the *Congressional Record*, 95th Congress, 1st session (1977), pp. 5327–30.

10. 42 U.S.C. 2000e-(g) (1).

11. 401 U.S. 424 (1971).

12. Uniform Guidelines on Employee Selection Procedures (1978), 29 C.F.R. Section 1607.4D (1989).

13. 490 U.S. 642 (1989). [See the case presentation below in this volume. Ed.]

# A Defense of Diversity Affirmative Action

*James P. Sterba*

As one might expect, lack of clarity as to how to characterize affirmative action has affected the debate over whether affirmative action can be justified. Frequently, the affirmative action that critics attack is not the affirmative action that most people defend. Accordingly, it would seem that if we are going to bring this debate any closer to a resolution, we need some agreement on what we should call affirmative action. In this regard, I think it is more appropriate for critics of affirmative action to take their characterization of affirmative action from those who defend it rather than devise characterizations of their own. In this way, critics of affirmative action, assuming there are any left once we get straight about its proper characterization, can then avoid missing their target. It would also be helpful if defenders of affirmative action were to formulate their definitions of affirmative action so as to avoid as much as possible the criticisms that have been directed against it. At least this is what I will try to do in this essay.

Here I propose to define affirmative action as a policy of favoring qualified women and minority candidates over qualified men or nonminority candidates, with the immediate goals of outreach, remedying discrimination, or achieving diversity, and the ultimate goals of attaining a color-blind (racially just) and

Reprinted with permission from Oxford University Press. Excerpted from *Affirmative Action and Racial Preference: A Debate*, by Carl Cohen and James P. Sterba, © 2003 OUP.

gender-free (sexually just) society (see diagram).

A color-blind society is a society in which race has no more significance than eye color has in most societies. A gender-free society is a society in which sex has no more significance than eye color has in most societies. It is a society in which the traits that are truly desirable and distributable in society are equally open to both women and men. The ultimate goals can be understood to be racial justice and sexual justice. Since our society is far from being either color-blind (racially just) or gender-free (sexually just), it is generally recognized that to make the transition to a racially just or a sexually just society, we will have to take race and sex into account. . . .

Even the strongest critics of affirmative action acknowledge that to advance toward a color-blind (racially just) and gender-free (sexually just) society, *we will sometimes have to depart from the status quo,* for example, *by favoring qualified women or minority candidates over qualified men or nonminority candidates when the qualified women or minority candidates have themselves directly suffered from proven past discrimination.* They will consider such cases to be justified uses of racial or sexual classifications, and *not* consider them to involve racial preferences. However, these critics will typically object to any use of any kind of sexual or racial proportionality as a means for achieving a color-blind (racially just) or gender-free (sexually just) society. . . .

As I define it, affirmative action can have a number of immediate goals. It can have the goal of outreach, with the purpose of searching out qualified women and minority candidates who would otherwise not know about or apply for the available positions, and then hiring or accepting only those who are actually the most qualified. Affirmative action can also attempt to remedy discrimination. Here, there are two possibilities. First, an affirmative action program can be designed simply to put an end to an existing discriminatory practice, and to create, possibly for the first time in a particular setting, a truly equal opportunity environment. Second, an affirmative action program can attempt to compensate for past discrimination and the effects of that discrimination. The idea here is that stopping discrimination is one thing and making up for past discrimination and the effects of that discrimination is another, and that both need to be done. Still another form of affirmative action has the goal of diversity, where the pursuit of diversity is, in turn, justified either in terms of its educational benefits or in terms of its ability to create a more effective workforce in such areas as policing or community relations. Here it might even be said that the affirmative action candidates are, in fact, the most qualified candidates overall, since candidates who do not bring diversity would not be as qualified. As it turns out, all other forms of affirmative action can be understood in terms of their immediate goals to be either outreach, remedial, or diversity affirmative action, where remedial affirmative action further divides into two subtypes; one subtype simply seeks to end present discrimination and create an equal playing field, the other subtype attempts to compensate for past discrimination and its effects. . . .

---

Affirmative Action
  Its Immediate Goals
   –Outreach
   –Remedying Discrimination
     Putting an End to Discrimination
     Compensating Past Discrimination
   –Diversity
  Its Ultimate Goals
   –A Color-Blind (Racially Just) and
     Gender-free (Sexually Just) Society

**Evidence of Racial Discrimination**

While native-born white males make up only 41 percent of the U.S. population, they comprise 80 percent of all tenured professors, 97 percent of all school superintendents, and 97 percent of senior managerial positions in Fortune 1000 industrial and Fortune 500 service companies. African Americans hold only 0.6 percent, Asian Americans 0.3 percent, and Hispanic Americans 0.4 percent of the senior managerial positions. For 1993, it was estimated that the failure to employ blacks in jobs using simply their *current* skills for that year represented a $137 billion loss to the U.S. economy. This means that rather than being in jobs for which they are underqualified, many blacks are actually *overqualified* for the jobs they hold. One study done in the Los Angeles area found that race and skin color affected the probability of obtaining employment by as much as 52 percent. While whites and light-skinned African Americans were relatively likely to find employment when searching for a job, dark-skinned men were not. In fact, dark-skinned men were twice as likely as others to remain unemployed. According to another study, only 10.3 percent of light-skinned African American men with 13 or more years of schooling were unemployed, compared with 19.4 percent of their dark-skinned counterparts with similar education. Among men who had participated in job-training programs, light-skinned blacks actually had a lower jobless rate than their white counterparts—11.1 percent, compared with 14.5 percent. Yet the rate for dark-skinned African American men with job training was 26.8 percent. Thus, there is plenty of evidence that, at least in the United States, African Americans and other minorities not only are discriminated against but also suffer from the continuing effects of past discrimination. . . .

## A DEFENSE OF DIVERSITY AFFIRMATIVE ACTION

There is [a] type of affirmative action, however, that is not grounded in the ideal of remedying discrimination, whether that discrimination is present or past. The goal of this type of affirmative action is diversity, which in turn is justified either in terms of its educational benefits or its ability to create a more effective workforce in such areas as policing and community relations. The legal roots of this form of affirmative action in the United States are found in *Bakke* (1978).

In *Bakke,* Justice Powell argued that the attainment of a diverse student body was clearly a constitutionally permissible goal for an institution of higher education. According to Powell, in an admissions program that aimed at diversity, "[r]ace or ethnic background may be deemed a 'plus' in a particular applicant's file, yet it does not insulate the individual from comparison with all other candidates for the available seats. . . . The applicant who loses out in the last available seat to another candidate receiving a 'plus' on the basis of ethnic background will not have been foreclosed from all consideration for that seat. . . . It will mean only that his combined qualifications . . . did not outweigh those of the other applicant." Furthermore, an admissions program may "pay some attention to distribution among many types and categories of students," as more than a "token number of blacks" is needed to secure the educational benefits that flow from a racially and ethnically diverse student body.

For almost 20 years, Powell's opinion in *Bakke,* supported by Justices Brennan, Marshall, Blackmun, and White, has been the rationale for the affirmative action used by most American colleges and universities. Even Justice O'Connor, who rejected diversity as a compelling interest for the broadcasting industry in *Metro Broadcasting v. FCC* (1990), has allowed that a state interest in the promotion of diversity has been found sufficiently compelling, at least in the context of higher education.

In 1995, however, the U.S. Court of Appeals for the Fifth Circuit held in *Hopwood v. Texas* that Powell's opinion in *Bakke* is not binding precedent. According to the court, the view that race may be used as a "plus" factor to obtain diversity "garnered only [Powell's] vote and has never represented the view of a majority of the Court in Bakke or any other case." However, it has been generally recognized that the Brennan group (which included Brennan, who wrote the opinion, and Marshall, Blackmun, and White, who endorsed it) did support Powell's view in *Bakke*. In fact, Brennan himself said as much in a subsequent decision. Moreover, the reason why no other case since *Bakke* has supported Powell's view on diversity in education is that no other case since Bakke has dealt with diversity in education.

The *Hopwood* court also ruled that evidence of discrimination in Texas's school system as a whole was not relevant to whether the affirmative action program of the University of Texas law school is justified. Even though, as of May 1994, desegregation suits remained pending against more than 40 Texas school districts, and at the time the *Hopwood* plaintiffs filed suit, the U.S. Office of Civil Rights had not yet determined that the state had desegregated its schools sufficiently to comply with federal civil rights laws, and most of the applicants to the law school had passed through that very same educational system with its alleged inequalities, the *Hopwood* court only allowed the law school at the University of Texas to use evidence of its *own* discrimination to justify engaging in affirmative action. But, as I have argued earlier, once sufficient evidence of discrimination has been provided, there seems to be no reason to impose the additional requirement that the agent engaged in the affirmative action program must be implicated in the discrimination it is seeking to correct.

Interestingly, the *Hopwood* court supported its overall decision on two contradictory claims about race. First, the court claimed that race does make a difference, that we can't assume there would be proportional participation in the absence of past discrimination. But then the court claimed that race does not make a difference, that race is not a good indicator of diversity. We might try to rescue the court from contradiction here by understanding its first claim to refer to an ideal society, and its second to refer to current U.S. society. So understood, the court would be claiming that in an ideal society, race would still make a difference, but in our present society, race does not make a difference. But this would only save the court from a contradiction by committing it to an absurdity. Surely, what we should believe here about actual and ideal societies is exactly the opposite of what the court appears to be claiming. What we should believe about the United States, on the basis of the evidence of past and present discrimination, is that race does make a difference in the kind of life people experience in U.S. society. And what we should believe, or at least hope for, about an ideal society is that in such a society, race will not make a difference because in such a society race will be no more significant than eye color is in most societies. Thus, the *Hopwood* court's decision, based as it is on two contradictory conceptions of race, is deeply flawed.

There have also been two recent district court cases in the state of Michigan that, it turns out, have reached diametrically opposed opinions about the legitimacy of using race as a factor to achieve diversity. In *Gratz v. Bollinger* (2000), the District Court for the Eastern District of Michigan held that under *Bakke*, diversity constitutes a compelling governmental interest that, in the context of education, justifies the use of race as one factor in the admissions process. The court ruled further that the university had provided solid evidence regarding the educational benefits that flow from a racially and ethnically diverse student body.[1] Accordingly, the court found that the university's undergraduate admissions program from 1999 onward satisfies the *Bakke* requirements for a permissible race-conscious affirmative action program. That program uses a 150-point scale and assigns 20 points for membership in one of the identified underrepresented minority categories, as well as points for other factors, such as athletics (20 points) and socioeconomic status (20 points), up to a total of 40 points for such factors. Interestingly, one cannot receive 20 points both for membership in one of the identified underrepresented minority categories and 20 points for socioeconomic disadvantage, but one can receive 20 points for being a nonminority who attended a predominantly minority high school, and one can receive 16 points just for being from the Upper Peninsula of Michigan. At the same time, the court found that an earlier program, which was in place between 1995 and 1998 and which protected a certain number of seats for such groups as athletes, foreign applicants, underrepresented minorities, ROTC candidates, and legacies, did fail the *Bakke* test, but only with respect to its *minority* set-aside. The other set-asides were legally permissible.

By contrast, another judge from the same district court ruled in *Grutter v. Bollinger* (2001) that using race as a factor to achieve diversity was not established as a compelling state interest in *Bakke;* the Brennan group, with its four votes, did not endorse the parts of Powell's opinion that discussed diversity. The court quotes the Brennan group as saying that it "joins Part I and V-C of . . . Powell's opinion." But it goes on to say, "We also agree with Justice Powell that a plan like the 'Harvard' plan is constitutional. . . ." Since the Harvard plan also sets

out the diversity rationale for racial preference, it seems unreasonable to claim that the Brennan group is not also endorsing this aspect of Powell's opinion. As one would expect, however, having denied that Powell's support of diversity in education is a controlling precedent, the court went on to reject the affirmative action program at the law school of the University of Michigan as unconstitutional.[2]

More recently, the *Grutter* district court decision was reversed by the U.S. Court of Appeals for the Sixth Circuit (2002). Earlier, in *Marks v. United States* (1977), the U.S. Supreme Court had argued that "when a fragmented Court decides a case and no single rationale explaining the result enjoys the assent of five Justices, the holding of the Court may be viewed as that position taken by those Members who concurred in the judgments on the narrowest grounds." Applying these instructions from *Marks* to the *Bakke* decision, the Sixth Circuit Court of Appeals found that Powell's opinion represents the holding of the court, arguing that Powell's use of strict scrutiny allows a more limited use of race than Brennan's use of intermediate scrutiny, and so is *Bakke*'s narrowest rationale. The court subsequently ruled that the Michigan law school's affirmative action program met the requirements that Powell set out in his opinion for a justified diversity affirmative action program.

In his dissent to this decision, Judge Boggs argues that Brennan's plurality opinion, rather than Powell's opinion, satisfies the instructions given in *Marks* because Brennan's opinion, not Powell's, would have "invalidated the smaller set of laws." Nevertheless, Boggs does not draw the conclusion that Brennan's plurality opinion is the proper holding for *Bakke*. Instead, he argues that still other interpretations of the instructions given in *Marks* are plausible, and so concludes that *Marks* fails to extract any holding from *Bakke* concerning the constitutionality of diversity affirmative action. Unlike the majority in this case, Boggs refuses to find in Powell's opinion the narrowest possible rationale for justified affirmative action.

Unfortunately, Boggs, as well as the majority in this case, fails to see that there is a straightforward application of *Marks* to *Bakke*. In *Marks,* the majority interpreted its plurality decision in *Memoirs v. Massachusetts* (1966). In that case, three justices wanted to reverse the censorship of a book depicting a prostitute's life on the grounds that while the book was hard-core pornography, the book had *not* been shown to be utterly without redeeming social value. Another justice wanted to reverse the censorship on the grounds that the book had not been shown to be hard-core pornography, and two other justices wanted to reverse the censorship on the grounds that they did not think that hard-core pornography should be prohibited. The U.S. Supreme Court in *Marks* determined that the holding in *Memoirs* was the view of the first three justices, because it would reverse the censorship of the book on the narrowest possible grounds.

If we look now to the *Bakke* case, I think we can find a straightforward application of the U.S. Supreme Court's instructions in *Marks*. In *Bakke,* both Powell and the Brennen group hold that race can be used as a factor in admissions programs for educational institutions. Powell thinks that race can be used as a factor when it is a means to achieving diversity in educational institutions, something he takes to be a constitutionally permissible goal. By contrast, the Brennan group thinks that race can be used as a factor in determining admissions for educational institutions on the grounds that it would help remedy the effects of societal discrimination, a goal the group also takes to be constitutionally permissible. According to *Marks,* the holding in *Memoirs* rejects censorship when hard-core pornography can be shown to have some redeeming social value, but allows censorship for the whole range of cases with respect to which the other members of the plurality opposed

censorship. Similarly, Powell's opinion as the holding in *Bakke* allows the use of race as a factor when it is a means to achieving diversity in educational institutions, but rejects any more sweeping use of race in educational institutions that the Brennan group might have favored. So we have here what seems to be a fairly straightforward application of the instructions in *Marks* to the *Bakke* case. One hopes that now that the U.S. Supreme Court has chosen to hear together the appeals of the *Grutter* decision from the Sixth Circuit and the *Gratz* decision from the district court, it will also recognize how its own instructions in *Marks* show that Powell's opinion is the holding in *Bakke*.

One also hopes that the court will be aware of the impact of shutting down affirmative action programs in education resulting from Proposition 209 and various lower court decisions. In 1996, before Proposition 209 took effect in California, there were 89 Hispanic Americans, 43 African Americans, and 10 American Indians enrolled as first-year students at the top three University of California law schools. In 1997, these numbers fell to 59, 16, and 4, respectively. That year saw only one African American enroll in the freshman law class at Berkeley, where there had been 20 enrolled in the first-year class the year before. At the University of Texas at Austin, whose admissions system was challenged in *Hopwood,* the percentage of African American law students entering dropped from 5.8 percent (29 students) in 1996 to 0.9 percent (6 students) in 1997. American Indian enrollment at the law school dropped from 1.2 percent (6 students) in 1996 to 0.2 percent (1 student) in 1997. Hispanic enrollment dropped from 9.2 percent (46 students) in 1996 to 6.7 percent (31 students) in 1997.

What is particularly disturbing about the criteria for admission that are being used once diversity affirmative action has been declared illegal—criteria that have the effect of significantly limiting minority enrollment—is that they are so tenuously related to the sort of graduates these educational institutions ultimately hope to produce. For example, LSAT scores at the University of Pennsylvania law school have only had a 14 percent correlation with students' first-year grades. Moreover, they do not correlate at all with conventional success in the profession, as measured in terms of income, self-reported satisfaction, and service contributions. Moreover, almost all Michigan law school minority graduates who pass a bar exam go on to have careers that are successful by these conventional measures, something that would not have happened for many of them without affirmative action. Interestingly, Harvard University, in a recent study of its graduates over a 30-year period, found only two correlates of its successful graduates, where success was similarly defined in terms of high income, community involvement, and a satisfying career. Those correlates were blue-collar background and *low* SAT scores.

In addition, following 9/11, the U.S. Justice Department under John Ashcroft has interviewed more than eight thousand people nationwide—the majority of them Middle Eastern men age 18 to 46 who came to the United States within the last two years on nonimmigrant visas—in search of information on terrorist organizations such as al Qaeda. The Justice Department denies that it is engaging in racial or ethnic profiling. According to Assistant Attorney General Michael Chertoff, "What we are looking to are characteristics like country of issuance of passport. . . ."[3] But as Justice Brennan pointed out in an analogous context, "The line between discrimination based on 'ancestry or ethnic characteristics' and discrimination based on 'place or nation of . . . origin' is not a bright one."[4] Thus, if the U.S. government can justify such large-scale uses of "racial and ethnic classifications" for the benefit of the general population, surely it can justify a much more limited use of racial and ethnic classifications to achieve diversity

affirmative action in higher education, given the benefits of such programs to their recipients and to the student body as a whole.

In light of these considerations, therefore, the U.S. Supreme Court should reaffirm the *Bakke* decision, which has been guiding educational institutions in the United States for almost 24 years. The case for nonremedial diversity affirmative action is as strong as it ever was; in fact, it is stronger now that we have studies and reports that prove the benefits of racial diversity in education. Accordingly, diversity affirmative action should be regarded as justified when

1. Race is used as a factor to select from the pool of applicants a sufficient number of qualified applicants to secure the educational benefits that flow from a racially and ethnically diverse student body; and
2. Proponents may admit only those candidates whose qualifications are such that when their selection is combined with a suitably designed educational enhancement program, they will normally turn out, within a reasonably short time, to be as qualified as, or even more qualified than, their peers. . . .

It is also important to distinguish between remedial affirmative action that seeks to compensate for past discrimination (which we have just been discussing) and remedial affirmative action that simply attempts to put an end to present discrimination. With regard to this latter form of affirmative action, there is no need to prove that those who benefit from the affirmative action are those who were discriminated against in the past. *Local 28 of the Sheetmetal Workers Union v. EEOC* (1986) provides us with a clear example of this kind of affirmative action. Similarly, we might view the Banneker Scholarship Program at the University of Maryland at College Park (UMCP) as part of an attempt to put an end to the present effects of past discrimination. Through its Banneker Program, what the UMCP was attempting to do, was improve its poor reputation among the African American community and also eliminate the hostile racial climate that existed on its campus, thereby creating, possibly for the first time, an equal educational opportunity environment for prospective African American students at UMCP. If the university had been successful, the main beneficiaries of its remedial affirmative action program would have been African American students who were subsequently admitted into the university; most of these beneficiaries would not have previously experienced discrimination from the university. This is just what we would expect, given that the main goal of the university's affirmative action program was to eliminate the current effects of past discrimination. Thus, there is no reason to think that those who would thereby benefit would be limited to persons whom the university had actually harmed in the past. Rather, they would be minorities who now, under conditions of equal opportunity, would be admitted to the university roughly in proportion to the availability of prospective African American students in the state of Maryland and in other areas from which the university draws its students. So it is possible to view the UMCP's Banneker Program as part of an attempt to create an equal opportunity playing field from which African Americans would rightly benefit, even if they hadn't been harmed by the university's past discriminatory practices or their effects. In this case, those who would benefit would be those who had just secured their right to equal educational opportunity at the UMCP.

## NOTES

1. Patricia Gurin, "The Compelling Need for Diversity in Higher Education"; *Gratz v. Bollinger* (2000). For additional evidence, see Thomas Weisskoff, "Consequences of Affirmative Action in U.S. Higher Education: A Review of Recent Empirical Studies," *Economic and Political Weekly* 22 (December 2001).

2. Recently, in *Johnson v. Board of Regents of the University System of Georgia* (2001), the U.S. Eleventh Circuit Court of Appeals struck down the Univerisity of Geogia's affirmative action program on the grounds that its pursuit of diversity was not sufficiently narrowly tailored. The court of appeals allowed that the University of Georgia (UG) had used seven factors to measure diversity in 1999, and had added two more—economic disadvantage and academic disadvantage—in 2000, but the court still argued that this was not enough to be narrowly tailored.

3. Michael Chertoff, Testimony before the Senate Judiciary Committee Hearing on Preserving Freedoms While Defending against Terrorism, Federal News Service, 28 November 2001.

4. *St. Francis College v. Al-Khazraji*, 481 U.S. 604 (1987).

# Diversity

*George Sher*

My topic in this article is the argument that preferential treatment is needed to increase diversity in educational institutions and the workplace. Although this argument has achieved considerable currency, and although it is often thought to sidestep the complications that arise when preferential treatment is viewed as a form of compensation, its normative basis has rarely been made explicit. Thus, one aim of my discussion is simply to explore the different forms that the diversity argument can take. However, a further and more substantive aim is to show that its alleged advantages are illusory—that in every version, the appeal to diversity raises difficult questions whose most plausible answers turn on tacit appeals to past wrongdoing.

# I

Justifications of preferential treatment come in two main types. Arguments of one type—often called backward-looking—make essential reference to the discrimination and injustice that blacks, women, and members of certain other groups have suffered in the past. These arguments urge that current group members be given preference in employment or admission to educational institutions to make amends for or rectify the effects of such wrongdoing— to put things right or, as far as possible, "make the victims whole." By contrast, the other type of justification—often called forward-looking—makes *no* essential reference to past wrongdoing, but instead defends preferential treatment entirely as a means to some desirable future goal. Even when the goal is to eliminate inequalities or disadvantages that *were in fact* caused by past wrongdoing, the reason for eliminating them is not *that* they were caused by past wrongdoing. Rather, their continued existence is said to violate some purely *non*historical principle or ideal—for example, the principle of utility or some ideal of equality.

Of the two types of argument, the forward-looking type is often viewed as more straightforward. Those who look exclusively to the future are spared both the daunting task of documenting the effects of past injustice on specific individuals and the even more diffi-

cult task of specifying *how much* better off any given individual would now be in its absence. In a more theoretical vein, they need not answer the troublesome question of whether (and if so why) we must compensate persons who would not even have existed, and so *a fortiori* would not be better off, if historical wrongs such as slavery had not taken place; and neither need they specify how many generations must elapse before claims to compensation lose their force. Perhaps for these reasons, defenders of preferential treatment seem increasingly inclined to eschew the backward-looking approach and to cast their lot with forward-looking arguments.

It seems to me, however, that this strategy is badly misguided for two distinct but related reasons: first, because the forward-looking defenses of preferential treatment are only superficially less problematic than their backward-looking counterparts, and, second, because the most promising way of rectifying their inadequacies is to reintroduce precisely the sorts of reference to the past that their proponents have sought to avoid. . . .

If selecting a less-than-best-qualified applicant is to be an acceptable way of promoting utility when the chosen applicant is black or female but not when that applicant is white male, the reason is very likely to be that blacks and women, but not white males, were often treated unjustly in the past. . . .

My topic here, however, is neither the general contrast between the forward- and backward-looking defenses of preferential treatment nor the prospects for mounting a successful utilitarian or egalitarian defense. Instead, I mention these matters only to frame what I want to say about a different forward-looking defense that has recently come to the fore. This new defense is, of course, the one I mentioned at the outset—the argument that preferential treatment is justified by the need to promote racial, sexual, and ethnic diversity in such crucial sectors of our society as the academy and the workplace. A bit more precisely, it is the argument that preferential treatment is justified when, and because, it moves us closer to a situation in which the holders of every (desirable) type of job and position include representatives of all racial, sexual, and ethnic groups in rough proportion to their overall numbers.

The rhetoric of this new argument is all around us . . . .

## II

I can envision four possible ways of arguing that racial, sexual, and ethnic diversity is morally important. To show this, someone might argue that such diversity is either (1) a requirement of justice or (2) intrinsically valuable or (3) conducive to the general welfare or (4) conducive to some value *other* than well-being. However, as we will see, each version of the diversity argument remains vulnerable to essentially the same objection that I advanced against the other forward-looking defenses of preferential treatment—namely, that when we ask why the argument focuses only on certain groups, we are invariably thrown back on the injustice or discrimination that their past members have suffered.

Consider first the claim that diversity is a requirement of justice. To defend this claim, one must first specify the relevant conception of justice and then show why it requires that every desirable job and position be distributed among all racial, sexual and ethnic groups in rough proportion to their numbers. Although there are obviously many ways of filling in the blanks, I shall consider only two that I think may actually exert some influence. Of these two proposals, one construes racial, sexual, and ethnic groups as morally fundamental entities with claims of justice of their own, while the other takes these groups to be only derivatively relevant.

Suppose, first, that racial, sexual, and ethnic groups do themselves have claims of justice; and suppose, further, that the best theory of justice is egalitarian. In that case, the best theory of justice will require that all racial, sexual, and ethnic groups be made roughly equally well off. Because such groups are not organized entities, and so are incapable either of having experiences or of pursuing goals, their well-being cannot reside either in the quality of their subjective states or in their success in achieving their goals. Instead, each group's well-being must be a function of the well-being of its individual members, which in turn can be expected to vary with the members' income and social standing. Because these connections hold, any society that wishes to implement a conception of justice that requires that all racial, sexual, and ethnic groups be made equally well off may indeed have to distribute all desirable jobs and positions among all relevant groups in rough proportion to their numbers.

Here, then, is one way of grounding the case for racial, sexual, and ethnic diversity in a broader conception of justice. But should we accept this argument? Elsewhere, I have contended that racial, sexual, and ethnic groups are in fact *un*likely to have independent claims of justice;[1] I also doubt that the best theory of justice is straightforwardly egalitarian. However, in the current discussion, I shall simply grant both premises and focus only on the argument's further assumption that not all groups, but only some subset that includes racial, sexual, and ethnic groups, have independent claims of justice.

Why exactly, must the argument make this further assumption? One answer is simply that if enough other groups *did* have independent claims of justice, then even distributing every desirable position among all racial, sexual, and ethnic groups in exact proportion to their numbers would at best eliminate only a small fraction of a society's unjust inequalities. However, while this answer is not wrong, it does not go far enough. The more decisive answer is that if enough other groups also had independent claims of justice, then no increase in a society's diversity could bring *any* increase in its overall justice . . . .

There are, of course, many other possible ways of arguing that mixed groups lack the moral status of racial, sexual, and ethnic groups. Thus, the mere fact that the cited arguments fail is hardly decisive. Still, in the absence of any better argument, the best explanation of the impulse to single out certain racial, sexual, and ethnic groups is again that it reflects a desire to make amends for (or rectify the lingering effects of) the discrimination that their past members have suffered. As Paul Taylor has put it, the guiding thought appears to be that the relevant groups were "as it were, *created* by the original unjust practice[s]."[2] I think, in fact, that this way of formulating the moral importance of past injustice is highly misleading, but I shall not argue that point here. Instead, in keeping with my broader theme, I shall simply observe that if anyone *were* to elaborate the diversity argument in these terms, he would be abandoning all pretense that his argument is purely forward-looking.

## III

What, next, of the suggestion that racial, sexual, and ethnic diversity is a requirement of justice for individuals? Unlike its predecessor, this suggestion does not presuppose a problematic moral ontology. Yet just because the suggestion does not construe groups as morally fundamental, it raises a difficult new question—namely, why should justice for individuals call for *any* special distribution of positions among groups?

Although this question, too, can be answered in various ways, I shall consider only the single answer that I think proponents of diversity would be most likely to give. Put most briefly, that answer is, first, that the operative principle of justice is one of equality of opportunity, and, second, that a lack of racial, sexual, and ethnic diversity is significant precisely because it shows that opportunities remain *un*equal. Even though legal barriers are a thing of a past, the fact that relatively few blacks, women, and members of other minorities hold well-paying, authoritative positions is often viewed as compelling evidence that the members of these groups have lacked, and continue to lack, equal opportunity. That in turn may be thought to show that using preferential treatment to bring about their representation within desirable professions in proportion to their numbers is justified by the fact that it will make opportunities *more* equal. . . .

This observation does not show that such uses of preferential treatment cannot make opportunities more equal; but it does show that any relevant gains must be long term rather than immediate. The point must be not that opportunities will be more equal *when* the preferential treatment is used, but rather that they will be more equal *afterward*. This will be true (the argument must run) because the proportional distribution of desirable positions among all racial, sexual, and ethnic groups will convey to the members of previously excluded groups the message that people like them can successfully acquire and hold such positions, and that in turn will raise the aspirations of many. Because this reasoning appeals to the effects of diversity upon the motivation of future group members, it is, in essence, a variant of the familiar "role model" argument. . . .

If all preferences and attitudes were either innate or else the results of past wrongdoing, we could end this part of our discussion here. However, in fact, these alternatives are not exhaustive. Many people have acquired their current attitudes from cultures that did *not* evolve in response to wrongdoing or oppression; and such attitudes, too, can lead the relevant groups to be underrepresented within professions. It may be, for example, that the reason relatively few members of a given group have pursued careers that require academic success or extended training is simply that the group's culture, which was shaped by its earlier agrarian lifestyle, does not attach much value to education. If internalizing this attitude also counts as being denied equal opportunity, and if increasing the group's presence within various professions would help eventually to dispel the attitude, then using preferential treatment to promote such diversity may indeed be justified on purely forward-looking grounds.

How significant is the challenge to my thesis that every ostensibly forward-looking defense of diversity has a backward-looking core? That depends I think, on the answers to several further questions. It depends, most obviously, on whether equal opportunity *does* require that no one be brought up in a culture that instills attitudes unconducive to success in the modern world; but it depends, as well, on whether equal opportunity trumps respect for ancestral cultures; whether increasing diversity would effectively diminish the transmission of counterproductive attitudes; and whether, even if it would, we can more effectively alter these attitudes in some other way. . . . Thus, pending further discussion, this issue must simply remain unresolved.

## IV

So far, I have discussed only the first of the four possible arguments for racial, sexual, and ethnic diversity. That argument, which construes such diversity as a requirement of justice, predictably raised a variety of complications. By contrast, the second and third arguments—that diversity is intrinsically valuable and that it is conducive to the general welfare—raise fewer new issues and so can be dealt with much more quickly.

The challenge to someone who holds that racial, sexual, and ethnic diversity is *intrinsically* valuable is to provide some justification of this claim that goes beyond the bare fact that he believes it. He cannot simply assert that the claim is self-evident because such assertions are equally available to his opponents; yet once we ask what else can be said, we almost immediately run out of argument. I say "almost immediately" because many of the metaphors that are commonly used in this connection—for example, descriptions of a diverse society as a tapestry or a "gorgeous mosaic"—can themselves be viewed as arguments that the relevant intrinsic values are familiar aesthetic ones. However, I hope it goes without saying that the aesthetic appeal of a given pattern of distribution is not a proper basis for any decision about social policy.

Because the appeal to intrinsic value is essentially a nonargument, I cannot pinpoint the exact place at which it goes historical. Yet just because that appeal has so little to recommend it, the best explanation of whatever influence it has—and, though I cannot prove it, I think it does have some influence—is again that it provides cover for a policy whose real aim is to benefit members of unjustly disadvantaged groups.

The third possible argument for diversity—that it is conducive to the general welfare—is very different; for unlike the appeal to intrinsic value, this argument can be developed in various ways. One obvious possibility is to exploit our earlier observation that the members of many racial, sexual, and ethnic groups identify strongly with the fortunes and accomplishments of other group members; for given this mutual identification, increasing diversity will benefit not only those group members who actually gain prestigious, well-paying positions, but also the many others who take pride and pleasure in their success. Alternatively or in addition, it can be argued that working closely with members of unfamiliar groups breaks down barriers and disrupts stereotypes, and that increasing racial, sexual, and ethnic diversity will therefore increase overall well-being by fostering understanding and harmony.

Because diversity yields these and other benefits, there is an obvious case for the use of preferential treatment to promote it. However, when the issue is framed in these terms, the diversity argument is no longer an alternative to a utilitarian defense of preferential treatment, but rather is itself such a defense. Despite its interposition of diversity, its essential message is precisely that preferential treatment is justified by its beneficial consequences. Thus, if my conjecture about the other utilitiarian defenses was correct—if the disparity between the difficulties they confront and the confidence with which they are advanced suggests that their proponents' real impulse is compensatory—then that conjecture must apply here too.

# V

That leaves only the fourth argument for diversity's importance—the argument that it promotes some value *other* than well-being. Although there are many nonwelfarist values to which appeal might theoretically be made, the only live version of this argument is one that appeals to the intellectual values of the academy.

That increasing racial, sexual, and ethnic diversity will advance the academic enterprise is an article of faith among many academics. Neil Rudenstine, the president of Harvard, expressed the conventional wisdom this way: "A diverse educational environment challenges [students] to explore ideas and arguments at a deeper level—to see issues from various sides, to rethink their own premises, to achieve the kind of understanding that comes only from testing their own hypotheses against those of people with other views."[3] Although these claims obviously do not support all forms of preferential treatment—they are, for example, irrelevant both to nonacademic hiring and to contractual "set-asides"—they do purport to justify, through an appeal to values internal to the academy's own mission, both preferential admission to many educational institutions and preferential hiring across the curricular spectrum.

Like many of the other arguments we have considered, this one can itself be fleshed out in various ways. Some of its proponents, including Rudenstine himself, stress the value *to students* of exposure to different perspectives, while others stress the value of diversity in research. Of those who focus on research, some argue that including hitherto excluded groups will open up new areas of investigation, while others emphasize the value of diverse challenges to all hypotheses, including, or especially, hypotheses in traditional, well-worked areas. Of those who emphasize challenges to hypotheses, some stress the importance of confronting all hypotheses with the broadest possible range of potentially falsifying tests, while others focus on exposing the hidden biases of investigators. Because the appeal to diversity's contribution to intellectual inquiry is so protean, I cannot work systematically through its variants, but will pose only a single question that applies to each. That question, predictably enough, is why we should single out the contributions of any small set of groups such as those on the official Affirmative Action list.

For even if diversity yields every one of the intellectual benefits that are claimed for it, why should we benefit most when the scholarly community contains substantial numbers of blacks, women, Hispanics, (American) Indians, Aleuts, and Chinese Americans? Why not focus instead, or in addition, on Americans of Eastern European, Arabic, or (Asian) Indian extraction? For that matter, can't we achieve even greater benefit by extending preference to *native* Africans, Asians, Arabs, and Europeans? And why understand diversity only in terms of gender, ethnicity, and national origin? Why should a population that is diverse in this dimension provide any more educational or scholarly benefit than one that is ethnically homogeneous but includes suitable number of gays, religious fundamentalists, the young, the old, the handicapped, ex-military officers, conservatives, Marxists, Mormons, and blue-collar workers? These groups, too, have characteristic concerns, types of experience, and outlooks on the world. . . .

The most salient feature of the groups on the official list is of course the discrimination they have suffered. This may not entirely explain why just these groups are included—that may in part be traceable to the play of political forces—but it does explain the prominence of such core groups as blacks and women. This strongly suggests that the current argument is also covertly backward-looking. However, before we can draw this conclusion, we must consider an important alternative—namely, that the real reason for concentrating on previously oppressed groups is not that their members alone are owed compensation, but rather that beliefs and attitudes shaped by oppression are better suited than others to advance educational or scholarly aims.

For although we obviously cannot assume that all the members of any group think alike, a history of discrimination may indeed affect the way many of a group's members tend to view the world. In addition to the already-noted high degree of collective identification, the perspective of the oppressed is often said to include a keen awareness of the motives, prejudices, and hidden agendas of others, a heightened sense of the oppressive effects of even seemingly benign social structures, and

a strong commitment to social change. As a corollary, that perspective may include a degree of antagonism toward received opinion and a certain impatience with abstraction. Thus, the question that remains to be addressed is whether, and if so how, any of these beliefs, attitudes, or traits might make a special contribution to education or research. . . .

Yet while such knowledge may contribute significantly to mutual understanding and social harmony, the beliefs, attitudes, traits, and experiences that are characteristic of oppressed groups are in the end only one class of facts among innumerable others. Considered simply as objects of study—and that is how we must consider them if the current argument is not to be yet another tributary of the great utilitarian river—the beliefs, attitudes, traits, and experiences of the oppressed are no more important than those of the nonoppressed, which in turn are no more important than indefinitely many other possible objects of inquiry.

Thus, to give their variant of the argument a fighting chance, those who attach special educational and scholarly value to the perspective of the oppressed must take the other path. They must locate its special educational or scholarly value not in anyone's *coming to know* that oppressed groups hold certain beliefs, attitudes, etc., but rather in the contribution of those beliefs and attitudes to the acquisition of *other* knowledge. Their argument must be that this perspective uniquely enhances our collective ability to pose or resolve questions across much of the intellectual spectrum. To show that the perspective of the oppressed generates new lines of inquiry, friends of diversity often cite the tendency of women to pursue scientific research with humanitarian rather than militaristic applications and the contributions that various minorities have made to history and other fields by studying their own past and present. To show that this perspective contributes to the investigation of established topics, they point out that black and female investigators tend to be specially attuned to the inclusion of blacks and women in experimental control groups, that black students bring to the study of law a well-founded mistrust of the police, and that enhanced sensitivity to power relations has opened up fruitful new ways of interpreting literary texts.

We certainly must agree that the beliefs, attitudes, and traits of oppressed groups have made important contributions to the way academic questions are now formulated and addressed. However, what friends of diversity must show is not merely that these beliefs, attitudes, and traits make *some* significant contribution to effective inquiry, but that they are *more* conducive to it, all things considered, than any of the alternative mixtures that would emerge if there were no Affirmative Action or if preference were given to other sorts of groups. . . .

My own view is that we will make the most progress if we simply stock the academy with persons who display the traditional academic excellences to the highest degree. The students and faculty members who are most likely to help us progress toward true beliefs, powerful explanations, deep understanding, and a synoptic worldview are just the ones with the greatest analytical ability, the most imagination, the best memory, and the strongest desire to pursue the truth wherever it leads. However, while these are things that I deeply believe, my argument does not require any premise this strong. Instead, it requires only the much weaker premise that indefinitely many traits of intellect or character are sometimes useful in advancing cognitive or pedagogical aims, and that we have no reason to expect the beliefs and attitudes of the oppressed to be preeminent among these.

This reasoning of course presupposes that the aims of the academy *are* to be understood in terms of truth, understanding, explanation, and the rest. If they are not—if, for example, the basic aim is instead to promote social change—then the case for favoring the beliefs and attitudes of the oppressed may well be stronger. However, if someone does take the basic aim to be social change, and if he urges the hiring and admission of more members of oppressed groups to expedite the desired changes, then he will no longer be appealing to the very academic values that even his opponents share. He will, instead, be mounting an appeal to some further conception of social justice—one whose evaluation must await its more precise articulation. Thus, pending further discussion, my main thesis—that every major defense of diversity is either incomplete or backward-looking—remains intact. . . .

## VI

The motivation I have stressed—a desire to rationalize the use of preferential treatment to benefit members of previously wronged groups—is a complex mixture of the admirable and the base. It is admirable because it reflects a high-minded conception of what justice requires, base because it substitutes the use of half-truths, half-arguments, and persuasive slogans for a frank willingness to acknowledge what is really at stake. In fact, compensatory justice *is* immensely problematic, and the moral status of preferential treatment is immensely problematic too. We do not advance the cause of justice, but only degrade public discourse, if we blur these difficulties instead of seeking to overcome them.

## NOTES

1. The argument appears in "Groups and Justice," *Ethics* 87, no. 1 (October 1977): 81–87; reprinted in *Approximate Justice*, pp. 55–64.

2. Paul W. Taylor, "Reverse Discrimination and Compensatory Justice," in *The Affirmative Action Debate,* ed. Steven M. Cahn (New York: Routledge, 1995), 14.

3. Neil L. Rudenstine, "Why a Diverse Student Body Is So Important." *Chronicle of Higher Education* (April 19, 1996): B1.

## SEXUAL HARRASMENT

# Sexual Harassment and Solidarity

*Larry May*

Sexual harassment, like rape, seems obviously wrong. Yet, many men are not as willing to condemn it as they are willing to condemn rape. In part, this is no doubt due to the fact that it is less clear what are the boundaries of the concept of harassment, where some putative forms of harassment are not easily distinguished from "horseplay" or pranksterism. But it may also be due to the fact that men are reluctant to condemn practices which have for so long functioned to build solidarity among men. The *Playboy* centerfold pinned to the bulletin board at a workplace has at least two functions. It is a constant source of erotic stimulation for the men who work there; and it is a constant source of embarrassment and annoyance for many of the women, a clear sign that this is not the kind of place for them, but that it is a place for men.

In this chapter I wish to examine sexual harassment in its various forms, seeking a basis for moral criticism of it. In addition to more standard criticisms, largely parallel to those developed in law, I offer a new critique that calls attention to the way that sexual harassment promotes male solidarity and also thereby often excludes women from full and equal participation in various practices and contexts. At the end of the chapter I discuss positive aspects of male solidarity and indicate why sexual

harassment is not a good basis for such solidarity. Men need to feel good about who they are as men, not on the model of little boys retreating to a clubhouse with a "no girls allowed" sign on the door, but on the model of reformed alcoholics who are now so changed that they are not afraid to discuss their past problems with others as well as among themselves.

## SEXUAL INTIMIDATION

The case of *Alexander v. Yale University* was the first sexual harassment lawsuit to concern an educational rather than a workplace setting.[1] The case concerned a female student at Yale University who alleged that one of her male political science professors threatened to *lower* her grade on a term paper (from a B to a C) unless she slept with him. The student, who was hoping to go to law school, felt intimidated by the proposal but did not capitulate. After her initial accusation, other women came forward with similar stories about this particular political science professor. The professor denied these other charges but admitted discussing grades with the student who sued. He claimed that he had offered to *raise* the student's grade (from a C to a B) if she slept with him, but that she had simply declined his offer. Since, on his view, the grade had remained what the student had earned, no harm had been done to the student. No foul, no harm.

This case raised difficulties with the way that sexual harassment had been previously understood. Previously, sexual harassment was thought by the courts to involve five elements:

1. a sexual advance
2. by a person in a more powerful position
3. made to a person in a less powerful position
4. against the second person's will
5. which adversely affected
   a. retention of job
   b. evaluation or
   c. promotion.

At least according to the version of the story told by the political science professor, the student had not been adversely affected, and so the fifth element of sexual harassment was not present.

Sexual harassment was understood to be harmful in that it constituted an unjustified form of intimidation, much like blackmail. But the attorneys who defended the Yale student felt that a different model was needed given the group-oriented nature of the offense. So they seized on the idea that sexual harassment like that directed at the student was a form of sex discrimination and thus harmful as a form of degradation. But what if the facts were as alleged by the professor, was there any discrimination against or degradation of the student? This seemed not to be like blackmail, since there was no clear indication that she would be rendered worse off if she turned down the professor's proposal.

If the facts were as the student alleged, then this was an egregious case of sexual intimidation. No one who understands the purpose of educational institutions would countenance the idea of a male professor threatening to give a student less than she deserved unless the student did something so utterly outside the realm of academic achievement as providing sexual favors. Worse than this is the idea of a male professor abusing his power and authority over often naive students for his own personal gain. And worse yet is the idea that a man could extort sex from an otherwise unwilling female by threatening to do something undeserved to harm her career prospects. For all these reasons, sexual harassment of the sort alleged by the student is clearly morally wrong.

If we believe the male political science professor, something morally wrong has occurred as well, although somewhat less clearly so. On his version he offered to give the student a grade better than she deserves, and so he seemingly did not threaten to harm her undeservedly. But there was an indication that the female student may have been harmed which can be seen in that she would not have wanted to have such proposals made in the first place. The student was put in the position of having her sexuality count as a basis of academic achievement. This had a negative impact on the educational environment in which the student resided. I have elsewhere argued that this was indeed a form of sex discrimination which effectively coerced the student, even though there was no direct threat to her, at least if we believe the professor's story.[2]

The professor's "offer" changes the range of options that the student previously had in a way which makes her post-offer situation worse than it was in the pre-offer state. The student could no longer proceed as before, thinking of her options in a purely academic way. And in this sense she is disadvantaged, perhaps even coerced, in that she is made to accept a set of options that she would not otherwise choose. When such proposals get made, the well is poisoned, and it is no longer possible for the student to think of herself as merely a student and not also as a sex object.[3] In the case of sexual harassment, seen as either a direct threat or as a seemingly innocent sexual offer, harm has occurred.

Laurence Thomas has challenged my analysis of sexual harassment in offer situation. He contends that not all examples of sexual offers contain veiled threats or can be characterized as situations that the woman would prefer not to be in. He gives an example: "Deborah is Peter's secretary. Peter offers to pay Deborah so many dollars per week, in addition to her present salary, if she would be his exclusive sexual partner. The money would come out of his own pocket."[4] Thomas stipulates that there is no veiled threat here, and no one is under psychological duress. In the case in question. Thomas "is not inclined to think that there is a moral wrong here." His rationale is expressed in this blunt statement: "It simply cannot be the case that we should not enter into any interaction if there is the possibility that it might become morally explosive."

It seems to me, however, that Peter has done something morally suspect by introducing sex into the workplace. Even though Deborah can take the offer or leave it, she cannot, on her own, return to a situation where her relationship with Peter was strictly professional. By turning the offer down, she does not return to the previous state of affairs because of the way that Peter's offer has changed the relationship between them and set the stage for abuse of Peter's authority. This much Thomas admits; yet he claims that we cannot stop acting just because it might turn out that abuse could occur. But he has focused on only one aspect of the problem, the possibility that things might turn ugly. What he has missed is that the relationship has changed, nearly irrevocably, in a way that is out of Deborah's control.

In some cases of sexual offers, or sexual innuendos, nothing straightforwardly coercive occurs, but there may be reason nonetheless to think that a moral wrong has occurred. The moral wrong concerns the way that a person's options are restricted against that person's will.

It is morally wrong not only to make a person's options worse than they were before, but also to limit them undeservedly if this is against the person's will. In this latter case, it is not the worsening of the situation but rather the way that it is undeservedly taken out of the control of the woman which makes it morally suspect. To put the point starkly, sexual harassment normally involves a restriction of options which also restricts autonomy. In the straightforwardly coercive cases of sexual harassment, autonomy is restricted because a woman is forced to accede to a man's wishes or risk harm to herself. In some subtler cases of sexual harassment, autonomy is restricted in that a change in relationship is effected against the wishes of the woman, possibly to her detriment. But even if it is not to her detriment, she has been undeservedly forced into a situation that she has not chosen. In the next sections I will explore in more detail the moral harms of some of the subtle cases of sexual harassment.

## HOSTILE ENVIRONMENTS

In 1993 the United States Supreme Court gave its clearest support to a relatively new basis for understanding the harm of sexual harassment which is closer to the basis I have just suggested than is the intimidation model, although with several important differences. The Court carefully enunciated a doctrine that held that sexual harassment can be harmful in that it produces a hostile or abusive work environment for a person because of her gender.[5] I want to explore various theoretical issues that are implicated in this new approach to sexual harassment, where the older model of intimidation and blackmail is by and large abandoned. I am especially interested in how this new model affects our understanding of male behavior in educational and workplace settings.

Here are some of the relevant facts of the case of *Harris v. Forklift Systems Inc.*

Teresa Harris worked as a manager at Forklift Systems Inc., an equipment rental company, from April 1985 until 1987. Charles Hardy was Forklift's president. The magistrate found that, throughout Harris's time at Forklift, Hardy often insulted her because of her gender and often made her the target of unwanted sexual innuendos. Hardy told Harris on several occasions, in the presence of other employees, "You're a woman, what do you know" and "We need a man as the rental manager"; at least once, he told her she was " a dumb ass woman." Again, in front of others, he suggested that the two of them "go to the Holiday Inn to negotiate [Harris's] raise." Hardy occasionally asked Harris and other female employees to get coins from his front pants pocket. He threw objects on the ground in front of Harris and other women, and asked them to pick them up. He made sexual innuendos about Harris's and other women's clothing.[6]

This pattern of harassment was not aimed at extracting a particular form of behavior, such as a sexual favor. It was not straightforwardly coercive, but nonetheless something seems morally wrong about Hardy's actions.

What Hardy did was to create an environment in which it was very difficult for his female employees to be taken seriously as equals to their male counterparts. Justice Sandra Day O'Connor, delivering the opinion of the court, considered this case an example of a "discriminatorily abusive work environment." This new standard "takes a middle path between making actionable any conduct that is merely offensive, and requiring the conduct to cause a tangible psychological injury." A hostile environment is, according to O'Connor, not something that can be defined with mathematical precision, but it can be determined by "looking at . . . the frequency of the discriminatory conduct; its severity; whether it is physically threatening or humiliating, or a more offensive utterance; and whether it unreasonably interferes with an employee's work performance."

The harm of a hostile work environment is relatively clear. Again, according to O'Connor, a "discriminatorily abusive work environment, even one that does not seriously affect employees' psychological well-being, can and often will detract from employees' job performance, discourage employees from remaining on the job, or keep them from advancing in their careers." Even without a showing of these specific harms, O'Connor rightly pointed to the denial of "workplace equality" which is broadly guaranteed by Title VII of the Civil Rights Act of 1964.[7] The key here is that this form of behavior treats men differently from women, subjecting only the women to these risks.

The chief harm of sexual harassment is indeed that it discriminates against women by subjecting women to "run a gauntlet of sexual abuse in return for the privilege of being allowed to work and make a living"[8] and thereby demeans them. Sexual harassment, even of the more subtle variety, normally changes the work environment against the wishes of the women. And this creates a difference between male and female employees. Women are forced to be seen as both workers and sexual objects, while men are free either to be seen as only workers or to be seen as workers and sexual objects. The environmental change effected by sexual harassment discriminates against women, generally to their detriment.

What if the changes in the work environment are welcome? What if a particular woman wishes to be able to advance by the use of sexual favors? To go back to Thomas's example, what if Deborah wishes to be able to supplement her income by doing sexual favors, on the side, for her boss? Does it still make sense to say that the environment is discriminatory? I believe the answer to this question is yes. But I'm not so sure that the environment is always hostile or abusive. In order to see this one needs to think about the way that women in the workplace, or in an educational setting, will be affected as a group. The environment is discriminatory because of the way that only women have had their options restricted in respect to the kind of relationships they can have with their male bosses. Normally only women, not men, are the ones whose appearance and sexual characteristics matter and who will be judged according to non-work-related, sexual criteria.

In my view the court has done well to focus on the discriminatory environment, rather than intimidation, created by even subtle examples of sexual harassment. But it has potentially led us astray by calling that environment hostile or abusive. Surely in the most egregious cases, such as that of Charles Hardy and Teresa Harris at Forklift Systems Inc., the discriminatory work environment does become abusive. But in the more subtle cases, this is not necessarily so, and yet the environment is still discriminatory, and morally suspect for that reason. When more subtle forms of sexual harassment occur, such as when a *Playboy* centerfold is displayed in a common room, women are treated in a way that men are not, and even if some women find this to be welcome it still puts them at a competitive disadvantage in terms of being taken as seriously as their male counterparts with regard to job performance. Their sexuality is considered, illegitimately, to be relevant to job performance, and other, legitimate, bases of job performance are put on the same level as this illegitimate basis, thereby tainting the legitimate bases. This situation has been forced upon them and is, generally speaking, contrary to the autonomy of the women in question.

Sex discrimination can be morally wrong on at least three counts: women are degraded; they are treated unfairly; or they are denied a certain amount of autonomy over their lives. When women seem to welcome differential status in a given context, as in the case of Deborah welcoming the opportunity to make more

money by sleeping with her boss, it can appear that women are gaining autonomy rather than losing it. But this is not the case. For what is being lost is the choice of whether to be treated only as a worker and not also as a sex object. In most contexts this loss of control brings more harm to the woman's autonomy than the possible gain from being given more attention or allowed to use one's sexuality to gain certain advantages. What counts as "job related" or "meritorious" has undergone a sometimes subtle shift, to the detriment of women workers.

## FEMALE EXCLUSION FROM FULL PARTICIPATION

One of the things often ignored in discussions of sexual harassment is how it promotes male solidarity, especially a solidarity that keeps women in an inferior position and excludes them from full and equal participation in a practice. Think of a very minor form of sexual harassment, at least as compared to that suffered in the *Harris* or *Alexander* cases, namely, a *Playboy* centerfold placed on a locker door in an employee work area. Such an act is not likely to cause serious psychological distress to female employees, and it is not some kind of quid pro quo attempt to extort sexual favors. Nevertheless it resembles these more egregious acts in excluding women from full and equal participation in a work environment with their male colleagues, as we will see.

How is it that even such seemingly innocuous acts as posting the *Playboy* centerfold in a common area can contribute to a form of male bonding and solidarity that is aimed at, or at least has the known effect of, making females feel unwelcome? My analysis is explicitly group oriented. The various forms of sexual harassment share, it seems to me, the effect of creating an environment in which women feel excluded. In this respect sexual harassment is best understood as a harm perpetrated by men against women. To see why this is a group-based problem as well as an interpersonal problem, one needs to recognize that putting the poster on the wall is a signal to any woman who enters the room that women are to be viewed as comparable to the woman in the centerfold picture—to be gawked at, drooled over, and reduced to the measurements of their breasts and buttocks—not welcome here as equals to men.

Even in the most egregious cases, sexual harassment often appears to be merely an interpersonal problem. One party, typically a male, is proposing sex to another party, typically a female, and the female does not welcome such a proposal. But again, one needs to realize that in many of these cases, including *Alexander v. Yale* and *Harris v. Forklift Systems Inc.,* the woman who sues is normally not the only one being harassed. Other female students or employees often come forward to allege the same behavior toward them by the same male. The multiple victims of sexual harassers make it unlikely that theirs is only an interpersonal problem between an individual male and an individual female.

The type of behavior characteristic of sexual harassment rarely relates to the differences of individual women. The underlying attitudes of the men in question are contempt or at least condescension toward all or most women, not merely toward the one who is currently being harassed. In the next section we will see in more detail how this works when we examine the case of a heterosexual male who harasses a homosexual male. The thing that links the two cases is that exclusion is occurring because a person fails to occupy a certain category, not because of one's unique characteristics. A group-based harm has occurred whenever there is harm directed at a person because of features that that person shares with other members of a group.

Indeed, it is common for sexual harassment to promote male solidarity in educational or employment contexts. Think again of the *Playboy* centerfold displayed in a prominent place in an auto mechanic's work area. If a woman should stray into the work area by mistake or in order to find the mechanic working on her car, she will be alerted right away that this is a male-only domain. Indeed, it may be the practice of the fellow mechanics to touch the breasts of the woman in the picture or to pat her buttocks as they enter or leave the work area, especially when women are present. Here is a good example of how pornographic images can be used to isolate women and separate them from men, but this image also solidifies bonds of men with men. Such a practice is obviously much less morally offensive than actually touching the breasts or patting the buttocks of real women in the workplace. But these practices serve as a reminder that the same thing could happen to women who stumble into the wrong place at the wrong time.

Here is another case. A male graduate student displays a *Playboy* centerfold on a bulletin board in an office that houses half a dozen teaching assistants in philosophy, some of whom are women. The male students gather and comment on the physical dimensions of the centerfold woman's breasts and buttocks, laughing and joking and comparing the dimensions of the centerfold woman to those of their fellow female graduate students. The women find this behavior either annoying or humiliating or both. One woman finds it increasingly difficult to go into the office, knowing that her male colleagues may be discussing the dimensions of her breasts and buttocks. Another woman who complains finds herself the subject of ridicule for her lack of camaraderie.

In both of these cases male bonding and solidarity are furthered by excluding women from full and equal participation. Of course, it is not necessarily the intention of these men or of these practices to exclude women, although this is at least a reasonable thing to expect. The exclusion is by and large the unintended, but foreseen, consequence of the practices that build solidarity. But this is not a necessary result of building male solidarity, as we will see in the final section of this chapter. Indeed, men often find themselves today under siege because their practices of bonding have so publicly excluded women in ways that have deprived women of opportunities to advance, compete, and cooperate in the larger society. Men have been challenged in this domain, both in the courts and in various other public forums. It is not male solidarity that is the culprit, but the forms of harassment that have both supported the bonding between men, and also excluded women from full and equal participation with males.

One may wonder if it is always wrong for one group to adopt practices that have the effect of excluding another group. To answer this question one needs to think seriously about the moral principles that would be implicated in such exclusion. Exclusion is not always morally wrong or even suspect. But when exclusion affects a whole category of people and there is no reasonable basis for it, then it is morally suspect. The principle of moral equality is implicated whenever like cases are not treated alike. Excluding one group of people from a domain without good reason is a paradigmatic example of morally suspicious treatment. While it is obviously quite common for one group of people to exclude another group, moral criticism is appropriate when the exclusion is done for arbitrary reasons, especially if it perpetuates a pattern of exclusion in the larger society.

Is it necessary that there be a past pattern of exclusion for a current particular instance of sexual harassment to constitute group-based harm to women? This is a complex question that cannot be easily answered. Implicated here is the question whether harassment of a man by a female superior would constitute harm to men as a group. In part the answer could be obvious. If the man is sexually harassed merely for being a man, where other men have been similarly treated, then the man is clearly harmed in a discriminatory way and, in some sense, so are men as a group. But without the pattern of adverse treatment it is unclear that men as a group are *significantly* harmed by this seemingly isolated act by a woman. What makes sexual harassment a form of morally harmful sexual discrimination is that it contributes to a particular pattern of subordination. . . .

## DISCRIMINATION AND HARASSMENT

I wish to investigate two cases of harassment that complicate the preceding analysis because of the sexual orientation of the people involved. I begin with a brief examination of a hypothetical case, then move on to a more developed treatment of an actual case and a variation on that case. The first case involves a bisexual man who harasses both men and women indifferently. The second case is that of a heterosexual man who harasses another man whom he believes to be a homosexual. A consideration of these cases will allow us to achieve a more adequate understanding of the moral harm involved in excluding someone on grounds of sexuality. A variation on the later case, where the supervisee is actually a homosexual, is especially interesting for even though it does not involve harassment by a man of a woman, it nonetheless involves harassment of one person whose group, homosexual males, is subordinated on grounds of sexuality, by another person whose group, heterosexual males, is dominant. A consideration of this case also relates to the previous section's discussion of how sexual harassment contributes to male solidarity.

In the case of a bisexual man who sexually harasses both men and women indifferently, we can begin to see whether it matters morally that the harassment is based on men's historical dominance of women. This harasser does not treat women differently from men, so there is no disparate treatment of women and therefore it appears that there is no sex discrimination occurring either. This case contrasts with the case of the male boss who simply harasses (in the sense of "gives a hard time to") every one of his employees equally; the harassment itself may be morally problematic, but not because of its connection with sexuality. The male bisexual harasser seemingly harasses men and women indiscriminately, but the harassment is on sexual grounds and takes a sexual form, either making sexual propositions or engaging in sexual jokes and ridicule that change the workplace environment.

It seems fair to say that the male bisexual harasser is engaging in sexual harassment since his behavior places both men and women in uncomfortable, and unwanted, positions, undeservedly restricting their autonomy. His propositions indicate that he views sexual favors as appropriate criteria in judging job performance. Insofar as the employees wish that this were not the case, the work environment has been rendered hostile. But the hostility is muted by the fact that this does not appear to be part of a larger pattern of hostile treatment by bisexuals in the larger society. What makes sexual harassment so problematic morally is that it contributes to a larger social problem, namely, the discriminatory treatment of women by men.

The male bisexual harasser does engage in sexual harassment, which creates a hostile work environment, but he does not engage in sex discrimination. Even though he sexually harasses women in the workplace, creating a hostile work environment for them, even sexually intimidating them in some cases, his behavior does not necessarily contribute to a society-wide pattern of sex discrimination. The main reason for this, of course, is that he does not treat the men in his employ any differently. This is not to deny that the women may respond quite differently from their male colleagues to his propositions, because of differential socialization. And this socialization may make things worse for the women, who find it harder to resist the propositions than the men. But the acts of the bisexual harasser are not themselves instances of sex discrimination and hence do not violate the moral principle of equal treatment and equal respect.

Now consider a case of a heterosexual male who harasses a male supervisee. A recent case arose in Springfield, Illinois.

> The suit alleges that the supervisor, John Trees, created "a sexually offensive and hostile work environment" at a Transportation Department facility in Springfield, repeatedly making comments in front of other workers indicating he believed that [Jim] Shermer was a homosexual. . . . Shermer isn't gay, the suit says. He alleges he "suffered emotional distress to his reputation, embarrassment, humiliation and other personal injuries," as a result of Tree's behavior. . . . A federal judge in Springfield dismissed the suit in August [1996], in part because of the state's novel argument: As a man on an all-male work crew, it was intrinsically impossible for Shermer to prove he was the victim of sexual discrimination, a necessary component of sexual harassment.

I am inclined to agree with the judge in this case. There is no sex discrimination here because not all, or any other, men are being treated similarly by the supervisor, and there is no indication that the supervisee is being harassed because he is male.

In a variation of the above case, where the heterosexual male supervisor was harassing a homosexual male, we can begin to see whether it matters morally that harassment is directed at women for it to be pernicious. Here the history of the discriminatory treatment of homosexual men by the larger society makes the act of sexual harassment of a homosexual man more like the standard cases of men harassing women than like the original case, one heterosexual male harassing another, or like the hypothetical case of the male bisexual harasser. But even in this case, sexual harassment is not a form of sex discrimination, because it is not directed at someone by virtue of being a member of a certain gender group. As long as heterosexual men are not subjected to the same mistreatment, then it is not clear that the mistreatment is based on belonging to a gender group. But it may be discriminatory nonetheless if it turns out that the harasser mistreats only homosexual men, and no others, and such mistreatment is arbitrary.

Illegal discrimination occurs whenever one group is arbitrarily and adversely treated differently from another. Harassment of homosexual men is a clear example of discrimination even though it is not a form of sex discrimination. Discrimination against homosexuals is still in the stage of being quite blatant in most of Western society. The acts of gay bashing and ridicule of gay lifestyles occur largely unabated and unchallenged. In this sense discrimination against homosexuals is in a different stage, and perhaps a worse stage, from that of discrimination against women. The main way to see that it is, is to think about discrimination as a form of exclusion from full and equal participation in social practices. Discrimination against homosexuals, especially men, is so virulent that it virtually excludes this group from mainstream society in ways that are not now true for the way discrimination against women works.

Discrimination against women and discrimination against homosexual men share this much: they are both instances of dominant males' excluding from full and equal participation those who are different from them and thereby building solidarity within the dominant group. But such solidarity is morally problematic, especially when it is purchased by virulent antihomosexual behavior and attitudes. When solidarity is purchased by strong exclusion, two sorts of moral wrong occur. First, of course, there is harm to the excluded group and its members. Second, the group that does the excluding is also morally harmed and, in this sense, harms itself by its irrational aggression and anger, emotional responses that make it much harder for its members to know and do what is right and hence to attain certain moral virtues.

Aggression and anger often block one's ability to perceive a moral situation correctly. Indeed, the kind of exclusion-oriented aggression and anger characteristic of discrimination against homosexual men have made it very difficult for heterosexual men to recognize their behavior as discriminatory and their attitudes as displaying a lack of respect for fellow humans. Exclusion of one group by another is not always, but quite often, associated with characterizing the excluded group as one which is deserving of its exclusion. In the case of discrimination against homosexual men in Western society, and also in many areas of the non-Western world, the exclusion has been joined by strong emotional reactions directed against the "pernicious" lifestyles of gay men. These strong emotional reactions have created moral harms both for those harassed but also, interestingly, for those who do the harassing.

What would it take for a society to restructure itself so that women and homosexuals were not excluded and vilified for failing to conform to heterosexual male standards? It is beyond the scope of my project to attempt to give a full answer to this question. But one thing does seem clear to me. If heterosexual men could find alternative mechanisms for building solidarity which did not rely on exclusion, then a major part of the motivation for discrimination might be eliminated.

## NOTES

1. *Alexander v. Yale University,* 459 F.Supp. 1 (D. Conn. 1977), 631 F.2d 178 (2d Cir. 1980). The courts ruled the case moot since the student had already graduated and other students were not clearly adversely affected by the harassment of one of their friends.

2. John C. Hughes and Larry May, "Sexual Harassment" *Social Theory and Practice* 6 (Fall 1980).

3. See Larry May and John C. Hughes, "Is Sexual Harassment Coercive?" in *Moral Rights in the Workplace,* ed. Gertrude Ezorsky (Albany: State University of New York Press, 1987).

4. Laurence Thomas, "On Sexual Offers and Threats," in *Moral Rights in the Workplace,* ed. Ezorsky, p. 125.

5. This doctrine was first embraced, by a unanimous Supreme Court, in *Meritor Savings Bank v. Vinson,* 477 U.S. 57, 106 S.Ct. 2399, 91 L.Ed.2d 49 (1986).

6. *Harris v. Forklift Systems Inc.* 114 S.Ct. 367 (1993).

7. Ibid.

8. This is a quotation from the Eleventh Circuit Court of Appeals ruling in *Henson v. Dundee,* quoted by Chief Justice William Rehnquist in *Meritor Savings Bank v. Vinson.*

# Normative Issues In Defining Sexual Harassment

*Jaimie Leeser and William O'Donohue*

Arriving at an acceptable conception or definition of sexual harassment is more difficult than arriving at acceptable conceptions of many other moral phenomena. Sexual harassment is still a relatively new construct, and thus far has been defined mostly by select groups needing to formulate laws or policies on sexual harassment for schools or places of employment. Thus, definitions vary widely, and disagreement may prevail about whether a given situation is an instance of sexual harassment. As a result, there are many controversial cases and few agreed-upon cases to use as a starting point for forging a conception of sexual harassment. In addition, Christensen (1994) has argued that "sexual harassment is an ill-conceived notion that should be discarded, since, given any group of alleged cases of sexual harassment, what the cases have in common (i.e., that they have

*something* to do with sexuality) has *nothing* to do with what makes the *wrong* action in each case *problematic*" (p. 1). Perhaps such a charge should be taken into account when attempting to elucidate an adequate conception of sexual harassment. For example, should we say that the sexual element in an instance of sexual harassment is a central part of the normative infraction that takes place, or is the sexual element merely an accidental property that accompanies a nonsexual wrongdoing? One's answer to this question will significantly govern the way one goes about defining sexual harassment.

Thus far, we can acknowledge that a common starting point for forging a conception of sexual harassment is the agreement that a normative infraction has occurred in instances of harassment, that is, that "something wrong" has happened, and that degree of wrongness should be made apparent in an adequate definition. But what is it about sexual harassment that makes it subject to our disapprobation while breaches of etiquette or unprofessional or immature behavior can be equally annoying and disagreeable but do not bear the same negative moral import? On what basis do we hold the sexual harasser more deserving of moral blame than one who simply lacks etiquette, and are we justified in doing so? To date, the nature of the wrongness of sexual harassment has not been adequately explicated in the literature, nor has the significance of the wrongness been adequately justified. . . .

Our purpose here is twofold. We intend . . . to evaluate three major conceptions of sexual harassment based on the nature of the wrongness they identify: sexual harassment as the oppression of women, as an abuse of power, and as a violation of privacy rights. While all three fall short as acceptable conceptions, for reasons we will see later, all of these conceptions identify important aspects of the wrongness of sexual harassment and help to move us closer to a more adequate conception of the wrongness of sexual harassment. . . .

In the final part of the chapter, we will examine moral principles from deontological ethics, which we take to be useful in the justification of the wrongness or disvalue in sexual harassment. In doing so, we will sketch our own conception of sexual harassment, which we believe encompasses and justifies the negative moral import of sexual harassment more successfully than the rival conceptions discussed in the chapter.

## THE FEMINIST CONCEPTION OF SEXUAL HARASSMENT: OPPRESSION OF WOMEN

The danger in evaluating a feminist conception of sexual harassment stems from the fact that there is no *single* feminist conception of

any phenomenon. Feminists have had a central role in the study of sexual harassment. . . . In this section we will discuss Anita Superson's article "A Feminist Definition of Sexual Harassment" and evaluate it as representative of many feminists' views.

Superson (1993) puts forth the following as a definition of sexual harassment: "Any behavior (verbal or physical) caused by a person, A, in the dominant class directed at another, B, in the subjugated class, that expresses and perpetuates the attitude that B or members of B's sex is/are inferior because of their sex, thereby causing harm to either B and/or B's sex" (p. 46). Superson remarks that the main benefit of her definition is that it pin-points "the group harm sexual harassment causes all women, thereby getting to the heart of what is wrong with sexual harassment" (p. 61). . . . But is the expression or perpetuation of a person's inferiority because of her sex what we ought to identify as the disvalue of sexual harassment? . . .

Superson maintains that women cannot harass men. . . . Although her reason for making such a claim (that women cannot dominate men and harm them as a group given the current social structure) may be correct, the claim itself immediately clashes with our intuitions. For example, imagine a 45-year-old female professor directing sexually bothersome behavior at a 22-year-old male graduate student. Let us assume that the graduate student is poor and desperately hoping to get an assistantship and the female professor has made an implicit threat that he must tolerate her unwanted behavior in order to receive the post. Let us also assume that she is a bodybuilder and he is very thin, small, and frequently ill. He is greatly disturbed by the professor's behavior, and she recognizes this fact and enjoys the power she has over young graduate students who are so financially strained that they will be forced to drop out of school if she does not recommend them for assistantships. We hypothesize that to most people such a situation would clearly appear to be one of sexual harassment; the woman is older and is physically, financially, and professionally superior to the man. . . . Superson, however, would have to maintain that this scenario is not an instance of sexual harassment because the professor's behavior cannot result in the harm or degradation of men *as a group.*

A denial of this scenario as an instance of sexual harassment reveals two striking but popular aspects of many feminist positions. First, since Superson claims that sexual harassment is about domination and abuse of power, and since our scenario obviously seems to involve domination and the abuse of power, we notice that Superson mistakenly sees the only "real" power as that which men (in general) have over women (in general). Superson does not provide a justification for such a strong claim; it is unlikely that any adequate justification for such a claim can be provided. Many factors determine power in relationships, including race, age, financial and professional status, physical strength, physical and mental health, intelligence, and so on. . . . We have no reason to think that the power one has in virtue of one's gender outweighs the power another has in any other area of life.

Second, . . . in the existing social structure, in which Superson maintains that no such group harm to men can occur, she does not seem to recognize that women like the professor still deserve our moral reproach. . . . While one may be correct and even justified in proclaiming that oppression and the abuse of social power are wrong, our moral intuitions tell us that, based on our scenario, there is still an element of wrongness present in sexual harassment for which one cannot fully account by appealing to the wrongness of an abuse of social power.

The belief that the power one holds on the basis of gender overrides other types of power also leads one to conflate sexual (erotic in nature) harassment and gender (or sexist)

harassment. . . . Superson . . . uses the phrase "sexual harassment" to denote both sexual harassment and gender harassment. . . .

The conflation of sexual harassment and gender harassment is . . . a common practice insofar as both are classified as sexual discrimination, and there is frequently an overlap between the two. . . . Although we regularly see sexual behavior linked with sexist behavior, we run into problems when we conflate the two. . . . If sexual harassment is a form of gender harassment and gender harassment can only be committed by males and against females, then sexual harassment cannot occur between two individuals of the same sex, nor can it be committed by women against men. . . . The wrongness . . . in sexual harassment differs from that in gender harassment and the conflation of the two results in a loss of meaning and moral import of either one or the other.

## THE WRONGNESS OF SEXUAL HARASSMENT AS ABUSE OF POWER

The abuse of power . . . can be identified in female-to-male sexual harassment and same-sex sexual harassment as well as male-to-female sexual harassment. . . . We need to examine whether the abuse of power in general is the essential factor resulting in the disvalue in sexual harassment. . . . "Abuse of power" is a muddy notion despite its frequency in common parlance. Power is a difficult thing to define and identify; one individual may have power over another in numerous ways. . . .

If we say that an abuse of power must occur in order for sexual harassment to occur, we must have some idea of which individual is in a more powerful position in any allegedly harassive situation. . . .

We need to look at cases in which it is fairly simple to discern which individual is in the position of power and then decide if an abuse of that power with sexual overtones constitutes sexual harassment. Consider the following scenario put forth by Crosthwaite and Swanton (1986) as an example in which there is a clear case of an abuse of power and the abuse is motivated by sexual attraction:

> Consider a lecturer whose passions are so excited by a student that he loses his sense of professional responsibilities. Out of excessive concern for her interests, and neither requesting nor expecting any response from her, he gives her an unwarranted pass in the subject. This is wrong, but it is hardly harassment. The woman concerned need know nothing at all of his motivation, and may be only favorably affected by his action. (p. 99)

This example qualifies as an abuse of power but does not qualify as an instance of sexual harassment. . . . Abuse of power, even when exercised for sexual reasons in some sense, is not a sufficient condition for sexual harassment. There are cases that are intuitively not sexually harassive in which sexually motivated abuses of power do occur. . . .

The wrongness of sexual harassment cannot be found solely, if at all, in the abuse of power; something with greater negative moral import must be missing from the assessment. . . .

There must be something more illustrative than the misuse of power that is central to the wrongness of sexual harassment. . . .

Perhaps the illustrative element we are looking for is that which is also similar to and closely associated with an abuse of power— namely, coercion. Part of the reason that the example of Crosthwaite and Swanton lacked negative moral import is that the scenario failed to identify specific *harm* committed by the perpetrator. Coercion, however, can be defined in terms of harm, since what often occurs in an instance of coercion is that the victim commits an action she would not otherwise commit with the belief that doing so will spare her some sort of threatened harm from the perpetrator. . . . We do not need to ver-

ify the existence of power between two or more individuals in order to determine whether coercion has taken place. Rather, we can simply use an objective standard to determine whether coercion has taken place and evaluate the wrongness of coercion and its relationship to sexual harassment, happily ridding ourselves of the bewildering search for a misuse of power. . . .

It will be helpful to explain what we mean by coercion so that we may see why it is or is not essential to the wrongness of sexual harassment. . . . Consider the following scenario, which [Edmund] Wall uses to stress the importance of the perpetrator's intentions in determining whether a situation is coercive:

> P is a homeless individual who happens to be a very large man. P approaches another man, Q, seeking some money for that night's meal. P goes about his request in a polite fashion. However, unknown to P, Q was once the victim of a serious and unprovoked assault. Similar to P, the assailant was a very large man dressed in soiled clothing. The thought of this terrible incident is recalled by Q when P approaches him, evoking a feeling of fear in Q. As a result of fear, Q feels threatened into performing the action (A) that P requests. He does, indeed, perform A. But, do we want to conclude that Q was coerced by P into doing A? I think not. (p. 76)

Wall mentions that although Q feels threatened, he is not actually threatened. Such a distinction applies to sexual harassment, as we often hear that sexual harassment is whatever makes the victim feel uncomfortable, or that we must define sexual harassment from a victim's point of view. While it may be perfectly normal for Q to feel threatened given his having previously been an assault victim, the proposition *Q was coerced by P* remains false. In Wall's example we can say that Q's reaction is normal or even justified and yet still maintain that coercion, or a moral infraction, did not occur.

The same attitude must be brought to instances of alleged sexual harassment. Too often those asked to judge whether sexual harassment has occurred are forced into a false dichotomy of deciding whether the victim's feelings are normal or abnormal and on that basis deciding whether sexual harassment did or did not occur. In brief, the victim's feelings are not ultimately decisive in ascertaining whether sexual harassment occurred, but they are a part of that decision, just as they are in coercion. . . . On the other hand, the *moral* status of an act does not fluctuate with the reaction of the victim of the act. Thus, even if the victim of an attempted sexually harassing action is not bothered by the action, we ought to still assign moral blame to the perpetrator. Again, because both coercion and sexual harassment are subject to our moral disapprobation, we must make sure we can point to a breach of a moral principle in such cases, and we must make sure that the perpetrator is a thinking, feeling, purposeful being who is at least *capable* of knowing the moral principle he violates. . . .

Other definitions of coercion, such as Robert Nozick's (1972), focus on whether the victim would have chosen to perform the action *had the threat not been made.* But, as Wall's example demonstrates, one may decide to perform a certain action before the threat is made, but still ultimately perform the action to avoid harm coming to oneself and be coerced. . . .

In instances of quid pro quo sexual harassment we frequently hear of cases of alleged harassment in which the victim had shown a sexual interest in the perpetrator before the sexually threatening or harassing behavior occurred. The victim's sexual interest is then sometimes incorrectly used as evidence that no sexual harassment could have occurred. However, the perpetrator may not *know* about the victim's interest and so may still attempt to coerce her into a sexual relationship. The perpetrator may threaten the victim with diminished promotional opportunities should she refuse to undertake a sexual relationship with him. In such cases the perpetrator deserves moral blame regardless of whether the victim had a previous sexual interest in him. . . .

Cases of hostile environment sexual harassment typically do not involve coercion unless we were to construe coercion broadly enough to include a forcible exposure to a certain environment. However, coercion is readily apparent in quid pro quo sexual harassment, and when coercion of a sexual nature occurs, we will almost certainly declare that action to be sexually harassive. Thus, sexual coercion is a sufficient condition for sexual harassment, although it is not a necessary one. Notice that the wrongness in quid pro quo sexual harassment lies primarily in the coercive nature of the phenomenon; the sexual aspect does not appear to play a role in the wrongness but is merely an accidental feature. That is, this harassment is wrong because it is coercion, not because it is sexual coercion. . . .

## THE WRONGNESS OF SEXUAL HARASSMENT AS A VIOLATION OF PRIVACY RIGHTS

In this section we will evaluate what Wall (1991) and others identify as the wrongness in sexual harassment. Although we found much of what Wall says about coercion applicable to at least some forms of sexual harassment, Wall makes no mention of coercion in his defense of the wrongness of sexual harassment; instead, he locates the disvalue of sexual harassment in a violation of the victim's privacy rights. In "The Definition of Sexual Harassment," Wall (1991, 374) sets up his own necessary and sufficient conditions for sexual harassment, which are as follows:

1. X does not attempt to obtain Y's consent to communicate to Y, X's or someone else's purported sexual interest in Y.

2. X communicates to Y, X's or someone else's purported sexual interest in Y. X's motive for communicating this is some perceived benefit that he expects to obtain through the communication.

3. Y does not consent to discuss with X, X's or someone else's purported sexual interest in Y.

4. Y feels emotionally distressed because X did not attempt to obtain Y's consent to this discussion and/or because Y objects to the content of X's sexual comments.

The first strength of Wall's set of conditions is that most of us agree that the right to privacy is a basic human right, and so the violation of it is likely to warrant moral censure. However, Wall's first condition seems overly stringent in requiring that X attempt to obtain Y's consent merely to communicate one's sexual interest in X. Of course, it depends on what Wall means by "sexual interest," which he does not make clear in his article. But since sexual interest is usually understood to include attraction, the condition seems too stringent. Most of us would not want to say that X would be violating Y's privacy rights merely by not attempting to obtain Y's consent to express to Y, X's or *someone else's* sexual attraction to Y. Asking someone out for a date, for example, could be a way of expressing sexual attraction/sexual interest. Under Wall's condition, however, X would be required to attempt to obtain Y's consent simply to *ask* Y out for a date. It is difficult to get permission to express sexual interest without inadvertently expressing one's interest in the process of asking for permission. A failure to obtain an individual's consent before asking her out for a date is not even severe enough to qualify as a breach of etiquette, much less a moral infraction.

The reason Wall makes the first condition so inclusive is to capture those cases in which Y has an interest in X but still objects to X's sexual behavior. As Wall (1991) notes, "Y may

actually agree to a sexual proposition made to her by X and still be sexually harassed by X's attempting to discuss it with her. . . . Y might not feel that it is the proper time or place to discuss such matters" (p. 375). Again, Wall holds that a failure to obtain consent to a certain type of communication (in this case, to discuss sexual matters with an individual) is a violation of one's privacy rights and is central to sexual harassment. He goes on to elaborate about the wrongness of sexual harassment in the following passage:

> What is inherently repulsive about sexual harassment is not the possible vulgarity of X's sexual comment or proposal, but his failure to show respect for X's rights. It is the obligation that stems from privacy rights that is ignored. Y's personal behavior and aspirations are protected by Y's privacy rights. The intrusion by X into this moral sphere is what is so objectionable about sexual harassment. If X does not attempt to obtain Y's approval to discuss such private matters, then he has not shown Y adequate respect. (p. 375)

Although Wall's conception of sexual harassment is too broad, he makes an important point: that vulgarity is less central to sexual harassment than the failure to show respect for X's rights. If coworkers, or even supervisors and subordinates, have an agreement that sexual joking and teasing is harmless and enjoyable, then it is not sexually harassive even though it may be unprofessional. However, less vulgar sexual joking directed at someone whom the perpetrator knows is distressed by such language can be sexually harassive.

The areas in which Wall's conception can be shown to be too broad are what he means by a victim's privacy rights and by "some perceived benefit" in the second condition. For instance, we know that Wall maintains that failure to gain consent to a certain type of communication violates a victim's privacy rights, but such communication is not only verbal; it includes "gestures, noises, stares, etc. that violate its recipient's privacy rights. Such behavior can be every bit as intrusive as verbal remarks" (1991, 375). We do not typically think of an individual's privacy rights as something that can be violated by noises, stares, and so on. It sounds as though Wall's idea of the right to privacy is more like a right to be left alone from all disturbances. The problem with such a broad conception of an individual's privacy rights is that it encroaches on other individuals' rights to free expression.

Also, Wall appears inconsistent in qualifying a failure to attempt to obtain consent as a *violation* of a victim's privacy rights. If one fails to attempt to gain consent, then it is more fitting that we should say he perhaps has been insensitive, negligent, or has *failed to show proper respect* to the victim's privacy rights. A *violation* of privacy rights should occur only if the perpetrator *acts against* (and, hence, violates) the victim's wishes. . . .

## THE WRONGNESS OF SEXUAL HARASSMENT AS TREATING PERSONS AS MERE SEX OBJECTS

Although we have not yet settled on a firm conception of what sexual harassment is, we have, it seems, come closer to deciding what is wrong with sexual harassment, and once we discover the wrongness of sexual harassment, we have at least one necessary condition in its definition. What is central to the wrongness of sexual harassment, we propose, is that it involves using another individual as a means only. The wrongness of using a human being as a means is a much defended and easily accepted principle in moral philosophy that first gained popularity as the principle of humanity in the categorical imperative of Immanuel Kant (1964): "Act in such a way that you always treat humanity, whether in your own person or in the person of any other, never simply

as a means, but always at the same time as an end" (pp. 32–33). . . .

The notion of respect for persons is relatively straightforward. As one would expect, respecting persons as persons entails respecting those characteristics about persons that make us persons as opposed to animals or automatons. For instance, persons make rational and moral judgments and act on the basis of those judgments, so we have a duty to respect a person's liberty to make such judgments. . . .

It is on the notion of respect for persons that the deontologists part with the utilitarians and consequentialists most drastically. Deontologists claim that utilitarians cannot recognize respect for persons as a fundamental ethical principle, because utilitarians cannot accept humans as having incalculable intrinsic worth. . . . As a result, deontological theories have greater explanatory and justificatory power for the wrongness of sexual harassment, since according to deontological theories, sexual harassment, insofar as it displays a lack of respect for persons, is always wrong, while in some utilitarian theories an act of sexual harassment may be justifiable. . . .

Sexual harassment involves treating someone as a means or not showing her the respect that is morally required of us. These are the fundamental ethical principles that are violated in the act of sexual harassment and that are the basis on which we are justified in passing a negative moral judgment on those who sexually harass. A violation of such principles, then, is a *necessary condition* of sexual harassment; that is, it is what we ought to look for as a minimum requirement in determining whether sexual harassment has occurred in a given situation.

The disvalue of sexual harassment, on our view, is that when A sexually harasses B, he displays a lack of respect for her as a person. We may say that he treats her as less than a person, and he uses her sexuality *as a means* of treating her as less than a person. Therefore, a second necessary condition of sexual harassment is that the *vehicle* for violating these ethical principles is something sexual. Put simply, we may say that sexual harassment involves treating someone as a sex object rather than as a sexual person. Let us examine briefly what it means to treat someone as a sex object by contrasting the meaning of "sex object" with the meaning of "a sexual person." . . .

Sexual persons seek after valuable sexual interactions, are capable of following rules or principles to which they have assented as guides for their sexual conduct, and have the ability to choose their sexual partners and the timing of their sexual interactions. There are, of course, other attributes that make sexual persons worthy of respect and distinguish them from animals or objects but these are some of the basic differences. . . .

Ways in which one might treat a sexual person as if she did not possess characteristics making her, *qua* sexual person, worthy of respect would include many of the cases already discussed, such as any type of action in which one individual coerces another into a sexual relationship, thereby not respecting the victim's ability to choose his or her own sexual interactions. In addition, a man who subjects a woman, against her interests, to listening to detailed reports of sexual fantasies he has about her would be in violation of these principles because we may construe one's ability to choose his or her own sexual interactions to include sexual conversation. . . .

Our proposed principle is not put forth as a necessary or sufficient condition of sexual harassment but is proposed as a general principle that tends to be violated in many instances of sexual harassment. . . .

## CONCLUSION

In the foregoing examination of various conceptions of the disvalue of sexual harassment, we have attempted to make several important points. First, an adequate conception of sexual harassment must make explicit what it posits the disvalue or wrongness in sexual harassment to be. Second, the wrongness identified in sexual harassment should coincide with our fundamental moral intuitions, or the principle that one claims is violated in sexual harassment should be a principle on which there is a general consensus. Third, deontological ethical theories give us a stronger basis than utilitarian or consequentialist theories from which to argue for the necessary wrongness of sexual harassment because deontological theories stress the incalculable worth of human beings and locate the wrongness of actions in the moral duty that is violated rather than in the contingent consequences of the action. Fourth, the principle that one claims is violated in sexual harassment must have the moral significance to enable us to differentiate cases of sexual harassment from cases of poor etiquette or mere unprofessional behavior.

## REFERENCES

Christensen, F. M. 1994. "'Sexual Harassment' Must Be Eliminated," *Public Affairs Quarterly* 8:1–17.

Crosthwaite, J., and C. Swanton. 1986. On the Nature of Sexual Harassment. *Australian Journal of Philosophy* 64:91–106.

Dodds, S., L. Frost, R. Pargetter, and E. Prior. 1988. "Sexual Harassment." *Social Theory and Practice* 14:111–30.

Downie, R. S., and E. Telfer. 1970. *Respect for Persons.* New York: Schocken Books.

Hampshire, S., and H. L. A. Hart. 1972. Decision, Intention, and Certainty. In *New Readings in Philosophical Analysis,* ed. H. Feigl, W. Sellars, and K. Lehrer. New York: Appleton-Century-Crofts.

Kant, T. 1964. *Groundwork of the Metaphysic of Morals,* trans. H. J. Paton. New York: Harper & Row.

Nozick, R. 1972. "Coercion." In P. Laslett, W. G. Runcimann, and Q. Skinner (Eds.), *Philosophy, Politics, and Society: Fourth Series.* Oxford: Blackwell.

Nozick, R. 1981. *Philosophical Explanations.* Cambridge, England: Belknap Press.

Peters, R. S. 1986. Respect for Persons and Fraternity. *Right and Wrong: Basic Reading in Ethics,* ed. C. Hoff Sommers. New York: Harcourt Brace Jovanovich.

Superson, A. M. 1993. "A Feminist Definition of Sexual Harassment," *Journal of Social Philosophy* 24:46–64.

Wall, E. 1988. "Intention and Coercion." *Journal of Applied Philosophy* 5:75–85.

Wall, E. 1991. "The Definition of Sexual Harassment." *Public Affairs Quarterly* 5:371–85.

## LEGAL PERSPECTIVES

# *Local 28 of the Sheet Metal Workers' International Association v. Equal Employment Opportunity Commission*

*United States Supreme Court*

In 1975, petitioners were found guilty of engaging in a pattern and practice of discrimination against black and Hispanic individuals (nonwhites) in violation of Title VII of the Civil Rights Act of 1964, 42 U.S.C. § 2000e *et seq.*, and ordered to end their discriminatory practices, and to admit a certain percentage of nonwhites to union membership by July 1981. In 1982 and again in 1983, petitioners were found guilty of civil contempt for disobeying the District Court's earlier orders. They now challenge the District Court's contempt finding, and also the remedies the court ordered both for the Title VII violation and for contempt. Principally, the issue presented is whether the remedial provision of Title VII, see 42 U.S.C. § 2000e-5(g), empowers a district court to order race-conscious relief that may benefit individuals who are not identified victims of unlawful discrimination.

Petitioner Local 28 of the Sheet Metal Workers' International Association (Local 28) represents sheet metal workers employed by contractors in the New York City metropolitan area. Petitioner Local 28 Joint Apprenticeship Committee (JAC) is a management–labor committee which operates a 4-year apprenticeship training program designed to teach sheet metal skills. . . .

Petitioners joined by the EEOC, argue that the membership goal, the [Employment, Training, Education and Recruitment Fund ("the Fund")] order, and other orders which require petitioners to grant membership preferences to nonwhites are expressly prohibited by § 706(g), 42 U.S.C. § 2000e-5(g), which defines the remedies available under Title VII. Petitioners and the EEOC maintain that § 706(g) authorizes a district court to award preferential relief only to the actual victims of

106 S.Ct. 3109 (1986).

unlawful discrimination. They maintain that the membership goal and the Fund violate this provision, since they require petitioners to admit to membership, and otherwise to extend benefits to, black and Hispanic individuals who are not the identified victims of unlawful discrimination. We reject this argument, and hold that § 706(g), does not prohibit a court from ordering, in appropriate circumstances, affirmative race-conscious relief as a remedy for past discrimination. Specifically, we hold that such relief may be appropriate where an employer or a labor union has engaged in persistent or egregious discrimination, or where necessary to dissipate the lingering effects of pervasive discrimination.

Section 706(g) states: "If the court finds that the respondent has intentionally engaged in or is intentionally engaging in an unlawful employment practice . . ., the court may enjoin the respondent from engaging in such unlawful employment practice, and order such affirmative action as may be appropriate, which may include, but is not limited to, reinstatement or hiring of employees, with or without back pay . . ., or any other equitable relief as the court deems appropriate. . . . No order of the court shall require the admission or reinstatement of an individual as a member of a union, or the hiring, reinstatement, or promotion of an individual as an employee, or the payment to him of any back pay, if such individual was refused admission, suspended, or expelled, or was suspended or discharged for any reason other than discrimination on account of race, color, religion, sex, or national origin in violation of . . . this title." 78 Stat. 261, as amended and as set forth in 42 U.S.C. § 2000e-5(g).

The language of § 706(g) plainly expresses Congress' intent to vest district courts with broad discretion to award "appropriate" equitable relief to remedy unlawful discrimination. . . . Nevertheless, petitioners and the EEOC argue that the last sentence of § 706(g)

prohibits a court from ordering an employer or labor union to take affirmative steps to eliminate discrimination which might incidentally benefit individuals who are not the actual victims of discrimination. This reading twists the plain language of the statute.

The last sentence of § 706(g) prohibits a court from ordering a union to admit an individual who was "refused admission . . . for any reason other than discrimination." It does not, as petitioners and the EEOC suggest, say that a court may order relief only for the actual victims of past discrimination. The sentence on its face addresses only the situation where a plaintiff demonstrates that a union (or an employer) has engaged in unlawful discrimination, but the union can show that a particular individual would have been refused admission even in the absence of discrimination, for example, because that individual was unqualified. In these circumstances, § 706(g) confirms that a court could not order the union to admit the unqualified individual. . . . In this case, neither the membership goal nor the Fund order required petitioners to admit to membership individuals who had been refused admission for reasons unrelated to discrimination. Thus, we do not read § 706(g) to prohibit a court from ordering the kind of affirmative relief the District Court awarded in this case.

The availability of race-conscious affirmative relief under § 706(g) as a remedy for a violation of Title VII also furthers the broad purposes underlying the statute. Congress enacted Title VII based on its determination that racial minorities were subject to pervasive and systematic discrimination in employment. . . . Title VII was designed "to achieve equality of employment opportunities and remove barriers that have operated in the past to favor an identifiable group of white employees over other employees. . . . In order to foster equal employment opportunities, Congress gave the lower courts broad power under § 706(g) to fashion "the most complete relief possible" to remedy past discrimination. . . .

In most cases, the court need only order the employer or union to cease engaging in discriminatory practices, and award make-whole relief to the individuals victimized by those practices. In some instances, however, it may be necessary to require the employer or union to take affirmative steps to end discrimination effectively to enforce Title VII. Where an employer or union has engaged in particularly longstanding or egregious discrimination, an injunction simply reiterating Title VII's prohibition against discrimination will often prove useless and will only result in endless enforcement litigation. In such cases, requiring recalcitrant employers or unions to hire and to admit qualified minorities roughly in proportion to the number of qualified minorities in the work force may be the only effective way to ensure the full enjoyment of the rights protected by Title VII. . . .

Affirmative race-conscious relief may be the only means available "to assure equality of employment opportunities and to eliminate those discriminatory practices and devices which have fostered racially stratified job environments to the disadvantage of minority citizens.". . .

Finally, a district court may find it necessary to order interim hiring or promotional goals pending the development of nondiscriminatory hiring or promotion procedures. In these cases, the use of numerical goals provides a compromise between two unacceptable alternatives: an outright ban on hiring or promotions, or continued use of a discriminatory selection procedure. . . .

Many opponents of Title VII argued that an employer could be found guilty of discrimination under the statute simply because of a racial imbalance in his work force, and would be compelled to implement racial "quotas" to avoid being charged with liability. *Weber*, 443 U.S., at 205. 99 S.Ct., at 2728. At the same time, supporters of the bill insisted that employers would not violate Title VII simply because of racial imbalance, and emphasized that neither the Commission nor the courts could compel employers to adopt quotas solely to facilitate racial balancing, *Id.*, at 207, n. 7, 99 S.Ct, at 2729, n. 7. The debate concerning what Title VII did and did not require culminated in the adoption of 703(j), which stated expressly that the statute did not require an employer of labor union to adopt quotas or preferences simply because of a racial imbalance. However, while Congress strongly opposed the use of quotas or preferences merely to maintain racial balance, it gave no intimation as to whether such measures should be acceptable as *remedies* for Title VII violations. . . .

The purpose of affirmative action is not to make identified victims whole, but rather to dismantle prior patterns of employment discrimination and to prevent discrimination in the future. Such relief is provided to the class as a whole rather than to individual members; no individual is entitled to relief, and beneficiaries need not show that they were themselves victims of discrimination. In this case, neither the membership goal nor the Fund order required petitioners to indenture or train particular individuals, and neither required them to admit to membership individuals who were refused admission for reasons unrelated to discrimination. . . .

The court should exercise its discretion with an eye toward Congress' concern that race-conscious affirmative measures not be invoked simply to create a racially balanced work force. In the majority of Title VII cases, the court will not have to impose affirmative action as a remedy for past discrimination, but need only order the employer or union to cease engaging in discriminatory practices and award make-whole relief to the individuals victimized by those practices. However, in some cases, affirmative action may be necessary in order effectively to enforce Title VII. As we noted before, a court may have to resort to race-conscious affirmative action when confronted with an employer or labor union that has engaged in persistent or egregious discrimination. Or such relief may be necessary to dissipate the lingering effects of pervasive discrimination. Whether there might be other circumstances that justify the use of court-ordered affirmative action is a matter that we need not decide here. We note only that a court should consider whether affirmative action is necessary to remedy past discrimination in a particular case before imposing such measures, and that the court should also take care to tailor to fit the nature of the violation it seeks to correct. In this case, several factors lead us to conclude that the relief ordered by the District Court was proper.

First, both the District Court and the Court of Appeals agreed that the membership goal and Fund order were necessary to remedy petitioners' pervasive and egregious discrimination. The District Court set the original 29 percent membership goal upon observing that "[t]he record in both state and federal courts against [petitioners] is replete with instances of their bad faith attempts to prevent or delay affirmative action." 401 F.Supp., at 488. The court extended the goal after finding petitioners in contempt for refusing to end their discriminatory practices and failing to comply with various provisions of RAAPO. In affirming the revised membership goal, the Court of Appeals observed that "[t]his court has twice recognized Local 28's long continued and egregious racial discrimination . . . and Local 28 has presented no facts to indicate that our earlier observations are no longer apposite." 753 F.2d, at 1186. In light of petitioners' long history of "foot-dragging resistance" to court orders, simply enjoining them from once again engaging in discriminatory practices would clearly have been futile. Rather, the District Court properly determined that affirmative race-conscious

measures were necessary to put an end to petitioners' discriminatory ways.

Both the membership goal and Fund order were similarly necessary to combat the lingering effects of past discrimination. In light of the District Court's determination that the union's reputation for discrimination operated to discourage nonwhites from even applying for membership, it is unlikely that an injunction would have been sufficient to extend to nonwhites equal opportunities for employment. Rather, because access to admission, membership, training, and employment in the industry had traditionally been obtained through informal contacts with union members, it was necessary for a substantial number of nonwhite workers to become members of the union in order for the effects of discrimination to cease. The Fund, in particular, was designed to insure that nonwhites would receive the kind of assistance that white apprentices and applicants had traditionally received through informal sources. On the facts of this case, the District Court properly determined that affirmative, race-conscious measures were necessary to assure the equal employment opportunities guaranteed by Title VII.

Second, the District Court's flexible application of the membership goal gives strong indication that it is not being used simply to achieve and maintain racial balance, but rather as a benchmark against which the court could gauge petitioners' efforts to remedy past discrimination. The court has twice adjusted the deadline for achieving the goal, and has continually approved of changes in the size of the apprenticeship classes to account for the fact that economic conditions prevented petitioners from meeting their membership targets; there is every reason to believe that both the court and the administrator will continue to accommodate *legitimate* explanations for petitioners' failure to comply with the court's orders. Moreover, the District Court expressly disavowed any reliance on petitioners' failure to meet the goal as a basis for the contempt finding, but instead viewed this failure as symptomatic of petitioners' refusal to comply with various subsidiary provisions of RAAPO. In sum, the District Court has implemented the membership goal as a means by which it can measure petitioners' compliance with its orders, rather than as a strict racial quota.

Third, both the membership goal and the Fund order are temporary measures. Under AAAPO "[p]referential selection of [union members] will end as soon as the percentage of [minority union members] approximates the percentage of [minorities] in the local labor force." *Weber*, 443 U.S., at 208–209, 99 S.Ct., at 2730; see *United States v. City of Alexandria*, 614 F.2d, at 1366. Similarly, the Fund is scheduled to terminate when petitioners achieve the membership goal, and the court determines that it is no longer needed to remedy past discrimination. The District Court's orders thus operate "as a temporary tool for remedying past discrimination without attempting to 'maintain' a previously achieved balance." *Weber*, 443 U.S., at 216, 99 S.Ct., at 2734 (Blackmun, J., concurring).

Finally, we think it significant that neither the membership goal nor the Fund order "unnecessarily trammel[s] the interests of white employees." *Id.*, 443 U.S., at 208, 99 S.Ct., at 2730; *Teamsters*, 431 U.S., at 352–353, 97 S.Ct., at 1863–1864. Petitioners concede that the District Court's orders did not require any member of the union to be laid off, and did not discriminate against existing union members. See *Weber, supra*, 443 U.S., at 208, 99 S.Ct., at 2729–2730; see also 30 St. Louis U.L.J., at 264. While whites seeking admission into the union may be denied benefits extended to their nonwhite counterparts, the court's orders do not stand as an absolute bar to such individuals; indeed, a majority of new union members have been white. See *City of Alexandria, supra*, at 1366. Many provisions of the court's orders

are race-neutral (for example, the requirement that the [Joint Apprenticeship Committee (JAC)] assign one apprentice for every four journeyman workers), and petitioners remain free to adopt the provisions of AAAPO and the Fund order for the benefit of white members and applicants.

Petitioners also allege that the membership goal and Fund order contravene the equal protection component of the Due Process Clause of the Fifth Amendment because they deny benefits to white individuals based on race. We have consistently recognized that government bodies constitutionally may adopt racial classifications as a remedy for past discrimination. . . . We conclude that the relief ordered in this case passes even the most rigorous test—it is narrowly tailored to further the Government's compelling interest in remedying past discrimination.

In this case, there is no problem . . . with a proper showing of prior discrimination that would justify the use of remedial racial classifications. Both the District Court and Court of Appeals have repeatedly found petitioners guilty of egregious violations of Title VII, and have determined that affirmative measures were necessary to remedy their racially discriminatory practices. More importantly, the District Court's orders were properly tailored to accomplish this objective. First, the District Court considered the efficacy of alternative remedies, and concluded that, in light of petitioners' long record of resistance to official efforts to end their discriminatory practices, stronger measures were necessary. . . . Again, petitioners concede that the District Court's orders did not disadvantage *existing* union members. While white applications for union membership may be denied certain benefits available to their nonwhite counterparts, the court's orders do not stand as an absolute bar to the admission of such individuals; again, a majority of those entering the union after entry of the court's orders have been white.

We therefore conclude that the District Court's orders do not violate the equal protection safeguards of the Constitution.

Finally, Local 28 challenges the District Court's appointment of an administrator with broad powers to supervise its compliance with the court's orders as an unjustifiable interference with its statutory right to self-governance. See 29 USC § 401(a). Preliminarily, we note that while AAAPO gives the administrator broad powers to oversee petitioners' membership practices, Local 28 retains complete control over its other affairs. Even with respect to membership, the administrator's job is to insure that petitioners comply with the court's orders and admit sufficient numbers of nonwhites; the administrator does not select the particular individuals that will be admitted, that task is left to union officials. In any event, in light of the difficulties inherent in monitoring compliance with the court's orders, and especially petitioners' established record of resistance to prior state and federal court orders designed to end their discriminatory membership practices, appointment of an administrator was well within the District Court's discretion. . . .

To summarize our holding today, six members of the Court agree that a district court may, in appropriate circumstances, order preferential relief benefiting individuals who are not the actual victims of discrimination as a remedy for violations of Title VII, . . . that the District Court did not use incorrect statistical evidence in establishing petitioners' nonwhite membership goal, that the contempt fines and Fund order were proper remedies for civil contempt, and that the District Court properly appointed an administrator to supervise petitioners' compliance with the court's orders. Five members of the Court agree that in this case, the District Court did not err in evaluating petitioners' utilization of the apprenticeship program, and that the membership goal and the Fund order are not violative of either Title VII or the Constitution. The judgment of the Court of Appeals is hereby *Affirmed.* . . .

# Barbara Grutter, Petitioner, v. Lee Bollinger et al.

*United States Supreme Court*

## JUSTICE SANDRA DAY O'CONNOR [OPINION OF THE COURT]

This case requires us to decide whether the use of race as a factor in student admissions by the University of Michigan Law School (Law School) is unlawful. . . . The hallmark of that policy is its focus on academic ability coupled with a flexible assessment of applicants' talents, experiences, and potential "to contribute to the learning of those around them." . . .

The Law School seeks "a mix of students with varying backgrounds and experiences who will respect and learn from each other." *Ibid.* In 1992, the dean of the Law School charged a faculty committee with crafting a written admissions policy to implement these goals. . . .

Petitioner Barbara Grutter is a white Michigan resident who applied to the Law School in 1996 with a 3.8 grade point average and 161 LSAT score. The Law School initially placed petitioner on a waiting list, but subsequently rejected her application. In December 1997, petitioner filed suit in the United States District Court for the Eastern District of Michigan against the Law School. . . . Petitioner alleged that respondents discriminated against her on the basis of race in violation of the Fourteenth Amendment; Title VI of the Civil Rights Act of 1964, 78 Stat. 252, 42 U.S.C. § 2000d; and Rev. Stat. § 1977, as amended, 42 U.S.C. § 1981. . . .

We last addressed the use of race in public higher education over 25 years ago. In the landmark *Bakke* case, we reviewed a racial set-aside program that reserved 16 out of 100 seats in a medical school class for members of certain minority groups. 438 U.S. 265 (1978). The decision produced six separate opinions, none of which commanded a majority of the Court. . . .

Since this Court's splintered decision in *Bakke*, Justice Powell's opinion announcing the judgment of the Court has served as the touchstone for constitutional analysis of race-conscious admissions policies. Public and private universities across the Nation have modeled their own admissions programs on Justice Powell's views on permissible race-conscious policies. . . .

First, Justice Powell rejected an interest in "'reducing the historic deficit of traditionally disfavored minorities in medical schools and in the medical profession'" as an unlawful interest in racial balancing. *Id.*, at 306–307. Second, Justice Powell rejected an interest in remedying societal discrimination because such measures would risk placing unnecessary burdens on innocent third parties "who bear no responsibility for whatever harm the beneficiaries of the special admissions program are thought to have suffered." *Id.*, at 310. Third, Justice Powell rejected an interest in "increasing the number of physicians who will practice in communities currently underserved," concluding that even if such an interest could be compelling in some circumstances the program under review was

not "geared to promote that goal." *Id.*, at 306, 310.

Justice Powell approved the university's use of race to further only one interest: "the attainment of a diverse student body." . . .

In the wake of our fractured decision in *Bakke*, courts have struggled to discern whether Justice Powell's diversity rationale, set forth in part of the opinion joined by no other Justice, is nonetheless binding precedent. . . .

We have held that all racial classifications imposed by government "must be analyzed by a reviewing court under strict scrutiny." *Ibid.* This means that such classifications are constitutional only if they are narrowly tailored to further compelling governmental interests. . . . When race-based action is necessary to further a compelling governmental interest, such action does not violate the constitutional guarantee of equal protection so long as the narrow-tailoring requirement is also satisfied. . . .

With these principles in mind, we turn to the question whether the Law School's use of race is justified by a compelling state interest. Before this Court, as they have throughout this litigation, respondents assert only one justification for their use of race in the admissions process: obtaining "the educational benefits that flow from a diverse student body." Brief for Respondents Bollinger et al. i. In other words, the Law School asks us to recognize, in the context of higher education, a compelling state interest in student body diversity.

We first wish to dispel the notion that the Law School's argument has been foreclosed, either expressly or implicitly, by our affirmative-action cases decided since *Bakke*. It is true that some language in those opinions might be read to suggest that remedying past discrimination is the only permissible justification for race-based governmental action. See, e.g., *Richmond v. J. A. Croson Co., supra*, at 493 (plurality opinion) (stating that unless classifications based on race are "strictly reserved for remedial settings, they may in fact promote notions of racial inferiority and lead to a politics of racial hostility"). But we have never held that the only governmental use of race that can survive strict scrutiny is remedying past discrimination. Nor, since *Bakke*, have we directly addressed the use of race in the context of public higher education. Today, we hold that the Law School has a compelling interest in attaining a diverse student body.

The Law School's educational judgment that such diversity is essential to its educational mission is one to which we defer. The Law School's assessment that diversity will, in fact, yield educational benefits is substantiated by respondents and their *amici*. . . .

Our conclusion that the Law School has a compelling interest in a diverse student body is informed by our view that attaining a diverse student body is at the heart of the Law School's proper institutional mission, and that "good faith" on the part of a university is "presumed" absent "a showing to the contrary." 438 U.S., at 318–319.

As part of its goal of "assembling a class that is both exceptionally academically qualified and broadly diverse," the Law School seeks to "enroll a 'critical mass' of minority students." Brief for Respondents Bollinger et al. 13. The Law School's interest is not simply "to assure within its student body some specified percentage of a particular group merely because of its race or ethnic origin.". . . Rather, the Law School's concept of critical mass is defined by reference to the educational benefits that diversity is designed to produce.

These benefits are substantial. As the District Court emphasized, the Law School's admissions policy promotes "cross-racial understanding," helps to break down racial stereotypes, and "enables [students] to better understand persons of different races." App. to Pet. for Cert. 246a. These benefits are "important and laudable," because "classroom discussion is livelier, more spirited, and simply more enlightening and interesting" when the students have "the greatest possible variety of backgrounds." *Id.*, at 246a, 244a.

The Law School's claim of a compelling interest is further bolstered by its *amici*, who point to the educational benefits that flow from student body diversity. In addition to the expert studies and reports entered into evidence at trial, numerous studies show that student body diversity promotes learning outcomes, and "better prepares students for an increasingly diverse workforce and society, and better prepares them as professionals.". . .

These benefits are not theoretical but real, as major American businesses have made clear that the skills needed in today's increasingly global marketplace can only be developed through exposure to widely diverse people, cultures, ideas, and viewpoints. Brief for 3M et al. as *Amici Curiae* 5; Brief for General Motors Corp. as *Amicus Curiae* 3–4. . . .

We have repeatedly acknowledged the overriding importance of preparing students for work and citizenship, describing education as pivotal to "sustaining our political and cultural heritage" with a fundamental role in maintaining the fabric of society. *Plyler v. Doe,* 457 U.S. 202, 221 (1982). . . .

In order to cultivate a set of leaders with legitimacy in the eyes of the citizenry, it is necessary that the path to leadership be visibly open to talented and qualified individuals of every race and ethnicity. All members of our heterogeneous society must have confidence in the openness and integrity of the educational institutions that provide this training. As we have recognized, law schools "cannot be effective in isolation from the individuals and institutions with which the law interacts.". . . diminishing the force of stereotypes is both a crucial part of the Law School's mission, and one that it cannot accomplish with only token numbers of minority students. Just as growing up in a particular region or having particular professional experiences is likely to affect an individual's views, so too is one's own, unique experience of being a racial minority in a society, like our own, in which race unfortunately still matters. The Law School has determined, based on its experience and expertise, that a "critical mass" of under-represented minorities is necessary to further its compelling interest in securing the educational benefits of a diverse student body.

Even in the limited circumstance when drawing racial distinctions is permissible to further a compelling state interest, government is still "constrained in how it may pursue that end: [T]he means chosen to accomplish the [government's] asserted purpose must be specifically and narrowly framed to accomplish that purpose." *Shaw v. Hunt,* 517 U.S. 899, 908 (1996) (internal quotation marks and citation omitted). The purpose of the narrow tailoring requirement is to ensure that "the means chosen 'fit' . . . th[e] compelling goal so closely that there is little or no possibility that the motive for the classification was illegitimate racial prejudice or stereotype." *Richmond v. J. A. Croson Co.,* 488 U.S., at 493 (plurality opinion). . . . purpose of strict scrutiny is to take such "relevant differences into account." 515 US., at 228 (internal quotation marks omitted).

To be narrowly tailored, a race-conscious admissions program cannot use a quota system. . . . Instead, a university may consider race or ethnicity only as a "'plus' in a particular applicant's file". . . .

We find that the Law School's admissions program bears the hallmarks of a narrowly tailored plan. As Justice Powell made clear in *Bakke,* truly individualized consideration demands that race be used in a flexible, non-mechanical way. It follows from this mandate that universities cannot establish quotas for members of certain racial groups or put members of those groups on separate admissions tracks. See *Id.,* at 315–316. Nor can universities insulate applicants who belong to certain racial or ethnic groups from the competition for admission. *Ibid.* Universities can, however, consider race or ethnicity more

flexibly as a "plus" factor in the context of individualized consideration of each and every applicant. . . .

Quotas "'impose a fixed number or percentage which must be attained, or which cannot be exceeded,'" *Sheet Metal Workers v. EEOC,* 478 U.S. 421, 495 (1986) (O'CONNER, J., concurring in part and dissenting in part), and "insulate the individual from comparison with all other candidates for the available seats." *Bakke, supra,* at 317 (opinion of Powell, J.). In contrast, "a permissible goal . . . require[s] only a good-faith effort . . . to come within a range demarcated by the goal itself," *Sheet Metal Workers v. EEOC, supra,* at 495, and permits consideration of race as a "plus" factor in any given case while still ensuring that each candidate "compete[s] with all other qualified applicants," *Johnson v. Transportation Agency, Santa Clara Cty.,* 480 U.S. 616, 638 (1987). . . .

That a race-conscious admissions program does not operate as a quota does not, by itself, satisfy the requirement of individualized consideration. When using race as a "plus" factor in university admissions, a university's admissions program must remain flexible enough to ensure that each applicant is evaluated as an individual and not in a way that makes an applicant's race or ethnicity the defining feature of his or her application. . . . By this flexible approach, the Law School sufficiently takes into account, in practice as well as in theory, a wide variety of characteristics besides race and ethnicity that contribute to a diverse student body. . . . Narrow tailoring does, however, require serious, good-faith consideration of workable race-neutral alternatives that will achieve the diversity the university seeks. . . .

We are mindful, however, that "[a] core purpose of the Fourteenth Amendment was to do away with all governmentally imposed discrimination based on race." *Palmore v. Sidoti,* 466 U.S. 429, 432 (1984). Accordingly, race-conscious admissions policies must be limited in time. This requirement reflects that racial classifications, however compelling their goals, are potentially so dangerous that they may be employed no more broadly than the interest demands. Enshrining a permanent justification for racial preferences would offend this fundamental equal protection principle. We see no reason to exempt race-conscious admissions programs from the requirement that all governmental use of race must have a logical end point. The Law School, too, concedes that all "race-conscious programs must have reasonable durational limits." Brief for Respondents Bollinger et al. 32. . . .

The requirement that all race-conscious admissions programs have a termination point assure[s] all citizens that the deviation from the norm of equal treatment of all racial and ethnic groups is a temporary matter, a measure taken in the service of the goal of equality itself." . . . We expect that 25 years from now, the use of racial preferences will no longer be necessary to further the interest approved today. . . .

The judgment of the Court of Appeals for the Sixth Circuit, accordingly, is affirmed.

*It is so ordered.*

# Dissending Opinion

## JUSTICE THOMAS, WITH WHOM JUSTICE SCALIA JOINS AS TO PARTS I–VII, CONCURRING IN PART AND DISSENTING IN PART

I believe blacks can achieve in every avenue of American life without the meddling of university administrators. Because I wish to see all students succeed whatever their color, I share, in some respect, the sympathies of those who sponsor the type of discrimination advanced by the University of Michigan Law School (Law School). The Constitution does not, however, tolerate institutional devotion to the status quo in admissions policies when such devotion ripens into racial discrimination. Nor does the Constitution countenance the unprecedented deference the Court gives to the Law School, an approach inconsistent with the very concept of "strict scrutiny."

No one would argue that a university could set up a lower general admission standard and then impose heightened requirements only on black applicants. Similarly, a university may not maintain a high admission standard and grant exemptions to favored races. The Law School, of its own choosing, and for its own purposes, maintains an exclusionary admissions system that it knows produces racially disproportionate results. Racial discrimination is not a permissible solution to the self-inflicted wounds of this elitist admissions policy. . . .

The Constitution abhors classifications based on race, not only because those classifications can harm favored races or are based on illegitimate motives, but also because every time the government places citizens on racial registers and makes race relevant to the provision of burdens or benefits, it demeans us all. . . .

The proffered interest that the majority vindicates today, then, is not simply "diversity." Instead the Court upholds the use of racial discrimination as a tool to advance the Law School's interest in offering a marginally superior education while maintaining an elite institution. Unless each constituent part of this state interest is of pressing public necessity, the Law School's use of race is unconstitutional. I find each of them to fall far short of this standard. . . .

Finally, even if the Law School's racial tinkering produces tangible educational benefits, a marginal improvement in legal education cannot justify racial discrimination where the Law School has no compelling interest in either its existence or in its current educational and admissions policies.

The interest in remaining elite and exclusive that the majority thinks so obviously critical requires the use of admissions "standards" that, in turn, create the Law School's "need" to discriminate on the basis of race. The Court validates these admissions standards by concluding that alternatives that would require "a dramatic sacrifice of . . . the academic quality of all admitted students," *ante,* at 27, need not be considered before racial discrimination can be employed. . . .

The Court's deference to the Law School's conclusion that its racial experimentation leads to educational benefits will, if adhered to, have serious collateral consequences. . . . The Court never acknowledges . . . . the growing evidence that racial (and other sorts) of heterogeneity actually impairs learning among black students. . . . Contained within today's majority opinion is the seed of a new constitutional justification for a concept I thought long and rightly rejected—racial segregation. . . .

The rallying cry that in the absence of racial discrimination in admissions there would be a true meritocracy ignores the fact that the entire process is poisoned by numerous exceptions to "merit." For example, in the national debate on racial discrimination in higher education admissions, much has been made of the fact that elite institutions utilize a so-called legacy preference to give the children of alumni an advantage in admissions. This, and other, exceptions to a "true" meritocracy give the lie to protestations that merit admissions are in fact the order of the day at the Nation's universities. The Equal Protection Clause does not, however, prohibit the use of unseemly legacy preferences or many other kinds of arbitrary admissions procedures. What the Equal Protection Clause does prohibit are classifications made on the basis of race. . . .

I believe what lies beneath the Court's decision today are the benighted notions that one can tell when racial discrimination benefits (rather than hurts) minority groups, see

*Adarand,* 515 U.S., at 239 (Scalia, J., concurring in part and concurring in judgment), and that racial discrimination is necessary to remedy general societal ills. This Court's precedents supposedly settled both issues, but clearly the majority still cannot commit to the principle that racial classifications are *per se* harmful and that almost no amount of benefit in the eye of the beholder can justify such classifications. . . .

The Court spends considerable time discussing the impressive display of *amicus* support for the Law School in this case from all corners of society. *Ante,* at 18–19. But nowhere in any of the filings in this Court is any evidence that the purported "beneficiaries" of this racial discrimination prove themselves by performing at (or even near) the same level as those students who receive no preferences. . . .

Beyond the harm the Law School's racial discrimination visits upon its test subjects, no social science has disproved the notion that this discrimination "engender[s] attitudes of superiority or, alternatively, provoke[s] resentment among those who believe that they have been wronged by the government's use of race." *Adarand,* 515 U.S., at 241 (Thomas, J., concurring in part and concurring in judgment). "These programs stamp minorities with a badge of inferiority and may cause them to develop dependencies or to adopt an attitude that they are 'entitled' to preferences." . . .

No one can seriously contend, and the Court does not, that the racial gap in academic credentials will disappear in 25 years. Nor is the Court's holding that racial discrimination will be unconstitutional in 25 years made contingent on the gap closing in that time. . . .

For the immediate future, however, the majority has placed its *imprimatur* on a practice that can only weaken the principle of equality embodied in the Declaration of Independence and the Equal Protection Clause. . . . I therefore respectfully dissent from the remainder of the Court's opinion and the judgment.

# Barbara Grutter, Petitioner, v. Lee Bollinger et al.

FEBRUARY 18, 2003

*United States Supreme Court*

## BRIEF FOR *AMICI CURIAE*: 65 LEADING AMERICAN BUSINESSES IN SUPPORT OF RESPONDENTS

This brief is filed on behalf of the following 65 businesses:

3M
Abbott Laboratories
Alcoa, Inc.
Alliant Energy Corporation
Altria Group, Inc.
American Airlines, Inc.
American Express Company
Amgen Corporation
Ashland, Inc.
Bank One Corporation
Baxter Healthcare Corporation
The Boeing Company
Charter One Financial, Inc.
ChevronTexaco Corporation
The Coca-Cola Company
Coca-Cola Enterprises Inc.
DaimlerChrysler Corporation
Deloitte Consulting L.P.
Deloitte & Touche LLP
The Dow Chemical Company
Eastman Kodak Company
Eaton Corporation
Eli Lilly & Company
Ernst & Young LLP
Exelon Corporation
Fannie Mae
General Dynamics Corporation
General Electric Company
General Mills, Inc.

John Hancock Financial Services
Harris Bankcorp, Inc.
Hewlett-Packard Company
Illinois Tool Works, Inc.
Intel Corporation
Johnson & Johnson
Kaiser Found. Health Plan, Inc.
Kellogg Company
KPMG Int'l for KPMG LLP
Kraft Foods, Inc.
Lockheed Martin Corporation
Lucent Technologies, Inc.
Medtronic, Inc.
Merck & Co., Inc.
Microsoft Corporation
Mitsubishi Motors North America
MSC. Software Corporation
Nationwide Mutual Insurance Co.
NetCom Solutions International
Nike, Inc.
Northrop Grumman Corporation
Pepsi Bottling Group, Inc.
PepsiCo, Inc.
Pfizer, Inc.
PPG Industries, Inc.
PricewaterhouseCoopers LLP
The Procter & Gamble Company
Reebok International
Sara Lee Corporation
Schering-Plough Corporation
Shell Oil Company
Steelcase, Inc.
Sterling Financial Group of Cos.
United Airlines, Inc.
Whirlpool Corporation
Xerox Corporation

## INTEREST OF *AMICI CURIAE*

*Amici* are global businesses that recruit at the University of Michigan or similar leading institutions of higher education. Collectively, *amici* have annual revenues well over a trillion dollars and hire thousands of graduates of the University of Michigan and other major public universities. *Amici* have a vital interest in who is admitted to our nation's colleges and universities, and what kind of education and training those students receive. Many of the *amici* have substantial business presences in the state of Michigan. . . .

The existence of racial and ethnic diversity in institutions of higher education is vital to *amici*'s efforts to hire and maintain a diverse workforce, and to employ individuals of all backgrounds who have been educated and trained in a diverse environment. . . .

Now more than ever, the ability of universities, such as the University of Michigan, to consider all of an applicant's attributes is essential to create the educational environment necessary to best train all their students to succeed. The students of today are this country's corporate and community leaders of the next half-century. For these students to realize their potential as leaders, it is essential that they be educated in an environment where they are exposed to diverse people, ideas, perspectives, and interactions. In the experience of the *amici* businesses, today's global marketplace and the increasing diversity in the American population demand the cross-cultural experience and understanding gained from such an education. Diversity in higher education is therefore a compelling government interest not only because of its positive effects on the educational environment itself, but also because of the crucial role diversity in higher education plays in preparing students to be the leaders this country needs in business, law, and all other pursuits that affect the public interest. . . .

As Justice Powell recognized in his controlling opinion in *Bakke,* a diverse student body promotes an atmosphere of "speculation, experiment and creation" that is "essential to the quality of higher education." *Id.* at 312 (internal quotations omitted). . . .

Justice Powell's recognition of the compelling nature of the state's interest in diversity was not limited to undergraduate admissions. "[E]ven at the graduate level, our tradition and experience lend support to the view that the contribution of diversity is substantial." . . .

Justice Powell emphasized that ethnic diversity is only one element in a range of factors a university properly may consider in attaining the goal of a heterogeneous student body. *Id.* "The diversity that furthers a compelling state interest encompasses a far broader array of qualification and characteristics of which racial or ethnic origin is but a single though important element.". . .

In the practical experience of the *amici* businesses, the need for diversity in higher education is indeed compelling. Because our population is diverse, and because of the increasingly global reach of American business, the skills and training needed to succeed in business today demand exposure to widely diverse people, cultures, ideas and viewpoints. Employees at every level of an organization must be able to work effectively with people who are different from themselves. *Amici* need the talent and creativity of a workforce that is as diverse as the world around it.

The population of the United States is increasingly defined by its diversity. . . . The nature of American business also is changing. Most of the *amici* are truly international companies, and virtually all are becoming so. *Amicus* 3M is a $16.7 billion diversified manufacturing and technology company with operations in more than 60 countries and customers in nearly 200 countries. *Amicus* Boeing makes 70 percent of its commercial airplane sales to international customers. *Amicus* Procter & Gamble sold a branded product to more than 2.5 billion people across the world last year, yielding more than $40 billion in sales. Similar figures could be provided for many of the *amici*: they operate and compete in a global environment, serving and working with people and cultures of all kinds.

In the experience of *amici*, individuals who have been educated in a diverse setting are more likely to succeed, because they can make valuable contributions to the workforce in several important and concrete ways. First, a diverse group of individuals educated in a cross-cultural environment has the ability to facilitate unique and creative approaches to problem-solving arising from the integration of different perspectives. Second, such individuals are better able to develop products and services that appeal to a variety of consumers and to market offerings in ways that appeal to those consumers. Third, a racially diverse group of managers with cross-cultural experience is better able to work with business partners, employees, and clientele in the United States and around the world. Fourth, individuals who have been educated in a diverse setting are likely to contribute to a positive work environment, by decreasing incidents of discrimination and stereotyping. Overall, an educational environment that ensures participation by diverse people, viewpoints and ideas will help produce the most talented workforce.

*Amici* attest to the validity of these claims through their actions. *Amici* are hiring an increasingly diverse workforce. Drawing upon the diverse student bodies that have existed at schools like the University of Michigan, *amicus* Microsoft has steadily increased its percentage of minority employees, from 16.8 percent in 1997 to 25.6 percent of Microsoft's domestic workforce today. Many of the *amici* spend millions of dollars each year to provide financial and other support for minority students to participate in undergraduate and graduate programs at the University of Michigan and other schools. For each of the *amici*, diversity is an increasingly critical component of their business, culture and planning.

There is not, and cannot be, serious debate about the importance of maintaining racial and ethnic diversity in our nation's leading colleges and universities. Whatever methodology is employed to select those who will be afforded the opportunity to obtain the best education and training available in America today, that methodology must operate in such a way that students of all races, cultures and ethnic backgrounds are in fact meaningfully included. . . .

What is critical to *amici* is that the leading colleges, universities, and graduate schools from which they recruit and hire their employees be diverse, and consist of the most qualified and talented diverse students as is possible. . . .

The experiences of *amici* in the 25 years since *Bakke* was decided confirm Justice Powell's holding that the pursuit of diversity in higher education is a compelling state interest. The reasons given by Justice Powell are just as valid today, if not more so. . . . Such consideration is vital to the interests of American business, and it is necessary to ensure that members of all segments of our society receive the education and training they need to become the leaders of tomorrow.

For these reasons, the Court should find that the pursuit of diversity in higher education is a compelling state interest, and that the University of Michigan may take appropriate, narrowly tailored actions to admit a student body that, among other things, is racially and ethnically diverse.

# *Meritor Savings Bank, FSB, v. Vinson et al.*

*United States Supreme Court*

This case presents important questions concerning claims of workplace "sexual harassment" brought under Title VII of the Civil Rights Act of 1964, 78 Stat. 253, as amended, 42 U.S.C. § 2000e *et seq.*

## I

In 1974, respondent Mechelle Vinson. . .started as a teller-trainee, and thereafter was promoted to teller, head teller, and assistant branch manager. She worked at the same branch for four years, and it is undisputed that her advancement there was based on merit alone. In September 1978, respondent notified her supervisor, Sidney Taylor, that she was taking sick leave for an indefinite period. On November 1, 1978, the bank discharged her for excessive use of that leave.

Respondent brought this action against Taylor and the bank, claiming that during her four years at the bank she had "constantly been subjected to sexual harassment" by Taylor in violation of Title VII. She sought injunctive relief, compensatory and punitive damages against Taylor and the bank, and attorney's fees.

At the 11-day bench trial, the parties presented conflicting testimony about Taylor's behavior during respondent's employment.* Respondent testified that during her probationary period as a teller-trainee, Taylor treated her in a fatherly way and made no sexual ad-

vances. Shortly thereafter, however, he invited her out to dinner and, during the course of the meal, suggested that they go to a motel to have sexual relations. At first she refused, but out of what she described as fear of losing her job she eventually agreed. According to respondent, Taylor thereafter made repeated demands upon her for sexual favors, usually at the branch, both during and after business hours; she estimated that over the next several years she had intercourse with him some 40 or 50 times. In addition, respondent testified that Taylor fondled her in front of other employees, followed her into the women's restroom when she went there alone, exposed himself to her, and even forcibly raped her on several occasions. These activities ceased after 1977, respondent stated, when she started going with a steady boyfriend.

Respondent also testified that Taylor touched and fondled other women employees of the bank, and she attempted to call witnesses to support this charge. But while some supporting testimony apparently was admitted without objection, the District Court did not allow her "to present wholesale evidence of a pattern and practice relating to sexual advances to other female employees in her case in chief, but advised her that she might well be able to present such evidence in rebuttal to the defendants' cases." *Vinson v. Taylor*, 22 EPD §30, 708, p. 14,693, n. 1, 23 FEP Cases 37, 38–39, n. 1 (DC 1980). Respondent did not offer such evidence in rebuttal. Finally, respondent testified that because she was afraid of Taylor she never reported his harassment to any of his supervisors and never attempted to use the bank's complaint procedure.

---

*Like the Court of Appeals, this Court was not provided a complete transcript of the trial. We therefore rely largely on the District Court's opinion for the summary of the relevant testimony.

---

Taylor denied respondent's allegations of sexual activity, testifying that he never fondled her, never made suggestive remarks to her, never engaged in sexual intercourse with her, and never asked her to do so. He contended instead that respondent made her accusations in response to a business-related dispute. The bank also denied respondent's allegations and asserted that any sexual harassment by Taylor was unknown to the bank and engaged in without its consent or approval.

The District Court denied relief and . . . ultimately found that respondent "was not the victim of sexual harassment and was not the victim of sexual discrimination" while employed at the bank.

Although it concluded that respondent had not proved a violation of Title VII, the District Court nevertheless went on to address the bank's liability. After noting the bank's express policy against discrimination, and finding that neither respondent nor any other employee had ever lodged a complaint about sexual harassment by Taylor, the court ultimately concluded that "the bank was without notice and cannot be held liable for the alleged actions of Taylor."

The Court of Appeals for the District of Columbia Circuit reversed. . . . The court stated that a violation of Title VII may be predicated on either of two types of sexual harassment: harassment that involves the conditioning of concrete employment benefits on sexual favors, and harassment that, while not affecting economic benefits, creates a hostile or offensive working environment. . . . Believing that "Vinson's grievance was clearly of the [hostile environment] type," and that the District Court had not considered whether a violation of this type had occurred, the court concluded that a remand was necessary.

The court further concluded that the District Court's findings that any sexual relationship between respondent and Taylor "was a voluntary one" did not obviate the need for a remand. . . .

As to the bank's liability, the Court of Appeals held that an employer is absolutely liable for sexual harassment practiced by supervisory personnel, whether or not the employer knew or should have known about the misconduct. The court relied chiefly on Title VII's definition of "employer" to include "any agent of such a person," 42 U.S.C. §2000e(b), as well as on the EEOC Guidelines. The court held that a supervisor is an "agent" of his employer for Title VII purposes, even if he lacks authority to hire, fire, or promote, since "the mere existence—or even the appearance—of a significant degree of influence in vital job decisions gives any supervisor the opportunity to impose on employees.". . .

In accordance with the foregoing, the Court of Appeals reversed the judgment of the District Court and remanded the case for further proceedings. . . .

## II

Title VII of the Civil Rights Act of 1964 makes it "an unlawful employment practice for an employer . . . to discriminate against any individual with respect to his compensation, terms, conditions, or privileges for employment, because of such individual's race, color, religion, sex, or national origin.". . . .

Respondent argues, and the Court of Appeals held, that unwelcome sexual advances that create an offensive or hostile working environment violate Title VII. Without question, when a supervisor sexually harasses a subordinate because of the subordinate's sex, that supervisor "discriminate[s]" on the basis of sex. . . .

First, the language of Title VII is not limited to "economic" or "tangible" discrimination. The phrase "terms, conditions, or privileges of employment" evinces a congressional intent "'to strike at the entire spectrum of disparate treatment of men and women'" in employment. . . .

Second, in 1980 the EEOC issued Guidelines specifying that "sexual harassment," as there defined, is a form of sex discrimination prohibited by Title VII. . . .

In defining "sexual harassment," the Guidelines first describe the kinds of workplace conduct that may be actionable under Title VII. These include "[u]nwelcome sexual advances, requests for sexual favors, and other verbal or physical conduct of a sexual nature." 29 CFR § 1604.11(a) (1985). Relevant to the charges at issue in this case, the Guidelines provide that such sexual misconduct constitutes prohibited "sexual harassment," whether or not it is directly linked to the grant or denial of an economic *quid pro quo*, where "such conduct has the purpose or effect of unreasonably interfering with an individual's work performance or creating an intimidating, hostile, or offensive working environment.". . .

In concluding that so-called "hostile environment" (i.e., non *quid pro quo*) harassment violates Title VII, the EEOC drew upon a substantial body of judicial decisions and EEOC precedent holding that Title VII affords employees the right to work in an environment free from discriminatory intimidation, ridicule, and insult. . . .

Since the Guidelines were issued, courts have uniformly held, and we agree, that a plaintiff may establish a violation of Title VII by proving that discrimination based on sex has created a hostile or abusive work environment. . . .

For sexual harassment to be actionable, it must be sufficiently severe or pervasive "to alter the conditions of [the victim's] employment and create an abusive working environment." *Ibid.* Respondent's allegations in this case—which include not only pervasive harassment but also criminal conduct of the most serious nature—are plainly sufficient to state a claim for "hostile environment" sexual harassment. . . .

The fact that sex-related conduct was "voluntary," in the sense that the complainant was not forced to participate against her will, is not a defense to a sexual harassment suit brought under Title VII. The gravamen of any sexual harassment claim is that the alleged sexual advances were "unwelcome." 29 CFR § 1604.11(a) (1985). While the question whether particular conduct was indeed unwelcome presents difficult problems of proof and turns largely on credibility determinations committed to the trier of fact, the District Court in this case erroneously focused on the "voluntariness" of respondent's participation in the claimed sexual episodes. The correct inquiry is whether respondent by her conduct indicated that the alleged sexual advances were unwelcome, not whether her actual participation in sexual intercourse was voluntary. . . .

## III

Although the District Court concluded that respondent had not proved a violation of Title VII, it nevertheless went on to consider the question of the bank's liability. Finding that "the bank was without notice" of Taylor's alleged conduct, and that notice to Taylor was not the equivalent of notice to the bank, the court concluded that the bank therefore could not be held liable for Taylor's alleged actions. The Court of Appeals took the opposite view, holding that an employer is strictly liable for a hostile environment created by a supervisor's sexual advances, even though the employer neither knew nor reasonably could have known of the alleged misconduct. The court held that a supervisor, whether or not he possesses the authority to hire, fire, or promote, is necessarily an "agent" of his employer for all Title VII purposes, since "even the appearance" of such authority may enable him to impose himself on his subordinates. . . .

The EEOC, in its brief as *amicus curiae*, contends that courts formulating employer liability rules should draw from traditional agency principles. Examination of those principles has led the EEOC to the view that where a supervisor exercises the authority actually delegated to him by his employer, by making or threatening to make decisions affecting the employment status of his subordinates, such actions are properly imputed to the employer whose delegation of authority empowered the supervisor to undertake them. . . . Thus, the courts have consistently held employers liable for the discriminatory discharges of employees by supervisory personnel, whether or not the employer knew, should have known, or approved of the supervisor's actions. . . .

The EEOC suggests that when a sexual harassment claim rests exclusively on a "hostile environment" theory, however, the usual basis for a finding of agency will often disappear. In that case, the EEOC believes, agency principles lead to

a rule that asks whether a victim of sexual harassment had reasonably available an avenue of complaint regarding such harassment, and, if available and utilized, whether that procedure was reasonably responsive to the employee's complaint. If the employer has an expressed policy against sexual harassment and has implemented a procedure specifically designed to resolve sexual harassment claims, and if the victim does not take advantage of that procedure, the employer should be shielded from liability absent actual knowledge of the sexually hostile environment (obtained, e.g., by the filing of a charge with the EEOC or a comparable state agency). In all other cases, the employer will be liable if it has actual knowledge of the harassment or if, considering all the facts of the case, the victim in question had no reasonably available avenue for making his or her complaint known to appropriate management officials." Brief for United States and EEOC as *Amici Curiae* 26.

As respondent points out, this suggested rule is in some tension with the EEOC Guidelines, which hold an employer liable for the acts of its agents without regard to notice. 29 CFR § 1604.11(c) (1985). The Guidelines do require, however, an "examin[ation of] the circumstances of the particular employment relationship and the job [f]unctions performed by the individual in determining whether an individual acts in either a supervisory or agency capacity."

We hold that the Court of Appeals erred in concluding that employers are always automatically liable for sexual harassment by their supervisors. For the same reason, absence of notice to an employer does not necessarily insulate that employer from liability. *Ibid.*

Finally, we reject petitioner's view that the mere existence of a grievance procedure and a policy against discrimination, coupled with respondent's failure to invoke that procedure, must insulate petitioner from liability. While those facts are plainly relevant, the situation before us demonstrates why they are not necessarily dispositive. Petitioner's general nondiscrimination policy did not address sexual harassment in particular, and thus did not alert employees to their employer's interest in correcting that form of discrimination. App. 25. Moreover, the bank's grievance procedure apparently required an employee to complain first to her supervisor, in this case Taylor. Since Taylor was the alleged perpetrator, it is not altogether surprising that respondent failed to invoke the procedure and report her grievance to him. Petitioner's contention that respondent's failure should insulate it from liability might be substantially stronger if its procedures were better calculated to encourage victims of harassment to come forward.

## IV

In sum, we hold that a claim of "hostile environment" sex discrimination is actionable under Title VII, that the District Court's findings were insufficient to dispose of respondent's hostile environment claim, and that the District Court did not err in admitting testimony about respondent's sexually provocative speech and dress. As to employer liability, we conclude that the Court of Appeals was wrong to entirely disregard agency principles and impose absolute liability on employers for the acts of their supervisors, regardless of the circumstances of a particular case.

Accordingly, the judgment of the Court of Appeals reversing the judgment of the District Court is affirmed, and the case is remanded for further proceedings consistent with this opinion.

# *Teresa Harris, Petitioner, v. Forklift Systems Inc.*

*United States Supreme Court*

In this case we consider the definition of a discriminatorily "abusive work environment" (also known as a "hostile work environment") under Title VII of the Civil Rights Act of 1964, 78 Stat. 253, as amended, 42 U.S.C. § 2000e *et seq.* (1988 ed., Supp. III).

Teresa Harris worked as a manager at Forklift Systems Inc., an equipment rental company, from April 1985 until October 1987. Charles Hardy was Forklift's president.

The Magistrate found that, throughout Harris' time at Forklift, Hardy often insulted her because of her gender and often made her the target of unwanted sexual innuendos. Hardy told Harris on several occasions, in the presence of other employees, "You're a woman, what do you know" and "We need a man as the rental manager"; at least once, he told her she was "a dumb ass woman." App. to Pet. for Cert. A-13. Again in front of others, he suggested that the two of them "go to the Holiday Inn to negotiate [Harris'] raise." *Id.*, at A-14. Hardy occasionally asked Harris and other female employees to get coins from his front pants pocket. *Ibid.* He threw objects on the ground in front of Harris and other women, and asked them to pick the objects up. *Id.*, at A-14 to A-15. He made sexual innuendos about Harris' and other women's clothing. *Id.*, at A-15.

In mid-August 1987, Harris complained to Hardy about his conduct. Hardy said he was surprised that Harris was offended, claimed he was only joking, and apologized. *Id.*, at A-16. He also promised he would stop, and based on this assurance Harris stayed on the job. *Ibid.* But in early September, Hardy began anew: While Harris was arranging a deal with one of Forklift's customers, he asked her, again in front of other employees, "What did you do, promise the guy . . . some [sex] Saturday night?" *Id.*, at A-17. On October 1, Harris collected her paycheck and quit.

Harris then sued Forklift, claiming that Hardy's conduct had created an abusive work environment for her because of her gender. The United States District Court for the Middle District of Tennessee, adopting the report and recommendation of the Magistrate, found this to be "a close case, " *id.*, at A-31, but held that Hardy's conduct did not create an abusive environment. The court found that some of Hardy's comments "offended [Harris], and would offend the reasonable woman, " *id.*, at A-33, but that they were not

> so severe as to be expected to seriously affect [Harris'] psychological well-being. A reasonable woman manager under like circumstances would have been offended by Hardy, but his conduct would not have risen to the level of interfering with that person's work performance.
>
> Neither do I believe that [Harris] was subjectively so offended that she suffered injury. . . . Although Hardy may at times have genuinely offended [Harris], I do not believe that he created a working environment so poisoned as to be intimidating or abusive to [Harris]." *Id.*, at A-34 to A-35. . . .

. . . Title VII of the Civil Rights Act of 1964 makes it "an unlawful employment practice for an employer . . . to discriminate against any individual with respect to his compensation, terms, conditions, or privileges of employment, because of such individual's race, color, religion, sex, or national origin." 42 U.S.C. § 2000e-2(a)(1). As we made clear in *Meritor Savings Bank, FSB, v. Vinson*, 477 U.S. 57, 91 L.Ed. 2d 49, 106 S.Ct. 2399 (1986), this language "is not limited to 'economic' or 'tangible' discrimination. The phrase 'terms, conditions, or privileges of employment' evinces a congressional intent 'to strike at the entire spectrum of disparate treatment of men and women' in employment, "which includes requiring people to work in a discriminatorily hostile or abusive environment. *Id.*, at 64, quoting *Los Angeles Dept. of Water and Power v. Manhart*, 435 U.S. 702, 707, n.13, 55 L.Ed.2d 657, 98 S.Ct. 1370 (1978) (some internal quotation marks omitted). When the workplace is permeated with "discriminatory intimidation, ridicule, and insult," 477 U.S. at 65, that is "sufficiently severe or per-

vasive to alter the conditions of the victim's employment and create an abusive working environment," *id.*, 67 (internal brackets and quotation marks omitted), Title VII is violated.

This standard, which we reaffirm today, takes a middle path between making actionable any conduct that is merely offensive and requiring the conduct to cause a tangible psychological injury. As we pointed out in *Meritor*, "mere utterance of an. . . epithet which engenders offensive feelings in a employee," *ibid.* (internal quotation marks omitted) does not sufficiently affect the conditions of employment to implicate Title VII. Conduct that is not severe or pervasive enough to create an objectively hostile or abusive work environment—an environment that a reasonable person would find hostile or abusive—is beyond Title VII's purview. Likewise, if the victim does not subjectively perceive the environment to be abusive, the conduct has not actually altered the conditions of the victim's employment, and there is no Title VII violation.

But Title VII comes into play before the harassing conduct leads to a nervous breakdown. A discriminatorily abusive work environment, even one that does not seriously affect employees' psychological well-being, can and often will detract from employees' job performance, discourage employees from remaining on the job, or keep them from advancing in their careers. Moreover, even without regard to these tangible effects, the very fact that the discriminatory conduct was so severe or pervasive that it created a work environment abusive to employees because of their race, gender, religion, or national origin offends Title VII's broad rule of workplace equality. The appalling conduct alleged in *Meritor*, and the reference in that case to environments "'so heavily polluted with discrimination as to destroy completely the emotional and psychological stability of minority group workers,'" *id.*, at 66, quoting *Rogers v. EEOC*, 454 F.2d 234, 238 (CA5 1971), cert. denied, 406 U.S. 957, 32 L. Ed. 2d 343, 92 S.Ct. 2058 (1972), merely present some especially egregious examples of harassment. They do not mark the boundary of what is actionable.

We therefore believe the District Court erred in relying on whether the conduct "seriously affected plaintiff's psychological well-being" or led her to "suffer injury." Such an inquiry may needlessly focus the factfinder's attention on concrete psychological harm, an element Title VII does not require. Certainly Title VII bars conduct that would seriously affect a reasonable person's psychological well-being, but the statute is not limited to such conduct. So long as the environment would reasonably be perceived, and is perceived, as hostile or abusive, *Meritor, supra*, at 67, there is no need for it also to be psychologically injurious.

This is not, and by its nature cannot be, a mathematically precise test. We need not answer today all the potential questions it raises, nor specifically address the Equal Employment Opportunity Commission's new regulations on this subject, see 58 Fed. Reg. 51266 (1993) (proposed 29 CFR § 1609.1, 1609.2); see also 29 CFR § 1604.11 (1993). But we can say that whether an environment is "hostile" or "abusive" can be determined only by looking at all the circumstances. These may include the frequency of the discriminatory conduct; its severity; whether it is physically threatening or humiliating, or a mere offensive utterance; and whether it unreasonably interferes with an employee's work performance. The effect on the employee's psychological well-being is, of course, relevant to determining whether the plaintiff actually found the environment abusive. But while psychological harm, like any other relevant factor, may be taken into account, no single factor is required.

Forklift, while conceding that a requirement that the conduct seriously affect psychological well-being is unfounded, argues that the District Court nonetheless correctly applied the *Meritor* standard. We disagree. Though the District Court did conclude that the work environment was not "intimidating or abusive to [Harris],"App. to Pet. for Cert. A-35, it did so only after finding that the conduct was not "so severe as to be expected to seriously affect plaintiff's psychological well-being," *id.*, at A-34, and that Harris was not "subjectively so offended that she suffered injury," *ibid.* The District Court's application of these incorrect standards may well have influenced its ultimate conclusion, especially given that the court found this to be a "close case," *id.*, at A-31.

We therefore reverse the judgment of the Court of Appeals, and remand the case for further proceedings consistent with this opinion.

So ordered.

# CASES

## CASE 1.   *How Would You Vote if You Lived in Michigan?*

In 2003 the U.S. Supreme Court heard two cases about racial preferences in admissions at the University of Michigan. The Court ruled that some limited forms of racial preference are allowable. (See *Grutter v. Bollinger*, in this chapter.) In response to the Supreme

This case was prepared by Patrick James Connolly.

Court cases, some citizens of Michigan proposed an amendment to the constitution, which came to be called the Michigan Civil Rights Initiative and "Proposal 2." The amendment would prohibit all state agencies in Michigan from giving preferences to individuals because of their race, ethnicity, color, country of origin, or gender. The proposed amendment would effectively dismantle all forms of affirmative action programs that were in place for public contracting, hiring, university admissions, and the like.

For Michigan, a state which is roughly 80 percent white, but is also among the most segregated in the country, the issue was an especially divisive one. A lagging economy, a recent influx of foreign immigrants, and competitive admissions at the state's universities all contributed to the import of the proposed amendment. In earlier years, California and Washington State had paved the way by passing similar measures.

Proponents of the amendment claimed that individual merit ought to be the sole factor in hiring and admissions decisions and that giving preference to minorities was reverse discrimination. They believed that all distinctions made along gender or racial lines are unjust. Opponents of the amendment claimed that diversity was itself valuable and that affirmative action programs were necessary to lessen racial inequalities in the state. They believed that the proposed amendment would severely hurt minorities and women and would result in fewer opportunities for members of these groups.

Voters in Michigan were therefore faced with a stark moral choice about what the law *should be* (not about what the law *is*). They were asked to evaluate the moral acceptability of the amendment and the likely effects of this amendment on diversity, social cohesion, and individual merit before deciding between strict equality of opportunity and programs designed to help underprivileged minorities.

The proposed amendment was ultimately passed with a 58 percent majority, thus banning affirmative action policies in the state. The University of Michigan, with great reluctance, changed its admissions policies to conform to the new law while vowing to fight for continued diversity. The university's students were divided over how they would have voted. On January 13, 2007, University of Michigan President Mary Sue Coleman reiterated the university's commitment to diversity and vowed to continue to create as much diversity as the law allows and to use outreach programs for recruitment of minorities.

## Questions

1. Is it ever acceptable for public institutions to engage in preferential treatment of minority groups? If so, under what conditions?

2. How much say should citizens have in determining the hiring practices of the state and state-funded institutions?

3. Is diversity in the workplace inherently valuable? Or is it valuable as a means to something else that is inherently valuable, such as protecting human rights?

4. Does minority racial preference entail reverse discrimination? If so, is reverse discrimination a form of invidious discrimination?

5. Is ending preferential treatment the best way to ensure that candidates are judged solely on personal merit? Would other criteria take its place?

## CASE 2.  *Sing's Chinese Restaurant*

The Bali Hai Corporation started as a small Chinese restaurant in Boston, Massachusetts, in 1959. The restaurant was an exact replica of a Chinese pagoda. Over the years, the restaurant, owned and managed by Arnold Sing, became known for its food and atmosphere. Customers were made to feel as if they were actually in China. In the last few years, Sing decided to incorporate and open other similar restaurants throughout the country. Sing, who had come to the United States from China in the early 1940s, was very strict in keeping up his reputation for good food and atmosphere. He had a policy of hiring only waiters of Asian descent. He felt this added to his customers' dining pleasure and made for a more authentic environment. For kitchen positions, though, Sing hired any qualified applicants.

About a year ago at Sing's Bali Hai in Washington, DC, there was a shortage of waiters. An advertisement was placed in the newspaper for waiters, and the manager of the store was instructed by Sing to hire only Asians. The manager was also reminded of Bali Hai's commitment to a reputation for good food and atmosphere. Two young men, one black and one white, both with considerable restaurant experience, applied for the waiter's jobs. The manager explained the policy of hiring only Asians to the young men, and he also told them he could get them work in his kitchen. The two men declined the positions and instead went directly to the area Equal Employment Office and filed a complaint. Sing's defense was that the policy was only to preserve the atmosphere of the restaurant. He said the Asian waiters were needed to make it more authentic. Sing also added that he hired blacks, whites, and persons of other races for his kitchen help.

### Questions

1. Is Sing's defense a good one under the law? Why or why not?
2. Is Sing's defense a good one under the standards of morality? Why or why not?
3. Is this a case of "preferential hiring"? Of "reverse discrimination"?

## CASE 3.  *Kaiser Aluminum and the United Steelworkers*

In 1974 the United Steelworkers of America, a labor union, and the Kaiser Aluminum & Chemical Corporation made an agreement seeking to solve an overwhelming racial inequality in the Kaiser workforce. Before the deal was struck fewer than 2 percent of the skilled workers at a Kaiser plant in Gramercy, Louisiana, were black. This was despite the fact that nearly 40 percent of the Gramercy area workforce was black.

Previously, Kaiser had hired its *skilled* laborers with experience from outside of the company. In an effort to correct historical inequalities of treatment, the company decided to begin a training program for skilled positions by recruiting directly from and providing training for *unskilled* Kaiser employees. It was agreed that those with the most seniority at the plant in Gramercy would be accepted into the program with the condition that at least half of the employees accepted would be black. In the agreement it was stated that this preferential treatment of black employees would be discontinued once the percentage of skilled black laborers at the Gramercy plant reached the level of the percentage of blacks in the Gramercy area's workforce.

In the year the program began, 13 workers from the Gramercy plant were chosen for the job training program. Of these, seven were black and six were white. However, two of the black workers chosen had less seniority than several white workers who had applied to and been rejected from the program. Brian Weber, a white worker, had not been selected, though he had more seniority than some of the black workers selected. Weber thought this was unfair treatment and filed a lawsuit.

Weber alleged that his civil rights had been violated and that, as a result of his race, he had been discriminated against. He claimed that this was illegal under Title VII of the Civil Rights Act and under the Fourteenth Amendment. In a 5–2 vote, the U.S. Supreme Court determined that because the agreement was voluntary, undertaken by private parties, and temporary, Weber was not a victim of unfair discrimination.

Kaiser was attempting to correct a glaring racial inequality that was the product of historical circumstances and its own unfair past practices. Weber, by contrast, thought that Kaiser engaged in objectionable racial discrimination by setting aside his position of seniority.

### Questions

1. Are the percentage figures in the case "quotas"? Are they justified under the circumstances?
2. Does Kaiser have a justified employment policy? If not, how should it be revised?
3. Does Kaiser's policy eventuate in reverse discrimination against Weber? If so, is it justified?
4. Does the fact that the agreement was voluntary and temporary make the case morally different?
5. How much should companies be willing to do to correct historical inequalities?

## CASE 4. *Promotions at Uptown Bottling and Canning Company*

Lincoln Grant, a 31-year-old African American employee, has been working for six years as a technician at Uptown Bottling and Canning Co. in Baltimore, Maryland. On four separate occasions, he has unsuccessfully sought a promotion to a managerial position. As the only member in his department who has completed graduate study, Grant questions how the company has treated him. He also knows that only four African American employees have been promoted during the previous nine years, compared with 41 white employees who have been offered promotions over the same period of time. Baltimore city is more than 50

This case was prepared by David Lawrence.

percent African American, and the surrounding metropolitan region is about 25 percent African American.

On one occasion, the company posted a listing for a managerial position and encouraged current employees to apply. According to the job description, eligible applicants should have at least five years of prior experience with the company and should hold a graduate degree in either business or engineering. Furthermore, each applicant would be required to take a written exam. Although Grant applied, the company awarded the position to Henry Thompson, a white male with only two years of experience and no graduate degree. Grant, as it turned out, was the only applicant with five years of prior experience and a graduate degree.

In making its final selections for jobs, Uptown Bottling and Canning considers test scores and leadership potential. Grant's test scores were significantly above average, but his supervisors told him that he lacked the leadership skills required of managers. Based on observed performance, they pointed out, Grant has never demonstrated leadership skills while working at Uptown. At the same time, Grant has also never been given any form of leadership training. Most of the 41 white employees who were promoted had been given leadership training within the first five years of their employment with the company.

**Questions**

1. Are the facts in this case sufficient to indicate that the Uptown Bottling and Canning Co. discriminated against Lincoln Grant on the basis of race?
2. Given the promotion statistics, should the company do more to see that African American employees are considered for both leadership training and promotions? Are statistics irrelevant, or do they point to underlying failures of fair employment?

## CASE 5.  *Freedom of Expression in the Workplace*

Barbara Hill was employed at American Plastic Products Co. beginning in June 1999. As a member of the engineering department, part of her job description included identifying defects in the equipment that formed the plastic products. She was expected to report on these defects at production meetings, which were held every morning.

In order to enter the engineering laboratory to perform this research, Barbara had to walk down a long corridor that was the only entrance to the room in which production meetings were held. As she walked down this hall every morning, she could not escape noticing pinup photographs and provocative calendars on the walls that had been placed there by male employees. Barbara complained to her supervisor, who proceeded to remove all the offending materials, including even a postcard located on a desk in an office with glass doors opening into the corridor.

The following day, as she was walking down the corridor to the laboratory, Barbara overheard a conversation between two male employees. Though not directed at her, she could not help but overhear that they were agreeing, with intensely expressed conviction, that women should not be given detail-oriented

This case was prepared by David Lawrence.

jobs, such as hers, because men are better able to focus in the workplace. Their conversation was punctuated with the language of "chicks," "bitches," and the like.

Barbara complained to her supervisor again, this time claiming that such behavior created a hostile work environment. When approached by the supervisor, the two male employees contended that they were simply expressing their political and business opinions—nothing more. The supervisor considered whether he should place the two men on probation and warn them to refrain from such conversations in the future. However, the supervisor decided to sit on this idea for a few days.

## Questions

1. Should the pinup photographs and calendars have been taken down? Why or why not? Why might a supervisor deem it necessary to do so?

2. Should employees be permitted to voice their opinions at work even if other employees find them misguided or offensive? Does the right to free expression outweigh the right to a nonhostile working environment?

## CASE 6.  *"Harassment" at Brademore Electric*

Maura Donovan is a recent graduate of UCLA who now works as a low-level administrative assistant for Keith Sturdivant at the Brademore Electric Corporation, a large Los Angeles electrical contractor. Keith interviewed and hired Maura to work directly under him.

Maura had been employed at Brademore only three weeks when Keith approached her to go out on the weekend. Maura was taken somewhat by surprise and declined, thinking it best not to mix business and pleasure. But two days later Keith persisted, saying that Maura owed him something in return for his "getting" her the job. Maura was offended by this comment, knowing that she was well qualified for the position, but Keith seemed lonely, almost desperate, and she agreed to go with him to the Annual Renaissance Fair on Saturday afternoon. As it turned out, she did not have an enjoyable time. She liked the fair but found Keith a bit crude and at times al-

most uncivil in the way he treated employees at the fair. She hoped he would not ask her out again.

But Monday morning he came back with the idea that they go on an overnight sailboat trip with some of his friends the next weekend. Maura politely declined. But Keith persisted, insisting that she owed her job to him. Maura found herself dreading the times she saw Keith coming down the corridor. What had been a very nice work environment for her had turned into a place of frequent dread. She spent a lot of time working to avoid Keith.

For four straight weeks, Keith came up with a different idea for how they might spend the weekend—always involving an overnight trip. Maura always declined. After the second week, she lied and told him that she was dating a number of other men. She said she was quite interested in two of these men and that she did not see any future with Keith. Keith's reaction was

This case was prepared by Tom L. Beauchamp.

to become even more insistent that they had a future together and to continue to ask her out.

Keith had become quite infatuated with Maura. He watched her every movement, whenever he had the opportunity. Sometimes he openly stared at her as she walked from one office to another. He began to have sexual fantasies about her, which he disclosed to two male supervisors. However, he never mentioned to Maura that he had in mind any form of sexual relationship.

Keith's direct supervisor, Vice President B. K. Singh, became aware of Keith's interest in Maura from two sources. First, he was told about the sexual fantasies by one of Keith's two male friends to whom Keith made the disclosures. Second, Maura had that same day come to his office to complain about what she considered sexual harassment. Mr. Singh became concerned about a possible contaminated work environment, but he did not think that he or Maura could make any form of harassment charge stick. The company had no corporate policy on harassment. Mr. Singh considered

the situation to be just another case of one employee asking another out and being overly persistent. Mr. Singh decided not to do anything right away, not even to discuss the problem with Keith. He was worried that if he did take up the matter with Keith at such an early stage, he would himself be creating a hostile work environment. He believed Keith's advances would have to worsen before he should intervene or take the problem to the president.

**Questions**

1. Is Keith's conduct a case of sexual harassment? Is it a clear case, a borderline case, or no case at all?
2. Is it justifiable for Mr. Singh to adopt a position of nonintervention? Should he speak with Keith? What would you do if you were in his position?
3. Does the fact that Maura agreed once to go out with Keith mean that she has encouraged him to make further requests? If so, was she sufficiently discouraging at a later point?

## Suggested Supplementary Readings

ALBERTS, ROBERT J., and LORNE H. SEIDMAN. 1994. "Sexual Harassment by Clients, Customers, and Suppliers: How Employers Should Handle an Emerging Legal Problem." *Employee Relations Law Journal* 20 (Summer): 85–100.

ACHAMPONG, FRANCIS. 1999. *Workplace Sexual Harassment Law: Principles, Landmark Developments, and Framework for Effective Risk Management.* Westport, CT: Quorum Books.

ANDERSON, ELIZABETH S. 2002. "Integration, Affirmative Action, and Strict Scrutiny." *New York University Law Review* 77 (November): 1195–1271.

BAUGH, S. GAYLE. 1997. "On the Persistence of Sexual Harassment in the Workplace." *Journal of Business Ethics* 16 (1997): 899–908.

BEAUCHAMP, TOM L. 1998. "In Defense of Affirmative Action." *Journal of Ethics* 2:143–58.

BERGMANN, BARBARA R. 1996. *In Defense of Affirmative Action.* New York: Basic Books.

BLOCH, FARRELL. 1994. *Antidiscrimination Law and Minority Employment: Recruitment Practices and Regulatory Constraints.* Chicago: The University of Chicago Press.

BOOKER, M. J. 1998. "Can Sexual Harassment Be Salvaged?" *Journal of Business Ethics* 17 (August): 1171–77.

BOYLAN, MICHAEL. 2002. "Affirmative Action: Strategies for the Future." *Journal of Social Philosophy* 33 (Spring): 117–30.

BOXILL, BERNARD. 1992. *Blacks and Social Justice.* Totowa, NJ: Rowman and Littlefield.

CAHN, STEVEN M., ed. 2002. *The Affirmative Action Debate.* New York: Routledge.

CARD, ROBERT F. 2005. "Making Sense of the Diversity-Based Legal Argument for Affirmative Action." *Public Affairs Quarterly* 19:11–24.

COHEN, CARL, and JAMES P. STERBA. 2003. *Affirmative Action and Racial Preference.* New York: Oxford University Press.

COKORINOS, LEE. 2003. *The Assault on Diversity: An Organized Challenge to Racial and Gender Justice.* Lanham, MD: Rowman & Littlefield.

CORLETT, ANGELO J. 2003. *Race, Racism, and Reparations.* Ithaca, New York: Cornell University Press.

CRAIN, KAREN A., and KENNETH A. HEISCHMIDT. 1995. "Implementing Business Ethics: Sexual Harassment." *Journal of Business Ethics* 14 (April): 299–308.

CROSBY, FAYE J. 2004. *Affirmative Action Is Dead; Long Live Affirmative Action.* New Haven, CT: Yale University Press.

CROUCH, MARGARET A. 1998. "The 'Social Etymology' of 'Sexual Harassment'." *Journal of Social Philosophy* 29:19–40.

———. 2001. *Thinking about Sexual Harassment: A Guide for the Perplexed.* New York: Oxford University Press.

DANDEKER, NATALIE. 1990. "Contrasting Consequences: Bringing Charges of Sexual Harassment Compared with Other Cases of Whistleblowing." *Journal of Business Ethics* 9.

DODDS, SUSAN M., LUCY FROST, ROBERT PARGETTER, and ELIZABETH W. PRIOR. 1988. "Sexual Harassment." *Social Theory and Practice* 14 (Summer): 111–30.

EGLER, THERESA DONAHUE. 1995. "Five Myths about Sexual Harassment." *HR Magazine* 40 (January): 27–30.

EPSTEIN, DEBORAH. "Freedom of Speech vs. Workplace Harassment." *Slate.* http://Slate.msn.com (September 17, 1997, and October 17, 1997).

EPSTEIN, RICHARD A. 2002. "A Rational Basis for Affirmative Action: A Shaky but Classical Liberal Defense." *Michigan Law Review* 100 (August): 2036–61.

ERLER, EDWARD J. 1997. "The Future of Civil Rights: Affirmative Action Redivivus." *Notre Dame Journal of Law and Ethics* 11:15–65.

European Commission. *Sexual Harassment at the Workplace in the European Union.* Belgium: European Communities, 1999.

EYRING, ALISON, and BETTE ANN STEAD. 1998. "Shattering the Glass Ceiling: Some Successful Corporate Practices." *Journal of Business Ethics* 17 (February): 245–51.

EZORSKY, GERTRUDE. 1991. *Racism and Justice.* Ithaca, NY: Cornell University Press.

FICK, BARBARA J. 1997. "The Case for Maintaining and Encouraging the Use of Voluntary Affirmative Action in Private Sector Employment." *Notre Dame Journal of Law and Ethics* 11:159–70.

FINE, LESLIE M., C. DAVID SHEPHERD, and SUSAN L. JOSEPHS. 1994. "Sexual Harassment in the Sales Force: The Customer Is NOT Always Right." *Journal of Personal Selling & Sales Management* 14 (Fall): 15–30.

FINKELMAN, PAUL. "Affirmative Action." encarta.msn.com/encyclopedia_761580666/Affirmative_Action.html Microsoft® Encarta® Online Encyclopedia 2006.

FORDE-MAZRUI, KIM. 2004. "Taking Conservatives Seriously: A Moral Justification for Affirmative Action and Reparations." *California Law Review* 92 (May): 683–753.

FOSTER, CARLEY, and SUE NEWELL. 2002. "Managing Diversity and Equal Opportunities—Some Practical Implications." *Business and Professional Ethics Journal* 21: 11–26.

FULLINWIDER, ROBERT K. "Affirmative Action." *Stanford Encyclopedia of Philosophy.* http://plato.stanford.edu/entries/affirmative-action/

———. 1997. "The Life and Death of Racial Preferences." *Philosophical Studies* 85:163–80.

———. 2002. "Diversity and Affirmative Action." In *Philosophical Dimensions of Public Policy,* ed. Verna V. Gehring and William A. Galston. New Brunswick, New Jersey: Transaction Publishers. 115–24.

GRIFFITH, STEPHEN. 1999. "Sexual Harassment and the Rights of the Accused." *Public Affairs Quarterly* 13:43–71.

GUINIER, LANI, and STURM, SUSAN. 2001. *Who's Qualified?* Boston: Beacon Press.

HOLMES, ROBERT L. 1996. "Sexual Harassment and the University." *Monist* 79:499–518.

HOPKINS, WILLIE E. 1997. *Ethical Dimensions of Diversity.* Thousand Oaks, CA: Sage.

HORNE, GERALD. 1992. *Reversing Discrimination: The Case for Affirmative Action.* New York: International Publishers.

IRVINE, WILLIAM B. "Beyond Sexual Harassment." 2000 *Journal of Business Ethics* 28 (December): 353–60.

KALANTARI, BEHROOZ. 1995. "Dynamics of Job Evaluation and the Dilemma of Wage Disparity in the United States." *Journal of Business Ethics* 14: 397–403.

KERSHNAR, STEPHEN. 1999. "Uncertain Damages to Racial Minorities and Strong Affirmative Action." *Public Affairs Quarterly* 13:83–98.

KEYTON, JOANN, and RHODES, STEVEN C. 1997. "Sexual Harassment: A Matter of Individual Ethics, Legal Definitions, or Organizational Policy?" *Journal of Business Ethics* 16:129–46.

LADENSON, ROBERT. 1995. "Ethics in the American Workplace." *Business and Professional Ethics Journal* 14:17–31.

LEAP, TERRY L., and LARRY R. SMELTZER. 1984. "Racial Remarks in the Workplace: Humor or Harassment?" *Harvard Business Review* 62.

LEMONCHECK, LINDA, and MANE HAJDIN. 1997. *Sexual Harassment: A Debate*. Lanham, MD: Rowman & Littlefield.

LICHTENBERG, JUDITH, and DAVID LUBAN. 2002. "The Merits of Merit." In *Philosophical Dimensions of Public Policy*, ed. Verna V. Gehring and William A. Galston. New Brunswick, New Jersey: Transaction Publishers, 101–13.

MACKINNON, CATHARINE A. 1979. *Sexual Harassment of Working Women: A Case of Sex Discrimination*. New Haven, CT: Yale University Press.

MOSLEY, ALBERT G., and NICHOLAS CAPALDI. 1996. *Affirmative Action: Social Justice or Unfair Preference?* Lanham, MD: Rowman & Littlefield.

MORRIS, CELIA. 1994. *Bearing Witness: Sexual Harassment and Beyond—Everywoman's Story*. Boston: Little, Brown & Co.

MOY, PATRICIA, DAVID DOMKE, and KEITH STAMM. 2001. "The Spiral of Silence and Public Opinion on Affirmative Action." *Journalism and Mass Communication Quarterly* 78 (Spring): 7–25.

O'DONOHUE, WILLIAM, ed. 1997. *Sexual Harassment: Theory, Research, and Treatment*. Boston: Allyn and Bacon.

ORFIELD, GARY, with MICHAEL KURLAENDER, eds. 2001. *Diversity Challenged: Evidence on the Impact of Affirmative Action*. Cambridge, MA: Harvard Education Publishing Group.

PACE, JOSEPH MICHAEL, and ZACHARY SMITH. 1995. "Understanding Affirmative Action: From the Practitioner's Perspective." *Public Personnel Management* 24:139–47.

PHILIPS, MICHAEL. 1991. "Preferential Hiring and the Question of Competence." *Journal of Business Ethics* 10.

PLATT, ANTHONY M. 1997. "The Rise and Fall of Affirmative Action." *Notre Dame Journal of Law and Ethics* 11:67–78.

POJMAN, LOUIS P. 1998. "The Case against Affirmative Action." *International Journal of Applied Philosophy* 12:97–115.

PURDY, LAURA. 1994. "Why Do We Need Affirmative Action?" *Journal of Social Philosophy* 25: 133–43.

ROSENFELD, MICHEL. 1991. *Affirmative Action and Justice: A Philosophical and Constitutional Inquiry*. New Haven, CT: Yale University Press.

ROTHMAN, STANLEY, SEYMOUR MARTIN LIPSET, and NEIL NEVITTE. 2003. "Racial Diversity Reconsidered." *Public Interest* 151 (Spring): 25–38.

SINGH, VAL, and SEBASTIEN POINT. 2006. "(Re)Presentations of Gender and Ethnicity in Diversity Statements on European Company Websites." *Journal of Business Ethics* 68 (November): 363–79.

SKRENTNY, JOHN DAVID. 1996. *The Ironies of Affirmative Action: Politics, Culture, and Justice in America*. Chicago: University of Chicago Press.

SEGRAVE, KERRY. 1994. *The Sexual Harassment of Women in the Workplace, 1600 to 1993*. Jefferson, NC: McFarland.

SOWELL, THOMAS. 2004. *Affirmative Action Around the World: An Empirical Study*. New Haven, CT: Yale University Press.

STOCKDALE, MARGARET S., and FAYE J. CROSBY. 2004. *The Psychology and Management of Workplace Diversity*. Malden, MA: Blackwell Publishing.

SUNSTEIN, CASS R. 1991. "The Limits of Compensatory Justice." *Nomos* 33:281–310.

SUPERSON, ANITA. 1993. "A Feminist Definition of Sexual Harassment." *Journal of Social Philosophy* 24.

VOLOKH, EUGENE. 1992. "Freedom of Speech and Workplace Harassment." *UCLA Law Review* 39.

———. 1997. "Freedom of Speech vs. Workplace Harassment." *Slate*: http://Slate.msn.com (September 23).

WALL, EDMUND, ed. 1992. *Sexual Harassment: Confrontations and Decisions*. Buffalo, NY: Prometheus Books.

WARNKE, GEORGIA. 1998. "Affirmative Action, Neutrality, and Integration." *Journal of Social Philosophy* 29:87–103.

WELLS, DEBORAH L., and BEVERLY J. KRACHER. 1993. "Justice, Sexual Harassment, and the Reasonable Victim Standard." *Journal of Business Ethics* 12:423–31.

WIKIPEDIA. "Sexual Harassment." en.wikipedia.org/wiki/Sexual_harassment

YORK, KENNETH M. 1989. "Defining Sexual Harassment in Workplaces: A Policy-Capturing Approach." *Academy of Management Journal* 32.

# Chapter 5

# Marketing and the Disclosure of Information

## INTRODUCTION

MARKETING ETHICS EXPLORES decision making that emerges at several different levels in corporate life, such as whether to place a new product on the market, how to price a product, how to advertise, and how to conduct sales. Marketing research, pricing, advertising, selling, and international marketing have all come under close ethical scrutiny in recent years. Ethical issues about marketing are often centered on obligations to disclose information. Advertising is the most visible way businesses present information to the public, but not the only or even the most important way. Sales information, annual reports containing financial audits, public relations presentations, educational seminars, physician office visits, warranties, trade secrets, and public education and public health campaigns are other vital means by which corporations manage, communicate, and limit information.

A classic defense of U.S. business practice is that business provides the public with products that the public wants; the consumer is king in the free-enterprise system, and the market responds to consumer demands. This response is often said to represent the chief strength of a market economy over a collectivist system. Freedom of consumer choice is unaffected by government and corporate controls. But consider the following controversy about freedom of choice. In the mid-1980s the Federal Trade Commission (FTC) "reconsidered" its rule prohibiting supermarket advertising of items when those items are not in stock. The rule had been enacted in 1971 to combat frustration among shoppers who found empty shelves in place of advertised goods and often wound up substituting more expensive items. FTC officials suggested that the rule may have been unduly burdensome for the supermarket industry and that "market forces" would eliminate or curtail those who dishonestly advertised. Consumer groups argued that relaxing the rule would permit more expensive stores to lure shoppers by advertising low prices leading many shoppers to spend more overall than they would have spent in a low-budget store. Mark Silbergeld of Consumers Union argued that the commission was acting in ignorance of the *real purpose* of supermarket advertising, which is to present a "come-on to get people into their stores."[1]

In the last 30 years or so it has been widely appreciated that this problem is only one among many that confronts marketers of goods and services. Some problems are commonplace—for example, withholding vital information, distorting data, and providing payments or gifts to individuals who can influence sales. Other problems of information control are more subtle; these include the use of flashy information to entice customers, the use of annual reports as public relations devices, and the use of calculated "news releases" to promote products. Rights of autonomy and free choice are at the center of these discussions. In some forms, withholding information and manipulating advertising messages threaten to undermine the free choice of consumers, clients, stockholders, and even colleagues. Deceptive and misleading statements can limit freedom by restricting the range of choice and can cause a person to do what he or she otherwise would not do.

Aside from these *autonomy*-based problems, there are *harm*-based problems that may have little to do with making a choice. For example, in a now classic case, the Nestlé corporation was pressured to suspend infant formula advertising and aggressive marketing tactics in developing countries. This controversy focused less on the freedom-based issue of the right to disseminate information than on preventing a population from harming itself through inadequate breastfeeding and inadequate appreciation of the risks of the use of infant formula. Such harm-based issues are mentioned in this chapter, but the restriction of free choice by manipulative influence is the central issue.

The inception of the problem is that consumers are frequently unable to evaluate information about the variety of goods and services available to them without assistance. There is a large "knowledge gap," as it is commonly called, between consumer and marketer. The consumer either lacks vital information or lacks the skills to evaluate the good or service. This circumstance leads to a situation in which the consumer must place trust in a service agency, producer, or retailer. Many marketers are well aware of this situation and feel acutely that they must not abuse their position of superior information. Many also engage in marketing their own trustworthiness while simultaneously marketing a product or service. When the felt or proclaimed trust is breached (whether intentionally or by accident), the marketer–consumer relationship is endangered.

### Advertising

Many critics deplore the values presented in advertising as well as the effects advertising has on consumers. Other critics are more concerned about specific practices of advertising directed at vulnerable groups such as children, the poor, and the elderly; advertising that exploits women or uses fear appeals; advertising that uses subliminal messages; and the advertising of liquor and tobacco products. Although critics have long denounced misleading or information-deficient advertising, the moral concerns and concepts underlying these denunciations have seldom been carefully examined. What is a deceptive or misleading advertisement? Is it, for example, deceptive or misleading to advertise a heavily sweetened cereal as "nutritious" or as "building strong bodies"? Are such advertisements forms of lying? Are they manipulative, especially when children are the primary targets or people are led to make purchases they do not need and would not have made had they not seen the advertising? If so, does the manipulation derive from some form of deception? For example, if an advertisement that touts a particular mouthwash as germ killing manipulates listeners into purchasing the mouthwash, does it follow that these consumers have been deceived?

Does such advertising represent a deprivation of free choice, or is it rather an example of how free choice determines market forces? Control over a person is exerted through various kinds of influences, but not all *influences* actually *control* behavior. Some forms of influence are desired and accepted by those who are influenced, whereas others are unwelcome. Many influences can easily be resisted by most persons; others are irresistible. Human reactions to influences such as corporate-sponsored information and advertising presentations cannot in many cases be determined or easily studied. Frank Dandrea, vice president of marketing for Schiefflin & Co., the importer of Hennessy's Cognac, once said that in their advertisements, "the idea is to show a little skin, a little sex appeal, a little tension."[2] This effect is accomplished by showing a scantily clad woman holding a brandy snifter and staring provocatively in response to a man's interested glance. Hennessy tries in a subtle manner to use a mixture of sex and humor, just as Coors beer uses the technique in less than subtle ways. Other companies use rebates and coupons. All these methods are attempts to influence, and it is well known that they are at least partially successful. However, the degree of influence of these strategies and the moral acceptability of these influences have been less carefully examined.

There is a continuum of controlling influence in our daily lives, running from coercion, at the most controlling end of the continuum, to persuasion and education, both of which are noncontrolling influences. Other points on the continuum include indoctrination, seduction, and the like. Coercion requires an intentional and successful influence through an irresistible threat of harm. A coercively induced action deprives a person of freedom because it entirely controls the person's action. Rational persuasion, by contrast, involves a successful appeal to reason to convince a person to accept freely what is advocated by the persuader. Like informing, persuading is entirely compatible with free choice.

Many choices are not substantially free, although we commonly think of them as free. These include actions under powerful family and religious influences, purchases made under partial ignorance of the quality of the merchandise, and deference to an authoritative physician's judgment. Many actions fall short of ideal free action either because the agent lacks critical information or because the agent is under the control of another person. The central question is whether actions are sufficiently or adequately free, not whether they are ideally or wholly free.

*Manipulation* is a general term that refers to the great gray area of influence. It is a catchall category that suggests the act of getting people to do what is advocated without resorting to coercion but also without appealing to reasoned argument. In the case of *informational* manipulation, on which several selections in this chapter concentrate, information is managed so that the manipulated person will do what the manipulator intends. Whether such uses of information necessarily compromise or restrict free choice is an unresolved issue. One plausible thesis is that some manipulations—for instance, the use of rewards such as free trips or lottery coupons in direct-mail advertising—are compatible with free choice, whereas others—such as deceptive offers or tantalizing ads aimed at young children—are not compatible with free choice. Beer, wine, and tobacco advertising aimed at teenagers and young adults has been under particularly harsh criticism in recent years, on grounds that sex, youth, fun, and beauty are directly linked in the advertising to dangerous products, with noticeable marketing success.

As Robert L. Arrington points out in his essay, these issues raise complex questions of moral responsibility in the advertising of products. Arrington notes that puffery, subliminal advertising, and indirect information transfer are typical examples of the problem. After he examines criticisms and defenses of such practices, he analyzes four of the central concepts at work in the debate: (1) autonomous desire, (2) rational desire, (3) free choice, and (4) control. He tries to show that, despite certain dangers, advertising should not be judged guilty of frequent violations of the consumer's autonomy in any relevant sense of this notion.

Many problems with advertising seem to fall somewhere between acceptable and unacceptable manipulation. Consider these two examples: Anheuser-Busch ran a television commercial for its Budweiser beer showing some working men heading for a brew at day's end. The commercial began with a shot of the Statue of Liberty in the background, included close-up shots of a construction crew working to restore the statue, and ended with the words "This Bud's for you; you know America takes pride in what you do." This statement may seem innocent, but the Liberty–Ellis Island Foundation accused Anheuser-Busch of a "blatant attempt to dupe [i.e., manipulate] consumers" by implying that Budweiser was among the sponsors helping repair the statue. The foundation was particularly annoyed because Anheuser-Busch had refused such a sponsorship when invited by the foundation, whereas its rival, Stroh Brewing Company, had subsequently accepted an exclusive brewery sponsorship.[3]

A second case comes from Kellogg's advertising for its All-Bran product. The company ran a campaign linking its product to the prevention of cancer, apparently causing an immediate increase in sales of 41 percent for All-Bran. Although many food manufacturers advertise the low-salt, low-fat, low-calorie, or high-fiber content of their products, Kellogg went further, citing a specific product as a way to combat a specific disease. It is illegal to make claims about the health benefits of a specific food product without Food and Drug Administration (FDA) approval, and Kellogg did not have this approval. Even so, officials at both the National Cancer Institute and the FDA were not altogether critical of the ads. On the one hand, officials at these agencies agree that a high-fiber, low-fat diet containing some of the ingredients in

All-Bran does help prevent cancer. On the other hand, no direct association exists between eating a given product and preventing cancer, and certainly no single food product can function like a drug as a preventive or remedy for such a disease.

The Kellogg ad strongly suggested that eating All-Bran is what one needs to do to prevent cancer. Such a claim is potentially misleading in several respects. The ad did not suggest how much fiber people should eat, nor did it note that people can consume too much fiber while neglecting other essential minerals. Further, no direct scientific evidence linked the consumption of this product with the prevention of cancer, and this product could not be expected to affect all types of cancer. Is the Kellogg promise manipulative, or is the ad, as Kellogg claims, basically a truthful, health-promotion campaign? Does it contain elements of both?

One of the court cases in this chapter—*Coca-Cola Co. v. Tropicana Products Inc.*—focuses on a central question of the ethics of advertising. In this case, the two main competitors in the United States for the chilled orange juice market came into a direct conflict. The Coca-Cola Co., maker of Minute Maid orange juice, sued Tropicana Products on grounds of false advertising. Tropicana had claimed in its advertisements that its brand of orange juice is "as it comes from the orange" and the only "brand not made with concentrate and water." Coke asserted that this claim was false and that Tropicana is pasteurized and sometimes frozen prior to packaging. Coke also claimed that it had lost sales of its product as a result of this misrepresentation. The court agreed with Coke both that the company had lost sales and that consumers had been misled by Tropicana's advertising campaign.

In a second case in the legal section, the United States Court of Appeals for the Seventh Circuit took up a set of issues presented in the case *B. Sanfield Inc. v. Finlay Fine Jewelry Corp.* The issues concerned one of the most commonly used forms of bargain advertising, which is to offer a percentage reduction from the advertiser's own former price for an article. Had the original price been a bona fide price at which the article was being offered to the public over the course of a substantial period of time, the price comparison would be a legitimate basis for an advertisement. But if the alleged "former price" was not bona fide but, rather, fictitious—for example, an inflated price that makes the subsequent offer appear to be a large reduction—then the "bargain" being advertised is itself fictitious. In this case, Sanfield (a locally owned retailer) contended that when Finlay (a nationwide retailer) advertised its jewelry at around 50 percent off the "regular" price, the ad was nothing more than a way of deceiving consumers; the "bargain" that Finlay advertised was no bargain at all, as Sanfield saw it. Sanfield believed that its business was suffering because of its competitors' misleading advertisements with phony discounting and fake percentage markdowns. Nonetheless, the court found in this case that "deception, like beauty, is in the eye of the beholder." Whether an ad is deceptive therefore turns entirely on the perception of the consumer, not the ad itself.

These examples illustrate the broad categories on the continuum of controlling influences that are under examination in this chapter. They indicate that the difference between *manipulation* and *persuasion* is the key matter. Of course, the question must be addressed whether *unjustifiably* manipulative advertising occurs frequently, or even at all.

## Sales

Some of these issues about disclosure, deception, and manipulation are as prominent in sales as in advertising. The attractive pricing of products is a first step in sales, and questions have been raised about pricing itself. For example, there have been accusations of price gouging of specific populations, such as the poor and the elderly. The more common problems, however, concern failures (intentional or not) to disclose pertinent information about a product's function, quality, or price. A simple example is the common practice of selling a product at a low price because it is the previous year's model, although it is not disclosed that the latest models are already out and in stock.

As the marketplace for products has grown more complex and the products themselves more sophisticated, buyers have become more dependent on salespersons to know their products and to tell the truth about them. The implicit assumption in some sales contexts is that bargaining and deception about a selling price are parts of the game, just as they are in real estate and labor negotiations. Nevertheless, this "flea-market" and "horse-trader" model of sales is unsuited to other contemporary markets. The salesperson is expected to have superior knowledge and is treated as an expert on the product, or at least as one who obtains needed information about a product. In this climate, it seems unethical for salespersons to take advantage of a buyer's implicit trust by using deceptive or manipulative techniques. But even if it is unethical to disclose too little, does it follow that the ethical salesperson has an obligation to disclose everything that might be of interest to the customer? For example, must the salesperson disclose that his or her company charges more than a competitor? What principles rightly govern the transfer of information during sales?

In an article on sales practices in this chapter, David M. Holley probes the social role of the salesperson. He concludes that there is a general obligation to disclose all information that a consumer would need to make a reasonable judgment about whether to purchase a product or service. Holley argues that this rule is superior to several alternatives that have been proposed in the literature. Changes in the climate of sales of the sort proposed in this article could potentially have a massive impact in business. More persons are employed in sales than any other area of marketing, and sales has commonly been criticized as a poorly monitored area of business activity. Salespersons appear to be more prone to unethical conduct if substantial portions of their income are dependent on commissions, competition is fierce and unregulated, dubious practices of disclosure are common, sales managers are removed from actual selling practices, and codes of ethics are disregarded.

## Bluffing and Disclosure

Whether marketing practices can be justified by the "rules of the game" in business is another major question. Some have argued that marketing strategies should be understood as by their nature attempts to influence us, but against which we should also be expected to protect ourselves—as in the proverbial case of purchasing a used automobile. By the very rules of the game, bluffing, bidding, and rhetorical overstatement invite similar countermoves. Although abuse and contempt are not tolerated, deception is tolerated and even encouraged as long as all players know the rules of the game and occupy roughly equal bargaining positions. This model suggests that some deceptive practices and sharp practices can be justifiable; however, limits must be set to restrict deception, manipulation, and cunning maneuvers that take advantage of a competitor's misfortune.

Manipulation can take many forms: offering rewards, threatening punishments, instilling fear, and so forth. The principal form discussed in this chapter is the manipulation of information. Here the manipulator modifies a person's sense of options by affecting the person's understanding of the situation. Deception, bluffing, and the like are used by the manipulator to change not the person's *actual* options but only the person's *perception* of the options. The more a person is deprived of a relevant understanding in the circumstances, the greater the effect on the person's free choice.

One does not need extensive experience in business to know that many deceptive practices, like bluffing and slick sales techniques, are widely practiced and widely accepted. It is common knowledge that automobile dealers do not expect people to pay the sticker price for automobiles, but it is a closely guarded secret as to how much can be knocked off that price. A certain amount of quoting of competitors, bargaining, moving "extras" under the basic price, and going to managers for approval is part of the game. A similar situation prevails in real estate transactions, in which the asking price for a house is seldom the anticipated selling price, as well as at bargaining sessions, in which labor leaders overstate wage demands and management understates the wage increases it is willing to grant. The intent is to manipulate, however gently.

The sophistication of the audience, standard practice in the business, and intention of the informer all need to be considered to decide whether gilded information is unacceptable. Manipulation and deception can result as much from what is not said as from what is said. For example, true information can be presented out of context and thereby be misleading.

A classic problem about disclosure of information appears in *Backman v. Polaroid Corporation*. In this case, investors alleged that Polaroid had obtained negative information about its product Polavision but had failed to disclose to investors unfavorable facts that were known about the product. In effect, the claim is that Polaroid manipulated investors into purchasing its stock at a higher value than its actual worth. A similar charge led to accusations against Salomon Inc., for both moral and legal failures to disclose properly to shareholders a stock option plan and cash bonus plan that benefited top corporate executives. Investors charged that the level of compensation diluted the value of the stock. Salomon responded that it had "followed the rules" of disclosure in its mailings to stockholders.[4]

Another advertising tactic related to disclosure is discussed in the case study "Advice for Sale." This case explains how companies such as Sony, Hewlett-Packard, and Wal-Mart pay "experts" to recommend their product during interviews on television news programs. The ethical problem lies in the fact that these "experts" fail to disclose to viewers, or to those conducting the interviews, that they have been paid to recommend specific products to viewers. Such deceptive practices have angered many consumers.

## Marketing and Vulnerable Populations

Marketing takes many forms and includes not just advertising and "stealth" practices such as the undisclosed use of paid experts but nearly all forms of corporate communication. In the recent California Supreme Court decision *Kasky v. Nike, Inc.* included in this chapter, it was found that corporations can be held accountable for the accuracy of statements made by public relations personnel regarding controversial issues such as their labor practices. Some have argued that the *Kasky v. Nike* decision will have a chilling affect on external corporate communications. Others have argued that the decision will help hold corporations accountable for the information they disclose to the public.

Certain segments of any given population are especially vulnerable to deceptive and manipulative marketing strategies. The elderly, children, and the economically impoverished are examples of such vulnerable groups. U.S. children, for example, are targeted by more than $15 billion in marketing annually.[5] One study estimated that children view in the range of 40,000 television commercials each year.[6] Unlike previous generations, U.S. children growing up in the twenty-first century are reached by marketers in nearly every facet of their lives. Advertisements reach them at home via television, radio, the Internet, and magazines and newspapers; on the way to and from school via billboards and vehicle placards; and in school via Channel One Network, paid advertisements in cafeterias, and vending machines. As the American Psychological Association has noted, children—especially children under the age of eight—typically lack the critical skills necessary to recognize advertisements as biased and tend to understand them as statements of fact.[7] Marketers who target children know this and use it to their advantage. Marketing to children can result in serious harms such as poor self-esteem, false notions of how to achieve happiness, a distorted world view, a poor diet leading to obesity and serious health problems, and poor money management skills leading to indebtedness in the teen years and beyond.

In his article in this chapter, "Marketing and the Vulnerable," George Brenkert notes that the concept of vulnerability is slippery, but he argues that we can gain enough clarity about the concept to make use of it in assessing marketing strategies. Brenkert argues that vulnerability is best understood as susceptibility to harm by others. He argues that marketing campaigns that target those, such as children, who are specially vulnerable must be designed so that those that are targeted are treated fairly. Marketing campaigns that fail to do so, he argues, are unethical.

Next to targeting children, one of the most controversial areas in marketing concerns the aggressive sales tactics of prescription drugs by pharmaceutical companies. The pharmaceutical industry is responsible for the creation of a wide range of drugs that have fundamentally improved the welfare of millions, perhaps billions, of people.

As we saw in Chapter 2, this includes the development and distribution of the drug Mectizan by Merck, a drug that has prevented millions of individuals from contracting river blindness. However, as described in the case "Merck & Company: The Vioxx Recall," Merck has recently been widely criticized for unintentional cardiac-related deaths caused by its painkiller Vioxx. Merck aggressively marketed this drug directly to consumers and to physicians, despite concerns raised by some physicians and researchers about the drug's safety. Merck ended up recalling the drug in 2004. As a result, its reputation has been significantly damaged and it is fighting a flood of lawsuits.

American consumers are nearly alone among the citizens of industrialized nations in being directly targeted by prescription drug advertising. Among industrialized nations, only New Zealand also allows direct-to-consumer (DTC) advertising. In 1997 the U.S. Food and Drug Administration altered its policy on DTC advertising in such a way as to make it possible for the widespread use of television commercials for prescription pharmaceutical advertising. Since that time spending on direct to consumer advertising has increased substantially. However, the practice of advertising directly to consumers has come under sustained criticism. Critics of DTC advertising argue that the practice undermines physician–patient relationships and drives up the cost of prescription drugs. In response, drug manufacturers, especially their trade group The Pharmaceutical Research and Manufacturers of America (PhRMA), argue that DTC advertisements empower consumers and have no impact on the cost of drugs.

In 2005 $4.2 billion was spent in the United States on DTC advertising, up from less than $1 billion in 1996. Nonetheless, such expenditures constituted only 14.2 percent of the $29.9 billion spent on prescription drug marketing in 2005. The majority of pharmaceutical marketing, approximately $25.6 billion in 2005, is targeted at physicians.[8] This marketing includes visits to physicians' offices by marketing representatives laden with free samples and gifts such as calculators, notepads, and lunch for the entire office staff; dinners at the best restuarants in town, typically with a presentation by a paid company spokesperson; and all-expenses-paid trips for physicians and their spouses to luxurious resorts, where they are typically offered research paid for by the company as evidence of the effectiveness of the company's latest drugs. In response to criticism of such practices, PhRMA issued guidelines for marketing to physicians in 2002. These voluntary guidelines, their "Code on Interactions with Health Care Professionals," are included in this chapter.

In "The Drug Pushers," the last article in this chapter, Carl Elliott, a medical doctor with a doctorate in philosophy, criticizes pharmaceutical companies for their aggressive marketing practices. He provides examples of the many sorts of gifts (some would say "bribes") that "drug reps" provide to physicians—expensive dinners, paid vacations, unrestricted grants—to get physicians to write more prescriptions for their companies' drugs. Elliott argues that truly innovative and safe drugs need no marketing. The billions of dollars spent annually in the United States alone to market pharmaceuticals are used, he argues, to sell "me too" drugs—drugs that companies develop mainly to take market share from a competitor's drug rather than because they provide new or innovative benefits to patients. These marketing expenditures, in turn, increase the cost of drugs and drive patient demand for unneeded medicine, thus driving up costs for individuals, employers who provide health insurance for their employees, and the state and federal governments that pay much of the cost of prescription drugs for their employees and for the poor or uninsured. An alternative to this model is to have physicians, relying on their training and experience, peer-reviewed journal articles, and non-industry-sponsored continuing medical education, determine what medications are appropriate for their patients. Elliott argues that pharmaceutical company marketing undermines the objectivity of prescribing decisions made by physicians and unduly interferes with physician–patient relationships. Further, he claims that PhRMA's guidelines for marketing to physicians have largely been ignored.

## NOTES

1. Sari Horwitz, "FTC Considers Letting Food Stores Advertise Out-of-Stock Items," *Washington Post* (December 27, 1984), p. E1.
2. As quoted in Amy Dunkin et al., "Liquor Makers Try the Hard Sell in a Softening Market," *Business Week* (May 13, 1985), p. 56.
3. "Anheuser-Busch Sued on Ad Showing Statue of Liberty," *Wall Street Journal* (November 28, 1984), p. 43.
4. Robert J. McCartney, "Investors Hit Salomon on Bonuses," *Washington Post* (October 23, 1991), pp. C1, C5.
5. Susan Linn, *Consuming Kids: The Hostile Takeover of Childhood* (New York: The New Press, 2004), 1.
6. American Psychological Association, "Television Advertising Leads to Unhealthy Habits in Children, Says APA Task Force," February 23, 2004. Available at www.apa.org/releases/childrenads.html.
7. Ibid.
8. Julie M. Donohue, Marisa Cevasco, and Meredith B. Rosenthal, "A Decade of Direct-to-Consumer Advertising of Prescription Drugs," *The New England Journal of Medicine,* 357 (2007), p. 676.

---

## ADVERTISING AND DISCLOSURE

# Advertising and Behavior Control

*Robert L. Arrington*

Consider the following advertisements:

1. "A woman in *Distinction Foundation* is so beautiful that all other women want to kill her."

2. Pongo Peach color from Revlon comes "from east of the sun . . . west of the moon where each tomorrow dawns." It is "succulent on your lips" and "sizzling on your finger tips (And on your toes, goodness knows)." Let it be your "adventure in paradise."

*Journal of Business Ethics* 1 (1982): 3–12. Copyright © 1982. Reprinted with permission from Kluwer Academic Publishers.

3. "Musk by English Leather—The Civilized Way to Roar."
4. "Increase the value of your holdings. Old Charter Bourbon Whiskey—The Final Step Up."
5. Last Call Smirnoff Style: "They'd never really miss us, and it's kind of late already, and its quite a long way, and I could build a fire, and you're looking very beautiful, and we could have another martini, and its awfully nice just being home . . . you think?"
6. A Christmas Prayer. "Let us pray that the blessings of peace be ours—the peace to build and grow, to live in harmony and sympathy with others, and to plan for the future with confidence." New York Life Insurance Company.

These are instances of what is called puffery—the practice by a seller of making exaggerated, highly fanciful, or suggestive claims about a product or service. Puffery, within ill-defined limits, is legal. It is considered a legitimate, necessary, and very successful tool of the advertising industry. Puffery is not just bragging; it is bragging carefully designed to achieve a very definite effect. Using the techniques of so-called motivational research, advertising firms first identify our often hidden needs (for security, conformity, oral stimulation) and our desires (for power, sexual dominance and dalliance, adventure) and then they design ads which respond to these needs and desires. By associating a product, for which we may have little or no direct need or desire, with symbols reflecting the fulfillment of these other, often subterranean interests, the advertisement can quickly generate large numbers of consumers eager to purchase the product advertised. What woman in the sexual race of life could resist a foundation which would turn other women envious to the point of homicide? Who can turn down an adventure in paradise, east of the sun where tomorrow dawns? Who doesn't want to be civilized and thoroughly libidinous at the same time? Be at the pinnacle of success—drink Old Charter. Or stay at home and dally a bit—with Smirnoff. And let us pray for a secure and predictable

future, provided for by New York Life, God willing. It doesn't take very much motivational research to see the point of these sales pitches. Others are perhaps a little less obvious. The need to feel secure in one's home at night can be used to sell window air conditioners, which drown out small noises and provide a friendly, dependable companion. The fact that baking a cake is symbolic of giving birth to a baby used to prompt advertisements for cake mixes which glamorized the 'creative' housewife. And other strategies, for example involving cigar symbolism, are a bit too crude to mention, but are nevertheless very effective.

Don't such uses of puffery amount to manipulation, exploitation, or downright control? In his very popular book *The Hidden Persuaders*, Vance Packard points out that a number of people in the advertising world have frankly admitted as much:

> As early as 1941 Dr. Dichter (an influential advertising consultant) was exhorting ad agencies to recognize themselves for what they actually were—"one of the most advanced laboratories in psychology." He said the successful ad agency "manipulates human motivations and desires and develops a need for goods with which the public has at one time been unfamiliar—perhaps even undesirous of purchasing." The following year *Advertising Agency* carried an ad man's statement that psychology not only holds promise for understanding people but "ultimately for controlling their behavior."[1]

Such statements lead Packard to remark: "With all this interest in manipulating the customer's subconscious, the old slogan 'let the buyer beware' began taking on a new and more profound meaning."

B. F. Skinner, the high priest of behaviorism, has expressed a similar assessment of advertising and related marketing techniques. Why, he asks, do we buy a certain kind of car?

> Perhaps our favorite TV program is sponsored by the manufacturer of that car. Perhaps we have

seen pictures of many beautiful or prestigeful persons driving it—in pleasant or glamorous places. Perhaps the car has been designed with respect to our motivational patterns: the device on the hood is a phallic symbol; or the horse-power has been stepped up to please our competitive spirit in enabling us to pass other cars *swiftly* (or, as the advertisements say, 'safely'). The concept of freedom that has emerged as part of the cultural practice of our group makes little or no provision for recognizing or dealing with these kinds of control.[2]

In purchasing a car we may think we are free, Skinner is claiming, when in fact our act is completely controlled by factors in our environment and in our history of reinforcement. Advertising is one such factor. . . .

Puffery, indirect information transfer, subliminal advertising—are these techniques of manipulation and control whose success shows that many of us have forfeited our autonomy and become a community, or herd, of packaged souls? The business world and the advertising industry certainly reject this interpretation of their efforts. *Business Week*, for example, dismissed the charge that the science of behavior, as utilized by advertising, is engaged in human engineering and manipulation. It editorialized to the effect that "it is hard to find anything very sinister about a science whose principle conclusion is that you get along with people by giving them what they want."[3] The theme is familiar: businesses just give the consumer what he/she wants; if they didn't they wouldn't stay in business very long. Proof that the consumer wants the products advertised is given by the fact that he buys them, and indeed often returns to buy them again and again.

The techniques of advertising we are discussing have had their more intellectual defenders as well. For example, Theodore Levitt, Professor of Business Administration at the Harvard Business School, has defended the practice of puffery and the use of techniques depending on motivational research.[4] What would be the consequences, he asks us, of deleting all exaggerated claims and fanciful associations from advertisements? We would be left literal descriptions of the empirical characteristics of products and their functions. Cosmetics would be presented as facial and bodily lotions and powders which produce certain odor and color changes; they would no longer offer hope or adventure. In addition to the fact that these products would not then sell as well, they would not, according to Levitt, please us as much either. For it is hope and adventure we want when we buy them. We want automobiles not just for transportation, but for the feelings of power and status they give us. Quoting T. S. Eliot to the effect that "Human kind cannot bear very much reality," Levitt argues that advertising is an effort to "transcend nature in the raw," to "augment what nature has so crudely fashioned." He maintains that "everybody everywhere wants to modify, transform, embellish, enrich, and reconstruct the world around him." Commerce takes the same liberty with reality as the artist and the priest—in all three instances the purpose is "to influence the audience by creating illusions, symbols, and implications that promise more than pure functionality." For example, "to amplify the temple in men's eyes, (men of cloth) have, very realistically, systematically sanctioned the embellishment of the houses of the gods with the same kind of luxurious design and expensive decoration that Detroit puts into a Cadillac." A poem, a temple, a Cadillac—they all elevate our spirits, offering imaginative promises and symbolic interpretations of our mundane activities. Seen in this light, Levitt claims, "Embellishment and distortion are among advertising's legitimate and socially desirable purposes." To reject these techniques of advertising would be "to deny man's honest needs and value."

Philip Nelson, a Professor of Economics at SUNY-Binghamton, has developed an interesting defense of indirect information advertising.[5] He argues that even when the message (the direct information) is not credible, the fact that the brand is advertised, and advertised frequently, is valuable indirect information for the consumer. The reason for this is that the brands advertised most are more likely to be better buys—losers won't be advertised a lot, for it simply wouldn't pay to do so. Thus even if the advertising claims made for a widely advertised product are empty, the consumer reaps the benefit of the indirect information which shows the product to be a good buy. Nelson goes so far as to say that advertising, seen as information and especially as indirect information, does not require an intelligent human response. If the indirect information has been received and has had its impact, the consumer will purchase the better buy even if his explicit reason for doing so is silly, e.g., he naively believes an endorsement of the product by a celebrity. Even though his behavior is overtly irrational, by acting on the indirect information he is nevertheless doing what he ought to do, i.e., getting his money's worth. "'Irrationality' is rational," Nelson writes, "if it is cost-free". . . .

The defense of advertising which suggests that advertising simply is information which allows us to purchase what we want, has in turn been challenged. Does business, largely through its advertising efforts, really make available to the consumer what he/she desires and demands? John Kenneth Galbraith has denied that the matter is as straightforward as this.[6] In his opinion the desires to which business is supposed to respond, far from being original to the consumer, are often themselves created by business. The producers make both the product and the desire for it, and the "central function" of advertising is "to create desires." Galbraith coins the term 'The Dependence Effort' to designate the way

wants depend on the same process by which they are satisfied.

David Braybrooke has argued in similar and related ways.[7] Even though the consumer is, in a sense, the final authority concerning what he wants, he may come to see, according to Braybrooke, that he was mistaken in wanting what he did. The statement 'I want *x*,' he tells us, is not incorrigible but is "ripe for revision." If the consumer had more objective information than he is provided by product puffing, if his values had not been mixed up by motivational research strategies (e.g., the confusion of sexual and automotive values), and if he had an expanded set of choices instead of the limited set offered by profit-hungry corporations, then he might want something quite different from what he presently wants. This shows, Braybrooke thinks, the extent to which the consumer's wants are a function of advertising and not necessarily representative of his real or true wants.

The central issue which emerges between the above critics and defenders of advertising is this: do the advertising techniques we have discussed involve a violation of human autonomy and a manipulation and control of consumer behavior, *or* do they simply provide an efficient and cost effective means of giving the consumer information on the basis of which he or she makes a free choice. Is advertising information, or creation of desire?

To answer this question we need a better conceptual grasp of what is involved in the notion of autonomy. This is a complex, multifaceted concept, and we need to approach it through the more determinate notions of (a) autonomous desire, (b) rational desire and choice, (c) free choice, and (d) control or manipulation. In what follows I shall offer some tentative and very incomplete analyses of these concepts and apply the results to the case of advertising.

(a)  *Autonomous Desire.* Imagine that I am watching TV and see an ad for Grecian Formula 16. The thought occurs to me that if I purchase some and apply it to my beard, I will soon look younger—in fact I might even be myself again. Suddenly I want to be myself! I want to be young again! So I rush out and buy a bottle. This is our question: was the desire to be younger manufactured by the commercial, or was it 'original to me' and truly mine? Was it autonomous or not?

F. A. von Hayek has argued plausibly that we should not equate nonautonomous desires, desires which are not original to me truly mine, with those which are culturally induced.[8] If we did equate the two, he points out, then the desires for music, art, and knowledge could not properly be attributed to a person as original to him, for these are surely induced culturally. The only desires a person would really have as his own in this case would be the purely physical ones for food, shelter, sex, etc. But if we reject the equation of the nonautonomous and the culturally induced, as von Hayek would have us do, then the mere fact that my desire to be young again is caused by the TV commercial—surely an instrument of popular culture transmission—does not in and of itself show that this is not my own, autonomous desire. Moreover, even if I never before felt the need to look young, it doesn't follow that this new desire is any less mine. I haven't always liked 1969 Aloxe Corton Burgundy or the music of Satie, but when the desires for these things first hit me, they were truly mine.

This shows that there is something wrong in setting up the issue over advertising and behavior control as a question whether our desires are truly ours *or* are created in us by advertisements. Induced and autonomous desires do not separate into two mutually exclusive classes. To obtain a better understanding of autonomous and nonautonomous desires, let us consider some cases of a desire which a person does not *acknowledge* to be his own even though he *feels* it. The kleptomaniac has a desire to steal which in many instances he repudiates, seeking by treatment to rid himself of it. And if I were suddenly overtaken by a desire to attend an REO concert, I would immediately disown this desire, claiming possession or momentary madness. These are examples of desires which one

might have but with which one would not identify. They are experienced as foreign to one's character or personality. Often a person will have what Harry Frankfurt calls a second-order desire, that is to say, a desire *not* to have another desire.[9] In such cases, the first-order desire is thought of as being nonautonomous, imposed on one. When on the contrary a person has a second-order desire to maintain and fulfill a first-order desire, then the first-order desire is truly his own, autonomous, original to him. So there is in fact a distinction between desires which are the agent's own and those which are not, but this is not the same as the distinction between desires which are innate to the agent and those which are externally induced. . . .

What are we to say in response to Braybrooke's argument that insofar as we might choose differently if advertisers gave us better information and more options, it follows that the desires we have are to be attributed more to advertising than to our own real inclinations? This claim seems empty. It amounts to saying that if the world we lived in, and we ourselves, were different, then we would want different things. This is surely true, but it is equally true of our desire for shelter as of our desire for Grecian Formula 16. If we lived in a tropical paradise we would not need or desire shelter. If we were immortal, we would not desire youth. What is true of all desires can hardly be used as a basis for criticizing some desires by claiming that they are nonautonomous.

(b)  *Rational Desire and Choice.* Braybrooke might be interpreted as claiming that the desires induced by advertising are often irrational ones in the sense that they are not expressed by an agent who is in full possession of the facts about the products advertised or about the alternative products which might be offered him. Following this line of thought, a possible criticism of advertising is that it leads us to act on irrational desires or to make irrational choices. It might be said that our autonomy has been violated by the fact that we are prevented from following our rational wills or that we have been denied the 'positive freedom' to develop our true, rational selves. It might be claimed that the desires induced in us by advertising are false desires in that they do not reflect our essential, i.e., rational, essence.

The problem faced by this line of criticism is that of determining what is to count as rational desire or rational choice. If we require that the desire or choice be the product of an awareness of *all* the facts about the product, then surely every one of us is always moved by irrational desires and makes nothing but irrational choices. How could we know all the facts about a product? If it be required only that we possess all of the *available* knowledge about the product advertised, then we still have to face the problem that not all available knowledge is *relevant* to a rational choice. If I am purchasing a car, certain engineering features will be, and others won't be, relevant, *given what I want in a car.* My prior desires determine the relevance of information. Normally a rational desire or choice is thought to be one based upon relevant information, and information is relevant if it shows how other, prior desires may be satisfied. It can plausibly be claimed that it is such prior desires that advertising agencies acknowledge, and that the agencies often provide the type of information that is relevant in light of these desires. To the extent that this is true, advertising does not inhibit our rational wills or our autonomy as rational creatures.

It may be urged that much of the puffery engaged in by advertising does not provide relevant information at all but rather makes claims which are not factually true. If someone buys Pongo Peach in anticipation of an adventure in paradise, or Old Charter in expectation of increasing the value of his holdings, then he/she is expecting purely imaginary benefits. In no literal sense will the one product provide adventure and the other increased capital. A purchasing decision based on anticipation of imaginary benefits is not, it might said, a rational decision, and a desire for imaginary benefits is not a rational desire. . . .

Some philosophers will be unhappy with the conclusion of this section, largely because they have a concept of true, rational, or ideal desire which is not the same as the one used here. A Marxist, for instance, may urge that any desire felt by alienated man in a capitalistic society is foreign to his true nature. Or an existentialist may claim that the desires of inauthentic men are themselves inauthentic. Such concepts are based upon general theories of human nature which are unsubstantiated and perhaps incapable of substantiation. Moreover, each of these theories is committed to a concept of an ideal desire which is normatively debatable and which is distinct from the ordinary concept of a rational desire as one based upon relevant information. But it is in the terms of the ordinary concept that we express our concern that advertising may limit our autonomy in the sense of leading us to act on irrational desires, and if we operate with this concept we are driven again to the conclusion that advertising may lead, but probably most often does not lead, to an infringement of autonomy.

(c) *Free Choice.* It might be said that some desires are so strong or so covert that a person cannot resist them, and that when he acts on such desires he is not acting freely or voluntarily but is rather the victim of irresistible impulse or an unconscious drive. Perhaps those who condemn advertising feel that it produces this kind of desire in us and consequently reduces our autonomy.

This raises a very difficult issue. How do we distinguish between an impulse we do not resist and one we *could* not resist, between freely giving in to a desire and succumbing to one? I have argued elsewhere that the way to get at this issue is in terms of the notion of acting for a reason.[10] A person acts or chooses freely if he does so for a reason, that is, if he can adduce considerations which justify in his mind the act in question. Many of our actions are in fact free because this condition frequently holds. Often, however, a person will act from habit, or whim, or impulse, and on these occasions he does not have a reason in mind. Nevertheless he often acts voluntarily in these instances, i.e., he could have acted otherwise. And this is because if there *had been* a reason for acting otherwise of which he was aware, he would in fact have done so. Thus acting from habit or impulse is not necessarily to act in an involuntary manner. If, however, a person is aware of a good reason to do *x* and still follows his impulse to do *y*, then he can be said to be impelled by irresistible impulse and hence to act involuntarily. Many kleptomaniacs can be said to act involuntarily, for in spite of their knowledge that they likely will be caught and their awareness that the goods they steal have little utilitarian value to them, they nevertheless steal.

Here their 'out of character' desires have the upper hand, and we have a case of compulsive behavior.

Applying these notions of voluntary and compulsive behavior to the case of behavior prompted by advertising, can we say that consumers influenced by advertising, act compulsively? The unexciting answer is: sometimes they do, sometimes not. I may have an overwhelming, TV-induced urge to own a Mazda RX-7 and all the while realize that I can't afford one without severely reducing my family's caloric intake to a dangerous level. If, aware of this good reason not to purchase the car, I nevertheless do so, this shows that I have been the victim of TV compulsion. But if I have the urge, as I assure you I do, and don't act on it, or if in some other possible world I could afford an RX-7, then I have not been the subject of undue influence by Mazda advertising. Some Mazda RX-7 purchasers act compulsively; others do not. The Mazda advertising effort *in general* cannot be condemned, then, for impairing its customers' autonomy in the sense of limiting free or voluntary choice. Of course the question remains what should be done about the fact that advertising may and does *occasionally* limit free choice. We shall return to this question later.

In the case of subliminal advertising we may find an individual whose subconscious desires are activated by advertising into doing something his calculating, reasoning ego does not approve. This would be a case of compulsion. But most of us have a benevolent subconsciousness which does not overwhelm our ego and its reasons for action. And therefore most of us can respond to subliminal advertising without thereby risking our autonomy. To be sure, if some advertising firm developed a subliminal technique which drove all of us to purchase Lear jets, thereby reducing our caloric intake to the zero point, then we would have a case of advertising which could properly be censured for infringing our right to autonomy. We should acknowledge that this is possible, but at the same time we should recognize that it is not an inherent result of subliminal advertising.

(d) *Control or Manipulation.* Briefly let us consider the matter of control and manipulation. Under what conditions do these activities occur? In a recent paper on 'Forms and Limits of Control' I suggested the following criteria:[11]

A person *C* controls the behavior of another person *P iff*

1. *C* intends *P* to act in a certain way *A*;
2. *C*'s intention is causally effective in bringing about *A*; and
3. *C* intends to ensure that all of the necessary conditions of *A* are satisfied.

These criteria may be elaborated as follows. To control another person it is not enough that one's actions produce certain behavior on the part of that person; additionally one must intend that this happen. Hence control is the intentional production of behavior. Moreover, it is not enough just to have the intention; the intention must give rise to the conditions which bring about the intended effect. Finally, the controller must intend to establish by his actions any otherwise unsatisfied necessary conditions for the production of the intended effect. The controller is not just influencing the outcome, not just having input; he is as it were guaranteeing that the sufficient conditions for the intended effect are satisfied.

Let us apply these criteria of control to the case of advertising and see what happens. Conditions (1) and (3) are crucial. Does the Mazda manufacturing company or its advertising agency intend that I buy an RX-7? Do they intend that a certain number of people buy the car? *Prima facie* it seems more appropriate to say that they *hope* a certain number of people will buy it, and hoping and intending are not the same. But the difficult term here is 'intend.' Some philosophers have argued that to intend *A* it is necessary only to desire that *A* happen and to believe that it will. If this is correct, and if marketing analysis gives the Mazda agency a reasonable belief that a certain segment of the population will buy its product, then, assuming on its part the desire that this happen, we have the conditions necessary for saying that the agency intends that a certain segment purchase the car. If I am a member of this segment of the population, would it then follow that the agency intends that I purchase an RX-7? Or is control referentially opaque? Obviously we have some questions here which need further exploration.

Let us turn to the third condition of control, the requirement that the controller intend to activate or bring about any otherwise unsatisfied necessary conditions for the production of the intended effect. It is in terms of this condition that we are able to distinguish brainwashing from liberal education. The brainwasher arranges all of the necessary conditions for belief. On the other hand, teachers (at least those of liberal persuasion) seek only to influence their students—to provide them with information and enlightenment which they may absorb *if they wish.* We do not normally think of teachers as controlling their students, for the students' performances depend as well on their own interests and inclinations. . . .

Let me summarize my argument. The critics of advertising see it as having a pernicious effect on the autonomy of consumers, as controlling their lives and manufacturing their very souls. The defense claims that advertising only offers information and in effect allows industry to provide consumers with what they want. After developing some of the philosophical dimensions of this dispute, I have come down tentatively in favor of the advertisers. Advertising may, but certainly does not always or even frequently, control behavior, produce compulsive behavior, or create wants which are not rational or are not truly those of the consumer. Admittedly it may in individual cases do all of these things, but it is innocent of the charge of intrinsically or necessarily doing them or even, I think, of often doing so. This limited potentiality, to be sure, leads to the question whether advertising should be abolished or severely curtailed or regulated because of its potential to harm a few poor souls in the above ways. This is a very difficult question, and I do not pretend to have the answer. I only hope that the above discussion, in showing some of the kinds of harm that can be done by advertising and by indicating the likely limits of this harm, will put us in a better position to grapple with the question.

## NOTES

1. Vance Packard, *The Hidden Persuaders* (Pocket Books, New York, 1958), 20–21.
2. B. F. Skinner, "Some Issues Concerning the Control of Human Behavior: A Symposium," in *Man Controlled*, ed. Karlins and Andrews (The Free Press, New York, 1972).
3. Quoted by Packard, *op. cit.*, p. 220.
4. Theodore Levitt, "The Morality (?) of Advertising," *Harvard Business Review* 48 (1970): 84–92.
5. Phillip Nelson, "Advertising and Ethics," in *Ethics, Free Enterprise and Public Policy*, ed. Richard T. De George and Joseph A. Pichler (Oxford University Press, New York, 1978), 187–98.
6. John Kenneth Galbraith, *The Affluent Society*; reprinted in *Ethical Theory and Business*, ed. Tom L. Beauchamp and Norman E. Bowie (Prentice Hall Englewood Cliffs, 1979), 496–501.
7. David Braybrooke, Skepticism of Wants, and Certain Subversive Effects of Corporation on American Values, in *Human Values and Economic Policy*, ed. Sidney Hook (New York University Press, New York, 1967); reprinted in Beauchamp and Bowie, eds., *op. cit.*, pp. 502–8.
8. F. A. von Hayek, The Non Sequitur of the "Dependence Effect," in *Southern Economic Journal* (1961); reprinted in Beauchamp and Bowie, eds. *op. cit.*, pp. 508–12.
9. Harry Frankfurt, "Freedom of the Will and the Concept of Person," *Journal of Philosophy* 68 (1971): 5–20.
10. Robert L. Arrington, "Practical Reason, Responsibility and the Psychopath," *Journal for the Theory of Social Behavior* 9 (1979): 71–89.
11. Robert L. Arrington, "Forms and Limits of Control", delivered at the annual meeting of the Southern Society for Philosophy and Psychology, Birmingham, Alabama, 1980.

# Information Disclosure in Sales

*David M. Holley*

The issue of information disclosure is an important topic for a number of areas of applied ethics. Discussions in medical ethics often deal with the question of how much information should be given to a patient by health-care professionals. A central topic of journalistic ethics is what kind of information the public has a right to know. In business ethics, discussions of information disclosure have dealt with areas such as disclosure of health and safety risks to employees, financial information to stockholders, and product safety information to consumers.[1]

One area of business ethics which seems inadequately explored, but holds both theoretical and practical interest, is the question of exactly how much information a salesperson is obligated to give to a potential customer in selling a product. Unlike the field of health care in which roles such as physician or nurse are paradigms of professions which carry with them clearly recognized responsibilities to serve the best interest of the patient, a salesperson is not generally thought to have such a professional responsibility to customers. In fact it is usually expected that the activity of sales will involve a primary pursuit of the interests of the seller. While there are legal obligations to disclose certain types of information, the question of what moral responsibilities a salesperson has is open to dispute.

An attempt to resolve the matter and specify a salesperson's moral responsibilities to disclose information raises two important theoretical questions: (1) To what extent can ethical argument help to define the moral responsibilities of a social role when these are only vaguely defined in a culture? and (2) How is empirical information about common practice relevant to making normative judgments? This paper considers these issues in the context of an examination of ethical responsibilities for information disclosure in sales. . . .

## MORAL GUIDELINES AND SOCIAL ROLES

Suppose we imagine the various options with regard to a salesperson's duty to disclose specific information in some situation to lie along a continuum with one end of the continuum representing a requirement for a high level of information disclosure and the other a requirement for a minimal level of information disclosure:

Low level                                    High level
```
■ ■ ■ ■ ■ ■ ■ ■ ■ ■ ■ ■ ■ ■ ■ ■ ■ ■ ■
```
  1          2          3          4          5

If we assume that a salesperson has a responsibility to answer a customer's questions nondeceptively, we could represent various points on the continuum as rules requiring particular levels of additional disclosure such as the following:

1. *Minimal Information Rule:* The buyer is responsible for acquiring information about the product. There is no obligation to give any information the buyer does not specifically ask about.

2. *Modified Minimal Information Rule:* The only additional information the seller is obligated to give is information a buyer might need to avoid risk of injury (safety information).

3. *Fairness Rule:* In addition to safety information, a seller is responsible for giving the buyer any information needed to make a reasonable judgment about whether to purchase the product which the buyer could not reasonably be expected to know about unless informed by the seller.

4. *Mutual Benefit Rule:* In addition to safety information, the seller is responsible for giving the buyer any information needed to make a reasonable judgment about whether to purchase the product which the buyer does not possess.

5. *Maximal Information Rule:* A seller is responsible for giving the buyer any information relevant to deciding whether to purchase the product.

What considerations might move us toward one end of the continuum or the other? One approach is to take the perspective of the buyer. A person attracted by the ideal of the golden rule might ask, "What would I want the salesperson to tell me if I were purchasing the product?" . . .

Trying to get a determinate answer from a moral ideal such as the golden rule also leads to some implausible conclusions. Suppose, for example, that what I would want as a buyer in some situation is an objective analysis of the merits and disadvantages of this product in relation to competing products. Does this automatically imply that the information should be supplied in the desired form by the salesperson? To think so is to disregard the salesperson's role as an advocate of the product. A jury member may need enough information to formulate a reasonable judgment of guilt or innocence, but it would be far-fetched to conclude that this gives the defense attorney a responsibility to provide all the necessary information. To think so overlooks the attorney's role as an advocate (as well as the responsibilities of others in the legal system).

These considerations suggest that deciding how much information a salesperson should provide depends upon an understanding of the nature of the salesperson's role. While there are various types of sales, we can say in general that a salesperson is supposed to act toward achieving a particular goal: getting people to purchase a product. Describing the activity as sales probably also implies that the method of achieving this goal is some type of persuasion rather than coercion. But determining the proper limits of this persuasion calls for some conception of the context of sales activities. If, for example, we viewed selling a product as a kind of game (a metaphor which has been applied to many business activities), then supplying or withholding information might plausibly be viewed as strategies employed to win (make the sale). If the game is like poker, we could even imagine that essentially deceptive strategies (bluffing) could be an accepted part of the game.[2] Someone adopting this picture might argue that a salesperson should disclose information only when it is strategically advantageous to do so.

However, this picture of sales activities is clearly deficient. Part of the problem is that it presupposes relatively equal parties who know that they are involved in a game and what the nature and goals of this game are. Even if this is adequate as an account of some business situations, it hardly seems to apply as a general picture of the buyer–seller relationship. Furthermore, efficient functioning of the buyer–seller relationship presupposes a higher degree of trust than game metaphors would suggest to be appropriate. Buyers must depend to some extent on information they receive from sellers, and if we imagine that the information is not reliable, we are imagining a situation which, if widespread enough, undermines the ends for which the marketplace exists.

On the other hand, the need of the buyer to depend on the seller is not as great as the need of a patient to rely on the objectivity and good judgment of a physician. In that case it seems necessary to build into the professional role a duty to seek the patient's well-being, which limits and overrides the physician's activities as a profit seeker. The professional requirement is connected with the extreme vulnerability of patients to the pure pursuit of economic self-interest by physicians.

While buyers are generally less vulnerable than patients, there are cases where the interest involved is significant enough to call for certain limits on self-interest in the pursuit of a sale. For example, suppose that use of a product involves some danger of physical injury which the buyer is unlikely to know about. Withholding the information is in effect subjecting the buyer to a risk of physical injury which she/he does not voluntarily agree to accept. Given the importance of avoiding physical injury and the vulnerability of virtually everyone to hidden dangers, there would be a strong moral reason for modifying the minimal information rule to require that such risks be revealed. The limit here could be stated in terms of applying a general principle of noninjury to sales situations, perhaps something like "Do not act in ways which are likely to result in injury to another person without the informed and reasonable consent (explicit or implicit) of that person." . . .

## REASONABLE EXPECTATIONS AND BUYER KNOWLEDGE

The moral credentials of what I have called the fairness rule rest upon the claim that this rule assures fair treatment of all parties. I shall interpret this to mean that a system utilizing this rule gives all parties to a transaction an adequate opportunity to protect their individual interests. If information is needed but unavailable, it should be revealed; if it is needed and available, the party who needs it can seek it out.

We should notice, however that applying this rule depends upon assessing what the buyer can reasonably be expected to know. How is this assessment to be made? Is the seller to think about what buyers in general can reasonably be expected to know, or about what some subgroup of buyers of which this buyer is a member can reasonably be expected to know, or perhaps about what this individual buyer can be expected to know? Different answers to this question yield different requirements about what information needs to be disclosed.

Suppose I am selling antiques, and I am dealing with a person I know to be a collector and retailer of antiques. It seems plausible to suggest that I would be justified in assuming this person to have a certain level of knowledge about the value of antiques. Suppose it becomes evident to me that this dealer is not aware of a distinction between the item I am selling and a more valuable item with which it might be confused. Do I have an obligation to enlighten him?

According to the mutual benefit rule, the answer would be yes. If we interpret the fairness rule to be relative to the individual person, we would have to determine whether this individual buyer could be expected to know this distinction, and it is unclear how such a determination is to be made. So perhaps the most promising way of applying the fairness rule is to regard "what a person can reasonably be expected to know" as applying relative to some relevant class membership. In this case I might have obligations to reveal to someone acting as an expert only what that person could not be expected to know, even with expertise in the field. Of course, in a particular case I might have good reason for revealing more: say, for example that I have a long-term relationship with this individual which has been mutually beneficial and that she would regard my withholding information I know she does not have negatively, possibly resulting in the disruption of the relationship, but this need not imply that there is a moral obligation to reveal the information.

If we interpret the fairness rule to apply relative to group membership and if we distinguish at least between cases in which the buyer is reasonably regarded as an expert in knowledge of some area from cases in which the buyer should not be regarded as an expert, the rule provides different guidance about what should be revealed to experts as opposed to what should be revealed to nonexperts. Should the class of nonexperts be subject to further division? Perhaps the general public could be divided into sophisticated consumers and unsophisticated or naive consumers. Given this distinction, the fairness rule would imply that a salesperson is obligated to reveal more when dealing with an unsophisticated consumer. The main problem with making this distinction is that it would be difficult in practice to determine the type of consumer being dealt with in a particular transaction. I might become aware that I am dealing with a particularly naive consumer, but how much effort must I expend in making such a determination?

From a practical point of view it would probably be more realistic to have some expectations of a level of information to be revealed to the general public which would result in informed and reasonable judgment in the vast majority of cases. Exactly how much information this is would depend on what level of informed judgment is high enough and what percentage of customers making such a judgment is good enough. Assuming that such a determination could be made, the fairness rule on this interpretation would require disclosure of information sufficient for a reasonable judgment by a high percentage of customers falling in the relevant class.

But what if in the course of a sales transaction it becomes evident that a particular buyer has not been given enough information to

judge reasonably (e.g., because this buyer is more uninformed or naive than might be expected of the average buyer)? Or what if the buyer is using misinformation which the seller did not cause but could correct? If the fairness rule is to be interpreted to require that information be supplied in such cases, then it is functionally equivalent to the mutual benefit rule in these cases. This would probably be distasteful to most advocates of the fairness rule, since the whole point of a rule less stringent than the mutual benefit rule is to place some responsibility for acquiring information on the buyer rather than the seller. To build in a requirement that misinformation or ignorance must be corrected seems to defeat much of the purpose of the rule.

If the seller could distinguish between those buyers who could have acquired the relevant information with an appropriate level of effort and those who could not because of unavoidable deficiencies or circumstantial difficulties, it would be possible to make allowances for the latter class, but not the former. But except in obvious cases, such a distinction would often be difficult to make. So a decision to act in accordance with the fairness rule probably means deciding to withhold information both from the culpably irresponsible as well as many of the unavoidably ignorant.

## VULNERABILITY AND DEPENDENCE

It is relatively easy to think of some cases in which withholding information seems unconscionable. The financial advisor who sells to an elderly widow with very limited resources a risky investment without making the risk clear surely exemplifies substandard ethics. The failure to disclose in such a case takes advantage of one who is in a vulnerable position. Whatever we might say about exchanges in which both parties have adequate opportunity to protect their interests, we must still take into account that some individuals may be relatively defenseless, either permanently or temporarily. A disclosure rule which allows such people to be exploited when their vulnerability is apparent would fail one of the most basic of ethical tests. So if the fairness rule is to be ethically defensible, some restrictions must be built in to limit the pursuit of self-interest at the expense of those who might be persuaded to act in ways which are clearly contrary to their interests.

Some writers have raised the general question of whether a salesperson needs to behave paternalistically.[3] This way of putting the question can be misleading, since paternalistic action involves overriding or limiting another's choice or ability to choose. While a salesperson may occasionally have such a responsibility when dealing with individuals who are incompetent or behaving in clearly irrational ways, there is ordinarily no obligation to refuse to sell a legitimate product because the purchase is judged not to be in the buyer's interest. However, the question of how hard to push a sale when it appears to diverge from a customer's interest can arise fairly often. It is all very well to say that the customer is the one who should decide what is in his/her interest, but if the salesperson is strategically withholding information crucial to making such a judgment, this defense seems hollow.

Consider the case of a person of very limited education, intelligence, and sophistication who lives on a small social security income and needs roof repairs. A salesperson recommends and makes the case for a total reroofing with the finest materials available, a choice which will mean using up a small savings account and acquiring a significant debt. The salesperson makes no attempt to explore cheaper alternatives, and the customer is not sufficiently astute to inquire about them. What seems to make nondisclosure objectionable in this case is the customer's limited capacity to protect his own interests. He relies on the salesperson

to provide not only information but a kind of guidance. To follow a policy or revealing only as much as an average customer would need in effect deprives this very vulnerable customer of what he needs to know, but is unable to learn without help.

Examples involving extremely vulnerable consumers suggest that even if the fairness rule were a sufficient guide to disclosure in some cases, there are situations in which the relationship between salesperson and customer involves such an imbalance of power that the customer is not adequately protected. In such cases the buyer is dependent on the seller for information, and failure to provide crucial information becomes more like a betrayal of trust than an admirable competitive move.

While cases involving extremely vulnerable individuals furnish the clearest illustrations of the limits of the fairness rule, we can see problems with this rule even in transactions involving more skillful buyers. Suppose Simon wants to buy a rocker-recliner. Because he has children who have been rough on furniture, Simon tells a salesperson that he is especially concerned about finding a piece that can endure their abuse. Simon notices that a particular manufacturer has advertised a "lifetime warranty" on its chairs. He assumes that this means that anything which goes wrong with the chair is covered. The salesperson knows that the lifetime warranty does not include the kind of damage children are likely to inflict on the chair, but does not mention this, nor does she mention that a cheaper chair of a lesser-known manufacturer with a more limited warranty is actually more likely to provide the kind of durability this customer seeks.

What is apparent from this kind of example is that ordinary customers often interpret the salesperson's role to be not merely an advocate for a particular product but a kind of consultant who can be relied upon to help the customer satisfy particular needs. Withholding information of relevance to attaining such satisfaction would often be a refusal to accept a role the customer is expecting to be performed.

While we can imagine the marketplace working without salespeople functioning as consultants, the complexity of the modern marketplace often makes it practically necessary, even if not absolutely necessary, to rely on sellers to provide information which could have been attained with enough effort but is not likely to be possessed by the average consumer because of a variety of limitations, including limitations of time. As a result the salesperson comes to be relied upon to provide the customer with enough information to enable him or her to satisfy particular needs.

This kind of dependence of customer on salesperson is avoidable only with great difficulty. It is a dependence brought about by complexities involved in navigating the marketplace under social conditions such as ours. The vulnerabilities brought about by such practical necessities create a need for building into the salesperson's role some degree of responsibility for providing information needed by the customer to judge how to satisfy his or her needs and desires.

Hence, the fairness rule is inadequate as a general account of what a salesperson is obligated to disclose. While there may be certain limited contexts in which such a rule can function, they would primarily involve individuals with significant expertise in a particular area and an implicit willingness to protect their own interests. Under such conditions it might be permissible to disregard the interests of the buyer, but we should not be misled into thinking of these as paradigmatic of the buyer–seller relationship generally.

## THE MUTUAL BENEFIT RULE

How far is a salesperson obligated to go in serving the customer's interests through information disclosure? The strongest kind of obligation which could be advocated would claim that a salesperson must seek to produce optimal benefit for the customer. Such a requirement would mean that a salesperson might often have to direct a customer to buy merchandise from a competitor offering superior or equal quality for a lower price. In effect it could virtually deny the salesperson's role as an advocate for her own company's products.

The maximal information rule calls upon the salesperson to provide any information relevant to deciding whether to purchase a product. Presumably this would include objective comparisons of the strengths and weaknesses of various alternatives. It would place on the salesperson the responsibility for supplying customers with the sort of analysis we expect from a *Consumer Reports* product test. While we can imagine such a requirement, it is difficult to see how it could work without undermining the competitive structure of the market.

What seems to be needed is a rule which could still allow the salesperson to function as a product advocate but limit that advocacy in ways conducive to fulfillment of the customer's needs. The mutual benefit rule requires the salesperson to disclose enough information to allow the customer to make a reasonable judgment about whether to purchase the product. How strict a requirement this is depends on how we interpret "reasonable." We need not interpret this term to designate an optimal choice. In most cases there are a range of products and purchases that could satisfy a particular customer's needs. Given varieties of product features, some may be better in some respects and worse in others, but equally satisfactory. Furthermore, there are many equally reasonable ways of evaluating how much money a particular product feature is worth or how much time and effort should be expended in shopping. It can be entirely reasonable to patronize a store with knowledgeable and reliable salespeople even if that occasionally means paying a higher price for comparable merchandise.

Thus, we could loosely interpret the mutual benefit rule to require that the salesperson provide enough information for a customer to make a judgment which is satisfactory, given his or her particular needs, desires, and budget. This need not imply a requirement to make extensive inquiries about the particular customer's situation (though some products such as life insurance or financial investments or home purchases might make such knowledge necessary). In most cases a salesperson could make general assumptions based on what most customers in the market for this kind of product are concerned about. As distinctive concerns or needs become apparent, however, this standard would require them to be taken into account. Hence, for example, in the rocker-recliner case described earlier, the customer's concern about damage children might cause is relevant to what information this customer needs.

The distinction between the mutual benefit rule and the maximal information rule is that the latter requires disclosure of all information relevant to a purchase decision, while the former requires disclosure only of enough information for a reasonable judgment. Suppose we compare the two with regard to disclosure of price information. All relevant information would probably include clear cost comparisons to products with similar features sold by competitors. But given the above interpretation of "reasonable," the mutual benefit rule would allow disclosure of the price of a product without comparative information as long as the price is not so much out of line that the purchase could not be judged competitive. Requiring that comparative information about price be furnished only when the price is clearly uncompetitive is probably equivalent to a requirement to price one's products competitively, something most merchants would say the market generally requires them to do anyway.

The mutual benefit rule, even with the permissive interpretation I have given it, builds in some protection of customer vulnerabilities.

The spirit of this rule of information disclosure would mean a salesperson should not knowingly encourage choices which would be against the interests of someone in the customer's position. Notice that is not the same as saying that the salesperson should always promote the choice he or she would have made in the customer's position. The salesperson is free under this rule, as I have interpreted it, to advocate a range of reasonable choices.

Such a rule would require the disclosure of defects which might significantly diminish the value of the product. Unlike the fairness rule, this requirement would apply regardless of whether the defects could be discovered with a reasonable amount of effort. It would not, however, require disclosure of all details which might be regarded as negative unless they clearly bear on a purchaser's central concerns. Hence, one selling a house ordinarily need not disclose that the next-door neighbors are obnoxious, but would be required to disclose that the city planned to construct a major freeway a hundred yards away or that the foundation has a crack which will soon need repair.

With a relatively loose interpretation of what counts as a reasonable judgment, the mutual benefit rule comes closest to satisfying the important ethical and practical concerns. Hence, there is good reason to regard this rule as our primary norm for information disclosure in sales This conclusion is consistent with the possibility of recognizing specialized contexts in which buyers need fewer protections. So, for example, we might regard the fairness rule as adequate for situations in which buyers are representing themselves as professionals in the relevant field.

## CONCLUSION

I have attempted to use ethical argument to render more precise the extent of a salesperson's obligation to disclose information to a customer. The argument takes into account features of the contemporary marketplace which call for locating the disclosure requirement somewhere in the neighborhood of a permissively interpreted mutual benefit rule. Even if my argument is correct, it does not establish precisely what information needs to be revealed in every case since the concept of "reasonableness" used in interpreting the mutual benefit rule can be highly elastic. Nevertheless, it does furnish a guideline for ruling out some clearly unethical conduct as well as some conduct which some people's moral intuitions would allow.

## NOTES

1. E.g., R. Faden. and Tom Beauchamp, "The Right to Risk Information and the Right to Refuse Workplace Hazards," in *Ethical Theory and Business*, 6th ed., ed. Tom Beauchamp and Norman Bowie (Prentice Hall, Englewood Cliffs, NJ, 1992). Frederick, Robert, and Michael Hoffman, "The Individual Investor in Securities Markets: An Ethical Analysis," *Journal of Business Ethics* 9 (1990): 579–89. Louis Stern, "Consumer Protection via Increased Information," *Journal of Marketing* 31 (1967): 48–52. Richard DeGeorge, "Corporate Disclosure" in *Business Ethics*, 4th ed. (Prentice Hall, Englewood Cliffs, NJ, 1995), 284–93.

2. Albert Carr, "Is Business Bluffing Ethical?" *Harvard Business Review* 46 (1968): 143–53.

3. James Ebejer, and Michael Morden, "Paternalism in the Marketplace: Should a Salesman Be His Buyer's Keeper?" *Journal of Business Ethics* 7 (1988): 337–39. Kerry Walters, "Limited Paternalism and the Pontius Pilate Plight," *Journal of Business Ethics* 8 (1989): 955–62. George Brockway, "Limited Paternalism and the Salesperson: A Reconsideration," *Journal of Business Ethics* 12 (1993): 275–79.

## MARKETING

# Marketing and the Vulnerable

*George G. Brenkert*

## INTRODUCTION

Contemporary marketing is commonly characterized by the marketing concept which enjoins marketers to determine the wants and needs of customers and then to try to satisfy them. This view is standardly developed, not surprisingly, in terms of normal or ordinary consumers. Much less frequently is attention given to the vulnerable customers whom marketers also (and increasingly) target. Though marketing to normal consumers raises many moral questions, marketing to the vulnerable

also raises many moral questions which are deserving of greater attention.

This paper has three objectives. First, it explores the notion of vulnerability which a target audience might (or might not) have. I argue that we must distinguish those who are specially vulnerable from normal individuals, as well as the susceptible and the disadvantaged—two other groups often distinguished in marketing literature. Second, I contend that marketing to the specially vulnerable requires that marketing campaigns be designed to ensure that these individuals are not treated unfairly, and thus possibly harmed. Third, I maintain that marketing programs which violate this preceding injunction are unethical or unscruplous whether or not those targeted are harmed in some further manner. Accordingly, social control over marketing to the vulnerable cannot simply look to consumer injury as the measure of unfair treatment of the vulnerable.

The upshot of my argument is that, just as we have a doctrine of product liability to which marketers are accountable, we also need a corresponding doctrine of targeted consumer liability to which marketers should be held. By this I refer to the moral liability of marketers for the manner in which they market to consumers. Marketing to the specially vulnerable without making appropriate allowances for their vulnerabilities is morally unjustified.

## ON BEING VULNERABLE

The notion of vulnerability is complex and slippery. Most simply, to be "vulnerable is to be susceptible to being wounded; liable to physical hurt" (Barnhart 1956). More generally, being vulnerable is being susceptible to some harm or other. One can be vulnerable to manmade or natural harms: one can also be vulnerable to harms from actions or omissions (Goodin 1985, 110). In each of these cases, the threatened harm is to one's "welfare" or "interests."

The vulnerability of the person who may be harmed by others may be a permanent, or temporary, condition. Clearly, vulnerability is a matter of degree. Typically only those who are subject to some substantial level of harm are referred to as "vulnerable." This vulnerability may arise due to their own peculiar characteristics, those of the agents who are said to impose the harm on them, or the system within which certain acts impose harm

on them. Accordingly, vulnerability is a four-place relation: Some person (P) is vulnerable to another (moral or causal) agent (A) with respect to some harm (H) in a particular context (C). As such "vulnerability is inherently object and agent specific" (Goodin 1985, 112).

The relation of vulnerability to two related concepts—susceptibility and disadvantage—used in marketing literature may serve to further clarify its nature.

Vulnerability is distinct from susceptibility, in that a person might be susceptible to something or someone and still not be vulnerable to that thing or person. "Susceptibility" merely implies that one is "capable of being affected, especially easily" by something or someone. It is true that one who is susceptible may also be vulnerable. Clearly, one who is vulnerable is susceptible. But one need not be vulnerable if one is susceptible, since one's susceptibility may not be to some harm or other. An overweight, underexercised adult might be susceptible through flattery or positive remarks to certain suggestions made by friends to exercise and moderate food intake. But this person would not, thereby, be vulnerable to such suggestions. Hence, vulnerability and susceptibility are different.

The vulnerable also differ from those with "unusual susceptibilities," a term of art in marketing for those "who have idiosyncratic reactions to products that are otherwise harmless when used by most people" (Morgan, Schuler, and Stoltman 1995, 267). People who are "unusually susceptible" are those who are atypically harmed by various products. Accordingly, "unusual susceptibility" has been linked with vulnerability. However, in any ordinary sense, a person might have "unusual susceptibilities" to some experiences (e.g., changes in air pressure or moisture), the suggestions of others, clothing styles, etc., and this might not involve harm to the person but, perhaps, that person's heightened sensitivity to those influences.

Further, people may be vulnerable in ways other than that they may be atypically harmed by the products they use. Vulnerable groups such as young children, the grieving, or the elderly are not necessarily atypically harmed by the products they use. Nevertheless, they are vulnerable.

Finally, the vulnerable are also distinct from the disadvantaged. Though marketers quite frequently speak of disadvantaged populations or market segments, they have given little analysis of this concept. Most discussants simply give examples of those whom they consider to be disadvantaged. This extensive, diverse and confused list includes the poor, immigrants, the young married, teenagers, the elderly, children, racial minorities, the physically handicapped, ethnic minorities, and even women shopping for automobiles.

Generally we are told that members of this list are disadvantaged because they are impaired in their transactions in the marketplace. For some this means not getting their full consumer dollar (Andreasen 1975, 6). For others this means confronting an imbalance in the marketplace (Barnhill 1972; Morgan and Riordan 1983). Andreasen says "the disadvantaged" are "those who are unequal in the marketplace because of characteristics that are not of their own choosing, including their age, race, ethnic minority status, and (sometimes) gender" (Andreasen 1993, 273).

It is clear, then, that the vulnerable and disadvantaged also constitute different, though overlapping, groups. The disadvantaged are impaired or unequal with regard to their attempt to obtain various goods and services. This may occur relative to other groups (normal consumers) competing for various goods, or to those from whom they seek to purchase those goods. On the contrary, those who are vulnerable are not vulnerable with regard to others who are competing for similar goods, but with regard to the harm they might suffer from those who market those goods to them. As such, the notion of vulnerability suggests the harm which one might receive, whether or not one is competing for a particular good, but due to the manner of obtaining some good (or service). Further, this harm need not come from paying more or being deceived. The vulnerable may get exactly what they want, but what they want may unwittingly and unfairly harm them (as well as their family and/or community).

Accordingly, the vulnerable are not simply the susceptible or the disadvantaged. They constitute a distinct group which deserves our close attention.

## VULNERABILITY AND MARKETING

What moral responsibilities do marketers have when they consider marketing to the vulnerable? Since one might be said to be vulnerable in a variety of ways, and since some people might willingly place themselves in competitive situations where their vulnerabilities are exposed, we must specify the manner(s) in which various forms of vulnerability are significant from the standpoint of marketing. Otherwise, if it were morally unjustified to market to those who are vulnerable in any sense, moral marketing would not exist. It would be an oxymoron. . . .

One standard to which we might turn for the responsibilities of marketers to the vulnerable refers not to the degree of their vulnerability but to the effects on all those relevantly affected by marketing to these individuals. In short, harm to the vulnerable by marketing programs might be balanced by countervailing benefits for all other consumers and competitors. Thus, the responsibilities of marketers to the vulnerable would depend upon which course of action would maximize all relevant utilities.

However, appeal to a simple utilitarian standard is ethically unacceptable in that it would allow a few vulnerable individuals to substantially suffer because a certain action or policy maximized total utilities. For example, it might be that other marketers are more vulnerable (they might go out of business) than some of the individuals (they might be harmed by the products or the form of marketing targeting them) to whom those marketers and others sought to sell their goods. Hence, in order to protect vulnerable marketers (and their employees, suppliers, etc.), the proposed standard might permit targeting various vulnerable market segments because the total harm they sustained was less than that of those *engaged* in producing and marketing products to them. This could unleash a tide of manipulative and exploitative marketing.

Similarly, suppose that a particular means of marketing did not make allowances for the fact that those targeted were vulnerable in that they significantly lacked a capacity to make judgments regarding economic exchanges (e.g., children, the senile, or the retarded). Though the marketing efforts took advantage of this vulnerability, it nevertheless maximized total utilities. We might suppose that these customers were not dissatisfied and the marketers were pleased with their successes. To argue that this means of marketing is, nevertheless, morally acceptable runs afoul of important moral and market principles. To begin with, those targeted are not competent to evaluate the product marketed to them. They might not be aware of problems with the products they use. As such, this justification of marketing to the vulnerable permits treating some individuals simply as means to the ends of others. It denies them moral respect. It runs afoul of basic ethical and market principles, even though those targeted do not suffer a direct harm.

The difficulty with Goodin's approach is that he treats vulnerability as simply a quantitative matter without recognizing that each form of vulnerability occurs within a particular context. The market is one such context. In it some individuals may justifiedly seek, in recognized forms of competition, to exploit the vulnerabilities of others. The problem with the consequential first approach is that it does not consider the nature of people's vulnerabilities except insofar as they portend certain consequences for everyone. Not the ability of the person to participate, but the effects on society are its concern. Instead, we need to be able to identify those who are specially vulnerable within a market situation, but whose vulnerability is not the occasion for justified competitive attacks. In short, we need a different approach which takes account both of the context within which marketers address the vulnerable as well as the nature of their vulnerabilities.

## MARKETING TO THE VULNERABLE

The necessary features for morally (not merely legally) justified market relations are commonly stated in terms of the nature of the relations or interactions which participants in the market enjoy.[1] Thus, we are told that among the relevant characteristics a morally justified market requires are the following: (a) Competition is free, i.e., participants in the market do so voluntarily, when each believes they can benefit; (b) Competition is open, i.e., "access to the market is not artificially limited by any power, government, or group" (DeGeorge 1982, 101); and (c) Deception or fraud are not used in market competition (Friedman 1962).

These conditions spell out some of the necessary conditions for a justified form of competition among those we may call "market participants," i.e., those who willingly and knowingly engage in market relations. The activity of these marketplace competitors is strongly determined by their need to derive a profit. To be a market participant is to place oneself in competition with other participant capitalists in which one recognizes that one may succeed or fail. It is to engage in these relations in order to produce various goods or services for sale. It is to acknowledge that all participants, including oneself, have strengths and weaknesses, formidable powers and vulnerabilities. The endeavor of each participant is to compete such that their own strengths and powers will outweigh those of others, or that their weaknesses and vulnerabilities are less significant than those of others.

Second, though these conditions are important for a morally justified market, they make no direct reference to the conditions or characteristics which those individuals who engage in market relations as ultimate consumers—call them "market clients"—must have in order to do so. However, morally and legally justified market relations also make assumptions about the nature of these participants, since not just anyone can be a market client. To take the most obvious cases, the severely mentally ill, incompetent elderly, and young children cannot be market visitors. Someone else must visit the market on their behalf.

Those who would visit the market as consumers do so not under a concern to derive a profit, but in order to satisfy various needs and wants they have. Accordingly, they must have certain market competencies such as the following: (a) They know they should shop around and are able to do so, (b) They are competent to determine differences in quality and best price, (c) They are aware of their legal rights (Schnapper 1967), (d) They have knowledge of the products and their characteristics, and (e) They have the resources to enter into market relations.[2]

These conditions, conjoined with the preceding, spell out essential requirements for individuals to be market clients. It is assumed that those who fulfill these conditions are able to protect their own interests and that their self-interested behavior in the market will work towards greater wealth or well-being for all. Accordingly, when these conditions are fulfilled (ceteris paribus), market relations between market participants and clients will be fair or just. Thus, these conditions for market clients (or consumers) have been recognized not simply as moral restrictions, but also as the source of various legal regulations regarding children, the elderly, and the grieving.

Third, the preceding market client conditions are not fulfilled by consumers wholly independently of marketers. On the contrary, marketers seek to foster the fulfillment of these conditions. "Ultimately," a marketing text reminds us, "the key objective [for marketers] must be to influence customer behavior" (Assael 1993, 592). Thus, marketers extend credit or loans to prospective individuals so that they may have the needed resources to enter the market. They advertise to foster the knowledge and desire of their products. They seek to identify unfulfilled needs, wants, and interests among potential consumers or clients and endeavor to find ways to satisfy them. Marketers seek to draw into the market those who might not otherwise enter the market, or do so only in different ways and under different conditions. Thus, one marketing researcher comments that "marketers have failed to develop strategies designed to attract the elderly consumer market" (Bailey 1987, 213). In short, marketers create not only products to sell to market clients (consumers), but seek to create consumers (clients) out of ordinary, nonmarket interested people. This is not to say that they create consumers out of whole cloth, it might seem that they do a product. Nor is it to say that they are always successful, or that whenever a person becomes a market client it is because of some specific action of a marketer. Still, marketers not only create products for consumers, but they also have a hand in creating consumers for their products.

In these various efforts, the marketer has a number of advantages over even the most reasonable consumer (client). These include greater knowledge of the product; expertise on how to market to individual customers and targeted groups; knowledge of what interests, fears, wants and/or needs motivate various market segments; and resources to bring that knowledge to bear on behalf of persuading a customer to buy a product. Indeed, the marketer may be aware of attributes of potential consumers of which they are themselves unaware. These special characteristics, powers, and abilities of marketers create special responsibilities for them in the relationships they create with consumers.[3]

Fourth, when marketers, or market participants, compete with each other, the fact that one has a vulnerability may be viewed as an opportunity for another who seeks to take advantage of that vulnerability. There are, obviously, legal and moral limits here. If one firm has temporarily lost its security force and its headquarters are unguarded one evening, this does not imply that another firm may use that opportunity to sneak into those headquarters to steal important files. Thus, competing firms ought not to try to exploit those vulnerabilities which would require illegal or immoral acts. On the other hand, vulnerabilities linked to market performance may be the occasion for other firms to try to outperform the vulnerable firm when the acts involved do not transgress the preceding limits. Accordingly, if market participants fail to compete aggressively out of laziness or are indifferent to quality differences, they may be harmed as a result. This is acceptable to the market, since it is intended to encourage participant competitiveness.

However, when a marketer confronts a market client, i.e., an ordinary consumer, the situation is different. Individuals must fulfill the above conditions to be market clients. Those that do so may also be lazy shoppers or indifferent to quality differences. As a consequence, they too may suffer. This is also acceptable within the market. However, some individuals may suffer not through such circumstances, but because they fail to fulfill, in ways which render them specially vulnerable, various conditions to be market clients.

I suggest that we may initially characterize this specially vulnerable group as being constituted by those individuals who are particularly susceptible to harm to their interests because the qualitatively different experiences and conditions that characterize them (and on account of which they may be harmed) derive from factors (largely) beyond their control.

Accordingly, there are three conditions for the specially vulnerable:

1.  They are those, in contrast to other normal adults, who are characterized by qualitatively different experiences, conditions, and/or incapacities which impede their abilities to participate in normal adult market activities. These characteristics may render them vulnerable in any of four different ways:

    A.  They may be **physically vulnerable** if they are unusually susceptible due to physical or biological conditions to products on the market, e.g., allergies or special sensitivity to the chemicals or substances which are marketed.

    B.  They may be **cognitively vulnerable** if they lack certain levels of ability to cognitively process information or to be aware that certain information was being withheld or manipulated in deceptive ways. Children, the senile elderly, and even those who lack education and shopping sophistication have been included here.[4]

    C.  They may be **motivationally vulnerable** if they could not resist ordinary temptations and/or enticements due to their own individual characteristics. Under the motivationally vulnerable might be brought the grieving and the gravely ill.[5]

    D.  They may be **socially vulnerable** when their social situation renders them significantly less able than others to resist various enticements, appeals, or challenges which may harm them. Some of those who have been included here are certain groups of the poor, the grieving, and new mothers in developing countries.

2. The qualitatively different conditions and incapacities of specially vulnerable individuals are ones they possess due to factors (largely) beyond their control. In addition, they may be largely unaware of their vulnerability(ies). In either case, they are significantly less able (in any normal sense) to protect themselves against harm to their interests as a result. Thus, the allergic, the child, the elderly, and the grieving all experience their vulnerabilities due to reasons (largely) beyond their control. In certain situations this may also be true of various racial groups. The fact that these factors are largely beyond their control may be due to the weaknesses or inabilities these individuals themselves possess, due to the greater power of marketers which render their characteristics specially weak or incapable, or due to the system within which they find themselves.

3. These special conditions render them particularly susceptible to the harm of their interests by various means which marketers (and others) use but which do not (similarly) affect the normal adult. In short, it is the combination of their special characteristics and the means or techniques which marketers use that render them specially vulnerable. This emphasizes the relational nature of vulnerability.

As so identified, the specially vulnerable are significantly less able than others to protect their own interests and, in some cases, even to identify their own interests. Consequently, they are considerably less able to take appropriate measures to satisfy or fulfill those interests. Central to these difficulties is the special liability (or susceptibility) they have to be swayed, moved, or enticed in directions which may benefit others but which may harm their interests.

Accordingly, when market participants face individuals who do not qualify or pass a certain threshold for market competition, the latter are unable to protect their interests in a manner comparable to that of ordinary market clients. If the fulfillment of these conditions or threshold is required to be treated as a market client, then these individuals may not morally be treated as other clients in the market. Further, when this situation arises because these individuals have special vulnerabilities then to market to them in ways which take advantage of their vulnerabilities, i.e., to seek to engage them in the competitive effort to sell them goods through the weaknesses characterizing their vulnerabilities, is to treat them unfairly. Regardless of whether they are actually harmed, they are being taken advantage of. They have little or no control over these features of their behavior. The fact that they may take fun or pleasure in being targeted by marketers is, then, irrelevant since they do not qualify, as market clients.[6] And it is this situation which has been cited as one of the criteria for determining unfairness in advertising, i.e., advertising (or marketing) makes unfair claims when those claims ". . . cause especially vulnerable groups to engage in conduct deleterious to themselves" (Cohen 1974, 13).[7]

Consequently, since moral marketing must exclude treating customers unfairly, marketers need to "qualify" those they propose to target as genuine market clients before they introduce marketing campaigns which target them. This might involve helping them to become qualified consumers, avoiding marketing to them, or marketing to them in ways which are compatible with their limited abilities and characteristics.

As such, moral marketing requires a theory of targeted consumer liability analogous to the product liability, to which marketers are presently held responsible. A theory of targeted consumer liability would elaborate on and operationalize the conditions noted above under which individuals may play full roles as market clients as well as what lesser roles they may play. In each case, it would tell us what relationships marketers might have with them.

## IMPLICATIONS

What are the implications of the preceding analysis? A first interpretation might be that marketers may not market to the specially vulnerable at all. This is mistaken. There are obviously cases in which those who are specially vulnerable, e.g., the elderly or the grieving, require various products and services and would benefit from learning about them. The preceding argument contends that any marketing to the vulnerable cannot morally be undertaken in a way which trades upon their vulnerabilities.

In cases when the special vulnerability is temporary, measures could be taken to restrain marketing to them until after such period. Accordingly, the legislatures of some states have introduced and/or passed legislation prohibiting lawyers from "soliciting the business of victims until 30 days after accidents, wrongful deaths, and workplace injuries" (Ferrar 1996). Similarly, for the grieving, some have suggested that "insurance companies may need to be restricted through legislation regarding the nature of their contacts with those in grief; specifically, the payoff of a life insurance policy should not be accompanied by an immediate attempt to encourage the survivor to reinvest. A period of time (i.e., at least a month) should elapse before the insurance company initiates a sales contact" (Gentry et al. 1994, 139). When it is desirable that individuals in this group have certain products or services prior to the vulnerability-creating situation's abating, other arrangements can be made for advisors to the specially vulnerable to be present or for restraints on marketing to them.

The situation is different when the vulnerability is not temporary or relatively short-term. In such cases, marketers may not target those who are specially vulnerable in ways such that their marketing campaign depends upon the vulnerabilities of that specially vulnerable group. That is, in the case of the specially vulnerable, no significant aspect of a marketing campaign may rely upon the characteristics that render those individuals specially vulnerable in order to sell a product. Hence, because children are cognitively vulnerable due to their undeveloped abilities, any marketing to children must be done in ways which do not presuppose those vulnerabilities. As such, the FCC's limit on the amount of advertising on children's television programming does not directly address this issue. Instead, the content of those advertisements must be monitored so that children's special vulnerabilities are not taken advantage of. The removal of ads for vitamins and drugs from children's television programming does directly respond to the present point (Guber and Berry 1993, 145). However, it does not go far enough. Since young children do not understand the purpose of ads (cf. McNeal 1987, 186), they do not fulfill the qualifications of market clients. Accordingly, it is mistaken to speak of restrictions on marketing to the vulnerable (and particularly children) as violating their rights as consumers (cf. McNeal 1987, 185). Since vulnerable children do not qualify as market clients or consumers, they cannot be said to have consumers' rights.

Admittedly, vulnerable individuals such as children will witness marketing to competent market clients. There is no way to stop this. Nor is it desirable to try to do so. But this does not mean that marketers can invoke images, symbols, etc., which are designed to persuade or influence this group of noncompetent vulnerable individuals to purchase products (or influence those who do) through the very characteristics which render them unfit to be market clients.

Accordingly, it is not morally acceptable to market goods to specially vulnerable individuals with the intention that they bring pressure to bear on genuine market clients to buy those products and with the expectation that those genuine clients will curb any problems which the use or possession of those products by the specially vulnerable would raise. Such marketing continues to target those who are not fully competent market clients. Further, to depend upon others to prevent harm which the marketing techniques may potentially engender through the purchase of various products is to seek to escape from the responsibility marketers have for the consequences of their actions. It is a case of displaced moral responsibility.

However, the interpretation of the above argument is still incomplete. What about those cases in which marketing takes place to genuine market clients, but the campaigns are (unavoidably) witnessed by the specially vulnerable who positively react upon these campaigns and seek out the marketers' products? Let us assume that R.J. Reynolds use of "Old Joe" is such an example.[8]

If the effects on the specially vulnerable in such cases were not harmful, then few moral problems would be raised. However, when they are harmful, one must ask whether there are other means of marketing the product which would not have these secondary effects? If marketers, as other individuals, are under the general obligation of doing no harm, or minimizing harm, then they should seek to alter those marketing methods even if the harm is an indirect result of the marketer's intentions. On the other hand, if it is not possible to alter the marketing methods, then means might be sought to limit the exposure of those who are specially vulnerable to these marketing measures. In short, moral marketing requires some response other than simply ignoring the harm done to the vulnerable.

I suggest, then, that a more complete account of marketers and the vulnerable is that marketers may not market their products to target groups (specially vulnerable or not) in such a way that their marketing campaigns significantly affect vulnerable groups through their vulnerabilities. That is, there is nothing in the preceding that says that we must limit the effects of marketers' programs to their intentional aims with regard to a particular target segment. When significant spillover effects arise, they too must be taken into account. In effect, this would be to apply a form of strict targeted consumer liability.

Finally, is it morally justified to use marketing techniques which take advantage of the vulnerabilities of the specially vulnerable but which promote products which members of this group are widely acknowledged to need? For example, may marketers use techniques which young children cannot understand in order to get them to exercise properly or to eat a healthy diet? Or, may marketers use fear appeals to get the elderly to use their medications in a proper manner? Bailey has suggested that public service appeals might use fear appeals to warn certain groups of the elderly about dangers to them (Bailey 1987, 242). But this misses the point three ways. First, if the use of such appeals violates those who have been rendered specially susceptible to it, then they ought not to be used for good (public service messages) or bad (confidence games) or even ordinary marketing. Second, if some of the elderly are so specially susceptible to messages including fear, then the use of ordinary messages concerning their problems should also reach them. Fear is not needed; they are already concerned about the content of the appeal. Third, public service messages are one kind of "communication," whereas those messages which seek to sell a product or a service are very different. Since the marketing concept speaks of marketers seeking to satisfy consumer needs, some seek to use this to slide over into the public message realm. However, this is a slide that rests on an equivocation: public messages solely for the good of the recipient and private messages for the good of the sender, which may also be good for the recipient. In short, if a group is specially vulnerable, the use of unfair techniques which would not ultimately cause them harm is still the use of techniques which treat such individuals unfairly through manipulating them through their vulnerabilities. Only in very special circumstances should such marketing techniques be employed. . . .

## ENDNOTES

1. I wish to capture here not the ideal market, but a morally justified imperfect market, filled with real participants. Further, I do not attempt to state all the necessary conditions for a capitalist market system, but only to highlight those most important for present purposes.

2. I intend that this allows for the use of credit, loans, and the like.

3. It is conceivable that they could transform the vulnerabilities of a normal consumer into special vulnerabilities.

4. Andreasen writes that "the swindler finds particularly good customers among the disadvantaged, since he expects the consumer not to understand much about contracts and 'formalities,' such as confessions of judgment, and to be unlikely to read legal language carefully or to peruse contracts disguised as receipts" (Andreasen 1975, 204).

5. Vulnerability, in the grieving, involves a transformation of the self that forces people to face new consumer of market roles when they are least prepared to do so because of the associated stresses (Gentry et al. 1994, 129). This state involves "traumatic confusion" (Ibid.); a passage between two worlds; a "marginalized experience often accompanied by isolation and suspension of social status" (Ibid.).

6. See McNeal, who notes the objection that limiting the market exposure of children would rob them of "the joy of being a consumer" or "the fun and pleasure that comes with being a consumer" (McNeal 1987, 183–84).

7. Among the members of these specially vulnerable groups which may be treated unfairly by

marketers Cohen lists "children, the Ghetto Dweller, the elderly, and the handicapped" (Cohen 1974, 11).

8. There is much dispute over whether this is the case. For present purposes I will assume that R.J. Reynolds has not directly targeted children.

## BIBLIOGRAPHY

Andreasen, A. R. 1975. *The Disadvantaged Consumer* (New York: The Free Press).

——. 1993. "Revisiting the Disadvantaged: Old Lessons and New Problems," *Journal of Public Policy & Marketing* 12:270–75.

Assael, H. 1993. *Marketing: Principles & Strategy,* 2nd edition (Fort Worth, TX: The Dryden Press).

Bailey, J. M. 1987. "The Persuasibility of Elderly Consumers." *Current Issues in Research in Advertising* 10 (1): 213–47.

Barnhill. J. A. 1972. "Market Injustice: The Case of the Disadvantaged Consumer." *Journal of Consumer Affairs* 6 (1): 78–83.

Barnhart, C. L., ed. 1956. *American College Dictionary* (New York: Random House).

Cohen, D. 1974. "The Concept of Unfairness as It Relates to Advertising Legislation." *Journal of Marketing* 38:8–13.

DeGeorge, R. T. 1982. *Business Ethics* (New York: Macmillan).

Ferrar, R. 1996. "Bill Seeks to Reduce 'Ambulance Chasing.'" *Knoxville News Sentinel* (January 18): A3.

Friedman, M. 1962. *Capitalism and Freedom* (Chicago: University of Chicago Press).

Gentry, J. W., P. F. Kennedy, K. Paul, and R. P. Hill. 1994. "The Vulnerability of Those Grieving the Death of a Loved One: Implications for Public Policy," *Journal of Public Policy & Marketing* 13 (2): 128–42.

Guber, S. S., and J. Berry. 1993. *Marketing to and Through Kids* (New York: McGraw-Hill).

McNeal, J. U. 1987. *Children as Consumers* (Lexington, MA: Lexington Books).

Morgan, F. W., and E. A. Riordan. 1983. "The Erosion of the Unusual Susceptibility Defense: The Case of the Disadvantaged Consumer." *Journal of the Academy of Marketing Science* 11 (2): 85–96.

Schnapper, R. 1967. " Consumer Legislation and the Poor," *Yale Law Journal,* 76 (4): 745–92.

# The Drug Pushers

*Carl Elliott*

Back in the old days, long before drug companies started making headlines in the business pages, doctors were routinely called upon by company representatives known as "detail men." To "detail" a doctor is to give that doctor information about a company's new drugs, with the aim of persuading the doctor to prescribe them. When I was growing up, in South Carolina in the 1970s, I would occasionally see detail men sitting patiently in the waiting room outside the office of my father, a family doctor. They were pretty easy to spot. Detail men were usually sober, conservatively dressed gentlemen who would not have looked out of place at the Presbyterian church across the street. Instead of Bibles or hymn books, though, they carried detail bags, which were filled with journal articles, drug samples, and branded knick-knacks for the office.

Today detail men are officially known as "pharmaceutical sales representatives," but everyone I know calls them "drug reps." Drug reps are still easy to spot in a clinic or hospital, but for slightly different reasons. The most obvious is their appearance. It is probably fair to say that doctors, pharmacists, and medical-school professors are not generally admired for their good looks and fashion sense. Against this backdrop, the average drug rep looks like a supermodel, or maybe an A-list movie star. Drug reps today are often young, well-groomed, and strikingly good-looking. Many are women. They are usually affable and sometimes very smart. Many give off a kind of glow, as if they had just emerged from a spa or salon. And they are always, hands down, the best-dressed people in the hospital.

Drug reps have been calling on doctors since the mid-nineteenth century, but during the past decade or so their numbers have increased dramatically. From 1996 to 2001 the pharmaceutical sales force in America doubled, to a total of 90,000 reps. One reason is simple: good reps move product. Detailing is expensive, but almost all practicing doctors see reps at least occasionally, and many doctors say they find reps useful. One study found that for drugs introduced after 1997 with revenues exceeding $200 million a year, the average return for each dollar spent on detailing was $10.29. That is an impressive figure. It is almost twice the return on investment in medical-journal advertising, and more than seven times the return on direct-to-consumer advertising.

But the relationship between doctors and drug reps has never been uncomplicated, for reasons that should be obvious. *The first duty of doctors, at least in theory, is to their patients.* Doctors must make prescribing decisions based on medical evidence and their own clinical judgment. Drug reps, in contrast, are salespeople. They swear no oaths, take care of no patients, and profess no high-minded ethical duties. Their job is to persuade doctors to prescribe their drugs. If reps are lucky, their drugs are good, the studies are clear, and their job is easy. But sometimes reps must persuade doctors to prescribe drugs that are marginally effective, exorbitantly expensive, difficult to administer, or even dangerously toxic. Reps that succeed are rewarded with bonuses or commissions. Reps that fail may find themselves unemployed.

Most people who work in health care, if they give drug reps any thought at all, regard them with mixed feelings. A handful avoid reps as if they were vampires, backing out of the room when they see one approaching. In their view, the best that can be said about reps is that they are a necessary by-product of a market economy. They view reps much as NBA players used to view Michael Jordan: as an awesome, powerful force that you can never really stop, only hope to control.

Yet many reps are so friendly, so easygoing, so much fun to flirt with that it is virtually impossible to demonize them. How can you demonize someone who brings you lunch and touches your arm and remembers your birthday and knows the names of all your children? After a while even the most steel-willed doctors may look forward to visits by a rep, if only in the self-interested way that they look forward to the UPS truck pulling up in their driveway. A rep at the door means a delivery has arrived: takeout for the staff, trinkets for the kids, and, most indispensably, drug samples on the house. Although samples are the single largest marketing expense for the drug industry, they pay handsome dividends: doctors who accept samples of a drug are far more likely to prescribe that drug later on. . . .

## THE KING OF HAPPY HOUR

Gene Carbona was almost a criminal. I know this because, 30 minutes into our first telephone conversation, he told me, "Carl, I was almost a criminal." I have heard ex–drug reps speak bluntly about their former jobs, but never quite so cheerfully and openly. These days Carbona works for the *Medical Letter,* a highly respected nonprofit publication (Carbona stresses that he is speaking only for himself), but he was telling me about his 12 years working for Merck and then Astra Merck, a firm initially set up to market the Sweden-based Astra's drugs in the United States. Carbona began training as a rep in 1988, when he was only 11 days out of college. He detailed two drugs for Astra Merck. One was a calcium-channel blocker he calls "a dog." The other

was the heartburn medication Prilosec, which at the time was available by prescription only. Prilosec is the kind of drug most reps can only dream about. The industry usually considers a drug to be a blockbuster if it reaches $1 billion a year in sales. In 1998 Prilosec became the first drug in America to reach $5 billion a year. In 2000 it made $6 billion. Prilosec's success was not the result of a massive heartburn epidemic. It was based on the same principle that drove the success of many other 1990s blockbusters, from Vioxx to Viagra: the restoration of an ordinary biological function that time and circumstance had eroded. In the case of Prilosec, the function was digestion. Many people discovered that the drug allowed them to eat the burritos and curries that their gastrointestinal systems had placed off-limits. So what if Prilosec was $4 a pill, compared with a quarter or so for a Tagamet? Patients still begged for it. Prilosec was their savior. Astra Merck marketed Prilosec as the "purple pill," but, according to Carbona, many patients called it "purple Jesus."

How did Astra Merck do it? Prilosec was the first proton pump inhibitor (a drug that inhibits the production of stomach acid) approved by the Food and Drug Administration, and thus the first drug available in its class. By definition this gave it a considerable head start on the competition. In the late 1990s Astra Merck mounted a huge direct-to-consumer campaign; ads for the purple pill were ubiquitous. But consumer advertising can do only so much for a drug, because doctors, not patients, write the prescriptions. This is where reps become indispensable.

Many reps can tell stories about occasions when, in order to move their product, they pushed the envelope of what is ethically permissible. I have heard reps talk about scoring sports tickets for their favorite doctors, buying televisions for waiting rooms, and arranging junkets to tropical resorts. One rep told me he set up a putting green in a hospital and gave a putter to any doctor who made a hole in one. A former rep told me about a colleague who somehow managed to persuade a pharmacist to let him secretly write the prescribing protocol for antibiotic use at a local hospital.

But Carbona was in a class of his own. He had access to so much money for doctors that he had trouble spending it all. He took residents out to bars. He distributed "unrestricted educational grants." He arranged to buy lunch for the staff of certain private practices every day for a year. Often he would invite a group of doctors and their guests to a high-end restaurant, buy them drinks and a lavish meal, open up the club in back, and party until 4:00 A.M. "The more money I spent," Carbona says, "the more money I made." If he came back to the restaurant later that week with his wife, everything would be on the house. "My money was no good at restaurants," he told me, "because I was the King of Happy Hour."

My favorite Carbona story, the one that left me shaking my head in admiration, took place in Tallahassee. One of the more important clinics Carbona called on was a practice there consisting of about 50 doctors. Although the practice had plenty of patients, it was struggling. This problem was not uncommon. When the movement toward corporate-style medicine got under way, in the 1980s and 1990s, many doctors found themselves ill-equipped to run a business; they didn't know much about how to actually make money. ("That's why doctors are such great targets for Ponzi schemes and real-estate scams," Carbona helpfully points out.) Carbona was detailing this practice twice a week and had gotten to know some of the clinicians pretty well. At one point a group of them asked him for help. "Gene, you work for a successful business," Carbona recalls them saying. "Is there any advice you could give us to help us turn the practice around?" At this point he knew he had stumbled upon an extraordinary opportunity.

Carbona decided that the clinic needed a "practice management consultant." And he and his colleagues at Astra Merck knew just the man: a financial planner and accountant with whom they were very friendly. They wrote up a contract. They agreed to pay the consultant a flat fee of about $50,000 to advise the clinic. But they also gave him another incentive. Carbona says, "We told him that if he was successful there would be more business for him in the future, and by 'successful,' we meant a rise in prescriptions for our drugs."

The consultant did an extremely thorough job. He spent 11 or 12 hours a day at the clinic for months. He talked to every employee, from the secretaries to the nurses to the doctors. He thought carefully about every aspect of the practice, from the most mundane administrative details to big-picture matters such as bill collection and financial strategy. He turned the practice into a profitable, smoothly running financial machine. And prescriptions for Astra Merck drugs soared.

When I asked Carbona how the consultant had increased Astra Merck's market share within the clinic so dramatically, he said that the consultant never pressed the doctors directly. Instead, he talked up Carbona. "Gene has put his neck on the line for you guys," he would tell them. "If this thing doesn't work, he might get fired." The consultant emphasized what a remarkable service the practice was getting, how valuable the financial advice was, how everything was going to turn around for them—all courtesy of Carbona. The strategy worked. "Those guys went berserk for me," Carbona says. Doctors at the newly vitalized practice prescribed so many Astra Merck drugs that he got a $140,000 bonus. The scheme was so successful that Carbona and his colleagues at Astra Merck decided to duplicate it in other practices.

I got in touch with Carbona after I learned that he was giving talks on the American Medical Student Association lecture circuit about his experiences as a rep. At that point I had read a fair bit of pharmaceutical sales literature, and most of it had struck me as remarkably hokey and stilted. Merck's official training materials, for example, instruct reps to say thing like, "Doctor, based on the information we discussed today, will you prescribe Vioxx for your patients who need once-daily power to prevent pain due to osteoarthritis?" So I was unprepared for a man with Carbona's charisma and forthright humor. I could see why he had been such an excellent rep: he came off as a cross between a genial con artist and a comedic character actor. After 2 hours on the phone with him I probably would have bought anything he was selling.

Most media accounts of the pharmaceutical industry miss this side of drug reps. By focusing on scandals—the kickbacks and the fraud and the lavish gifts—they lose sight of the fact that many reps are genuinely likeable people. The better ones have little use for the canned scripts they are taught in training. For them, effective selling is all about developing a relationship with a doctor. If a doctor likes a rep, that doctor is going to feel bad about refusing to see the rep, or about taking his lunches and samples but never prescribing his drugs. As Jordan Katz, a rep for Schering-Plough until two years ago, says, "A lot of doctors just write for who they like."

A variation on this idea emerges in *Side Effects*, Kathleen Slattery-Moschau's 2005 film about a fictional fledgling drug rep. Slattery-Moschau, who worked for 9 years as a rep for Bristol-Myers Squibb and Johnson & Johnson, says the carefully rehearsed messages in the corporate training courses really got to her. "I hated the crap I had to say to doctors," she told me. The heroine of *Side Effects* eventually decides to ditch the canned messages and stop spinning her product. Instead, she is brutally honest. "Bottom line?" she says to one doctor. "Your patients won't shit for a week." To her amazement, she finds that the blunter she is, the higher her

market share rises. Soon she is winning sales awards and driving a company BMW.

For most reps, market share is the yardstick of success. The more scripts their doctors write for their drugs, the more the reps make. Slattery-Moschau says that most of her fellow reps made $50,000 to $90,000 a year in salary and another $30,000 to $50,000 in bonuses, depending on how much they sold. Reps are pressured to "make quota," or meet yearly sales targets, which often increase from year to year. Reps who fail to make quota must endure the indignity of having their district manager frequently accompany them on sales calls. Those who meet quota are rewarded handsomely. The most successful reps achieve minor celebrity within the company.

One perennial problem for reps is the doctor who simply refuses to see them at all. Reps call these doctors "No Sees." Cracking a No See is a genuine achievement, the pharmaceutical equivalent of a home run or a windmill dunk. Gene Carbona says that when he came across a No See, or any other doctor who was hard to influence, he used "Northeast–Southwest" tactics. If you can't get to a doctor, he explains, you go after people surrounding that doctor, showering them with gifts. Carbona might help support a little league baseball team or a bowling league. After a while, the doctor would think, Gene is doing such nice things for all these people, the least I can do is give him 10 minutes of my time. At that point, Carbona says, the sale was as good as made. "If you could get ten minutes with a doctor, your market share would go through the roof." For decades the medical community has debated whether gifts and perks from reps have any real effect. Doctors insist that they do not. Studies in the medical literature indicate just the opposite. Doctors who take gifts from a company, studies show, are more likely to prescribe that company's drugs or ask that they be added to their hospital's formulary. The pharmaceutical industry has managed this debate skillfully, pouring vast resources into gifts for doctors while simultaneously reassuring them that their integrity prevents them from being influenced. For example, in a recent editorial in the journal *Health Affairs*, Bert Spilker, a vice president for PhRMA, the pharmaceutical trade group, defended the practice of gift giving against critics who, he scornfully wrote, "fear that physicians are so weak and lacking in integrity that they would 'sell their souls' for a pack of M&M candies and a few sandwiches and doughnuts."

Doctors' belief in their own incorruptibility appears to be honestly held. It is rare to hear a doctor—even in private, off-the record conversation—admit that industry gifts have made a difference in his or her prescribing. In fact, according to one small study of medical residents in the *Canadian Medical Association Journal*, one way to convince doctors that they cannot be influenced by gifts may be to give them one; the more gifts a doctor takes, the more likely that doctor is to believe that the gifts have had no effect. This helps explain why it makes sense for reps to give away even small gifts. A particular gift may have no influence, but it might make a doctor more apt to think that he or she would not be influenced by larger gifts in the future. A pizza and a penlight are like inoculations, tiny injections of self-confidence that make a doctor think, I will never be corrupted by money.

Gifts from the drug industry are nothing new, of course. William Helfand, who worked in marketing for Merck for 33 years, told me that company representatives were giving doctors books and pamphlets as early as the late nineteenth century. "There is nothing new under the sun," Helfand says. "There is just more of it." The question is: Why is there so much more of it just now? And what changed during the past decade to bring about such a dramatic increase in reps bearing gifts?

## AN ETHICS OF SALESMANSHIP

One morning last year I had breakfast at the Bryant-Lake Bowl, a diner in Minneapolis, with a former Pfizer rep named Michael Oldani. Oldani grew up in a working-class family in Kenosha, Wisconsin. Although he studied biochemistry in college, he knew nothing about pharmaceutical sales until he was recruited for Pfizer by the husband of a woman with whom he worked. Pfizer gave him a good salary, a company car, free gas, and an expense account. "It was kind of like the Mafia," Oldani told me. "They made me an offer I couldn't refuse." At the time, he was still in college and living with his parents. "I knew a good ticket out of Kenosha when I saw one," he says. He carried the bag for Pfizer for 9 years, until 1998.

Today Oldani is a Princeton-trained medical anthropologist teaching at the University of Wisconsin at Whitewater. He wrote his doctoral dissertation on the anthropology of pharmaceutical sales, drawing not just on ethnographic fieldwork he did in Manitoba as a Fulbright scholar but also on his own experience as a rep. This dual perspective—the view of both a detached outsider and a street-savvy insider—gives his work authority and a critical edge. I had invited Oldani to lecture at our medical school, the University of Minnesota, after reading his work in anthropology journals. Although his writing is scholarly, his manner is modest and self-effacing, more Kenosha than Princeton. This is a man who knows his way around a diner.

Like Carbona, Oldani worked as a rep in the late 1980s and the 1990s, a period when the drug industry was undergoing key transformations. Its ethos was changing from that of the country-club establishment to the aggressive, new-money entrepreneur. Impressed by the success of AIDS activists in pushing for faster drug approvals, the drug industry increased pressure on the FDA to let companies bring drugs to the market more quickly. As a result, in 1992 Congress passed the Prescription Drug User Fee Act, under which drug companies pay a variety of fees to the FDA, with the aim of speeding up drug approval (thereby making the drug industry a major funder of the agency set up to regulate it). In 1997 the FDA dropped most restrictions on direct-to-consumer advertising of prescription drugs, opening the gate for the eventual Levitra ads on Super Bowl Sunday and Zoloft cartoons during daytime television shows. The drug industry also became a big political player in Washington: by 2005, according to The Center for Public Integrity, its lobbying organization had become the largest in country.

Many companies started hitting for the fences, concentrating on potential blockbuster drugs for chronic illnesses in huge populations: Claritin for allergies, Viagra for impotence, Vioxx for arthritis, Prozac for depression. Successful drugs were followed by a flurry of competing me-too drugs. For most of the 1990s and the early part of this decade, the pharmaceutical industry was easily the most profitable business sector in America. In 2002, according to Public Citizen, a nonprofit watchdog group, the combined profits of the top 10 pharmaceutical companies in the Fortune 500 exceeded the combined profits of the other 490 companies.

During this period reps began to feel the influence of a new generation of executives intent on bringing market values to an industry that had been slow to embrace them. Anthony Wild, who was hired to lead Parke-Davis in the mid-1990s, told the journalist Greg Critser, the author of *Generation Rx,* that one of his first moves upon his appointment was to increase the incentive pay given to successful reps. Wild saw no reason to cap reps' incentives. As he said to the company's older executives, "Why not let them get rich?" Wild told the reps about the change at a meeting in San Francisco. "We announced that we were taking off the caps," he told Critser, "and the sales force went nuts!"

It was not just the industry's ethos that was changing; the technology was changing, too. According to Oldani, one of the most critical changes came in the way that information was gathered. In the days before computers, reps had to do a lot of legwork to figure out whom they could influence. They had to schmooze with the receptionists, make friends with the nurses, and chat up the pharmacists in order to learn which drugs the local doctors were prescribing, using the right incentives to coax what they needed from these informants. "Pharmacists are like pigeons," Jamie Reidy, a former rep for Pfizer and Eli Lilly, told me. "Only instead of bread crumbs, you toss them pizzas and sticky notes."

But in the 1990s, new information technology made it much simpler to track prescriptions. Market-research firms began collecting script-related data from pharmacies and hospitals and selling it to pharmaceutical companies. The American Medical Association collaborated by licensing them information about doctors (including doctors who do not belong to the AMA), which it collects in its "Physician Masterfile." Soon reps could find out exactly how many prescriptions any doctor was writing and exactly which drugs those prescriptions were for. All they had to do was turn on their laptops and download the data.

What they discovered was revelatory. For one thing, they found that a lot of doctors were lying to them. Doctors might tell a rep that they were writing prescriptions for, say, Lipitor, when they weren't. They were just being polite, or saying whatever they thought would get the rep off their back. Now reps could detect the deception immediately. (Even today many doctors do not realize that reps have access to script-tracking reports.)

More important, script-tracking helped reps figure out which doctors to target. They no longer had to waste time and money on doctors with conservative prescribing habits; they could head straight to the "high prescibers," or "high writers." And they could get direct feedback on which tactics were working. If a gift or a dinner presentation did not result in more scripts, they knew to try another approach.

But there was a rub: the data were available to every rep from every company. The result was an arms race of pharmaceutical gift giving, in which ways to exert influence. If the Eli Lilly rep was bringing sandwiches to the office staff, you brought Thai food. If GSK flew doctors to Palm Springs for a conference, you flew them to Paris. Oldani used to take residents to major league baseball games. "We did beer bongs, shots, and really partied," he told me. "Some of the guys were incredibly drunk on numerous occasions. I used to buy half barrels for their parties, almost on a retainer-like basis. I never talked product once to any of these residents, and they took care of me in their day-to-day practice. I never missed quota at their hospital."

Oldani says that script-tracking data also changed the way that reps thought about prescriptions. The old system of monitoring prescriptions was very inexact, and the relationship between a particular doctor's prescriptions and the work of a given rep was relatively hard to measure. But with precise script-tracking reports, reps started to feel a sense of ownership about prescriptions. If their doctors started writing more prescriptions for their drugs, the credit clearly belonged to them. However, more precise monitoring also invited micromanagement by the reps' bosses. They began pressuring reps to concentrate on high prescribers, fill out more paperwork, and report more frequently back to management.

"Script tracking, to me at least, made everyone a potentially successful rep," Oldani says. Reps didn't need to be nearly as resourceful and street savvy as in the past; they just needed the script-tracking reports. The industry began hiring more and more reps, many with backgrounds in sales (rather than, say, pharmacy, nursing, or biology). Some older reps say that during this period the industry replaced the serious detail man with "Pharma Barbie" and "Pharma Ken," whose medical knowledge was exceeded by their looks and catering skills. A newer, regimented style of selling began to replace the improvisational, more personal style of the old-school reps. Whatever was left of an ethic of service gave way to an ethic of salesmanship.

Doctors were caught in a bind. Many found themselves being called on several times a week by different reps from the same company. Most continued to see reps, some because they felt obligated to get up to speed with new drugs, some because they wanted to keep the pipeline of free samples open. But seeing reps has a cost, of course: the more reps a doctor sees, the longer the patients sit in the waiting room. Many doctors began to feel as though they deserved whatever gifts and perks they could get because reps were such an irritation. At one time a few practices even charged reps a fee for visiting.

Professional organizations made some efforts to place limits on the gifts doctors were allowed to accept. But these efforts were half-hearted, and they met with opposition from indignant doctors ridiculing the idea that their judgment could be bought. One doctor, in a letter to the *American Medical News*, confessed, "every time a discussion comes up on guidelines for pharmaceutical company gifts to physicians, I feel as if I need to take a blood pressure medicine to keep from a having a stroke." In 2001 the AMA launched a campaign to educate doctors about the ethical perils of pharmaceutical gifts, but it undercut its message by funding the campaign with money from the pharmaceutical industry.

Of course, most doctors are never offered free trips to Monaco or even a weekend at a spa; for them an industry gift means a Cialis pen or a Lexapro notepad. Yet it is a rare rep who cannot tell a story or two about the extravagant gifts doctors have requested. Oldani told me that one doctor asked him to build a music room in his house. Phyllis Adams, a former rep in Canada, was told by a doctor that he would not prescribe her product unless her company made him a consultant. (Both said no.) Carbana arranged a $35,000 "unrestricted educational grant" for a doctor who wanted a swimming pool in his back yard. "It was the Wild West," says Jamie Reidy, whose frank memoir about his activities while working for Pfizer in the 1990s, *Hard Sell: The Evolution of a Viagra Salesman*, recently got him fired from Eli Lilly. "They cashed the check, and that was it. And hopefully they remembered you every time they turned on the TV, or bought a drink on the cruise, or dived into the pool."

The trick is to give doctors gifts without making them feel that they are being bought. "Bribes that aren't considered bribes," Oldani says. "This, my friend, is the essence of pharmaceutical gifting." According to Oldani, the way to make a gift feel different from a bribe is to make it personal. "Ideally, a rep finds a way to get into a script-writer's psyche," he says. "You need to have talked enough with a script-writer—or done enough recon with gatekeepers—that you know what to give." When Oldani found a pharmacist who liked to play the market, he gave him stock options. When he wanted to see a resistant oncologist, he talked to the doctor's nurse and then gave the oncologist a $100 bottle of his favorite cognac. Reidy put the point nicely when he told me, "You are absolutely buying love."

Such gifts do not come with an explicit quid pro quo, of course. Whatever obligation doctors feel to write scripts for a rep's products usually comes from the general sense of reciprocity implied by the ritual of gift giving. But it is impossible to avoid the hard reality informing these ritualized exchanges: reps would not give doctors free stuff if they did not expect more scripts.

My brother Hal, a psychiatrist currently on the faculty of Wake Forest University, told me about an encounter he had with a drug rep from Eli Lilly some years back, when he was in private practice. This rep was not one of his favorites; she was too aggressive. That day she had insisted on bringing lunch to his office staff, even though Hal asked her not to. As he tried to make polite conversation with her in the hall, she reached over his shoulder into his drug closet and picked up a couple of sample packages of Zoloft and Celexa. Waving them in the air, she asked, "Tell me, Doctor, do the Pfizer and Forest reps bring lunch to your office staff?" A stony silence followed. Hal quietly ordered the rep out of the office and told her to never come back. She left in tears.

It's not hard to understand why Hal got so angry. The rep had broken the rules. Like an abrasive tourist who has not caught onto the code of manners in a foreign country, she had said outright the one thing that, by custom and common agreement, should never be said: that the lunches she brought were intended as a bribe. What's more, they were a bribe that Hal had never agreed to accept. He likened the situation to having somebody drop off a bag of money in your garage without your consent and then ask, "So what about our little agreement?"

When an encounter between a doctor and a rep goes well, it is a delicate ritual of pretense and self-deception. Drug reps pretend that they are giving doctors impartial information. Doctors pretend that they take it seriously. Drug reps must try their best to influence doctors, while doctors must tell themselves that they are not being influenced. Drug reps must act as if they are not salespeople, while doctors must act as if they are not customers. And if, by accident, the real purpose of the exchange is revealed, the result is like an elaborate theatrical dance in which the masks and costumes suddenly drop off and the actors come face to face with one another as they really are. Nobody wants to see that happen.

## THE NEW DRUG REPS?

Last spring a small group of first-year medical students at the University of Minnesota spoke to me about a lecture on erectile dysfunction that had just been given by a member of the urology department. The doctor's PowerPoint slides had a large, watermarked logo in the corner. At one point during the lecture a student raised his hand and, somewhat disingenuously, asked the urologist to explain the logo. The urologist, caught off-guard, stumbled for a moment and then said that it was the logo for Cialis, a drug for erectile dysfunction that is manufactured by Eli Lilly. Another student asked if he had a special relationship with Eli Lilly. The urologist replied that yes, he was on the advisory board for the company, which had supplied the slides. But he quickly added that nobody needed to worry about the objectivity of his lecture because he was also on the advisory boards of the makers of the competing drugs Viagra and Levitra. The second student told me, "A lot of people agreed that it was a pharm lecture and that we should have gotten a free breakfast."

This episode is not as unusual as it might appear. Drug company–sponsored consultancies, advisory-board memberships, and speaking engagements have become so common, especially among medical-school faculty, that the urologist probably never imagined that he would be challenged for lecturing to medical students with materials produced by Eli Lilly. According to a recent study in the *Journal of the American Medical Association,* 9 out of 10 medical students have been asked or required by an attending physician to go to a lunch sponsored by a drug company. As of 2003, according to the Accreditation Council for Continuing Medical education, pharmaceutical companies were providing 90 percent of the $1 billion spent annually on continuing medical education events, which doctors must attend in order to maintain their licensure.

Over the past year or two pharmaceutical profits have started to level off, and a backlash against reps has been felt; some companies have actually reduced their sales forces. But the industry as a whole is hiring more and more doctors as speakers. In 2004, it sponsored nearly twice as many educational events led by doctors as by reps. Not long before, the numbers had been roughly equal. This raises the question, Are doctors becoming the new drug reps?

Doctors are often the best people to market a drug to other doctors. Merck discovered this when it was developing a campaign for Vioxx, before the drug was taken off the market because of its association with heart attacks and strokes. According to an internal study by Merck, reported in the *Wall Street Journal,* doctors who attended a lecture by another doctor subsequently wrote nearly four times more prescriptions for Vioxx than doctors who attended an event led by a rep. The return on investment for doctor-led events was nearly twice that of rep-led events, even after subtracting the generous fees Merck paid to the doctors who spoke.

These speaking invitations work much like gifts. While reps hope, of course, that a doctor who is speaking on behalf of their company will give their drugs good PR, they also know that such a doctor is more likely to write prescriptions for their drugs. "If he didn't write, he wouldn't speak," a rep who has worked for four pharmaceutical companies told me. The semi-official industry term for these speakers and consultants is "thought leaders," or "key opinion leaders." Some thought leaders do not stay loyal to one company but rather generate a tidy supplemental income by speaking and consulting for a number of different companies. Reps refer to these doctors as "drug whores."

The seduction, whether by one company or several, is often quite gradual. My brother Hal explained to me how he wound up on the speakers' bureau of a major pharmaceutical company. It started when a company rep asked him if he'd be interested in giving a talk about clinical depression to a community group. The honorarium was $1,000. Hal thought, Why not? It seemed almost a public service. The next time, the company asked him to talk not to the public but to practitioners at a community hospital. Soon company reps were making suggestions about content. "Why don't you mention the side-effect profiles of the different antidepressants?" they asked. Uneasy, Hal tried to ignore these suggestions. Still, the more talks he gave, the more the reps became focused on antidepressants rather than depression. The company began giving him PowerPoint slides to use, which he also ignored. The reps started telling him, "You know, we have you on the local circuit giving these talks, but you're medical-school faculty; we could get you on the national circuit. That's where the real money is." The mention of big money made him even more uneasy. Eventually the reps asked him to lecture about a new version of their antidepressant drug. Soon after that, Hal told them, "I can't do this anymore."

Looking back on this trajectory, Hal said, "It's kind of like you're a woman at a party, and your boss says to you, 'look, do me a favor: be nice to this guy over there.' And you see the guy is not bad-looking, and you're unattached, so you say, 'Why not? I can be nice.'" The problem is that it never ends with that party. "Soon you find yourself on the way to a Bangkok brothel in the cargo hold of an unmarked plane. And you say, 'Whoa, this is not what I agreed to.' But then you have to ask yourself, 'When did the prostitution actually start? Wasn't it at that party?'"

Thought leaders serve an indispensable function when it comes to a potentially very lucrative marketing niche: off-lable promotion, or promoting a drug for uses other than those for which it was approved by the FDA—something reps are strictly forbidden to do. The case of Neurontin is especially instructive. In 1996 a whistle-blower named David Franklin, a medical-science liaison with Parke-Davis (now a division of Pfizer), filed suit against the company over its off-label promotion of this drug. Neurontin was approved for the treatment of epilepsy, but according to the lawsuit, Parke-Davis was promoting it for other conditions—including bipolar disorder, migraines, and restless legs syndrome—for which there was little or no scientific evidence that it worked. To do so the company employed a variety of schemes, most involving a combination of rep ingenuity and payments to doctors. Some doctors signed ghostwritten journal articles. One received more than $300,000 to speak about Neurontin at conferences. Others were paid just to listen. Simply having some of your thought leaders in attendance at a meeting is valuable, Kathleen Slattery-Moschkau explains, because they will often bring up off-label uses of a drug without having to be prompted. "You can't get a better selling situation than that," she says. In such circumstances all she had to do was pour the wine and make sure everyone was happy.

The litigation over Neurontin cost Pfizer $430 million in criminal fines and civil damages for the period 1994 to 2002. It was well worth it. The drug's popularity and profitability soared. In spite of the adverse publicity, Neurotin generated more than $2.7 billion in revenues in 2003, more than 90 percent of which came from off-label prescriptions.

Of course, sometimes speakers discover that the drug they have been paid to lecture about is dangerous. One of the most notorious examples is Fen-Phen, the diet-drug combination that has been linked to primary pulmonary hypertension and valvular heart disease. Wyeth, the manufacturer of Redux, or dexfenfluramine—the "Fen" in Fen-Phen—

has put aside $21 billion to cover costs and liabilities from litigation. Similar events played-out, on a lesser scale, with Parke-Davis's diabetes drug Rezulin, and Wyeth's pain reliever Duract, which were taken off the market after being associated with life-threatening complications.

And what about reps themselves? Do they trust their companies to tell them about potential problems with their drugs? Not exactly. As one veteran rep, voicing a common sentiment, told me, "Reps are the last to know." Of course, for a rep to be detailing a drug enthusiastically right up to the day it is withdrawn from the market is likely to erode that rep's credibility with doctors. Yet some reps say they don't hear about problems until the press gets wind of them and the company launches into damage control. At that point, Slattery-Moschau explains, "Reps learn verbatim how to handle the concern or objection in a way that spins it back in the drug's favor."

Some believe that the marketing landscape changed dramatically for both reps and doc-

tors in 2002, after the Office of the Inspector General in the Department of Health and Human Services announced its intention to crack down on drug companies' more notorious promotional practices. With the threat of prosecution in the air, the industry began to take the job of self-policing a lot more seriously, and PhRMA issued a set of voluntary marketing guidelines.

Although most reps agree that the PhRMA code has changed things, not all of them agree that it changed things for the better. Some say that as long as reps feel pressure to meet quota, they will find ways to get around the rules. As one former rep pointed out, not all drug companies belong to PhRMA, and those that don't are, of course, not bound by PhRMA's guidelines. Jordan Katz says that things actually got worse after 2002. "The companies that tried to follow the guidelines lost a ton of market share, and the ones who didn't gained it," he says. "The bottom line is that if you don't pay off the doctors, you will not succeed in pharmaceuticals. Period."

## LEGAL PERSPECTIVES

# *Irving A. Backman v. Polaroid Corporation*

*United States Court of Appeals for the First Circuit*

This is a class action brought by Irving A. Backman on behalf of himself and all other persons who purchased shares of stock of defendant Polaroid Corporation on the open market between January 11 and February 22, 1979, allegedly misled by defendant's conduct that violated Section 10 (b) of the Securities Exchange Act of 1934 and Rule 10b-5 of the regulations promulgated thereunder. Suit was filed

in June 1979. . . . The improprieties asserted, both in the complaint and in plaintiffs' opening to the jury, as responsible for plaintiffs' purchasing shares before a substantial drop in the market, were defendant's failure to disclose unfavorable facts about its new product, Polavision, an instant movie camera. Following trial on liability, the jury found for plaintiffs. . . . On appeal, a divided panel . . . granted a new trial.

910 F.2d 10 (1st Cir. 1990).

On this rehearing en banc we reverse and order judgment for defendant. . . .

In their amended complaint plaintiffs alleged that defendant failed to disclose that Polavision, introduced in the spring, had been unprofitable throughout 1978, and would continue so, significantly, at least through 1979; that it had been excessively inventoried and had suffered lagging sales; that little, if any, information had been made public; that defendant knew that this undisclosed information was material to investors, and that major investment research firms had publicly projected defendant's earnings based on assumptions defendant knew were contrary to the true facts, all of which nondisclosure was in violation of the securities laws.

Secondly, plaintiffs re-alleged the above and added that over the years defendant had advertised that it was a growth company, and that, through its successes, the investment community had come to consider it the best of the growth companies, and that its failing to make the above disclosures operated as a fraud and deceit on the investing public, was a "fraud on the market," and constituted an unlawful manipulation thereof. . . .

However, mere market interest is no basis for imposing liability. We said [in a former case] the materiality of the information claimed not to have been disclosed . . . is not enough to make out a sustainable claim of securities fraud. Even if information is material, there is no liability under Rule 10b-5 unless there is a duty to disclose it.

A duty to disclose "does not arise from the mere possession of non-public information." . . .

In a twelve day trial [the plaintiffs] precisely followed their opening, alleging, simply, nondisclosure of material information. As summarized in their final argument,

> Polaroid . . . violated the federal securities laws which require full disclosure so that people who purchase and sell securities do so on a fair playing field; that people have the same information and people can make their investment decisions based on having all of the information and having truthful information. . . . [Y]ou have to find that Polaroid had adverse information, that information was material—i.e., that it was important—and that Polaroid knowingly and deliberately withheld it. *And that's all we're asking you to do here.* (Emphasis supplied.)

The summation was not an inadvertence, but was in accord with plaintiffs's own testimony.

> Q.    Now, Mr. Backman, in this action you are not claiming, are you, that the financial information put out by Polaroid was in any way false and misleading, are you?
> A.    I think you'll have to refer to the complaint. I believe the failure to disclose is just as improper as providing false information. And I believe the essence of my suit deals with the failure to disclose. . . . I do claim it was false and misleading because the failure to disclose is just as misleading a (sic) improper disclosure.
>
> This, of course, is not so, "Silence, absent a duty to disclose, is not misleading under Rule 10b-5." . . .

We have gone into this at length, not so much to show the emptiness of plaintiff's first claim—agreed to by the full panel—but to accent our finding that there had been no falsity or misleading by defendant in any respect. In eight years of preparation and twelve days of trial, the words misrepresentation and misleading never crossed plaintiffs' lips. . . .

It appeared that Dr. Edwin H. Land, the founder and at all times president or C.E.O. of Polaroid, had added to his invention of the world-famous instant still camera another exceptional invention—an instant movie camera, Polavision. It appeared throughout the case, however, that Polavision's sales appeal did not correspond with the quality of the invention. Launched in early 1978 with great fanfare, the estimates for fall, to which production had been geared, proved to be substantially excessive. As a result, in late October, Eumig, the Austrian manufacturer, having earlier been told to increase production, was instructed to reduce by 20,000. In mid-November Euming was told to take out another 90,000 sets, and to halt production. Plaintiffs' panel brief, quoting the fortuitous language of Eumig's cable acknowledgment, "to now finally stop production entirely," gives the impression that the halt was intended to be permanent. Conveniently, from plaintiffs' standpoint, dots in the quotation replace the subsequent sentence, "Steps have been taken to ensure a quick new start-up of production on a reduced scale." This omission aids plaintiffs in their recitation, the regrettable incorrectness of which we will come to, that "management knew that Polavision was a commercial failure." Thereafter, fourth-quarter internal figures, not publicly released, confirmed that the original Polavision estimates (also not released) had been substantially excessive.

The next event was a newspaper release published on January 9, 1979, that Rowland Foundation, a charitable trust established by Dr. and Mrs. Land, was to sell 300,000 shares of Polaroid, in part for funds for a new project, and in part to diversify its portfolio. Defendant participated in the preparation of the release, but not in the action itself. It is not claimed that the release was in any way untrue. Plaintiff's claim is misleading because additional information should then have been given the public. The sale was consummated on January 11. . . .

On February 22, 1979, immediately following the annual meeting, defendant announced further facts about Polavision's lack of success, and the market fell, shortly, by some 20%. . . .

Plaintiffs' brief now finds assisted misrepresentation because "Polaroid featured Polavision on the cover," plaintiffs point out that after President McCune "announced record worldwide sales and earnings for both the third quarter and the first nine months of 1978, . . .

Mr. McCune noted that the Company's worldwide manufacturing facilities continue to operate at close to maximum capacity," whereas, in fact, Polavision's contract supplier, Eumig, was told, shortly before the report, to hold up on 20,000 units. We note, first, that the statement, taken as a whole, was true; it expressly recognized an absence of totality. Of more specific importance, it flagged, on three of its three and half pages of text, that Polavision's effect on earnings was negative. . . . With this emphasized three times, we ask did this report mislead investors to buy stock because Polavision was doing so well?

Plaintiffs quote *Roeder,* 814 F.2d at 26, that even a voluntary disclosure of information that a reasonable investor would consider material must be "complete and accurate." This, however, does not mean that by revealing one fact about a product, one must reveal all others, that, too, would be interesting, marketwise, but means only such others, if any, that are needed so that what was revealed would not be "so incomplete as to mislead." . . . Disclosing that Polavision was being sold below cost was not misleading by reason of not saying how much below. Nor was it misleading not to report the number of sales, or that they were below expectations. . . .

We come, next, to the January 9 Rowland Foundation sale release. There was nothing untrue or misleading in the release itself, but plaintiffs say, with support from the panel opinion, that it should have contained additional information in order to keep the November report from being misleading. . . .

Obviously, if a disclosure is in fact misleading when made, and the speaker thereafter learns of this, there is a duty to correct it. . . . In special circumstances, a statement, correct at the time, may have a forward intent and connotation upon which parties may be expected to rely. If this is a clear meaning, and there is a change, correction, more exactly, further disclosure, may be called for. . . . Fear that statements of historical fact might be claimed to fall within it, could inhibit disclosures altogether. And what is the limit? In the present case if the shoe were on the other foot, and defendant could have, and had, announced continued Polavision profits, for how long would it have been under a duty of disclosure if the tide turned? Plaintiffs' contention that it would be a jury question is scarcely reassuring. . . .

After indicating reluctance to accept plaintiffs' contention that the Third Quarter Report was misleading when made, the panel opinion, in holding that it could be found misleading in light of late developments, said as follows.

[E]ven if the optimistic Third Quarter Report was not misleading at the time of its issuance, there is sufficient evidence to support a jury's determination that the report's relatively brief mention of Polavision difficulties *became* misleading in light of the subsequent information acquired by Polaroid indicating the seriousness of Polavision's problems. This subsequent information included . . . Polaroid's decision to . . . stop Polavision production by its Austrian manufacturer, Eumig, *and its instruction to its Austrian supplier to keep this production cutback secret.* We feel that a reasonable jury could conclude that this subsequent information rendered the Third Quarter Report's brief mention of Polavision expenses misleading, triggering a duty to disclose on the part of Polaroid. (Emphasis in orig.)

At the time of the Rowland sale, while selling the stock had absolutely nothing to do with

Polaroid's financial health . . . some might find it less than forthcoming for the press release not to have at least mentioned Polavision's difficulties so that the investing public could assess for themselves the reasons behind the sale.

That this was an improper mix was made conspicuous by plaintiffs' oral argument.

[W]e've cited the specific passages of Mr. Mc-Cune's testimony in our brief, where Mr. Mc-Cune testified that the expression, "continued to reflect substantial expenses" was intended to convey that that condition would continue in the future. . . . What we're saying is that a jury could find that this statement, even if it wasn't misleading when issued, became misleading because of the forward-looking nature.

This is a failure to recognize that what Mr. Mc-Cune said was a single, simple, statement, that substantial expenses had made Polavision's earnings negative. Though the panel opinion characterized it as "relatively brief," it was precisely correct, initially. Even if forward-looking, it remained precisely correct thereafter. . . . In arguing that the statement did not "remain true," plaintiffs' brief, unabashedly, points solely to matters outside the scope of the initial disclosure, in no way making it incorrect or misleading, originally, or later.

The shells in plaintiffs' gun at trial . . . are all percussion cap and no powder. . . . Plaintiffs have no case.

# B. Sanfield Inc. v. Finlay Fine Jewelry Corp.

*United States Court of Appeals for the Seventh Circuit*

## I.

Sanfield is a locally owned retailer. At its one and only store in Rockford, it offers jewelry, floral arrangements, plants, and other gifts for sale

to the public. Finlay is a nationwide retailer that also sells jewelry to the public. It does so through fine jewelry departments that it leases from host department stores such as Bergner's, which has 13 stores in Illinois, including two in Rockford.

No. 98–1873, 168 F.3d 967 (1999). September 16, 1998, Argued. February 17, 1999, Decided.

Among other items, Sanfield and Finlay each sell gold earrings, gold chains, gold bangles, and gold charms; and this suit centers upon Finlay's efforts to advertise and promote the sale of those four categories of jewelry. Although Finlay prices these items in the first instance at about 5.5 times their cost, it frequently offers them for sale at 40 to 60 percent off the original price, with 50 percent being the most common discount. In fact, Finlay sells the vast majority of these types of jewelry in Rockford at the discounted, rather than the original, price. See R. 183 Ex. 77 PP 9, 10.

The premise of Sanfield's suit is that the "regular" price that Finlay sets for its gold earrings, chains, bangles, and charms is a sham. Finlay sets the original price high, Sanfield alleges, with no expectation that it will make substantial sales at that price. The truly regular price is, in practice, the discounted price. Yet, Sanfield emphasizes, although reduced, even the discounted price of a given piece of Finlay jewelry may in fact be substantially higher than the regular, nondiscounted price at which other retailers, including Sanfield, customarily offer that same item. Rational consumers who take the time to price shop would, of course, opt to buy the jewelry at the regular prices offered by the other retailers. Sanfield believes, however, that "50 percent off" has such an alluring ring that many consumers are misled into thinking that Finlay's sale prices are really better than the nondiscounted prices at which Sanfield offers its own jewelry. As a result, customers are enticed away from Sanfield.

Consistent with Sanfield's theory, state and federal regulations (which we will set out in full below) both recognize the possibility that the advertising and promotion of discount prices can be deceptive. Like a number of other states, Illinois has adopted a regulation which provides that it is deceptive for a seller to compare the discounted price of an item with the regular price, unless the seller has either (1) sold a substantial number of that item at a price equal to or greater than the regular price or (2) has offered the item openly and actively at the regular price for a reasonably substantial time in good faith with the genuine intent of selling the item at that price. 14 Ill. Admin. Code § 470.220; see generally Alan M. Komensky & Mark D. Wegener, When Is a Sale Not a Sale? State Regulation of Price Comparison Advertising, 5 Antitrust 28 (Summer 1991). The federal counterpart likewise recognizes the deceptive potential of advertising a reduction in a product's former price when the former price is fictitious; and it poses a similar question for the purpose of assessing whether the regular price is bona fide—has the seller in good faith offered the item at the regular price openly and actively for a reasonably substantial period of time in the regular, recent course of its business? . . .

Only if there were proof that consumers actually believe that Finlay regularly and in good faith offered its jewelry for sale at the regular price could one conclude that Finlay's advertising and promotional practices are deceptive, the court reasoned. Sanfield offered some evidence on that score (as did Finlay), but the court found it insufficient to show that consumers were actually misled. Consequently, the court found that Sanfield had not carried its burden in establishing the first element of its claim under the Illinois consumer fraud statute—that Finlay had engaged in a deceptive act or practice and the first and second elements of its Lanham Act claim—that Finlay had issued false or misleading advertisements which are actually deceiving or likely to deceive. Having so concluded, the court believed it unnecessary to consider whether Finlay's ads comported with the state and federal regulations. . . .

## II.

## A.

Exercising the regulatory authority granted him by the consumer fraud act, 815 ILCS 505/4, the Illinois Attorney General has determined that "the use of misleading price comparisons is injurious to both the consuming public and competitors and is an unfair or deceptive act and an unfair method of competition under Section 2 of the Consumer Fraud and Deceptive Practices Act. . . ." 14 Ill. Admin. Code—470.110. The following regulation identifies the circumstances under which a seller's comparison of a discounted price to its own regular price amounts to a deceptive act for purposes of the statute: It is unfair or deceptive for a seller to compare current price with its former (regular) price for any product or service (for example: "$99, now $69 Save $30"; "regularly $99, Now $69"; "Originally $99, Now $69"; "Save $30, Now $69") unless one of the following criteria are [sic] met:

(a) the former (regular) price is equal to or below the price(s) at which the seller made a substantial number of sales of such products in the recent regular course of its business; or

(b) the former (regular) price is equal to or below the price(s) at which the seller offered the product for a reasonably substantial period of time in the recent regular course of its business, openly and actively and in good faith, with an intent to sell the product at that price(s). . . .

One of the most commonly used forms of bargain advertising is to offer a reduction from the advertiser's own former price for an article. If the former price is the actual, bona fide price at which the article was offered to the public on a regular basis for a reasonably substantial period of time, it provides a legitimate basis for the advertising of a price comparison. Where the former price is genuine, the bargain being advertised is a true one. If, on the other hand, the former price being advertised is not bona fide but fictitious—for example, where an artificial, inflated, price was established for the purpose of enabling the subsequent offer of a large reduction—the "bargain" being advertised is a false one; the purchaser is not receiving the unusual value he expects. In such a case, the reduced price is, in reality, probably just the seller's regular price.

Taking its cue from these regulatory provisions, Sanfield contends that when Finlay advertises its jewelry at 50 percent (or some other percentage) off the "regular" price, it is deceiving consumers, because in fact Finlay rarely if ever sells the jewelry at that price and (as Sanfield sees it) makes no good-faith effort to do so. The "bargain" that Finlay purports to offer prospective customers is therefore no bargain at all, as Sanfield sees it, because the ostensibly discounted price is the price at which Finlay makes (and expects to make) the vast majority of its sales. . . .

Deception, like beauty, is in the eye of the beholder. If consumers generally understand that a retailer makes little or no concerted effort to sell at a stated regular price, then stating the price as regular would be neither deceptive nor misleading. It might impact the efficacy of the promoted sale, but it would not deceive. If the consuming public held the opposite belief, that is, that [the] regular price is the price that defendant regularly and genuinely offers the advertised items for sale at, then that would evidence deception. Absent consumer perceptions, however, whether defendant actually offers or sells the items at [the] regular price proves little, if anything, in this context.

# Coca-Cola Company v. Tropicana Products Inc.

*United States Court of Appeals for the Second Circuit*

A proverb current even in the days of ancient Rome was "seeing is believing." Today, a great deal of what people see flashes before them on their TV sets. This case involves a 30-second television commercial with simultaneous audio and video components. We have no doubt that the byword of Rome is as valid now as it was then. And, if seeing something on TV has a tendency to persuade a viewer to believe, how much greater is the impact on a viewer's credulity when he both sees and hears a message at the same time?

In mid-February of 1982 defendant Tropicana products, Inc. (Tropicana) began airing a new television commercial for its Premium Pack orange juice. The commercial shows the renowned American Olympic athlete Bruce Jenner squeezing an orange while saying "It's pure, pasteurized juice as it comes from the orange," and then shows Jenner pouring the fresh-squeezed juice into a Tropicana carton while the audio states "It's the only leading brand not made with concentrate and water."

Soon after the advertisement began running, plaintiff Coca-Cola Company (Coke, Coca-Cola), maker of Minute Maid orange juice, brought suit in the United States District Court for the Southern District of New York, 538 F. Supp. 1091, against Tropicana for false advertising in violation of section 43(a) of the Lanham Act. The statute provides that anyone who uses a false description or representation in connection with goods placed in commerce "shall be liable to a civil action by [anyone]. . . . Who believes that he is or is likely to be damaged by the use of . . . such false description or representation." 15 U.S.C. § 1125(a) (1976). Coke claimed the commercial is false because it incorrectly represents

that Premium Pack contains unprocessed, fresh-squeezed juice when in fact the juice is pasteurized (heated to about 200 degrees Fahrenheit) and sometimes frozen prior to packaging. The court below denied plaintiff's motion for a preliminary injunction to enjoin further broadcast of the advertisement pending the outcome of this litigation. In our view preliminary injunctive relief is appropriate.

Perhaps the most difficult element to demonstrate when seeking an injunction against false advertising is the likelihood that one will suffer irreparable harm if the injunction does not issue. It is virtually impossible to prove that so much of one's sales will be lost or that one's goodwill will be damaged as a direct result of a competitor's advertisement. Too many market variables enter into the advertising-sales equation. Because of these impediments, a Lanham Act plaintiff who can prove actual lost sales may obtain an injunction even if most of his sales decline is attributable of factors other than a competitor's false advertising. In fact, he need not even point to an actual loss or diversion of sales.

The Lanham Act plaintiff must, however, offer something more than a mere subjective belief that he is likely to be injured as a result of the false advertising, Id. at 189; he must submit proof which provides a reasonable basis for that belief. The likelihood of injury and causation will not be presumed, but must be demonstrated in some manner.

Two recent decisions of this Court have examined the type of proof necessary to satisfy this requirement. Relying on the fact that the products involved were in head-to-head competition, the Court in both cases directed the issuance of a preliminary injunction under the

Lanham Act. Vidal Sassoon, 661 F.2d at 227; Johnson & Johnson, 631 F.2d at 189–91. In both decisions the Court reasoned that sales of the plaintiffs' products would probably be harmed if the competing products' advertising tended to mislead consumers in the manner alleged. Market studies were used as evidence that some consumers were in fact misled by the advertising in issue. Thus, the market studies supplied the causative link between the advertising and the plaintiffs' potential lost sales, and thereby indicated a likelihood of injury.

Applying the same reasoning to the instant case, if consumers are misled by Tropicana's commercial, Coca-Cola probably would suffer irreparable injury. Tropicana and Coca-Cola are the leading national competitors for the chilled (ready-to-serve) orange juice market. If Tropicana's advertisement misleads consumers into believing that Premium Pack is a more desirable product because it contains only fresh-squeezed, unprocessed juice, then it is likely that Coke will lose a portion of the chilled juice market and thus suffer irreparable injury.

Evidence in the record supports the conclusion that consumers are likely to be misled in this manner. A consumer reaction survey conducted by ASI Market Research, Inc. and a Burke test, measuring recall of the commercial after it was aired on television, were admitted into evidence, though neither one was considered by the district court in reference to irreparable injury. The trial court examined the ASI survey regarding the issue of likelihood of success on the merits, and found that it contained various flaws which made it difficult to determine for certain whether a large number of consumers were misled. We do not disagree with those findings. We note, moreover, that despite these flaws the district court ruled that there were at least a small number of clearly deceived ASI interviewees. Our examination of the Burke test results leads to the same conclusion, i.e., that a not insubstantial

number of consumers were clearly misled by the defendant's ad. Together these tests provide sufficient evidence of a risk of irreparable harm because they demonstrate that a significant number of consumers would be likely to be misled. The trial court should have considered these studies on the issue of irreparable injury. . . .

Once the initial requisite showing of irreparable harm has been made, the party seeking a preliminary injunction must satisfy either of the two alternatives regarding the merits of his case. We find that Coca-Cola satisfies the more stringent first alternative because it is likely to succeed on the merits of its false advertising action.

Coke is entitled to relief under the Lanham Act if Tropicana has used a false description or representation in its Jenner commercial. When a merchandising statement or representation is literally or explicitly false, the court may grant relief without reference to the advertisement's impact on the buying public. When the challenged advertisement is implicitly rather than explicitly false, its tendency to violate the Lanham Act by misleading, confusing, or deceiving should be tested by public reaction.

In viewing defendant's 30-second commercial at oral argument, we concluded that the trail court's finding that this ad was not facially false is an error of fact. Since the trial judge's finding on this issue was based solely on the inference it drew from reviewing documentary evidence, consisting of commercial, we are in as good a position as it was to draw an appropriate inference. We find, therefore, that the squeezing-pouring sequence in the Jenner commercial is false on its face. The visual component of the ad makes an explicit representation that Premium Pack is produced by squeezing oranges and pouring the freshly squeezed juice directly into the carton. This is not a true representation of how the product is prepared. Premium Pack juice is heated and sometimes frozen prior to packaging. Additionally, the simultaneous audio component of the ad states that Premium Pack is "pasteurized juice as it comes from the oranges." This statement is blatantly false—pasteurized juice does not come from oranges. Pasteurization entails heating the juice to approximately 200 degrees Fahrenheit to kill certain natural enzymes and microorganisms which cause spoilage. Moreover, even if the addition of the word "pasteurized" somehow made sense and effectively qualified the visual image, Tropicana's commercial nevertheless represented that the juice is only squeezed, heated, and packaged when in fact it may actually also be frozen.

Hence, Coke is likely to succeed in arguing that Tropicana's ad is false and that it is entitled to relief under the Lanham Act. The purpose of the Act is to insure truthfulness in advertising and to eliminate misrepresentations with reference to the inherent quality or characteristic of another's product. The claim that Tropicana's Premium Pack contains only fresh-squeezed, unprocessed juice is clearly a misrepresentation as to that product's inherent quality or characteristic. Since the plaintiff has satisfied the first preliminary injunction alternative, we need not decide whether the balance or hardships tips in its favor.

Because Tropicana has made a false representation in its advertising and Coke is likely to suffer irreparable harm as a result, we reverse the district court's denial of plaintiff's application and remand this case for issuance of a preliminary injunction preventing broadcast of the squeezing-pouring sequence in the Jenner commercial.

# Kasky v. Nike, Inc.

*Supreme Court of California*

Acting on behalf of the public, plaintiff brought this action seeking monetary and injunctive relief under California laws designed to curb false advertising and unfair competition. Plaintiff alleged that defendant corporation, in response to public criticism, and to induce consumers to continue to buy its products, made false statements of fact about its labor practices and about working conditions in factories that make its products. Applying established principles of appellate review, we must assume in this opinion that these allegations are true.

The issue here is whether defendant corporation's false statements are commercial or noncommercial speech for purposes of constitutional free speech analysis under the state and federal constitutions. Resolution of this issue is important because commercial speech receives a lesser degree of constitutional protection than many other forms of expression, and because governments may entirely prohibit commercial speech that is false or misleading.

Because the messages in question were directed by a commercial speaker to a commercial audience, and because they made representations of fact about the speaker's own business operations for the purpose of promoting sales of its products, we conclude that these messages are commercial speech for purpose of applying state laws barring false and misleading commercial messages. Because the Court of Appeal concluded otherwise, we will reverse its judgment.

Our holding, based on decisions of the United States Supreme Court, in no way prohibits any business enterprise from speaking

45 P.3d 243 (2002). Opinion by Judge J. Jacobs.

out on issue of public importance or from vigorously defending its own labor practices. It means only that when a business enterprise, to promote and defend its sales and profits, makes factual representations about its own products or its own operations, it must speak truthfully. Plaintiff Marc Kasky is a California resident suing on behalf of the general public of the State of California. Defendant Nike, Inc. (Nike) is an Oregon corporation with its principal place of business in that state; Nike is authorized to do business in California and does promote, distribute, and sell its products in this state.

Nike manufactures and sells athletic shoes and apparel. In 1997, it reported annual revenues of $9.2 billion, with annual expenditures for adverting and marketing of almost $1 billion. Most of Nike's products are manufactured by subcontractors in China, Vietnam, and Indonesia. Most of the workers who make Nike products are women under the age of 24. Since March 1993, under a memorandum of understanding with its subcontractors, Nike has assumed responsibility for its subcontractors' compliance with applicable local laws and regulations concerning minimum wage, overtime, occupational health and safety, and environmental protection.

Beginning at least in October 1996 with a report on the television news program *48 Hours,* and continuing at least through November and December of 1997 with the publication of articles in the *Financial Times,* the *New York Times,* the *San Francisco Chronicle,* the *Buffalo News,* the *Oregonian,* the *Kansas City Star,* and the *Sporting News,* various persons and organizations alleged that in the factories where Nike products are made workers were paid less than the applicable local minimum wage; required to work overtime; allowed and encouraged to work more overtime hours than applicable local law allowed; subjected to physical, verbal, and sex-

ual abuse; and exposed to toxic chemicals, noise, heat, and dust without adequate safety equipment, in violation of applicable local occupational health and safety regulations.

In response to this adverse publicity, and for the purpose of maintaining and increasing its sales and profits, Nike and the individual defendants made statements to the California consuming public that plaintiff alleges were false and misleading. Specifically, Nike and the individual defendants said that workers who make Nike products are protected from physical and sexual abuse, that they are paid in accordance with applicable local laws and regulations governing wages and hours, that they are paid on average double the applicable local minimum wage, that they receive a "living wage," that they receive free meals and health care, and that their working conditions are in compliance with applicable local laws and regulations governing occupational health and safety. Nike and the individual defendants made these statements in press releases, in letters to newspapers, in a letter to university presidents and athletic directors, and in other documents distributed for public relations purposes. Nike also bought full-page advertisements in leading newspapers to publicize a report that GoodWorks International, LLC., had prepared under a contract with Nike. The report was based on an investigation by former United States Ambassador Andrew Young, and it found no evidence of illegal or unsafe working conditions at Nike factories in China, Vietnam, and Indonesia.

Plaintiff alleges that Nike and the individual defendants made these false and misleading statements because of their negligence and carelessness and "with knowledge or reckless disregard of the laws of California prohibiting false and misleading statements.". . .

The United States Supreme Court has not adopted an all-purpose test to distinguish commercial from noncommercial speech under the First Amendment, nor has this court adopted such a test under the state constitution, nor do we propose to do so here. A close reading of the high court's commercial speech decisions suggests, however, that it is possible to formulate a limited-purpose test. We conclude, therefore, that *when a court must decide whether particular speech may be subjected to laws aimed at preventing false advertising or other forms of commercial deception,* categorizing a particular statement as commercial or noncommercial speech requires consideration of three elements: the speaker, the intended audience, and the content of the message. . . .

Here, the first element—a commercial speaker—is satisfied because the speakers—Nike and its officers and directors—are engaged in commerce. Specifically, they manufacture, import, distribute, and sell consumer goods in the form of athletic shoes and apparel.

The second element—an intended commercial audience—is also satisfied. Nike's letters to university presidents and directors of athletic departments were addressed directly to actual and potential purchasers of Nike's products, because college and university athletic departments are major purchasers of athletic shoes and apparel. Plaintiff has alleged that Nike's press releases and letters to newspaper editors, although addressed to the public generally, were also intended to reach and influence actual and potential purchasers of Nike's products. Specifically, plaintiff has alleged that Nike made these statements about its labor policies and practices "to maintain and/or increase its sales and profits.". . .

The third element—representations of fact of a commercial nature—is also present. In describing its own labor policies, and the practices and working conditions in factories where its products are made, Nike was making factual representations about its own business operations. In speaking to consumers about working conditions and labor practices in the factories where its products are made, Nike addressed matters within its own knowledge. The wages paid to the factories' employees, the hours they work, the way they are treated, and whether the environmental conditions under which they work violate local health and safety laws, are all matters likely to be within the personal knowledge of Nike executives, employees, or subcontractors. Thus, Nike was in a position to readily verify the truth of any factual assertions it made on these topics.

Because in the statements at issue here Nike was acting as a commercial speaker, because its intended audience was primarily the buyers of its products, and because the statements consisted of factual representations about its own business operations, we conclude that the statements were commercial speech for purposes of applying state laws designed to prevent false advertising and other forms of commercial deception.

Nike argues that its allegedly false and misleading statements were not commercial speech because they were part of "an international media debate on issues of intense public interest." This argument falsely assumes that speech cannot properly be categorized as commercial speech if it relates to a matter of significant public interest or controversy. As the United States Supreme Court has explained, commercial speech commonly concerns matters of intense public and private interest. The individual, consumer's interest in the price, availability, and characteristics of products and services "may be as keen, if not keener by far, than his interest in the day's most urgent political debate."

We also reject Nike's argument that regulating its speech to suppress false and misleading statements is impermissible because it would restrict or disfavor expression of one point of view (Nike's) and not the other point of view (that of the critics of Nike's labor practices).

The argument is misdirected because the regulations in question do not suppress points of view but instead suppress false and misleading statements of fact. As we have explained, to the extent Nike's speech represents expression of opinion or points of view on general policy questions such as the value of economic "globalization," it is noncommercial speech subject to full First Amendment protection. Nike's speech loses that full measure of protection only when it concerns facts material to commercial transactions—here, factual statements about how Nike makes its products. . . .

As the United States Supreme Court has explained, false and misleading speech has no constitutional value in itself and is protected only in circumstances and to the extent necessary to give breathing room for the free debate of public issues. Commercial speech, because it is both more readily verifiable by its speaker and more hardy than noncommercial speech, can be effectively regulated to suppress false and actually or inherently misleading messages without undue risk of chilling public debate. With these basic principles in mind, we conclude that when a corporation, to maintain and increase its sales and profits, makes public statements defending labor practices and working conditions at factories where its products are made, those public statements are commercial speech that may be regulated to prevent consumer deception.

# The Pharmaceutical Research and Manufacturers of America Code on Interactions with Health-Care Professionals

## 1. BASIS OF INTERACTIONS

Our relationships with health-care professionals are intended to benefit patients and to enhance the practice of medicine. Interactions should be focused on informing health-care professionals about products, providing scientific and educational information, and supporting medical research and education.

## 2. INFORMATIONAL PRESENTATIONS BY OR ON BEHALF OF A PHARMACEUTICAL COMPANY

Informational presentations and discussions by industry representatives and others speaking on behalf of a company provide valuable scientific and educational benefits. In connection with such presentations or discussions, occasional meals (but no entertainment/recreational events) may be offered so long as they (a) are modest as judged by local standards and (b) occur in a venue and manner conducive to informational communication and provide scientific or educational value. Inclusion of a health-care professional's spouse or other guests is not appropriate. Offering takeout meals or meals to be eaten without a company representative's being present (such as "dine & dash" programs) is not appropriate.

## 3. THIRD-PARTY EDUCATIONAL OR PROFESSIONAL MEETINGS

- Continuing medical education (CME) or other third-party scientific and educational conferences or professional meetings can contribute to the improvement of patient care and therefore, financial support from companies is permissible. Since the giving of any subsidy directly to a health-care professional by a company may be viewed as an inappropriate cash gift, any financial support should be given to the conference's sponsor, which, in turn, can use the money to reduce the overall conference registration fee for all attendees. In addition, when companies underwrite medical conferences or meetings other than their own, responsibility for and control over the selection of content, faculty, educational methods, materials, and venue belongs to the organizers of the conferences or meetings in accordance with their guidelines.

- Financial support should not be offered for the costs of travel, lodging, or other personal expense of nonfaculty health-care professionals attending CME or other third-party scientific or educational conferences or professional meetings, either directly to the individuals attending the conference or indirectly to the conference's sponsor (except as set out in section 6 below). Similarly, funding should not be offered to compensate for the time spent by health-care professionals attending the conference or meeting.
- Financial support for meals or receptions may be provided to the CME sponsors, who, in turn, can provide meals or receptions for all attendees. A company also may provide meals or receptions directly at such events if it complies with the sponsoring organizations, guidelines. In either of the above situations, the meals or receptions should be modest and be conducive to discussion among faculty and attendees, and the amount of time at the meals or receptions should be clearly subordinate to the amount of time spent at the educational activities of the meeting.
- A conference or meeting shall mean any activity, held at an appropriate location, where (a) the gathering is primarily dedicated, in both time and effort, to promoting objective scientific and educational activities and discourse (one or more educational presentations(s) should be the highlight of the gathering), and (b) the main incentive for bringing attendees together is to further their knowledge on the topic(s) being presented.

## 4. CONSULTANTS

It is appropriate for consultants who provide services to be offered reasonable compensation for those services and to be offered reimbursement for reasonable travel, lodging, and meal expenses

incurred as part of providing those services. Compensation and reimbursement that would be inappropriate in other contexts can be acceptable for bona fide consultants in connection with their consulting arrangements. Token consulting or advisory arrangements should not be used to justify compensating health-care professionals for their time or their travel, lodging, and other out-of-pocket expenses. The following factors support the existence of a bona fide consulting arrangement (not all factors may be relevant to any particular arrangement):

- A written contract specifies the nature of the services to be provided and the basis for payment of those services.
- A legitimate need for the services has been clearly identified in advance of requesting the services and entering into arrangements with the prospective consultants.
- The criteria for selecting consultants are directly related to the identified purpose, and the persons responsible for selecting the consultants have the expertise necessary to evaluate whether the particular health-care professionals meet those criteria.
- The number of health-care professionals retained is not greater than the number reasonably necessary to achieve the identified purpose.
- The retaining company maintains records concerning and makes appropriate use of the services provided by consultants.
- The venue and circumstances of any meeting with consultants are conducive to the consulting services, and activities related to the services are the primary focus of the meeting, and any social or entertainment events are clearly subordinate in terms of time and emphasis.

It is not appropriate to pay honoraria or travel or lodging expenses to nonfaculty and nonconsultant attendees at company-sponsored meetings, including attendees who participate in interactive sessions.

## 5. SPEAKER TRAINING MEETINGS

It is appropriate for health-care professionals who participate in programs intended to recruit and train speakers for company-sponsored speaker bureaus to be offered reasonable compensation for their time, considering the value of the type of services provided, and to be offered reimbursement for reasonable travel, lodging, and meal expenses, when (1) the participants receive extensive training on the company's drug products and on compliance with FDA regulatory requirements for communications about such products, (2) this training will result in the participants' providing a valuable service to the company, and (3) the participants meet the criteria for consultants (as discussed in part 4.a. above).

# 6. SCHOLARSHIPS AND EDUCATIONAL FUNDS

Financial assistance for scholarships or other educational funds to permit medical students, residents, fellows, and other health-care professionals in training to attend carefully selected educational conferences may be offered so long as the selection of individuals who will receive the funds is made by the academic or training institution. "Carefully selected educational conferences" are generally defined as the major educational, scientific, or policy-making meetings of national, regional, or specialty medical associations.

# 7. EDUCATIONAL AND PRACTICE-RELATED ITEMS

- Items primarily for the benefit of patients may be offered to health-care professionals if they are not of substantial value ($100 or less). For example, an anatomical model for use in an examination room primarily involves a patient benefit, where-

as a VCR or CD player does not. Items should not be offered on more than an occasional basis, even if each individual item is appropriate. Providing product samples for patient use in accordance with the Prescription Drug Marketing Act is acceptable.

- Items of minimal value may be offered if they are primarily associated with a health-care professional's practice (such as pens, notepads, and similar "reminder" items with company or product logos).
- Items intended for the personal benefit of health-care professionals (such as floral arrangements, artwork, music CDs, or tickets to a sporting event) should not be offered.
- Payments in cash or cash equivalents (such as gift certificates) should not be offered to health-care professionals either directly or indirectly, except as compensation for bona fide services (as described in parts 4 and 5). Cash or equivalent payments of any kind create a potential appearance of impropriety or conflict of interest.

# 8. INDEPENDENCE AND DECISION MAKING

No grants, scholarships, subsidies, support, consulting contracts, or educational or practice-related items should be provided or offered to a health-care professional in exchange for prescribing products or for a commitment to continue prescribing products. Nothing should be offered or provided in a manner or on conditions that would interfere with the independence of a health-care professional's prescribing practices.

# 9. ADHERENCE TO CODE

Each member company is strongly encouraged to adopt procedures to assure adherence to this Code.

## CASES

# CASE 1.  *More HorsePOWER?*

A television advertisement praises next year's model of the popular pickup truck, the Mammoth, claiming that "This sleek and stylish truck is the most powerful in its class." The company that produces the truck traditionally sells luxury sedans and sports cars, which are among the best rated and the safest in the industry. While trucks like the Mammoth are often used for hauling heavy equipment, this model has a smaller capacity and is not well suited for hauling, though it does have a powerful engine. Critics have pointed out, probably correctly, that if the Mammoth were produced by any other company, few consumers would have interest in it because of its limited capacity and decidedly awkward design.

The ad begins with a young man preparing himself for a night at the opera. Dressed in a tuxedo, he looks in the mirror and appears uncomfortable and without confidence. He then gets behind the wheel of the Mammoth, which is beautifully styled on the inside with wood interior and leather seats. The next scene presents the same man as he arrives at the opera house. Reporters and photographers, interviewing the music director, suddenly flock toward the Mammoth and surround it. As the man exits the truck, five well-known models flock to his side and escort him inside the theater. The once unconfident man is now the guest of honor, and appears suave and collected. As the commercial ends, a narrator comments, "The Mammoth. Power, Beauty, Style."

**Questions**

1. Is this a case of puffery in advertising? Does the advertisement unduly focus on qualities not necessarily connected with the product?
2. Is it permissible for advertisements to use "hidden human needs" in order to sell products? Should they simply state the facts?

This case was prepared by David Lawrence and Dianna Spring.

# CASE 2.  *Advice for Sale: How Companies Pay TV Experts for On-Air Product Mentions*

In November, *Child* magazine's Technology Editor James Oppenheim appeared on a local television show in Austin, Texas, and reviewed educational gadgets and toys. He praised "My ABC's Picture Book," a personalized photo album from Eastman Kodak Co.

"Considering what you showed me, kids' games really don't have to be violent," said the anchor for KVUE, an ABC affiliate and the no. 1-rated television station in its market.

"If . . . you're not careful, they will be," Mr. Oppenheim replied. "That's why I've shown you some of the best."

There was one detail the audience didn't know: Kodak paid Mr. Oppenheim to mention the photo album, according to the company

James Bandler, *Wall Street Journal* (19 April 2005), A1.

and Mr. Oppenheim. Neither Mr. Oppenheim nor KVUE disclosed the relationship to viewers. During the segment, Mr. Oppenheim praised products from other companies, including Atari Inc., Microsoft Corp., Mattel Inc., Leapfrog Enterprises Inc. and RadioShack Corp. All paid for the privilege, Mr. Oppenheim says.

One month later, Mr. Oppenheim went on NBC's *Today* show, the U.S.'s biggest national morning news program, which is part of NBC's news division. "Kodak came out with a great idea," he said to host Ann Curry, before proceeding to talk about the same product he'd been paid to discuss on KVUE. Ms. Curry called it a "nice gift for a little child." Kodak says it didn't pay for the *Today* show mention. But neither Mr. Oppenheim nor NBC disclosed the prior arrangement to tout the product on local TV.

In the *Today* segment, Mr. Oppenheim talked about products made or sold by 15 companies. Nine were former clients, and eight of those had paid him for product placement on local TV during the preceding year.

KVUE says it didn't know about Mr. Oppenheim's business deal. An NBC spokeswoman says the network is looking into what it knew about Mr. Oppenheim's relationship with Kodak and the other manufacturers.

Mr. Oppenheim is part of a little-known network that connects product experts with advertisers and TV shows. The experts pitch themselves to companies willing to pay for a mention. Next, they approach local-TV stations and offer themselves up to be interviewed. Appearances frequently coincide with trade shows, such as the Consumer Electronics Show, or holidays, including Christmas or Valentine's Day.

The segments are often broadcast live via satellite from a trade event and typically air during regular news programming in a way that's indistinguishable from the rest of the show. One reviewer may conduct dozens of interviews with local stations over the course of a day in what the industry calls a "satellite media tour." While this circuit is predominantly focused on the local television market, the big prize for marketers is a mention on national television shows, which carry far more clout with viewers.

The familiar faces on this circuit include Mr. Oppenheim, *Today* Tech Editor Corey Greenberg, and trend spotter Katlean de Monchy. They are among an army of experts who have risen to prominence as news organizations everywhere, seeking to expand their audiences, have branched into reviewing consumer products ranging from home furnishings to personal finance.

A long-standing principle of journalism holds that reporters cannot have financial relationships with the people or companies they cover. TV shows present these gurus' recommendations as unbiased and based solely on their expertise. But that presentation is misleading if the experts have been paid to mention products on network or local TV.

Mr. Oppenheim's pitch is typical. Late last year, he invited electronics and game companies to join two satellite tours, according to a copy of his solicitation. "We expect these tours to sell out fast," Mr. Oppenheim wrote, "so please contact us as soon as possible to reserve a spot." The $12,500 fee per company, he explained, covered development, production, and "spokesperson expenses."

On his Web site, Mr. Oppenheim used to describe himself as a consumer advocate. "My pledge is to tell the unvarnished truth about the products reviewed," he wrote. "The good, the bad, and the ugly." He recently changed his biographical description to "technology expert and industry spokesperson."

In an interview, Mr. Oppenheim says getting paid by the companies he reviews on local television doesn't influence his judgment. He says his main purpose is to educate the public about nonviolent games. Renting studio and satellite time, he says, is expensive. Mr. Oppenheim says he, too, needs to be paid.

"My motives are the highest: to get information out to parents about what they can be doing to advance children through technology," he says.

Mr. Oppenheim has a different set of standards when it comes to getting paid to go on national television. He says he notifies clients in writing that his *Today* appearances are off-limits, in part because the show bars such payments. According to a copy of Mr. Oppenheim's pitch, his tour "does not run on the *Today* show."

Kodak, one of the companies that hired Mr. Oppenheim, is happy with its relationship with the reviewer but thinks their financial relationship ought to have been disclosed, according to spokesman Mike McDougal. Mr. McDougal says disclosing the payments is the responsibility of local television stations.

Some production companies say they inform stations about the financial relationship beforehand. By contrast, Frank Volpicella, executive news director of KVUE, the station which hosted Mr. Oppenheim last year, says it didn't know about the payments and wouldn't have aired the segment if it had.

"There's an appearance that he compromised his integrity by promoting a product in which he has a financial interest," Mr. Volpicella says.

NBC, the General Electric Co. unit that broadcasts the *Today* show, says it tightened its conflicts-of-interest policies after receiving questions about the matter from the *Wall Street Journal.* It now specifically says any payments for local-TV appearances via satellite tours should be disclosed to the network.

David McCormick, executive producer for broadcast standards at NBC, says an expert might be allowed to talk about a product on *Today* even if he had a financial conflict. "Some products that they might talk about might be quite topical," Mr. McCormick says, "and to avoid them would be peculiar." In this case, Mr. McCormick says he believes Mr. Oppenheim picked the Kodak photo album on its merits.

The use of TV consumer experts is the latest way marketers have tried to disguise their promotions as real news, often with the aid of media outlets. Magazines accept "advertorials" designed to look like editorial features, not ads. TV stations often use "video news releases" produced by companies, which are designed to look like news segments. Last week, the Federal Communications Commission told broadcasters they must inform viewers about the origins of these video releases.

For advertisers, these techniques help keep their messages from getting lost in an increasingly crowded sea of ads. An example is the camera maker Olympus Optical Corp. Along with Canon Inc. and Nikon Inc., it paid last year to be on a satellite tour operated by DWJ Television that featured John Owens, the editor-in-chief of *Popular Photography & Imaging* magazine, according to Michael Friedman, DWJ's executive vice president. The DWJ tour was timed to coincide with a 2004 photography trade show.

Chris Sluka, an Olympus spokesman, says the tour "secured me some broadcast coverage that's hard to get in a cluttered atmosphere." He says local stations probably wouldn't air the segments if they knew manufacturers paid to be mentioned. "I know when these are pitched, they're pitched as news," he says.

For example, KFMB Local 8, a CBS affiliate in San Diego, aired an interview with Mr. Owens from that tour but didn't disclose the payments. Fred D'Ambrosi, news director at KFMB, says the station assumed Mr. Owens's magazine paid for the tour. He says the station will do a better job finding out who the actual sponsors are in the future.

Mr. Owens also didn't disclose the financial ties when he went on CBS's *Early Show* in December and talked about Nikon and Canon products, among others. Leigh Farris, a spokes-woman for CBS News, says the network is revising its rules to include such conflicts of interest.

Mr. Owens didn't respond to repeated requests seeking comment. Mr. Friedman says Mr. Owens wouldn't endorse products he didn't believe in.

While most satellite media tours take place on local television, the biggest prize is a mention on a national television show. The publicity value of a brief *Today* appearance is estimated at about $250,000, according to Multivision Inc., a company that tracks TV broadcasts. Multivision bases its estimate on ad rates, audience size, and other factors. *Today* is watched by an average of 6.1 million people each weekday. A mention on a local news show is valued at anywhere from a few hundred to a few thousand dollars, depending on audience size.

The exact relationship between paid local tours and mentions on national television is unclear. Many reviewers say national shows are off-limits because of stricter ethics rules enforced by top news organizations.

But some advertisers say one of the key reasons they pay for local media tours is the hope—and sometimes the expectation—that they'll get a mention on the national shows, even if there isn't an explicit financial arrangement to do so.

For several years, Wal-Mart Stores Inc.'s Sam's Club paid trend and fashion expert Katlean de Monchy to get its jewelry mentioned on local TV. Ms. de Monchy's company, Nextpert News, charges $25,000 for a "special option" that includes Ms. de Monchy touting products on local shows, according to a copy of one of its pitches.

Then in January, Ms. de Monchy appeared as a guest on a *Good Morning America* segment explaining how to replicate fashions worn at the Golden Globe awards. "It's the accessories that really caught my eye, though. A lot of bling-bling," Ms. de Monchy told host Diane Sawyer, singling out a pair of diamond earrings available at Sam's Club.

Dee Breazeale, Sam's Club's vice president and divisional merchandise manager for jewelry, says the company didn't pay to get on ABC's *Good Morning America* but that the mention was "the icing on the cake." Ms. Breazeale adds that Sam's Club would probably not hire Ms. de Monchy if the payments were disclosed, because that would make her appearance seem too much like an infomercial. Ms. Breazeale says the paid segments are more effective than buying an ad. "It brings [the product] more to life," she says.

During the same *Good Morning America* segment, Ms. de Monchy showed off a pair of pointy-toed pumps, sold by another paying customer, shoe retailer DSW. Mike Levison, DSW's vice president of marketing, says he believed his company paid to get on *Good Morning America* as part of the satellite tour. With 10 being the ultimate marketing coup, he described the appearance as a "9 or 10."

A third client, prom-dress maker Faviana International Inc., had two dresses mentioned on the show. Omid Morady, a principal at Faviana, says getting on *Good Morning America* was the main appeal of hiring Ms. de Monchy and was part of his contract. "Millions of people see it," he says. "It creates more credibility with customers."

Ms. de Monchy did not respond to requests for comment. David Post, executive producer for Ms. de Monchy's company, says the payments help defray their company's high production expenses, which include hiring models. He says Nextpert doesn't recommend particular items and adds that *Good Morning America* is "absolutely not in the tour. It's as clear as a bell."

Asked why the paying relationships weren't disclosed on local TV, Mr. Post says: "It's soft news . . . we would never do anything on drugs or political issues; it's like where do you get a prom dress." He says TV stations wouldn't air the segments if they weren't newsworthy.

Bridgette Maney, a spokeswoman for *Good Morning America* says ABC, a unit of Walt Disney

Co., requires that regular contributors disclose conflicts of interest. She says Ms. de Monchy isn't a regular contributor. "We were unaware of her affiliation with these other companies," Ms. Maney says. "Now that we're aware of it I do not think she'll be on the program."

One of the most coveted TV consumer experts is Corey Greenberg, the *Today* show's main tech-product reviewer. He came to NBC in 2000 with little television experience. Previously, he was a well-regarded editor and writer at a number of audio-equipment magazines.

Quick on his feet, witty, and able to talk about complicated technology in a simple way, Mr. Greenberg quickly became a regular, doing dozens of segments a year. NBC pays Mr. Greenberg a nominal fee per segment and also gave him the title of Tech Editor.

Mr. Greenberg has charged companies $15,000 per tour to get their products on local news programs, according to a copy of one of his contracts. Mr. Greenberg says paying clients he has mentioned on local shows include Sony Corp., Hewlett-Packard Co., Seiko Epson Corp., and Energizer Holdings Inc.

Mr. Greenberg has also appeared on national shows, including *The Wall Street Journal Report with Maria Bartiromo,* a weekly syndicated business program produced by CNBC, a division of NBC. In a February broadcast about digital music, Mr. Greenberg mentioned products made by Apple Computer Inc. and Creative Technology Ltd. Mr. Greenberg says Apple was a client more than a year ago. He did paid work for Creative last November, both sides say. Neither relationship was disclosed on CNBC.

"It should have been disclosed. He was bound by our policies, which require contributors to disclose such payments to the network," says Amy Zelvin, a CNBC spokeswoman. Mr. Greenberg says he didn't solicit the appearance and was invited by CNBC to talk about that topic.

Rachel Branch, a Sony public-relations official, says one of the things Sony likes about Mr. Greenberg is his credibility. "Viewers like him because he's able to communicate about a product without showing bias," she says. Mr. Greenberg also comes cheaper than some of his competitors, Ms. Branch adds, without elaborating.

Mr. Greenberg defends his local paid work, saying he's providing valuable news to consumers. He says he wouldn't do paid work for a product he didn't believe in. Mr. Greenberg says his business resembles a magazine that collects money from advertisers and then reviews products marketed by the same companies. He says he can maintain a wall between his business and editorial practices. "I am a one-man magazine," he says.

Mr. Greenberg says he labors to keep his *Today* appearances distinct from the paid work. He says on *Today* he is giving specific recommendations; on satellite tours, Mr. Greenberg says, he talks generally about gadget-related issues, such as battery life. As a general rule, he says he won't mention a product on *Today* until 6 months after a paid mention. He says he's rebuffed "high five-figure" offers "to place a product on *Today*."

Mr. McCormick, the NBC executive, says the network has "a lot of confidence" in Mr. Greenberg.

Executives at some companies have the impression there is a connection between Mr. Greenberg's paid tours and his *Today* appearances. Jacqueline E. Burwitz, vice president of investor relations for Energizer, said she's "absolutely sure" that when Energizer hired Mr. Greenberg for a local tour in late 2003, the company believed he would mention its products on *Today*.

A few weeks after the local tour, Mr. Greenberg mentioned Energizer's lithium batteries on *Today*.

"So, buy them," said the *Today* host Ms. Curry.

"Exactly," said Mr. Greenberg.

Neither NBC nor Mr. Greenberg mentioned that he had recently been hired by Energizer.

**Questions**

1. Are the stealth marketing practices described in this case ethically legitimate means of marketing to consumers? Why, or why not? Explain.

2. Should consumer experts be required to disclose their financial relationships with manufactures when they appear on television? Why, or why not? Explain. If so, who should enforce such a requirement?

# CASE 3.    *Sales at World Camera and Electronics*

Sales personnel at World Camera and Electronics are given a financial incentive to sell overstocked cameras; each week, the management identifies a particular camera that salespeople should try to sell over other brands. When such cameras are sold, the salesperson receives a 20 percent commission instead of the usual 10 percent.

Matthew Anderson, a college student, wishes to purchase a camera. After carefully researching different styles, he decides to buy a digital camera that he believes is ideal for student photographers. He finds the exact model that he desires at World Camera. The salesperson agrees that this model would be a fine purchase.

However, rather than simply sell this camera, the salesperson shows Matthew another camera. This one is far more expensive and a bit less practical for his needs. The salesperson has a financial incentive to sell this camera and convinces Matthew that it is indeed a better buy. While this model is widely recognized as having numerous advanced features,

Matthew does not require these additions—and is not likely in the future to need such sophisticated options. In the end, Matthew buys the more expensive camera believing that the salesperson's expertise is valuable in finding the "perfect fit" for his future needs.

**Questions**

1. Is this a case of deceptive sales? Does the fact that the salesperson sold a "better" camera with sophisticated features justify the sale? Is the fact that she will receive a financial bonus relevant to a moral assessment of her actions?

2. Does the salesperson's "steering" toward a particular product, in this case a more expensive camera, represent a "significant harm" to the customer? Should customers expect salespeople to be objective, with the customer's best interest in mind, or should they accept the principle "buyer beware"?

This case was prepared by David Lawrence.

# CASE 4.    *Hucksters in the Classroom*

Increased student loads, myriad professional obligations, and shrinking school budgets have

sent many public school teachers scurrying for teaching materials to facilitate their teaching.

From William H. Shaw and Vincent Barry, *Moral Issues in Business*, 10th ed. (Belmont, CA: Wadsworth, 2007).

They don't have to look far. Into the breach has stepped business, which is ready, willing, and able to provide print and audiovisual materials for classroom use. These industry-supplied teaching aids are advertised in educational journals, distributed directly to schools, and showcased at educational conventions. Clearasil, for example, distributes a teaching aid and color poster called "A Day in the Life of Your Skin." Its message is hard to miss: Clearasil is the way to clear up your pimples. Domino's Pizza supplies a handout that is supposed to help kids learn to count by tabulating the number of pepperoni wheels on one of the company's pizzas. Chef Boyardee sponsors a study program on sharks based on its "fun pasta," which is shaped like sharks and pictured everywhere on its educational materials.

The list goes on. General Mills supplies educational pamphlets on Earth's "great geothermic 'gushers'" along with the company's "Gushers" snack (a candy filled with liquid). The pamphlets recommend that teachers pass the "Gushers" around and then ask the students as they bite the candy, "How does this process differ from that which produces erupting geothermic phenomena?" In an elementary school in Texas, teachers use a reading program called "Read-A-Logo." Put out by Teacher Support Software, it encourages students to use familiar corporate names such as McDonald's, Hi-C, Coca-Cola, or Cap'n Crunch to create elementary sentences, such as, "I had a hamburger and a Pepsi at McDonld's." In other grade schools, children learn from Exxon's Energy Cube curriculum that fossil fuels pose few environmental problems and that alternative energy is costly and unattainable. Similarly, materials from the American Coal Foundation teach them that the "earth could benefit rather than be harmed from increased carbon dioxide." Courtesy of literature from the Pacific Lumber Company, students in California learn about forests; they also get Pacific Lumber's defense of its forest-clearing activities: "The Great

American Forest . . . is renewable forever." At Pembroke Lakes elementary school in Broward County, Florida, 10-year-olds learned how to design a McDonald's restaurant and how to apply and interview for a job at McDonald's, thanks to a 7-week company-sponsored class intended to teach them about the real world of work.

"It's a corporate takeover of our schools," says Nelson Canton of the National Education Association. "It has nothing to do with education and everything to do with corporations making profits and hooking kids early on their products." "I call it the phantom curriculum" adds Arnold Fege of the National PTA, "because the teachers are often unaware that there's subtle product placement." There's nothing subtle, however, about the product placement in *Mathematics Applications and Connections*, a textbook used by many sixth graders. It begins its discussion of the coordinate system with an advertisement for Walt Disney: "Have you ever wanted to be the star of a movie? If you visit Walt Disney–MGM Studios Theme Park, you could become one." Other math books are equally blatant. They use brand-name products like M&Ms, Nike shoes, and Kellogg's Cocoa Frosted Flakes as examples when discussing surface area, fractions, decimals, and other concepts.

All this is fine with Lifetime Learning Systems, a marketing firm that specializes in pitching to students the products of its corporate customers. "[Students] are ready to spend and we reach them," the company brags, touting its "custom-made learning materials created with your [company's] specific marketing objectives in mind." Today's 43 million school-children have tremendous buying power. Elementary schoolchildren spend $15 billion a year and influence another $160 billion in spending by parents. Teenagers spend $57 billion of their own money and $36 billion of their families' money. It's not surprising, then, that many corporations clearly see education marketing as a cost-effective way to build brand loyalty.

Corporate America's most dramatic venture in the classroom, however, began in 1990, when Whittle Communications started beaming into classrooms around the country its controversial Channel One, a television newscast for middle- and high-school students. The broadcasts are 12 minutes long—10 minutes of news digest with slick graphics and 2 minutes of commercials for Levi's jeans, Gillette razor blades, Head & Shoulders shampoo, Snickers candy bars, and other familiar products. Although a handful of states have banned Channel One, 40 percent of American teens see it every school day.

Primedia, which now owns Channel One, provides cash-hungry schools with thousands of dollars worth of electronic gadgetry, including TV monitors, satellite dishes, and video recorders, if the schools agree to show the broadcasts. In return, the schools are contractually obliged to broadcast the program in its entirety to all students at a single time on 90 to 95 percent of the days that school is in session. The show cannot be interrupted, and teachers do not have the right to turn it off.

For their part, students seem to like Channel One's fast-paced MTV-like newscasts. "It was very interesting and it appeals to our age group," says student Angelique Williams. "One thing I really like was the reporters were our own age. They kept our attention." But educators wonder how much students really learn. A University of Michigan study found that students who watched Channel One scored only 3.3 percent better on a 30-question test of current events than did students in schools without Channel One. Although researchers called this gain so small as to be educationally unimportant, they noted that all the Channel One students remembered the commercials. That, of course, is good news for Primedia, which charges advertisers $157,000 for a 30-second spot. That price sounds high, but companies are willing to pay it because Channel One delivers a captive, narrowly targeted audience.

That captive audience is just what worries the critics. Peggy Charren of Action for Children's Television calls the project a "great big, gorgeous Trojan horse. . . . You're selling the children to the advertisers. You might as well auction off the rest of the school day to the highest bidders." On the other hand, Principal Rex Stooksbury of Central High School in Knoxville, which receives Channel One, takes a different view. "This is something we see as very, very positive for the school," he says. And as student Danny Diaz adds, "We're always watching commercials" anyway.

## Questions

1. Have you had any personal experience with industry-sponsored educational materials? What moral issues, if any, are involved in the affiliation between education and commercial interests? Does commercial intrusion into schools change the nature of education? What values and beliefs does it instill in children?

2. Do you think students have a "moral right" to an education free of commercial indoctrination? If you were a parent of school-age children, would you be concerned about their exposure to commercials and corporate propaganda?

3. If you were a member of a school board contemplating the use of either industry-sponsored materials or Channel One, what would you recommend?

4. Do you think industry in general and Channel One in particular are intentionally using teachers and students as a means to profit? Or do they have a genuine concern for the education process? On the other hand, if teachers and students benefit from these educational materials or from viewing Channel One, is there any ground for concern?

# CASE 5. *Kraft Foods Inc.: The Cost of Advertising on Children's Waistlines*

The room fell silent as Dr. Ellen Wartella, Dean of the College of Communications at the Univeristy of Texas at Austin, gave Kraft executives her opinions on a presentation they had just made regarding Kraft and advertising to children. Wartella characterized Kraft's online marketing as *"indefensible"* and concluded that Kraft's claim that it was not advertising to children under the age of six was *"at best disingenuous and at worst a downright lie."*[1] The executives in the room were visibly shaken by her comments.

In late 2003, Kraft formed the Worldwide Health & Wellness Advisory Council, comprising 10 nutritionists and media experts, including Wartella, to investigate allegations that Kraft had been knowingly advertising unhealthy foods and to help address the rise in obesity, among other health issues.[2] The pressure for Kraft to review its advertising policies came amidst increasing criticism from congressional panels, parent groups and other concerned citizens, that food corporations, such as Kraft Foods and McDonald's Corporation, have been knowingly targeting young children (up to age 12) in their advertising campaigns. The concern surrounding childhood obesity stems from statistics showing a 200 percent increase in childhood obesity since the 1980s. Between the 1960s and the 1980s, the percentage of overweight children hovered around 6 percent, but in the last two decades, this rate has leapt to 16 percent.[3] Despite this, Kraft decided to keep marketing to children under 12. One Kraft executive admitted, "We didn't want to give up the power of marketing to kids."[4]

This "power" is villainizing the company, however. Currently, Kraft is a trusted brand, but that reputation is already slipping. According to the Reputation Quotient study conducted in 2005 by research firm Harris Interactive, Kraft is ranked in the 50th slot.[5] While this is a small drop from the 48th spot Kraft held the previous year, it is a far distance from the 8th position occupied by competitor General Mills. This survey is based on consumer perception of various factors, including a company's quality of products and services, social responsibility, and vision and leadership. Depending on what Kraft chooses to do about its food marketing issue, the company may rise higher in subsequent Reputation Quotient studies, or it may fall further down.

Kraft Foods is a company that values quality and safety in its products. One of Kraft's key strategies is to "build superior consumer brand value" through "great-tasting products, innovative packaging, consistent high quality, wide availability, helpful services and strong brand image."[6] With products in more than 99 percent of U.S. households, Kraft certainly has earned the trust of its consumers.[7] With the recent feedback from the Health and Wellness Advisory Council and public concerns about childhood obesity due to aggressive food marketing, however, Kraft must take action

---

This case was prepared by Research Assistants Pauline Hwa and Timothy Housman under the direction of James S. O'Rourke, Concurrent Professor of Management, as the basis for class discussion rather than to illustrate either effective or ineffective handling of an administrative situation. Information was gathered from corporate as well as public sources.

before it loses consumers' loyalty and trust in its products.

## KRAFT FOODS INC.

Kraft Foods Inc., the largest food and beverage company in North America, has grown considerably from its humble beginnings in 1903. With only $65, a rented wagon, and a horse named Paddy, J. L. Kraft started the company by purchasing cheese from a wholesale market and reselling it to local merchants.[8] These cheeses were packaged with Kraft's name. A decade later, Kraft improved the cheese by processing the product, which prolonged its shelf life. The processed cheese became such a success that a patent for the "Process of Sterilizing Cheese and an Improved Product Produced by Such Process" was issued to Kraft in 1916.[9] Over the years, the company went on to create other new cheese products that are familiar to homes today including *Velveeta* and *Cheez Whiz*, as well as expanding beyond cheese to introduce salad dressings, packaged dinners, barbecue sauce, and other products.

Tobacco giant Philip Morris acquired General Foods Corporation in 1985 and then Kraft three years later for $12.9 billion.[10] Through the acquisition of these two major food companies, Philip Morris formed Kraft General Foods, which put products such as *Velveeta*, *Post* cereals, *Oscar Mayer*, and *Jell-O* pudding all under the same food division. Kraft General Foods further expanded its household reach by acquiring Nabisco, home of well-known brands including *Oreo* cookies, *Ritz* crackers, and *Planters* nuts in 2000. The next big step for Kraft occurred in 2001 when Philip Morris conducted an initial public offering of Kraft's shares (NYSE: KFT). The following year, Philip Morris shareholders accepted a proposal to change the company's name to Altria Group. As of January 27, 2003, Altria Group became the parent company to Kraft Foods.

## KRAFT'S TROUBLES IN ADVERTISING

There are many reasons why Kraft should be concerned about further criticism of its advertising practices. As a leader in the food industry, Kraft is both large and very visible, and the company has experienced repeated controversy and criticism of its advertising campaigns over the years. A few recent issues include:

- Kraft's advertisement of Post cereal in *National Geographic Kids* was not focused on the food but rather on the premium of Postokens instead, which is a violation of The Children's Advertising Review Unit's Self-Regulatory Guidelines for Children's Advertising.[11]
- Kraft had previously announced its intention to reduce portion size and then later backed out of that commitment, saying that consumers wanted to choose their portion sizes for themselves.[12]
- Kraft pulled an *Oreo* commercial directed at teenagers that promoted a "slothlike" lifestyle because the company realized that such an ad would hurt its image and instead opted for promoting "a more active lifestyle."[13]

## OBESITY IN THE COURTS: THE McLAWSUIT

The food industry became visibly worried about food marketing and childhood obesity in 2002. It was then that McDonald's Corporation faced a lawsuit, *Pelham v. McDonald's Corporation,* in which the company was charged with marketing food products that contribute to the rise of obesity in children and teenagers. Although the judge threw out the class-action lawsuit against McDonald's, he made it very clear that he supports the plaintiffs' position. He encouraged them to redraft and refile the suit with stronger evidence, and went so far as to provide advice on what to look for. One of his recommendations was to show how McDonald's advertising campaigns encouraged overconsumption by promoting its food products for "everyday" eating.[14]

McDonald's Corporation still stands behind their standards in marketing to children. According to David Green, Senior Vice President of Marketing for McDonald's, even though 20 percent of McDonald's commercials are targeted at children, the company follows a strict set of guidelines. The Golden Arches Code, according to company spokesmen, "conforms with the major network Broadcasting Standards and the guidelines of the Children's Unit of the National Advertising Division Council of Better Business Bureaus Inc., as well as establishing additional standards applicable only to McDonald's advertising."[15] Green says that the Golden Arches Code "states that in our advertising we should never promote the sale of food items to children that might be too large for them to consume realistically at one sitting nor should children be depicted as coming to McDonald's on their own, as they must always be accompanied by an adult."

A month prior to *Pelham v. McDonald's Corporation*, Sam Hirsch, the attorney who filed the suit for the overweight children and teenagers, had filed another class-action suit against McDonald's and other leading fast-food establishments.[16] This suit was filed not only against McDonald's Corporation, but also Burger King, Kentucky Fried Chicken, and Wendy's. Observers speculated the driving force behind these two suits was the prospect of a large financial settlement. Hirsch remained adamant about his clients' intentions, saying "we are not looking to get rich from a large money settlement. We are proposing a fund that will educate children about the nutritional facts and contents of McDonald's food."[17] These suits intensified fears in the food industry of a future of "tobacco-like" litigation against restaurants and food manufacturers.[18]

In January 2005, the second U.S. Circuit Court of Appeals reinstated claims that McDonald's falsely advertised the health benefits of its fast food, a violation of the New York's Consumer Protection Act.[19] Unquestionably, the plaintiffs had the full attention of quick service restaurant operators and food manufacturers worldwide.

## STUDIES SHOW. . .

### Fewer Ads

In July 2005, the Federal Trade Commission (FTC) released its findings that children today watch fewer food commercials than they did almost three decades ago. Children today watch 13 food advertisements on television per day, a significant reduction from the 18 television commercials per day in 1977.[20] The FTC also reported that kids today are exposed to fewer ads for cereal, candy, and toys but more ads for restaurants and fast-food chains, other television shows, movies, video games, and DVDs. Wally Snyder, president of the American Advertising Federation, believed this study was proof that food marketing is not culpable for the rise of obesity in children, which he blamed on a "lack of exercise and moderation in the diet."

### More Ads

A year later in 2004, the Kaiser Family Foundation released a study with contrary information, claiming "the number of ads children see on TV has doubled from 20,000 to 40,000 since the 1970s, and the majority of ads targeted to kids are for candy, cereal, and fast food."[21] The study suggested that this increase in food advertising was correlated to the rise in obesity in children aged 6 to 11. In 1963–1970, only 4.2 percent of children in this age group were listed as overweight compared with 1999–2000, when the number spiked to 15.3 percent.

**The Tie-Breaker**

Perhaps because of the conflicting findings or because of rising concerns about food marketing to children and its effects, Congress requested a study of its own from the National Academy of Sciences, which was created by the federal government to advise on scientific issues.[22] In December 2005, The Institute of Medicine (IOM), a private, nongovernmental division of the National Academy of Sciences, released the latest study on the subject, *Food Marketing to Children and Youth: Threat or Opportunity?* Based upon individual findings, the IOM committee responsible for the study came to the following five conclusions:[23]

---

### Broad Conclusions

1. Along with many other intersecting factors, food and beverage marketing influences the diets and health prospects of children and youth.
2. Food and beverage marketing practices geared to children and youth are out of balance with healthful diets and contribute to an environment that puts their health at risk.
3. Food and beverage companies, restaurants, and marketers have underutilized potential to devote creativity and resources to develop and promote food, beverages, and meals that support healthful diets for children and youth.
4. Achieving healthful diets for children and youth will require sustained multisectoral and integrated efforts that include industry leadership and initiative.
5. Public-policy programs and incentives do not currently have the support or authority to address many of the current and emerging marketing practices that influence the diets of children and youth.

---

The study also suggested there was "strong evidence" that food marketing influences the preferences, purchase requests, and short-term consumption of children between the ages of 2 and 11. This information combined with the fact that a "preponderance of television food and beverage advertising relevant to children and youth promotes high-calorie and low-nutrient products, it can be concluded that television advertising influences children to prefer and request high-calorie and low-nutrient foods and beverages."[24] Wartella, who served not only on Kraft's advisory council but also as a member of the committee that produced the IOM study, said "We can't any more argue whether food advertising is related to children's diets. It is."[25]

The Institute of Medicine's recommendations for the food industry included promoting and supporting healthier products and working with government, public health, and consumer goods "to establish and enforce the highest standards for the marketing" of food and beverage products to children.[26] In general, many food companies had already started programs to promote healthier products. The problem was with the latter recommendation in marketing standards. IOM believed this meant licensed characters should be "used only for the promotion of foods and beverages that support healthful diets for children and youth."[27] Most companies, Kraft included, were reluctant to give this up. Licensed characters were typically familiar faces to children. How does a company replace a spokesperson or promoter that already has the trust of the audience, is affordable, and will never get into any real-life trouble?

## THE ANNOUNCEMENT

In January 2005, Kraft announced that it would stop advertising certain products to children under 12. These products include regular *Kool-Aid* beverages, *Oreo* and *Chips Ahoy* cookies, several *Post* children's cereals, and some varieties of its *Lunchables* lunch packages.[28] These favorites will still be found in stores, but Kraft said it will no longer be targeting children with television, radio, and print ads for these products. The initial cost of implementing these new guidelines included an estimated $75 million in lost profits, though this figure continued to change several times.[29] While this estimate may seem high, Michael Mudd, a member of Kraft's obesity strategy team said, "If the tobacco industry could go back 20 or 30 years, reform their marketing, disarm their critics, and sacrifice a couple of hundred million in profits, knowing what they know today, don't you think they'd take that deal in a heartbeat?"[30] Kraft, learning the lessons of Philip Morris, was eager for the deal.

Shortly after Kraft made its announcement, however, the company joined competitors General Mills and Kellogg to form a lobbying group to keep the government from regulating food marketing to children. The group's mission statement states its belief that "there is not a correlation between advertising trends and recent childhood obesity."[31] General Mills had always argued for this point. In fact, instead of stopping ads to children, Tom Forsythe, General Mills vice president, announced that the company "launched a vigorous defense of cereal," to support its health benefits.[32] The company also decided to promote "balanced moderation and exercise," believing that such lifestyle choices affect obesity as much as food selection.[33] Thus, General Mills' participation in this group was expected, but for Kraft, joining this group appeared to be a hypocritical move. David S. Johnson, Kraft's Chief of North America, defended the action, "We believe self-regulation of the marketing of food products can and does work, and we are collaborating with the industry to strengthen efforts in this area."[34]

## CONCLUSION

Since the announcement, Kraft has still struggled with child advertising and obesity issues. Margo G. Wootan, Director of Nutrition for the Center for Science in the Public Interest, has called Kraft's new marketing plan only "a really good step forward."[35] The problem is that there will always be critics who will demand for more. For instance, although Kraft has taken a huge leap in minimizing television, radio, and print ads, the company has yet to act on Wartella's criticism for its online advertising.

Kraft has spent a great deal of time to respond to critics and potential threats of government regulation. What Kraft really needs at this point is to put the focus back on its customers and communicate with them. The question is how to go about doing this without appearing to go back on its promises of not saturating the market with advertisements.

### Questions

1. What are the critical issues of this case? Who are the stakeholders (primary, secondary and indirect)?
2. What should Kraft do to maintain the already declining trust of the consumers?
3. Can the public believe in Kraft's commitment to control food marketing to children?
4. What are Kraft's options concerning its marketing tactics?

## NOTES

1. Ellison, Sarah, "Why Kraft Banned Some Food Ads," *Wall Street Journal* (November 1, 2005).
2. http://164.109.46.215/newsroom/09032003.html.
3. http://www.childstats.gov/americaschildren/index.asp.
4. Ellison, Sarah, "Why Kraft Banned Some Food Ads," *Wall Street Journal* (November 1, 2005).

5.  http://www.foodprocessing.com/industrynews/2006/018.html.

6.  http://kraft.com/profile/company_strategies.html.

7.  http://www.altria.com/about_altria/01_00_01_kraftfoods.asp.

8.  http://kraft.com/profile/factsheet.html.

9.  http://kraft.com/100/founders/JLKraft.html.

10. http://www.altria.com/about_altria/1_2_5_1_altriastory.asp.

11. http://www.caru.org/news/2004/kraft.asp.

12. Callahan, Patricia, and Delroy Alexan, "As Fat Fears Grow, Oreo Tries a New Twist," *Chicago Tribune* (August 22, 2005).

13. Callahan, Patricia, and Delroy Alexan, "As Fat Fears Grow, Oreo Tries a New Twist," *Chicago Tribune,* (August 22, 2005).

14. Weiser, Benjamin, "Your Honor, We Call Our Next Witness: McFrankenstein," *New York Times* (January 26, 2003).

15. "McLibel" Case—Green, David B., Witness Statement, http://www.mcspotlight.org/people/witnesses/advertising/green.html.

16. Summons, http://news.findlaw.com/cnn/docs/mcdonalds/barbermcds72302cmp.pdf.

17. Wald, Jonathan, "McDonald's Obestiy Suit Tossed," *CNNmoney.com* (February 17, 2003). http://money.cnn.com/2003/01/22/news/companies/mcdonalds/.

18. Reuters article: http://onenews.nzoom.com/onenews_detail/0,1227,218579-1-6,00.html.

19. http://www.law.com/jsp/article.jsp?id=1106573726371.

20. Mayer, Caroline E., "TV Feeds Kids Fewer Food Ads, FTC Staff Study Finds," *Washington Post* (July 15, 2005).

21. "Ads Rapped in Child Obesity Fight," http://www.cbsnews.com/stories/2004/02/24/health/main601894.shtml.

22. http://www.iom.edu/?id=5774.

23. Institute of Medicine, "Food Marketing to Children and Youth: Threat or Opportunity?" 2006, Box 7-1, p. 317.

24. Institute of Medicine, "Food Marketing to Children and Youth: Threat or Opportunity?" 2006, p. 322.

25. Ellison, Sarah, and Janet Adamy, "Panel Faults Food Packaging for Kid Obesity," *Wall Street Journal,* (December 7, 2005).

26. Institute of Medicine, "Food Marketing to Children and Youth: Threat or Opportunity?" 2006, pp. 325–26.

27. Institute of Medicine, "Food Marketing to Children and Youth: Threat or Opportunity?" 2006, p. 326.

28. "Kraft to Curb Some Snack Food Advertising," Associated Press (January 12, 2005); http://msnbc.msn.com/id/6817344/.

29. Ellison, Sarah, "Why Kraft Decided to Ban Some Food Ads to Children," *Wall Street Journal* (November 1, 2005).

30. Ellison, Sarah, "Why Kraft Decided to Ban Some Food Ads to Children," *Wall Street Journal* (November 1, 2005).

31. Callahan, Patricia, and Delroy Alexan, "As Fat Fears Grow, Oreo Tries a New Twist," *Chicago Tribune* (August 22, 2005).

32. Ellison, Sarah, and Janet Adamy, "Panel Faults Food Packaging For Kid Obesity," *Wall Street Journal* (December 7, 2005).

33. Ellison, Sarah, "Divided, Companies Fight for Right to Plug Kids' Food," *Wall Street Journal* (January 26, 2005).

34. Callahan, Patricia, and Delroy Alexan, "As Fat Fears Grow, Oreo Tries a New Twist," *Chicago Tribune* (August 22, 2005).

35. Mayer, Caroline E., "Kraft to Curb Snack-Food Advertising," *Washington Post* (January 12, 2005).

# CASE 6.    *Marketing Malt Liquor*

During the summer of 1991, the surgeon general of the United States and advocacy groups led by the Center for Science in the Public In-terest (CSPI) launched a campaign to remove G. Heileman Brewing Company's malt liquor PowerMaster from store shelves. The LaCrosse,

Wisconsin–based brewer had experienced a series of financial setbacks. In January 1991 the company filed for protection from creditors in a New York bankruptcy court, claiming to be "struggling under a huge debt load." (Alix Freedman, "Heileman Will Be Asked to Change Potent Brew's Name," *Wall Street Journal,* June 20, 1991, p. B1.) In an attempt to reverse its financial decline, Heileman introduced PowerMaster with a 5.9 percent alcohol content. Most malt liquors (defined by law as beers with alcohol levels above 4 percent) have a 5.5 percent average content, as compared with the typical 3.5 percent alcohol level of standard beers.

PowerMaster came under fire from both anti-alcohol and African American activists. These groups charged that Heileman had created the name and the accompanying advertising campaign, which featured a black male model, with the intent of targeting young black men, who consume roughly one-third of all malt liquors. U.S. Surgeon General Antonia Novello joined the Heileman critics, calling the PowerMaster marketing campaign insensitive. Citing the economic burden that a legal contest to retain the brand name would entail, the company discontinued the product. However, beer industry executives and members criticized the government's role in the controversy. One newspaper columnist cited race as the critical factor in the campaign to remove PowerMaster, noting that the "It's the power" advertising slogan used in the marketing of Pabst Brewing Co.'s Olde English 800 malt liquor had gone unchallenged. James Sanders, president of the Washington, DC–based Beer Institute, contended that the government focused on the PowerMaster label to avoid having to focus on other factors such as unemployment and poverty, the real problems that the black community confronts.

### Questions

1. Would it be deceptive or manipulative advertising to call your beer "PowerMaster" and to use black male models?
2. Is it ethically insensitive for a company to target a specific market identified by race and gender?

## CASE 7.    *Merck & Company: The Vioxx Recall*

On the afternoon of September 23, 2004, Raymond V. Gilmartin, president, chairman, and chief executive officer of Merck and Co. Inc. sat in his office intently focused on reviewing the firm's strategic direction. Gilmartin had guided Merck and Co. through unprecedented growth within the pharmaceutical industry. During the 1990's Merck launched six blockbuster drugs, which drove the increased revenue, stock, and value of the company. Merck had been the darling of Wall Street and earned an irreproachable ethical reputation in a risky and complex market.

However, times had been changing for Merck. Merck had lost its market leadership position and had fallen to number six within the industry. In the last few years, five patents had expired, significantly impacting their revenue

This case was prepared for educational puposes by Frank Eichman, Mike Hanahoe, Mike Good, Jake Kulzer, Terry Griffith, and Steve Manlove under the supervison of Norman Bowie © 2007.

stream. To complicate matters, Merck cancelled work on two major research and development initiatives in the fight against depression and diabetes. The depression drug failed a critical clinical trial, and the diabetes drug increased the risk of cancer when tested in laboratory animals. Merck had been positioning the two drugs as the next blockbuster to propel Merck back into their leadership position. The product pipeline, which was once continuously stocked, was not meeting Gilmartin's expectations.

Despite these setbacks Gilmartin was committed to "staying the course" on the corporate strategy.[1] He had confidence that his leadership team and the innovation of his employees would overcome these setbacks. The research and development conducted by Merck's employee base was the lifeblood of the company. Only last week Merck had dedicated its newest research facility near the Harvard Medical School. It would facilitate research for the treatment of Alzheimer's, cancer and obesity. This exemplified Merck's commitment to improving the quality of life of people worldwide.

What Gilmartin had not prepared for was the news Research and Development Chief Peter Kim would deliver that afternoon. Kim called to inform Gilmartin that outside investigators had recommended Merck discontinue the APPROVe (Adenomatous Polyp Prevention on Vioxx) study. APPROVe was a long-term study on Vioxx's efficacy in reducing size and frequency of colon polyps. In parallel Merck had decided to utilize the study to determine whether Vioxx produced increased cardiovascular risk to its users. The result demonstrated that Vioxx increased risk of heart attack for patients who had regularly used the prescription for greater than 18 months. For several years external researchers had charged that Vioxx was a cardiovascular risk. However, Merck vehemently defended the drug and was confident in their internal testing procedures and trial results.

Did other factors play a role in Merck's zealous defense of Vioxx, or did they base it purely on objective scientific evidence?

The results of the APPROVe study added credence to the external researcher's accusations and required Merck to make some critical decisions. Merck had spent nearly $500 million annually in their direct-to-customer advertising of Vioxx. Gilmartin now had to determine the appropriate response to notify customers. Based on Food and Drug Administration (FDA) policies, Merck was under no obligation to withdraw the product from the market or conduct a full-scale recall. Updating the FDA on the new clinical findings and amending the prescription warning criteria was all that was required. However, Merck had always relied in its ethical principles to guide it. Gilmartin's commitment was "to make a decision about Vioxx totally in the interest of the patients' safety."[2]

On September 30, 2004, Gilmartin informed the FDA of Merck's intention to recall Vioxx from the market. Withdrwing the $6 billion-a-year drug would have unprecedented financial and legal ramifications.

## THE VIOXX STORY

In 1994 Merck scientists discovered Vioxx, one of a new class of painkillers called COX-2 inhibitors. COX-2 inhibitors reduce pain and inflammation without causing ulcers and gastrointestinal bleeding, side effects often seen from nonsteroidal anti-inflammatory drugs (NSAIDs), such as ibuprofen. These older painkillers such as aspirin and Aleve, known generically as naproxen, block two enzymes—COX-1 and COX-2—that are involved in inflammation and pain. Blocking COX-1 can damage the stomach and intestines, but it also may prevent blood clots. Vioxx and another drug, Pfizer Inc.'s Celebrex, were designed to block only COX-2.

From early on, companies developing COX-2 inhibitors faced a dilemma. The drugs seemed to offer clear benefits to arthritis and other pain sufferers who couldn't stand the stomach damage of aspirin, naproxen, or ibuprofen. But that was a relatively small market. The real bonanza lay with the general mass of pain patients.[3]

Merck was facing the loss of patent protection on its largest revenue-producing drugs over the next 5 years and needed a new blockbuster. Merck felt that it would be difficult to penetrate the pain management market if patients did not receive a cardiovascular benefit provided by COX-1 inhibitors. Merck underwent trials attempting to prove that there was a clear benefit to the stomach without increased risk to the heart.

Study participants were not able to take aspirin, and Merck researchers were concerned "there is a substantial chance that significantly higher rates" of heart problems in the Vioxx control group. This concern was voiced again in February 1997 by a Merck official who said that "thrombotic events" will "kill [the] drug."[4]

By 1998 Merck had completed the multiphase development and research for Vioxx. They submitted a New Drug Application (NDA) for Vioxx to the U.S. Food and Drug Administration. The mood at Merck was upbeat. Recent drug releases had propelled Merck's stock to new highs with no end in sight. With the successful release of Vioxx, Merck intended to take a leadership position in the long-term anti-inflammatory drug market. However, in the autumn of 1998, a group of University of Pennsylvania researchers discovered that COX-2 inhibitors interfere with enzymes thought to play a key role in preventing cardiovascular disease. Merck vehemently opposed the study and said that it found the evidence to be inconclusive.[5] That year Merck's net income was $5.24 billion, making them the number one pharmaceutical company in the world.

During the following year there were three important events for Merck: The first was the initiation of the Vioxx Gastrointestinal Outcomes Research (VIGOR) trial, the purpose of which was to show that Vioxx posed less gastrointestinal risk than older NSAIDs. In the study patients were given high doses of Vioxx and not allowed to take aspirin. It excluded patients at risk for heart problems. The second event occurred in May 1999. The FDA approved Vioxx for marketing. It took only 6 months of review, whereas the typical drug review periods for drugs from other pharmaceutical companies typically averaged 2 years. This quick turnaround is alleged to be a result of a "cozy" relationship between Merck and the FDA and payment of a large fee. Merck touted its release as "the biggest, fastest, and best launch ever." Merck marketed Vioxx directly to consumers with tremendous success. The third was the impending retirement of Dr. Edward Scolnick, head of Merck Research Laboratories. Scolnick was leaving just as Merck was facing several looming drug patent expirations. Its drug development pipeline was dwindling, and Merck found itself banking on only a small number of potential new drug releases—the most significant of which was Vioxx.

In February 2000, the Merck-sponsored Adenomatous Polyp Prevention on Vioxx (APPROVe) trial was initiated. The purpose of the study was to show whether the use of Vioxx would reduce colon polyps. This study was unique in that it was the first true controlled study comparing Vioxx with a placebo instead of another drug. In March, the VIGOR results were published internally. The study showed Vioxx patients suffered fewer stomach problems, but more blood clot problems, than the naproxen group. The heart attack rate was five times higher. This significant disparity caused Scolnick to write an internal email confirming cardiovascular events "are clearly there." Dr. Scolnick went on to say that he wanted more data before results were presented publicly. The research chief recalled that some of his greatest drugs had side effects. He wrote, "We have a great drug, but just like angioedema with Vasotec, seizures with Primaxin, and myopathy with Mevacor, there is always a hazard. The class will do well and so will we."[6]

In a news release later in March, no mention of the research chief's message was given. Merck maintained that the VIGOR results were consistent with expectations. A month later another news release touted "No difference in the incidence of cardiovascular events" between Vioxx and older painkillers. The *New England Journal of Medicine* published the VIGOR study results in November of the same year. The article was authored by academics, some of whom received funding from Merck. The paper discussed Vioxx's benefits to the digestive system and the cardiac problems. In addition, the paper maintained that patients who were not at high risk for heart problems did not show an increase in heart problems.

The pressures of the dwindling drug pipeline were taking their toll on Dr. Scolnick however. Several potential "inside" successors had left the company, complaining of an "emperor's new clothes" mentality that was developing in Scolnick's wake. Despite these problems, Merck's net income was up $930 million to $6.82 billion, and their stock was selling at $93.63 a share, up 38 percent from the previous year. This year would later prove to be Merck's high mark in both market share and stock price. At year-end, Peter Kim joined Merck as head of its internal research operations.

By early 2001 the VIGOR results caused the debate to shift to whether the drug was fundamentally safe. In February, an advisory committee recommended that the FDA require a label warning of the possible link to cardiovascular problems. Merck ignored the recommendation, approaching the same committee

later that month in order to convince them to allow Merck to drop an unrelated digestive tract warning.[7] In the end, a compromise was reached with the warning label showing good news about fewer stomach problems and bad news about possibly more heart attacks and strokes. The FDA warned Merck to stop misleading doctors about Vioxx's effect on the cardiovascular system, requiring them to send doctors a letter "to correct false or misleading impressions and information" about Vioxx's effect on the cardiovascular system.[8]

By year end Merck's net income was $7.28 billion. Expiring patents, as well as overall market conditions were blamed for a decline in the stock price. The impact of the Vioxx concerns had yet to reach Wall Street or the general population.

In April 2002, Merck was spending more than $100 million a year in direct-to-consumer advertising. This investment was successfully sustaining Vioxx's "blockbuster" status. Merck went on the offensive, taking on the critics of Vioxx's safety.

## CRITICISM MOUNTS

The first of these was Gurkirpal Singh from Stanford University. A prominent COX-2 researcher, he gave lectures sponsored by Merck and said he repeatedly asked Merck for more safety data. When the company refused his request, Dr. Singh added a portion to his presentation depicting a man hiding under a blanket. This was aimed to represent missing safety data. Merck cancelled several lectures by Dr. Singh, and Merck officials lodged complaints with the school that Dr. Singh was "irresponsibly anti-Merck and anti-Vioxx." Merck suggested that if this continued, there would be consequences for Dr. Singh and Stanford. When news of the threats was brought to the attention of CEO Gilmartin, he responded that Merck had a "deep and abiding commitment to the highest ethical standards in all our dealings with physicians and other healthcare providers." Merck took steps to repair the relationship and eventually Dr. Singh stopped using the controversial slide. A similar threat was made to Dr. M. Thomas Stillman of the University of Minnesota. When he discussed data on high blood pressure and swelling as a result of Vioxx in his lectures, he was fired from the Merck-sponsored lecture program.

At the end of 2002, Edward Scolnick retired as President, Merck Research Laboratories. As planned, Peter Kim was named his successor. Merck had failed to launch any significant new drugs, and patents continued to expire on their existing products. Merck's net income was down $130 million.

In 2003, Merck suspended research on four costly Phase III drug trials. By year-end, Merck's net income was $6.83 billion (down $320 million) and their stock was selling at $46.20/share, down 18 percent from the previous year.

The FDA approved Vioxx for the treatment of juvenile rheumatoid arthritis in August of 2004. Since this indication involves using the product for children, Vioxx was put through a particularly rigorous review.

On August 25, 2004, an FDA researcher presented the results of a data analysis of 1.4 million patients, which concluded that Vioxx users were more likely to suffer a heart attack than those taking Celebrex or older NSAIDs. Though the evidence was now mounting, Merck relentlessly stuck to its guns and issued a news release strongly disagreeing with the FDA study. "Merck stands behind the efficacy, overall safety and cardiovascular safety of Vioxx."

On September 23, 2004, Peter Kim called Ray Gilmartin, telling him that the APPROVe study was showing that patients using Vioxx have a demonstrably higher incidence of heart attack, after 18 months of regular use. The APPROVe researchers had recommended to Kim that the study be stopped because of cardiovascular concerns. Both Gilmartin and Kim report that they were "stunned and shocked" at the news.[9]

Merck pulled Vioxx from the market on September 30. By this time, Merck had spent more than $500 million on direct-to-consumer advertising. Twenty million Americans had taken the drug, which was generating $2.5 billion in annual sales in the United States. Vioxx was the second-best-selling COX-2 inhibitor. Merck lost $33 billion in market capitalization (33% of its total) over the next several days. On December 7, 2004, Merck's stock was selling at $27.89 a share, down 60 percent since the first of the year.

## Questions

1. What, if anything, was ethically wrong about Merck's development and introduction of Vioxx? Explain.
2. Should a pharmaceutical company control the information physicians disclose about their products when those physicians are hired as consultants? Why or why not? Explain.
3. Merck spent $500 million dollars advertising Vioxx to the general public before the company pulled the drug off the market because of health concerns. Should pharmaceutical companies market prescription drugs directly to consumers? Why, or why not? Explain.
4. The U.S. Congress is considering legislation that would ban direct-to-consumer advertising on new classes of drugs until their safety can be better assessed and doctors have had an opportunity to learn about the new drug. This law would have prevented Merck from marketing Vioxx to consumers. Proponents argue that this policy will promote patient welfare, whereas critics argue that it unjustly limits free speech. Do you support such legislation? Why, or why not? Explain.

## NOTES

1. John Simons, "Will Merck Survive Vioxx?" *Fortune* (November 1, 2004).

2. Ibid.

3. Anna Wilde Mathews and Barbara Martinez, "Warning Signs: Merck Knew Vioxx Dangers at Early Stage" *Wall Street Journal* (November 1, 2004).

4. Ibid.

5. Simon, "Will Merck Survive Vioxx?"

6. Anna Wilde Mathews and Barbara Martinez, "Warning Signs: E-mails Suggest Merck Knew Vioxx's Dangers at Early Stage," *Wall Street Journal* (November 1, 2004).

7. Rita Rubin, "How Did Vioxx Debacle Happen?" *USA Today* (October 12, 2004).

8. Ibid.

9. Matthew Herper, "Behind Merck's Fall" *Forbes* (October 1, 2004).

## Suggested Supplementary Readings

ABRAMSON, JOHN. 2005. *Overdosed America: The Broken Promise of American Medicine.* New York: Harper Collins.

ALLMON, DEAN E., and JAMES GRANT. 1990. "Real Estate Sales Agents and the Code of Ethics." *Journal of Business Ethics* 9 (October).

ANGELL, MARCIA. 2004. *The Truth About the Drug Companies.* New York, Random House.

ARNOLD, DENIS G. 2009. The Ethics of Direct to Consumer Pharmaceutical Advertising. In *Ethics and the Business of Biomedicine,* ed. Denis G. Arnold. Cambridge: Cambridge University Press.

ATTAS, DANIEL. 1999. "What's Wrong with 'Deceptive' Advertising?" *Journal of Business Ethics* 21:49–59.

BEAUCHAMP, TOM L. 1984. "Manipulative Advertising." *Business and Professional Ethics Journal* 3 (Spring–Summer): 1–22.

———. 2004. *Case Studies in Business, Society, and Ethics,* 5th ed., chaps. 2, 4. Upper Saddle River, NJ: Prentice Hall.

BISHOP, JOHN DOUGLAS. 2000. "Is Self-Identity Image Advertising Ethical?" *Business Ethics Quarterly* 10:371–98.

BOWIE, NORMAN, and RONALD F. DUSKA. 1990. Applying the Moral Presuppositions of Business to Advertising and Hiring. In *Business Ethics,* 2nd ed., ed. Norman E. Bowie and Ronald F. Duska. Englewood Cliffs, NJ: Prentice Hall.

BRENKERT, G. G. 1998. "Marketing to Inner-City Blacks: PowerMaster and Moral Responsibility." *Business Ethics Quarterly* 8:1–18.

BROCKWAY, GEORGE. 1993. "Limited Paternalism and the Salesperson: A Reconsideration." *Journal of Business Ethics* 12 (April): 275–80.

*Business and Professional Ethics Journal* 1984. 3 (Spring–Summer). The entire issue is devoted to ethical issues in advertising.

*Business Ethics Quarterly* 2006. 16 (July). Special forum devoted to marketing and technology.

*Business Ethics Quarterly* 2007. 17 (January). Special section on commercial speech.

CARR, ALBERT Z. 1968. "Is Business Bluffing Ethical?" *Harvard Business Review* 46 (January/February).

CARSON, THOMAS L. 1993. "Second Thoughts about Bluffing." *Business Ethics Quarterly* 3 (October): 317–41.

———. 1998. "Ethical Issues in Sales: Two Case Studies." *Journal of Business Ethics* 17 (May): 725–28.

———. 2001. "Deception and Withholding Information in Sales." *Business Ethics Quarterly* 11 (April): 275–306.

COHAN, JOHN ALAN. 2001. "Towards a New Paradigm in the Ethics of Women's Advertising." *Journal of Business Ethics* 33 (October): 323–37.

DABHOLKAR, PRATIBHA A., and JAMES J. KELLARIS. 1992. "Toward Understanding Marketing Students' Ethical Judgment of Controversial Personal Selling Practices." *Journal of Business Research* 24 (June): 313–29.

DE CONINCK, J. B., and D. J. GOOD. 1989. "Perceptual Differences of Sales Practitioners and Students Concerning Ethical Behavior." *Journal of Business Ethics* 8 (September): 667–76.

EBEJER, JAMES M., and MICHAEL J. MORDEN. 1998. "Paternalism in the Marketplace: Should a Salesman Be His Buyer's Keeper?" *Journal of Business Ethics* 7:337–39.

GREENLAND, LEO. 1974. "Advertisers Must Stop Conning Consumers." *Harvard Business Review* (July/August): 18–28, 156.

HAMILTON III, J. B., JAMES R. LUMPKIN, and DAVID STRUTTON. 1997. "An Essay on When to Fully Disclose in Sales Relationships: Applying Two Practical Guidelines for Addressing Truth-Telling Problems." *Journal of Business Ethics* 16 (April): 545–60.

HARE, R. M. 1984. "Commentary on Beauchamp's 'Manipulative Advertising'." *Business Professional Ethics Journal* 3 (Spring–Summer): 23–28.

HITE, ROBERT E., JOSEPH A. BELLIZZI, and CYNTHIA FRASER. 1988. "A Content Analysis of Ethical Policy Statements Regarding Marketing Activities." *Journal of Business Ethics* 7 (October).

HOLLEY, DAVID M. 1986–87. "A Moral Evaluation of Sales Practices." *Business and Professional Ethics Journal* 5:3–21.

KAUFMANN, PATRICK J., N. CRAIG SMITH, and GWENDOLYN K. ORTMEYER. 1994. "Deception in Retailer High-Low Pricing: A 'Rule of Reason' Approach." *Journal of Retailing* 70 (Summer): 115–38.

KOEHN, DARYL. 1997. "Business and Game-Playing: The False Analogy." *Journal of Business Ethics* 16:1447–52.

KING, CAROLE. 1990. "It's Time to Disclose Commissions." *National Underwriter* 94 (November 19).

LACZNICK, GENE R. 1993. "Marketing Ethics: Onward Toward Greater Expectations." *Journal of Public Policy and Marketing* 12:91–96.

LACZNICK, GENE R., and PATRICK E. MURPHY. 1993. *Ethical Marketing Decisions: The Higher Road.* Boston: Allyn and Bacon.

LEVITT, THEODORE. 1995. The Morality (?) of Advertising. In *Ethical Issues in Business,* ed. Michael Boylan. Fort Worth, TX: Harcourt Brace.

LIPPKE, RICHARD L. 1989. "Advertising and the Social Conditions of Autonomy." *Business and Professional Ethics Journal* 8:35–58.

———. 1990. "The 'Necessary Evil' Defense of Manipulative Advertising." *Business and Professional Ethics Journal* 18:3–21.

MAES, JEANNE D., ARTHUR JEFFERY, and TOMMY V. SMITH. 1998. "The American Association of Advertising Agencies (4As) Standards of Practice: How Far Does this Professional Association's Code of Ethics Influence Reach?" *Journal of Business Ethics* 17:1155–61.

MCCLAREN, NICHOLAS. 2000. "Ethics in Personal Selling and Sales Management: A Review of the Literature Focusing on Empirical Findings and Conceptual Foundations." *Journal of Business Ethics* 27 (October): 285–303.

MICHALOS, ALEX C. 1995. Advertising: Its Logic, Ethics, and Economics. In *A Pragmatic Approach to Business Ethics.* Thousand Oaks, CA: Sage.

MURPHY, PATRICK E. 2005. "Sustainable Marketing." *Business and Professional Ethics Journal* 24 (Spring–Summer): 171–98.

MURPHY, PATRICK E., and PRIDGEN, M. D. 1991. "Ethical and Legal Issues in Marketing," *Advances in Marketing and Public Policy* 2:185–244.

OAKES, G. 1990. "The Sales Process and the Paradoxes of Trust." *Journal of Business Ethics* 9 (August): 67–79.

PERKINS, ANNE G. 1994. "Advertising: The Costs of Deception." *Harvard Business Review* 72 (May–June): 10–11.

PETERSON, ROBIN T. 1996 "Physical Environment Television Advertisement Themes." *Journal of Business Ethics* 10 (March).

POLONSKY, MICHAEL JAY, JUDITH BAILEY, HELEN BAKER, CHRISTOPHER BASCHE, CARL JEPSON, and LENORE NEATH. 1998. "Communicating Environmental Information: Are Marketing Claims on Packaging Misleading?" *Journal of Business Ethics* 17:281–94.

PHILLIPS, BARBARA J. 1997. "In Defense of Advertising: A Social Perspective." *Journal of Business Ethics* 16:109–18.

PHILLIPS, MICHAEL J. 1994. "The Inconclusive Case against Manipulative Advertising." *Business and Professional Ethics Journal* 13.

PREDMORE, CAROLYN E., and TARA J. RADIN. 2002. "The Myth of the Salesperson: Intended and Unintended Consequences of Product-Specific Sales Incentives." *Journal of Business Ethics* 36 (March): 79–92.

QUINN, JOHN F. 1989. "Moral Theory and Defective Tobacco Advertising and Warnings." *Journal of Business Ethics* 8 (November).

SMITH, N. CRAIG, and JOHN A. QUELCH. 1992. *Ethics in Marketing Management.* Homewood, IL: Irwin.

SNEDDON, ANDREW. 2001. "Advertising and Deep Autonomy." *Journal of Business Ethics* 33 (September): 15–28.

SULLIVAN, ROGER J. 1984. "A Response to 'Is Business Bluffing Ethical?'" *Business and Professional Ethics Journal* 3 (Winter).

VALLANCE, ELIZABETH. 1995. *Business Ethics at Work.* New York: Cambridge University Press.

WONG, KENMAN L. 1996. "Tobacco Advertising and Children: The Limits of First Amendment Protection." *Journal of Business Ethics* 15:1051–64.

# Chapter 6

# Ethical Issues in Finance and Accounting

## INTRODUCTION

No areas of business are more important in market economies than finance and accounting. Without accurate and transparent financial accounting and auditing, investors will lose faith in companies, share values will decline rapidly, and financial markets may collapse as a result. In the beginning years of the twenty-first century the faith of many investors was shaken by financial scandals at Enron, WorldCom, Arthur Andersen and the numerous other companies that misstated earnings during this dark period in the history of market economies. At the time, most investors trusted the accounting systems that were in place. Internal accountants at publicly held companies, such as Enron and WorldCom, would accurately state their earnings and expenses and then turn over their accounting books to external auditors at one of the "Big Five" international accounting firms such as Arthur Andersen. The firm's auditors, well versed in the American Institute of Certified Public Accountants' Code of Professional Conduct (included in this chapter) would scrutinize the books, root out and rectify any errors, and certify the books as accurately representing the finances of the company under review. When auditors at Arthur Andersen acted in ways that systematically contradicted the professional standards of the accounting profession, they undermined the integrity of financial markets and eventually caused the demise of their own firm.

## AUDITING AFTER ENRON

As Ronald Duska and Brenda Shay Duska argue in their essay "Ethics in Auditing: The Auditing Function," the primary function of independent accountants is to determine whether a corporation's financial reports are prepared in accordance with generally accepted accounting principles and fairly represent the financial position of the corporation for the relevant time period. To accomplish this goal, Duska and Duska argue, accountants must be trustworthy, must be willing and able to report fraud, and must in all cases have total independence. By "total independence" Duska and Duska mean both independence in fact and the appearance of independence from anyone or any group or organization that has a vested interest in the outcome of the audit. They go on to articulate four basic principles for assessing auditor independence.

The public's faith in the accounting profession was shaken when auditors at Arthur Andersen misrepresented the financial status of companies such as Enron, WorldCom, Qwest, and Halliburton, merely because it was in their financial interest to do so. At the root of Andersen's failure were conflicts of interest that undermined the independence of Andersen's auditors and corrupted the independent auditing process. First, Andersen's consulting business made much more money working for these individual companies than did the accounting unit at Andersen. To retain the lucrative consulting business, Andersen applied pressure to its auditors to ignore fraudulent practices. Second, companies such as Enron actively recruited employees from Andersen for well-compensated management positions within their organizations. Thus, in many cases the company being audited employed former Andersen employees. In addition, the prospect of obtaining such jobs in the future is alleged to have influenced the behavior of current Andersen employees, especially junior auditors (called "articling students" in Canada).

After the systematic misrepresentation of the earnings of these companies was discovered, investors suffered huge losses. Large, respected companies had failed to act on generally accepted principles of financial accounting, and one of the most respected accounting firms in the world had failed in its core mission of providing trustworthy independent audits. In the face of such substantial failures of self-regulation, and in response to a growing chorus of outrage from individual and institutional investors, Congress passed the Sarbanes-Oxley Act in 2002. This act was designed to help curb the worst abuses by holding executives directly responsible for accounting fraud and by enhancing sanctions so that executives would be deterred from approving fraudulent activity.

In his essay "The Structural Origins of Conflicts of Interest in the Accounting Profession," Colin Boyd explains how the conflicts of interest that destabilized the accounting profession and financial markets came about via the consolidation of accounting services by the Big Five accounting firms and the subsequent diversification of those firms into a variety of lucrative consulting services. Boyd explains that when the conflicts of interest within the accounting industry became apparent in the 1990s, regulators sought to put in place rules that would curtail such conflicts. However, regulators were confronted with stiff resistance from the Big Five including significant increases in political donations and paid political lobbying. Boyd argues that although Sarbanes-Oxley has reduced the likelihood of some conflicts of interest, it does not go far enough to prohibit the full range of conflicts present in the accounting industry. In conclusion, he argues that the accounting industry has lost its integrity by failing to meet the most important responsibility of any profession:

self-regulation. As a result, he argues that future evolution of the accounting industry lies with external regulators.

John Boatright offers a different analysis of the Sarbanes-Oxley Act in his first contribution to this chapter: "Individual Responsibility in the American Corporation System: Does Sarbanes-Oxley Strike the Right Balance?" Boatright argues that Sarbanes-Oxley places too much legal responsibility for corporate wrongdoing on corporate executives. He argues that if we take seriously the role of managers as agents, and transaction cost economics, we should conclude that corporate misconduct is primarily due to a conflict of interest between managers and shareholders and that from this perspective misconduct can best be prevented by placing primary responsibility for wrongdoing on corporations and their shareholders.

## FINANCIAL SERVICES

Financial service firms provide a variety of services to their customers in addition to auditing such as financial planning, insurance, investment vehicles, and tax advice. In his second contribution to this chapter, "Ethical Issues in Financial Services," John Boatright begins by discussing some of the unethical practices that are commonly observed in the financial services industry. These include deception; churning, or the inappropriate trading of a client's assets by a broker with the intent to generate commissions rather than benefit the client; and recommending inappropriate securities and financial products relative to the risk tolerance of the client. He argues that financial service professionals have a moral obligation to refrain from such behavior. Boatright then turns his attention to insider trading, where he argues that the fiduciary duties of managers and other insiders to shareholders provide a strong basis for a prohibition on insider trading. In the 1997 U.S. Supreme Court decision *U.S. v. O'Hagan*, also reprinted in the legal perspectives section of this chapter, insider trading was found to be illegal when it involves the misappropriation of confidential information by an insider, even if the insider is not directly employed by the company in question. It is enough, the Court ruled, if the insider has fiduciary ties to the company and makes inappropriate use of confidential information.

In the concluding essay of this chapter, "Applying Ethics to Insider Trading," Robert W. McGee argues that a prohibition against insider trading is unwarranted. He argues that there is little empirical evidence to support the claim that insider trading harms anyone. Until such evidence is produced, he argues, the legal ban on insider trading should be lifted because, in his view, insider trading constitutes a morally legitimate expression of the right to buy and sell property at will. He points to the Martha Stewart case to illustrate his point. In this case (see the case study "Martha Stewart Living Omnimedia Inc.: An Accusation of Insider Trading" included in this chapter) Ms. Stewart was convicted of lying to prosecutors about a crime that she was not found guilty of committing. McGee regards this case as an example of the perils of unneeded and unethical restriction on individual liberty.

AUDITING AFTER ENRON

# Ethics in Auditing: The Auditing Function

*Ronald F. Duska and Brenda Shay Duska*

Given the way financial markets and the economic system have developed, society has carved out a role for the independent auditor, which is absolutely essential for the effective functioning of the economic system. If accounting is the language of business, it is the auditor's job to see the language is used properly so that the relevant message is communicated properly. This means that, in the system, the role of the independent auditor is "to see whether the company's estimates are based on formulas that seem reasonable in the light of whatever evidence is available and that choice formulas are applied consistently from year to year."[1]

Most times, when people talk about the ethics of public accounting, they are talking about the responsibilities of the independent auditor. Auditing the financial statements of publicly owned companies is certainly not the only role of an accountant, but an argument can be made that it is one of the, if not *the*, most important roles in the current economic system. . . .

This function and responsibility is not new; it has only come under the harsh glare of public scrutiny with the eruption of the Enron/Arthur Andersen debacle. The classic statement of this function and responsibility of the auditor is the opinion given by Justice Burger in the 1984 landmark Arthur Young case.[2]

Corporate financial statements are one of the primary sources of information available to guide the decisions of the investing public. In an effort to control the accuracy of the financial data available to investors in the securities markets, various provisions of the federal securities laws require publicly held companies to file their financial statements with the Securities and Exchange Commission. Commission regulations stipulate that these financial reports must be audited by an independent CPA in accordance with generally accepted auditing standards. *By examining the corporation's books and records, the independent auditor determines whether the financial reports of the corporation have been prepared in accordance with generally accepted accounting principles. The auditor then issues an opinion as to whether the financial statements, taken as a whole, fairly present the financial position and operations of the corporation for the relevant period.* [Authors' italics.]

Burger puts the responsibility of the auditor clearly—to issue an opinion as to whether the financial statement *fairly* presents the financial position of the corporation. Performance of this role attesting that the financial positions and operations of the corporation are fairly presented requires the auditor to have as much integrity and honesty as possible. Further, to assure that an accurate picture has been presented it is essential that the integrity and honesty of the auditor not be imperiled by the presence of undue influence. To bolster integrity and honesty the auditor must have as much independence as possible. For the market to function efficiently those who need to make decisions about the company based on as true and accurate information as possible must be able to trust the accountants' pictures. But such trust is eroded if there is even an appearance of a conflict of interest. . . .

Excerpted From Ronald F. Duska and Brenda Shay Duska, *Accounting Ethics* (Malden, MA: Blackwell, 2003).

## TRUST

We can understand all this if we apply Immanuel Kant's first categorical imperative, the universalizability principle: "Act so you can will the maxim of your action to be a universal law." As we saw, the imperative demands that an action be capable of being universalized—that is, we need to consider what would occur if everyone acted the same way for the same reason. Consider the reasons people have for not giving the most accurate picture possible of the financial status of a company. As we saw, one generally gives a false picture to get another party to act in a way other than they would act given full and truthful information. For example, a CFO misrepresents his company's profits to get a bank loan, thinking that if the bank had the true picture, no loan would be forthcoming. In the Enron case it was more complicated, the aim being to buoy up the price of the stock, which was then used as collateral to float loans to cover (bad?) debts. What would happen if such behavior were universalized, that is, if everybody misrepresented the financial health of their company when it was to their advantage to lie?

In such a situation two things would happen. First, trust in business dealings that required information about the financial picture would be eroded. This certainly happens, as Der Hovanesian relates. Chaos would ensue, because financial markets cannot operate without trust. Cooperation is essential, and trust is a precondition of cooperation. We engage in hundreds of transactions daily, which demand that we trust other people with our money and our lives. If misrepresentation were to become a universal practice such trust, and consequently such cooperation, would be impossible.

Secondly, universalizing misrepresentation, besides leading to mistrust, chaos, and consequently inefficiencies in the market,

would make the act of misrepresentation impossible. When universalizing misrepresentation makes trust impossible, it simultaneously makes the very act of misrepresenting impossible, because misrepresentation can only occur if the person lied to trusts the person lying. Since prudent people don't trust known liars, if everyone lied, no one would trust another and it would be impossible to lie. So universalized lying makes lying impossible. Do we trust the defendant in a murder case to tell the truth? Do we trust young children who are worried about being punished to tell the truth? Of course not. Once we recognize that certain people are unreliable or untrustworthy it becomes impossible for them to misrepresent things to us, because we don't believe a word they're saying. Hence the anomaly—if misrepresentation became universalized in certain situations, it would be impossible to misrepresent in those situations, since no one would trust what was being represented. This makes the universalizing of lying irrational or self-contradictory.

The contradiction here, according to Kant, is a will contradiction, and the irrationality lies in the fact that you are simultaneously willing the possibility of misrepresentation and the impossibility of misrepresentation, by willing out of existence the conditions (trust) necessary to perform the act you will to perform. Face it, people who lie don't want lying universalized. Liars are free riders. Liars want an unfair advantage. They don't want others to lie—to act like the liars are acting. Liars want others to tell the truth and be trusting so that the liars can lie to those trusting people. Liars want the world to work one way for them and differently for all others. In short, liars want a double standard. They want their cake and want to eat it too. But such a selfish self-serving attitude is the antithesis of the ethical. In this case auditing would become a useless function. As a matter of fact, in an issue of *Accounting Today,* Rick Teleberg thinks this has already happened: "CPA firms long ago became more like insurance companies—complete with their focus on assurances and risk-managed audits—than attesters." We won't risk telling the public what your financial state looks like; we'll just guarantee that your presentation won't be subject to charges of illegal behavior. They serve the client and not the public.

In this discussion we can see another important aspect of trust. Only a fool trusts someone who gives all the appearances of being a liar. Only a fool trusts someone who puts themselves in positions where they seem likely to have their integrity compromised. These are the reasons why people take precautions against getting involved with those who give even the appearance of being caught in a conflict of interest. Because trust is necessary, even the *appearance* of honesty and integrity of accountants becomes important. So the auditor must not only be trustworthy, he or she must also appear trustworthy, for the prudent manager as the prudent accountant has an obligation to be sufficiently skeptical in order to protect the legitimate claims of stakeholders.

## THE AUDITOR'S RESPONSIBILITY TO THE PUBLIC

This role and the consequent duty to attest to the fairness of the financial statements gives the accountant special responsibilities to the public. As we saw in the chapters on codes of ethics, possessing these responsibilities puts the accountant in a different relationship with the client who hires him or her than the client relationships found in the other professions. Justice Burger mentions this in his classic statement of auditor responsibility.

The auditor does not have the same relationship to his client that a private attorney who has a role as ". . . a confidential advisor and advocate, a loyal representative whose duty it is to present the client's case in the most favorable possible light. An independent CPA performs a different role. *By certifying the public reports that collectively depict a corporation's financial status, the independent auditor assumes a public responsibility transcending any employment relationship with the client* [authors' italics]. The independent public accountant performing this special function owes ultimate allegiance to the corporation's creditors and stockholders, as well as to the investing public. This 'public watchdog' function demands that the accountant maintain total independence from the client at all times and requires complete fidelity to the public trust. To insulate from disclosure a CPA's interpretations of the client's financial statements would be to ignore the significance of the accountant's role as a disinterested analyst charged with public obligations."[3]

Given the conflict of interests between the public and clients, it is clear that auditors face conflicting loyalties. To whom are they primarily responsible, the public or the client who pays the bill? We have seen that accountants are professionals and, consequently, should behave as professionals. Like most other professionals, they offer services to their clients. But the public accounting profession, because it includes operating as an independent auditor, has another function. The independent auditor acts not only as a recorder, but also as an evaluator of other accountants' records. The auditor has what Justice Burger calls "a public watchdog function."

As we have seen, over time, the evaluation of another accountant's records has developed into a necessary component of capitalist societies, particularly that part of society that deals in money markets and offers publicly traded stocks and securities. In such a system, it is imperative for potential purchasers of financial products to have an accurate picture of the companies in which they wish to invest, to whom they are willing to loan money, or with whom they wish to merge. In such a system there needs to be a procedure for verifying the accuracy of the financial picture of companies. The role of verifier fell to the public accountant—the auditor. . . .

In short, while auditors' clients are the ones who pay the fees for the auditor's services, the auditor's primary responsibility is to look out for the interest of a third party, the public, and not to look out primarily for the interests of the one who employs the accountant.

Since the auditor is charged with public obligations, he or she should be a disinterested analyst. The auditor's obligations are to certify that the public reports depicting a corporation's financial status *fairly* present the financial position and operations of the corporation for the relevant period. In short, the fiduciary responsibility of the auditor is to the public trust, and "independence" from the client is demanded for that trust to be honored. The importance of this can be seen in the emphasis the Securities and Exchange Commission puts on the independence factor.

> In January of 2000, partners and employees at Pricewaterhouse-Coopers were found by the SEC to have routinely violated rules forbidding their ownership of stock in companies they were auditing. The investigation found 8,064 violations at the firm, which then dismissed five partners. Pricewaterhouse said at the time that it did not believe that the integrity of any audit had been compromised by the violations.[4]

The fact that the auditor's role requires "transcending any employment relationship with the client" quite often creates dilemmas for the auditor. Since dilemmas arise because of conflicts of responsibility, it will be helpful to specify the particular responsibilities of an auditor.

## THE AUDITOR'S BASIC RESPONSIBILITIES

While the first responsibility of the auditor is to certify or attest to the truth (as far as one is able) of financial statements, an auditor has other responsibilities specified in the AICPA's statements on auditing standards. In Statement of Auditing Standards No. 1, the *Codification of Auditing Standards and Procedures,* the Auditing Standards Board specifies the *generally accepted auditing standards* (the GAAS). These consist in three general standards, three standards of field work and four standards of reporting. They call for (1) proficiency on the part of the auditor; (2) independence in fact and in appearance; (3) due professional care, which involves a sense of "professional skepticism;" (4) adequately planned and properly supervised field work; (5) a sufficient understanding of the internal control structure of the audited entity; (6) sufficient inspection, observation, and inquiries to afford a "reasonable basis" for an opinion; (7) a report stating whether the financial statements are in accord with generally accepted accounting principles (GAAP); (8) identification of circumstances in which the principles have not been consistently observed; (9) disclosures (including notes and wordings) in the financial statements are to be regarded as reasonably adequate unless otherwise stated; and (10) a report shall contain either an opinion of the statement taken as a whole, or an assertion to the effect that an opinion cannot be expressed . . .[5]

It will help us understand the major areas of responsibility if we go back a quarter of a century to a document known as the Cohen Report.[6]

In 1974, the AICPA's Commission on Auditor's Responsibilities (the Cohen Commission) was established to develop conclusions and recommendations regarding the appropriate responsibilities of independent auditors, and to examine the gap between public expectations and needs and what auditors can reasonably accomplish. If gaps existed, the commission was to determine how the disparity between the public's expectations and needs and the realistic capabilities of the accountant could be resolved.

The report defined the independent auditor's primary role in society as that of an intermediary between the financial statements and the users of those statements. Because the auditor is a third party between the client and the public, he or she has an accountability relationship between the issues covered in financial statements and users who rely on those statements. The Cohen Commission made it clear that the primary responsibility of auditors is to the user of the financial statements, not to their clients.

But the report did more than reiterate the primary responsibility of the auditor to attest to fair financial pictures. It examined the gap between public expectations of auditors and what auditors, given the restraints of time and business pressures, can reasonably be expected to accomplish. The report took pains to point out some areas that *are not* the responsibility of the independent auditor.

For example, there is an erroneous belief among some of the public that auditors are responsible for the actual preparation of the financial statements. Others erroneously believe that an audit report indicates that the business being audited is sound. Auditors are not responsible for attesting to the soundness of the business. In fact management, and not auditors, are responsible for the preparation of the financial statements. Indeed, in most cases, management accountants will prepare the financial statements, but that is a different role for the accountant.

Auditors are responsible for forming an opinion about whether the financial statements are presented in accord with appropri-

ately utilized accounting principles. This raises a controversial subject in the accounting ethics literature. The traditional attest statement stated that the financial statements were "presented fairly in accordance with generally accepted accounting principles." In the 1960s a committee of the AICPA had raised the following questions about the fairness claim.

> In the standard report of the auditor, he generally says that financial statements "present fairly" in conformity with generally accepted accounting principles—and so on. What does the auditor mean by the quoted words? Is he saying: (1) that the statements are fair *and* in accordance with GAAP; or (2) that they are fair *because* they are in accordance with GAAP; or (3) that they are fair only *to the extent* that GAAP are fair; or (4) that whatever GAAP may be, the *presentation* of them is fair? [Emphasis in original.][7]

The Cohen Report pointed out that "fairness" is an ambiguous word and hence it is imprudent to hold auditors accountable for the fairness of the report, if that means accuracy of material facts. Rather, the responsibility of the auditors is to determine whether the judgments of managers in the selection and application of accounting principles were appropriate or inappropriate for use in the matter at hand. Note that this differs from Justice Burger's notion that the auditor attests to the "fairness" of the picture.

The Cohen Report would find Burger's requirement too rigid, for three reasons. In some situations there may be no detailed principles that are applicable, in others alternative accounting principles may be applicable, and at times there need to be evaluations of the cumulative effects of the use of a principle. The report called for more guidance for auditors in these three areas. Still, that is hardly the end of the matter, for there seems to be a sense in which the notion of "fairly" presented means the report that is being audited will give the reasonable person a fairly good picture of the financial status of the entity being pictured. One can argue that the GAAP can be used by artful dodgers to hide the real health or sickness of a company. Indeed, many accountants have suggested that accounting is an art, and a truly proficient artist can by the skillful use of GAAP make the same company look to be dizzyingly successful or failing miserably.

Consider the opinion of a federal judge in *Herzfeld v. Laventhol:*

Compliance with generally accepted accounting principles is not necessarily sufficient for an accountant to discharge his public obligation. Fair presentation is the touchstone for determining the adequacy of disclosure and financial statements. While adherence to generally accepted accounting principles is a tool to help achieve that end, it is not necessarily a guarantee of fairness.

Too much attention to the question whether the financial statements formally complied with principles, practices and conventions accepted at the time should not be permitted to blind us to the basic question whether the financial statements performed the function of enlightenment, *which is their only reason for existence.*[8]

Finally, consider the words of former SEC Commissioner A. A. Sommer, Jr.

More disturbingly to the accounting profession . . . was the language in which Judge Henry J. Friendly, surely one of the most knowledgeable of federal judges in financial and accounting matters, scrapped the affirmance (in *Continental Vending*). He said in effect that the first law for accountants was not compliance with generally accepted accounting principles, but rather full and fair disclosure, fair presentation, and if the principles did not produce this brand of disclosure, accountants could not hide behind the principles but had to go beyond them and make whatever additional disclosures were necessary for full disclosure. In a word, "present fairly" was a concept separate from "generally accepted accounting principles," and the latter did not necessarily result in the former.[9]

Whatever the meaning of fairness, it seems to require that the picture presented be such that it gives as accurate a picture as possible to third parties that have a market interest in the financial statements. Thus whatever would fulfill the misrepresentation criteria that we suggested earlier in the chapter would determine what counted as "unfair."

Besides the difficulties the Cohen Report had with the ambiguity of the word "fairly" it went on to examine some further important responsibilities of auditors, responsibilities that have been reiterated in subsequent AICPA statements of auditing standards.

**The evaluation of internal auditing control:** The Cohen Report also insisted that it was a responsibility of the auditor to express an opinion on internal accounting control. The auditor is responsible for determining whether the internal auditing system and controls are adequate. Expressing an opinion on internal accounting controls necessarily leads to a claim that auditors have an obligation to examine the internal workings of the company's accounting procedures, and the safeguards from risks that are in place. It is interesting to contemplate how Arthur Andersen, who served as both the internal and external auditor of Enron, could possibly in an objective manner fulfill the role of critiquing the internal auditing of the company.

But what specifically is an internal auditor to do? To discuss that will require an articulation of the obligations of the management accountants, to see if those are adhered to. We will examine those obligations in the next chapter, but the point here is that the auditor is responsible for evaluating whether the management accountant is living up to his or her obligations and whether the internal auditing controls are adequate and adhered to.

**Responsibility to detect and report errors, irregularities, and or fraud:** A further area that the Cohen Report claimed was an area of responsibility was the auditor's responsibility to report on significant uncertainties that were detected in the financial statements. Further, in a most important area, the report went on to clarify the responsibility of auditors for the detection of fraud and the detection of errors and irregularities.

To more clearly ascertain auditors' responsibilities, let's consider the following situation:

Lawyers for the Allegheny health system's creditors have sued Allegheny's longtime auditors, Pricewaterhouse-Coopers, asserting that the accounting firm "ignored the sure signs" of the system's collapse and failed to prevent its demise.

The suit called Pricewaterhouse-Coopers, "the one independent entity that was in a position to detect and expose" Allegheny's "financial manipulations." Yet the system's financial statements audited by the firm "consistently depicted a business conglomerate in sound financial condition," even after Allegheny's senior officials were fired in 1998.

A spokesman for Pricewaterhouse-Coopers, Steven Silber, said, "We believe this lawsuit to be totally without merit. We intend to defend ourselves vigorously and we're fully confident that we will prevail. Accounting firms are considered to be deep pockets and lawsuits happen to auditors with great frequency."[10]

What was Pricewaterhouse-Coopers' responsibility to detect and expose Allegheny's financial manipulations? How much time, effort and money needed to be expended to detect the signs of the system's collapse? Does the public have a right to expect that an audit should turn up such matters and, if it does, to report them when detected?

To report such errors and irregularities seems to be one of the most serious and perplexing responsibilities of an auditor. In the first place it seems prima facie to run counter to the accountant's responsibility of confidentiality.[11]

John E. Beach, in an article entitled "Code of Ethics: The Professional Catch 22,"[12] gives two examples showing how the accountant's responsibility to the public, when in conflict with the responsibility to keep the client's affairs confidential, can lead to accounting firms' getting sued, and losing lawsuits. According to Beach:

> In October of 1981, a jury in Ohio found an accountant guilty of negligence and breach of contract for violating the obligation of confidentiality mandated in the accountant's code of ethics, and awarded the plaintiffs approximately $1,000,000. At approximately the same time, a jury in New York awarded a plaintiff in excess of $80,000,000 based in part on the failure of an accountant to disclose confidential information.

Without wrestling with this complex issue, which involves deciding when it is permissible for auditors to report certain inappropriate activities of their clients as well as when it is required to report those activities, suffice it to say there is legal opinion that the duty of confidentiality is not absolute and "overriding public interests may exist to which confidentiality must yield."[13]

> Due professional care requires the auditor to exercise *professional skepticism* . . . an attitude that includes a questioning mind and a critical assessment of audit evidence. The auditor uses the knowledge, skill, and ability called for by the profession of public accounting to diligently perform, in good faith and with integrity, the gathering and objective evaluation of evidence.[14]
>
> An audit of financial statements in accordance with generally accepted auditing standards should be planned and performed with an attitude of professional skepticism. The auditor neither assumes that management is dishonest nor assumes unquestioned honesty. Rather, the auditor recognizes that conditions observed and evidential matter obtained, including information from prior audits, need to be objectively evaluated to determine whether the financial statements are free of material misrepresentation.[15]

## INDEPENDENCE

Thus far we have looked at the responsibilities of the auditor. But to meet those responsibilities it is imperative that the auditor maintains independence. Let's recall Justice Burger's statement:

> The independent public accountant performing this special function owes ultimate allegiance to the corporation's creditors and stockholders, as well as to the investing public. *This 'public watchdog' function demands that the accountant maintain total independence from the client at all times and requires complete fidelity to the public trust.*

"Total independence" is the key phrase that Burger uses. But what does total independence require? Obviously an external auditor should be *independent* from the client. But must independence be *total*, as Justice Burger says? If so, what exactly does *total independence* require? What does "complete" fidelity to the public trust require? We need to examine whether total independence is a possibility or even a necessity. How much independence should an auditor maintain and how should the auditor determine that?

Let us suggest that what is usually meant by total independence is independence not only in fact, but also in appearance. . . . The AICPA code of ethics recognizes these two kinds of independence: independence in fact and independence in appearance. Independence in fact is applicable to all accountants, for if the function of the accountant is to render accurate pictures of the financial situation, then conflicts of interest that cause inaccurate pictures do a disservice to whomever is entitled to and in need of the accurate picture. . . .

The most recent thinking about independence has been carried on by the Independence Standards Board, which has recently published *A Statement of Independence Concepts: A Conceptual Framework for Auditor Independence.* The Independence Standards Board (ISB) was established in 1997 by Securities and Exchange Commission Chairman Arthur Levitt in concert with the American Institute of Certified Public Accountants. . . .

The ISB defined auditor independence as "freedom from those pressures and other factors that compromise, or can reasonably be expected to compromise, an auditor's ability to make unbiased audit decisions." This, of course, does not mean freedom from all pressures, only those that are "so significant that they rise to a level where they compromise, or can reasonably be expected to compromise, the auditor's ability to make audit decisions without bias." By "reasonably be expected," the

report has in mind the rationally based beliefs of well-informed investors and other users of financial information. For example, if I stood to gain from a company to which I give a favorable attestation, because I am a shareholder in that company, or because the company is planning on hiring my firm to do extensive consulting work when it gets a loan from a bank which is contingent upon a favorable audit, the reasonable person would be somewhat skeptical of my ability to be unbiased in that case, not because I was a dishonorable person, but because human beings in general can be unduly influenced by such pressures.

But what sorts of pressures are there? To begin with, there are pressures that can come from relationships such as those with family, friends, acquaintances or business contacts. Standard-setting bodies issue rules that limit certain activities and relationships which they believe represent "potential sources of bias for auditors generally." As we noted, some auditors might be able to remain unbiased in such situations, but the rules apply to them also because "it is reasonable to expect audit decisions to be biased in those circumstances." "Accordingly, noncompliance with those rules might not preclude a particular auditor from being objective, but it would preclude the auditor from claiming to be independent," at least in appearance if not in reality.

Finally, not every situation can be identified or covered by a rule, so the absence of a rule covering a certain relationship does not mean the independence is not jeopardized by the relationship, if the audit decision could reasonably be expected to be compromised as a result of that relationship. "Compliance with the rules is a necessary, but not a sufficient, condition for independence."

The report then turned to the goal of auditor independence, using that goal as the focal point to determine what the auditor needs to do to achieve that independence. That is what the report meant by a conceptual framework.

The goal is "to support user reliance on the financial reporting process and to enhance management efficiency." Hence, independence is an instrumental good while the main goal to keep in mind is management efficiency.

The report next delineated four basic principles and four concepts that could be used as guidelines for deciding what interferes with or aids independence. In that context it discusses four concepts that relate to independence: (1) threats, (2) safeguards, (3) independence risk, and (4) significance of threats/effectiveness of safeguards. . . .

After setting out the four concepts, the framework turns to four basic activities necessary to evaluate auditor independence, which are called principles.

**Principle 1. Assessing the level of independence risk:** *Independence decision makers should assess the level of independence risk by considering the types and significance of threats to auditor independence and the types and effectiveness of safeguards.*
To help with this assessment, the report suggests auditors can examine five levels of independence risk. There is the level of *no independence risk*, where compromised objectivity is *virtually impossible.* There is a level of *remote independence risk*, where compromised objectivity is *very unlikely.* There is the level of *some independence risk*, where compromised objectivity is *possible.* There is the level of *high independence risk*, where compromised objectivity is *probable.* Finally, there is the level of *maximum independence risk*, where compromised objectivity is *virtually certain.*

While none of these levels can be measured precisely, there is the opportunity to describe a specific threat as belonging to one of the segments or at one of the "end points of the continuum." Thus the continuum offers a tool that enables an auditor to fulfill the obligation to assess the risk to independence.

**Principle 2. Determining the acceptability of the level of independence risk:** *After assessing the level of risk the auditor needs to determine "whether the level of independence is at an acceptable position on the independence risk continuum."*

**Principle 3. Considering benefits and costs:** *Independence decision makers should ensure that the bene-* *fits resulting from reducing independence risk by imposing additional safeguards exceed the costs of those safeguards.*

**Principle 4. Considering interested parties' views in addressing auditor independence issues:** *Independence decision makers should consider the views of investors, other users and others with an interest in the integrity of financial reporting when addressing issues related to auditor independence and should resolve those issues based on the decision makers' judgment about how best to meet the goal of auditor independence.*

Recognizing that there is no such thing as total independence, the report provides auditors with a framework that can be used in judging whether the amount of independence they have is sufficient for allowing them to avoid the risks to independence that would jeopardize their judgment or audit. . . .

Thus, in summary, the reasons for avoiding even the appearance of having a conflict of interest, which might affect one's independence, are obvious. In order for people to make their best judgments they need faith in the representations upon which they make those judgments. And representations made by those who have—or even appear to have—conflicting interests do not inspire such faith. Reasonable people, taking a commonsense approach to human behavior, would think that certain relationships would affect one's behavior. A skepticism that believes where there's smoke, there's fire, serves one well. It may be that where there appears to be a conflict, there is none, but there may also be self-delusion, and where the appearance of conflict is the only thing to exist, such a situation presents a temptation, that while currently is being resisted, sooner or later will probably prevail.

People respond on the basis of what they think. If we think someone is angry, we will respond differently to him or her than if we think they are in pain. Similarly, if we trust someone, we will respond differently than if we suspect him or her. Contrast the perceptions we have of an independent prosecutor with those we have of one appointed by the justice department. Whom do we trust more? Compare the perceptions we have of a police department report clearing officers of illicit behavior with a report of an independent panel of judges clearing those same officers. The appearance of dependence will have major effects on the estimation of the worth of all sorts of financial entities. . . .

## NOTES

1. *Encyclopedia Britannica Micropaedia,* "Accounting."

2. *United States v. Arthur Young and Co. et al.,* 104 S.Ct, 465 US 805, 1984.

3. As quoted in Abraham J. Briloff, "The 'Is' and the 'Ought'," *Accounting Today* (September 26, 1999), 6ff.

4. Gretchen Morgenson, "SEC Seeks Increased Scrutiny And New Rules for Accountants," *New York Times* (May 11, 2000), Thursday, late edition, section C Business/Financial Desk, p. 1.

5. AICPA, *Professional Standards,* Vol. 1.

6. The Commission on Auditors' Responsibilities, "Report, Conclusion and Recommendations" (New York: Commission on Auditors' Responsibilities, 1978), 3.

7. Quoted in Abraham J. Briloff, *The Truth about Corporate Accounting* (Harper & Row, 1980), 6.

8. Quoted in Briloff, ibid., 5.

9. Quoted in Briloff, ibid., 4–5.

10. Karl Stark, "Lawsuit Is Filed against Auditors for Allegheny," *Philadelphia Inquirer* (April 13, 2000), sec. D, p. 1.

11. See AICPA Code, Rule 301: Confidential client information.

12. John E. Beach, "Code of Ethics: The Professional Catch 22," *Journal of Accounting and Public Policy* 3 (1984): 311–23.

13. Appellate *Wagenheim, J.S. (Consolidated Services, Inc.) v. Grant & Co.,* 1983. 10th District, Court of Appeals, Ohio 3393.l.

14. SAS no. 1, sec. 230.

15. SAS 53.16.

# The Structural Origins of Conflicts of Interest in the Accounting Profession

*Colin Boyd*

*Accountancy is believed by its practitioners to be a profession, not a commercial venture.*

(Magill Previts, and Robinson 1998, 4)

The spectacular collapse of Enron in 2001 and the subsequent disintegration of their auditors, Arthur Andersen, was arguably the most significant scandal in modern U.S. business history. The debacle has provided enough analytical fodder to engage the minds of scores of academics, and there will no doubt be many theories advanced for the reasons behind the fraud and for the failure of the audit firm to perform its role properly.

In this paper I wish to advance my own particular theory. I suggest that a substantial contribution to the Enron collapse came from the failings of Enron's audit firm, which was itself affected by a general buildup of tensions related to conflicts of interest in large audit firms and within the accounting profession itself. These ethical tensions, like pressures between tectonic plates in geology, had built up over decades as the structure of the accounting profession evolved.

This paper will argue that there was a systemic failure to note and correct the increasing range of new conflicts of interest that were emerging from the way in which the industrial structure of the accounting profession's delivery of services evolved in the latter part of the twentieth century. These conflicts of interest placed intolerable pressures on the ethical judgments of experienced professionals employed by accounting firms that presumably otherwise espoused adherence to the highest levels of ethical integrity. . . .

## THE MODERN EVOLUTION OF PUBLIC ACCOUNTING FIRMS

For much of the twentieth century the public accounting industry had a stable industrial structure. Most professional public accountants worked in public-practice accounting firms that provided tax and accounting services to businesses, other organizations, and to that small proportion of private individuals whose financial affairs were complex. The scope of most firms was local, with operations typically confined to one office servicing one town or city and its hinterland.

Larger accounting firms operated as partnerships rather than as sole proprietorships. Recruits to the profession entered accounting firms as "articling" students ("junior auditors" in the U.S.), with each firm usually admitting only the number of students that would be required by the turnover of individuals within the firm (e.g., by death or retirement) or as required for internal business growth. In countries with a federal structure, the regulation of professional accountants and the organization of their professional institutes took place at the regional (state or provincial) level. In other countries professional institutes operated at the national level.

The structure of the accounting profession was stable up until the 1960s or so. The profession enjoyed a rather insulated and protected environment—many public accounting firms had a local or regional focus, and were employed by a solid base of permanent local clients. Accountants were historically perceived by the public to be part of a solid, conservative profession with an impeccable reputation for ethical integrity. . . .

The late 1950s and 1960s saw changes in the transport and communications infrastructures of developed countries that enabled many business organizations to expand the geographic scope of their operations from a local base to a regional and then to a national level. As the accounting profession's major clients changed their geographic scope, then so it became advantageous for ambitious accounting firms to themselves expand from a local to a regional to a national level so as to match the scope of their largest clients.

The means for accomplishing this change in geographic scope was the merger of partnerships based in different cities and towns. For example, KPMG Canada was formed from merging "more than 115 firms in communities across Canada." The evolution of national firms via successions of mergers naturally increased the degree of concentration of the industry. . . .

Global growth via international mergers was achievable for the major accounting firms because the services they offer are more or less homogeneous across national boundaries, reflecting the degree of homogeneity of accounting standards across nations. By contrast, the relative lack of homogeneity of laws across nations has obstructed the possible parallel evolution of major multinational firms in the legal profession.

Successive waves of mergers first produced the "Big Eight" accounting firms, to be followed by the "Big Six," and finally by the "Big Five." The failure of the proposed merger of KPMG and Ernst and Young in 1997 prevented further consolidation down to a "Big Four." The major structural change in public accounting in the past couple of decades has therefore been the emergence of this dominating small number of large global accounting firms.

Some statistics from 1996 demonstrate their dominance: 93 percent of the revenues earned by the top 18 accounting firms in the United States in that year went to the Big Six, while 91 percent of the employees were Big Six employees. The revenue of the smallest of the Big Six firms was one and a half times the combined revenue of the seventh- through the eighteenth-largest firms.

These data show a degree of extreme concentration of power and ownership in the accounting profession that has had no parallel in any other profession. One significant consequence is that a large proportion of the members of national or regional accounting institutes are the employees of these few giant global accounting firms. This strong concentration of interests within the membership of each accounting institute will be discussed later on in this paper. During this period of tumultuous change in the industrial structure of the profession, there was no parallel change in the basic institutional structure of the profession.

Another parallel dramatic change in the profession was the transformation of auditing from being the profession's most conspicuous and prestigious service to its later state as a low profit activity within a constellation of other far more profitable services offered by the major accounting firms.

The sequences of successive mergers may have been one of a number of factors that reduced the loyalty of clients to their auditors in the 1970s and 1980s as audit services became to be increasingly recognized to be an undifferentiated commodity product. Clients became sophisticated purchasers, shopping around for the best deal and putting intense pressure on audit prices, and thus on profits. The traditional long-term auditor–client relationship appeared to become lost in the process. Audit prices declined steadily from the 1980s onward.

A darker side of the increased instability of auditor–client relationships emerged when some companies began to resort to a practice known as "opinion shopping" (Magill and Previts 1991, 124). Here, the audit client would not just approach other accounting firms to gain price quotations but would also attempt to ascertain the degree to which each firm might interpret accounting standards so as to present the client's financial statements in the manner that management most preferred. Accounting standards are flexible, and there are alternative standards that can conceivably be validly applied to the circumstances of any client. Given that the application of different standards can produce quite different financial pictures on any given day, some clients began to see just how far they could persuade an auditor to apply a particular desired standard.

In the price-shopping and opinion-shopping turbulence of the 1980s the audit increasingly became a commodity business which had declining margins and which placed increased stress on the ability of audit firms to maintain a high level of professional integrity independent of these market forces. We thus see the first signs of newly evolving forms of conflicts of interest arising in the accounting profession.

## THE PRESSURES ON LABOR INPUTS

In the face of the propensity of clients to shop for audit services, individual accounting firms found that the only competitive variable at their disposal was price. Magill and Previts note that competitive bidding by CPA firms gradually became commonplace after a removal of a ban on the practice by the American Institute of Certified Public Accountants (AICPA) in 1972, and that "bids significantly below any reasonable measure of cost or profitability (lowballing) were generating heated criticism" (1991, 124).

If price is used as a means of attracting business, then this must either reduce the audit firm's margins, or else put pressure on the costs of providing audit services. Given that labor is the main cost of auditing, then there are only two major ways of reducing the cost of an audit in the absence of increased automation—either reduce the total labor-hours put into an audit, or else reduce the average cost of a labor-hour. It would be difficult to determine if large accounting firms did explicitly cut costs by cutting the total labor-hours put into the average audit, because part of the period when they perhaps were doing this was indeed also the time when audits were becoming partially automated via the increased use of computers.

However, as with any reduction in the cost of an audit labor-hour that comes from reducing the amount of expensive senior supervision of a particular audit, any reduction in overall audit labor-hours would be expected to automatically lower the quality of audits. Some indirect evidence of reduced audit quality did surface in the 1970s and 1980s, when there was a general increase in the number of audit failures, a subsequent increase in litigation against the major accounting firms, and consequent sharp increases in their malpractice insurance premiums.

The other means of reducing the average labor cost per hour of an audit is to increase the proportion of low-cost employees assigned to any given audit. In the case of accounting firms, the low-cost employees are the articling students, or junior auditors. One major transformation in the evolution of the modern accounting profession has been a change in the approach to the use of junior employees. In the past, as was noted above, articling students were taken on primarily to meet the internal needs of the accounting firm, either as future replacements for normal labor turnover, or else to meet the needs of internal business growth.

The 1970s and 1980s saw the major accounting firms beginning to employ many more ar-

ticling students than they had historically needed to replace retirees and to accommodate growth. There appeared to be no adverse reactions to this phenomenon, either from the professional institutes (who stood to gain more revenues from the resultant inflation in their membership numbers) or from undergraduate business schools (who were pleased to see the demand for their accounting students increase).

One of the reasons there was no concern for the increase in employment of articling students was the fact that there was an increasing demand for accountants in industry and commerce, outside of public practice. Large proportions of articling students in the big accounting firms ended up taking up offers of employment as accountants with the firms' audit clients relatively early on in their careers with the accounting firms. It may even be that the accounting firms *had* to employ more articling students in the first place because of this new form of erosion of their employee numbers.

Whatever the origins of this new phenomenon, the resulting strategy proved to be very positive for the big accounting firms. The shedding of the newly excessive numbers of articling students to clients not only produced both happy clients and happy students (who had now given up on any ambition to be public practice partners), but it also seeded the business sector with friends of the big accounting firms so as to ensure a high probability of future business relationships with these "biased" clients. It was a clever strategy that had the added benefit of providing the big firms with cheap labor at the very time when price competition increased the pressure to reduce audit costs.

In her recent book about Arthur Andersen, Barbara Ley Toffler notes the existence of this general labor strategy: "like the other big accounting firms, [it] made its money by using young, low-paid staff to do the majority of its work" (2003, 31–32). Elsewhere, she describes the motivation of the firm's new junior auditing recruits, and of Andersen's explicit strategy for their use:

> They all knew that their chance of making partner was slim, and that they were in for a rigorous, exhausting few years as the "grunts." But there was that big fat brass ring at the end. Even if they did not make partner, the opportunities for an Arthur Andersen-trained accountant were many and choice. We would "tell them that they should find other employment because their future was limited," said Spacek in an oral history, "but . . . help them get into good jobs because they were what I call our "fifth column." When they got into the business, they remembered their alma mater, that's all." The point was to maintain goodwill, so that even the people who didn't make it remembered their experience fondly and would go out of their way to steer business to the good old Firm. (Toffler 2003, 25–26, quoting from Spacek 1989, 124. Leonard Spacek was the most famous managing partner in the history of Arthur Andersen.)

The ethics of this strategy of the big accounting firms encouraging former audit team members to transfer to employment within the organizations that they were continuing to audit did not appear to be a matter for widespread concern in the immediate period leading up to the Enron scandal. If these kinds of transfers were perceived to be only from within the junior ranks of accountants being shaken out from the big firms, then this practice might not have been considered to be anything other than mildly questionable.

The Enron case, however, revealed employee transfers between the auditor and the audit client on a huge scale, and at senior levels from within Arthur Andersen's Enron audit team. A *New York Times* article described the closeness of the relationship, and hinted that Andersen indeed encouraged these employee transfers as a way to gain more nonaudit business from Enron:

> Investigators . . . are looking at Arthur Andersen, which so thoroughly blended its corporate DNA with its client's that a steady stream of Andersen employees came to work for Enron at the trading company's futuristic downtown tower. . . . One Enron vice president, who was laid off in December, said Andersen often had as many as 250 employees working inside Enron's 50-story skyscraper. "They were involved in about everything there," the vice president said. . . . This physical proximity was accentuated by the fact that so many Enron employees had once worked at Andersen: . . . the company's chief accounting officer, Richard A. Causey, had started at Andersen. . . . "I remember them saying that once you got to a certain level at Andersen, they would suggest you tried to get hired by a lot of clients like Enron," the former Enron vice president said. "This would provide them with access to more accounting jobs." (Van Natta, Schwartz, and Yardley 2002)

Another article in the same edition of the *New York Times* indicates one type of additional nonaudit accounting work that Enron was giving to Arthur Andersen: "Moreover, Enron turned over to Andersen some responsibility for its internal bookkeeping, blurring a fundamental division of responsibilities that companies employ to assure the honesty and completeness of their financial figures. Further obscuring the line between an independent auditor and corporate management, many of Enron's financial executives had moved there from Andersen" (Stevenson and Gerth 2002).

The revelation that many members of Andersen's Enron audit team had moved into financial management positions at Enron has provoked the consideration of placing stronger restrictions on individual accountants making such moves from audit team to audit client. As noted above, the big accounting firms had encouraged this type of transfer for many years as a part of the modern evolution of the industry. There were no prior prohibitions on such transfers, even though Congress had actually queried the ethics of this practice back in 1976.

## THE STRATEGY OF HORIZONTAL INTEGRATION

Auditing was becoming remarkably unattractive to the major accounting firms: audits offered declining margins, produced difficult ethical dilemmas, cost a fortune to insure, and produced risks of time-consuming litigation which at the extreme could bankrupt a firm. But in the 1980s, against all intuition, the competition for audit clients began to intensify. Why did competition remain so intense?

The reason why the audit business remained desirable was because of the spin-off benefits that an audit could produce. An audit allowed an accounting firm to enter the client's business and to discover how the client's various business systems operated. If the accounting firm tangentially detected aspects of the client's systems that could be improved, then there would be an opportunity for the selling of consulting services to fix the client's problems. These services could be priced so as to give a high margin, thus offsetting the low margin audit business that enabled the firm to access the high margin business opportunity in the first place. The audit effectively became a "loss-leader" product for the accounting firms, producing at the extreme a stimulus for "lowball" bids for audits.

The predominant strategic response of public accounting firms to the price/cost pressures of audit competition in the profession was thus the offering of other parallel services to audit customers: "Firms are branching out into consulting practices and other nontraditional specialties as the one-time staple of audit services is being squeezed" (Conrad 1994).

The big accounting firms began to offer a wider range of business advisory services (eventually including even legal services, as noted above) and began to view themselves primarily as high-level business advisors rather than as accounting firms focused primarily on auditing.

## CONFLICTS OF INTEREST BETWEEN AUDITING AND CONSULTING

The emergence of possible conflicts of interest for audit firms related to the simultaneous sale of consulting services to audit clients was widely recognized by critics of the accounting profession, but this core problem remained substantially unrecognized and uncorrected by the profession itself.

Arthur Levitt, one of the profession's leading critics, and former head of the U.S. Securities and Exchange Commission (SEC) claims that "conflicts of interest . . . inevitably occur when a company pays an accounting firm consulting fees that far outweigh the audit fee" (Levin 2002a, 15). Elsewhere in his recent book he writes that "More and more, it became clear that the auditors did not want to do anything to rock the boat with clients, potentially jeopardizing their chief source of income. Consulting contracts were turning accounting firms into extensions of management—even cheerleaders at times" (Levitt 2002a, 116). . . .

In the case of Enron, it was widely noted that Arthur Andersen provided consulting services to Enron alongside its audit service: "In recent years, concerns have mounted about whether auditors are truly independent of their clients. Accounting firms have come to rely more on consulting work rather than on traditional audits for their revenues, raising questions about their ability to stand up to clients if improper bookkeeping is suspected. . . . In Enron's case, consulting work accounted for slightly more than half of the $52 million that Andersen received in fees in 2000" (Abelson and Glater 2002).

For Enron, the press suspected a conflict of interest within Arthur Andersen because the revenue split between consulting and audit revenues was 1 to 1. In the later case of the collapse of WorldCom (where Andersen was again the auditor) the revenue split between Andersen's consulting and audit revenues from WorldCom was 3 to 1, suggesting an even greater likelihood of a conflict of interest influencing Andersen's audit independence.

The splits between audit and consulting revenues from the same client that are typically quoted in the press do not in fact reveal the full scale of the conflicts of interest that might actually have existed in these cases. The business journalists (and critics such as Arthur Levitt) have overlooked the fact that the profit margin from consulting can be as much as three times the margin from auditing. Such a differential in margins would imply that Andersen's annual consulting profit from World-Com was about nine times higher than their annual WorldCom auditing profit.

In a context where the power of audit partners had declined because of diversification into consulting, it is not surprising that there was intense pressure on the audit team to not rock the boat. The consulting profits were simply too high to be able to consider sacrificing them for the sake of adhering to a professional principle in auditing that no one in the outside world might ever hear about. . . .

The Big Five and the AICPA had consistently claimed that auditor independence was particularly unaffected by consulting. They argued that since there was no empirical evidence of conflicts of interest between auditing and consulting, then such conflicts could not be presumed to exist. Levitt refers to this as the "no smoking gun" argument (2002a, 129). A number of research studies had sought to produce empirical evidence of a conflict of interest between audit and consulting work provided for the same client, but these had generally been inconclusive.

Enron has provided the "smoking gun" evidence, indicating that the profession had reached the stage where commercial interests simply overwhelmed allegiance to professional integrity. The outcome has been catastrophic for the profession. This begs the question as to why, when the problem of conflicts of interest had been known about for so long, had so little

been done to protect the sanctity of the profession's core activity?

## THE POWER AND INFLUENCE OF THE BIG FIVE

The Big Five have without doubt had an enormous direct influence on the accounting institutes via representation of their employees both on the directing boards of the institutes, and as elected officials. However, there are other less obvious ways in which the Big Five almost certainly influenced the institutes.

Earlier in this paper I suggested that the evolution of a few giant accounting firms had a parallel pattern of influence within the membership of accounting institutes. The most obvious form of influence on institute affairs relates to pure scale. As the Big Five became so large and dominant within the accounting profession, then the sheer number of accountants that they employed who were also members of accounting institutes gave the Big Five an effective dominant voice within each institute. . . .

The growing conflicts of interest between auditing and consulting within the Big Five's business activities would thus have been mirrored in subtle ways within the accounting institutes themselves, most obviously manifest by their reluctance to support initiatives designed to eliminate these conflicts of interest. There are a fair number of examples of such reluctance, but I shall only deal with two of these.

In the United Kingdom back in 1992 the Auditing Practices Board (APB) produced a discussion paper proposing several initiatives as a means of preventing any reoccurrence of the 1989/90 accounting scandals in the UK. Two of the APB proposals were:

1. The compulsory periodic rotation of auditors through individual audit clients to prevent a close relationship from developing. One suggested plan was that an auditor, once appointed, must be retained by the client for

5 years, and then must be compulsorily replaced by another auditor who would then remain in place for another 5 years.

2. That any firm auditing a client should not simultaneously provide any non-audit services for that client. (Auditing Practices Board 1992)

The profession successfully lobbied against these initiatives in the UK.

A more recent example came in 2000, when Arthur Levitt's legislative proposals were similarly thwarted by the profession: "When I was chairman of the Securities and Exchange Commission, we put into place a number of reforms to improve audits and minimize conflicts of interest. But we were largely unsuccessful in persuading accounting firms to separate their auditing businesses from their consulting businesses and in convincing the auditing profession to do a better job of policing itself" (Levitt 2002b).

Levitt's failure was attributable to intense political lobbying: "The profession has succeeded in fighting off tougher regulation over the decades, but it reached its apex in political power only in the last few years, a reflection of the industry's mushrooming campaign contributions and increased lobbying. . . . At the height of the fight between the industry and Mr. Levitt in the second half of 2000, all the Big Five accounting firms sharply increased their political donations and spending on lobbying. Andersen doubled its lobbying budget, to $1.6 million. . . . The investment paid off" (Labaton 2002).

We therefore see that the Big Five had not just become powerful within the accounting institutes themselves, but that their power and influence had extended deep into the external political sphere as well.

To all intents and purposes, by the end of the twentieth century the Big Five had overwhelmed the accounting profession to such an extent that the profession no longer appeared to have any voice independent of the interests of the Big Five (Kliegman 1999). And unfortunately for the whole profession, when the commercial interests of these big firms conflicted with the protection of the integrity of the core activity of the profession, then the profession's interests were apparently sacrificed.

## WILL THE SARBANES-OXLEY ACT WORK?

The Enron scandal directly prompted the passing of the Sarbanes-Oxley Act in the United States in 2002, in the face of strong lobbying by the accounting profession. Those sections of that act that deal with the issues that I have raised in this paper will be discussed below.

With regard to audit team members joining the audit client, section 206 of the Sarbanes-Oxley Act directs that "The CEO, Controller, CFO, Chief Accounting Officer or person in an equivalent position cannot have been employed by the company's audit firm during the 1-year period preceding the audit" (U.S. House of Representatives 2002, 31).

This measure will to some extent prevent conflicts of interest arising from the transfers of employees at the highest levels, although it does not bar the transfer of audit team members into intermediate or transitory positions within audit clients. The fact that the ban is just for 1 year seems to be insufficient—the financial rewards may be such that an employee subject to the transfer ban may be willing to step out of the ring for 1 year. A 1-year ban is also far too short a time for the audit team's work practices to have changed sufficiently so as to render a former audit team member's knowledge of these practices obsolete.

Section 203 of the Sarbanes-Oxley Act directs that "the lead audit or coordinating partner and the reviewing partner must rotate off of the audit every 5 years" (U.S. House of Representatives 2002, 30). This compulsory rotation of the audit leaders falls far short of the full rotation of the audit firm itself that was originally proposed in the United Kingdom, as noted above.

However, Section 207 of the Sarbanes-Oxley Act does direct the Comptroller General of the United States to conduct a study and review of the potential effects of requiring the mandatory rotation of registered public accounting firms within 1 year of the enactment of the act (U.S. House of Representatives 2002, 31). This study may, of course, be the subject of intensive lobbying by the accounting profession, and so it remains to be seen if this deferred study will result in any change in the status quo.

From the perspective of this paper, the most relevant element of the Sarbanes-Oxley Act is Section 201, which limits the range of services an auditor can offer to a client alongside the audit. The prohibited services include:

(1) bookkeeping or other services related to the accounting records or financial statements of the audit client; (2) financial information systems design and implementation; (3) appraisal or valuation services, fairness opinions, or contribution-in-kind reports; (4) actuarial services; (5) internal audit outsourcing services; (6) management functions or human resources; (7) broker or dealer, investment adviser, or investment banking services; (8) legal services and expert services unrelated to the audit; (9) any other service that the [Public Company Accounting Oversight] Board determines, by regulation, is impermissible. (U.S. House of Representatives 2002, 28)

The prohibited activities in the list seem to be drawn up as if the conflict of interest with auditing are perceived to mostly take the form of operational or production conflicts of interest for the auditor. A number of the conflicts of interest that I have presented in this paper originate within the marketing and sales activities of the big accounting firms, encouraged by internal reward systems and cultural norms. Accordingly, the Sarbanes-Oxley Act may have missed the mark here by not considering those audit conflicts of interest that are marketing-related.

With the proviso that item (9) above allows the oversight board to add anything to the list, it is of interest to note that this list does not explicitly ban the offering of consulting services alongside audit services. The act does however place a minor limitation on the offering of such services, in that they must all be preapproved by the client's audit committee, and then openly reported. The degree to which client audit committees will be effective as a moral screen to eliminate consulting conflicts of interest remains to be seen.

## THE FUTURE EVOLUTION OF THE PROFESSION

Both prior to and following the rapid demise of Arthur Andersen, three of the four remaining big accounting firms distanced themselves from their original consulting divisions to varying degrees. However, given that there is no outright legal prohibition on their offering many consulting services to audit clients, it is conceivable that if the profession experiences a few years of negligible levels of controversy in the immediate future, then some firms may be tempted to start to use the audit as a lever to expand consulting again.

The utter commercial logic of consulting being an automatic companion to auditing was, as noted above, illustrated by the regrowth of a new consulting division within Arthur Andersen following the splitting off of Andersen Consulting. In the light of that commercial logic I remain skeptical about the effectiveness of any rule other than a complete prohibition on the offering of consulting services to audit clients as the means of preventing commercial pressures from affecting audit independence and integrity.

It appears almost inevitable, given the profession's apparent inability to police itself, and given that audit firms will still be allowed to offer some consulting services in the future, that some further scandal will eventually occur, prompting an externally dictated prohibition on the simultaneous provision of consulting and audit services to the same client. . . .

As with a prohibition on the offering of consulting services, and the reform of accounting firm cultures, it is difficult to conceive of how any reduction of the degree of concentration in the accounting profession could ever be initiated from within the profession itself. All of the evidence suggests that the modern evolution of the accounting profession has been down a one-way street, and that a voluntary reversal of this evolution back toward an era of greater professional integrity would be extremely hard to effect. The future evolution of the profession would appear to lie in the hands of external regulators and legislators, implying that the fundament of any profession, self-regulation, is forever lost to the accounting profession.

## REFERENCES

Abelson, R., and J. D. Glater. 2002. "Who's Keeping the Accountants Accountable?" *New York Times* (January 15), p. 1.

Conrod, M. 1994. "The Bottom Line Top 30 Accounting Firms," *The Bottom Line* (April): 1.

Kliegman, E. J. 1999. "The Demise of the Profession." *Accounting Today* (January 27): 6, 12–13.

Labaton, S. 2002. "Auditing Firms Exercise Power In Washington." *New York Times* (January 19), 1.

Levitt, A. 2002a. *Take On the Street.* New York: Pantheon Books.

———. 2002b. "Who Audits the Auditors?" *New York Times* (January 17), p. 29.

Magill, H. T., and G. J. Previts. 1991, *CPA Professional Responsibilities: An Introduction.* Cincinnati: South-Western Publishing.

Magill, H. T., G. J. Previts, and T. R. Robinson. 1998. *The CPA Profession: Oportunities, Responsibilities and Services.* Upper Saddle River, NJ: Prentice Hall.

Spacek, L. 1989. *The Growth of Arthur Andersen & Co., 1928–1973; An Oral History.* New York: Garland Publishing.

Stevenson, R. W., and J. Gerth. 2002. "Web of Safeguards Failed as Enron Fell." *New York Times* (January 20), p. 1.

Toffler, B. L. 2003. *Final Accounting: Ambition, Greed, and the Fall of Arthur Andersen.* New York: Broadway Books.

U.S. House of Representatives, 107th Congress 2d Session, Report 107–610. 2002. The Sarbanes-Oxley Act of 2002. Available from the Senate Banking Committee Web site at http://banking.senate.gov/pss/acctrfm/conf_rpt.pdf

Van Natta, Jr., D., J. Schwartz, and J. Yardley. 2002. "In Houston, the Lines Dividing Politics, Business, and Society Are Especially Blurry." *New York Times* (January 20), p. 25.

# Individual Responsibility in the American Corporate System: Does Sarbanes-Oxley Strike the Right Balance?

*John R. Boatright*

In *The Devil's Dictionary,* the American journalist Ambrose Bierce defines a corporation as "An ingenious device for obtaining individual profit without individual responsibility."[1] This famous quip expresses a recurring theme among critics of the modem corporation, that individual responsibility has been eroded and ought to be restored. This is especially true in the aftermath of the scandals at Enron, WorldCom, Tyco, and other companies. The resulting public outrage reflects a deep sense of injustice at the possibility

© John R. Boatright, *Business & Professional Ethics Journal* 23, nos. 1 and 2.

that top executives could inflict such great losses on investors and employees without suffering greater personal consequences. Many people believe that Kenneth Lay, Jeffrey Skilling, and Andrew Fastow—to name only key figures at Enron—deserve to be locked up for an extended period of time and forced to give up their ill-gotten gains. A similar sentiment is often expressed about the accountants at Arthur Andersen and the various bankers and lawyers who provided crucial assistance.

The legal process has not yet run its course, and perhaps in the end justice will be done. This prospect presumes, however, that we know what justice requires. But to what extent should executives be held personally responsible when corporations engage in significant misconduct? And what is the responsibility of accountants, bankers, and attorneys who, in legal terms, "aid and abet" wrongful conduct? These questions have received extensive attention in American law, and a certain balance has been achieved that places limits on the responsibility of individuals in corporations. However, a widespread feeling that existing law has failed to satisfy the demands of justice prompted Congress to include several key provisions in the Sarbanes-Oxley Act that address individual responsibility.

In signing this legislation, President George W. Bush claimed that it ushers in a "new ethic of personal responsibility in the business community,"[2] and he emphasized the personal consequences for executives by saying, "No more easy money for corporate criminals, just hard time."[3] Despite this tough language, the Sarbanes-Oxley Act does not appear to increase significantly the responsibility of individuals. This result, I believe, is for the best, because the prevailing legal treatment of individual responsibility is generally sound. I argue that the American corporate system requires a certain separation of individual responsibility from an executive's corporate role and that, for this reason, we should be cautious about efforts to hold executives more accountable or liable personally for their actions. One danger posed by the recent scandals is that public outrage at some admittedly egregious conduct might create pressures for unwise reforms.

The responsibility at issue here is that of individuals who are acting within their role in an organization, which is to say within the scope of their authority. Individuals in business enterprises, acting on their own, can also commit crimes and other misdeeds for which they bear full responsibility. Thus, executives who loot or defraud their own company or who engage in obstruction of justice or insider trading deserve to be prosecuted and punished. The allegations against Dennis Kozlowski at Tyco, Bernie Ebbers at WorldCom, and the Rigas family at Adelphia, for example, address criminal conduct for which these individuals are personally liable. Although some criminal conduct took place at Enron—such as Fastow's unauthorized personal benefit from partnerships he managed—the collapse of the company was not due to criminal wrongdoing but to excessive risk taking. In assessing the responsibility of Skilling and Lay, then, we need to distinguish between their flawed pursuit of a plausible business plan and their criminal actions, if any. It is responsibility for the former kind of conduct that is at issue here, not for the latter.[4]

## THE SARBANES-OXLEY ACT

The Sarbanes-Oxley Act contains four provisions that bear on individual responsibility. Section 302, the certification provision, requires that the chief executive officer and the chief financial officer of companies subject to Securities and Exchange Commission (SEC) jurisdiction personally certify certain reports submitted to the commission. Specifically, the signing officer is required to certify that he or she has reviewed the report; that to the best of the officer's knowledge the report is complete and accurate; that it fairly represents the financial situation of the company; that effective internal controls have been established and evaluated; and that any deficiencies in the control system and any fraud involving management or those involved in the control system have been disclosed to the auditors and the audit committee of the board.

Section 304, the forfeiture provision, mandates that in the event the corporation is forced to restate its earnings due to misconduct with regard to financial reporting requirements, the chief executive officer and the chief financial officer shall return to the company any bonus or incentive compensation and any profits from the sale of securities in the 12-month period following the issuance or filing of the report that contains the misreported earnings. Potentially the most burdensome requirement of the Sarbanes-Oxley Act is Section 404, which requires management to assume responsibility for establishing and maintaining an adequate system of internal control and assessing the effectiveness of this system annually.

Title IX of the Sarbanes-Oxley Act, known as the White-Collar Crime Penalty Enhancement Act of 2002 (WCCPEA), significantly increases the fines and sentences of a number of offences, including fraud and conspiracy. The increases range from a factor of 4 to a factor of 10 the number of years to which an executive may be imprisoned, and some fines are increased by factors ranging from 5 to 20. The act instructs the United States Sentencing Commission to revise the Federal Sentencing Guidelines to reflect these increased penalties and the seriousness of these offenses. Section 906 of the WCCPEA also contains penalties for violating the certification provision. Anyone who certifies a report knowing that it does not conform to all requirements of the Securities Exchange Act shall be fined up to $1 million and/or imprisoned up to 10 years or both. A "willful" viola-

tion increases the fine to a maximum of $5 million and the prison term to a maximum of 20 years.

Whether these provisions of Sarbanes-Oxley succeed in increasing the individual responsibility of corporate executives remains to be seen. Much depends on how the rules are interpreted and enforced. However, legal scholars who have addressed this question tend to be pessimistic, describing these provisions as efforts by Congress to express outrage and impress the public without significantly altering the existing legal obligations of officers.

CEOs and CFOs are already liable under the Securities Exchange Act for documents filed by their companies if they are aware of material discrepancies, even if they do not sign them. Thus, the certification requirement adds little beyond a formal requirement that the officer personally sign certain documents. Moreover, the officer is still signing not as an individual but on behalf of the corporation, and what is being certified is only that the information contained in the documents is accurate to the best of that person's knowledge. No officer is in a position to verify fully the financial data in corporate reports and must, of necessity, rely on the work of others. In addition, chief executive and chief financial officers have a preexisting fiduciary duty under corporate law to ensure that adequate internal controls are in place. Signing a document may focus an officer's attention on this legal obligation, but this effect, whatever its force, is largely psychological and symbolic.

The forfeiture provision is innovative inasmuch as it allows a prosecutor to enforce restitution to the corporation, but such restitution can already be sought by the corporation through suits for fraud. There is nothing in Sarbanes-Oxley that would prevent a corporation and its shareholders from forgoing such restitution or from reimbursing or indemnifying officers for any losses under this provision. Prosecutors already have the power to force an executive to give up ill-gotten gains as part of a legal settlement of criminal charges.

The WCCPEA does not change the legal elements of fraud and conspiracy—the charges under which most white-collar prosecutions are brought—nor does it significantly ease the main impediments to successful prosecutions. In particular, the difficulties of showing knowledge and intent on the part of the white-collar defendants remain. The increased penalties under the WCCPEA can be effective only if prosecutors seek and judges impose sentences that take advantage of the new law. The fact that maximum penalties have seldom been imposed in the past gives scant assurance that the increased penalties will provide much deterrent effect.

Regardless of whether the Sarbanes-Oxley Act makes any changes with respect to individual responsibility, the question of how much responsibility officers and directors and other corporate personnel should bear must be answered. This is not an empirical question about what impact the law will have but a normative question about what the law should be. The answer depends on considerations not only of justice but also of public policy, and these two considerations may require some trade-off. For example, attempts to hold executives more liable as a matter of justice might make corporations less efficient and productive and thus be undesirable as a matter of public policy. In any event, we need to clarify what it means to hold officers, directors, and others more responsible and what we want to achieve by doing so.

## PROBLEMS IN ASSIGNING RESPONSIBILITY

The word "responsibility" has several meanings, but I use it here in the sense of being answerable or accountable for what one has done.[5] This sense, which has received exten-

sive treatment in moral philosophy and legal theory, assumes that a person has failed to perform some moral or legal obligation and deserves to be blamed or punished. The main concern in both the philosophical and legal literatures has been to determine the conditions under which one can rightfully be blamed or punished. These conditions for responsibility are generally held to be that a person acts freely and has the appropriate mental state. When an individual is responsible in the sense of being answerable or accountable, justice requires that there be consequences for a failure to act appropriately, and an injustice has occurred if a person does not bear these consequences.

In business, the consequences in question are often legal consequences, such as paying compensation or fines or serving time in prison. However, consequences may also be imposed in the market by various corporate constituencies. Thus, errant executives may suffer loss of compensation and reputation when they are dismissed for misconduct. Shareholders can drive down the price of a company's stock and with it the executives' compensation. Customers may also punish an executive by ceasing to do business with the company. Any consideration of individual responsibility, then, must take account of the disciplining effects of both law and the market.

The law and the market represent, respectively, the public and private realms in which corporations operate. Insofar as the law determines the responsibility of corporate personnel, it reflects the judgment of public officials—legislators, judges, and regulators—about how best to control the corporation in the interests of society. The market, on the other hand, settles questions about individual responsibility through contracting among private parties. Not only can shareholders impose responsibility on executives and other employees above that set by law, but they can also relieve these persons of legally imposed responsibility by indemnifying or insuring them for any settlements or fines. Public regulation and private contracting work together inasmuch as the law often reflects the contracts that individuals would make in an effort to achieve efficiency. Indeed, that law should attempt to secure efficient market outcomes is a central tenet of the law and economics movement.

The modern corporation creates a number of different problems with holding individuals responsible in the sense of being answerable or accountable. One problem, which is addressed by the standard philosophical and legal treatments of responsibility, is the need to show that a person performed a wrongful act (or omission) with the necessary mental state. In law, these are the elements of *actus reus* (the "guilty act") and *mens rea* (the "guilty mind"). Although corporations can act only through persons, the fragmentation of decision making and action and the diffusion of knowledge in organizations often makes it difficult to place responsibility on any given individual or group of individuals. Even though a wrong has been done and some response is required as a matter of justice, it may be unjust to blame or punish specific individuals. Under such conditions it may be appropriate to assign only collective or corporate responsibility.

A second problem, which is not commonly addressed in moral philosophy but has been extensively considered in the legal literature, concerns the assignment of responsibility when business is done in the corporate form. The source of this problem is the use of contracts to define the obligations and duties of one party to the other and specifically the use of agency relations. By means of contracts, individuals become bound to serve the will of others and to carry out their objectives. Thus, insofar as a corporate officer, such as a CEO, is an agent of the shareholders, a question arises as to whether that individual or the corporation itself should be held responsible for any misconduct. Does an agent, who is pledged

to serve the interests of another, thereby cease to be a responsible person?

The legal answer to this question is complex and has changed over time, but an enduring principle of law is that no one can evade responsibility for a crime merely by acting as an agent or a member of a corporation. Individuals are also generally held accountable as an accomplice whenever they aid, counsel or otherwise facilitate a person in the commission of a crime. However, in cases of less serious conduct, such as reckless harm, the legal principle of *respondeat superior* has been applied, whereby the principal is responsible for the actions of an agent, provided that the agent is acting within the scope of his or her authority. Furthermore, individuals may be held accountable by law for failing to control the behavior of subordinates when they have an obligation to do so in virtue of their position in the corporate hierarchy.

The law's treatment of individual responsibility results from the pursuit of at least three different objectives. One objective is to deter actions that cause harm to the public, as when the law imposes a responsibility with regard to safe and properly branded products, safe and healthy working conditions, and fair and efficient markets. These matters are the subjects of the law in such areas as consumer protection, occupational health and safety, antitrust, and securities markets. A second objective is to secure compensation for wrongful harms, which is the subject matter of tort law, and the third is to seek appropriate punishment for criminal conduct by means of fines and imprisonment. These three objectives may be summarized as deterrence, compensation, and retribution.

These three objectives of the law are often pursued together. For example, product liability law seeks both to deter companies from producing defective products and to compensate the victims of such products on the market. However, the effects of imposing individual responsibility may be different for each of these objectives. Personal liability might have a greater deterrent effect than imposing liability on the corporation, but a corporation usually has deeper pockets for providing adequate compensation. A critical question in law is the extent to which we should criminalize undesirable economic behavior and seek to impose criminal penalties, whether they be on individuals or corporations. For example, should antitrust violations, such as price-fixing, or securities violations, such as insider trading, be subject to criminal prosecution as opposed to civil action? Generally, criminal prosecution is appropriate only for actions that are regarded as morally wrong (*mala in se*), and its use for the enforcement of economic regulation, which involves actions that, for the most part, are wrong only in virtue of some legislation (*mala prohibita*), may undermine the integrity of the legal system.

In considering the extent to which we should attempt to hold individuals responsible in the sense of answerable or accountable for misconduct that occurs within a corporate setting, we need, first, to identify our objectives. In holding individuals responsible, are we trying to achieve deterrence, compensation, retribution or some combination of these objectives? Second, we need to separate what justice requires from what is socially desirable as a matter of public policy. In particular, compensation and retribution are required by justice, but deterrence is primarily a matter of achieving a social good and, thus, belongs to the realm of public policy.

Whatever our objective in holding individuals responsible, we must have a full understanding of the nature of corporate misconduct and the consequences of the various alternatives designed to prevent it. This is especially true in view of Forrester's law, which holds that complex systems operate in counterintuitive ways and that, as a result, plausible interventions tend to have unexpected outcomes. The lesson of Forrester's law for corporate misconduct is that attempting to hold individuals more responsible may be ineffective and may even have unintended and undesirable consequences. This lesson has particular application to the development of the law that bears on corporate misconduct.

The question of individual versus organizational sanctions has a long history in law. During the formative period of corporations, individuals had sole and unlimited liability for corporate conduct for reasons already explained. The possibility of corporate punishment had to await the development of a suitable legal theory of enterprise or vicarious liability that was done first in the context of torts and then in the regulation of corporate conduct generally. However, the development of this theory proceeded primarily by the application of existing legal doctrines. That is, it sought above all to make the law coherent rather than morally justified.

Moreover, the development of the law has paid little attention to the practical effect of punishment for individuals and corporations. The main body of work, which is identified with the Chicago School, has applied neoclassical economic theory, which treats both individuals and corporations as rational economic actors. The result is a theory of optimal fines for corporations, according to which the fine should be a function of the monetary gain to the corporation (or the loss to the victim, if greater) and the probability of detection and successful prosecution. A drawback of this approach is that the corporation is regarded as a "black box," which produces a rational response to the threat of punishment. What takes place inside the corporation itself is taken to be either unknowable or irrelevant. As long as the corporation is the rational economic actor of neoclassical economic theory, this "black-box" view is adequate, but ample evidence exists to show that individuals and corporations do not always respond as economic theory predicts.

More promising theoretical approaches to the question of individual and corporate sanctions are agency theory and transaction cost economics, which analyze behavior within a firm, and the behavioral approach to law and economics, which focuses on how people actually behave in markets. The former approach is an extension of the Chicago School insofar as agency theory and transaction costs economics retain the principle that individuals and corporations behave rationally. However, these tools enable economic analysis to get inside the "black box" and explain the internal workings of firms. Although the behavioral approach rejects the assumption of economic rationality, it is intended by its advocates to advance the economic analysis of law with a more realistic account of human behavior. The two approaches agree that economic analysis of whatever kind provides the best descriptive and prescriptive guide to the law.

In what follows, I apply the insights provided by agency theory, transaction cost economics, and behavioral law and economics to the question of individual responsibility within the American system of corporate governance. The provisions of the Sarbanes-Oxley Act that seek to hold individuals more responsible reflect an understandable moralistic response, to the current scandals. However, my main thesis is that we ought to temper our outrage with a realistic understanding of the practical effects of different assignments of responsibility. We need to strike a balance between the responsibility placed on individuals and that applied to the corporation itself.

## AN AGENCY THEORY, TRANSACTION COST PERSPECTIVE

Questions about individual responsibility are part of a larger, ongoing debate about how best to regulate corporations so as to prevent misconduct like the accounting frauds that occurred at Enron, WorldCom, and other companies. Whether to impose penalties primarily on individuals or the corporation is one question, but another, equally important one is whether to use government regulation, including the criminal law, or to rely on market mechanisms.

The main objective of both government and market regulation is deterrence. Retribution is achieved by existing laws that hold executives criminally liable for actions that are not within the scope of their authority. However, most corporate misconduct involves white-collar offenses in which individuals are pursuing legitimate business goals, albeit in unethical or illegal ways. For such misconduct, deterrence rather than retribution is more appropriate. Furthermore, most corporate misconduct involves regulatory violations (*mala prohibita*), which are not commonly regarded as morally reprehensible (*mala in se*) and thus not deserving of retributive punishment. The objective of compensation can generally be secured most readily by holding corporations responsible inasmuch as they usually have deeper pockets than individuals. In examining the question of individual responsibility, then, I focus primarily on deterrence as the objective.

If deterrence is the objective, then the choice between individual and corporate responsibility and the choice of sanctions or penalties are based primarily on considerations of effectiveness and cost. Agency theory enables us to assess these factors. In corporations with a separation of ownership and control, the shareholders are principals who hire managers to serve as their agents. This arrangement creates an agency problem because the managers, although under a commitment to act in the shareholders' interest, may pursue their own, divergent interest. Shareholders and managers also have different risk preferences that need to be reconciled. The expenses incurred by shareholder-principals in controlling their manager-agents constitute agency costs.

From an agency perspective, if managers were perfect agents, always acting in the shareholders' interest, corporate misconduct would be rare. The reason is that managers, who hold an undiversified investment in a firm, can be expected to be more risk averse than shareholders, who are easily able to diversify their portfolio. Risk-averse managers would be unlikely to engage in misconduct solely for the benefit of shareholders in view of the uncompensated risk that they would incur. . . .

Corporate misconduct does occur, and so in order to explain it, we must drop the assumption that managers are perfect agents and assume instead that misconduct is sufficiently in the manager's interest to overcome the risk. From an agency theory perspective, then, corporate misconduct must be understood as a form of conflict of interest in which managers make rational choices that advance their own interest in the organization. Some misconduct may benefit shareholders, especially if it is undetected, but there is no reason to believe that misconduct necessarily benefits shareholders, much less that such benefits are the intended aim of corporate actors. Even if misconduct is committed by managers out of self-interest, though, it is still difficult to understand why, being generally risk averse, they would engage in misconduct that courts dismissal and even criminal prosecution.

One situation in which senior managers would have a strong incentive to engage in misconduct occurs when the firm is faced with insolvency and the accompanying threat of job loss for the whole managerial team. Faced with such a dire situation, any means for remaining solvent would be attractive, especially since the misconduct is unlikely to be discovered if management's efforts succeed in saving the firm. This so-called "last period" problem is exacerbated if the consequences for such misconduct are borne primarily by the corporation and its shareholders.

The incentives in the "last period," which were certainly present at Enron and World-Com, can also be found in solvent companies in which managers cannot realize the full value of enormous compensation packages without engaging in misconduct. For such managers, the difference between the incentive effects of insolvency and of subpar performance may be small. Pressure can also be applied to lower-level employees that make misconduct a rational choice, especially when the risk of criminal prosecution and organizational sanctions for misconduct are slight and the threat of job loss from not engaging in misconduct is great.

Given this agency analysis of misconduct, the question of whether to hold individuals or corporations responsible is one to which the Coase theorem is applicable. On the Coase theorem, if transaction costs were negligible, these two different assignments of liability would be equally efficient in preventing misconduct. If full responsibility for misconduct were placed on corporations, then they would seek to transfer some of the burden to managers, who would then have an incentive not to engage in misconduct or else bear the consequences themselves. Similarly, if full responsibility were placed on managers, they would transfer some of the risk to the corporation in the form of demands for higher compensation or indemnification. In either case, the result would be the same assignment of liability, one that is Pareto optimal for both parties and hence one that they would reach by contracting.

Of course, transaction costs are significant in this context, and they largely determine the answer to the question about individual versus corporate responsibility. A standard argument for placing liability on the corporation rather than the individual is that any fine that can be imposed on an individual is likely to outstrip his or her ability to pay. This is known as the "deterrence trap." According to optimal penalty theory, any fine capable of deterring must exceed a person's expected return divided by the probability of successful prosecution. If this amount exceeds a person's total assets, then the deterrent value of any fine is significantly reduced. A corporation, on the other hand, is more likely to have assets sufficient to pay an optimal fine.

The effectiveness of corporate sanctions, on the other hand, depends on the ability of corporations to deter individual behavior. Holding corporations responsible is more efficient only if corporations are better able than the law to prevent misconduct *ex ante* or to punish it *ex post*. *Ex post*, a corporation can provide greater deterrence either by imposing greater penalties than the law can or by increasing the probability of apprehension and punishment. The standard argument holds that corporations are better able to deter both *ex ante* and *ex post* and to do so at a lower cost than legal actions brought against individuals. In addition, corporate liability creates greater incentives for a corporation to screen and monitor their employees more carefully. Overall, then, transaction costs make the use of corporate sanctions more efficient than sanctions imposed on individuals. Holding corporations rather than individuals responsible provides a more effective deterrent at a lower cost.

A second argument in favor of corporate responsibility is that it results in an optimal sharing of risk that is beneficial to society. First, shareholders, who generally hold diversified portfolios, are assumed to be risk neutral, whereas managers, whose wealth is tied up in the corporation, can be expected to be risk averse. If managers were held responsible for misconduct, especially of the kind that is hardly distinguishable from legitimate business practices, then they would face increased

risk for which they would demand compensation in the form of higher pay, indemnification, insurance or some combination of these. Insofar as managers are risk averse, then, it would cost more for shareholders to provide compensation than for them to assume the risk themselves. It is the role of shareholders to assume the preponderance of risk precisely because they can bear it at lower cost. Insofar as an inefficient allocation of risk raises costs and reduces profitability, it will also raise the cost of capital. So, in sum, a greater assignment of individual responsibility would involve an inefficient allocation of risk, which in turn would result in an increase in the cost of capital and a subsequent reduction in profits.

Second, if managers bore risk from individual responsibility that was not compensated by shareholders, they would use corporate assets to protect themselves. This would take the form of putting controls in place to prevent misconduct as well as of avoiding more risky projects that might create the possibility of wrongdoing. The result would be corporations that are less risky than shareholders would prefer, and this outcome would create less wealth for society. Indeed, an often overlooked reason for high executive compensation is to encourage top executives to be less risk averse and to operate the corporation at the level of risk that is most beneficial to diversified shareholders.

Although executives may resent the burden that Sarbanes-Oxley places on them, the overall effect of the act is to force corporations to devote more resources to measures that serve to protect managers. Ironically, an act that is intended to protect investors and the public, by appearing to place greater responsibility on executives, may end up protecting executives instead, without creating any greater risk for them. Without the Sarbanes-Oxley Act, shareholders and executives would be free to negotiate about the desirable level of risk for the firm and how much should be spent on internal controls to prevent misconduct. With this act, Congress is preventing any negotiation over these matters and inserting its own judgment.

A third argument for holding corporations rather than individuals responsible is that the more responsibility is shifted from the shareholders to managers, the less incentive the shareholders have to select and monitor managers' activities and to invest in internal controls. Also, the more that responsibility falls on lower-level employees, the greater incentive executives have to encourage those under them to engage in misconduct that benefits the corporation, secure in the knowledge that the consequences will not flow upward. Individual responsibility, in other words, creates a moral hazard problem in that shareholders and executives may reap the benefits for misconduct, the consequences of which are borne by others lower in the organization. This phenomenon has been labeled by William Laufer as "the paradox of compliance."[6] He writes, "The purchase of compliance sufficient to shift the risk of liability and loss, in certain firms, has the effect of decreasing levels of care . . . . This acceptance, coupled with the constant pressure on middle management to produce results, has led to increased deviance throughout the corporate hierarchy."[7] In short, more emphasis on compliance, paradoxically, creates greater deviance.

A fourth agency theory argument views a loss of control over agents as a function of corporate structure. The agency problem in corporate governance arises initially from the separation of ownership and control, which occurs in business organizations because of the greater efficiency and wealth-creating power of large, capital-intensive firms under professional management. The next step is the multidivision or M-form organization, in which each division is run like a separate company. In M-form organizations, the controls over the constituent businesses are primarily financial. Financial controls create strong pressures on employees lower in the organization to achieve financial targets with little regard

for the practical problems they face. As a result, these employees may perceive the risks of not achieving the financial goals to be greater than an internal or external sanction for wrongdoing.

## A BEHAVIORAL LAW AND ECONOMICS APPROACH

Agency theory and the Chicago School generally have limitations that require us to supplement their valuable insights with other theoretical approaches. In particular, individuals do not always behave as rational decision makers who engage in misconduct only after a rational assessment of the gains and losses. There are other explanations for corporate misconduct that challenge the rationality assumption and assume instead some forms of irrationality. For example, managers may not be aware that conduct they are considering is unethical or illegal; they may be misled into believing that their conduct, although unethical or illegal, is permissible in the current climate; and they may underestimate the likelihood of detection or the severity of the consequences.

Additional explanations are provided by research in social psychology which shows, first, that people are vulnerable to many cognitive biases that distort their decision-making abilities and produce unintended unethical and illegal conduct. Second, people also make decisions on the basis of heuristic devices or rules of thumb that may work well in many cases but can lead to systematic errors. Third, managers may not be risk averse, as agency theory holds, but, in fact, risk seekers. These factors all suggest that predictions about the effectiveness of sanctions to deter managers under more realistic assumptions about rationality may differ markedly from those derived from a neoclassical economics, rational actor model. . . .

To say this is not to excuse their behavior and deny that they have any responsibility. However, if the objective in holding individuals or the corporation responsible is to deter this kind of behavior, how effective can sanctions on individual managers be as a deterrent? Some managers may be less vulnerable to these cognitive impediments and better able to make sound decisions. However, much decision making is done in groups, so that an executive at the top still receives information and recommendations from those below. Individual managers cannot easily insulate themselves from flaws in the organizational decision-making process. Imposing sanctions on individuals, therefore, is unlikely to have much deterrent effect.

The remedy, insofar as there is one, is for business organizations to develop decision-making processes that compensate for the distorting effects of biases and heuristics and produce sound decisions. Steps might include systematic information gathering, multiple lines of communication, and the involvement of people with diverse perspectives. Changes might also be needed in the corporate culture and belief system. These kinds of reforms, which involve organizational processes, belief systems, and cultures, are best brought about by sanctions applied to the corporation. Only the threat of loss to the shareholders provides a sufficient inducement for the corporation to undertake the necessary measures. In addition to fines imposed by law, the market will punish firms that do not succeed in overcoming the detrimental effect of these biases and heuristics. Over time, there should be an evolution of corporate decision-making procedures, cultures, and belief systems that compensate for human cognitive limitations.

Although cognitive biases can produce flawed decision making, some of them are also valued characteristics of successful business leaders. We expect executives to be optimistic, highly confident risk takers, and these features are often responsible for their success. The biases identified by social psychologists are of two kinds: those that arise from bounded rationality (the confirmation bias and cognitive dissonance, for example) and those that relate to motivation (overoptimism and overconfidence). The former kind may have no offsetting benefits, but the latter do. Great optimism and confidence and even an illusion of control, for example, can enable an entrepreneur to pursue a promising idea in spite of formidable obstacles. Leaders with these characteristics can also inspire others and help a team recover after serious setbacks. Occasional misconduct may be a price that we have to pay for the added value that such individuals bring to our economy.

These characteristics of strong leaders are also valuable for organizations. A high level of optimism encourages employees to invest more of themselves in a firm and to cooperate for the sake of expected future rewards. . . .

## RESPONSIBILITY IN AIDING AND ABETTING

Many accounts of Enron's collapse and the other recent scandals cite the failure of gatekeeper institutions—most notably accounting firms, law firms, and investment banks—to exercise their oversight function. This failure has prompted calls for greater responsibility on the part of these firms and individual accountants, lawyers, and bankers.

For many decades, securities regulators and victims of securities fraud have been able to bring action not only against corporations and their officers and directors but also against the accounting firms, law firms, and investment bankers that provide crucial assistance. The legal basis for such actions against these professional service providers has been a doctrine of liability for aiding and abetting under Section 10(b) of the 1934 Securities Exchange Act, which prohibits fraud and other misconduct in securities transactions. Aiding and abetting liability is an application of the common-law principle that an accessory to a crime can rightfully be prosecuted along with the principal. This doctrine is also supported by moral notions of responsibility for acts committed by others, as in the case of a person who provides a weapon to a murderer knowing the intended use.

However, the ability of investors and the SEC to bring actions against firms for aiding and abetting has been severely limited by a controversial 1994 Supreme Court decision in the case *Central Bank of Denver v. First Interstate Bank of Denver.* The 5–4 ruling by the Supreme Court, which overturned a long line of decisions that had found an implied right of action for aiding and abetting, has brought howls of protest for the apparent removal of responsibility from key gatekeeper institutions. It is widely perceived as a step away from holding accountants, lawyers, and investment bankers responsible for wrongdoing by their clients.[8]

However, public policy considerations properly belong to Congress. If abandoning a right of action is not good public policy, then Congress could easily amend Section 10(b) to include the necessary language, but so far Congress has allowed the Supreme Court decision to stand. In the Sarbanes-Oxley Act, Congress has placed renewed emphasis on individual responsibility, albeit with more show than substance. So should Congress have taken this opportunity to reconsider the responsibility of the gatekeeper institutions that are in a position to aid and abet? What is the responsibility of these professional service providers when they aid and abet fraud and other misconduct?

Aiding and abetting liability is similar to the liability of corporate personnel inasmuch as they both involve the responsibility of agents. Insofar as these agents incur risk to benefit a principal, aiding and abetting, like corporate crime, should be, according to agency theory, a rare form of altruism. However, aiding and abetting, again like corporate crime, must be understood from an agency point of view to involve an agent acting for some gain. Some incentive, usually a fee, creates a conflict of interest. A conflict of interest may exist in a professional service firm not only with respect to a client-corporation but also with respect to its own members. That is, an individual accountant, lawyer or banker may, for the sake of personal advancement, enable a fraud that is not in the interest of the firm. Thus, professional service providers, like corporations, face a moral hazard problem.

If action can be brought against a professional service for aiding and abetting, then the firm, like a corporation, has an incentive to monitor and control individuals so as to deter misconduct. Agency theory would thus appear to support aiding and abetting liability for the same reason it would provide an argument for action against a corporation and its shareholders for corporation misconduct. Again, the Coase theorem would suggest that the assignment of liability is immaterial as long as transaction costs are minimal. With any initial assignment of liability, a corporation and its professional service providers could contract to produce an optimal apportionment. However, aiding and abetting liability involves considerable costs, leading to the conclusion that it is not desirable. On the whole, the *Denver Bank* decision may turn out to be good public policy despite the outcry against it.

First, there are considerations of fairness. Justice or fairness requires that victims of fraud and other misconduct be compensated.

However, except in cases of bankruptcy, there is no reason why compensation could not be provided by the primary violator, which is to say the corporation involved. The inclusion of secondary violators, such as accounting firms, law firms, and investment banks, provides deep pockets, which benefit plaintiffs by ensuring sufficient funds for recovery. However, another benefit of deep pockets for plaintiffs is that a professional service firm may be induced to settle lest they be forced to pay the full amount. Thus, an opportunity for coercion exists insofar as a firm may face a liability that is out of proportion to what it stands to gain from any misconduct. By contrast, a corporation is under less pressure to settle a baseless case because it is more likely to have realized the benefit of the conduct in question and thus be able to pay the full amount if required to do so. This element of coercion is a source of unfairness to professional service providers, which may also have the undesirable effect of encouraging frivolous suits.

Another source of unfairness is that aiding and abetting liability, in effect, makes agents responsible for actions of a principal, which is unfair on its face because it involves responsibility without control. This responsibility has a benefit inasmuch as a corporation's professional service providers have much better knowledge than shareholders about the conduct of managers and thus are in a better position to monitor their activities. This is why these professional service firms are assigned a gatekeeper function, not only by shareholders but also by regulators. However, to induce firms to be monitors or gatekeepers by holding them responsible for misconduct by their clients is unfair for the reason that they may have little control over the use that a corporation makes of their professional services.

Fairness requires that firms have an opportunity to protect themselves or to be compensated for the risk they incur. In order for firms to protect themselves, though, they would have to gain substantial knowledge about a corporation's operations, knowledge that would be both costly to acquire and difficult to obtain. The cost, moreover, would be largely a deadweight loss inasmuch as its purpose would be merely to protect a firm against liability and not to enable the firm to better serve a client. In addition, corporations might be less inclined to use professional services if they were forced to share more information merely to reduce a firm's liability or to pay more to compensate firms for the greater (avoidable) risk.

Although aiding and abetting liability induces professional service providers to be more vigilant monitors or gatekeepers, there are more effective ways of achieving the same end. Liability is an *ex post* incentive, a penalty that is imposed after misconduct has occurred and that serves as a deterrent. As a deterrent, though, liability is not very effective for at least two reasons. One is that the conduct that constitutes aiding and abetting is often unclear and difficult to distinguish from legitimate business activity. The second reason is that the imposition of a penalty is uncertain and subject to unpredictable factors. Incentives that operate *ex ante*—such as measures to increase auditor independence and to provide oversight of auditing performance, which are called for in the Sarbanes-Oxley Act—are apt to be more effective.

Even when investors with meritorious suits deserve to be compensated, their claims must be weighed against the costs that a system of compensation imposes on the operations of the securities market, which is so crucial to our economic well being. Aiding and abetting liability creates a number of costs that may outweigh the benefits to investors and society as a whole. The most obvious costs are those of frivolous suits, which are passed on to the client-corporation and ultimately to shareholders and the public. If these costs exceed the benefit, then there is no net gain for investors as a class or for society.

Other costs are more indirect. The vagueness of aiding and abetting creates a great deal of uncertainty that is unsettling in securities markets, which require predictability. The Supreme Court observed that excessive litigation combined with uncertain outcomes can have "ripple effects" that may prevent new and smaller companies, which are crucial for job creation and technological advances, from obtaining professional advice. Both direct and indirect costs raise the cost of capital, which not only inhibits domestic growth but also places American firms at a competitive disadvantage with other countries that do not impose these costs. The result, according to one writer, is a "litigation tax," which if retained, will lead to "higher cost of capital, fewer new jobs, and fewer innovative products, culminating in a diminished global competitive presence."[9]

Although these arguments are scarcely sufficient to resolve such a complex issue, they do serve to show that fears about the elimination of aiding and abetting liability by the *Denver Bank* decision are not well founded. It is possible that the decision may send the message to professional service providers that they will bear no consequences for their clients' misconduct, which will undermine the deterrent effect of the law. However, some commentators express the view that the SEC still possesses sufficient resources to effectively deter aiding and abetting, and investors can still bring action by alleging that a defendant is primary rather than a secondary violator.

## NOTES

1. Ambrose Bierce, *The Devil's Dictionary* (New York: World, 1911).
2. Press Release, Office of the Press Secretary, July 9, 2002, at http://www.whitehouse.gov/news/releases/2002/07/20020709-4.html (last visited December 17, 2003).
3. Press Release, Office of the Press Secretary, July 30, 2002, at http://www.whitehouse.gov/news/releases/2002/07/20020730.html (last visited December 17, 2003).
4. This distinction, which is rough at best, is complicated by the fact that what conduct is criminalized is subject to social and political factors. The risk taking at Enron, for example, is different only in degree from the financial structures at many reputable companies, such as General Electric. What risk is permissible, as opposed to reckless, and what risk ought to be disclosed to prevent charges of fraud involve fine lines. The lines may be drawn differently depending on whether the risk taking pays off. If Enron had succeeded, then Fastow's conflicts of interest in managing the LJM partnerships, for example, might be viewed differently, as they were beforehand when the Enron board approved his dual role.
5. Michael J. Zimmerman distinguishes three senses of "responsibility." One is causal responsibility in the sense of causally bringing about some state of affairs; a second is prospective responsibility in the sense of having a responsibility that one is expected to fulfill; and the third is retrospective responsibility in the sense of having failed to fill some duty or obligation. See Michael J. Zimmerman, *An Essay on Moral Responsibility* (Totowa, NJ: Rowman and Littlefield, 1988). "Responsibility" is being used here in the retrospective sense.
6. William S. Laufer, "Corporate Liability, Risk Shifting, and the Paradox of Compliance," *Vanderbilt Law Review* (1999): 1343–420.
7. Laufer, "Corporate Liability, Risk Shifting, and the Paradox of Compliance," 1415.
8. The decision in *Central Bank of Denver* turned on the narrow legal issue of whether the wording of Section 10(b) that prohibits the making of a material misstatement covers those who aid and abet that activity. Read literally, the act applies only to the parties that actually make a material misstatement (the primary violator) and not those engaged merely in aiding and abetting (the secondary violator). For many years, however, the courts had held that a right to bring action against aiders and abettors was implied by the act. A minority of the justices in the *Central*

*Bank* decision held that the failure of Congress to respond to the numerous decisions that recognized a right of action indicated tacit acceptance, but the majority believed that the failure of Congress to explicitly include aiding and abetting language was controlling. Neither side considered whether the

abandonment of aiding and abetting liability represents good public policy.

9. Anthony J. Jorgenson, "The Supreme Court Abolishes Aiding and Abetting Liability under Section 10(b): The End of an Era, or a Break in the Action?" *Oklahoma Law Review* 47 (1994): 660.

## FINANCIAL SERVICES

# Ethical Issues in Financial Services

*John. R. Boatright*

Some cynics jokingly deny that there is any ethics in finance, especially on Wall Street. This view is expressed in a thin volume, *The Complete Book of Wall Street Ethics,* which claims to fill "an empty space on financial bookshelves where a consideration of ethics should be."[1] Of course, the pages are all blank! However, a moment's reflection reveals that finance would be impossible without ethics. The very act of placing our assets in the hands of other people requires immense trust. An untrustworthy stockbroker or insurance agent, like an untrustworthy physician or attorney, finds few takers for his or her services. Financial scandals shock us precisely because they involve people and institutions that we should be able to trust.

Finance covers a broad range of activities, but the two most visible aspects are financial markets, such as stock exchanges, and the financial services industry, which includes not only commercial banks, but also investment banks, mutual fund companies, pension funds, both public and private, and insurance. Less visible to the public are the financial operations of a corporation, which are the responsibility of the chief financial officer (CFO). . . .

## FINANCIAL SERVICES

The financial services industry still operates largely through personal selling by stockbrokers, insurance agents, financial planners, tax advisers, and other finance professionals. Personal selling creates innumerable opportunities for abuse, and although finance professionals take pride in the level of integrity in the industry, misconduct still occurs. However, customers who are unhappy over failed investments or rejected insurance claims are quick to blame the seller of the product, sometimes with good reason.

For example, two real-estate limited partnerships launched by Merrill Lynch & Co. in 1987 and 1989 lost close to $440 million for 42,000 investor-clients. Known as Arvida I and Arvida II, these highly speculative investment vehicles projected double-digit returns on residential developments in Florida and California, but both stopped payments to investors in 1990. At the end of 1993, each $1,000 unit of Arvida I was worth $125, and each $1,000 unit of Arvida II, a mere $6.

The Arvida partnerships were offered by the Merrill Lynch sales force to many retirees

From John R. Boatright, *Ethics and the Conduct of Business.* Adapted by permission of Pearson Education Inc., Upper Saddle River, NJ.

of modest means as safe investments with good income potential. The brokers themselves were told by the firm that Arvida I entailed only "moderate risk," and company-produced sales material said little about risk while emphasizing the projected performance. Left out of the material was the fact that the projections included a return of some of the investors' own capital, that the track record of the real-estate company was based on commercial, not residential projects, and that eight of the top nine managers of the company had left just before Arvida I was offered to the public.

This case raises questions about whether investors were *deceived* by the brokers' sales pitches and whether material information was *concealed*. In other cases, brokers have been accused of *churning* client accounts in order to generate higher fees and of selecting *unsuitable* investments for clients. Other abusive sales practices in the financial services industry include *twisting*, in which an insurance agent persuades a policyholder to replace an older policy with a newer one that provides little if any additional benefit but generates a commission for the agent, and *flipping*, in which a loan officer persuades a borrower to repay an old loan with a new one, thereby incurring more fees. In one case, an illiterate retiree, who was flipped 10 times in a 4-year period, paid $19,000 in loan fees for the privilege of borrowing $23,000.

This section discusses three objectionable practices in selling financial products to clients, namely, deception, churning, and suitability.

## Deception

The ethical treatment of clients requires salespeople to explain all of the relevant information truthfully in an understandable, nonmisleading manner. One observer complains that brokers, insurance agents, and other salespeople

have developed a new vocabulary that obfuscates rather than reveals.

> Walk into a broker's office these days. You won't be sold a product. You won't even find a broker. Instead, a "financial adviser" will "help you select" an "appropriate planning vehicle," or "offer" a menu of "investment choices" or "options" among which to "allocate your money." . . . [Insurance agents] peddle such euphemisms as "private retirement accounts," "college savings plans," and "charitable remainder trusts." . . . Among other linguistic sleights of hand in common usage these days: saying tax-free when, in fact, it's only tax-deferred; high yield when it's downright risky; and projected returns when it's more likely in your dreams.[2]

Salespeople avoid speaking of commissions, even though they are the source of their compensation. Commissions on mutual funds are "front-end" or "back-end loads"; and insurance agents, whose commissions can approach 100 percent of the first year's premium, are not legally required to disclose this fact—and they rarely do. The agents of one insurance company represented life insurance policies as "retirement plans" and referred to the premiums as "deposits."[3]

Deception is often a matter of interpretation. Promotional material for a mutual fund, for example, may be accurate but misleading if it emphasizes the strengths of a fund and minimizes the weaknesses. Figures of past performance can carefully be selected and displayed in ways that give a misleading impression. Deception can also occur when essential information is not revealed. Thus, an investor may be deceived when the sales charge is rolled into the fund's annual expenses, which may be substantially higher than the competition's, or when the projected hypothetical returns do not reflect all charges. As these examples suggest, true claims may lead a typical investor to hold a mistaken belief.

Deception aside, what information *ought* to be disclosed to a client? The Securities Act of

1933 requires the issuer of a security to disclose all material information, which is defined as information about which an average prudent investor ought reasonably to be informed or to which a reasonable person would attach importance in determining a course of action in a transaction. The rationale for this provision of the Securities Act is both fairness to investors, who have a right to make decisions with adequate information, and the efficiency of securities markets, which requires that investors be adequately informed. Most financial products, including mutual funds and insurance policies, are accompanied by a written prospectus that contains all of the information that the issuer is legally required to provide.

In general, a person is deceived when that person is unable to make a rational choice as a result of holding a false belief that is created by some claim made by another. That claim may be either a false or misleading statement or a statement that is incomplete in some crucial way.

Consider two cases of possible broker (mis)conduct:

1. A brokerage firm buys a block of stock prior to issuing a research report that contains a "buy" recommendation in order to ensure that enough shares are available to fill customer orders. However, customers are not told that they are buying stock from the firm's own holdings, and they are charged the current market price plus the standard commission for a trade.

2. A broker assures a client that an initial public offering (IPO) of a closed-end fund is sold without a commission and encourages quick action by saying that after the IPO is sold, subsequent buyers will have to pay a 7 percent commission. In fact, a 7 percent commission is built into the price of the IPO, and this charge is revealed in the prospectus but will not appear on the settlement statement for the purchase.

In the first case, one might argue that if an investor decides to purchase shares of stock in response to a "buy" recommendation, it matters little whether the shares are bought on the open market or from a brokerage firm's holdings. The price is the same. An investor might appreciate the opportunity to share any profit that is realized by the firm (because of lower trading costs and perhaps a lower stock price before the recommendation is released); but the firm is under no obligation to share any profit with its clients. On the other hand, the client is buying the stock at the current market price and paying a fee as though the stock were purchased at the order of the client. The circumstances of the purchase are not explained to the client, but does the broker have any obligation to do so? And would this knowledge have any effect on the client's decision?

In the second case, however, a client might be induced to buy an initial offering of a closed-end mutual fund in the mistaken belief that the purchase would avoid a commission charge. The fact that the commission charge is disclosed in the prospectus might ordinarily exonerate the broker from a charge of deception except that the false belief is created by the broker's claim, which, at best, skirts the edge of honesty. Arguably, the broker made the claim with an intent to deceive, and a typical, prudent investor is apt to feel that there was an attempt to deceive.

### Churning

Churning is defined as excessive or inappropriate trading for a client's account by a broker who has control over the account with the intent to generate commissions rather than to benefit the client. Although churning occurs, there is disagreement on the frequency or the rate of detection. The brokerage industry contends that churning is a rare occurrence and is easily detected by firms as well as clients. No statistics are kept on churning, but complaints to the SEC and various exchanges about unauthorized trading and other abuses have risen sharply in recent years.

The ethical objection to churning is straightforward: it is a breach of a fiduciary duty to trade in ways that are not in a client's best interests. Churning, as distinct from unauthorized trading, occurs only when a client turns over control of an account to a broker, and by taking control, a broker assumes a responsibility to serve the client's interests. A broker who merely recommends a trade, is not acting on behalf of a client or customer and is more akin to a traditional seller, but a broker in charge of a client's portfolio thereby pledges to manage it to the best of his or her ability.

Although churning is clearly wrong, the concept is difficult to define. Some legal definitions offered in court decisions are: "excessive trading by a broker disproportionate to the size of the account involved, in order to generate commissions,"[4] and a situation in which "a broker, exercising control over the frequency and volume of trading in the customer's account, initiates transactions that are excessive in view of the character of the account."[5] The courts have held that for churning to occur a broker must trade with the *intention* of generating commissions rather than benefiting the client. The legal definition of churning contains three elements, then: (1) the broker controls the account; (2) the trading is excessive for the character of the account; and (3) the broker acted with intent.

The most difficult issue in the definition of churning is the meaning of "excessive trading." First, whether trading is excessive depends on the character of the account. A client who is a more speculative investor, willing to assume higher risk for a greater return, should expect a higher trading volume. Second, high volume is not the only factor; pointless trades might be considered churning even if the volume is relatively low. Third, churning might be indicated by a pattern of trading that con-

sistently favors trades that yield higher commissions. Common to these three points is the question of whether the trades make sense from an investment point of view. High-volume trading that loses money might still be defended as an intelligent but unsuccessful investment strategy, whereas investments that represent no strategy beyond generating commissions are objectionable, no matter the amount gained or lost.

A 1995 SEC report concluded that the compensation system in brokerage firms was the root cause of the churning problem. The report identified some "best practices" in the industry that might prevent churning, including ending the practice of paying a higher commission for a company's own products, prohibiting sales contests for specific products, and tying a portion of compensation to the size of a client's account, regardless of the number of transactions. However, an SEC panel concluded that the commission system is too deeply rooted to be significantly changed and recommended better training and oversight by brokerage firms.

## Suitability

In general, brokers, insurance agents, and other salespeople have an obligation to recommend only suitable securities and financial products. However, suitability, like churning, is difficult to define precisely. The rules of the National Association of Securities Dealers include the following:

> In recommending to a customer the purchase, sale, or exchange of any security, a member shall have reasonable grounds for believing that the recommendation is suitable for such customer upon the basis of the facts, if any, disclosed by such customer as to his other security holding and as to his financial situation and needs.[6]

The most common causes of unsuitability are (1) *unsuitable types of securities,* that is, recommending stocks, for example, when bonds would better fit the investor's objectives; (2) *unsuitable grades of securities,* such as selecting lower-rated bonds when higher-rated ones are more appropriate; (3) *unsuitable diversification,* which leaves the portfolio vulnerable to changes in the markets; (4) *unsuitable trading techniques,* including the use of margin or options, which can leverage an account and create greater volatility and risk; and (5) *unsuitable liquidity.* Limited partnerships, for example, are not very marketable and are thus unsuitable for customers who may need to liquidate the investment.

The critical question, of course, is, when is a security unsuitable? Rarely is a single security unsuitable except in the context of an investor's total portfolio. Investments are most often deemed to be unsuitable because they involve excessive risk, but a few risky investments may be appropriate in a well-balanced, generally conservative portfolio. Furthermore, even an aggressive, risk-taking portfolio may include unsuitable securities if the risk is not compensated by the expected return.

Ensuring that a recommended security is suitable for a given investor thus involves many factors, but people in the financial services industry offer to put their specialized knowledge and skills to work for us. We expect suitable recommendations from physicians, lawyers, and accountants. Why should we expect anything less from finance professionals?

## INSIDER TRADING

Insider trading is commonly defined as trading in the stock of publicly held corporations on the basis of material, nonpublic information. In a landmark 1968 decision, executives of Texas Gulf Sulphur Company were found guilty of insider trading for investing heavily in their own company's stock after learning of the discovery of rich copper ore deposits in

Canada. The principle established in the *Texas Gulf Sulphur* case is that corporate insiders must refrain from trading on information that significantly affects stock price until it becomes public knowledge. The rule for corporate insiders is, reveal or refrain!

Much of the uncertainty in the law on insider trading revolves around the relation of the trader to the source of the information. Corporate executives are definitely "insiders," but some "outsiders" have also been charged with insider trading. Among such outsiders have been a printer who was able to identify the targets of several takeovers from legal documents that were being prepared; a financial analyst who uncovered a huge fraud at a high-flying firm and advised his clients to sell; a stockbroker who was tipped off by a client who was a relative of the president of a company and who learned about the sale of the business through a chain of family gossip; a psychiatrist who was treating the wife of a financier who was attempting to take over a major bank; and a lawyer whose firm was advising a client planning a hostile takeover. The first two traders were eventually found innocent of insider trading; the latter three were found guilty (although the stockbroker case was later reversed in part). From these cases a legal definition of insider trading is slowly emerging.

The key points are that a person who trades on material, nonpublic information is engaging in insider trading when (1) the trader has violated some legal duty to a corporation and its shareholders; or (2) the source of the information has such a legal duty and the trader knows that the source is violating that duty. Thus, the printer and the stock analyst had no relation to the corporations in question and so had no duty to refrain from using the information that they had acquired. The stockbroker and the psychiatrist, however, knew or should have known that they were obtaining inside information indirectly from high-level executives who had a duty to keep the information confidential. The corresponding rule for outsiders is,

Don't trade on information that is revealed in violation of a trust. Both rules are imprecise, however, and leave many cases unresolved.

## Arguments against Insider Trading

The difficulty in defining insider trading is due to disagreement over the moral wrong involved. Two main rationales are used in support of a law against insider trading. One is based on *property rights* and holds that those who trade on material, nonpublic information are essentially stealing property that belongs to the corporation. The second rationale is based on *fairness* and holds that traders who use inside information have an unfair advantage over other investors and that, as a result, the stock market is not a level playing field. These two rationales lead to different definitions, one narrow, the other broad. On the property rights or "misappropriation" theory, only corporate insiders or outsiders who bribe, steal, or otherwise wrongfully acquire corporate secrets can be guilty of insider trading. The fairness argument is broader and applies to anyone who trades on material, nonpublic information no matter how it is acquired.

*Inside Information as Property.* One difficulty in using the property rights or misappropriation argument is determining who owns the information in question. The main basis for recognizing a property right in trade secrets and confidential business information is the investment that companies make in acquiring information and the competitive value that some information has. Not all insider information fits this description, however. Advance knowledge of better-than-expected earnings would be an example. Such information still has value in stock trading, even if the corporation does not use it for that purpose. For

this reason, many employers prohibit the personal use of any information that an employee gains in the course of his or her work. This position is too broad, however, since an employee is unlikely to be accused of stealing company property by using knowledge of the next day's earning report for any purpose other than stock trading.

A second difficulty with the property rights argument is that if companies own certain information, they could then give their own employees permission to use it, or they could sell the information to favored investors or even trade on it themselves to buy back stock. Giving employees permission to trade on insider information could be an inexpensive form of extra compensation that further encourages employees to develop valuable information for the firm. Such an arrangement would also have some drawbacks; for example, investors might be less willing to buy the stock of a company that allowed insider trading because of the disadvantage to outsiders. What is morally objectionable about insider trading, according to its critics, though, is not the misappropriation of a company's information but the harm done to the investing public. So the violation of property rights in insider trading cannot be the sole reason for prohibiting it. Let us turn, then, to the second argument against insider trading, namely the argument from fairness.

*The Fairness Argument.* Fairness in the stock market does not require that all traders have the same information. Indeed, trades will take place only if the buyers and sellers of a stock have different information that leads them to different conclusions about the stock's worth. It is only fair, moreover, that a shrewd investor who has spent great time and money studying the prospects of a company should be able to exploit that advantage. Otherwise there would be no incentive to seek out new information. What is objectionable about using inside information is that other traders are barred from obtaining it no matter how diligent they may be. The information is unavailable not for lack of *effort* but for lack of *access*. Poker also pits card players with unequal skill and knowledge without being unfair, but a game played with a marked deck gives some players an unfair advantage over others. By analogy, then, insider trading is like playing poker with a marked deck.

The analogy may be flawed, however. Perhaps a more appropriate analogy is the seller of a home who fails to reveal hidden structural damage. One principle of stock market regulation is that both buyers and sellers of stock should have sufficient information to make rational choices. Thus, companies must publish annual reports and disclose important developments in a timely manner. A CEO who hides bad news from the investing public, for example, can be sued for fraud. Good news, such as an oil find, need not be announced until a company has time to buy the drilling rights, and so on; but to trade on that information before it is public knowledge might also be described as a kind of fraud.

Insider trading is generally prosecuted under SEC Rule 10b-5, which merely prohibits fraud in securities transactions. In fraudulent transactions, one party, such as the buyer of the house with structural damage, is wrongfully harmed for lack of knowledge that the other party concealed. So too—according to the fairness argument—are the ignorant parties to insider trading transactions wrongfully harmed when material facts, such as the discovery of copper ore deposits in the *Texas Gulf Sulphur* case, are not revealed.

The main weakness of the fairness argument is determining what information ought to be revealed in a transaction. The reason for requiring a homeowner to disclose hidden structural damage is that doing so makes for a more efficient housing market. In the absence of such a requirement, potential home buyers would pay less because they are not sure what they are getting, or they would invest in costly home inspections. Similarly—the argument goes—requiring insiders to reveal before trading makes the stock market more efficient.

The trouble with such a claim is that some economists argue that the stock market would be more efficient *without* a law against insider trading. If insider trading were permitted, they claim, information would be registered in the market more quickly and at less cost than the alternative of leaving the task to research by stock analysts. The main beneficiaries of a law against insider trading, critics continue, are not individual investors but market professionals who can pick up news "on the street" and act on it quickly. Some economists argue further that a law against insider trading preserves the illusion that there is a level playing field and that individual investors have a chance against market professionals.

Economic arguments about market efficiency look only at the cost of registering information in the market and not at possible adverse consequences of legalized insider trading, which are many. Investors who perceive the stock market as an unlevel playing field may be less inclined to participate or will be forced to adopt costly defensive measures. Legalized insider trading would have an effect on the treatment of information in a firm. Employees whose interest is in information that they can use in the stock market may be less concerned with information that is useful to the employer, and the company itself might attempt to tailor its release of information for maximum benefit to insiders. More important, the opportunity to engage in insider trading might undermine the relation of trust that is essential for business organizations. A prohibition on insider trading frees employees of a corporation to do what they are supposed to be doing—namely, working for the interests of the shareholders—not seeking ways to advance their own interests.

The harm that legalized insider trading could do to organizations suggests that the strongest argument against legalization might be the breach of fiduciary duty that would result. Virtually everyone who could be called an "insider" has a fiduciary duty to serve the interests of the corporation and its shareholders, and the use of information that is acquired while serving as a fiduciary for personal gain is a violation of this duty. It would be a breach of professional ethics for a lawyer or an accountant to benefit personally from the use of information acquired in confidence from client, and it is similarly unethical for a corporate executive to make personal use of confidential business information.

The argument that insider trading constitutes a breach of fiduciary duty accords with recent court decisions that have limited the prosecution of insider trading to true insiders who have a fiduciary duty. One drawback of the argument is that "outsiders," whom federal prosecutors have sought to convict of insider trading, would be free of any restrictions. A second drawback is that insider trading, on this argument, is no longer an offense against the market but the violation of a duty to another party. And the duty not to use information that is acquired while serving as a fiduciary prohibits more than insider trading. The same duty would be violated by a fiduciary who buys or sells property or undertakes some other business dealing on the basis of confidential information. That such breaches of fiduciary duty are wrong is evident, but the authority of the SEC to prosecute them under a mandate to prevent fraud in the market is less clear.

***The** O'Hagan **Decision.*** In 1997, the U.S. Supreme Court ended a decade of uncertainty over the legal definition of insider trading. The SEC has long prosecuted insider trading using the misappropriation theory, according to which an inside trader breaches a fiduciary duty by misappropriating confidential information for personal trading. In 1987, the high court split 4–4 on an insider trading case involving a reporter for the *Wall Street Journal* and thus left standing a lower court decision that found the reporter guilty of misappropriating information. However, the decision did not create a precedent for lack of a majority. Subsequently, lower courts rejected the misappropriation theory in a series of cases in which the alleged inside trader did not have a fiduciary duty to the corporation whose stock was traded. The principle applied was that the trading must itself constitute a breach of fiduciary duty. This principle was rejected in *U.S. v. O'Hagan.*

James H. O'Hagan was a partner in a Minneapolis law firm that was advising the British firm Grand Metropolitan in a hostile takeover of Minneapolis-based Pillsbury Company. O'Hagan did network on Grand Met business but allegedly tricked a fellow partner into revealing the takeover bid. O'Hagan then reaped $4.3 million by trading in Pillsbury stock and stock options. An appellate court ruled that O'Hagan did not engage in illegal insider trading because he had no fiduciary duty to Pillsbury, the company in whose stock he traded. Although O'Hagan misappropriated confidential information from his own law firm—to which he owed a fiduciary duty—trading on this information did not constitute a fraud against the law firm or against Grand Met. Presumably, O'Hagan would have been guilty of insider trading only if he were an insider of Pillsbury.

In a 6–3 decision, the Supreme Court reinstated the conviction of Mr. O'Hagan and affirmed the misappropriation theory. According to the decision, a person commits securities fraud when he or she "misappropriates confidential information for securities trading purposes, in breach of a fiduciary duty owed to the source of the information." Thus, an inside trader need not be an insider (or a temporary insider, like a lawyer) of the corporation whose stock is traded. Being an insider in Grand Met is sufficient in this case to hold that insider trading occurred. The majority opinion observed that "it makes scant sense" to hold a lawyer like O'Hagan to have violated the law "if he works for a law firm representing the target of a tender offer, but not if he works for a law firm representing the bidder." The crucial point is that O'Hagan was a fiduciary who misused information that had been entrusted to him. This decision would also apply to a person who receives information from an insider and who knows that the insider source is violating a duty of confidentiality. However, a person with no fiduciary ties who receives information innocently (by overhearing a conversation, for example) would still be free to trade.

### Conclusion

Ethical issues in finance are important because they bear on our financial well-being. Ethical misconduct, whether it be by individuals acting alone or by financial institutions, has the potential to rob people of their life savings. Because so much money is involved in financial dealings, there must be well-developed and effective safeguards in place to ensure personal and organizational ethics. Although the law governs much financial activity, strong emphasis must be placed on the integrity of finance professionals and on ethical leadership in our financial institutions. Some of the principles in finance ethics are common to other aspects of business, especially the duties of fiduciaries and fairness in sales practices and securities markets. However, such activities as insider trading and hostile takeover raise unique issues that require special consideration.

## NOTES

1. Jay L. Walker [pseudonym], *The Complete Book of Wall Street Ethics* (New York: William Morrow and Company, 1987).
2. Ellen E. Schultz, "You Need a Translator for Latest Sales Pitch," *Wall Street Journal* (February 14, 1994), p. C1.
3. Michael Quint, "Met Life Shakes Up Its Ranks," *New York Times* (October 29, 1994), p. C1.
4. *Marshak v. Blyth Eastman Dillon & Co. Inc.*, 413 F. Supp. 377, 379 (1975).
5. *Kaufman v. Merrill Lynch, Pierce, Fenner & Smith*, 464 F. Supp. 528, 534 (1978).
6. *NASD Rules of Fair Practice*, art. III, sec. 2.

# Applying Ethics to Insider Trading

*Robert W. McGee*

People profit from using inside information all the time. Tax preparers use their expert knowledge of the tax law to save their clients' money in the preparation of their tax returns and charge professional fees for this service. Yet no one complains or accuses the service provider of performing an unethical activity. Both sides benefit by the transaction. The taxpayer benefits because the preparer helps satisfy the legal requirement to file the tax return and probably also benefits by having his tax liability reduced. The tax preparer also benefits

*Journal of Business Ethics* 17, no. 6 (2007).

because he earns a fee for such services. It is a win-win situation because both parties to the transaction benefit. There are no losers, except perhaps the tax authority, but if the tax preparer does not violate any rules in the preparation of the tax return, the tax authority does not fail to receive what it is legally entitled to receive. It just does not receive more than it is legally entitled to receive because the tax preparer has applied the law in such a way as to minimize the amount of the tax liability.

What could be said about tax return preparers could also be said about all other professions. Medical doctors use their inside information, which was gained through years of study and practice, to cure or alleviate suffering. The general public does not possess the information that these doctors possess. Thus, they are profiting from the use of nonpublic information. Plumbers, chefs and airline pilots also make their living by applying the inside, non-public information they have acquired through study and work, yet no one accuses these people of acting unethically merely because they profit from applying the information they have acquired along the way.

Another common beneficial use of inside information occurs whenever a shopper takes advantage of a department store sale. Let's say that a shopper visits a department store to purchase a certain item and, upon arrival, reads a sign that states that all merchandise will go on sale tomorrow at a 30 percent discount. The only people who know about the pending sale are the people who visited the store and read the sale signs. Let's say that as a result of reading the sale sign, the shopper decides to go home and return the next day to take advantage of the 30 percent discount. The next day the shopper buys items costing $70 that would otherwise have cost $100, thus saving $30 as a result of using this inside information.

Is there anything unethical about profiting from the use of such information? The cus-

tomer benefits and so does the store. True, the store would have benefited by an additional $30 if the shopper would have made the purchases yesterday instead of today, but the store still benefited by making the sale today. Otherwise it would not have made the sale. Furthermore, it was the store management's decision to put its goods on sale, so the store cannot be labeled as a victim of insider trading, since it was the store that initiated the sale. The fact that only a small percentage of the local community read the sale signs, and thus benefited because of this sale information, is completely irrelevant. The percentage of the community that is aware of any particular economic information has absolutely nothing to do with the determination of whether a trade constitutes ethical or unethical conduct.

Let's change the fact situation. Let's say that no signs were posted to alert shoppers to the pending sale, but that a sales clerk told a shopper "You should put that back on the shelf and come back tomorrow when it will be on sale." Does this change in the fact situation alter the ethics of the transaction? In either case the shopper benefits and so does the store. The only difference is that the information is not public information, in the sense that there were no signs posted to alert the public of the existence of the sale. But the only people who would know about the sale anyway were the people who happened to be in the store. So the subset of potential shoppers is smaller if no signs are posted, but no one is harmed by trading on this information regardless of how many or how few people know what will happen the next day when the sale begins.

From the perspective of utilitarian ethics, any transaction is ethical provided the gains exceed the losses. Therefore, since both the customer and the store benefited by the sales, the transaction is ethical. There were two winners and no losers, so the gains exceeded the losses. Whether signs were posted or whether a shopper learned of the pending sale from a sales clerk is irrelevant as far as the ethics of the matter is concerned. There were two winners and no losers as a result of this use of nonpublic information.

If there is nothing unethical about shoppers, doctors, chefs, airline pilots and tax return preparers trading on insider information, can it be said that trading on stock information is also not unethical, or are there other issues that need to be explored?

These examples could be criticized by those who take a narrow view of insider trading. The criticism might go something like this. Inside information is the information held by the board of directors, auditors and management of a corporation that is available to them solely due to their role inside the organization. Such information is not available to the public through any legal means. Tax preparers use expert information to prepare a tax return and save the client some money. However, such expert information used by the tax preparer is not known only to the tax preparers. It is public knowledge and is available to anybody who wants to spend the time and energy to locate it. The knowledge held by the doctors, chefs, and plumbers, and the like, is part of the public body of knowledge that is supplemented by the experience earned by these individuals through years of practice. Anybody who is willing to spend the money and time and practice the profession can earn similar knowledge. Such knowledge cannot be equated to what we commonly understand as "insider information."

This line of reasoning has some plausibility, at least on the surface. But the real issue is not whether it is ethical for privileged groups or individuals to profit from information that is not available to the general public, but whether it is ethical to profit from asymmetric information. There are at least two ways to determine whether profiting from such information is ethical. The utilitarian ethics approach looks at results. If the winners exceed the losers or if the result is a positive-sum game, then profiting from the use of such information is ethical.

The other approach is to look at the process and to ignore the results. If the process is ethical, then profiting from the use of the information is ethical regardless of whether the result is a positive-sum game, a negative-sum game or a zero-sum game. This article explores both views.

Whenever the term "insider trading" is used, the average listener/reader immediately classifies it as a bad practice, or something that is immoral or unethical. Inside traders are viewed as common criminals. The purpose of this paper is to explore the nature of insider trading and analyze the issues to determine the positive and negative aspects of insider trading, and how policy should be changed, if at all.

## IS INSIDER TRADING FRAUDULENT?

Whether insider trading is fraudulent is questionable. St. Thomas Aquinas said that fraud can be perpetrated in three ways, either by selling one thing for another or by giving the wrong quality or quantity. A more modern definition is "intentional deception to cause a person to give up property or some lawful right" (Webster 1964).

A typical case of insider trading occurs when a buyer with inside information calls his stock broker and tells him to buy, knowing that the stock price is likely to rise as soon as the inside information becomes public. In this case, the buyer does not deceive the seller into giving up property. Indeed, the buyer does not even know who the seller is, and the seller would have sold anyway, anonymously, through the same broker. The seller's action would have been the same whether an inside trader was the other party to the transaction or not. If the inside trader had not purchased the stock, someone else would have. Yet this "someone else" would not be accused of reaping unjust profits, even if the identical stock was purchased for the same price the insider would have paid.

Insider trading does not seem to fit the definition of fraud, so there does not seem to be anything fraudulent about it. Furthermore, according to Aquinas, if you are a seller, there is no moral duty for you to inform a potential buyer that the price of the good you are trying to sell is likely to decline in the near future.

In the case Aquinas discusses, a wheat merchant

> . . . carries wheat to a place where wheat fetches a high price, knowing that many will come after him carrying wheat . . . if the buyers knew this they would give a lower price. But . . . the seller need not give the buyer this information . . . the seller, since he sells his goods at the price actually offered him, does not seem to act contrary to justice through not stating what is going to happen. If however he were to do so, or if he lowered his price, it would be exceedingly virtuous on his part: although he does not seem to be bound to do this as a debt of justice. (Acquinas)

Based on this view, an insider who knows the stock price is likely to rise in the near future has no moral duty to inform potential sellers of this fact. Where there is no moral duty, certainly there should be no legal duty either. In fact, the U.S. Supreme Court has ruled at least twice that those in possession of nonpublic information do not have a general duty to disclose the information to the marketplace.

## WHO IS HARMED BY INSIDER TRADING?

While the transaction of buying and selling stock by an insider does not meet either the dictionary's or Aquinas' definition of fraud, the question of justice still remains. If no one is harmed, the act is not unjust; if someone who does not deserve to be harmed is harmed, the act is unjust. The obvious question to be raised is: Who is harmed by insider trading?

The most obvious potential "victims" of insider trading are the potential sellers who sell their stock anonymously to an inside trader. But as was mentioned above, they would have sold anyway, so whether the inside trader buys from them or not does not affect the proceeds they receive from the sale. If the sellers are hurt by having an inside trader in the market, it is difficult to measure the damage, and it appears that there is no damage. In fact, the academic literature recognizes that insider trading does not result in any harm to any identifiable group and those who sell to inside traders may actually be helped rather than harmed because they received a better price, so it appears illogical to allow them to sue for damages if, in fact, there are no damages. From the perspective of utilitarian ethics, sellers are no worse off as a result of having sold to an insider than they would have been if they had sold to a noninsider. Thus, there is nothing wrong with the practice from the perspective of utilitarian ethics. Of course, utilitarian ethics has been criticized for having certain structural flaws, but time and space do not permit an adequate analysis of those arguments.

It has been argued that employers are harmed by insider trading because employees misappropriate corporate information for personal gain. Yet employers whose employees misappropriate information for personal gain have a remedy at law already. If anyone sues, it should be the employer that sues the employee. Government should not be a party to such a lawsuit, since it is a private harm rather than a public harm that has been committed, if in fact any harm has been committed at all.

## WHAT ARE THE BENEFICIAL EFFECTS OF INSIDER TRADING?

Insider trading serves as a means of communicating market information, which makes markets more efficient. When insiders are seen trading, it acts as a signal to others that a stock's price will likely move in a certain direction. If a director of General Motors purchases a large quantity of General Motors stock, that act reveals evidence that the stock's price is likely to rise in the near future. Likewise, if the director sells, it is likely that the price will soon fall. A chain reaction will take place as the brokerage firm handling the transaction alerts other brokers and clients, and the stock price will start moving in the correct direction, closer to its true value. There is no need to make a public announcement, because the market reacts almost immediately. Even if the insider is anonymous, an increase (or decrease) in demand for a particular stock will be noticed by the market, and the price will move accordingly. Placing prohibitions on insider trading has the effect of blocking this flow of information. Insiders will attempt to hide their trades, or perhaps not make them at all, thus preventing the market from learning this valuable information.

The potential acquirer in a takeover attempt may also benefit by insider trading. The investment banker hired by the acquirer may leak information to arbitragers, who then accumulate shares in the target company with the intent of tendering them shortly thereafter. The result is that the takeover's chances of success are increased, and the acquirer may actually benefit as a result of the investment banker's misconduct.

The shareholders who sell at the time the arbitragers are buying may also benefit. The increased demand generated by the arbitragers increases the price the sellers receive when they sell. Without the leakage of the insider information to the arbitragers, the demand for the stock in question would have been lower, so the sellers (who would probably have sold anyway) would have received a somewhat lower price for their stock. Shareholders who do not sell also benefit, since the price of their shares rises as a result of insider trading.

A goal of most corporate managements is to increase shareholder wealth—in other words, increase the stock's price. Since insider trading has a tendency to increase the stock's price, inside traders assist management to achieve its goal. Inside traders may benefit the corporation in another way as well.

> A decision by the board or its delegates to "tip" inside corporate information to certain outsiders, to facilitate trading by them, could also be in the best interests of the corporation. For example, where the corporation has received valuable services from an outsider, one way of providing indirect compensation for those services is by providing the outsider with the authorized use of inside information owned by the corporation. Thus, if one accepts the notion that inside information is property of the corporation, even the tipping of that information to others ought not to be regarded as improper, if the board of directors or other authorized corporate decision maker has determined that such tipping is in the best interests of the corporation. (Morgan 1987, 98)

## WHO IS HARMED BY PROHIBITIONS ON INSIDER TRADING?

Outlawing or restricting insider trading may have long-term adverse effects on the economy. The market certainly will operate less efficiently, since insider trading increases market efficiency. Hostile takeovers will be more difficult to make, so shareholders will lose, since shareholders tend to benefit by hostile takeovers.

Having insider trading laws on the books will result in compliance and escape costs. The legal and accounting fees involved in complying with or circumventing the law can be fairly expensive, an expense that would not be incurred in the absence of insider trading laws. Using indirect means to accomplish what could otherwise be accomplished directly also leads to unnecessary costs. The delay in disclosure that results from using indirect means of accomplishing the goal also increases market inefficiency. There may also be other transaction costs, such as using an obscure mutual fund or a foreign bank or broker, when a more direct purchase would be less costly.

Taxpayers are adversely affected by insider trading laws, since enormous resources must be placed at the disposal of the police power to do any kind of policing. The resources used to police the insider trading laws might be better used to prevent some real criminal activity from being committed. For any use of government resources, there is a cost and a benefit. Since insider trading is regarded as a victimless crime if, indeed, it is a crime at all, an argument can be made that the resources government uses to enforce the insider trading laws can be better employed elsewhere. Furthermore, the risk of being caught is small, and the potential gain from using insider information can be enormous, so having an insider trading law on the books will not stop the practice or even reduce it significantly.

## THE LEVEL PLAYING FIELD ARGUMENT

The underlying philosophical argument of the level playing field argument is fairness. The market should be fair to all participants, meaning that the asymmetry of information should be minimized, in the case of insider trading. The level playing field argument has been used to justify any number of economic regulations, including prohibitions on insider trading. Trade cannot be free, it must be fair, whatever that means.

The problem with this level playing field argument is that it is not possible or desirable to ever have a level playing field in the realm of economics. The level playing field argument is appropriate to apply to sporting events but not to economics. It would not be fair for one football team to have to run uphill for the entire game while its opponent can run downhill. It is not fair for one basketball team to have a larger hoop to shoot at than its opponent. But there is nothing unfair about allowing banana farmers in Alaska to compete with banana farmers in Honduras. Alaska banana farmers should not be subsidized so that they can compete more effectively with banana farmers from Honduras, and banana farmers from Honduras should not have to comply with punitive regulations or higher tax burdens to make them less able to compete with banana farmers from Alaska. Likewise, there is nothing unfair about allowing experts who work 60 hours a week to gather financial information as part of their job to profit from that information. What is unfair is to force them to disclose such information to people who have done nothing to earn it.

Ricardo's theory of comparative advantage (1871/1996) is at work here. Some individuals or groups are naturally better at some things than others, and some individuals or groups develop skills that are better than those of their competitors. Penalizing those who are better at something or subsidizing those who are worse at something results in inefficient outcomes and is unfair to some groups. Thus, the level playing field argument is inappropriate when discussing economics.

Comparative advantage works to the benefit of the vast majority of the population. It allows specialization and division of labor, which Smith pointed out in his pin factory example (1776/1953) leads to far greater efficiency, higher quality and lower prices. Not allowing individuals to use their special talents harms the entire community as well as the individuals who are being held back by some government law or regulation. Forcing a level playing field on people is always harmful because it reduces efficiency and violates rights. Using the level playing field argument to prevent individuals from using their insider knowledge for personal gain does not hold up under analysis. If insider trading is to be made illegal and if inside traders are to be punished, some other justification must be found.

## PROPERTY AND CONTRACT RIGHTS

One of the major criticisms of utilitarian ethics is that it is difficult, or perhaps impossible, to precisely measure gains and losses. Indeed, it is not always possible to even identify the winners and the losers in many cases. Leland (1992) attempted to measure gains and losses resulting from insider trading and came up with mixed results. He found that insider trading accelerates the resolution of uncertainty, which is a good thing. He also found that where insider trading is permitted, stock prices better reflect information, a conclusion that others have drawn a priori without the need for mathematical models. He also found that insider trading tends to lead to higher stock prices than would otherwise be the case, which is good for existing shareholders, but that outside investors and liquidity traders tend to be harmed. His conclusion is that total welfare may either be enhanced or reduced by insider trading. The policy conclusion from this and similar studies might be that insider trading should be permitted when the result is a positive-sum game and prohibited when the result is a negative-sum game.

There are several problems with taking such a policy position. For one, it is not always possible to determine, even after the event, whether the gains exceed the losses. Outright prohibitions on certain kinds of insider trading that would, if permitted, result in positive-sum games, result in reduced welfare. They also have a chilling effect on the practice, thus causing the economy to operate less efficiently, with the result that welfare is guaranteed to be reduced. Furthermore, having a policy that prohibits insider trading in cases where no one's rights have been violated is itself a violation of rights. Using a utilitarian approach has its dangers, since there is a tendency to overlook other issues, such as the violation of rights that would result from prohibiting the practice.

Machan (1996) rightly points out the danger of applying utilitarian ethics. The underlying premise of all utilitarian ethics is that the end justifies the means. Thus, according to this logic, insider trading should be permitted if the result is a positive-sum game and prohibited if it is not. The problem with this philosophical view is that property rights are totally ignored. Someone's property rights or even the right to life can be violated if there is an overall benefit to society according to this view. . . .

## THE MARTHA STEWART CASE

The Martha Stewart case provides an excellent example of how prohibitions against insider trading can do more harm than good. Martha Stewart, a female billionaire who has brought many useful products to market and who has created thousands, if not tens of thousands of jobs, was investigated for violating the insider trading laws because her stockbroker gave her a tip that the stock of another company she held shares in was probably going to decline in price in the very near future. She acted on this nonpublic information by selling her shares, thus avoiding a loss, which surely would have occurred if she had waited until the nonpublic information became public.

The government investigated her action for insider trading violations but never prosecuted her for insider trading. That is because her sale did not violate any insider trading laws. What she was prosecuted for, and what she was found guilty of, was altering records and lying to federal prosecutors to cover up a crime she did not commit. Furthermore, and what is even more outrageous from the perspective of civil liberties, is that the government attempted to convict her of manipulating the price of the stock in her own company merely because she declared that she was innocent of the other charges the government had brought against her.

Their reasoning was rather curious. Basically, they argued that she declared her innocence against selling shares in the other company so that the market value of the shares in her own company would rebound, since her company's share price declined when it became public that she was being investigated for insider trading. In effect, she was being prosecuted for exercising her First Amendment right to declare her innocence. True, declaring her innocence caused the price of her company's stock to increase, but that is beside the point. Luckily, this charge was thrown out. If it had not been thrown out, any future corporate executive could be punished for declaring his or her innocence if the effect would be to increase the price of the stock in which the executive holds a material interest.

There was also a certain air of populism and envy involved in both the prosecution and the press coverage of the Martha Stewart case. Some commentators accused the prosecutors of going after her just because she was rich and arrogant. The prosecution's actions were referred to as a "Witch Hunt." One economist stated that she was prosecuted for "outsider" trading, since she was not clas-

sified as being within the category of an inside trader. The hunt for inside traders has been referred to as an example of socialism in capital markets because advocates press for the socialization of information. Martha Stewart has been called a political prisoner because she did not commit a crime against any individual but was prosecuted because of power-hungry prosecutors. Some commentators have called insider trading a noncrime, since it has no identifiable victims. Economists are continuing to call for the legalization of insider trading.

## REFERENCES

Aquinas, St. Thomas. Summa Theologica, II-II, Q.77.

Leland, H. E. 1992. "Insider Trading: Should It Be Prohibited?" *Journal of Political Economy* 100 (4): 859–87.

Machan, T. 1996. "What is Morally Right with Insider Trading?" *Public Affairs Quarterly* 10 (2): 135–41.

Morgan, R. J. 1987. "Insider Trading and the Infringement of Property Rights," *Ohio State Law Journal* 48:79–116.

*Webster's New World Dictionary of the American Language, College edition.* 1964. (Cleveland and New York: World Co.).

## LEGAL PERSPECTIVES

# United States Supreme Court

Justice Ginsburg delivered the opinion of the Court.

Respondent James Herman O'Hagan was a partner in the law firm of Dorsey & Whitney

*United States, Petitioner v. James Herman O'Hagan*

in Minneapolis, Minnesota. In July 1988, Grand Metropolitan PLC (Grand Met), a company based in London, England, retained Dorsey & Whitney as local counsel to represent

Grand Met regarding a potential tender offer for the common stock of the Pillsbury Company, headquartered in Minneapolis. Both Grand Met and Dorsey & Whitney took precautions to protect the confidentiality of Grand Met's tender offer plans. O'Hagan did no work on the Grand Met representation. Dorsey & Whitney withdrew from representing Grand Met on September 9, 1988. Less than a month later, on October 4, 1988, Grand Met publicly announced its tender offer for Pillsbury stock.

On August 18, 1988, while Dorsey & Whitney was still representing Grand Met, O'Hagan began purchasing call options for Pillsbury stock. Each option gave him the right to purchase 100 shares of Pillsbury stock by a specified date in September 1988. Later in August and in September, O'Hagan made additional purchases of Pillsbury call options. By the end of September, he owned 2,500 unexpired Pillsbury options, apparently more than any other individual investor. O'Hagan also purchased, in September 1988, some 5,000 shares of Pillsbury common stock, at a price just under $39 per share. When Grand Met announced its tender offer in October, the price of Pillsbury stock rose to nearly $60 per share. O'Hagan then sold his Pillsbury call options and common stock, making a profit of more than $4.3 million.

The Securities and Exchange Commission (SEC or Commission) initiated an investigation into O'Hagan's transactions, culminating in a 57-count indictment. The indictment alleged that O'Hagan defrauded his law firm and its client, Grand Met, by using for his own trading purposes material, nonpublic information regarding Grand Met's planned tender offer.

According to the indictment, O'Hagan used the profits he gained through this trading to conceal his previous embezzlement and conversion of unrelated client trust funds.

O'Hagan was charged with 20 counts of mail fraud, 17 counts of securities fraud, 17 counts of fraudulent trading in connection with a tender offer, and 3 counts of violating federal money laundering statutes. A jury convicted O'Hagan on all 57 counts, and he was sentenced to a 41-month term of imprisonment.

A divided panel of the Court of Appeals for the Eighth Circuit reversed all of O'Hagan's convictions. Liability under §10(b) and Rule 10b-5, the Eighth Circuit held, may not be grounded on the "misappropriation theory" of securities fraud on which the prosecution relied. The Court of Appeals also held that Rule 14e-3(a)—which prohibits trading while in possession of material, nonpublic information relating to a tender offer—exceeds the SEC's §14(e) rulemaking authority because the rule contains no breach of fiduciary duty requirement. The Eighth Circuit further concluded that O'Hagan's mail fraud and money laundering convictions rested on violations of the securities laws, and therefore could not stand once the securities fraud convictions were reversed. Judge Fagg, dissenting, stated that he would recognize and enforce the misappropriation theory, and would hold that the SEC did not exceed its rulemaking authority when it adopted Rule 14e-3(a) without requiring proof of a breach of fiduciary duty. . . .

We hold, in accord with several other Courts of Appeals that criminal liability under §10(b) may be predicated on the misappropriation theory.

In pertinent part, §10(b) of the Exchange Act provides:

> It shall be unlawful for any person, directly or indirectly, by the use of any means or instrumentality of interstate commerce or of the mails, or of any facility of any national securities exchange . . .
>
> (b) To use or employ, in connection with the purchase or sale of any security registered on a national securities exchange or any security not so registered, any manipulative or deceptive device or contrivance in contravention of such rules and regulations as the [Securities and Exchange] Commission may prescribe as necessary

or appropriate in the public interest or for the protection of investors. 15 U.S.C. §78j(b)

The statute thus proscribes (1) using any deceptive device (2) in connection with the purchase or sale of securities, in contravention of rules prescribed by the Commission. The provision, as written, does not confine its coverage to deception of a purchaser or seller of securities; rather, the statute reaches any deceptive device used "in connection with the purchase or sale of any security."

Pursuant to its §10(b) rulemaking authority, the Commission has adopted Rule 10b-5, which, as relevant here, provides:

> It shall be unlawful for any person, directly or indirectly, by the use of any means or instrumentality of interstate commerce, or of the mails or of any facility of any national securities exchange,
> (a) To employ any device, scheme, or artifice to defraud, [or] . . .
> (c) To engage in any act, practice, or course of business which operates or would operate as a fraud or deceit upon any person,
> in connection with the purchase or sale of any security.

Under the "traditional" or "classical theory" of insider trading liability, §10(b) and Rule 10b-5 are violated when a corporate insider trades in the securities of his corporation on the basis of material, nonpublic information. Trading on such information qualifies as a "deceptive device" under §10(b), we have affirmed, because "a relationship of trust and confidence [exists] between the shareholders of a corporation and those insiders who have obtained confidential information by reason of their position with that corporation." That relationship, we recognized, "gives rise to a duty to disclose [or to abstain from trading] because of the 'necessity of preventing a corporate insider from . . . tak[ing] unfair advantage of . . . uninformed . . . stockholders.'" The classical theory applies not only to officers, directors, and other permanent insiders of a corporation, but also to attorneys, accountants, consultants, and others who temporarily become fiduciaries of a corporation.

The "misappropriation theory" holds that a person commits fraud "in connection with" a securities transaction, and thereby violates §10(b) and Rule 10b-5, when he misappropriates confidential information for securities trading purposes, in breach of a duty owed to the source of the information. Under this theory, a fiduciary's undisclosed, self serving use of a principal's information to purchase or sell securities, in breach of a duty of loyalty and confidentiality, defrauds the principal of the exclusive use of that information. In lieu of premising liability on a fiduciary relationship between company insider and purchaser or seller of the company's stock, the misappropriation theory premises liability on a fiduciary turned trader's deception of those who entrusted him with access to confidential information.

The two theories are complementary, each addressing efforts to capitalize on nonpublic information through the purchase or sale of securities. The classical theory targets a corporate insider's breach of duty to shareholders with whom the insider transacts; the misappropriation theory outlaws trading on the basis of nonpublic information by a corporate "outsider" in breach of a duty owed not to a trading party, but to the source of the information. The misappropriation theory is thus designed to "protec[t] the integrity of the securities markets against abuses by 'outsiders' to a corporation who have access to confidential information that will affect th[e] corporation's security price when revealed, but who owe no fiduciary or other duty to that corporation's shareholders."

In this case, the indictment alleged that O'Hagan, in breach of a duty of trust and confidence he owed to his law firm, Dorsey & Whitney, and to its client, Grand Met, traded on the basis of nonpublic information regarding Grand Met's planned tender offer for Pillsbury common stock. This conduct, the Government charged, constituted a fraudulent device in connection with the purchase and sale of securities.

We agree with the Government that misappropriation, as just defined, satisfies §10(b)'s requirement that chargeable conduct involve a "deceptive device or contrivance" used "in connection with" the purchase or sale of securities. We observe, first, that misappropriators, as the Government describes them, deal in deception. A fiduciary who "[pretends] loyalty to the principal while secretly converting the principal's information for personal gain," "dupes" or defrauds the principal. . . .

Deception through nondisclosure is central to the theory of liability for which the Government seeks recognition. As counsel for the Government stated in explanation of the theory at oral argument: "To satisfy the common law rule that a trustee may not use the property that [has] been entrusted [to] him, there would have to be consent. To satisfy the requirement of the Securities Act that there be no deception, there would only have to be disclosure." . . .

The misappropriation theory targets information of a sort that misappropriators ordinarily capitalize upon to gain no risk profits through the purchase or sale of securities. Should a misappropriator put such information to other use, the statute's prohibition would not be implicated. The theory does not catch all conceivable forms of fraud involving confidential information; rather, it catches fraudulent means of capitalizing on such information through securities transactions.

The dissent's charge that the misappropriation theory is incoherent because information, like funds, can be put to multiple uses, misses the point. The Exchange Act was enacted in part "to insure the maintenance of fair and honest markets," and there is no question that fraudulent uses of confidential information fall within §10(b)'s prohibition if the fraud is "in connection with" a securities transaction. It is hardly remarkable that a rule suitably applied to the fraudulent uses of certain kinds of information would be stretched beyond reason were it applied to the fraudulent use of money. . . .

In sum, it is a fair assumption that trading on the basis of material, nonpublic information will often involve a breach of a duty of confidentiality to the bidder or target company or their representatives. The SEC, cognizant of the proof problem that could enable sophisticated traders to escape responsibility, placed in Rule 14e-3(a) a "disclose or abstain from trading" command that does not require specific proof of a breach of fiduciary duty. That prescription, we are satisfied, applied to this case, is a "means reasonably designed to prevent" fraudulent trading on material, nonpublic information in the tender offer context. . . .

The judgment of the Court of Appeals for the Eighth Circuit is reversed, and the case is remanded for further proceedings consistent with this opinion.

*It is so ordered.*

---

# American Institute of Certified Public Accountants Code of Professional Conduct

## PREAMBLE

1. Membership in the American Institute of Certified Public Accountants is voluntary. By accepting membership, a certified public accountant assumes an obligation of self-discipline above and beyond the requirements of laws and regulations.

2. These Principles of the Code of Professional Conduct of the American Institute of Certified Public Accountants express the profession's recognition of its responsibilities to the public, to clients, and to colleagues. They guide members in the performance of their professional responsibilities and express the basic tenets of ethical and professional conduct. The Principles call for an unswerving commitment to honorable behavior, even at the sacrifice of personal advantage.

# ARTICLE I: RESPONSIBILITIES

*In carrying out their responsibilities as professionals, members should exercise sensitive professional and moral judgments in all their activities.*

1. As professionals, certified public accountants perform an essential role in society. Consistent with that role, members of the American Institute of Certified Public Accountants have responsibilities to all those who use their professional services. Members also have a continuing responsibility to cooperate with each other to improve the art of accounting, maintain the public's confidence, and carry out the profession's special responsibilities for self-governance. The collective efforts of all members are required to maintain and enhance the traditions of the profession.

# ARTICLE II: PUBLIC INTEREST

*Members should accept the obligation to act in a way that will serve the public interest, honor the public trust, and demonstrate commitment to professionalism.*

1. A distinguishing mark of a profession is acceptance of its responsibility to the public. The accounting profession's public consists of clients, credit grantors, governments, employers, investors, the business and financial community, and others who rely on the objectivity and integrity of certified public accountants to maintain the orderly functioning of commerce. This reliance imposes a public interest responsibility on certified public accountants. The public interest is defined as the collective well-being of the community of people and institutions the profession serves.

2. In discharging their professional responsibilities, members may encounter conflicting pressures from among each of those groups. In resolving those conflicts, members should act with integrity, guided by the precept that when members fulfill their responsibility to the public, clients' and employers' interests are best served.

3. Those who rely on certified public accountants expect them to discharge their responsibilities with integrity, objectivity, due professional care, and a genuine interest in serving the public. They are expected to provide quality services, enter into fee arrangements, and offer a range of services—all in a manner that demonstrates a level of professionalism consistent with these Principles of the Code of Professional Conduct.

4. All who accept membership in the American Institute of Certified Public Accountants commit themselves to honor the public trust. In return for the faith that the public reposes in them, members should seek continually to demonstrate their dedication to professional excellence.

# ARTICLE III: INTEGRITY

*To maintain and broaden public confidence, members should perform all professional responsibilities with the highest sense of integrity.*

1. Integrity is an element of character fundamental to professional recognition. It is the quality from which the public trust derives and the benchmark against which a member must ultimately test all decisions.

2. Integrity requires a member to be, among other things, honest and candid within the constraints of client confidentiality. Service and the public trust should not be subordinated to personal gain and advantage. Integrity can accommodate the inadvertent error and the honest difference of opinion; it cannot accommodate deceit or subordination of principle.

3. Integrity is measured in terms of what is right and just. In the absence of specific rules, standards, or guidance, or in the face of conflicting opinions, a member should test decisions and deeds by asking: "Am I doing what a person of

integrity would do? Have I retained my integrity?" Integrity requires a member to observe both the form and the spirit of technical and ethical standards; circumvention of those standards constitutes subordination of judgment.

4. Integrity also requires a member to observe the principles of objectivity and independence and of due care.

## ARTICLE IV: OBJECTIVITY AND INDEPENDENCE

*A member should maintain objectivity and be free of conflicts of interest in discharging professional responsibilities. A member in public practice should be independent in fact and appearance when providing auditing and other attestation services.*

1. Objectivity is a state of mind, a quality that lends value to a member's services. It is a distinguishing feature of the profession. The principle of objectivity imposes the obligation to be impartial, intellectually honest, and free of conflicts of interest. Independence precludes relationships that may appear to impair a member's objectivity in rendering attestation services.

2. Members often serve multiple interests in many different capacities and must demonstrate their objectivity in varying circumstances. Members in public practice render attest, tax, and management advisory services. Other members prepare financial statements in the employment of others, perform internal auditing services, and serve in financial and management capacities in industry, education, and government. They also educate and train those who aspire to admission into the profession. Regardless of service or capacity, members should protect the integrity of their work, maintain objectivity, and avoid any subordination of their judgment.

3. For a member in public practice, the maintenance of objectivity and independence requires a continuing assessment of client relationships and public responsibility. Such a member who provides auditing and other attestation services should be independent in fact and appearance. In providing all other services, a member should maintain objectivity and avoid conflicts of interest.

4. Although members not in public practice cannot maintain the appearance of independence, they nevertheless have the responsibility to maintain objectivity in rendering professional services. Members employed by others to prepare financial statements or to perform auditing, tax, or consulting services are charged with the same responsibility for objectivity as members in public practice and must be scrupulous in their application of generally accepted accounting principles and candid in all their dealings with members in public practice.

## ARTICLE V: DUE CARE

*A member should observe the profession's technical and ethical standards, strive continually to improve competence and the quality of services, and discharge professional responsibility to the best of the member's ability.*

1. The quest for excellence is the essence of due care. Due care requires a member to discharge professional responsibilities with competence and diligence. It imposes the obligation to perform professional services to the best of a member's ability with concern for the best interest of those for whom the services are performed and consistent with the profession's responsibility to the public.

2. Competence is derived from a synthesis of education and experience. It begins with a mastery of the common body of knowledge required for designation as a certified public accountant. The maintenance of competence requires a commitment to learning and professional improvement that must continue throughout a member's professional life. It is a member's individual responsibility. In all engagements and in all responsibilities, each member should undertake to achieve a level of competence that will assure that the quality of the member's services meets the high level of professionalism required by these Principles.

3. Competence represents the attainment and maintenance of a level of understanding and knowledge that enables a member to render services with facility and acumen. It also establishes the limitations of a member's capabilities by dictating that consultation or referral may be required when a professional

engagement exceeds the personal compe-tence of a member or a member's firm. Each member is responsible for assessing his or her own competence—of evaluating whether ed-ucation, experience, and judgment are ade-quate for the responsibility to be assumed.

4. Members should be diligent in discharging re-sponsibilities to clients, employers, and the public. Diligence imposes the responsibility to render services promptly and carefully, to be thorough, and to observe applicable technical and ethical standards.

5. Due care requires a member to plan and su-pervise adequately any professional activity for which he or she is responsible.

## ARTICLE VI: SCOPE AND NATURE OF SERVICES

*A member in public practice should observe the Principles of the Code of Professional Conduct in determining the scope and nature of services to be pro-vided.*

1. The public interest aspect of certified public ac-countants' services requires that such services be consistent with acceptable professional be-havior for certified public accountants. Integri-ty requires that service and the public trust not be subordinated to personal gain and advan-tage. Objectivity and independence require that members be free from conflicts of interest in discharging professional responsibilities. Due care requires that services be provided with competence and diligence.

2. Each of these Principles should be considered by members in determining whether or not to provide specific services in individual circum-stances. In some instances, they may represent an overall constraint on the nonaudit services that might be offered to a specific client. No hard-and-fast rules can be developed to help members reach these judgments, but they must be satisfied that they are meeting the spirit of the Principles in this regard.

3. In order to accomplish this, members should

   • Practice in firms that have in place internal quality-control procedures to ensure that services are competently delivered and ad-equately supervised.

   • Determine, in their individual judgments, whether the scope and nature of other ser-vices provided to an audit client would cre-ate a conflict of interest in the performance of the audit function for that client.

   • Assess, in their individual judgments, whether an activity is consistent with their role as professionals.

## CASES

# CASE 1.   *An Auditor's Dilemma*

As she sorts through a stack of invoices, Alison Lloyd's attention is drawn to one from Ace Glass Company. Her responsibility as the new internal auditor for Gem Packing is to verify all expenditures, and she knows that Ace has al-ready been paid for the June delivery of the jars that are used for Gem's jams and jellies. On closer inspection, she notices that the in-voice is for deliveries in July and August that have not yet been made. Today is only June 10. Alison recalls approving several other invoices lately that seemed to be misdated, but the amounts were small compared with the $130,000 that Gem spends each month for glass jars. I had better check this out with pur-chasing, she thinks.

Over lunch, Greg Berg, the head of purchasing, explains the system to her. The jam and jelly division operates under an incentive plan whereby the division manager and the heads of the four main units—sales, production, distribution, and purchasing—receive substantial bonuses for meeting their quota in pretax profits for the fiscal year, which ends on June 30. The bonuses are about half of annual salary and constitute one-third of the managers' total compensation. In addition, meeting quota is weighted heavily in evaluations, and missing even once is considered to be a death blow to the career of an aspiring executive at Gem. So the pressure on these managers is intense. On the other hand, there is nothing to be gained from exceeding a quota. An exceptionally good year is likely to be rewarded with an even higher quota the next year, since quotas are generally set at corporate headquarters by adding 5 percent to the previous year's results.

Greg continues to explain that several years ago, after the quota had been safely met, the jam and jelly division began prepaying as many expenses as possible—not only for glass jars but for advertising costs, trucking charges, and some commodities, such as sugar. The practice has continued to grow, and sales also helps out by delaying orders until the next fiscal year or by falsifying delivery dates when a shipment has already gone out. "Regular suppliers like Ace Glass know how we work," Greg says, "and they sent the invoices for July and August at my request." He predicts that Alison will begin seeing more irregular invoices as the fiscal year winds down. "Making quota gets easier each year." Greg observes, "because the division gets an ever increasing head start, but the problem of finding ways to avoid going too far over quota has become a real nightmare." Greg is not sure, but he thinks that other divisions are doing the same thing. "I don't think corporate has caught on yet," he says. "But they created the system, and they've been happy with the results so far. If they're too dumb to figure out how we're achieving them, that's their problem."

Alison recalls that on becoming a member of the Institute of Internal Auditors, she agreed to abide by the IIA code of ethics. This code requires members to exercise "honesty, objectivity, and diligence" in the performance of their duties, but also to be loyal to the employer. However, loyalty does not include being a party to any "illegal or improper activity." As an internal auditor, she is also responsible for evaluating the adequacy and effectiveness of the company's system of financial control. But what is the harm of shuffling a little paper around? she thinks. Nobody is getting hurt, and it all works out in the end.

### Questions

1. Is the IAA code of ethics really helpful in resolving Alison's dilemma? Why or why not?
2. Greg blames the incentive system for the dilemma. Is he right?

## CASE 2.  *Accounting for Enron*

Enron Corporation has come to symbolize the worst of recent corporate corruption scandals. Billions of dollars were lost by investors, and thousands of people lost their jobs and their retirement savings when the one-time seventh-largest United States corporation went bankrupt, the largest bankruptcy in history at the time, as a result of the fraud

From Joseph R. DesJardins and John J. McCall, *Contemporary Issues in Business Ethics*, 5th ed. (Belmont, CA: Thompson Wadsworth, 2005).

created by its highest-ranking executives. But the story of Enron is also the story of a failed watchdog system designed to prevent such fraud. Auditors, attorneys, and government officials who had responsibilities to protect investors and ensure the integrity of financial markets systematically failed to live up to their responsibilities.

Enron's collapse began in 2001 when some independent stock analysts and journalists publicly raised questions about the value of Enron's stock. At that time, Enron's stock was trading at more than $80 a share, and Enron's CEO Jeffrey Skilling was publicly claiming that it ought to be valued at well over $100 a share. During the summer of 2001, several Enron insiders, including Vice Chair Clifford Baxter, Treasurer Jeff McMahon, and Vice President Sherron Watkins, all expressed doubts internally about Enron's financial practices. During this same period, other Enron insiders, including CEO Skilling and Board Chair and former CEO Kenneth Lay, Enron's corporate counsel, and several board members were selling millions of shares of Enron stock.

In October 2001 when Arthur Andersen auditors finally reversed their previous decisions and restated Enron's financial situations, the collapse of Enron began in earnest. By December, when its stock was worth just pennies a share, Enron declared bankruptcy and dismissed over 4,000 employees.

Enron's collapse was mirrored by the collapse of its auditing firm, Arthur Andersen. Once one of the "Big Five" accounting firms, Arthur Andersen was driven out of business by its role in the Enron scandal. On January 9, 2002, the United States Justice Department announced that it had begun a criminal investigation into Arthur Andersen's activities related to Enron. At the time, Arthur Andersen was already on probation by the SEC for its questionable accounting practices in previous scandals at Sunbeam Corporation and Waste Management. The next day, Andersen admit-

ted that it had shredded thousands of documents related to its Enron audits. Five days later, Andersen fired David Duncan, an Andersen partner and head auditor for Enron. Soon after, the Justice Department indicted Arthur Andersen on charges of obstruction of justice. Finally, on June 15, 2002, Arthur Andersen was found guilty in a criminal trial of obstructing justice by shredding evidence relating to the Enron scandal and, as a result, the firm agreed to cease auditing public companies by August 31.

Records show that as early as May 1998, Andersen's auditors were expressing grave concerns about Enron's financial practices. On that date, in an e-mail to David Duncan, Benjamin Neuhausen, a member of Andersen's Professional Standards Group, expressed his thoughts on the Special Purpose Entities (SPEs) that were at the heart of the Enron scandal. "Setting aside the accounting, [sic] idea of a venture entity managed by CFO is terrible from a business point of view. Conflicts of interest galore. Why would any director in his or her right mind ever approve such a scheme?" Neuhausen then went on to highlight the many accounting problems with the SPEs being managed by Enron CFO Andrew Fastow. Duncan replied, "But first, on your point 1 (i.e. the whole thing is a bad idea), I really couldn't agree more." Nevertheless, the Andersen auditors continued to cooperate with Enron by attesting to the soundness of Enron's financial statements.

In February 2001, more than a dozen Andersen auditors once again met to discuss the financial status of Enron's SPEs. Evidence shows that Andersen's auditors had serious concerns about the validity of Enron's financial self-portrait. In light of these concerns, they considered dropping Enron as an audit client. Michael Jones, one of Andersen's Houston employees, summarized the meeting in an e-mail to David Duncan, who also participated. Jones' notes reveal "significant discussion was held regarding the related party transactions with LJM" (one of Enron's Special Purpose Entities). Apparently, several Andersen auditors thought that LJM costs should not be kept off of Enron's books. Jones goes on to say, "The discussion focused on Fastow's conflicts of interest in his capacity as CFO and the LJM manager, the amount of earnings that Fastow receives for his services and participation in LJM, the disclosures of the transaction in the financial footnotes, and Enron's BOD's [Board of Directors] views regarding the transactions." Enron's activities were described as "intelligent gambling," and Andersen's auditors acknowledged "Enron's reliance on its current credit rating to maintain itself," its "dependence" on a supporting audit to meet its financial objectives, and "the fact that Enron often is creating industries and markets and transactions for which there are no specific rules [and therefore] which requires significant judgment." Enron was also described as "aggressive" in the way it structured its financial statements.

But the risks of Enron were not the only issues discussed at that meeting. Andersen's auditors realized that Andersen was also doing significant consulting business with Enron, business that could be jeopardized by an unfavorable audit. "We discussed whether there would be a perceived independence issue solely considering our level of fees. We discussed that the concerns should not be on the magnitude of the fees but in the nature of the fees. We discussed that it would not be unforeseeable that fees could reach $100 million per year. Such amounts did not trouble the participants as long as the nature of the services was not an issue." In the end, Andersen decided that the risks were worth taking. "Ultimately the conclusion was reached to retain Enron as a client citing that it appeared that we had the appropriate people and processes in place to serve Enron and manage our risks."

Less than a year later, Enron's third-quarter financial report would reflect Andersen's new and different judgment concerning the SPEs. On October 16, Enron reported a quarterly loss of $618 million and announced that as a result of Andersen's auditing decisions, they would take a $1.2 billion reduction in shareholder equity. Within one week, the SEC announced that it had opened an investigation into Enron's accounting practices. By the end of October, Enron's stock was trading at just $10 per share, an almost a 90% drop in 18 months.

It is fair to say that Andersen overestimated their ability to manage the risks of Enron. Several decisions made by Andersen's professional staff during October proved to be disastrous for the company. On October 12, as Andersen prepared for the public release of the new financial statements, Andersen attorney Nancy Temple advised head auditor David Duncan to get "in compliance" with Andersen's document retention policy. Because Andersen's document retention policy included directions to destroy documents that were no longer needed, Duncan interpreted that advice to mean that he should have Enron-related documents destroyed. Duncan then instructed Andersen employees to shred Enron documents. Duncan has acknowledged that he and others at Andersen were aware of a possible SEC investigation at the time.

Four days later, on October 16, Duncan shared a draft of a press release on Enron with Temple. In her role as Andersen attorney, Temple advised changing the press release to delete some language that might suggest that Andersen's audit was not in compliance with Generally Accepted Accounting Principles (GAAP), as well as certain references to discussions within Andersen's legal group concerning Enron. Temple concluded her e-mail by promising to "consult further within the legal group as to whether we should do anything more to protect ourselves from potential Section 10 issues" (Section 10 refers to SEC rules that require auditors to report illicit client activity). In early November, two weeks after they began shredding documents, Andersen received a federal subpoena for documents related to Enron. Only at this point did Temple advise Andersen to write a memo advising auditors at Andersen to "keep everything, do not destroy anything." By the end of November, the SEC investigation was officially expanded to include Arthur Andersen.

At one time, Sherron Watkins was an Arthur Andersen auditor who worked on the Enron account. In 1993, she left Andersen to join Enron, working for Andrew Fastow in Enron's finance, international, broadband, and finally, its corporate development division. Thus, for 18 years she participated in a wide range of Enron's business activities. In August 2001, shortly after Jeffrey Skilling resigned as Enron's CEO, she wrote a memo to Kenneth Lay. Watkins became widely known as the Enron whistle-blower as a result of this memo, despite the fact that she had not expressed concerns earlier and she did not share her concerns with anyone outside of the company. In part, her memo to Lay reads as follows:

> Has Enron become a risky place to work? For those of us who didn't get rich over the last few years, can we afford to stay?
>
> Skilling's abrupt departure will raise suspicions of accounting improprieties and valuation issues. Enron has been very aggressive in its accounting—most notably the Raptor transactions and the Condor vehicle. We do have valuation issues with our international assets and possibly some of our EES MTM positions.
>
> The spotlight will be on us, the market just can't accept that Skilling is leaving his dream job. I think that the valuation issues can be fixed and reported with other good will write-downs to occur in 2002. How do we fix the Raptor and Condor deals? They unwind in 2002 and 2003, we will have to pony up Enron stock and that won't go unnoticed. . . .

> It sure looks to the layman on the street that we are hiding losses in a related company and will compensate that company with Enron stock in the future. I am incredibly nervous that we will implode in a wave of accounting scandals. My 8 years of Enron work history will be worth nothing on my résumé, the business world will consider the past successes as nothing but an elaborate accounting hoax. Skilling is resigning now for "personal reasons" but I would think he wasn't having fun, looked down the road and knew this stuff was unfixable and would rather abandon ship now than resign in shame in 2 years. . . .
>
> Is there a way our accounting gurus can unwind these deals now? I have thought and thought about a way to do this, but I keep bumping into one big problem—we booked the Condor and Raptor deals in 1999 and 2000, we enjoyed wonderfully high stock price, many executives sold stock, we then try and reverse or fix the deals in 2001, and it's a bit like robbing the bank in one year and trying to pay it back two years later. Nice try, but investors were hurt, they bought at $70 and $80 a share looking for $120 a share and now they're at $38 or worse. We are under too much scrutiny and there are probably one or two disgruntled "redeployed" employees who know enough about the "funny" accounting to get us in trouble. What do we do? I know this question cannot be addressed in the all-employee meeting, but can you give some assurances that you and Causey will sit down and take a good hard objective look at what is going to happen to Condor and Raptor in 2002 and 2003? . . .
>
> I realize that we have had a lot of smart people looking at this and a lot of accountants including AA & Co. have blessed the accounting treatment. None of that will protect Enron if these transactions are ever disclosed in the bright light of day. (Please review the late 90s problems of Waste Management where AA paid $130 million plus in litigation re questionable accounting practices.) . . .
>
> I firmly believe that executive management of the company must have a clear and precise knowledge of these transactions and they must have the transactions reviewed by objective experts in the fields of securities law and accounting. I believe Ken Lay deserves the right to judge for himself what he believes the probabilities of discovery to be and the estimated damages to the company from those discoveries and decide one of two courses of action:

1. The probability of discovery is low enough and the estimated damage too great; therefore we find a way to quietly and quickly reverse, unwind, write down these positions/transactions.

2. The probability of discovery is too great, the estimated damages to the company too great; therefore, we must quantify, develop damage containment plans and disclose.

I firmly believe that the probability of discovery significantly increased with Skilling's shocking departure. Too many people are looking for a smoking gun. . . . There is a veil of secrecy around LJM and Raptor. Employees question our accounting propriety consistently and constantly. This alone is cause for concern. . . . I have heard one manager-level employee from the principal investments group say, "I know it would be devastating to all of us, but I wish we would get caught. We're such a crooked company." . . .[1]

Another group of Enron insiders who were in position and had a responsibility to protect investors from fraud was Enron's Board of Directors, and particularly the Board's audit committee. In theory and in law, the board's primary responsibility is to represent the interests of shareholders. In practice, the board seemed less than vigilant in fulfilling these responsibilities. Enron's board approved of Andrew Fastow's violation of the corporate conflicts of interest prohibition when he negotiated contracts between Enron and the SPEs in which he was heavily invested and from which he profited tremendously. As Benjamin Neuhausen, one of Andersen's Enron accountants, claimed, the "idea of a venture entity managed by CFO is terrible from a business point of view. Conflicts of interest galore. Why would any director in his or her right mind ever approve such a scheme?"

The final line of defense against corporate fraud should be government officials and regulators. Arthur Levitt, chairman of the SEC throughout the 1990s, strongly criticized the dual auditing and consulting activities of the big accounting firms as involving conflicts of interest. Congress ignored his advice, apparently convinced by the lobbying efforts of the accounting profession to allow audit firms to continue working as consultants to the firms they audited.

The federal government was also actively dismantling a wide range of financial regulatory protections during the 1990s. During the first Bush Administration, the federal government deregulated the energy industry, ostensibly to spur economic growth according to free market principles. One of the leading advocates for this deregulation was Wendy Gramm, who at the time was chairwoman of the U.S. Commodity Futures Trading Commission. Gramm's husband is Phil Gramm, then U.S. Senator from Texas and a member of the Senate banking, finance, and budget committees that supported this deregulation. Senator Gramm had received over $100,000 in campaign contributions from Enron during his last two Senate campaigns. When Wendy Gramm left government in 1992, she joined Enron's Board of Directors as a member of their audit committee.

## Questions

1. What responsibilities did David Duncan owe to Arthur Andersen? To Enron's management? To Enron's stockholders? To the accounting profession?

2. What are the ethical responsibilities of a corporate attorney, such as Nancy Temple, who works for an "aggressive" client wishing to push the envelope of legality?

3. Under what conditions should an employee such as Sherron Watkins blow the whistle to outside authorities? To whom did she owe loyalty?

4. To whom does the board of directors owe their primary responsibility? Can you think of any law or regulations that would help ensure that boards meet their primary responsibilities?

5. What responsibilities do government regulators owe to business? To the market? To the
general public?
6. Are accounting and law professions or businesses? What is the difference?

## NOTES

1. From a report released by the U.S. House of
Representatives Energy Committee, February
2002.

## CASE 3.   *Enron and Employee Investment Risk*

To determine appropriate and acceptable levels of risk in their retirement funds, employee-
investors must be knowledgeable about how
those funds are invested. Often employees are
unaware of the level of risk taken by their employers in maintaining a fund. A famous recent case of the problem emerged from the
ashes of the collapse of Enron.

After greatly expanding its operations during
the 1990s, Enron, an energy broker, experienced
unprecedented financial growth and soaring
stock prices. Much of this growth, however, was
not legitimate, and the details, as a result, were
not disclosed to investors or to employees.

Using the lawful practice of "mark-to-market"
accounting, Enron's financial analysts and
advisors were able to record potential future
profits as immediate gains. To boost these
apparent profits even more, Enron also created
businesses and partnerships to hide its debt.
These practices inflated stock prices while falsely
establishing the company's financial position
and stability. The success and prominence of
the company seemed to minimize concerns
about investment risk in Enron stock. Seeing
immediate and extensive gains, however, such
employee-investors saw little incentive in questioning the risk of their investments. They were
not concerned when Enron used company
stock as the sole unit of deposit in employee

401(k) earnings. While this involved tremendous risk, given Enron's true instability, the details of the company's financial state remained
undisclosed. Only after uncovering the fraudulent accounting practices was the true level of
the risk assessed. By this time, however, employee-investors and employees with retirement
savings invested in stock had lost all of their investments and all of their retirement funds.

Enron-style investing is commonplace in
employee retirement accounts, where diversification in types of investment is not generally
recognized as a legal or a moral requirement.
While the collapse of Enron is everywhere recognized to be a scandal, the underlying questions of investor risk in company retirement
plans is one feature of this scandal that remains largely unaddressed.

### Questions

1. Should businesses, like Enron, encourage
employees to buy stock in their own companies? Why or why not? What are some
of the risks involved in permitting such
practices?
2. Although legally not all information must
be disclosed, should companies be obligated to reveal the true nature of investor

---

This case was prepared by David Lawrence and Tom L. Beauchamp.

risk? Or are investors individually responsible for determining such risk?

3. Did Enron's overstating of profit amount to a manipulation of investors? Was the manipulation intentional? Should investors assume a high level of risk unless expressly told otherwise?

# CASE 4. *The Conventions of Lying on Wall Street*

Salomon Brothers is among an elite group authorized to purchase U.S. Treasury notes from the U.S. government for resale to private investors. These notes are sold periodically at Treasury auctions. Before each auction, a firm receives "buy" orders from customers. The firm then tries to buy securities at the lowest possible price. The government places some restrictions on the bidding. First, a firm may purchase no more than 35 percent of the notes offered at a given auction for its portfolio. Second, if a firm holds large orders from an investor, it can buy bonds directly for that customer, and these bonds are *not* included in the 35 percent limit. If a firm is unable to purchase enough securities to fill the orders from its customers, the firm must then buy from competing firms at a higher rate than the auction rate.

In July 1991 Salomon Brothers Inc. confessed to illegally purchasing U.S. Treasury notes on three separate occasions. They exploited the system in two ways. First, at the December, February, and May auctions, Salomon used customers' names to submit false bids. That is, they ordered bonds for customers who had *not* placed orders and did not know their names were being used. After the auction, Salomon added these bonds to its own portfolio. On the second occasion, Salomon worked with a customer to purchase a large quantity of bonds in the customer's name. Salomon then bought back a portion of the bonds, effectively making a net purchase from the auction greater than 35 percent. Using this strategy, Salomon purchased 46 percent of Treasury notes sold on one occasion and 57 percent of the securities sold on another occasion.

Treasury auctions are also affected by the prevalent practice of sharing information. Current and former traders at several prominent Wall Street investment banks admit they regularly have shared "secrets" about the size and price of their bids at government auctions. This collusion to create a low bidding strategy results in firms paying less to the federal government. Consequently, the government makes less money to finance debt, causing an increase in taxes and interest rates.

This collusion is further complicated by strategies of deception. Lying has been tolerated and indeed has been expected for many years as part of the competition for trading. "It is part of the playing field. It's ingrained in the way the Street operates," one industry executive says, "I've stood out there on that trading floor and they lie to each other (before the auctions). That's part of the game. It was an exception when traders actually told the truth to each other about their bidding strategy." He adds, "They lie through their teeth to each other. You want to catch the [other] guy in an awkward position and pick him off."

This case was prepared by Tom L. Beauchamp and revised by Jeff Greene.

In a report to the U.S. Congress, the Federal Home Mortgage Company claimed that two-thirds of Wall Street firms that it regularly deals with have lied to the agency to increase the chances of buying as many of the agency's securities as possible. Such deceit is so pervasive and routine on Wall Street that it has come to be regarded as the preferred and accepted way of doing business—the "standard of practice," as some put it. The common practice of submitting inflated orders has come under scrutiny from securities firms and the Federal Trade Commission, but the practice is so pervasive that it cannot be easily remedied. A small group of dealers holds purchasing power on the market and has long operated with financial success and with no serious challenges to its mode of operation.

One bond market specialist says, "I'm not condoning it or excusing it or saying it didn't go to an extreme . . . but people forget that the markets which are under the spotlight are part of that kind of distribution activity which for centuries has [been] associated with a fair amount of caveat emptor and puffery." The traditions of bluffing, deception, and puffery have created an environment in which every player in the "game" expects deception as the condition for playing.

**Questions**

1. Is Wall Street actually a "game," and can these allegations and expectations be applied equally to every participant?
2. Should the FTC ignore deceit and collusion on Wall Street, since it is ingrained in the system? Why or why not?
3. Does Wall Street have a valid standard of practice for disclosing information?

## CASE 5.  *Martha Stewart Living Omnimedia Inc.: An Accusation of Insider Trading*

The sun shone brightly as the private jet touched down in San Antonio to refuel before heading on to San José del Cabo, Mexico. Martha Stewart flipped open a cell phone to check her messages. After discovering that someone from brokerage firm Merrill Lynch was trying to contact her, she returned the call. Within minutes, she placed a sell order on her entire holding of ImClone shares. Her call was made at 1:41 P.M., Eastern Standard Time (EST). Just 2 minutes later, at 1:43 P.M., Merrill Lynch trading assistant Douglas Faneuil executed the order, selling 3,928 shares of ImClone Systems Inc. common stock for $58 per share.[1]

### THE MAKING OF MARTHA STEWART LIVING OMNIMEDIA

In July 1991, Martha Stewart and Time Publishing Venture Inc. printed the first issue of *Martha Stewart Living,* a monthly lifestyle magazine. Martha later teamed up with Sharon Patrick, a graduate of Stanford University and the Harvard Business School. A business plan

This case was prepared by Arianne R. Westby and Mary P. Moulton under the supervision James S. O'Rourke. © 2002 Fanning Centers For Business Communication.

for Martha's company emerged during an adventurous trip in which the two climbed Africa's Mount Kilimanjaro. The plan included a strategy to buy back her magazine with a combination of cash and stock (unregistered stock at the time of the arrangement). Within 2 years, on October 19, 1999, Martha Stewart Living Omnimedia was born. As she stood on the balcony overlooking the main trading floor of the New York Stock Exchange, Martha watched her net worth soar instantly from $614.7 million to $1.27 billion.[2]

Martha Stewart Living Omnimedia is a leading creator of "how to" content and related products for homemakers and other consumers. It was valued at $295 million in 2001 and produced $21.9 million in profit. Leveraging the well-known "Martha Stewart" brand name across a broad range of media and retail outlets, the company provided consumers with ideas, products and other resources to raise their quality of living. Martha Stewart Living Omnimedia (commonly known by its ticker symbol as MSO) owns and manages multiple media, including four core magazines, an Emmy award–winning domestic arts television program, a weekly segment on *CBS This Morning,* and 34 book titles, which together have sold more than 10 million copies. Additionally, MSO manages a weekly ask Martha® newspaper column, syndicated in more than 230 newspapers; a radio program, airing on more than 330 stations throughout the United States, and a Web site, marthastewart.com, with more than 1.7 million registered users.[3] From 1994 to 2002, Martha earned countless accolades ranging from winning six Daytime Emmy Awards to being counted among "America's 25 Most Influential People" in *Time* magazine's June 1996 issue. The most relevant accomplishment in light of the issue at hand, however, was when Martha Stewart was elected to the NYSE Board of Directors on June 6, 2001.[4]

Known widely as the "Diva of Domesticity" or "Domestic Doyenne," Martha combined the attributes of a skilled businesswoman with the culinary instincts of Julia Child by the 1990s. With such notoriety, however, come both admirers and abhorrers. She appeals to some as the girl next door, while others think she will do literally anything to get ahead. Proxy statements filed in April 2001 show that Martha Stewart Living Omnimedia paid about $2.7 million to Martha in salary and bonuses. In addition, she received another $2 million in royalties for allowing her name to appear in various company publications and television programming. And then there are the $30.6 million in Class B shares of which Ms. Stewart is the sole owner, giving her ultimate control of the company.[5]

## MERRILL LYNCH

Peter Bacanovic joined Merrill Lynch Pierce Fenner and Smith as a broker in 1993. He had previously worked for two years as a Marketing Director at ImClone Systems Inc. His personal and professional contacts quickly grew, as Peter used his good looks and social savvy to gain entry into the fast-paced, heady world of New York's *Social Register.* By the mid-1990s, his client list featured a number of New York's social elite, including members of the Waksal family (Samuel, Aliza and Jack) as well as Martha Stewart, whom he had met shortly after coming to New York.[6] In 2001, Bacanovic hired a young man named Douglas Faneuil as his assistant at Merrill Lynch. Faneuil, who graduated from Vassar in 1997, was also visible in another of New York's social scenes. He fit Bacanovic's requirement for an assistant who understood both the financial and social needs of his clients. According to *New York Times* reporter Alex Kuczynski, "People who know Mr. Faneuil and Mr. Bacanovic . . . all said that Mr. Faneuil was considered an easygoing person who looked to Mr. Bacanovic as a role model."[7]

On December 27, 2001, Douglas Faneuil executed a trade for Martha Stewart, selling 3,928 shares of ImClone Systems Inc. The sale was based on what Stewart claimed was a standing stop-loss order of $60.[8] Mr. Faneuil later changed his official statement to federal investigators on June 19, 2002, contradicting the prior claim of a stop-loss order. Just 2 days later, Merrill Lynch suspended both Faneuil and his boss, Bacanovic, with pay and declined to comment on the details of the internal investigation. Bacanovic's tight network of clients, which at times was his strength, would soon prove to be a liability.[9]

## IMCLONE SYSTEMS INC.

ImClone Systems Inc. was founded by Dr. Samuel Waksal in 1984 as a biopharmaceutical company dedicated to developing breakthrough biologic medicines in the field of oncology.[10] In addition to his role as chief executive officer of ImClone Systems, Dr. Waksal founded Scientia Health Group in late 2000, an incubator for biotechnology firms.[11] During 2001, two issues were emerging concurrently at ImClone and Scientia. At ImClone Systems, a promising new colon cancer drug, Erbitux, was under review by the U.S. Food and Drug Administration (FDA). And at Scientia Health Group, leadership issues were tearing at the structure of the firm.

Dr. Waksal's brother, Harlan, assumed the role of ImClone CEO in the autumn of 2001, just weeks before indications surfaced in early December that the FDA might reject Erbitux.[12] Just 1 month earlier, Samuel Waksal had fired Scientia President James Neal after just 8 months with the firm. For his part, Neal claims the reason for his termination was that Dr. Waksal "felt hampered in his ability to engage in illegal, unethical and fraudulent conduct." The reason for the termination offered earlier by Dr. Waksal involved Neal's compensation plan and its interference with potential investments in the company.[13] By the time ImClone learned that the FDA rejection was "99 percent likely," Sam Waksal was $80 million in debt, with his ImClone shares staked as collateral.[14]

## THE CASE UNFOLDS

In late October 2001, Bristol-Myers Squibb made a tender offer of $70 per share for ImClone stock. At that time, Martha Stewart was interested in unloading her nearly 5,000 shares of the stock. Because the offer was oversubscribed, however, she was able to sell just 1,000 shares.[15] Apparently, just 1 month later in November, Martha told her broker to affix a $60 stop-loss order to her remaining ImClone shares. Her broker, Peter Bacanovic remembers the request to have taken place sometime in December.[16]

On December 4, 2001, Lily Lee, an ImClone employee, met with the FDA to discuss issues facing the company's new oncology drug, Erbitux. After her meeting, Lee wrote an internal memo detailing her discussions with FDA officials, suggesting that the drug might not receive approval. At this point, news of the decision was neither official nor public, and some within the company still held out hope for Erbitux.[17] ImClone CEO Harlan Waksal was apparently not among them. He sold his shares for $50 million just 2 days later. He later claimed that the Board of Directors knew of his intention to sell those shares weeks before he executed the trade.[18]

## HOW THE GRINCH STOLE CHRISTMAS

The holiday season turned ugly for the Waksal family, as Harlan learned on Christmas Day from Brian Markison of Bristol-Myers Squibb that the rejection of Erbitux was "99 percent likely." He waited until the next day, Wednesday, December 26th, to share the news with his brother, Samuel. Harlan has said that he did not share the news sooner with others because he "did not feel it was appropriate to wreck Christmas for the people of the company."[19]

Sam Waksal flew home immediately from his vacation in the Caribbean. Knowing that he could not sell the shares himself without approval from the ImClone General Counsel, Sam instructed his accountant to transfer 79,797 shares to his daughter, Aliza. That night, he also called his father. He also knew that the company did not plan to announce the FDA rejection until after the markets closed on Friday, December 28th. According to a federal complaint filed later against Dr. Waksal, he also knew there would be a "blackout" that day, a period during which no insiders could sell their shares before the news became public.[20]

It is not clear how quickly the accountant reached anyone at Merrill Lynch or to whom he spoke. Public documents show that Dr. Waksal, his daughter Aliza, and his father, Jack, raced to unload more than $15 million of the company's shares in trading on December 27th. Merrill Lynch was unable to execute Dr. Waksal's trade order without specific authorization from the ImClone General Counsel, however. Desperate to save his investment, Sam then shifted his 79,797 shares of stock to Bank of America, only to find that they, too, would not execute the trade. One bad decision led to another, and Sam forged the signature of the ImClone General Counsel in a last-ditch effort to sell his shares, which later led to charges of bank fraud.[21]

That same day, in the midst of all this turmoil in the Waksal family, Martha Stewart and some friends cruised through the clear, blue skies over Texas in her private plane, en route to San José del Cabo, Mexico. About midday, the corporate jet landed in San Antonio to refuel before continuing on to its destination. The exact sequence of events that took place next is still unclear. What is known is that Martha Stewart responded to a message from either her broker or his office. Who spoke with whom, and what mechanisms for communication were used (laptop, cell phone, etc.) is still subject to investigation. At the time of her trip, Peter Bacanovic was in Miami, and his assistant Douglas Faneuil was in the office at Merrill Lynch in New York City. What is also known is that Martha placed a call at 1:41 P.M. (EST), and her trade of ImClone stock was executed by Douglas Faneuil at 1:43 P.M. for $58 per share.[22]

What actually led to the sale of ImClone stock by Martha Stewart on December 27, 2001, is among the questions that have come under scrutiny. Whom did she talk to and what exactly did they say? Did she know that the Waksal family was simultaneously dumping their shares? Did she know why? Martha contends that the sale was in response to the alleged $60 stop-loss order that she claims to have placed in November 2001 with her broker, Bacanovic. If this is true, why was her stock not sold immediately when the share price dipped below $60 for the first time since placing the order, to $59.98 at 11:07 A.M. that same morning? At the same time that her shares were being sold, Martha placed a call to Sam Waksal and left a message, which was recorded on his phone log as "something is going on at ImClone and she [Martha] wants to know what." Her call was never returned.[23]

Also on the plane with Martha that fateful day was Mariana Pasternak. Early the next morning, Mariana's ex-husband, Bart, sold 10,000 shares of ImClone stock. Later that same day, at 2:55 P.M., ImClone received official notification from the FDA that it was, indeed, rejecting Erbitux. The company waited to release this information to the public until 4:30 P.M., when the markets closed.[24]

On Monday, December 31st, 18.5 million shares of ImClone were traded, leaving the closing price at $46.46 per share.[25] About a week later, the SEC requested documents from the company regarding its investigation into possible insider trading by the Waksal family. In the midst of this investigation, Waksal was also sued by a former executive at Scientia concerning issues of "illegal and unethical conduct."[26]

## HANDS IN THE COOKIE JAR

In early June 2002, news broke of the investigation into Martha Stewart's ImClone trade. On June 12th, Martha released a statement asserting that she had no insider information and sold the stock simply because of a preexisting agreement with Merrill Lynch and broker, Peter Bacanovic. She claimed that the sale was "entirely proper and lawful.[27]

At about the same time, information also began to leak out regarding sales of MSO stock by both Martha and her associates totaling approximately $79 million.[28] Some shareholders became disgruntled because these trades were made prior to information about Martha's investigation being made public. MSO stock began a steady fall and closed on June 25, 2002, at $13.60 per share, an all-time low since her company went public in 1999. Her paper losses were approximated at nearly $200 million.[29]

## "I JUST WANT TO FOCUS ON MY SALAD"

Soon after news of the investigation was made public, Martha made her regularly scheduled appearance on the CBS Television Network's *The Early Show,* in a segment on how to prepare appetizing summer salads. Jane Clayson,

the show's anchor, asked Martha a pointed question about ImClone. Stewart continued to chop cabbage in between gestures made with a knife in hand. She replied that she hoped "the scandal would be resolved soon" and that she would be "exonerated of any ridiculousness." After this appearance, she canceled future segments on the show.[30]

By mid-July 2002, Martha Stewart was the subject of three separate investigations. The U.S. Department of Justice was looking into the possibility of obstruction of justice, which carries a maximum prison term of 5 years. The SEC was investigating the possibility of insider trading, with securities fraud carrying a prison term of as many as 10 years. A separate investigation began in the U.S. House of Representatives Committee on Energy and Commerce. Prosecutors wanted to know precisely what Stewart knew when she sold the shares. The committee had already combed through phone logs, cell phone records and a flight log for Stewart, as well as transaction documents.[31]

### Questions

1. What are the critical ethical issues in the case and how would you rank order them?
2. What, if anything, did Ms. Stewart do wrong? Be as specific as possible.
3. What, if anything, ought Ms. Stewart have done differently?

## NOTES

1. Constance L. Hays and Patrick McGeehan, "A Closer Look at Martha Stewart's Trade," *New York Times* (July 15, 2002), pp. C1, C9.
2. Christopher M. Byron, *Martha Inc.,* 2002, pp. 219, 316.
3. www.marthastewart.com.
4. www.nyse.com.

5. Constance L. Hays and Richard A. Oppel Jr., "Stewart Inquiry Is Said to Focus on Words Used," *New York Times* (June 29, 2002), p. C1.

6. Constance L. Hays and Patrick McGeehan, "A Closer Look at Martha Stewart's Trade," *New York Times* (July 15, 2002), pp. C1, C9.

7. Alex Kuczynski, "A Swift Detour from the Fast Lane," *New York Times* (June 30, 2002), p. ST6.

8. Constance L. Hays and Patrick McGeehan. "A Closer Look at Martha Stewart's Trade," *New York Times* (July 15, 2002), pp. C1, C9.

9. Alex Kuczynski, "A Swift Detour from the Fast Lane," *New York Times* (June 30, 2002), p. ST6.

10. www.imclone.com.

11. Andrew Pollack, "Stewart, Icahn, and Others Invested in Venture Fund," *New York Times* (July 2, 2002), p. C3.

12. Constance L. Hays and Patrick McGeehan, "A Closer Look at Martha Stewart's Trade," *New York Times* (July 15, 2002), pp. C1, C9.

13. Andrew Pollack, "Stewart, Icahn, and Others Invested in Venture Fund," *New York Times* (July 2, 2002), p. C3.

14. Constance L. Hays and Patrick McGeehan, "A Closer Look at Martha Stewart's Trade," *New York Times* (July 15, 2002), pp. C1, C9.

15. Jerry Markon, "Stewart, Broker Differ on Imclone Sale," *Wall Street Journal* (June 17, 2002), p. A4.

16. "Martha's Survival Is on the Chopping Block," www.fortune.com (June 25, 2002).

17. Constance L. Hays and Patrick McGeehan, "A Closer Look at Martha Stewart's Trade," *New York Times* (July 15, 2002), pp. C1, C9.

18. Jerry Markon, "Stewart, Broker Differ on Imclone Sale," *Wall Street Journal* (June 17, 2002), p. A4.

19. Constance L. Hays and Patrick McGeehan, "A Closer Look at Martha Stewart's Trade," *New York Times* (July 15, 2002), pp. C1, C9.

20. Ibid, C9.

21. Ibid.

22. Ibid.

23. Ibid.

24. Ibid.

25. Ibid.

26. Andrew Pollack, "Stewart, Icahn, and Others Invested in Venture Fund," *New York Times* (July 2, 2002), p. C3.

27. www.marthastewart.com.

28. Andrew Pollack, "Stewart, Icahn, and Others Invested in Venture Fund," *New York Times* (July 2, 2002), p. C3.

29. www.fortune.com (June 25, 2002).

30. *New York Times* (August 6, 2002), pp. C1, C2.

31. *Wall Street Journal* (August 9, 2002), pp. A1, A5.

## Suggested Supplementary Readings

ALMEDER, ROBERT F., and MILTON SNOEYENBOS. 1987. "Churning: Ethical and Legal Issues." *Business and Professional Ethics Journal* 6 (Spring).

ALMEDER, ROBERT F., and DAVID CAREY. 1991. "In Defense of Sharks: Moral Issues in Hostile Liquidating Takeovers." *Journal of Business Ethics* 10:471–84.

BOATRIGHT, JOHN. 2007. *Ethics in Finance,* 2nd ed. Malden Mills, MA: Blackwell.

BROWN, DONNA. 1990. "Environmental Investing: Let the Buyer Beware." *Management Review* 79 (June).

BRUNER, ROBERT F., and LYNN SHARP PAINE. 1988. "Management Buyouts and Managerial Ethics." *California Management Review* 30 (Winter): 89–106.

*Business Ethics Quarterly.* 2004. Special Issue: Accounting Ethics. 14, no. 3 (July).

*Business & Professional Ethics Journal.* 2004. Special Issue: Ethics in the Financial Services after Sarbanes-Oxley. 12, nos. 1 and 2 (Spring/Summer).

DUSKA, RONALD F., and BRENDA SHAY DUSKA. 2003. *Accounting Ethics,* Malden Mills, MA: Blackwell.

FRANKS, JULIAN, and COLIN MAYER. 1989. *Risk, Regulation, and Investor Protection: The Case of Investment Management.* Oxford: Clarendon Press.

HEACOCK, M. V., K. P. HILL, and S. C. ANDERSON. 1987. "Churning: An Ethical Issue in Finance." *Business and Professional Ethics Journal* 6 (Spring).

HOFFMAN, W. MICHAEL, and RALPH J. McQUADE. 1986. "A Matter of Ethics." *Financial Strategies and Concepts* 4.

KESTER, W. C., and T. A. LUEHRMAN. 1995. "Rehabilitating the Leveraged Buyout." *Harvard Business Review.* 73 (May–June): 119–30.

MACKENZIE, CRAIG, and ALAN LEWIS. 1999. "Morals and Markets: The Case of Ethical Investing." *Business Ethics Quarterly.* 9 (July): 439–52.

SCHADLER, F. P., and J. E. KARNS. 1990. "The Unethical Exploitation of Shareholders in Management Buyout Transactions." *Journal of Business Ethics* 9 (July): 595–602.

WILLIAMS, OLIVER, FRANK REILLY, and JOHN HOUCK. 1989. *Ethics and the Investment Industry.* Savage, MD: Rowman and Littlefield.

# Chapter 7

# Ethical Issues Regarding Emerging Technologies

## INTRODUCTION

College students in the twenty-first century take for granted recent advances in information technology such as computers, the World Wide Web, and iPods, as well as recent advances in medical technology such as magnetic resonance imaging (MRI), endoscopic surgery, and cutting-edge pharmaceuticals such as Accutane (isotretinoin) for severe acne, and Gardasil for the prevention of genital warts and cervical cancer. However, these emerging technologies often raise new ethical issues that businesses must confront. Consider two recent examples. First, the rights of Internet users to have their identities and e-mail messages protected from third parties by their Internet service providers (ISPs) has recently gained new attention as the Chinese government has sought the help of U.S. ISPs such as Yahoo to silence political activists who use the Internet to network, raise funds, and promote their political agendas.[1] Second, Merck—the U.S. distributor of Gardasil—has received sustained criticism for lobbying state governments to require the vaccination of young girls. Merck executives, and many physicians, believe such vaccination will save many lives. Merck's critics argue that vaccination will encourage early sexual activity.[2]

The ethical issue regarding emerging technologies that may be most familiar to readers of this text is the downloading of music. In 2007 students at Arizona State, North Carolina State, Ohio, and Syracuse Universities; the Universities of South Florida, Southern California, Massachusetts, Nebraska, Tennessee, and Texas; and other universities received letters threatening lawsuits from the Recording Industry Association of America

(RIAA). The students were alleged to have downloaded songs illegally.[3] These students reportedly used the Donkey, Kazaa, and LimeWire Web sites to illegally share copyrighted music. The recording industry, facing declining sales of compact disks, has targeted file sharing as a cause of this decline in sales. At the University of Tennessee at Knoxville, for example, 15 students were given the choice to settle out of court for between $3,750 and $4,500 each or face federal prosecution.[4] Sharing music online may be illegal, but is it unethical? If a student buys a music album in compact disk format, transfers the songs from that disk to her computer, and then shares those songs online, in what way are her actions unethical?

Intellectual property is one of the most ethically contentious business issues of the twenty-first century. Just as the RIAA vigorously defends copyrighted music, so too, the pharmaceutical industry vigorously defends patents on new drugs to protect their intellectual property. By retaining a virtual monopoly on individual drugs during the period of patent protection pharmaceutical companies are able to charge whatever the market will tolerate for these products. At the same time, in nearly all developing nations, the poor, and many of their elected representatives, believe that they have a moral right to affordable access to lifesaving drugs. Who is right?

## INFORMATION AND THE WORLD WIDE WEB

There is no doubt that the computer and the World Wide Web were two of the most significant inventions of the twentieth century. Perhaps the most important feature of computers and the Web is that they allow quick access to information. Computers and the Web also enable business firms to store and transmit large quantities of information regarding most aspects of their stakeholder relations. The way businesspeople work with information has been transformed. Entire textbooks are now devoted to ethical issues in information technology. In this business ethics text, we limit our discussion to two issues regarding information technology: privacy and intellectual property rights. Protecting privacy and protecting intellectual property were a challenge before the computer and the Web came into widespread use; however, information technology has vastly complicated when and how privacy and intellectual property should be protected. Information technology has changed the scale of information gathering, the kind of information that can be gathered, and the scale of information exchange.

In her contribution to this chapter Deborah Johnson provides an overview of the many privacy issues that face computer users. She begins with a series of scenarios that present specific issues requiring theoretical ethical resolution. Johnson points out that the normal way of addressing these issues is to speak of trade-offs between the right to privacy of those individuals whom the information is about and the needs of those who use the information. Those who want the information argue that it makes for better decision making. What is needed, Johnson believes, are arguments on behalf of privacy that counterbalance the benefits of information gathering. Because improved decision making is a social good, Johnson is attracted to arguments that make privacy a social good as well. The exercise of autonomy is a social good, and since privacy is necessary for one to exercise his or her autonomy, Johnson believes that she has the argument that will best counterbalance the improved decision-making argument.

Privacy is seldom protected on the Internet. Many Web sites that have privacy policies enable you to indicate that you do not want to receive ads from the site or have your information sold to third parties. This is called *opting out.* Privacy advocates would require a strategy called *opting in.* Only if you opted in could you receive ads, and you would have to explicitly agree to have the site sell your information to third parties. Some privacy advocates argue that the United States should adopt strict privacy laws similar to those adopted by the European Union. Others argue that self-regulation through the use of privacy seals or technical fixes is sufficient to protect a person's right to privacy on the Internet.

In 2006, representatives from Google, Yahoo, Cisco Systems, and Microsoft were summoned to testify before Congress regarding their complicity with the Chinese government's efforts to monitor and censor the Internet. For example, Yahoo provided Chinese authorities with information that led to the 10-year imprisonment of journalist Shi Tao. Tao's crime was to disclose Chinese censorship practices on domestic reporters to the foreign press.[5] The chair of the congressional subcommittee that held the hearings characterized the actions of the Internet companies as "sickening collaboration."[6] In their defense, Yahoo and the other companies argued that they are required to adhere to Chinese laws and that they are providing a net benefit to the Chinese people.

In his contribution to this chapter, Jeffery Smith examines the recent practices of Internet content providers (ICPs) in China and concludes that ICPs are *actively* engaged in supporting the Chinese government's suppression of the rights to expression, association, and privacy. Smith argues that ICPs should be *passive* in response to the supression of human rights. For example, he argues that ICPs should wait for court orders before complying with requests and should appeal such requests when they are made. In this way ICPs can provide Chinese citizens with many of the benefits of the Internet age without actively contributing to human rights violations.

In nearly all industrial nations students believe they have a moral right to share music files they have purchased. In 2001 the courts declared that Napster, a company that facilitated the free exchange of music online, infringed on copyrights and was ordered to change its way of doing business. Its new business model failed and Naptster declared bankruptcy. At the bankruptcy auction the Napster brand name and trademarks were purchased by the software company Roxio, which used the Napster name to rebrand its own online music service.[7] It is interesting to note that it is legal to tape a program on your VCR, but it is illegal to download a song under copyright protection. Selections from the two court cases, *Sony Corp. v. Universal City Studios Inc.*, and *A&M Records v. Napster,* are included in this chapter. The concern of Universal City Studios was unauthorized copying. Suppose you recorded a program and then gave your tape to others to copy. The court found that the impact on individual viewers would be too great to justify forbidding the copying. However, the sharing of music would have a great impact on those who held copyright. Presumably, the sales of CDs would plunge if one could download a song for free and then share it with anyone else on the Internet.

Issues such as these are the concern of Richard De George in his article "Intellectual Property and the Information Age." De George notes three characteristics of intellectual property: (1) it is infinitely sharable, and one person's having the property is compatible with many other persons' having it as well; (2) any expression of an idea builds on prior knowledge that is not one's own creation; and (3) it is fundamentally social in the sense that it can be further developed when shared. There are good reasons not to have a property right in such knowledge. Indeed, that idea was behind the Linux operating system and Shareware. De George then examines the ethical justification for copyright. There is a utilitarian argument that copyright protection is necessary to encourage the production of these works. There is also a fairness argument that says that those who take the time, energy, and money to develop the ideas should be compensated. De George then looks at the issue of whether or not intellectual property deserves copyright protection from four different perspectives: (1) the view of scholars and authors who are concerned about honesty and proper attribution; (2) the view of the entrepreneur who views copying as taking one's property and in so doing increasing the risk that the entrepreneur will be driven out of business; (3) the view of the buyers; and (4) the view of society as a whole. De George then considers what would be right with respect to copying programs for personal use and the peer-to-peer exchange of copyrighted material. Although protection may be more justified for the latter, De George points out the difficulty with enforcing this copyright protection.

**Pharmaceutical Patents**

Pharmaceutical companies research, manufacture, and market valuable—often lifesaving—drugs, and they employ hundreds of thousands of skilled employees in well-paid jobs. The industry itself is consistently among the most profitable for investors. Despite these accomplishments, the industry has come under sustained criticism from physicians, consumer advocates, human rights activists, and governments. As we saw in Chapter 5, the marketing practices of the pharmaceutical industry have been criticized as unethical, and the industry has begun to respond to such criticism with voluntary marketing guidelines. The industry has also been criticized for its agressive defense of patent protection for lifesaving drugs despite the desperate need of citizens in developing nations for these drugs. For example, Africa is home to 70 percent of those living with AIDS, and almost none of these individuals can afford to purchase the drugs necessary for survival. African governments are in little better position to be able to afford the expensive drugs needed by their citizens.[8] When the government of South Africa passed a law encouraging the use of cheap, generic drugs it was sued by 39 pharmaceutical companies who alleged that their patents were at risk. The pharmaceutical companies later dropped the lawsuit in response to worldwide criticism.[9] Partly in response to these events the World Trade Organization, at its Ministerial Conference in Doha, Qatar, declared that the Trade-Related Aspects of Intellectual Property Rights (TRIPS Agreement) should be interpreted as ensuring the right of member nations to promote access to medicines for all when public health crises result in national emergencies. Relevant portions of the TRIPS Agreement and the Doha Declaration are included in this chapter.

In his essay "Intellectual Property and Pharmaceutical Drugs: An Ethical Analysis," Richard De George argues that the response of pharmaceutical companies to criticism regarding their patents and the nonaccessibility of lifesaving drugs has been to invoke legal and economic arguments. De George points out that these arguments have been unpersuasive to critics of the industry because they fail to adequately take account of ethical concerns regarding the right to health care and the obligation to help others in desperate need. De George argues that the standard arguments used by pharmaceutical companies to defend vigorous patent protection are unpersuasive and that the companies have far greater obligations than they have previously acknowledged.

In their contribution to this chapter, Patricia Werhane and Michael Gorman point out that intellectual property is nearly always the result of a long history of scientific or technological development by many individuals and groups of people. Legally a company may be able to secure a patent on an innovative drug; however, Werhane and Gorman claim that in typical cases many other researchers and organizations will have a legitimate moral basis for claiming some ownership of the drug. For example, many drugs patented by pharmaceutical companies relied on previous research conducted in university or government laboratories, and that research itself relied on overlapping content with other research. Given the nature of networks of creativity, they argue that it makes more sense to think in terms of shared rights. They argue that because of these networks of discovery, pharmaceutical companies have an obligation to share their intellectual property with those who have a desperate need for access to their drugs. Further, they argue that the best means of ensuring that the obligations of the pharmaceutical industry are met is to develop a network model whereby companies work alongside governments and nongovernmental organizations to ensure that the needs of desperately poor and sick individuals are met. The case study that concludes this chapter, "Aventis: Partnerships for Health," describes just such a program.

## NOTES

1. "The Party, the People, and the Power of Cyber-Talk: China and the Internet," *Economist* (April 27, 2006).
2. Andrew Pollack and Stephanie Saul, "Merck to Halt Lobbying for Vaccine for Girls," *New York Times* (February 21, 2007).
3. Brock Read, "Recording Industry Will Again Sue College Students—Unless They Agree to Settlement Terms," *Chronicle of Higher Education* (March 1, 2007).

4. Andrew Eder, "15 Students Hit with Lawsuits," *Knoxville News Sentinel* (April 13, 2007).

5. Peter S. Goodman, "Yahoo Says It Gave China Internet Data," *Washington Post* (September 11, 2005).

6. Tom Zeller, "Web Firms Are Grilled on Dealings in China," *New York Times* (February 16, 2006).

7. "Roxio Buys Napster Assets," *New York Times* (November 28, 2002).

8. David Shook, "The Drugmakers' AIDS Dilemma in Africa," *Business Week* (March 7, 2001).

9. Rachel L. Swarns, "Drug Makers Drop South Africa Suit over AIDS Medicine," *New York Times* (April 20, 2001).

## INFORMATION AND THE WORLD WIDE WEB

# Privacy

*Deborah G. Johnson*

## SCENARIO 5.1 FUND-RAISING AND POTENTIAL DONORS

Jan Perez began college as a computer science major. She loves computers and has always been very good at figuring out how to do things on the Internet and the Web. However, after a year and a half of college, Jan decides that as much as she likes computing, she doesn't want to major in it; she chooses, instead, a major that is more likely to lead to a career involving contact and interaction with people. She also wants something that involves public service or promoting good causes.

After college, Jan is delighted to find that the development office of a large, private university wants to hire her. She accepts the job enthusiastically, thinking she will do some good by raising money for a great university.

Jan's supervisor is extremely pleased to find out how much Jan knows about computers and the Internet. Within a few months of starting the job, Jan is asked to find out all she can about a Frank Doe. Mr. Doe has never been approached by the university; Jan's supervisor only recently heard from another donor that Mr. Doe has a very positive impression of the university and has the capacity to make a major contribution.

The fund-raising unit needs to know how wealthy Mr. Doe is to determine what kind of contribution to ask for. They need to know about his life and interests to know which of their projects he might want to support. And, they need to know about him personally so they can approach him, put him at ease, and not offend him in any way. Jan is given some suggestions about where to look, but she is also told to find out whatever she can.

Using the Internet, Jan does the following:

1. She searches a variety of public databases which give her information about his real estate holdings, his memberships on the boards of public corporations, a list of corporations for which he is a major stockholder.

2. She searches other databases to find out if he has made contributions to political parties or campaigns.

3. She searches archives of newspapers to see if Mr. Doe has ever been written about in the news.

4. She searches other databases to see if he has had any encounters with law enforcement agencies.

5. She searches other databases to find out what religious organizations he supports.

6. She contacts credit agencies and requests his credit history.

7. Jan wonders if Amazon.com would tell her what types of books, if any, Mr. Doe purchases.

8. Jan wonders which Internet service provider Mr. Doe uses; she contemplates what she could learn about Mr. Doe if his service provider would tell her about his online activities. For example, he may keep a portfolio of stock holdings in his account.

9. Mr. Doe is a local resident. Jan's supervisor mentions in passing that Mr. Doe, she has been told, uses the university's medical complex for all his medical treatment. Jan decides to see whether she can access patient files at the university medical complex. Much to her surprise, she is able to access Mr. Doe's insurance records and this tells her that in the last several years, he has been receiving frequent treatment for a kidney ailment. She wonders if this will make him interested in contributing to the hospital or for kidney research.

At the end of several weeks of research, Jan has an enormous amount of information about Mr. Doe. As she acquired each bit of information from a separate database, there didn't seem anything wrong with doing that; now, however, the cumulative effect of putting all of this information together makes Jan feel uncomfortable. She wonders if this is right. She feels a bit like a voyeur or stalker.

Has Jan done anything wrong?

## SCENARIO 5.2 TAKING DATA HOME

Max Brown works in the Department of Alcoholism and Drug Abuse of a northeastern state. The agency administers programs for individuals with alcohol and drug problems and maintains huge databases of information on the clients who use their services. Max has been asked to take a look at the track records of the treatment programs. He is to put together a report that contains information about such factors as number of clients seen in each program each month for the past 5 years, length of each client's treatment, number of clients who return after completion of a program, criminal histories of clients, and so on.

To put together this report, Max has been given access to all files in the agency's mainframe computer. It takes Max several weeks to find the information he needs because it is located in a variety of places in the system. As he finds information, he downloads it to the computer in his office; that is, he copies the information from the mainframe onto the hard disk of his office microcomputer.

Under pressure to get the report finished by the deadline, Max finds that he is continuously distracted at work. He decides that he will have to work at home over the weekend to finish on time. This will not be a problem. He copies the information (containing, among other things, personal information on clients) onto several disks and takes them home. He finishes the report over the weekend. To be safe, he leaves a copy of the report on his home computer as well as copying it onto a disk which he takes up to work.

Was Max wrong in moving personal information from the mainframe to his office computer? In moving the information from his office computer to a disk? To his home computer? In leaving the information on his computer at home? What could happen as a result of Max's treatment of the data? Should the agency for which Max works have a policy on use of personal information stored in its system? What might such a policy specify?

## SCENARIO 5.3 WORKPLACE MONITORING

Estelle Cavello was recently hired to supervise a large unit of a medical insurance company. Estelle will be in charge of a unit responsible for processing insurance claims. When she was hired, the vice president made it clear to Estelle that he expects her to significantly increase the efficiency of the unit. The company has targets for the number of claims that should be processed by each unit and Estelle's unit has never been able to meet its target.

One of the first things Estelle does when she starts this job is to install a software system that will allow her to monitor the work of each and every claims processor. The software allows Estelle to record the number of keystrokes made per minute on any terminal in the unit. It also allows her to bring the work of others up on her computer screen so that she can watch individual work as it is being done. As well, Estelle can access copies of each employee's work at the end of each day. She can find out how much time each worker spent with the terminal off; she can see what correspondence the person prepared; she can review e-mail that the worker sent or received; and so on.

Should Estelle use this software to monitor her employees?

## SCENARIO 5.4 DATA MINING

Ravi Singh works for one of the major credit card companies in their data-processing center. The company is continuously developing new products to offer to customers and add revenue to the corporation. He is an avid reader of computer magazines and recently has been reading about data-mining tools that are now available for a reasonable cost. Ravi goes to his supervisor with the suggestion that their unit purchase one of these tools and use it to find out more about their customers. The information may be telling in terms of customer interest and capability.

The supervisor likes the idea. After exploring the systems that are available, the unit purchases one and Ravi is assigned to explore patterns in the database of information on the company's customers and their purchasing habits.

Ravi discovers that certain zip codes are highly correlated with loan defaults. These zip codes must be in low-income areas, for the mined and analyzed data indicate that the company could reduce its losses significantly by refusing to extend credit to anyone living in 25 zip codes while at the same time not significantly reducing their revenues. In other words, on average, losses due to default generated by individuals in those zip codes were greater than revenue generated.

Ravi continues with his data mining. Next he discoverers a correlation between those who use their credit cards to make contributions to Hindu charitable organizations and those who charge over $40,000 a year on their credit cards. This information seems important. If the company made a special effort to solicit Hindus as customers, it might be able to increase its revenues significantly.

Ravi goes to his supervisor with the suggestion that they adopt these strategies. Has Ravi done anything wrong? If his company adopts these strategies, have they done anything wrong?

These scenarios depict just a few of the ways that information can be created, gathered, moved, and used with computer technology. Of all the social and ethical concerns surrounding computer technology, the threat to personal privacy was probably the first to capture public attention. And this issue persists in drawing public concern and leading to action by policy makers. One hears about it frequently in the popular media; major studies continue to be undertaken; new books continue to be written; and new legislation continues to be passed to regulate electronic information. It will be helpful to begin by laying out just why and how computer technology facilitates information gathering and seems to threaten personal privacy.

## IS THERE ANYTHING NEW HERE?

I suggest that computer and information technology, like other new technologies, creates new possibilities; it creates possibilities for behavior and activities that were not possible before the technology. Public concern about computers and privacy arises for precisely this reason. Computers make it possible (and in many cases, cheap and easy) to gather detailed information about individuals to an extent never possible before. Federal, state, and local government agencies now maintain extensive records of individual behavior including such things as any interactions with criminal justice agencies, income taxes, employment history for social security, use of human services agencies, motor vehicle registration, and so on. As well, private organizations maintain extensive databases of information on individual purchases, airline travel, credit worthiness, health records, telephone or cellular phone usage, employment, and so on.

We have the technological capacity for the kind of massive, continuous surveillance of individuals that was envisioned in such frightening early twentieth-century science fiction works as George Orwell's *1984* (1949) and Zamyatin's *We* (1920). The only differences between what is now possible and what was envisioned then is that much of the surveillance of individuals that takes place now is done by private institutions (marketing firms, insurance companies, credit agencies), *and* much of the surveillance now is via electronic records instead of by direct human observation or through cameras. . . .

We can ask whether there is anything fundamentally different about today as compared to 50 years ago or a century ago. Record keeping is far from a new phenomenon. Government agencies and private corporations have been keeping records for thousands of years and using this information in a variety of ways. So, is there anything different about the kind or degree of privacy that we have today as compared to 50 or 100 years ago?

Computer technology has changed record-keeping activities in a number of undeniable and powerful ways. First, the *scale of information gathering* has changed. Second, the *kind of information* that can be gathered has changed.

And, third, the *scale of exchange* of information has changed enormously.

In the precomputer, "paper-and-ink" world, the mere fact that records were paper and stored in file cabinets, imposed some limitations on the amount of data gathered, who had access, how long records were retained, and so on. Electronic records do not have these limitations. We can collect, store, manipulate, exchange, and retain practically infinite quantities of data. The point is that technology no longer limits what can be done; now only time and money and, perhaps, human capabilities impose limits on the quantity of information that can be gathered and processed.

The kind of information that it is now possible to collect and use is also new. Think about the workplace monitoring scenario at the beginning of this chapter. Employers can keep records of every keystroke an employee makes. Before computers, finger movements of this kind would not have been thought to be important, let alone the kind of thing that could be recorded. Employers can monitor their employees' uses of the Web, their participation in chat rooms, not to mention their e-mail.

One particularly important new form of information is referred to as transaction generated information (TGI). TGI includes purchases made with a credit card, telephone calls, entry and exit from intelligent highways, and so on. As you move about in the world, your activities (transactions) are automatically recorded. . . .

There is no single government or private organization accumulating all of the information. TGI gathering seems to be fragmented and, therefore, seems not to pose the threat of Big Brother.

Indeed, in the very early days of computing, especially in the 1960s and 1970s, many social commentators expressed concern about the information gathering potential of computer technology and these fears were articulated as fears of Big Brother—fears that all the information would be funneled to a highly centralized U.S. government. The fear was that electronic information gathering practices would give too much power to government. It would create a potentially totalitarian government, a surveillance society. Those fears waned in part because legislation was passed that restricted government information gathering.

Fear also weakened because computer technology changed. It became smaller and cheaper, and, consequently, became available much more widely. On the one hand, this diffused fear of Big Brother because it promised computer power in the hands of "many" rather than just big government. At the same time, however, smaller computers in the hands of many companies and individuals facilitated the exchange of information to an extent previously unimaginable. Typically information of one kind will be gathered and stored separately from information of another kind; for example, marketing firms will gather and store information on buying habits, one government agency will record income tax information, another government agency will record criminal justice activities, and so on.

With computer technology, however, it is technically possible to combine all this information. In the private sector this is done routinely. Think of the fund-raising example at the beginning of this chapter. Within government this happens less frequently because the Privacy Act of 1974 restricted data matching. . . .

The restriction on matching mentioned in the Privacy Act of 1974 did not apply to private organizations, just to the federal government. What was called "matching" in the 1970s is today called data mining and is quite common in private organizations. Indeed, you can now purchase data-mining tools, sometimes called knowledge discovery instruments (kdi) that help find patterns of behavior among groups of individuals. Their use is described in Scenario 5.4.

Add to these changes in the scale and kind of information gathered with computer technology, a further element. Because computerized information is electronic, it is easy to copy and distribute. Before computers were connected by telephone lines, information could be fairly easily copied using tapes or disks. Now that computers are connected via telecommunication lines, information can go anywhere in the world where there are telephone lines. Hence, the extent to which information can be exchanged is now practically limitless. Once information about an individual is recorded in a machine or on a disk, it can be easily transferred to another machine or disk. It can be bought and sold, given away, traded, and even stolen. The information can spread instantaneously from one company to another, from one sector to another, and from one country to another.

The Max Brown case (Scenario 5.2) is illustrative here. He takes sensitive data home on a disk. From a technical point of view, he could have simply accessed the data from home. But in either case, the data moves around. Once it moves out of its source, it is very difficult to keep track of all the places it might exist, be it on disks or hard drives.

Movement of data happens when you subscribe to a magazine and your name and address are sold to a marketing firm. The marketing firm infers from the subscription that you have certain tastes and begins sending you a variety of opportunities to buy the things you like. Forester and Morrison (1990) report the case of a woman who took her landlord to court after he refused to do anything about the pest problem in her apartment. He did not show up for court but evicted her shortly after the court date. When she went looking for another apartment, she found that she was repeatedly turned down by landlords. She would look at an apartment, notify the landlord that she wanted it, and within a few days hear back that the apartment was already rented to someone else. It turned out that a database of names of individuals who take landlords to court is maintained and the information is sold to landlords. Needless to say, landlords don't want to rent to individuals who may take them to court.

As far as the technology goes, the distribution of information can take place with or without the knowledge of the person whom the information is about, and it can take place intentionally as well as unintentionally. There is an unintentional distribution when records are provided that contain more information than is requested. As well, when information is stolen, the exchange is unintentional from the point of view of the agency that gathered or maintained the records. Think again of the Max Brown scenario; Brown's wife, children, or friends might (while using his home computer) inadvertently access the data on individuals in the state's treatment programs and see the names of clients in the state programs.

If all of this were not cause enough for concern, there is more. Information stored in a computer can be erroneous, and, at the same time, can be readily distributed. The effect of a small error can be magnified enormously. Information can be erroneous due to unintentional human error or because someone has intentionally altered it to harm a competitor or enhance their own records. It is important to remember that databases of information are not always as secure as we would like them to be. When computers are connected via telecommunications lines, the possibilities of data's being tampered with or stolen are increased. . . .

Suppose John A. Smith's file is inadvertently combined with John B. Smith's. John A. Smith is turned down for a loan on the basis of erroneous information since John A. has *never* failed to pay his debts, has a good job, and has a sizeable holding of stocks, but John B. has a low-paying job, declared bankruptcy 3 years ago, and is once again deeply in debt. John A.

is wronged when he is turned down for a loan. Moreover, suppose that after a series of inquires and complaints by John A., the error is identified, and John A.'s file is corrected. (This is not always as easy as it sounds. Companies are often very slow in responding to complaints about errors in records.) John A. asks his bank to send for the updated report, and the bank changes its mind about the loan when it sees the accurate information. It would appear that the injury to John A. has been remedied. Not necessarily. The inaccurate information may have been given to other companies before it was corrected, and they, in turn, may have given it to others. As a result, it may be difficult, if not impossible, to track down all the databases in which the error is now stored. It may be impossible to completely expunge the erroneous information from John A.'s records.

When information is stored in a computer, there is little incentive to get rid of it; hence, information may stay with an individual for a long period of time. Information stored in a computer takes up very little space and is easy to maintain and transfer. Because of this, details can be carried in a record forever. Something insignificant that happened to an individual when he was 10 years old may easily follow him through life because the information has been recorded once and there is little motivation to delete it. In the past, the inconvenience of paper served to some degree as an inhibitor to keeping and exchanging apparently useless information.[1]

Because it is so easy to keep information, some fear that individuals will get categorized and stigmatized at early stages in their lives. One way to see this is to imagine what it would be like if elementary and secondary school records were put into a national database where prospective employers, government agencies, or insurance companies could get access. We might find decisions being made about us on the basis of testing done when we were in elementary school or on the basis of disciplinary incidents in our teenage years.

When decision makers are faced with making decisions about individuals, they want data. They want data both to insure a good decision and to justify their decision to others. When they must choose between making a decision on the basis of little or no data, and making it on the basis of lots of data known to be unreliable, many prefer the latter. Hence, information tends to get used if it is available even though it may not be relevant or reliable.

In summary, while record keeping is, by no means, a new activity, it appears that computer and information technology has changed record-keeping activities in the following ways: (1) it has made a *new scale* of information gathering possible; (2) it has made *new kinds* of information possible, especially transaction generated information; (3) it has made *a new scale of* information *distribution and exchange* possible; (4) the *effect* of erroneous information can be *magnified*; and (5) information about events in one's life may *endure* much longer than ever before. These five changes make the case for the claim that the world we live in is more like a panopticon than ever before.

As an aside here, you may be tempted to say that computers are not really the problem or the cause of the problem. It is individuals and organizations that are creating, gathering, exchanging, and using information. Computers, according to this line of argument, are simply tools: if there is a problem, the problem is the people who use computers, not the computers themselves.

While there is some truth to this, it is important to remember that computer technology facilitates certain kinds of activities. Computer technology makes it possible for individuals to do things they could not do before. Individuals and organizations are more likely to engage in activities when they are possible (not to speak of easy and inexpensive).

For example, in Scenario 5.4, Estelle would not have monitored employees to the extent she did or in quite the way that she did if computers and the monitoring software were not available. Individuals choose actions because they find themselves in a world which has certain possibilities; in a world with different possibilities, they would behave differently. Insofar as computer technology changes what it is possible for human beings to do, it can be a major factor in determining what people do and the kind of society in which we live.

## UNDERSTANDING THE "COMPUTERS AND PRIVACY" ISSUE

### Uses of Information

Information about individuals would not exist if organizations did not have an interest in using it. Information is created, collected, and exchanged because organizations can use it to further their interests and activities. Information about individuals is used to make decisions about those individuals, and often the decisions profoundly affect the lives of those individuals whom the information is about. Information about you, stored in a database, may be used to decide whether or not you will be hired by a company; whether or not you will be given a loan; whether or not you will be called to the police station for interrogation, arrest, or prosecution; whether or not you will receive education, housing, social security, unemployment compensation, and so on.

The computers and privacy issue is often framed as an issue that calls for a balancing of the needs of those who use information about individuals (typically government agencies and private institutions) *against* the needs or rights of those individuals whom the information is about. Later in this chapter, I will argue against this framing of the issue on grounds that it is biased in favor of information gathering, but for the moment it is important to understand why organizations want information.

In general, those who want information about individuals want it because they believe that it will help them to make better decisions. Several examples quickly illustrate this point. Banks believe that the more information they have about an individual, the better they will be able to make judgments about that individual's ability to pay back a loan or about the size of the credit line the individual can handle. The FBI's National Crime Information Center (NCIC) provides criminal histories of individuals to all the states. Law enforcement agencies justify the existence of this database on grounds that the more information they have about individuals, the better they will be able to identify and capture criminals. We might also bring in examples from the insurance industry where decisions are made about which individuals to insure at what rate, or from the Department of Health and Human Services where decisions are made about who qualifies for various welfare and medical benefits. And, of course, don't forget the fund-raising organization, data-mining, and workplace monitoring scenarios at the beginning of this chapter. In theory, the more and better the information these organizations have, the better their decision making will be.

Companies also claim that they need information about their customers to serve them better. If a company like Amazon.com keeps track of the books that you buy, it can infer from this information what new books you are likely to be interested in. When they send you information on these new books, they claim they are providing a service to you (even if it is one that you didn't ask for and one that happens also to serve their interest in selling more books). If an advertising firm knows what I buy at the grocery store, it can use that information to send me coupons for items I am likely to buy. If television stations know what I watch on television and when I change the channel,

they can use that information to develop programming more suited to my tastes. If marketing companies know about my income level and my tastes in clothes, food, sports, and music, they can send me catalogues or special offers for products and services that fit my precise tastes.

In the standard understanding of the computers and privacy issue we have public and private institutions that want information about individuals. They make a powerful case for how this information improves their decision making and helps them to do their job better and more efficiently. In theory, all of that means better serving us, as consumers and citizens. It means, for example, better law enforcement; more efficient government; better, more customized services; and so on.

Personal privacy is generally put on the other side of the balancing scales. The issue is framed so that we have to balance all the good things that are achieved through information gathering and exchange *against* the desire or need for personal privacy. Some even claim that we have a right to personal privacy for if that were true, the scales would weigh heavily on the side of personal privacy. From a legal and constitutional point of view, however, we have, at most, a limited and complex right to privacy.

This framing of the issue seems to be skewed heavily in favor of information gathering and exchange. The only way to counter the powerful case made on behalf of information gathering and exchange is, it would seem, to make a more powerful case for protecting and ensuring privacy in the lives of individuals. Either we must show that there is a grave risk or danger to these information-gathering activities—a danger so great that it counterbalances the benefits of the activity. Or we must show that there is a greater benefit to be gained from constraining these activities. To put this another way, once the benefits of information gathering and exchange are on the table, the burden of proof is on privacy advocates to show either that there is something harmful about information gathering and exchange or that there is some benefit to be gained from constraining information gathering. Either way, there is a daunting hurdle to overcome.

Many of us feel uncomfortable with the amount of information that is gathered about us. We do not like not knowing who has what information about us and how it is being used. Why are we so uncomfortable? What do we fear? Part of the fear is, no doubt, related to our mistrust of large, faceless organizations, and part of it is related to mistrust of government. The challenge is to translate this discomfort and fear into an argument that counterbalances the benefits of information gathering.

Odd as it may seem, the case for protecting personal privacy has not been easy to make. From the point of view of public policy, arguments on behalf of personal privacy have not "won the day." I am going to discuss a number of ways that the case for individual privacy can be and has been made, but I am also going to argue for a somewhat different framing of the issue. At least part of the problem, I believe, lies in framing the issue as a matter of balancing the interests of private and public institutions against the interests of individuals. We ought, instead, to recognize that privacy is both an individual and a social good, one that goes to the heart of the kind of beings we are and important to the realization of a democratic society.

## Personal Privacy

Two big questions have dominated the philosophical literature on privacy: What is it and why is it valuable? Needless to say, the two questions are intertwined. Neither has been easy to answer. The term *privacy* seems to be used to refer to a wide range of social practices and domains, for example, what we do in the privacy of our own homes, domains of life in which the government should not interfere, things about ourselves that we tell only our closest friends. Privacy seems, also, to overlap other concepts such as freedom or liberty, seclusion, autonomy, secrecy, and controlling information about ourselves. So, privacy is a complex and, in many respects, elusive concept. A variety of arguments have been put forward to explain the value of personal privacy.

As we review several of these, it will be helpful to keep in mind a distinction between privacy as an instrumental good and privacy as an intrinsic good. When privacy is presented as being valuable because it leads to something else, then it is cast as an instrumental good. In such arguments, privacy is presented as a means to an end. Its value lies in its connection to something else. On the other hand, when privacy is presented as good in itself, it is presented as a value in and of itself. As you might predict, the latter argument is harder to make for it requires showing that privacy has value even when it leads to nothing else or even when it may lead to negative consequences.

The most important arguments on behalf of privacy as an instrumental good have focused either on its being necessary for special relationships or on its being necessary for democracy. Charles Fried (1968), for example, argued that we have to have privacy to have relationships of intimacy and trust. In a society in which individuals were always being observed (as in the panopticon), he argued, friendship, intimacy, and trust could not develop. If we want such relationships, we must create domains of privacy. Others argue that privacy is necessary for democracy. Here the important idea is that if individuals are constantly being observed, they will not be able to exercise the kind of independent thinking that is essential for democracy to work.

The arguments on behalf of privacy as an instrumental good begin to cross over into privacy as an intrinsic good when they suggest a connection between privacy and autonomy. You'll remember from the discussion of Kantian theory that autonomy is not just one among many values; autonomy is fundamental to what it means to be human, to our value as human beings. If privacy is essential to autonomy, then the loss of privacy would be a threat to our most fundamental values. But the connection between privacy and autonomy is often presented not exactly as a means–ends relationship. Rather the suggestion is that autonomy is inconceivable without privacy.

It will take us too far afield to explore all of these arguments. In what follows, I am going to explore several of the most salient arguments on behalf of privacy, and I will move from a focus on privacy as an individual good to privacy as a *social good.*

## Information Mediates Relationships

To begin with what seems most clear, information about an individual seems to be a fundamental precondition for establishing a relationship with that individual. Moreover, the information determines the character of the relationship. James Rachels (1975) has argued that people need to control information about themselves in order to maintain a diversity of relationships. His insight is that individuals maintain a variety of relationships (e.g., with parents, spouses, employers, friends, casual acquaintances, and so on), and each of these relationships is different because of the different information that each party has. Think, for example, about what your best friend knows about you as compared with what your teacher, your employer, or your dentist knows about you. These diverse relationships are a function of differing information.

Take your relationship with your dentist. Suppose she has been your dentist for 5 years

but she knows relatively little about you, except, of course, for what she knows about your teeth. Now suppose you need extensive work done on your teeth, and you begin to go to her office regularly at a time of the day when she is not rushed. You strike up conversations about your various interests. Each time you talk to her, she learns more about you and you learn more about her. Suppose you discover you have several hobbies and sports interests in common. She suggests that if you schedule your appointment next week so you are her last appointment, you could go out and play tennis afterward. The story can go on about how this relationship might develop from one of patient–professional, to good friends, perhaps to one of intimate friends. The changes in the relationship will in large measure be a function of the amount and kind of information you acquire about one another.

Rachels uses this insight to argue that privacy is important because it allows us to maintain a diversity of relationships. If everything were open to all (that is, if everyone knew the same things about you), then diversity would not be possible. You would have similar relationships with everyone.

Rachels seems right about the way information affects relationships. We control relationships by controlling the information that others have about us. When we lose control over information, we lose significant control over how others perceive and treat us. However, while Rachels seems right about this, his analysis does not quite get at what is worrisome about all the information gathering that is facilitated by computer technology. That is, the information gathering and exchange that goes on via computer technology does not seem, on the face of it, to threaten the diversity of personal relationships each of us has. For example, despite the fact that huge quantities of data now exist about my purchases, phone calls, medical condition, work history, and so on, I am able to maintain a diversity of personal relationships. Rachels seems slightly off target in putting the emphasis on the diversity of relationships, rather than simply on the loss of control of relationships that comes with loss of control of information. Perhaps, this is not surprising given that Rachels focused on personal relationships rather than relationships between individuals and organizations.

What happens when you lose control of information is better thought of on the model of an everyday case in which gossip generates some (false) information about you and the information is spread from one person to another. You are interested in being viewed and treated in a certain way and you know the information (true or false) will affect the way people see you and treat you. Once the information begins to move from person to person, you have no way of knowing who has heard it. If it is false information, you have no way contacting everyone and correcting their repository of information about you. Even if the information is true, there may be individuals that will treat you unfairly on the basis of this information and yet since you don't know who has it, you can't protect yourself. So, loss of control of information reduces your ability to establish and influence the relationships you have and the character of those relationships.

### Individual–Organization Relationships

In trying to understand the threat to privacy posed by the new type and scale of personal information gathering made possible by computer technology, the relationships most at issue are those between *individuals and formal organizations*.[2] In these relationships what is important to the individual is that the individual have some power or control in establishing or shaping the relationship (not that he or she has a diversity of such relationships). Information about us is what allows an organization

such as a marketing firm, a credit card company, or a law enforcement agency to establish a relationship with us. And information determines how we are treated in that relationship. One is sent an offer to sign up for a credit card when the credit card company gets your name and address and finds out how much you earn and/or own. How much credit is extended depends on the information. Similarly, a relationship between you and your local police force is created when the police force receives information about you; the nature of the relationship depends on the information received.

Currently, organizations may establish (or try to establish) a relationship with you without any action on your part. That is, you may subscribe to a magazine or open a bank account and establish a relationship with one organization, but when that organization sells information about you, another organization creates a file on you and begins to evaluate you for their purposes.

As an aside, let me point out that the twentieth century was a period of enormous growth in the size of public and private organizations (facilitated in part by the development of computer and information technology). This growth is likely to continue in the twenty-first century on a global scale. What this trend means is that instead of interacting with small, local, family-owned businesses wherein one might know or come to know the decision makers personally, most of us now (and in the future will) interact mostly with large national or international organizations operating with complex rules and regulations. Indeed, it is often a computer that makes the decision about our credit line or loan application. We may shop at grocery stores, department stores, or franchises that are local units of national companies. We may purchase items from catalogs or on the Internet and have no idea where the offices of the company are located. We may deal with banks that are national or international, go to large impersonal agencies for government services such as driver's licenses or building permits, attend colleges of 2,000 to 40,000 students, and so on. While our dealings with these organizations may have the most powerful effects on our lives, we may know little about these organizations and the people who own or manage them. Yet they will have (or have access to) an enormous amount of information about us—be it accurate or relevant. And unless we make an exerted effort, we are not likely to know what information they have about us to use when making decisions.

Everything that I have said here was recognized in the 1977 report of the Privacy Protection Study Commission when computer technology was in its early stages of development (i.e., when record-keeping practices were relatively primitive as compared with today's practices). Contrasting face-to-face relationships with relationships to record-keeping organizations, the report explains:

> What two people divulge about themselves when they meet for the first time depends on how much personal revelation they believe the situation warrants and how much confidence each has that the other will not misinterpret or misuse what is said. If they meet again, and particularly if they develop a relationship, their self-revelation may expand both in scope and detail. All the while, however, each is in a position to correct any misrepresentation that may develop and to judge whether the other is likely to misuse the personal revelations or pass them on to others without asking permission. Should either suspect that the other has violated the trust on which the candor of their communication depends, he can sever the relationship altogether, or alter its terms, perhaps by refusing thereafter to discuss certain topics or to reveal certain details about himself. Face-to-face encounters of this type, and the human relationships that result from them, are the threads from which the fabric of society is woven. The situations in which they arise are inherently social, not private, in that the disclosure of information about oneself is expected.

An individual's relationship with a record-keeping organization has some of the features of his face-to-face relationships with other individuals. It, too, arises in an inherently social context, depends on the individual's willingness to divulge information about himself or to allow others to do so, and often carries some expectation as to its practical consequences. Beyond that, however, the resemblance quickly fades.

By and large it is the organization's sole prerogative to decide what information the individual shall divulge for its records or allow others to divulge about him and the pace at which he must divulge it. If the record-keeping organization is a private-sector one, the individual theoretically can take his business elsewhere if he objects to the divulgences required of him. Yet in a society in which time is often at a premium, in which organizations performing similar functions tend to ask similar questions, and in which organizational record-keeping practices and the differences among them are poorly perceived or understood, the individual often has little real opportunity to pick and choose. Moreover, if the record-keeping organization is a public-sector one, the individual may have no alternative but to yield whatever information is demanded of him.

So, private and public organizations are powerful actors in the everyday lives of most individuals in our society, and yet it would seem that individuals have very little power in those relationships. One major factor making this possible is that these organizations can acquire, use, and exchange information about us, without our knowledge or consent. . . .

## REFRAMING THE COMPUTERS AND PRIVACY ISSUE—PRIVACY AS A SOCIAL GOOD

A major part of the problem seems to come from the combination of taking a piecemeal approach and then framing the computers and privacy issue as one involving a trade-off between social goods, such as law enforcement and government efficiency, and the interests of individuals in controlling information about themselves. Instead of thinking comprehensively about what record keeping and exchanging practices would be best for our society, the problem has been framed as one in which interests are pitted against one another and business and government seem to be pitted against individuals. This is odd when one remembers that ultimately business and government are justified in terms of their service to individuals as consumers and citizens.

In her 1995 book, *Legislating Privacy*, Priscilla M. Regan examined three privacy policy debates that took place in the United States in recent years—information privacy, communications privacy, and psychological privacy. She concludes that when individual privacy is pitted against social goods such as law enforcement or government efficiency, personal privacy loses. Regan suggests that privacy should be seen not as an individual good but rather as a social good. As an important social good, privacy would be on par with other social goods such as law enforcement or government efficiency. Instead of a social good outweighing an individual good, it would be clear that we have two social goods at stake. In reframing the issue in this way, privacy would be more likely to be treated as equally important, if not more important, than other social goods.

How, then, can the case be made for privacy as a social good? Earlier I argued that loss of control of information about us significantly reduces our autonomy—our power in relationships with formal organizations. Now I want to push this line of thinking even further. Instead of emphasizing loss of control, however, I want to return to the idea of the panopticon. If most everything that we do is recorded, then it would seem that the world that we live in is fundamentally changed from the world that existed in the past. And with this change comes an extremely important loss of freedom. We are unable to go places or do things without a record being created. The act of making a phone call is now the act of making a phone call *and* creating a record. We no longer have the option of making a phone call and not creating a record. Therefore, we have lost a degree of freedom. The loss of this freedom might be justified if you are in prison after having been fairly prosecuted and found guilty. But it hardly seems justified if you have done nothing wrong.

Even more important are the changes that take place in individuals as a result of constant surveillance. When persons are being watched, they tend to take on the perspective of the observer. When you know that decisions will be made about you on the basis of your activities (e.g., your educational records, work records, political activities, criminal activities), you think about that fact before you act. You take on the view of the private and public institutions that will make decisions about you. This can have a powerful effect both on how individuals behave and on how they see themselves. Individuals may come more and more to view themselves as they are viewed by those who watch them.

You may think of this as a good thing insofar as it means more social control and perhaps fewer crimes, fewer loan defaults, people working harder, and so on. The consequences of this kind of social control are, however, insidious. For one thing, it means that formal organizations exert an enormous amount of social control that may or may not be justified. Individuals may be inhibited about what they buy at the grocery store when they learn that their purchases are being recorded and analyzed. Remember that freedom is one of the most fundamental aspects of democracy. Yet freedom is eroded (or at least threatened) when every move is recorded. The result may be individuals who are ill-equipped to live in a democracy.

Consider how Jeffrey Reiman (1995), drawing on other authors, describes the situation:

> To the extent that a person experiences himself as subject to public observation, he naturally experiences himself as subject to public review. As a consequence, he will tend to act in ways that are publicly acceptable. People who are shaped to act in ways that are publicly acceptable will tend to act in safe ways, to hold and express and manifest the most widely-accepted views, indeed, the lowest-common denominator of conventionality.... Trained by society to act conventionally at all times, people will come so to think and so to feel.... As the inner life that is subject to social convention grows, the still deeper inner life that is separate from social convention contracts and, given little opportunity to develop, remains primitive.... You lose both the practice of making your own sense out of your deepest and most puzzling longings, and the potential for self-discovery and creativity that lurk within a rich inner life.... To say that people who suffer this loss will be easy to oppress doesn't say enough. They won't have to be oppressed, since there won't be anything in them that is tempted to drift from the beaten path.

The idea of democracy is the idea of citizens having the freedom to exercise their autonomy and in so doing to develop their capacities to do things that have not been thought of and to be critical. All of this makes for a citizenship that is active and pushing the world forward progressively. But if the consequences of trying something new, expressing a new idea, acting unconventionally are too negative, then there is no doubt that few citizens will take the risks. Democracy will diminish.

When the argument for privacy is framed in this way, privacy is shown to be something which is not just an individual good that can be diminished for the sake of a social good; rather, it is shown to be a social good in its own right and more important than other social goods such as efficiency and better consumer services. . . .

## CONCLUSION

Privacy is, perhaps, the most important of the ethical issues surrounding computer and information technology. I have tried to show this by making clear the importance of privacy to democratic society and the subtle ways in which our lives are changed when we are being watched. Individuals who walk through life knowing that each step creates a record that may or may not end up in a database somewhere are very different from individuals who walk through life feeling free and confident that they live in a open society in which the rules are known and fair.

Protecting personal privacy is not easy and is not likely to get easier. The most effective approach to privacy protection is a many-pronged approach. One thing is for sure, the use of personal information is not going to diminish of its own accord. Information about individuals is extremely valuable both in the private and in the public sector. This issue is not going to go away until we do something about it.

## REFERENCES

Fried, Charles. 1968. "Privacy," *Yale Law Journal* 77:477.

Orwell, George. 1949. *1984* New York: Harcourt, Brace & World.

Rachels, James. 1975. "Why Privacy Is Important." *Philosophy and Public Affairs*, 4 (Summer): 323–33.

Regan, Pricilla M. 1995. *Legislating Privacy, Technology, Social Values, and Public Policy.* Chapel Hill, NC: University of North Carolina Press.

Reiman, Jeffrey. 1995. "Hl. Driving to the Panopticon: A Philosophical Exportation of the Risks to Privacy Posed by the Highway Technology of the Future." *Computer and High Technology Law Journal* 11:27–44.

Zamyatin, Yl. 1972. *We.* Harmonsworth, England: Penguin Books. Originally published in Russia, 1920.

## NOTES

1. Ironically, it can work the other way as well. Sometimes, that is, changes in technology may result in data's being forgotten. In other words, where paper records stored in boxes in an archive may be obtained (even with difficulty), data stored on an old computer may be much more difficult to access because the technology is obsolete.

2. Of course, information stored in databases could affect personal relationships and gossip can spread on the Internet, but most large-scale, massive databases are maintained by formal organizations who make powerful decisions about individuals.

# Internet Content Providers and Complicity in Human Rights Abuse

*Jeffery D. Smith*

Internet content providers (ICPs) such as Yahoo, Google, and Microsoft host popular Internet search engines and provide a wide range of information services such as e-mail, chat rooms, blog hosting, and Web page authoring. These ICPs have recently experienced public scrutiny for their involvement in censoring information available through the Internet and disclosing sensitive information about the activities of their service subscribers. This scrutiny came to the foreground with the testimony of senior managers from Yahoo, Google, and Microsoft and Cisco Systems before the U.S. House of Representatives Committee on International Relations on February, 10, 2006. The focus of this testimony was on the compliance of ICPs in China with an elaborate system of laws and regulations that restrict Internet access within China and proscribe the Internet activity of Chinese citizens.

There are two central problems raised by these cases of Internet censorship in China. First, the regulatory efforts of the Chinese government to block access to Web sites, filter information, shut down information portals, and gather information about the Internet activities of particular individuals are an abridgement of basic human rights. The regulations suppress the right to expression, preclude political association, and where information is gathered to prosecute Chinese dissidents, it often interferes with the entitlement to privacy in matters of legitimate, peaceful social action.[1] Second, ICPs have been instrumental in carrying forth the directives of the Chinese government to limit the kind of information and activity of Chinese Internet users. In some cases, for example, ICPs have dutifully complied with directives to filter content from search engine queries. In other cases ICPs have turned over user information to Chinese agencies who are seeking to prosecute Chinese citizens for unlawful political speech.[2]

This essay will focus on the second problem. If one acknowledges that the rights to expression, association, and privacy are undermined by Chinese Internet censorship, then it remains an important task to determine how, and if, ICPs can legitimately do business in China without being implicated in violating these rights. Thus, while there is much to be said about the scope and justification of the human rights in question, this essay will take it for granted that there have been, and continue to be, violations of basic human rights that result from Chinese Internet censorship. I am more interested in exploring the extent to which ICPs bear moral responsibility for their compliance with Chinese directives. More specifically, these cases are an interesting opportunity to examine what it means for corporations to be *complicit* in moral wrongdoing, in this case the duty not to infringe upon the legitimate human rights of others.[3]

After an initial presentation of the extent and scope of ICP involvement in Chinese Internet censorship, I will present a conceptual examination of different forms of complicity in the infringement of human rights. I will offer a set of distinctions designed to clarify what it means to ascribe moral responsibility to corporate actors based upon their complicit involvement in activities that violate human rights. These observations will be applied to a number of recent instances drawn from ICPs and their presence in the Chinese market. I will argue in subsequent sections that while it is tempting to think of ICPs as passively involved in the violation of human rights, their behavior is more active once further details are examined. I conclude with some tentative remarks as to how ICPs can shift to a more passive presence in the Chinese Internet market that preserves their competitive position and does not assist the Chinese government in the suppression of the rights of expression, association, and privacy.

## HUMAN RIGHTS AND MULTINATIONAL BUSINESS

The rights to expression, association, and privacy have been recognized as fundamental rights under international law and a growing consensus of multinational business leaders. The United Nations *International Covenant on Civil and Political Rights*, signed by China and ratified by the United States, explicitly acknowledges the right to expression and association in Articles 19 and 21, respectively:

> Everyone shall have the right to freedom of expression; this right shall include freedom to seek, receive and impart information and ideas of all kinds, regardless of frontiers, either orally, in writing or in print, in the form of art, or through any other media of his choice.
>
> The right of peaceful assembly shall be recognized. No restrictions may be placed on the exercise of this right other than those imposed in conformity with the law and which are necessary in a democratic society in the interests of national security or public safety, public order, the protection of public health or morals or the protection of the rights and freedoms of others.[4]

Article 22 of the *International Covenant* also protects association in other forms: "everyone shall have the right to freedom of association with others, including the right to form and join trade unions for the protection of his interests."[5] The *International Covenant* has served as the primary international instrument for the development of constitutionally recognized rights by nation-states. Its legal authority can be traced to the United Nations *Universal Declaration of Human Rights*, which also codifies the rights of expression and association.[6]

It is more difficult to find mention and use of the right of privacy in international law; however, a working group of the United Nations Sub-Commission on Human Rights has called for a recognition of the right to privacy in its *Draft Norms of Responsibilities of Transnational Corporations and Other Business Enterprises with Regard to Human Rights*.[7] This step represents a recognition among international lawyers and business leaders that the protection of privacy should be a guiding norm of multinational businesses to regulate businesses' interactions with workers, customers, and members of the community so as to assure that the content of interpersonal communication, personal data, and memberships or affiliations will not be disclosed to outside parties without due process. The United Nations *Global Compact*, too, has served as an international instrument to recognize and protect the human rights of various stakeholders. The *Global Compact* is an ongoing group of United Nations agencies, labor organizations, and business leaders that has attempted to implement the norms of the *Universal Declaration of Human Rights* within business contexts. The *Global Compact*'s Business Leaders Initiative has worked diligently to articulate strategies for multinational businesses to institutionalize human rights standards in their operations, including the right to privacy.[8]

It is important to note that this legal and institutional recognition of the rights of expression, association, and privacy is not what gives these rights their moral authority. The legal recognition of human rights is important from a practical point of view in assuring the protection of rights; however, their authority is prior to their legal protection because nation-states and corporations have a moral duty to not abridge these rights regardless of the extent to which they may, or may not, be positively recognized and protected by governments.[9]

The moral authority of human rights, including the rights of expression, association, and privacy, has been defended from a number of philosophically credible perspectives. Kantian scholars have argued that respect for personhood requires, among other things, guarantees of autonomy or the ability to fully self-determine one's life in accordance with one's own choices.[10] Human rights are one means toward securing this kind of autonomy. Libertarian and utilitarian schools of thought provide fertile ground to defend the importance of rights, especially so-called liberty rights that require noninterference by others in areas of speech, thought, and association.[11] Other scholars have more recently focused on conceptions of human well-being to defend the notion that core human goods are secured only when central human capabilities are protected. Martha Nussbaum and Amartya Sen have maintained, for instance, that human life requires physical safety, health, creativity, education, social membership, and control over their external environment. Rights are instrumental in securing these constituents of a complete life.[12]

It is not the intent of this essay to examine these philosophical justifications. It is also too large of a task to systematically explore the prospects of the *Draft Norms* or the *Global Compact* in securing the rights of current and future stakeholders. My efforts in the remaining portions of this essay are instead focused on what it means for corporations to be complicit in violating these rights. In order to accomplish this task we need to first review the activities of ICPs in China that impact the rights of expression, association, and privacy and, second, develop a typology of different forms of complicity.

## INTERNET CENSORSHIP IN CHINA

There are three primary levels at which Internet content is censored in China.[13] First, there is the censorship of content at the point where Chinese Internet access providers (IAPs) are connected to other regions of the Internet. These state-licensed IAPs sell access to this so-called international backbone of the Internet to hundreds of smaller Internet service providers (ISPs) which, in turn, sell access to individual customers. IAPs make frequent use of routers, primarily designed and sold by Cisco Systems, which screen and block specific information hosted by sources both within and outside of China.[14] IAPs block access to specific Web addresses (URLs) or Web addresses that are known to host objectionable content. They also selectively filter content on Web pages if such content is thought to be in conflict with norms established by the Ministry of Information, its main administrative arm, the State Council of Information Office, or the propaganda agency of the Communist Party. Filtering content is more difficult to accomplish because it requires a much finer examination of the content displayed on particular Web pages on an ongoing basis, whereas blocking access to URLs can be accomplished effectively once URLs with prohibited content have been identified, collected, and passed on to ISPs.

Second, ISPs must also comply with a series of directives issued by the Ministry of Information and other state and local agencies that prohibit the hosting of content that is deemed to be harmful to state security or social stability. These orders are far reaching. Managers of ISPs are legally required to monitor the exchange of information among their customers and routinely examine and report the content of e-mails, Web pages, and other forms of communication on the Internet. Dissident political activity, discussions initiated by banned organizations, references to specific historical events, and Western news sources are prime targets for ISP monitoring and censorship.

Finally, the entry of multinational ICPs into the Chinese market has brought an additional layer of censorship that essentially conditions the operation of ICPs in China upon compliance with the aims of the Ministry of Information's "Public Pledge on Self-Discipline of the Chinese Internet Industry."[15] ICPs are licensed prior to operation and are held legally responsible for all content hosted through their services, including blogs, e-mail, personal Web sites, and chat rooms. Although the "Public Pledge" is not itself legally required, there are an array of specific laws that require ICPs to refrain from "disseminating pernicious in-

formation that may jeopardize state security or disrupt social stability."[16] ICPs are specifically required to delist Web sites and filter content that contain words, phrases, names, and addresses that are intended to be blocked at the IAP or ISP level but which may escape censorship. ICPs have discretion over how they identify sites to delist and content to filter. They also are responsible for directing internal compliance with the censorship directives of the Chinese government.

## COMPLICITY IN INTERNET CENSORSHIP

ICPs play an increasingly central role in managing information available on the Internet. While ISPs provide access to the infrastructure of the Internet, ICPs are the primary way in which individuals search, gain access, and share information. Accordingly, the proliferation of ICPs and the commercial opportunities for ICPs in China have produced a competitive landscape where ICPs are faced with the difficult challenge of complying with Chinese directives regarding Internet censorship or risk losing access to the most promising information systems market in the world. This reality has been mentioned time and time again by senior executives of the key ICPs like Yahoo, Google, and Microsoft.

On the assumption that there are basic human rights of expression, association, and privacy, and that the coordinated efforts of the Chinese government and ICPs constitute a violation of these rights, then it is natural to ask, To what extent, if any, are ICPs morally responsible for those violations? One common way that this type of problem is addressed in human rights circles is to probe whether we can say ICPs are *complicit* in the violation of human rights.

The International Center on Human Rights Policy holds that complicity in human rights violations involves "participating or assisting abuses committed by others," whether by armies, government agencies, or other non-governmental organizations.[17] There are numerous considerations in determining whether a corporate actor is complicit in the violation of a human right: the corporation's knowledge of the violations, their intentions, the causal significance of the corporation's activities in producing the violation, and the directness of the relationship between the corporation, the victims and the principal perpetrators all seem like relevant pieces of information in making determinations of complicity.[18] These factors are essential in understanding the extent to which corporations can be said to participate or assist in abuse.

The Office of the United Nations High Commissioner for Human Rights (OHCHR) defines the term "complicity" in the context of applying the norms outlined in the United Nations Global Compact:

> A company is complicit in human rights abuses if it authorizes, tolerates, or knowingly ignores human rights abuses committed by an entity associated with it, or if the company knowingly provides practical assistance or encouragement that has a substantial effect on the perpetration of human rights abuse. The participation of the company need not actually cause the abuse. Rather the company's assistance or encouragement has to be to a degree that, without such participation, the abuses most probably would not have occurred to the same extent or in the same way.[19]

Here complicity includes authorization, toleration, or neglect of abuses in addition to a provision of assistance to a principal perpetrator. The implication of this passage is that any one of these facilitating acts serves as a sufficient condition for a complicit violation of human rights. The OHCHR definition extends complicity beyond assistance to forbearance and involvement in practices that involve the violation of human rights. Complicity does not require the corporation to be causally implicated in the violation; that is, the complicit corporation is not necessarily one that causes the abuse but simply facilitates or accentuates a violation that might still have otherwise occurred.

To say that a corporation has been complicit in the violation of human rights is to ascribe a level of moral blameworthiness in failing to respect the basic entitlements of other human beings. The level of blame or the extent of the moral failure, however, may not rise to the level of direct violations of human rights. There is therefore a basic distinction that needs to be drawn between acts that violate human rights because of an intentional, deliberate decision to do so and acts that violate human rights because of an intentional, nondeliberate decision to do so.

All intentional actions that violate human rights can be divided into two categories: those that are performed by actors with the purpose of violating human rights and those that are performed by actors who are responding to the directives issued by other authoritative parties to engage in the violation of human rights. I will call the former category of actions *direct* acts that violate human rights and the latter category *indirect* acts that violate human rights. Direct violations are deliberate in that they are essentially characterized by the intention to deprive an individual of some human right, whereas indirect violations are nondeliberate in the sense that while they may intentionally violate a human right, they would not be performed but for adherence to a directive issued by some authoritative individual, organization, or agency.

Direct violations are noncomplicit deprivations of some human right. Indirect violations are complicit deprivations because an indirect violation can be described as a knowledgeable act of tolerance, compliance, acquiescence, assistance, support, or encouragement of an authoritative directive to deprive an individual of some human right.

Within this category of indirect violations there is another important distinction to be drawn between *active* and *passive* responses to authoritative directives that deprive individuals of some human right. This difference is subtle but important. Active indirect violations are acts that take positive steps to deprive individuals of their rights where the extent and methods used in the violation are at the discretion of the secondary party. I describe such acts as *active* because the techniques used in the deprivation of rights are developed and implemented by the secondary party. There are clearly norms and implied expectations communicated by principal authorities that condition the indirect party's intentional act to implement the techniques used in depriving individuals of their rights. This is what makes this category of violations indirect; but these violations are active in the sense that indirect parties are not merely compliant with specific directives issued by the principal authority but take initiative on their own to develop policies that uphold the spirit of the principal's goal of violating some basic right. Active indirect acts involve intentional acts of assistance that qualitatively strengthen the principal authority's efforts to deprive an individual of some human right.

Passive indirect violations are indirect violations that are merely compliant to a specific directive issued by a principal authority. There is no meaningful effort at a creative implementation of some overarching norm established by the principal authority; instead, passive indirect actors remain poised simply to respond to particular edicts handed down through authoritative channels.

To illustrate this difference, consider examples from the recent past. There were a number of documented cases in apartheid South Africa where companies took positive steps to report the activities of individual employees that were seen as a challenge to the authority of the apartheid government.[20] By targeting political speech for eventual suppression by government, these South African companies can be understood as committing an indirect yet active effort to deprive individual employees of the right of expression. Consider, too, the recent revelation that Deutsche Bank branches financed the construction of certain concentration camp buildings, most notably the crematorium at Auschwitz.[21] Absent the Nazi regime, this act would not have taken place; however, within the political and business climate of the Third Reich, Deutsche Bank took active steps to enable the final solution and the deprivation of rights to life, property, and personhood. In both of these cases the companies in question exercised discretion over their relationship with the principal authority's interest in suppression of rights.

Indirect passive violations have routinely occurred. Suppose a telecommunications company responds to a specific court order to hand over individual phone records in order to facilitate an investigation as to whether someone belonged to an underground, dissident political organization. Although intentional, this act would not have occurred but for the court order. The company is merely responsive or compliant even though it can be said to facilitate the infringement of the right to association. To the extent that it facilitates the investigation and mangers have knowledge of the investigation it can be said to be complicit in the violation of the right to association.

Human rights organizations extend further the class of actions that are said to be complicit. The International Council on Human Rights Policy has applied the analysis provided under the UN Global Compact to include two additional kinds of complicit acts that, I believe, are not intentional and therefore do not involve indirect violations of rights in the way I have been describing.

First, companies can be complicit in human rights abuse when they are "silent enablers" of abuse. This means that companies that engage in activities with separate, legitimate business purposes may be implicated through these activities in providing resources, technology, or expertise that are used by principal authorities to deprive individuals of their human rights. The term "silent" refers to the fact that the companies in question have knowledge, or could reasonably be expected to have knowledge, about the use of their resources, technology, or expertise in the deprivation of human rights. It is natural to describe these silent enabling acts as morally negligent as opposed to intentional because the intention to deprive an individual of some right is not a deliberate or nondeliberate intention of the company's managers. It is simply that their actions with legitimate business purposes provide the principal authority with the derivate ability to deprive individuals of their rights. This difference separates acts that silently enable human rights abuse from secondary acts that are, by definition, intentional in their deprivation of human rights. Acts that silently enable human rights violations are therefore complicit but not indirect.

The case of the Canadian oil firm Talisman Energy and its joint venture with the Sudanese government to extract and transport oil to the Red Sea serves as a nice illustration. The Canadian Foreign Ministry confirmed through various investigations that the Heglig oil field, constructed and managed by Talisman, was used by the Sudanese government to coordinate and launch military raids against Christian and tribal populations in the southern part of the country as part of Sudan's ongoing civil war.[22] Although the oil field had legitimate business purposes that were part of the explicit provisions of the joint venture, critics rightly claimed that Talisman either knew, or should have known, that the Sudanese military was using their resources as a tool to gain a geographic advantage over other factions in the civil war. To the extent that independent moni-

tors verified that such bombing raids targeted civilian populations, it was argued that Talisman was a silent yet significant contributor to the violation of the right of noncombatants not to become military targets.

A final category of complicit acts that is often highlighted in the human rights literature concerns instances where corporations derive benefits from their engagement with a principal authority. Corporations that are derivative beneficiaries of human rights violations receive business-related benefits from actions taken by a principal authority to deprive individuals of their rights. Unocal's operations in Burma depended heavily on the existence of infrastructure and pipelines that were constructed, in part, with the use of forced labor under auspices of the Burmese government.[23] In this case Unocal knowingly tolerated the abuse of human rights as an ongoing condition of operating in the Burmese commercial environment, even though there was neither intentional assistance provided to the government (actively or passively) nor an unintentional but negligent provision of support.

This conceptual mapping has produced the following results (see Figure 1). Direct violations of human rights are intentional, deliberate, and have the specific purpose of depriving an individual or individuals of a right. These acts are not complicit. They are direct in that there is a principal authority that has the discretion and power to carry forth the violations. Indirect acts that result in the violation of human rights are intentional, nondeliberate and have the purpose of responding to norms established by some other principal authority. Indirect acts would not take place but for the existence of a principal authority demanding that the indirect party to commit actions that result in the violation of some human right. Indirect actors are complicit in the violation of a human right because they provide practical assistance to a principal

**FIGURE 1**    Classification of Human Rights Violation.

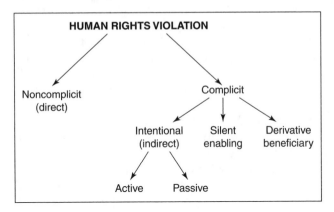

authority who directs the violation. There are active and passive secondary instances of indirect violations; the former are positive acts taken to deprive an individual of some right where the means and methods used in the deprivation are at the discretion of the secondary actor. Passive violations are merely acts of compliance with a specific order issued by the principal authority.

Not all complicit acts are indirect violations. Examples of these include situations where corporations enable other principal authorities to violate human rights and times when corporations benefit from ongoing human rights violations committed by principal authorities. Corporations that silently enable or derive benefit from the violation of human rights can potentially be morally negligent even though their actions do not fall into the category of indirect (intentional, nondeliberate) violations of human rights.

## COMPLICIT ICPS

The extent to which ICPs have been complicit in the violation of rights to expression, association, and privacy in China has been widely discussed. In the remaining portions of this paper I will outline the nature of these complicit acts bringing to bear the aforementioned distinctions as a way of helping us understand the morally relevant features of these complicit acts. I will conclude in the following section by offering a tentative explanation as to how the different forms of complicity reviewed in this section impact the moral assessment of actions taken by ICPs in China.

The event that has garnered the most attention from critics of ICPs in China has been the case of Shi Tao, the imprisoned Chinese journalist who was found by Chinese courts to have disclosed state secrets by reporting the Communist Party's intention to limit media reports about the 15th anniversary of the Tiananmen Square massacre.[24] Shi Tao apparently took notes on a memorandum to be enforced by Chinese media agencies entitled "A Notice Regarding Current Stabilizing Work" that included recommendations that journalists not report on commemorations or other prodemocracy events at the time of the anniversary. Shi Tao sent details of this memorandum to the "Democracy Forum" under a pseudonym that was subsequently linked to Shi Tao after Yahoo provided the Chinese government the Internet protocol (IP) address from which the e-mails were sent. This established that Shi Tao's personal e-mail account was accessed by a computer located in the news office of his employer, *Contemporary Business News*.[25] Once this connection was verified, the Chinese authorities also requested the content of Shi Tao's communications with the "Democracy Forum" and used this as evidence in the trial where he was convicted of "divulging state secrets abroad." He is now serving a 10-year prison sentence.

In response to the Shi Tao case, Yahoo took the official position that their managers are required to adhere to the laws, regulations, and customs of the country in which they are based. In his testimony before the U.S. House of Representatives, Senior Vice President Michael Callahan asserted that Yahoo had no option but to conform to the requests made by Chinese law enforcement agencies for the IP addresses and user data that were eventually used in Shi Tao's case.[26] In response to criticisms leveled by human rights organizations, Yahoo has claimed that it hands over such private information only when there are specific, targeted requests made through official Chinese government channels, e.g., law enforcement agencies or courts. They also asserted that they have no way of knowing the nature of the investigations and whether there are any reliable appeal procedures for rejecting a government request for information.[27]

All of this would appear upon first blush to be an instance of what I have labeled above a passive, indirect act that violates the right of expression and privacy. Absent the government's demand for information, Yahoo would not have supplied such information. Moreover, from the perspective of Yahoo management, Yahoo was providing information in a very limited fashion, responding only to the narrow request for IP addresses and, once Shi Tao's identity had been established, specific communications of a particular user.

There are some complications with this analysis. First, although senior executives at Yahoo have confirmed that user data for Yahoo's Chinese Internet services is housed on servers in China, the information identified in court records appears to have originated from Yahoo's Hong Kong affiliate, Yahoo Holdings of Hong Kong.[28] This has led to speculation that collaboration between management in China and Hong Kong was instrumental in producing the information used to prosecute Shi Tao. Michael Callahan has denied any such information exchange between Yahoo Hong Kong and Yahoo China.[29]

If it is true that user data in Hong Kong was handed over at the request of Chinese authorities, then Yahoo's complicit action may not simply be passive in the way defined above. It could be construed as an active complicity because there is no evidence that the Chinese government either requested information on non-Chinese servers or had jurisdiction over information housed in Hong Kong. To be truly passive in their complicity Yahoo would need to demonstrate that their involvement in the investigation was specifically demanded by Chinese authorities; otherwise, the means and methods used to respond to the Chinese investigation were determined by Yahoo, rather than the principal authorities.

Second, even if this was a truly passive act of complicity with the Chinese government, Yahoo had a clear awareness of the potential problems associated with investigations of the sort illustrated in the Shi Tao case. Yahoo management clearly understood the nature of Chinese censorship of speech and the repression of political activities. While it is true that Yahoo has no way of knowing whether investigations may be criminal or political in nature, this fact provides an even stronger reason to avoid business models that may possibly implicate Yahoo in the violation of expression and privacy. Without the rule of law a company like Yahoo can easily foresee that the information gathered by the Chinese government may vary from time to time or may be arbitrary depending upon edicts of the Communist Party or the Ministry of Information. This was exactly the rationale offered by Google and Microsoft as to why they have made the decision not to offer Chinese mail, Web, and blogging services. Keeping these services in the United States has meant that user information remains located on servers outside of China.

Another set of problems has to do with the ways that Internet content in China is censored by ICPs. Here the main issue has to do with how we classify the complicity of ICPs in censorship. Are they passively responding to Chinese demands or is there an active dimension to their censorship practices?

ICPs engage in two practices that they claim are required by their operating licenses in China. First, ICPs routinely block access or "delist" Web sites that contain content that is deemed to be politically sensitive, destabilizing or threatening, to state security. In many cases delisting Web sites is redundant because such sites will be blocked by routers at the ISP and IAP level. Given the fact that ICP search engines will often display abstracted information, however, it is required that ICPs undertake their own delisting in order to prevent certain descriptions of Web sites from appearing before Chinese users. Examples include the *New York Times*, Radio Free Asia, Amnesty International, and Falun Gong news sites. Second, in addition to censoring certain URLs, ICPs filter content containing words or phrases that contravene norms established by the Ministry of Information. This means that Web sites containing dissident political themes such as Tibet, Tiananmen Square, and human rights are censored from normal search queries when those searches are performed through platforms hosted in China. When Chinese users use search phrases like "Wu Hao" (a detained filmmaker) or "June 4th 1989 crackdown" (referring to Tiananmen Square) they receive a list of Web resources and addresses that are substantially shorter than those generated by comparable searches through ICP search engines operating in other countries.[30]

Based upon studies performed by organizations such as OpenNet Initative (ONI), Human Rights Watch, and the *Washington Post,* Yahoo, Google, and MSN all engage in delisting of URLs and Web content filtering. The extent and scope of these censorship efforts vary widely. Yahoo appears to be more aggressive in its delisting and filtering. Out of 25 URLs examined by Human Rights Watch on August 9, 2006, from stations in China, Yahoo delisted 15 sites, 14 of which were censored without explanation or notification to the user that the search result had been censored. In these nontransparent cases Yahoo's Chinese search engine simply turned up a "no results found" message in response to searches for particular URLs. Google delisted 8 URLs all with a standard notification that "according to local laws, regulations, and policies, a portion of the search results do not appear." MSN was more aggressive in its delisting than Google but provided greater levels of transparency in identifying that some search results had been removed. Interestingly enough, Baidu, a main Chinese-based ICP, did not delist any of the 25 URLs on the Human Rights Watch survey; instead, Baidu simply provides a message indicating that no results have been found and a clickable URL link that is subsequently blocked by ISPs.[31]

There appears to be greater parity when looking at keyword filtering. Both Yahoo and Google filtered content from all 25 keyword searches with the addendum that some search results may not appear due to relevant laws and regulations. The number of information links available through censored searches varies according to the ICP used. In some cases the discrepancy is quite large. The keyword search for "Tibet Independence" turned up 75,200 sites in Google and 38,900 sites in Yahoo. It is difficult to determine with great accuracy the extent to which these differences result from filtering or from the search technologies employed by Google and Yahoo, respectively. Both search engines' results were dominated by pro-Chinese sources.[32]

Filtering occurs on other levels as well. MSN has taken the initiative to remove postings from blogs that use words and phrases that MSN takes to be prohibited by the spirit of the Chinese ICP licensing requirements. Google News now has a Chinese language platform that filters results that it has learned would be blocked by Chinese ISPs. Google has opted in this case not to display links to news stories or organizations that would lead to blocked searches or error pages. Google News users are neither informed that there has been blocked content nor the specific URLs or names of news organization from which the blocked content would normally appear.[33] The rationale for this move, like the rationale to filter regular Web search results, is that a limited Google presence in China is instrumental to the long-term presence of an open Internet in China. Some Internet access through non-Chinese ICPs is better than none.

Delisting and filtering sites appears to be another instance of passive complicity where ICPs are adhering to the directives issued by Chinese authorities. ICP executive leaders, such as Google's senior counsel Andrew McLaughlin and Google CEO Eric Schmidt, have stressed that absent adherence to China's censorship program it is likely that Google's services would be blocked altogether.[34] There is precedent to believe this is true. Google's U.S. search engine and news platform were routinely inaccessible in China before the launch of Google's Chinese operations when specific licensing requirements were accepted as a condition for its operation. These requirements included delisting and filtering.[35]

The problem with classifying delisting and filtering as passive complicity is that it belies the methods used by ICPs to comply with Chinese licensing requirements. There is no official published list of URLs, words, phrases or news stories that is handed down from Chinese

officials to the managers of ICPs.[36] ICPs have developed lists of content to be censored based upon a careful extrapolation of what would fall into the broad categories of banned content identified by the Chinese government.[37] Yahoo has voluntarily signed the "Public Pledge on Self-Discipline for the Chinese Internet Industry," which specifies that Yahoo will block or filter all words, phrases, and addresses that are censored at the ISP and IAP levels. There are no guidelines, however, as to how ICPs should achieve this goal. They exercise discretion over how to monitor what is blocked by ISPs and the diagnostic tests used to determine what content Chinese routers are blocking at the point where IAPs link to the central arteries of the Internet.[38] From this effort ICPs make inferences about what content the Chinese authorities intend to block and, in turn, develop their lists of censored information. Obtaining these lists has proven to be very difficult.

ICP censorship is clearly responsive to the demands of Chinese authorities. Nonetheless, in an effort to avoid conflict with Chinese authorities and a strong motive to assure a strong competitive position within the Chinese market, American ICPs have been instrumental in improving the effectiveness of Chinese Internet censorship policies. They have deployed technology and committed resources to blocking information that has not been precisely mandated by Chinese authorities. This is an active step of complicity that requires moral justification.

A final act of complicity that should be mentioned concerns the use of Cisco System's routers in the maintenance of China's information networks. Cisco is not intentionally engaging in conduct that either actively or passively deprives individuals of their human rights, unless one assumes (as some have) that Cisco provides technical expertise in the use of routers for filtering purposes.[39] The act of selling network technology may be an instance of silently enabling the Chinese government to suppress rights. This may be morally negligent in that Cisco managers could foresee the use of their technology in this way. If it turns out that Cisco has intentionally designed their routers for censorship purposes, or provided technical guidance in achieving these ends, then their actions may reasonably be said to be an example of an indirect yet active violation of the rights in question. Mark Chandler, Senior Vice President and General Counsel for Cisco Systems, has specifically denied that Cisco provides special technology or expertise for the specific purpose of filtering content or delisting URLs.[40]

## RESISTANCE THROUGH PASSIVITY

Although I have argued that ICPs have been actively complicit in their decisions to disclose user information and filter Internet content, I have not engaged in a comparative moral assessment of active and passive varieties of what I have been calling indirect violations of human rights. Most will find the active variety more morally problematic than the passive variety. A commitment not to actively pursue methods of censorship may make the Chinese effort at censorship more difficult to accomplish. The success of the Chinese system to block all impermissible content has had, at best, mixed results; thus, if ICPs were to take a more deliberate stand to verify requests for information, explore appeal processes, wait for court orders, refrain from employing technology to enable more efficient filtering, and block URLs only upon official request, then it is more likely that ICPs could claim allegiance to the values that support basic human rights. Responding to such official requirements would help ICPs make the case that they are merely compliant actors and not assistants through their discretionary acts.

Others, including individuals representing organizations such as the Berkeley-China Internet Project and the Oxford Internet Institute, have maintained that ICPs should adopt principles that ensure greater passivity, in the technical way that I have been classifying complicit acts.[41] Greater passivity does not require inaction; indeed, refusing to initiate censorship through new technology, keeping user data offshore, waiting for written court orders, pursuing appeals, using maximal security techniques at all times, and the like, should be viewed as a kind of limited refusal to provide practical assistance in the censorship effort.

The underlying motivation for this call for greater passivity is the inability of ICPs to claim that they simply do not have a choice in how they do business in China. They are intimately familiar with the technical aspects of the Internet as well as the complicated social and political environment of China. This knowledge demands not a withdraw from the Chinese market but a constructive engagement with it that at once refuses to provide practical assistance to censorship efforts and presses for regulatory reform through industry partners and China's trading partners. This resistance to censorship acknowledges the significance of stakeholders' rights while also accepting the claims of ICPs that their presence in China is a positive force for greater openness in an otherwise closed society.

## NOTES

1. For a more detailed discussion of human rights standards and their application to business see Denis Arnold, "Human Rights and Business: An Ethical Analysis," and Bennett Freeman, "Managing Risk and Building Trust: The Challenge of Implementing the Voluntary Principles on Security and Human Rights," both in *Business and Human Rights: Dilemmas and Solutions*, ed. Rory Sullivan (Sheffield: Greenleaf Publishers, 2003).

2. Tom Zeller, "Internet Firms Are Grilled on Dealings in China," *New York Times* (February 16, 2006). Retrieved from http://www.nytimes.com on August 15, 2006.

3. "Group Alleges Yahoo! Complicit in China Arrest," February 8, 2006. Retrieved from http://money.cnn.com/2006/02/08/technology/yahoo_china/index.htm?cnn=yes on September 23, 2006.

4. International Covenant on Civil and Political Rights. Retrieved from http://www.ohchr.org/english/law/ccpr.htm on September 20, 2006.

5. Ibid.

6. Universal Declaration of Human Rights. Retrieved from http://www.un.org/Overview/rights.html on September 20, 2006.

7. David Weissbrodt and Muria Kruger, "Norms on the Responsibilities of Transnational Corporations and Other Business Enterprises with Regard to Human Rights," *American Journal of International Law*, 97, no. 4 (2003): 901–22. For the complete text of the document see the Draft Norms on the Responsibilities of Transnational Corporations and Other Business Enterprises with Regard to Human Rights, retrieved from http://www1.umn.edu/humanrts/links/NormsApril2003.html on January 3, 2007.

8. United Nations Global Compact, "The Principles of the Global Compact." Retrieved from http://www.un.org/Depts/ptd/global.htm on November 11, 2006. See also Business Leader's Forum on Human Rights, "A Guide for Integrating Human Rights into Business Management," 2006. Retrieved from http://www.blihr.org/Pdfs/GIHRBM.pdf on September 2, 2006.

9. Denis Arnold, "Human Rights and Business: An Ethical Analysis," pp. 71–75.

10. See Onora O'Neill, *Constructions of Reason: Explorations of Kant's Practial Philosophy* (Cambridge: Cambridge University Press, 1989), 187–205; Thomas E. Hill, *Dignity and Practical Reason in Kant's Moral Theory* (Ithaca, NY: Cornell University Press, 1992), 38-57; and John Rawls, *Political Liberalism* (New York: Columbia University Press, 1993), 289–372.

11. See John Stuart Mill, *"On Liberty" and Other Writings,* ed. Stefan Collini (Cambridge: Cambridge University Press, 1989) and Loren Lomasky, *Persons, Rights, and the Moral Community* (New York: Oxford University Press, 1987).

12. Martha Nussbaum, *Women and Human Development* (Cambridge: Cambridge University Press, 2001) and Amartya Sen, *Development and Freedom* (New York: Random House Books, 1999).

13. This summary and the associated acronyms are drawn, in large part, from Human Rights Watch, "Race to the Bottom: Corporate Complicity in Chinese Internet Censorship," 18, no. 8 (August 2006): 9–24.

14. "Material Submitted for the Hearing Record," *China and the Internet: Tool for Freedom or Suppression*, pp. 181–82.

15. Human Rights Watch, "Race to the Bottom," p. 30.

16. This pledge is monitored by the Internet Society of China. See Human Rights Watch, "Race to the Bottom," p. 12, and the Internet Society of China, "Public Pledge of Self-Regulation and Professional Ethics for China Internet Industry." Retrieved from http://www.isc.org.cn/20020417/ca102762.htm on September 10, 2006.

17. International Council on Human Rights Policy, "Beyond Voluntarism: Human Rights and the Developing International Legal Obligations of Companies," 2002. Retrieved from http://www.ichrp.org/paper_files/107_p_01.pdf on October 16, 2006.

18. Ibid., 121.

19. Business Leader's Forum on Human Rights, "A Guide for Integrating Human Rights into Business Management," 2006. Retrieved from http://www.blihr.org/Pdfs/GIHRBM.pdf on September 2, 2006.

20. International Council on Human Rights Policy, "Beyond Voluntarism," p. 126.

21. "Holocaust Reparations: German CEOs Unlock Their Vaults," *Business Week* (February 22, 1999). Retrieved from http://www.businessweek.com/1999/99_11/b3620148.htm on October 27, 2006. I owe this example to the International Council on Human Rights Policy, "Beyond Voluntarism," p. 126.

22. John Harker, "Human Security in Sudan: The Report of a Canadian Assessment Mission," Canadian Ministry of Foreign Affairs, 2000.

23. International Council on Human Rights Policy, "Beyond Voluntarism," pp. 131–32.

24. "Yahoo 'Helped Jail China Writer'," BBC News, September 7, 2005. Retrieved from http://news.bbc.co.uk/1/hi/world/asia-pacific/4221538.stm on October 1, 2006.

25. Human Rights Watch, "Race to the Bottom," pp. 107–8.

26. Michael Callahan, Testimony before the Sub-committees on Africa, Global Human Rights, and International Operations before the Committee on International Relations, U.S. House of Representatives, February 15, 2006, pp. 3–4.

27. Human Rights Watch, "Race to the Bottom," pp. 32–33.

28. Ibid., 34.

29. Michael Callahan, Testimony before the Committee on International Relations, p. 4

30. Human Rights Watch, "Race to the Bottom," pp. 11–14. See also "The Great Firewall of China," *Washington Post* (February 18, 2006). Retrieved from http://www.washingtonpost.com/wpdyn/content/article/2006/02/18/AR2006021800554.html on September 23, 2006.

31. Human Rights Watch, "Race to the Bottom," pp. 142–45.

32. Ibid.

33. Open Net Initiative, "Google.cn Filtering: How It Works," January 25, 2006. Retrieved from http://www.opennetinitiative.net/blog/?=87 on November 27, 2006.

34. Human Rights Watch, "Race to the Bottom," p. 55.

35. Philip Pan, "U.S. Firms Balance Morality and Commerce," *Washington Post* (February 18, 2006). Retrieved from http://www.washingtonpost.com/wp-dyn/content/article/2006/02/18/AR2006021801397.html on September 6, 2006.

36. Human Rights Watch, "Race to the Bottom," p. 12.

37. Ibid., 3–4.

38. Open Net Initiative, "Google.cn Filtering: How It Works."

39. Mark Chandler, Testimony before the Sub-committees on Africa, Global Human Rights, and International Operations before the Committee on International Relations, U.S. House of Representatives, February 15, 2006, p. 1.

40. For a response see Declan McCullah, "U.N. Blasts Cisco, Others on China Cooperation," CNet News.com, October 31, 2006. Retrieved from http://news.com.com/U.N.+blasts+Cisco,+others+on+China+cooperation/2100-1028_3-6131010.html on November 17, 2006.

41. These organizations have focused their efforts on a voluntary code of conduct for ICPs. See Human Rights Watch, "Race to the Bottom," pp. 73–76.

# Intellectual Property and the Information Age

*Richard T. De George*

When VCRs first became available in the United States, both the movie and the TV industries felt them as a threat to their commercial interests. They sued to block the use of VCRs, arguing they were a tool devised to violate copyright laws. The courts ruled otherwise, finding that VCRs had many legitimate uses, even though they might be used to violate copyright laws, and holding that users could legally make copies of material pre-sented on TV for personal viewing and use at a later time. They justified this under the "fair use" clause of the copyright law, which allows individuals to make certain reasonable use of copyrighted material for personal use. The commercial use of such copies is illegal, as is the copying of rented movies and other copyrighted material available in tape format. The movie and TV industries responded creatively by turning the presence of home VCRs into an additional profit stream through the sale and rental of movies and TV programs.

Last evening Joe taped the popular movie *Sound of Music*, which was playing on one of the TV channels. He was away for the evening and intended to look at the movie when it better fit his schedule. This is both common and legal. He may tape as many programs and movies as he wishes for later viewing. His taped version is his to use, even though the same movie is also available for rent or sale at his local video rental store. His friend, Richard, intended to tape the movie but by mistake set his VCR to the wrong channel, and hence taped some other program instead. When he learned this, he asked Joe if he could copy Joe's tape. He reasoned that since it was legal for him to copy the movie directly from the TV, and he would have if he had not made a mistake, there seems to be no difference in principle for him to copy Joe's tape. Another friend, Tom, also meant to tape the movie but forgot to set his machine. Rather than phone friends to see if any of them had taped it, he simply went to the Internet and asked if anyone had made a copy from the TV broadcast that they would let him copy. His reasoning was similar to Richard's. It was legal for him to make a copy from the TV—there is no difference in principle between his recording it directly or his getting it from someone else who recorded it directly, and it does not make any difference whether or not the person he copies it from is a friend, as long as he or she copied it legally. Now whether this reasoning is correct from a legal point of view is questionable, since lending a copy of one's tape for someone else to copy does not seem to be "personal use." Yet the reasoning of Richard and Tom does seem to have some plausibility. For if they could have made legal copies directly themselves, then there is nothing wrong in their having the copy from that source, and getting it secondhand rather than firsthand does not seem pertinent from an ethical point of view. No harm is done

to the commercial interests of any of the parties. The small number of viewers who did not tape directly and got their copy secondhand would not likely change the station's Nielsen ratings, and neither Richard nor Tom would buy or rent the film, nor would Joe. They simply wanted a copy of that and other films to look at when the TV offerings on a given evening were not to their liking.

In addition to taping the *Sound of Music*, Joe also taped some songs that were being played on MTV. He not only videotaped them, but he also taped just the audio part on his tape recorder. Since he could tape the whole video, it seems he is also allowed to tape only a portion of it. Richard and Tom, having the same tastes as Tom and being in the same situations as they were with the movie, copy from Joe or from whoever has a copy and is willing to share the videos and the songs.

Since he may make copies for his personal use, Joe reasons that he may also make copies of music played by DJs on the radio or that he gets via the Internet. The principle of fair use seems to be the same, whether one uses a VCR or a CD writer on one's computer.

Napster is a firm that carried this scenario one step further. It developed technology that would allow anyone using the Internet to request a certain song, and Napster would serve as an intermediary between the requester and someone willing to supply the song. There were two important differences, however, from the cases of Joe, Richard, and Tom. First, although some of the songs that were supplied and copied were not covered by copyright, others were so covered. They were copies on CDs that the owner had purchased. And purchasing the CD gives one a right to listen to the songs on it, but it does not give one the right to copy the songs or to allow others to copy them. The same is true of rented or purchased tapes of movies. They may not legally be copied and such copying does not come under the doctrine of fair use. The second important difference is that the service provided by Napster proved to be so attractive that it was used by millions of people to download music free that they would otherwise have paid for. Why buy a CD when one can get the same songs free? Why buy all the songs on a CD when one is interested in only one song and one can download it free?

The rock band Mettalica sued Napster for copyright infringement. A U.S. District Court ordered Napster to shut down its services. In October 2000, a U.S. Appellate Court affirmed the lower court's action and ruled that Napster could provide access to only those songs that were not protected by copyright, and that it had a way to do this before it could continue its operation. Some music companies then sought to enter into various agreements with Napster whereby they would get a fee for each of their songs downloaded. On July 1, 2001, Napster shut down to integrate the technology the courts mandated it have installed to block the trading of copyrighted material.

In the meantime, however, other programmers devised programs that did not require an intermediary such as Napster, and that allowed individuals to contact each other and trade or download music on a peer-to-peer basis. Gnutella was one of these programs, which users could download for free and then use to contact and trade music with others who used the program. Gnutella, like Napster, can be used to download the newest amateur band that wants to get an audience by giving its music away, as well as copyrighted music. By mid-July 2001, six alternative services had sprung up and were providing peer-to-peer copying capabilities involving no intermediary. Over 1 million users downloaded Music City's program Morpheus, and over 900,000 downloaded Audiogalaxy' Satellite program. The companies, which hope to make money by running banner ads, claim that they are not responsible for what users do with the programs they provide.

Two questions arise. First, is the development of such technology itself ethically defensible, and does the same kind of argument that justifies the use of VCRs justify their use as well? Second, is the copying of material, such as music, from someone else's hard drive using this technology ethically defensible if the material, for instance, is played over streaming audio sites on the Internet?

Central to answering these questions is the notion of intellectual property and its ethical and legal status.

Intellectual property refers to certain products of the mind or intellect that a society decides can be owned in some sense. One trait that distinguishes intellectual property from other types of property is that intellectual property is infinitely shareable. If I have an idea I can give it away and still have it. Unlike other kinds of property, someone can borrow or take or steal my idea and I still have it. I no longer have exclusive use of it if others have it as well; but their having it does not preclude my also having it. It is this key feature of products of the mind that makes discussions of intellectual property significantly different from discussions about other kinds of property. One may have the right to exclusive use, but not the right to destroy it (which would make no sense), and one's possession of the intellectual property is compatible with others' having the same property. Because I can have an idea and you may independently come to have a similar idea, ideas in general are not considered the type of thing that can be owned. There would be no way of knowing if someone else had an idea first and if so, whether the idea belonged to that person. There would be no social utility in trying to have ownership of ideas. Nor would there be any social utility in trying to assign ownership rights to mathematics or to facts or to scientific discoveries and theories. But 'idea' is a very broad term and covers some things to which some societies give property rights. What is usually proprietary is the expression of an idea in some tangible form, such as a book or an invention, although this is a rough characterization, since it is debatable whether one can have an idea that one does not express in some sense.

A second feature that influences the bundle of rights that constitutes intellectual property is the fact that any expression of an idea builds on prior knowledge that is not of one's creation. Newton and Leibniz hit upon the calculus independently, and there was a dispute about who had the idea first. But it makes no difference to others who had the idea first since both shared their insight and made their mathematical discoveries available to all. The more or less simultaneous development of the calculus demonstrates the notion that ideas are built on other ideas. By the time of Newton and Leibniz mathematical knowledge had developed to the level where the next step was the calculus. Had Leibniz and Newton not developed it, someone else within a reasonable amount of time would undoubtedly have done so. We each stand on the shoulders of others who have gone before us and who have passed on their ideas. We absorb them and in turn build on them before passing them on. So we cannot make complete claim to them, the way we might with physical objects we build or make or own.

The third aspect of intellectual property that makes it distinctive is that such property is fundamentally social. It is not only socially developed, but information and knowledge are most useful when shared, because sharing allows others to develop them further. For this reason some societies do not and have not recognized any property right to the products of the mind or to any claimed sort of intellectual property. Those that do recognize intellectual property must balance the social nature against individual claims to certain rights with respect to it, and this directly influences the bundle of rights any society assigns to intellectual property.

These three characteristics form the foundation for the widely held belief that each gen-

eration has the responsibility to pass on to the next generation the knowledge that has been socially acquired and developed. It is this aspect of human beings—the ability to develop and pass on knowledge—that clearly separates them from other species. Colleges and universities in turn are established in order to preserve, transmit, and develop the social knowledge base, and they have the responsibility to do so.

This social view of knowledge informed the early development of the computer and the mind set of the early programmers, who freely shared their work. It similarly was an important aspect in the early development of the Internet, which was seen as free and open to all. . . .

## PROTECTION OF INTELLECTUAL PROPERTY

In the United States, the legal basis for the protection of intellectual property comes from the U.S. Constitution, Article 1, Section 8, which includes under the Powers of Congress the power "To promote the Progress of Science and useful Arts, by securing for limited Times to Authors and Inventors the exclusive Right to their respective Writings and Discoveries." Two aspects of this basis for the protection of intellectual property are noteworthy. The first is that the main purpose of the protection of intellectual property is not the right of the author or inventor but the progress of science and the useful arts. The purpose of the protection is the benefit of the common good. The second is that unlike other property rights which exist indefinitely, the rights granted for intellectual property are limited in time. . . .

### Copyright

*Copyright*, as the name implies, governs the exclusive right of the author to reproduce or copy the work, distribute it, display or perform it publicly, prepare derivative works based upon it, and authorize others to do these things. We have seen that ideas cannot be owned. What one can have a legal right to is the protection of the expression of one's ideas, and it is this that copyright grants. We can express our ideas in a variety of ways. Language is the most obvious, and copyright covers verbal expressions in books, articles, plays, poetry, and other written media. Copyright includes also the expression of ideas in other forms—music, film, video, painting, and recordings. It protects authorship in that it makes it illegal for anyone but the author to claim authorship. It also gives the author the exclusive right to sell the expression of his idea or to otherwise profit from it. This in turn prohibits others from copying it or from selling or profiting from it without the author's permission. The exception is fair use, which allows certain uses, such as quoting a portion of a work in a review or in a scholarly publication (giving appropriate attribution), or making a partial copy for legitimate personal use. . . .

The ethical justification for copyright is twofold. The first is a basically utilitarian justification. This says that since society wishes to encourage the production of such works, the best way to promote such production is by making it possible for those who produce them to benefit financially therefrom. We have the history of the development of works that are covered by copyright that tends to show the result has been to society's benefit. Of course, we do not know what would have been produced without the financial incentives copyright provides, and we do know that people continue to have ideas, to develop mathematics, to develop scientific formulas, and to produce knowledge that cannot be protected by copyright. There are some societies that deny any protection for ideas in any form and hence do not recognize the validity of claims of intellectual property rights. For centuries

there was no copyright protection, yet works of art, literature, music, and so on were produced. Shakespeare borrowed many of his plots from others and had no copyright protection for what he produced. Nonetheless, in modern societies the financial inducement is certainly at least one motivating force encouraging the production of literary, artistic, and other works.

The second justification for copyright is one of fairness. It says that those who expend time, energy, and money on developing the expression of their ideas, deserve recompense for that time, energy, and money. Moreover, if such protection did not exist, and the item were sold commercially, then those who did not expend the time, energy, and money would reap the rewards instead of the originator of the work. The one who did profit without the prior effort and expense would be a free rider, and since the free rider had no prior expenses to be recouped, could undersell the legitimate producer. This would be clearly unfair.

This argument is challenged by some who contend that the claim of authorship is legitimate, but that there is no inherent right to any reward from the production of any such work. Despite the possible and actual objections by some, the justifications are widely accepted and ground the legitimacy of copyright worldwide. . . .

If one asks about the relation of intellectual property, ethics, and copyright protection, four different moral intuitions are applicable and represent four different perspectives. The perspectives represent the four major parties involved in copyright issues.

The first intuition is that from an ethical point of view what is appropriate in this domain is not property rights but honesty of attribution. This is the view of scholars and of some authors. One should not claim that an idea is one's own when it comes from another. But ideas are not the sort of thing that we can or should in general restrict. They can be shared and if useful can be built upon and developed. Since ideas and knowledge are infinitely shareable, the general rule is that we all benefit from correct ideas and knowledge, and the way to make sure the ideas and knowledge are correct is to test them against other ideas and knowledge claims that are contrary to them. This is the view of ideas prevalent in most areas of a university, where ideas are usually shared rather than sold or traded. To take one area, in a university teachers of philosophy share their philosophical ideas with their colleagues, in their classes, at meetings and conventions, in articles, and in books. They do not steal each others ideas by using, criticizing, or developing them. But they cannot ethically claim them as their own when they are not. Most philosophy journals do not pay for the articles they publish, and most books in philosophy are not written with the intent of making a great deal of money. If that is the goal, it is rarely achieved. That does not prevent articles and books from being written and published. This is the point of view adopted by many of the writers of programs, who argue that software should be treated the same as many other products of intellectual activity and that this is the best way to guarantee their development.

A second widely shared ethical intuition is that of the entrepreneur. Just as someone should not copy another's work and claim it is one's own, if a product is sold it is prima facie wrong simply to copy that product and sell it as if it were one's own. Selling it while acknowledging that it is not one's own satisfies the criterion of honesty of attribution. It violates property rights if these have been developed in a legal system of property, such as the one we have. Vendors of software want people to buy their products and are not interested in simply having others acknowledge the source. They spend money to develop and market the product, and they want a return on that investment. It is blatantly unfair for some other

company simply to copy and market the product, under the same or a different name, and get the profit without having invested in the development. Even worse is undercutting the original producer and driving it out of business. Hence if a society wants commercial products, they should be protected at least until the original producers can recoup their expenses. This intuition is part of the basis for the claim of legal protection by the commercial vendors of software. They argue in addition for continuous protection for as long as possible for them to reap profits—a claim that goes beyond the moral intuition.

The third intuition is that of the buyers of software that what they buy is their own to use in any way they like comparable to their use of other products they buy. Thus if I have three computers in my home and I buy a word-processing program, I tend to feel I have the right to use it on all three machines rather than buying three copies, or physically carrying the program from machine to machine and loading it each time, as some software vendors claim I should. The rights I have with respect to most of the other items I buy are not restricted, except insofar as they violate the second intuition. But if I do not engage in selling the product or copying it for sale, it is mine to do with as I like.

The fourth group is society as a whole. And the appropriate intuition is that intellectual knowledge and intellectual products are essentially social for the reasons we have already seen. They should be used for the common good. And if there is a conflict between the common good and individual claims to property rights in intellectual property, the former may well take precedence over the latter.

Although the interests of the four groups overlap to some extent, in many ways they are importantly different. To argue either in ethics or law from only one of these perspectives is not to do justice to the others. The law has tended to favor the interests of the marketers of software, since the law has been formed in part by the claims of the marketers and the cases have involved primarily suits brought by them.

## UNAUTHORIZED COPYING OF SOFTWARE

The four intuitions are applicable in considering the unauthorized copying of software. . . .

### Copying Programs for Personal Use

Some of the writers of programs have opted for free exchange of software or for shareware. This is perfectly appropriate. It is interesting to note that authors of books have not objected to copyright laws, while programmers have. The reasons for the difference in attitude are significant and should be taken more seriously than they have by the courts and legislatures. Although the coexistence of shareware and commercial programs is not obviously unfair or counterproductive to the needs of society, the protection given commercial programs must not be such as to stifle or preclude the development of shareware or of software. Claims that they do stifle or preclude the development of some software have so far fallen on deaf legislative and judicial ears.

The views of marketers rather than the views of many writers of software who did not market their products but shared them became the accepted legal norm in areas where those two intuitions conflict.

The views of marketers have also trumped the views of the users of software marketed on a large scale or of the recipients of custom-designed software, and the marketers' views have been written into law. The views of the marketers of software concerning their legal claims were also put forth as morally binding.

Those views almost uncritically have become the conventional ethical norm that is preached, even though widely flouted. Users of programs such as WordPerfect and Lotus 1-2-3 are told that it is unethical to share such programs with others, and there is even an attempt to make users feel guilty if they use a program they buy on more than one machine within their own homes.

Lending a book to a friend is not unethical. Lending a program is said to be. Why? The usual answer is that lending a program to a friend is not considered comparable to lending a book to a friend, since typically one retains the use of one's copy of the program. Hence lending a program is compared to photocopying a book. The argument against lending software is based on an analogy with books, copyrights of written material, and fair-use doctrines established to protect written material. Although the items lent (books and programs) are very different, the analogy of copying rather than of lending or sharing has come to dominate ethical discussions. Yet the analogy between books and software breaks down at various points, and only some of these are considered, despite the arguable importance of some of the other differences. The ease of copying software is a technological boon to users and to society that one could argue should be capitalized on as a means of transferring knowledge and technology broadly. Yet that aspect of technology is precisely what mass producers of software with the help of copyright wish to stem. Insufficient thought has been given to the results.

Focusing on the preceding third intuition, the users of programs would like the right to use what they buy. By analogy with many other products, how one uses the product after one buys it is up to the owners. They may sell it, change it, and so on. What is precluded is copying it and selling it in competition with the original seller. What copyright grants in most cases is the right of initial sale. Thus if a student buys a textbook for a class, for instance, he or she may sell it after the course is over, and it is then resold to another student. Neither the publisher nor the author receives any compensation beyond the initial sale. Soon publishers find that the market becomes saturated with secondhand copies of the book, and sales fall dramatically. To protect their interests many textbook publishers and authors come out with a new edition of the book after 3 or so years, forcing the sale of the new edition and rendering the old edition obsolete and unsalable. But the sellers of software make more radical claims for ownership and wish to prevent resale on the basis of the claim that they did not sell the product but only licensed it on certain conditions which they specify.

From a legal point of view they place a great deal of emphasis on the fact that one signs an agreement that comes with purchased software—which one does not do when one buys a book. However, the agreement is one that is forced by the seller on the buyer after having paid one's $400 or $500 if one wants to get technical support and the options to upgrade when new versions of the program come out. The borrower of a program gets neither the documentation nor the servicing—items that do not come with books, and that help justify the higher prices of programs. One typically buys a program to use it, not to read it. The extension of copyright laws to programs ignores these and other very important differences.

Since the marketers of software cannot effectively police or enforce the agreements or prevent such violations of copyright, they attempt to protect their products through moral claims. Indirectly through the agreements that are included with software there has been an attempt to inculcate a view on the morality of copying software. The moral claims do not automatically follow from the developments in the legal realm. It is not necessarily the case

that everything that is illegal is immoral. Copying or lending software is not in itself immoral. It is claimed to be immoral primarily because it is illegal. But whether a law that is neither enforced nor enforceable has the force of law, and hence whether one is ethically bound by such a legal statute in this case is at least open to question. The argument from analogy with other items one buys provides grounds for arguing the moral justifiability of lending and copying software for personal use. . . .

The legal property rights one has in software are a function of the system of property and law in which the software develops and becomes embedded. It is the commercial possibilities that drive the analogies and definitions. For this reason the proper question is not some abstract notion of rights or of intellectual property. The right questions are whether the present state of affairs is satisfactory to all concerned and to society's best interests, and if not how it can be improved. . . .

## PEER-TO-PEER EXCHANGE OF COPYRIGHTED MATERIAL

This brings us to the kind of case with which we started and exemplified by the legal charges brought against Napster.

When it comes to downloading MP3 music files (or eventually other copyrighted material such as movies in digital format), most people do not consider it the same as placing commercial programs on the Web for the taking. Two of their intuitions, they feel, conflict. The one is that making a copyrighted item freely available for downloading by anyone is unethical as well as illegal; the other is that one has a moral if not a legal right to share whatever one buys with a friend if one so chooses.

The courts found Napster guilty of abetting the violation of copyright law by serving as an intermediary between those wishing to swap or share copyrighted as well as noncopyrighted music. It was not seen as comparable to a VCR, which might be used for copyright violation but also had legitimate uses. It was Napster, not its 80 million individual users, that was targeted for legal action. But shutting Napster down even temporarily did not solve the problem because users quickly developed and shared peer-to-peer programs that eliminated the need for a middle man who could be identified, sued, and shut down.

Moral suasion and possible legal action has not stopped the downloading by millions of copyrighted music. While lending a copy of a song to a friend might plausibly be claimed to be covered by fair use, and while the 1992 Audio Home Recording Act allows the taping of a CD on a tape for personal use, e.g., in a car, the indiscriminate copying of copyrighted material from unknown peers on the Internet is arguably hardly comparable.

The defense of the practice that is often given is not that those who produce the music and who market it do not deserve any return for their effort. Many who engage in the practice claim that they would be willing to pay what they consider a reasonable amount for the music they wish. But the music distributors had not made available the music they want for purchase online, and the marketing strategy of many music companies has been to mix on a single CD a popular song with many that the customer does not want. The customer must buy the whole CD to get the item he or she wants, and to the customer the cost of the CD is greater than the perceived value of the one song. In addition, those who defend the practice argue, the music industry itself gives its music away on MTV, for instance, or by providing it on the radio or other formats available over the Internet. Vendors of computer programs do not do this. If music is provided free to the listener in these ways, and if taping videos is legally fair use, by analogy taping or downloading music should be fair use.

These arguments do not, of course, show that downloading the music one wants freely is justifiable either legally or ethically. But they do indicate that the music industry and its marketing techniques have not kept pace with technology and that there are anomalies in the way music is distributed. With the advent of VCRs, movie makers found they had to adopt a different marketing strategy from the one on which they previously relied and found that they could use the prevalence of VCRs to their commercial interests by renting movies at a very reasonable rate.

The extent to which music companies and artists are harmed is a matter of controversy. One side argues that obviously those who download won't buy the music; this deprives the companies and artists of legitimate income. They will be adversely affected. Furthermore, the incentive for other companies and artists to produce more music is diminished, since the rewards are less. This in turn means less music available for society and for music lovers themselves who do the downloading. The other side argues that in many cases those who download would not buy the disk anyway, so there is no lost revenue in those cases. Others download to listen. If they like what they hear, then they buy that artist's CDs, which increases rather than decreases sales. Forrester Research claimed that Napster increased sales. CD sales jumped 8 percent in the first quarter of 2000 over 1999. Both sides can point to some statistics. Similarly, the results on society are speculative. One side argues the demise of the music industry, the other the freeing up of creativity from the straight jacket of the big five record companies. Hence the utilitarian arguments are not decisive. But neither is the argument based on property rights, except insofar as they are presently reflected in copyright law and judicial decisions based thereon.

The problem facing the music industry and legislators in the face of the rising peer-to-peer technology that is replacing Napster is that the law is all but unenforceable. Prosecuting even a small fraction of those who download copyrighted music using the new technology from the Internet is unfeasible. Even if the worse perpetrators were caught and fined, the chance of any individual's being caught would be slight, unless more resources were put into policing and prosecuting such action than it seems socially responsible to do. The alternative seems to find some solution that does justice to both intuitions, that protects the legitimate commercial interests of those in the music industry, and that makes available at a reasonable price—determined as in most cases by the market—the music that consumers wish to download. While some question whether anyone will pay even a nominal price to download music when they can download the same music free, there are built-in incentives for users to do so. Peer-to-peer technology opens one's computer to access by anyone on the Internet, and those who download music from unknown sources take the risk of downloading viruses or other dangers. Students who download music using the fast Internet access provided by their colleges and universities open up their institutions to possible lawsuit, as well as opening themselves up to various penalties if the institution prohibits such downloading, as the institutions might do both to avoid possible suit and to avoid the need of expanding its bandwidth to accommodate the traffic and difficulties that massive downloading of music by students can create. Burning one's own CDs, moreover, requires that one buy a CD-write drive, which might more than offset what one saves from free downloads. Those who download to their hard drives do not have the portability that makes music CDs so popular.

Only so much can be legislated. It would be a great cost to society to try to outlaw any technology, such as peer-to-peer, which holds great promise as a means of easy, inexpensive exchange of all things digital.

At this stage it seems likely that accommodation will be made, that present copyright laws with reference to music and other products on the Internet are inadequate, and that changes are both necessary and will be forthcoming. The important thing is to make sure that all affected parties and their claims and arguments are adequately heard and taken into account, and that no one of the intuitions or groups is given special privilege, consideration, or legislative preference.

The great advantage of information is that it is infinitely shareable with others while it is retained by oneself. Everyone in the world is thus a potential recipient of information and all can share in these benefits without depriving others of them. The information age thus provides an opportunity to move from individuality to community, away from private ownership rights and toward concern for sharing for the common good. Yet, paradoxically, the information age, by focusing on the importance of information, has highlighted its commercial value. A result has been an attempt not to share freely but to control information for commercial purposes. Technology and ownership rules are at odds in the case of the copying of software and anything else in digitalized form, in the development of peer-to-peer exchanges, in the open source code movement, and in the trend toward licensing rather than the ownership acquired in purchasing.

The problem then becomes twofold. The first issue is whether the present law can be enforced if millions of users are trading copyrighted material, even if it is illegal. Is an unenforceable law a law? There is a long tradition that claims it is not. The problem is exacerbated by the fact that downloading material easily crosses borders. If something comparable to Napster is located in a country that does not prohibit its activities, the server outlawed in the United States can perform its function from a different jurisdiction. . . .

PHARMACEUTICAL PATENTS

# Intellectual Property and Pharmaceutical Drugs: An Ethical Analysis

*Richard T. De George*

The notion of intellectual property (IP) is contentious. Nonetheless there is justification for granting exclusive rights to some original useful products or processes if the result benefits the common good. This is recognized in Article 1, Section 8 of the U.S. Constitution, which establishes the power of Congress "to promote the progress of science and useful arts, by securing for limited times to authors and inventors the exclusive right to their respective writings and discoveries." The length of time is somewhat arbitrary, has varied over the past century, and is vastly different for copyright than for patents, the latter offering much stronger protection for a shorter period of time.

## THE MORAL JUSTIFICATION OF INTELLECTUAL PROPERTY

Because intellectual property is significantly different from other kinds of property,[1] the ethical defenses of intellectual property differ from the defenses—such as the Lockean—of other kinds of property, and traditions in different parts of the world treat intellectual property differently. Nonetheless, there is a two-part argument in defense of the ethical legitimacy of limited intellectual property rights that is intuitively attractive, widely held, and, I believe, sound.

The first part is a fairness, or justice, argument that says that, within the economic system of free enterprise, those who spend time and/or money in developing a product or the expression of an idea deserve a chance to receive recompense if the result they achieve is useful and beneficial to others who are willing to pay for it. It would be unfair or unjust for others to take that result, market it as their own, and profit from it without having expended comparable time or money in development, before the original developer has a chance to recoup his investment and possibly make a profit. Intellectual property protection gives innovators this chance.

The second part of the argument is based on consequences. It states that unless developers are allowed a period during which to recoup their investment and make a profit, the incentive to produce new products beneficial to society will be greatly reduced. Society benefits from new products, both initially and after they are no longer protected and fall into the public domain. Hence, the greatest benefit to the common good or to society is achieved by offering inventors and developers of new products a period during which they can make their profits without the competition of free riders. Both arguments together lead to the conclusion that protection of intellectual property for a limited period of time is just and produces more good for society than an absence of such protection.

I shall call the two arguments together the Standard Argument (SA). For the sake of argument, let us accept SA as a valid moral justification for intellectual property. It is general in form, and applies to pharmaceutical products as well as to inventions, machines, and other types of intellectual property. There have been many studies by economists to support the second part of the Standard Argument. The pharmaceutical industry and some economist have persuasively argued that more new drugs are developed when pharmaceutical companies make sufficient profits to invest in research and development, and the pharmaceutical industry argues that the large profits for which the industry is known are necessary to underwrite both the high cost of developing a new drug and the large number of initial attempts that never turn into successful, marketable drugs.

The industry then builds on the Standard Argument to develop what I shall call the Status Quo Approach (SQA), which is a legal-economic approach, to reply to critics of their policies who adopt not an economic but a moral approach to pharmaceuticals. The Status Quo Approach takes existing intellectual property law, especially patent law, as setting the appropriate parameters within which to view and answer all challenges to the practices of pharmaceutical companies. Taking this approach leads to concentration on using the law to help these companies protect and increase their profits so that they can develop new drugs. Thus they defend their techniques to extend the time before which generic drugs can be introduced, to extend patent protection on an international level through the World Trade Organization (WTO), to produce me-too drugs or drugs that are only marginally different from existing drugs rather than concentrating on breakthrough drugs, and so on. Morally based attacks that make a link between patents and the availability of drugs for the poor are rejected as misconceived. Nonetheless, there is an attempt to diffuse the latter attacks by giving away some drugs in some circumstances. These giveaway programs are presented as the industry's or a particular company's living up to its social responsibility. Social responsibility is the surrogate for moral responsibility, is part of the Status Quo Approach, and is seen by the industry as answering morally based criticism.

The SQA is an approach that pharmaceutical companies are comfortable with, as well as one that is widely accepted. It has the benefits of tradition, of requiring no change in current practices or law, and of having produced beneficial results in the past. Hence, one can argue, it is more likely than untried alternative schemes of intellectual property protection to produce beneficial results in the future. The approach thus entrenches and sanctifies the status quo.

Both the Standard Argument and the Status Quo Approach, however, are coming under increased strain and attack, and in this paper I shall attempt to examine the direction of those strains and the validity of these attacks. Only if we fully appreciate the Standard Argument and the Status Quo Approach, and their shortcomings, can we make sense of the continuing charges made by critics and the responses made by the pharmaceutical industry. My aim is to bring some order to a very confused and confusing public discussion on the actions of pharmaceutical companies, the obligations attributed to them, and the claimed right of the public with respect to needed drugs. Although clarifying the discussion is my main purpose, I shall also make some suggestions for improving the situation.

## THE LIMITS OF THE STANDARD ARGUMENT

Patents, I have argued, can be justified from an ethical point of view. But that justification is limited. Despite the constitutionally stated basis for patents, neither common good (nor utilitarian) considerations form part of what is required for a patent. Nor have ethical considerations been a dominant consideration in changes that have been made in patent law. Hence the details of how patent protection has developed do not follow from the ethical justification. It is not that the way in which patent law has developed is unethical, but that it is only one of many sets of ethically justifiable ways of protecting pharmaceuticals.

Discussions of intellectual property are very complex and involve knowledge of convoluted laws, legal decisions, and economic and business analyses. Typically, at any negotiation involving intellectual property prior to the drafting of legislation, the parties are government officials, lawyers, and corporate representatives. Thus the best defense of those policies is given not in ethical but in legal and economic terms. This is why the SQA uses these. Critics, however, fail to be convinced by such considerations. It is not clear to them who, if anyone, represents the general public in the general process. It is difficult for any government to represent both the consumer and the industry, and the public's trust in government as representing the public's interest is lessened when the industry present in the negotiations is the pharmaceutical industry, which is known for being one of the most successful lobbying groups and for being among the top spenders of lobbying money.

The complaint about the Standard Argument is not that it is wrong, but that it is taken to prove too much and to respond to all objections. The mantra that is repeated by industry representatives in every context and in reply to every criticism with respect to intellectual property protection, pricing, and access is that unless the pharmaceutical companies are profitable enough to have the funds to do so and can expect future profits from their products, they will not engage in R&D and will not develop new drugs, which, of course, benefit society as a whole. When critics point to the fact that the industry has the highest rate of profit of any industry year after year, this is the primary answer. When critics complain about the high cost of drugs and the fact that the price of drugs increases much faster than the inflation rate, this is their answer. When the critics claim that the developed nations are forcing the less-developed ones to adopt standards of intellectual protection that go against their traditions and may not be in their best interests, this is their answer. When critics say that the reason for intellectual property protection is not private profit but the common good, this is the answer. And all this makes some sense because there is ample evidence that, without profits, there are few new drugs developed. Yet the answer covers over a good deal, as I shall try to show. . . .

## THE RIGHT-TO-HEALTH-CARE ARGUMENT

Just as the Standard Argument is often assumed by the pharmaceutical industry, the defense of the right to health care is often assumed by its critics. The critics do not deny the overall validity of the SA and the SQA, but at its limits the critics challenge the application of the argument and the defenses of their practices given by representatives of the pharmaceutical industry. The central claim is that although the Standard Argument justifies the right to intellectual property, the right is only a prima facie and not an absolute right. In many cases the right holds sway and trumps other considerations. But in the case of pharmaceuticals it comes up against other prima facie rights, namely the right to life, the right to adequate health care, and the right to access essential lifesaving drugs; it comes up against the obligation to aid those in need; and it comes up against competing claims made in the name of the common good. The right to life, the right to adequate health care, the right to access to essential lifesaving drugs, and the obligation to aid those in need, critics note, must be given at least as much consideration as intellectual property rights. Not only do IP rights not necessarily trump those other rights, but they are in fact often trumped by them. The pharma industry tends to argue that intellectual property rights are always sacrosanct, when they are not. Although critics sometimes give too little weight to the actual strength of

IP rights, the rights to health and to health care raise serious issues in certain circumstances about the pharma industry's claims. Hence the discussion does not end with simply asserting the Standard Argument and the SQA.

What then are the arguments in support of the right to health and health care and the right to access, and how can they be weighed against the right to intellectual property?

There is considerable confusion in the literature, and although the basic ethical claims are usually fairly clear, how they are justified is not.

We can start by distinguishing two different rights that are often confused. They are related but are not identical. One is the right to health; the other is the right to health care. The UN Declaration of Human Rights, Article 25, states

> (1) Everyone has the right to a standard of living adequate for the health and well-being of himself and of his family, including food, clothing, housing, and medical care and necessary social services, and the right to security in the event of unemployment, sickness, disability, widowhood, old age, or other lack of livelihood in circumstances beyond his control.

Although there are a number of different rights included in this sentence, for our purposes two are central. One is the right to health; the other is the right to medical or health care. It is generally agreed that the rights stated in the Declaration are primarily rights that members of a state enjoy vis-à-vis their governments. Thus, the primary obligation that is correlative to the right to health falls on the state. The right to health has perhaps received so little attention in developed nations because in its most plausible sense these nations face no problem with respect to it. Most plausibly the right to health is analogous to the right to life. The state cannot give anyone health. Its obligation, rather, is to ensure that the conditions necessary for maintaining good health are provided and to prevent any party from damaging the health of

another. Understood in this way, the state has the obligation to provide those conditions that promote the health of its citizens, such as ensuring clean water and air, providing sewers and sanitation, and taking other basic measures necessary to promote and protect the health of its members. But although states may have that general obligation, their obligation does not exhaust the obligation of others. The rights impose obligations on business, individuals, and others as well. It is a violation of the human right to health, for instance, for manufacturers to dump toxic waste that will infiltrate a community's water supply and cause people to fall ill. The obligation not to cause harm to people's health and thus not to act in this way is a negative obligation. Positively, companies are bound to provide safe and healthy working conditions for their employees. Providing these conditions is an obligation imposed on them by their employees' right to health, whether or not it is also required by law. And positively, the government has the obligation to pass and enforce such laws.

If one reads the right to health care in the same way, then it is an obligation of states or governments to see that medical care is available to their people, whether or not the governments actually provide it. Although states are generally held responsible for protecting the health of their citizens by providing the common goods of clean drinking water and sewers and other general sanitation facilities, they are not usually held responsible for providing health care in the same way. The reason is that the principle of subsidiarity comes into play. The principle of subsidiarity states that one does not call on a higher level to do a job that can be done at a lower level. With respect to health care, it is usually applied intuitively, even by those who do not use that term. Thus, when children get sick, for instance, it is typical for their parents to care for them, and family members usually are the primary caregivers, rather than the state. When a family is unable to adequately care for someone who needs medical care, they might first go to the circle of friends, or to the larger community. When the community cannot handle the need, they go to the city or the state or federal level. Although in a developed society the structures are in place to handle the needs of people at the appropriate level, they are considerably different in a country that has a socialized medicine program than in a country that does not. If a government is unable to handle the need or needs it faces, it might appeal to the international community. Also assumed by this process is that individuals have not only the right to health and health care, but they also have the obligation to do what they can to preserve their health and to care for themselves to the extent they are able to do so. Thus the rights to health and to health care impose correlative obligations on many parties. So far the obligations of pharmaceutical companies are no different from the obligations of other companies. But this is only part of the story.

Another argument comes into play here that develops the obligation to help others in serious need to the extent that one can do so. There are two versions of this. One is a weak version which says that one has the obligation to help others in serious need to the extent that one can do so with little or moderate cost to oneself. A stronger version says that one must do so even at great expense to oneself, although one does not have to make oneself worse off than the person or persons one is helping. The obligation to aid others in serious need can be justified by either a rule-utilitarian approach, which argues that more good is achieved overall if this rule is followed than if it is not; or by a deontological approach, which bases it on the respect due others as persons and beings worthy of respect. The obligation is one that is widely acknowledged. Intuitively, if one sees a child drowning and one can save the child's life by extending a hand, one has the obligation to do so. Not to do so would be

characterized by most people as inhuman or barbaric. The obligation holds even if one will be late to an appointment, or if one will get one's shoes wet in the process of saving the child. The obligation becomes less clear as the cost to oneself increases, and most would agree that one is not obliged to save the child at the risk of one's drowning oneself.

The application of this principle with respect to an individual vis-à-vis a drowning child is straightforward. It becomes more and more problematic as the case becomes more complex. What if the child is drowning in the water of a crowded beach, with a thousand people on it? Is it the obligation of each of the thousand to save the child? Is the obligation greater for those closer? Is it exculpatory for someone who is dressed to say that the obligation falls on those in bathing suits? Would all be equally blameworthy if no one did anything and the child drowned? Now increase the number of children drowning, say from an overturned boat, to twenty. Each person on the beach can save at most one of the children. Is it the obligation of every person on the beach to save all the children, or to save only one, and, if the latter, which one? When we then move to millions of people in danger of death from the lack of medical care in the world and ask what is the obligation of developed countries, of those living in developed countries, of NGOs, and of pharmaceutical companies with respect to the needy, the arguments tend to get more and more tenuous. This is not to say that there is no obligation to help based on the right of the people to health or medical care. But the complexity of the situation suggests the need for action by many parties on many levels.

If one accepts the obligation of aid, then it is not difficult to argue that those in the best position to help have the greatest obligation to do so. Now join that with the fact that those in the health professions have special obligations with respect to health and health care. They have these special obligations because of the field they have freely chosen, because they are related to health care in a way others are not, because they have the expertise that others lack, and because they make their living or profit from health-related activities. A doctor, for instance, has a greater obligation to help an accident victim if other aid is not available, than does someone without medical training. A hospital has a greater obligation to help an accident victim brought through its doors than does a bank or a department store, and people naturally would bring such victims to a hospital rather than to some other kind of enterprise. . . .

With this background we can develop the right to access to needed medicines. But the argument works differently with respect to lifesaving medicines, to those which are necessary for health but which treat non-life-threatening illnesses, and to those that are neither and are simply life-enhancing.

The strongest case can be made for the right to access to those drugs that are essential for the preservation of life. If one has the right to life, then one has the right to that which is necessary to sustain one's life—be it food and shelter, or medicines and medical care. Medicines, obviously, are included in medical care. The right of access to available lifesaving medicine has both a negative and a positive aspect. Negatively, all have the obligation not to prevent anyone from having access to what they need to sustain their lives. The positive obligation to ensure that access is available, as in the earlier case, falls on a variety of parties (applying the principle of subsidiarity) and is practically limited by the goods and resources available in a given situation. . . .

I shall call the set of arguments I have sketched out above the Moral Argument.

People typically invoke something like the above general arguments with respect to the drug industry and drug companies. The various claims are that the industry as a whole and the individual companies that make it up have special obligations; that these are related to

what they produce, namely pharmaceutical drugs; that they are in a special position to help and that therefore they have the special obligation to do so; and that those in dire need, because of their right to health care, impose obligations on those able to help, including the pharmaceutical industry.

We can apply this claimed right to access both on the international and on the national level in the United States and see how we can weigh it against the right to intellectual property.

We should note that approaching ethical issues relating to the pharmaceutical industry from the perspective of the Moral Right to Access dramatically changes the issues that rise to the surface as opposed to those that arise when taking the Standard Argument and the Status Quo Approach. To see how, we can start with the pharmaceutical companies' use of the term "social responsibility."

## THE MORAL RESPONSIBILITY OF PHARMACEUTICAL COMPANIES

With this background, we can now ask: What are the obligations, from an ethical point of view, of the pharmaceutical industry as a whole and of individual pharmaceutical companies? The above discussion forms the background that is generally understood by critics, even though they do not often articulate their arguments very clearly. Can we come up with general obligations that stem from the rights of those in need of medical care? Clearly, pharmaceutical companies are not the only healthcare providers and the entire obligation to fulfill the rights in question does not fall on them. And clearly if they have special obligations, that does not mean that governments, individuals, families, NGOs, and so on do not also have obligations. Since governments have the primary responsibility to provide for the health care of their citizens, they bear the primary obligation. They may either meet this obligation directly or indirectly by ensuring the needs of the public are met in some other way.

Given present structures, the pharmaceutical industry, as part of the health-care system, arguably has two basic ethical obligations. I shall call the first the Production Obligation and the second the Access Obligation. The obligations of the industry with respect to health care are broader and more general than the obligations of any particular pharmaceutical company. The industry's obligations can only be met to the extent that individual companies take the appropriate action. Yet the two levels—industry and company—should be kept distinct, even though many critics conflate the two.

## The Production Obligation

The Production Obligation consists in the obligation to develop and produce beneficial drugs. This is the area of the industry's expertise and it is that which the companies in the industry can do that others cannot. Moreover, in this regard one can argue that the pharmaceutical industry as well as individual companies have the obligation to pursue needed new lifesaving drugs more than to pursue alternatives to drugs that already exist and are effective, namely, so-called me-too drugs. Benefit to the patient, and hence to the public and the common good, should play a greater role in the case of health care than in other industries, just as safety is paramount in the engineering industries, whether it be in airplane or building and bridge safety. This first obligation is not an unjust imposition by society, but simply reflects part of the role of pharmaceutical companies in society. The obligation is one that is arguably shared by governments also. The United States Government funds billions of dollars worth of medical research, and it is appropriate that it does so because of its obligation to fulfill the rights of its citizens to health and to health care. In a free enterprise system governments do not engage directly in production, although they can encourage and promote production through their system of intellectual property protection and their tax system, among others. To the extent that the pharmaceutical industry fails to produce needed drugs, it is up to governments to ensure that they are produced.

Many pharma companies and the industry in general, as well as government-sponsored programs, are engaged in the search for cures or remedies for cancer, various kinds of heart disease, new and improved antibiotics to fight infections, and so on. The industry as a whole, therefore, not only is actively engaged in fulfilling this obligation, but individual pharmaceutical companies have an economic interest in pursuing breakthrough and essential new drugs. The market for such drugs, if they treat diseases suffered by large numbers of people in the developed countries, is potentially lucrative.

Nonetheless the market incentive fails with respect to orphan drugs. Diseases which are lifethreatening but in which the market is either small or the potential recipients poor, require a different approach.

In the United States the Orphan Drug Act has proven to be a successful marriage of government and pharmaceutical companies. The government provides tax incentives and guarantees 7 years of exclusivity (after FDA approval) to encourage drug makers to develop drugs that affect fewer than 200,000 people and are generally unprofitable. The result has been, on the whole, positive, despite abuses. . . .

The market similarly fails with respect to the development of drugs for diseases restricted to those living in tropical countries. Although the governments in such countries have the responsibility for providing for the health of their people, they have insufficient funds to promote research and in addition they lack the facilities and the expertise needed. With minimal budgets for health care, they have difficulty providing the bare essentials of clean water and sanitation and developing an adequate delivery system for health care, regardless of the cost of drugs. Under these conditions the obligation of aid comes to the surface. In this case the appropriate aid is the development of drugs for the diseases in question. The obligation does not clearly fall on any particular pharmaceutical company, and how it is to be apportioned among countries and the pharmaceutical industry worldwide is a topic that urgently needs addressing. The first step in any solution, however, is to recognize the obligation. Perhaps something comparable to an international orphan drug act can be agreed upon; perhaps governments can subsidize special research in these areas; perhaps companies can agree to fund joint research for drugs that would not be covered by patents and would be produced and distributed at cost. The actual action taken should be the result of negotiations among all the interested and affected parties. The pharmaceutical industry clearly has an important role to play in any such negotiations. But approaching the problem from the point of view of the Moral Argument brings to the fore obligations in this regard that the Standard Argument and the Status Quo Approach do not.

Although I have indicated the financial incentive that drug companies have to pursue important new drugs, critics of the pharmaceutical industry have concentrated on whether the drug industry is actually doing either all it can and should do, or all it claims to be doing with respect to the development of new drugs. The issue arises in part because of the industry's use of the Standard Argument and the Status Quo Approach. The many tactics used by pharmaceutical companies to produce profits are justified, the SA and SQA claim, because these profits are necessary to fund the research that has led to and will lead to the development of new essential drugs. The industry thus implicitly acknowledges that the production of such drugs is its goal, even if it does not acknowledge that it is also its obligation.

It is in this context that some critics claim that the amount that the industry spends on R&D is less than the amount that it spends on marketing (including advertising, free samples to doctors, etc.), that the amount may even be less than the amount it spends on lobbying government officials; that most of the profits it makes are not in fact plowed back into research but distributed as dividends to shareholders; and that most of the research that leads to new drugs comes from government-funded research, the results of which are appropriated for private gain. All of this may be appropriate. But it is not self-evidently so, and this is what most concerns the critics. The industry in its blanket claims fails to be convincing.

According to a 2002 study of the National Institute for Health Care Management Research and Educational Foundation for the period 1989–2000, only 35 percent of new drug applications contained new active ingredients (of which only 15 percent were considered to provide "significant improvement over existing drugs"), while 54 percent were incremental modifications of existing drugs (and under Hatch-Waxman get up to 3 years of market exclusivity) and 11 percent were identical to existing drugs.[2] Although these facts by themselves prove nothing with respect to the obligation to provide new drugs, they are used by critics to offset the image that the pharmaceutical industry suggests by its use of the SA to justify its approach to the development of new drugs.

To be convincing the industry must first acknowledge its obligations; but even more important it must be willing to show why the above activities are necessary to produce new drugs. Simply pointing to new drugs as proof is an instance of a logical fallacy. Simply because new drugs have been produced and the industry has been profitable using its advertising, lobbying, and other techniques, does not show that these techniques are necessary to produce new drugs.

If one takes the obligation to produce new lifesaving drugs seriously, then one might consider changes in the status quo with respect to IP. Essential, lifesaving drugs can and arguably should be distinguished from other drugs for a variety of purposes. Me-too drugs and incremental changes, as well as cosmetic changes, do not clearly deserve the same protection or the same encouragement and inducement on the part of government. . . .

## The Access Obligation

The second obligation, the Access Obligation, is the obligation to make the drugs the industry or a company develops available to those who need them. Simply developing them would not serve any purpose otherwise. Fulfilling this obligation may be compatible with the existing structures relating to existing practices concerning intellectual property, pricing, government regulation, charity, and so on. Yet critics claim that both the industry and the market fail to some extent with regard to this obligation, and they claim that if and when current practices impede the fulfillment of this obligation, then the right to access and the concomitant obligation to provide access take precedence over IP and other rights.

The argument as we have developed it so far imposes a stronger obligation on governments to ensure access than it does on the pharmaceutical industry. As we have developed the argument to aid, it comes into play most clearly in times of dire need. This would apply most clearly with respect to essential lifesaving drugs. The obligation to help those in need in less dire circumstances is proportionately weaker. But the obligation of governments is not to ensure access only for lifesaving drugs, but for all drugs needed for health. Governments are obliged to ensure their people have access, whether by actually buying and supplying the drugs or by other means—such as making sure the price of drugs makes them accessible. The right to access puts a strain on any strong claim to intellectual property rights in drugs, if what stands

in the way of people receiving lifesaving drugs is maximizing corporate profit.

(a) Let us look at the poor countries first. The question of access to many medicines is a pressing need. Although governments have the responsibility to enable or provide access, it is beyond the ability of many of them to do so. Hence the obligation falls on others able to do so. Included in that number are pharmaceutical companies, especially those that manufacture the needed drugs. The issue was brought to global attention by the AIDS epidemic. The drugs in question are very expensive and only a few are on the current WHO list of essential drugs because of that. The most widely used such drug in poor countries is a combination of three generic drugs produced by the Indian pharmaceutical company Cipla. Nonetheless, it is clear from the Moral Argument that when millions of people are dying and can benefit substantially from available medicines, they have a right to access with respect to them. A consensus is emerging that many parties are ethically responsible for access—the patient, the local government, other governments that can help, NGOs, international organizations, and the drug companies. The problem is clearly not only the result of practices of pharmaceutical companies. Even if the drugs were given away free, access by many of the needy would still be a problem. And a number of pharmaceutical companies have instituted plans to give away antiretroviral drugs, to sell them at cost, or to license them for production by generic manufacturers in less developed countries under certain conditions. Arguably they are at least to some extent meeting their obligation to be part of the solution. (We have already seen the arguments of critics to the industry's approach that it is being socially responsible by its programs.)

Both nations and companies seem to acknowledge in principle the obligation to respond in case of dire need. Thus, for instance, a provision of the TRIPS agreement states that mandatory licensing of necessary medicines is justifiable in times of extreme national emergencies (such as epidemics) as decided by the country in question. Yet despite the Agreement the right to access is not being met and the pharmaceutical industry bears part of the blame. The TRIPS Agreement, despite its recognition of the obligation to aid, has in practice had little effect and has been faulted for a number of reasons. In 2001 PhRMA and a group of pharmaceutical companies charged South Africa with violating the WTO's rules on patents by producing the drugs needed by their people and 40 companies filed suit. After much adverse publicity, the charges and the suit were withdrawn. But neither the industry nor the companies involved ever acknowledged the right of the South African government to provide access to the needed life saving drugs in accord with the spirit of TRIPS, if not with its letter.

The TRIPS Agreement requires that poor countries adopt the type of IP protection found in the developed countries. They must do so whether or not it impedes the government of the country in question from meeting its obligation to provide access to needed drugs for its people. In this way it fails to consider the common good of the people of the country in question. For instance, while strong defenses of intellectual property with respect to pharmaceuticals may produce the best results overall for developed countries, they do not seem to do so for poor and developing countries, such as India. If, as drug companies claim, new drugs cost $800,000,000 to develop, then developing countries are probably not able to develop any. They are better served by developing generic drugs or by requiring compulsory licensing of drugs or by some other strategy. Compulsory licensing and parallel importing policies—with measures adopted to prevent the development of a gray market—would arguably benefit poor countries more than present arrangements. The Moral Argument puts these as well as other suggestions on the table for consideration, while the Standard Argument and the Status Quo Approach—used in negotiating TRIPS—in effect prevent their being raised. . . .

(b)  As opposed to poor countries that cannot afford drugs, the United States can afford to pay for drugs. In fact the United Stated both pays more for drugs and contributes more to the profit of the pharmaceutical companies than any other nation. So the aspect of the right to access that has received the greatest attention is the barrier of high prices to access, even though access and price are not the same thing. Even if drugs were free, access requires that the drugs be transported, distributed, and administered to patients. At issue is accessibility, especially of the newer drugs for which no competitive generic drug is available. Although

the lack of accessibility for the poor and elderly on restricted incomes gets most publicity, more and more people are complaining that the high cost of drugs is limiting accessibility by putting the cost of insurance out of their reach. As insurance prices rise, employers are less and less willing to pay the escalating costs and are forcing employees to bear a larger and larger portion of the cost. The complaints against the pharmaceutical industry focus especially on two issues that are seen as limiting access. One is the high and ever increasing price of new drugs covered by patents. Not only the poor and elderly, but even middle-class families find that the "co-pay" portion of medicines is increasing at a rate so much faster than inflation that they are having a harder time keeping up. The second is what is seen as illegitimate attempts by drug companies to "extend" their patents and to prevent generic drugs from entering the market, thereby keeping prices high and restricting access for those who can afford only the lower cost of the generics.

The Status Quo Approach simply applies market economics, assuming the force of law in protecting intellectual property rights with respect to patents, and adding that the overall result is not only fair but produces the most good for society. A rights approach to health care yields a different focus. If the right to access to needed drugs is more important than the right to property, then the status quo is up for evaluation and becomes a candidate for change, rather than for passive acceptance. The issue then is not what does market economics prescribe, but how should the status quo be changed to do justice to the right to access to needed drugs. This means once again that intellectual property rights with respect to pharmaceutical drugs should be carefully scrutinized and perhaps changed. . . .

*i. Access and the Cost of Drugs.* My earlier argument distinguished between those drugs that are necessary for life and those that are important for illnesses that are not life-threatening. In the United States critics of pharmaceutical industry pricing are critical of both, and for the most part insurance plans do not distinguish clearly between the two kinds of drugs. The assumption—and as we have seen a dubious assumption—of most Americans is that they are entitled or have a right to the best drugs available for their condition. The relation between the cost of health insurance and the price of medicines and between the cost of health care and the price of medicines is complicated. But the cost of medicines has increased much faster than the cost of health care generally, and the justification for the increase in not obvious, except if one invokes market economics and produces the not-surprising result that the market has been willing to pay the higher prices.

The right to access argument in the U.S. is joined to a fairness argument. That argument says that fairness involves all parties paying their fair share for medicines, including paying sufficient amounts so that drug companies have a continuing incentive to produce more beneficial drugs. The complaint is not that American consumers are subsidizing drugs for the poor countries, or even that they are subsidizing the pharmaceutical companies' compassionate programs. That would be acceptable, and the better off—such as Americans in general—may well have the obligation to bear this cost. But under the Status Quo Approach, in effect, Americans are subsidizing not only poor countries but also seem to bear a disproportionate load. Japan, Canada, and the countries of Europe all negotiate much lower prices than are available in the United States. Americans are increasingly finding it not only ironic but unfair that U.S. drugs cost more in the United States than in other developed countries. This leads to such anomalies as the U.S. government presently prohibiting the importation of U.S.-made drugs from Canada for personal use. while various state governments attempt to find ways of making it legal for senior U.S. citizens to buy U.S.-made drugs from Canada, where the government helps keep the price lower than it is in the United States. . . .

The standard reply to all questions about the high cost of drugs is to appeal to the SA and the SQA and claim that unless there are the profits brought about by high prices, there will be many fewer future drugs. The Status Quo Approach tends to present a questionable dichotomy: either protect drugs and drug pricing to the maximum or face a future with fewer new innovative drugs. The claim is made no matter what the percent of profit, no matter what the prices, no matter how much the industry spends on lobbying and advertising to consumers. The claims are blanket, the justification is blanket, and the public is asked to take the claims on faith. The consuming public must take it on faith that money spent on the recently developed technique of advertising prescription drugs to the general public, for instance, is necessary to produce the profits that will lead to new drugs. They must take it on faith that money spent on researching minor changes in existing drugs is necessary to produce the profits that will lead to new drugs. They must take it on faith that the various tactics that seek loopholes in legislation—whether with respect to the Orphan Drug Act to garner windfall profits or Hatch-Waxman or other legislation to keep competition at bay as long as possible—are necessary to produce the profits that will lead to new drugs.

That faith has been shaken. Because there is very little transparency in drug pricing economics, the claims have worn thin. That the industry needs the highest rate of profit of any industry is not obvious, even for the production of new products.[3] The lack of adequate transparency exacerbates the communication gap and hinders fruitful dialogue. Abuses and attempts at gaming the system further erode trust. . . .

***ii. Access and Patents.*** If there is a difference between different kinds of drugs, and if people have a greater right to access to the more essential drugs than to the less essential ones, then at least it becomes an open question what the best means of protecting the different kinds is. If one takes seriously the Moral Argument, then the assumption of the SQA that all drugs deserve the same length or strength of protection and that they should be treated the same as all other patents in all other areas, is on the table for discussion. Although the laws governing patents are uniform for all products and processes, the range of processes and products is extensive, the differences among them considerable, and so the argument for a one-size-fits-all approach is questionable. Moreover, the pressure on pharmaceutical patents is different from the pressure on patents in general. No one has a right to a better mouse trap, and the market may legitimately determine who gets one; but the right to access to essential medicines places an obligation on all those who can satisfy that right to come up with an equitable means of doing so. . . .

Since access and price are related, attempts to extend the protected life of a drug by introducing slight modifications to get new patents or to delay the entry of generic competitors—which would lower the price and increase accessibility—are not justified by the Standard Argument and are more appropriately seen as taking advantage of the system. . . .

The task with respect to pharmaceutical products is to balance claims to intellectual property rights against the rights to access to needed medicines, the common good, and the obligation to aid. The economic argument that unless companies can make a profit from their research in discovering, developing, and producing drugs, they will not produce them, is only a partial defense of the existing patent system and one that focuses only on property rights. It is only a partial defense because patent protection is not the only conceivable way of either protecting intellectual property or of guaranteeing profits. It does not show that other alternatives—public financing of research and development, cooperation instead of competition on some drug development, government regulation of prices or guarantees of profits at a certain level for certain drugs, and so on, are not viable alternatives. In particular, the SA and SQA do not show that intellectual property rights, no matter how strong and justifiable, trump the right to basic health care and

the right of access to needed medicines or that the right to profits trumps these, the common good, or the obligation to aid. . . .

## NOTES

1. Unlike other property, intellectual property is infinitely shareable. It can be stolen, borrowed, copied, and one still has it. Intellectual property refers to some products of the mind. But arguably the most important products—ideas—cannot be claimed as one's property. Only the expressions of ideas or their embodiment in some product or process can with any plausibility be said to constitute property in any sense. Even in these cases, no expression or invention is developed completely independently. In the realm of knowledge one always builds on what has gone and has been developed before and is part of the public domain.

2. NIHCM, "Changing Patterns of Pharmaceutical Innovation," p. 3 at http://www.nihcm.org/innovations.pdf.

3. According to the Fortune 500 Report, in 2001, the pharmaceutical industry was the most profitable industry again for several years running. In 2001 the profit of the top 10 drug makers increased 33 percent, and drug prices increased 10 percent, even though the rate of inflation was only 1.6 percent. *The Public Citizen* (April 18, 2002, "Pharmaceutical Industry Ranks as Most Profitable Industry—Again" at http://www.citizen.org/congress/reform/drug_industry/profits) notes that "The drug industry maintains that it needs extraordinary profits to fuel risky R&D into new medicines. But companies plow far more into profits than into R&D. Fortune 500 drug companies channeled 18.5 percent of revenue into profits last year. Yet they spent just 12.5 percent of revenue on R&D." It also reports that for 2002 the industry had return on assets of 14.1 percent (compared with a median of 2.3 percent for Fortune 500 companies); that it spent 30.8 percent of its revenue on marketing and administration, but only 14.1 percent on R&D; and that its direct-to-consumer advertising increased from $800 million in 1996 to $2.7 billion in 2001. (Public Citizen, Congress Watch, June 2003, "2002 Drug Industry Profits: Hefty Pharmaceutical Company Margins Dwarf Other Industries," at http://www.citizen.org/congress/reform/drug_industry/r_d/articles.cfm?ID=9923).

# Intellectual Property Rights, Moral Imagination, and Access to Life-Enhancing Drugs

*Patricia H. Werhane and Michael E. Gorman*

## INTRODUCTION

Although the idea of intellectual property (IP) rights—proprietary rights to what one invents, writes, paints, composes or creates—is firmly embedded in Western thinking, these rights are now being challenged across the globe in a number of areas. These challenges include:

- Widespread copying of music and other works of art without permission
- "Knock-off" copies of designer products
- Counterfeit versions of well-known drugs and other products
- The copying of products by reverse engineering
- Challenges to gene patenting and genetic engineering
- Conflicting ownership claims to products developed from tacit knowledge of indigenous populations
- Government-sanctioned copying of patented drugs without permission or license of the patent owner in the name of national security, in health emergencies, or in life-threatening epidemics.

This paper will focus on the last challenge. It will weigh two seemingly opposing values: the value of intellectual property protection and the value of increasing access to anti-retroviral drugs for HIV/AIDS to indigent infected patients. It will examine three different models of intellectual property rights. Part I will discuss two models of intellectual property rights apparently embraced by the pharmaceutical industry, the first grounded in traditional Western defenses of property rights and the second appealing to well-defended

utilitarian justifications. In part II we shall present another way to think about intellectual property that both challenges and preserves this Western tradition. We shall then apply our arguments to the issue at hand: the protection of intellectual property rights garnered by new drug development in light of pandemics such as HIV/AIDS. How does one fund new drug development if patents are threatened and at the same time take on corporate responsibilities to provide access to HIV drugs in less developed countries?

## PART I: THE "TRADITIONAL INTELLECTUAL PROPERTY RIGHTS" MENTAL MODEL

Enlightenment Age thinkers, including Locke, Hume, Smith, and Jefferson, recognized property rights among other fundamental rights of human beings. With the advent of the industrial revolution and the expansion of technology it became apparent that ideas as well as material property needed to be protected. Jefferson, in particular, defended patent protection because it encourages invention and creativity by protecting ownership of new ideas and allows the inventor or creator to reap benefits from that idea, just as the farmer benefits from good agricultural practices on her land. Unlike the farmer, the inventor should be encouraged to make public her or his innovation while protecting the right to copy or reproduce the invention. Jefferson defended intellectual property protection on two rather different grounds. The first, from the rights perspective of Locke, held that inventors have rights to what they create. If a person or company creates a patentable (i.e., new, usable and not obvious) process or product, because of the creativity and work involved, the person or organization has rights to that process or product, just as she has right to land she has bought and developed. The second defense was on more utilitarian grounds that without protection of intellectual property, inventers will be less likely to be creative, since they would not be able to reap honor or other benefits from their inventions. Jefferson contended that these should be time-limited protections so that others could eventually use those inventions to develop other things.

Thus there evolved a set of patent and copyright laws that "protect some (or most) products of the human mind *for varying periods of time*, against use by others of those products in various ways" (Vaver 2000, 621; our italics). Many nations, including the United States, have developed complex trademark, copyright, and patent laws to protect intellectual property. Genetically engineered products, designs, trade secrets, plant breeder rights, databases, and a variety of other forms of intellectual property are also protected by various laws, at least in most Western developed countries.[1]

Despite the legal treatment of intellectual property (IP) rights as time-limited protected claims in most Western countries, these rights are sometimes assumed to be perfect rights, a view that violation or destruction of copyrights, trademarks, or patents are always wrong without exception. Ayn Rand argues for one version of this view:

> Patents and copyrights are the legal implementation of the base of all property rights: man's right to the product of his mind. . . . [P]atents are the heart and core of property rights, and once they are destroyed, the destruction of all other rights will follow automatically, as a brief postscript. (Rand 1966, 125, 128)

Rand contends that IP rights are the most basic rights; without them all other rights are threatened. If this is true, then intellectual property rights might even preempt other important rights, say, to life and liberty. Thus, Rand's defense of the critical nature of IP rights as the basis of the protection of other rights would seem to argue against any action that would dilute intellectual property rights, even, for example, to save the lives of people afflicted with HIV/AIDS.

## UTILITARIAN ARGUMENTS FOR INTELLECTUAL PROPERTY RIGHTS

There are a number of strong arguments for the protection of intellectual property from a utilitarian point of view. It is commonly argued that protection of intellectual property is critical for the continued discovery, creation, and development of new ideas. Few people will write new material, create new art, or invent new products without such protections, because there would be little in the way of honor, recognition, or profit in such activities. Many inventers and companies argue that they have rights to patent protection to control access to that process and product because without such protections there will be few incentives for new product or idea development.

There are other facets of a utilitarian defense of intellectual property. Patent protection, for example, is contended to be particularly important to pharmaceutical companies, whose survival and creativity depends on large amounts of money for research and development. Patent protection allows companies to develop ideas, to profit from that development, and thus to gain funds for further research and development. Without this protection, pharmaceutical companies argue, there would be less incentive to take risk and fewer breakthrough drugs in the future.

Patients and consumers would be the ultimate losers, companies contend.

In a paper titled "'Napsterizing' Pharmaceuticals," Hughes, Moore, and Snyder consider the view that, in the short term, consumers would be much better off if we eliminated present patents on drugs, thereby increasing competition with generic products. Costs of all drugs would be lower. However, as they demonstrate, in the long run we would all be worse off. This is because with lower revenues, pharmaceutical companies could not put as much money into the research and development that is critical for the development of new products. So gradually the development of new drugs would decline, and fewer new lifesaving and life-enhancing treatments would be available to future generations.

There is a fourth set of utilitarian arguments defending IP protections. C. L. Clemente, a senior vice president at Pfizer Corporation, contends that without intellectual property protection, companies such as Pfizer, which depend on patent protection for profits and product development, will not go into countries such as India because through reverse engineering, Indian companies could copy their products (Clemente 2001). Indeed, according to Clemente, one early 1990s World Bank survey of international executives shows that tax rates and intellectual property protection were the main factors in determining global corporate investment decisions. Thus, lack of intellectual property protection, by discouraging investment and development, will widen the gap between the developed and developing countries. As Dr. Harvey Bale of the International Federation of Pharmaceutical Manufacturers Associations (IFPMA) put it:

> [w]ithout strong and effective global intellectual property rules, the gap between developed and developing countries will only grow in the future. (Bale 2002)

This is also the argument of the World Intellectual Property Organization (WIPO). In a new book sponsored by the WIPO, Director General Kamil Idris argues that the transformation of natural resources and products produced by indigenous populations into intellectual property and the protection of those ideas and others with a rule of law can contribute substantially to the wealth of any nation (Idris 2003).

## PART II: A "NETWORK OF INTELLECTUAL PROPERTY RELATIONSHIPS" MENTAL MODEL

Before continuing our discussion, let us step back and outline a set of assumptions from which our analysis derives. As we have argued at length elsewhere, all our experiences are socially constructed through a series of mental models or mind sets that frame our experiences. We do not simply take in experiences as if our minds were receptacles or "blank tablets." Rather, we focus, organize, select, and censor even our simplest perceptions so that all our experiences are framed by complex socially learned mind-sets or cognitive schema. Mental models take the form of schema that frame the experience through which individuals process information, conduct experiments, and formulate theories. This conclusion is based on a commonly (although not universally) held assumption that human beings deal with the world through mind-sets or mental models. Although the term is not always clearly defined, "mental model" encompasses the notion that human beings have mental representations, or cognitive frames, that structure the stimuli or data with which they interact, and these frameworks set up parameters though which experience, or a certain set of experiences, is organized or filtered.

The "traditional intellectual property rights" model is one way to frame our thinking, a mind-set or mental model, a social construction of experiences that predominates in developed countries. But it is only one worldview, and it raises at least three sets of problems. While protection of IP is important because of the proprietary rights to what one discovers or creates, to argue that intellectual property rights are inviolable or should not be destroyed is less plausible, *particularly* from a human rights perspective. If the most basic rights are those of life, liberty, and/or the right not to be harmed (or, as Henry Shue has argued, these rights are to survival, security and liberty [Shue 1996]) these most basic rights override property rights, or should do so, such as during crises such as the threat of death by HIV/AIDS. Even in the United States, where patent laws grant "exclusive" rights, health and security concerns have "trumped" intellectual property rights on occasion. For example, after the anthrax scares in 2001 and 2002, the allegedly inviolable nature of IP rights was brought into question by the U.S. government. The antidote for anthrax is a highly powerful antibiotic called Cipro, patented and manufactured exclusively by Bayer. During the anthrax scare, on the grounds of a national emergency, the U.S. government threatened to override Bayer's patent of Cipro and license its manufacture elsewhere. Thus, even in a country that espouses the traditional-rights model of IP protection, patents can be overridden in cases of national emergencies or life-threatening events. Accordingly, from a traditional rights perspective, IP is a prima facie time-limited right that can and should be overridden, particularly when rights to life or liberty are at stake.

In addition, there are two other interrelated problems with a traditional view of IP. First, when do individual and, by extension, corporate intellectual property rights interfere with innovation? That is, when is an inventor prohibited from using the ideas of others to develop his own? Second, how do we acknowledge and give credit for the myriad of scientific developments and discoveries that precede and influence the development of a particular idea? Most new ideas do not drop out of the sky; they are the result of years, perhaps centuries of investigations that led to the latest invention. So how do we account for these connections? These questions are not merely of intellectual importance; how one deals with them affects our conclusions concerning aid to indigent and dying HIV patients. . . .

Control (or not) of what one has patented is clearly linked to ownership, and exclusive control of what one has discovered or created depends on exclusive ownership rights. But that may be an issue. IP protection is allegedly granted to the source of the innovative idea. But what is that source? Is it the person who created or discovered the idea? The innovator of an idea or the person or company who developed it? Some companies, universities, and other institutions, through employee agreements, receive patents for products and processes their researchers develop on the grounds that they funded the project and will market it.

But ownership of IP as depicted as "mine" or as the sole proprietorship of a company presents an overly simplistic picture. The development of IP—a so-called new idea or creation—is a result of a network of interrelationships, discoveries, research and development, and exchanges of ideas, some passed down over time. IP phenomena are not single or even corporate creations; they are results of a buildup of research and exchange of ideas. Centuries of research made the discovery of DNA possible; the idea did not merely come from the minds of Watson and Crick. Out of the discovery of DNA came years of research and networking relationships underlying the human genome projects. This is the case of every "new" scientific discovery or technological innovation. IP claims, at least in science, are derived from series of other intellectual property developments and a complex chain of human creativity. Even if only two people discovered DNA (and that in itself is a questionable conclusion), the discovery could not have been possible without the contributions of thousands of researchers, foundations, dollars, and companies, and a long history of overlapping and interrelated research.

While credit for the final "aha" might be given to the person or group of persons who brought the idea to fruition, simple patent protection may not be the proper vehicle for protecting this discovery or creation, since the property in question has many ancestral "owners." IP is a result of numbers of inputs, not all of which can ever be acknowledged or traced. AZT, for example, was first synthesized in 1964 by Dr. Jerome Horwitz at the Detroit Institute of Cancer Research as a cancer drug. Since it was ineffective for cancer, the compound was shelved and never patented by Dr. Horwitz. Later, Drs. Samuel Broder and Hiroaki Mitsuya at the National Institutes of Health tested the efficacy of the product on humans after it was rediscovered at Burroughs Wellcome (now GlaxoSmithKline). Other contributors include Dr. Janet Rideout, who isolated the compound, and Dr. Martha St. Clair, who tested the drug in mice. These women were helped by Phillip Furman and Sandra Lehrman at Burroughs Wellcome. Then Burroughs Wellcome patented AZT as a marketable HIV drug.

Recognizing how IP develops from a complex web of interrelationships tracks its causal origins. At the same time the nature of these relationships might help us in recrafting our normative views about that kind of property. Part of this recrafting is parsing out the distinction between ownership, control, and sharing that is different from the traditional IP rights view. This parsing out, in turn, requires that we challenge the traditional IP model, and such challenges require a great deal of moral imagination. . . .

## PART III: IP RIGHTS, CORPORATE RESPONSIBILITIES, AND ACCESS TO HIV DRUGS IN LESS-DEVELOPED COUNTRIES

### The Dilemmas

By law, IP rights are time-limited conventions. If IP rights are not the most basic rights that can "trump" others, they can be overridden in life-threatening emergencies or worldwide epidemics, and indeed we have seen examples of that. IP develops out of, and is dependent upon networks of relationships rather than being a result of a one-time discovery. It would appear, then, that we should arrive at the following conclusions. In times of life-threatening epidemics such as the worldwide HIV epidemic IP rights can be overridden with justification. Moreover, since IP develops from a network of interlocking relationships and shares critical characteristics with other IP, rights to IP are, in some sense, shared rights. It follows that the owner of those rights has some obligations to share that information or its outcomes since the owner's discovery came out of a network of shared ideas *and* shares overlapping content. If that conclusion is applied to thinking about the distribution of antiretroviral drugs, what are pharmaceutical companies ethically required to do to increase access to these medicines in the developing world?

Patents are not protected in at least two-thirds of those less-developed countries with high HIV infections. These countries, then, *could*, in theory, make generic versions of antiretroviral drugs without violating their own laws. So either the IP issue is a "red herring" in this debate, or the problem is much more complex.

The reality is that most countries with high rates of HIV/AIDS have no money to buy medicines. In most sub-Saharan African countries with HIV infections, countries that account for two-thirds of worldwide infections, the question of whether or not they have laws protecting intellectual property is irrelevant. There is little in the way of financial resources, except in South Africa, to underwrite the manufacture of drugs, even generic drugs. There is also no money to finance the purchase of HIV drugs. Worse, in most of these countries, with the possible exceptions of Botswana and South Africa, there is little in the way of medical infrastructure in place to distribute and monitor the use of these drugs. Ideally, one's government should be the first resort for such protections. But in most sub-Saharan countries there is little in the way of funding for health care and almost no enforcement of a rule of law. So the responsibilities of less-developed country governments to their citizens have to be reconceived for each country involved in this crisis, and the responsibility for addressing the pandemic becomes expanded beyond borders.

Even if pharmaceutical companies sacrifice some revenues and stop worrying about patent infringement, companies dealing in the developing world cannot simply give away HIV drugs: There is no place to send the medicines, no central authority, no distribution channels, and no competent health-care professionals to administer and monitor drug use, nor are adequate delivery and follow-up systems in place in most of these countries. Even if the drugs reached the ill, without medical assistance, the medicines might be misused. Giving away the drugs even in countries with a semblance of a medical system is dangerous because often these drugs get into the black market. They are then diluted and/or sold back to developed countries at discount prices. For instance, according to one report, as much as two-thirds of the AZT now virtually given away in many African countries by Glaxo-SmithKline, finds its way back to Europe through black markets. This reduces revenues

for pharmaceutical companies in major markets and reduces funds available for R&D on new treatments.

Another complication arises out of the mission of pharmaceutical companies. These companies are in the business of reducing pain and/or curing disease. This is what they do, and if they do it well, focusing on customers as their primary stakeholders, they are ordinarily profitable. These companies are always faced with a series of dilemmas. Which research should they fund? Which diseases should they concentrate on? And if they have a drug or set of drugs that are effective, how do they serve infected communities that have no money to pay for these drugs? The dilemma is acute in the case of HIV. Although HIV/AIDS is fatal, we have effective life-prolonging and life-enhancing drugs to address this disease. Isn't the responsibility of companies that have these drugs to give them away to their indigent patients? Isn't that part of their mission?

**Networks, Moral Imagination, and an Alliance Model**

The previous discussion of issues surrounding the HIV pandemic in sub-Saharan Africa, like the initial analysis of IP, was too simplistic. We have presented the pandemic as either-or dilemmas, but the issues are much more interrelated and intractable. This pandemic presents unique challenges. It presents challenges to pharmaceutical companies, not to their expertise or to the quality of their products, but to their way of thinking through IP and its implication for these ethical issues. The pandemic presents similar challenges to those governments, donor organizations, and NGOs that deal with these issues on a daily basis and to other individuals, governments, and international organizations that at least pay lip service to the problem.

To wrestle with this issue requires that companies, governments, donor organizations, and NGOs rethink their traditional approaches to problems in less-developed countries and revise their standard operating procedures or traditional mind-sets that have worked well in other situations. What is needed is a networked approach to thinking about intellectual property and IP protection and new thinking about drug distribution and disease control, along with a great deal of moral imagination. Such an approach could create a template for future corporate, government and donor activities for this pandemic.

Dealing in a creative way with the HIV/AIDS pandemic, like our analysis of IP, involves appealing to [the use of] moral imagination. This pandemic is embedded in a complex network of relationships themselves embedded in a complex set of systems and subsystems, including the diverse cultures and practices of indigenous people in every infected country; distribution issues; financing and funding challenges; pressures from shareholders, the media, and NGOs, and the ever-present worry about protection of patents. For pharmaceutical companies with antiretroviral drugs, to protect their patents and address this crisis requires more of companies than we ordinarily expect. It requires developing and implementing a truly systemic approach to IP and to the HIV pandemic that gives good moral reasons for addressing this issue and then engages companies, donor organizations, NGOs, local villages, and countries. Such a multiple-perspectives systems approach should include the following:

1. There are a number of good moral reasons why pharmaceutical companies with antiretroviral drugs have responsibilities to impoverished communities with widespread infection rates of HIV/AIDS. First, and most obviously, from the point of view of rights and justice, responding to the needs of infected and impoverished communities is the right thing to do. Unless one imagines that IP rights override the right to life, it is difficult to justify ignoring this pandemic. The Good Samaritan argument, while not applicable to every situation, suggests that if we see someone in need and we are capable of helping, we have obligations to do so. This is because we all live in an interdependent global community [no longer separate communities, if they ever were] where interactive involvement is necessary for survival, preventing the spread of disease, and well-being. Analogously, no new drug could have ever been developed without these social interactions; thus obligations also arise because of the intellectual debts we have to each other. This does not imply, however, that companies should give away their HIV/AIDS drugs until they go bankrupt. Their responsibilities to employees, paying customers, shareholders, and future generations who will benefit from new drug development must be weighed as well. But to do nothing is unacceptable, and today almost every pharmaceutical company with antiretroviral drug protocols is engaged in some philanthropic project in Africa

2. If, as we suggested in part II, drug development like all IP, is a result of an interactive networking set of processes and overlapping ideas, then obligations, at least imperfect obligations, exist to continue that sharing activity, since a company's ownership of an idea is in fact a shared dependency on predecessor discoveries. There is no practical means to recognize all or even very many of the ancestors of any idea. Yet one has intellectual debts that can be translated into a forward-projecting set of obligations to other scientists and to communities in which drug development is encouraged, permitted, and needed. In an interdependent global community these obligations become more widespread.

3. In dealing with the pandemic 'on the ground,' a multiperspective analysis, spelling out the networks of relationships and viewing them from the perspective of each kind of relationship is critical. This would include an attempt to understand these issues from the point of view of pharmaceutical companies with antiretroviral drugs, from country and cultural perspectives, from the perspectives of traditions, funding agencies, NGOs and delivery mechanisms, and from the global perspective of the pandemic.

Consider, for example, the alliance model developed by Mary Ann Leeper, COO of the Female Health Company, a for-profit company that distributes female condoms to protect women against HIV infection in over 100 less-developed countries. The model was developed in response to a huge demand by women first in Zimbabwe and now in many other countries for protection against infection in cultures where men are averse to condom use. The dilemma for this small company was obvious. The company had a fine product, a large customer demand for the female condom, and adequate supplies. But, the customer base was extremely poor, and as we have mentioned, governments in countries with high infection rates, at least in Africa, have little or no funds for this or any other product. So Dr. Leeper began finding donor organizations to support supplying this product. She solicited monies from UNAID, USAID, DFID, social marketing organizations that deeply discount products such as condoms, and other international organizations. But even with funding for the product, the company was faced with a second challenge: getting governments in these countries to support or at least not oppose the distribution of the product. And there was a third challenge: training villagers and local health personnel on how to use the product and how to instruct others. By working with NGOs, the Female Health Company is gradually overcoming this problem through training and education, village by village in the 100 countries where it distributes it product.

4. An evaluative perspective, prioritizing the value priorities of each stakeholder and of the pandemic.

This evaluative approach has been adapted by Merck and the Gates Foundation. Merck has partnered with the Botswana government and Gates Foundation in its HIV project in Botswana. It could not merely give its HIV drug, Crixivan, away, even if it were willing to do so. Although Botswana has better medical facilities and a more stable government than most of the rest of sub-Saharan Africa, its complex culture is such that education, medical infrastructures, and monitoring are not adequate, nor are tribal traditions aligned with modern medical treatment.

5. A multistakeholder model for structural change that will attack and work to alleviate the pandemic by distributing [but not avoiding] the risks and responsibilities.

In Tanzania, Abbott Laboratories Fund has partnered with the Tanzanian government and the Axios Foundation (a U.S. NGO) in a multiyear multimillion dollar project to upgrade and improve the medical care infrastructure, to train health-care professionals, and to expand access to treatment for HIV infected citizens.

An alliance model entails thinking of IP as a shared right and the enterprise of distribution as a program, not merely as delivering a product. Employing this model requires proactive corporate initiatives, because these initiatives have not been forthcoming by those countries with widespread epidemics. One has to find international donor organizations for funding, elicit government cooperation in the countries most afflicted with HIV, and work with NGOs to set up delivery, medical, and monitoring systems. The model requires developing alliances with local and state governments, NGOs, and donor organizations, and it requires hands-on interaction in the infected communities. It requires training local villagers to deliver and monitor drug intake. This is currently being done in Haiti, where hundreds of local people are being trained in the rudiments of drug delivery and sent out to villages daily to deliver and monitor drug use by the HIV infected. This model is also being tried by the World Health Organization in a number of other countries. And of course, companies have to provide the drugs and monitor the process of delivery and use themselves. Otherwise the drugs will go onto the black market or into the hands of unscrupulous people. Without a systems approach the Female Health Company, Merck, Abbott, and even the Gates Foundation will fail, whether or not IP is preserved. And such an approach requires a great deal of moral imagination to think "out of the box" so to speak, that one's consumers are not paying customers, that product distribution requires more than merely marketing or sales, and that even charity—giving products away—is not always a good solution

A hands-on alliance approach to drug distribution in LDCs protects company patents and insures that products are to be used properly and by those for whom the program is aimed, because companies are in control of distribution and use. At the same time it acknowledges limits to IP rights by sharing its products (and in some cases, as in Brazil, its processes). But is it unfair to those of us who pay full price for drugs or who pay for this giveaway through buying other expensive drugs? We would argue that it would be unfair if we lived in a global egalitarian society where everything is distributed equally and if we adapted that model as the fairest for distributive justice. But we neither live nor will live in such a society, nor, as Ronald Dworkin argued some years ago, is equal distribution always the fairest method. Dworkin argues, in brief, that the fairest means of societal distribution is not based merely on equality but rather on the principle of treating every individual as an equal. So for example, if I have a small supply of medicine and three children, I give the medicine to the sickest. This is because that sick child is disadvantaged and needs

to be brought up to the healthy status of the others (Dworkin 1977, 273). Similarly providing transportation to people who otherwise cannot get to the voting booths is not unfair to those who can for the same reasons. So those indigent people dying of HIV/AIDS are owed more than the rest of us just to bring them up to the same level, that is, the level of the living. This would be unfair only if they could provide for themselves; but they cannot. . . .

## NOTE

1. Copyright laws protect the ownership name, but give the right to copy, with the proper citation. But patent laws are different, since with a patent one controls the right to share or copy the information! Similarly, registered trademarks protect the trademark for owner use only.

## REFERENCES

Bale, Harvey E., Jr. 2002. "Patents and Public Health: A Good or Bad Mix?" *Pfizer Forum*, www.pfizerforum.com

Clemente, C. L. 2001. "Intellectual Property: The Patent on Prosperity." *Pfizer Forum*, www.pfizerforum.com/english/clemente/shtml

Dworkin, Ronald. 1977. *Taking Rights Seriously*. Cambridge, MA: Harvard University Press.

Hughes, James, W., Michael J. Moore, and Edward A. Snyder. 2002. "'Napsterizing' Pharmaceuticals Access, Innovation, and Consumer Welfare." National Bureau of Economic Research Working Paper 9229.

Idris, Kamil. 2003. *Intellectual Property: A Tool for Economic Growth*. Geneva: World Intellectual Property Organization.

Rand, Ayn. 1966. *Capitalism: The Unknown Ideal*. New York: New American Library.

Shue, Henry. 1996. *Basic Rights*, 2nd ed. Princeton, N.J.: Princeton University Press.

Vaver, David. 2000. "Intellectual Property: State of the Art." *Law Quarterly Review* 116:621–37.

## LEGAL PERSPECTIVES

# Sony Corp. v. Universal City Studios Inc.

*United States Supreme Court*

Petitioners manufacture and sell home video-tape recorders. Respondents own the copyrights on some of the television programs that are broadcast on the public airwaves. Some members of the general public use videotape recorders sold by petitioners to record some of these broadcasts, as well as a large number of other broadcasts. The question presented is whether the sale of petitioners' copying equipment to the general public violates any of the rights conferred upon respondents by the Copyright Act.

Respondents commenced this copyright infringement action against petitioners in the United States District Court for the Central District of California in 1976. Respondents alleged that some individuals had used Betamax video tape recorders (VTRs) to record some of respondents' copyrighted works which had been exhibited on commercially sponsored television and contended that these individuals had thereby infringed respondents' copyrights. Respondents further maintained that petitioners were liable for the copyright infringement allegedly committed by Betamax consumers because of petitioners' marketing of the Betamax VTRs. Respondents sought no relief against any Betamax consumer. Instead, they sought money damages and an equitable accounting of profits from petitioners, as well as an injunction against the manufacture and marketing of Betamax VTRs.

After a lengthy trial, the District Court denied respondents all the relief they sought and entered judgment for petitioners. The United States Court of Appeals for the Ninth Circuit reversed the District Court's judgment on respondents' copyright claim, holding petitioners liable for contributory infringement and ordering the District Court to fashion appropriate relief. We granted certiorari, since we had not completed our study of the case last Term, we ordered reargument. We now reverse.

An explanation of our rejection of respondents' unprecedented attempt to impose copyright liability upon the distributors of copying equipment requires a quite detailed recitation of the findings of the District Court. In summary, those findings reveal that the average member of the public uses a VTR principally to record a program he cannot view as it is being televised and then to watch it once at a later time. This practice, known as "time-shifting," enlarges the television viewing audience. For that reason, a significant amount of television programming may be used in this manner without objection from the owners of the copyrights on the programs. For the same reason, even the two respondents in this case, who do assert objections to time-shifting in this litigation, were unable to prove that the practice has impaired the commercial value of their copyrights or has created any likelihood of future harm. Given these findings, there is no basis in the Copyright Act upon which respondents can hold petitioners liable for distributing VTRs to the general public. The Court of Appeals' holding that respondents are entitled to enjoin the distribution of VTR's, to collect royalties on the sale of such equipment, or to obtain other

464 U.S. 417 (1984). Majority opinion by Justice Stevens.

relief, if affirmed, would enlarge the scope of respondents' statutory monopolies to encompass control over an article of commerce that is not the subject of copyright protection. Such an expansion of the copyright privilege is beyond the limits of the grants authorized by Congress.

# I

The two respondents in this action, Universal City Studios Inc., and Walt Disney Productions, produce and hold the copyrights on a substantial number of motion pictures and other audiovisual works. In the current marketplace, they can exploit their rights in these works in a number of ways: by authorizing theatrical exhibitions, by licensing limited showings on cable and network television, by selling syndication rights for repeated airings on local television stations, and by marketing programs on prerecorded videotapes or videodiscs. Some works are suitable for exploitation through all of these avenues, while the market for other works is more limited.

Petitioner Sony manufactures millions of Betamax videotape recorders and markets these devices through numerous retail establishments, some of which are also petitioners in this action. Sony's Betamax VTR is a mechanism consisting of three basic components: (1) a tuner, which receives electromagnetic signals transmitted over the television band of the public airwaves and separates them into audio and visual signals; (2) a recorder, which records such signals on a magnetic tape; and (3) an adapter, which converts the audio and visual signals on the tape into a composite signal that can be received by a television set.

Several capabilities of the machine are noteworthy. The separate tuner in the Betamax enables it to record a broadcast off one station while the television set is tuned to another

channel, permitting the viewer, for example, to watch two simultaneous news broadcasts by watching one "live" and recording the other for later viewing. Tapes may be reused, and programs that have been recorded may be erased either before or after viewing. A timer in the Betamax can be used to activate and deactivate the equipment at predetermined times, enabling an intended viewer to record programs that are transmitted when he or she is not at home. Thus a person may watch a program at home in the evening even though it was broadcast while the viewer was at work during the afternoon. The Betamax is also equipped with a pause button and a fast-forward control. The pause button, when depressed, deactivates the recorder until it is released, thus enabling a viewer to omit a commercial advertisement from the recording, provided, of course, that the viewer is present when the program is recorded. The fast-forward control enables the viewer of a previously recorded program to run the tape rapidly when a segment he or she does not desire to see is being played back on the television screen.

The respondents and Sony both conducted surveys of the way the Betamax machine was used by several hundred owners during a sample period in 1978. Although there were some differences in the surveys, they both showed that the primary use of the machine for most owners was "time-shifting"—the practice of recording a program to view it once at a later time, and thereafter erasing it. Timeshifting enables viewers to see programs they otherwise would miss because they are not at home, are occupied with other tasks, or are viewing a program on another station at the time of a broadcast that they desire to watch. Both surveys also showed, however, that a substantial number of interviewees had accumulated libraries of tapes. Sony's survey indicated that over 80% of the interviewees watched at least as much regular television as they had before owning a Betamax. Respondents offered no evidence of decreased television viewing by Betamax owners.

Sony introduced considerable evidence describing television programs that could be copied without objection from any copyright holder, with special emphasis on sports, religious, and educational programming. For example, their survey indicated that 7.3 percent of all Betamax use is to record sports events, and representatives of professional baseball, football, basketball, and hockey testified that they had no objection to the recording of their televised events for home use.

Respondents offered opinion evidence concerning the future impact of the unrestricted sale of VTRs on the commercial value of their copyrights. The District Court found, however, that they had failed to prove any likelihood of future harm from the use of VTRs for time-shifting. . . .

## II

Article I, 8, of the Constitution provides:

> The Congress shall have Power . . . To Promote the Progress of Science and useful Arts, by securing for limited Times to Authors and Inventors the exclusive Right to their respective Writings and Discoveries.

The monopoly privileges that Congress may authorize are neither unlimited nor primarily designed to provide a special private benefit. Rather, the limited grant is a means by which an important public purpose may be achieved. It is intended to motivate the creative activity of authors and inventors by the provision of a special reward, and to allow the public access to the products of their genius after the limited period of exclusive control has expired. . . .

As the text of the Constitution makes plain, it is Congress that has been assigned the task of defining the scope of the limited monopoly

that should be granted to authors or to inventors in order to give the public appropriate access to their work product. Because this task involves a difficult balance between the interests of authors and inventors in the control and exploitation of their writings and discoveries on the one hand, and society's competing interest in the free flow of ideas, information, and commerce on the other hand, our patent and copyright statutes have been amended repeatedly.

From its beginning, the law of copyright has developed in response to significant changes in technology. Indeed, it was the invention of a new form of copying equipment—the printing press—that gave rise to the original need for copyright protection. Repeatedly, as new developments have occurred in this country, it has been the Congress that has fashioned the new rules that new technology made necessary. . . .

The judiciary's reluctance to expand the protections afforded by the copyright without explicit legislative guidance is a recurring theme. Sound policy, as well as history, supports our consistent deference to Congress when major technological innovations alter the market for copyrighted materials. Congress has the constitutional authority and the institutional ability to accommodate fully the varied permutations of competing interests that are inevitably implicated by such new technology.

In a case like this, in which Congress has not plainly marked our course, we must be circumspect in construing the scope of rights created by a legislative enactment which never contemplated such a calculus of interests. . . .

## III

If vicarious liability is to be imposed on Sony in this case, it must rest on the fact that it has sold equipment with constructive knowledge of the fact that its customers may use that equipment to make unauthorized copies of copyrighted material. There is no precedent in the law of copyright for the imposition of vicarious liability on such a theory. . . .

## IV

The question is . . . whether the Betamax is capable of commercially significant noninfringing uses. . . .

### A. Authorized Time-Shifting

Each of the respondents owns a large inventory of valuable copyrights, but in the total spectrum of television programming their combined market share is small. The exact percentage is not specified, but it is well below 10 percent. If they were to prevail, the outcome of this litigation would have a significant impact on both the producers and the viewers of the remaining 90 percent of the programming in the Nation. . . .

### B. Unauthorized Time-Shifting

Even unauthorized uses of a copyrighted work are not necessarily infringing. An unlicensed use of the copyright is not an infringement unless it conflicts with one of the specific exclusive rights conferred by the copyright statute. Moreover, the definition of exclusive rights in 106 of the present Act is prefaced by the words "subject to sections 107 through 118." Those sections describe a variety of uses of copyrighted material that "are not infringements of copyright" "notwithstanding the provisions of section 106." The most pertinent in this case is 107, the legislative endorsement of the doctrine of "fair use."

That section identifies various factors that enable a court to apply an "equitable rule of reason" analysis to particular claims of infringement. Although not conclusive, the first factor requires that "the commercial or nonprofit character of an activity" be weighed in any fair use decision. If the Betamax were used to make copies for a commercial or profit-making purpose, such use would presumptively be unfair. The contrary presumption is appropriate here, however, because the District Court's findings plainly establish that time-shifting for private home use must be characterized as a noncommercial, nonprofit activity. Moreover, when one considers the nature of a televised copyrighted audiovisual work, and that time-shifting merely enables a viewer to see such a work which he had been invited to witness in its entirety free of charge, the fact that the entire work is reproduced, see 107(3), does not have its ordinary effect of militating against a finding of fair use.

This is not, however, the end of the inquiry because Congress has also directed us to consider "the effect of the use upon the potential market for or value of the copyrighted work." The purpose of copyright is to create incentives for creative effort. Even copying for noncommercial purposes may impair the copyright holder's ability to obtain the rewards that Congress intended him to have. But a use that has no demonstrable effect upon the potential market for, or the value of, the copyrighted work need not be prohibited in order to protect the author's incentive to create. The prohibition of such noncommercial uses would merely inhibit access to ideas without any countervailing benefit.

Thus, although every commercial use of copyrighted material is presumptively an unfair exploitation of the monopoly privilege that belongs to the owner of the copyright, noncommercial uses are a different matter. A challenge to a noncommercial use of a copyrighted work requires proof either that the particular use is harmful, or that if it should become widespread, it would adversely affect the potential market for the copyrighted work. Actual present harm need not be shown; such a requirement would leave the copyright holder with no defense against predictable damage. Nor is it necessary to show with certainty that future harm will result. What is necessary is a showing by a preponderance of the evidence that some meaningful likelihood of future harm exists. If the intended use is for commercial gain, that likelihood may be presumed. But if it is for a noncommercial purpose, the likelihood must be demonstrated. . . .

There was no need for the District Court to say much about past harm. "Plaintiffs have admitted that no actual harm to their copyrights has occurred to date."

On the question of potential future harm from time-shifting, the District Court offered a more detailed analysis of the evidence. It rejected respondents' "fear that persons 'watching' the original telecast of a program will not be measured in the live audience and the ratings and revenues will decrease," by observing that current measurement technology allows the Betamax audience to be reflected. It rejected respondents' prediction "that live television or movie audiences will decrease as more people watch Betamax tapes as an alternative," with the observation that "[t]here is no factual basis for [the underlying] assumption." It rejected respondents' "fear that time-shifting will reduce audiences for telecast reruns," and concluded instead that "given current market practices, this should aid plaintiffs rather than harm them." And it declared that respondents' suggestion that "theater or film rental exhibition of a program will suffer because of time-shift recording of that program" "lacks merit."

After completing that review, the District Court restated its overall conclusion several times, in several different ways. "Harm from time-shifting is speculative and, at best, minimal." "The audience benefits from the time-

shifting capability have already been discussed. It is not implausible that benefits could also accrue to plaintiffs, broadcasters, and advertisers, as the Betamax makes it possible for more persons to view their broadcasts." "No likelihood of harm was shown at trial, and plaintiffs admitted that there had been no actual harm to date." "Testimony at trial suggested that Betamax may require adjustments in marketing strategy, but it did not establish even a likelihood of harm." "Television production by plaintiffs today is more profitable than it has ever been, and, in 5 weeks of trial, there was no concrete evidence to suggest that the Betamax will change the studios' financial picture."

The District Court's conclusions are buttressed by the fact that to the extent time-shifting expands public access to freely broadcast television programs, it yields societal benefits. In *Community Television of Southern California v. Gottfried*, we acknowledged the public interest in making television broadcasting more available. Concededly, that interest is not unlimited. But it supports an interpretation of the concept of "fair use" that requires the copyright holder to demonstrate some likelihood of harm before he may condemn a private act of time-shifting as a violation of federal law.

When these factors are all weighed in the "equitable rule of reason" balance, we must conclude that this record amply supports the District Court's conclusion that home time-shifting is fair use. In light of the findings of the District Court regarding the state of the empirical data, it is clear that the Court of Appeals erred in holding that the statute as presently written bars such conduct.

In summary, the record and findings of the District Court lead us to two conclusions. First, Sony demonstrated a significant likelihood that substantial numbers of copyright holders who license their works for broadcast on free television would not object to having their broadcasts time-shifted by private viewers. And second, respondents failed to demonstrate that time-shifting would cause any likelihood of nonminimal harm to the potential market for, or the value of, their copyrighted works. The Betamax is, therefore, capable of substantial noninfringing uses. Sony's sale of such equipment to the general public does not constitute contributory infringement of respondents' copyrights.

**V**

> The direction of Art. I is that Congress shall have the power to promote the progress of science and the useful arts. When, as here, the Constitution is permissive, the sign of how far Congress has chosen to go can come only from Congress. [*Deepsouth Packing Co. v. Laitram Corp.*]

One may search the Copyright Act in vain for any sign that the elected representatives of the millions of people who watch television every day have made it unlawful to copy a program for later viewing at home, or have enacted a flat prohibition against the sale of machines that make such copying possible.

It may well be that Congress will take a fresh look at this new technology, just as it so often has examined other innovations in the past. But it is not our job to apply laws that have not yet been written. Applying the copyright statute, as it now reads, to the facts as they have been developed in this case, the judgment of the Court of Appeals must be reversed.

It is so ordered.

# A&M Records v. Napster

*United States District Court for the Northern District of California*

The matter before the court concerns the boundary between sharing and theft, personal use and the unauthorized worldwide distribution of copyrighted music and sound recordings. On December 6, 1999, A&M Records and 17 other record companies ("record company plaintiffs") filed a complaint for contributory and vicarious copyright infringement, violations of the California Civil Code section 980(a)[1], and unfair competition against Napster Inc., an Internet start-up that enables users to download MP3 music files without payment. On January 7, 2000, plaintiffs Jerry Leiber, Mike Stoller, and Frank Music Corporation filed a complaint for vicarious and contributory copyright infringement on behalf of a putative class of similarly situated music publishers ("music publisher plaintiffs") against Napster Inc. and former CEO Eileen Richardson. . . . Now be-

fore this court is the record company and music publisher plaintiffs' joint motion to preliminarily enjoin Napster Inc. from engaging in or assisting others in copying, downloading, uploading, transmitting, or distributing copyrighted music without the express permission of the rights owner.

In opposition to this motion, defendant seeks to expand the "fair use" doctrine articulated in *Sony Corp. of America v. Universal City Studios Inc.*, 464 U.S. 417 (1984), to encompass the massive downloading of MP3 files by Napster users. Alternatively, defendant contends that, even if this third-party activity constitutes direct copyright infringement, plaintiffs have not shown probable success on the merits of their contributory and vicarious infringement claims. Defendant also asks the court to find that

114 F. Supp 2d 896 (2001). Opinion by Chief Judge Marilyn Hall Patel.

copyright holders are not injured by a service created and promoted to facilitate the free downloading of music files, the vast majority of which are copyrighted.

Having considered the parties' arguments, the court grants plaintiffs' motion for a preliminary injunction against Napster Inc. The court makes the following Findings of Fact and Conclusions of Law to support the preliminary injunction under Federal Rules of Civil Procedure 65(d).

## I. FINDINGS OF FACT

### A. MP3 Technology

*1.* Digital compression technology makes it possible to store audio recordings in a digital format that uses less memory and may be uploaded and downloaded over the Internet. MP3 is a popular, standard format used to store such compressed audio files. Compressing data into MP3 format results in some loss of sound quality. However, because MP3 files are smaller, they require less time to transfer and are therefore better suited to transmission over the Internet.

*2.* Consumers typically acquire MP3 files in two ways. First, users may download audio recordings that have already been converted into MP3 format by using an Internet service such as Napster. Second, "ripping" software makes it possible to copy an audio compact disc ("CD") directly onto a computer hard drive; ripping software compresses the millions of bytes of information on a typical CD into a smaller MP3 file that requires a fraction of the storage space.

### B. Defendant's Business

*1.* Napster Inc. is a start-up company based in San Mateo, California. It distributes its pro-prietary file-sharing software free of charge via its Internet Web site. People who have downloaded this software can log on to the Napster system and share MP3 music files with other users who are also logged on to the system. It is uncontradicted that Napster users currently upload or download MP3 files without payment to each other, defendant, or copyright owners. According to a Napster Inc. executive summary, the Napster service gives its users the unprecedented ability to "locate music by their favorite artists in MP3 format." Defendant boasts that it "takes the frustration out of locating servers with MP3 files" by providing a peer-to-peer file-sharing system that allows Napster account holders to conduct relatively sophisticated searches for music files on the hard drives of millions of other anonymous users.

*2.* Although Napster was the brainchild of a college student who wanted to facilitate music swapping by his roommate, it is far from a simple tool of distribution among friends and family. According to defendant's internal documents, there will be 75 million Napster users by the end of 2000. At one point, defendant estimated that even without marketing, its "viral service" was growing by more than 200 percent per month. Approximately 10,000 music files are shared per second using Napster, and every second more than 100 users attempt to connect to the system.

*3.* Napster Inc. currently collects no revenues and charges its clientele no fees; it is a free service. However, it has never been a nonprofit organization. It plans to delay the maximization of revenues while it attracts a large user base. The value of the system grows as the quantity and quality of available music increases. Defendant's internal documents reveal a strategy of attaining a "critical mass" of music in an "ever-expanding library" as new members bring their MP3 collections online.

Defendant eventually plans to "monetize" its user base. Potential revenue sources include targeted e-mail; advertising; commissions from links to commercial Web sites; and direct marketing of CDs, Napster products, and CD burners and rippers. Defendant also may begin to charge fees for a premium or commercial version of its software. The existence of a large user base that increases daily and can be "monetized" makes Napster Inc. a potentially attractive acquisition for larger, more established firms. . . .

*4.* The evidence shows that virtually all Napster users download or upload copyrighted files and that the vast majority of the music available on Napster is copyrighted. Eighty-seven percent of the files sampled by plaintiffs' expert, Dr. Ingram Olkin, "belong to or are administered by plaintiffs or other copyright holders." After analyzing Olkin's data, Charles J. Hausman, antipiracy counsel for the RIAA, determined that 834 out of 1,150 files in Olkin's download database belong to or are administered by plaintiffs; plaintiffs alone own the copyrights to more than 70 percent of the 1,150 files. Napster users shared these files without authorization.

*5.* Napster Inc. has never obtained licenses to distribute or download, or to facilitate others in distributing or downloading, the music that plaintiffs own. . . .

## D. Plaintiffs' Business

*1.* The music publisher plaintiffs compose music and write songs. They depend financially upon the sale of sound recordings because they earn royalties from such sales.

However, they do not get a royalty when a Napster user uploads or downloads an MP3 file of their compositions without payment or authorization. The record company plaintiffs' sound recordings also result from a substantial investment of money, time, manpower, and creativity.

In contrast, defendant invests nothing in the content of the music which means that,

compared with plaintiffs, it incurs virtually no costs in providing a wide array of music to satisfy consumer demand.

*2.* To make a profit, the record company plaintiffs largely rely on the success of "hit" or popular recordings, which may constitute as little as 10 or 15 percent of albums released. Many, or all, of their top recordings have been available for free on Napster.

*3.* The record company plaintiffs have invested substantial time, effort, and funds in actual or planned entry into the digital downloading market. . . .

## E. Effect of Napster on the Market for Plaintiffs' Copyrighted Works

*1.* The court finds that Napster use is likely to reduce CD purchases by college students, who defendant admits constitute a key demographic. Plaintiffs' expert, Dr. E. Deborah Jay, opined that 41 percent of her college-student survey respondents "gave a reason for using Napster or described the nature of its impact on their music purchases in a way which either explicitly indicated or suggested that Napster displaces CD sales." She also found that 21 percent of the college students surveyed revealed that Napster helped them make a better selection or decide what to buy. However, Jay's overall conclusion was that "[t]he more songs Napster users have downloaded," the more likely they are to admit or imply that such use has reduced their music purchases. The report of Soundscan CEO Michael Fine lends support to Jay's findings. After examining data culled from three types of retail stores near college or university campuses,[2] Fine concluded that "online file sharing has resulted in a loss of album sales within college markets."

For the reasons discussed in the court's separate order, the report by defendant's expert, Dr. Peter S. Fader, does not provide credible evidence that music file-sharing on Napster stimulates more CD sales than it displaces. Nor do the recording industry documents that defendant cites reliably show increased music sales due to Napster use. . . .

*2.* Because plaintiffs entered the digital download market very recently, or plan to enter it in the next few months, they are especially vulnerable to direct competition from Napster Inc. The court finds that, in choosing between the free Napster service and pay-per-download sites, consumers are likely to choose Napster. . . .

*3.* Downloading on Napster also has the potential to disrupt plaintiffs' promotional efforts because it does not involve any of the restrictions on timing, amount, or selection that plaintiffs impose when they offer free music files. Even if Napster users sometimes download files to determine whether they want to purchase a CD, sampling on Napster is vastly different than that offered by plaintiffs. On Napster, the user—not the copyright owner—determines how much music to sample and how long to keep it.

## II. CONCLUSIONS OF LAW

### A. Legal Standard

*1.* The Ninth Circuit authorizes preliminary injunctive relief for "a party who demonstrates either (1) a combination of probable success on the merits and the possibility of irreparable harm, or (2) that serious questions are raised and the balance of hardships tips in its favor."

*2.* The standard is a sliding scale which requires a greater degree of harm the lesser the probability of success. In a copyright infringement case, demonstration of a reasonable likelihood of success on the merits creates a presumption of irreparable harm.

### B. Proof of Direct Infringement

*1.* To prevail on a contributory or vicarious copyright infringement claim, a plaintiff must show direct infringement by a third party. As a threshold matter, plaintiffs in this action must demonstrate that Napster users are engaged in direct infringement.

*2.* Plaintiffs have established a prima facie case of direct copyright infringement. As discussed above, virtually all Napster users engage in the unauthorized downloading or uploading of copyrighted music; as much as 87 percent of the files available on Napster may be copyrighted, and more than seventy percent may be owned or administered by plaintiffs.

### C. Affirmative Defense of Fair Use and Substantial Noninfringing Use

*1.* Defendant asserts the affirmative defenses of fair use and substantial noninfringing use. The latter defense is also known as the staple article of commerce doctrine. . . .

*2.* For the reasons set forth below, the court finds that any potential noninfringing use of the Napster service is minimal or connected to the infringing activity, or both. The substantial or commercially significant use of the service was, and continues to be, the unauthorized downloading and uploading of popular music, most of which is copyrighted.

*3.* Section 107 of the Copyright Act provides a nonexhaustive list of fair-use factors. These factors include:

1. the purpose and character of the use, including whether such use is of a commercial nature or is for nonprofit educational purposes;
2. the nature of the copyrighted work;
3. the amount and substantiality of the portion used in relation to the copyrighted work as a whole; and
4. the effect of the use upon the potential market for or value of the copyrighted work.

*4.* In the instant action, the purpose and character of the use militates against a finding of fair use. . . .

**5.** Under the first factor, the court must also determine whether the use is commercial. In *Acuff-Rose*, the Supreme Court clarified that a finding of commercial use weighs against, but does not preclude, a determination of fairness.

**6.** If a use is noncommercial, the plaintiff bears the burden of showing a meaningful likelihood that it would adversely affect the potential market for the copyrighted work if it became widespread.

**7.** Although downloading and uploading MP3 music files is not paradigmatic commercial activity, it is also not personal use in the traditional sense. Plaintiffs have not shown that the majority of Napster users download music to sell—that is, for profit. However, given the vast scale of Napster use among anonymous individuals, the court finds that downloading and uploading MP3 music files with the assistance of Napster are not private uses. At the very least, a host user sending a file cannot be said to engage in a personal use when distributing that file to an anonymous requester. Moreover, the fact that Napster users get for free something they would ordinarily have to buy suggests that they reap economic advantages from Napster use.

**8.** The court finds that the copyrighted musical compositions and sound recordings are creative in nature; they constitute entertainment, which cuts against a finding of fair use under the second factor.

**9.** With regard to the third factor, it is undisputed that downloading or uploading MP3 music files involves copying the entirety of the copyrighted work. The Ninth Circuit held prior to Sony that "wholesale copying of copyrighted material precludes application of the fair-use doctrine." Even after Sony, wholesale copying for private home use tips the fair-use analysis in plaintiffs' favor if such copying is likely to adversely affect the market for the copyrighted material.

**10.** The fourth factor, the effect on the potential market for the copyrighted work, also weighs against a finding of fair use. Plaintiffs have produced evidence that Napster use harms the market for their copyrighted musical compositions and sound recordings in at least two ways. First, it reduces CD sales among college students. Second, it raises barriers to plaintiffs' entry into the market for the digital downloading of music. . . .

### D. Contributory Copyright Infringement

**1.** Once they have shown direct infringement by Napster users, plaintiffs must demonstrate a likelihood of success on their contributory infringement claim. A contributory infringer is "one who, with knowledge of the infringing activity, induces, causes or materially contributes to the infringing conduct of another." Courts do not require actual knowledge; rather, a defendant incurs contributory copyright liability if he has reason to know of the third party's direct infringement.

**2.** Plaintiffs present convincing evidence that Napster executives actually knew about and sought to protect use of the service to transfer illegal MP3 files. For example, a document authored by cofounder Sean Parker mentions the need to remain ignorant of users' real names and IP addresses "since they are exchanging *pirated* music." The same document states that, in bargaining with the RIAA, defendant will benefit from the fact that "we are not just making *pirated* music available but also pushing demand." These admissions suggest that facilitating the unauthorized exchange of copyrighted music was a central part of Napster Inc.'s business strategy from the inception.

Plaintiffs also demonstrate that defendant had actual notice of direct infringement because the RIAA informed it of more than

12,000 infringing files. Although Napster Inc. purportedly terminated the users offering these files, the songs are still available using the Napster service, as are the copyrighted works which the record company plaintiffs identified in Schedules A and B of their complaint. . . .

### E. Vicarious Copyright Infringement

*1.* Even in the absence of an employment relationship, a defendant incurs liability for vicarious copyright infringement if he "has the right and ability to supervise the infringing activity and also has a direct financial interest in such activities."

*2.* In Fonovisa, the swap meet operator satisfied the first element of vicarious liability because it had the right to terminate vendors at will; it also controlled customers' access and promoted its services. Although Napster Inc. argues that it is technologically difficult, and perhaps infeasible, to distinguish legal and illegal conduct, plaintiffs have shown that defendant supervises Napster use. Indeed, Napster Inc. itself takes pains to inform the court of its improved methods of blocking users about whom rights holders complain. This is tantamount to an admission that defendant can, and sometimes does, police its service. . . .

Moreover, a defendant need not exercise its supervisory powers to be deemed capable of doing so. The court therefore finds that Napster Inc. has the right and ability to supervise its users' infringing conduct.

*3.* Plaintiffs have shown a reasonable likelihood that Napster Inc. has a direct financial interest in the infringing activity. Citing several non-governing cases from other districts, they contend that direct financial benefit does not require earned revenue, so long as the defendant has economic incentives for tolerating unlawful behavior.

Although Napster Inc. currently generates no revenue, its internal documents state that it "will drive [sic] revenues directly from increases in user base." The Napster service attracts more and more users by offering an increasing amount of quality music for free. It hopes to "monetize" its user base through one of several generation revenue models noted in the factual findings. . . .

*4.* Plaintiffs have shown a reasonable likelihood of success on their vicarious infringement claims. . . .

### J. Irreparable Harm

*1.* Because plaintiffs have shown a reasonable likelihood of success on the merits of their contributory and vicarious copyright infringement claims, they are entitled to a presumption of irreparable harm.

*2.* The court rejects defendant's contention that it has rebutted this presumption by demonstrating that any harm is *de minimis*. The declarations of record company executives, combined with the Teece Report, establish that plaintiffs have invested in the digital downloading market and that their business plans are threatened by a service that offers the same product for free. Moreover, while the court recognizes the limitations of a survey that only targets college students, the Jay Report suggests the tendency of Napster use to suppress CD purchases, especially among heavy users.

### K. Balance of the Hardships

*1.* The court cannot give much weight to defendant's lament that the requested relief will put it out of business. Although even a narrow injunction may so fully eviscerate Napster Inc. as to destroy its user base or make its service technologically infeasible, the business interests of an infringer do not trump a rights holder's entitlement to copyright protection. Nor does defendant's supposed inability to separate infringing and noninfringing elements of its service constitute a valid reason for denying plaintiffs relief or for issuing a stay.

Any destruction of Napster Inc. by a preliminary injunction is speculative compared to the statistical evidence of massive, unauthorized downloading and uploading of plaintiffs' copyrighted works—as many as 10,000 files per second, by defendant's own admission. The court has every reason to believe that, without a preliminary injunction, these numbers will mushroom as Napster users, and newcomers attracted by the publicity, scramble to obtain as much free music as possible before trial. . . .

### III. Conclusion

For the foregoing reasons, the court GRANTS plaintiffs' motion for a preliminary injunction against Napster Inc. Defendant is hereby preliminarily ENJOINED from engaging in, or facilitating others in copying, downloading, uploading, transmitting, or distributing plaintiffs' copyrighted musical compositions and sound recordings, protected by either federal or state law, without express permission of the rights owner. This injunction applies to all such works that plaintiffs own; it is not limited to those listed in Schedules A and B of the complaint.

Plaintiffs have shown persuasively that they own the copyrights to more than 70 percent of the music available on the Napster system. Because defendant has contributed to illegal copying on a scale that is without precedent, it bears the burden of developing a means to comply with the injunction. Defendant must insure that no work owned by plaintiffs which neither defendant nor Napster users have permission to use or distribute is uploaded or downloaded on Napster. The court ORDERS plaintiffs to cooperate with defendant in identifying the works to which they own copyrights. To this end, plaintiffs must file a written plan no later than September 5, 2000, describing the most expedient method by which their rights can be ascertained. The court also ORDERS plaintiffs to post a bond for the sum of $5,000,000.00 to compensate defendant for its losses in the event that this injunction is reversed or vacated.

IT IS SO ORDERED.

## NOTES

1. The court's memorandum and order regarding the admissibility of expert reports includes a detailed discussion of flaws in the Fader Report. Among the shortcomings the court noted are Fader's heavy reliance on journalistic articles and studies that he did not conduct, the fact the centerpiece of his repor is a survey that he only distantly supervised, and the lack of tables offering statistical breakdowns of survey respondents and their answers.

2. Fine's study tracked retail music sales trends in three types of stores in the United States: (1) all stores located within 1 mile of any college or university on a list acquired from Quality Education Data; (2) all stores located within 1 mile of any college or university on a list of colleges and universities that have banned Napster use; (3) all stores within 1 mile of any college or university listed among the "Top 40 Most Wired Colleges in 1999," according to Yahoo Internet Life. Researchers working on the Fine Report used Soundscan Point of Sale data to compare music sales totals from the latter two categories with (1) national totals and (2) sales from the first category, "All College Stores." The report tracked retail sales in the first quarter ("Q1") of 1997, 1998, 1999, and 2000.

# World Trade Organization

## I. AGREEMENT ON TRADE–RELATED ASPECTS OF INTELLECTUAL PROPERTY RIGHTS

*Desiring* to reduce distortions and impediments to international trade, and taking into account the need to promote effective and adequate protection of intellectual property rights, and to ensure that measures and procedures to enforce intellectual property rights do not themselves become barriers to legitimate trade;

*Recognizing*, to this end, the need for new rules and disciplines concerning:

(a) the applicability of the basic principles of GATT 1994 and of relevant international intellectual property agreements or conventions;

(b) the provision of adequate standards and principles concerning the availability, scope and use of trade-related intellectual property rights;

(c) the provision of effective and appropriate means for the enforcement of trade-related intellectual property rights, taking into account differences in national legal systems;

(d) the provision of effective and expeditious procedures for the multilateral prevention and settlement of disputes between governments; and

(e) transitional arrangements aiming at the fullest participation in the results of the negotiations;

*Recognizing* the need for a multilateral framework of principles, rules and disciplines dealing with international trade in counterfeit goods;

*Recognizing* that intellectual property rights are private rights;

*Recognizing* the underlying public policy objectives of national systems for the protection of intellectual property, including developmental and technological objectives;

*Recognizing* also the special needs of the least-developed country Members in respect of maximum flexibility in the domestic implementation of laws and regulations in order to enable them to create a sound and viable technological base;

*Emphasizing* the importance of reducing tensions by reaching strengthened commitments to resolve disputes on trade-related intellectual property issues through multilateral procedures;

*Desiring* to establish a mutually supportive relationship between the WTO and the World Intellectual Property Organization (referred to in this Agreement as "WIPO") as well as other relevant international organizations;

*Hereby agree* as follows:

## PART I GENERAL PROVISIONS AND BASIC PRINCIPLES

### Article 1 Nature and Scope of Obligations

1. Members shall give effect to the provisions of this Agreement. Members may, but shall not be obliged to, implement in their law more extensive protection than is required by this Agreement, provided that such protection does not contravene the provisions of this Agreement. Members shall be free to determine the appropriate method of implementing the provisions of this Agreement within their own legal system and practice. . . .

### Article 7 Objectives

The protection and enforcement of intellectual property rights should contribute to the promotion of technological innovation and to the transfer and dissemination of technology, to the mutual advantage of producers and

Annex 1C of the *Marrakesh Agreement Establishing the World Trade Organization*, April 15, 1994.

users of technological knowledge and in a manner conducive to social and economic welfare, and to a balance of rights and obligations.

### Article 8 Principles

1. Members may, in formulating or amending their laws and regulations, adopt measures necessary to protect public health and nutrition, and to promote the public interest in sectors of vital importance to their socioeconomic and technological development, provided that such measures are consistent with the provisions of this Agreement.
2. Appropriate measures, provided that they are consistent with the provisions of this Agreement, may be needed to prevent the abuse of intellectual property rights by right holders or the resort to practices which unreasonably restrain trade or adversely affect the international transfer of technology.

## PART II STANDARDS CONCERNING THE AVAILABILITY, SCOPE AND USE OF INTELLECTUAL PROPERTY RIGHTS

## SECTION 1: COPYRIGHT AND RELATED RIGHTS

### Article 11 Rental Rights

In respect of at least computer programs and cinematographic works, a Member shall provide authors and their successors in title the right to authorize or to prohibit the commercial rental to the public of originals or copies of their copyright works. A Member shall be excepted from this obligation in respect of cinematographic works unless such rental has led to widespread copying of such works which is materially impairing the exclusive right of reproduction conferred in that Member on authors and their successors in title. In respect of computer programs, this obligation does not

apply to rentals where the program itself is not the essential object of the rental.

### Article 12 Term of Protection

Whenever the term of protection of a work, other than a photographic work or a work of applied art, is calculated on a basis other than the life of a natural person, such term shall be no less than 50 years from the end of the calendar year of authorized publication, or, failing such authorized publication within 50 years from the making of the work, 50 years from the end of the calendar year of making.

### Article 13 Limitations and Exceptions

Members shall confine limitations or exceptions to exclusive rights to certain special cases which do not conflict with a normal exploitation of the work and do not unreasonably prejudice the legitimate interests of the right holder.

### Article 14 Protection of Performers, Producers of Phonograms (Sound Recordings) and Broadcasting Organizations

1. In respect of a fixation of their performance on a phonogram, performers shall have the possibility of preventing the following acts when undertaken without their authorization: the fixation of their unfixed performance and the reproduction of such fixation. Performers shall also have the possibility of preventing the following acts when undertaken without their authorization: the broadcasting by wireless means and the communication to the public of their live performance.
2. Producers of phonograms shall enjoy the right to authorize or prohibit the direct or indirect reproduction of their phonograms.
3. Broadcasting organizations shall have the right to prohibit the following acts when undertaken without their authorization: the fixation, the reproduction of fixations, and the

rebroadcasting by wireless means of broadcasts, as well as the communication to the public of television broadcasts of the same. . . .

5. The term of the protection available under this Agreement to performers and producers of phonograms shall last at least until the end of a period of 50 years computed from the end of the calendar year in which the fixation was made or the performance took place. The term of protection granted pursuant to paragraph 3 shall last for at least 20 years from the end of the calendar year in which the broadcast took place. . . .

# SECTION 2: TRADEMARKS

## Article 15 Protectable Subject Matter

1. Any sign, or any combination of signs, capable of distinguishing the goods or services of one undertaking from those of other undertakings, shall be capable of constituting a trademark. Such signs, in particular words including personal names, letters, numerals, figurative elements and combinations of colors as well as any combination of such signs, shall be eligible for registration as trademarks. Where signs are not inherently capable of distinguishing the relevant goods or services, Members may make registrability depend on distinctiveness acquired through use. Members may require, as a condition of registration, that signs be visually perceptible. . . .

## Article 16 Rights Conferred

1. The owner of a registered trademark shall have the exclusive right to prevent all third parties not having the owner's consent from using in the course of trade identical or similar signs for goods or services which are identical or similar to those in respect of which the trademark is registered where such use would result in a likelihood of confusion. In case of the use of an identical sign for identical goods or services, a likelihood of confusion shall be presumed. The rights described above shall not prejudice any existing prior rights, nor shall they affect the possibility of Members making rights available on the basis of use. . . .

# SECTION 5: PATENTS

## Article 27 Patentable Subject Matter

1. Subject to the provisions of paragraphs 2 and 3, patents shall be available for any inventions, whether products or processes, in all fields of technology, provided that they are new, involve an inventive step and are capable of industrial application. . . .

2. Members may exclude from patentability inventions, the prevention within their territory of the commercial exploitation of which is necessary to protect *ordre public* or morality, including to protect human, animal or plant life or health or to avoid serious prejudice to the environment, provided that such exclusion is not made merely because the exploitation is prohibited by their law.

3. Members may also exclude from patentability:

   (a) diagnostic, therapeutic and surgical methods for the treatment of humans or animals;

   (b) plants and animals other than microorganisms, and essentially biological processes for the production of plants or animals other than nonbiological and microbiological processes. However, Members shall provide for the protection of plant varieties either by patents or by an effective *sui generis* system or by any combination thereof. The provisions of this subparagraph shall be reviewed 4 years after the date of entry into force of the WTO Agreement.

## Article 28 Rights Conferred

1. A patent shall confer on its owner the following exclusive rights:

   (a) where the subject matter of a patent is a product, to prevent third parties not having the owner's consent from the acts of: making, using, offering for sale, selling, or importing for these purposes that product;

   (b) where the subject matter of a patent is a process, to prevent third parties not having the owner's consent from the act of using the process, and from the acts of: using, offering for sale, selling, or importing for these purposes at least the product obtained directly by that process.

2. Patent owners shall also have the right to assign, or transfer by succession, the patent and to conclude licensing contracts.

## Article 30 Exceptions to Rights Conferred

Members may provide limited exceptions to the exclusive rights conferred by a patent, provided that such exceptions do not unreasonably conflict with a normal exploitation of the patent and do not unreasonably prejudice the legitimate interests of the patent owner, taking account of the legitimate interests of third parties. . . .

## Article 31 Other Use Without Authorization of the Right Holder

Where the law of a Member allows for other use of the subject matter of a patent without the authorization of the right holder, including use by the government or third parties authorized by the government, the following provisions shall be respected:

(a) authorization of such use shall be considered on its individual merits;

(b) such use may only be permitted if, prior to such use, the proposed user has made efforts to obtain authorization from the right holder on reasonable commercial terms and conditions and that such efforts have not been successful within a reasonable period of time. This requirement may be waived by a Member in the case of a national emergency or other circumstances of extreme urgency or in cases of public noncommercial use. In situations of national emergency or other circumstances of extreme urgency, the right holder shall, nevertheless, be notified as soon as reasonably practicable. In the case of public noncommercial use, where the government or contractor, without making a patent search, knows or has demonstrable grounds to know that a valid patent is or will be used by or for the gov-

ernment, the right holder shall be informed promptly;

(c) the scope and duration of such use shall be limited to the purpose for which it was authorized. . . .

(f) any such use shall be authorized predominantly for the supply of the domestic market of the Member authorizing such use;

(g) authorization for such use shall be liable, subject to adequate protection of the legitimate interests of the persons so authorized, to be terminated if and when the circumstances which led to it cease to exist and are unlikely to recur. The competent authority shall have the authority to review, upon motivated request, the continued existence of these circumstances;

(h) the right holder shall be paid adequate remuneration in the circumstances of each case, taking into account the economic value of the authorization;

(i) the legal validity of any decision relating to the authorization of such use shall be subject to judicial review or other independent review by a distinct higher authority in that Member.

(j) any decision relating to the remuneration provided in respect of such use shall be subject to judicial review or other independent review by a distinct higher authority in that Member;

# II. DECLARATION ON THE TRIPS AGREEMENT AND PUBLIC HEALTH

1. We recognize the gravity of the public health problems afflicting many developing and least-developed countries, especially those resulting from HIV/AIDS, tuberculosis, malaria and other epidemics.

2. We stress the need for the WTO Agreement on Trade-Related Aspects of Intellectual Property Rights (TRIPS Agreement) to be part of the wider national and international action to address these problems.

3. We recognize that intellectual property protection is important for the development of new medicines. We also recognize the concerns about its effects on prices.

4. We agree that the TRIPS Agreement does not and should not prevent Members from taking

measures to protect public health. Accordingly, while reiterating our commitment to the TRIPS Agreement, we affirm that the Agreement can and should be interpreted and implemented in a manner supportive of WTO Members' right to protect public health and, in particular, to promote access to medicines for all.

In this connection, we reaffirm the right of WTO Members to use, to the full, the provisions in the TRIPS Agreement, which provide flexibility for this purpose.

5. Accordingly and in the light of paragraph 4 above, while maintaining our commitments in the TRIPS Agreement, we recognize that these flexibilities include:

   (a) In applying the customary rules of interpretation of public international law, each provision of the TRIPS Agreement shall be read in the light of the object and purpose of the Agreement as expressed, in particular, in its objectives and principles.

   (b) Each Member has the right to grant compulsory licences and the freedom to determine the grounds upon which such licences are granted.

   (c) Each Member has the right to determine what constitutes a national emergency or other circumstances of extreme urgency, it being understood that public health crises, including those relating to HIV/AIDS, tuberculosis, malaria and other epidemics, can represent a national emergency or other circumstances of extreme urgency.

   (d) The effect of the provisions in the TRIPS Agreement that are relevant to the exhaustion of intellectual property rights is to leave each Member free to establish its own regime for such exhaustion without challenge, subject to the MFN and national treatment provisions of Articles 3 and 4.

# CASES

# CASE 1.   *Privacy Pressures: The Use of Web Bugs at HomeConnection*

As Matthew Scott, president of HomeConnection, sat in his office waiting for several members of his executive team to arrive, he grew more worrisome about a story featuring his company in the morning paper. His impulse was to fight back and go on the defensive, but Scott knew that he had to be careful. However, he did not accept the article's implicit conclusion that HomeConnection had no regard for the privacy rights of its customers, and he was anxious to hear what his colleagues had to say about the matter.

HomeConnection was an Internet Service Provider (ISP) with several million customers, primarily clustered in the mid-West. An ISP links people and businesses to the Internet, usually for a monthly fee. HomeConnection was much smaller than the industry leader, America OnLine (AOL), but it was still seen as a formidable player in this industry. Thanks to Scott's management, the company had recorded increasing profits for the past 3 years, 1999 through 2002. One feature that attracted customers was the opportunity to create their own personal Web page. HomeConnection made this process easy and convenient.

In the past year HomeConnection had devised an innovative promotion to help increase its subscriber base. The company encouraged its users with their own personal Web pages to carry an ad for HomeConnection. The ad would offer new subscribers a heavily discounted rate for the first year of membership. In addition, as an incentive to display the ad on their personal Web pages, the company agreed to pay its users $25 for any new members who signed up for a subscription by clicking on the ad. The response to the promotion was stronger than expected, and HomeConnection's membership had risen by over 6.5 percent since the program's inception 8 months ago. Scott was quite enthused about the results, and he did not anticipate that one aspect of the program would attract some negative attention.

In consultation with his marketing manager, Scott had authorized the use of Web bugs so that when users placed the ad on their Web pages they would also get a Web bug. A Web bug is embedded as a minuscule and invisible picture on the screen and it can track everything one does on a particular Web site. Web bugs, also called "Web beacons," are usually deployed to count visitors to a Web site or to gather cumulative data about visitors to those sites without tracking any personal details. In this case the Web bug transmitted information to a major online ad agency, DoubleDealer. DoubleDealer would collect data about those who visited these Web pages, which ads they clicked on, and so forth.

The newspaper report cited HomeConnection as well as other ISPs and e-commerce sites for using this protocol without the permission of their customers. They quoted a well-known privacy expert: "It's extremely disturbing that these companies are using technology to gather information in such a clandestine manner; I don't see how it can be morally justified." The article had clearly resonated with some of HomeConnecton's users, and the switchboard had been busy most of the afternoon with calls from irate customers. Some wanted to cancel their subscription.

Scott felt that the company had done nothing wrong but was a victim of a pervasive paranoia about privacy. HomeConnection was not using these bugs for any untoward purposes—its purpose was to track the results of the advertising promotion, that is, how many people were clicking on these ads. Also, Scott himself had modified the company's privacy policy to indicate that Web bugs might be used sometimes. (However, there was no indication that Web bugs would be placed on the personal Web pages of its user base.)

As several of his managers made their way into the conference room adjoining his office, Scott made one last check with customer service. By now it was late in the day and the volume of calls and e-mails was dying down. It was now up to Scott to determine a response—did the company face a serious problem or was this just a tempest in a teapot?

### Questions*

1. Has HomeConnection's use of the Web bug violated the privacy of those who agreed to display the ad on their personal computers? Has the privacy of those who visit the site and click on the ad been violated?

2. Should those who display the ad on their personal computers have the right to refuse to have the Web bugs attached? In other words should they be allowed to have the right to opt-out of this arrangement?

3. Suppose a person who displays the ad agrees to the Web bug. Should that person be required to place a statement on his or her personal Web site indicating that persons clicking on the ad may receive further advertisements from a number of sources?

*Questions added by the editor.

# CASE 2.   *Spiders at the Auction*

eBay Inc. is one of the largest and most successful commercial sites on the entire World Wide Web. Founded in 1995, eBay introduced consumers to a consumer business model that brings buyers and sellers together in an engaging auction format in order to buy and sell many different items such as coins, consumer electronics, antiques, appliances, and so forth. Products sold on the Web site can range from a $1 baseball card to a $578,000 Shoeless Joe Jackson's baseball bat. With 38 million customers, sales for 2002 were projected to be $1 billion returning a net income of $150 million. eBay carries no inventory so it can keep costs low. But the biggest reason for success derives from the fact that eBay is "a master at harnessing the awesome power of the Net—not just to let customers sound off directly in the ears of the big brass, but to track their every movement so new products and services are tailored to just what customers want."[1]

eBay has had several disputes with auction aggregator services which accumulate data from different auction sites so that a consumer can see what is available at all these different sites. The advantage for the buyer is the ability to see if a product available on eBay might be available at a lower asking price on a different site. One such dispute occurred in 1999 with an aggregator service known as AuctionWatch. The AuctionWatch site offers a "Universal Search Function" which allows users to access the price, product, description, and bidding history from popular auction sites such as eBay, Yahoo, and amazon.com. For example, if a user was interested in Boston Red Sox baseball memorabilia, that individual could check the AuctionWatch site to ascertain all of the Red Sox memorabilia available for auction across multiple sites.

AuctionWatch relied on spider technology to locate this data at these different auction sites. A spider is a robotic search engine that can crawl through sites many times a day to extract shopping data. According to Karen Solomon, "The benefits of bots for consumers are indisputable, but some merchants are less than thrilled about the technology's parasitic presence."[2]

eBay officials were certainly "less than thrilled" with AuctionWatch's constant forays into its computer system. They asked the company to stop, but it refused to contain its auction bot activities. eBay claimed that its auction data was proprietary, though that data was not eligible for any copyright protection. eBay also argued that the auction bots burdened its servers and perhaps impeded performance for its regular customers.

Given AuctionWatch's categorical refusal to curtail its intrusive activities, eBay executives met with their lawyers to discuss the next step. Should they simply allow the auction bot to continue? Should they pursue legal action? One possible legal angle to deter AuctionWatch was to accuse it of "trespass to chattels." Trespass to chattels represents a tort action for the unauthorized theft, use, or interference with another's tangible property.[3] But was this bot really "trespassing" on eBay's property, including its servers? Hasn't eBay made its Web site available to the public on this public network?

---

*Case Studies in Information Technology Ethics*, 2nd ed., by Richard A. Spinello, copyright 2002. Reprinted by permission of Pearson Education, Inc., Upper Saddle River, NJ.

# NOTES

1. R. Hof, "The People's Company," *Business Weeke.biz* (December 3, 2001): 15.
2. K. Solomon, "Revenge of the Bots," *Industry Standard* (November 29, 1999): 263.
3. Restatement (Second) of Torts, Sections 217–18 (1965).

## Questions*

1. Does the fact that eBay can track the movements of those who visit their site violate the visitor's right to privacy?

2. Should eBay's auction data be considered proprietary and thus be protected as intellectual property? Or should that data be considered public property, since eBay's data are available to eBay's customers?

3. Would you agree with eBay that these "spiders" are thieves?

*Questions supplied by the editor.

# CASE 3.  *Ditto.Com*

Ditto.com, a small company formerly known as Arriba Software, operates a popular visual search engine at the Web site www.ditto.com. In response to queries from users, Ditto.com will retrieve images instead of text. It produces a list of "thumbnail" pictures that are relevant to the user's query. While this functionality provides a valuable service to consumers, it has generated considerable controversy about the scope of intellectual property protection for online photographs and images.

Ditto.com's Web site includes a massive search index with over 6 million entries. Each entry is a thumbnail image that has been acquired through the use of Ditto's spider,[1] which crawls its way through media Web sites that collect and store photographs or other images. According to the company's Web site, once the crawler does its work, "we then select, rank, weight, filter, and rate pictures, illustrations, clipart, photographs, drawings and other image-related material; next we index the images

from the Web site."[2] All of this is done without the permission of the artist or photographer who created the image. When a user initiates a query, he or she receives the list of reduced thumbnail pictures ranked and in order of relevance. When the user clicks on one of these retrieved thumbnail images, two windows appear on the user's screen: The first is a stand-alone copy of a full-size image and the second contains the complete originating Web page where that image appeared.

The Ditto.com program presents two sets of problems for some artists and photographers. Some object to the fact that their works were indexed by Ditto.com without their knowledge or permission. They argue that when search engines like Ditto.com display images without their permission and out of context, there is copyright infringement. There are also objections to Ditto's "deep linking" to the originating Web page for the image; this deep linking bypasses the home page which often includes advertisements and other promotional messages.

And there has been at least one lawsuit filed against Ditto.com. Leslie Kelly is a photographer from Huntington California who operates a Web site called www.goldrush1849.com. This site provides users with a virtual photographic tour of Sacramento and the California gold rush country. According to court documents, 35 of Kelly's photographs have been indexed in the Ditto.com image database with thumbnail versions made available to Ditto's users. Kelly filed suit for copyright infringement, arguing that Ditto.com had no right to copy and distribute his copyrighted photos without his explicit permission. In late 1999 a federal judge ruled in Ditto.com's favor, but the case has been appealed to the United States Court of Appeals for the Ninth Circuit.

At issue is whether the reduced size of the images (i.e., thumbnail versions) exempts them from copyright infringement. Specifically, is Ditto.com's use of these images tantamount to "fair use"? In copyright law fair use is a limitation on the copyright owner's exclusive right "to reproduce the copyrighted work in copies."[3] There are four factors to be considered in a fair-use decision:

1. Purpose and character of the use. (Is the use commercial or for nonprofit or educational purposes?; in general, there is a bias against commercial use.)
2. Nature of the copyrighted work. (Creative works tend to receive more protection than factual ones.)
3. Amount and "substantiality of the portion used in relation to the copyrighted work as a whole."
4. Effects on the potential market for the copyrighted work.[4]

In this controversial case, the judge concluded that the search engine's activities amounted to "fair use" of the copyrighted images for several reasons. Judge Taylor concluded that while the use was commercial, "it was also

of a somewhat more incidental and less exploitative nature than more traditional types of commercial use."[5] The judge also found that Ditto.com's use was significantly transformative, that is, it adds something new or alters the original with a new expression. This is a highly significant factor given the Supreme Court's ruling in *Campbell v. Acuff-Rose.* "The more transformative the new work, the less will be the significance of other factors, like commercialism, that may weigh against a finding of fair use."[6] According to Judge Taylor, Ditto.com's use is notably different from the use for which the images were created: "Plaintiff's photographs are artistic works used for illustrative purposes. Defendant's visual search engine is designed to catalog and improve access to images on the Internet."[7] Judge Taylor also found that there would most likely not be a negative commercial impact, since Ditto.com's activities would actually bring more users to the Web sites where the images are located. While factors (2) and (3) did weigh against the fair-use defense, Judge Taylor felt that on the whole this case passed the fair use test especially because the "defendant's purposes were and are inherently transformative."[8]

Despite Judge Taylor's ruling, this case raises some nagging moral and legal questions. Is Ditto.com's functionality similar to Napster's as some have alleged? Does it allow users to steal online art, since they can view and download images without even visiting the originating Web site? Does it support wholesale visual plagiarism? Does the reduced size of the image represent a real transformation of the original as Judge Taylor has maintained? If not, is the fair-use defense really tenable here? Is the deep linking to the originating Web site morally acceptable in this case?

## NOTES

1. A spider is an automated program that "crawls" through Web sites looking for certain information.

2. Available at www.ditto.com/about_us.asp.
3. 17 U.S.C. §106 (1).
4. 17 U.S.C. §107.
5. *Leslie A. Kelly et al. v. Arriba Soft Corp.*, 77 F. Supp. 2d 1116; U.S. Dist. (1999).
6. *Campbell v. Acuff-Rose*, 510 U.S. 569 (1994).
7. *Kelly v. Arriba.*
8. Ibid.

**Questions***

1. Should the photographs that are "found" on the Internet and reduced in size by Ditto.com be considered the intellectual property of the photographer and thus subject to copyright protection?

2. Do you agree with the cited court opinions that reducing the image is sufficient for a transformation such that the photographs do not deserve copyright protection?

3. Is Ditto.com's indexing of the photographs without the permission of the artists who made them a violation of the artist's property rights in the photographs he or she takes?

*Questions supplied by editor.

# CASE 4.   *Patents and the African AIDS Epidemic*

## INTRODUCTION

Today, more than 38.6 million people are suffering from AIDS. In 2005, AIDS killed more than 3 million people. One-third of those killed lived in sub-Saharan Africa.[1] In an attempt to garner such much needed economic stimulation and improve trade relations with the developed world, most sub-Saharan African nations have joined the World Trade Organization, an offshoot of the United Nations. One of the qualifications for membership in the WTO, is ratification of the Agreement on Trade-Related Aspects of Intellectual Property Rights (TRIPS). TRIPS requires member nations "to make patents available for any inventions, whether products or processes, in all fields of technology without discrimination, subject to the normal tests of novelty, inventiveness and industrial applicability."[2]

## DRUG PATENTS

One major consequence of this agreement is that these countries must honor patents covering antiretroviral (ARV) drugs used for the treatment of AIDS. Unfortunately, the pharmaceutical companies who own the patents on these drugs have found it most profitable to sell a relatively small number of their drugs at a large premium in the developed world. Consequently, patients in developing countries are often denied treatment because they cannot afford to purchase drugs at first world prices and the monopoly protection granted by these patents precludes the production of generic alternatives. If such generic alternatives were available at a reasonable price, the impact would be enormous. In the United States, ARV drugs have reduced the AIDS mortality rate by 75 percent in three years.[3]

## COMPULSORY LICENSING

In response to pressure from AIDS-afflicted nations and human rights groups, several large pharmaceutical companies dramatically reduced prices on patented ARV drugs in May 2000. However no drugs were actually sold until October and it was found that even these reduced prices were much more than what most nations could afford.[4] In an attempt to make generic drugs available, several countries began to issue "compulsory" patent licenses. TRIPs permits these licenses to be issued without consent of the patent holder in situations of "national crisis". The Pharmaceutical industry responded by intensifying their lobbying efforts in the United States and the European Union. At the behest of the industry, the United States made several attempts to strongarm South Africa and Thailand into agreements that would curtail compulsory drug licenses. At one point South Africa and Thailand were even placed on the U.S. trade sanctions "watch list."[5]

## DOHA DECLARATION

Finally in November of 2001, the WTO released the Doha declaration to remedy the compulsory licensing situation. The Doha declaration clarifies parts of the TRIPS agreement to give countries more power to issue compulsory patent licenses in emergency situations. Under this declaration, sub-Saharan African nations were reassured of their ability to issue compulsory licenses for ARV drug patents so that generic alternatives could be made available.[6]

## FTAA AND TRIPS-PLUS

However, the battle between intellectual property holders and AIDS-afflicted nations wages on. Lobbyist pressure has caused the United States to continue to pursue more restrictive AIDS patent licensing measures in more recent agreements such as the U.S.–Jordan Free Trade Agreement and the Latin American Free Trade Agreement of the Americas. Meanwhile, Brazil has demonstrated the promise of generic ARV drugs. AIDS infection rates have been reduced to 1995 levels, and the cost of ARVs have been reduced by up to 80 percent over their patented equivalents.[7]

## NOTES

1. Wikipedia, AIDS, http://en.wikipedia.org/wiki/AIDS
2. World Trade Organization, TRIPS Overview, http://www.wto.org/english/tratop_e/trips_e/intel2_e.htm
3. World Intellectual Property Organization, Patent Protection and Access to HIV/AIDS Pharmaceuticals in sub-Saharan Africa, http://www.wipo.org/about-ip/en/studies/pdf/iipi_hiv.pdf
4. Ibid.
5. Human Rights News, "The FTAA, Access to HIV/AIDS Treatment, and Human Rights," http://www.hrw.org/press/2002/10/ftaa1029-bck.htmIII.%20TRIPS%20and%20Doha
6. Ibid.
7. World Intellectual Property Organization.

# CASE 5.  *Aventis: Partnerships for Health*

Pharmaceutical company Aventis focuses on the discovery and development of products such as prescription drugs, vaccines, and therapeutic proteins through it's business units Aventis Pharma and Aventis Pasteur.

Aventis's products are increasingly becoming essential tools in dealing with the many emerging and reemerging epidemics that threaten people the world over. However, in places where many of these epidemics are prevalent, the fight requires more than products. A lack of clinics and skilled personnel, insufficient supply chains, missing health insurance systems, and in some cases political unrest and violence make provision of health products complex.

However, there are institutions such as the World Health Organization (WHO) that have the capabilities and regional knowledge required, and it makes sense for companies like Aventis to share competencies with such bodies. Thus, Aventis teamed up with WHO and other groups to ensure that the products needed to tackle such epidemics reach those in need. Partnerships include the Global Alliance for Vaccines and Immunization (GAVI), the Global Polio Eradication Initiative, and the recently formed partnership to tackle African sleeping sickness.

Concerned about the disparity between the quantity and types of vaccines supplied in developed countries and those made available in developing countries, Aventis has become a partner in GAVI, which includes others in the vaccine industry, WHO, Unicef, the World Bank, governments of developing countries, and many OECD governments. The alliance was founded on the belief that protecting the health of children through immunization is a fundamental cornerstone for economic development and global security. Its goals are to improve access to sustainable immunization services; expand the use of safe, cost-effective vaccines where needed; accelerate the development and introduction of new vaccines and technologies; accelerate research and development efforts for vaccines needed primarily in developing countries; and make immunization coverage a centerpiece of international development efforts.

"For Aventis Pasteur, industry participation in the alliance is necessary to help ensure supply for these markets—and to make vaccines available to the 40 million to 70 million children born each year who would otherwise not have access to this preventive intervention," says Jacques Berger, Aventis Pasteur's senior vice president for corporate public policy. He points out that the vaccine industry is the only one that supplies large volumes of products to the poorest segment of the population at highly discounted prices. "This private–public alliance is a model for other basic-needs markets," he adds.

Aventis is also a partner in the Global Polio Eradication Initiative, launched in 1988 by WHO, Rotary International, the U.S. Centers for Disease Control, and UNICEF, with the goal of eliminating polio worldwide. Aventis Pasteur has launched a Web site (www.polio-vaccine.com) devoted to polio eradication. The trilingual site (in French, English and Spanish) provides current information about the disease. Between 2000 and 2002, Aventis Pasteur will be donating 50 million doses of oral polio vaccine to Angola, Liberia, Sierra Leone,

Somalia, and Southern Sudan. Since 1997, Aventis Pasteur has donated nearly 90 million doses of oral polio vaccine to African countries. "As the largest historical producer of polio vaccines, we have an obligation to contribute to the final assault on polio," says Jean-Jacques Bertrand, chairman and chief executive officer of Aventis Pasteur. "Today, when now more than ever polio eradication is within our reach, we believe that we must sustain this momentum and intensify our fight."

There is a dramatic resurgence of African trypanosomiasis, more commonly known as sleeping sickness, in sub-Saharan Africa. The disease is spreading in some of the poorest Central African communities, threatening more than 60 million people in 36 countries. It has become one of the greatest causes of mortality, ahead of HIV/AIDS in some provinces.

Aventis and WHO, working with medical humanitarian organization Médecins sans Frontières (MSF), designed a large-scale program to combat the disease. "This partnership is an example of a public–private partnership wanting to find viable solutions for life-threatening diseases," said Richard J. Markham, CEO of Aventis Pharma.

Aventis Pharma has committed $25 million to support WHO's activities in the field of African trypanosomiasis over a 5-year period. This is not a simple donation of products but rather a structured partnership that involves three related efforts to tackle the epidemic. Key pharmaceuticals will be provided to WHO, to be distributed by MSF. Aventis will also finance the acceleration of disease surveillance, control activities, and support new research. For any undertaking to be successful, it is necessary to address the integrated considerations of drug manufacturing and provision, as well as the ongoing treatment and needs of patients.

Aventis could not have tackled such programs alone. The company lacks the experience of working with patients in such affected areas; neither does it possess the capabilities to conduct the necessary surveillance and control of activities. The administration of drugs in some cases is also very demanding on the provider. For example, those affected by sleeping sickness require treatment four times a day, at 6-hour intervals for 1 month. WHO, however, possesses the capacity and experience and knows the affected regions. But they do not possesses the capacity to manufacture the treatment drugs. Clearly then, partnerships that bring together these necessary skills, experience, and capacities are required.

## Suggested Supplementary Readings

ANGELL, MARCIA. 2004. *The Truth About the Drug Companies.* New York: Random House.

AGRE, PHILIP, and MARC ROTENBERG, eds. 1997. *Technology and Privacy: The New Landscape.* Cambridge, MA: MIT Press.

ALDERMAN, JOHN. 2001. *Sonic Boom: Napster, MP3 and the New Pioneers of Music.* Cambridge, MA: Perseus.

BENNETT, CALON J., and REBECCA GRANT. 1999. *Visions of Privacy: Policy Choices for the Digital Age.* Toronto: University of Toronto Press.

BRANDEIS, LOUIS, and SAMUEL WARREN. "The Right to Privacy." *4, 193 Harvard Law Review,* 193 (1890).

BRIN, DAVID. 1998. *The Transparent Society.* Reading, MA: Addison-Wesley.

BURK, DAN L. 1994. "Transborder Intellectual Property Issues on the Electronic Frontier." *Stanford Law & Policy Review* 6 (1):9–16.

CHALYKOFF, JOHN, and NITIN NOHIRA. 1990. "Note on Electronic Monitoring." Boston, MA: *Harvard Business School Publications.*

DAVIS, RANDALL, PAMELA SAMUELSON, MITCHELL KAPOR, and JEROME REICHMAN. 1996. "A New View of Intellectual Property and Software." *Communications of the ACM* 39 (3) (March):21–30.

DeCew, Judith Wagner. 2003. *In Pursuit of Privacy, Law, Ethics and the Rise of Technology*. Ithaca, NY: Cornell University Press.

De George, Richard. 2003. *The Ethics of Information Technology and Business*. Oxford: Blackwell.

Etzioni, Amitai. 1999. *The Limits of Privacy*. New York: Basic Books.

Lessig, Lawrence. 2002. *The Future of Ideas: The Fate of the Commons in a Connected World*. New York: Vintage.

———. 2006. *Code: Version 2.0*. New York: Basic Books.

Lyon, David, and Elia Zureik, eds. 1996. *Computers, Surveillance, and Privacy*. Minneapolis: University of Minnesota Press.

Mason, Richard, and Mary Culnan. 1995. *Information and Responsibility: The Ethical Challenge*. Thousand Oaks, CA: Sage.

Moor, James. 1990. "The Ethics of Privacy Protection." *Library Trends* 39 (1–2):69–82.

Rosen, Jonathan. 2000. *The Unwanted Gaze*. New York: Random House.

Santoro, Michael A., and Thomas M. Gorrie, eds. 2005. *Ethics and the Pharmaceutical Industry*. Cambridge: Cambridge University Press.

Spinello, Richard. 2002. E-Mail and Panoptic Power in the Workplace. In *Perspectives on Business Ethics*, ed. L. Hartman. New York: McGraw-Hill.

"Symposium: Drugs for the Developing World." 2001. *Developing World Bioethics* 1 (1).

U.S. Congress, Office of Technology Assessment. 1992. "Finding a Balance: Computer Software, Intellectual Property, and the Challenge of Technological Change," OTA-TCT-527. Washington, DC: U.S. Government Printing Office.

Westin, Alan. 1967. *Privacy and Freedom*. New York: Atheneum.

Wright, Marie, and John Kahalik. 1997. "The Erosion of Privacy" *Computers and Society*, 27 (4) (December):22–26.

Chapter *8*

# Ethical Issues Regarding the Natural Environment

## INTRODUCTION

It is now widely recognized that we are in an environmental crisis. There is nearly unanimous agreement that the earth is getting warmer, and the consensus in the scientific community is that human activity, especially through activities that emit hydrocarbons, is the chief cause of climate change. Former Vice President Al Gore's documentary *An Inconvenient Truth* has raised public awareness of the dangers presented by global climate change. However, climate change is only the most prominent of the environmental issues facing us. Some species of fish, such as Atlantic cod, have been overfished to the extent that vast areas of the ocean that once contained millions of the species are now barren. Other fish popular with consumers, such as Chilean sea bass, swordfish, and orange roughy, are near extinction. Scientists predict that if present practices continue, all fisheries will collapse—falling below a critical mass that will not allow recovery—by 2048.[1] The dangers confronting fish populations are but one example of concerns about the future extinction of many plants and animals. In the United States and in most other nations old-growth forests, and the unique animal species that depend on such habitats for their survival, continue to be lost. The declining supply of freshwater is yet another concern. Overdevelopment in the Southwest and in Southern California has severely taxed the available water supply. The situation in the Southwest is similar to that in many parts of the world. Some believe that future wars will be fought over access to adequate water supplies. Lastly, the steady rise of gas prices over the past few years has awakened everyone to concerns about the future supply of oil and the changes we must make as the supply of oil inevitably declines.

In Europe, dealing with the environmental crisis is addressed at the highest levels of the European Union (EU). The EU has decreed that capitalism, and hence business practices within capitalism, should be environmentally sustainable. Financial success by itself is no longer sufficient. The sustainable corporation must be financially successful, but it must also be environmentally friendly and socially responsible. Thus, in the EU environmentally friendly business practices are considered a moral norm and consequently a moral obligation.

Although the United States has not made sustainable business a matter of public policy, many business leaders have argued that business must take a leadership role in responding to the environmental crisis. For example, in 2007 a group of 27 corporations and environmental organizations formed the United States Climate Action Partnership (USCAP) in response to inaction on the part of the Bush administration on climate change. USCAP is calling for national legislation that would require significant reductions in greenhouse gas emissions. Members of USCAP include Alcoa, BP America, General Electric, DuPont, PepsiCo and Shell. Also in 2007, the *Economist* magazine—whose normal editorial stance is consistent with Milton Friedman's stockholder view—published a special 15-page report on how businesses are responding to climate change.[2] The article pointed out that "very few serious businessmen will say publicly either that climate change is not happening or that it is not worth tackling."[3]

## ENVIRONMENTAL OBLIGATIONS

The view that business has an obligation to respond to environmental crises is becoming increasingly accepted. But what are the specific moral obligations of businesses regarding that natural environment? In the 1990s business contributions to a more sustainable environment began to emerge. Many practices of business had been wasteful and inefficient. Business leaders saw that waste was a cost and thus that eliminating waste, through recycling or alternative product development, was a good way to be more environmentally friendly and more profitable, not only in the long run but immediately. Even now there are many areas in which business could change its practices and be more profitable as a result. For instance, many escalators run day and night, yet there is technology that would have them on standby until an electronic eye sensed someone approaching. A similar technology would allow lights to be turned off in hallways and other public areas until people were actually present in the public space. Recently there has been a revolution in the technology of lightbulbs. Replacing incandescent bulbs with long-lasting compact fluorescent bulbs saves energy and money over the long run. Businesses would appear to have an obligation on grounds of both increasing profits and protecting the environment to switch to the new technology.

What other obligations do businesses have? In his article Norman Bowie offers a minimalist account of business obligations. He points out that business has a moral as well as legal obligation to obey all environmental laws. Although obedience to law is well recognized as a genuine obligation, there are many instances where environmental contamination has occurred that was in violation of the law. Beyond obedience to law, Bowie places much of the responsibility for protecting the environment on consumers. He argues that if consumers want more environmentally friendly products—products that are usually more costly—they will demand them. If there is a demand, business will step in to fulfill the demand. One of the problems facing business—especially in the United States— is that consumers traditionally have not been willing to pay the extra costs for environmentally friendly products and thus there has been insufficient demand. Beyond obeying environmental law and meeting consumer demand for environmentally friendly products, Bowie argues that businesses have two obligations with respect to the environment. First, business should not lobby against proposed environmental legislation. Bowie points out that environmental problems are nearly always public goods problems, and thus the political process is the appropriate place for consumers to express their preferences for a clean environment. Second, businesses have an obligation to utilize their considerable expertise regarding the causes of environmental harm to educate consumers about best practices regarding environmental protection.

Other writers have found Bowie's set of business obligations to protect the environment to be too narrow. In their contribution to this chapter, "Business, Ethics, and Global Climate Change," Denis Arnold and Keith Bustos criticize Bowie's position on numerous grounds. Arnold and Bustos use the example of the harm caused to the earth's environment by businesses via greenhouse gas emissions as the focal point of their analysis. They point out that there is a consensus among the world's scientists that anthropogenic carbon emissions are altering the earth's climate in ways that are harmful to present and future generations. They then argue that Bowie's argument fails for five reasons. Among these are that it is inapplicable in nondemocratic nations, that it fails to take into account harms caused to those who are powerless to change current practices, and that it overestimates the power of consumers to influence the environmental practices of businesses. Arnold and Bustos go on to argue that businesses ought to be held historically accountable for their greenhouse gas emissions from the point in recent history when anthropogenic climate change was discovered. They conclude with public policy recommendations intended to restrain those businesses that have not taken responsibility for their emissions.

In his essay "Sustainability: Business's New Environmental Obligation" Joseph DesJardins also criticizes Bowie's arguments. DesJardins argues that Bowie's position is the wrong way to think about the environmental obligations of business in the twenty-first century. Whereas Bowie seems to believe that environmentally friendly business practices typically impede profits, DesJardins argues for a model of sustainable business practices that include environmentally sustainable practices that are also profitable. His claim is not merely that this is good business but that businesses have an ethical obligation to conduct business in a sustainable manner. In support of his arguments he cites numerous examples of businesses that are already acting on the practices he advocates. Case studies on Unilever and Interface Corporation included in this chapter also highlight such proactive corporate responses to the global environmental crisis.

Dennis Cooley's contribution to this chapter concerns an environmental issue of paramount concern to many consumers in the United States, Canada, the United Kingdom, and Europe. This is the issue of genetically modified organisms (GMOs). Advances in genetic science now allow researchers to alter the genetic make-up of plants and animals. In crops these modifications can result in greater yields, pest resistance, drought resistance, and other properties beneficial to producers. However, many consumers fear negative consequences from consuming GMOs as well as the potential negative impact these technologies may have on citizens in the developing world. The EU has effectively banned the import of GMOs in response to pressure from European consumers and as a protectionist measure intended to keep out cheaper foreign crops. Cooley points out that the ethical debate over GMOs has mainly involved utilitarian arguments. Taking up the issues he argues that the best available scientific evidence supports the view that GMOs are on balance beneficial and that most fears about them are unjustified. His main conclusion is that there are good utilitarian reasons for supporting the use and sale of GMOs.

This chapter also includes two landmark environmental law cases from the U.S. Supreme Court. The 1998 case *U.S. v. Bestfoods et al.* deals with the issue of whether a parent corporation may be held liable for the polluting activities of one of its subsidiaries. The court maintained that liability depends on the level of active participation and control by the corporation, especially where wrongful purposes are involved (most notably fraud). This opinion explores several levels of corporate responsibility to avoid disposal of hazardous materials. The 2001 case *Whitman v. American Trucking Associations Inc.* concerns the issue of whether the administrator of the U.S. Environmental Protection Agency may take into consideration the cost to businesses of implementing congressionally mandated environmental standards. In this case trucking companies sought to weaken the enforcement of enhanced air quality standards. In ruling against the trucking companies the court maintained that in most cases involving congressional legislation the costs of implementation may not be taken into account. This case illustrates an increasingly rare business response to the environmental crisis that focuses on defeating legislation intended to protect the environment and human health. As we have seen, an alternative response is to seek proactive solutions that are simultaneously environmentally and economically sustainable.

## NOTES

1. Cornelia Dean, "Study Sees 'Global Collapse' of Fish Species," *New York Times* (November 2, 2006).
2. "Cleaning Up: A Special Report on Business and Climate Change," *Economist* (June 2, 2007).
3. Ibid., 3.

## BUSINESS AND ENVIRONMENTAL OBLIGATIONS

# Morality, Money, and Motor Cars

*Norman E. Bowie*

Environmentalists frequently argue that business has special obligations to protect the environment. Although I agree with the environmentalists on this point, I do not agree with them as to where the obligations lie. Business does not have an obligation to protect the environment over and above what is required by law; however, it does have a moral obligation to avoid intervening in the political arena in order to defeat or weaken environmental legislation. In developing this thesis, several points are in order. First, many businesses have violated important moral obligations, and the violation has had a severe negative impact on the environment. For example, toxic waste haulers have illegally dumped hazardous material, and the environment has been harmed as a result, One might argue that those toxic waste haulers who have illegally dumped have violated a special obligation to the environment. Isn't it more accurate to say that these toxic waste haulers have violated their obligation to obey the law and that in this case the law that has been broken is one pertaining to the environment? Businesses have an obligation to obey the law—environmental laws and all others. Since there are many well-publicized cases of business's having broken environmental laws, it is easy to think that business has violated some special obligations to the environment. In fact, what business has done is to disobey the law. Environmentalists do not need a special obligation to the environment to protect the environment against illegal business activity; they need only insist that business obey the laws.

Business has broken other obligations besides the obligation to obey the law and has harmed the environment as a result. Consider the grounding of the Exxon oil tanker *Valdez* in Alaska, That grounding was allegedly caused by the fact that an inadequately trained crewman was piloting the tanker while the captain was below deck and had been drinking. What needs to be determined is whether Exxon's policies and procedures were sufficiently lax so that it could be said Exxon was morally at fault. It might be that Exxon is legally responsible for the accident under the doctrine of respondent superior, but Exxon is not thereby morally responsible. Suppose, however, that Exxon's policies were so lax that the company could be characterized as morally negligent. In such a case, the company would violate its moral obligation to use due care and avoid negligence. Although its negligence was disastrous to the environment, Exxon would have violated no special obligation to the environment. It would have been morally negligent.

A similar analysis could be given to the environmentalists' charges that Exxon's cleanup procedures were inadequate. If the charge is true, either Exxon was morally at fault or not. If the procedures had not been implemented properly by Exxon employees, then Exxon is legally culpable, but not morally culpable. On the other hand, if Exxon lied to government officials by saying that its policies were in accord with regulations and/or were ready for emergencies of this type, then Exxon violated its moral obligation to tell the truth. Exxon's immoral conduct would have harmed the

---

From W. M. Hoffman, R. Frederick, and E. S. Petry Jr., eds. *Business, Ethics, and the Global Environment* (New York: Quosum Books, 1990), 89–97.

environment, but it violated no special obligation to the environment. More important, none is needed. Environmentalists, like government officials, employees, and stockholders, expect that business firms and officials have moral obligations to obey the law, avoid negligent behavior, and tell the truth. In sum, although many business decisions have harmed the environment, these decisions violated no environmental moral obligations. If a corporation is negligent in providing for worker safety, we do not say the corporation violated a special obligation to employees; we say that it violated its obligation to avoid negligent behavior.

The crucial issues concerning business obligations to the environment focus on the excess use of natural resources (the dwindling supply of oil and gas, for instance) and the externalities of production (pollution, for instance). The critics of business want to claim that business has some special obligation to mitigate or solve these problems. I believe this claim is largely mistaken. If business does have a special obligation to help solve the environmental crisis, that obligation results from the special knowledge that business firms have. If they have greater expertise than other constituent groups in society, then it can be argued that, other things being equal, business's responsibilities to mitigate the environmental crisis are somewhat greater. Absent this condition, business's responsibility is no greater than and may be less than that of other social groups. What leads me to think that the critics of business are mistaken?

William Frankena distinguished obligations in an ascending order of the difficulty in carrying them out; avoiding harm, preventing harm, and doing good.[1] The most stringent requirement, to avoid harm, insists no one has a right to render harm on another unless there is a compelling, overriding moral reason to do so. Some writers have referred to this obligation as the moral minimum. A corporation's

behavior is consistent with the moral minimum if it causes no avoidable harm to others.

Preventing harm is a less stringent obligation, but sometimes the obligation to prevent harm may be nearly as strict as the obligation to avoid harm. Suppose you are the only person passing a 2-foot-deep working pool where a young child is drowning. There is no one else in the vicinity. Don't you have a strong moral obligation to prevent the child's death? Our obligation to prevent harm is not unlimited, however. Under what conditions must we be good samaritans? Some have argued that four conditions must exist before one is obligated to prevent harm: capability, need, proximity, and last resort.[2] These conditions are all met with the case of the drowning child. There is obviously a need that you can meet since you are both in the vicinity and have the resources to prevent the drowning with little effort; you are also the last resort.

The least strict moral obligation is to do good—to make contributions to society or to help solve problems (inadequate primary schooling in the inner cities, for example). Although corporations may have some minimum obligation in this regard based on an argument from corporate citizenship, the obligations of the corporation to do good cannot be expanded without limit. An injunction to assist in solving societal problems makes impossible demands on a corporation because, at the practical level, it ignores the impact that such activities have on profit.

It might seem that even if this descending order of strictness of obligations were accepted, obligations toward the environment would fall into the moral minimum category. After all, the depletion of natural resources and pollution surely harm the environment. If so, wouldn't the obligations business has to the environment be among the strictest obligations a business can have?

Suppose, however, that a businessperson argues that the phrase "avoid harm" usually applies to human beings. Polluting a lake is not like injuring a human with a faulty product. Those who coined the phrase *moral minimum* for use in the business context defined harm as "particularly including activities which violate or frustrate the enforcement of rules of domestic or institutional law intended to protect individuals against prevention of health, safety or basic freedom."[3] Even if we do not insist that the violations be violations of a rule of law, polluting a lake would not count as a harm under this definition. The environmentalists would respond that it would. Polluting the lake may be injuring people who might swim in or eat fish from it. Certainly it would be depriving people of the freedom to enjoy the lake. Although the environmentalist is correct, especially if we grant the legitimacy of a human right to a clean environment, the success of this reply is not enough to establish the general argument.

Consider the harm that results from the production of automobiles. We know statistically that about 50,000 persons per year will die and than nearly 250,000 others will be seriously injured in automobile accidents in the United States alone. Such death and injury, which is harmful, is avoidable. If that is the case, doesn't the avoid-harm criterion require that the production of automobiles for profit cease? Not really. What such arguments point out is that some refinement of the moral minimum standard needs to take place. Take the automobile example. The automobile is itself a good-producing instrument. Because of the advantages of automobiles, society accepts the possible risks that go in using them. Society also accepts many other types of avoidable harm. We take certain risks—ride in planes, build bridges, and mine coal—to pursue advantageous goals. It seems that the high benefits of some activities justify the resulting harms. As long as the risks are known, it is not wrong that some avoidable harm be permitted so that other social and individual goals

can be achieved. The avoidable-harm criterion needs some sharpening.

Using the automobile as a paradigm, let us consider the necessary refinements for the avoid-harm criterion. It is a fundamental principle of ethics that "ought" implies "can." That expression means that you can be held morally responsible only for events within your power. In the ought-implies-can principle, the overwhelming majority of highway deaths and injuries are not the responsibility of the automaker. Only those deaths and injuries attributable to unsafe automobile design can be attributed to the automaker. The ought-implies-can principle can also be used to absolve the auto companies of responsibility for death and injury from safety defects that the automakers could not reasonably know existed. The company could not be expected to do anything about them.

Does this mean that a company has an obligation to build a car as safe as it knows how? No. The standards for safety must leave the product's cost within the price range of the consumer ("ought implies can" again). Comments about engineering and equipment capability are obvious enough. But for a business, capability is also a function of profitability. A company that builds a maximally safe car at a cost that puts it at a competitive disadvantage and hence threatens its survival is building a safe car that lies beyond the capability of the company.

Critics of the automobile industry will express horror at these remarks, for by making capability a function of profitability, society will continue to have avoidable deaths and injuries; however, the situation is not as dire as the critics imagine. Certainly, capability should not be sacrificed completely so that profits can be maximized. The decision to build products that are cheaper in cost but are not maximally safe is a social decision that has widespread support. The arguments occur over the line between safety and cost. What we have is a classical trade-off situation. What is desired is some appropriate mix between engineering safety and consumer demand. To say there must be some mix between engineering safety and consumer demand is not to justify all the decisions made by the automobile companies. Ford Motor Company made a morally incorrect choice in placing Pinto gas tanks where it did. Consumers were uninformed, the record of the Pinto in rear-end collisions was worse than that of competitors, and Ford fought government regulations.

Let us apply the analysis of the automobile industry to the issue before us. That analysis shows that an automobile company does not violate its obligation to avoid harm and hence is not in violation of the moral minimum if the trade-off between potential harm and the utility of the products rests on social consensus and competitive realities.

As long as business obeys the environmental laws and honors other standard moral obligations, most harm done to the environment by business has been accepted by society. Through their decisions in the marketplace, we can see that most consumers are unwilling to pay extra for products that are more environmentally friendly than less friendly competitive products. Nor is there much evidence that consumers are willing to conserve resources, recycle, or tax themselves for environmental causes.

Consider the following instances reported in the *Wall Street Journal*.[4] The restaurant chain Wendy's tried to replace foam plates and cups with paper, but customers in the test markets balked. Procter and Gamble offered Downey fabric softener in concentrated form that requires less packaging than ready-to-use products; however the concentrate version is less convenient because it has to be mixed with water. Sales have been poor. Procter and Gamble manufactures Vizir and Lenor brands of detergents in concentrate form, which the customer mixes at home in reusable bottles.

Europeans will take the trouble; Americans will not. Kodak tried to eliminate its yellow film boxes but met customer resistance. McDonald's has been testing mini-incinerators that convert trash into energy but often meets opposition from community groups that fear the incinerators will pollute the air. A McDonald's spokesperson points out that the emissions are mostly carbon dioxide and water vapor and are "less offensive than a barbecue." Exxon spent approximately $9,200,000 to "save" 230 otters ($40,000 for each otter). Otters in captivity cost $800. Fishermen in Alaska are permitted to shoot otters as pests.[5] Given these facts, doesn't business have every right to assume that public tolerance for environmental damage is quite high, and hence current legal activities by corporations that harm the environment do not violate the avoid-harm criterion?

Recently, environmentalists have pointed out the environmental damage caused by the widespread use of disposable diapers. Are Americans ready to give them up and go back to cloth diapers and the diaper pail? Most observers think not. Procter and Gamble is not violating the avoid-harm criterion by manufacturing Pampers. Moreover, if the public wants cloth diapers, business certainly will produce them. If environmentalists want business to produce products that are friendlier to the environment, they must convince Americans to purchase them. Business will respond to the market. It is the consuming public that has the obligation to make the trade-off between cost and environmental integrity.

Data and arguments of the sort described should give environmental critics of business pause. Nonetheless, these critics are not without counterresponses. For example, they might respond that public attitudes are changing. Indeed, they point out, during the Reagan deregulation era, the one area where the public supported government regulations was in the area of environmental law. In addition,

*Fortune* predicts environmental integrity as the primary demand of society on business in the 1990s.[6]

More important, they might argue that environmentally friendly products are at a disadvantage in the marketplace because they have public good characteristics. After all, the best situation for the individual is one where most other people use environmentally friendly products but he or she does not, hence reaping the benefit of lower cost and convenience. Since everyone reasons this way, the real demand for environmentally friendly products cannot be registered in the market. Everyone is understating the value of his or her preference for environmentally friendly products. Hence, companies cannot conclude from market behavior that the environmentally unfriendly products are preferred.

Suppose the environmental critics are right that the public goods characteristic of environmentally friendly products creates a market failure. Does that mean the companies are obligated to stop producing these environmentally unfriendly products? I think not, and I propose that we use the four conditions attached to the prevent-harm obligation to show why not. There is a need, and certainly corporations that cause environmental problems are in proximity. However, environmentally clean firms, if there are any, are not in proximity at all, and most business firms are not in proximity with respect to most environmental problems. In other words, the environmental critic must limit his or her argument to the environmental damage a business actually causes. The environmentalist might argue that Procter and Gamble ought to do something about Pampers; I do not see how an environmentalist can use the avoid-harm criterion to argue that Procter and Gamble should do something about acid rain. But even narrowing the obligation to damage actually caused will not be sufficient to establish an obligation to pull a product from the market because it

damages the environment or even to go beyond what is legally required to protect the environment. Even for damage actually done, both the high cost of protecting the environment and the competitive pressures of business make further action to protect the environment beyond the capability of business. This conclusion would be more serious if business were the last resort, but it is not.

Traditionally it is the function of the government to correct for market failure. If the market cannot register the true desires of consumers, let them register their preferences in the political arena. Even fairly conservative economic thinkers allow government a legitimate role in correcting market failure. Perhaps the responsibility for energy conservation and pollution control belongs with the government.

Although I think consumers bear a far greater responsibility for preserving and protecting the environment than they have actually exercised, let us assume that the basic responsibility rests with the government. Does that let business off the hook? No. Most of business's unethical conduct regarding the environment occurs in the political arena.

Far too many corporations try to have their cake and eat it too. They argue that it is the job of government to correct for market failure and then use their influence and money to defeat or water down regulations designed to conserve and protect the environment. They argue that consumers should decide how much conservation and protection the environment should have, and then they try to interfere with the exercise of that choice in the political arena. Such behavior is inconsistent and ethically inappropriate. Business has an obligation to avoid intervention in the political process for the purpose of defeating and weakening environmental regulations. Moreover, this is a special obligation to the environment since business does not have a general obligation to avoid pursuing its own parochial interests in the political arena. Business need do nothing wrong when it seeks to influence tariffs, labor policy, or monetary policy. Business does do something wrong when it interferes with the passage of environmental legislation. Why?

First, such a noninterventionist policy is dictated by the logic of the business's argument to avoid a special obligation to protect the environment. Put more formally:

1. Business argues that it escapes special obligations to the environment because it is willing to respond to consumer preferences in this matter.
2. Because of externalities and public goods considerations, consumers cannot express their preferences in the market.
3. The only other viable forum for consumers to express their preferences is in the political arena.
4. Business intervention interferes with the expression of these preferences.
5. Since point 4 is inconsistent with point 1, business should not intervene in the political process.

The importance of this obligation in business is even more important when we see that environmental legislation has special disadvantages in the political arena. Public choice reminds us that the primary interest of politicians is being reelected. Government policy will be skewed in favor of policies that provide benefits to an influential minority as long as the greater costs are widely dispersed. Politicians will also favor projects where benefits are immediate and where costs can be postponed to the future. Such strategies increase the likelihood that a politician will be reelected.

What is frightening about the environmental crisis is that both the conservation of scarce resources and pollution abatement require policies that go contrary to a politician's self-interest. The costs of cleaning up

the environment are immediate and huge, yet the benefits are relatively long range (many of them exceedingly long range). Moreover, a situation where the benefits are widely dispersed and the costs are large presents a twofold problem. The costs are large enough so that all voters will likely notice them and in certain cases are catastrophic for individuals (e.g., for those who lose their jobs in a plant shutdown).

Given these facts and the political realities they entail, business opposition to environmental legislation makes a very bad situation much worse. Even If consumers could be persuaded to take environmental issues more seriously, the externalities, opportunities to free ride, and public goods characteristics of the environment make it difficult for even enlightened consumers to express their true preference for the environment in the market. The fact that most environmental legislation trades immediate costs for future benefits makes it difficult for politicians concerned about reelection to support it. Hence it is also difficult for enlightened consumers to have their preferences for a better environment honored in the political arena. Since lack of business intervention seems necessary, and might even be sufficient, for adequate environmental legislation, it seems business has an obligation not to intervene. Nonintervention would prevent the harm of not having the true preferences of consumers for a clean environment revealed. Given business's commitment to satisfying preferences, opposition to having these preferences expressed seems inconsistent as well.

The extent of this obligation to avoid intervening in the political process needs considerable discussion by ethicists and other interested parties. Businesspeople will surely object that if they are not permitted to play a role, Congress and state legislators will make decisions that will put them at a severe competitive disadvantage. For example, if the

United States develops stricter environmental controls than other countries do, foreign imports will have a competitive advantage over domestic products. Shouldn't business be permitted to point that out? Moreover, any legislation that places costs on one industry rather than another confers advantages on other industries. The cost to the electric utilities from regulations designed to reduce the pollution that causes acid rain will give advantages to natural gas and perhaps even solar energy. Shouldn't the electric utility industry be permitted to point that out?

These questions are difficult, and my answer to them should be considered highly tentative. I believe the answer to the first question is "yes" and the answer to the second is "no." Business does have a right to insist that the regulations apply to all those in the industry. Anything else would seem to violate norms of fairness. Such issues of fairness do not arise in the second case. Since natural gas and solar do not contribute to acid rain and since the costs of acid rain cannot be fully captured in the market, government intervention through regulation is simply correcting a market failure. With respect to acid rain, the electric utilities do have an advantage they do not deserve. Hence they have no right to try to protect it.

Legislative bodies and regulatory agencies need to expand their staffs to include technical experts, economists, and engineers so that the political process can be both neutral and highly informed about environmental matters. To gain the respect of business and the public, its performance needs to improve. Much more needs to be said to make any contention that business ought to stay out of the political debate theoretically and practically possible. Perhaps these suggestions point the way for future discussion.

Ironically business might best improve its situation in the political arena by taking on an additional obligation to the environment.

Businesspersons often have more knowledge about environmental harms and the costs of cleaning them up. They may often have special knowledge about how to prevent environmental harm in the first place. Perhaps business has a special duty to educate the public and to promote environmentally responsible behavior.

Business has no reticence about leading consumer preferences in other areas. Advertising is a billion-dollar industry. Rather than blaming consumers for not purchasing environmentally friendly products, perhaps some businesses might make a commitment to capture the environmental niche. I have not seen much imagination on the part of business in this area. Far too many advertisements with an environmental message are reactive and public relations driven. Recall those by oil companies showing fish swimming about the legs of oil rigs. An educational campaign that encourages consumers to make environmentally friendly decisions in the marketplace would limit the necessity for business activity in the political arena. Voluntary behavior that is environmentally friendly is morally preferable to coerced behavior. If business took greater responsibility for educating the public, the government's responsibility would be lessened. An educational campaign aimed at consumers would likely enable many businesses to do good while simultaneously doing very well.

Hence business does have obligations to the environment, although these obligations are not found where the critics of business place them. Business has no special obligation to conserve natural resources or to stop polluting over and above its legal obligations. It does have an obligation to avoid intervening in the political arena to oppose environmental regulations, and it has a positive obligation to educate consumers. The benefits of honoring these obligations should not be underestimated.

# NOTES

1. William Frankena, *Ethics*, 2nd ed. (Englewood Cliffs, NJ: Prentice Hall, 1973), 47. Actually Frankena has four principles of prima facie duty under the principle of beneficence: one ought not to inflict evil or harm; one ought to prevent evil or harm; one ought to remove evil; and one ought to do or promote good.

2. John G. Simon, Charles W. Powers, and Jon P. Gunneman, *The Ethical Investor: Universities and Corporate Responsibility* (New Haven, CT: Yale University Press, 1972), 22–25.

3. Ibid., 21.

4. Alicia Swasy, "For Consumers, Ecology Comes Second," *Wall Street Journal* (August 23, 1988): B1.

5. Jerry Alder, "Alaska after Exxon." *Newsweek* (September 18, 1989): 53.

6. Andrew Kupfer, "Managing Now for the 1990s," *Fortune* (September 26, 1988): 46–47.

# Business, Ethics, and Global Climate Change

*Denis G. Arnold and Keith Bustos*

In years past, there was substantial debate over the existence of global warming. Today, the debate is largely over. A consensus has emerged in the global scientific community that global climate change (GCC) is occurring and that it will have a dramatic and adverse impact on ecosystems, nonhuman species populations, and human populations. In a recent review essay in *Ethics*, Stephen Gardiner notes that despite the fact that GCC is widely regarded by scientists, policy analysts, and politicians as an ethical issue, the philosophical literature on the ethics of GCC is surprisingly underdeveloped. The primary subjects of ethical analysis identified by Gardiner are states, and the primary ethical issues he identifies are the fair distributions of burdens among states in reducing emissions. However, what ethical obligations, if any, the business organizations that produce these emissions—either directly or indirectly—have regarding GCC is not addressed. This is not surprising, for the possibility that business organizations can have ethical obligations concerning GCC is almost entirely absent from the existing literature on the ethics of GCC.

The organization of this essay is as follows. First, an overview and brief history of the discovery of GCC is provided. Second, the influential position that holds that free markets and responsive democracies relieve business organizations of any special obligations to protect the environment is explained. Next, five objections to this "free market solution" to environmental problems, concerning GCC, are presented with special attention given to the transportation and electricity generation sectors' contribution to GCC. Finally, the ethical obligations of business in the transportation and energy sectors are identified with regard to their contribution to GCC, and preliminary policy recommendations are offered.

## GLOBAL CLIMATE CHANGE

There is a vast amount of conflicting information concerning GCC available to anyone surfing the Web, browsing headline articles in

© *Business & Professional Ethics Journal* 24:1 & 2 (Summer/Fall 2005): 103–130.

national newspapers, or scanning library collections. When trying to determine the scientific facts concerning GCC, it can be difficult to know which sources to trust. However, the most widely cited, peer-reviewed sources are the assessment reports produced by the Intergovernmental Panel on Climate Change (IPCC). In 1988, the IPCC was jointly established by the World Meteorological Organization (WMO) and the United Nations Environment Programme (UNEP) with the purpose of assessing the available scientific and socioeconomic information on climate change in order to provide expert advice to the Conference of the Parties to the United Nations Framework Convention on Climate Change.[1] Since 1990, the IPCC has relied upon hundreds of expert scientists to produce a series of reports and papers that have become standard works of reference used by policy makers, scientists, and other agencies such as the Energy Information Administration (EIA), a division of the United States Department of Energy.

Before getting to the IPCC's position on GCC, we should be clear about what factors contribute to this phenomenon. As solar radiation enters the earth's atmosphere, atmospheric greenhouse gases (GHGs) (such as water vapor, carbon dioxide, methane, and others) trap some of this radiation as it travels back out of the atmosphere, retaining heat much like glass in a greenhouse. Even though water vapor is by far the most abundant greenhouse gas in the earth's atmosphere, human activities have a negligible effect on the atmospheric concentrations of water vapor, and for this reason, it is not figured into national greenhouse gas emission inventories. Many of the GHGs (carbon dioxide, methane, nitrous oxide) are produced by both natural and anthropogenic processes, and there are natural mechanisms that remove significant amounts of GHGs from the atmosphere. However, anthropogenic emissions have increased the total concentration of GHGs beyond the earth's natural capacity to remove these gases from the atmosphere. Of these GHGs, $CO_2$ (carbon dioxide) is the most abundant in the earth's atmosphere due to burning fossil fuels. $CO_2$ is the most recalcitrant of the GHGs, since it does not decompose easily in the atmosphere (taking anywhere from 50 to 200 years to decompose). This means that a significant decrease in atmospheric $CO_2$ levels will not be realized for many years after anthropogenic $CO_2$ emissions drop. Incidentally, the United States has ranked first in the world for $CO_2$ emissions for several decades and has been responsible for about 24 percent of the total world $CO_2$ emissions for the past decade and is projected to hover between 23 percent and 24 percent until 2025.

According to the IPCC, approximately 75 percent of the atmospheric $CO_2$ stemming from human activity (worldwide) over the past 20 years is due to burning fossil fuel, and the other 25 percent is largely due to changes in land use, mainly deforestation. Due to an increase in atmospheric concentrations of $CO_2$, "the globally averaged surface temperatures have increased by $0.6 \pm 0.2°C$ over the twentieth century."[2] Furthermore, the IPCC projects that "the globally averaged surface air temperature is projected . . . to warm 1.4 to 5.8°C by 2100 relative to 1990."[3] This warming trend is projected to continue at a rate of about 0.1 to 0.2°C per decade for the next few decades. The IPCC has also found evidence indicating that regional changes in temperature have already affected a variety of physical and biological systems worldwide, such as shrinking glaciers, lengthening of mid- to high-latitude growing seasons, poleward migration of plant and animal ranges, and declines of some plant and animal populations.

Generally speaking, an increase in average global temperatures is likely (60 to 90 percent chance) to lead to altered weather patterns resulting in a greater risk of droughts (due to extreme drying) and floods (due to intense rainfall events) in many different regions, and the global mean sea level is projected to rise between 0.09 to 0.88 meters by 2100. Also, natural systems (such as coral reefs, mangroves, boreal and tropical forests, and prairie wetlands to name a few) are vulnerable to climate changes due to their inability to adapt to rapid environmental changes. Some of the more vulnerable species risk extinction, and the extent of damage or loss of biodiversity is sure to increase with the magnitude and rate of climate change.

The human systems that are highly susceptible to climate change are water resources, agriculture, forestry, fisheries, energy production, industry, insurance and other financial services, and human health (particularly a net increase in the geographic range of malaria and dengue). A nation's ability to cope with and adapt to climate change depends on such factors as wealth, available technology, education, access to information, skills, infrastructure, access to resources, and management capabilities. The most important thing to note is that the impacts of future climate changes will be disproportionately borne by the world's poor.

As for the impact on the global financial sector, the extreme weather events anticipated to accompany climate change would increase actuarial uncertainty in risk assessment, which would result in increased insurance premiums or could possibly lead to the withdrawal of coverage in certain situations altogether. In either case, the need for government-funded compensation following natural disasters is sure to increase (particularly in the United States).

Since many of the IPCC's claims have been met by staunch skeptics in industry and politics, a brief history of the discovery of GCC may be helpful.[4] By the late 1980s many scientists and other well-informed people were aware that the phenomenon of GCC was not a myth. However, no one really knew how severe this problem actually was or could become, nor did they completely understand what should be done about it.[5] The IPCC was formed partially in response to the growing concern that GCC could be worsening. Once formed in the late 1980s, the IPCC quickly gained credibility as supporting a moderate view concerning the reality of GCC, and its potential ecological effects. The IPCC gained credibility by offering cautious conclusions concerning GCC—ones that were extremely well supported by rigorous scientific studies. The third IPCC climate change report, released in 2001, confirmed that the vast majority of the scientific community was certain that GCC was happening and that the release of anthropogenic GHGs exacerbated its further onset. GCC had been discovered. The main uncertainty that remains concerns the appropriate response to GCC, which continues to stand as a major problem that the global community must address.

## THE MARKET "SOLUTION"

In his classic and widely reprinted essay "Money, Morality and Motor Cars" Norman Bowie takes on environmentalists who believe that businesses have special obligations to protect the environment.[6] Bowie is skeptical that an adequate defense of the environmentalist position has been mounted, and so he assumes the role of "devil's advocate" in arguing that businesses have no special obligation to protect the environment above and beyond what is required by law. Bowie begins by endorsing the commonly accepted principle that "no one has a right to render harm on another unless there is a compelling, overriding moral reason to do so."[7] He points out that this prima facie duty is commonly understood to apply to individual persons, not ecosystems, species, or even individual animals. Bowie next points out that when it comes to the manufacture and marketing of consumer goods, businesses must factor the cost of avoiding harm into the price of the product. He illustrates this claim with the example of automobiles. In 2003 there were 33,471 passenger fatalities in the U.S. Death is an obvious harm. When it comes to passenger safety, all cars are not created equal. Inexpensive cars typically have fewer safety features than more expensive cars. Customers who cannot afford to pay for safer, more expensive cars, buy inexpensive ones with comparatively few safety features. Other customers may prefer to pay more for a car that has particular engine performance or style qualities, despite the fact that it has a poor safety record. While still other consumers will emphasize safety as an overriding preference and purchase their vehicles from companies that emphasize safety such as the Volvo division of Ford. If many automobile manufacturers emphasized safety in all their models, then on Bowie's analysis, consumers would not buy as many cars from those manufacturers and those automobile companies would lose money. Given the varied preferences of consumers, Bowie concludes that "an automobile company does not violate its obligation to avoid harm and hence is not in violation of the moral minimum if the trade-off between potential harm and the utility of the products rests on social consensus and competitive realities."[8]

Bowie then extends this analysis to the question of harm to the environment. He points out that consumers often rebuff businesses that embrace environmentally friendly practices. For example,

> The restaurant chain Wendy's tried to replace foam plates and cups with paper, but customers in the test markets balked. Procter and Gamble offered Downey fabric softener in a concentrated form that requires less packaging than ready-to-use products; however the concentrate version is less convenient because it has to be mixed with water. Sales have been poor. Procter

and Gamble manufactures Vizar and Lenor brands of detergents in concentrate form, which the customer mixes at home in reusable bottles. Europeans will take the trouble, Americans will not. Kodak tried to eliminate its yellow film boxes but met customer resistance.[9]

Given this type of consumer behavior, Bowie concludes that legal harm to the environment caused by businesses is regarded as morally permissible by society. As such, he believes that "current legal activities by business organizations that harm the environment do not violate the avoid-harm criterion."[10]

In cases of market failure, where citizens recognize that their individual preference satisfaction is harming the environment in undesirable ways, Bowie points out that citizens in democracies have the ability to imposes regulations to correct market failures. For example, when consumers purchase SUVs and conventional automobiles, their use of those vehicles contributes to GCC. Citizens who choose to purchase such vehicles may nonetheless grant tax relief for purchasers of hybrid electric vehicles, thereby encouraging others to purchase low-emission vehicles that contribute much less to GCC. Given the importance of this ability to correct for market failures, together with the fact that businesses justify their environmental practices by appealing to consumer preferences, Bowie concludes that businesses have an obligation to refrain from opposing the preferences of consumers regarding environmental protection.

Bowie does not explicitly take up the issue of GCC. However, it is not difficult to extrapolate the obligations of business with regard to GCC, at least in democracies, according to his analysis. These are, first, to obey the law. Second, to refrain from opposing the collective will of citizens as expressed through the legislative process and the law regarding GCC. Third, to respond to consumer demand regarding GCC. Businesses that do these things will have no ethical obligations regarding GHG emissions and GCC beyond those stipulated by law.

## MARKET FAILURES AND ETHICAL OBLIGATIONS

Bowie's arguments have received surprisingly little criticism in the literature. However, there are serious difficulties with his defense of the market solution to environmental problems. In what follows we raise five of the most substantial objections, focusing in particular on the roles of business organizations in the transportation and electricity generation sectors regarding GCC.

### Objection One: The Absence of Democracy

This objection has two parts. First, many of the nations in which MNCs conduct business lack important democratic institutions such as equal voting rights, multiple political parties, democratic elections, politically neutral militaries, and an independent judiciary. Thirty-eight percent of the world's sovereign states and colonial units—home to 42 percent of the world's population—have nondemocratic forms of government. Bowie's defense of the ethical obligations of business concerning the environment are conceptually incoherent when applied to MNCs that operate in nondemocratic nations. It is conceptually incoherent because in order to provide normative guidance it must assume the existence of democratic institutions where they do not exist. Second, the elevated GHG emissions that are permitted in the United States will harm not merely U.S. citizens, but the entire population of the planet. Yet the preferences regarding the potential harm to non-U.S. citizens remain unaccounted for on Bowie's analysis. The fact

that voters accept a particular level of harm does not make such harm morally legitimate. This might be the case if the harm is restricted to those who accept it, but GCC will not only affect U.S. citizens, but the entire population of the planet and future generations of persons who cannot yet register their preferences in the market or in the political process. Yet the preferences regarding the potential harm to non-U.S. citizens and future generations remain unaccounted for on Bowie's analysis.

### Objection Two: The Roles of Consumers

It is unreasonable to believe that most consumers have an accurate understanding of the causes of global climate change, or an accurate understanding of the role of their own consumer choices regarding global climate change. With regard to complex environmental problems such a GCC, it is reasonable to conclude that most consumers lack an understanding of the causes of climate change or its likely harm to their welfare and the welfare of future generations. However, the large businesses that dominate the transportation and electricity sectors of the global economy typically have a sophisticated understanding both of GCC and the extent to which their own production, products, and services contribute to GCC. This sophisticated knowledge allows them to make changes regarding their practices and to develop environmentally friendly products and services, which consumer preference satisfaction by itself could never achieve. Bowie cites examples of failed environmentally friendly initiatives on the part of businesses. However, as with any new product offering, marketing the initiative to consumers must be regarded as an important priority. And just as the marketing of a new toothpaste or soda flavor can be a failure, so too can the marketing of an environmentally friendly product. Not all environmentally friendly products will be successful. However, we should not become too cynical as a result of failed product launches. There are many examples of businesses that have brought environmentally friendly products to market successfully. And it is worth noting that despite modest initial resistance from consumers, Wendy's and nearly all fast-food restaurants have successfully switched from foam plates and cups to paper.

### Objection Three: Consumer Choice

Bowie's analysis presumes that if businesses are to protect the environment above and beyond the law, it must be as a result of consumer preferences. However, there are two difficulties with this claim. First, consumer preferences are not always satisfied by businesses. For example, consumers who are concerned about GCC and wish to purchase hybrid electric vehicles (HEV) currently have few options. There are waiting lists for many HEV vehicles. But as automobile manufacturers are well aware, consumers purchase vehicles based on the ability of the vehicle to meet a variety of needs. Fuel efficiency and emissions may be important to a consumer, but so are things like passenger capacity, acceleration, and luxury qualities. At present there are no HEV minivans or HEV luxury sedans, so consumers who would prefer more environmentally friendly minivans or luxury sedans are left without options.

Second, consumers often have little or no influence with regard to the environmental practices of businesses. For example, a consumer who recognizes that coal-fired power plants emit harmful levels of GHGs into the atmosphere may strongly prefer to purchase electricity from an energy provider that relies more on wind, solar, or hydroelectric energy sources. However, energy providers typically have a monopoly over consumers, so the consumer cannot take her business elsewhere. Furthermore, the consumer *qua* citizen typically has no direct way to regulate energy providers.

### Objection Four: Harm to Others

As noted above, the impact of GCC will affect every person on Earth, and not merely the consumers of specific products or services. The atmosphere is a common resource, one that U.S. consumers share with the global community. As Will Kymlicka and Henry Shue have argued, preferences typically entail a claim on resources. The preference satisfaction of U.S. consumers, for example, makes use of a per capita disproportionate level of atmospheric resources. At the same time, the harm caused to present generations of non-U.S. consumers will be disproportionate to their use of atmospheric resources. So too, presumably, will be the harm to future generations. These future persons will have preferences that require due consideration. The mere preference satisfaction of present-day U.S. consumers cannot by itself justify this harm to others.

### Objection Five: Responsibility for the Past

A basic principle of justice holds that it is unfair to require others to pay for the costs of benefits one has secured for oneself without their uncoerced consent. Those who enjoy the benefits resulting from burning fossil fuels, and thereby contribute to GCC, ought to pay more for such benefits than those who do not enjoy such benefits. In the U.S. the transportation sector and the electricity generation sector are the two most carbon-intensive sectors, and thus the two sectors that contribute the most to the total U.S. $CO_2$ emissions. The reason for these two sectors' being so carbon intensive is due to their heavy dependence upon fossil fuel combustion. The transportation sector is more carbon intensive than the electricity generation sector because the former is almost completely dependent upon petrofuels.

Between 1990 and 2003, the transportation end-use sector contributed an average of about 31 percent of total $CO_2$ emissions from fossil fuel combustion in the U.S. In 2003 the U.S. emitted approximately 5,781.4 million metric tons (mmt) of $CO_2$ due to burning fossil fuels, with transportation accounting for approximately one-third of those emissions. The energy consumed by the transportation sector is predominantly petroleum-based, with slightly more than 61 percent of the $CO_2$ emissions resulting from burning gasoline, about 21 percent from diesel, and approximately 13 percent from jet fuels. In 2002, the transportation end-use sector consumed almost 97 percent of the total U.S. consumption of petroleum. The amount of energy consumed by automobiles within this sector accounted for more than 33 percent and light trucks (pickups, minivans, sport-utility vehicles, and vans) almost 25 percent. Even though automobiles consume more energy than light trucks (because there are fewer trucks on the road), the latter have had the greatest increase in energy consumption over the past decade due to their growing popularity.

In the United States, fossil fuels are the primary fuel used to power many sectors of our economy, especially the electric power industry. In 2003, the United States generated and sold 3,488 billion kWh of electricity—approximately 1,273 billion kWh (36 percent) was consumed by the residential end-use sector, roughly 1,151 billion kWh (34 percent) consumed by the commercial sector, about 1,008 billion kWh (29 percent) went to the industrial sector, and 7 billion kWh (less than 1 percent) was used by transportation.[11] In this same year, more than half the electricity produced in the U.S. was from coal (51 percent), 20 percent from nuclear, and 17 percent from natural gas. In order to produce 3,488 billion kWh, the electric generating

facilities burned slightly more than 1 billion tons of coal, about 207 million barrels of petroleum, and a little more than 5.5 billion metric cubic feet of natural gas. The generation of electricity in the United States released 2,279.3 million metric tons (mmt) of $CO_2$ into the atmosphere, which is the highest level since 2000. . . .[12]

Given the transportation and electricity generation sectors' large contribution to GCC, it is reasonable to hold them accountable for the proportional harm to the atmosphere that they have caused historically. In particular, there are good reasons for holding them accountable for the impact of at least some of their GHG emissions on GCC to date. While purely theoretical discussions of historical accountability are of interest, we wish to focus on an account of historical accountability that is useful for policy making. Our concern is to provide tools for policy makers who may need to use the coercive power of the law to encourage business organizations to fulfill their moral obligations regarding GCC.

Eric Neumayer offers a compelling moral position that may be helpful in establishing the level of culpability a business organization deserves regarding GHG emissions.[13] Neumayer's arguments pertain to nation states, whereas the present project deals with corporate environmental responsibility. Although these two groups play drastically different roles within society, the actual responsibilities regarding GHG abatement are quite similar. Neumayer gives three reasons in defense of historical accountability as it pertains to global GHG emissions. First, indisputable science has demonstrated that an increase in GHG emissions exacerbates the onset of GCC, and human activities (namely the burning of fossil fuels) have greatly contributed to the atmospheric concentrations of GHGs over the past century. And for this reason, to reject historical accountability would be to reject the phenomenon of GCC. (This tacit assumption has been embraced by business organizations such as ExxonMobil.) Second, Neumayer contends that the polluter-pays principle (PPP) helps to justify the historical accountability approach. The PPP supports the claim that GCC is predominantly caused by the GHG emissions of developed countries and these countries should pay for mitigating GCC. By rejecting historical accountability, we would reward rich industrial nations by not making them pay for the GHGs they have emitted while disadvantaging poor, less industrialized nations. Third, he argues that by adopting historical accountability we would ensure that all present and future individuals would have the equality of opportunity to use the global atmospheric commons, no matter where they live or will live. So, according to Neumayer, historical accountability should be adopted as morally preferable approach in assigning responsibility for the current and future harm resulting from GCC.

Although we are sympathetic to Neumayer's position, we do not accept full historical accountability, which assigns responsibility to GHG-emitting nations possibly as far back as the late 1800s when Svante Arrhenius first detected a warming trend in the Earth's atmosphere. Instead, we support a truncated version of historic accountability that is effective only back to 2001. Granted, many corporate leaders knew about their respective organizations' potential contribution to GCC as early as 1995 (and possibly as early as the mid-1980s); however, at that time the scientific evidence remained relatively uncertain. Business organizations cannot reasonably be held responsible for responding to every potentially alarming situation concerning their business practices. Even after GCC was determined to be likely in the late 1990s, there was still a significant amount of controversy concerning the science behind those findings. But by 2001 the IPCC was able to claim with a very high level of certainty that $CO_2$ emissions constituted a significant contribution to the further onset of

GCC. It was not until 2001 that GCC was an undeniable fact. It is reasonable to hold business organizations morally responsible for their negligent contribution to GCC once it became abundantly clear that their respective GHG emissions contributed greatly to GCC. . . .

## POLICY IMPLICATIONS

How should we determine the appropriate level of GHG abatement? What would an appropriate abatement plan look like? What time frame should it have? The two extremes that set our boundaries are (1) do too little, and cause substantial harm to future generations; or (2) take drastic action too soon thus incurring unnecessary costs. It seems reasonable to suggest that we adopt a moderate approach, which means that if we are to avoid the predicted catastrophes related to GCC, then we need to reduce $CO_2$ emissions below 1990 levels within a few decades, and then continue to decrease $CO_2$ steadily thereafter. The long-term goal is to reduce $CO_2$ emissions to a small fraction of what they are today. The need to engage in aggressive, but not frantic, $CO_2$ abatement is due to the fact that this GHG has an atmospheric lifetime of 50–200 years. This means that even an aggressive plan of action will not reverse GCC, it will only stabilize it since the $CO_2$ we produce today can continue to contribute to GCC for up to 200 years into the future. So, we contend that business organizations that are responsible for substantial $CO_2$ emissions have a moral obligation to be engaged in aggressive proactive measures to abate their $CO_2$ emissions, and that this obligation has been effective since 2001. Any business organization that has not taken proactive measures to abate $CO_2$ emissions is deserving of disapprobation.

Before discussing what sort of punishments and incentives might be invoked to help business organizations comply with such a moral duty, it must be noted that we do not believe that merely complying with current U.S. regulations satisfies the duties of business organizations regarding GHG abatement and GCC mitigation. In order to avoid censure, a business organization must go beyond mere compliance, for current U.S. legislation does not bode well for mitigating GCC.

The problem with determining the actual degree and type of proactive measures that a business organization must engage in, so as to meet this moral demand, is that there are numerous ways to go beyond compliance and still miss the mark. That is, just because a firm engages in beyond-compliance practices does not necessarily mean that it is doing all that it is morally obligated to do regarding GCC. Conversely, just because a business organization is guilty of a few environmental transgressions does not mean that it is failing to take appropriate action regarding GCC. Just as there are "shades of green" within the corporate world, there are also shades of brown.

The ambiguity in abatement actions illuminates the need for diagnostic tools that can help to make a distinction between green and brown organizations. It is challenging to gather neutral information from the business organizations themselves, as they tend to put their best environmental projects forward. Nonetheless, distinctions between the environmental practices of companies can be made. Take for example the difference between Toyota and General Motors (GM). Toyota is currently at the forefront of HEV vehicle production. It currently offers consumers a variety of high fuel economy vehicles, while GM currently manufactures no such vehicles. GM specializes mostly in producing larger vehicles that consume more fuel such as the Hummer brand, whereas Toyota primarily produces midsize cars and smaller vehicles. Another important reason for this disparity is that Toyota has invested heavily in hybrid technology, whereas GM chose to invest in hydrogen technology research.

Toyota's investment is currently paying off, allowing them to be a leader in the race to decrease the fuel demand of the transportation industry. GM's activities reflect a lack of concern with the current state of GHG emissions.

Writing in *Foreign Affairs*, Lord Browne, Group Chief Executive of British Petroleum, points out that "BP found that it was able to reach its initial target of reducing emissions by 10 percent below its 1990 levels without cost. Indeed, the company added around $650 million of shareholder value, because the bulk of the reductions came from the elimination of leaks and waste."[14] Morally imaginative companies, such as BP and Royal Dutch Shell, have already begun to assume responsibility for their impact on the global environment. However, it is reasonable to conclude that businesses that decline to fulfill their minimal ethical duties regarding GCC, such as ExxonMobile, should be provided with incentives for doing so by governments. One such incentive in meeting the duty to mitigate GCC would be imposing a tax on carbon emissions. The actual cost of the tax has been hotly contested and has yet to be settled. Setting a specific tax rate is beyond the scope of this paper; however, we suggest that this rate should reflect the fact that the future global climate is just as valuable as it is today. . . .

Those firms that failed to take proactive measures from 2001 on should be penalized for their negligence. Such a penalty might involve a compounding interest rate, meaning that each year past 2001 that a firm fails to take appropriate proactive measures, it will not only incur an interest expense, but for each year that the fine is unpaid, the accrued interest itself becomes part of the principle and also accrues interest. Here, for illustrative purposes, is an example. If the carbon tax were set at $450/toc (ton of carbon) for 2005, business organizations that only began abating their carbon emissions this year would be required to pay $450 per year that has passed ($450 × 4).[15]

This penalty would also include an interest rate of 10 percent. As a result, a firm that has only begun to engage in proactive measures to abate their $CO_2$ emissions in 2005 would have to pay \$495/toc for 2001, \$544.50/toc for 2002, \$598.95/toc for 2003, and \$658.85/toc for 2004.

The position that we have argued for is that individual business organizations are morally responsible for their contribution to GCC and the resulting harm. And, in order for firms to reduce their contribution to the harm that will inevitably befall persons in the future due to the extreme and chaotic weather events caused by GCC, they must take aggressive proactive measure to abate their respective $CO_2$ emissions. Ideally, this is a moral obligation that should be voluntarily embraced by individual firms. However, we realize that placing such a moral responsibility on firms may be too much to ask of them on their own, so we also call for the help of the government in abating industrial $CO_2$ emissions. Such governmental assistance would come in the form of imposing a tax on carbon emissions, and this expense can then be internalized by individual firms and incorporated in the price of their goods, thereby requiring consumers to bear a fair price for the pollution produced when manufacturing the goods that they consume. Also, the revenue generated from the carbon tax can be used to fund or subsidize further abatement measures so as to help the U.S. reduce its contribution to GCC.

## NOTES

1. Intergovernmental Panel on Climate Change, *Climate Change 2001: Impacts, Adaptation, and Vulnerability* (New York: Cambridge University Press, 2001), foreword.

2. Intergovernmental Panel on Climate Change, *Climate Change 2001: Impacts, Adaptation, and Vulnerability*, p. 3.

3. Ibid., 3.

4. One of the most well known skeptics is the self-proclaimed skeptical environmentalist Bjørn Lomborg. Bjørn Lomborg, *The Skeptical Environmentalist* (Cambridge: Cambridge University Press, 2001).

5. Spencer R. Weart, *The Discovery of Global Warming* (Cambridge: Cambridge University Press, 2003), 160.

6. Norman E. Bowie, "Money, Morality and Motor Cars," in *Business, Ethics, and the Global Environment*, ed. W. M. Hoffman, R. Frederic, and E. Petry (New York: Quorum Books, 1990), 89–97. Reprinted in this chapter.

7. Ibid., 90.

8. Ibid., 92.

9. Ibid., 93.

10. Ibid., 93.

11. Energy Information Administration, *Electric Power Annual 2003* (Washington, DC: Office of Coal, Nuclear, Electric and Alternative Fuels, 2004), 3, 39.

12. Energy Information Administration, *Emissions of Greenhouse Gases in the US 2003* (Washington, DC: 2004), 28. Available at http://www.eia.doe.gov/oiaf/1605/ggrpt/index.html; Energy Information Administration, *Electric Power Annual 2003* (Washington, DC: Office of Coal, Nuclear, Electric and Alternative Fuels, 2004), 2.

13. Eric Neumayer, "In Defense of Historical Accountability for Greenhouse Gas Emissions," *Ecological Economics* 33 (2000): 185–92.

14. John Browne, "Beyond Kyoto," *Foreign Affairs* 83, no. 4 (July/August 2004): 26.

15. This is the carbon tax suggested by William R. Cline, which, according to his calculations, is an appropriately risk-averse tax aimed at quickly reducing $CO_2$ emissions. Ideally, this tax would start at \$450/ton in 2005 and rise as high as \$1,900/ton by 2205. William R. Cline, "Climate Change," in *Global Crises, Global Solutions*, ed. Bjørn Lomborg (Cambridge University Press, 2004), 13–43. A summary of Cline's article along with responses to his views can be accessed on the Web at http://www.copenhagenconsensus.com/Default.asp?ID=415

16. The 10 percent interest rate reflects the philosophy behind choosing a private discount rate instead of a social discount rate. That is, a private discount rate reflects a greater degree

of impatience than does a social discount rate because individuals tend to be more myopic than societies when dealing with consumption—individuals place more value on immediate consumption than on future consumption. Private interest rates are generally higher than social interest rates and can be as high as 10 percent. We have deliberately set the interest rate at such a high percentage to reflect a high degree of impatience, in order to entice firms to quickly come into compliance. Ahmed M. Hussen, *Principles of Environmental Economics: Economics, Ecology and Public Policy* (New York, NY: Routledge, 2000), 324.

*Editors' note:* Seventy-six notes were deleted from this essay because of space constraints. Readers interested in detailed citations should consult the original article.

# Sustainability: Business's New Environmental Obligation

*Joseph DesJardins*

## INTRODUCTION

Does business have any special obligations to protect the environment? In an essay that has become a classic within the business ethics literature, Norman Bowie concludes that business does not have any special environmental obligations, at least not in the normal understanding of this phrase. In Bowie's words: "Business does not have an obligation to protect the environment over and above what is required by law."[1]

Bowie's conclusion is typical of mainstream theories of corporate environmental responsibility. These views hold that business is free to pursue profit as long as it complies with the law and causes no avoidable harm to others. From the classical model of corporate social responsibility associated with Milton Friedman to the more recent stakeholder theory, environmental concerns function as side constraints upon business's pursuit of profit. Business may have some negative duties regarding the environment, duties not to pollute and not to cause other avoidable harm, but business has no positive duty to conduct itself in ways that contribute to long-term ecological and environmental well-being.

Under this standard model of corporate environmental responsibility, society gets two opportunities to shape business's activities in respect to the environment. We can press for environmental responsibility through the products we demand as consumers, or we can pass legislation requiring business to act in environmentally responsible ways. Absent consumer demand and legal mandates, business itself has no ethical responsibility to consider the environment and is free to pursue profits even if this might otherwise be judged environmentally harmful.

Given his philosophical and environmental starting points, Bowie's argument is well reasoned and persuasive. However, I believe that the entire framework in which his position is developed is misguided. Simply put, this is the wrong way to think about business, the environment, and ethical responsibility. A range of economic, environmental, and ethical realities at the start of the twenty-first century require that we reconceptualize business's environmental obligations and redesign business institutions to meet standards of sustainability. Before explaining this claim, let us review the state of the world at the beginning of the twenty-first century.

## THE NEED FOR A NEW PARADIGM

Why the need to reconceptualize and redesign business? Several undeniable facts about the world in which we live make this case. First, a large percentage of the world's population, mostly children and the overwhelming majority of them morally innocent in every way, lack the basic requirements of a decent human life. Lack of clean drinking water, nutritious food, health care, education, work, shelter, clothing, and hope is a daily reality for billions of people. Population growth, even at the most conservative rates, will significantly exacerbate these problems in the near future. Because population growth is highest in those areas in which people are already most at risk due to the effects of poverty and oppression, these ethical challenges will only worsen in the future.

To meet these fundamental human needs on such a grand scale, the world's economy must produce substantial amounts of food, clothing, shelter, health care, and jobs and distribute these goods and services to those in need. Clearly, then, significant worldwide economic activity must occur if these harms are to be addressed at all.

Furthermore, these challenges will impact the nature and practice of virtually every business. An increasingly integrated global economy means that fewer and fewer business decisions anywhere can be made in isolation of the social, political, environmental, and economic events happening throughout the rest of the world. Gone are the days when business decisions in the United States or Western Europe could be made in ignorance and independence of financial markets in China, labor markets in India, or resource markets in the Middle East. Economic activity aimed at meeting the needs of the expanding world's population has already shifted the economic center of gravity away from the United States and Western Europe and towards Asia.

The extensive economic activity required to address these goals must rely on the productive capacity of the earth's biosphere. Two facts about that biosphere are at the core of my argument. First, the economy is but a subsystem within earth's biosphere, and therefore the biosphere establishes the biophysical parameters of economic growth. Second, that very biosphere is already under stress due to the level and type of activity that characterizes the present world economy.

Given these realities, those of us living in the consumerist economies of the developed world are faced with three alternative conclusions. First, we can have faith in the assumption that the world's economy can continue to grow indefinitely and that the world's poor will be able to satisfy their basic needs and even attain prosperous lives and a higher standard of living. We can assume, in other words, that there are no practical biophysical limits to economic growth and that business as usual can be expanded globally and into the long-term future without catastrophic environmental consequences. Second, we can conclude that the world's poor will not, cannot, or should not strive to satisfy their basic needs or for prosperous lifestyles and that they will or should remain poor. Third, we can conclude that alternative economic institutions must be created to meet world demand without further destroying the biosphere.

We have good reasons to doubt the legitimacy of the first option. Imagine the present American and Western European paradigm of economic growth and consumerism expanding to the earth's entire population of slightly more than 6 billion people. Envision a world in which the 1.3 billion people presently living in China used as many resources and created as many wastes as the 300 million people of the United States. One estimate has it that if China consumed oil at the rate of the United States, it would consume 80 million barrels of oil each day, which alone is more than the world's total production of 74 million barrels a day. If the Chinese economy ever reached the level of $CO_2$ emissions as the present U.S. economy, China alone would produce double the present worldwide $CO_2$ pollution.[2] The earth's climate is already reacting to the present levels of $CO_2$ and other greenhouse gas emissions caused by modern industrial society. Imagine that same world in which not only China, but the 1 billion people of India join the economic party at the same rates. Add to that another billion people living in Indonesia, Brazil, Russia, Pakistan, Bangladesh, and Nigeria.

The second option is not a real choice either. Believing that the world's poor will not, cannot, or should not strive for more prosperous lifestyles is, at best, a policy of self-deception.

This leaves the third as the only realistic and ethically satisfactory option. Unless a model of business can be created that allows significant economic activity without further depletion of the biosphere's ability to support both life and the very economic activity on which it depends, humans are facing a global ecological, economic, political, and ethical tragedy.

A background assumption of most mainstream theories of corporate environmental responsibility is that profits and the environment represent a zero-sum game. Resources devoted to protecting the environment come at the expense of profitability, the pursuit of profit excludes environmentally responsible practices. But this assumption is unwarranted.

Consider how this assumption plays out in Bowie's view. Business cannot be expected to

act in environmentally responsible ways unless consumers demand it or the law requires it. Requiring business to do otherwise violates the "ought implies can" maxim: ethics cannot require us to act in ways that we cannot. In the business context in which Bowie applies this maxim, this means that business cannot be required to act in ways that would put itself out of business by being unprofitable. If consumers demand environmentally responsible products, then business can be both environmentally responsible and profitable. If the law requires it, then environmentally responsible businesses are not at a competitive disadvantage with less responsible businesses. Absent consumer demand or legal mandates, business cannot be expected to put itself at risk by pursuing environmental goals.

But this background assumption underestimates the range of managerial discretion. Independently of environmental issues, business managers and executives enjoy a wide range of decision-making discretion. There are countless ways to pursue and attain profitability even within a single firm or industry. We should abandon the assumption that environmental responsibilities are side constraints on "the" pursuit of profit, as if there is only one way to pursue profits and ethical obligations are a barrier to that. Rather, we should recognize that some avenues to profitability are environmentally risky, others environmentally prudent and sensible. Sustainable societies generate both new responsibilities and new opportunities for business in the twenty-first century.

This model is what I refer to as sustainable business.

## SUSTAINABLE BUSINESS

For some observers, these considerations might suggest a "doom and gloom," pessimistic outlook. While we should not underestimate the real and significant ecological dangers we face, this is also the time to call forth human creativity, imagination, and ingenuity. The call for sustainability should also be understood as a call for entrepreneurs to imagine the future and help create the sustainable business firm of the twenty-first century.

Business in the twenty-first century must be practiced in a way that is *economically* vibrant enough to address the real needs of billions of people, yet *ecologically* informed so that the earth's capacity to support life is not diminished by that activity and *ethically* sensitive enough that fundamental human needs are met in the process. Economics, ecology, and ethics form the three pillars of a sustainable society.

Fortunately, some early versions of such a model of business are beginning to appear. What has been called, alternatively, "sustainable business," "the next industrial revolution," or "natural capitalism" provide models for business which can, in the words of the U.N. Commission on Sustainability, "meet the needs of the present without jeopardizing the ability of future generations to meet their own."[3] It is a new business model that emerges out of a paradigm shift in economics, management, and ethics. We must, to borrow the phrase of economist Herman Daly, abandon the economic model that takes unguided *growth* as the economic goal and replace it with one that targets economic *development*.[4]

What is the model of business that emerges from this new economics? First, we should recognize that there is not a single, unique way in which a sustainable business should be organized. Several models have been described in the literature, but we can abstract some common aspects of these various models.[5] The first aspect is a significant increase in economic efficiency brought about by design changes inspired by biological processes. This alternative business model should be based on a principle of biomimicry in which wastes of the production cycle are recycled back into a closed loop.

"Waste equals food," in the words of William McDonough and Michael Braungart. Just as the detritus of decomposed material is turned back into fertile soil within biological systems, sustainable business must be designed so that its by-products are themselves the resources for new productivity.

A second feature of sustainable business shifts the goal of production from goods and products to services. Human beings *need* surprisingly very few *products*: food, water, and clean air are obvious examples, and so far at least, only the first two have become commodities. Human beings do need many *services*: education, health care, shelter, security. As consumers, we need very few of the products purchased in the marketplace. What we actually *want*, although we often do not fully understand ourselves, are services. As the popularity of auto leasing shows, consumers want convenient personal transportation, not necessarily ownership of an automobile. As the information technology industry is showing, consumers want easy access to software, Internet, and e-mail, not ownership of a soon-to-be-outdated piece of computer hardware or software written on 3½-inch floppies. As Interface Corporation has shown, people want floor-covering services, not carpet ownership. This list goes on.

This focus on services rather than products has important implications for both business and consumers. By emphasizing services rather than products, business has strong financial incentives to create longer-lasting, more durable products that are easily recycled back into the product stream. Significant entrepreneurial opportunities exist here for creative business leaders to seize this initiative in creating a service economy. Significant economic opportunity also exists as one-time-product purchasers become long-term-service lessees. Consumers benefit if they are helped to escape what has been called a commodity fetish.

Another aspect of this alternative model requires business to invest in natural capital. For too long, business (and growth-based economics) has treated the productive capacity of the earth's biosphere as an unending revenue stream. Earth's productivity was something that could be spent without cost. Only in the last few decades have the true costs of spending down our natural capital been understood. The better metaphor is to think of the earth's productivity as capital, as something capable of generating revenue in the form of interest but not something that should be spent to the point where it is incapable of continuing to be a source of income. A prudent financial strategy is to spend interest but not capital. The earth has demonstrated a remarkable ability to produce life-sustaining necessities indefinitely, but only if we maintain sufficient savings in reserve to generate these necessities indefinitely.

One of the most interesting things about this alternative model of sustainable business is the huge potential it holds for entrepreneurial activity. Creative business leaders will find vast opportunities for new business ventures that transform business from the old industrial model to the new sustainable model. Thus, Bowie's fear that doing good is too much to ask of profit-seeking institutions is ill-founded. Sustainable business does not ask mangers to forego profits (although it would require that profits from ecologically destructive activities be abandoned); it only requires that profits be obtained in ecologically sustainable ways.

The ecological guidelines for this new approach to business are, in their most general form, relatively straightforward. The entire economic production process takes resources from the biosphere, turns them into products and services, and generates by-products (or wastes) in the process. The ecological guidelines for sustainable business mirror the two sides of this production cycle. Resources going

into the production process should be used only at the rate at which they can be replenished by the productive capacity of the biosphere. By-products and wastes of this production process should be generated no faster than the earth's capacity to absorb them.

More specifically, we can recognize that economic resources come in a variety of types. Some are nonrenewable, either in principle or in practice. Once a species becomes extinct, humans will never again have the ability to use it. Once oil or coal is burned, it is gone forever, in any practical sense of the word. Thus, use of nonrenewable resources ought, eventually, to be eliminated but should, in the meantime, be reduced to a minimum.

Other resources are renewable, some only within certain parameters, others practically without limit. Agriculture, fisheries, and forests are renewable, but only if we use them at moderate rates. Used wisely, the earth can produce biological resources at a sustainable rate indefinitely. Other resources—energy produced by the sun, hydrogen, wind, tides, and geothermal sources—are for all practical purposes infinite. An efficient, wise, and ethical sustainable business will use these infinitely available resources first, moderate its use of other renewables, and wean itself from reliance on nonrenewables.

Similar guidelines can be developed on the waste and by-product side of business. Waste is a bad thing, both economically and ecologically. Sustainable business must strive to eliminate all of the wastes created along each step of the production cycle. In general, all wastes are sent back into the earth's biosphere and, to be sustainable, must not be put there beyond the capacity of the biosphere to absorb them. For some by-products that will be easy. Much agricultural waste, for example, can be recycled back into the earth as mulch. For other by-products, the pollutants of much of the petrochemical or nuclear industry for example, that will be impossible. Such wastes will need to be eliminated. But, to emphasize, business wastes are not only an ecological harm, they are also an economic harm. As the word itself suggests, wastes are unused resources and any business that has a lot of waste is an inefficient and poorly run business. Great economic opportunities exist for discovering ways to transform this waste into useful resources.

## THE BUSINESS CASE FOR SUSTAINABILITY

As previously outlined, both history and ethics can encourage us to think of sustainability and business as a zero-sum game: environmentally sustainable decision comes at a cost of profitability; pursuing profits requires business managers to forgo environmental responsibility. But the possibility exists that what is right in terms of sustainability, may also be right in terms of business performance. One of the three pillars of sustainability, after all, is economic sustainability. If we expect business to address the significant global economic and environmental challenges of the twenty-first century, we need vibrant and stable, i.e., profitable, businesses. Simply put, a sustainable business must be a profitable business.

Concluding that business should not produce environmentally responsible goods and services unless and until consumers demand them also misrepresents the dynamics of the marketplace. Consumers cannot demand what doesn't exist and what they do not know about. For example, Toyota did not wait until consumers demanded hybrid cars before they began designing and manufacturing the Prius. Toyota itself helped create the market for hybrid cars. In contrast, by concentrating on past demand patterns, American automobile manufacturers were left behind in the hybrid market.

Similarly, waiting for legal mandates out of a fear of being placed at a competitive disadvantage has itself proven to be a competitive disadvantage. Business at the cutting edge of sustainable products and services will enjoy the advantages that go along with being the first to market. They are also likely to be the one who help establish future standards.

The sustainability paradigm starts with the assumption that the time is approaching when business institutions will either evolve into more sustainable enterprises or will simply cease to exist. The two forces of increasing social demand for goods and services and the decreasing ability of the biosphere to provide resources to meet that demand are approaching a point at which they will merge. That assumption is less a prediction of doom than it is an observation of present realities. But forward-looking, creative, and entrepreneurial companies will recognize this trend as offering tremendous opportunities rather than as creating barriers.

Barring a catastrophe, society will survive and vibrant businesses must play a role in that survival. All models for sustainable development envision a central role for business in a sustainable future. It will, after all, be the businesses of the next industrial revolution that meet the real needs of the billions of people living in that sustainable future. The businesses that survive in this sustainable world will be businesses that anticipate this change and adapt to it on their own terms.

So, can a "business case" be made for the move towards sustainability? In fact, some persuasive reasons can be offered to the business community for why it should move in the direction of sustainability. First, of course, is the huge market represented by the billions of human beings who face unmet needs on a daily basis. All too often economists and business managers conceptualize consumer demand in ways that ignore the needs of the billions of human beings who lack food, clothing, shelter, medical care, jobs. There are enormous opportunities waiting for the businesses who respond to this market.

A convincing and detailed case for how this might happen has been made by business scholar C. K. Prahalad in his book *The Fortune at the Bottom of the Pyramid.*[6] Prahalad and others have argued that entrepreneurial and creative businesses are finding ways to develop markets among the world's poorest people. The 4 billion people comprising the base of the pyramid (the phrase changed by Stuart Hart to avoid the pejorative-sounding "bottom"[7]) provide a market so large and diverse that it can be addressed only in ways that are environmentally sustainable. It will simply be impossible to meet those needs with products and services that are resource and energy intensive, environmentally destructive, or socially insensitive. Sustainable enterprises will find huge markets at the base of the pyramid that unsustainable business and industry will be unable to satisfy.

Beyond the unlimited opportunity for new markets, there are many potential cost savings available from the move towards sustainability. Significant savings can follow from eliminating wastes, reducing operating expenses, and striving towards ecoefficiency. Waste is a bad thing, both ecologically and financially. A company that reduces and eliminates its wastes will reduce its costs. A company that finds ways to turn waste into a new resource will increase its revenues from already existing assets.

Sustainability also creates opportunities to decrease capital costs in building or remodeling facilities. Buildings designed from the start to be energy efficient, with bright, airy, and well-ventilated space will decrease costs and improve efficiencies over the long term. William McDonough and Michael Braungart's work with a new manufacturing plant for Herman Miller, a large office furniture maker, is a case in point. Herman Miller has a long tradition of socially responsible practices and has worked with McDonough and Braungart's cradle-to-cradle design protocol to develop truly sustainable furniture products. But in the early 1990s, Herman Miller also worked with McDonough to design and build their new manufacturing plant in Michigan. The new design has paid dividends in the form of lower energy costs and increased worker productivity. Herman Miller has also been instrumental in creating the United States Green Building Council (USGBC) in 1993. The council describes itself as "the nation's foremost coalition of leaders from across the building industry working to promote buildings that are environmentally responsible, profitable, and healthy places to live and work."[8]

Sustainable companies can also acquire competitive advantages. Not only would increased savings, revenues, and efficiencies place a company in a better position relative to its competitors, but sustainable companies are poised to take advantage of "green" and sustainable markets. Sustainable practices should not be only a marketing tool, of course, but one should not underestimate the growing consumer market for sustainable and environmentally beneficial products and services.

Another aspect of the competitive advantages of sustainability lies in the labor market. Herman Miller discovered that their green building became very popular with employees. Improved morale, increased employee loyalty and, simply, healthier and more attractive working conditions for employees were added benefits of McDonough's sustainable design principles.

Business should also recognize the real possibility of future government regulation that may well require steps towards sustainability. The companies already involved in sustainable practices are likely to play leadership roles in fashioning future standards. Again, Herman Miller provides an excellent example. In 1993, Herman Miller was a founding sponsor of the United States Green Building Council. The USGBC is a nonprofit organization of architects, construction companies, engineering firms, and others in the building industry committed to promoting "environmentally responsible, and healthy buildings for business and homes." The USGBC developed the LEED rating system (Leadership in Energy and Environmental Design), a voluntary classification system of common standards for creating and measuring sustainable buildings. The USGBC used Herman Miller's manufacturing plant designed by Bill McDonough as a model for the LEED certification and rating process. Today, there is a growing movement, especially among state and local governments, to require new construction to conform to minimal LEED standards.

In the past, many companies waited until environmental regulations coerced them into action. At that point, many were overwhelmed by the costs of cleanup and compensation. Companies that wait will likely deal with sustainability as a compliance issue take similar risks. By taking the initiative in designing and constructing a sustainable building, Herman Miller helped create and set the standards that less innovative companies will now be challenged to meet.

Finally, avoiding future legal liability provides another business reason for the move towards sustainability. There is no better means for managing both regulatory and legal risks than by being proactive in taking steps to prevent problems from occurring. The legal concepts of negligence and forseeability are just waiting to be exploited in holding business liable for the entire life cycle of its products. As municipalities struggle to find ways to dispose of solid wastes or clean up old polluted landfills, an obvious strategy will be to turn to the businesses who designed, manufactured, and sold those products and hold them accountable to take back their products, or pay for their proper disposal and cleanup.

Legal developments in Europe and elsewhere already foreshadow this future. Beginning in the early 1990s, several countries have passed legislation mandating producer responsibility for the wastes created by their products. Variously referred to as "take-back" laws or "extended producer responsibility," such laws require that business be responsible financially, if not physically, for the eventual disposal or recycling of products that they place into the market.

Spurred on by the European Union's Waste Electrical and Electronic Equipment (WEEE) and Restriction of Hazardous Substances (RoHS) directives, over 20 European countries have already passed laws which encourage or require manufacturers to take responsibility for the eventual disposal of such products as batteries, electronics, fluorescent lights, appliances such as refrigerators and air conditioners, televisions, and automobiles. Japan, South Korea, and Taiwan have similar legislation.

Business executives who do not anticipate such developments on a wider scale by beginning to redesign their products in ways that make reuse and recycling easier and even profitable are not acting as very prudent risk managers.

## FINAL REFLECTIONS

The concept of sustainability has grown out of the recognition that economic development on a global level cannot be separated from questions of social justice and from ecological stability. The new worldview emerging as an alternative to the reigning paradigm of economic growth and free markets holds that long-term sustainability is the criterion of successful economic and social development. Sustainability involves three equally vital dimensions: economic, ecological, and ethical. Business, within this conceptualization, is no longer understood as having a primary economic goal, with ethical and environmental considerations functioning as side constraints. Business has three equally compelling goals that must be balanced over the long term.

Environmental responsibility functions less as a side constraint on normal business activities and more as a central part of the very mission of business in the twenty-first century.

## NOTES

1. Norman Bowie, *Morality, Money, and Motor Cars,* reprinted in this chapter.
2. These estimates are from Lester Brown, *Eco-Economy: Building an Economy for the Earth* (New York: W.W. Norton & Co., 2001).
3. This definition of sustainability comes from the United Nations World Commission on Environment and Development (the "Brundtland Commission"), which published its findings on economic development and the environment in *Our Common Future* (New York: Oxford University Press, 1987).
4. Herman Daly, *Beyond Growth* (Boston: Beacon Press, 1996).
5. My own thinking on this has been particularly influenced by three approaches: Herman

Daly's writing on ecological economics and especially in *Beyond Growth*; Amory Lovin, Hunter Lovins, and Paul Hawken's *Natural Capitalism* (Boston: Little, Brown, 1999); and William McDonough and Michael Braungart's, "The Next Industrial Revolution," *Atlantic Monthly* (October 1998).

6. *The Fortune at the Bottom of the Pyramid: Eradicating Poverty through Profits,"* by C. K. Prahalad (Upper Saddle River, NJ: Wharton School Publishing, 2005). See also Prahalad and Stuart Hart, "The Fortune at the Bottom of the Pyramid," *Strategy and Business* 26 (2002): 54–67; and Prahalad and Allen Hammond, "Serve the World's Poor, Profitably," *Harvard Business Review* (September, 2002).
7. Stuart Hart, *Capitalism at the Crossroads* (Upper Saddle River, NJ: Wharton School Publishing, 2005), 108, footnote 4.
8. Information about Herman Miller's long tradition of working towards sustainability can be found on the company's Web site: http://www.hermanmiller.com/. The United States Green Building Council also maintains a helpful Web site, with links to local affiliates, at http://www.usgbc.org/.

# Genetically Modified Organisms and Business Duties

*Dennis R. Cooley*

New technology is one of the principal areas in which businesses struggle to find ethical solutions to moral dilemmas. Genetically modified organisms (GMOs) are one case in point.[1] In general, a genetically modified organism results from splicing foreign genetic material—a transgene—into a target organism's DNA to create an organism exhibiting at least one new genetic characteristic. There are already a vast array of GMOs for medical and food purposes in the marketplace including goats that

produce spider's silk in their milk, enormous cows that give gallons of milk, and pigs, mice, and fish that glow in the dark. Plants have also been modified. Monsanto's Roundup Ready™ crops, for example, are insusceptible to the company's Roundup pesticide (glyphosate). Most plants die when sprayed with glyphosate because it blocks a key enzyme—EPSP synthase—in an amino acid pathway. Roundup Ready crops have a bacterium's DNA that is unaffected by glyphosate thereby allowing them to continue to manufacture the enzyme and survive, while nearby weeds die.

Although some estimate that 60–70 percent of food on grocery store shelves contains at least one GMO ingredient, GMOs are not without their market problems. Monsanto's 2004 decision to withdraw its Roundup Ready wheat approval applications is an example of when a company makes a decision to forgo introducing a product even though it has spent millions of dollars on research and development. Syngenta will face the same decision with its GM fusarium-resistant wheat in the near future.

In this work, the moral permissibility for companies to develop and market GMOs will be examined. I will first develop a practical utilitarian principle that businesses, such as Monsanto and Syngenta, can use to defend their general and particular positions on GMOs. The second section is an overview of standard arguments for and against GMOs, and the final section draws the conclusion that the permissibility of developing and marketing any GMO rests on the action's consequences and whether or not all stakeholders affected by the action are respected. My main conclusion is that Monsanto and other companies have acted ethically by pursuing GMO technology in general, but that there are moral pitfalls that need to be avoided.

## UTILITARIAN FOUNDATIONS

Two moral theories are fundamental to ethical business decision making: Kantianism and utilitarianism. When making difficult decisions or performing actions affecting many people, we should respect all people affected by our actions as ends in themselves, and if we do not, then the action is unethical (Kant 1956, 62–63). In order to respect a person, one must not only respect her for being an autonomous agent but her autonomous choices as well, as long as

the latter do not illicitly harm others. Kantianism has an important role in business ethics, however, in the GMO debates, both opponents and proponents of GMOs typically appeal to utilitarian reasoning. Fortunately, there is a form of utilitarianism that is consistent with important strains of contemporary Kantian ethics. *Reasonable person utilitarianism* holds that:

> An action is morally right only if a reasonable person would believe that the action would probably have at least as much utility as any alternative to the action, where utility is defined as the value found by subtracting the amount of evil or harm produced by an act from the amount of good produced by the act.

In general, a reasonable person is someone who desires and works toward achievable ends in order to make himself and other intrinsically valuable entities better, provided that doing so does not surrender something of greater moral value. In addition, the reasonable person correctly and consistently analyzes the value of the data available to him for the particular situation in the time available and incorporates all relevant facts about society's rules, practices, and customs; rules and responsibilities associated with specific roles the agent is playing at the time; claims that others have on the agent and the agent has on others; value of consequences; and all relevant things into their decision process (Holmes 2007, 227–28). If new relevant information becomes available, the reasonable person reanalyzes the situation to see if his position should be altered accordingly.

Finally, although all reasonable people consider precautions in making their decisions, they are unlikely always to use the precautionary principle—and for good reasons. From even a cursory review of the literature on GMOs, it is clear the precautionary principle is more than one principle. What is held in common by all invocations of these principles is the intuitively appealing idea of maintaining the status quo until certain risks from the product have been identified and dealt with adequately. There is a great deal of variation on what entities are covered by the principle.[2] The more serious problem is that the precautionary principle is ill-defined and gives inaccurate ethical classifications in many business cases. For example, according to Greenpeace the principle means that based on the available evidence, caution should be taken for all activities that might harm human health or the environment even if the full extent of the harm has not been scientifically established. In practice, Greenpeace's principle entails that any belief about a risk is adequate to prevent the approval of GMOs until a point in time when they can be made to pose no risk to any living thing whatsoever. If this is the case, then no product would enter the market because all products that have ever existed or will exist have some risk.

The European Union's (EU's) more moderate political version of the principle is to achieve a high level of protection "when there are reasonable grounds for concern that potential hazards may affect the environment or human, animal or plant health, and when at the same time the available data preclude a detailed risk evaluation" (CEC 2000, 9). The EU has argued that because of their inherent character, GMOs require "particular scrutiny" and a stringent precautionary approach. The EU's principle is weaker than that of Greenpeace because of the reasonable-person standard, but it still does not give adequate guidance for making business decisions. After all, reasonable people can reasonably disagree about risk. What is unwarranted risk in one person's evaluation might be acceptable to another. Given this fact, when applying the EU's principle, it is unclear which reasonable person is supposed to win the argument. If Monsanto states that reasonable grounds do not exist but a EU politician who knows nothing about the science says there are reasonable grounds, then does

the EU's precautionary principle allow the product to be delayed, labeled, or banned from the market? In practice, the answer is a very strong affirmative as evidenced by the EU's de facto moratorium on GMO releases imposed before 2003 and the restrictive regulatory framework in place today. Any imagined concern about risk is often counted as equally legitimate to contradictory beliefs well grounded in scientific evidence. Reliance on the precautionary principle makes technological progress virtually impossible.

Given our discussion of the precautionary principle and other forms of regulation, a reasonable person will use general rules about risk assessment, management, and communication rather than basing decisions on an impractical precautionary principle. First, he evaluates technology risks knowing that:

> For any given level of benefit, people are prepared to tolerate a greater level of risk for activities that rate more highly in point of being: voluntary; avoidable; controllable; familiar (i.e., not particularly striking, memorable, shocking); well understood; not dreaded; not potentially disastrous; remote (not immediate or near-term). (Rescher 1983, 123)

Once risk has been adequately determined, then the reasonable person is more reluctant to impose it on others than he is on himself because he thinks people should decide for themselves how much they are willing to take. He would take greater precaution for them than he automatically does for himself.

## TRANSGENICS AND REASONABLE PERSON UTILITARIANISM

In order to determine if marketing and selling GMOs in general is likely to maximize utility according to a reasonable person, both the potential positives and negatives of the plausible alternatives have to be examined. That is, reasonable people must decide if the overall outcome of marketing and selling GMOs is likely to be better than doing something else. In what follows, I will alternate between the potential positives and their corresponding negatives. A reasonable person would consider each in making a decision about probable utility.

First, transgenic plants and animals can be part of healthier diets and provide relatively sustainable medical benefits to both wealthy and poor countries. Golden rice, for example, contains vitamin A, which conventional rice varieties cannot. By adding adequate vitamin A to rice-based diets there is a potential to help prevent 50,000 cases of blindness or death per year. In addition, a banana plant is in development which will produce fruit that will immunize those who eat it from *E. coli* infection. Since the plants will be able to continue to produce the genetically altered fruit, developing countries will always have an inexpensive supply, thereby allowing them to focus resources on other pressing issues. Other GMOs beneficial to consumers are in the pipeline. If transgenics can feed and medically treat people more efficiently than is the case with conventional and organic products, then an attractive consequence for GMOs is preserving more lives and increasing social goods.

There are negative potential outcomes to human health, however, to consider in the utilitarian calculus. Opponents to GMOs cite a number of studies conducted purporting to show that GMOs are unsafe for human and animal consumption. For example, Pustazi is alleged to have demonstrated that rats eating Monsanto GMO corn had changes to their blood composition and reduction of kidney size (Wisner 2006, 12). However, evidence for GMO safety is often not as extensive as many people would like for the purpose of making utility calculations. Clark states that the trials that are conducted tend to be scientifically incomplete or suspect (1994, 4–5). The result is

that in some cases, insufficient information makes it impossible to answer with certainty many questions about GMOs health impact.

Even though better information is something GMO producers should pursue for consumers and themselves for the purpose of better decision making, there are several different factors that help reasonable people perform adequate cost-benefit analysis without having perfect knowledge. First, many GMOs are genetically recognized as safe (GRAS) or have undergone a rigorous decision/testing procedure by their owners and the regulatory agencies governing the markets in which the transgenics will be sold if approved. The World Trade Organization stated in its ruling against the EU's restrictive GMO laws that many of the EU's risk concerns were unlikely to happen or were just as likely to happen with non-biotech crops (WTO 2006, 8.5). Moreover, the EU's own experts had "evaluated the potential risks to human health and/or the environment prior to the granting approval and had provided a positive opinion" (WTO 2006, 8.9). The findings are supported by the fact that people have been exposed for a number of years to this technology without ill effect.

In addition, conventional and organic plants and animals have never been subjected to the testing being demanded of GMOs, even though the former might have ill effects on people. Although it is assumed that they are safe, without adequate scientific trials, there is literally no reason to believe they are any less risky than GMOs. In fact, non-GMOs can be more dangerous than GMOs. Consider peanut allergies in children. If a GMO peanut is created that susceptible children can eat without having a deadly reaction—these are in development—then it is safer than conventional and organic products. Therefore, until there is more information to show that one of the three types of products and their respective production techniques is safer than the others, a reasonable person would believe that GMOs have no greater risks than non-GMOs.

A second positive aspect of GMOs is the potential to increase environmental diversity. Instead of a species' variations being limited by evolution and other natural forces, new variations and even species can be developed to better fit ecological niches. It is true that *Homo sapiens sapiens* have eliminated quite a few species, but transgenic engineering allows us to create new ones. Genetic engineering has already saved certain crops from becoming extinct, such as papaya which lacked variations that would make it immune to the papaya ringspot virus. Bananas are also being rescued. Due to 10,000 years of conventional propagation methods for bananas, there is too little DNA variation in the species; therefore, all the members can be wiped out by a single disease. Genetic engineering can create greater variation to improve the species' survival probability. In addition, as scientists become more adept at creating GMOs, the time and resources required for new products will be reduced. This will limit development costs and generate greater flexibility in situations in which an unforeseeable genetic problem with conventional and organic species must be overcome quickly else the species is lost.

The diversity benefit's correlating negative consequence is that there is a very good chance that biodiversity can be reduced by the corporations producing transgenics. For example, since the seed market is essentially controlled by an oligopoly, diversity is generally the last thing served by genetically modified organisms. Given the expense of creating and marketing new GMOs—sometimes having to overcome fierce resistance to their introduction in certain markets—profits are maximized by developing fewer species. Agricultural producers, as a result, have fewer choices, and monoculture becomes a greater possibility with the environmental fragility that using one variety of a species always brings with it. Moreover, because

the research and development costs of transgenics is prohibitive for start-up companies a few corporations control the market; hence, there is little good reason to believe alternatives to the major companies or their offerings are likely to happen soon enough to benefit consumers, marketplaces, or the environmental diversity (Tabor 1989, 333).

Although a lack of diversity is a strong concern, it is not the responsibility of companies to promote it. Maintaining biodiversity and competitive markets is the responsibility of governments who have the legitimate authority to regulate. First, if insufficient market competition is a problem, the same ethical approaches to making markets more competitive by government agencies can be used on transgenic producers, including but not limited to breaking up the companies or encouraging start-ups with tax credits or other incentives. Second, if biodiversity is a social concern, then governments can encourage it through greater production of transgenics and conservation of existing species through sustainable practices. Third, from the fact that transgenics have been used to enhance biodiversity, it should be clear that transgenics are not inherently in conflict with diversity.

GMOs' third benefit is that agricultural producers and those relying upon them can receive adequate returns on their investments. . . . .

The final positive benefit from transgenics is the potential profit for those who control the patents on the new species or sell genetically engineered products. Two-thirds of corn and three-quarters of soybean seed sold by Novartis Seeds, Inc.,[3] one of the three largest seed companies, are genetically engineered technology. In the United States, 34 percent of corn, 75 percent of soybeans, and 71 percent of cotton grown in 2002 were GMO. GMO crops have found worldwide producer acceptance if the 8.5 million farmers, over 90 percent of them in the developing world, using them is any indication. Of the 222 million acres planted worldwide with GMOs over 33 percent are accountable to developing world farmers. With more extensive adoption, corporate profits increase, which in turn helps the company executives to continue making the company competitive.

Mitigating the good market news are concerns about consumer acceptance and regulations. Although the studies purporting to show GMO health risks have been called into question on scientific grounds, the fact of the matter is poor science often has a greater impact on consumers' belief than does good science.[4] It all depends on what the consumer wants to believe. Many consumers make decisions based on partial information or even poor evidence made stronger by their fear of being harmed, motivated, perhaps, by an almost inherent distrust of new technology. Good products can be killed merely by consumer fear and businesses' responses to that fear. The Canadian Wheat Board, for example, stated that 87 percent of Canada's wheat buyers required guarantees that the wheat they were receiving was not GMO. This and pressure from Canadian officials helped Monsanto decide against Roundup Ready wheat release in Canada, even though the wheat is GRAS. In addition, if consumers are afraid, then they are more likely to pressure politicians into placing restrictions on GMOs and other technology. The EU's past and current restrictive regulatory frameworks are prime examples of what consumer fears can do to businesses.

In 2006 the WTO ruled against the EU's moratorium on GMO approvals and releases. The WTO found that the EU had violated the WTO's trade Agreement on the Application of Sanitary and Phytosanitary Measures by using its version of the precautionary principle in spite of the fact the EU's own scientists had stated GMOs pose no greater hazard than their non-GMO counterparts. This ruling would seem to be good news to Monsanto and other companies. . . .

Weighing all potential costs and benefits for GMOs is difficult given the number of them in the global market and their enormous impact. However, one can justifiably state that a reasonable person that considered the available evidence would conclude that the benefits outweigh the costs, thereby making marketing GMOs in general likely to have positive utility.

## REFERENCES

Clark, E. Ann. 2000. "Food Safety of GM Crops in Canada: Toxicity and Allergenicity," http://www/canadians.org/ge-alert/clark-foodsafety.pdf.

Clark, Stephen R. L. 1994. "New Issues: Genetic and Other Engineering", *Journal of Applied Philosophy* 11 (no. 2): 233–37.

Commission of the European Communities (CEC). 2002. Communication from the Commission on the Precautionary Principle, COM(2000) 1, Brussels, February 2.

Cooley, Dennis. 2002. "So Who's Afraid of Frankenstein Foods?" *Journal of Social Philosophy* 33, no. 3 (Fall): 442–63.

Holmes, Robert L. 2007. *Basic Moral Philosophy*. Belmont, CA: Thomson Wadsworth.

Kant, Immanuel. 1956. *Groundwork of the Metaphysic of Morals*, trans. H. J. Paton. New York: Harper & Row.

Rescher, Nicholas. 1983. *Risk*. Lanham, MD: University Press of America.

Tabor, John M., ed. 1989. *Genetically Modified Organisms Technology in Industrial Pharmacy: Principles and Applications*. New York: Marcel Dekker.

Wisner, Robert, and Western Organization of Resource Councils. 2006. "Potential Market Impacts for Commercializing Roundup Ready Wheat (September); update, http://www.wroc.org/pdfs/Market%20Risks%20Update%20Final%208-06.pdf.

World Trade Organization, EC—Approval and Marketing of Biotech Products, DS291, DS292, DS293, September 29, 2006.

## NOTES

1. These are actually transgenic organisms. Genetically modified organisms, on the other hand, are any human altered/created

organism through conventional breeding or transgenic technology.

2. For example, both the European Community Treaty and Rio Declaration versions mention only the environment, whereas the Commission of the European Communities has expanded the principle's scope to include human, animal, and plant health.

3. Novartis has combined with AstraZeneca to become Sygenta.

4. Some of the citations seem to be twisting the results to conclusions attacking Roundup Ready crops that are unsupported by the researchers, as in the case of Benbrook and the studies of glyphosate and human placental cells by Richard et al. (Benbrook, p. 3)

## LEGAL PERSPECTIVES

# United States, Petitioner, v. Bestfoods et al.

*United States Supreme Court*

JUSTICE SOUTER delivered the opinion of the Court.

The United States brought this action for the costs of cleaning up industrial waste generated by a chemical plant. The issue before us, under the Comprehensive Environmental Response, Compensation, and Liability Act of 1980 (CERCLA), 94 Stat. 2767, as amended, 42 U.S.C. §9601 *et seq.*, is whether a parent corporation that actively participated in, and exercised control over, the operations of a subsidiary may, without more, be held liable as an operator of a polluting facility owned or operated by the subsidiary. We answer no, unless the corporate veil may be pierced. But a corporate parent that actively participated in, and exercised control over, the operations of the facility itself may be held directly liable in its own right as an operator of the facility.

I

In 1980, CERCLA was enacted in response to the serious environmental and health risks

posed by industrial pollution. See *Exxon Corp. v. Hunt*, 475 U.S. 355, 358–359 (1986). "As its name implies, CERCLA is a comprehensive statute that grants the President broad power to command government agencies and private parties to clean up hazardous waste sites" *Key Tronic Corp. v. United States*, 511 U.S. 809, 814 (1994). If it satisfies certain statutory conditions, the United States may, for instance, use the "Hazardous Substance Superfund" to finance cleanup efforts, see 42 U.S.C. §§9601 (11), 9604; 26 U.S. C. §9507, which it may then replenish by suits brought under §107 of the Act against, among others, "any person who at the time of disposal of any hazardous substance owned or operated any facility." 42 U.S.C. §9607(a) (2). So, those actually "responsible for any damage, environmental harm, or injury from chemical poisons [may be tagged with] the cost of their actions," S. Rep. No. 96-848, p. 13 (1980). The term "person" is defined in CERCLA to include corporations and other business organizations, see 42 U.S.C. §9601 (21), and the term "facility" enjoys a broad and detailed definition as well, see §9601 (9). The phrase "owner or operator" is defined only by tautology, however, as "any person owning or operating" a facility, §9601 (20) (A) (ii), and it is this bit of circularity that prompts our review. Cf. *Exxon Corp. v. Hunt, supra*, at 363 (CERCLA, "unfortunately, is not a model of legislative draftsmanship").

## II

It is a general principle of corporate law deeply "ingrained in our economic and legal systems" that a parent corporation (so called because of control through ownership of another corporation's stock) is not liable for the acts of its subsidiaries. Douglas & Shanks, Insulation from Liability Through Subsidiary Corporations, 39 Yale L. J. 193 (1929) (hereinafter Douglas) . . . Thus it is hornbook law that "the exercise of the 'control' which stock ownership gives to the stockholders . . . will not create liability beyond the assets of the subsidiary. That 'control' includes the election of directors, the making of by-laws . . . and the doing of all other acts incident to the legal status of stockholders. Nor will a duplication of some or all of the directors or executive officers be fatal." Douglas 196 (footnotes omitted). Although this respect for corporate distinctions when the subsidiary is a polluter has been severely criticized in the literature, see, e.g., Note, Liability of Parent Corporations for Hazardous Waste Cleanup and Damages, 99 Harv. L. Rev. 986 (1986), nothing in CERCLA purports to reject this bedrock principle, and against this venerable common-law backdrop, the congressional silence is audible. Cf. *Edmonds v. Compagnie Generale Transatlantique*, 443 U.S. 256, 266–267 (1979) ("silence is most eloquent, for such reticence while contemplating an important and controversial change in existing law is unlikely"). The Government has indeed made no claim that a corporate parent is liable as an owner or an operator under §107 simply because its subsidiary is subject to liability for owning or operating a polluting facility.

But there is an equally fundamental principle of corporate law, applicable to the parent-subsidiary relationship as well as generally, that the corporate veil may be pierced and the shareholder held liable for the corporation's conduct when, *inter alia*, the corporate form would otherwise be misused to accomplish certain wrongful purposes, most notably fraud, on the shareholder's behalf. . . . Nothing in CERCLA purports to rewrite this well-settled rule, either. CERCLA is thus like many another congressional enactment in giving no indication "that the entire corpus of state corporation law is to be replaced simply because a plaintiff's cause of action is based upon a federal statute," *Burks v. Lasker*, 441 U.S. 471, 478 (1979), and the failure of the statute to speak to a matter as fundamental as the liability implications of corporate ownership demands application of the rule that "[i]n order to abrogate a common-law principle, the statute must speak directly to the question addressed by the common law," *United States v. Texas*, 507 U.S. 529, 534 (1993) (internal quotation marks omitted). The Court of Appeals [for the Sixth Circuit] was accordingly correct in holding that when (but only when) the corporate veil may be pierced, may a parent corporation be charged with derivative CERCLA liability for its subsidiary's actions.

## III

### A

If the act rested liability entirely on ownership of a polluting facility, this opinion might end here; but CERCLA liability may turn on operation as well as ownership, and nothing in the statute's terms bars a parent corporation from direct liability for its own actions in operating a facility owned by its subsidiary. As Justice (then-Professor) Douglas noted almost 70 years ago, derivative liability cases are to be distinguished from those in which "the alleged wrong can seemingly be traced to the parent through the conduit of its own personnel and management" and "the parent is directly a participant in the wrong complained of." Douglas 207, 208. In such instances, the parent is directly liable for its own actions. . . . The fact that a corporate subsidiary happens to own a polluting facility operated by its parent does nothing, then, to displace the rule that the parent "corporation is [itself] responsible for the wrongs committed by its agents in the course of its business," *Mine Workers v. Coronado Coal Co.*, 259 U.S. 344, 395 (1922), and whereas the rules of veil-piercing limit derivative liability for the actions of another corporation, CERCLA's "operator" provision is concerned primarily with direct liability for one's own actions. See, e.g., *Sidney S. Arst Co. v. Pipefitters Welfare Ed. Fund*, 25 F. 3d 417, 420 (CA7 1994) ("the direct, personal liability provided by CERCLA is distinct from the derivative liability that results from piercing the corporate veil") (internal quotation marks omitted). It is this direct liability that is properly seen as being at issue here.

Under the plain language of the statute, any person who operates a polluting facility is directly liable for the costs of cleaning up the pollution. See 42 U.S.C. §9607 (a) (2). This is so regardless of whether that person is the facility's owner, the owner's parent corporation or business partner, or even a saboteur who sneaks into the facility at night to discharge its poisons out of malice. If any such act of operating a corporate subsidiary's facility is done on behalf of a parent corporation, the existence of the parent-subsidiary relationship under state corporate law is simply irrelevant to the issue of direct liability. See *Riverside Market Dev. Corp. v. International Bldg. Prods., Inc.*, 931 F. 2d 327, 330 (CA5) ("CERCLA prevents individuals from hiding behind the corporate shield when, as 'operators,' they themselves actually participate in the wrongful conduct

prohibited by the Act"), cert. denied, 502 U.S. 1004 (1991); *United States v. Kayser-Roth Corp.*, 910 F.2d 24, 26 (CA1 1990) ("a person who is an operator of a facility is not protected from liability by the legal structure of ownership").

This much is easy to say; the difficulty comes in defining actions sufficient to constitute direct parental "operation." Here of course we may again rue the uselessness of CERCLA's definition of a facility's "operator" as "any person . . . operating" the facility, 42 U.S.C. §9601(20)(A)(ii), which leaves us to do the best we can to give the term its "ordinary or natural meaning." *Bailey v. United States*, 516 U.S. 137, 145 (1995) (internal quotation marks omitted). In a mechanical sense, to "operate" ordinarily means "[t]o control the functioning of; run: *operate a sewing machine.*" *American Heritage Dictionary* 1268 (3d ed. 1992); see also *Webster's New International Dictionary* 1707 (2d ed. 1958) ("to work; as, to *operate* a machine"). And in the organizational sense more obviously intended by CERCLA, the word ordinarily means "[t]o conduct the affairs of; manage: *operate a business.*" *American Heritage Dictionary*, supra, at 1268; see also *Webster's New International Dictionary*, supra, at 1707 ("to manage"). So, under CERCLA, an operator is simply someone who directs the workings of, manages, or conducts the affairs of a facility. To sharpen the definition for purposes of CERCLA's concern with environmental contamination, an operator must manage, direct, or conduct operations specifically related to pollution, that is, operations having to do with the leakage or disposal of hazardous waste, or decisions about compliance with environmental regulations.

## B

In our enquiry into the meaning Congress presumably had in mind when it used the verb "to operate," we recognized that the statute obviously meant something more than mere mechanical activation of pumps and valves, and must be read to contemplate "operation" as including the exercise of direction over the facility's activities. . . . The Court of Appeals recognized this by indicating that a parent can be held directly liable when the parent operates the facility in the stead of its subsidiary or alongside the subsidiary in some sort of a joint venture. See 113 F. 3d, at 579. We anticipated a further possibility . . . that a dual officer or director might depart so far from the norms of parental influence exercised through dual officeholding as to serve the parent, even when ostensibly acting on behalf of the subsidiary in operating the facility. . . . Yet another possibility, suggested by the facts of this case, is that an agent of the parent with no hat to wear but the parent's hat might manage or direct activities at the facility.

Identifying such an occurrence calls for line drawing yet again, since the acts of direct operation that give rise to parental liability must necessarily be distinguished from the interference that stems from a normal relationship between parent and subsidiary. Again norms of corporate behavior (undisturbed by any CERCLA provision) are crucial reference points. Just as we may look to such norms in identifying the limits of the presumption that a dual officeholder acts in his ostensible capacity, so here we may refer to them in distinguishing a parental officer's oversight of a subsidiary from such an officer's control over the operation of the subsidiary's facility. . . . The critical question is whether, in degree and detail, actions directed to the facility by an agent of the parent alone are eccentric under accepted norms of parental oversight of a subsidiary's facility. . . .

---

# Christine Todd Whitman, Administrator of Environmental Protection Agency, et al., Petitioners, v. American Trucking Associations, Inc., et al.

*United States Supreme Court*

These cases present the following questions: (1) Whether §109(b)(1) of the Clean Air Act (CAA) delegates legislative power to the Administrator of the Environmental Protection Agency (EPA). (2) Whether the Administrator may consider the costs of implementation in setting national ambient air quality standards (NAAQS) under §109(b)(1). (3) Whether the Court of Appeals had jurisdiction to review the EPA's interpretation of Part D of Title I of the CAA, 42 U.S.C. §§7501–7515, with respect

to implementing the revised ozone NAAQS. (4) If so, whether the EPA's interpretation of that part was permissible.

## I

Section 109(a) of the CAA, as added, 84 Stat. 1679, and amended, 42 U.S.C. §7409(a), requires the Administrator of the EPA to promulgate NAAQS for each air pollutant for which "air quality criteria" have been issued under §108, 42 U.S.C. §7408. Once a NAAQS has been promulgated, the Administrator must review the standard (and the criteria on which it is based) "at five-year intervals" and make "such revisions . . . as may be appropriate." CAA §109(d)(1), 42 U.S.C. §7409(d)(1). These cases arose when, on July 18, 1997, the Administrator revised the NAAQS for particulate matter (PM) and ozone. . . . American Trucking Associations, Inc., and its co-respondents in No. 99-1257—which include, in addition to other private companies, the States of Michigan, Ohio, and West Virginia—challenged the new standards in the Court of Appeals for the District of Columbia Circuit, pursuant to 42 U.S.C. §7607(b)(1).

The District of Columbia Circuit accepted some of the challenges and rejected others. It agreed with the No. 99-1257 respondents (hereinafter respondents) that §109(b)(1) delegated legislative power to the Administrator in contravention of the United States Constitution, Art. I, §1, because it found that the EPA had interpreted the statute to provide no "intelligible principle" to guide the agency's exercise of authority. *American Trucking Assns., Inc. v. EPA*, 175 F. 3d 1027, 1034 (1999). The court thought, however, that the EPA could perhaps avoid the unconstitutional delegation by adopting a restrictive construction of §109(b)(1), so instead of declaring the section unconstitutional the court remanded the NAAQS to the agency. . . . On the second issue that the Court of Appeals addressed, it unanimously rejected respondents' argument that the court should depart from the rule of *Lead Industries Assn., Inc. v. EPA*, 647 F. 2d 1130, 1148 (CADC 1980), that the EPA may not consider the cost of implementing a NAAQS in setting the initial standard. It also rejected respondents' argument that the implementation provisions for ozone . . . were so tied to the existing ozone

standard that the EPA lacked the power to revise the standard. . . .

The Administrator and the EPA petitioned this Court for review of the first, third, and fourth questions described in the first paragraph of this opinion. Respondents conditionally cross-petitioned for review of the second question. We granted certiorari on both petitions, 529 U.S. 1129 (2000); 530 U.S. 1202 (2000), and scheduled the cases for argument in tandem. We have now consolidated the cases for purposes of decision.

## II

In *Lead Industries Assn., Inc. v. EPA, supra*, at 1148, the District of Columbia Circuit held that "economic considerations [may] play no part in the promulgation of ambient air quality standards under Section 109" of the CAA. In the present cases, the court adhered to that holding, 175 F. 3d, at 1040–1041, as it had done on many other occasions. . . . Respondents argue that these decisions are incorrect. We disagree; and since the first step in assessing whether a statute delegates legislative power is to determine what authority the statute confers, we address that issue of interpretation first and reach respondents' constitutional arguments in Part III, *infra*.

Section 109(b)(1) instructs the EPA to set primary ambient air quality standards "the attainment and maintenance of which . . . are requisite to protect the public health" with "an adequate margin of safety." 42 U.S.C. §7409(b)(1). Were it not for the hundreds of pages of briefing respondents have submitted on the issue, one would have thought it fairly clear that this text does not permit the EPA to consider costs in setting the standards. The language, as one scholar has noted, "is absolute." D. Currie, Air Pollution: Federal Law and Analysis 4–15 (1981). The EPA, "based on" the information about health effects contained in the technical "criteria" documents compiled under §108(a)(2), 42 U.S.C. §7408(a)(2), is to identify the maximum airborne concentration of a pollutant that the public health can tolerate, decrease the concentration to provide an "adequate" margin of safety, and set the standard at that level. Nowhere are the costs of achieving such a standard made part of that initial calculation.

Against this most natural of readings, respondents make a lengthy, spirited, but ultimately unsuccessful attack. They begin with the object of §109(b)(1)'s focus, the "public health." When the term first appeared in federal clean air legislation—in the Act of July 14, 1955 (1955 Act), 69 Stat. 322, which expressed "recognition of the dangers to the public health" from air pollution—its ordinary meaning was "[t]he health of the community." *Webster's New International Dictionary* 2005 (2d ed. 1950). Respondents argue, however, that §109(b)(1), as added by the Clean Air Amendments of 1970 (1970 Act), 84 Stat. 1676, meant to use the term's secondary meaning: "[t]he ways and means of conserving the health of the members of a community, as by preventive medicine, organized care of the sick, etc." *Ibid.* Words that can have more than one meaning are given content, however, by their surroundings, and in the context of §109(b)(1) this second definition makes no sense. Congress could not have meant to instruct the Administrator to set NAAQS at a level "requisite to protect" "the art and science dealing with the protection and improvement of community health." *Webster's Third New International Dictionary* 1836 (1981). We therefore revert to the primary definition of the term: the health of the public.

Even so, respondents argue, many more factors than air pollution affect public health. In particular, the economic cost of implementing a very stringent standard might produce health losses sufficient to offset the health gains achieved in cleaning the air—for example, by closing down whole industries and thereby impoverishing the workers and consumers dependent upon those industries. That is unquestionably true, and Congress was unquestionably aware of it. Thus, Congress had commissioned in the Air Quality Act of 1967 (1967 Act) "a detailed estimate of the cost of carrying out the provisions of this Act; a comprehensive study of the cost of program implementation by affected units of government; and a comprehensive study of the economic impact of air quality standards on the Nation's industries, communities, and other contributing sources of pollution." §2, 81 Stat. 505. The 1970 Congress, armed with the results of this study, see The Cost of Clean Air, S. Doc. No. 91-40 (1969) (publishing the results of the study), not only anticipated that compliance costs could injure the public health, but provided for that precise exigency. Section 110(f)(1) of the CAA permitted the Administrator to waive the compliance deadline for stationary sources if, *inter alia*, sufficient control measures were simply unavailable and "the continued operation of such sources is *essential . . . to the public health* or welfare." 84 Stat. 1683 (emphasis added). Other provisions explicitly permitted or required economic costs to be taken into account in implementing the air quality standards. Section 111(b)(1)(B), for example, commanded the Administrator to set "standards of performance" for certain new sources of emissions that as specified in §111(a)(1) were to "reflec[t] the degree of emission limitation achievable through the application of the best system of emission reduction which (taking into account the cost of achieving such reduction) the Administrator determines has been adequately demonstrated." Section 202(a)(2) prescribed that emissions standards for automobiles could take effect only "after such period as the Administrator finds necessary to permit the development and application of the requisite technology, giving appropriate consideration to the cost of compliance within such period." 84 Stat. 1690. See also §202(b)(5)(C) (similar limitation for interim standards); §211(c)(2) (similar limitation for fuel additives); §231(b) (similar limitation for implementation of aircraft emission standards). Subsequent amendments to the CAA have added many more provisions directing, in explicit language, that the Administrator consider costs in performing various duties. See, e.g., 42 U.S.C. §7545(k)(1) (reformulate gasoline to "require the greatest reduction in emissions . . . taking into consideration the cost of achieving such emissions reductions"); §7547(a)(3) (emission reduction for nonroad vehicles to be set "giving appropriate consideration to the cost" of the standards). We have therefore refused to find implicit in ambiguous sections

of the CAA an authorization to consider costs that has elsewhere, and so often, been expressly granted. . . .

To summarize our holdings in these unusually complex cases: (1) The EPA may not consider implementation costs in setting primary and secondary NAAQS under §109(b) of the CAA. (2) Section 109(b)(1) does not delegate legislative power to the EPA in contravention of Art. I, §1, of the Constitution. (3) The Court of Appeals had jurisdiction to review the EPA's interpretation of Part D of Title I of the CAA, relating to the implementation of the revised ozone NAAQS. (4) The EPA's interpretation of that Part is unreasonable.

The judgment of the Court of Appeals is affirmed in part and reversed in part, and the cases are remanded for proceedings consistent with this opinion.

*It is so ordered.*

---

## CASES

## CASE 1.  *Royal Caribbean: Exotic Promises and Toxic Waters*

Royal Caribbean Cruises Ltd., which operates the Royal Caribbean International, Celebrity Cruises, and Pullmantur lines, is one of the world's largest cruise companies. Currently they utilize 34 vessels, with a maximum passenger capacity of nearly 68,000, and visit approximately 200 locations

worldwide. By 2010, those numbers are expected to rise to 40 ships with a total capacity of almost 90,000. In 2006, Royal Caribbean Cruises Ltd. reported $5,229,584 in revenues. The company is headquartered in Miami, Florida, United States, and is publicly traded.

© 2007 by Todd Johnson and Denis Arnold. This case study was prepared by Todd M. Johnson under the supervision of Denis G. Arnold. The case is based on Robert Trigaux, "To Keep Waters Pristine, Punish the Polluters," *St. Petersburg Times* (May 19, 2002); Eliza Strickland, "Making a Stink: What Effect Does Ship Waste Have on Our Coastal Waters? As New Orleans embraces the cruise line industry, it's time to ask the No. 1 question about No. 2," *Gambit Weekly* (November 11, 2003), accessed at http://www.bestofneworleans.com/dispatch/2003-11-18/cover_story.html (15 February 2007); Morgan O'Rourke, "Cruise Line Forced to Address Pollution," *Risk Management* 51 (July 1, 2004) 8; "Pollution and Environmental Violations and Fines, 1992–2007 (Only those reported in the media or public documents)," http://www.cruisejunkie.com/envirofines.html (February 15, 2007); "Corporate Governance—Code of Business Conduct and Ethics," http://www.rclinvestor.com/phoenix.zhtml?c=103045&p=irol-govconduct (February 15, 2007); "Plan a Cruise >Activities," http://www.royalcaribbean.com/findacruise/experiencetypes/home.do;jsessionid=0000hfqnfoilghcBjIVE7jeyEGq:10ktdmlju?cS=NAVBAR (February 15, 2007); "Oceana, "http://oceana.org/index.php?id=1769&no_cache=1 (February 16, 2007).

Often called "floating cities," cruise ships are advertised as opportunities for travelers to visit exotic destinations, experience "once in a lifetime" scenery, and relax with a myriad of fun and games. Passengers are strongly encouraged to partake in such activities as swimming, snorkeling, scuba diving, interacting with dolphins, kayaking, rafting, fishing, and surfing, among other things.

According to Oceana, an organization that "campaigns to protect and restore the world's oceans," cruise liners can generate in excess of 30,000 gallons of sewage, or "black water," 250,000 gallons of water from sinks, showers, laundries, etc., known as "gray water," 7,500 gallons of oily bilge water, and 7–10 tons of garbage and solid waste in a single day. A study by the Department of Environmental Conservation concluded that of 42 samples of discharged water taken over the course of 2001 by various cruise companies voyaging in Alaskan waters, nine exceeded the fecal bacterial standards by 50,000 times, and only one sample was in full compliance with all regulations.

The Royal Caribbean Cruise's *Code of Business Conduct and Ethics* states the company's priority to, "Commit to a comprehensive environmental protection program focusing on the key elements of reduction of waste, recycling, and proper disposal." However, despite this inclusion in their corporate governance, from 1998 to 2000 the company was ordered by the U.S. government to pay roughly $30,500,000 in fines to state and national agencies as a result of their intentional environmental degradation and subsequent attempted cover-ups. The first offense in 1998 led to a $1 million fine, for falsifying records regarding oil-water discharged into the waters off the coast of Miami, Florida, by the *Nordic Empress* cruise ship. A second fine in 1998, of $8 million, resulted from similar activity off the coast of Puerto Rico by five different liners, *Sovereign of the Seas, Monarch of the Seas, Song of America, Nordic Prince,* and *Nordic Empress.* In addition to the dumping itself, the employees on all the ships admitted to falsifying the records and lying to the Coast Guard to conceal the dumping. Royal Caribbean Cruises Ltd. was placed on 5 years' probation. The largest fine came in 1999, when the company was ordered to pay $18 million because of similar activities, including illegal dumping by *Grandeur of the Seas, Majesty of the Seas, Monarch of the Seas, Nordic Empress, Nordic Prince, Song of America, Song of Norway, Sovereign of the Seas,* and *Sun Viking.* Many of these ships were found guilty of, in addition to bypassing mandated water purification systems for oily water, dumping human wastewater and other chemicals, as well as fabricating relevant records and providing false testimony to officials. Another fine of $3.5 million came in a 2000 plea agreement with the state of Alaska, for dumping oil, waste, dry-cleaning chemicals, and other toxins into the state's waters. It is important to note that a large majority of each of the fines over this span were caused by the deliberate and multiple attempts to cover up or obscure the activities when investigated by the Coast Guard and other state agencies, and not for the environmental damage itself.

In general, it is difficult to supervise and regulate the activities of cruise ships for at least two reasons. The first is that, unlike Royal Caribbean Cruises Ltd., many cruises lines are based in other countries. This is problematic for proper regulation because of the variance in environmental laws. The second is that many cruise liners travel in international waters, where no immediate oversight is present, and most laws protecting the environment are inapplicable. For example, the Clean Water Act is designed to regulate land-based activities, whereas the cruise ships' discharges are water-based.

Because of the inadequacies of the Clean Water Act concerning cruise ship pollution, Congress introduced and passed the Clean Cruise Ships Act of 2004. This legislation illegalized the dumping of black water, gray water, and oily bilge waste within 12 miles of U.S. banks. Additionally, any dumping of these materials outside of 12 miles, but still in U.S. waters, requires advanced treatment processes. Also included in the Act are mandated regular inspections of treatment and discharging operations, including equipment. Finally, the provision called for independent observers to monitor and police strict compliance with environmental laws and codes over the course of 3 years. Another means by which cruise ship dumping is being reduced, it is hoped, comes from the Act to Prevent Pollution from Ships, which offers financial compensation for information leading to the conviction of fraudulent behavior, that is, illegal dumping. This incentive was collected after a whistle-blower reported wrongful activities by Norwegian Cruise Lines off the coast of Florida from 1997 to 2000. The company was subsequently convicted and fined $1.5 million (the fine was modest, given the numerous violations, because the company reported its unlawful activities directly to the U.S. Department of Justice).

In all, the cruise line industry has spent an estimated $53,000,000 on fines owing to environmental destruction (and cover-up) since 1992, with Royal Caribbean and Carnival Cruises Lines commanding around 75 percent of that total. The latest fine for Royal Caribbean was ordered in November 2006, when one of its Celebrity Cruise ships was found guilty of dumping untreated wastewater multiple times in 2005. Royal Caribbean initially denied responsibility, but later it was discovered that documents onboard the ship verified the acts, and the company rescinded its original denial and took full responsibility.

**Questions:**

1. Given that Royal Caribbean and other cruise companies use images of excursions in pristine waters in their marketing campaigns, how should one ethically assess their illegal dumping in such waters? Explain.
2. Given that illegal activities and subsequent fines continue to occur despite the numerous punishments already handed out, what responsibility, if any, do customers have to ensure illegal dumping ceases? Explain.
3. What are the best moral arguments *supporting* the legislation and laws making certain levels of black water, gray water, and oily bilge discharge illegal? What are the best moral arguments *opposing* them? Explain.
4. Given the two stated problems of international regulation, who should ultimately be responsible for bringing environmental offenders "to justice?" Explain.

# CASE 2.  *Texaco in the Ecuadorean Amazon*

Ecuador is a small nation on the northwest coast of South America. During its 173-year history, Ecuador has been one of the least politically stable South American nations. In 1830 Ecuador achieved its independence from Spain. Ecuadorean history since that time has

This case was prepared by Denis G. Arnold and is based on James Brooke, "New Effort Would Test Possible Coexistence of Oil and Rain Forest," *New York Times* (February 26, 1991); Dennis M. Hanratty, ed., *Ecuador: A Country Study*, 3rd ed. (Washington DC: Library of Congress, 1991); Anita Isaacs, *Military Rule and Transition in Ecuador, 1972–92* (Pittsburgh: University of Pittsburgh Press, 1993); *Ecuador Poverty Report* (Washington DC: The World Bank, 1996); Joe Kane, *Savages* (New York: Vintage Books, 1996); Eyal Press, "Texaco on Trial," *Nation*, (May 31, 1999); and "Texaco and Ecuador," *Texaco: Health, Safety & the Environment* (September 27, 1999), www.texaco.com/she/index.html (December 16, 1999); and *Aguinda v. Texaco Inc.*, 142 F. Supp. 2d 534 (S.D.N.Y. 2001). © 2008.

been characterized by cycles of republican government and military intervention and rule. The period from 1960 to 1972 was marked by instability and military dominance of political institutions. From 1972 to 1979 Ecuador was governed by military regimes. In 1979 a popularly elected president took office, but the military demanded and was granted important governing powers. The democratic institutional framework of Ecuador remains weak. Decreases in public sector spending, increasing unemployment, and rising inflation have hit the Ecuadorean poor especially hard. World Bank estimates indicate that in 1994, 35 percent of the Ecuadorean population lived in poverty, and an additional 17 percent were vulnerable to poverty.

The Ecuadorean Amazon is one of the most biologically diverse forests in the world and is home to an estimated 5 percent of Earth's species. It is home to cicadas, scarlet macaws, squirrel monkeys, freshwater pink dolphins, and thousands of other species. Many of these species have small populations, making them extremely sensitive to disturbance. Indigenous Indian populations have lived in harmony with these species for centuries. They have fished and hunted in and around the rivers and lakes; and they have raised crops of cacao, coffee, fruits, nuts, and tropical woods in *chakras*, models of sustainable agroforestry.

Ten thousand feet beneath the Amazon floor lies one of Ecuador's most important resources: rich deposits of crude oil. Historically, the Ecuadorean government regarded the oil as the best way to keep up with the country's payments on its $12 billion foreign debt obligations. For 20 years American oil companies, lead by Texaco, extracted oil from beneath the Ecuadorean Amazon in partnership with the government of Ecuador. (The United States is the primary importer of Ecuadorean oil.) They constructed 400 drill sites and hundreds of miles of roads and pipelines, including a primary pipeline that extends for 280 miles across the Andes. Large tracts of forest were clear-cut to make way for these facilities. Indian lands, including *chakras*, were taken and bulldozed, often without compensation. In the village of Pacayacu the central square is occupied by a drilling platform.

Officials estimate that the primary pipeline alone has spilled more than 16.8 million gallons of oil into the Amazon over an 18-year period. Spills from secondary pipelines have never been estimated or recorded; however, smaller tertiary pipelines dump 10,000 gallons of petroleum per week into the Amazon, and production pits dump approximately 4.3 million gallons of toxic production wastes and treatment chemicals into the forest's rivers, streams, and groundwater each day. (By comparison, the Exxon Valdez spilled 10.8 million gallons of oil into Alaska's Prince William Sound.) Significant portions of these spills have been carried downriver into neighboring Peru.

Critics charge that Texaco ignored prevailing oil industry standards that call for the reinjection of waste deep into the ground. Rivers and lakes were contaminated by oil and petroleum; heavy metals such as arsenic, cadmium, cyanide, lead, and mercury; poisonous industrial solvents; and lethal concentrations of chloride salt, and other highly toxic chemicals. The only treatment these chemicals received occurred when the oil company burned waste pits to reduce petroleum content. Villagers report that the chemicals return as black rain, polluting what little freshwater remains. What is not burned off seeps through the unlined walls of the pits into the groundwater. Cattle are found with their stomachs rotted out, crops are destroyed, animals are gone from the forest, and fish disappear from the lakes and rivers. Health officials and community leaders report adults and children with deformities, skin rashes, abscesses, headaches, dysentery, infections, respiratory ailments, and disproportionately high rates of cancer. In 1972 Texaco signed a contract requiring it to turn over all of its operations to Ecuador's national oil company, Petroecuador, by 1992. Petroecuador inherited antiquated equipment, rusting pipelines, and uncounted toxic waste sites. Independent estimates place the cost of cleaning up the production pits alone at $600 million. From 1995 to 1998 Texaco spent $40 million on cleanup operations in Ecuador. In exchange for these efforts the government of Ecuador relinquished future claims against the company.

Numerous international accords—including the 1972 Stockholm Declaration on the Human Environment signed by over 100 countries, including the United States and Ecuador—identify the right to a clean and healthy environment as a fundamental human right and prohibit both state and private actors from endangering the needs of present and future generations. Ecuadorean and Peruvian plaintiffs, including several indigenous tribes, have filed billion-dollar class-action lawsuits against Texaco in U.S. courts under the Alien Tort Claims Act (ACTA). Enacted in 1789, the law was designed to provide noncitizens access to U.S. courts in cases involving a breach of international law, including accords. Texaco maintains that the case should be tried in Ecuador. However, Ecuador's judicial system does not recognize the concept of a class-action suit and has no history of environmental litigation. Furthermore, Ecuador's judicial system is notoriously corrupt (a poll by George Washington University found that only 16 percent of Ecuadoreans have confidence in their judicial system) and lacks the infrastructure necessary to handle the case (e.g., the city in which the case would be tried lacks a courthouse). Texaco defended its actions by arguing that it is in full compliance with Ecuadorean law and that it had full approval of the Ecuadorean government.

In May 2001 U.S. District Judge Jed Rakoff rejected the applicability of the ACTA and dismissed the case on grounds of forum non conveniens. Judge Rakoff argued that since "no act taken by Texaco in the United States bore materially on the pollution-creating activities," the case should be tried in Ecuador and Peru. In October 2001 Texaco completed a merger with Chevron Corporation. Chevron and Texaco are now known as ChevronTexaco Corporation. In August 2002 the U.S. Court of Appeals for the Second Circuit upheld Judge Rakoff's decision.

## Questions

1. Given the fact that Texaco operated in partnership with the Ecuadorean government, is Texaco's activity in the Amazon morally justifiable? Explain.
2. Does Texaco (now ChevronTexaco) have a moral obligation to provide additional funds and technical expertise to clean up areas of the Amazon it is responsible for polluting? Does it have a moral obligation to provide medical care for the residents of the Amazon region who are suffering from the effects of the pollution? Explain.
3. Does the fact that the military plays a dominant role in Ecuadorean political life undermine Texaco's claim that its environmental practices are justified because the government of Ecuador permitted them? Explain.
4. Does the example of Texaco's conduct in Ecuador indicate a need for enforceable regulations governing transnational corporate activity? Explain.

# CASE 3.    *BP: Beyond Petroleum Spills?*

*"I understand if people want to say 'how can you have something like this happen and you are supposedly a green company?' But I would say if you shut down for environmental reasons you are a pretty green company."*
—Robert Malone, BP America President and Chairman, 2006

## BP'S RECENT HISTORY

BP (British Petroleum) first entered Alaska around 1960, and after a decade of exploration discovered commercial-quantity oil in Prudhoe Bay in 1969. This discovery proved to be the largest existing oil field in North America, and BP soon set up refineries in the United States. Following the Prudhoe Bay discovery, BP signed an agreement with Standard Oil Company of Ohio that gave Standard the lease in Prudhoe Bay, and in return BP received a 25 percent equity share in Standard.

Owing to BP's 25 percent share in Standard Oil and the interest in Prudhoe Bay, BP survived the oil crisis of the 1970s. The oil crisis mainly affected companies that dealt predominately in the Middle East. The Trans-Alaska Pipeline was completed in 1977 and has delivered 15 billion barrels of oil to date. This pipeline completed the infrastructure BP needed to maximize the value of the Alaska oil fields. In 1987, BP bought the rest of Standard Oil and the portion of their stock that the British Government still owned.

BP currently has one-third of its fixed assets in the United States. It merged with Amoco in 1998, and kept the BP-Amoco name until 2002, when it dropped the Amoco. BP has tried to lead the way for other oil companies to take on environmental issues such as global warming. However, this positive image has been dwarfed by recent negative publicity stemming from an explosion at a BP refinery in Texas in 2005. The explosion killed 15 people. One year later, one of the BP pipelines in Alaska ruptured and dumped oil onto the frozen tundra for several days.

## HOW THE SPILL HAPPENED

Despite the finance and technology at BP's disposal, the spill was discovered in a decidedly low-tech manner. Operators first claimed to have suspected the leak when they detected the smell of oil vapor during a ride along the pipe. They were unable to see the leak, but they could hear a strange gurgling sound. Deep below the snow a dime-sized hole was found to be leaking oil. Later investigations revealed that the flow rates inside the pipe were unresolved to approximately the volume of oil that hemorrhaged from the line unnoticed over the course of several days. State regulations placed the minimum need for automatic loss detection to be 1 percent of the flow. The BP-operated line was configured to detect a 0.5 percent loss of flow and tripped 4 straight days prior to the discovery of the spill. BP technicians claimed that the condition of the line made it prone to false alarms and dismissed the warnings without investigation.

At the time of discovery of the leak, BP was spending the absolute minimum in maintenance cost to maintain the 22 miles of pipeline

---

This case study was written for educational purposes by Bryan Bollinger, Tarek El-Messidi, David Ralston, Kevin Rayburn, and Thomas Smith under the supervision of Denis G. Arnold © 2007.

in Prudhoe Bay. There were only two preventive measures in place. First was a series of chemical additives mixed into the slurry of crude in pipe, which are used to help break up sedimentation. The other measure BP claimed to be employing was a series of spot-checks of the thickness of the pipe walls using ultrasound. The checks were conducted at what the technicians felt were the most probable points of corrosion. However, the operation possessed a much more sophisticated line inspection device called a *pipeline inspection gauge* or "pig," which earned its name from the squealing sound it makes while traversing the pipe. Pigs act like a giant squeegee for the pipeline. They are inserted into the pipe during flow and seal to the inside of the pipeline. Sediment is then scraped from the inner wall as fluid pressure from product flow is exerted behind it. This process is critical to pipeline health because the slow-moving slurry allows deposits to form on the inner walls of the system. These deposits shield the metal from fresh slurry and create a haven for bacteria to grow and feed on the pipe.

The problem with pigging is the restriction it places on the pipeline. Some pigs require special flow conditions inside the pipe that do not always coincide with the operation of the field. Thus, in addition to the cost per kilometer of operating a pig, which is often in the thousands of dollars per kilometer depending on the pig's capabilities, production sometimes must be slowed (Short, Hak, and Smith 2006). More advanced pigs can run in tandem to coat the inner walls of the pipeline with composite repair material. Still other pigs can use ultrasound to provide precise thickness measures of both degraded walls and sediment deposits over the entire length of the pipeline, giving the operators notice of weakening pipe long before failure.

BP admitted at the time of the incident that a pig hadn't run in the line since 1998. Compare this schedule with that of the Trans-Alaska Pipeline, which is pigged every 14 days. Ronnie Chappell, a spokesman for BP, claimed the reason for this was that the pipes were already too clogged with sludge to allow the pig to pass. Bill Hedges, BP's North Slope corrosion manager added that the pipes were not believed to be at risk for corrosion-related leaks because the lines carried only oil that had corrosive water removed. However, the 1998 pig run through the pipe revealed no fewer than six weaknesses in the vicinity of the leak, and one of those places was where the fissure occurred. After the incident, the entire stretch of pipe was inspected using a smart pig. There was more than 80 percent corrosion of the ⅜-inch thick walls in some sections, and 16 miles of feeder pipe had to be replaced.

## THE MARCH 2006 SPILL

The March 2006 spill of 270,000 gallons was the largest in the North Slope's history. The leak started at a caribou crossing. The affected area is about 2 acres of tundra hundreds of miles north of Anchorage and includes the edge of a frozen-over lake. No one saw the spilled oil because the line is covered—it's above ground level but covered in gravel so caribou can cross. And the pipe, gravel, and ground were all covered in snow, with the oil hiding beneath the snow cover. As the hot oil melted the snow, it sank farther out of sight.

Winter conditions helped partially mitigate the impact on wildlife from the 2-acre oil spill. "It certainly would have been a lot worse (in the summer). We have probably 2 months to work on this thing, and it happened at the right time of year," said Ed Meggert, an on-scene response coordinator for the state. Wildlife is scarce in the region at that time of year but do return when the snow melts in the spring and summer (Rosen 2006).

Despite the timing, the spill did occur in a very sensitive area, one of several caribou-crossing areas where pipes are laid underground and covered with gravel to allow passage by migratory animals. These crossing areas always attract water (which exacerbated the pipe corrosion). Leftover oil traces after the cleanup operation can mix with the water that animals stop to drink while migrating. There is likely to be lots of oil residue where the spill occurred, since windchill at Prudhoe Bay was less than −40°F at times in March. "Right now, they are collecting a few hundred gallons a day basically, because it's so cold," said Brandon of the Alaska Wilderness League. "So that's just longer and longer the oil will be sitting out there" (Roach 2006).

There is a criminal investigation into whether BP was consistently negligent in pipeline maintenance. This probe was triggered by Chuck Hamel, an oil worker advocate, who went public with accusations of deliberate maintenance lapses and falsified documentation. As a result, the Environmental Protection Agency launched a probe into whether BP properly maintained its pipeline and into whether it violated the Clean Water Act. The U.S. Department of Justice is also considering charges.

Oil spills are not cheap, and BP is paying a considerable amount of money to clean up the spill and prevent future pipeline failures. "BP has earmarked an additional $550 million to improve the integrity of its 1,500 miles of pipes, along with wells and gathering centers. The entire system of transit lines that failed this summer will be replaced at a cost of $150 million, and 21 new corrosion and safety specialists are being hired" (Schwartz 2006).

BP is not the only party suffering the financial impact of the oil spill. Shutting down the pipeline translated into a loss of 400,000 barrels of oil a day. The Union of Concerned Scientists estimated that the United States would spend at least an additional $24 million a day on oil as a direct result of this pipeline spill and the subsequent price spike.

## IMPACT ON PUBLIC RELATIONS

BP had prided itself on being a more ethical company than its competitors. Only a couple of weeks before news of the pipeline issue broke, CEO John Browne had compared himself to Exxon and said, "It is not a matter of competition, it is a matter of character" (Mufson 2006). BP portrayed itself as a company that cared about the ramifications of its actions and was about more than the bottom line. It had a strong environmental public relations campaign that emphasized its concern for the environment, with add slogans like "It's time to turn up the heat on global warming" and "It's time to think outside the barrel" (Mufson 2006).

In 2000, BP spent $200 million and hired Ogilvy & Mather Worldwide to rebrand itself as an environmentally conscious or "green" company. Although the oil industry had a negative environmental image, BP wanted to be a different type of company. Its espousal of a commitment to the environment won praise and recognition in many circles. The campaign won the *PRWeek* 2001 "Campaign of the Year" award. This campaign won over many of its environmental critics, though not all. There were still articles published that criticized its explorations in the Artic National Wildlife Refuge and other environmentally sensitive areas. BP also admitted to hiring detectives to spy on some of its stronger critics in 2001, such as Greenpeace and the Body Shop.

BP's "green" image has become severely damaged owing to the Prudhoe Bay oil spill. Critics are accusing BP of knowing about this problem for years and claiming it fostered a corporate culture in which this was bound to happen. Members of Congress are calling for investigations, and the public image of BP as a socially and environmentally conscious leader has been smeared.

## Questions

1. How would you explain BP's lack of attention to maintenance of the Trans-Alaska Pipeline given its environmental commitments?
2. How would you characterize BP's public relations campaign from an ethical perspective? Explain.
3. Is BP's response to the pipeline spill adequate from an ethical perspective? Why or why not?
4. How, if at all, is this pipeline spill linked to the 2005 BP oil refinery explosion and fire in Texas City, Texas (see Chapter 3)? Explain.

## REFERENCES

"Alaska Pipeline Spill Amount Debated." *Associated Press. MSNBC.com.* March 6, 2006. November 28, 2006 <http://www.msnbc.msn.com/id/11696601/>.

"BP Pipeline Shutdown Highlights Nation's Oil Dependence." 2006. Union of Concerned Scientists. (August 7), <http://www.ucsusa.org/news/press_release/bp-pipeline-shutdown.html>

"Investigations into BP's Pipeline Operations in Alaska Widen." 2006. *Sentido.tv Ecology & Environment.* (August 10), <http://www.casavaria.com/sentido/usnews/environment/06-0810-bp-alaska.htm>

Kraus and Peters. 2006. "Biggest Oil Field in US Is Forced to Stop Pumping." *New York Times.* (August 8, 2006); *The Ledger.com,* <http://www.theledger.com/apps/pbcs.ll/article?AID=/20060808/ZNYT01/608080426/1001/BUSINESS> (November 28).

Leopold, Jason. 2006. "GOP Bids to Take ANWR While Region Was Ravaged by Major Oil Spill." *Free Press* (March 18, 2006) <http://www.freepress.org/departments/display/3/2006/1868>

Loy and Richtmyer. 2006. "Massive Repairs on North Slope." *Anchorage Daily News.* (August 8); <http://www.adn.com/front/picture_inset/story/8054990p-7948041c.html> (November 28).

Loy, Wesley. "Spill Alerts Rang, Dismissed as False." *Anchorage Daily News.* (April 26); <http://www.adn.com/money/industries/oil/story/7647852p-7559388c.html> (November 28).

Miller, Pamela. m.d. "The Impact of Oil Development on Prudhoe Bay." *Arctic Connections.* <http://arcticcircle.uconn.edu/ANWR/arcticconnections.htm>

Mufson, Steve, and Eilperin, Juliet. 2006. "Along with Pipeline, BP Has an Image to Fix." *Washington Post* (August 9).

"Myths and Facts." Alaska Wilderness League. <http://www.alaskawild.org/pressroom_mythsfacts.html#myth8>

Schwartz, Nelson. 2006. "Can BP Bounce Back?" *CNNMoney.com* (October 31); <http://money.cnn.com/magazines/fortune/fortune_archive/2006/10/16/8388595/index.htm> (November 28).

Roach, John. 2006. "Alaska Oil Spill Fuels Concerns over Arctic Wildlife, Future Drilling." *National Geographic News* (March 20). <http://news.nationalgeographic.com/news/2006/03/0320_060320_alaska_oil.html>

Rosen, Yereth. 2006. "Prudhoe Bay Restart on Hold for Oil Spill Cleanup." (March 9). <http://www.planetark.com/dailynewsstory.cfm/newsid/35545/newsDate/9-Mar-2006/story.htm>

Rostom, Aram, et al. 2006. "Was the BP Pipeline Problem Preventable". *MSNBC.Com* (August 9). <http://www.msnbc.msn.com/id/14251436/>

Shah, Saeed. 2006. "BP Facing Criminal Charges over Alaskan Oil Spill." *Independent* (London). (August 7).

Short, Hak, Gordon, John and George Smith. 2000. "Low-Cost Smart Pigging Comes of Age." Rstprojects.co.uk/. (February 1); <http://www.rstprojects.co.uk/pages/065256r1.pdf> (November 30, 2006).

# CASE 4.   *Maintaining a Seat at the Table*

## THE SHELL GROUP

Royal Dutch Shell, like all major oil producers, finds itself at the heart of the debate over climate change. In 2005, Shell's own operations emitted 105 million metric tons of $CO_2$ equivalents ($CO_2e$). The downstream combustion of the fossil fuels it produces emits another 763 million metric tons. Together these emissions account for some 3.6 percent of global fossil-fuel $CO_2$ emissions in any year—a total greater than that of the entire United Kingdom. But rather than sit on the sidelines and wait for carbon constraints to alter the company's business environment, Shell took an early position on the issue and engaged in actions that began to manage its carbon footprint. These actions have earned the company credibility and a powerful voice within policy, advocacy, and market circles. And this voice grants the company a measure of control over its future business environment. In the words of David Hone, Group Climate Change Advisor, "To validly have a seat at the table, you have to bring experience. You cannot just take a seat because you are interested."

In order to maintain that seat, the company must continue to develop the breadth and depth of its climate change program. The company now finds itself facing the challenge of integrating what had historically been treated as two separate tracks—energy strategy and climate change strategy. Shell is seeking ways to merge the two tracks into one synergistic approach that helps them explore new business opportunities. This harmonization of strategies must also coordinate the activities of units stretched around the globe, ensuring information sharing that takes advantage of Shell's wide and varied technical expertise.

## CLIMATE CHANGE PROGRAM IMPLEMENTATION

Shell has been watching climate change since the early 1990s through its Issues Management team, a group within Corporate Affairs that monitors issues that may impact the business units. In 1998, Jeroen van der Veer, then a group managing director (and now CEO), championed a more formal study of climate change and its potential impact on Shell businesses globally. This study came after the 1997 signing of the Kyoto Protocol and at a time when the company was feeling bruised over its 1996 fight with Greenpeace over the disposal of the Brent Spar oil platform. A cross-functional team that spanned the company was put together and made the business case for implementation of a greenhouse gas (GHG) management strategy. This study raised the bar for climate action and, as a result, created resistors—"There's always a challenge to what you create," Hone says, "but building a strong business case is key to overcoming this resistance." The business case revolved around the trio of ideas that the company would eventually face a real price for carbon, that a leadership position on climate change would be a business opportunity in terms of building brand and reputation, and that a seat at the table with the governments that would set the rules was important for the company's future. Out of this initiative emerged the goal of "Securing Shell's future by seizing opportunities that arise from

We would like to thank David Hone for his contributions to this case study. From Andrew Hoffman, *Getting Ahead of the Curve: Corporate Strategies that Address Climate Change* (Arlington, VA: The Pew Center on Global Climate Change, 2006), 111–20.

the climate change issue." Achieving this goal has historically followed two tracks.

The first track, energy strategy, considers the Shell energy portfolio. Planning for energy diversification is led in part by the company's well-established long-range planning tools like the Shell Scenarios. Like Alcoa, Shell has long thought in time horizons of half a century or more. And climate change requires a similarly long-term focus. "You can't look at this issue in a 5-year time frame, it's almost meaningless," says Hone. "But you can look at it in a 25-year time frame—there's the scope for it to be different."

The second track, climate change strategy, focuses on managing the carbon footprint of Shell, sharing experience and validating the company's position on climate change with governments, the NGO community and the general public. The goals of this track are to build capacity for action within the company and to participate in policy development. Recognizing that carbon would have value in the future, the company began by first, taking inventory of GHG emissions, second, developing a proficiency in carbon trading and third, integrating carbon values into financial decision-making. The logic is that there will be a business benefit to both developing the experience of operating in a carbon market and working with governments to help develop those markets.

Following the 1998 study, Shell set a long-term goal of matching the Kyoto standards of a 5 percent reduction in GHG emissions by 2010. The first target within that goal was a 10 percent GHG reduction by 2002. This was the first hard target for Shell and it was achieved through the elimination of associated gas venting at oil production units and the reduction of associated gas disposal by continuous flaring. The second hard target (remaining 5 percent below 1990 emissions through the year 2010) was a more difficult sell than the first. To address internal sentiments that the company had done enough and that further public action was unwise, meetings with the company's various business units as well as discussions with senior leaders were arranged. The workshops considered various target-setting and implementation options for the units themselves. The greatest resistance to the idea came from business units with significant growth opportunities in their forward plans. As such, a point of significant debate centered on whether to measure emission reductions targets through an absolute (for example, $MMtonsCO_2e$) or indexed approach (for example, $MMtonsCO_2e$ per unit of revenue or product). Shell decided that setting one universal standard for such a large company would be impractical, as it overlooked the company's very size and the challenge that size creates. The company chose a blend of these two approaches. Individual business units would use indexed or energy efficiency measures while the Group as a whole faced an absolute target.

To reach its first target, Shell looked first at the lowest-hanging fruit, achieving a sizable portion of its pre-2002 emissions reductions by ending the venting of associated gas (methane) from its exploration and production facilities and, most significantly, from its Nigerian operations. As the company heads toward its 2010 target, the emphasis has shifted to ending the flaring of the same gas. The company devotes energy and resources into capturing these gases and either pumping them back underground or feeding them into nearby facilities for small power stations. When the economics are right, these gases can also be converted into LNG, a major growth area for the company. . . .

But to realize the full benefits of carbon shadow pricing and monetize the cost of carbon, emissions trading has become an important prong of Shell's strategy. "It is an enabler of energy efficiency projects," states Hone. For that reason, the company was one of the early innovators in both internal and external GHG emissions allowance trading. These experiences are a good example of how the climate change issue started at the periphery of the company and moved to the core of its operations. . . .

The results of Shell's internal trading experience are mixed. They show less-than-satisfactory results on its intended outcome: gaining the greatest reductions at the lowest cost. But the company feels that internal trading was successful in making people aware of the need to reduce GHG emissions and the use of trading mechanisms to do it. . . .

In a January 2006 *Financial Times* editorial, Shell CEO Jeroen van der Veer articulated Shell's conclusion that future production of liquid fossil fuels would increasingly depend on unconventional sources, such as oil sands, gas-to-liquids, oil shale, and coal gasification. The days of "easy oil" are over. The more difficult oil is "dirtier" and the company will subsequently have to address its associated higher GHG output. Van der Veer stresses the importance of carbon sequestration—both underground and combined with other materials to make inert materials, as a technical solution. It has become clear that the energy portfolio will have a significant impact on its GHG profile. Conversely, the company's climate change strategy has created the expectation of a company able to manage GHG emissions and government action has created carbon value in the market. These two tracks must now be intertwined. The Group's future depends on it. . . .

However, as advances are made, the company finds that some renewables clash with the existing business model. For example, electricity generation is not part of Shell's core business, yet wind power is fundamentally an electricity business. Similarly, Shell Solar has undergone both expansions and contractions, buying Siemens Solar in 2001 and then selling its silicon-based solar activities in 2006 to Solar World AG. The remaining thin-film business line has sought a partner in the form of Saint-Gobain, a company with "film-on-glass" technology expertise. And, as Hone puts it, "Can an oil company like Shell compete in a market where an electronics company like Sony or Sharp can bring a lot of R&D and manufacturing expertise to bear?" . . .

## ORGANIZATIONAL INTEGRATION

To help diffuse and incentivize climate change initiatives, Shell has incorporated climate change related goals into individual business scorecards. Scorecards use a number of criteria to evaluate performance of business units and individual managers, and focus on two or three principal metrics, such as financial performance. A particular climate change initiative (e.g. preparation for the EU ETS by EU refineries) might account for 5 percent of a given score in a particular year—an amount Hone describes as "modest". But the measures are constantly changing, reflecting a particular year's goals. The scorecards are used for calculating bonuses more so than promotions and are revised each year to reflect new concerns. . . .

## CHALLENGES AHEAD

In looking over its initiatives thus far on climate change, Hone sees the failure of the company's internal trading system as one useful lesson. While its failure was a surprise, he feels the company should have seen its limitations beforehand. But rather than dismissing the entire venture as lost, he sees benefits in the way it helped the company develop the expertise to become a leader in emissions trading in Europe.

Reflecting on all his company has done, Hone ponders, "When addressing climate change, the question is not just how will you manage your own GHGs, but how will you change the game? Ultimately, we'll have to get out of fossil fuels, but that is almost certainly many decades away. Maybe hydrogen is the answer. But you have to make the right change at the right time and in the right way. People will not get rid of cars and people will always want more energy. The key is both influencing the rules of the game and timing your shift to a new carbon-constrained strategy. It's knowing what the next technology for energy production is, and shifting when the market is ready to reward it. We're not going to get out of the oil business in the near term." But you have to ask, says Hone, "What is the iPod® for energy? Is it out there? You have to be on watch."

# CASE 5.   *Interface Corporation and Sustainable Business*

Carpet manufacturing would not normally be thought of as an environmentally praiseworthy industry. Most carpet fibers are derived from petroleum, a nonrenewable resource, and synthesized with fiberglass and PVC—two known carcinogens—to create the fibers used to manufacture carpeting. The carpeting is then dyed, and the waste produced from this process contains various toxins and heavy metals. Carpet manufacturing factories are heavy industrial producers of $CO_2$ emissions. Used carpet, especially nylon-based products, are not recycled and therefore end up in landfills. This carpet waste is often toxic and nonbiodegradable.

Reflecting on the environmental record of the carpeting industry, Ray Anderson, the founder, CEO, and chairman of Interface, a $1 billion-a-year carpeting and floor-covering corporation, suggested that "In the future, people like me will go to jail." That now seems unlikely given recent changes at Interface. Over the last decade under Anderson's leadership, Interface has become a leader in the movement to make business environmentally sustainable.

"Sustainability" and "sustainable development" have become something of a mantra among many in the environmental community. The concept of sustainable business can be traced to a UN report authored by then-Prime Minister Gro Bruntland of Norway in which sustainability was defined as the ability "to meet the needs of the present without compromising the ability of future generations to meet their own needs." Since the mid-1990s, Anderson has moved to make Interface a model of sustainable business practices.

Perhaps the most significant change at Interface involves a redefinition of their business. Interface is making a transition from selling carpeting to leasing floor-covering services. On a traditional business model, carpet is sold to consumers who, once they become dissatisfied with the color or style or once the carpeting becomes worn, dispose of the carpet in landfills. There is little incentive here to produce long-lasting or easily recyclable carpeting. Once Interface shifted to leasing floor-covering services, incentives are created to produce long-lasting, easily replaceable and recyclable carpets. Interface thereby accepts responsibility for the entire life cycle of the product it markets. Because they retain ownership and are responsible for maintenance, Interface strives to produce carpeting that can be easily replaced in sections rather than in its entirety, that is more durable, and that can eventually be remanufactured. Redesigning their carpets and shifting to a service lease has also improved production efficiencies and reduced material and energy costs significantly. Consumers benefit by getting what they truly desire at lower costs and fewer burdens.

But Interface has also committed itself to wider-ranging changes. Interface has set seven distinct corporate goals on its road to sustainability. One goal is to continue to redesign their business to focus on delivering services rather than material. This produces incentives to create products that are long-lasting and recyclable rather than products with "planned obsolescence." A second goal is to eliminate, and not simply reduce, all forms of waste. A third goal is to make any and all products that are emitted from the production process nontoxic. Fourth, Interface seeks to reduce energy use and move to renewable and nonpollution sources of energy. Their fifth goal is to "close the loop" of the production process, so that everything that comes out of the process can be recycled back into productive uses. Sixth, Interface strives for resource efficiencies, seeking to transport information rather than products and people. This goal encourages plants to be located near suppliers and retailers and supports information technology, videoconferencing, e-mail, and telecommuting. Finally, Interface is committed to raising community awareness of natural systems and our impact upon them.

**Discussion Questions**

1. Some critics argue that sustainability is popular only because it allows industrialized countries to believe, falsely, that consumer-driven lifestyles can continue indefinitely. In what ways do you believe your own lifestyle is sustainable? Unsustainable?

2. Should manufacturers be legally liable for "cradle to grave" responsibility for their products? Should manufacturers be responsible to recycle their products after consumers are finished with them? Who should pay for disposal of consumer goods at the end of their product life?

3. What government policies might encourage other businesses to follow Interface's lead? What government policies hinder such activities?

4. What responsibilities, if any, do we have to future generations? How might these responsibilities change contemporary business?

# CASE 6.  *Monsanto's Roundup Ready Wheat*

Monsanto is one of the world's largest agricultural companies specializing in conventional and genetically modified organism (GMO) seeds and other products. Its Web site states that the company's key values include a commitment to safety, environmental protection, customer service, the highest standards for research, product stewardship, and attention to and inclusion of stakeholders' views in the company's decision-making procedure. Monsanto's "Pledge" asserts that the company wants to pursue profits and other goals in ways that respect all those affected by its actions, including making better seeds, offering a greater number of choices to agricultural producers, and improving food security and economic opportunities in the developing world and elsewhere. This effort involves creating seeds that are engineered to fit environmental niches for which there is limited choice, such as in the case of the company's drought-resistant maize, so that more food and other agricultural products can be produced in areas incapable of sustaining them now.[1]

Although there are many genetically modified organisms (GMOs) in the marketplace that do not bother most consumers, Monsanto's Roundup Ready® wheat created a

This case was written by Dennis R. Cooley © 2007.

moral dilemma for the company. Monsanto's line of GMO seeds, called Roundup Ready, allows the crops grown from it to survive direct applications of Monsanto's Roundup pesticide. When Roundup is sprayed on fields containing the crop, non-Roundup Ready plants die because they cannot make one of their key enzymes, whereas the wheat, which has a bacterial gene immune to the pesticide, remains healthy. The moral question was whether Monsanto should introduce the wheat, delay it, or drop it entirely.

There are a number of potential benefits to Roundup Ready wheat. First, in 2004, based on the testing data and other information supplied by Monsanto, the U.S. Food and Drug Administration (FDA) affirmed the wheat as generally recognized as safe (GRAS) as non-GMO wheat. The FDA's decision means that there is no greater risk to human and livestock consumption than that caused by non-GMO wheat. Second, in the 6 years of field testing by the company and researchers it was found that the wheat has the potential to increase crop yields by 5 percent to 15 percent and perform well under the most difficult production environments for spring-planted wheat. Of course, with increased yields come greater food resources and other market benefits. Third, producers benefit in a number of ways. GMO options allow producers more alternatives than merely organic and conventional seed from which to choose. In addition, since fields have to be sprayed with pesticides less than conventional crops to achieve the same result, pollution is reduced and producers have to pay less for pesticides and have to spend less time in their fields, thereby freeing them for other activities, such as jobs off the farms. One of the most significant advantages of any new technology is how it sets the stage for the second generation of technology, which tends to bring greater benefits for both producers and consumers. Finally, through GMO wheat, Monsanto might be able to increase its presence in

the wheat market as well as expand into oats, barley, and other small grain markets.

Although the technology looked promising for producers and Monsanto, many groups were opposed to the release of Roundup Ready wheat into production. The Organic Consumers Association stated that there wasn't a system in place that could maintain adequate segregation of GMO and non-GMO wheat. This is still the case. Given the outright refusal of certain governments and businesses to allow GMO wheat imports, any GMO presence over 1 percent in conventional or organic varieties will cause the latter producers to lose their markets through no fault of their own. Even if there is no actual mixing, there is still a potential for market loss. For all wheat producers, there is a possible reduction of one-third to a half of the U.S. hard red spring wheat exports, and large percentage losses for durum and white wheat exports.[2] The obvious solution is to create a segregated system similar to that in place for organic and conventional crops, but the cost of creating and maintaining strict GMO and non-GMO wheat segregation is likely to be high for limited beneficial results, if it can be achieved at all.

The Western Organization of Resource Councils—a seven-state coalition of farmers and environmentalists—opposes the wheat for additional reasons. It includes in its list of possible problems the cross-pollination with non-GMO wheat and weeds and consequent creation of a "superweed" resistant to the pesticide; environmental degradation through overuse of pesticides; health concerns for people eating the wheat; and most important, committed market resistance to Roundup Ready or any GMO wheat, including that of the European Union. According to some economists, the market's wheat resistance is unlikely to change anytime soon because of deep-seated distrust of GMOs and cultural dietary beliefs. Unlike the GMO corn and soybeans eaten by livestock, in many countries, food made from wheat has a central emotional place in everyday lives. Food is special; therefore, many consumers in these countries want to keep wheat the way it has always been.

Adding to the reluctance to embrace GMO wheat is consumer fear and worry. A 2006 study found that 62 percent of EU consumers believed that food safety as related to foods had worsened over the last 10 years. In addition, a review of U.S. approvals and scientific studies by several European scientists has supported these fears. The researchers claim that the U.S. system is scientifically flawed and does not support the safety of GMOs. Although the review may be scientifically flawed as well and contradicts the findings of the EU's official scientific assessment organization, the European Food Safety Authority, the important fact is the EU public believes it to be accurate. The belief state shows an important fact about markets. Some consumers do not want evidence merely showing that GMOs are unlikely to be harmful; they want absolute certainty that each GMO product is safe before it enters their marketplace. Since consumer perceptions—regardless of whether they are right or wrong—drive markets, if they do not want to eat GMOs, as can be seen by the fact 45 countries require strict farm-to-fork traceability and labeling, then they will not buy GMO or products containing them.

Finally, if consumers will not buy GMO wheat, then producers face great losses. The wheat market is not as flexible and forgiving as that of other GMO crops. If the market is lost for wheat because of consumer rejection, then unlike corn and soybeans, which can be used in ethanol and biodiesel, wheat will remain unsold.

In 2004, after repeated attempts to introduce Roundup Ready wheat into production in the United States, Canada, Australia, New Zealand, Russia, South Africa, and Columbia, Monsanto chose to focus much more attention on its other products. The company stated its reasons for the decision include spring wheat's 25 percent production decline since 1997, the lower need to control weeds for wheat in comparison with

other crops, and most important, insufficient demand for the product to make it profitable. Even though the U.S. Department of Agriculture (USDA) values the wheat market at over $800 million per year, wheat is a low-value crop compared with cotton, rice, and soybeans. It is an open question whether a costly genetic approach to wheat can be justified in the market, especially since the genome of wheat is 10 to 20 times larger than that of crops like cotton or rice, thereby making the improvement of wheat by biotechnology a far more complex and time-consuming challenge than for the other crops.[3] An unstated reason in the company's press release was major opposition to the product.

However, Monsanto claims it will continue to monitor markets to determine if and when they are ready to accept GMO wheat. If China, which is less sensitive about importing GMOs, increases wheat imports, then there might be an adequate market for Roundup Ready wheat. Given time and the safe use of other GMOs, other markets might lose their opposition to GMO wheat. To pave the way for smoother market introduction, the company will be working with regulatory agencies of all wheat markets to take appropriate steps with regard to regulatory submission. If market conditions change adequately, Monsanto will immediately be able to sell its product.

Although Monsanto will be ready for it, the chance that market conditions will improve seems low, even if Monsanto manages to create GMO wheat that offers benefits to both producer and consumer. Roundup Ready wheat is better for some producers but offers no feature that directly benefits consumers. Building on first-generation technology, Monsanto could develop GMO wheat that is more efficient to produce— a benefit for the producer—while giving something new to the consumer—better taste quality, durability or less gluten, for example.

What has happened to consumer value–added soybeans' relative market failure might provide guidance in the GMO wheat case.

These soybeans have low trans fat and are Roundup Ready. The first characteristic is good for consumers' health, and the latter makes their production more efficient for some producers. Because such appealing soybeans have not been a success, and there is less resistance to soybeans than there is to GMO wheat, it could be concluded that dual-benefit GMO wheat has a bleak prospect.

After careful consideration of the situation, Monsanto decided to concentrate on less complex and controversial crops that are replacing wheat in certain production areas. Corn, cotton, and soybeans have been increasing market share for a number of years. As a result, the company realigned its research portfolio to limit research and development money on wheat to $5 million of its $500 million budget and deferred development of the crop.[4] By focusing on stress tolerance, yield improvement, agronomic pest resistance traits, and food and feed improvement traits, such as improved health profile vegetable oil traits, the company can introduce products that will not face as much market resistance. Given the price of fossil fuels, the company might decide to pursue crops that can be converted efficiently into biodiesel.

### Questions

1. Did Monsanto act ethically by developing GMO wheat? Why or why not? Explain.
2. Did Monsanto make the correct ethical decision when it minimized its focus on GMO wheat in favor of other products? Why or why not? Explain.
3. Did the EU, its consumers, and others opposing GMO wheat act ethically toward Monsanto? Why or why not? Explain.

### NOTES

1. In the past, Monsanto has acted in ways showing commitment to its pledge. The most representative is what the company did in Malawi to help drought-ravaged farmers. Working in conjunction with the Malawian government, the company donated its hybrid maize seed, and the government contributed fertilizer. Monsanto did not give handouts because it wanted the farmers to produce their own crops instead of receiving more costly food aid that does not enable them to care for themselves. The result was a total harvest of grain that could feed 1 million people for a year. Each ton of maize raised through Monsanto's effort cost $40 to grow, while each donated ton of maize would have cost $400 to purchase and deliver. Not only were Monsanto's actions respectful of those affected, it was also efficient.
2. Robert Wisner and Western Organization of Resource Councils, "Potential Market Impacts for Commercializing Roundup Ready Wheat (September 2006); update, http://www.wroc.org/pdfs/Market%20Risks%20Update%20Final%208-06.pdf
3. http://filebox.vt.edu/cals/cses/chagedor/wheat.html
4. Other potential wheat GMOs include wheat that might grow back faster following grazing, more overall forage vigor, more leaf rust resistant wheat, and more drought-tolerant wheat; http://filebox.vt.edu/cals/cses/chagedor/wheat.html

## Suggested Supplementary Readings

*Business Ethics Quarterly.* The Ruffin Series No. 2, "Environmental Challenges to Business," (2000).

*Business & Professional Ethics Journal.* 2005. Special Issue: The Roots of the Obligation of Business to Preserve the Environment 13, nos. 1 and 2.

COOLEY, DENNIS. 2002. "So Who's Afraid of Frankenstein Foods?" *Journal of Social Philosophy* 33 (no. 3): 442–63.

———. 2004. "Transgenic Orgnisms and the Failure of a Free Market Argument," *Business Ethics: A European Review*, 13:354–71.

DALLMEYER, DORINDA, and ALBERT F. IKE, eds. 1998. *Environmental Ethics and the Global Marketplace.* Athens: University of Georgia Press.

DES JARDINS, JOSEPH R. 2005. *Environmental Ethics: An Introduction to Environmental Philosophy.* Belmont, CA: Wadsworth.

ENGEL, J. RONALD, and JOAN GIBB ENGEL, eds. 1991. *Ethics of Environment and Development.* Tucson: University of Arizona Press.

*Environmental Ethics:* "An Interdisciplinary Journal Dedicated to the Philosophical Aspects of Environmental Problems."

FREEMAN, R. EDWARD, JESSICA PIERCE, and RICHARD DODD. 2000. *Environmentalism and the New Logic of Business.* New York: Oxford University Press.

GIBSON, MARY. 1985. *To Breathe Freely: Risk, Consent, and Air.* Totowa, NJ: Rowman and Littlefield.

HOFFMAN, W. MICHAEL, ROBERT FREDERICK, and EDWARD S. PETRY JR., eds. 1990. *Business, Ethics, and the Environment: The Public Policy Debate.* New York: Quorum Books.

————. eds. 1990. *The Corporation, Ethics, and the Environment.* New York: Quorum Books.

LEDGERWOOD, GRANT. 1999. *Environmental Ethics and the Corporation.* Basingstoke, UK: Macmillan.

LOTZ, MARIANNE. 2002. "Colliding Worlds: Indigenous Rights, Traditional Knowledge, and Plant Intellectual Property," *Business & Professional Ethics Journal* 21.

LUDWIG, DEAN C., and JUDITH A. LUDWIG. 1992. "The Regulation of Green Marketing: Learning Lessons from the Regulation of Health and Nutrition Claims." *Business and Professional Ethics Journal* 11:73–91.

MCEWAN, TOM. 2001. "Environmental Protection." In *Managing Values and Beliefs in Organizations.* New York: Prentice Hall, 247–68.

NAESS, ARNE. 1990. *Ecology, Community, and Lifestyle,* trans. D. Rothenberg. New York: Cambridge University Press.

NEWTON, LISA H., CATHERINE DILLINGHAM, and JOANNE CHOLY. 2005. *Business Ethics and the Natural Environment.* Malden, MA. Blackwell.

————. 2006. *Watersheds 4: Ten Cases in Environmental Ethics.* Belmont, CA: Wadsworth.

ROLSTON, HOLMES, III. 1991. *Philosophy Gone Wild: Environmental Ethics.* Buffalo, NY: Prometheus Books.

ROSENTHAL, SANDRA B., and R. A. BUCHHOLZ. 1998. "Bridging Environmental and Business Ethics: A Pragmatic Framework." *Environmental Ethics* 20:393–408.

SAGOFF, MARK. 1990. *The Economy of the Earth.* New York: Cambridge University Press.

SINGH, JANG B., and EMILY F. CARASCO. 1996. "Business Ethics, Economic Development and Protection of the Environment in the New World Order." *Journal of Business Ethics* 15:297–307.

SINGH, JANG B., and V. C. LAKHAN. 1989. "Business Ethics and the International Trade in Hazardous Wastes." *Journal of Business Ethics* 8:889–99.

SMITH, DENIS, ed. 1993. *Business and the Environment: Implications of the New Environmentalism.* New York: St. Martin's Press.

STARIK, MARK. 1995. "Should Trees Have Managerial Standing? Toward Stakeholder Status for Non-Human Nature." *Journal of Business Ethics* 14:207–17.

VANDEVEER, DONALD, and CHRISTINE PIERCE. 1994. *Environmental Ethics and Policy Book: Philosophy, Ecology and Economics.* Belmont, CA: Wadsworth.

# Ethical Issues in International Business

## INTRODUCTION

There is no question that markets are international and that a failure to recognize this fact could be fatal. Most firms realize that competitors for their market share could come from any corner of the globe. Even fairly small regional firms often attempt to market their products internationally. Of course, there is much more to the awareness of international issues than the development of international markets. As people in all parts of the world travel outside their own countries, they discover that countries differ on many matters of right and wrong. In some instances what is considered right or acceptable in one country is considered wrong or unacceptable in another. In addition, many of the problems that affect one country have an impact on other nations. Two excellent examples come to us from two very different problems—maintaining the integrity of financial markets and protecting the world environment. Global financial markets are tied to one another in such a way that widespread fraud in U.S. markets, for example, has a direct impact on Asian and European markets. So, too, the phenomenon of anthropogenic climate change is inherently global in scope—Chinese carbon emissions have a direct impact on the United States and vice versa. Thus, we are all forced to think internationally whether we want to or not.

And there is plenty to think about. Bribery, extortion, and the issue of facilitating payments remain common problems. When firms try to take advantage of a lower cost structure, whether it be lower wages or lower taxes, they are often accused of exploitation. Consumers in developed countries have become increasingly aware of the alleged sweatshop conditions under which the goods they purchase are manufactured and assembled. And many would argue that the more developed countries and the companies that do business there have an obligation to help resolve the social problems, especially the problem of poverty that affects other parts of the world. However, before we can address these specific issues with much authority, an overarching problem needs to be addressed.

## Are Any Universal Moral Norms Applicable to International Business?

There is a wide variety of opinion on what is acceptable conduct in international business, and many doubt whether there are any universal norms for ethical business practice. An international company involved in business abroad must face the question, When in Rome, should I behave as the Romans do? For the purposes of this discussion, the home country of a business firm is where it has its headquarters or where it has its charter of incorporation. A host country is any other country where that firm does business.

When the norms of the home country and the norms of the host country are in conflict, a multinational corporation has four options: (1) Follow the norms of the home country because that is the patriotic thing to do; (2) follow the norms of the host country to show proper respect for the host country's culture; (3) follow whichever norm is most profitable; (4) follow whichever norm is morally best. (The four alternatives are not mutually exclusive.)

To choose option (4) requires an appeal to international moral norms for business practice. In his article Norman Bowie shows the importance of establishing the existence and content of these international norms. Bowie bases his argument for international norms on three considerations. First, widespread agreement already exists among nations, as illustrated by the large number of signatories to the United Nations Declaration of Human Rights and by the existence of a number of international treaties establishing norms of business practice. Two excellent examples of the latter are the "Guidelines for Multinational Enterprises," adopted by the Organization of Economic Cooperation and Development, and the Caux Roundtable Principles of Business. The United Nations itself is engaged in a voluntary cooperative project to improve the social responsibility of corporations. Corporations first participate by endorsing the 10 general principles of the U.N. Social Compact (reprinted in this chapter). Additionally, corporations may participate in the Global Reporting Initiative whereby corporations report on their progress in adopting and implementing the 10 principles. It should also be added that there are a number of industry-wide codes or agreements on the proper conduct of business matters. Industry-wide codes cover a number of important areas. A survey by the Organization for Economic Cooperation and Development has found that there are more than 240 codes of conduct and that roughly half cover the environment and roughly half cover labor rights. Many are individual company codes, but 26 codes from associations of companies and nonprofit groups require independent inspections. For example, the U.S.-based Chocolate Manufacturers Association and British chocolate makers have signed an agreement with antislavery groups and the International Labor Organization to monitor cocoa farms after allegations of child slavery in West Africa.[1] In the human rights area a group of energy companies and human rights organizations have adopted a set of voluntary guidelines for respecting human rights while protecting overseas operations.[2] In some parts of the world, corporations need security forces to protect their employees and property. However, these security forces have often been accused of human rights abuses as they carry out their tasks. Sometimes corporations are seen as wittingly or unwittingly supporting governments in human rights abuses. These guidelines have been criticized on the grounds that they are voluntary and will not be monitored for compliance.[3]

Second, Bowie argues that certain moral norms must be endorsed if society is to exist at all. Corporations ought to accept the moral norms that make society and hence business itself possible. This argument is a powerful argument against the view known as ethical relativism. *Ethical relativism* asserts that whatever a country says is right or wrong for a country, *really* is right or wrong for that country. But if there are ethical norms that must be adopted if a country is to exist at all, then obviously the rightness of these norms is not justified by being endorsed in any particular country.

Third, Bowie uses certain Kantian arguments to show that business practice presupposes certain moral norms if it is to exist at all. Bowie refers to these norms as the *morality of the marketplace*. For example, there must be a moral obligation for business to keep its contracts if business is to exist at all. Bowie's argument is not merely theoretical. Russia had great difficulty in adopting a capitalist economy because businesspersons and business firms were either unwilling or unable to pay their bills. Without institutions to enforce contracts, business practice is fragile at best. It should also be pointed out that similar arguments could be used by utilitarians. If certain moral rules or traits such as truth telling or honesty give a multinational corporation a competitive advantage, then eventually these moral norms or traits will be adopted by all multinationals, because those that do not will not survive.

Many argue that the notion of human rights provides a set of universal standards that both individuals and organizations, including business organizations, should respect. After all, nearly all countries in the world belong to the United Nations and thus have in principle endorsed the U.N. Declaration on Human Rights. (We acknowledge that countries differ on the interpretation and implementation of these rights.) However, as Thomas Donaldson has pointed out, there are three distinct ways to honor human rights: (1) to avoid depriving, (2) to help protect from deprivation, and (3) to aid the deprived.[4] Donaldson maintains that while human rights should be honored in all three senses, it is not clear that it is the obligation of business to honor all human rights in all three ways. For example, if a right to an education is a human right, that does not mean that it is the obligation of a corporation to provide it.

Working out what is morally required for firms engaged in international business is a complex activity that would require a full book. However, in addition to the U.N. Declaration on Human Rights, we also endorse the 10 principles of the U.N. Social Compact as a starting point for determining what can be morally expected of corporations. In addition, philosophers can provide a normative ground for human rights that can serve as a justification for claiming that business firms engaged in international business ought to take human rights issues into account.

In his article "The Human Rights Obligations of Multinational Corporations," Denis Arnold provides the required normative grounding. First, he distinguishes between human rights and legal rights, pointing out that human rights are not contingent on the existence of particular legal institutions. Second, he criticizes the United Nations "Draft Norms on the Responsibilities of Transnational Corporations and Other Business Enterprises with Regard to Human Rights" (reprinted in this chapter) on the grounds that the duties these draft norms attribute to corporations are too broad and too demanding. He sets out to defend an alternative set of human rights duties for corporations. Next, he shows that the often-invoked distinction between negative and positive rights is untenable. This is important because it undermines the arguments of libertarians and others who argue that corporations have a duty to protect only negative rights and not positive rights. Fourth, he provides a Kantian argument in defense of certain basic human rights duties on the part of corporations. Finally, he defends this account of basic rights against the claim that it is an inherently Western view with no applicability in non-Western nations.

The claim that there are universal human rights or moral norms that should be followed by all multinationals is not inconsistent with the idea that there is a wide range of situations where variations in conduct are permissible. In her article "Exporting Mental Models: Global Capitalism in the Twenty-First Century," Patricia Werhane points out that to some extent our view of the world is constructed from the society in which we live. Werhane refers to these images as mental models and she argues that we should not impose our mental models about capitalism and business practice on other cultures. Thus, the task of the manager of an international firm is to avoid a rigid imposition of his or her views on foreign subsidiaries while at the same time avoiding a relativism that would ensnare the firm in violations of legitimate universal norms.

Finally, this discussion of "When in Rome Should We Do as the Romans Do?" has legal ramifications as well. What about the rights of foreigners who are injured abroad by U.S. corporations? Do they have any rights to relief in American courts? Normally, they do not under the doctrine of *forum non conveniens* (it is not the convenient forum). It makes more practical sense for foreigners to seek relief in the country where the injury took place. But in *Dow Chemical Company and Shell Oil Company v. Domingo Castro Alfaro et al.,* the Supreme Court of Texas disagreed. The Texas Supreme Court in a majority opinion pointed out that the chief effect of the doctrine of *forum non conveniens* was to give an unjust advantage to multinationals. However, *forum non conveniens* is still the prevailing law in most states.

Recently, foreign nationals have sued American companies alleging human rights abuses. One landmark case, *John Doe I et. al., v. Unocal,* granted summary judgment on behalf of Unocal in a case involving alleged human rights violations in Myanmar (formerly Burma). The government of Myanmar supplied labor to Unocal that the plaintiffs claimed was forced labor or slavery. The court found that

Unocal knew about and benefited from forced labor in Myanmar. But Unocal was not a willing partner, since it could not control the Myanmar military and thus was not liable under federal law. However, the U.S. Court of Appeals disagreed in part and argued that trial against Unocal could go ahead on the issues of whether Unocal aided and abetted the Myanmar military in subjecting workers to forced labor. Selections from the appeals court decision are included in this chapter.

Most recently the Bush administration has attempted to create new hurdles for those who seek to sue American firms for human rights abuses. A U.S. State Department representative urged a federal judge to dismiss a case against the Exxon Mobil Corporation, which was accused of complicity in the murder, rape, and torture of villagers living near its natural gas operations in Indonesia. Allowing the case to go forward would compromise U.S. diplomatic efforts including efforts to fight the war on terrorism.[5] Nonetheless claims continue to be filed under an ancient law—the 1789 Alien Tort Claims Act, and early court victories have gone to the plaintiffs.[6]

## Sweatshops and Bribery

Perhaps the international business ethics issue that has received the most attention on college campuses in recent years is the issue of sweatshops. Foreign suppliers to such companies as Nike have been accused of operating sweatshops. The sweatshop issue has become the chief activist cause on college campuses, and there have been calls for universal standards and the monitoring of their implementation. Some calls have already been successful. Mattel, the Gap, adidas (formerly adidas-Salamon), and Nike have now implemented vigorous programs to ensure that the rights of workers in their global supply chains are protected. Not all activists are satisfied with these programs, but there can be no doubt that the negative publicity associated with abusive working conditions has led to significant improvements in the labor practices of many multinationals.

Monitoring is not limited to individual companies. The Fair Labor Association is made up of industry and human rights representatives. This group was created by a presidential task force and includes such companies as adidas, Levi Strauss and Co., Nike, Reebok, Liz Claiborne, and Phillips-Van Heusen.[7]

Not everyone is so quick to condemn the practices of multinationals in this area. Several prominent economists have spoken out claiming that the wages paid to the workers of foreign suppliers in the third world are hardly immoral "slave wages" but rather represent an increase in the standard of living. These arguments are summarized and defended in the article by Ian Maitland included in this chapter. Maitland argues that multinationals are wrong to improve working conditions and wages because doing so will lead to higher unemployment in developing nations. He argues that corporate executives should explain to activists and others that improving working conditions will be bad for workers and bad for developing economies, since it will slow economic growth. In their article "Sweatshops and Respect for Persons" Denis Arnold and Norman Bowie defend a different view.

They use Kantian arguments to show that multinational enterprises have a moral obligation to ensure that their suppliers follow local labor laws, refrain from coercion, meet minimum safety standards, and provide a living wage for employees. Arnold and Bowie bring forth considerations that call into question the economic arguments invoked by Maitland and, if successful, they undermine Maitland's moral arguments that depend on them.

One emerging international norm is a prohibition against bribery. Such a norm received legal recognition in the United States with the passage of the Foreign Corrupt Practices Act (FCPA) in 1977. That act, which was amended in 1988, makes it illegal for U.S. companies to pay bribes to do business abroad. Spokespersons for some American businesses have long criticized the law on the grounds that it puts American firms at a competitive disadvantage. Other countries operate under no such restrictions. Although the United States did take the lead in this respect, more and more organizations are passing rules outlawing bribery. For example, the European Union has done so.

Another criticism of the Foreign Corrupt Practices Act was that it was an example of American moral imperialism—a charge that is often leveled against American regulations. However, in this case, the charge of moral imperialism is false, since the FCPA does not force other countries or the multinationals of other countries to follow America's lead. It simply requires U.S. companies to follow American moral norms with respect to bribery when doing business abroad.

A third criticism of the FCPA is more telling, however. That criticism is that the act does not adequately distinguish among gift giving, facilitating payments, bribery, and extortion. The FCPA does allow for facilitating payments, and that allowance was expanded when the law was amended in 1988. However, the law does not sufficiently distinguish between bribery and extortion. The chief difference between bribery and extortion is who initiates the act. A corporation pays a bribe when it offers to pay or provide favors to a person or persons of trust to influence the latter's conduct or judgment. A corporation pays extortion money when it yields to a demand for money to have accomplished what it has a legal right to have accomplished without the payment. The difference between extortion and a facilitating payment is one of degree. It is also often difficult to distinguish a gift from a bribe.

In their essay "Taking Responsibility for Bribery," Thomas Dunfee and David Hess explain the connection between bribery and human rights violations. After reviewing international efforts to combat corruption they articulate and defend a corporate principles approach to bribery, one that relies on rigorous internal guidelines and controls. They point to Shell as an example of a company that has had great success at implementing such a program. They also point to the business case for antibribery efforts, concluding that combating bribery is both pro-business and pro–human rights.

Globalization and the increase in international business competition it brings forth continue to spark a number of debates in international business ethics. Multinationals need to find a way to harmonize the core values of the firm with universal ethical norms. At the same time, they need to respect the legitimate ethical norms and values of the countries in which they do business. The effort to be an ethical and profitable business at home becomes even more complicated when a business enters the international arena.

## NOTES

1. "Do-It-Yourself Labor Standards," *Business Week* (November 19, 2001): 74, 76.
2. Yochi J. Dreazen, "Global Standards of Human Rights are Released," *Wall Street Journal* (December 21, 2000), p. A6.
3. Ibid.
4. Thomas Donaldson, *The Ethics of International Business* (New York: Oxford University Press, 1989).
5. Peter Waldman and Timothy Mapes. "Administration Sets New Hurdles for Human-Rights Cases," *Wall Street Journal* (August 7, 2002), pp. B1, 3.
6. Paul Magnusson, "Making a Federal Case Out of Overseas Abuses," *Business Week* (November 22, 2002).
7. Aaron Bernstein, "Sweatshops: No More Excuses." *Business Week* (November 7, 1999): 104–6.

## UNIVERSALISM, RELATIVISM, AND HUMAN RIGHTS

# Relativism and the Moral Obligations of Multinational Corporations

*Norman E. Bowie*

In this essay, I will focus on the question of whether U.S. multinationals should follow the moral rules of the United States or the moral rules of the host countries (the countries where the U.S. multinationals do business). A popular way of raising this issue is to ask whether U.S. multinationals should follow the advice "When in Rome, do as the Romans do." In discussing that issue I will argue that U.S. multi-nationals would be morally required to follow that advice if the theory of ethical relativism were true. On the other hand, if ethical universalism is true, there will be times when the advice would be morally inappropriate. In a later section, I will argue that ethical relativism is morally suspect. Finally, I will argue that the ethics of the market provide some universal moral norms for the conduct of multinationals.

This piece is composed of selections from Norman Bowie, "The Moral Obligations of Multinational Corporations," *Problems of International Justice* (edited by Steven Luper-Foy), 1988 and Norman Bowie "Relativism, Cultural and Moral," *The Blackwell Encyclopedic Dictionary of Business Ethics* (edited by Patricia Werhane and R. Edward Freeman) Blackwell, Cambridge, MA, 1997. Reprinted with permission of the author and Blackwell Publishers.

## RELATIVISM

*Cultural relativism* is a descriptive claim that ethical practices differ among cultures; that, as a matter of fact, what is considered right in one culture may be considered wrong in another. Thus the truth or falsity of cultural relativism can be determined by examining the world. The work of anthropologists and sociologists is most relevant in determining the truth or falsity of cultural relativism, and there is widespread consensus among social scientists that cultural relativism is true.

*Moral relativism* is the claim that what is really right or wrong is what the culture says is right or wrong. Moral relativists accept cultural relativism as true, but they claim much more. If a culture sincerely and reflectively adopts a basic moral principle, then it is morally obligatory for members of that culture to act in accordance with that principle.

The implication of moral relativism for conduct is that one ought to abide by the ethical norms of the culture where one is located. Relativists in ethics would say, "One ought to follow the moral norms of the culture." In terms of business practice, consider the question, Is it morally right to pay a bribe to gain business? The moral relativists would answer the question by consulting the moral norms of the country where one is doing business. If those norms permit bribery in that country, then the practice of bribery is not wrong in that country. However, if the moral norms of the country do not permit bribery, then offering a bribe to gain business in that country is morally wrong. The justification for that position is the moral relativist's contention that what is really right or wrong is determined by the culture.

Is cultural relativism true? Is moral relativism correct? As noted, many social scientists believe that cultural relativism is true as a matter of fact. But is it?

First, many philosophers claim that the "facts" aren't really what they seem. Early twentieth-century anthropologists cited the fact that in some cultures, after a certain age, parents are put to death. In most cultures such behavior would be murder. Does this difference in behavior prove that the two cultures disagree about fundamental matters of ethics? No, it does not. Suppose the other culture believes that people exist in the afterlife in the same condition that they leave their present life. It would be very cruel to have one's parents exist eternally in an unhealthy state. By killing them when they are relatively active and vigorous, you insure their happiness for all eternity. The *underlying* ethical principle of this culture is that children have duties to their parents, including the duty to be concerned with their parents' happiness as they approach old age. This ethical principle is identical with our own. What looked like a difference in ethics between our culture and another turned out, upon close examination, to be a difference based on what each culture takes to be the facts of the matter. This example does, of course, support the claim that as a matter of fact ethical principles vary according to culture. However, it does not support the stronger conclusion that *underlying* ethical principles vary according to culture.

Cultures differ in physical setting, in economic development, in the state of their science and technology, in their literacy rate, and in many other ways. Even if there were universal moral principles, they would have to be applied in these different cultural contexts. Given the different situations in which cultures exist, it would come as no surprise to find universal principles applied in different ways. Hence we expect to find surface differences in ethical behavior among cultures even though the cultures agree on fundamental universal moral principles. For example, one commonly held universal principle appeals to the public good; it says that social institutions and individual behavior should be ordered so that they lead to the greatest good for the greatest number. Many different forms of social organization and individual behavior are consistent with this principle. The point of these two arguments is to show that differences among cultures on ethical behavior may not reflect genuine disagreement about underlying principles of ethics. Thus it is not so obvious that any strong form of cultural relativism is true.

But are there universal principles that are accepted by all cultures? It seems so; there does seem to be a whole range of behavior, such as torture and murder of the innocent, that every culture agrees is wrong. A nation-state accused of torture does not respond by saying that a condemnation of torture is just a matter of cultural choice. The state's leaders do not respond by saying, "We think torture is right, but you do not." Rather, the standard response is to deny that any torture took place. If the evidence of torture is too strong, a finger will be pointed either at the victim or at the morally outraged country: "They do it too." In this case the guilt is spread to all. Even the Nazis denied that genocide took place. What is important is that *no* state replies that there is nothing wrong with genocide or torture.

In addition, there are attempts to codify some universal moral principles. The United Nations Universal Declaration of Human Rights has been endorsed by the member states of the UN, and the vast majority of countries in the world are members of the UN. Even in business, there is a growing effort to adopt universal principles of business practice. In a study of international codes of ethics, Professors Catherine Langlois and Bodo B. Schlegelmilch[1] found that although there certainly were differences among codes, there was a considerable area of agreement. William Frederick has documented the details of six

international compacts on matters of international business ethics. These include the aforementioned UN Universal Declaration of Human Rights, the European Convention on Human Rights, the Helsinki Final Act, the OECD Guidelines for Multinational Enterprises and Social Policy, and the United Nations Conduct on Transnational Corporations (in progress). The Caux Roundtable, a group of corporate executives from the United States, Europe, and Japan, is seeking worldwide endorsement of a set of principles of business ethics. Thus there are a number of reasons to think that cultural relativism, at least with respect to basic moral principles, is not true, that is, that it does not accurately describe the state of moral agreement that exists. This is consistent with maintaining that cultural relativism is true in the weak form, that is, when applied only to surface ethical principles.

But what if differences in fundamental moral practices among cultures are discovered and seem unreconcilable? That would lead to a discussion about the adequacy of moral relativism. The fact that moral practices do vary widely among countries is cited as evidence for the correctness of moral relativism. Discoveries early in the century by anthropologists, sociologists, and psychologists documented the diversity of moral beliefs. Philosophers, by and large, welcomed corrections of moral imperialist thinking, but recognized that the moral relativist's appeal to the alleged truth of cultural relativism was not enough to establish moral relativism. The mere fact that a culture considers a practice moral does not mean that it is moral. Cultures have sincerely practiced slavery, discrimination, and the torture of animals. Yet each of these practices can be independently criticized on ethical grounds. Thinking something is morally permissible does not make it so.

Another common strategy for criticizing moral relativism is to show that the consequences of taking the perspective of moral relativism are inconsistent with our use of moral language. It is often contended by moral relativists that if two cultures disagree regarding universal moral principles, there is no way for that disagreement to be resolved. Since moral relativism is the view that what is right or wrong is determined by culture, there is no higher appeal beyond the fact that culture endorses the moral principle. But we certainly do not talk that way. When China and the United States argue about the moral rights of human beings, the disputants use language that seems to appeal to universal moral principles. Moreover, the atrocities of the Nazis and the slaughter in Rwanda have met with universal condemnation that seemed based on universal moral principles. So moral relativism is not consistent with our use of moral language.

Relativism is also inconsistent with how we use the term "moral reformer." Suppose, for instance, that a person from one culture moves to another and tries to persuade the other culture to change its view. Suppose someone moves from a culture where slavery is immoral to one where slavery is morally permitted. Normally, if a person were to try to convince the culture where slavery was permitted that slavery was morally wrong, we would call such a person a moral reformer. Moreover, a moral reformer would almost certainly appeal to universal moral principles to make her argument; she almost certainly would not appeal to a competing cultural standard. But if moral relativism were true, there would be no place for the concept of a moral reformer. Slavery is really right in those cultures that say it is right and really wrong in those cultures that say it is wrong. If the reformer fails to persuade a slaveholding country to change its mind, the reformer's antislavery position was never right. If the reformer is successful in persuading a country to change its mind, the reformer's antislavery views would be wrong—until the country did in fact change

its view. Then the reformer's antislavery view would be right. But that is not how we talk about moral reform.

The moral relativist might argue that our language should be reformed. We should talk differently. At one time people used to talk and act as if the world were flat. Now they don't. The relativist could suggest that we can change our ethical language in the same way. But consider how radical the relativists' response is. Since most, if not all, cultures speak and act as if there were universal moral principles, the relativist can be right only if almost everyone else is wrong. How plausible is that?

Although these arguments are powerful ones, they do not deliver a knockout blow to moral relativism. If there are no universal moral principles, moral relativists could argue that moral relativism is the only theory available to help make sense of moral phenomena.

An appropriate response to this relativist argument is to present the case for a set of universal moral principles, principles that are correct for all cultures independent of what a culture thinks about them. This is what adherents of the various ethical traditions try to do. The reader will have to examine these various traditions and determine how persuasive she finds them. In addition, there are several final independent considerations against moral relativism that can be mentioned here.

First, what constitutes a culture? There is a tendency to equate cultures with national boundaries, but that is naive, especially today. With respect to moral issues, what do U.S. cultural norms say regarding right and wrong? That question may be impossible to answer, because in a highly pluralistic country like the United States, there are many cultures. Furthermore, even if one can identify a culture's moral norms, it will have dissidents who do not subscribe to those moral norms.

How many dissidents can a culture put up with and still maintain that some basic moral principle is the cultural norm? Moral relativists have had little to say regarding criteria for constituting a culture or how to account for dissidents. Unless moral relativists offer answers to questions like these, their theory is in danger of becoming inapplicable to the real world.

Second, any form of moral relativism must admit that there are some universal moral principles. Suppose a culture does not accept moral relativism, that is, it denies that if an entire culture sincerely and reflectively adopts a basic moral principle, it is obligatory for members of that culture to act in accord with that principle. Fundamentalist Muslim countries would reject moral relativism because it would require them to accept as morally permissible blasphemy in those countries where blasphemy was permitted. If the moral relativist insists that the truth of every moral principle depends on the culture, then she must admit that the truth of moral relativism depends on the culture. Therefore the moral relativist must admit that at least the principle of moral relativism is not relative.

Third, it seems that there is a set of basic moral principles that every culture must adopt. You would not have a culture unless the members of the group adopted these moral principles. Consider an anthropologist who arrives on a populated island: How many tribes are on the island? To answer that question, the anthropologist tries to determine if some people on some parts of the island are permitted to kill, commit acts of violence against, or steal from persons on other parts of the island. If such behavior is not permitted, that counts as a reason for saying that there is only one tribe. The underlying assumption here is that there is a set of moral principles that must be followed if there is to be a culture at all. With respect to those moral principles, adhering to them determines whether there is a culture or not.

But what justifies these principles? A moral relativist would say that a culture justifies them. But you cannot have a culture unless the members of the culture follow the principles. Thus it is reasonable to think that justification lies elsewhere. Many believe that the purpose of morality is to help make social cooperation possible. Moral principles are universally necessary for that endeavor.

## THE MORALITY OF THE MARKETPLACE

Given that the norms constituting a moral minimum are likely to be few in number, it can be argued that the argument thus far has achieved something—that is, multinationals are obligated to follow the moral norms required for the existence of a society. But the argument has not achieved very much—that is, most issues surrounding multinationals do not involve alleged violations of these norms. Perhaps a stronger argument can be found by making explicit the morality of the marketplace. That there is an implicit morality of the market is a point that is often ignored by most economists and many businesspersons.

Although economists and businesspersons assume that people are basically self-interested, they must also assume that persons involved in business transactions will honor their contracts. In most economic exchanges, the transfer of product for money is not simultaneous. You deliver and I pay or vice versa. As the economist Kenneth Boulding put it: "without an integrative framework, exchange itself cannot develop, because exchange, even in its most primitive forms, involves trust and credibility."[2]

Philosophers would recognize an implicit Kantianism in Boulding's remarks. Kant tried to show that a contemplated action would be immoral if a world in which the contemplated act was universally practiced was self-defeating. For example, lying and cheating would fail Kant's tests. Kant's point is implicitly recognized by the business community when corporate officials despair of the immoral practices of corporations and denounce executives engaging in shady practices as undermining the business enterprise itself.

Consider what John Rawls says about contracts:

> Such ventures are often hard to initiate and to maintain. This is especially evident in the case of covenants, that is, in those instances where one person is to perform before the other. For this person may believe that the second party will not do his part, and therefore the scheme never gets going. . . . Now in these situations there may be no way of assuring the party who is to perform first except by giving him a promise, that is, by putting oneself under an obligation to carry through later. Only in this way can the scheme be made secure so that both can gain from the benefits of their cooperation.[3]

Rawls's remarks apply to all contracts. Hence, if the moral norms of a host country permitted practices that undermined contracts, a multinational ought not to follow them. Business practice based on such norms could not pass Kant's test.

In fact, one can push Kant's analysis and contend that business practice generally requires the adoption of a minimum standard of justice. In the United States, a person who participates in business practice and engages in the practice of giving bribes or kickbacks is behaving unjustly. Why? Because the person is receiving the benefits of the rules against such activities without supporting the rules personally. This is an example of what John Rawls calls freeloading. A freeloader is one who accepts the benefits without paying any of the costs.

In everyday life an individual, if he is so inclined, can sometimes win even greater benefits for himself by taking advantage of the cooperative efforts of others. Sufficiently many persons may be doing their share so that when special circumstances allow him not to contribute (perhaps his omission will not be found out), he gets the best of both worlds. . . . We cannot preserve a sense of justice and all that this implies while at the same time holding ourselves ready to act unjustly should doing so promise some personal advantage.[4]

This argument does not show that if bribery really is an accepted moral practice in country X, that moral practice is wrong. What it does show is that practices in country X that permit freeloading are wrong and if bribery can be construed as freeloading, then it is wrong. In most countries I think it can be shown that bribery is freeloading, but I shall not make that argument here.

The implications of this analysis for multinationals are broad and important. If activities that are permitted in other countries violate the morality of the marketplace—for example, undermine contracts or involve freeloading on the rules of the market—they nonetheless are morally prohibited to multinationals that operate there. Such multinationals are obligated to follow the moral norms of the market. Contrary behavior is inconsistent and ultimately self-defeating.

Our analysis here has rather startling implications. If the moral norms of a host country are in violation of the moral norms of the marketplace, then the multinational is obligated to follow the norms of the marketplace. Systematic violation of marketplace norms would be self-defeating. Moreover, whenever a multinational establishes businesses in a number of different countries, the multinational provides something approaching a universal morality—the morality of the marketplace itself. If Romans are to do business with the Japanese, then whether in Rome or Tokyo, there is a morality to which members of the business community in both Rome and Tokyo must subscribe—even if the Japanese and Romans differ on other issues of morality.

## NOTES

1.  C. Langlois and B. B. Schlegelmilch, "Do Corporate Codes of Ethics Reflect National Character? Evidence from Europe and the United States," *Journal of International Studies* 21(a): 519–39.

2.  Kenneth E. Boulding, "The Basis of Value Judgments in Economics," in *Human Values and Economic Policy*, ed. Sidney Hook (New York: New York University Press, 1967), 68.

3.  John Rawls, *A Theory of Justice* (Cambridge, MA: Harvard University Press, 1971), 569.

4.  Ibid., 497.

# The Human Rights Obligations of Multinational Corporations

*Denis G. Arnold*

We live in an era of increasing economic globalization. Although trade among nations has been an important feature of the global economy for centuries, recent years have seen a rapid increase in international trade. Multinational corporations (MNCs) operate in a multitude of political jurisdictions and so are subject to a multitude of legal frameworks. Frequently, the laws regarding such matters as the treatment of customers, the treatment of employees, and protection for the environment are significantly different in different host nations. In the case of developing economies, consumer protection, worker safety, and environmental safeguards are often poorly developed or nonexistent. Even when such laws exist in developing nations, the law enforcement and judicial apparatus necessary to ensure compliance often does not exist. MNCs operating in such nations are often free to determine for themselves whether they will adhere to host nation laws. As a result, MNCs must determine for themselves what minimum moral standards

ought to be adhered to in their global operations. One standard that is increasingly being used to determine the minimum ethical obligations to which MNCs should adhere in their global operations is that of human rights.

## HUMAN RIGHTS VERSUS LEGAL RIGHTS

Human rights differ from legal rights in that, unlike legal rights, the existence of human rights is not contingent on any institution. Many nations grant their citizens certain constitutional or legal rights via foundational documents or legal precedent. However, the rights that are protected vary among nations. Some nations ensure that the rights of citizens are protected via effective policing and an independent judiciary. Frequently, however, poor citizens and disfavored groups are not provided with the same level of protection for their legal rights as the economic and political elite. Persons who are deprived of their rights do not thereby cease to have those rights. As A. I. Melden has argued (1977, 167–68):

> the complaint that persons are deprived of their human rights when, for example, they are subjected to forced indenture by their employers, is a complaint that their rights have been violated and implies, clearly, that they have rights they are unjustly prevented from exercising. If one were deprived of one's rights in the sense in which one would be deprived of things in one's physical possession by having them taken away, one would no longer have the rights, and there would be no grounds for the complaint. So it is with the denial of a person's right—this does not consist in denying that he has the right but, rather, in denying him, by withholding from him, that to which he has the right or the means or opportunity for its exercise.

Employers may deny employees or other stakeholders their rights whether or not local governments are complicit, but in doing so they in no way diminish the legitimacy of the claims of their employees to those rights. However, by virtue of their failure to properly respect these stakeholders, such employers succeed in diminishing their own standing in the community of rights holders.

In the weak and failed states where many multinational corporations operate, they are often the most powerful institutions in existence. In such cases, corporate mangers are uniquely situated to help ensure that the basic rights of individuals within their spheres of influence are protected. Many corporations have embraced this obligation. For example, Mattel ensures that all of the factories in its global supply chains meet basic human rights standards. Nike provides microloans to community members in the areas where it has large contract factories, thus providing additional help to improve the economic well-being of these communities. And adidas ensures that the basic rights of workers in its contract factories are respected and uses its occupational safety expertise to help noncontract factories

in those same communities improve working conditions.

## The United Nations "Draft Norms"

The promulgation of the United Nations Universal Declaration of Human Rights, together with the advocacy of organizations such as Amnesty International and Human Rights Watch, has led to the widespread acceptance of human rights as a basic tool of moral evaluation by individuals of widely divergent political and religious beliefs. However, the U.N. Universal Declaration has well-known conceptual limitations and is of limited use in assessing the ethical obligations of multinational corporations. First, it presents a list of rights that would ideally be granted to individuals (e.g., the right to paid vacation time) rather than a rigorously grounded set of core ethical obligations. In a world of scarce resources and competitive markets, such an ideal list fails to provide clear ethical standards for the conduct of business. Second, the U.N. Universal Declaration does not distinguish among the ethical obligations of different global actors and instead implicitly concerns itself with the obligations of nation-states to their citizens. In particular, it does not distinguish among individuals, corporations, nongovernmental organizations, and states.

Recently, the U.N. Working Group on the Methods and Activities of Transnational Corporations has produced "Draft Norms on the Responsibilities of Corporations and Other Business Enterprises with Respect to Human Rights." These draft norms articulate a robust list of ethical obligations and specifically identify MNCs as responsible for their fulfilment. Furthermore, once adapted, adherence to these norms on the part of corporations is to be monitored and verified by the U.N. The list of basic rights identified by the working group include rights that enjoy relatively universal acknowledgement in a wide range of regional and international codes and agreements such as equal opportunity, nondiscrimination, collective bargaining, and safe and healthy working environments. However, the Draft Norms go well beyond this, stipulating, for example, that corporations must:

- Seek to ensure that "the goods and services they provide will not be used to abuse human rights."
- Contribute to "the highest attainable standard of physical and mental health; adequate housing; privacy; education; freedom of thought; conscience and religion" for all people.
- Ensure that "human rights, public health and safety, bioethics, and the precautionary principle" are respected in all of their environmental practices.

Unsurprisingly, the Draft Norms have met with strenuous resistance from business interests. Part of this resistance is due to the fact that the Draft Norms attribute such a wide and imprecise range of obligations to MNCs and do so without the benefit of a conceptual scheme for distinguishing between the basic ethical obligations of MNCs on one hand and states on the other. The Draft Norms seem to be aspirational in the same manner as the Universal Declaration. However, it is important that a clear distinction be drawn between the minimum duties of MNCs and their managers and those actions that it would be good to perform but that are not morally required. The latter sort of activities, if performed consistently over time, might serve as a basis for describing an MNC as a good global citizen—or a good citizen of those nations in which it operates—but the failure to perform such actions does not mean that an MNC fails to meet its minimum moral duties. What is needed, then, is an account of the basic human right obligations of MNCs.

## BASIC RIGHTS

Human rights are moral rights that apply to all persons in all nations, regardless of whether

the nation in which a person resides acknowledges and protects those rights. It is in this sense that human rights are said to be *inalienable.* To gain clarity about basic human rights, it is necessary to answer certain philosophical questions about their nature. Two of the most basic questions are the following: How can basic human rights be justified? What basic human rights exist? Let us consider each question in turn.

Human rights are rights enjoyed by humans not because we are members of the species *Homo sapiens sapiens* but because fully functional members of our species are persons. Personhood is a metaphysical category that may or may not be unique to *Homo sapiens sapiens*. To be a person one must be capable of reflecting on one's desires at a second-order level and one must be capable of acting in a manner consistent with one's considered preferences (Frankfurt 1988; Dworkin 1988). The capacity to reflect on one's competing preferences and to act in a manner consistent with one's second-order preferences is a key feature of personhood and one that distinguishes persons from mere animals. It is in this sense that the idea of personhood is properly understood as metaphysical rather than biological (Melden 1977).

Theorists with a wide range of commitments readily agree that persons enjoy a basic right to individual freedom, and that other persons have a duty not to restrict or constrain the freedom of others without strong justification (Nozick 1974, Lomasky 1987; O'Neil 2000). This right is grounded in Kant's second formulation of the categorical imperative: "Act so that you treat humanity, whether in your own person or in that of another, always as and end and never as a means only" (Kant 1990, 46). The popular expression of this principle is that morality requires that we respect people. Kant provides a sustained defense of the doctrine of respect for persons, and he and his interpreters specify in detail its practical implications. Respecting other persons requires that one refrain from interfering with their decisions and actions. Typically one person is justified in limiting the freedom of another only when her own freedom is unjustly restricted by that person. One traditional way of capturing this sense of a liberty right is that individuals should be free to as much liberty or freedom as is compatible with like liberty or freedom for all.

There is little controversy regarding the negative right to liberty or freedom. However, there is significant controversy over whether or not there are positive rights to certain economic and social goods. Positive rights entail not merely negative obligations on the part of others to refrain from certain actions, but a positive obligation to fulfill the right of the rights holder. For example, if individuals have a right to employment or health care to ensure their subsistence and well-being, then others have an obligation to provide them with health care or employment. The state may be called on to fulfill these duties, but in weak or corrupt states such duties may be neglected. And in states where market values trump consideration for basic human rights, such rights may also be neglected. Under such conditions the burden of fulfilling such obligations seems to fall on individuals, but most individuals are not well positioned to meet such obligations. Furthermore, even in cases where the state does meet such alleged obligations, traditional libertarians would argue that it is illegitimate to tax some citizens to ensure the subsistence and well-being of others. Have we then reached an impasse?

Arguably there are at least two philosophically sound reasons for thinking that we can move beyond this apparent impasse. First, there is an influential and persuasive argument against the idea that the distinction between negative and positive rights is sustainable. Second, there is a widely influential set of positive arguments that can be used to support both a right to freedom and minimal welfare rights such as the right to subsistence. Let us consider each argument in turn.

Henry Shue has famously argued that the very distinction between negative and positive rights that the preceding analysis presumes is artificial and inconsistent with social reality (1996). For example, consider the right to physical security (i.e., the right not to be harmed). It is possible to avoid violating a person's right not to be harmed by refraining from certain actions. However, it is not possible to protect a person from harm without taking proactive steps. At a minimum, law enforcement agencies and a criminal justice system are required so that individuals are not left to defend themselves against forces that they are unable to defeat on their own. The existence of these social institutions is predicated on positive actions in the forms of design, implementation, administration, and taxation. In this way it can be seen that the protection of a prototypical negative right requires positive actions, and not merely the avoidance of particular actions. Since negative rights entail both negative and positive duties, the notion of negative versus positive rights loses its meaning. There are only rights and corresponding obligations, but the obligations that correspond to these rights are both negative and positive. There is then a strong argument against a theory of rights that includes negative but not positive rights.

Now let us turn to the positive arguments. Much of the most important and influential work on human rights has been produced by Kantians. Rather than beginning with rights claims, Kantians begin with obligations or duties to respect other persons. These duties constrain the pursuit of ends, whether they are self-interested goals or projects pursued on behalf of other parties such as shareholders. Respecting persons involves both negative obligations, such as refraining from using others as mere tools via physical force, coercion, or manipulation, and positive obligations such as supporting physical well-being and the development of basic human capacities. When they stand in the appropriate relationship to an obligation-bearer, persons have rationally justified rights-claims against them. Rights take the form of side constraints that bound the moral space in which agents may pursue ends without unjustified interference by other agents or institutions. For example, a minor child has legitimate rights-claims against her parents regarding her physical well-being and the development of her human capacities by virtue of her relation to them. The morally legitimate ends of parents do not include actions that substantially undermine the physical well-being or normal development of their child. Similarly, a convenience store owner has a rights-claim against those in his community to be free from assault and robbery. The morally legitimate ends of other community members do not include actions that would undermine the freedom of the store owner.

Wherever corporations do business they are already in special relationships with a variety of stakeholders, such as workers, customers, and local communities. In their global operations and in their global supply chains, corporations have a duty to respect those with whom they have relationships. Corporate managers, then, have obligations to ensure that they do not illegitimately undermine the liberty of any persons and the additional obligation to help ensure that minimal welfare rights to physical well-being and the development of basic human capacities are met within their spheres of influence. For example, corporations have sufficient power and coercive influence to ignore the labor and environmental laws in many developing nations. These host nations typically lack the police and judicial infrastructure necessary to enforce such laws. Host nation governments may also be fearful that if they enforce their own laws, then the corporations may move their operations to nations th.   willing to ignore local laws. However, such laws are essential for the protection of the basic rights of the citizens of developing nations. For this reason, corporate managers have an obligation to ensure that local host nations laws are respected.

## THE MINIMUM MORAL DUTIES OF MNCs

For pragmatic purposes it will be helpful to specify the minimal moral duties of MNCs. Let us begin with those duties regarding liberty or freedom rights. Previously we characterized freedom as controlling one's behavior via one's unforced choice while having knowledge of relevant circumstances.

Possessing freedom entails having the general abilities and conditions required for a person to be able to act in a manner consistent with his or her second-order preferences. A right to freedom, then, involves the right to pursue one's own goals and preferences without interference from others. Specifically, it includes control over one's own physical integrity, freedom of belief and expression, and freedom of association. Traditionally, the right to freedom is thought to be as extensive as is compatible with a like right to freedom for all. Such freedom is not, however, unlimited. It may be rightfully curtailed if a person's actions illegitimately infringe on the rights of others.

The rights one enjoys as a person are not unlimited in the sense that one is free to exercise all of them under any circumstances. Legitimate restrictions may be placed on the exercise of one's rights by both the state and private enterprise. It is, for example, not an illegitimate infringement of one's right to freedom of expression if an employer prohibits proselytizing on behalf of one's religious convictions while at work. Such activity is typically disruptive and as such incompatible with the purposes for which employees are hired. Furthermore, employees are typically free to engage in such activity when they are not working. Restricting employee activity in this manner does not infringe on an employee's dignity as a person. There are, however, certain restrictions on employee freedom that always violate human dignity because they treat the employee as a tool rather than as a person. Control over one's physical integrity is one such example. This freedom could, for example, be violated by a rule that permitted only one bathroom break each day.

As we have seen, physical and psychological well-being are required for a person to be able to act autonomously. The most important human needs in this regard concern basic goods. Basic goods are the general physical and psychological capabilities necessary for human functioning. In recent years, the relationship between well-being and human functioning has received a great deal of attention from economists and philosophers. Some of the most important work on this topic has been produced by Amartya Sen and Martha Nussbaum. Their distinctive variety of quality of life assessment, known as the *capabilities approach*, had become increasingly influential. . . .

Nussbaum identifies the capabilities necessary for humans to enjoy well-being. Drawing from Nussbaum's work we may identify the most important of these as life, physical health and integrity, freedom of thought and expression, freedom of affiliation, and the ability to exercise practical reason and pursue one's conception of the good. The argument defended here is not that MNCs have an obligation to ensure that stakeholders function well. Instead, the argument is that MNC managers have an obligation to ensure that they do not inhibit employees, customers, community members, and other stakeholders, from the opportunity to pursue their basic capabilities.

Given the duty to respect persons with whom they interact, we may conclude that MNCs have minimal duties to ensure that the following rights are respected in their global operations.

- The right to physical security and freedom of movement,
- The right to nondiscrimination on the basis of arbitrary characteristics such as race, sex, religion, ethnicity, and sexual orientation,
- The right to freedom of association and collective bargaining,
- The right to fair treatment,
- The right to subsistence, and
- The right to develop basic human capabilities.

The first four rights that must be respected are comparatively straightforward. There is little disagreement over whether employees cannot legitimately be forced to work or locked into factories or whether customers may legitimately be discriminated against because of their race or sex. And despite the strenuous efforts of companies such as Wal-Mart to resist a union presence in its stores, there is little disagreement that it is morally illegitimate to prohibit employees from collective organizing. With respect to fair treatment, few would disagree that employee evaluations ought to be based on performance and not on personal relationships and that executive compensation ought to be based on merit and fair market comparisons rather than on membership in "good old boys" networks. The right to subsistence is somewhat more controversial. If it is taken to mean—as it must be—that employees are sometimes entitled to wages above both the legally mandated minimum wage and the prevailing market wage, then there is substantial disagreement about whether this is a duty.

Finally, some might object that a duty not to interfere with the development of basic human capacities is far too broad to be regarded as a duty of MNCs. For example, it might be objected that if poor people cannot afford a

MNC's products, for example, a potable water filter, then the MNC undermines access to potable water, and clearly water is a necessary good for the development of human capacities. This is not the case. To see this we need to notice the distinction between refraining from providing someone with the partial means for functioning and interfering with their ability to function. The arguments provided thus far do not support the conclusion that MNCs have obligations to provide citizens in the communities in which they operate with goods or services they need to function. This is an example of an action that might be morally praiseworthy but is not morally required. It is to be differentiated from, for example, the case of selling a potable water filter to people in the rural sectors of developing nations, people who if they could afford the filters at all could do so only after months and perhaps years of savings, only to have the filters fail to perform as advertised because of errors on the manufacturing processes or design flaws. In such cases the MNC would have a duty to compensate customers for the harm it caused and retrieve and either repair or destroy all faulty filters.

## ARE HUMAN RIGHTS A WESTERN CONCEPT?

At this point in our discussion, it is worthwhile to consider an objection to the foregoing argument concerning human rights. This criticism stems from the observation that the idea of human rights emerged from the Western philosophical tradition but is taken to be universal in its applicability. The claim is then made that human rights are of less importance in the value systems of other cultures. For example, it is argued that "Asian values" emphasize order, discipline, and social harmony, as opposed to individual rights. In this view,

the freedom and well-being of individuals should not be allowed to interfere with the harmony of the community, as might be the case, for example, when workers engage in disruptive collective action in an effort to secure their rights. This view might also be used to defend the claim that the moral norms that govern Asian factory operations should emphasize order and discipline, not freedom and well-being.

Several points may be made in reply to this objection. First, Asia is a large region with a vast and heterogeneous population. As Amartya Sen and others have argued, to claim that all, or even most, Asians share a uniform set of values is to impose a level of uniformity that does not exist at present and has not existed in the past (Donnely 1999; Sen 1999, 2000). Second, in secular democratic Asian societies such as India, respect for individual rights has a long tradition. Indeed, there are significant antecedents in the history of the civilizations of the Indian subcontinent that emphasise individual freedom and well-being. For example, in the third century B.C., the Emperor Ashoka granted his citizens the freedom to embrace whatever religious or philosophical system they might choose, while at the same time he emphasized the importance of tolerance and respect for philosophical and religious beliefs different from one's own (Sen 1999). Third, even if it was the case that Asian cultures shared a uniform set of values that de-emphasized human rights, this would not by itself provide good reasons for denying or disrespecting the rights to freedom and well-being. This is because the justification of human rights provided above is grounded in rational arguments that are valid across cultures. The critic is likely to retort that such a view reflects Western prejudices grounded in Enlightenment ideals. This response is unpersuasive. Diverse intellectual traditions have emphasized the importance of values derived from reason, rather than mythology, traditionalism, mere sentiment, or some other source.

## REFERENCES

Arnold, Denis G. 2009. *The Ethics of Global Business.* Malden, MA: Blackwell.

Donnely, Jack. 1999. Human Rights and Asian Values: A Defense of "Western" Universalism. In *The East Asian Challenge for Human Rights,* ed. Joanne R. Bauer and Daniel A. Bell, 60–87. Cambridge: Cambridge University Press.

Dworkin, Gerald. 1988. *The Theory and Practice of Autonomy.* Cambridge: Cambridge University Press.

Frankfurt, Harry. 1988. *The Importance of What We Care About.* Cambridge: Cambridge University Press.

Gewirth, Alan. 1982. *Human Rights: Essays on Justification and Applications.* Chicago: University of Chicago Press.

Hartman, Laura, Denis G. Arnold, and Richard E. Wokutch. 2003. *Rising Above Sweatshops: Innovative Approaches to Global Labor Challenges.* Westport, CT.

Kant, Immanuel. 1990. *The Foundations of the Metaphysics of Morals,* 2nd ed., trans. Lewis White Beck. New York: Macmillan.

Lomasky, Loren. 1987. *Persons, Rights, and the Moral Community.* New York: Oxford University Press.

Melden, A. I. 1977. *Rights and Persons* Berkeley: University of California Press.

Nozick, Robert. 1974. *Anarchy, State, and Utopia.* New York: Basic Books.

Nussbaum, Martha. 2001. *Women and Human Development.* New York: Cambridge University Press.

O'Neill, Onora. 2000. *Bound of Justice.* Cambridge: Cambridge University Press.

Sen, Amartya. 1985. " Well-being, Agency and Freedom: The Dewey Lectures 1984." *Journal of Philosophy* 82 (April).

———. 1999. "Human Rights and Asian Values." In *Business Ethics in the Global Marketplace,* ed. Tibor Machan, 37–62. Stanford, CA: Hoover Institution Press.

Shue, Henry. 1996. *Basic Rights: Subsistence, Affluence, and U.S. Foreign Policy,* 2nd ed. Princeton: Princeton University Press.

# Exporting Mental Models: Global Capitalism in the Twenty-First Century

*Patricia H. Werhane*

When one is asked to enumerate the most challenging ethical issues business will face in the next century, the list is long. Environmental sustainability, international trade, exploitation, corruption, unemployment, poverty, technology transfer, cultural diversity (and thus relativism) are a few obvious candidates. Underlying these and other issues is a more serious global phenomenon: the exportation of Western capitalism.

There is a mental model of free enterprise, a model primarily created in the United States, that is being exported, albeit unconsciously, as industrialized nations expand commerce through the globalization of capitalism. This model is not one of greedy self-interested cowboy capitalists eagerly competing to take advantage of resources, low-priced employment, or offshore regulatory laxity. Rather I am referring to another model, one that has worked

From Patricia H. Werhane, "Exporting Mental Models: Global Capitalism in the 21st Century," *Business Ethics Quarter,* 10, no. 1 (2000): 353–62. Reprinted with permission of the author and *Business Ethics Quarterly.*

and worked well in most of North America and Western Europe for some time. This model contends that industrialized free enterprise in a free trade global economy, where businesses and entrepreneurs can pursue their interests competitively without undue regulations or labor restrictions, will produce growth and well-being, i.e., economic good, in every country or community where this phenomenon is allowed to operate. . . .

What is wrong with adapting a model for global capitalism out of the highly successful American model for free enterprise? What is wrong with economic growth and improved standards of living, particularly in developing countries? Isn't reduction of poverty a universally desirable outcome? The tempting answer is that there is nothing wrong with this model. In this paper I shall suggest that a more thoughtful reply requires some qualifications.

To begin, let me explain the notion of mental models. Although the term is not always clearly defined, "mental model" connotes the idea that human beings have mental representations, cognitive frames, or mental pictures of their experiences, representations that model the stimuli or data with which they are interacting, and these are frameworks that set up parameters through which experience, or a certain set of experiences, is organized or filtered (Werhane 1991, 1998, 1999).

> Mental models are the mechanisms whereby humans are able to generate descriptions of system purpose and form, explanations of system functioning and observed system states, and predictions of future system states. (Rouse and Morris 1986, 351)

Mental models might be hypothetical constructs of the experience in question or scientific theories; they might be schema that frame the experience, through which individuals process information, conduct experiments, and formulate theories; or mental models may simply refer to human knowledge about a particular set of events or a system. Mental models account for our ability to describe, explain, and predict, and may function as protocols to account for human expectations that are often formulated in accordance to these models.

Mental models function as selective mechanisms and filters for dealing with experience. In focusing, framing, organizing, and ordering what we experience, mental models bracket and leave out data, and emotional and motivational foci taint or color experience. Nevertheless, because schema we employ are socially learned and altered through religion, socialization, culture, educational upbringing, and other experiences, they are shared ways of perceiving, organizing, and learning.

Because of the variety and diversity of mental models, none is complete, and "there are multiple possible framings of any given situation" (Johnson 1993, 9). By that I mean that each of us can frame any situation, event, or phenomenon in more than one way, and that same phenomenon can also be socially constructed in a variety of ways. It will turn out that the way one frames a situation is critical to its outcome, because "[t]here are . . . different moral consequences depending on the way we frame the situation" (Johnson 1993).

Why is the notion of mental models of concern for business, and in particular, for global business? Let me explain by using some illustrations. One of the presuppositions of Western free enterprise, a supposition that fueled and made possible the industrial revolution, is that feudalism, at least as it is exhibited through most forms of serfdom, is humiliating, it demeans laborers, and worse, it does not allow serfs, in particular, to create or experience any sense of what it would mean to be free, free to live and work where one pleases (or to be lazy), to own property, and choose how one lives. Adam Smith even argued that feudalism is inefficient as well. It is commonly, although not universally, argued that individual property ownership is a social good. In agriculturally based economies, in particular, owning one's own farm land is considered a necessary step toward freedom and self-reliance. The industrial revolution, coupled with free commerce, wage labor, and property ownership, changes the feudal mental model, and, it is commonly argued, improves the lives of serfs, farm workers, and tenant farmers, in particular.

However, as Akiro Takahashi points out in a recent article in *Business Ethics Quarterly*, even twentieth-century feudal arrangements are complex social institutions. One cannot simply free the serfs or sharecroppers, engage in redistributive land reform, and hope that a new economic arrangement will work out. Takahashi's example is from a 1960s rice-growing community in Luzon in the Philippines. From as long as anyone can remember until land reforms in the 1970s the village had operated as a fiefdom. There were a few landholders and the rest of the villagers were tenant farmers. In order to work the land, each year the tenant farmers paid rents equal to half the net production of their farms. But because the tenant farmers were always in debt to the landlords, they usually owed all the net production to the landlords. The tenant farmers in fact never paid their debts, but because of high interest rates, as much as 200 percent, their debt increased each year so that they really could never leave the property. Since in fact what was owed the landlord was the *net* produce, each sharecropper was allowed to hire workers to farm the land they rented. So tenant farmers hired workers from other landlords or from other communities to till and harvest. Each sharecropper, in turn, went to work for another landlord's sharecropper. In addition, it was common practice for the harvesters not to do a perfect job, leaving often as much as 20 to 25 percent of the rice unharvested. Gleaning was not allowed by tenant

farmers or their families on the land they rented. But the wives of the farm workers and rest of the community "gleaned" the rest of the rice for themselves. In this way the poor were supported by the landlord and tenant farmers got some rice. The landlords pretended none of this occurred, still demanding the net product from each of its tenant farmers (Takahaski 1997, 39–40).

The value of private ownership (as linked to personal freedom) is a perfectly fine idea in principle. But abstracting that idea and universalizing it as a mental model for all reform has severe negative moral consequences, as the following example illustrates.

> Seven years ago, the prayers of 39 families were answered when the government [of Mexico] gave them this 1,000-acre communal farm in southern Mexico to raise livestock. Today the exhausted pastures are a moonscape of dust and rock. Cattle here don't graze quietly; they root like pigs as they yank rare blades of grass from the parched earth. . . . All arable land has been split into 5-acre patches of corn per family. To stay alive, the men earn 21 cents an hour cutting sugar cane in nearby fields.
>
> Farms like this one, known as *ejidos*, have helped the government win political support in the countryside by answering peasant demands for "land and liberty" that date back to the revolution of 1910. Unfortunately, this continuing land-redistribution plan has done a better job of carving farmland into small, barren plots than it has of growing food or providing a decent living for farmers.
>
> . . . Farmers tend to split their parcels among their sons, and with two-thirds of farms already smaller than 12.5 acres, there isn't any room in the countryside for the next generations. (Frazier 1984, 1, 18)

Another example: the Neem tree is a wild scraggly tree that grows well throughout India. For thousands of years, in hundreds of villages throughout that country the Neem tree has had a special place in the community. The tree has special religious meaning in some Hindu sects. Its leaves are used as pesticides, spread on plants to protect them from insects. Various herbal medicines are made from Neem leaves and bark, its products are used as contraceptives and for skin ailments, and many Indians brush their teeth with small Neem branches. Because of its effectiveness as a pesticide, recently the W. R. Grace Company began studying the tree, and in 1992 they developed a pesticide, Neemix. Neemix works as effectively as Neem leaves and has a long shelf life, thus making it more desirable as a pesticide than the leaves. Following the guidelines of the Indian government regarding patenting, Grace patented Neemix, opened a plant in India, and manufactured the product.

However, there have been mass protests against this patenting, both from Indians and from the Foundation on Economic Trends, a biotechnology watchdog organization. The argument is that Grace committed "biopiracy" because the Neem tree belongs to Indians, and products from the tree cannot be patented. Moreover, such patenting and manufacture of Neemix and other products drives up prices of Neem such that the indigenous poor, to whom the tree belongs, can no longer have access to the trees (Severence, Spiro, and Werhane 1999; Vijayalakshmi, Radha, and Shiva, 1995).

A fourth illustration: SELF, the Solar Electric Light Fund, a United States-based NGO, for some time has been developing a project aimed at electrifying rural communities in China. SELF has promoted a small photovoltaic (PV) solar unit that produces about 20 to 60 watts of energy. SELF has a policy of not giving away its photovoltaic units. This is because, it argues, if people have to pay something, even a small amount, for this service, they will value it more. So SELF has set up complex long-term lending schemes so that some poor rural people in China can afford electricity and own their own units as well (Sonenshein et al. 1997a).

SELF has been highly successful in some rural communities in China, so it decided to export that project to South Africa, concentrating on small Zulu villages. Working with village leaders in one community, SELF tried a pilot project, with the aim of providing electricity for 75 homes in a small village of Maphephethe. Six units were installed and were well received, and those receiving the units were delighted to have reliable power. However, one serious problem developed. Previous to the introduction of PV technology all the villagers lived modest but similar lives in a fairly egalitarian community. Now, those who have PV units are able to improve their social and economic status by operating manual sewing machines at night. The distribution of PV technology has upset a very delicate social balance by creating social stratification within this community (Sonenshein, Gorman, and Werhane 1997b).

What do these examples tell us? They tell us something very simple, something we should have learned years ago from the Nestle infant formula cases. American (or in Nestle's case, Western European) mental models of property and free enterprise cannot be exported uniformly to every part of the world without sometimes producing untoward consequences. This is because the notion of what is good or a social good is a socially constructed idea that is contextually and culturally relative. Abstract ideas such as autonomy, equality, private property, ownership, and community create mental models that take on different meanings depending on the social and situational context. Differing notions of community, ownership, intellectual property, exchange, competition, equality, and fairness, what Walzer calls social goods, create cultural anomalies that cannot be overcome simply by globalizing private free enterprise and operating in the same way everywhere (see Walzer 1983, chap. 1).

Land reform based on the notion of private ownership will not be successful in every community without making drastic social changes that alter communal relationships, family traditions, and ancient practices. This does not mean that land reform is wrong-headed; it suggests that it must be reconceived in each situation, so that what falls under the rubric of "reform" is contextually relevant such that change does not destroy the cultural fabric underlying what is to be changed.

It is tempting to argue that what is needed in remote communities or in some developing countries is a rule of law, similar to Anglo-Saxon law, that respects rights and property ownership, enforces contracts, protects equal opportunity, and the like, along with adequate mechanisms for enforcement. Indeed, it has been argued, I think with some merit, that one of the difficulties in Russia today is inadequate commercial laws or means to enforce them. But this argument, too, needs qualification. For example, intellectual property rights, already under siege with the electronic revolution, cannot merely be spelled out in every instance using a Western notion of ownership without infringing on some deeply rooted traditions and customs. An Anglo-Saxon model of patent protection, adapted in Indian law, may not be appropriate in many parts of rural India.

Do these examples, and there are thousands of others, point to the conclusion that because of the relativity of custom and culture, we should either abandon the ideal of global economic well-being, or, alternately, simply continue to convert the world into versions of Dallas? Is the aim a television in every village? Or is John Gray correct when he declares in his recent book that "the global economy system [based on Western *laissez-faire* free enterprise] is immoral, inequitable, unworkable, and unstable" (Zakaria 1999, 16)?

These two alternatives, as I have crudely stated them, present us with unnecessary dilemmas as if there were only two sorts of responses to problems of globalizing free enterprise. I want to suggest that there are other ways to deal with these issues.

The existence of widespread complex cultural, social, community, and even religious differences along with differing social goods does not imply that we can neither operate in those settings if they are alien to our own nor merely export Western versions of capitalism. To appeal again to Michael Walzer, despite the plurality and incommensurability of cross-cultural social goods, there is a thin thread of agreement, across cultures and religious difference, about the "bads," what cannot be tolerated or should not be permitted in any community. Walzer also calls these thin threads of agreement "moral minimums" (Walzer 1994). Human suffering, abject poverty, preventable disease, high mortality, and violence are abhorred wherever they occur. We are uncertain about the constitution of the "good life," but there is widespread agreement about deficient or despicable living conditions, indecencies, violations of human rights, mistreatment, and other harms.

Given that perspective, almost everyone will agree that poverty, however contextually defined, disease, high infant mortality, and violence are bads. Alleviating suffering of these sorts is surely a good. Improving economic conditions, in most cases, alleviates poverty and human suffering, if not violence. Then, is not economic value added in the form economic growth the proper solution to those evils?

We must cautiously reach that conclusion. Economic growth is not a "bad." Indeed, in most cultures it is considered a social good. But the notion cannot be identified without qualification with a Western idea of free enterprise. The model of economic growth in each context has to be framed in terms of each particular culture and its social goods. Free enterprise and private ownership, as practiced in most industrialized nations, can be, in many contexts, viable options, but only if they are modified so as not to destroy the fabric of a particular set of social goods, or replace that fabric with a new "good" that destroys, without replacing, all the elements of that culture. For example, land reform and the redistribution of property, apparently worthwhile projects to free tenant farmers from feudal bonds, will be successful only if the new landholders have means to function as economically viable farmers and in ways that do not threaten age-old traditions. As the Philippines example demonstrates, the fragile distributive system in the feudal community cannot be dismantled merely for the sake of independence and private ownership without harming complex communal relationships that maintained this system for centuries.

As purveyors of free enterprise, when moving into new communities and alien cultures corporate managers need to test their business mental models, *especially* if a particular system, service, or product has been successful in a number of markets. One needs to examine one's own mental models and try to fathom which models are operating in the community in which a company is planning to operate. In particular, it is important to find out what the operative social structures and community relationships are, what it is that this community values as its social goods, and try to imagine how those might be different given the introduction of a new kind of economic system. Because it is *not* just "the economy, stupid." What matters are social relationships; family, religious, and community traditions; and values—deeply held values about what is important and treasured—that is, those social goods a community cannot give up without sacrificing more than its lack of material well-being. If endemic poverty is an evil, we must create new ways to engage in free enterprise that takes into account, and even celebrates, cultural difference. . . .

In a new article in the *Harvard Business Review*, Stuart Hart and C. K. Prahalad make a different kind of argument for this same point. Hart and Prahalad contend that it happens to be in the long-term self-interest of global multinational companies to tread cautiously and

with respect in alien cultural contexts. This is because, in brief, developing countries represent 80 percent of the population of the world and thus are an as yet untapped source of growth and development. If that growth is done carefully through working within indigenous constraints, the result could be the creation of exciting new products and services that enhance rather than destroy communities while at the same time benefiting the companies in question (Hart and Prahalad 1999).

The challenge is to create new mental models for global business that achieve the aims Hart and Prahalad propose. There is at least one such attempt by a large transnational corporation to do exactly this. Unilever is a multi-billion-dollar global company with over 300,000 employees operating in almost 100 countries. Its main products are foods, fish, chemicals, and household products. Because it was founded in the Netherlands, a country one-third of which is reclaimed from the seas, Unilever has always been concerned with questions of environmental sustainability. In addition, the more recent expansion of its agricultural and fishing operations in remote communities has made Unilever increasingly aware of cultural difference. Beginning in 1993, Unilever began a process that resulted in a corporate-wide initiative that they call The Triple Bottom Line (Vis 1997). The rationale for this initiative is that if Unilever is going to continue to be successful in the next century, its success depends on its worldwide financial, ecological, and social assets. So Unilever changed the definition of "economic value added" to an expanded triple bottom line that measures economic, ecological, and community assests, liabilities, profits (or benefits), and losses. According to Unilever in its statement of corporate purpose and practice, each of these assets is of equal importance, and its aim is to be able to quantify the corporate contributions to each of these three areas. This may sound Pollyannaish, but Unilever's defense of this initiative could have been written by Milton Friedman.

> Each type of asset represents a source of value to the company and its shareholders. The sustained development of each of these sources of value ensures that the overall value accruing to shareholders is built up sustainably over the long term. This is in essence the significance of sustainable development to a company that aims at sustainable profit growth and long-term value creation for its shareholders, [customers], and employees. (Vis 1997, 3)

As part of this Triple Bottom Line initiative, Unilever is currently engaged in a series of small enterprises in a few small villages in India to develop new products aimed at the rural poor. These are microdevelopment projects, because the products they are supporting require little capital, they are locally produced, and of only indigenous interest. Unilever's goal, however, is to make those villages and their inhabitants economically viable managers, entrepreneurs, and customers as those notions are defined and make sense within a particular village culture and in ways that are not environmentally threatening. Whether this example will be a success story remains to be seen. There is to date no outcomes data, since the case events are still unfolding, and it will be some years before one can determine whether these projects are successes.

Is this stretching the limits of what we should expect from global corporations? Not according to Unilever. It argues that human flourishing in diverse settings creates needs for a diversity of products and services, products and services that Unilever will be able to provide. At the same time human well-being creates long-term economic value added, both for Unilever and for the cultures and communities in which it operates.

# BIBLIOGRAPHY

Frazier, Steve. 1984. "Peasant Politics: Mexican Farmers Get Grants of Small Plots, But Output is Meager." *Wall Street Journal* (June 4), pp. 1, 18.

Hart, Stuart, and Prahalad, C. K. 1999. "Strategies for the Bottom of the Pyramid: Creating Sustainable Development." *Harvard Business Review* (November–December).

Johnson, Mark. 1993. *Moral Imagination*. Chicago: University of Chicago Press.

Rouse, William B., and Morris, Nancy M. 1986. "On Looking Into the Black Box: Prospects and Limits in the Search for Mental Models." *Psychological Bulletin* 100:349–63.

Severence, Kristi, Lisa Spiro, and Patricia H. Werhane. 1999. "W. R. Grace Co. and the Neemix Patent," *Darden Case Bibliography:* UVA-E-0157. Charlottesville: University of Virginia Press.

Sonenshein, Scott, Michael E. Gorman, and Patricia H. Werhane. 1997a. "SELF." *Darden Case Bibliography:* UVA-0112. Charlottesville: University of Virginia Press.

———. 1997b. "Solar Energy in South Africa." *Darden Case Bibliography:* UVA-E-0145. Charlottesville: University of Virginia Press.

Takahashi, Akiro, "Ethics in Developing Economies of Asia." *Business Ethics Quarterly,* 7:33–45.

Vijayalakshmi, K, K. S. Radha, and Vandana Shiva. 1996. *Neem: A User's Manual.* Madras: Centre for Indian Knowledge Systems.

Vis, Jan-Kees. 1997. *Unilever: Putting Corporate Purpose Into Action.* Unilever Publication.

Walzer, Michael. 1983. *Spheres of Justice.* New York: Basic Books.

———. 1994. *Thick and Thin.* Notre Dame: Notre Dame University Press.

Werhane, Patricia H. 1991. "Engineers and Management: The Challenge of the Challenger Incident." *Journal of Business Ethics,* 1:605–16.

———. 1998. "Moral Imagination and Management Decision Making." *Business Ethics Quarterly,* Special Issue No. 1: 75–98.

———. 1999. *Moral Imagination and Management Decision Making.* New York: Oxford University Press.

Zakaria, Fareed. 1999. "Passing the Bucks [a review of Gray's *False Dawn*]." *New York Times Book Review* (April 25), pp. 16, 18.

## SWEATSHOPS AND BRIBERY

# The Great Non-Debate
# over International Sweatshops

*Ian Maitland*

In recent years, there has been a dramatic growth in the contracting out of production by companies in the industrialized countries to suppliers in developing countries. This globalization of production has led to an emerging international division of labor in footwear and apparel in which companies like Nike and Reebok concentrate on product design and marketing but rely on a network of contractors in Indonesia, China, Central America, and the like, to build shoes or sew shirts according to exact specifications and deliver a high-quality good according to precise delivery schedules. As Nike's vice president for Asia has put it, "We don't know the first thing about manufacturing. We are marketers and designers."

The contracting arrangements have drawn intense fire from critics—usually labor and human rights activists. These "critics" (as I will refer to them) have charged that the companies are (by proxy) exploiting workers in the plants (which I will call "international sweatshops") of their suppliers. Specifically the companies stand accused of chasing cheap labor around the globe, failing to pay their workers living wages, using child labor, turning a blind eye to abuses of human rights, being complicit with repressive regimes in denying workers the right to join unions and failing to enforce minimum labor standards in the workplace, and so on.

The campaign against international sweatshops has largely unfolded on television and,

to a lesser extent, in the print media. What seems like no more than a handful of critics has mounted an aggressive, media-savvy campaign which has put the publicity-shy retail giants on the defensive. The critics have orchestrated a series of sensational "disclosures" on prime time television exposing the terrible pay and working conditions in factories making jeans for Levi's or sneakers for Nike or Pocahontas shirts for Disney. One of the principal scourges of the companies has been Charles Kernaghan who runs the National Labor Coalition (NLC), a labor human rights group involving 25 unions. It was Kernaghan who, in 1996, broke the news before a Congressional committee that Kathie Lee Gifford's clothing line was being made by 13- and 14-year-olds working 20-hour days in factories in Honduras. Kernaghan also arranged for teenage workers from sweatshops in Central America to testify before congressional committees about abusive labor practices. At one of these hearings, one of the workers held up a Liz Claiborne cotton sweater identical to ones she had sewn since she was a 13-year-old working 12-hour days. According to a news report, "[t]his image, accusations of oppressive conditions at the factory and the Claiborne logo played well on that evening's network news." The result has been a circus-like atmosphere—as in Roman circus where Christians were thrown to lions.

Kernaghan has shrewdly targeted the companies' carefully cultivated public images. He

From Ian Maitland, "The Great Non-Debate Over International Sweatshops," *British Academy of Management Annual Conference Proceedings,* September, pp. 240–65, 1997. Reprinted with permission of the author.

has explained: "Their image is everything. They live and die by their image. That gives you a certain power over them." As a result, he says, "these companies are sitting ducks. They have no leg to stand on. That's why it's possible for a tiny group like us to take on a giant like Wal-Mart. You can't defend paying someone 31 cents an hour in Honduras. . . ."[1] Apparently most of the companies agree with Kernaghan. Not a single company has tried to mount a serious defense of its contracting practices. They have judged that they cannot win a war of soundbites with the critics. Instead of making a fight of it, the companies have sued for peace in order to protect their principal asset—their image.

Major U.S. retailers have responded by adopting codes of conduct on human and labor rights in their international operations. Levi-Strauss, Nike, Sears, J.C. Penney, Wal-Mart, Home Depot, and Philips Van-Heusen now have such codes. As Lance Compa notes, such codes are the result of a blend of humanitarian and pragmatic impulses: "Often the altruistic motive coincides with 'bottom line' considerations related to brand name, company image, and other intangibles that make for core value to the firm."[2] Peter Jacobi, President of Global Sourcing for Levi-Strauss has advised: "If your company owns a popular brand, protect this priceless asset at all costs. Highly visible companies have any number of reasons to conduct their business not just responsibly but also in ways that cannot be portrayed as unfair, illegal, or unethical. This sets an extremely high standard since it must be applied to both company-owned businesses and contractors. . . ."[3] And according to another Levi-Strauss spokesman, "In many respects, we're protecting our single largest asset: our brand image and corporate reputation."[4] Nike recently published the results of a generally favorable review of its international operations conducted by former American U.N. Ambassador Andrew Young.

Recently a truce of sorts between the critics and the companies was announced on the White House lawn with President Clinton and Kathie Lee Gifford in attendance. A presidential task force, including representatives of labor unions, human rights groups and apparel companies like L.L.Bean and Nike, has come up with a set of voluntary standards which, it hopes, will be embraced by the entire industry. Companies that comply with the code will be entitled to use a "No Sweat" label.

## OBJECTIVE OF THIS PAPER

In this confrontation between the companies and their critics, neither side seems to have judged it to be in its interest to seriously engage the issue at the heart of this controversy, namely: What are appropriate wages and labor standards in international sweatshops? As we have seen, the companies have treated the charges about sweatshops as a public relations problem to be managed so as to minimize harm to their public images. The critics have apparently judged that the best way to keep public indignation at boiling point is to oversimplify the issue and treat it as a morality play featuring heartless exploiters and victimized Third World workers. The result has been a great nondebate over international sweatshops. Paradoxically, if peace breaks out between the two sides, the chances that the debate will be seriously joined may recede still further. Indeed, there exists a real risk (I will argue) that any such truce may be a collusive one that will come at the expense of the very Third World workers it is supposed to help.

This paper takes up the issue of what are appropriate wages and labor standards in international sweatshops. Critics charge that the present arrangements are exploitative. I proceed by examining the specific charges of exploitation from the standpoints of both (a) their factual and (b) their ethical sufficiency. However, in the absence of any well-established consensus among business ethicists (or other thoughtful observers), I simultaneously use the investigation of sweatshops as a setting for trying to adjudicate between competing views about what those standards should be. My examination will pay particular attention to (but will not be limited to) labor conditions at the plants of Nike's suppliers in Indonesia. I have not personally visited any international sweatshops, and so my conclusions are based entirely on secondary analysis of the voluminous published record on the topic.

## WHAT ARE ETHICALLY APPROPRIATE LABOR STANDARDS IN INTERNATIONAL SWEATSHOPS?

What are ethically acceptable or appropriate levels of wages and labor standards in international sweatshops? The following three possibilities just about run the gamut of standards or principles that have been seriously proposed to regulate such policies.

*1. Home-country standards:* It might be argued (and in rare cases has been) that international corporations have an ethical duty to pay the same wages and provide the same labor standards regardless of where they operate. However, the view that home-country standards should apply in host countries is rejected by most business ethicists and (officially at least) by the critics of international sweatshops. Thus Thomas Donaldson argues that "[b]y arbitrarily establishing U.S. wage levels as the benchmark for fairness one eliminates the role of the international market in establishing salary levels, and this in turn eliminates the incentive U.S. corporations have to hire foreign workers."[5] Richard DeGeorge makes much the same argument: If there were a rule that said that "that American MNCs [multinational corporations] that wish to be ethical must pay the same wages abroad as they do at home, . . . [then]

MNCs would have little incentive to move their manufacturing abroad; and if they did move abroad they would disrupt the local labor market with artificially high wages that bore no relation to the local standard or cost of living."[6]

*2. "Living wage" standard:* It has been proposed that an international corporation should, at a minimum, pay a "living wage." Thus DeGeorge says that corporations should pay a living wage "even when this is not paid by local firms."[7] However, it is hard to pin down what this means operationally. According to DeGeorge, a living wage should "allow the worker to live in dignity as a human being." In order to respect the human rights of its workers, he says, a corporation must pay "at least subsistence wages and as much above that as workers and their dependents need to live with reasonable dignity, given the general state of development of the society."[8] As we shall see, the living wage standard has become a rallying cry of the critics of international sweatshops. Apparently, DeGeorge believes that it is preferable for a corporation to provide no job at all than to offer one that pays less that a living wage. . . .

*3. Classical liberal standard:* Finally, there is what I will call the classical liberal standard. According to this standard a practice (wage or labor practice) is ethically acceptable if it is freely chosen by informed workers. For example, in a recent report the World Bank invoked this standard in connection with workplace safety. It said: "The appropriate level is therefore that at which the costs are commensurate with the value that informed workers place on improved working conditions and reduced risk."[9] Most business ethicists reject this standard on the grounds that there is some sort of market failure or the "background conditions" are lacking for markets to work effectively. Thus for Donaldson full (or near-full) employment is a prerequisite if workers are to make sound choices regarding workplace safety: "The average level of unemployment in the developing countries today exceeds 40 percent, a figure that has frustrated the application of neoclassical economic principles to the international economy on a score of issues. With full employment, and all other things being equal, market forces will encourage workers to make trade-offs between job opportunities using safety as a variable. But with massive unemployment, market forces in developing countries drive the unemployed to the jobs they are lucky enough to land, regardless of the safety."[10] Apparently there are other forces, like Islamic fundamentalism and the global debt "bomb," that rule out reliance on market solutions, but Donaldson does not explain their relevance.[11] DeGeorge, too, believes that the necessary conditions are lacking for market forces to operate benignly. Without what he calls "background institutions" to protect the workers and the resources of the developing country (e.g., enforceable minimum wages) and/or greater equality of bargaining power exploitation is the most likely result.[12] "If American MNCs pay workers very low wages . . . they clearly have the opportunity to make significant profits."[13] DeGeorge goes on to make the interesting observation that "competition has developed among multinationals themselves, so that the profit margin has been driven down" and developing countries "can play one company against another."[14] But apparently that is not enough to rehabilitate market forces in his eyes.

# THE CASE AGAINST INTERNATIONAL SWEATSHOPS

To many of their critics, international sweatshops exemplify the way in which the greater openness of the world economy is hurting workers. . . . Globalization means a transition from (more or less) regulated domestic economies to an unregulated world economy. The superior mobility of capital, and the essentially fixed, immobile nature of world labor, means a fundamental shift in bargaining power in favor of large international corporations. Their global reach permits them to shift production almost costlessly from one location to another. As a consequence, instead of being able to exercise some degree of control over companies operating within their borders, governments are now locked in a bidding war with one another to attract and retain the business of large multinational companies.

The critics allege that international companies are using the threat of withdrawal or withholding of investment to pressure governments and workers to grant concessions. "Today [multinational companies] choose between workers in developing countries that compete against each other to depress wages to attract foreign investment." The result is a race for the bottom—a "destructive downward bidding spiral of the labor conditions and wages of workers throughout the world. . . ."[15] Thus, critics charge that in Indonesia wages are deliberately held below the poverty level or subsistence in order to make the country a desirable location. The results of this competitive dismantling of worker protections, living standards and worker rights are predictable: deteriorating work conditions, declining real incomes for workers, and a widening gap between rich and poor in developing countries. I turn next to the specific charges made by the critics of international sweatshops.

## Unconscionable Wages

Critics charge that the companies, by their proxies, are paying "starvation wages" and "slave wages." They are far from clear about what wage level they consider to be appropriate. But they generally demand that companies pay a "living wage." Kernaghan has said that workers should be paid enough to support their families and they should get a "living wage" and "be treated like human beings."[16] . . . According to Tim Smith, wage levels should be "fair, decent or a living wage for an employee and his or her family." He has said that wages in the maquiladoras of Mexico averaged $35 to $55 a week (in or near 1993) which he calls a "shockingly substandard wage," apparently on the grounds that it "clearly does not allow an employee to feed and care for a family adequately."[17] In 1992, Nike came in for harsh criticism when a magazine published the pay stub of a worker at one of its Indonesian suppliers. It showed that the worker was paid at the rate of $1.03 per day which was reportedly less than the Indonesian government's figure for "minimum physical need."[18]

### Immiserization Thesis

Former Labor Secretary Robert Reich has proposed as a test of the fairness of development policies that "Low-wage workers should become better off, not worse off, as trade and investment boost national income." He has written that "[i]f a country pursues policies that . . . limit to a narrow elite the benefits of trade, the promise of open commerce is perverted and drained of its rationale."[19] A key claim of the activists is that companies actually impoverish or immiserize developing country workers. They experience an absolute decline in living standards. This thesis follows from the claim that the bidding war among developing countries is depressing wages. . . .

### Widening Gap Between Rich and Poor

A related charge is that international sweatshops are contributing to the increasing gap between rich and poor. Not only are the poor being absolutely impoverished, but trade is generating greater inequality within developing countries. Another test that Reich has proposed to establish the fairness of international trade is that "the gap between rich and poor should tend to narrow with development, not widen."[20] Critics charge that international sweatshops

flunk that test. They say that the increasing GNPs of some developing countries simply mask a widening gap between rich and poor. "Across the world, both local and foreign elites are getting richer from the exploitation of the most vulnerable."[21] And, "The major adverse consequence of quickening global economic integration has been widening income disparity within almost all nations. . . ."[22] There appears to be a tacit alliance between the elites of both first and third worlds to exploit the most vulnerable, to regiment and control and conscript them so that they can create the material conditions for the elites' extravagant lifestyles.

### Collusion with Repressive Regimes

Critics charge that, in their zeal to make their countries safe for foreign investment, Third World regimes, notably China and Indonesia, have stepped up their repression. Not only have these countries failed to enforce even the minimal labor rules on the books, but they have also used their military and police to break strikes and repress independent unions. They have stifled political dissent, both to retain their hold on political power and to avoid any instability that might scare off foreign investors. Consequently, critics charge, companies like Nike are profiting from political repression. "As unions spread in [Korea and Taiwan], Nike shifted its suppliers primarily to Indonesia, China and Thailand, where they could depend on governments to suppress independent union-organizing efforts."[23]

## EVALUATION OF THE CHARGES AGAINST INTERNATIONAL SWEATSHOPS

The critics' charges are undoubtedly accurate on a number of points: (1) There is no doubt that international companies are chasing cheap labor. (2) The wages paid by the international sweatshops are—by American standards—shockingly low. (3) Some developing country governments have tightly controlled or repressed organized labor in order to prevent it from disturbing the flow of foreign investment. Thus, in Indonesia, independent unions have been suppressed. (4) It is not unusual in developing countries for minimum wage levels to be lower than the official poverty level. (5) Developing country governments have winked at violations of minimum wage laws and labor rules. However, most jobs are in the informal sector and so largely outside the scope of government supervision. (6) Some suppliers have employed children or have subcontracted work to other producers who have done so. (7) Some developing country governments deny their people basic political rights. China is the obvious example; Indonesia's record is pretty horrible but had shown steady improvement until the last two years. But on many of the other counts, the critics' charges appear to be seriously inaccurate. And, even where the charges are accurate, it is not self-evident that the practices in question are improper or unethical, as we see next.

## Wages and Conditions

Even the critics of international sweatshops do not dispute that the wages they pay are generally higher than—or at least equal to—comparable wages in the labor markets where they operate. According to the International Labor Organization (ILO), multinational companies often apply standards relating to wages, benefits, conditions of work, and occupational safety and health, which both exceed statutory requirements and those practiced by local firms."[24] The ILO also says that wages and working conditions in so-called Export Processing Zones (EPZs) are often equal to or higher than jobs outside. The World Bank says that the poorest workers in developing countries work in the informal sector where they often earn less than half what a formal sector employee earns. Moreover, "informal and rural workers often must work under more hazardous and insecure conditions than their formal sector counterparts.[25]

The same appears to hold true for the international sweatshops. In 1996, young women working in the plant of a Nike supplier in Serang, Indonesia, were earning the Indonesian legal minimum wage of 5,200 rupiahs, or about $2.28 each day. As a report in the *Washington Post* pointed out, just earning the minimum wage put these workers among higher-paid Indonesians: "In Indonesia, less than half the working population earns the minimum wage, since about half of all adults here are in farming, and the typical farmer would make only about 2,000 rupiahs each day."[26] The workers in the Serang plant reported that they save about three-quarters of their pay. A 17-year-old woman said: "I came here one year ago from central Java. I'm making more money than my father makes." This woman also said that the she sent about 75 percent of her earnings back to her family on the farm.[27] Also in 1996, a Nike spokeswoman estimated that an entry-level factory worker in the plant of a Nike supplier made five times what a farmer makes.[28] Nike's chairman, Phil Knight, likes to teasingly remind critics that the average worker in one of Nike's Chinese factories is paid more than a professor at Beijing University.[29] There is also plentiful anecdotal evidence from non-Nike sources. A worker at the Taiwanese-owned King Star Garment Assembly plant in Honduras told a reporter that he was earning seven times what he earned in the countryside.[30] In Bangladesh, the country's fledgling garment industry was paying women who had never worked before between $40 and $55 a month in 1991. That compared with a national per capita income of about $200 and the approximately $1 a day earned by many of these women's husbands as day laborers or rickshaw drivers.[31]

The same news reports also shed some light on the working conditions in sweatshops. According to the *Washington Post*, in 1994 the Indonesian office of the international accounting firm Ernst & Young surveyed Nike workers concerning worker pay, safety conditions, and attitudes toward the job. The auditors pulled workers off the assembly line at random and asked them questions that the workers answered anonymously. The survey of 25 workers at Nike's Serang plant found that 23 thought the hours and overtime hours too high. None of the workers reported that they had been discriminated against. Thirteen said the working environment was the key reason they worked at the Serang plant while eight cited salary and benefits.[32] The *Post* report also noted that the Serang plant closes for about 10 days each year for Muslim holidays. It quoted Nike officials and the plant's Taiwanese owners as saying that 94 percent of the workers had returned to the plant following the most recent break. . . .

There is also the mute testimony of the lines of job applicants outside the sweatshops in Guatemala and Honduras. According to Lucy Martinez-Mont, in Guatemala the sweatshops are conspicuous for the long lines of young people waiting to be interviewed for a job.[33] Outside the gates of the industrial park in Honduras that Rohter visited "anxious onlookers are always waiting, hoping for a chance at least to fill out a job application [for employment at one of the apparel plants]."[34]

The critics of sweatshops acknowledge that workers have voluntarily taken their jobs, consider themselves lucky to have them, and want to keep them. . . . But they go on to discount the workers' views as the product of confusion or ignorance, and/or they just argue that the workers' views are beside the point. Thus, while "it is undoubtedly true" that Nike has given jobs to thousands of people who wouldn't be working otherwise, they say that "neatly skirts the fundamental human-rights issue raised by these production arrangements that are now spreading all across the world."[35] Similarly the NLC's Kernaghan says that "[w]hether workers think they are better off in the assembly plants than elsewhere is not the real issue."[36] Kernaghan, and Jeff Ballinger of the AFL-CIO, concede that the workers desperately need these jobs. But "[t]hey say they're not asking that U.S. companies stop operating in these countries. They're asking that workers be paid a living wage and treated like human beings."[37] Apparently these workers are victims of what Marx called false consciousness, or else they would grasp that they are being exploited. According to Barnet and Cavanagh, "For many workers . . . exploitation is not a concept easily comprehended because the alternative prospects for earning a living are so bleak."[38]

**Immiserization and Inequality**

The critics' claim that the countries that host international sweatshops are marked by growing poverty and inequality is flatly contradicted by the record. In fact, many of those countries have experienced sharp increases in living standards—for all strata of society. In trying to attract investment in simple manufacturing, Malaysia and Indonesia and, now, Vietnam and China, are retracing the industrialization path already successfully taken by East Asian countries like Taiwan, Korea, Singapore and Hong Kong. These four countries got their start by producing labor-intensive manufactured goods (often electrical and electronic components, shoes, and garments) for export markets. Over time they graduated to the export of higher-value-added items that are skill-intensive and require a relatively developed industrial base.[39]

As is well known, these East Asian countries achieved growth rates exceeding 8 percent for a quarter century. . . . The workers in these economies were not impoverished by growth.

The benefits of growth were widely diffused: These economies achieved essentially full employment in the 1960s. Real wages rose by as much as a factor of four. Absolute poverty fell. And income inequality remained at low to moderate levels. It is true that in the initial stages the rapid growth generated only moderate increases in wages. But once essentially full employment was reached, and what economists call the Fei-Ranis turning point was reached, the increased demand for labor resulted in the bidding up of wages as firms competed for a scarce labor supply.

Interestingly, given its historic mission as a watchdog for international labor standards, the ILO has embraced this development model. It recently noted that the most successful developing economies, in terms of output and employment growth, have been "those who best exploited emerging opportunities in the global economy."[40] An "export oriented policy is vital in countries that are starting on the industrialization path and have large surpluses of cheap labour." Countries which have succeeded in attracting foreign direct investment (FDI) have experienced rapid growth in manufacturing output and exports. The successful attraction of foreign investment in plant and equipment "can be a powerful spur to rapid industrialization and employment creation." "At low levels of industrialization, FDI in garments and shoes and some types of consumer electronics can be very useful for creating employment and opening the economy to international markets; there may be some entrepreneurial skills created in simple activities like garments (as has happened in Bangladesh). Moreover, in some cases, such as Malaysia, the investors may strike deeper roots and invest in more capital-intensive technologies as wages rise."

According to the World Bank, the rapidly growing Asian economies (including Indonesia) "have also been unusually successful at sharing the fruits of their growth."[41] In fact, while inequality in the West has been growing, it has been shrinking in the Asian economies. They are the only economies in the world to have experienced high growth *and* declining inequality, and they also show shrinking gender gaps in education. . . .

## Profiting from Repression?

What about the charge that international sweatshops are profiting from repression? It is undeniable that there is repression in many of the countries where sweatshops are located. But economic development appears to be relaxing that repression rather than strengthening its grip. The companies are supposed to benefit from government policies (e.g., repression of unions) that hold down labor costs. However, as we have seen, the wages paid by the international sweatshops already match or exceed the prevailing local wages. Not only that, but incomes in the East Asian economies, and in Indonesia, have risen rapidly. . . .

The critics, however, are right in saying that the Indonesian government has opposed independent unions in the sweatshops out of fear they would lead to higher wages and labor unrest. But the government's fear clearly is that unions might drive wages in the modern industrial sector *above* market-clearing levels— or, more exactly, further above market. It is ironic that critics like Barnet and Cavanagh would use the Marxian term "reserve army of the unemployed." According to Marx, capitalists deliberately maintain high levels of unemployment in order to control the working class. But the Indonesian government's policies (e.g., suppression of unions, resistance to a higher minimum wage, and lax enforcement of labor rules) have been directed at achieving exactly the opposite result. The government appears to have calculated that high unemployment is a greater threat to its hold on power. I think we can safely take at face value its claims that its policies are genuinely intended to help the economy create jobs to absorb the massive numbers of unemployed and underemployed.[42]

## LABOR STANDARDS IN INTERNATIONAL SWEATSHOPS: PAINFUL TRADE-OFFS

Who but the grinch could grudge paying a few additional pennies to some of the world's poorest workers? There is no doubt that the rhetorical force of the critics' case against international sweatshops rests on this apparently self-evident proposition. However, higher wages and improved labor standards are not free. After all, the critics themselves attack companies for chasing cheap labor. It follows that if labor in developing countries is made more expensive (say, as the result of pressures by the critics), then those countries will receive less foreign investment, and fewer jobs will be created there. Imposing higher wages may deprive these countries of the one comparative advantage they enjoy, namely low-cost labor.

We have seen that workers in most "international sweatshops" are already relatively well paid. Workers in the urban, formal sectors of developing countries commonly earn more than twice what informal and rural workers get. Simply earning the minimum wage put the young women making Nike shoes in Serang in the top half of the income distribution in Indonesia. Accordingly, the critics are in effect calling for a *widening* of the economic disparity that already greatly favors sweatshop workers.

By itself that may or may not be ethically objectionable. But these higher wages come at the expense of the incomes and the job opportunities of much poorer workers. As economists explain, higher wages in the formal sector reduce employment there and (by in-

creasing the supply of labor) depr
in the informal sector. The case against re quiring above-market wages for international sweatshop workers is essentially the same as the case against other measures that artificially raise labor costs, like the minimum wage. In Jagdish Bhagwati's words: "Requiring a minimum wage in an overpopulated, developing country, as is done in a developed country, may actually be morally wicked. A minimum wage might help the unionized, industrial proletariat, while limiting the ability to save and invest rapidly which is necessary to draw more of the unemployed and nonunionized rural poor into gainful employment and income."[43] The World Bank makes the same point: "Minimum wages may help the most poverty-stricken workers in industrial countries, but they clearly do not in developing nations. . . . The workers whom minimum wage legislation tries to protect—urban formal workers—already earn much more than the less favored majority. . . . And inasmuch as minimum wage and other regulations discourage formal employment by increasing wage and nonwage costs, they hurt the poor who aspire to formal employment."[44]

The story is no different when it comes to labor standards other than wages. If standards are set too high, they will hurt investment and employment. The World Bank report points out that "[r]educing hazards in the workplace is costly, and typically the greater the reduction the more it costs. Moreover, the costs of compliance often fall largely on employees through lower wages or reduced employment. As a result, setting standards too high can actually lower workers' welfare. . . ."[45] Perversely, if the higher standards advocated by critics retard the growth of formal sector jobs, then that will trap more informal and rural workers in jobs which are far more hazardous and insecure than those of their formal sector counterparts.

The critics consistently advocate policies that will benefit better-off workers at the expense of worse-off ones. If it were within their power, it appears that they would reinvent the labor markets of much of Latin America. Alejandro Portes' description seems to be on the mark: "In Mexico, Brazil, Peru, and other Third World countries, [unlike East Asia], there are powerful independent unions representing the protected sector of the working class. Although their rhetoric is populist and even radical, the fact is that they tend to represent the better-paid and more stable fraction of the working class. Alongside, there toils a vast, unprotected proletariat, employed by informal enterprises and linked, in ways hidden from public view, with modern sector firms." . . .

Of course, it might be objected that trading off workers' rights for more jobs is unethical. But, so far as I can determine, the critics have not made this argument. Although they sometimes implicitly accept the existence of the trade-off (we saw that they attack Nike for chasing cheap labor), their public statements are silent on the lost or forgone jobs from higher wages and better labor standards. At other times, they imply or claim that improvements in workers' wages and conditions are essentially free. . . .

In summary, the result of the ostensibly humanitarian changes urged by critics are likely to be (1) reduced employment in the formal or modern sector of the economy, (2) lower incomes in the informal sector, (3) less investment and so slower economic growth, (4) reduced exports, (5) greater inequality and poverty.

## CONCLUSION: THE CASE FOR NOT EXCEEDING MARKET STANDARDS

It is part of the job description of business ethicists to exhort companies to treat their workers better (otherwise what purpose do they serve?). So it will have come as no surprise that both the business ethicists whose views I summarized

at the beginning of this paper—Thomas Donaldson and Richard DeGeorge—objected to letting the market alone determine wages and labor standards in multinational companies. Both of them proposed criteria for setting wages that might occasionally "improve" on the outcomes of the market.

Their reasons for rejecting market determination of wages were similar. They both cited conditions that allegedly prevent international markets from generating ethically acceptable results. Donaldson argued that neoclassical economic principles are not applicable to international business because of high unemployment rates in developing countries. And DeGeorge argued that, in an unregulated international market, the gross inequality of bargaining power between workers and companies would lead to exploitation.

But this paper has shown that attempts to improve on market outcomes may have unforeseen tragic consequences. We saw how raising the wages of workers in international sweatshops might wind up penalizing the most vulnerable workers (those in the informal sectors of developing countries) by depressing their wages and reducing their job opportunities in the formal sector. Donaldson and DeGeorge cited high unemployment and unequal bargaining power as conditions that made it necessary to bypass or override the market determination of wages. However, in both cases, bypassing the market in order to prevent exploitation may aggravate these conditions. As we have seen, above-market wages paid to sweatshop workers may discourage further investment and so perpetuate high unemployment. In turn, the higher unemployment may weaken the bargaining power of workers vis-à-vis employers. Thus such market imperfections seem to call for more reliance on market forces rather than less. Likewise, the experience of the newly industrialized East Asian economies suggests that the best cure for the ills of sweatshops is more sweatshops. But most of the well-intentioned policies that improve on market outcomes are likely to have the opposite effect.

Where does this leave the international manager? If the preceding analysis is correct, then it follows that it is ethically acceptable to pay market wage rates in developing countries (and to provide employment conditions appropriate for the level of development). That holds true even if the wages pay less than so-called living wages or subsistence or even (conceivably) the local minimum wage. The appropriate test is not whether the wage reaches some predetermined standard but whether it is freely accepted by (reasonably) informed workers. The workers themselves are in the best position to judge whether the wages offered are superior to their next-best alternatives. (The same logic applies *mutatis mutandis* to workplace labor standards).

Indeed, not only is it ethically acceptable for a company to pay market wages, but it may be ethically unacceptable for it to pay wages that exceed market levels. That will be the case if the company's above-market wages set precedents for other international companies which raise labor costs to the point of discouraging foreign investment. Furthermore, companies may have a social responsibility to transcend their own narrow preoccupation with protecting their brand image and to publicly defend a system which has greatly improved the lot of millions of workers in developing countries.

## NOTES

1. Steven Greenhouse, "A Crusader Makes Celebrities Tremble." *New York Times* (June 18, 1996), p. B4.

2. Lance A. Compa and Tashia Hinchliffe Darricarrere, "Enforcement Through Corporate Codes of Conduct," in *Human Rights, Labor Rights, and International Trade* ed. Compa and Stephen F. Diamond (Philadelphia: University of Pennsylvania Press, 1996), 193.

3. Peter Jacobi in Martha Nichols, "Third-World Families at Work: Child Labor or Child Care." *Harvard Business Review* (January–February 1993).

4. David Sampson in Robin G. Givhan, "A Stain on Fashion; The Garment Industry Profits from Cheap Labor." *Washington Post* (September 12, 1995), p. B1.

5. Thomas Donaldson, *Ethics of International Business* (New York: Oxford University Press, 1989), 98.

6. Richard DeGeorge, *Competing with Integrity in International Business* (New York: Oxford University Press, 1993), 79.

7. Ibid., 356–57.

8. Ibid., 78.

9. World Bank, *World Development Report 1995*, "Workers in an Integrating World Economy" (Oxford University Press, 1995), 77.

10. Donaldson, *Ethics of International Business*, p. 115.

11. Ibid., 150.

12. DeGeorge, *Competing with Integrity*, 48.

13. Ibid., 358.

14. Ibid.

15. Terry Collingsworth, J. William Goold, Pharis J. Harvey, "Time for a Global New Deal," *Foreign Affairs* (January–February 1994): 8.

16. William B. Falk, "Dirty Little Secrets," *Newsday* (June 16, 1996).

17. Tim Smith, "The Power of Business for Human Rights." *Business & Society Review* (January 1994): 36.

18. Jeffrey Ballinger, "The New Free Trade Heel." *Harper's Magazine* (August 1992): 46–47. "As in many developing countries, Indonesia's minimum wage, . . . , is less than poverty level." Nina Baker, "The Hidden Hands of Nike," *Oregonian* (August 9, 1992).

19. Robert B. Reich, "Escape from the Global Sweatshop; Capitalism's Stake in Uniting the Workers of the World." *Washington Post* (May 22, 1994). Reich's test is intended to apply in developing countries "where democratic institutions are weak or absent."

20. Ibid.

21. Kenneth P. Hutchinson, "Third World Growth." *Harvard Business Review* (November–December 1994).

22. Robin Broad and John Cavanagh, "Don't Neglect the Impoverished South." *Foreign Affairs* (December 22, 1995).

23. John Cavanagh & Robin Broad, "Global Reach; Workers Fight the Multinationals." *Nation* (March 18, 1996): 21. See also Bob Herbert, "Nike's Bad Neighborhood." *New York Times* (June 14, 1996).

24. International Labor Organization, *World Employment 1995* (Geneva: ILO, 1995), 73.

25. World Bank, *Workers in an Integrating World Economy*, p. 5.

26. Keith B. Richburg, Anne Swardson, "U.S. Industry Overseas: Sweatshop or Job Source?: Indonesians Praise Work at Nike Factory." *Washington Post* (July 28, 1996).

27. Richburg and Swardson, "Sweatshop or Job Source?" The 17-year-old was interviewed in the presence of managers. For other reports that workers remit home large parts of their earnings see Seth Mydans, "Tangerang Journal; For Indonesian Workers at Nike Plant: Just Do It." *New York Times* (August 9, 1996), and Nina Baker, "The Hidden Hands of Nike."

28. Donna Gibbs, Nike spokeswoman on ABC's *World News Tonight,* June 6, 1996.

29. Mark Clifford, "Trading in Social Issues; Labor Policy and International Trade Regulation," *World Press Review* (June 1994): 36.

30. Larry Rohter, "To U.S. Critics, a Sweatshop; for Hondurans, a Better Life." *New York Times* (July 18, 1996).

31. Marcus Brauchli, "Garment Industry Booms in Bangladesh." *Wall Street Journal* (August 6, 1991).

32. Richburg and Swardson, "Sweatshop or Job Source?"

33. Lucy Martinez-Mont, "Sweatshops Are Better Than No Shops." *Wall Street Journal* (June 25, 1996).

34. Rohter, "To U.S. Critics a Sweatshop."

35. Barnet & Cavanagh, *Global Dreams,* p. 326.

36. Rohter, "To U.S. Critics a Sweatshop."

37. William B. Falk, "Dirty Little Secrets," *Newsday* (June 16, 1996).

38. Barnet and Cavanagh, "Just Undo It: Nike's Exploited Workers." *New York Times* (February 13, 1994).

39. Sarosh Kuruvilla, "Linkages between Industrialization Strategies and Industrial Relations/Human Resources Policies: Singapore, Malaysia, The Philippines, and India." *Industrial & Labor Relations Review* (July 1996): 637.

40. The ILO's Constitution (of 1919) mentions that: ". . . . the failure of any nation to adopt humane conditions of labour is an obstacle in the way of other nations which desire to improve the conditions in their own countries." ILO, *World Employment 1995*, p. 74.

41. World Bank, *The East Asian Miracle* (New York: Oxford University Press, 1993), 2.

42. Gideon Rachman, "Wealth in Its Grasp, a Survey of Indonesia." *Economist* (April 17, 1993): 14–15.

43. Jagdish Bhagwati & Robert E. Hudec, eds. *Fair Trade and Harmonization*, vol. 1 (Cambridge: MIT Press, 1996): 2.

44. World Bank, *Workers in an Integrating World Economy*, p. 75.

45. Ibid., 77. As I have noted, the report proposes that the "appropriate level is therefore that at which the costs are commensurate with the value that informed workers place on improved working conditions and reduced risk. . . ."

---

# Sweatshops and Respect for Persons

*Denis G. Arnold and Norman E. Bowie*

In recent years labor and human rights activists have been successful at raising public awareness regarding labor practices in both American and offshore manufacturing facilities. Organizations such as Human Rights Watch, United Students Against Sweatshops, the National Labor Coalition, Sweatshop Watch, and the Interfaith Center on Corporate

---

From Denis G. Arnold and Norman E. Bowie "Sweatshops and Respect for Persons," *Business Ethics Quarterly* 13 (2003). Reprinted with permission of authors and *Business Ethics Quarterly*.

Responsibility have accused multinational enterprises (MNEs), such as Nike, Wal-Mart, and Disney, of the pernicious exploitation of workers. Recent violations of American and European labor laws have received considerable attention.[1] However, it is the offshore labor practices of North American- and European-based MNEs and their contractors that have been most controversial. This is partly due to the fact that many of the labor practices in question are legal outside North America and Europe, or are tolerated by corrupt or repressive political regimes. Unlike the recent immigrants who toil in the illegal sweatshops of North America and Europe, workers in developing nations typically have no recourse to the law or social service agencies. Activists have sought to enhance the welfare of these workers by pressuring MNEs to comply with labor laws, prohibit coercion, improve health and safety standards, and pay a living wage in their global sourcing operations. Meanwhile, prominent economists wage a campaign of their own in the opinion pages of leading newspapers, arguing that because workers for MNEs are often paid better when compared with local wages, they are fortunate to have such work. Furthermore, they argue that higher wages and improved working conditions will raise unemployment levels.

One test of a robust ethical theory is its ability to shed light on ethical problems. One of the standard criticisms of Immanuel Kant's ethical theory is that it is too abstract and formal to be of any use in practical decision making. We contend that this criticism is mistaken and that Kantian theory has much to say about the ethics of sweatshops.[2] We argue that Kant's conception of human dignity provides a clear basis for grounding the obligations of employers to employees. In particular, we argue that respecting the dignity of workers requires that MNEs and their contractors adhere to local labor laws, refrain from coercion, meet minimum safety standards, and provide a liv-

ing wage for employees. We also respond to the objection that improving health and safety conditions and providing a living wage would cause greater harm than good.

## I. RESPECT FOR PERSONS

Critics of sweatshops frequently ground their protests in appeals to human dignity and human rights. Arguably, Kantian ethics provides a philosophical basis for such moral pronouncements. The key principle here is Kant's second formulation of the categorical imperative: "Act so that you treat humanity, whether in your own person or in that of another, always as an end and never as a means only."[3] The popular expression of this principle is that morality requires that we respect people. One significant feature of the idea of respect for persons is that its derivation and application can be assessed independently of other elements of Kantian moral philosophy. Sympathetic readers need not embrace all aspects of Kant's system of ethics in order to grant the merit of Kant's arguments for the second formulation of the categorical imperative. This is because Kant's defense of respect for persons is grounded in the uncontroversial claim that humans are capable of rational, self-governing activity. We believe that individuals with a wide range of theoretical commitments can and should recognize the force of Kant's arguments concerning respect for persons.

Kant did not simply assert that persons are entitled to respect; he provided an elaborate argument for that conclusion. Persons ought to be respected because persons have dignity. For Kant, an object that has dignity is beyond price. Employees have a dignity that machines and capital do not have. They have dignity because they are capable of moral activity. As free beings capable of self-governance they are responsible beings, since freedom and self-governance are the conditions for responsibility. Autonomous responsible beings are capable of making and following their own laws; they are not simply subject to the causal laws of nature. Anyone who recognizes that he or she is free should recognize that he or she is responsible (that he or she is a moral being). As Kant argues, the fact that one is a moral being entails that one possesses dignity.

> Morality is the condition under which alone a rational being can be an end in himself because only through it is it possible to be a lawgiving member in the realm of ends. Thus morality, and humanity insofar as it is capable of morality, alone have dignity.[4]

As a matter of consistency, a person who recognizes that he or she is a moral being should ascribe dignity to anyone who, like him- or herself, is a moral being.

Although it is the capacity to behave morally that gives persons their dignity, freedom is required if a person is to act morally. For Kant, being free is more than freedom from causal necessity. This is negative freedom. Freedom in its fullest realization is the ability to guide one's actions from laws that are of one's own making. Freedom is not simply a spontaneous event. Free actions are caused, but they are caused by persons acting from laws they themselves have made. This is positive freedom. Onora O'Neill puts the point this way.

> Positive freedom is more than independence from alien causes. It would be absent in lawless or random changes, although these are negatively free, since they depend on no alien causes. Since will is a mode of causality it cannot, if free at all, be merely negatively free, so it must work by non-alien causality . . . it [free will] must be a capacity for self-determination or autonomy.[5]

When we act autonomously we have the capacity to act with dignity. We do so when we act on principles that are grounded in morality rather than in mere inclination. Reason requires that any moral principle that is freely derived must be rational in the sense that it is universal. To be universal in this sense means that the principle can be willed to be universally binding on all subjects in relevantly similar circumstances without contradiction. The fact that persons have this capability means that they possess dignity. And it is as a consequence of this dignity that a person "exacts respect for himself from all other rational beings in the world."[6] As such, one can and should "measure himself with every other being of this kind and value himself on a footing of equality with them."[7]

Respecting people requires honoring their humanity; which is to say it requires treating them as ends in themselves. In Kant's words,

> Humanity itself is a dignity; for a man cannot be used merely as a means by any man . . . but must always be used at the same time as an end. It is just in this that his dignity . . . consists, by which he raises himself above all other beings in the world that are not men and yet can be used, and so over all *things*.[8]

Thomas Hill, Jr. has discussed the implication of Kant's arguments concerning human dignity at length.[9] Hill argues that treating persons as ends in themselves requires supporting and developing certain human capacities, including the capacity to act on reason; the capacity to act on the basis of prudence or efficiency; the capacity to set goals; the capacity to accept categorical imperatives; and the capacity to understand the world and reason abstractly.[10] Based on Kant's writings in the *Metaphysics of Morals*, we would make several additions to the list. There Kant argues that respecting people means that we cannot be indifferent to them. Indifference is a denial of respect.[11] He also argues that we have an obligation to be concerned with the physical welfare of people and their moral well being. Adversity, pain, and want are temptations to vice and inhibit the ability of individuals to develop their rational and moral capacities.[12] It is these rational and moral capacities that distinguish people from mere animals. People who are not free to develop these capacities may end up leading lives that are closer to animals than to moral beings. Freedom from externally imposed adversity, pain, and want facilitate the cultivation of one's rational capacities and virtuous character. Thus, treating people as ends in themselves means ensuring their physical well being and supporting and developing their rational and moral capacities.

With respect to the task at hand, what does treating the humanity of persons as ends in themselves require in a business context—specifically in the context of global manufacturing facilities? In an earlier work Bowie has spelled out the implications of the Kantian view for businesses operating in developed countries.[13] Here we apply the same strategy in order to derive basic duties for MNEs operating in developing countries. Specifically, we derive duties that apply to MNEs that are utilizing the vast supplies of inexpensive labor currently available in developing economies. To fully respect a person one must actively treat his or her humanity as an end. This is an obligation that holds on every person *qua* person, whether in the personal realm or in the marketplace. As Kant writes, "Every man has a legitimate claim to respect from his fellow men and is *in turn* bound to respect every other."[14] There are, of course, limits to what managers of MNEs can accomplish. Nonetheless, we believe that the analysis we have provided entails that MNEs operating in developing nations have an obligation to respect the humanity of their employees. We discuss the implications of this conclusion next.

It is noteworthy that an application of the doctrine of respect for persons to the issue of the obligations of employers to employees in developing economies results in conclusions similar to the capabilities approach developed by Amartya Sen.[15] Over the last 20 years

Sen has argued that development [is] more than an increase in people's [income] and the GNP of the country. He argues that we should be concerned with certain basic human capabilities, the most important of which is freedom. Sen's perspective is similar in important respects to our own because both are concerned with providing work that enhances the positive freedom of the worker. The United Nations utilizes both the Kantian view and the capabilities view as a dual theoretical foundation for its defense of human rights. Among the rights identified by the UN are freedom from injustice and violations of the rule of law; freedom to decent work without exploitation; and the freedom to develop and realize one's human potential. It argues that all global actors, including MNEs, have a moral obligation to respect basic human rights.[16] . . .

## II. OUTSOURCING AND THE DUTIES OF MNES

One significant feature of globalization that is of particular relevance to our analysis is the increase in outsourcing by MNEs. Prior to the 1970s most foreign production by MNEs was intended for local markets. In the 1970s new financial incentives led MNEs to begin outsourcing the production of goods for North American, European, and Japanese markets to manufacturing facilities in developing countries. Encouraged by international organizations such as the World Bank and the International Monetary Fund, developing nations established "free trade zones" to encourage foreign investment via tax incentives and a minimal regulatory environment. In the 1980s the availability of international financing allowed entrepreneurs to set up production facilities in developing economies in order to meet the growing demand by

MNEs for offshore production.[17] Outsourcing production has many distinct advantages from the perspective of MNEs. . . . Outsourcing has been especially popular in consumer products industries, and in particular in the apparel industry. Nike, for example, outsources all of its production.

Are MNEs responsible for the practices of their subcontractors and suppliers? We believe that they are. Michael Santoro has defended the view that MNEs have a moral duty to ensure that their business partners respect employees by ensuring that human rights are not violated in the workplace. Santoro argues as follows:

> multinational corporations are morally responsible for the way their suppliers and subcontractors treat their workers. The applicable moral standard is similar to the legal doctrine of *respondeat superior,* according to which a principal is "vicariously liable" or responsible for the acts of its agent conducted in the course of the agency relationship. The classic example of this is the responsibility of employers for the acts of employees. Moreover, ignorance is no excuse. Firms must do whatever is required to become aware of what conditions are like in the factories of their suppliers and subcontractors, and thereby be able to assure themselves and others that their business partners don't mistreat those workers to provide a cheaper source of supply.[18]

We concur with Santoro's judgment and offer the following twofold justification for the view that MNEs have a duty to ensure that the dignity of workers is respected in the factories of subcontractors. First, an MNE, like any other organization, is composed of individual persons and since persons are moral creatures, the actions of employees in an MNE are constrained by the categorical imperative. This means MNE managers have a duty to ensure that those with whom they conduct business are properly respected.[19] Second, as Kant acknowledges, individuals have unique duties as a result of their unique circum-

stances. One key feature in determining an individual's duties is the power they have to render assistance. For example, Kant famously argues that a wealthy person has a duty of charity that an impoverished person lacks. Corollary duties apply to organizations. Researchers have noted that the relationship of power between MNEs and their subcontractors and suppliers is significantly imbalanced in favor of MNEs:

> As more and more developing countries have sought to establish export sectors, local manufacturers are locked in fierce competitive battles with one another. The resulting oversupply of export factories allows U.S. companies to move from one supplier to another in search of the lowest prices, quickest turnaround, highest quality and best delivery terms, weighted according to the priorities of the company. In this context, large U.S. manufacturer-merchandisers and retailers wield enormous power to dictate the price at which they will purchase goods.[20]

MNEs are well positioned to help ensure that the employees of its business partners are respected because of this imbalance of power. In addition, MNEs can draw upon substantial economic resources, management expertise, and technical knowledge to assist their business partners in creating a respectful work environment.

## III. THE RULE OF LAW

Lawlessness contributes to poverty[21] and is deeply interconnected with human and labor rights violations. One important role that MNEs can play to help ensure that the dignity of workers is properly respected is encouraging respect for the rule of law. . . . It is commonplace for employers in developing nations to violate worker rights in the interest of economic efficiency and with the support of state institutions. Violations of laws relating to wages and benefits, forced overtime, health and safety, child labor, sexual harassment, discrimination, and environmental protection are legion. Examples include the following:

1. Human Rights Watch reports that in Mexican maquiladoras, or export processing zones, U.S. companies such as Johnson Controls and Carlisle Plastics require female job applicants to submit to pregnancy screening; women are refused employment if they test positive. Employment discrimination based on pregnancy is a violation of Mexican law.[22]
2. A Guatemalan Ministry of the Economy study found that less than 30 percent of maquiladora factories that supply MNEs make the legally required payments for workers into the national social security system which gives workers access to health care. The report was not made public by the Ministry of the Economy due to its "startling" nature.[23]
3. An El Salvadoran Ministry of Labor study funded by the United States Agency for International Development found widespread violation of labor laws, including flagrant violation of the freedom to organize and unionize, in maquiladora factories that supply MNEs. The report was suppressed by the Ministry of Labor after factory owners complained.[24]
4. In North and Central Mexico widespread violation of Mexican environmental laws by MNEs and their contractors has been documented by both U.S. and Mexican nongovernmental organizations, and local Mexican governmental officials.[25]
5. In Haiti, apparel manufacturers such as L.V. Myles Corporation, producing clothing under license with the Walt Disney Company in several contract factories, paid workers substantially less than the Haitian minimum wage. These clothes were sold in the United States at Wal-Mart, Sears, J. C. Penney and other retailers. This practice continued until the National Labor Committee documented and publicized this violation of Haitian law.[26]

Furthermore, in many nations in which MNEs operate those responsible for administering justice are violators of the law. Factory workers frequently have no legal recourse when their legal rights are violated.

The intentional violation of the legal rights of workers in the interest of economic efficiency is fundamentally incompatible with the duty of MNEs to respect workers. Indifference to the plight of workers whose legal rights are systematically violated is a denial of respect. At a minimum MNEs have a duty to ensure that their offshore factories, and those of their suppliers and subcontractors, are in full compliance with local laws. Failure to honor the dignity of workers by violating their legal rights—or tolerating the violation of those rights—is also hypocritical. In Kantian terms, it constitutes a pragmatic contradiction. A pragmatic contradiction occurs when one acts on a principle that promotes an action that would be inconsistent with one's purpose if everyone were to act upon that principle. In this case, the principle would be something like the following: "It is permissible to violate the legal rights of others when doing so is economically efficient." MNEs rely on the rule of law to ensure, among other things, that their contracts are fulfilled, their property is secure, and their copyrights are protected. When violations of the legal rights of MNEs take place, MNEs and business organizations protest vociferously. Thus, MNEs rely on the rule of law to ensure the protection of their own interests. Without the rule of law, MNEs would cease to exist. Therefore, it is inconsistent for an MNE to permit the violation of the legal rights of workers while at the same time it demands that its own rights be protected.

## IV. COERCION

We have shown why it is reasonable to believe that all persons possess dignity and that this dignity must be respected. The obligation that we respect others requires that we not use people as a means only, but instead that we treat other people as capable of autonomous law guided action. The requirement not to use people can be met passively, by not treating them in certain ways. However, the requirement to treat them as ends in themselves entails positive obligations. We will explore these positive obligations as they relate to sweatshops in Section VI. In this section and the next, we explore the requirement that we not use people as a means only. One common way of doing so recognized by Kant is coercion. Coercion violates a person's negative freedom. Coercion is prima facie wrong because it treats the subjects of coercion as mere tools, as objects lacking the rational capacity to choose for themselves how they shall act.

Are sweatshops in violation of the no coercion requirement? An answer to this question depends both on the definition of the concepts in question and on the facts of the particular case. Elsewhere Arnold has provided accounts of physical and psychological coercion.[27] Physical coercion occurs when one's bodily movements are physically forced. In cases where one person (P) physically coerces another person (Q), Q's body is used as an object or instrument for the purpose of fulfilling P's desires. We assume that readers of this essay will agree that using physical coercion to keep people working in sweatshops against their will is disrespectful and morally wrong. While comparatively rare, physical coercion (or the threat of physical coercion) does take place. For example, at a shoe factory in Guangdong, China, it is reported that 2,700 workers were prevented from leaving the factory by 100 live-in security guards that patrolled the walled factory grounds.[28]

For psychological coercion to take place, three conditions must hold. First, the coercer must have a desire about the will of his or her victim. However, this is a desire of a particular kind because it can only be fulfilled through the will of another person. Second, the coercer must have an effective desire to compel his or her victim to act in a manner that makes efficacious the coercer's other

regarding desire. The distinction between an other regarding desire and a coercive will is important because it provides a basis for delineating between cases of coercion and, for example, cases of rational persuasion. In both instances a person may have an other regarding desire, but in the case of coercion that desire will be supplemented by an effective first-order desire which seeks to enforce that desire on the person, and in cases of rational persuasion it will not. What is of most importance in such cases is that P intentionally attempts to compel Q to comply with an other regarding desire of P's own. These are necessary, but not sufficient conditions of coercion. In order for coercion to take place, the coercer must be successful in getting his or her victim to conform to his or her other regarding desire. In all cases of coercion P attempts to violate the autonomy of Q. When Q successfully resists P's attempted coercion, Q retains his or her autonomy. In such cases P retains a coercive will.

In typical cases, people work in sweatshops because they believe they can earn more money working there than they can in alternative employment, or they work in sweatshops because it is better than being unemployed. In many developing countries, people are moving to large cities from rural areas because agriculture in those areas can no longer support the population base. When people make a choice that seems highly undesirable because there are no better alternatives available, are those people coerced? On the definition of coercion employed here, having to make a choice among undesirable options is not sufficient for coercion. We therefore assume that such persons are not coerced even though they have no better alternative than working in a sweatshop.

Nonetheless, the use of psychological coercion in sweatshops appears widespread. For example, coercion is frequently used by supervisors to improve worker productivity. Workers throughout the world report that they are forced to work long overtime hours or lose their jobs. In Bangladesh, factory workers report that they are expected to work virtually every day of the year. Overtime pay, a legal requirement, is often not paid. Employees who refuse to comply are fired.[29] In El Salvador, a government study of maquiladora factories found that

in the majority of companies, it is an obligation of the personnel to work overtime under the threat of firing or some other kind of reprisal. This situation, in addition to threatening the health of the workers, causes family problems in that [the workers] are unable to properly fulfill obligations to their immediate family.

On some occasions, because the work time is extended into the late hours of the night, the workers find themselves obligated to sleep in the factory facilities, which do not have conditions necessary for lodging of personnel.[30]

Bangladesh, El Salvador, and other developing economies lack the social welfare programs that workers in North America and Europe take for granted. If workers lose their jobs, they may end up without any source of income. Thus, workers are understandably fearful of being fired for noncompliance with demands to work long overtime hours. When a worker is threatened with being fired by a supervisor unless she agrees to work overtime, and when the supervisor's intention in making the threat is to ensure compliance, then the supervisors actions are properly understood as coercive. Similar threats are used to ensure that workers meet production quotas, even in the face of personal injury. For example, a 26-year-old worker who sews steering wheel covers at a Mexican maquila owned by Autotrim reports the following:

We have to work quickly with our hands, and I am responsible for sewing 20 steering wheel covers per shift. After having worked for 9 years at the plant, I now suffer from an injury in my right hand. I start out the shift okay, but after about 3 hours of work, I feel a lot of sharp pains in my fingers. It gets so bad that I can't hold the steering wheel correctly. But still the supervisors keep

pressuring me to reach 100 percent of my production. I can only reach about 70 percent of what they ask for. These pains began a year ago and I am not the only one who has suffered from them. There are over 200 of us who have hand injuries and some have lost movement in their hands and arms. The company has fired over 150 people in the last year for lack of production. Others have been pressured to quit. . . .[31]

We do not claim that production quotas are inherently coercive. Given a reasonable quota, employees can choose whether or not to work diligently to fill that quota. Employees who choose idleness over industriousness and are terminated as a result are not coerced. However, when a supervisor threatens workers who are ill or injured with termination unless they meet a production quota that either cannot physically be achieved by the employee, or can only be achieved at the cost of further injury to the employee, the threat is properly understood as coercive. In such cases the employee will inevitably feel compelled to meet the quota. Still other factory workers report being threatened with termination if they seek medical attention. For example, when a worker in El Salvador who was 3 months pregnant began hemorrhaging she was not allowed to leave the factory to receive medical attention. She subsequently miscarried while in the factory, completed her long work day, and took her fetus home for burial.[32] Other workers have died because they were not allowed to leave the factory to receive medical attention.[33] In cases where workers suffer miscarriages or death, rather than risk termination, we believe that it is reasonable to conclude that the workers are coerced into remaining at work.

According to the analysis provided here, workers choose to work in sweatshops because the alternatives available to them are worse. However, once they are employed coercion is often used to ensure that they will work long overtime hours and meet production quotas. Respecting workers requires that they be free to decline overtime work without fear of being fired. It also requires that if they are injured or ill—especially as a result of work-related activities—they should be allowed to consult health-care workers and be given work that does not exacerbate their illnesses or injuries. Using coercion as a means of compelling employees to work overtime, to meet production quotas despite injury, or to remain at work while in need of medical attention is incompatible with respect for persons because the coercers treat their victims as mere tools. It is important to note that even if the victim of coercion successfully resisted in some way, the attempted coercion would remain morally objectionable. This is because the coercer acts as if it is permissible to use the employees as mere tools.

## V. WORKING CONDITIONS

Critics of MNEs argue that many workers are vulnerable to workplace hazards such as repetitive motion injuries, exposure to toxic chemicals, exposure to airborne pollutants such as fabric particles, and malfunctioning machinery. One of the most common workplace hazards concerns fire safety. In factories throughout the world workers are locked in to keep them from leaving the factory. When fires break out workers are trapped. This is what happened in 1993 when a fire broke out at the Kader Industrial Toy Company in Thailand. Over 200 workers were killed and 469 injured. The factory had been producing toys for U.S. companies such as Hasbro, Toys "R" Us, J.C. Penney, and Fisher-Price.[34] In Bangladesh alone, there have been 17 fires that have resulted in fatalities since 1995. A recent fire at Chowdhury Knitwears claimed 52 lives.[35]

Workers are also exposed to dangerous toxic chemicals and airborne pollutants. For example, a Nike-commissioned Ernst & Young Environmental and Labor Practices Audit of the Tae Kwang Vina factory outside Ho Chi Minh City, Vietnam, was leaked to the press. Among the many unsafe conditions reported by Ernst & Young at this 10,000-person facility was exposure to toluene (a toxic chemical used as a solvent in paints, coatings, adhesives, and cleaning agents) at 6 to 177 times that allowed by Vietnamese law.[36] . . . In addition to toluene, workers at the Tae Kwang Vina factory were exposed to airborne fabric particles and chemical powders at dangerous levels. It is implausible to think that the (mainly) young women who work in the Tae Kwang Vina factory were informed about these health risks before they were hired. Ernst & Young reports that the employees received no training concerning the proper handling of chemicals after they were hired. Since that time Nike has overseen substantial health and safety improvements at the Tae Kwang Vina factory, and at the other Southeast Asian factories with which it contracts. Nonetheless, available evidence indicates that unsafe workplace conditions remain common among MNE factories.[37] Consider, for example, the report of Mexican maquila worker Omar Gil:

> Back in 1993 I got my first job in a maquiladora, at Delphi Auto Parts. They paid 360 pesos a week (about $40). There was a lot of pressure from the foreman on the assembly lines to work hard and produce, and a lot of accidents because of the bad design of the lines. The company didn't give us adequate protective equipment to deal with the chemicals—we didn't really have any idea of the dangers, or how we should protect ourselves. The Union did nothing to protect us.
>
> From Delphi I went to another company, National Auto parts. In that plant we made car radiators for Cadillacs and Camaros, and there was a lot of sickness and accidents there too. I worked in the area with the metal presses. There were not ventilators to take the fumes out of the plant, and they didn't give us any gloves. We had to handle the parts with our bare hands, and people got cut up a lot. I worked in an area with a lot of lead. If you worked with lead, you're supposed to have special clothing and your clothes should be washed separately. But the company

didn't give us any of that. We had to work in our street clothes.

For all of that they paid 400 pesos a week (about $43). We had no union, and there was the same pressure for production from the fore-man and the group leaders as I saw at Delphi.

Now I work at TRW, where I've been for about a month and a half. There's really no dif-ference in the conditions in any of these plants— if anything, my situation now is even worse.[38]

If our analysis is correct, then those MNEs that tolerate such health and safety risks have a duty to improve those conditions. Lax health and safety standards violate the moral re-quirement that employers be concerned with the physical safety of their employees. A failure to implement appropriate safeguards means that employers are treating their employees as disposable tools rather than as beings with unique dignity.

We cannot provide industry specific health and safety guidelines in the space of this essay. However, we believe that the International Labour Organization's carefully worked out Conventions and Recommendations on safety and health provide an excellent template for minimum safety standards.[39] For example, the ILO provides specific recommendations re-garding airborne pollutants in "Occupational Exposure to Airborne Substances Harmful to Health" (1980) and exposure to chemicals in "Safety in the Use of Chemicals at Work" (1993). Ethicists, business people, and labor leaders with widely divergent views on a num-ber of issues can agree on a minimum set of health and safety standards that should be in place in factories in the developing world. We return to this issue in Section VII.

## VI. WAGES

One of the most controversial issues con-cerning sweatshops is the demand that em-ployers raise the wages of employees in order to provide a "living wage." Workers from all over the world complain about low wages. For example,

employees of a maquiladora in Ciudad Acuna, Mexico, owned by the Aluminum Company of America (Alcoa), calculated that to buy the most basic food items needed by a factory worker— items such as beans, tortilla, rice, potatoes, onions and cooking oil, and excluding such "lux-uries" as milk, meat, vegetables and cereal—cost U.S. $26.87 per week. At the time, weekly wages at the plant ranged only from $21.44 to $24.60.[40]

While a living wage is difficult to define with pre-cision, one useful approach is to use a method similar to that used by the U.S. government to de-fine poverty. This method involves calculating the cost of a market basket of food needed to meet minimum dietary requirements and then adding the cost of other basic needs. The Council on Economic Priorities uses this ap-proach to define a wage that meets basic needs in different countries. Their formula is as follows:

1. Establish the local cost of a basic food basket needed to provide 2100 calories per person.
2. Determine the share of the local household income spent on food. Divide into 1 to get total budget multiplier.
3. Multiply that by food spending to get the total per person budget for living expenses.
4. Multiply by half the average number of house hold members in the area. (Use a higher share if there are many single-parent households.)
5. Add at least 10 percent for discretionary income.[41]

The United Nations Development Programme employs a similar method to distinguish be-tween three different levels of poverty (see Table 1).[42]

It is our contention that, at a minimum, re-spect for employees entails that MNEs and their suppliers have a moral obligation to ensure that employees do not live under conditions of overall poverty by providing adequate wages for a 48-hour workweek to satisfy both basic

**TABLE 1**

| Types of Poverty | Deficiencies | Measures |
|---|---|---|
| Extreme Poverty (also known as Absolute Poverty) | Lack of income necessary to satisfy basic food needs | Minimum caloric intake and a food basket that meets that requirement |
| Overall Poverty (also known as Relative Poverty) | Lack of income necessary to satisfy basic nonfood needs | Ability to secure shelter, energy, transportation, and basic health care |
| Human Poverty | Lack of basic human capabilities | Access to goods, services, and infrastructure |

food needs and basic nonfood needs. Doing so helps to ensure the physical well-being and independence of employees, contributes to the development of their rational capacities, and provides them with opportunities for moral development. This in turn allows for the cultivation of self-esteem.[43] It is difficult to specify with precision the minimum number of hours per week that employees should work in order to receive a living wage. However, we believe that a 48-hour workweek is a reasonable compromise that allows employees sufficient time for the cultivation of their rational capacities while providing employers with sufficient productivity. In addition, MNEs and their suppliers have an obligation to pay appropriate host nations taxes and meet appropriate codes and regulations to ensure that they contribute in appropriate ways to the creation and maintenance of the goods, services, and infrastructure necessary for the fulfillment of human capabilities. Anything less than this means that MNEs, or their suppliers, are not respecting employees as ends in themselves.

## VII. ECONOMIC CONSIDERATIONS

. . . In a recent paper, Ian Maitland criticizes both the labor and human rights activists who have accused MNEs of unjust labor practices, as well as MNEs, such as Nike, that have re-

sponded by acquiescing to some of the activists' demands.[44] . . . In addition to assessing the veracity of claims regarding worker exploitation, he sets out to determine "the ethically appropriate levels of wages and labor standards in international sweatshops."[45] He argues that philosophers . . . who object to letting market determinations alone set wage standards, are misguided on the grounds that "attempts to improve on market outcomes may have unforeseen tragic consequences."[46] Maitland's arguments regarding ethically appropriate levels of wages and labor standards may be summarized as follows:

1. Workers in the urban, formal sector of developing nations earn better wages than do workers in the rural, informal sector.
2. The imposition of wages or labor standards greater than that demanded by the market increases costs.
3. Increased costs result in layoffs and slow investment in the formal sector.
4. Formal sector layoffs result in a surplus supply of labor in the informal sector.
5. A surplus of informal sector workers depresses income in the informal sector.
   **Conclusion:** higher wages or labor standards increase poverty and limit economic growth in developing nations.

Appealing as it does to textbook economic theory, Maitland's conclusion retains an authoritative quality. Naive critics of MNEs fail to take into consideration rudimentary economic theory, and cynical corporate managers ignore these economic realities in order to preserve their brand images and corporate reputations. Maitland has done a valuable service by raising issues of central importance to the welfare of millions of powerless and impoverished people. However, is his conclusion correct? In the remaining portion of essay we argue that it is not.

First, despite his faith in the ability of international markets alone to generate ethically acceptable wage and labor standards for MNEs and their contractors . . . Maitland does not himself defend an unrestricted market approach. It is not clear, however, that Maitland recognizes this fact. The most obvious evidence in support of this conclusion is his criticism of corporate managers who, he believes, merely seek to appease their critics. "Not a single company has tried to mount a serious defense of its contracting practices. They have judged that they cannot win a war of soundbites with the critics. Instead of making a fight of it, the companies have sued for peace in order to protect their principal asset—their image."[47] Thus, according to Maitland, corporate managers have made the strategic decision to respond to market forces—in this case consumers' preferences and other marketing considerations—in the manner they deem most consistent with profitability. Given Maitland's faith in the free market, one might expect him to criticize this strategy because it is inefficient.[48] However, Maitland does not pursue this approach. Instead, he argues that managers should not appease their critics—even if managers regard this as the strategy most consistent with profitability—because doing so will have undesirable economic and moral outcomes, namely, higher unemployment and slower economic growth. There is, then, a contradiction at the heart of Maitland's analysis. He argues in favor of improvements to current market outcomes, while at the same time he argues against

attempts to improve on market outcomes on the grounds that doing so will result in undesirable moral consequences.[49]

Second, some of the most compelling evidence in support of the proposition that MNEs can improve workplace health and safety conditions while avoiding "tragic outcomes" comes from MNEs themselves. Companies such as Levis Strauss, Motorola, and Mattel have expended considerable resources to ensure that employees in their global sourcing operations work in healthy and safe environments. For example, Levis Strauss & Company stipulates that "We will only utilize business partners who provide workers with a safe and healthy environment."[50] Levis is known for acting in a manner consistent with this policy. Motorola explicitly endorses the idea of respect for persons in their Code of Business Conduct. The Code is built on two foundations:

> **Uncompromising integrity** means staying true to what we believe. We adhere to honesty, fairness and "doing the right thing" without compromise, even when circumstances make it difficult.
> **Constant respect for people** means we treat others with dignity, as we would like to be treated ourselves. Constant respect applies to every individual we interact with around the world.[51]

The physical instantiation of these principles can be seen at a Motorola's factory in Tianjin, China:

> In the company cafeteria, workers queue up politely for a variety of free and nutritious meals. One area is set aside for a pregnancy well-care program. A booth is open at which appointments can be made with the company medical staff. There is a bank branch dedicated to employee needs. It is a scene that one might expect in a Fortune 500 corporate campus in the United States. The overwhelming sense is of a pleasant, orderly place in which people are fulfilled in their work.[52]

Recently Mattel announced the creation of a global code of conduct for its production facilities and contract manufactures. It has spent millions of dollars to upgrade its manufacturing facilities in order to improve worker safety and comfort. Furthermore, it has invited a team of academics lead by S. Prakash Sethi to monitor its progress in complying with its self-imposed standards and to make their findings public.[53] This is believed to be the first time that a major MNE has voluntarily submitted to external monitoring. The examples set by Levis, Motorola, and Mattel provide evidence that MNEs are capable of improving worker health and safety without causing further hardship in the communities in which they operate.

Finally, it is not clear that improving employee wages will inevitably lead to the "tragic consequences" that Maitland and others predict. The economic issues under consideration are complex and we cannot address them here in the detail they deserve. Nonetheless, several reasons may be provided for thinking that Maitland's conclusion is incorrect. With regard to the lowest paid formal sector wage earners in developing countries, the assumption that productivity is independent of wage levels is dubious.

> As exceptionally low wages are raised, there may be increases in productivity either because of induced management improvements or because of greater labour efficiency due to a decrease in wasteful labour turnover and industrial disputes and to improvements in workers morale and nutrition resulting, in turn, in an increase in the workers willingness and capacity to work and a reduction in the incidence of debilitating diseases, time off due to illness and accidents caused by fatigue. If higher wages, at least over a certain range, are accompanied by certain improvements in labour productivity, it is conceivable that labour costs could decrease rather than increase and to such an extent that employment would not fall.[54]

Put simply, workers whose minimum daily caloric intakes are met, and who have basic nonfood needs met, will have more energy and better attitudes at work; will be less likely to come to work ill; and will be absent with less frequency. Workers are thus likely to be more productive and loyal. Economists refer to a wage that if reduced would make the firm worse off because of a decrease in worker productivity as the efficiency wage. Empirical evidence supports the view that increased productivity resulting from better nutrition offsets the cost of higher wages.[55] Thus, if workers are being paid less than the efficiency wage in a particular market there are good economic reasons, in addition to moral reasons, for raising wages. Higher productivity per hour could also help alleviate the need for overtime work and facilitate a 48-hour workweek.

One might object that our analysis implies that MNE managers are unaware of the correlation between wages and productivity, and that such ignorance on the part of MNE managers is implausible. Our reply is twofold. First, workers in developing nations *are* frequently paid less than the efficiency wage in those labor markets. Second, findings from an El Salvadoran Ministry of Labor study of maquiladora factories are instructive. Researchers found that "According to the production managers interviewed, some companies use North American and Asian efficiency and productivity levels as a parameter for establishing production goals, without considering the different nutritional conditions and technical capacity of our workers."[56] We believe that such erroneous assumptions have been widespread among MNE managers.

Part of Maitland's analysis rests on the assumption that increased labor costs will inevitably result in higher unemployment in competitive markets. Maitland is correct to identify this view as a common belief among many economists, especially as it relates to minimum wage legislation.[57] However, this view has been challenged in recent years. In their influential recent book-length study of the impact of minimum wage increases on employment, David Card and Alan Krueger argue that their reanalysis of the evidence from the United States, Canada, the United Kingdom, and Puerto Rico indicates that the existing data do not provide compelling evidence for the textbook view.[58] In addition, Card and Krueger analyzed new data for recent increases in the minimum wage in the United States. Their analysis is complex, but the results of their analysis are straightforward. "In every case . . . the estimated effect of the minimum wage was either zero or positive."[59] Increased labor costs appear to have been passed on to consumers in the form of higher prices without increasing unemployment. Again, these data undermine the textbook view regarding the impact of increases in the minimum wage. Economist Richard Freeman summarizes the impact of Card and Krueger's work as follows:

> the Card-Krueger work is essentially correct: the minimum wage at levels observed in the United States has had little or no effect on employment. At the minimum, the book has changed the burden of proof in debates over the minimum, from those who stressed the potential distributional benefits of the minimum to those who stress the potential employment losses.[60] After evaluating recent work on the impact of minimum wages, economists William Spriggs and John Schmitt reached a more determinate conclusion: "The overwhelming weight of recent evidence supports the view that low-wage workers will benefit overwhelmingly from a higher federal minimum."[61]

Two points concerning wages should be distinguished. First, conclusions concerning the impact of U.S. minimum wage legislation on unemployment cannot automatically be assumed to apply to developing nations. Careful study of the unique conditions of those labor markets is necessary before corollary claims can be assessed. Nonetheless, the textbook view rests significantly on studies concerning the U.S. labor market. As such, we believe that the burden of proof remains with those who maintain that increased labor costs must inevitably result in higher unemployment. Second, we wish to emphasize that we are not taking a position in this essay on increasing federally mandated minimum wages in developing nations. Rather, our contention is that it is economically feasible for MNEs to voluntarily raise wages in factories in developing economies without causing increases in unemployment. MNEs may choose to raise wages while maintaining existing employment levels. Increased labor costs that are not offset by greater productivity may be passed on to consumers, or, if necessary, absorbed through internal cost cutting measures such as reductions in executive compensation.

## VIII. CONCLUSION

As Kant argues, it is by acting in a manner consistent with human dignity that persons raise themselves above all things. Insofar as we recognize the dignity of humanity, we have an obligation to respect both ourselves and others.[62] We have argued that MNE managers that encourage or tolerate violations of the rule of law; use coercion; allow unsafe working conditions; and provide below subsistence wages, disavow their own dignity and that of their workers. In so doing, they disrespect themselves and their workers. Further, we have argued that this moral analysis is not undermined by economic considerations. Significantly, MNEs are in many ways more readily able to honor the humanity of workers. This is because MNEs typically have well-defined internal decision structures that, unlike individual moral agents, are not susceptible to weakness of the will.[63] For this reason, MNE managers who recognize a duty to respect their employees, and those of their subcontractors, are well positioned to play a constructive role in ensuring that the dignity of humanity is respected.

## NOTES

1. See, for example, Susan Chandler, "Look Who's Sweating Now," *BusinessWeek* (October 16, 1995); Steven Greenhouse, "Sweatshop Raids Cast Doubt on an Effort By Garment Makers to Police the Factories," *New York Times* (July 18, 1997); and Gail Edmondson et al., "Workers in Bondage," *BusinessWeek* (November 27, 2000).

2. For the purposes of this paper we define the term as any workplace in which workers are typically subject to two or more of the following conditions: income for a 48-hour workweek less than the overall poverty rate for that country (see Table 1); systematic forced overtime; systematic health and safety risks that stem from negligence or the willful disregard of employee welfare; coercion; systematic deception that places workers at risk; and underpayment of earnings.

3. Immanuel Kant, *Foundations of the Metaphysics of Morals,* trans. Lewis White Beck (New York: Macmillan, 1990), 46.

4. Kant, *Foundations of the Metaphysics of Morals,* p. 52.

5. Onora O'Neill, *Constructions of Reason* (Cambridge: Cambridge University Press, 1989), 53.

6. Immanuel Kant, *The Metaphysics of Morals,* trans. Mary Gregor (Cambridge: Cambridge University Press, 1991), 230.

7. Ibid.

8. Ibid., 255.

9. Thomas Hill, Jr., *Dignity and Practical Reason in Kant's Moral Theory* (Ithaca: Cornell University Press, 1992).

10. Ibid., 40–41.

11. Kant, *Metaphysics of Morals,* p. 245.

12. Ibid., 192–93 and 196–97.

13. Norman E. Bowie, *Business Ethics: A Kantian Perspective* (Malden, MA: Blackwell, 1999). See pp. 41–81 for further discussion of the second categorical imperative.

14. Kant, *Metaphysics of Morals,* p. 255.

15. His latest book is *Development as Freedom* (New York: Anchor Books, 1999). Martha Nussbaum has developed her own version of the capabilities approach, one that pays particular attention to the unique circumstances of women's lives. *Women and Human Development: The Capabilities Approach* (Cambridge: Cambridge University Press, 2000).

16. United Nations Development Programme, *Human Development Report 2000* (New York: Oxford University Press, 2000).

17. Pamela Varley, ed., *The Sweatshop Quandary: Corporate Responsibility on the Global Frontier* (Washington DC, Investor Responsibility Research Center, 1998), 185–86.

18. Michael A. Santoro, *Profits and Principles: Global Capitalism and Human Rights in China* (Ithaca: Cornell University Press, 2000), 161.

19. For a fuller discussion of this matter, see Bowie, *Business Ethics: A Kantian Perspective,* esp. chap. 2.

20. Varley, ed., *The Sweatshop Quandary,* p. 95.

21. Better rule of law is associated with higher per capita income. See *World Development Report 2000/2001: Attacking Poverty* (New York: Oxford University Press, 2000), 103.

22. Human Rights Watch, "A Job or Your Rights: Continued Sex Discrimination in Mexico's Maquiladora Sector," 10 (1)(B) December 1998. Available at http://www.hrw.org/reports98/women2/

23. Varley, ed., *The Sweatshop Quandary,* p. 131.

24. Republic of El Salvador, Ministry of Labor, Monitoring and Labor Relations Analysis Unit, "Monitoring Report on Maquilas and Bonded Areas" (July 2000). Available at http://www.nlcnet.org/elsalvador/0401/translation.htm

25. Edward J. Williams, "The Maquiladora Industry and Environmental Degradation in the United States–Mexican Borderlands." Paper presented at the annual meeting of the Latin American Studies Association, Washington, DC, September 1995. Available at http://www.natlaw.com/pubs/williams.htm. See also, Joan Salvat, Stef Soetewey, and Peter Breuls, *Free Trade Slaves,* 58 min. (Princeton, NJ: Films for the Humanities and Sciences, 1999), videocassette.

26. National Labor Committee, "The U.S. in Haiti: How to Get Rich on 11 Cents an Hour" (1995). Available at http://www.nlcnet.org/Haiti/0196/index.htm

27. Denis G. Arnold, "Coercion and Moral Responsibility," *American Philosophical Quarterly* 38 (2001): 53–67. The view of psychological coercion employed here is a slightly revised version of the view defended in that essay. In particular, the condition that cases of psychological coercion always involve psychological compulsion has been replaced with the condition that cases

of psychological coercion always involve the victim's compliance with the threat.

28. Varley, ed., *The Sweatshop Quandary*, p. 72.

29. Barry Bearak, "Lives Held Cheap In Bangladesh Sweatshops," *New York Times* (April 15, 2001).

30. Republic of El Salvador, Ministry of Labor, Monitoring and Labor, Relations Analysis Unit, "Monitoring Report on Maquilas and Bonded Areas."

31. Varley, ed., *The Sweatshop Quandary*, p. 68.

32. Salvat et al., *Free Trade Slaves*.

33. Ibid.

34. Varley, ed., *The Sweatshop Quandary*, p. 67.

35. Bearak, "Lives Held Cheap in Bangladesh Sweatshops."

36. "Ernst & Young Environmental and Labor Practice Audit of the Tae Kwang Vina Industrial Ltd. Co., Vietnam." Available at http://www.corpwatch.org/trac/nike/ernst/audit.html

37. See, for example, Varley, ed., *The Sweatshop Quandary*, esp. pp. 59–98.

38. Campaign for Labor Rights, "The Story of a Maquiladora Worker: Interview with Omar Gil by David Bacon," (September 6, 2000). Available at www.summersault.com/~agj/clr/alerts/thestoryofamqquiladoraeworker.html

39. International Labour Organization, "SafeWork: ILO Standards on Safety and Health." Available at http://www.ilo.org/public/english/protection/safework/standard.htm

40. After the complaint was raised in a shareholder meeting, Alcoa raised the wages of the workers by 25 percent. Pamela Varley, ed., *The Sweatshop Quandary*, p. 63.

41. Aaron Bernstein, "Sweatshop Reform: How to Solve the Standoff," *BusinessWeek* (May 3, 1999).

42. *Poverty Report 2000: Overcoming Human Poverty* (New York: United Nations Development Programme, 2000).

43. Self-esteem is grounded in the conscious recognition of one's dignity as a rational being.

44. Ian Maitland, "The Great Non-Debate Over International Sweatshops," reprinted in *Ethical Theory and Business, 6th ed.*, ed. Tom L. Beauchamp and Norman E. Bowie (Englewood Cliffs: Prentice Hall, 2001), 595. First published in *British Academy of Management Conference Proceedings* (September 1997): 240–65.

45. Ibid.

46. Ibid., 603.

47. Ibid., 594.

48. Such an argument would likely maintain that corporate managers fail to recognize that a public relations strategy that includes higher wages and improved workplace standards is more costly than an alternative strategy that does not. The details of such a strategy would then need to be worked out.

49. Maitland, "The Great Non-Debate Over International Sweatshops," p. 602.

50. Ibid., 539.

51. Motorola, "Code of Business Conduct." Available at http://www.motorola.com/code/code.html

52. Santoro, *Profits and Principles*, p. 6.

53. S. Prakash Sethi, "Codes of Conduct for Multinational Corporations: An Idea Whose Time Has Come," *Business and Society Review* 104, no. 3 (1999): 225–41.

54. Gerald Starr, *Minimum Wage Fixing* (Geneva: International Labour Organization, 1981), 157.

55. C. J. Bliss and N. H. Stern, "Productivity, Wages, and Nutrition, 2: Some Observations." *Journal of Development Economics* 5 (1978): 363–98. For theoretical discussion, see C. J. Bliss and N. H. Stern, "Productivity, Wages, and Nutrition, 1: The Theory." *Journal of Development Economics*, 5 (1978): 331–62.

56. Republic of El Salvador, Ministry of Labor, Monitoring and Labor Relations Analysis Unit, "Monitoring Report on Maquilas and Bonded Areas." Available at http://www.nlcnet.org/elsalvador/0401/translation.htm

57. See, for example, the essays collected in Simon Rottenberg, ed., *The Economics of Legal Minimum Wages* (Washington DC: The American Enterprise Institute, 1981).

58. See David Card and Alan B. Krueger, *Myth and Measurement: The New Economics of the Minimum Wage* (Princeton: Princeton University Press, 1995. See also the special symposium on *Myth and Measurement* in *Industrial & Labor Relations Review* (July 1995) with contributions by Charles Brown, Richard Freeman, Daniel Hamermesh, Paul Osterman, and Finis Welch; David Neumark and William Wascher, "Minimum Wages and Employment: A Case Study of the Fast-Food Industry in

New Jersey and Pennsylvania: Comment,"
*American Economic Review* (December 2000):
1362–96; and David Card and Alan B.
Krueger, "Minimum Wages and Employment:
A Case Study of the Fast-Food Industry in
New Jersey and Pennsylvania: Reply," *American
Economic Review* (December 2000): 1397–1420.
For a discussion of the living wage issue in
the context of the U.S. economy, see Robert
Pollin and Stephanie Luce, *The Living Wage:
Building a Fair Economy* (New York: The New
Press, 1998).

59. Card and Krueger, *Myth and Measurement,*
p. 389.

60. Richard B. Freeman, "In Honor of David Card:
Winner of the John Bates Clark Medal," *Journal
of Economic Perspectives* (Spring 1997): 173.

61. William Spriggs and John Schmitt, "The Minimum Wage: Blocking the Low-Wage Path," in
Todd Schafer and Jeff Faux, *Reclaiming Prosperity: A Blueprint for Progressive Economic Reform*
(Armonk, NY: ME Sharpe, 1996), 170.

62. Kant, *Foundations of the Metaphysics of Morals,*
p. 255.

63. For a fuller defense of this position see Peter
A. French, *Corporate Ethics* (Fort Worth, TX:
Hartcourt Brace: 1995), pp. 79–87.

# Taking Responsibility for Bribery:
# The Multinational Corporation's
# Role in Combating Corruption

*David Hess and Thomas Dunfee*

Corruption is an underappreciated impediment
to the realization of human rights in developing countries. While government officials profit
from bribes taken from multinational corporations and others, many citizens' rights are compromised. Like any economic transaction,
corruption has both a demand side and a supply side. Public officials demand bribes, and private citizens or organizations, such as businesses,
supply the bribes. Any system to control corruption by attacking only one side of the transaction will surely fail. An effective anticorruption
system requires a variety of measures attacking
corruption from all sides. In this essay, we focus
on the attempts made to control the supply side.

The essay proceeds by reviewing the impact
of corruption on human rights. In the following section, we evaluate the international efforts
to outlaw corruption and their effectiveness

to date. Next, we discuss a corporate principles approach to controlling bribery in international business transactions and review
current corporate practices. The final section
looks specifically at Royal Dutch/Shell's efforts
at combating corruption.

## CORRUPTION AS AN IMPEDIMENT
## TO THE REALIZATION OF HUMAN
## RIGHTS

A common understanding of international
human rights laws and obligations is established
in international treaties and declarations. The
most well known of these are the Universal Declaration of Human Rights (UDHR), the International Covenant on Economic, Social, and
Cultural Rights (ICESCR), and the International

From Rory Sullivan, ed., *Business and Human Rights: Dilemmas and Solutions* (Sheffield, UK: Greenleaf, 2003). Reprinted
with permission.

Covenant on Civil and Political Rights (ICCPR) (Green 2001). In addition to establishing the content of substantive human rights, such agreements also place obligations on states to allow the realization of these rights. For example, the ICESCR proclaims:

> Each State Party to the present Covenant undertakes to take steps, individually and through international assistance and co-operation, especially economic and technical, to the maximum of its available resources, with a view to achieving progressively the full realization of the rights recognized in the present Covenant by all appropriate means.

One of the greatest impediments to the realization of rights recognized under such international agreements is corruption. Corruption's pernicious impact takes many forms. Most directly, corruption diverts critical resources in ways that personally enrich public officials, instead of being used to promote human rights. The scope of diversion can be mind-boggling. As just one example, in the 1990s, two South Korean presidents were convicted for corruptly amassing a fund of over U.S. $900 million. International assistance may be diverted to private hands in a gross distortion of its humanitarian purposes. Foreign aid sent to Zaire (now known as the Democratic Republic of Congo) in the 1980s and 1990s was allegedly sent to the offshore accounts of President Mobutu Sese Seko. While Seko accumulated one of the world's largest fortunes, ever-increasing numbers of his country's citizens were reduced to abject poverty. Locally, funds intended for domestic development may be skewed toward projects where bribes can be extracted, such as construction, and away from public projects that would allow the realization of the rights to education and health. In addition, these construction projects can be so heavily influenced by corruption that they fail to provide the citizens with any benefit. For example, the corrupted 'bean curd'

bridges of China were collapsing on completion, causing numerous deaths and injuries.

Corruption also prevents a country from developing its economy. In addition to rights recognized under the ICCPR and the ICESCR, the United Nations adopted the Declaration on the Right to Development in 1986. While the right to development has been controversial in the past—the United States voted against the 1986 declaration—the Vienna Declaration at the 1993 UN World Conference on Human Rights, and similar actions at subsequent intergovernmental conferences, have established this right as an "undeniable fact" (Sengupta 2002, 842). Included in this right is a process of development whereby the underprivileged can have their "living standard raised and capacity to improve their position strengthened" (Sengupta 2002, 848). Although the obligations and duties of governments are not necessarily to provide the realization of development, they must establish the conditions for individuals to realize that right.

By engaging in corruption, governments are not creating the conditions necessary to allow its citizens to realize their right to development. In addition to the factors discussed above, corruption significantly hinders a country's economic development. A recent study found that corruption acts as a significant 'tax' on foreign direct investment and reduces such investment (Wei 2000). Due to its secrecy, corruption acts more as a distortion to the economy rather than as a simple tax. For example, allocative efficiency is likely to be distorted when country leaders accept payments to limit entry by certain firms or to grant monopolies. The reduction of corruption makes it more likely that economic development will not simply lead to greater income inequalities and a continued reduction of the income-earning potential of underprivileged citizens. Instead, the benefits of economic development are more likely to be fairly distributed.

## INTERNATIONAL EFFORTS TO COMBAT CORRUPTION

The worldwide focus on combating corruption has increased tremendously in the past 10 years. Most significantly, the members of the Organization for Economic Cooperation and Development (OECD) signed the Convention on Combating Bribery of Foreign Public Officials in International Business Transactions in 1997, which entered into force in February 1999. This convention requires the signatory countries to criminalize the payment of bribes to foreign officials and to prohibit practices that allow the concealment of bribe payments (e.g. off-the-books accounts). As of October 2002, 34 countries have passed legislation ratifying the convention.

The OECD Convention, apparently, has not had a major impact on multinational firms. In 2002, Transparency International conducted a survey of executives of foreign and domestic corporations operating in 15 emerging market economies. Only 19 percent of the respondents to this survey stated that they were either familiar with the Convention or at least knew something about it. In addition, only 27 percent of respondents stated that the level of corruption by foreign companies of senior public officials had decreased in the past 5 years. The private sector's (and general public's) limited awareness of the international efforts to outlaw bribery restricts the effectiveness of these attempts.

Ending the entrenched practice of bribery will require aggressive enforcement of the new antibribery legal regime. Although it is too soon to know whether there will be adequate prosecutorial effort, there is some heartening evidence of a willingness to prosecute bribe-paying companies. In Lesotho in 2002, the government prosecuted a Canadian company, Acres International Ltd, and imposed a U.S. $3.5 million fine. Acres was charged with paying U.S. $320,000 to the engineer overseeing the Lesotho Highlands Water Project. The case has gained notoriety because it is one of the few times local authorities have attempted to prosecute the corporation paying the bribe, as they typically focus only on the official receiving the bribe. In this case, the official receiving the bribe from Acres was sentenced to 18 years in jail. It is important to note that, at the time of writing, Acres was appealing its conviction.

While the Acres case is encouraging, enforcement of anticorruption laws will require a significant amount of resources by various countries. It is yet to be seen how many countries are willing and able to expend these resources. In addition, many think that corrupt practices will simply adapt around these laws and continue to thrive. For example, in Transparency International's index of countries whose corporations are perceived as most likely to pay bribes, the United States (where the Foreign Corrupt Practices Act has been in place since 1977) ranked 13th out of 21 countries in a ranking from least likely to pay bribes to the most likely. This placed the United States behind such countries as Canada, the UK, and Australia.

To eradicate corruption, a criminal law approach by itself is not likely to work. Instead, the government must work with the private sector and civil society. Only with various initiatives attacking corruption from different angles will it be possible to reach a "tipping point," after which we will see a continuous and increasing decline in corruption. The remainder of this essay focuses on the initiatives of the private sector.

## A CORPORATE PRINCIPLES APPROACH TO COMBATING CORRUPTION

Corporations know where they are paying their bribes, or, at a minimum, know where they are at the greatest risk of their agents paying bribes. By this fact alone, the private sector is a crucial element in ending corruption. Corporations must be able to stand up to demands for bribes and must also reward employees for doing so. To do this, corporations need assurances that their competitors are behaving in the same manner.

Two recent initiatives to achieve this goal are the $C^2$ Principles (Combating Corruption) adopted by the Caux Round Table (see Box 1) and the Business Principles for Countering Bribery published jointly by Social Accountability International and Transparency International. The Business Principles consists of two simple principles: namely, "The enterprise shall prohibit bribery in any form whether direct or indirect" and "The enterprise shall commit to implementation of a Program to counter bribery." These principles are accompanied by a list of areas a company's anticorruption program should cover and the requirements for implementing the program. While the $C^2$ Principles require a company to publicly adopt the principles, the Business Principles do not, as they are meant only for purposes of creating a "starting point" for companies and establishing benchmarks for best practices.

To simplify matters, we have classified the $C^2$ Principles into the basic themes of policies, procedures, and publication. Principles 1–4 establish required policies, Principles 5, 8, 9, 10, and 12 set forth necessary procedures, while Principles 1, 6, 7, and 11 set forth required disclosures

---

# $C^2$ Principles

1. To disclose publicly and make widely known its endorsement of the $C^2$ Principles
2. To establish a clearly articulated written policy prohibiting any of the firm's employees from paying or receiving bribes or "kickbacks"
3. To implement the policy with due care and take appropriate disciplinary action against any employee discovered to have made payments in violation of the policy
4. To provide training for employees to carry out the policy, and to provide continuing support, such as help-lines, to assist employees to act in compliance with the firm's policy
5. To record all transactions fully and fairly, in accordance with clearly stated record-keeping procedures and accounting controls, and conduct internal audits to assure no improper payments are made
6. To report annually on the firm's bribery and corruption policy, along with a description of the firm's experiences implementing and enforcing the policy
7. To have the annual report in Principle 6 audited either by an independent financial auditor or an independent social auditor, or both
8. To require all agents of the firm to affirm that they have neither made nor will make any improper payments in any business venture or contract to which the firm is a party
9. To require all suppliers of the firm to affirm that they have neither made nor will make any improper payments in any business venture or contract to which the firm is a party
10. To establish a monitoring and auditing system to detect any improper payments made by the firm's employees and agents
11. To report publicly any solicitations for payments, or report privately to a monitoring organization or a social auditor
12. To establish a system to allow any employee or agent of the firm to report any improper payment without fear of retribution for their disclosures

**Box 1** $C^2$ Principles

that the organization should publish or otherwise make known. In general, these themes also apply to the anticorruption program recommendations of the Business Principles.

The theme of policies refers to the establishment of an antibribery policy for the company. This includes establishing a code of conduct that clearly articulates a prohibition on bribery. Currently, many companies address the issue of bribery in their codes of conduct, but the depth of treatment the topic receives can vary greatly from company to company. One reason for this disparity in treatment is the lack of a universal agreement on what constitutes corruption owing to the absence of a dialogue on the topic. For example, in the year of Transparency International's founding (1993), few governments would even openly discuss the issues of bribery and corruption. Now, with the recent OECD convention and other intergovernmental initiatives, a consensus is developing to provide companies with guidance.

Two recent studies on the treatment of bribery in multinational corporations' codes of conduct provide insight into extant practices. Gordon and Miyake (2001) considered 118 codes issued by individual firms and 128 codes issued by industry associations and NGOs, while Berenbeim (2000) surveyed companies on their anticorruption practices and received 151 responses from corporations headquartered all over the world. In these studies, while corporations appear to find it easy to provide a general definition of corruption, they find it significantly more difficult to define a workable standard to guide employees (Gordon and Miyake 2001). Among the difficulties in providing a working definition of bribery are: how to deal with such matters as gifts and entertainment; facilitation payments (small payments to lower-level public officials to encourage them to perform their duties more quickly, such as providing a licence to conduct business); and how to operate in different cultural environments. For example, for gifts,

Gordon and Miyake (2001) find that some companies establish specific monetary limits, others direct their employees to follow local law, and others simply leave discretion to the employee (e.g., "not excessive"). In response to these difficulties, many codes provide only a general prohibition on bribery, without further defining it or providing guidance to the company's employees. A 1995 study of 109 U.S. companies found that, while 36 percent of the companies had antibribery provisions, only 14 percent defined "grease" payments (Spalding and Reinstein 1995).

The legal environment of a company also affects its choice of definitions. Berenbeim (2000) found that, owing to the Foreign Corrupt Practices Act (FCPA), U.S. companies are more likely to provide a detailed definition of bribery based on the statute. Non-U.S. companies, on the other hand, are more likely to use only general terms. Presumably, as the OECD Convention gains more recognition, it will influence non-U.S. corporations' definitions of bribery for their employees.

To ensure that employees comply with these policies, the next theme—procedures—is required. The necessary procedures include appropriate accounting and auditing processes, as well as procedures to ensure that all agents employed by the firm are aware of the firm's antibribery policies and that management uses due diligence when selecting these agents (e.g., avoid the hiring of agents with a reputation for paying bribes). Finally, procedures must be in place to allow employees to report any violations of the company's policy.

Corporations seeking to reduce corruption recognize the importance of these procedures. Gordon and Miyake (2001) found that company codes mentioning bribery are twice as likely to discuss issues of record-keeping, whistle-blowing, and internal monitoring than company codes that do not mention bribery. These basic compliance measures were found to be similar to other financial control practices, thus allowing managers to use existing knowledge to implement antibribery procedures. Such firms were also commonly seen to require local managers to certify that they have complied with the corporation's policies. In addition, Berenbeim's (2000) study found that companies with more effective anticorruption programs often require joint-venture partners and agents to explicitly accept compliance with their corporate antibribery policies. These companies recognized a duty to prevent corruption and not to pass that obligation on to another actor in the channel of distribution.

Unfortunately, many of these practices are not currently widespread. For example, Spalding and Reinstein's (1995) study of U.S. corporations found that, while 93 percent of the companies had codes of ethics, only 20 percent monitored compliance with the code and only 35 percent had compliance with the code certified annually by management. With respect to the FCPA, only 26 percent of companies had their compliance efforts independently audited and only 11 percent reported FCPA compliance to the board's audit committee. Many view these controls as necessary because it is common in FCPA violations for management to override internal accounting controls (Spalding and Reinstein 1995).

One of the most valued procedures in the fight against corruption is a whistle-blowing program. These programs encourage employees to report violations of the company's policies and to ask questions about antibribery rules without fear of punishment. To achieve these goals, company programs typically allow the anonymous reporting of violations. While whistle-blowing has been a valuable tool for U.S. companies, it faces significant challenges in other parts of the world. Berenbeim (2000) reports a resistance to whistle-blowing in Western Europe. Some suggest that this is due to concern about returning to an 'informer society'. Likewise, Husted (2002) argues that whistle-blowing works well in countries with

cultures like the United States, but will not work as well in Latin American cultures. The specific cultural factors that Husted considers are individualism/collectivism and power–distance relationships. In Latin America, Husted argues, the cultures are more collectivist and leaders are accorded more power compared with the United States. These factors work against whistle-blowing, as trust in leadership will only be undermined by extreme cases of abuse of power and members of society will work to protect the in-group, rather than follow an obligation to society in general.

On the other hand, others argue that an appreciation and acceptance of whistle-blowing can become an effective tool against corruption throughout the world if implemented appropriately (Berenbeim 2000). The key is for management to understand the potential cultural barriers to effective implementation and to develop sound policies to address those concerns. Creating an organizational culture accepting of whistle-blowing is one of the challenges facing global business in establishing an effective anticorruption culture.

The final theme is publication, which is a requirement of disclosure. Included in this theme are a public commitment to upholding the principles and the disclosure of company efforts in implementing an anticorruption program. This theme works to control both the supply of corruption and the demand. To reduce the demand side of bribery, Principle 11 of the $C^2$ Principles requires the disclosure of bribe solicitations. This is consistent with the recent Publish What You Pay initiative, which has gained the support of numerous NGOs and UK Prime Minister Tony Blair. Under this initiative, oil, gas and mining companies are encouraged to disclose all payments made to developing-country governments (including taxes, fees, and royalties). Through this disclosure, citizens and other interested parties can better determine where these payments are going and work to increase government accountability. For example, in Angola, some estimate that U.S. $1 billion of oil payments to the government goes missing every year. At the same time, the country receives U.S. $200 million annually in foreign aid to help reduce hunger.

On the supply side, publication works to establish best practices for combating corruption. By publishing a detailed code of conduct for operations in a certain country, a company provides assistance to its employees in resisting bribery. With disclosure, however, such codes can also assist other companies in combating corruption. For example, managers attempting to promote nondiscrimination in apartheid South Africa in the 1980s stated that the disclosure of company practices under the Sullivan Principles allowed them to better implement their own policies (Hess and Dunfee 2000). In other words, these managers were not forced to reinvent the wheel, but could build on the experiences of others. In addition, disclosure provides information to the public, which encourages a dialogue to develop on appropriate norms of behavior.

Overall, the adoption of anticorruption principles works to push all corporations to develop anticorruption cultures. Through a principles approach, corporations do not have to worry that they will be acting alone in the fight against corruption. Those corporations that are serious in their attempts to reduce bribe payments should start with industry-wide initiatives to adopt the principles. An industry-based strategy will ensure that a corporation's competitors are playing by the same rules, as any firms attempting to free-ride on the "no bribes" policies of others should be easily identifiable. Industry-based initiatives are also of value because the publication aspect furthers the transfer of knowledge on fighting corruption. This sharing of experiences allows best practices to emerge, which is to the benefit of all in the industry. In addition to pressure from industry associations, NGOs and other parties can also play a significant role. For example, some argue

that the World Bank could have considerable influence by requiring all firms bidding on World Bank–financed contracts to have an appropriate code of conduct.

The $C^2$ Principles and the Business Principles both push companies to go beyond simply having a compliance culture with respect to corruption and toward a culture of integrity. Key to establishing such a culture is the active involvement of senior management, coupled with an emphasis on communicating the importance of the program to all employees. For example, management must acknowledge and actively reassure employees that lost business may be the consequence of following an antibribery policy, but employees will only be punished for not following the policy. That is, any incentives must reward resisting corruption and not obtaining a contract at any cost. . . .

## THE ANTICORRUPTION EFFORTS OF SHELL

The Royal Dutch/Shell corporation is often praised for its "no bribes" policy. Shell is an oil, gas, and chemical company operating in over 100 countries. In response to various public relations crises in the mid-1990s (including the controversy surrounding the disposal of the Brent Spar and the execution of Ken Saro-Wiwa in Nigeria), Shell recommitted itself to operating under a set of business principles of appropriate behavior and to greater transparency in its actions. Through this recommitment, Shell established its "no bribes" policy. This policy clearly states that bribery will not be tolerated and that employees engaging in corruption will have their employment terminated and will, if possible, be prosecuted. To implement this policy, Shell developed a program based in part on its study of best practices at 15 multinational corporations. Overall, Shell's anticorruption program (see Box 2) is based on a set of practices similar to the $C^2$ Principles.

## Shell's Policies and Procedures

| | |
|---|---|
| 1. Senior management commitment | • Set the ethical tone at the top |
| 2. Written policies | • Company-wide policies should be supplemented by codes for local conditions |
| 3. Internal controls and record-keeping | • Including an "ethics ledger" of requested facilitation payments |
| 4. Auditing | • Ensure that employees and third parties are complying with the "no bribes" objectives |
| 5. Communication channels | • Hotlines to report corruption problems and assurances that employees will not suffer for reporting problems or losing business due to adherence to integrity principles |
| 6. Accountability | • Require managers to certify compliance with the principles |
| 7. Training | • Include extra training for employees in positions of high risk for corruption |
| 8. Third-party checks | • Due diligence processes for selecting and continuing relationships with suppliers and contractors |
| 9. Investigations | • Investigate allegations of bribery |

**Box 2** Shell's Policies and Procedures
*Source:* Royal Dutch/Shell 1999.

As part of this effort, Shell published its policies on bribery in a booklet entitled *Dealing with Bribery and Corruption: A Management Primer*. This document provides its employees with an understanding of what constitutes bribery and distinguishes bribery from facilitation payments and gifts. For example, to help employees distinguish between a bribe and a gift, the *Management Primer* notes that gifts can be given directly and openly, while bribes must be given in secret and often through intermediaries. With respect to facilitation payments, Shell does not condone them, but also does not place an absolute prohibition on them. Instead, it instructs the individual Shell companies to address these matters in their local business guidelines for employees ("with the aim of eliminating it") and at all times to obey local law. In recognition of the difficulty

of establishing bright line rules in such areas of bribery, Shell provides short case studies of actual situations from the company's experience to assist employees in their training.

Company compliance with the policies is monitored by the Audit Committee and Social Responsibility Committee, which oversees the implementation of Shell's business principles and control mechanisms. One such control procedure is the letter of representation. A letter of representation is a formal document signed by the chief executive officer and chief financial officer of that country's company and sent to the Shell Group's comptroller. In the document, these officers state that all transactions have been recorded properly and that no bribes have been paid. In situations where facilitation payments have been made or bribes discovered, these payments are included in the document and the officers are required to provide follow-up reports on how they have attempted to deal with the problem.

Shell also publishes its efforts. Each year, Shell distributes a report entitled *People, Planet and Profits,* which details its performance on environmental and social matters. KPMG and PricewaterhouseCoopers verify components of this report. Included in *People, Planet and Profits* reports are details of the bribery solicitations received or offered by the company's employees for the year. In 2001, Shell reported that its employees either solicited bribers or were offered bribes in 13 situations (with a total estimated financial value of U.S. $26,000), up from only four cases in 2000 (total estimated financial value of U.S. $89,000). Shell also reported that employees had refused bribes in nine cases, employees were dismissed in three cases, and one case was not yet settled. In addition, Shell reported two cases where nonemployee agents offered or solicited bribes. The accuracy of these numbers can be challenged, however, as they do not reflect allegations of corruption that the company could not prove, and, of course, instances that were not detected or reported. Overall, though, Shell has demonstrated a willingness to combat corruption and to begin the process of obtaining the experience necessary to remove all forms of bribery in its business transactions throughout the world.

## CONCLUSION

Reducing corruption is a win-win situation in that it is simultaneously pro-business and pro-human rights. The reduction of corruption reduces barriers to investment in foreign countries, allows a more efficient use of capital and promotes economic growth. This provides a more conducive environment for business while, at the same time, improving the human rights conditions in developing countries, including the right to development. To attain these benefits, corporations must play a vital role in ending corruption. As indicated in our review of corporate codes of conduct, many corporations are demonstrating a willingness to get out of a cycle of corruption. These companies are experimenting with policies and procedures to ensure that corruption does not exist at any point along the chain of distribution of their goods or services. While many companies' efforts may be seen as potentially ineffective, best practices are emerging. In addition to developing successful anticorruption programs, a key challenge facing these companies is reining in those competitors that persist in supplying bribes. To achieve all these goals, adopting anticorruption principles is an important first step.

## REFERENCES

Berenbeim, R. E. 2000. *Company Programs for Resisting Corrupt Practices: A Global Study.* Conference Board Report No. 1279-00 RR; New York: The Conference Board.

Gordon, K., and M. Miyake 2001. "Business Approaches to Combating Bribery: A Study of Codes of Conduct." *Journal of Business Ethics* 34 (3–4): 161–73.

Green, M. 2001. "What We Talk About When We Talk About Indicators: Current Approaches to Human Rights Measurement." *Human Rights Quarterly* 23 (4): 1062–97.

Hess, D., and T. Dunfee. 2000. "Fighting Corruption: A Principled Approach." *Cornell International Law Journal* 33 (3): 593–626.

Husted, B. 2002. "Culture and International Anti-Corruption Agreements in Latin America." *Journal of Business Ethics* 37 (1): 413–22.

Sengupta, A. 2002. "On the Theory and Practice of the Right to Development." *Human Rights Quarterly* 24 (4): 837–89.

Spalding, A., and A. Reinstein. 1995. "The Audit Committee's Role Regarding the Provisions of the Foreign Corrupt Practices Act." *Journal of Business Strategies* 12 (1): 23–35.

Wei, S. 2000. "How Taxing Is Corruption on International Investors?" *Review of Economics and Statistics* 82 (1): I–II.

LEGAL PERSPECTIVES

# Dow Chemical Company and Shell Oil Company v. Domingo Castro Alfaro et al.

*Supreme Court of Texas*

Because its analysis and reasoning are correct I join in the majority opinion without reservation. I write separately, however, to respond to the dissenters who mask their inability to agree among themselves with competing rhetoric. In their zeal to implement their own preferred social policy that Texas corporations not be held responsible at home for harm caused abroad, these dissenters refuse to be restrained by either express statutory language or the compelling precedent, previously approved by this very court, holding that *forum non conveniens* does not apply in Texas. To accomplish the desired social engineering, they must invoke yet another legal fiction with a fancy name to shield alleged wrongdoers, the so-called doctrine of *forum non conveniens*. The refusal of a Texas corporation to confront a Texas judge and jury is to be labeled "inconvenient" when what is really involved is not convenience but connivance to avoid corporate accountability.

The dissenters are insistent that a jury of Texans be denied the opportunity to evaluate the conduct of a Texas corporation concerning decisions it made in Texas because the only ones allegedly hurt are foreigners. Fortunately Texans are not so provincial and narrow-minded as these dissenters presume. Our citizenry recognizes that a wrong does not fade away because its immediate consequences are first felt far away rather than close to home. Never have we been required to forfeit our membership in the human race in order to maintain our proud heritage as citizens of Texas.

The dissenters argue that it is *inconvenient* and *unfair* for farmworkers allegedly suffering permanent physical and mental injuries, including irreversible sterility, to seek redress by suing a multinational corporation in a court three blocks away from its world headquarters and another corporation, which operates in Texas this country's largest chemical plant. Because the "doctrine" they advocate has nothing to do with fairness and convenience and everything to do with immunizing multinational corporations from accountability for their alleged torts causing injury abroad, I write separately.

## THE FACTS

Respondents claim that while working on a banana plantation in Costa Rica for Standard Fruit Company, an American subsidiary of Dole Fresh Fruit Company, headquartered in Boca Raton, Florida, they were required to handle dibromochloropropane ["DBCP"], a pesticide allegedly manufactured and furnished to Standard Fruit by Shell Oil Company ["Shell"] and Dow Chemical Company ["Dow"]. The Environmental Protection Agency issued a notice of intent to cancel all food uses of DBCP on September 22, 1977. 42 Fed. Reg. 48026 (1977). It followed with an order suspending registrations of pesticides containing DBCP on November 3, 1977. 42 Fed. Reg. 57543 (1977). Before and after the EPA's ban of DBCP in the United States, Shell and Dow apparently

---

786 S.W. 2d 674 (Tex. 1990); concurring opinion by Judge Doggett.

shipped several hundred thousand gallons of the pesticide to Costa Rica for use by Standard Fruit. The Respondents, Domingo Castro Alfaro and other plantation workers, filed suit in a state district court in Houston, Texas, alleging that their handling of DBCP caused them serious personal injuries for which Shell and Dow were liable under the theories of products liability, strict liability, and breach of warranty.

Rejecting an initial contest to its authority by Shell and Dow, the trial court found that it had jurisdiction under Tex. Civ. Prac. & Rem. Code Ann. § 71.031 (Vernon 1986), but dismissed the cause on the grounds of *forum non conveniens*. The court of appeals reversed and remanded, holding that Section 71.031 provides a foreign plaintiff with an absolute right to maintain a death or personal injury cause of action in Texas without being subject to *forum non conveniens* dismissal. 751 S.W.2d 208. Shell and Dow have asked this court to reverse the judgment of the court of appeals and affirm the trial court's dismissal.

Shell Oil Company is a multinational corporation with its world headquarters in Houston, Texas. Dow Chemical Company, though headquartered in Midland, Michigan, conducts extensive operations from its Dow Chemical USA building located in Houston. Dow operates this country's largest chemical manufacturing plant within 60 miles of Houston in Freeport, Texas. The district court where this lawsuit was filed is three blocks away from Shell's world headquarters, One Shell Plaza in downtown Houston.

Shell has stipulated that all of its more than 100,000 documents relating to DBCP are located or will be produced in Houston. Shell's medical and scientific witnesses are in Houston. The majority of Dow's documents and witnesses are located in Michigan, which is far closer to Houston (both in terms of geography and communications linkages) than to Costa Rica. The respondents have agreed to be available in Houston for independent medical examinations, for depositions and for trial. Most of the respondents' treating doctors and co-workers

have agreed to testify in Houston. Conversely, Shell and Dow have purportedly refused to make their witnesses available in Costa Rica.

The banana plantation workers allegedly injured by DBCP were employed by an American company on American-owned land and grew Dole bananas for export soley to American tables. The chemical allegedly rendering the workers sterile was researched, formulated, tested, manufactured, labeled, and shipped by an American company in the United States to another American company. The decision to manufacture DBCP for distribution and use in the third world was made by these two American companies in their corporate offices in the United States. Yet now Shell and Dow argue that the one part of this equation that should not be American is the legal consequences of their actions.

## FORUM NON CONVENIENS—"A COMMON LAW DOCTRINE OUT OF CONTROL"

As a reading of Tex. Civ. Prac. & Rem. Code Ann. § 71.031 (Vernon 1986) makes clear, the doctrine of *forum non conveniens* has been statutorily abolished in Texas. The decision in *Allen v. Bass,* . . . approved by this court, clearly holds that, upon a showing of personal jurisdiction over a defendant, article 4678, now section 71.031 of the Texas Civil Practice & Remedies Code, "opens the courts of this state to citizens of a neighboring state and gives them an absolute right to maintain a transitory action of the present nature and to try their cases in the courts of this state."

Displeased that *Allen* stands in the way of immunizing multinational corporations from suits seeking redress for their torts causing injury abroad, the dissenters doggedly attempt to circumvent this precedent. Unsuccessful with arguments based upon Texas law, they criticize the court for not justifying its result on public policy grounds.

## Using the "Doctrine" to Kill the Litigation Altogether

Both as a matter of law and of public policy, the doctrine of *forum non conveniens* is without justification. The proffered foundations for it are "considerations of fundamental fairness and sensible and effective judicial administration." . . . In fact, the doctrine is favored by multinational defendants because a *forum non conveniens* dismissal is often outcome-determinative, effectively defeating the claim and denying the plaintiff recovery. . . .

Empirical data available demonstrate that less than 4 percent of cases dismissed under the doctrine of *forum non conveniens* ever reach trial in foreign court.[1] A *forum non conveniens* dismissal usually will end the litigation altogether, effectively excusing any liability of the defendant. The plaintiffs leave the courtroom without having had their case resolved on the merits.

## The *Gulf Oil* Factors—Balanced Toward the Defendant

Courts today usually apply *forum non conveniens* by use of the factors set forth at length in *Gulf Oil Corp. v. Gilbert* . . . . Briefly summarized, those factors are (i) the private interests of the litigants (ease and cost of access to documents and witnesses); and (ii) the public interest factors (the interest of the forum state, the burden on the courts, and notions of judicial comity). In the 43 years in which the courts have grappled with the *Gulf Oil* factors, it has become increasingly apparent that their application fails to promote fairness and convenience. Instead, these factors have been used by defendants to achieve objectives violative of public policy. . . .

*The Public Interest Factors.* The three public interest factors asserted by Justice Gonzalez may be summarized as (1) whether the interests of the jurisdiction are sufficient to justify entertaining the lawsuit; (2) the potential for docket backlog; and (3) judicial comity. . . .

The next justification offered by the dissenters for invoking the legal fiction of "inconvenience" is that judges will be overworked. Not only will foreigners take our jobs, as we are told in the popular press; now they will have our courts. The xenophobic suggestion that foreigners will take over our courts "forcing our residents to wait in the corridors of our courthouses while foreign causes of action are tried," Gonzalez's dissent, 786 S.W.2d at 690, is both misleading and false.

It is the height of deception to suggest that docket backlogs in our state's urban centers are caused by so-called "foreign litigation." This assertion is unsubstantiated empirically both in Texas and in other jurisdictions rejecting *forum non conveniens*.[2] Ten states, including Texas, have not recognized the doctrine. Within these states, there is no evidence that the docket congestion predicted by the dissenters has actually occurred. The best evidence, of course, comes from Texas itself. Although foreign citizens have enjoyed the statutory right to sue defendants living or doing business here since the 1913 enactment of the predecessor to Section 71.031 of the Texas Civil Practice and Remedies Code, reaffirmed in the 1932 decision in *Allen,* Texas has not been flooded by foreign causes of action.

Moreover, the United States Supreme Court has indicated that docket congestion "is a wholly inappropriate consideration in virtually every other context." . . . If we begin to refuse to hear lawsuits properly filed in Texas because they are sure to require time, we set a precedent that can be employed to deny Texans access to these same courts.

Nor does *forum non conveniens* afford a panacea for eradicating congestion:

Making the place of trial turn on a largely imponderable exercise of judicial discretion is extremely costly. Even the strongest proponents of the most suitable forum approach concede that it is inappropriately time-consuming and wasteful for the parties to have to "litigate in order to determine where they shall litigate." If forum non conveniens outcomes are not predictable, such litigation is bound to occur. . . . In terms of delay, expense, uncertainty, and a fundamental loss of judicial accountability, the most suitable forum version of forum non conveniens clearly costs more than it is worth. Robertson, *supra,* 103 L.Q.Rev. at 414, 426.

Comity—deference shown to the interests of the foreign forum—is a consideration best achieved by rejecting forum non conveniens. Comity is not achieved when the United States allows its multinational corporations to adhere to a double standard when operating abroad and subsequently refuses to hold them accountable for those actions. As S. Jacob Scherr, Senior Project Attorney for the Natural Resources Defense Counsel, has noted:

> There is a sense of outrage on the part of many poor countries where citizens are the most vulnerable to exports of hazardous drugs, pesticides, and food products. At the 1977 meeting of the UNEP Governing Council, Dr. J.C. Kiano, the Kenyan minister for water development, warned that developing nations will no longer tolerate being used as dumping grounds for products that had not been adequately tested "and that their peoples should not be used as guinea pigs for determining the safety of chemicals." Comment, *U.S. Exports Banned For Domestic Use, But Exported to Third World Countries,* 6 Int'l Tr.L.J. 95, 98 (1980–81) [hereinafter *"U.S. Exports Banned"*].

Comity is best achieved by "avoiding the possibility of 'incurring the wrath and distrust of the Third World as it increasingly recognizes that it is being used as the industrial world's garbage can." Note, *Hazardous Exports from a Human Rights Perspective,* 14 Sw. U.L. Rev. 81, 101 (1983) [hereinafter *"Hazardous Exports"*] (quoting Hon. Michael D. Barnes (Representative in Congress representing Maryland)).[3] . . .

## PUBLIC POLICY AND THE TORT LIABILITY OF MULTINATIONAL CORPORATIONS IN UNITED STATES COURTS

The abolition of *forum non conveniens* will further important public policy considerations by providing a check on the conduct of multinational

corporations (MNCs). *See Economic Approach,* 22 Geo. Wash.J. Int'l L. & Econ. at 241. The misconduct of even a few multinational corporations can affect untold millions around the world.[4] For example, after the United States imposed a domestic ban on the sale of cancer-producing TRIS-treated children's sleepwear, American companies exported approximately 2.4 million pieces to Africa, Asia, and South America. A similar pattern occurred when a ban was proposed for baby pacifiers that had been linked to choking deaths in infants. *Hazardous Exports, supra,* 14 Sw. U.L.Rev. at 82. These examples of indifference by some corporations towards children abroad are not unusual.[5]

The allegations against Shell and Dow, if proven true, would not be unique, since production of many chemicals banned for domestic use has thereafter continued for foreign marketing.[6] Professor Thomas McGarity, a respected authority in the field of environmental law, explained:

> During the mid-1970s, the United States Environmental Protection Agency (EPA) began to restrict the use of some pesticides because of their environmental effects, and the Occupational Safety and Health Administration (OSHA) established workplace exposure standards for toxic and hazardous substances in the manufacture of pesticides. . . .[I]t is clear that many pesticides that have been severely restricted in the United States are used without restriction in many Third World countries, with resulting harm to fieldworkers and the global environment.

McGarity, *Bhopal and the Export of Hazardous Technologies,* 20 Tex.Int'l L.J. 333, 334 (1985) (citations omitted). By 1976, "29 percent, or 161 million pounds of all the pesticides exported by the United States were either unregistered or banned for domestic use." McWilliams, *Tom Sawyer's Apology: A Reevaluation of United States Pesticide Export Policy,* 8 Hastings Int'l & Comp.L.Rev. 61, 61 & n. 4 (1984). It is estimated that these pesticides poison 750,000 people in developing countries each year, of which 22,500 die. *Id.* at 62. Some estimates place the death toll from the "improper marketing of pesticides at 400,000 lives a year." *Id.* at 62 n. 7.

Some United States multinational corporations will undoubtedly continue to endanger human life and the environment with such activities until the economic consequences of these actions are such that it becomes unprofitable to operate in this manner. At present, the tort laws of many Third World countries are not yet developed. *An Economic Approach, supra,* 22 Geo. Wash.J.Int'l L. & Econ. at 222–23. Industrialization "is occurring faster than the development of domestic infrastructures necessary to deal with the problems associated with industry." *Exporting Hazardous Industries, supra,* 20 Int'l L. & Pol. at 791. When a court dismisses a case against a United States multinational corporation, it often removes the most effective restraint on corporate misconduct. *See An Economic Approach, supra,* 22 Geo. Wash.J.Int'l L. & Econ. at 241.

The doctrine of *forum non conveniens* is obsolete in a world in which markets are global and in which ecologists have documented the delicate balance of all life on this planet. The parochial perspective embodied in the doctrine of *forum non conveniens* enables corporations to evade legal control merely because they are transnational. This perspective ignores the reality that actions of our corporations affecting those abroad will also affect Texans. Although DBCP is banned from use within the United States, it and other similarly banned chemicals have been consumed by Texans eating foods imported from Costa Rica and elsewhere. *See* D. Weir & M. Schapiro, *Circle of Poison* 28–30, 77, 82–83 (1981). In the absence of meaningful tort liability in the United States for their actions, some multinational corporations will continue to operate without adequate regard for the human and environmental costs of their actions. This result cannot be allowed to repeat itself for decades to come.

As a matter of law and of public policy, the doctrine of *forum non conveniens* should be abolished. Accordingly, I concur. . . .

## NOTES

1. Professor David Robertson of the University of Texas School of Law attempted to discover the subsequent history of each reported transnational case dismissed under forum non conveniens from *Gulf Oil v. Gilbert,* 330 U.S. 501, 67 S.Ct. 839, 91 L.Ed. 1055 (1947) to the end of 1984. Data was received on 55 personal injury cases and 30 commercial cases. Of the 55 personal injury cases, only one was actually tried in a foreign court. Only two of the 30 commercial cases reached trial. *See* Robertson, *supra,* at 419.

2. Evidence from the most recent and largest national study ever performed regarding the pace of litigation in urban trial courts suggests that there is no empirical basis for the dissenters' argument that Texas dockets will become clogged without *forum non conveniens.* The state of Massachusetts recognizes *forum non conveniens. See Minnis v. Peebles,* 24 Mass.App. 467, 510 N.E.2d 289 (1987). Conversely, the state of Louisiana has explicitly not recognized *forum non conveniens* since 1967. . . . Nevertheless, the study revealed the median filing-to-disposition time for tort cases in Boston to be 953 days; in New Orleans, with no *forum non conveniens,* the median time for the disposition of tort cases was only 405 days. The study revealed the median disposition time for contract cases in Boston to be 1580 days, as opposed to a mere 271 days in New Orleans where *forum non conveniens* is not used. J. Goerdt, C. Lomvardias, G. Gallas & B. Mahoney, Examining Court Delay—The Pace of Litigation in 26 Urban Trial Courts, 1987 20, 22 (1989).

3. A senior vice president of a U.S. multinational corporation acknowledged that "[t]he realization at corporate headquarters that liability for any [industrial] disaster would be decided in the U.S. courts, more than pressure from Third World governments, has forced companies to tighten safety procedures, upgrade plants, supervise maintenance more closely and educate workers and communities." Wall St. J., Nov. 26, 1985, at 22, col. 4 (quoting Harold Corbett, senior vice president for environmental affairs at Monsanto Co.).

4. As one commentator observed, U.S. multinational corporations "adhere to a double standard when operating abroad. The lack

of stringent environmental regulations and worker safety standards abroad and the relaxed enforcement of such laws in industries using hazardous processes provide little incentive for [multinational corporations] to protect the safety of workers, to obtain liability insurance to guard against the hazard of product defects or toxic tort exposure, or to take precautions to minimize pollution to the environment. *This double standard has caused catastrophic damages to the environment and to human lives.*"

Note, *Exporting Hazardous Industries: Should American Standards Apply?*, 20 Int'l L. & Pol. 777, 780–81 (1988) (emphasis added) (footnotes omitted) [hereinafter *"Exporting Hazardous Industries"*]. *See also* Diamond, *The Path of Progress Racks the Third World, New York Times*, Dec. 12, 1984, at B1, col. 1.

5. A subsidiary of Sterling Drug Company advertised Winstrol, a synthetic male hormone severely restricted in the United States since it is associated with a number of side effects that the FDA has called "virtually irreversible," in a Brazilian medical journal, picturing a healthy boy and recommending the drug to combat poor appetite, fatigue, and weight loss. *U.S. Exports Banned, supra,* 6 Int'l Tr.L.J. at 96. The same company is said to have

marketed Dipyrone, a painkiller causing a fatal blood disease and characterized by the American Medical Association as for use only as "a last resort," as "Novaldin" in the Dominican Republic. "Novaldin" was advertised in the Dominican Republic with pictures of a child smiling about its agreeable taste. *Id.* at 97. "In 1975, 13 children in Brazil died after coming into contact with a toxic pesticide whose use had been severely restricted in this country." *Hazardous Exports, supra,* 14 Sw. U.L. Rev. at 82.

6. Regarding Leptophos, a powerful and hazardous pesticide that was domestically banned, S. Jacob Scherr stated that "In 1975 alone, Velsicol, a Texas-based corporation exported 3,092,842 pounds of Leptophos to 30 countries. Over half of that was shipped to Egypt, a country with no procedures for pesticide regulation or tolerance setting. In December 1976, the *Washington Post* reported that Laptophos use in Egypt resulted in the death of a number of farmers and illness in rural communities. . . . But despite the accumulation of data on Leptophos' severe neurotoxicity, Velsicol continued to market the product abroad for use on grain and vegetable crops while proclaiming the product's safety." *U.S. Exports Banned,* 6 Int'l Tr.L.J. at 96.

---

# *Doe 1 vs. Unocal*

*United States Court of Appeals for the Ninth Circuit*

## OPINION

This case involves human rights violations that allegedly occurred in Myanmar, formerly known as Burma. Villagers from the Tenasserim region in Myanmar allege that the Defendants directly or indirectly subjected the villagers to forced labor, murder, rape, and torture when the Defendants constructed a gas pipeline through the Tenasserim region.

The villagers base their claims on the Alien Tort Claims Act, 28 U.S.C. § 1350, and the Racketeer Influenced and Corrupt Organizations Act, 18 U.S.C. § 1961 *et seq.,* as well as state law.

The District Court, through dismissal and summary judgment, resolved all of Plaintiffs' federal claims in favor of the Defendants. For the following reasons, we reverse in part and affirm in part the District Court's rulings.

---

963 F Supp (2002); opinion by Circuit Judge Pregerson.

# I. FACTUAL AND PROCEDURAL BACKGROUND

## A. Unocal's Investment in a Natural Gas Project in Myanmar

Burma has been ruled by a military government since 1958. In 1988, a new military government, Defendant-Appellee State Law and Order Restoration Council ("the Myanmar Military"), took control and renamed the country Myanmar. The Myanmar Military established a state owned company, Defendant-Appellee Myanmar Oil and Gas Enterprise ("Myanmar Oil"), to produce and sell the nation's oil and gas resources.

In 1992, Myanmar Oil licensed the French oil company Total S.A. ("Total") to produce, transport, and sell natural gas from deposits in the Yadana Field off the coast of Myanmar ("the Project"). Total set up a subsidiary, Total Myanmar Exploration and Production ("Total Myanmar"), for this purpose. The Project consisted of a Gas Production Joint Venture, which would extract the natural gas out of the Yadana Field, and a Gas Transportation Company, which would construct and operate a pipeline to transport the natural gas from the coast of Myanmar through the interior of the country to Thailand.

Also in 1992, Defendant-Appellant Unocal Corporation and its wholly owned subsidiary Defendant-Appellant Union Oil Company of California, collectively referred to below as "Unocal," acquired a 28 percent interest in the Project from Total. Unocal set up a wholly owned subsidiary, the Unocal Myanmar Offshore Company ("the Unocal Offshore Co."), to hold Unocal's 28 percent interest in the Gas Production Joint Venture half of the Project. Similarly, Unocal set up another wholly owned subsidiary, the Unocal International Pipeline Corporation ("the Unocal Pipeline Corp."), to hold Unocal's 28 percent interest in the Gas Transportation Company half of the Project. Myanmar Oil and a Thai government entity,

the Petroleum Authority of Thailand Exploration and Production, also acquired interests in the Project. Total Myanmar was appointed Operator of the Gas Production Joint Venture and the Gas Transportation Company. As the Operator, Total Myanmar was responsible, *inter alia,* for "determin[ing] . . . the selection of . . . employees [and] the hours of work and the compensation to be paid to all . . . employees" in connection with the Project.

## B. Unocal's Knowledge that the Myanmar Military Was Providing Security and Other Services for the Project

It is undisputed that the Myanmar Military provided security and other services for the Project, and that Unocal knew about this. The pipeline was to run through Myanmar's rural Tenasserim region. The Myanmar Military increased its presence in the pipeline region to provide security and other services for the Project. A Unocal memorandum documenting Unocal's meetings with Total on March 1 and 2, 1995 reflects Unocal's understanding that "[f]our battalions of 600 men each will protect the [pipeline] corridor" and "[f]ifty soldiers will be assigned to guard each survey team." A former soldier in one of these battalions testified at his deposition that his battalion had been formed in 1996 specifically for this purpose. In addition, the Military built helipads and cleared roads along the proposed pipeline route for the benefit of the Project.

There is also evidence sufficient to raise a genuine issue of material fact whether the Project *hired* the Myanmar Military, through Myanmar Oil, to provide these services, and whether Unocal knew about this. A Production Sharing Contract, entered into by Total Myanmar and Myanmar Oil before Unocal acquired an interest in the Project, provided that "[Myanmar Oil] shall . . . supply[ ] or mak[e] available . . . security protection . . . as may be requested by

[Total Myanmar and its assigns]," such as Unocal. Unocal was aware of this agreement. Thus, a May 10, 1995, Unocal "briefing document" states that "[a]ccording to *our contract,* the government of Myanmar is responsible for protecting the pipeline." (Emphasis added.) Similarly, in May 1995, a cable from the U.S. Embassy in Rangoon, Myanmar, reported that Unocal On-Site Representative Joel Robinson ("Unocal Representative Robinson" or "Robinson") "stated forthrightly that *the companies have hired* the Burmese military to provide security for the project." (Emphasis added.)

Unocal disputes that the Project hired the Myanmar Military or, at the least, that Unocal knew about this. For example, Unocal points out that the Production Sharing Contract quoted in the previous paragraph covered only the offshore Gas Production Joint Venture but not the Gas Transportation Company and the construction of the pipeline which gave rise to the alleged human rights violations. Moreover, Unocal President John Imle ("Unocal President Imle" or "Imle") stated at his deposition that he knew of "no . . . contractual obligation" requiring the Myanmar Military to provide security for the pipeline construction. Likewise, Unocal CEO Roger Beach ("Unocal CEO Beach" or "Beach") stated at his deposition that he also did not know "whether or not Myanmar had a contractual obligation to provide . . . security." Beach further stated that he was not aware of "any support whatsoever of the military[,] . . . either physical or monetary." These assertions by Unocal President Imle and Unocal CEO Beach are called into question by a briefing book which Total prepared for them on the occasion of their April 1996 visit to the Project. The briefing book lists the "numbers of villagers" working as "local helpers hired by battalions," the monthly "amount paid in Kyats" (the currency of Myanmar) to "Project Helpers," and the "amount in Kyats" expended by the Project on "food rations (Army + Villages)."

Furtermore, there is evidence sufficient to raise a genuine issue of material fact whether the Project directed the Myanmar Military in these activities, at least to a degree, and whether Unocal was involved in this. In May 1995, a cable from the U.S. Embassy in Rangoon reported:

> [Unocal Representative] Robinson indicated . . . Total/Unocal uses [aerial photos, precision surveys, and topography maps] to show the [Myanmar] military where they need helipads built and facilities secured. . . . Total's security officials meet with military counterparts to inform them of the next day's activities so that soldiers can ensure the area is secure and guard the work perimeter while the survey team goes about its business.

A November 8, 1995, document apparently authored by Total Myanmar stated that "[e]ach working group has a security officer . . . to control the army positions." A January 1996 meeting document lists "daily security coordination with the army" as a "working procedure." Similarly, the briefing book that Total prepared for Unocal President Imle and Unocal CEO Beach on the occasion of their April 1996 visit to the Project mentions that "daily meeting[s]" were "held with the tactical commander" of the army. Moreover, on or about August 29, 1996, Unocal (Singapore) Director of Information Carol Scott ("Unocal Director of Information Scott" or "Scott") discussed with Unocal Media Contact and Spokesperson David Garcia ("Unocal Spokesperson Garcia" or "Garcia") via e-mail how Unocal should publicly address the issue of the alleged movement of villages by the Myanmar Military in connection with the pipeline. Scott cautioned Garcia that "[b]y saying *we* influenced the army not to move a village, you introduce the concept that they would do such a thing; whereas, by saying that no villages have been moved, you skirt the issue of whether it could happen or not." (Emphasis added.) This e-mail is some evidence that

Unocal could influence the army not to commit human rights violations, that the army might otherwise commit such violations, and that Unocal knew this.

## C. Unocal's Knowledge that the Myanmar Military Was Allegedly Committing Human Rights Violations in Connection with the Project

Plaintiffs are villagers from Myanmar's Tenasserim region, the rural area through which the Project built the pipeline. Plaintiffs allege that the Myanmar Military forced them, under threat of violence, to work on and serve as porters for the Project. For instance, John Doe IX testified that he was forced to build a helipad near the pipeline site in 1994 that was then used by Unocal and Total officials who visited the pipeline during its planning stages. John Doe VII and John Doe X, described the construction of helipads at Eindayaza and Po Pah Pta, both of which were near the pipeline site, were used to ferry Total/Unocal executives and materials to the construction site, and were constructed using the forced labor of local villagers, including Plaintiffs. John Roes VIII and IX, as well as John Does I, VIII and IX testified that they were forced to work on building roads leading to the pipeline construction area. Finally, John Does V and IX, testified that they were required to serve as "pipeline porters"—workers who performed menial tasks such as hauling materials and cleaning the army camps for the soldiers guarding the pipeline construction.

Plaintiffs also allege in furtherance of the forced labor program just described, the Myanmar Military subjected them to acts of murder, rape, and torture. For instance, Jane Doe I testified that after her husband, John Doe I, attempted to escape the forced labor program, he was shot at by soldiers, and in retaliation for his attempted escape, that she and her baby were thrown into a fire, resulting in injuries to her and the death of the child. Other witnesses described the summary execution of villagers who refused to participate in the forced labor program, or who grew too weak to work effectively. Several Plaintiffs testified that rapes occurred as part of the forced labor program. For instance, both Jane Does II and III testified that while conscripted to work on pipeline-related construction projects, they were raped at knifepoint by Myanmar soldiers who were members of a battalion that was supervising the work. Plaintiffs finally allege that Unocal's conduct gives rise to liability for these abuses.

The successive military governments of first Burma and now Myanmar have a long and well-known history of imposing forced labor on their citizens. . . . As detailed below, even before Unocal invested in the Project, Unocal was made aware—by its own consultants and by its partners in the Project—of this record and that the Myanmar Military might also employ forced labor and commit other human rights violations in connection with the Project. And after Unocal invested in the Project, Unocal was made aware—by its own consultants and employees, its partners in the Project, and human rights organizations—of allegations that the Myanmar Military was actually committing such violations in connection with the Project. . . .

## II. ANALYSIS

### Liability Under the Alien Tort Claims Act

#### 1. Introduction

*1.* The Alien Tort Claims Act confers upon the federal district courts "original jurisdiction of any civil action by an alien for a tort only, committed in violation of the law of nations." We have held that the ATCA also provides a cause of action, as long as "plaintiffs . . . allege a violation of 'specific, universal, and obligatory' international norms as part of [their] ATGA claim." . . . Plaintiffs allege that Unocal's conduct gave rise to ATCA liability for the forced labor, murder, rape, and torture inflicted on them by the Myanmar Military. . . . We must determine whether, viewing the evidence in the light most favorable to the nonmoving party, there are any genuine issues of material fact and whether the district court correctly applied the relevant substantive law.

*2.* One threshold question in *any* ATCA case is whether the alleged tort is a violation of the law of nations. We have recognized that torture, murder, and slavery are *jus cogens* violations and, thus, violations of the law of nations.[1] . . . Rape can be a form of torture. Moreover, forced labor is so widely condemned that it has achieved the status of a *jus cogens* violation. *See,* e.g., Universal Declaration of Human Rights. . . . Accordingly, all torts alleged in the present case are *jus cogens* violations and, thereby, violations of the law of nations. . . .

*4.* In light of these authorities,[2] we conclude that forced labor is a modern variant of slavery that, like traditional variants of slave trading, does not require state action to give rise to liability under the ATCA.

(b) Unocal may be liable under the ATCA for aiding and abetting the Myanmar Military in subjecting Plaintiffs to forced labor.

Plaintiffs argue that Unocal aided and abetted the Myanmar Military in subjecting them to forced labor. We hold that the standard for aiding and abetting under the ATCA is, as discussed below, knowing practical assistance or encouragement that has a substantial effect on the perpetration of the crime. We further hold that a reasonable factfinder could find that Unocal's conduct met this standard. . . .

We however agree with the District Court that in the present case, we should apply international law as developed in the decisions by international criminal tribunals such as the Nuremberg Military Tribunals for the applicable substantive law. "The law of nations 'may be ascertained by consulting the works of jurists, writing professedly on public law; or by the general usage and practice of nations; *or by judicial decisions recognizing and enforcing that law.*'" . . .

*7.* International human rights law has been developed largely in the context of criminal prosecutions rather than civil proceedings. . . .

*8.* The *Furundzija* standard for aiding and abetting liability under international criminal law can be summarized as knowing practical assistance, encouragement, or moral support which has a substantial effect on the perpetration of the crime. At least with respect to assistance and encouragement, this standard is similar to the standard for aiding and abetting under domestic tort law. Thus, the Restatement of Torts states: "For harm resulting to a third person from the tortious conduct of another, one is subject to liability if he . . . (b) knows that the other's conduct constitutes a breach of duty and gives *substantial assistance or encouragement* to the other so to conduct himself. . . ." *Restatement (Second) of Torts* § 876 (1979) (emphasis added). Especially given the similarities between the *Furundzija* international criminal standard and the Restatement domestic tort standard, we find that application of a slightly modified *Furundzija* standard is appropriate in the present case. In particular, given that there is—as discussed below—sufficient evidence in the present case that Unocal gave assistance and encouragement to the Myanmar Military, we do not need to decide whether it would have been enough if Unocal had only given moral support to the Myanmar Military. Accordingly, we may impose aiding and abetting liability for knowing practical assistance or encouragement which has a substantial effect on the perpetration of the crime, leaving the question whether such liability should also be imposed for moral support which has the required substantial effect to another day.

**9.** First, a reasonable factfinder could conclude that Unocal's alleged conduct met the *actus reus* requirement of aiding and abetting as we define it today, that is, practical assistance or encouragement which has a substantial effect on the perpetration of the crime of, in the present case, forced labor.

**10.** Unocal's weak protestations notwithstanding, there is little doubt that the record contains substantial evidence creating a material question of fact as to whether forced labor was used in connection with the construction of the pipeline. Numerous witnesses, including a number of Plaintiffs, testified that they were forced to clear the right of way for the pipeline and to build helipads for the project before construction of the pipeline began. For instance, John Doe IX testified that he was forced to build a helipad near the pipeline site in 1994 that was then used by Unocal and Total officials who visited the pipeline during its planning stages. Other Plaintiffs and witnesses, including John Doe VII and John Roe X, described the construction of helipads at Eindayaza and Po Pah Pta, both of which were near the pipeline site, were used to ferry Total/Unocal executives and materials to the constructed site, and were constructed using the forced labor of local villagers, including Plaintiffs. Other Plaintiffs, such as John Roes VIII and IX, as well as John Does I, VIII and IX, testified that they were forced to work on building roads leading to the pipeline construction area. Finally, yet other Plaintiffs, such as John Does V and IX, testified that they were required to serve as "pipeline porters"—workers who performed menial tasks such as hauling materials and cleaning the army camps for the soldiers guarding the pipeline construction. These serious allegations create triable ques-

tions of fact as to whether the Myanmar Military implemented a policy of forced labor in connection with its work on the pipeline.

**11.** The evidence also supports the conclusion that Unocal gave practical assistance to the Myanmar Military in subjecting Plaintiffs to forced labor. The practical assistance took the form of hiring the Myanmar Military to provide security and build infrastructure along the pipeline route in exchange for money or food. The practical assistance also took the form of using photos, surveys, and maps in daily meetings to show the Myanmar Military where to provide security and build infrastructure.

**12.** This assistance, moreover, had a "substantial effect" on the perpetration of forced labor, which "most probably would not have occurred in the same way" without someone hiring the Myanmar Military to provide security, and without someone showing them where to do it. This conclusion is supported by the admission of Unocal Representative Robinson that "[o]ur assertion that [the Myanmar Military] has not *expanded and amplified its usual methods* around the pipeline *on our behalf* may not withstand much scrutiny," and by the admission of Unocal President Imle that "[i]f forced labor goes hand and glove with the military yes there will be *more forced labor*." (Emphasis added.)

**13.** Second, a reasonable factfinder could also conclude that Unocal's conduct met the *mens rea* requirement of aiding and abetting as we define it today, namely, actual or constructive (i.e., reasonable) knowledge that the accomplice's actions will assist the perpetrator in the commission of the crime. The District Court found that "[t]he evidence does suggest that Unocal knew that forced labor was being utilized and that the Joint Venturers benefitted from the practice." Moreover, Unocal knew or should reasonably have known that its conduct—including the payments and the instructions where to provide security and build infrastructure—would assist or encourage the Myanmar Military to subject Plaintiffs to forced labor.

*14.* Viewing the evidence in the light most favorable to Plaintiffs, we conclude that there are genuine issues of material fact whether Unocal's conduct met the *actus reus* and *mens rea* requirements for liability under the ATCA for aiding and abetting forced labor. Accordingly, we reverse the District Court's grant of Unocal's motion for summary judgment on Plaintiffs forced labor claims under the ATCA.

## NOTES

1. *Jus cogens* norms are norms of international law that are binding on nations even if they do not agree to them.
2. From Section [3], which has been omitted.

# United Nations Draft Norms on the Responsibilities of Transnational Corporations and Other Business Enterprises with Regard to Human Rights (2003)

## A. GENERAL OBLIGATIONS

1. States have the primary responsibility to promote, secure the fulfilment of, respect, ensure respect of, and protect human rights recognized in international as well as national law, including assuring that transnational corporations and other business enterprises respect human rights. Within their respective spheres of activity and influence, transnational corporations and other business enterprises have the obligation to promote, secure the fulfilment of, respect, ensure respect of, and protect human rights recognized in international as well as national law.

## B. RIGHT TO EQUAL OPPORTUNITY AND NON-DISCRIMINATORY TREATMENT

2. Transnational corporations and other business enterprises shall ensure equality of opportunity and treatment, as provided in the relevant international instruments and national legislation as well as international human rights law, for the purpose of eliminating discrimination based on race, color, sex, language, religion, political opinion, national or social origin, social status, indigenous status, disability, age (except for children who may be given greater protection), or other status of the individual unrelated to the inherent requirements to perform the job, or complying with special measures designed to overcome past discrimination against certain groups.

## C. RIGHT TO SECURITY OF PERSONS

3. Transnational corporations and other business enterprises shall not engage in nor benefit from war crimes; crimes against humanity; genocide; torture; forced disappearance; forced or compulsory labor; hostage-taking; extrajudicial, summary or arbitrary executions; other violations of humanitarian law;

Source: University of Minnesota Human Rights Library; http://www1.umn.edu/humanrts/links/NormsApril2003.html (accessed May 20, 2007).

and other international crimes against the human person as defined by international law, in particular human rights and humanitarian law.

4. Security arrangements for transnational corporations and other business enterprises shall observe international human rights norms as well as the laws and professional standards of the country or countries in which they operate.

## D. RIGHTS OF WORKERS

5. Transnational corporations and other business enterprises shall not use forced or compulsory labor as forbidden by the relevant international instruments and national legislation as well as international human rights and humanitarian law.

6. Transnational corporations and other business enterprises shall respect the rights of children to be protected from economic exploitation as forbidden by the relevant international instruments and national legislation as well as international human rights and humanitarian law.

7. Transnational corporations and other business enterprises shall provide a safe and healthy working environment as set forth in relevant international instruments and national legislation as well as international human rights and humanitarian law.

8. Transnational corporations and other business enterprises shall provide workers with remuneration that ensures an adequate standard of living for them and their families. Such remuneration shall take due account of their needs for adequate living conditions with a view towards progressive improvement.

9. Transnational corporations and other business enterprises shall ensure the freedom of association and effective recognition of the right to collective bargaining by protecting the right to establish and, subject only to the rules of the organization concerned, to join organizations of their own choosing without distinction, previous authorization, or interference, for the protection of their employment interests and for other collective bargaining purposes as provided in national legislation and the relevant ILO conventions.

## E. RESPECT FOR NATIONAL SOVEREIGNTY AND HUMAN RIGHTS

10. Transnational corporations and other business enterprises shall recognize and respect applicable norms of international law; national laws; regulations; administrative practices; the rule of law; the public interest; development objectives; social, economic, and cultural policies including transparency, accountability, and prohibition of corruption; and authority of the countries in which the enterprises operate.

11. Transnational corporations and other business enterprises shall not offer, promise, give, accept, condone, knowingly benefit from, or demand a bribe or other improper advantage. Nor shall they be solicited or expected to give a bribe or other improper advantage to any government, public official, candidate for elective post, any member of the armed forces or security forces, or any other individual or organization. Transnational corporations and other business enterprises shall refrain from any activity which supports, solicits, or encourages States or any other entities to abuse human rights. They shall further seek to ensure that the goods and services they provide will not be used to abuse human rights.

12. Transnational corporations and other business enterprises shall respect civil, cultural, economic, political, and social rights, and contribute to their realization, in particular the rights to development; adequate food and drinking water; the highest attainable standard of physical and mental health; adequate housing; privacy; education; freedom of thought, conscience, and religion; and freedom of opinion and expression; and refrain from actions which obstruct or impede the realization of those rights.

## F. OBLIGATIONS WITH REGARD TO CONSUMER PROTECTION

13. Transnational corporations and other business enterprises shall act in accordance with fair business, marketing, and advertising practices and shall take all necessary steps to ensure the safety and quality of the goods and services they provide, including observance of the precautionary principle. Nor shall they

produce, distribute, market, or advertise potentially harmful or harmful products for use by consumers.

## G. OBLIGATIONS WITH REGARD TO ENVIRONMENTAL PROTECTION

14. Transnational corporations and other business enterprises shall carry out their activities in accordance with national laws, regulations, administrative practices, and policies relating to the preservation of the environment of the countries in which they operate as well as in accordance with relevant international agreements, principles, objectives, responsibilities, and standards with regard to the environment as well as human rights, public health and safety, bioethics, and the precautionary principle; and shall generally conduct their activities in a manner contributing to the wider goal of sustainable development.

## H. GENERAL PROVISIONS OF IMPLEMENTATION

15. As an initial step towards implementing these Norms each transnational corporation or other business enterprise shall adopt, disseminate, and implement internal rules of operation in compliance with the Norms. Further, they shall periodically report on and take other measures fully to implement the Norms and to provide at least for the prompt implementation of the protections set forth in the Norms. Each transnational corporation or other business enterprise shall apply and incorporate these Norms in their contracts or other arrangements and dealings with contractors, subcontractors, suppliers, licensees, distributors, or natural or other legal persons that enter into any agreement with the transnational corporation or business enterprise in order to ensure respect for and implementation of the Norms.

16. Transnational corporations and other businesses enterprises shall be subject to periodic monitoring and verification by United Nations, other international, and national mechanisms, already in existence or yet to be created, regarding application of the Norms. This monitoring shall be transparent, independent, and take into account input from stakeholders (including nongovernmental organizations) and as a result of complaints of violations of these Norms. Further, transnational corporations and other businesses enterprises shall conduct periodic evaluations concerning the impact of their own activities on human rights under these Norms.

17. States should establish and reinforce the necessary legal and administrative framework for assuring that the Norms and other relevant national and international laws are implemented by transnational corporations and other business enterprises.

18. Transnational corporations and other business enterprises shall provide prompt, effective, and adequate reparation to those persons, entities, and communities that have been adversely affected by failures to comply with these Norms through, inter alia, reparations, restitution, compensation, and rehabilitation for any damage done or property taken. In connection with determining damages, and in all other respects, these Norms shall be enforced by national courts and/or international tribunals if appropriate.

19. Nothing in these Norms shall be construed as diminishing, restricting, or adversely affecting the human rights obligations of States under national and international law. Nor shall they be construed as diminishing, restricting, or adversely affecting more protective human rights norms. Nor shall they be construed as diminishing, restricting, or adversely affecting other obligations or responsibilities of transnational corporations and other business enterprises in fields other than human rights.

## I. DEFINITIONS

20. The term "transnational corporation" refers to an economic entity operating in more than one country or a cluster of economic entities operating in two or more countries—whatever their legal form, whether in their home country or country of activity, and whether taken individually or collectively.

21. The phrase "other business enterprise" includes any business entity, regardless of the international or domestic nature of its activities, including a transnational corporation; the corporate, partnership, or other legal

form used to establish the business entity; and the nature of the ownership of the entity. These Norms shall be presumed to apply, as a matter of practice, if the business enterprise has any relation with a transnational corporation, the impact of its activities is not entirely local, or the activities involve violations of the right to security as indicated in paragraphs three and four.

22. The term "stakeholder" includes stockholders, other owners, workers, and their representatives, as well as any other individual or group that is affected by the activities of transnational corporations or other business enterprises. The term "stakeholder" shall be interpreted functionally in light of the objectives of these Norms and include indirect stakeholders when their interests are or will be substantially affected by the activities of the transnational corporation or business enterprise. In addition to parties directly affected by the activities of business enterprises, stakeholders can include parties which are indirectly affected by the activities of transnational corporations or other business enterprises such as consumer groups, customers, governments, neighboring communities, indigenous peoples and communities, nongovernmental organizations, public and private lending institutions, suppliers, trade associations, and others.

23. The phrases "internationally recognized human rights" and "international human rights" include civil, cultural, economic, political, and social rights, as set forth in the International Bill of Human Rights and other human rights treaties, as well as the right to development and rights recognized by international humanitarian law, international refugee law, international labor law, and other relevant instruments adopted within the United Nations system.

## UNITED NATIONS GLOBAL COMPACT

The Global Compact's 10 principles in the areas of human rights, labor, the environment and anticorruption enjoy universal consensus and are derived from:

*The Universal Declaration of Human Rights*
*The International Labor Organization's Declaration on Fundamental Principles and Rights at Work*
*The Rio Declaration on Environment and Development*
*The United Nations Convention against Corruption*

The Global Compact asks companies to embrace, support and enact, within their sphere of influence, a set of core values in the areas of human rights, labor standards, the environment, and anticorruption:

## HUMAN RIGHTS

Principle 1: Businesses should support and respect the protection of internationally proclaimed human rights; and
Principle 2: make sure that they are not complicit in human rights abuses.

## LABOR STANDARDS

Principle 3: Businesses should uphold the freedom of association and the effective recognition of the right to collective bargaining;
Principle 4: the elimination of all forms of forced and compulsory labor;
Principle 5: the effective abolition of child labor; and
Principle 6: the elimination of discrimination in respect of employment and occupation.

## ENVIRONMENT

Principle 7: Businesses should support a precautionary approach to environmental challenges;

*Source:* United Nations, http://www.unglobalcompact.org/AboutTheGC/TheTenPrinciples/index.html (accessed May 20, 2007).

Principle 8: undertake initiatives to promote greater environmental responsibility; and Principle 9: encourage the development and diffusion of environmentally friendly technologies

# ANTI-CORRUPTION

Principle 10: Businesses should work against all forms of corruption, including extortion and bribery.

---

# CASES

# CASE 1.  *Foreign Assignment*

Sara Strong graduated with an MBA from UCLA four years ago. She immediately took a job in the correspondent bank section of the Security Bank of the American Continent. Sara was assigned to work on issues pertaining to relationships with correspondent banks in Latin America. She rose rapidly in the section and received three good promotions in 3 years. She consistently got high ratings from her superiors, and she received particularly high marks for her professional demeanor.

In her initial position with the bank, Sara was required to travel to Mexico on several occasions. She was always accompanied by a male colleague even though she generally handled similar business by herself on trips within the United States. During her trips to Mexico she observed that Mexican bankers seemed more aware of her being a woman and were personally solicitous to her, but she didn't discern any major problems. The final decisions on the work that she did were handled by male representatives of the bank stationed in Mexico.

A successful foreign assignment was an important step for those on the "fast track" at the bank. Sara applied for a position in Central or South America and was delighted when she was assigned to the bank's office in Mexico City. The office had about 20 bank employees and was headed by William Vitam. The Mexico City office was seen as a preferred assignment by young executives at the bank.

After a month, Sara began to encounter problems. She found it difficult to be effective in dealing with Mexican bankers—the clients. They appeared reluctant to accept her authority, and they would often bypass her in important matters. The problem was exacerbated by Vitam's compliance in her being bypassed. When she asked that the clients be referred back to her, Vitam replied, "Of course, that isn't really practical." Vitam made matters worse by patronizing her in front of clients and by referring to her as "my cute assistant" and "our lady banker." Vitam never did this when only Americans were present and in fact treated her professionally and with respect in internal situations.

Sara finally complained to Vitam that he was undermining her authority and effectiveness; she asked him in as positive a manner as possible to help her. Vitam listened carefully to Sara's complaints, then replied, "I'm glad that you brought this up, because

---

This case was prepared by Thomas Dunfee and Diana Robertson, the Wharton School.

I've been meaning to sit down and talk to you about my little game playing in front of the clients. Let me be frank with you. Our clients think you're great, but they just don't understand a woman in authority, and you and I aren't going to be able to change their attitudes overnight. As long as the clients see you as my assistant and deferring to me, they can do business with you. I'm willing to give you as much responsibility as they can handle your having. I *know* you can handle it. But we just have to tread carefully. You and I know that my remarks in front of clients don't mean anything. They're just a way of playing the game Latin style. I know it's frustrating for you, but I really need you to support me on this. It's not going to affect your promotions. You just have to act like it's my responsibility." Sara replied that she would try to cooperate, but that basically she found her role demeaning.

As time went on, Sara found that the patronizing actions in front of clients bothered her more and more. She spoke to Vitam again, but he was firm in his position and urged her to try to be a little more flexible, even a little more "feminine."

Sara also had a problem with Vitam over policy. The Mexico City office had five younger women who worked as receptionists and secretaries. They were all situated at work stations at the entrance of the office. They were required to wear standard uniforms that were colorful and slightly sexy. Sara protested the requirement that uniforms be worn because (1) they were inconsistent to the image of the banking business and (2) they were demeaning to the women who had to wear them. Vitam just curtly replied that he had received a lot of favorable comments about the uniforms from clients of the bank.

Several months later, Sara had what she thought would be a good opportunity to deal with the problem. Tom Fried, an executive vice president who had been a mentor for her since she arrived at the bank, was coming to Mexico City; she arranged a private conference with him. She described her problems and explained that she was not able to be effective in this environment and that she worried that it would have a negative effect on her chance of promotion within the bank. Fried was very careful in his response. He spoke of certain "realities" that the bank had to respect, and he urged her to "see it through" even though he could understand how she would feel that things weren't fair.

Sara found herself becoming more aggressive and defensive in her meetings with Vitam and her clients. Several clients asked that other bank personnel handle their transactions. Sara has just received an Average rating, which noted "the beginnings of a negative attitude about the bank and its policies."

## Questions

1. What obligations does an international company have to ensure that its employees are not harmed, for instance, by having their chances for advancement limited by the social customs of a host country?

2. What international moral code, if any, is being violated by Security Bank of the American Continent?

3. Has the bank made the correct decision by opting to follow the norms of the host country?

4. What steps can be taken on the part of the internationals and their employees to avoid or resolve situations in which employees are offended or harmed by host country practices?

5. In this situation does morality require respect for Mexican practices, or does it require respect for Sara Strong? Are these incompatible?

# CASE 2.   *Facilitation or Bribery: Cultural and Ethical Disparities*

Geletex Inc., is a U.S. telecommunications corporation attempting to expand its operations worldwide. As Geletex begins its operations in other countries, it has discovered cultural, governmental, and ethical standards that differ significantly from country to country and from those in the United States. Geletex has had a code of ethics for its U.S. operations since 1975. The company's director of compliance, Jed Richardson, provides ongoing training for employees, runs a hotline through which employees can report problems and is well known and respected throughout the company for his high standards and trustworthiness. As Geletex's international operations grow, Jed is becoming increasingly uncomfortable with what appear to be double standards for the company's U.S. operations and its operations in other countries. Jed, who has been traveling to each of the Geletex international offices, has found the following situations, which since have been causing him some sleepless nights:

- In the Lima, Peru, office, Jed, in reviewing financial records, discovered that the commissions expense for the branch is unusually high. Geletex pays its salespeople commissions for each commercial customer they recruit for cellular or long-distance services. Jed knows from experience that some companies pay unusually high sales commissions to disguise the fact that salespeople are paying kickbacks in exchange for contracts. In the United States, such payments would be commercial bribery and a violation of Geletex's code of ethics. When Jed confronted the Lima, Peru, district manager and questioned him about the high commissions, he responded, "Look, things are different down here. We've got a job to do. If the company wants results, we've got to get things moving any way we can."

- In the Stockholm, Sweden, office, Jed noted a number of college-age student employees who seemed to have little work to do. Again, Jed questioned the district manager, who responded, "Sure, Magnus is the son of a telecommunications regulator. Caryl is the daughter of a judge who handles regulatory appeals in utilities. Andre is a nephew of the head of the governing party. They're bright kids, and the contacts don't hurt us. In the Scandanavian culture, giving jobs to children is part of doing business."

- In the Bombay, India, office, Jed noted that many different payments had been made to both the Indian government and government officials. When Jed voiced his concern, the district manager responded, "I can explain every payment. On this one, we needed the utilities [water and electricity] for our offices turned on. We could have waited our turn and had no services for 90 days, or we could pay to get moved to the top of the list and have our utilities turned on in 48 hours. On the check for licensing, again, we could have waited 6 months to get licensed or pay to expedite it and be licensed."

Jed is an expert on the Foreign Corrupt Practices Act (FCPA). The act permits "facilitation" or "grease" payments but prohibits bribes. Facilitation opens doors or expedites processes; it does not purport to influence outcomes. Jed is unsure about Geletex's international operations and compliance with the law. He is very unsure about Geletex having an international code of ethics.

### Questions

1. Do any of the offices' actions violate the FCPA?
2. Must a business adopt the ethical standards of a host culture in order to succeed?

3. Are all of the actions in the various offices ethical?

4. If you were Jed, what ethical standards would you develop for international operations?

5. Does Jed's firm create any internal problems by allowing different conduct in different countries and cultures?

6. The American Bar Association reports that there have been only 16 bribery prosecutions under the FCPA since 1977. However, thousands of others have settled voluntarily rather than go to trial. Is the FCPA necessary for international business operations? Does it impede U.S. businesses' success in other countries?

## CASE 3.    *Chrysler and Gao Feng: Corporate Responsibility for Religious and Political Freedom in China*

Michael A. Santoro

## INTRODUCTION

For multinational corporations, doing business in China presents many complex ethical issues. The Gao Feng incident exemplifies the challenging decisions that confront corporate executives trying to run a business in a country run by a totalitarian government that violates the human rights of its own citizens.

## THE GAO FENG INCIDENT

In May 1994, Gao Feng, a devout Christian, was arrested in Beijing for planning a private worship service and candlelight vigil to commemorate the fifth anniversary of the Tiananmen Square massacre. Gao was a 26-year employee of Beijing Jeep, Chrysler's joint venture with the Chinese government. Gao was accused of violating Chinese laws against the practice of religion outside of a state-authorized venue.

Technically, Gao appears to have violated Chinese law. Article 36 of the Chinese Constitution nominally provides for freedom of religious belief. However, the government restricts religious practice to government-sanctioned organizations in order to control the growth and scope of activity of religious groups. State Council Regulation 145, signed into law by then Premier Li Peng in January 1994, requires all places of worship to register with government religious affairs bureaus and come under the supervision of official "patriotic" religious organizations. There are almost 85,000 approved venues for religious activities in China. Many religious groups, however, have been reluctant to comply with the regulation either out of principled opposition to state control of religion or due to fear of adverse consequences if they reveal, as the regulations require, the names and addresses of church leaders.

The Universal Declaration of Human Rights, endorsed by a resolution of the United Nations General Assembly in 1948, contains the following relevant provisions:

*Article 18.* Everyone has the right to freedom of thought, conscience and religion; this right includes freedom to change his religion or belief, and freedom, either alone or in community with others and in public or private, to manifest his religion or belief in teaching, practice, worship and observance.

*Article 19.* Everyone has the right to freedom of opinion and expression; this right includes freedom to hold opinions without interference and to seek, receive and impart information and ideas through any media and regardless of frontiers.

*Article 20.* (1) Everyone has the right to freedom of peaceful assembly and association. (2) No one may be compelled to belong to an association.

According to press reports, Gao remained under administrative detention for 5 weeks. He was never formally charged. In early July, Gao returned to work at Beijing Jeep and told his supervisor that the Chinese Public Safety Bureau had imprisoned him for over a month. Chrysler asked Gao to produce proof of his detention. The Chinese police gave Gao a note that said that he had been detained for 3 days and then released without trial.

Beijing Jeep's general manager was faced with a tough decision. The Chinese joint venture partner was pressuring Chrysler to fire Gao Feng. If he did not fire him, millions of dollars of Chrysler's invested capital in China would be put at risk. If, however, Chrysler fired Gao Feng, the company would become complicit in the violation of his right to religious freedom and political expression.

The commercial interests at stake for Chrysler cannot be ignored. One of the keys to success in the Chinese markets is good relations with the Communist Party, which keeps rigid control over the economy. Multinational corporations spend years cultivating good *guanxi* or connections in China. They are thus extremely vulnerable to retaliation. Even powerful corporations such as Motorola, Hewlett-Packard, and General Motors are well aware that they could jeopardize billions of dollars of investments if they take a position on human rights that angers the Chinese government. At the time of the Gao Feng incident, for example, Chrysler was very aware that failure to accede to the government's request could result in losing a valuable minivan

contract to its German competitor Daimler-Benz. (United States–based Chrysler subsequently merged its worldwide businesses with the Germany-based Daimler-Benz.) As a consequence, the basic instinct of most foreign businesspeople in China is to stay as far away from the subject of human rights as possible. However, when a situation like the Gao Feng incident arises, corporate executives must make a decision and take action. Avoidance is simply not an option.

## THE DECISION

Put yourself in the position of Chysler's general manager. How would you handle the situation? Would you fire Gao Feng? Would you refuse to fire him? Is there some other course of action you would consider?

Would it be a sign of "cultural imperialism" if Chrysler refused to fire Gao Feng? After all, didn't Gao Feng violate Chinese law on the practice of religion? Does it matter that the enforcement of the law would appear to be in violation of the Universal Declaration of Human Rights?

How much should you factor in the financial consequences of your decision? What if your refusal to fire Gao Feng cost Chrysler millions of dollars in potential profits? Is there some way of handling the situation that would minimize the potential financial consequences?

When asked how he would handle the Gao Feng scenario, one executive with many years of business experience in China replied as follows: "The first thing I would do is to tell my secretary to hold my calls and then I would close my door to think. Because this would be a very serious situation, which, if not handled properly, could have serious repercussions for my company. I would take this very seriously."

# OUTCOME

Chrysler, presumably reasoning that Gao Feng had no documented reason for failing to report to work for the bulk of the time he was missing, fired him for poor attendance. Gao Feng's case became widely publicized when the advocacy group Human Rights Watch took up his cause. Due to the personal intervention of Chrysler's chairman, Robert J. Eaton, Gao was eventually reinstated, but his case dramatically illustrates the moral and financial pitfalls of operating in a country where there are serious and pervasive human rights abuses.

Gao's freedom was, however, short-lived once the publicity surrounding his case subsided. A few months after his reinstatement at Chrysler, Gao was rearrested and without benefit of a legal proceeding sent to a reeducation through labor camp. Gao Feng was again released in 1998 following the highly publicized visit of a interdenominational group of clergy appointed by President Clinton to investigate religious freedom in China.

## Questions

1. Was Chrysler's decision to fire Gao Feng right? Why, or why not? Explain.
2. What other options did Chrysler have in this situation? Explain.
3. Should Chrysler lobby the Chinese government to change its laws regarding religious freedom? Why or why not? Explain.

# CASE 4.    *Should Wal-Mart Do More?: A Case Study in Global Supply Chain Ethics*

*Respect for the Individual*
*Service to our Customers*
*Strive for Excellence*

—Sam Walton

## SHOULD WAL-MART DO MORE?

Wal-Mart's Global Procurement Organization was formed in 2002 and took ownership of Wal-Mart's Global Factory Certification Program, which had existed for 10 years and managed the ethical conduct of Wal-Mart's supply chain. By 2005, this program, renamed the Ethical Standards Program, was one of the largest, most extensive efforts by a multinational firm to enforce ethical conduct throughout its supply chain. In July 2006, Global Procurement Organization President and Chief Executive Officer Lawrence Jackson announced that Wal-Mart had conducted 13,600 factory audits in 2005—more than any other multinational firm ("2005 Report on Ethical Sourcing," 2006). He pointed out that

This case study was written for educational purposes by Ellery Hanlin, Amy Lambert, Chris M. Miller, Joel Riddle, and Ritchey Young under the supervision of Denis G. Arnold © 2007.

the program collaborated with suppliers, even training and assisting them in their compliance with ethical standards.

In a 2006 article entitled"Secrets, Lies, and Sweatshops: How Chinese Suppliers Hide the Truth from U.S. Companies" *BusinessWeek* reported that a Wal-Mart supplier in China falsified reports and faked inspections to defy both local labor laws and Wal-Mart's own standards (Roberts et al. 2006). Around the same time a class-action lawsuit was filed by the Washington, DC–based advocacy group International Labor Rights Fund. Filed on behalf of Wal-Mart employees from Bangladesh, China, Indonesia, Nicaragua, and Swaziland, the lawsuit accused Wal-Mart of knowingly allowing their code of conduct to be broken by overseas suppliers. Specifically, the lawsuit complained that employees were paid less than minimum wage, did not receive equitable compensation for overtime, were denied the right to associate freely, and suffered abusive managers and working conditions (Greenhouse 2005).

## WAL-MART'S ETHICAL STANDARDS PROGRAM

The November 2006 *BusinessWeek* article focused on Ningbo Beifa Group, a Chinese supplier to Wal-Mart of pens, highlighters, and other writing instruments. After failing three of Wal-Mart's audits, Beifa feared losing its largest customer permanently. Out of desperation, Beifa resorted to hiring a "consulting firm," who advised the company to cover up its practices through fake documentation and forcing employees to display ethical labor practices on the days of audit (Roberts et al. 2006).

The November 2006 *BusinessWeek* article was certainly not the first time Wal-Mart had received widespread negative publicity about its supply-chain practices. As far back as 1992,

NBC's *Dateline* accused Wal-Mart of not monitoring its Asian suppliers' illegal use of child labor and sweatshops. Nearly 14 million Americans tuned into the broadcast, the highest rated episode of the season, and Americans were shocked by the images of 11-year-old children sewing garments in sweatshops. Consumers had long associated Wal-Mart with Sam Walton's American values, and many now questioned these values. Wal-Mart's then president and chief executive officer, David D. Glass, responded by rejecting the accusations, claiming they had recently audited the factories in question and had not discovered inappropriate use of child labor (Hayes 1992).

While Mr. Glass maintained his position that Wal-Mart monitored its suppliers closely, the *Dateline* broadcast was a wake-up call that Wal-Mart needed to actively set forth an ethical code of conduct. With that realization, he set forth the initiative to begin a Factory Certification Program, including written Standards for Suppliers ("2005 Report on Ethical Sourcing," 2006). These standards were based on Wal-Mart's core values laid out by its founder, Sam Walton. While this laid an ethical foundation for Wal-Mart to build on, its scope was limited to the areas of China and Bangladesh (the two countries highlighted in the *Dateline* broadcast) and addressed labor issues such as safety, compensation, working hours, and minimum age standards. While the program included an audit plan, it did not include a comprehensive plan to actively build relationships with its suppliers ("2005 Report on Ethical Sourcing," 2006).

Since 1992, Wal-Mart's Factory Certification Program has expanded to all its suppliers, domestic and global. The scope of the program now covers issues such as protecting the natural environment, freedom of association and collective bargaining, and rights of foreign contract workers ("2005 Report on Ethical Sourcing," 2006).

Not only has Wal-Mart expanded the scope of the program's geographic boundaries and guidelines, it has evolved its approach. Many suppliers did not even fully understand the laws and regulations in the country where they operated, much less Wal-Mart's comprehensive standards. Beginning in 2003, Wal-Mart began a program to build relationships with its suppliers and train their managers on how to operate in compliance with Wal-Mart's ethical standards ("2005 Report on Ethical Sourcing," 2006). In its "2005 Report on Ethical Sourcing," Wal-Mart referred to this as a change from a "policing approach to a coaching approach." In addition, Wal-Mart very clearly communicates its standards on its corporate Web site.

Jackson stated his strong belief in the program's success in his message appended to Wal-Mart's "2005 Report on Ethical Sourcing." In addition to performing over 13,000 audits in 2005, Wal-Mart trained over 11,000 suppliers on ethical practices regarding health, safety, the natural environment, and labor. This increased from 8,000 trained suppliers in 2004. Wal-Mart has also segmented its suppliers by level of risk and focused its auditing efforts on higher-risk companies. Furthermore, high-risk suppliers are subject to unannounced audits, which contributed 20 percent of the audits in 2005. Still, Wal-Mart acknowledges the challenges of hidden violations in its "2005 Report on Ethical Sourcing." Wal-Mart has reacted to this issue through information gathering and further collaboration, but as the Beifa incident shows, this may not sufficiently uncover hidden violations.

## THE CHALLENGES OF OVERSEAS AUDITS

Over the past 10 years, society has demanded answers from American importers for the abusive work conditions of their overseas suppliers. In order to address these accusations,

many corporations developed auditing systems and eloquent codes of ethics. While there is proof that substantial improvements have been made, it is clear that many companies have just improved their ability to conceal abuse (Roberts et al. 2006). Some auditors estimate that as many as half of all contract factories in China are committing some kind of deception. As a result, the positive assurances of certain corporations on behalf of supply-chain partners are often based on faulty information (Foster and Harney 2005).

Some of the most common methods for misleading labor auditors include keeping double books, training employees on scripted responses, and maintaining hidden production areas. Factory managers are reluctant to explain their methods, and many corporations are reluctant to persuade them for fear of negative publicity. The few details that have leaked out include factory managers retaining teams of employees that falsify records and forge documents (Foster and Harney 2005). Some companies even go so far as bribery to assure a successful audit (Roberts et al. 2006).

When questioned, overseas factory managers complain about the pressure put on them to meet production quotas and control costs while balancing the costs of compliance. For many of these factories, failing an audit means the loss of a contract and potential bankruptcy. On the other hand, compliance is costly and often requires a cultural overhaul. Faced with those choices, many factory owners result to illegal activities. As one Asian manager put it,

> We are under enormous stress, customers place late orders, they change their orders part way through manufacturing, and they pay their bills late. At the same time, they ask us to provide better training for our staff, better health and safety, and better accommodation. We just can't do it all (Foster and Harney 2005).

So far, the answer has not been more auditing. As the level and number of audits increases, the time of auditors has been spread over more and more factories. Additionally, those auditors want to avoid embarrassing public relations fiascos for their employers, often issuing only warnings or even turning a blind eye. Even as auditors get more effective, factories employ "consultants" that help them beat audits. They see the cost of these consultants as less than the cost for compliance.

## JOHN AND JANE DOE ET AL. v. WAL-MART STORES INC.

On September 13, 2005, the International Labor Rights Fund (ILRF) filed a class-action lawsuit in the Los Angeles Superior Court on the grounds that Wal-Mart had a breach of contract violation with employees of overseas suppliers (Appendix 7). ILRF's complaint laid out the case that Wal-Mart's Standards for Suppliers created a contractual obligation between Wal-Mart and overseas contractors. As a result of failing to enforce those standards, the ILRF argued that Wal-Mart is violating the contract at the cost of working conditions for thousands of workers around the globe.

The executive director of ILRF, Terry Collingsworth, claimed that the lawsuit was filed in California because Wal-Mart had violated that state's laws regarding employment standards. In addition, he reported that the lawsuit could not be filed in the employees' local countries because they would face the threat of arrest, physical attacks, and hostile judicial systems that favor corporations. Mr. Collingsworth addressed Wal-Marts' Standards for Suppliers by saying, "Our premise here is that Wal-Mart and many other companies issued these codes of conduct as public relations devices. They never expected that someone would take it seriously and use it as an affirmative tool to actually make them do what they promised to do" (Ecker 2005).

## Questions

1. Are Wal-Mart's critics correct in believing that Wal-Mart has an ethical obligation to ensure that the factories in its supply chain adhere to local labor laws and treat employees in an ethically appropriate manner? Why or why not? Explain.
2. Should Wal-Mart do more to ensure that the factories in its supply chain adhere to local labor laws and treat employees in an ethically appropriate manner? If so, what should they do and why? If not, why not? Explain.
3. What obligations, if any, do consumers have regarding working conditions in supply chains? Explain.

## References

"2005 Report on Ethical Sourcing," 2006. *Wal-Mart Stores* (July 31), www.walmartstores.com (accessed November 28, 2006).

Ecker, Keith. 2005. "Labor Group Holds Wal-Mart to Code of Conduct." *Corporate Legal Times* (November). Accessed November 28, 2006, via LexisNexis.

Foster, Lauren, and Alexandra Harney. 2005. "Why Ethical Sourcing Means Show and Tell." *Financial Times* (April 22). Accessed November 28, 2006, via LexisNexis.

Greenhouse, Steven. 2006. "Suit Says Wal-Mart is Lax on Labor Abuses Overseas." *New York Times* (September 14). Accessed November 28, 2006, via LexisNexis.

Hayes, Thomas. 1992. "Wal-Mart Disputes Report on Labor." *New York Times* (December 24). Accessed November 28, 2006, via LexisNexis.

Roberts, Dexter, Pete Engardio, Aaron Bernstein, Stanley Holmes. 2006. "Secrets, Lies, And Sweatshops: How Chinese Suppliers Hide the Truth from U.S. Companies." *BusinessWeek* 4,011:50 (November 27).

# CASE 5.   *adidas¹: Application of Standards of Engagement to Child Labor Dilemma*

Adidas, formerly called adidas-Salomon was founded in 1949 and was named after its founder Adolf (Adi for short) Dassler. Most of us know adidas for its shoe production but the firm also produces clothing and sports equipment.[2] This diversification helped adidas to earn a net income of 208 million euros (approximately $183 million) on net sales of 6.11 billion euros (approximately $5.35 billion) in 2001.[3] Shoes accounted for approximately 44 percent of sales during that year.[4]

Adidas does not actually manufacture any of its products but instead contracts with approximately 950 suppliers worldwide.[5] Though it is not the case with its contract apparel factories, most of adidas' footwear suppliers produce almost exclusively for adidas. This allows the firm great leverage in footwear factories to demand compliance with certain standards with regard to labor practices or issues surrounding safety, health, and the environment. Given its leverage with suppliers, adidas asserts that "outsourcing supply does not mean outsourcing social responsibility."[6]

## ADIDAS-SALOMON'S STANDARDS OF ENGAGEMENT

Many firms have created and have published codes of conduct and other like statements *subsequent* to targeted attacks by activists. Adidas had been subject to similar attacks but also had discovered through its own internal mechanisms that some of its supplier operations were not operating at standards equivalent to its own operations. In 1998, adidas published its Standards of Engagement (SoE) with the aim of ensuring that all of its suppliers' factories are safe, fair places to work. Updated in 2001, the SoE are patterned after the ILO conventions and the model code of conduct of the World Federation of Sporting Goods Industries and reflect attention to the following labor, safety, health, and environmental issues:

- forced labor
- child labor
- discrimination
- wages and benefits
- hours of work
- freedom of association and collective bargaining
- disciplinary practices
- health and safety
- environmental requirements
- community involvement

Since their inception, the most widely encountered problems in Asian supplier factories are the payment of recruitment fees, poor age documentation, wages lower than minimum wage, maximum working hours ignored, working rules not published, wages docked as punishment for violating working rules, confiscation of passports, abuse of migrant workers, and illegal status of unions.[7]

Once informed by its sourcing division that adidas will be using a new supplier, adidas's SoE division schedules a first-time audit to determine compliance with the SoE. At the conclusion of this or other annual audits, suppliers are informed about areas needing attention, are given performance rating for (1) health, safety, and environment; and (2) labor

Reprinted with permission of the author, Laura P. Hartman. This case was developed based on research that serves as the foundation for *Rising above Sweatshops: Innovative Management Responses to Global Labor Challenges*, edited by L. Hartman, D. Arnold, and R. Wokutch (Praeger Publishers, 2003).

standards, and are ranked using the adidas 5-star approach. It was during one of these first-time audits that adidas discovered a pervasive problem with child labor in one of its new Asian suppliers.

### Children Found in Supplier Factory

Adidas faced this particularly challenging dilemma when it performed a first-time audit of a footwear supplier in Vietnam. On her audit of the factory, the auditor found documents that did not seem to make sense and confirmed these inconsistencies through worker interviews. At the conclusion of her investigation, the auditor identified just under 200 of the factory's 2000 workers as underage, according to adidas's SoE.

The auditor found both child workers (under 16) as well as juveniles (16–18 years old). Both groups were subject to the same responsibilities, pay, hours, and overtime requirements as other workers, in violation of adidas's SoE. According to the SoE and its Guidelines on Employment Standards, child laborers are not permitted at all: Business partners may not employ children who are less than 15 years old, or who are younger than the age for completing compulsory education in the country of manufacture where such age is higher than 15. Adidas also requires that juvenile workers must be assigned to age-appropriate, safe duties, with a maximum of 7 hours per day with no overtime.[8]

### Next Steps

After reporting this information, the adidas auditor realized that the solution was more complicated than simply letting the supplier terminate all of these youths. However, during the time the SoE division was contemplating its response, several dozen child workers were immediately terminated without

the knowledge of adidas. Adidas SoE staff now knew that some-thing had to be done—and quickly—to avoid losing contact with other youth workers, which might force these kids into alternatives far worse than the work environment they were forced to leave.

Adidas senior production staff immediately told the factory manager that no more youths could be encouraged to leave, under any circumstances. Adidas felt incredible pressure to act without delay in establishing some parameters for the situation, even though a more drawn out process might have resulted in greater buy-in and participation from the factory, and a longer consultation period with the youths. Adidas hired a Vietnamese education coordinator through an NGO called Verité. At the same time, adidas drafted some basic notices to the children, on behalf of the factory. The notices explained that the factory would offer a program of educational classes and vocational training to the workers under 18. The students had to decide whether they would commit to the program. The notice required them to discuss the issue with family members and to give their consent to enter into the program. It was clear to the adidas SoE team members that most of the students did not have a full understanding of what was going to happen and many of them were naturally suspicious.

### Possible Solutions?

Working with Verité and the education coordinator, adidas was able to develop what later became adidas's global policy for managing similar situations, that is, a global vision:

> The supplier meets with the worker and tries to persuade them to go back to school. If the worker agrees to return to school, schooling fees and other costs are paid for by the factory until the worker completes compulsory education. Any continued employment is conditional on enrolling the workers in a work study program of continued education.

The factory continues to pay the average monthly wage for the worker until the worker finishes school. This will make up for any lost income that the worker's family depends on in order to cover the basic needs of the family. The worker is required to provide the personnel manager proof of enrollment in school in order to continue receiving the monthly salary and school payments.

Finally, the factory agrees to provide a job for the worker once the worker has completed compulsory education.[9]

For children up to 16 years of age, in cooperation with teachers from the local government schools, the factory put into place a full-day education program with coverage similar to that covered in local schools. Topics included math, literature, chemistry, physics, biology, and history. Children would arrive and depart from the factory at the same times they originally traveled, but would spend the workday in a large classroom in a space specifically designated for the program by the factory. Preprogram assessments were completed to accurately place each student in an education-appropriate program, and teachers were hired to conduct the classes from a local province.

For juveniles who are 16 and 17 years of age, adidas felt that it was important to offer them continuing education programs in "lifestyle skills" subjects such as topics including computer skills, the Vietnamese Labor Code, the environment, safety (both personal and in the workplace, with a focus on fire safety), AIDS/HIV, sexual education, and hygiene. Not only would these programs assist the juveniles in areas of personal development, but adidas felt that it was necessary to occupy the workers in the afternoons so they wouldn't seek other work in alternate factories, thus subverting the current efforts.

## Assessment

When the program began, they had 13 students enrolled in the younger program and 133 students in the juvenile program. As of June 2001, only 56 students remained involved in the program since many had already reached the age of 18. Eleven of these students are less than 16 years old (following an academic program equivalent to the 6th, 7th, and 8th grade levels); 43 are juveniles participating in the lifestyle education programs and two are older workers who have chosen to participate in these latter courses.

While adidas was of tremendous assistance in the establishment of the programs themselves, they did not contribute to the programs on a financial level. "We wanted them to know that we believed this was their responsibility and not a 'rescue'" says the adidas auditor. In order to facilitate payments, and because it was Verité's policy to enter into a contractual relationship with the multinational rather than the factory (to ensure payments and assure leverage between the MNE and the factory), adidas paid to Verité a quarterly advance for the work anticipated while the factory paid adidas retrospectively on a monthly basis for work performed. Under these arrangements, the risk was carried in full by adidas; but this arrangement also afforded adidas the leverage it needed in order to ensure compliance by the factory. In the final months of the program, an assessment by another NGO and local Vietnamese researches will be conducted. The assessment will be fully funded by adidas, but the results of, and any recommendations in, the assessment will be available to all the parties involved in the program.

## Questions

1. If a supplier is not in compliance with the SoE, what is the most effective way for adidas to respond? Under what circumstances would you suggest that adidas work to resolve the issues versus terminating the relationship with the supplier?

2. Do you believe that adidas's, response to the child labor challenge in its supplier was effective? What alternatives did it have in terms of a response?

3. If you were the auditor, in hindsight, what lessons could be learned from this experience?

## NOTES

1. Note: adidas-Salomon customarily uses a lower-case "a" to begin its name.
2. http://www.adidas-salomon.com/en/overview/
3. adidas-Salomon, "Overview, History," *infra* n. 3.
4. adidas-Salomon, "Overview, History," *infra* n. 3.
5. adidas-Salomon, "Clearer: Social and Environmental Report 2001." Herzogenaurach, Germany: adidas-Salomon, 2000, p. 20.
6. adidas-Salomon, "Our World: Social and Environmental Report 2000," *infra* n. 5, p. 14.
7. adidas-Salomon. "Our world: Social and Environmental Report 2000," *infra* n. 5, pp. 26–27.
8. adidas-Salomon Guidelines on Employment Standards, (2001), pt. 2, chap. 3, pp. 1–8.
9. adidas-Salomon Guidelines on Employment Standards *infra* at n. 8, at pt. 2, chap. 3, p. 5.

## APPENDIX

# Adidas Standards of Engagement

## AUTHENTICITY. INSPIRATION. COMMITMENT. HONESTY.

These are some of the core values of the adidas brand. We measure ourselves by these values, and we measure our business partners in the same way.

Consistent with these brand values, we expect our partners—contractors, subcontractors, suppliers, and others—to conduct themselves with the utmost fairness, honesty, and responsibility in all aspects of their business.

These Standards of Engagement are tools that assist us in selecting and retaining business partners that follow workplace standards and business practices consistent with our policies and values. As a set of guiding principles, they also help identify potential problems so that we can work with our business partners to address issues of concern as they arise.

Specifically, we expect our business partners to operate workplaces where the following standards and practices are followed:

### I.   General Principle

Business partners shall comply fully with all legal requirements relevant to the conduct of their businesses.

### II.   Employment Standards

We will only do business with partners who treat their employees fairly and legally with regard to wages, benefits, and working conditions. In particular, the following guidelines apply:

**Forced labor:** Business partners shall not employ forced labor, whether in the form of prison labor, indentured labor, bonded labor, or otherwise.

**Child labor:** Business partners shall not employ children who are less than 15 years old (or 14 years old where the law of the country of manufacture allows), or who are younger than the age for completing compulsory education in the country of manufacture where such age is higher than 15.

**Discrimination:** While we recognize and respect cultural differences, we believe that workers should be employed on the basis of their ability to do the job, rather than on the basis of personal characteristics or beliefs. We will seek business partners that share this value, and that do not discriminate in hiring and employment practices on grounds of race, national origin, gender, religion, age, disability, sexual orientation, or political opinion.

**Wages and benefits:** Business partners shall pay their employees the minimum wage required by law or the prevailing industry wage, whichever is higher, and shall provide legally mandated benefits. Wages shall be paid directly to the employee in cash or check or the equivalent, and information relating to wages shall be provided to employees in a form they understand. Advances and deductions from wages shall be carefully monitored, and shall comply with law.

**Hours of work:** Employees shall not be required to work more than 60-hours per week, including overtime, on a regular basis and shall be compensated for overtime according to law. Employees shall be allowed at least 24 consecutive hours off per week, and should receive paid annual leave.

**Right of association:** Business partners shall recognize and respect the right of workers to join and organize associations of their own choosing.

**Disciplinary practices:** Every employee shall be treated with respect and dignity. No employee shall be subject to any physical, sexual, psychological, or verbal harassment or abuse.

### III. Heath and Safety

Business partners shall provide a safe and healthy working environment, including protection from fire, accidents, and toxic substances. Lighting, heating and ventilation systems should be adequate. Employees should have access at all times to sanitary facilities, which should be adequate and clean. When residential facilities are provided for employees, the same standards should apply.

### IV. Environmental Requirements

Business partners shall comply with all the applicabel environmental laws and regulations.

### V. Community Involvement

We will favor business partners who make efforts to contribute to improving conditions in the countries and communities in which they operate.

## CASE 6.   *Tackling HIV/AIDS: Unilever Tea Kenya*

At the end of 2003, UNAIDS estimated that Kenya had more than 1 million adults living with HIV/AIDS and was home to 650,000 AIDS orphans. Unilever Tea Kenya has implemented a workplace program to fight the disease.

### PERSONNEL

With more than 20,000 workers, Unilever Tea Kenya is the country's single largest private-sector employer.

Source: World Business Council for Sustainable Development. Case study provided courtesy of the Global Business Coalition on HIV/AIDS, Tuberculosis, and Malaria (GBC), which honors outstanding business action on HIV/AIDS at its Annual Awards for Business Excellence Gala.

## LOCATION GUIDE

Kericho district, which neighbors Nyanza, the Kenyan province most affected by HIV/AIDS with infection rates up to 15 percent.

## MINDING ITS BUSINESS

Officially formed in 1930, Unilever represents a conglomeration of companies that were well established before the start of the twentieth century. Its founding companies produced products made of oils and fats, principally margarine and soap.

Today, the company has 400 brands in more than 100 countries, offering a variety of products for cooking and eating, healthy living, beauty and style, and home care.

## FIRST AID

Employees and their families live on company estates, making Unilever Tea responsible for some 80,000 people.

Published in May 2002, the company's HIV/AIDS policy provides education and communication programs; medical care policies that treat HIV/AIDS infected and affected people in a manner consistent with the treatment of people with other life-threatening diseases; and best-practice strategies from within Unilever.

The company deems routine HIV screening, either in the pre-employment process or of existing employees, impermissible without informed consent.

## FLASH POINT

In 1999, Kenya's government declared HIV/AIDS a national disaster. At the end of 2003, UNAIDS estimated that Kenya had more than 1 million adults living with HIV/AIDS and was home to 650,000 AIDS orphans.

## UNILEVER'S RESPONSE

With an annual medical budget of U.S. $1.4 million, Unilever Tea Kenya owns and operates 22 dispensaries, four health centers, and an 85-bed hospital.

Its internal activities fall into four areas: awareness and education; prevention; care and support; and capacity building. It offers mobile clinics; AIDS-awareness messages on paychecks; drama, music, and poster competitions; youth and school programs; health talks; and nutritional support.

In-house trainers schooled by the National Organization of Peer Educators in turn have prepared 275 Unilever peer educators. In compliance with Kenya's 2000–2005 strategic plan, the company makes a concerted effort to have greater involvement of people living with HIV (GIPA) in the creation and maintenance of company HIV programs.

The HIV prevention programs focus on the distribution of male and female condoms, the prevention of mother-to-child transmission, and postexposure prophylaxis.

People living with HIV/AIDS benefit from a nondiscrimination policy, support groups, highly active antiretroviral therapy (HAART),voluntary counseling and testing (VCT), and registration in the HIV wellness program, which has already enrolled 750 individuals.

Externally, the company collaborates with a variety of partners—Kenya HIV Aids Business Council, Kenya Tea Growers Association, Walter Reed, National Organization of Peer Educators, GTZ, World Economic Forum Global Health Initiative Taskforce, and schools—to bring its programs into the local community.

## Suggested Supplementary Readings

ARNOLD, DENIS G. 2003. "Libertarian Theories of the Corporation and Global Capitalism." *Journal of Business Ethics* 48 (December): 155–73.

———. 2009. *The Ethics of Global Business*. Malden, MA. Blackwell.

ARNOLD, DENIS G., and LAURA P. HARTMAN. 2005. "Beyond Sweatshops: Positive Deviancy and Global Labor Practices." *Business Ethics: A European Review* 14, no. 3 (July): 206–22.

———. 2006 "Worker Rights and Low Wage Industrialization: How to Avoid Sweatshops." *Human Rights Quarterly* 28, no. 3 (August): 676–700.

ABENG, TANRI. 1997. "Business Ethics in Islamic Context: Perspectives of a Muslim Business Leader." *Business Ethics Quarterly* 7:47–54

AVIVA, GEVA. 1999. "Moral Problems of Employing Foreign Workers." *Business Ethics Quarterly* 9:381–403.

BRENKERT, GEORGE C. 1992. "Can We Afford International Human Rights?" *Journal of Business Ethics* 11 (July): 515–21.

BRENNAN, BARTLEY A. 1990. "The Foreign Corrupt Practices Act Amendments of 1988: The Death of a Law." *North Carolina Journal of International Law & Commerce Regulation* 15:229–47.

*Business Ethics Quarterly*. 2006. Special Forum: "Voluntary Codes of Conduct for Multinational Corporations." 16:2.

CARSON, THOMAS L. 1985. "Bribery, Extortion, and 'The Foreign Corrupt Practices Act.'" *Philosophy and Public Affairs* 14 (Winter): 66–90.

DEGEORGE, RICHARD. 1993. *Competing with Integrity in International Business*. New York: Oxford University Press.

———. 1993. "International Business Ethics: Russia and Eastern Europe." *Social Responsibility: Business, Journalism, Law and Medicine* 19:5–23.

DOLLINGER, MARC J. 1988. "Confucian Ethics and Japanese Management Practices." *Journal of Business Ethics* 7 (August): 575–83.

DONALDSON, THOMAS. 1989. *The Ethics of International Business*, New York: Oxford University Press.

———. 1992. "The Language of International Corporate Ethics." *Business Ethics Quarterly* 2 (July): 271–81.

———. 1996. "Values in Tension: Ethics Away from Home," *Harvard Business Review* (September/October): 48–62.

FILATOTCHEV, IGOR, KEN STARKEY, and MIKE WRIGHT. 1994. "The Ethical Challenge of Management Buy-outs as a form of Privatization in Central and Eastern Europe." *Journal of Business Ethics* 13 (July): 523–32.

FREDERICK, WILLIAM C. 1991. "The Moral Authority of Transnational Corporate Codes." *Journal of Business Ethics* 10:165–77.

GETZ, KATHLEEN. 1999. "International Codes of Conduct: An Analysis of Ethical Reasoning." *Journal of Business Ethics* 9:567–77.

GILLESPIE, KATE. 1987. "Middle East Response to the Foreign Corrupt Practices Act." *California Management Review* 29 (Summer): 9–30.

HAZERA, ALEJANDRO. 1995. "A Comparison of Japanese and U.S. Corporate Financial Accountability." *Business Ethics Quarterly* 5 (July): 479–97.

HINDMAN, HUGH D., and CHARLES G. SMITH. 1999. "Cross-Cultural Ethics and the Child Labor Problem." *Journal of Business Ethics* 19 (March): 21–33.

HOFFMAN W., Michael, A. E. LANGE, and D. A. FEDO, eds. 1985. *Ethics and the Multinational Enterprise*. Washington, DC: University Press of America.

HSIEH, NIEN-HE. 2006. "The Obligations of Transnational Corporations: Rawlsian Justice and the Duty of Assistance." *Business Ethics Quarterly* 14:643-61.

HUSTED, BRYAN W. 1994. "Honor Among Thieves: A Transaction-Cost Interpretation of Corruption in Third World Countries." *Business Ethics Quarterly* 4 (January): 17–27.

———. 2002. "Culture and International Anti-Corruption Agreements in Latin America," *Journal of Business Ethics* 37, no. 4 (June): 413–22.

IP, PO-KEUNG. 2002. "The Weizhi Group of Xian: A Chinese Virtuous Corporation." *Journal of Business Ethics*. 35, no. 1 (January): 15–26.

KOEHN, DARYL. 1999. "What Can Eastern Philosophy Teach Us about Business Ethics?" *Journal of Business Ethics* 19:71–79.

LANE, HENRY W., and DONALD G. SIMPSON. 1984. "Bribery in International Business: Whose

Problem Is It?" *Journal of Business Ethics* 3 (February): 35–42.

LANGLOIS, CATHERINE C., and BODO B. SCHLEGELMILCH. 1990. "Do Corporate Codes of Ethics Reflect National Character? Evidence from Europe and the United States." *Journal of International Business Studies* 21 (Fall): 519–39.

NOONAN, JOHN T. JR. 1984. *Bribes.* New York: Macmillan.

O'NEILL, O. 2000. "Agents of Justice." *Metaphilosophy* 32:180–95.

PACINI, CARL, JUDYTH A. SWINGEN, and HUDSON ROGERS. 2002. "The Role of the OECD and EU Conventions in Combating Bribery in Foreign Public Officials," *Journal of Business Ethics* 37, no. 4 (June): 385–405.

SANTORO, MICHAEL. 2000. *Profits and Principles: Global Capitalism and Human Rights in China.* Ithaca: Cornell University Press.

SETHI, S. PRAKASH. 2003. *Setting Global Standards: Guidelines for Creating Codes of Conduct in Multinational Corporations.* Hoboken, NJ. Wiley.

SEN, AMRTYA. 1997. "Human Rights and Asian Values." New York: Carnegie Council on Ethics and International Affairs.

STEIDLMEIER, PAUL. 1993. "The Moral Legitimacy of Intellectual Property Claims: American Business and Developing Country Perspectives." *Journal of Business Ethics* 12 (February): 157–64.

SU, CHENTING, and JAMES E. LITTLEFIELD. 2001. "Entering Guanxi: A Business Ethical Dilemma in Mainland China?" *Journal of Business Ethics* 33:199–210.

TAKA, IWAO. 1994. "Business Ethics: A Japanese View." *Business Ethics Quarterly* 4 (1).

Transparency International Corruption Reports, http://www.transparency.de

TUBBS, WALTER. 1993. "Karoushi: Stress-death and the Meaning of Work." *Journal of Business Ethics* 12 (November): 869–77.

VELASQUEZ, MANUEL. 1992. "International Business, Morality, and the Common Good." *Business Ethics Quarterly* 2 (January): 26–40.

WOKUTCH, RICHARD E., and JON M. SHEPARD. 1999. "The Maturing of the Japanese Economy: Corporate Social Responsibility Implications." *Business Ethics Quarterly* 9:541–58.

# Chapter *10*

# Social and Economic Justice

## INTRODUCTION

Economic disparities among individuals and nations have generated heated controversy over systems for distributing and taxing income and wealth. Sustained moral and political conflicts in the United States and other nations concern the justification of structures of taxation, international debt relief, corporate profits, corporate gifts, executive salaries and bonuses, plant closings, and exploitative conditions in factories.

Several well-reasoned and systematic answers to these and related questions have been grounded in theories of justice—that is, theories of how social and economic benefits, protections, services, and burdens should be distributed. In Chapter 1 we briefly analyzed some problems of ethical theory and justice. In the present chapter, the major distinctions, principles, and methods of moral argument in theories of justice are treated. The first three articles address the question, Which general system of social and economic organization is most just? Later articles (and cases at the end of the chapter) address the issue of executive compensation and justice in relation to economic globalization.

### Theories of Distributive Justice

What a person deserves or is entitled to is often decided by specific rules and laws, such as those governing state lotteries, food stamp allocation, health-care coverage, admission procedures for universities, and the like. These rules may be evaluated, criticized, and revised by reference to moral principles such as equality of persons, nondiscriminatory treatment, property ownership, protection from harm, compensatory justice, and retributive justice. The word *justice* is used broadly to cover both these principles and specific rules derived from the same principles, but developed for specific situations.

Economists have sometimes complained about philosophers' approaches to justice, on grounds that a "fair price" or "fair trade" is not a matter of moral fairness: prices may be low or high, affordable or not affordable, but not fair or unfair. It is simply unfortunate, not unfair, if one cannot afford to pay for something or if another person is paid 40 times what you are paid. The basis of this exclusion of price as a consideration of justice is the market-established nature of prices and salaries. To speak of "unfair" prices, trade, or salaries is to express a negative opinion, of course; but these economists reason that from a market perspective any price is fair as long as it is determined by a fair market. Salaries must be treated in the same way.

However, the economist may be missing the philosopher's point. The philosopher is often asking whether the market itself is a fair arrangement. If so, what makes it fair? If not, what makes it unfair? If coercion is used in the market to set prices, is this maneuver unfair, or does it render the market not a free market? If health care and education are distributed nationally or internationally with vast inequality, can high prices on essential items such as health care goods and university tuition be fair? If a multinational company has a monopoly on an essential foodstuff, is there no such thing as a price that is too high? These questions of fairness fall under the topic of distributive justice.

The term *distributive justice* refers to the proper distribution of social benefits and burdens. A theory of distributive justice attempts to establish a connection between the properties or characteristics of persons and the morally correct distribution of benefits and burdens in society. *Egalitarian* theories emphasize equal access to primary goods (see John Rawls's article); *libertarian* theories emphasize rights to social and economic liberty and deemphasize collective control (see Robert Nozick's essay); and *utilitarian* theories emphasize a mixed use of such criteria resulting in the maximization of both public and individual interests (see Peter Singer's article).

Systematic theories of justice attempt to elaborate how people should be compared and what it means to give people what they are due. Philosophers attempt to achieve the needed precision by developing material principles of justice, so called because they put material content into a theory of justice. Each material principle of justice identifies a relevant property on the basis of which burdens and benefits should be distributed. The following list includes the major candidates for the position of principles of distributive justice.

1. To each person an equal share
2. To each person according to individual need
3. To each person according to that person's rights
4. To each person according to individual effort
5. To each person according to societal contribution
6. To each person according to merit

A theory of justice might accept more than one of these principles. Some theories accept all six as legitimate. Many societies use several, in the belief that different rules are appropriate to different situations.

## Utilitarian Theory

In utilitarianism (which is examined in detail in Chapter 1), problems of justice are viewed as one part of the larger problem of maximizing value, and it is easy to see how a utilitarian might use all these material principles to this end. The ideal distribution of benefits and burdens is simply the one having this maximizing effect. According to utilitarian Peter Singer, in his essay in this chapter, a heavy element of political planning and economic redistribution is required to ensure that justice is done. Because utilitarianism was treated in Chapter 1, detailed considerations will be given in this introduction only to egalitarian and libertarian theories.

## Egalitarian Theory

Equality in the distribution of social benefits and burdens has a central place in several influential ethical theories. For example, in utilitarianism different people are equal in the value accorded their wants, preferences, and happiness, and in Kantian theories all persons are considered equally worthy and deserving of respect as ends in themselves. Egalitarian theory treats the question of how people should be considered equal in some respects (for example, in their basic political and moral rights and obligations), yet unequal in others (for example, in wealth and social burdens such as taxation).

*Radical and Qualified Egalitarianism.* In its radical form, egalitarian theory proposes that individual differences are always morally insignificant. Distributions of burdens and benefits in a society are just to the extent that they are equal, and deviations from absolute equality in distribution are unjust. For example, the fact that in the United States more than 35 percent of the wealth is owned by less than 1 half of 1 percent of the population makes U.S. society unjust, according to this theory, no matter how relatively "deserving" the people at both extremes might be.

However, most egalitarian accounts are guardedly formulated, so that persons are not entitled to equal shares of all social benefits and so that individual merit justifies some differences in distribution. Egalitarianism, so qualified, is concerned only with basic equalities among individuals. For example, egalitarians generally prefer *progressive* tax rates (higher incomes taxed more heavily than lower) rather than *proportional* rates (each unit taxed the same). This preference may seem odd, since a proportional rate treats everyone equally. However, qualified egalitarians often reason that progressive rates tax the wealthy more and thereby distribute wealth more evenly.

*John Rawls's Theory.* In recent years a qualified egalitarian theory in the Kantian tradition has enjoyed wide discussion. John Rawls's *A Theory of Justice* maintains that all economic goods and services should be distributed equally except when an unequal distribution would work to everyone's advantage (or at least to the advantage of the worst off in society). Rawls presents this egalitarian theory as a direct challenge to utilitarianism. He argues that social distributions produced by maximizing utility permit violations of basic individual liberties and rights. Being indifferent to the distribution of satisfactions among individuals, utilitarianism permits the infringement of people's rights and liberties to produce a proportionately greater utility for all concerned.

Rawls defends a hypothetical social contract procedure that is strongly indebted to what he calls the "Kantian conception of equality." Valid principles of justice are those to which all persons would agree if they could freely and impartially consider the social situation. Impartiality is guaranteed by a conceptual device Rawls calls the "veil of ignorance." Here each person is imagined to be ignorant of all his or her particular characteristics, for example, the person's sex, race, IQ, family background, and special talents or handicaps. Theoretically, this veil of ignorance would prevent the adoption of principles biased toward particular groups of persons.

Rawls argues that under these conditions people would unanimously agree on two fundamental principles of justice. The first requires that each person be permitted the maximum amount of basic liberty compatible with a similar liberty for others. The second stipulates that once this equal basic liberty is assured, inequalities in social primary goods (for example, income, rights, and opportunities) are to be allowed only if they benefit everyone. Rawls considers social institutions to be just if and only if they conform to these principles of the social contract. He rejects radical egalitarianism, arguing that inequalities that render everyone better off by comparison to being equal are desirable.

Rawls formulates what is called the *difference principle:* inequalities are justifiable only if they maximally enhance the position of the "representative least advantaged" person, that is, a hypothetical individual particularly unfortunate in the distribution of fortuitous characteristics or social advantages. Rawls is unclear about who might qualify under this category, but a worker incapacitated from exposure to asbestos and living in poverty clearly would qualify. Formulated in this way, the difference principle could allow, for instance, extraordinary economic rewards to business entrepreneurs, venture capitalists, and corporate takeover artists if the resulting economic situation were to produce improved job opportunities and working conditions for the least advantaged members of society, or possibly greater benefits for pension funds holding stock for the working class.

The difference principle rests on the moral viewpoint that because inequalities of birth, historical circumstance, and natural endowment are undeserved, persons in a cooperative society should make more equal the unequal situation of its naturally disadvantaged members.

### Libertarian Theory

What makes a libertarian theory *libertarian* is the priority given to distinctive procedures or mechanisms for ensuring that liberty rights are recognized in social and economic practice, typically the rules and procedures governing economic acquisition and exchange in capitalist or free-market systems.

***The Role of Individual Freedom.*** The libertarian contends that it is a basic violation of justice to ensure equal economic returns in a society. In particular, individuals are seen as having a fundamental right to own and dispense with the products of their labor as they choose, even if the exercise of this right leads to large inequalities of wealth in society. Equality and utility principles, from this perspective, sacrifice basic liberty rights to the larger public interest by exploiting one set of individuals for the benefit of another. The most apparent example is the coercive extraction of financial resources through taxation.

***Robert Nozick's Theory.*** Libertarian theory is defended in this chapter by Robert Nozick, who refers to his view as an "entitlement theory" of justice. Nozick argues that a theory of justice should work to protect individual rights and should not propound a thesis intended to "pattern" society through arrangements such as those in socialist and (impure) capitalist countries in which governments take pronounced steps to redistribute wealth.

Nozick's libertarian position rejects all distributional patterns imposed by material principles of justice. He is thus committed to a form of *procedural* justice. That is, for Nozick there is no pattern of just distribution independent of fair procedures of acquisition, transfer, and rectification; in this view he is joined by Milton Friedman (see Chapter 2). Their claims have been at the center of controversy over the libertarian account, and competing theories of justice often react to their uncompromising commitment to pure procedural justice.

## Capitalism: Is There Justice beyond the Free Market?

Many philosophers argue that an adequate theory of economic justice must recognize a set of individual rights that is more inclusive than those acknowledged in theories of capitalist markets. *Capitalism* is here understood as a market-based economic system governed by capital, that is, the wealth of an individual or an establishment accumulated by or employed in its business activities. Entrepreneurs and the institutions they create generate the capital with which businesses provide goods, services, and payments to workers. Defenders of capitalism argue that this system maximally distributes social freedoms and desirable resources, resulting in the best economic outcomes for everyone in society. All libertarians, but also many utilitarians, egalitarians, and communitarians, have defended capitalism using this general conception.

Critics of capitalism believe that owners and managers unfairly allocate high wages for themselves while distributing only low wages to workers, who are not able to move freely from one job to another in many capitalist markets. Critics of capitalism generally acknowledge that capitalists do often take significant economic risks (a justification advanced for their higher wages); however, critics maintain that capitalists rarely have to assume the burdens of deprivation that workers do. The avoidance of deprivation is a major reason why some writers propose interventions in capitalist markets; they seek to secure stronger economic rights for workers—such as a higher minimum wage, continuous health insurance, and unemployment insurance (or protections against economic disaster in the circumstance of job layoffs).

Every year American business magazines such as *Fortune* and *BusinessWeek* run exposés on excessive executive compensation. The editors argue that in the worst cases—poor corporate performances together with excessive executive compensation—there is no possible justification other than greed, and that in many cases with good corporate performance, the salaries are still excessive. Critics of capitalism point to ever-increasing executive compensation and declining real wages for workers as evidence of the need for reform. In his contribution to this chapter, "Do CEOs Get Paid Too Much?" Jeffery Moriarty assesses executive compensation packages and considers various arguments that might be used to justify them. He argues that neither a free market defense, a defense grounded in what executives deserve as a result of their labors, or a utility-based argument justify current compensation packages. His conclusion is that the popular view that CEOs are overpaid is correct.

Critics of capitalism argue that its proponents must answer the following questions: Why should we assume that people's economic rights extend only to the acquisition and dispensation of private property according to free-market rules? Is it not equally plausible to posit more substantive moral rights in the economic sphere—say, rights to health care, decent levels of education, decent standard of living, and limits on compensation?

The capitalist ideal is widely agreed to be plausible for free transactions among informed and consenting parties who start as equals in the bargaining process. However, this conception has come under significant criticism in circumstances in which contractual bargaining among equals is impossible or unlikely. Contracts, voting privileges, individuals investing in the stock market, and family relationships may involve bluffing, differentials of power and wealth, manipulation, and the like. These factors can and often do work systematically to disadvantage vulnerable individuals. For example, over the course of time in the working of capitalist markets, one group in society may gain considerable wealth and political influence, by comparison with other groups in society. Even if the *transactions* leading to this imbalance may have been legitimate, the *outcome* may not be acceptable. If an individual's bargaining position has been deeply eroded, does he or she have a right to protection from social inequalities that have emerged? If he or she is destined to poverty as a result of social conditions, is there a legitimate claim of justice, as several authors in this chapter propose?

If people have a right to a minimal level of material means (a right libertarians do not acknowledge), it seems to many writers that their rights are violated whenever economic distributions leave persons with less than that minimal level. A commitment to individual economic rights, then, may go hand in hand with a theory of justice that requires a more activist role for government. This may be true even if one starts with free-market assumptions. Many philosophers agree with libertarian premises that economic freedom is a value deserving of respect and protection, but they disagree with the claim that the principles and procedures of unmitigated capitalist markets adequately protect the basic values of individual and public welfare.

In reaction to these problems, some reject the pure procedural commitments of pure capitalist (often libertarian or utilitarian) theories and replace them with a principle specifying human need as the relevant respect in which people are to be compared for purposes of determining social and economic justice. Much turns here on how the notion of need is defined and implemented. For purposes of justice, a principle of need would be least controversial if it were restricted to fundamental needs. If malnutrition, bodily injury, and the withholding of certain information involve fundamental harms, we have a fundamental need for nutrition, health-care facilities, and education. According to theories based on this material principle, justice places the satisfaction of fundamental human needs above the protection of economic freedoms or rights (or at least at the same level of importance).

This construal of the principle of need has been used to support rights that reach well beyond capitalism. Yet there may be room for reconciliation between the principle of need and the principles that underlie capitalist systems. Many advanced industrial countries have the capacity to produce more than is strictly necessary to meet their citizens' fundamental needs. One might argue that *after* everyone's fundamental needs have been satisfied, *then* justice requires no particular pattern of distribution. For example, some current discussions of the right to health care and the right to a job are rooted in the idea of meeting basic medical and economic needs—but *only basic* needs. In this way, a single unified theory of justice might require the maintenance of certain patterns in the distributions of basic goods (for example, a decent minimum level of income, education, and health care) while allowing the market to determine distributions of goods beyond those that satisfy fundamental needs.

This approach accepts a two-tiered system of access to goods and services: (1) social coverage for basic and catastrophic needs and (2) private purchase of other goods and services. On the first tier, distribution is based on need, and everyone's basic needs are met by the government. Better services may be made available for purchase in an economic system on the second tier. This proposal seems to present an attractive point of convergence and negotiation for libertarians, utilitarians, and egalitarians. It provides a premise of equal access to basic goods while allowing additional rights to economic freedom. Theories such as utilitarianism may also find the compromise particularly attractive because it serves to minimize public dissatisfaction and to maximize community welfare. The egalitarian finds an opportunity to use an equal-access principle, and the libertarian retains free-market production and distribution. However, the system would involve compromise by proponents of each of these theories of justice.

## Global Justice

Concerns regarding the global distribution of economic resources have come to dominate much of the most interesting work by theorists of justice in recent years. The facts that inform much of this debate over global justice are increasingly well known. Nearly 1 billion people are malnourished and without access to safe drinking water. Approximately 50,000 human deaths per day are attributable to poverty-related causes.[1] This remains true despite the fact that Article 25 of the Universal Declaration of Human Rights (included in this chapter) stipulates that all people have "the right to a standard of living adequate for . . . health and well-being, for themselves and their families."[2]

Current foreign direct investment (FDI) outflows are approximately U.S. $730 billion annually, up from $53 billon in 1980. Approximately one-third of that investment is finding its way into developing economies. This remarkable increase in FDI is one indicator of a steady increase in economic globalization. Trade economists typically argue that such FDI enhances job creation in the world's poorest nations. Using broadly utilitarian reasoning, they argue that the exploitation by multinational corporations of cheap labor supplies, abundant natural resources, and lax regulatory regimes allows developing countries to expand export activities and to improve their economies. This economic growth brings much-needed jobs, which cause labor markets to tighten, which eventually force corporations to improve working conditions in order to attract workers. As wages rise, workers spend more and local economies expand, thus creating more jobs and wealth.

Critics of economic globalization argue that rather than improving overall welfare, economic globalization increases inequality and poverty by depressing the wages of the poor and middle class while enhancing the wealth of economic elites, thus increasing the gap bewtween the "haves" and the "have nots." In their view, economic globalization undermines rather than enhances human rights. Further, they argue that workers are often treated as disposable tools, and local environments are often polluted in ways that harm human welfare and inhibit future well-being. Critics of "neo-liberal" strategies for alleviating global poverty point out that the global labor supply is so vast that the theoretically sound idea that tighter labor markets alone will lead to improved working conditions is, in practicality, implausible. In his contribution to this chapter, economist Martin Wolf argues that most critics of globalization are wrong. He argues that both the number and the percentage of the world's population in poverty has declined since 1980 as a result of economic globalization. Broadly construed, Wolf argues, the economic welfare of the world's population has improved as a result of globailization.

Thomas Pogge criticizes the sort of position defended by Wolf and other economists. Cosmopolitans, such as Pogge, maintain that a system of global socioeconomic justice must be grounded in core ethical norms such as respect for basic human rights. Cosmopolitans see political institutions as a means to ensure respect for such universal norms. Nation-states that contribute to the violation of basic rights, or merely tolerate the violations of such rights, are problems that must be overcome. Proponents of this view typically call for the creation of institutions that have both the power and legitimate authority to compensate for failed states; stabilize weak states; and successfully coerce successful states into respecting relevant ethical norms. In his contribution to this chapter, "Priorities of Global Justice," Pogge argues that wealthy nations of the world are not doing enough to eradicate severe poverty. He does not challenge the facts that Wolf deploys, rather he develops three aguments in support of the conclusion that wealthy nations, and their corporations, are culpable for the circumstances of the world's poor. First, he argues that wealthy nations are stingy with respect to development assistance, despite having ample resources and a duty of assistance to poorer nations and their peoples. Second, he argues that the existing global economic order—one dominated by wealthy nations—consigns hundreds of millions of people to grinding poverty from which it is all but impossible to extricate oneself. Finally, he argues that corporations routinely corrupt officials in developing nations, thereby gaining unfair and illegitimate access to national resources and undermining the welfare of the vast majority of citizens of those nations. For these reasons, he concludes that we have an obligation to reform the global economic order.

## Conclusion

Rawls, Nozick, and the other theorists we consider in this chapter all capture some intuitive convictions about justice. Rawls's difference principle, for example, describes a widely shared belief about justified inequalities. Nozick's theory makes a strong appeal in the domains of property rights and liberties. Utilitarianism is widely used in Western nations in the development of public policy. And Pogge's cosmopolitan view supports many international agreements and protocols such as the Universal Declaration of Human Rights.

Perhaps, then, there are several equally valid, or at least equally defensible, theories of justice. There could be, based on this analysis, libertarian societies, egalitarian societies, utilitarian societies, and cosmopolitan global community, as well as societies based on mixed theories or derivative theories of taxation and redistribution. However, this possibility raises other problems in ethical theory discussed in Chapter 1—in particular, relativism and moral disagreement, and before this conclusion is accepted, the details of the arguments in this chapter's selections should be carefully assessed.

### NOTES

1. Thomas Pogge, "Priorities of Global Justice," reprinted in this chapter.
2. United Nations Universal Declaration of Human Rights, reprinted in this chapter.

# THEORIES OF SOCIAL JUSTICE

# An Egalitarian Theory of Justice

*John Rawls*

## THE ROLE OF JUSTICE

Justice is the first virtue of social institutions, as truth is of systems of thought. A theory however elegant and economical must be rejected or revised if it is untrue; likewise laws and institutions no matter how efficient and well-arranged must be reformed or abolished if they are unjust. Each person possesses an inviolability founded on justice that even the welfare of society as a whole cannot override. For this reason justice denies that the loss of freedom for some is made right by a greater good shared by others. It does not allow that the sacrifices imposed on a few are outweighed by the larger sum of advantages enjoyed by many. Therefore in a just society the liberties of equal citizenship are taken as settled; the rights secured by justice are not subject to political bargaining or to the calculus of social interests. The only thing that permits us to acquiesce in an erroneous theory is the lack of a better one; analogously, an injustice is tolerable only when it is necessary to avoid an even greater injustice. Being first virtues of human activities, truth and justice are uncompromising.

These propositions seem to express our intuitive conviction of the primacy of justice. No doubt they are expressed too strongly. In any event I wish to inquire whether these contentions or others similar to them are sound, and if so how they can be accounted for. To this end it is necessary to work out a theory of justice in the light of which these assertions can be interpreted and assessed. I shall begin by considering the role of the principles of justice. Let us assume, to fix ideas, that a society is a more or less self-sufficient association of persons who in their relations to one another recognize certain rules of conduct as binding and who for the most part act in accordance with them. Suppose further that these rules specify a system of cooperation designed to advance the good of those taking part in it. Then, although a society is a cooperative venture for mutual advantage, it is typically marked by a conflict as well as by an identity of interests. There is an identity of interests since social cooperation makes possible a better life for all than any would have if each were to live solely by his own efforts. There is a conflict of interests, since persons are not indifferent as to how the greater benefits produced by their collaboration are distributed, for in order to pursue their ends they each prefer a larger to a lesser share. A set of principles is required for choosing among the various social arrangements which determine this division of advantages and for underwriting an agreement on the proper distributive shares. These principles are the principles of social justice: they provide a way of assigning rights and duties in the basic institutions of society and they define the appropriate distribution of the benefits and burdens of social cooperation. . . .

# THE MAIN IDEA OF THE THEORY OF JUSTICE

My aim is to present a conception of justice which generalizes and carries to a higher level of abstraction the familiar theory of the social contract as found, say, in Locke, Rousseau, and Kant. In order to do this we are not to think of the original contract as one to enter a particular society or to set up a particular form of government. Rather, the guiding idea is that the principles of justice for the basic structure of society are the object of the original agreement. They are the principles that free and rational persons concerned to further their own interests would accept in an initial position of equality as defining the fundamental terms of their association. These principles are to regulate all further agreements; they specify the kinds of social cooperation that can be entered into and the forms of government that can be established. This way of regarding the principles of justice I shall call justice as fairness.

Thus we are to imagine that those who engage in social cooperation choose together, in one joint act, the principles which are to assign basic rights and duties and to determine the division of social benefits. Men are to decide in advance how they are to regulate their claims against one another and what is to be the foundation charter of their society. Just as each person must decide by rational reflection what constitutes his good, that is, the system of ends which it is rational for him to pursue, so a group of persons must decide once and for all what is to count among them as just and unjust. The choice which rational men would make in this hypothetical situation of equal liberty, assuming for the present that this choice problem has a solution, determines the principles of justice.

In justice as fairness the original position of equality corresponds to the state of nature in the traditional theory of the social contract. This original position is not, of course, thought of as an actual historical state of affairs, much less as a primitive condition of culture. It is understood as a purely hypothetical situation characterized so as to lead to a certain conception of justice. Among the essential features of this situation is that no one knows his place in society, his class position or social status, nor does any one know his fortune in the distribution of natural assets and abilities, his intelligence, strength, and the like. I shall even assume that the parties do not know their conceptions of the good or their special psychological propensities. The principles of justice are chosen behind a veil of ignorance. This ensures that no one is advantaged or disadvantaged in the choice of principles by the outcome of natural chance or the contingency of social circumstances. Since all are similarly situated and no one is able to design principles to favor his particular condition, the principles of justice are the result of a fair agreement or bargain. For given the circumstances of the original position, the symmetry of everyone's relations to each other, this initial situation is fair between individuals as moral persons, that is, as rational beings with their own ends and capable, I shall assume, of a sense of justice. The original position is, one might say, the appropriate initial status quo, and thus the fundamental agreements reached in it are fair. This explains the propriety of the name "justice as fairness": it conveys the idea that the principles of justice are agreed to in an initial situation that is fair. The name does not mean that the concepts of justice and fairness are the same, any more than the phrase "poetry as metaphor" means that the concepts of poetry and metaphor are the same.

Justice as fairness begins, as I have said, with one of the most general of all choices which persons might make together, namely, with the choice of the first principles of a conception of justice which is to regulate all subsequent criticism and reform of institutions. Then, having chosen a conception of justice, we can suppose that they are to choose a constitution and a legislature to enact laws, and so on, all in accordance with the principles of justice initially agreed upon. Our social situation is just if it is such that by this sequence of hypothetical agreements we would have contracted into the general system of rules which defines it.

. . . It may be observed, however, that once the principles of justice are thought of as arising from an original agreement in a situation of equality, it is an open question whether the principle of utility would be acknowledged. Offhand it hardly seems likely that persons who view themselves as equals, entitled to press their claims upon one another, would agree to a principle which may require lesser life prospects for some simply for the sake of a greater sum of advantages enjoyed by others. Since each desires to protect his interests, his capacity to advance his conception of the good, no one has a reason to acquiesce in an enduring loss for himself in order to bring about a greater net balance of satisfaction. In the absence of strong and lasting benevolent impulses, a rational man would not accept a basic structure merely because it maximized the algebraic sum of advantages irrespective of its permanent effects on his own basic rights and interests. Thus it seems that the principle of utility is incompatible with the conception of social cooperation among equals for mutual advantage. It appears to be inconsistent with the idea of reciprocity implicit in the notion of a well-ordered society. Or, at any rate, so I shall argue.

I shall maintain instead that the persons in the initial situation would choose two rather different principles: the first requires equality in the assignment of basic rights and duties, while the second holds that social and economic inequalities, for example inequal-

ities of wealth and authority, are just only if they result in compensating benefits for everyone, and in particular for the least advantaged members of society. These principles rule out justifying institutions on the grounds that the hardships of some are offset by a greater good in the aggregate. It may be expedient but it is not just that some should have less in order that others may prosper. But there is no injustice in the greater benefits earned by a few provided that the situation of persons not so fortunate is thereby improved. The intuitive idea is that since everyone's well-being depends upon a scheme of cooperation without which no one could have a satisfactory life, the division of advantages should be such as to draw forth the willing cooperation of everyone taking part in it, including those less well situated. Yet this can be expected only if reasonable terms are proposed. The two principles mentioned seem to be a fair agreement on the basis of which those better endowed, or more fortunate in their social position, neither of which we can be said to deserve, could expect the willing cooperation of others when some workable scheme is a necessary condition of the welfare of all. Once we decide to look for a conception of justice that nullifies the accidents of natural endowment and the contingencies of social circumstance as counters in the quest for political and economic advantage, we are led to these principles. They express the result of leaving aside those aspects of the social world that seem arbitrary from a moral point of view. . . .

## THE ORIGINAL POSITION AND JUSTIFICATION

. . . The idea here is simply to make vivid to ourselves the restrictions that it seems reasonable to impose on arguments for principles of justice, and therefore on these principles themselves. Thus it seems reasonable and generally acceptable that no one should be advantaged or disadvantaged by natural fortune or social circumstances in the choice of principles. It also seems widely agreed that it should be impossible to tailor principles to the circumstances of one's own case. We should insure further that particular inclinations and aspirations, and persons' conceptions of their good, do not affect the principles adopted. The aim is to rule out those principles that it would be rational to propose for acceptance, however little the chance of success, only if one knew certain things that are irrelevant from the standpoint of justice. For example, if a man knew that he was wealthy, he might find it rational to advance the principle that various taxes for welfare measures be counted unjust; if he knew that he was poor, he would most likely propose the contrary principle. To represent the desired restrictions one imagines a situation in which everyone is deprived of this sort of information. One excludes the knowledge of those contingencies which sets men at odds and allows them to be guided by their prejudices. In this manner the veil of ignorance is arrived at in a natural way. . . .

## TWO PRINCIPLES OF JUSTICE

I shall now state in a provisional form the two principles of justice that I believe would be chosen in the original position. . . .

The first statement of the two principles reads as follows.

> **First:** each person is to have an equal right to the most extensive basic liberty compatible with a similar liberty for others.
>
> **Second:** social and economic inequalities are to be arranged so that they are both (a) reasonably expected to be to everyone's advantage, and (b) attached to positions and offices open to all. . . . [The Difference Principle]

By way of general comment, these principles primarily apply, as I have said, to the basic structure of society. They are to govern the assignment of rights and duties and to regulate the distribution of social and economic advantages. As their formulation suggests, these principles presuppose that the social structure can be divided into two more or less distinct parts, the first principle applying to the one, the second to the other. They distinguish between those aspects of the social system that define and secure the equal liberties of citizenship and those that specify and establish social and economic inequalities. The basic liberties of citizens are, roughly speaking, political liberty (the right to vote and to be eligible for public office) together with freedom of speech and assembly; liberty of conscience and freedom of thought; freedom of the person along with the right to hold (personal) property; and freedom from arbitrary arrest and seizure as defined by the concept of the rule of law. These liberties are all required to be equal by the first principle, since citizens of a just society are to have the same basic rights.

The second principle applies, in the first approximation, to the distribution of income and wealth and to the design of organizations that make use of differences in authority and responsibility, or chains of command. While the distribution of wealth and income need not be equal, it must be to everyone's advantage, and at the same time, positions of authority and offices of command must be accessible to all. One applies the second principle by holding positions open, and then, subject to this constraint, arranges social and economic inequalities so that everyone benefits.

These principles are to be arranged in a serial order with the first principle prior to the second. This ordering means that a departure from the institutions of equal liberty required by the first principle cannot be justified, or compensated for, by greater social and economic advantages. The distribution of wealth and income, and the hierarchies of authority must be consistent with both the liberties of equal citizenship and equality of opportunity.

It is clear that these principles are rather specific in their content, and their acceptance rests on certain assumptions that I must eventually try to explain and justify. A theory of justice depends upon a theory of society in ways that will become evident as we proceed. For the present, it should be observed that the two principles (and this holds for all formulations) are a special case of a more general conception of justice that can be expressed as follows.

> All social values—liberty and opportunity, income and wealth, and the bases of self-respect— are to be distributed equally unless an unequal distribution of any, or all, of these values is to everyone's advantage.

Injustice, then, is simply inequalities that are not to the benefit of all. Of course, this conception is extremely vague and requires interpretation.

As a first step, suppose that the basic structure of society distributes certain primary goods, that is, things that every rational man is presumed to want. These goods normally have a use whatever a person's rational plan of life. For simplicity, assume that the chief primary goods at the disposition of society are rights and liberties, powers and opportunities, income and wealth. These are the social primary goods. Other primary goods such as health and vigor, intelligence and imagination, are natural goods; although their possession is influenced by the basic structure, they are not so directly under its control. Imagine, then, a hypothetical initial arrangement in which all the social primary goods are equally distributed: everyone has similar rights and duties, and income and wealth are evenly shared. This state of affairs provides a benchmark for judging improvements. If certain inequalities of wealth and organizational powers would make everyone better off than in this hypothetical starting situation, then they accord with the general conception.

Now it is possible, at least theoretically, that by giving up some of their fundamental liberties men are sufficiently compensated by the resulting social and economic gains. The general conception of justice imposes no restrictions on what sort of inequalities are permissible; it only requires that everyone's position be improved. . . .

Now the second principle insists that each person benefit from permissible inequalities in the basic structure. This means that it must be reasonable for each relevant representative man defined by this structure, when he views it as a going concern, to prefer his prospects with the inequality to his prospects without it. One is not allowed to justify differences in income or organizational powers on the ground that the disadvantages of those in one position are outweighed by the greater advantages of those in another. Much less can infringements of liberty be counterbalanced in this way. Applied to the basic structure, the principle of utility would have us maximize the sum of expectations of representative men (weighted by the number of persons they represent, on the classical view); and this would permit us to compensate for the losses of some by the gains of others. Instead, the two principles require that everyone benefit from economic and social inequalities. . . .

## THE TENDENCY TO EQUALITY

I wish to conclude this discussion of the two principles by explaining the sense in which they express an egalitarian conception of justice. Also I should like to forestall the objection to the principle of fair opportunity that it leads to a callous meritocratic society. In order to prepare the way for doing this, I note several aspects of the conception of justice that I have set out.

First we may observe that the difference principle gives some weight to the considerations singled out by the principle of redress. This is the principle that undeserved inequalities call for redress; and since inequalities of birth and natural endowment are undeserved, these inequalities are to be somehow compensated for. Thus the principle holds that in order to treat all persons equally, to provide genuine equality of opportunity, society must give more attention to those with fewer native assets and to those born into the less favorable social positions. The idea is to redress the bias of contingencies in the direction of equality. In pursuit of this principle greater resources might be spent on the education of the less rather than the more intelligent, at least over a certain time of life, say the earlier years of school.

Now the principle of redress has not to my knowledge been proposed as the sole criterion of justice, as the single aim of the social order. It is plausible as most such principles are only as a prima facie principle, one that is to be weighed in the balance with others. For example, we are to weigh it against the principle to improve the average standard of life, or to advance the common good. But whatever other principles we hold, the claims of redress are to be taken into account. It is thought to represent one of the elements in our conception of justice. Now the difference principle is not of course the principle of redress. It does not require society to try to even out handicaps as if all were expected to compete on a fair basis in the same race. But the difference principle would allocate resources in education, say, so as to improve the long-term expectation of the least favored. If this

end is attained by giving more attention to the better endowed, it is permissible; otherwise not. And in making this decision, the value of education should not be assessed only in terms of economic efficiency and social welfare. Equally if not more important is the role of education in enabling a person to enjoy the culture of his society and to take part in its affairs, and in this way to provide for each individual a secure sense of his own worth.

Thus although the difference principle is not the same as that of redress, it does achieve some of the intent of the latter principle. It transforms the aims of the basic structure so that the total scheme of institutions no longer emphasizes social efficiency and technocratic values. . . .

. . . The natural distribution is neither just nor unjust; nor is it unjust that men are born into society at some particular position. These are simply natural facts. What is just and unjust is the way that institutions deal with these facts. Aristocratic and caste societies are unjust because they make these contingencies the ascriptive basis for belonging to more or less enclosed and privileged social classes. The basic structure of these societies incorporates the arbitrariness found in nature. But there is no necessity for men to resign themselves to these contingencies. The social system is not an unchangeable order beyond human control but a pattern of human action. In justice as fairness men agree to share one another's fate. In designing institutions they undertake to avail themselves of the accidents of nature and social circumstance only when doing so is for the common benefit. The two principles are a fair way of meeting the arbitrariness of fortune; and while no doubt imperfect in other ways, the institutions which satisfy these principles are just. . . .

There is a natural inclination to object that those better situated deserve their greater advantages whether or not they are to the benefit of others. At this point it is necessary to be clear about the notion of desert. It is perfectly true that given a just system of co-operation as a scheme of public rules and the expectations set up by it, those who, with the prospect of improving their condition, have done what the system announces that it will reward are entitled to their advantages. In this sense the more fortunate have a claim to their better situation; their claims are legitimate expectations established by social institutions, and the community is obligated to meet them. But this sense of desert presupposes the existence of the cooperative scheme; it is irrelevant to the question whether in the first place the scheme is to be designed in accordance with the difference principle or some other criterion.

Perhaps some will think that the person with greater natural endowments deserves those assets and the superior character that made their development possible. Because he is more worthy in this sense, he deserves the greater advantages that he could achieve with them. This view, however, is surely incorrect. It seems to be one of the fixed points of our considered judgments that no one deserves his place in the distribution of native endowments, any more than one deserves one's initial starting place in society. The assertion that a man deserves the superior character that enables him to make the effort to cultivate his abilities is equally problematic, for his character depends in large part upon fortunate family and social circumstances for which he can claim no credit. The notion of desert seems not to apply to these cases. Thus the more advantaged representative man cannot say that he deserves and therefore has a right to a scheme of co-operation in which he is permitted to acquire benefits in ways that do not contribute to the welfare of others. There is no basis for his

making this claim. From the standpoint of common sense, then, the difference principle appears to be acceptable both to the more advantaged and to the less advantaged individual. . . .

## BACKGROUND INSTITUTIONS FOR DISTRIBUTIVE JUSTICE

The main problem of distributive justice is the choice of a social system. The principles of justice apply to the basic structure and regulate how its major institutions are combined into one scheme. Now, as we have seen, the idea of justice as fairness is to use the notion of pure procedural justice to handle the contingencies of particular situations. The social system is to be designed so that the resulting distribution is just however things turn out. To achieve this end it is necessary to get the social and economic process within the surroundings of suitable political and legal institutions. Without an appropriate scheme of these background institutions the outcome of the distributive process will not be just. Background fairness is lacking. I shall give a brief description of these supporting institutions as they might exist in a properly organized democratic state that allows private ownership of capital and natural resources. . . .

In establishing these background institutions the government may be thought of as divided into four branches.[1] Each branch consists of various agencies, or activities thereof, charged with preserving certain social and economic conditions. These divisions do not overlap with the usual organization of government but are to be understood as different functions. The allocation branch, for example, is to keep the price system workably competitive and to prevent the formation of unreasonable market power. Such power does not exist as long as markets cannot be made more competitive consistent with the requirements of efficiency and the facts of geography and the preferences of households. The allocation branch is also charged with identifying and correcting, say by suitable taxes and subsidies and by changes in the definition of property rights, the more obvious departures from efficiency caused by the failure of prices to measure accurately social benefits and costs. To this end suitable taxes and subsidies may be used, or the scope and definition of property rights may be revised. The stabilization branch, on the other hand, strives to bring about reasonably full employment in the sense that those who want work can find it and the free choice of occupation and the deployment of finance are supported by strong effective demand. These two branches together are to maintain the efficiency of the market economy generally.

The social minimum is the responsibility of the transfer branch. . . . The essential idea is that the workings of this branch take needs into account and assign them an appropriate weight with respect to other claims. A competitive price system gives no consideration to needs and therefore it cannot be the sole device of distribution. There must be a division of labor between the parts of the social system in answering to the common sense precepts of justice. Different institutions meet different claims. Competitive markets properly regulated secure free choice of occupation and lead to an efficient use of resources and allocation of commodities to households. They set a weight on the conventional precepts associated with wages and earnings, whereas a transfer branch guarantees a certain level of well-being and honors the claims of need. . . .

It is clear that the justice of distributive shares depends on the background institutions and how they allocate total income, wages and other income plus transfers. There is with reason strong objection to the competitive determination of total income, since this ignores the claims of need and an appropriate standard of life. From the standpoint of the legislative stage it is rational to insure oneself and one's descendants against these contingencies of the market. Indeed, the difference principle presumably requires this. But once a suitable minimum is provided by transfers, it may be perfectly fair that the rest of total income be settled by the price system, assuming that it is moderately efficient and free from monopolistic restrictions, and unreasonable externalities have been eliminated. Moreover, this way of dealing with the claims of need would appear to be more effective than trying to regulate income by minimum wage standards, and the like. It is better to assign to each branch only such tasks as are compatible with one another. Since the market is not suited to answer the claims of need, these should be met by a separate arrangement. Whether the principles of justice are satisfied, then, turns on whether the total income of the least advantaged (wages plus transfers) is such as to maximize their long-run expectations (consistent with the constraints of equal liberty and fair equality of opportunity).

Finally, there is a distribution branch. Its task is to preserve an approximate justice in distributive shares by means of taxation and the necessary adjustments in the rights of property. Two aspects of this branch may be distinguished. First of all, it imposes a number of inheritance and gift taxes, and sets restrictions on the rights of bequest. The purpose of these levies and regulations is not to raise revenue (release resources to government) but gradually and continually to correct the distribution of wealth and to prevent concentrations of power detrimental to the fair value of political liberty and fair equality of opportunity. For example, the progressive principle might be applied at the beneficiary's end.[2] Doing this would encourage the wide dispersal of property which is a necessary condition, it seems, if the fair value of the equal liberties is to be maintained.

## NOTES

1. For the idea of branches of government, see R. A. Musgrave, *The Theory of Public Finance* (New York: McGraw-Hill, 1959), chap. 1.
2. See Meade, *Efficiency, Equality and the Ownership of Property* , pp. 56ff.

# The Entitlement Theory

*Robert Nozick*

The term *distributive justice* is not a neutral one. Hearing the term "distribution," most people presume that some thing or mechanism uses some principle or criterion to give out a supply of things. Into this process of distributing shares some error may have crept. So it is an open question, at least, whether *re*distribution should take place; whether we should do again what has already been done once, though poorly. However, we are not in the position of children who have been given portions of pie by someone who now makes last-minute adjustments to rectify careless cutting. There is no *central* distribution, no person or group entitled to control all the resources, jointly deciding how they are to be doled out. What each person gets, he gets from others who give to him in exchange for something, or as a gift. In a free society, diverse persons control different resources, and new holdings arise out of the voluntary exchanges and actions of persons. . . .

The subject of justice in holdings consists of three major topics. The first is the *original acquisition of holdings*, the appropriation of unheld things. This includes the issues of how unheld things may come to be held, the process, or processes, by which unheld things may come to be held, the things that may come to be held by these processes, the extent of what comes to be held by a particular person, and so on. We shall refer to the complicated truth about this topic, which we shall not formulate here, as the principle of justice in acquisition. The second topic concerns the *transfer of holdings* from one person to another. By what processes may a person transfer holdings to another? How may a person acquire a holding from another who holds it? Under this topic come general descriptions of voluntary exchange, and gift and (on the other hand) fraud, as well as reference to particular conventional details fixed upon in a given society. The complicated truth about this subject (with placeholders for conventional details) we shall call the principle of justice in transfer. (And we shall suppose it also includes principles governing how a person may divest himself of a holding, passing it into an unheld state.)

If the world were wholly just, the following inductive definition would exhaustively cover the subject of justice in holdings.

---

From Robert Nozick, *Anarchy, State, and Utopia* (New York: Basic Books, Inc., Publishers, 1974), pp. 149–54, 156–57, 159–63, 168, 174–75, 178–79, 182. Copyright © 1974 by Basic Books, Inc., Publishers, New York. Reprinted by permission of Basic Books, Inc., a member of Perseus Books, L.L.C.

1. A person who acquires a holding in accordance with the principle of justice in acquisition is entitled to that holding.
2. A person who acquires a holding in accordance with the principle of justice in transfer, from someone else entitled to the holding, is entitled to the holding.
3. No one is entitled to a holding except by (repeated) applications of 1 and 2.

The complete principle of distributive justice would say simply that a distribution is just if everyone is entitled to the holdings they possess under the distribution. . . .

Not all actual situations are generated in accordance with the two principles of justice in holdings: the principle of justice in acquisition and the principle of justice in transfer. Some people steal from others, or defraud them, or enslave them, seizing their product and preventing them from living as they choose, or forcibly exclude others from competing in exchanges. None of these are permissible modes of transition from one situation to another. And some persons acquire holdings by means not sanctioned by the principle of justice in acquisition. The existence of past injustice (previous violations of the first two principles of justice in holdings) raises the third major topic under justice in holdings: the rectification of injustice in holdings. If past injustice has shaped present holdings in various ways, some identifiable and some not, what now, if anything, ought to be done to rectify these injustices? . . .

## HISTORICAL PRINCIPLES AND END-RESULT PRINCIPLES

The general outlines of the entitlement theory illuminate the nature and defects of other conceptions of distributive justice. The entitlement theory of justice in distribution is *historical*; whether a distribution is just depends upon how it came about. In contrast, *current time-slice principles* of justice hold that the justice of a distribution is determined by how things are distributed (who has what) as judged by some *structural* principle(s) of just distribution. A utilitarian who judges between any two distributions by seeing which has the greater sum of utility and, if the sums tie, applies some fixed equality criterion to choose the more equal distribution, would hold a current time-slice principle of justice. As would someone who had a fixed schedule of trade-offs between the sum of happiness and equality. According to a current time-slice principle, all that needs to be looked at, in judging the justice of a distribution, is who ends up with what; in comparing any two distributions one need look only at the matrix presenting the distributions. No further information need be fed into a principle of justice. It is a consequence of such principles of justice that any two structurally identical distributions are equally just. . . .

Most persons do not accept current time-slice principles as constituting the whole story about distributive shares. They think it relevant in assessing the justice of a situation to consider not only the distribution it embodies, but also how that distribution came about. If some persons are in prison for murder or war crimes, we do not say that to assess the justice of the distribution in the society we must look only at what this person has, and that person has, and that person has, . . . at the current time. We think it relevant to ask whether someone did something so that he deserved to be punished, *deserved* to have a lower share. . . .

## PATTERNING

. . . Almost every suggested principle of distributive justice is patterned: to each according to his moral merit, or needs, or marginal product, or how hard he tries, or the weighted sum of the foregoing, and so on. The principle of entitlement we have sketched is *not* patterned. There is no one natural dimension or weighted sum or combination of a small number of natural dimensions that yields the distributions generated in accordance with the principle of entitlement. The set of holdings that results when some persons receive their marginal products, others win at gambling, others receive a share of their mate's income, others receive gifts from foundations, others receive interest on loans, others receive gifts from admirers, others receive returns on investment, others make for themselves much of what they have, others find things, and so on, will not be patterned. . . .

To think that the task of a theory of distributive justice is to fill in the blank in "to each according to his _____" is to be predisposed to search for a pattern; and the separate treatment of "from each according to his _____" treats production and distribution as two separate and independent issues. On an entitlement view these are *not* two separate questions. Whoever makes something, having bought or contracted for all other held resources used in the process (transferring some of his holdings for these cooperating factors), is entitled to it. . . .

So entrenched are maxims of the usual form that perhaps we should present the entitlement conception as a competitor. Ignoring acquisition and rectification, we might say:

> From each according to what he chooses to do, to each according to what he makes for himself (perhaps with the contracted aid of others) and what others choose to do for him and choose to give him of what they've been given previously (under this maxim) and haven't yet expended or transferred.

This, the discerning reader will have noticed, has its defects as a slogan. So as a summary and great simplification (and not as a maxim with any independent meaning) we have:

*From each as they choose, to each as they are chosen.*

## HOW LIBERTY UPSETS PATTERNS

It is not clear how those holding alternative conceptions of distributive justice can reject the entitlement conception of justice in holdings. For suppose a distribution favored by one of these nonentitlement conceptions is realized. Let us suppose it is your favorite one and let us call this distribution $D_1$; perhaps everyone has an equal share, perhaps shares vary in accordance with some dimension you treasure. Now suppose that Wilt Chamberlain is greatly in demand by basketball teams, being a great gate attraction. (Also suppose contracts run only for a year, with players being free agents). He signs the following sort of contract with a team: In each home game, 25 cents from the price of each ticket of admission goes to him. (We ignore the question of whether he is "gouging" the owners, letting them look out for themselves.) The season starts, and people cheerfully attend his team's games; they buy their tickets, each time dropping a separate 25 cents of their admission price into a special box with Chamberlain's name on it. They are excited about seeing him play; it is worth the total admission price to them. Let us suppose that in one season 1 million persons attend his home games, and Wilt Chamberlain winds up with $250,000, a much larger sum than the average income and larger even than anyone else has. Is he entitled to this income? Is this new distribution $D_2$, unjust? If so, why? There is *no* question about whether each of the people was entitled to the control over the resources they held in $D_1$; because that was the distribution (your favorite) that (for the purposes of argument) we assumed was acceptable. Each of these persons *chose* to give 25 cents of their money to Chamberlain. They could have spent it on going to the movies, or on candy bars, or on copies of *Dissent* magazine, or of *Monthly Review*. But they all, at least 1 million of them, converged on giving it to Wilt Chamberlain in exchange for watching him play basketball. If $D_1$ was a just distribution, and people voluntarily moved from it to $D_2$, transferring parts of their shares they were given under $D_1$ (what was it for if not to do something with?), isn't $D_2$ also just? If the people were entitled to dispose of the resources to which they were entitled (under $D_1$) didn't this include their being entitled to give it to, or exchange it with, Wilt Chamberlain? Can anyone else complain on grounds of justice? Each other person already has his legitimate share under $D_1$. Under $D_1$, there is nothing that anyone has that anyone else has a claim of justice against. After someone transfers something to Wilt Chamberlain, third parties *still* have their legitimate shares; *their* shares are not changed. By what process could such a transfer among two persons give a rise to a legitimate claim of distributive justice on a portion of what was transferred, by a third party who had no claim of justice on any holding of the others *before* the transfer? To cut off objections irrelevant here, we might imagine the exchanges occurring in a socialist society, after hours. After playing whatever basketball he does in his daily work, or doing whatever other daily work he does, Wilt Chamberlain decides to put in *overtime* to earn additional money. (First his work quota is set; he works time over that.) Or imagine it is a skilled juggler people like to see, who puts on shows after hours. . . .

The general point illustrated by the Wilt Chamberlain example is that no end-state principle or distributional patterned principle of justice can be continuously realized without continuous interference with people's lives. Any favored pattern would be transformed into one unfavored by the principle, by people choosing to act in various ways; for example, by people exchanging goods and services with other people, or giving things to other people, things the transferrers are entitled to under the favored distributional pattern. To maintain a pattern one must either continually interfere to stop people from transferring resources as they wish to, or continually (or periodically) interfere to take from some person's resources that others for some reason chose to transfer to them. . . .

Patterned principles of distributive justice necessitate *re*distributive activities. The likelihood is small that any actual freely arrived-at set of holdings fits a given pattern; and the likelihood is nil that it will continue to fit the pattern as people exchange and give. From the point of view of an entitlement theory, redistribution is a serious matter indeed, involving, as it does, the violation of people's rights. (An exception is those takings that fall under the principle of the rectification of injustices.) . . .

## LOCKE'S THEORY OF ACQUISITION

. . . [Let us] introduce an additional bit of complexity into the structure of the entitlement theory. This is best approached by considering Locke's attempt to specify a principle of justice in acquisition. Locke views property rights in an unowned object as originating through someone's mixing his labor with it. This gives rise to many questions. What are the boundaries of what labor is mixed with? If a private astronaut clears a place on Mars, has he mixed his labor with (so that he comes to own) the whole planet, the whole uninhabited universe, or just a particular plot? Which plot does an act bring under ownership? . . .

Locke's proviso that there be "enough and as good left in common for others" is meant to ensure that the situation of others is not worsened. . . .

. . . I assume that any adequate theory of justice in acquisition will contain a proviso similar to [Locke's]. . . .

I believe that the free operation of a market system will not actually run afoul of the Lockean proviso. . . . If this is correct, the proviso will not . . . provide a significant opportunity for future state action.

# Rich and Poor

*Peter Singer*

One way of making sense of the nonconsequentialist view of responsibility is by basing it on a theory of rights of the kind proposed by John Locke or, more recently, Robert Nozick. If everyone has a right to life, and this right is a right *against* others who might threaten my life, but not a right *to* assistance from others when my life is in danger, then we can understand the feeling that we are responsible for acting to kill but not for omitting to save. The former violates the rights of others, the latter does not.

Should we accept such a theory of rights? If we build up our theory of rights by imagining, as Locke and Nozick do, individuals living independently from each other in a "state of nature," it may seem natural to adopt a conception of rights in which as long as each leaves the other alone, no rights are violated. I might, on this view, quite properly have maintained my independent existence if I had wished to do so. So if I do not make you any worse off than you would have been if I had had nothing at all to do with you, how can I have violated your rights? But why start from such an unhistorical, abstract and ultimately inexplicable idea as an independent individual? We now know that our ancestors were social beings long before they were human beings, and could not have developed the abilities and capacities of human beings if they had not been social beings first. In any case we are not, now, isolated individuals. If we consider people living together in a community, it is less easy to assume that rights must be restricted to rights against interference. We might, instead, adopt the view that taking rights to life seriously is incompatible with standing by and watching people die when one could easily save them. . . .

## THE OBLIGATION TO ASSIST

### The Argument for an Obligation to Assist

The path from the library at my university to the Humanities lecture theatre passes a shallow ornamental pond. Suppose that on my way to give a lecture I notice that a small child has fallen in and is in danger of drowning. Would anyone deny that I ought to wade in and pull the child out? This will mean getting my clothes muddy, and either cancelling my lecture or delaying it until I can find something dry to change into; but compared with the avoidable death of a child this is insignificant.

A plausible principle that would support the judgment that I ought to pull the child out is this: if it is in our power to prevent something very bad happening, without thereby sacrificing anything of comparable moral significance, we ought to do it. This principle seems uncontroversial. It will obviously win the assent of consequentialists; but nonconsequentialists should accept it too, because the injunction to prevent what is bad applies only when nothing comparably significant is at stake. Thus the principle cannot lead to the kinds of actions of which nonconsequentialists strongly disapprove—serious violations of individual rights, injustice, broken promises, and so on. If a nonconsequentialist regards any of these as comparable in moral significance to the bad thing that is to be prevented, he will automatically regard the principle as not applying in those cases in which the bad thing can only be prevented by violating rights, doing injustice, breaking promises, or whatever else is at stake.

From Peter Singer, "Rich and Poor," in *Practical Ethics* (New York: Cambridge University Press, 1979), pp. 166, 168–79. Reprinted with permission of the publisher.

Most nonconsequentialists hold that we ought to prevent what is bad and promote what is good. Their dispute with consequentialists lies in their insistence that this is not the sole ultimate ethical principle: that it is *an* ethical principle is not denied by any plausible ethical theory.

Nevertheless the uncontroversial appearance of the principle that we ought to prevent what is bad when we can do so without sacrificing anything of comparable moral significance is deceptive. If it were taken seriously and acted upon, our lives and our world would be fundamentally changed. For the principle applies, not just to rare situations in which one can save a child from a pond, but to the everyday situations in which we can assist those living in absolute poverty. In saying this I assume that absolute poverty, with its hunger and malnutrition, lack of shelter, illiteracy, disease, high infant mortality and low life expectancy, is a bad thing. And I assume that it is within the power of the affluent to reduce absolute poverty, without sacrificing anything of comparable moral significance. If these two assumptions and the principle we have been discussing are correct, we have an obligation to help those in absolute poverty which is no less strong than our obligation to rescue a drowning child from a pond. Not to help would be wrong, whether or not it is intrinsically equivalent to killing. Helping is not, as conventionally thought, a charitable act which it is praiseworthy to do, but not wrong to omit; it is something that everyone ought to do.

This is the argument for an obligation to assist. Set out more formally, it would look like this.

**First premise:** If we can prevent something bad without sacrificing anything of comparable significance, we ought to do it.
**Second premise:** Absolute poverty is bad.
**Third premise:** There is some absolute poverty we can prevent without sacrificing anything of comparable moral significance.

**Conclusion:** We ought to prevent some absolute poverty.

The first premise is the substantive moral premise on which the argument rests, and I have tried to show that it can be accepted by people who hold a variety of ethical positions.

The second premise is unlikely to be challenged. Absolute poverty is, as [Robert] McNamara put in, "beneath any reasonable definition of human decency" and it would be hard to find a plausible ethical view which did not regard it as a bad thing.

The third premise is more controversial, even though it is cautiously framed. It claims only that some absolute poverty can be prevented without the sacrifice of anything of comparable moral significance. It thus avoids the objection that any aid I can give is just "drops in the ocean" for the point is not whether my personal contribution will make any noticeable impression on world poverty as a whole (of course it won't) but whether it will prevent some poverty. This is all the argument needs to sustain its conclusion, since the second premise says that any absolute poverty is bad, and not merely the total amount of absolute poverty. If without sacrificing anything of comparable moral significance we can provide just one family with the means to raise itself out of absolute poverty, the third premise is vindicated.

I have left the notion of moral significance unexamined in order to show that the argument does not depend on any specific values or ethical principles. I think the third premise is true for most people living in industrialized nations, on any defensible view of what is morally significant. Our affluence means that we have income we can dispose of without giving up the basic necessities of life, and we can use this income to reduce absolute poverty. Just how much we will think ourselves obliged to give up will depend on what we consider to be of comparable moral significance to the poverty we could prevent: color television, stylish clothes, expensive dinners, a sophisticated stereo system, overseas holidays, a (second?) car, a larger house, private schools for our children. . . . For a utilitarian, none of these is likely to be of comparable significance to the reduction of absolute poverty; and those who are not utilitarians surely must, if they subscribe to the principle of universalizability, accept that at least *some* of these things are of far less moral significance than the absolute poverty that could be prevented by the money they cost. So the third premise seems to be true on any plausible ethical view—although the precise amount of absolute poverty that can be prevented before anything of moral significance is sacrificed will vary according to the ethical view one accepts.

### Objections to the Argument

*Taking Care of Our Own.* Anyone who has worked to increase overseas aid will have come across the argument that we should look after those near us, our families and then the poor in our own country, before we think about poverty in distant places.

No doubt we do instinctively prefer to help those who are close to us. Few could stand by and watch a child drown; many can ignore a famine in Africa. But the question is not what we usually do, but what we ought to do, and it is difficult to see any sound moral justification for the view that distance, or community membership, makes a crucial difference to our obligations.

Consider, for instance, racial affinities. Should whites help poor whites before helping poor blacks? Most of us would reject such a suggestion out of hand, [by appeal to] the principle of equal consideration of interests: people's needs for food has nothing to do with their race, and if blacks need food more than whites, it would be a violation of the principle of equal consideration to give preference to whites.

The same point applies to citizenship or nationhood. Every affluent nation has some relatively poor citizens, but absolute poverty is limited largely to the poor nations. Those living on the streets of Calcutta, or in a drought-stricken region of the Sahel, are experiencing poverty unknown in the West. Under these circumstances it would be wrong to decide that only those fortunate enough to be citizens of our own community will share our abundance.

We feel obligations of kinship more strongly than those of citizenship. Which parents could give away their last bowl of rice if their own children were starving? To do so would seem unnatural, contrary to our nature as biologically evolved beings—although whether it would be wrong is another question altogether. In any case, we are not faced with that situation, but with one in which our own children are well fed, well clothed, well educated, and would now like new bikes, a stereo set, or their own car. In these circumstances any special obligations we might have to our children have been fulfilled, and the needs of strangers make a stronger claim upon us.

The element of truth in the view that we should first take care of our own lies in the advantage of a recognized system of responsibilities. When families and local communities look after their own poorer members, ties of affection and personal relationships achieve ends that would otherwise require a large, impersonal bureaucracy. Hence it would be absurd to propose that from now on we all regard ourselves as equally responsible for the welfare of everyone in the world; but the argument for an obligation to assist does not propose that. It applies only when some are in absolute poverty, and others can help without sacrificing anything of comparable moral significance. To allow one's own kin to sink into absolute poverty would be to sacrifice something of comparable significance; and before that point had been reached, the breakdown of the system of family and community responsibility would be a factor to weigh the balance in favor of a small degree of preference for family and community. This small degree of preference is, however, decisively outweighed by existing discrepancies in wealth and property.

*Property Rights.* Do people have a right to private property, a right which contradicts the view that they are under an obligation to give some of their wealth away to those in absolute poverty? According to some theories of rights (for instance, Robert Nozick's) provided one has acquired one's property without the use of unjust means like force and fraud, one may be entitled to enormous wealth while others starve. This individualistic conception of rights is in contrast to other views, like the early Christian doctrine to be found in the works of Thomas Aquinas, which holds that since property exists for the satisfaction of human needs, "whatever a man has in superabundance is owed, of natural right, to the poor for their sustenance." A socialist would also, of course, see wealth as belonging to the community rather than the individual, while utilitarians, whether socialist or not, would be prepared to override property rights to prevent great evils.

Does the argument for an obligation to assist others therefore presuppose one of these other theories of property rights, and not an individualistic theory like Nozick's? Not necessarily. A theory of property rights can insist on our *right* to retain wealth without pronouncing on whether the rich *ought* to give to the poor. Nozick, for example, rejects the use of compulsory means like taxation to redistribute income, but suggests that we can achieve the ends we deem morally desirable by voluntary means. So Nozick would reject the claim that rich people have an "obligation" to give to the poor, in so far as this implies that the poor have a right to our aid, but might accept that giving is something we

ought to do and failure to give, though within one's rights, is wrong—for rights is not all there is to ethics.

The argument for an obligation to assist can survive, with only minor modifications, even if we accept an individualistic theory of property rights. In any case, however, I do not think we should accept such a theory. It leaves too much to chance to be an acceptable ethical view. For instance, those whose forefathers happened to inhabit some sandy wastes around the Persian Gulf are now fabulously wealthy, because oil lay under those sands; while those whose forefathers settled on better land south of the Sahara live in absolute poverty, because of drought and bad harvests. Can this distribution be acceptable from an impartial point of view? If we imagine ourselves about to begin life as a citizen of either Kuwait or Chad—but we do not know which—would we accept the principle that citizens of Kuwait are under no obligation to assist people living in Chad?

*Population and the Ethics of Triage.* Perhaps the most serious objection to the argument that we have an obligation to assist is that since the major cause of absolute poverty is overpopulation, helping those now in poverty will only ensure that yet more people are born to live in poverty in the future.

In its most extreme form, this objection is taken to show that we should adopt a policy of "triage." The term comes from medical policies adopted in wartime. With too few doctors to cope with all the casualties, the wounded were divided into three categories: those who would probably survive without medical assistance, those who might survive if they received assistance, but otherwise probably would not, and those who even with medical assistance probably would not survive. Only those in the middle category were given medical assistance. The idea, of course, was to use limited medical resources as effectively as possible. For those in the first category, medical treatment was not strictly necessary; for those in the third category, it was likely to be useless. It has been suggested that we should apply the same policies to countries, according to their prospects of becoming self-sustaining. We would not aid countries which even without our help will soon be able to feed their populations. We would not aid countries which, even with our help, will not be able to limit their population to a level they can feed. We would aid those countries where our help might make the difference between success and failure in bringing food and population into balance.

Advocates of this theory are understandably reluctant to give a complete list of the countries they would place into the 'hopeless' category; but Bangladesh is often cited as an example. Adopting the policy of triage would, then, mean cutting off assistance to Bangladesh and allowing famine, disease and natural disasters to reduce the population of that country (now around 80 million) to the level at which it can provide adequately for all.

In support of this view Garrett Hardin has offered a metaphor: we in the rich nations are like the occupants of a crowded lifeboat adrift in a sea full of drowning people. If we try to save the drowning by bringing them aboard our boat will be overloaded and we shall all drown. Since it is better that some survive than none, we should leave the others to drown. In the world today, according to Hardin, "lifeboat ethics" apply. The rich should leave the poor to starve, for otherwise the poor will drag the rich down with them. . . .

Anyone whose initial reaction to triage was not one of repugnance would be an unpleasant sort of person. Yet initial reactions based on strong feelings are not always reliable guides. Advocates of triage are rightly concerned with the long-term consequences of our actions. They say that helping the poor

and starving now merely ensures more poor and starving in the future. When our capacity to help is finally unable to cope—as one day it must be—the suffering will be greater than it would be if we stopped helping now. If this is correct, there is nothing we can do to prevent absolute starvation and poverty, in the long run, and so we have no obligation to assist. Nor does it seem reasonable to hold that under these circumstances people have a right to our assistance. If we do accept such a right, irrespective of the consequences, we are saying that, in Hardin's metaphor, we would continue to haul the drowning into our lifeboat until the boat sank and we all drowned.

If triage is to be rejected it must be tackled on its own ground, within the framework of consequentialist ethics. Here it is vulnerable. Any consequentialist ethics must take probability of outcome into account. A course of action that will certainly produce some benefit is to be preferred to an alternative course that may lead to a slightly larger benefit, but is equally likely to result in no benefit at all. Only if the greater magnitude of the uncertain benefit outweighs its uncertainty should we choose it. Better one certain unit of benefit than a 10 percent chance of 5 units; but better a 50 percent chance of 3 units than a single certain unit. The same principle applies when are we trying to avoid evils.

The policy of triage involves a certain, very great evil: population control by famine and disease. Tens of millions would die slowly. Hundreds of millions would continue to live in absolute poverty, at the very margin of existence. Against this prospect, advocates of the policy place a possible evil which is greater still: the same process of famine and disease, taking place in, say, 50 years time, when the world's population may be three times its present level, and the number who will die from famine, or struggle on in absolute poverty, will be that much greater. The question is: How probable is this forecast that continued assistance now will lead to greater disasters in the future?

Forecasts of population growth are notoriously fallible, and theories about the factors which affect it remain speculative. One theory, at least as plausible as any other, is that countries pass through a "demographic transition" as their standard of living rises. When people are very poor and have no access to modern medicine their fertility is high, but population is kept in check by high death rates. The introduction of sanitation, modern medical techniques and other improvements reduces the death rate, but initially has little effect on the birth rate. Then population grows rapidly. Most poor countries are now in this phase. If standards of living continue to rise, however, couples begin to realize that to have the same number of children surviving to maturity as in the past, they do not need to give birth to as many children as their parents did. The need for children to provide economic support in old age diminishes. Improved education and the emancipation and employment of women also reduce the birthrate, and so population growth begins to level off. Most rich nations have reached this stage, and their populations are growing only very slowly.

If this theory is right, there is an alternative to the disasters accepted as inevitable by supporters of triage. We can assist poor countries to raise the living standards of the poorest members of their population. We can encourage the governments of these countries to enact land reform measures, improve education, and liberate women from a purely childbearing role. We can also help other countries to make contraception and sterilization widely available. There is a fair chance that these measures will hasten the onset of the demographic transition and bring population growth down to a manageable level. Success cannot be guaranteed; but the evidence that improved economic security and education reduce population growth is strong enough to make triage ethically unacceptable. We cannot allow millions to die from starvation and disease when there is a reasonable probability that population can be brought under control without such horrors.

Population growth is therefore not a reason against giving overseas aid, although it should make us think about the kind of aid to give. Instead of food handouts, it may be better to give aid that hastens the demographic transition. This may mean agricultural assistance for the rural poor, or assistance with education, or the provision of contraceptive services. Whatever kind of aid proves most effective in specific circumstances, the obligation to assist is not reduced.

One awkward question remains. What should we do about a poor and already overpopulated country which, for religious or nationalistic reasons, restricts the use of contraceptives and refuses to slow its population growth? Should we nevertheless offer development assistance? Or should we make our offer conditional on effective steps being taken to reduce the birthrate? To the latter course, some would object that putting conditions on aid is an attempt to impose our own ideas on independent sovereign nations. So it is—but is this imposition unjustifiable? If the argument for an obligation to assist is sound, we have an obligation to reduce absolute poverty; but we have no obligation to make sacrifices that, to the best of our knowledge, have no prospect of reducing poverty in the long run. Hence we have no obligation to assist countries whose governments have policies which will make our aid ineffective. This could be very harsh on poor citizens of these countries—for they may have no say in the government's policies—but we will help more people in the long run by using our resources where they are most effective.

COMPENSATION

# Do CEOs Get Paid Too Much?

*Jeffrey Moriarty*

America's corporate executives get paid huge sums of money. *BusinessWeek* estimates that, in 2003, CEOs of the 365 largest U.S. corporations were paid on average $8 million, 301 times as much as factory workers (Lavelle 2004).[1] CEOs' pay packages, including salary, bonus, and restricted stock and stock option grants, increased by 340 percent from 1991 to 2001, while workers' paychecks increased by only 36 percent (Byrne 2002). What, if anything, is wrong with this?

Although it has received a great deal of attention in management and economics journals and in the popular press, the topic of executive compensation has been virtually ignored by philosophers. As a result, its normative dimensions have been largely ignored. Organizational theorists and economists tend to be more interested in what the determinants of CEO pay *are* than in what they *should be*. What is needed, I suggest, is an general ethical framework for thinking about justice in pay. After elaborating this framework, I will argue that CEOs get paid too much.

## THREE VIEWS OF JUSTICE IN WAGES

To determine whether CEOs get paid too much, we first need to consider what, in general, makes a wage just. In this section, I will sketch three views of justice in wages, each of which is based on a widely recognized moral value. I do not claim that these are the only views of justice in wages possible. But the values from which they derive are the ones most frequently appealed to in the debates about

CEO pay. It is unlikely that any other view would be as attractive.

According to what I will call the "agreement view," just prices for goods are obtained through arm's-length negotiations between informed buyers and informed sellers. In our case, the good is the CEO's services, the seller is the CEO, and the buyer(s) is (are) the company's owner(s). Provided there are no imperfections (e.g., fraud, coercion) in the bargaining process, the agreement view says, the wage that comes out of it is just. Owners are free to do what they want with their money, and CEOs are free to do what they want with their services.

The "desert view" appeals to independent standards for justice in wages. It says that people deserve certain wages for performing certain jobs, whatever they might agree to accept for performing them. The wages people deserve may depend on facts about their jobs (e.g., their difficulty or degree of responsibility), people's performances in them (e.g., how much effort they expend, how much they contribute to the firm), or both. According to the desert view, the CEO should be paid $8 million per year if and only if he deserves to be paid $8 million per year.

What I will call the "utility view" conceives of wages not as rewards for past work, but as incentives for future work. The purpose of wages on this view is to maximize firm wealth by attracting, retaining, and motivating talented workers. If, in our case, the CEO's position is not compensated adequately, few talented candidates will apply or remain on the job for long, and the company as a whole will suffer. On the other hand, an expensive CEO can easily earn his keep through even small increases in the price of the company's stock. According to the utility view, then, a compensation package of $8 million per year is just if and only if it maximizes firm wealth by attracting, retaining, and optimally motivating a talented CEO.[2]

Too often in discussions of executive compensation, the separateness of these views is overlooked. But if we do not distinguish among them, we run the risk of talking past each other. P's belief that CEOs do not deserve, by any standard of deservingness, $8 million per year may lead him to the conclusion that CEOs make too much money. Q's belief that the pay negotiations between CEOs and owners are fair may lead him to conclusion that CEOs do not make too much money. In fact, both P and Q may agree that CEOs do not deserve $8 million per year and that the pay negotiations between CEOs and owners are fair. They may simply disagree about what is morally more important: deserts or agreements. Understanding this, of course, does not solve the debate. But it does help to clarify what it might be about.

To solve the debate about CEO pay, we must determine which view of justice in wages is correct. It is unlikely (for reasons given below) that agreement theorists, desert theorists, and utility theorists will all come to the same conclusion about how much CEOs should be paid. I will not try to do this here. There is deep disagreement about the relative importance of these values. A full defense of one of them against the others is beyond the scope of this paper. Fortunately, it is not necessary to determine which view of justice in wages is correct to draw *any* conclusions about CEO pay. Below I will argue that its current level cannot be justified by the agreement view, the desert view, or the utility view. No matter which one is correct, CEOs get paid too much. It is possible, as I indicated, that new theories of justice in wages will be developed. But the theories

we have sketched are based on the most common moral values, and it is not at all clear what these new theories would look like. Until it is, we have reason to believe that the current level of CEO pay cannot be justified *simpliciter*.

## THE AGREEMENT VIEW

According to this view, a just price for the CEO's services is one that results from an arm's-length negotiation between an informed CEO and informed owners. I will show that these negotiations are not, in general, conducted at arm's length. If they were, CEOs would be paid on average less than $8 million per year.[3]

The problem occurs mainly on the "buy" side of the equation, so we will focus our attention there. Traditionally, shareholders are represented in negotiations with the CEO by a subset of the members of the company's board of directors. This may seem promising to those who would appeal to the agreement view to justify the current level of CEO compensation. Since directors are elected by shareholders, they might say, it is likely that the directors who negotiate with the CEO—those who form the board's "compensation committee"—are in fact independent and informed. If shareholders did not elect independent and informed directors, they would risk paying too much to an incompetent CEO, or too little to an exceptional one.

This hope is unfounded. It is well known that shareholders do not, in fact, elect directors in any meaningful way. When a seat on the board opens up, usually there is just one person who "runs" in the "election." Once a candidate is nominated, her election is a formality. The group that controls the nomination process, then, controls the board's membership. In most cases this is not the shareholders but the board itself, whose chairman in 84 percent of American firms is the

694       Social and Economic Justice

firm's CEO (Shivdasani & Yermack 1999). Although there has been a trend away from direct CEO involvement in the nominating process in recent years, most CEOs still wield considerable informal influence over it (Main, O'Reilly, and Wade 1995).

This is worrisome. Whereas shareholders may elect, out of apathy or ignorance, directors who are unfamiliar with the industry and friendly with the CEO, CEOs can encourage the appointment of such directors. Do they? The fact that CEOs who are appointed *before* the appointment of their compensation committee chairs are paid more, on average, than CEOs who are appointed *after* suggests that they do (Main et al. 1995). Examining the composition of boards of directors more carefully, we see that, in general, directors may be informed, but they are not independent.

Three factors compromise directors' independence from their CEOs. The first is gratitude. The board member's job is prestigious, lucrative, and undemanding. Directors of the 200 largest American corporations receive on average $179,000 for 20 days of work per year (Jaffe 2003). They may also be given life and medical insurance, retirement benefits, and the use of company property such as automobiles and vacation homes. In addition, there is the considerable "social capital" directors acquire in the form of connections with influential people. Thus getting an appointment to a board is like getting a large gift. This is problematic, for it is natural for gift-recipients to feel grateful to gift-givers. The larger the gift is, the more grateful, and more inclined to "return the favor," the gift-recipient will be. Since CEOs have a great deal of influence over who gets appointed to the board, the directors will feel grateful to him. To represent properly shareholders' interests, then, they will have to fight against this feeling. There is reason to believe they have not been successful. Recent research shows a positive correlation between director and CEO pay (Boyd 1994).[4]

Self-interest is the second factor compromising the independence of directors in pay negotiations with CEOs. To determine how much to pay their CEO, the board will usually find out how much CEOs of comparable firms are being paid. The more those CEOs make, the more the board will pay their CEO (Ezzamel and Watson 1998). The problem is that many boards have members who are CEOs of comparable firms (Main et al. 1995). This is good from the point of view of having knowledgeable directors. But CEO-directors have a self-interested reason to increase the pay of the CEO with whom they are negotiating. Suppose CEO A sits on CEO B's board, and A and B run comparable firms. The more pay A agrees to give to B, the more pay A himself will later receive. For, when it comes time to determine A's pay package, B's pay package will be used as one of the reference points.

The third factor is not a reason directors have to favor CEOs; it is the absence of a reason directors should have to favor shareholders. Since they are paying with their own money, shareholders have a powerful incentive not to overpay the CEO. The more they pay the CEO, the less they have for themselves. Directors, by contrast, are not paying with their own money. Although they are often given shares in the company as compensation, directors are rarely required to buy them. So their incentive not to overpay the CEO is less powerful. It might be wondered whether shareholders can make it more powerful by threatening to recall overly generous directors. They cannot. Shareholders in most firms lack this power. In fact, not only will directors have nothing to fear if they *do* overpay the CEO, they will have something to fear if they *do not*. Shareholders cannot recall generous directors, but CEOs can use their power to force them out.

Let me sum up. According to the agreement view, a wage of $8 million per year is just if and only if it results from an arm's-length negotiation between an informed CEO and an informed group of owners. We argued that these negotiations are not, in general, conducted at arm's length. It follows that $8 million per year is not a just (average) wage. Because the independence condition is violated in a way that favors the CEO, we can be confident that the just average wage on this view is less than $8 million per year. Speculation about how much less, however, would be premature. A different view of justice in wages may be correct, and it may justify the current level of CEO pay. In the next section I will examine the desert view.

## THE DESERT VIEW

A familiar complaint about CEO pay is that it has increased in years when firms have performed badly. This complaint is grounded in the desert view of justice in wages. It assumes that a CEO should get the wage he deserves, that the wage a CEO deserves is determined by his contribution to the firm, and that the proper measure of contribution is firm performance. If the firm performs worse in year two than in year one, the argument goes, the CEO deserves to make less, and therefore should make less, in year two than in year one. The agreement and utility views of justice in wages cannot account, except indirectly, for this intuition.[5]

Determining how much pay CEOs deserve involves us in two difficulties. The first is identifying the standard(s) for deservingness. Above I noted that economic contribution is often taken to be the basis of desert of wages. But a variety of others have been offered, including (i) the physical effort exerted by the worker, (ii) the amount of ability, skill, or training his job requires, (iii) its difficulty, stress, dangerousness, or unpleasantness, and (iv) its degree of responsibility or importance. Desert may be determined by one or several of these

factors. The second problem is connected to the first. Once we identify the desert base(s) for wages, then we must find a way of matching desert levels to pay levels. Suppose contribution is the basis of desert, and suppose, as a direct result of key decisions by the CEO, the firm's profits increase 20 percent in a year. We might think that the CEO's desert level increases by 20 percent and therefore that he deserves a 20 percent raise. But what should his initial salary have been? Without a way of matching desert levels to pay levels, we cannot answer this question. However, from the point of view of desert, the absolute amount of the CEO's pay raise matters as much as its percentage increase.

For the purposes of this paper, both of these problems may be avoided. The first questions our ability to identify the base(s) of desert. In response, I will assume, as most parties to the debate about CEO pay do, that the basis for desert of pay is contribution. Indeed, of all the desert bases mentioned above, this is the one most likely to justify the current level of CEO pay. The second questions our ability to identify what it is exactly that people deserve. In response, I will not argue that CEOs deserve to make less than $8 million per year *absolutely*. Instead, I will argue that they deserve to make less than $8 million per year *given that* their employees make on average $27,000 per year. CEOs are not 301 times as deserving as their employees.

Under the assumption that contribution is the sole desert base for pay, the CEO deserves to be paid 301 times what the average worker is paid if and only if his contribution is 301 times as valuable as the worker's. For every $1 in revenue the worker generates, the CEO must generate $301. If the worker generates $100,000 in a year, the CEO must generate $30.1 million. Does this happen?

Some will deny that this question can be answered. They will say that employees are not Robinson Crusoes, each at work on their own self-contained projects. Instead, many people work together on the same complex projects. As a result, it is difficult or impossible to tell where one person's contribution ends and another's begins.

This is not, of course, an objection that will be advanced by those who appeal to the desert view to justify the current level of CEO pay. They need a way to measure contribution accurately. If the stronger form of this objection is true, however, and we cannot tell how much each employee contributes to the firm, then we cannot tell how much each deserves to be paid. So this conclusion is not unwelcome from the point of view of this paper. But it is weak. A thoroughgoing skepticism about the accuracy of contribution measurements yields the conclusion that we *cannot tell* whether CEOs deserve to make 301 times as much as their employees, not that they *do not* deserve to make this much. As far as this view is concerned, CEOs may deserve to make *more* than 301 times as much as their employees.

This kind of skepticism about the accuracy of contribution measurements is, I believe, unwarranted. Although it may be impossible to determine exactly how much each employee contributes to the firm, rough estimates are possible. The popular view, of course, is that CEOs matter enormously to their firms. The CEOs of successful corporations are glorified in news stories and biographies. Witness, for example, the flurry of books written by and about Jack Welch, the former chief executive of General Electric. If we accept this view, we will conclude that CEOs' contributions are at least 301 times as valuable as their employees'.

But we should not. To be sure, some scholars endorse the popular view, but an increasing number reject it. Summarizing the current state of the debate, Khurana says the "overall evidence" points to "at best a contingent and relatively minor cause-and-effect relationship between CEOs and firm performance . . ." (2002, 23). He explains: "a variety of internal and external constraints inhibit CEOs' abilities to affect firm performance . . . [including] internal politics, previous investments in fixed assets and particular markets, organizational norms, and external forces such as competitive pressures and barriers to exit and entry" (2002, 22). It cannot be denied that CEOs' decisions at times make a difference to firm performance. These leaders may deserve bonuses for strategic thinking. But, if Khurana is right, cases such as these are exceptions to the rule. Factors outside of the CEO's control normally "contribute" more to the firm's success than the CEO does.

Some will reject the research on which this result is founded. Others will point out that it is compatible with the claim that CEOs contribute 301 times as much to their firms as their employees. These claims are not irrational. No theorist is willing to say exactly how much, compared with the average employee, the average CEO contributes. But they are unreasonable. There is mounting evidence that CEOs are not as important as they were once thought to be, and average employees are far from useless. We have ample evidence for a negative conclusion, namely, the claim that CEOs deserve to be paid 301 times as much as their employees is *unjustified*. But I think the evidence licenses a tentative positive conclusion as well, namely, that CEOs are *less* than 301 times as deserving as their employees, and so deserve *less* than 301 times as much pay. The desert view clearly does not support, and probably condemns, the current level of CEO pay.

## THE UTILITY VIEW

Having considered the agreement and desert views of justice in wages, let us now turn to the utility view. To recall, this view says that a just wage for a CEO is one that maximizes firm wealth by attracting, retaining, and motivating a talented leader. This is perhaps the most important of the three views of justice in wages. Boards of directors frequently appeal to utility-based arguments to defend the pay packages they give to their CEOs. I will argue that these defenses fail. I begin by discussing pay as a tool of attraction and retention. I then consider its role in motivation.

**Attraction and Retention**

Several of the desert bases discussed above might be cited as reasons an employer has to pay more to fill a certain job. The most important of these are effort, skill, and difficulty (including stress, dangerousness, and unpleasantness).[6] Since, other things equal, an employee will choose an easier job over a harder job, employers will have to make other things unequal, by offering higher wages for the harder job. Similarly, employers will offer higher wages for jobs that require rare and valuable skills or long periods of training, and for jobs that are comparatively difficult.[7]

The CEO's job has some of these characteristics. It does not require much physical effort, but it requires skill and training, and it is difficult and stressful. The question, of course, is not *if* the CEO's job has these characteristics, but *to what degree* it has them. Is the CEO's job *so* difficult and stressful, and does it require *so* much skill and training, that offering $8 million per year is necessary to get talented people to become CEOs? Those convinced by my argument that CEOs do not deserve to be paid 301 times what their employees are paid may think not. But notice we are now asking a different question: not what people deserve for performing the CEO's job, but what would make them willing to perform it.

The answer, however, is similar. There is no evidence that offering $8 million per year is necessary to get talented people to become CEOs. Indeed, we have reason to believe that much less will do. Consider the jobs of university presidents and U.S. military generals. They are no less difficult, and require no less skill and training, than the jobs of CEOs. But the wages offered to presidents and generals are many times lower than the wages offered to CEOs. The median compensation of presidents of private research universities is $385,000 per year (Basinger 2003); U.S. military generals earn $143,000 per year (Bureau of Labor Statistics 2004). Despite this, there is no shortage of talented university presidents and military generals. The fact that people can be attracted to difficult, specialized, and high-skill managerial jobs that pay "only" several hundred thousand dollars per year suggests that talented people will still want to become CEOs even if they are paid less than $8 million per year.

Three objections might be advanced against this conclusion. It might be admitted that the CEO's job is about as difficult, and requires about as much skill and training, as the university president's job or the military general's job. But, it might be said, the CEO's job is in one important way more unpleasant than these jobs. Military generals get, in addition to a paycheck, the satisfaction of knowing that they are protecting their country. University presidents get, in addition to a paycheck, the satisfaction of knowing that they are helping to increase human understanding. There is no comparable benefit, according to this objection, for CEOs.

I suspect that many CEOs find their jobs immensely intrinsically rewarding, and would find this suggestion mildly insulting. But let us grant, for the sake of argument, that CEOs' jobs are less intrinsically rewarding than university presidents' and military generals' jobs. Are they *that* much less rewarding—as many as 21 times so? For the objection to succeed, they would have to be. But it is implausible to suppose that they are. While the extra unpleasantness of the CEO's job may make it necessary to offer more than $385,000 per year to attract talented candidates, it is hardly plausible to suppose that it makes it necessary to offer $8 million.

The second objection grants that talented people would still be attracted to the CEO's job even if they were offered less than $8 million per year. But, it says, when this much pay is offered, truly exceptional people become interested. Analogously, the people who are now university presidents are talented, but truly exceptional people would become university presidents if they were offered, instead of several hundred thousand dollars per year, several million dollars per year.

Pay does matter to people when they are choosing a profession. So it is reasonable to assume that the people who become CEOs because corporations offer $8 million per year are, on average, more talented than the people who would become CEOs if corporations offered $1 million per year. But there are two reasons to think that they are not *that much* more talented, and so not worth the extra pay. First, the spectrum of managerial talent is only so wide. And $1 million per year is more than enough to attract a talented person to a difficult and important managerial job, as is demonstrated by the high talent level found among military generals and university presidents. Thus the $8 million-per-year CEO simply *cannot be* that much more talented than the $1 million-per-year CEO. Second, as we said in our discussion of the desert view, firms' performances do not usually depend heavily on the contributions of their CEOs. So it is unlikely that the modest difference in talent between the $8 million-per-year CEO and the $1 million-per-year CEO will translate into a $7 million difference in firm performance. In support of this, note that while American CEOs significantly outearn Japanese and British CEOs, American firms do not generally outperform Japanese and British firms (Abowd and Kaplan 1999).

It might be said—as a third objection—that I am missing the point. The fact is that the going rate *now* for CEOs is $8 million per year. In this market, it is necessary for any one firm to offer $8 million per year to get a talented person to become its CEO. This argument defies free-market economic sense. It says, in effect, that the market cannot correct itself. This is pessimistic.

Our discussion has focused on attraction; we have said nothing about retention. Could it be the case that while $8 million per year is not necessary to *attract* talented people to the CEO's job, it is necessary to *retain* them in the face of competing offers? The answer is no. In the first place, it is unlikely that there will be many competing offers. According to a study by Challenger, Gray, and Christmas Inc., of the 67 CEO departures in December 2003, in only one case was "position elsewhere" given as the reason for the departure. If CEOs were paid less, this number might increase. But even if it did, firms should not be alarmed. The difficulty of retention is a function of the difficulty of attraction. If it is not difficult to get a qualified person to take the CEO's job in the first place, it will not be difficult—or, more to the point, necessary—to retain him in the face of competing offers. The company can simply hire a new one.[8]

## Motivation

Attraction and retention are not the only utility-based reasons for paying employees certain wages. There is also motivation. Employees who are talented *and* motivated create more wealth for their firms than employees who are only talented. There are three ways paying CEOs $8 million per year might be thought—mistakenly, I will argue—to maximize firm wealth through motivation.

First, it might motivate the CEO himself. The CEO knows that if he does not do an excellent job, he will be fired. Since he wants to keep making $8 million per year, he will work as hard as he can. If CEOs were paid less money, they would work less hard, and firms would be worse off.

In this respect also, pay matters. It motivates people to work hard. It is thus arguable that the CEO who is paid $8 million per year will work harder than the CEO who is paid $1 million per year. But this, as we know by now, is not what needs to be shown. What needs to be shown is that the extra amount of hard work put in by the $8 million-per-year CEO is worth an extra $7 million. It is unlikely that it is. There is no guarantee that extra hard work will translate into extra revenue, and there is only so hard an executive can work. One might think that an extra $7 million per year would be worth it if one thought that CEOs would put in very little effort if they were paid only $1 million per year. But this takes a pessimistic view of CEOs' characters, as if only money—and only a lot of it—could get them to do anything. There is no empirical evidence to support this view. To the contrary, studies show that money is not the only, or even the primary, reason people work hard (Annis and Annis 1986). Instead of trying to further motivate their CEOs with more money, then, firms would do better to use the extra money to increase revenue in other ways, such as advertising more.

The second motivation-based reason for paying CEOs $8 million per year is, in effect, a slightly different version of the first. It has been said that CEOs' compensation packages should be structured so that CEOs' and owners' interests are *aligned* (Jensen and Murphy 1990). Owners want the stock price to go up. So CEOs should be paid in a way that makes them want the stock price to go up. This is typically achieved by paying CEOs mostly in restricted stock and stock options. Since, it is assumed, the CEO wants to make more money rather than less, this will give him an incentive to try to make the company's stock price go up. The idea is not just to make sure that CEOs do what investors want; it is to make sure that they do

*only* what investors want. If the CEO is paid mostly in stock, he has little to gain from pursuing alternative courses of action.

Let us grant, for the sake of argument, that CEOs' interests should be aligned exclusively with investors' interests. Let us also grant that offering CEOs $5 million per year in restricted stock and stock options accomplishes this (Khurana 2002). Does this prove that CEOs should be paid $5 million in stock? It does only if there is no cheaper way of achieving this goal. But there is: monitoring and dismissal. The interests of most employees are aligned with investors' interests this way. Employees are monitored. If they promote interests other than those (ultimately) of the investors, they are dismissed. Would anyone seriously propose, as an alternative to this practice, giving each employee several million dollars in stock options? To be sure, doing so would align their interests with investors' interests. But it is expensive and unnecessary. The same is true of paying CEOs $5 million in stock. There is no reason to give away so much of the firm's wealth when the CEO can simply be fired for poor performance. Owners could secure the same level of loyalty at a fraction of the price.

We have examined two ways that paying CEOs $8 million per year might maximize firm wealth through motivation. Both focus on the effects of high pay on the CEO. The third focuses on the effects of high pay on other employees. According to some, a firm's job hierarchy can be seen as a tournament, with the CEO's job as top prize. Many of the firm's employees, they say, want this prize and will work hard to get it. The better the prize is, the harder they will work. If the CEO is paid $8 million per year, the rest of the employees will work very hard indeed. The consequent increase in productivity will be good for the firm as a whole. Ehrenberg and Bognanno (1990) find evidence for this hypothesis in the field of professional golf. They observe that golfers' scores are negatively correlated with potential earnings. The larger the tournament's purse is, and hence the more money the golfers could win, the better they play.

This is the most sophisticated of the utility-based attempts to justify the current level of CEO pay. Still, the argument in its present form has several problems. In the first place, not every employee wants to be CEO, no matter how much the job pays. So paying the CEO $8 million per year provides an incentive to work hard to only some of the firm's employees. Second, there is evidence that this practice will have unintended negative effects. Since there is only one CEO's job, employees must compete with each other to get it. The more the job pays, the more intense the competition will be. This is problematic, for competition fosters jealousy and hostility, which can hinder communication and cooperation (Annis and Annis 1986). This will not matter to golfers; they play alone. But employees often work together; a decline in communication and cooperation may lead to a decline in productivity. In support of this, Cowherd and Levine (1992) find that pay inequality between workers and managers is negatively correlated with product quality. Thus, while paying CEOs $8 million per year may increase hard work, it may also increase competition. The benefit of the former may be outweighed by the cost of the latter.

Even if it is not, this does not suffice to prove that CEOs should be paid $8 million per year. My objection is familiar. That is, while paying CEOs $8 million per year might be an effective motivational tool, it is likely not a *cost*-effective one. Above we said that the $8 million-per-year CEO is likely to be only slightly more productive than the $1 million-per-year CEO. Similar reasoning suggests that $8 million-per-year CEO hopefuls are likely to be only slightly more productive than $1 million-per-year CEO hopefuls. From the point of view of utility, then, firms would do better to use the extra $7 million to increase revenue in other ways.

# CONCLUSION

To structure the debate about executive compensation, I distinguished three views of justice in wages: the agreement view, the desert view, and the utility view. No matter which one is right, I argued, CEO pay is too high. Owners may "agree" to pay CEOs $8 million per year, but the negotiations are not conducted at arm's length. If they were, CEOs would be paid less. The evidence suggests also that CEOs do not deserve to make 301 times what workers make, and that paying CEOs $8 million per year does not maximize firm wealth. New evidence may emerge that challenges these conclusions. Alternatively, new theories of justice in wages may be developed. Until then, it is reasonable to believe that CEO pay is too high.

This result is important. It supports the popular suspicion that CEOs are overpaid. But our inquiry leaves an important question unanswered, namely, exactly how much should CEOs be paid? Answering this question will truly be an interdisciplinary effort. First, we must determine what the correct view of justice in wages is. That is, we must determine which of these values, in this context, is most important. Here the writings of moral and political philosophers will be relevant. Second, we must apply the correct theory of justice in wages to the problem of CEO pay. That is, we must identify the wage that maximizes firm wealth, gives the CEO what he deserves, or would be the result of an arm's-length negotiation between the CEO and the owners. Here the writings of economists and organizational theorists will be relevant. Each of these tasks will be difficult and will require a full discussion of its own. In the meantime, what should be done? CEO pay should be kept from increasing; ideally, it should decrease. Space considerations prevent a detailed discussion of how this can be accomplished. I conclude, however, with two preliminary suggestions.

First, CEOs should be removed from the director election process. Directors feel obligated to those who put them on the board. If this is the CEO, they will feel obligated to him, and be more inclined to overpay him. Directors should feel obligated to the people they are actually representing: the shareholders. Letting shareholders elect them will help to create this feeling. It is possible that it will also make being a director a more demanding job. It may end the era in which an individual can serve on several corporate boards and still hold a full time job. This would be a good thing. Being a director is an important job: directors oversee entities whose actions can impact the welfare of thousands of people. It should feel like one.

Second, directors should be required to make meaningful investments in the firms that they direct. They need not all own a certain percentage of the firm's total stock. What matters is that they own an amount that is meaningful for them. This promotes the first objective: directors will feel more obligated to shareholders if they are themselves shareholders. It is useful for another reason as well. Above we said that a problem with the pay negotiations between directors and CEOs is that directors feel as if they are not paying with their own money. Making them buy stock would help to ameliorate this problem. An implication of this view is that other kinds of compensation that seem "free" to directors should be eliminated. This includes stock options insofar as they are not counted against firm earnings. If options are given as compensation, they should be expensed.[9]

## NOTES

1. For convenience, the figures for average CEO pay and average factory worker pay are rounded off in the text. The more precise figures— $8.1 million and $26,899, respectively—are used in the calculation of the ratio of CEO pay to worker pay.

2. Some might deny that it makes sense to speak of an "agreement view" or "utility view" of *justice* in wages. We can talk about whether utility or agreements should determine the wages workers get, all things considered. But, according to this objection, justice is *defined* in terms of desert; the just wage, by definition, is the wage the worker deserves. I do not want to engage in a terminological dispute. What the objection describes as a debate about the wages workers should get, all things considered, *just is* what I describe as a debate about justice in wages.

3. More precisely, CEOs would be paid *on average* less than $8 million per year. It is possible that some CEOs are not overpaid according to any of the three views of justice in wages. But even if some—or as I suspect, most—are, it follows that average CEO pay is too high.

4. This contradicts the intuitively plausible view that since most directors are rich already, the money they get paid for being a director will not influence them.

5. Most researchers believe CEO pay is not, in fact, tied closely to performance. See, for example, Jensen and Murphy 1990.

6. I do not include on this list degree of responsibility. While some people may not want to hold jobs in which they could have a significant impact on people's lives, I suspect there are equally many, if not more, who do. I also do not include contribution. Instead I understand "skill" expansively to include all of the talents and traits taken by firms to be positively correlated with contribution.

7. Nichols and Subramanian (2001) suggest that high CEO pay is justified, in part, because CEOs' jobs are risky. When the company performs poorly, CEOs are more likely than average workers to be fired. But this ignores the fact that CEOs have less to fear from job loss than average workers. CEOs are wealthy, whereas most employees cannot afford to be out of work for long.

8. This is not to suggest that companies should make *no* effort to keep their CEOs. There is debate about whether CEO succession events disrupt firm performance, but most writers agree that they tend to lower the price of the firm's stock.

9. A draft of this paper was presented at Georgetown University. I wish to thank members

of that audience, and also George Brenkert, Edwin Hartman, Kelly Moriarty, Jeffrey Wilder, and two anonymous *Business Ethics Quarterly* referees for helpful comments and discussion.

# REFERENCES

Abowd, J. M., and D. S. Kaplan. 1999. "Executive Compensation: Six Questions that Need Answering." *Journal of Economic Perspectives* 13:145–68.

Annis, D. B., and L. F. Annis. 1986. "Merit Pay, Utilitarianism, and Desert." *Journal of Applied Philosophy* 3:33–41.

Basinger, J. 2003. "Soaring Pay, Big Questions." *Chronicle of Higher Education* 50 (12): S9–S11.

Boyd, B. K. 1994. "Board Control and CEO Compensation." *Strategic Management Journal* 15:335–44.

Bureau of Labor Statistics. 2004. *Occupational Outlook Handbook, 2004–05 Edition.* Washington, DC: U.S. Department of Labor.

Byrne, J. A. 2002. "How to Fix Corporate Governance." *BusinessWeek* (May 6): 68–75.

Cowherd, D. M., and D. I. Levine. 1992. "Product Quality and Pay Equity between Lower-Level Employees and Top Management: An Investigation of Distributive Justice Theory." *Administrative Science Quarterly* 37:302–20.

Ehrenberg, R., and M. L. Bognanno. 1990. "Do Tournaments Have Incentive Effects?" *Journal of Political Economy* 98:1307–24.

Ezzamel, M., and R. Watson. 1998. "Market Comparison Earnings and the Bidding-up of Executive Cash Compensation: Evidence from the United Kingdom." *Academy of Management Journal* 41:221–31.

Jaffe, M. 2003. "Average CEO Pay at Big Firms Held Steady at $11.3 Million." *Mercury News* (December 30); http://www.mercurynews.com/mld/mercurynews/business/7597346.htm.

Jensen, M. C., and K. J. Murphy. 1990. "Performance Pay and Top Management Incentives." *Journal of Political Economy* 98:225–64.

Khurana, R. 2002. *Searching for a Corporate Savior: The Irrational Quest for Charismatic CEOs.* Princeton, NJ: Princeton University Press.

Lavelle, L. 2004. "Executive Pay." *BusinessWeek.* (April 19): 106–19.

Main, B. G., C. A. O'Reilly, and J. B. Wade. 1995. "The CEO, the Board of Directors and Executive Compensation: Economic and Psychological Perspectives." *Industrial and Corporate Change* 4:292–332.

Nichols, D., and C. Subramanian. 2001. Executive Compensation: Excessive or Equitable? *Journal of Business Ethics* 29:339–51.

Shivdasani, A., and D. Yermack. 1999. "CEO Involvement in the Selection of New Board Members: An Empirical Analysis." *Journal of Finance* 54:1829–53.

## GLOBAL JUSTICE

# Why Globalization Works

*Martin Wolf*

*Globalization has dramatically increased inequality between and within nations, even as it connects people as never before. A world in which the assets of the 200 richest people are greater than the combined income of the more than 2 billion people at the other end of the economic ladder should give everyone pause.*

Jay Mazur, president of the Union of Needletrades, Industrial and Textile Employees.[1]

From Martin Wolf, *Why Globalization Works* (New Haven, CT: Yale University Press, 2004).

Jay Mazur is not alone. Ignacio Ramonet has written on similar lines, in *Le Monde Diplomatique*, that:

> the dramatic advance of globalization and neoliberalism . . . has been accompanied by an *explosive growth in inequality* and a return of mass poverty and unemployment. The very opposite of everything which the modern state and modern citizenship is supposed to stand for.
>
> The net result is a *massive growth in inequality*. The United States, which is the richest country in the world, has more than 60 million poor. The world's foremost trading power, the European Union, has over 50 million. In the United States, 1 percent of the population owns 39 percent of the country's wealth. Taking the planet as a whole, the combined wealth of the 358 richest people (all of them dollar billionaires) is greater than the total annual income of 45 percent of the world's poorest inhabitants, that is, 2.6 billion people.[2]

Let us, for a moment, ignore the assumption that the number of poor (how defined?) in two of the richest regions in the world tells one anything about global inequality, or about poverty for that matter, or even about inequality within the United States and the European Union. Let us also ignore the comparison between the *assets* of one group of people, the richest, and the *incomes* of another, the poor, which is a comparison of apples and oranges. (In order to obtain the permanent incomes of the rich, one would need to divide the value of their assets by at least 20.) These absurdities merely make Ramonet's diatribe representative of the empty rhetoric of many critics of globalization. But the questions that underlie his remarks need to be tackled. Here are seven propositions that can be advanced about what has happened in the age of so-called neoliberal globalization over the past two decades.

First, the ratio of average incomes in the richest countries to those in the poorest has continued to rise.

Second, the absolute gap in living standards between today's high-income countries and most developing countries has also continued to rise.

Third, global inequality among individuals has risen.

Fourth, the number of people in extreme poverty has risen.

Fifth, the proportion of people in extreme poverty in the world's population has also risen.

Sixth, the poor of the world are worse off not just in terms of incomes, but in terms of a wide range of other indicators of human welfare.

Seventh, income inequality has risen in every country and particularly in countries most exposed to international economic integration.

In the rest of this essay I will consider what we know about these propositions and how the answers relate to international economic integration. Before examining them, however, we need to ask what matters to us. Most of the debate has been either about whether inequality has risen between the world's rich and poor or about whether the number of people in income poverty has risen. But critics of globalization have themselves often rightly argued that there is more to life than income. What is most important must be the living standards of the poor, not just in terms of their incomes, narrowly defined, but in terms of their health, life expectancy, nourishment and education.

Equally, we need to understand that rises in inequality might occur in very different ways. Three possibilities come to mind at once; a rise in the incomes of the better off, at the expense of the poor; a rise in the incomes of the better off, with no effects on the welfare of the poor; or rises in incomes of the better off that, in various ways, benefit the poor, but not by proportionately as much as they benefit the better off. It seems clear that the first of these is malign, the second desirable, unless the welfare of the better off counts for nothing, and the third unambiguously desirable, though one might wish more of the gains to accrue to the poor. True egalitarians would differ on these judgments, of course. Indeed, an extreme egalitarian might take the view that a world in which everybody was an impoverished subsistence farmer would be better than the world we now have, because it would be less unequal. Most people—including, I imagine, many protesters against globalization—would regard this as crazy. Few are that egalitarian. Most people are not even as egalitarian as the late philosopher John Rawls, who argued that inequality was permissible only to the extent that it benefited the poor.

We need to be equally careful in considering the role of globalization in relation to inequality and poverty. International economic integration may affect global inequality in several different ways. Here are a few possibilities: it may increase inequality by lowering the incomes of the poor; it may raise the incomes of the better off, without having any impact on the incomes of the poor; it may raise the incomes of the poor by proportionately less than it raises the incomes of the better off; or it may raise the incomes of the poor by proportionately more than it raises those of the better off. Only the first is unambiguously bad, but all of the first three would be associated with increasing inequality. Yet both of the last two mean higher living standards for the poor.

Again, it may not be globalization, as such, that delivers these outcomes, but a combination of globalization with nonglobalization. Globalization may raise incomes of globalizers, while nonglobalization lowers the incomes of nonglobalizers. Then an era of globalization may be associated with rising inequality that is caused not by globalization, but by its opposite, the refusal (or inability) of some countries to participate.

The most important questions to bear in mind in the discussions below are, therefore, these. Is human welfare, broadly defined, rising? Is the proportion of humanity living in desperate misery declining? If inequality is rising, are the rich profiting at the expense of the poor? Is globalization damaging the poor or is it rather nonglobalization that is doing so? To answer all these questions, one must start at the beginning, with economic growth.

## ECONOMIC GROWTH AND GLOBALIZATION

In the mid-1970s I was the World Bank's senior divisional economist on India during the country's worst postindependence decade. After a spurt of growth in the early phase of its inward-looking development, growth in incomes per head had ground virtually to a halt. Hundreds of millions of people seemed, as a result, to be mired in hopeless and unending poverty. In a book published in 1968, a well-known environmentalist doomsayer, Paul Ehrlich, had written the country off altogether.[3] For a young man from the UK, work in India as an economist was both fascinating and appalling: so much poverty; so much frustration; so much complacency. Yet I was convinced then, as I am now, that, with perfectly feasible policy changes, this vast country could generate rapid rates of economic growth and reductions in poverty. No iron law imposed levels of real output (and so real incomes) per head at only 10 percent of those in high-income countries.

Since those unhappy days, India has enjoyed the fruit of two revolutions: the green revolution, which transformed agricultural productivity; and a liberalizing revolution, which began, haltingly, under Rajiv Gandhi's leadership, in the 1980s and then took a "great leap forward" in 1991, in response to a severe foreign exchange crisis, under the direction of one of the country's most remarkable public servants, Manmohan Singh, the then finance minister. Slowly, India abandoned the absurdities of its pseudo-Stalinist "control raj" in favor of individual enterprise and the market. As a result, between 1980 and 2000, India's real GDP per head more than doubled. Stagnation has become a thing of the past.

India was not alone. On the contrary, it was far behind a still more dynamic and even bigger liberalizing country—China, which achieved a rise in real incomes per head of well over 400 percent between 1980 and 2000. China and India, it should be remembered, contain almost two-fifths of the world's population. China alone contains more people than Latin America and sub-Saharan Africa together. Many other countries in east and south Asia have also experienced rapid growth. According to the *2003 Human Development Report* from the United Nations Development Programme, between 1975 and 2001, GDP per head rose at 5.9 percent a year in east Asian developing countries (with 31 percent of the world's population in 2000). The corresponding figure for growth of GDP per head for south Asia (with another 22 percent of the world's population) was 2.4 percent a year. Between 1990 and 2001, GDP per head rose at 5.5 percent a year in east Asia, while growth rose to 3.2 percent a year in south Asia.

Never before have so many people—or so large a proportion of the world's population— enjoyed such large rises in their standards of living. Meanwhile, GDP per head in high-income countries (with 15 percent of the world's population) rose by 2.1 percent a year between 1975 and 2001 and by only 1.7 percent a year between 1990 and 2001. This then was a period of partial convergence: the incomes of poor developing countries, with more than half the world's population, grew substantially faster than those of the world's richest countries.

This, in a nutshell, is why Mazur and the many people who think like him are wrong. Globalization has not increased inequality. It has reduced it, just as it has reduced the incidence of poverty. How can this be, critics will demand? Are absolute and proportional gaps in living standards between the world's richest and poorest countries not rising all the time? Yes is the answer. And is inequality not rising in most of the world's big countries? Yes, is again the answer. So how can global inequality be falling? To adapt Bill Clinton's campaign slogan, it is the growth, stupid. Rapid economic growth in poor countries with half the world's population has powerful effects on the only sort of inequality which matters, that among individuals. It has similarly dramatic effects on world poverty. . . .

What, the reader may ask, has this progress to do with international economic integration? In its analysis of globalization, published in 2002, the World Bank divided 73 developing countries, with aggregate population, in 1997, of 4 billion (80 percent of all people in developing countries), into two groups: the third that had increased ratios of trade to GDP, since 1980, by the largest amount and the rest.[4] The former group, with an aggregate population of 2.9 billion, managed a remarkable combined increase of 104 percent in the ratio of trade to GDP. Over the same period, the increase in the trade ratio of the high-income countries was 71 percent, while the 'less globalized' two-thirds of countries in the sample of developing countries experienced a decline in their trade ratios.

The average incomes per head of these 24 globalizing countries rose by 67 percent (a compound rate of 3.1 percent a year) between 1980 and 1997. In contrast, the other 49 countries managed a rise of only 10 percent (a compound rate of 0.5 percent a year) in incomes per head over this period. . . .

What then do we learn from the success of the countries picked out as globalizers by the World Bank? We can say, with confidence, that the notion that international economic integration necessarily makes the rich richer and the poor poorer is nonsense. Here is a wide range of countries that increased their integration with the world economy and prospered, in some cases dramatically so. A subtler question is precisely what policies relatively successful developing countries have followed. Critics are right to argue that success has not required adoption of the full range of so-called neoliberal policies—privatization, free trade, and capital-account liberalization. But, in insisting upon this point, critics are wilfully mistaking individual policy trees for the market- oriented forest. What the successful countries all share is a move toward the market economy, one in which private property rights, free enterprise, and competition increasingly took the place of state ownership, planning, and protection. They chose, however haltingly, the path of economic liberalization and international integration. This is the heart of the matter. All else is commentary. . . .

## GROWTH AND INEQUALITY

Now what does the performance of those who have succeeded in growing through economic integration mean for inequality? Inequality is a measure of relative incomes. If the average real incomes of poor countries containing at least half of the world's population have been rising faster than those of the relatively rich, inequality among countries, weighted by population, will have fallen. This will be true even if the ratio of the incomes of the world's richest to the world's poorest countries and the absolute gaps in average incomes per head between rich countries and almost all developing countries have risen (as they have).

These two points may need a little explanation. First, compare, say, the United States with China. Between 1980 and 2000, according to the World Bank, Chinese average real incomes rose by about 440 per cent. Over the same period, U.S. average real incomes per head rose by about 60 percent. The ratio of

Chinese real incomes per head, at purchasing power parity, to those of the United States rose, accordingly, from just over 3 percent in 1980 to just under 12 percent in 2000. This is a big reduction in relative inequality. But the absolute gap in real incomes between China and the United States rose from $20,600 to $30,200 per head (at PPP). The reason is simple: since China's standard of living was, initially, about a thirtieth of that of the U.S., the absolute gap could have remained constant only if China's growth had been 30 times faster than that of the United States. That would have been impossible. If China continues to grow faster than the United States, however, absolute gaps will ultimately fall, as happened with Japan in the 1960s and 1970s.

Second, while the *ratio* of the average incomes per head in the richest country to those in the world's least successful countries is rising all the time, the *proportion* of the world's population living in the world's poorest countries has, happily, been falling. Thirty years ago, China and India were among the world's poorest countries. Today, the poorest seems to be Sierra Leone, a country with a population of only 5 million. China's average real income per head is now some 10 times higher than Sierra Leone's. The largest very poor country today is Nigeria, with a population of 127 million in 2000 and a real income, at PPP, just a fortieth of that of the United States (and a fifth of China's). Again, this means that rising ratios between the average incomes of the world's richest and poorest countries are consistent with declining inequality among countries, weighted by their populations. Moreover, it is also perfectly possible for inequality to have risen in every single country in the world (as Mazur alleges, wrongly) while global inequality has fallen. Unless the increase in inequality among individuals within countries offsets the reduction in population-weighted inequality among countries, not only inequality among (population-weighted) inequality among countries, not only inequality among (population-weighted) countries, but also inequality among individuals will have declined. . . .

## GROWTH AND POVERTY

On all measures, global inequality rose until about the early 1980s. Since then, it appears, inequality among individuals has declined as a result of the rapid growth of much of Asia and, above all, China. But it is also important to understand what drove the long-term trend toward global inequality over almost two centuries. It is the consequence of the dynamic growth that spread, unevenly, from the UK in the course of the nineteenth and twentieth centuries. In the process a growing number of people became vastly better off than any one had ever been before, but few can have become worse off. Such dynamic growth is bound to be uneven. Some regions of the world proved better able to take advantage of the new opportunities for growth, because of superior climates, resources and policies. In just the same way, some parts of countries, particularly huge countries such as China or India, are today better able to take advantage of new opportunities than others. To bemoan the resulting increase in inequality is to bemoan the growth itself. It is to argue that it would be better for everybody to be equally poor than for some to become significantly better off, even if, in the long run, this will almost certainly lead to advances for everybody.

For this reason, it makes more sense to focus on what has happened to poverty than to inequality. Again, the statistical debate is a vexed one. But some plausible conclusions can be reached.

The World Bank has, for some time, defined extreme poverty as an income of a dollar a day at 1985 international prices (PPP).

Bourguignon and Morrison also used that figure in an analysis of extreme poverty since 1820, on the same lines as their analysis of inequality.[5] It comes to three intriguing conclusions. First, the number of desperately poor people rose from about 900 million in 1820 to a peak of from 1.3 to 1.4 billion between 1960 and 1980, before falling, modestly, to just under 1.3 billion in 1992. Second, the proportion of the world's population living on less than a dollar a day fell dramatically, over time, from over 80 percent in 1820, a time when living on the margins of subsistence was the norm, to about two-thirds at the beginning of the twentieth century, to close to 50 percent by 1950, then 32 percent in 1980 and, finally, 24 percent by 1992. The contrast between rising numbers and falling proportions of the world's population in extreme poverty reflects the race between higher output and rising population, particularly in poor countries. In 1820, the world's population was a little over a billion. By 1910 it was 1.7 billion and by 1992 it had risen to 5.5 billion.

Again, the results from Bourguignon and Morrison are cause for qualified optimism. From being universal, extreme poverty has become, if not rare, the affliction of less than a quarter of a vastly increased human population. . . .

Professors Thomas Pogge and Sanjay Reddy, also of Columbia University, like Professor Sala-I-Martin, argue that the Bank's numbers, if not necessarily too optimistic, are unsoundly based. They suggest, in particular, that this admittedly heroic attempt to compare poverty across the globe with the use of one measuring rod ($1.08 a day at PPP, in 1993 prices) is fundamentally flawed, in three ways. First, the international poverty line used by the Bank "fails to meet elementary requirements of consistency." As a result, "the Bank's poverty line leads to meaningless poverty estimates." Second, "the Bank's poverty line is not anchored in any assessment of the basic resource requirements of human beings." And third, "the poverty estimates currently available are subject to massive uncertainties because of their sensitivity to the values of crucial parameters that are estimated on the basis of limited data or none at all."[6]

Let us grant most of this. It is evident that converting national data with PPP exchange rates that are themselves both averages for economies and variable from year to year is a rough-and-ready procedure, to put it mildly. Equally, the dollar-a-day line is both inherently arbitrary and bound to mean different things in different countries. It is also true, as Pogge and Reddy argue, that PPP adjustments, which are largely for the relative price of nontradable services, will create large, and growing, mismeasurement of the real incomes of the poor, since the latter consume commodities more intensively than the better off. That could well justify higher poverty lines. At the same time, it might mean that the rate of decline in poverty is higher than estimated by the Bank, since relative prices of commodities normally fall in fast-growing countries.

The big question, however, is whether it would be easy to do better. Pogge and Reddy suggest that the exercise should be conducted in terms not of arbitrary levels of income, but of capabilities—"calories and essential nutrients." They argue that "the income persons need to avoid poverty at some particular time and place can then be specified in terms of the least expensive locally available set of commodities containing the relevant characteristics needed to achieve the elementary human capabilities."[7] This sounds straightforward. In fact, long experience suggests that reaching agreement on such poverty levels across countries is nigh on impossible.

Pogge and Reddy provide a warning. All poverty estimates are inherently arbitrary. Certainly, there is no good reason to believe in anybody's estimates of the levels of poverty at any moment. Trends are another matter. It is certain that the share of those in extreme (absolute, as opposed to relative) income poverty in the world's population has fallen enormously over the last two centuries, a decline that has, equally certainly, continued since 1980. It is almost equally certain that the numbers in extreme income poverty fell in east Asia over the past few decades and particularly over the past two. That is likely, though less certain, for India. Encouragingly, both China and India show enormous declines in estimates of numbers in extreme poverty on their different national measures (about 100 million for India, between 1980 and 2000, and 220 million for China, between 1978 and 1999, despite large increases in population in both countries over this period). Given these changes in east and south Asia, it is plausible, though not certain, that numbers in absolute income poverty declined worldwide. What is more than merely plausible is the proposition that, where numbers in extreme poverty have declined, the cause has been accelerated growth. This is as true of regions within countries (especially where mobility is hindered, as in China) as among them.

## POVERTY AND HUMAN WELFARE

In the absence of any of the internationally comparable measures of capabilities that Pogge and Reddy call for, one has to look at other supporting evidence. It is here that we find unambiguous good news. For it is clear that human welfare has improved greatly in recent decades.[8] As an independent analyst, Indur Goklany, persuasively argues, it is possible, in addition, for people to enjoy better health and longer lives, at lower incomes, than before.[9] This is the result of technological and organizational improvements that have come from the world's rich countries.

In 1913, life expectancy at birth in the United States was 52 years. U.S. GDP per head, at PPP, was then about 50 percent higher than China's would be in 2000, and 150 percent higher than India's. Yet, in 2000, life expectancy in China was 70 and in India 63. In 1900, Sweden seems to have had the world's highest life expectancy, at 56. In 2000, only very poor countries, mostly in Africa, had life expectancy as low as (or lower than) this. As Goklany shows, the curve relating life expectancy to average GDP per head has shifted upward over time. Similarly, the curve relating infant mortality to incomes has shifted downward over time. Much the same desirable pattern can be observed for the relationship between other indicators of human welfare and income.

In the developing world as a whole, life expectancy rose by 4 months each year after 1970, from 55 years in 1970 to 64 years in 2000. It rose from 49 in 1970 to 62 in south Asia and from 59 to 69 in east Asia. Tragically, life expectancy fell in 32 countries in the 1990s, mostly because of the AIDS epidemic, or the gross incompetence (or worse) of governments, as in North Korea and Zimbabwe. It also fell because of Western hysteria about DDT, which removed the only effective way of controlling that dreadful curse, malaria. Improvements in life expectancy have meant a decline in global inequality as well. In 1950, average life expectancy in developing countries was two-thirds of the levels in high-income countries (44 and 66 years of age, respectively). By 2000, it was 82 percent (64 and 78).

Meanwhile, in the developing world as a whole, infant mortality rates have fallen from 107 per thousand in 1970 to 87 in 1980 and 58 in 2000. In east Asia, the region with the fastest-growing economy, they have fallen from 56 in 1980 to 35 in 2000. In south Asia, infant mortality fell from 119 in 1980 to 73 in 2000. In sub-Saharan Africa progress was, once again,

slower. But infant mortality fell even there, from 116 in 1980 to 91 in 2000.

Losing a child must inflict the sharpest grief human beings can suffer. The decline in infant mortality is thus a tremendous blessing in itself. So, too, is the rise in life expectancy. But these improvements also mean that it makes sense to invest in education. The world increasingly produces smaller families with much better-educated children. On average, adult literacy in developing countries rose from 53 percent in 1970 to 74 percent in 1998. By 2000, adult male illiteracy was down to 8 percent in east Asia, though it was still 30 percent in sub-Saharan Africa and (a real scandal this) 34 percent in south Asia. Adult female illiteracy was more widespread than that for men, but was also improving. Between 1990 and 2000, female illiteracy fell from 29 percent to 21 percent in east Asia. In south Asia, it fell from 66 percent to 57 percent (an even worse scandal than the low rate for men), while in sub-Saharan Africa it fell from 60 to 47 percent. Illiteracy is much lower among the young. This guarantees that rates will continue to fall, as time passes.

The reduction in fertility rates has also been remarkable. In the developing world as a whole, births per woman (the fertility rate) have fallen from 4.1 in 1980 to 2.8 in 2000. In east Asia, the fertility rate, down from 3.0 to 2.1, is already at close to the replacement rate. In Latin America, the fertility rate has fallen from 4.1 to 2.6. Even in south Asia it has fallen from 5.3 in 1980 to 3.3 in 2000. Again, progress has been slowest in sub-Saharan Africa, where the birth rate has only fallen from 6.6 in 1980 to 5.2 in 2000. But, in all, these reductions tell us of improved control by women of their fertility, of fewer children with more parental investment in each and of far stronger confidence that children will survive to maturity. The demographic transition that is now under way in the developing world is immensely encouraging. It is also an indication—as well as a source—of rising welfare.

Now, let us look at hunger. Growth in food production has substantially outpaced that of population. Between 1961 and 1999, the average daily food supply per person increased 24 percent globally. In developing countries, it rose by 39 percent, to 2,684 calories. By 1999, China's average daily food supply had gone up 82 percent, to 3,044 calories, from a barely subsistence level of 1,636 in 1961. India's went up by 48 percent to 2,417 calories, from 1,635 calories in 1950–51. According to estimates by the United Nations Food and Agricultural Organization, the average active adult needs between 2,000 and 2,310 calories per person. Thus the developing-country food supply has gone, on average, from inadequate to adequate. Hunger persists. But the FAO estimates that the number of people suffering from chronic undernourishment fell from 920 million in 1969–71 to 790 million in 1997–99, or from 35 to 17 percent of the population of developing countries. Trends in sub-Saharan Africa, the continent that did not grow, were far worse. Between 1979–81 and 1997–99, the share of the population that was undernourished declined from 38 to 34 percent, but absolute numbers, in a rapidly growing population, rose from 168 million to 194 million.

Now, turn to what has become one of the most controversial indicators: child labor. One would expect that more prosperous parents, with fewer children, who are also expected to live longer, would wish to see their children being educated rather than at work. So, happily, it has proved. The proportion of children aged 10 to 14 in the labor force has, according to the World Bank, fallen from 23 percent in all developing countries in 1980 to 12 percent in 2000. The fall in east Asia has, once again, been astonishing, from 26 to 8 percent. In south Asia, it has fallen from 23 to 15 percent. In sub-Saharan Africa, the decline has been

less impressive, from 35 to 29 percent. China's transformation has been breathtaking, with a fall from 30 percent in 1980 to just 8 percent in 2000. In lagging India, the fall was from 21 to 12 percent. Thus, just as one would expect, countries whose economies have done well in the era of globalization have been ones in which parents have chosen to withdraw their children from the labor force. Parents have never put their children to work out of indifference or malevolence, but only out of necessity.

Finally, let us remember some of the other features of the last two decades: the worldwide shift to democracy, however imperfect; the disappearance of some of the worst despotisms in history; the increase in personal economic opportunity in vast swaths of the world, notably China and India; and the improving relative position of women almost, although not quite, everywhere.

All these are very encouraging trends. People in developing countries and, particularly, in the fast-growing ones are enjoying longer and healthier lives than before. They are better fed and better educated. They treat their fewer children better. All these good things have not happened only because of rising incomes. Learning from the high-income countries has helped. Developing countries are reaching higher levels of social progress at lower levels of income than the high-income countries of today. But, as one would expect, social progress has been greatest where incomes have risen fastest. It remains "the growth, stupid."

## CONCLUSION

Let us return then to the propositions with which this exploration of growth, poverty and inequality began. Here they are, together with what we now know.

First, the ratio of average incomes in the richest countries to those in the very poorest has continued to rise in the age of globalization. Response: correct.

Second, the absolute gap in living standards between today's high-income countries and the vast proportion of developing countries has continued to rise. Response: also correct and inevitably so, given the starting point two decades ago.

Third, global inequality among individuals has risen. Response: false. Global inequality among individuals has, in all probability, fallen since the 1970s.

Fourth, the number of people in extreme income poverty has also risen. Response: probably false. The number of people in extreme poverty may well have fallen since 1980, for the first time in almost two centuries, because of the rapid growth of the Asian giants.

Fifth, the proportion of people in extreme poverty in the world's population has also risen. Response: false. The proportion of the world's population in extreme poverty has certainly fallen.

Sixth, the poor of the world are worse off not just in terms of incomes, but in terms of a wide range of indicators of human welfare and capability. Response: unambiguously false. The welfare of humanity, judged by life expectancies, infant mortality, literacy, hunger, fertility and the incidence of child labor has improved enormously. It has improved least in sub-Saharan Africa, partly because of disease and partly because of the continent's failure to grow.

Seventh, income inequality has risen in every country and particularly in countries most exposed to international economic integration. Response: false. Income inequality has not risen in most of the developing countries that have integrated with the world economy, though it has risen in China. Inequality has apparently risen in the high-income countries, but the role of globalization in this change is unclear and, in all probability, not decisive.

We can also make some propositions of our own. Human welfare, broadly defined, has risen. The proportion of humanity living in desperate misery is declining. The problem of the poorest is not that they are exploited, but that they are almost entirely unexploited: they live outside the world economy. The soaring growth of the rapidly integrating developing economies has transformed the world for the better. The challenge is to bring those who have failed so far into the new web of productive and profitable global economic relations.

## NOTES

1. "Labor's New Internationalism," *Foreign Affairs* 79 (January–February 2000).

2. Ignacio Ramonet, *Le Monde Diplomatique* (May 1998). Cited in Xavier Sala-I-Martin, "The Myth of Exploding Income Inequality in Europe and the World," in *Europe and Globalization* ed. Henryk Kierzkowski (Basingstoke: Palgrave Macmillan, 2002), 11.

3. Paul Ehrlich, *The Population Bomb* (New York: Ballantine Books, 1968).

4. World Bank, *Globalization, Growth and Poverty: Building an Inclusive World Economy* (Washington DC: 2002), table 1.1, p. 34.

5. François Bourguignon and Christian Morrison, "Inequality among World Citizens," *American Economic Review,* 92, no. 4 (September 2002): 727–44.

6. See Thomas W. Pogge and Sanjay G. Reddy, "Unknown: The Extent, Distribution and Trend of Global Income Poverty," July 16, 2003, mimeo, pp. 1–2.

7. Ibid., 12.

8. Where not otherwise indicated, data in this section come from World Bank, *World Development Indicators 2002* (Washington DC: World Bank, 2002).

9. Indur M. Goklany, "The Globalization of Human Well-Being," Policy Analysis No. 447, Cato Institute, Washington DC, August 22, 2002.

# Priorities of Global Justice

*Thomas Pogge*

Looking back on the post-Cold War period, the greatest surprise for me was that the affluent states have done so very little toward eradicating global poverty. This is surprising, because the conditions for a major effort were exceptionally favorable. The demise of the Soviet bloc gave the affluent states greatly enhanced opportunities to incorporate their moral values and concerns into their foreign policy and into the rapidly evolving international institutional order. It also enabled these states to cut their military expenditures as a share of gross domestic product (GDP) from 4.1 percent of their combined GDPs in 1985 to 2.2 percent in 1998 (UNDP 1998, 197; UNDP 2000, 217), which is still roughly the present level (yearbook2005.sipri.org/ch8/ch8), resulting in an annual "peace dividend" of about $675 billion.[1] Maintaining healthy economic and technological growth throughout the period, the affluent states thus had both the power and the funds to make a major effort toward poverty eradication.

However, no such effort took place. The affluent states, during the same period, actually cut their official development assistance (ODA) as a share of gross national product (GNP) by one-third.[2] They have also reduced their allocations to multilateral development efforts, revised Part XI of the 1982 United Nations Convention on the Law of the Sea to the disadvantage of poor countries, and imposed onerous terms of trade and intellectual property right requirements on the latter in the context of the Uruguay Round.[3]

To be sure, the affluent states have been more willing to appeal to moral values and to use such appeals in justification of initiatives—such as the NATO bombing of Yugoslavia and the invasion of Iraq—that would have been unthinkable during the Cold War. But these appeals only heighten the puzzle. If it makes sense to spend billions and to endanger thousands of lives in order to rescue a million people from Serb oppression, would it not make more sense to spend similar sums, without endangering any lives, on leading many millions out of life-threatening poverty?

To appreciate the force of this question about priorities, one must know some of the salient facts about global poverty. About one-sixth of all human beings alive, 1,089 million, live below $1/day, that is, their income or consumption expenditure per day has less purchasing power than $1.075 had in the United States in 1993.[4] According to this extremely low poverty line, persons need only $560 annually to count as nonpoor in the United States (www.bls.gov/cpi/home.htm), or $140 annually to avoid poverty in a typical poor country.[5]

Such severe poverty has grave consequences: some 850 million human beings lack adequate nutrition, 1,037 million lack access to safe water, and 2,600 million lack basic sanitation (UNDP 2005, 24, 44, 49), more than 2,000 million lack access to essential drugs (www.fic.nih.gov/about/summary.html), 1,000 million are without adequate shelter, and 2,000 million without electricity (UNDP 1998, 49). One hundred seventy-nine million children under 18 are involved in the "worst forms of child labor" including hazardous work in agriculture, construction, textile, or carpet production as well as "slavery, trafficking, debt

From *Metaphilosophy* 32, nos. 1–2 (January 2001): 6–24 and updated by the author for this book in 2007. Reprinted with the permission of the publisher and the author.

bondage, and other forms of forced labor, forced recruitment of children for use in armed conflict, prostitution, and pornography, and illicit activities" (ILO 2002, 9, 11, 18). Some 799 million adults are illiterate (www. uis.unesco.org). Roughly one-third of all human deaths, some 50,000 daily, are due to poverty-related causes and thus avoidable insofar as poverty is avoidable (WHO 2004, Annex Table 2).

Severe poverty causes not only massive underfulfillment of social and economic human rights, such as the "right to a standard of living adequate for the health and well-being of oneself and one's family, including food, clothing, housing, and medical care."[6] Severe poverty and economic inequality also contribute significantly to the underfulfillment of civil and political human rights associated with democratic government and the rule of law. Desperately poor people, often stunted from infancy, illiterate, and heavily preoccupied with the struggle to survive, can do little by way of either resisting or rewarding their local and national rulers, who are therefore likely to rule them oppressively while catering to the interests of other (often foreign) agents more capable of reciprocation. The income and staying power of such rulers often depends less on their poor subjects than on a small local elite or on a few foreign companies and governments, to whom they can sell the country's natural resources and from whom they can obtain grants and loans and weapons. Such rulers have little need for popular support and many of them use torture, restrict freedom of expression, and perpetuate their rule by force.

Severe poverty is by far the greatest source of human misery today. Deaths and harms from direct violence around the world—in Chechnya, East Timor, Congo, Bosnia, Kosovo, Ethiopia and Eritrea, Rwanda, Somalia, Iraq, Afghanistan, and so on—provoke more pub-

licity and hand-wringing. But they are vastly outnumbered by deaths and harms due to poverty. In 2002, for example, some 172,000 deaths were due to war; other homicides and violence caused some 559,000 more. Starvation and preventable diseases, by contrast, claimed about 18 million human lives.[7] The few years since the end of the Cold War have seen over 300 million deaths due to poverty-related causes.

While the data about global poverty may be daunting, it is in fact becoming more and more feasible for the affluent countries to eradicate such poverty. The reason is the dramatic long-term trend of rising global economic inequality (Milanovic 2005). Today, the 1,089 million persons reported below $1/day together live on about $109 billion annually, with an aggregate gap of about $44 billion to the $1/day poverty line.[8] This aggregate gap is only one-eighth of 1 percent of the gross national incomes of the high-income economies. And even if we take a less measly poverty line, twice as high, the poverty problem looks surprisingly manageable: the 2,735 million persons reported below $2/day together live on about $440 billion annually, with an aggregate gap of about $330 billion to the $2/day poverty line. Even this much larger aggregate gap is under 1 percent of the gross national incomes of the high-income economies.[9] For the first time in human history it is quite feasible, economically, to wipe out hunger and preventable diseases worldwide without real inconvenience to anyone—all the more so because the affluent countries no longer face any serious military threat.

The moral upshot of all this seems obvious: we should provide a path out of poverty to that great majority of all poor people whom we can reach without the use of force. When we can save so many millions from hunger, disease, and premature death, then the affluent states should be willing to spend certainly 1 percent of our gross national incomes ($355 billion annually) specifically on poverty eradication—and even more, if we can do so effectively. We should make this effort so as to ensure that the poor, especially poor children, have secure access to food and shelter, vaccines, safe water, basic health services and sanitation, primary education, electricity, and road or rail links and will thus be able to fend for themselves in the new global economy. If we can make so huge a difference to hundreds of millions at so little cost to ourselves, we must not refuse to make this effort.

While this call for greater solidarity is plausible in what it directs us to do, it is misleading in the grounds it suggests for this directive. It appeals to a positive duty to protect persons from great harms and risks if one can do so at little cost.[10] I have no doubt that we have such a moral duty and that this duty requires us to make a serious effort toward poverty reduction. And yet, it would be misleading to characterize our present and future failure to make such an effort as a lack of beneficence. We are not bystanders who find ourselves confronted with foreign deprivations whose origins are wholly unconnected to ourselves. In fact, there are at least three morally significant connections between us and the global poor: First, their social starting positions and ours have emerged from a single historical process that was pervaded by massive grievous wrongs. The same historical injustices, including genocide, colonialism, and slavery, play a crucial role in explaining both their poverty and our affluence. Second, they and we depend on a single natural resource base from the benefits of which they are largely, and without compensation, excluded. The affluent countries and the elites of the poorer countries divide these resources on mutually agreeable terms without leaving "enough and as good" for the remaining majority of humankind. Third, they and we coexist within a single global eco-

nomic order that has a strong tendency to perpetuate and even to aggravate global economic inequality.[11]

Given these connections, our failure to make a serious effort toward poverty reduction may constitute not merely a lack of beneficence, but our active impoverishing, starving, and killing millions of innocent people by economic means. To be sure, we do not intend these harms, and we are thus not on a par with Stalin who used economic policies and institutions specifically in order to impoverish and kill segments of the population he deemed hostile to the Soviet regime. We may not even have foreseen these harms when, beginning in the late 1980's, we constructed today's freer, more global economic architecture. Now that we do know, our moral situation is more akin to that of Mao Tse-Tung in 1959. Mao did not foresee that his Great Leap Forward, begun in 1958, would acutely aggravate poverty in China. But when the catastrophic effects of these policies became evident, he continued his policies and declined foreign help. Twenty to 30 million Chinese perished in 1959–62 as a direct consequence of this moral failure. Continuing our current global economic structures and policies unmodified would manifest a similar moral failure. Perhaps we had reason to believe our own persistent pronouncements that the new global economic architecture would cease the reproduction of poverty. So perhaps we just made an innocent and blameless mistake. But it is *our* mistake nonetheless, and we must not allow it to kill yet further tens of millions in the poorer countries.

The call for greater beneficence in the face of world hunger is one that politicians, diplomats, international bankers, and economists are willing to entertain. Most of them will even agree with it, blaming our failure to do more on other politicians, diplomats, bankers, economists, or the voting public. The idea that our economic policies and the global economic institutions we impose make us causally and morally responsible for the perpetuation—even aggravation—of world poverty, by contrast, is an idea rarely taken seriously by established intellectuals and politicians in the developed world. But this subversive idea nonetheless plays an important role in that theorists of poverty and justice, consciously and unconsciously, expend much intellectual energy on making invisible this idea and the three connections that support it. Focusing on the third of these connections, let me briefly indicate some of the distortions arising from our interest in obscuring the role that the design of the global economic order plays in perpetuating and aggravating poverty.

A good example of such distortion in philosophical work is provided by John Rawls. When discussing the economic order of a single society, Rawls pays great attention to the fact that economic cooperation can be structured in many ways and that such structural alternatives have diverse distributional effects (cf. Rawls 1996, 265–67). In response to this fact, he not only insists that the shaping and reshaping of a national economic order should be controlled by all adult participants through a democratic political process, but also argues that justice requires citizens to aim for a national economic order that satisfies the difference principle, that is, allows social and economic inequalities to arise only insofar as they tend to optimize the lowest socioeconomic position (Rawls 1999a, secs. 11, 12, 17).

What is true of a domestic economic order is clearly true of the international economic order as well: alternative ways of organizing global economic cooperation have diverse distributional effects and differ, in particular, in how supportive or obstructive they are of economic development in the poorest countries and areas. In his recent treatment of international justice, Rawls seems briefly to acknowledge this point when he calls for correction of any "unjustified distributive effects" of

cooperative organizations (Rawls 1999b, 43). But how is this vague demand to be specified? Rawls endorses "fair standards of trade to keep the market free and competitive" (ibid.)—but, as he stresses himself (Rawls 1996, 267), free and competitive markets are quite compatible with huge and ever increasing inequality. What is needed is a principle that assesses alternative global economic orders in terms of their distributive effects as his difference principle assesses alternative ways of structuring a national economy. Yet in the international case Rawls specifically rejects any such principle without "a target and a cutoff point" (Rawls 1999b, 115–19). He also rejects any international analogue to a democratic process which, at least in theory, allows a majority of citizens in a liberal society to restructure its economic order if it favors the rich too much.

Like the existing global economic order, that of Rawls's Society of Peoples is then shaped by free bargaining.[12] There is one crucial constraint, however, as Rawls insists on a universal minimum: "Peoples have a duty to assist other peoples living under unfavorable conditions that prevent their having a just or decent political and social regime" (Rawls 1999b, 37). This duty is unobjectionable and hugely important: If existing affluent societies honored it, malnutrition and preventable diseases would be much less common. And yet, making this duty the only distributive constraint on global economic institutions is nonetheless implausible. Imposition by affluent and powerful societies of a skewed global economic order that hampers the economic growth of poor societies and further weakens their bargaining power—such imposition is not made right by the fact that the former societies also keep the latter from falling below the minimum. Moreover, making this duty the only distributive constraint also misleads us into perceiving the injustice of the status quo as insufficient assistance to the poorer societies, when it really consists in the imposition of a skewed global order that aggravates international inequalities and makes it exceedingly hard for the weaker and poorer populations to secure a proportional share of global economic growth. Rawls obscures then the important causal role that the global economic order plays in the reproduction of poverty and inequality, suggesting that each society bears sole responsibility for its own place in the economic rank-order: "The causes of the wealth of a people and the forms it takes lie in their political culture and in the religious, philosophical, and moral traditions that support the basic structure, as well as in the industriousness and cooperative talents of its members, all supported by their political virtues. . . . Crucial also is the country's population policy" (ibid., 108). Thus, he goes on, a society may be poor because of high population growth or low investment (ibid., 117–18) and, in any case, "if it is not satisfied, it can continue to increase savings, or, if this is not feasible, borrow from other members of the Society of Peoples" (ibid., 114). In these ways, Rawls's account of international justice renders all but invisible the question whether the global economic order we currently impose is harming the poor by unjustly creating a headwind against economic development in the poorest areas.

We find similar distortions in economic work. Our international bankers and economists tell us that our global economic order is fine and that protests against it are actually harming the poor. The same bankers and economists also dutifully tell us about the horrendous conditions among the poor and about the lack of progress, lest anyone suspect them of not knowing or not caring enough.[13] So why does a global economic order designed with so much tender loving concern for the global poor not improve their condition? The official answer in unison: because their own governments in the less developed countries are not pursuing optimal policies. Our bankers

and economists differ on what the optimal policies are and hence on how their common claim should be elaborated. The more libertarian types on the right tell the story of the Asian tigers—Hong Kong, Taiwan, Singapore, and South Korea—as showing how misery disappears under governments that allow free enterprise to flourish with a minimum in taxes and regulations. The more social-democratic types tell the story of Kerala, a state in India with a traditionally socialist government, as showing how misery can be abolished even at low income levels if only governments make a serious effort to this end.[14] The stories vary, but the lesson is the same: With the right policies, any poor state can over time meet the basic needs of its people; so there is nothing wrong with the global economic order as it is.

These stories have the familiar ring of the Horatio Alger stories often appealed to in celebration of the unbridled American capitalism before the New Deal: in America, even a farm boy can become rich.[15] Left aside in such celebrations is the crucial question why nearly all the relevant agents fail even while (supposedly) they can succeed. Once this question is asked, there are two obvious and complementary answers: first, what is possible for each may not be possible for all. Even if each farm boy could have become a millionaire in the world of Alger's stories, it was still quite impossible for more than a few to succeed. So we can indeed say that each farm boy who failed had himself to blame, for he could have succeeded. But we cannot blame the fact that over 99 percent failed on the farm boys themselves. In the system as it was, they could not have changed this fact, either individually or collectively. Similarly with unemployment: it does not follow from the fact that *each* person willing to work can find work that *all* such persons can. And similarly also for poor countries. There was indeed a profitable niche in the world economy (better technology than other poor countries and lower labor costs than more affluent countries), which the Asian tigers exploited, but this niche would not have been so profitable if many poor states had scrambled to occupy it all at once.

Second, there may be systemic reasons for why many of the relevant agents do not make the necessary effort. Most farm boys may have lacked stamina and initiative because, having grown up in grinding poverty, they were suffering the lasting effects of childhood malnutrition and disease or of primitive schools stifling ambition. With the governments of poor countries, the problem most often is not merely inability, but also unwillingness to reduce domestic poverty. Yet this unwillingness, the corruption endemic to many of these governments, does not show that such poverty cannot be traced back to the existing global economic order. To the contrary, the prevalence of official corruption may itself be a consequence of our economic policies, of the global economic order we impose and of the extreme international inequalities that have accumulated over two centuries. Let me develop this point a bit further.

A paradigm case of corruption is bribery. Bribes are a major factor in the awarding of public contracts in the less developed countries, which suffer staggering losses as a result. These losses arise in part from the fact that bribes are "priced in": bidders on contracts must raise their price in order to get paid enough to pay the bribes. Additional losses arise as bidders can afford to be noncompetitive, knowing that the success of their bid will depend on their bribes more than on the price they offer. The greatest losses probably arise from the fact that officials focused on bribes pay little attention to whether the goods and services they purchase in their country's behalf are of good quality or even needed at all. Much of what poor countries have imported over the years has been of no use to them—or even harmful, by promoting environmental degradation or violence (bribery is

especially pervasive in the arms trade). May we then conclude that poverty in less developed societies is the fault of their own tolerance of corruption and of their own leaders' venality?

This comfortable conclusion is upset by the fact that the developed states have permitted their companies not merely to pay bribes, but even to deduct these from their taxes. By providing financial inducements and moral support, these states have made a vital contribution to promoting and entrenching a culture of corruption in poorer societies. Fortunately, this contribution is now being phased out. The first major step was the U.S. Foreign Corrupt Practices Act of 1977, enacted after the Lockheed Corporation was found to have paid a $2 million bribe not to a Third World potentate, but to Japanese Prime Minister Kakuei Tanaka. It took another 20 years until 32 affluent states, under OECD auspices and under public pressure generated by a new NGO (Transparency International), signed a Convention on Combating Bribery of Foreign Officials in International Business Transactions, which requires them to criminalize the bribery of foreign officials (www.oecd.org). It remains to be seen whether this convention will produce serious enforcement efforts and thus will reduce bribery and undermine the now deeply entrenched culture of corruption in many of the poorer countries.[16]

Surveying the ruling elites of many less developed countries, one may well surmise that they would have done their best to enrich themselves, and done little for the eradication of poverty in their countries, even if they had not been bribed by foreigners. Many of these countries have not managed to become genuinely democratic, and their rulers can therefore hang on by force even if opposed by the vast majority of the population. Does this support the view that the persistence of severe poverty in many societies is their own fault after all?

To see how this conclusion is problematic, consider a very central feature of the current global institutional order: any group controlling a preponderance of the means of coercion within a country is internationally recognized as the legitimate government of this country's territory and people—regardless of how that group came to power, of how it exercises power, and of the extent to which it may be supported or opposed by the population it rules. That such a group exercising effective power receives international recognition means not merely that we engage it in negotiations. It means also that we accept this group's right to act for the people it rules, that we, most significantly, confer upon it the privileges freely to borrow in the country's name (international borrowing privilege) and freely to dispose of the country's natural resources (international resource privilege).[17]

The international borrowing privilege includes the power to impose internationally valid legal obligations upon the country at large. Any successor government that refuses to honor debts incurred by an ever so corrupt, brutal, undemocratic, unconstitutional, repressive, unpopular predecessor will be severely punished by the banks and governments of other countries; at minimum it will lose its own borrowing privilege by being excluded from the international financial markets. Such refusals are therefore quite rare, as governments, even when newly elected after a dramatic break with the past, are compelled to pay the debts of their ever so awful predecessors.

The international borrowing privilege has three important negative effects on human rights fulfillment in the less developed countries. First, this privilege facilitates borrowing by destructive governments. Such governments can borrow more money and can do so more cheaply than they could do if they alone, rather than the entire country, were obliged to repay. In this way, the borrowing privilege helps such governments stay in power even against near-universal popular discontent and opposition. Second, the international borrowing privilege imposes upon democratic successor regimes the often huge debts of their corrupt predecessors. It thereby saps the capacity of such democratic governments to implement structural reforms and other political programs, thus rendering such governments less successful and less stable than they would otherwise be.[18] Third, the international borrowing privilege provides incentives toward coup attempts: whoever succeeds in bringing a preponderance of the means of coercion under his control gets the borrowing privilege as an additional reward.

The international resource privilege enjoyed by a group in power is much more than our mere acquiescence in its effective control over the natural resources of the country in question. This privilege includes the power to effect legally valid transfers of ownership rights in such resources. Thus a corporation that purchases resources from a wholly illegitimate tyrant, junta, or ruling family thereby becomes entitled to be—and actually *is*—recognized anywhere in the world as the legitimate owner of these resources. This is a remarkable feature of our global institutional order. A group that overpowers the guards and takes control of a warehouse may be able to give some of the merchandise to others, accepting money in exchange. But the fence who pays them becomes merely the possessor, not the owner, of the loot. Contrast this with a group that overpowers an elected government and takes control of a country. Such a group, too, can give away some of the country's natural resources, accepting money in exchange. In this case, however, the purchaser acquires not merely possession, but all the rights and liberties of ownership, which are supposed to be—and actually *are*—protected and enforced by all other states' courts and police forces. The international resource privilege, then, is the power to confer globally valid ownership rights in the country's resources.

The international resource privilege has disastrous effects in many poor countries, whose resource sector often constitutes a large segment of the national economy. Whoever can take power in such a country by whatever means can maintain his rule, even against widespread popular opposition, by buying the arms and soldiers he needs with revenues from the export of natural resources (and funds borrowed abroad in the country's name). This fact in turn provides a strong incentive toward the undemocratic acquisition and unresponsive exercise of political power in these countries. The international resource privilege also gives foreigners strong incentives to corrupt the officials of such countries who, no matter how badly they rule, continue to have resources to sell and money to spend. We see here how the local causal chain—persistent poverty caused by corrupt government caused by natural resource wealth—can itself be traced back to the international resource privilege, which renders resource-rich developing countries more likely to experience coup attempts and civil wars and more likely also to be ruled by corrupt elites, so that—despite considerable natural wealth—poverty in these countries tends to decline only slowly, if at all.[19]

These brief remarks on bribery and on the international borrowing and resource privileges show at least in outline how the current global order we uphold shapes the national culture and policies of the poorer and weaker countries. It does so in four main ways: it crucially affects what sorts of persons exercise political power in these countries, what incentives these persons face, what options they have, and what impact the implementation of any of their options would have on their impoverished compatriots. In many ways, our global order is disadvantageous to the global poor by sustaining oppression, corruption, and hence poverty, in their countries. It is hardly surprising that this order reflects the interests of the wealthy and powerful states. Their governments, dependent on our votes and taxes, work hard on shaping the international rules for our benefit. To be sure, the global poor have their own governments. But almost all of them are too weak to exert real influence on the organization of the global economy. More important, these governments have little incentive to attend to the needs of their poor compatriots, as their continuation in power depends on the local elite and on foreign governments and corporations. Such rulers—able to sell the country's resources, to buy arms and soldiers to maintain their rule, and to amass personal fortunes—like the global order just the way it is. And so do we: if ownership rights in natural resources could not be acquired from illegitimate and repressive regimes, for example, the resources we need to import would be scarcer and hence more expensive.

The conclusion is once again that the underfulfillment of human rights in the less developed countries is not an entirely homegrown problem, but one we greatly contribute to through the policies we pursue and the international order we impose. We have then not merely a positive responsibility with regard to global poverty, like Rawls's "duty of assistance," but a negative responsibility to stop imposing (i.e., to reform) the existing global order[20] and to prevent and mitigate the harms it continually causes for the world's poorest populations. Because our responsibility is negative and because so much harm can be prevented at so little cost to ourselves, the reduction of severe global poverty should be our foremost moral priority.

# BIBLIOGRAPHY

Baker, Raymond. 2005. *Capitalism's Achilles Heel.* New York: Wiley.

Chen, Shaohua, and Martin Ravallion. 2004. "How Have the World's Poorest Fared since the Early 1980s?" *World Bank Research Observer* 19:141–69; also at wbro.oupjournals.org/cgi/content/abstract/19/2/141

ILO (International Labor Organization). 2002. *A Future without Child Labour.* Geneva: ILO; also at www.ilo.org/public/english/standards/decl/publ/reports/report3.htm

Lam, Ricky, and Leonard Wantchekon. 1999. "Dictatorships as a Political Dutch Disease." Unpublished working paper, Yale University, <http://econpapers.hhs.se/paper/wopyalegr/>

Milanovic, Branko. 2005. *Worlds Apart: Measuring International and Global Inequality.* Princeton, NJ: Princeton University Press.

Pogge, Thomas. 2002. *World Poverty and Human Rights.* Cambridge: Polity Press.

———. 2005. "Human Rights and Global Health: A Research Program." In *Global Institutions and Responsibilities,* ed. Christian Barry and Thomas Pogge. Oxford: Blackwell.

Rawls, John. 1996 [1993]. *Political Liberalism.* New York: Columbia University Press.

———. 1999a [1971]. *A Theory of Justice.* Cambridge, MA: Harvard University Press.

———. 1999b. *The Law of Peoples.* Cambridge MA: Harvard University Press.

Reddy, Sanjay, and Thomas Pogge. 2007. "How *Not* to Count the Poor." In *Measuring Global Poverty,* ed. Sudhir Anand and Joseph Stiglitz. Oxford: Oxford University Press; also at www.socialanalysis.org

Singer, Peter. 1972. "Famine, Affluence and Morality." *Philosophy and Public Affairs* 1:229–43.

Unger, Peter. (1996). *Living High and Letting Die: Our Illusion of Innocence.* Oxford: Oxford University Press.

UNICEF (United Nations Children's Fund). 2005. *The State of the World's Children 2005.* New York: UNICEF; also at www.unicef.org/publications/files/SOWC_2005_ (English).pdf

UNDP (United Nations Development Programme). 1998. *Human Development Report 1998.* New York: Oxford University Press.

———. 2000. *Human Development Report 2000.* New York: Oxford University Press.

———. 2002. *Human Development Report 2002.* New York: Oxford University Press.

———. 2005. *Human Development Report 2005.* New York: UNDP.

World Bank. 2006. *World Development Report 2007.* Washington: The World Bank.

WHO (World Health Organization). 2004. *The World Health Report 2004.* Geneva: WHO Publications; <www.who.int/whr/2004>

## NOTES

1. This is 1.9 percent of their combined GDPs of $35,529 billion in 2005 (World Bank 2006, 289).

2. From 0.33 percent of their combined GNPs in 1990 to 0.22 percent in 2000 (UNDP 2002, 202). The United States led the decline by reducing ODA from 0.21 percent to 0.10 percent of GNP in a time of great prosperity culminating in enormous budget surpluses (ibid.). In the aftermath of September 11, ODA has grown back to 0.33 percent of GNP ($106.5 billion) in 2005 due to dramatic growth in spending on Musharraf's Pakistan and post-occupation Afghanistan and Iraq (www.oecd.org/dataoecd/52/18/37790990.pdf).

3. For details, see Pogge 2002, introduction and chap. 5, and Pogge 2005.

4. Chen and Ravallion 2004, 147 and 153. (Martin Ravallion and Shaohua Chen have managed the World Bank's income poverty assessments for well over a decade. These latest data are for 1998.) Because life expectancy among the very poor is much lower than average, they account for far more than one-sixth of all human lives—and deaths. Conventional measures of the incidence of poverty may thus distort what is morally significant by assigning lower weight to the poor in proportion to their lower life expectancy. Suppose, for example, as is approximately true, that the poor live, on average, half as long as the non-poor. The number of lives and deaths among the poorest sixth would then be twice the average number of lives and deaths among the other five-sixths: 29 percent of all human lives and deaths would occur among the poor, even while these poor, at any given time, make up only 17 percent of the world's population. This distortion affects most conventional statistics I cite in this essay, though not of course the statement that one-third of all human deaths are due to poverty-related causes.

5. To assess the incomes of poor people in poor countries, the World Bank uses official purchasing power parities (PPPs). These are typically two to nine times higher than market exchange rates: India's per capita gross national income of $720 is equated to $3,460 PPP, China's $1,740 to $6,600 PPP, Nigeria's $560 to $1,040 PPP, Pakistan's $690 to $2,350 PPP,

Bangladesh's $470 to $2,090 PPP, Ethiopia's $160 to $1,000 PPP, Vietnam's $620 to $3,010 PPP, and so on (World Bank 2006, 288–89). Inflating the incomes of the poor according to these PPPs is deeply problematic, because PPPs are based on the prices of all goods and services worldwide, whereas the poor are compelled to concentrate their expenditures on a narrow subset of such commodities. These basic necessities are cheaper in the poor countries, but not nearly as much cheaper as general PPPs would suggest. Using general PPPs to inflate the incomes of the poor abroad thus greatly exaggerates their consumption possibilities in terms of basic necessities. See Reddy and Pogge 2007 for a comprehensive analysis.

6. *Universal Declaration of Human Rights*, sec. 25.

7. WHO 2004, Annex Table 2. The total number of human deaths in 2002 was 57 million (ibid.). Among these, 10.6 million were deaths of children under 5 (UNICEF 2005, inside front cover).

8. On average, the poor live 28.4 percent below the $1/day poverty line. See Chen and Ravallion 2004, 152 and 158, dividing the poverty gap index by the headcount index. Calculated at market exchange rates, gross national incomes per person in the affluent countries are about 350 times what typical poor persons live on. Inequalities in wealth are much greater still, as poor persons typically own much less than one annual income and rich persons typically much more.

9. Those below $2/day live, on average, 42 percent below that line. See Chen and Ravallion 2004, 152 and 158, again dividing the poverty gap index by the headcount index.

10. The problem of world hunger has often been addressed in these terms, for example, in Singer 1972 and in Unger 1996.

11. For detailed explication of these three connections, cf. Pogge 2002, sec. 8.2.

12. His second and third laws state: "Peoples are to observe treaties and undertakings. . . . Peoples are equal and are parties to the agreements that bind them" (Rawls 1999b, 37).

13. The World Bank recently interviewed 60,000 poor people in less developed countries and published snippets of their responses in a series of *Voices of the Poor* volumes.

14. Amartya Sen has mentioned Kerala in many of his writings, and references to this state are now common in the literature (e.g., Rawls 1999b, 110).

15. Horatio Alger (1832–99) was a highly successful U.S. writer of stories about the rise to prosperity of boys from poor backgrounds.

16. The record after the first few years has not been encouraging: "Plenty of laws exist to ban bribery by companies. But big multinationals continue to sidestep them with ease" ("The Short Arm of the Law," *Economist* 2 (March 2002): 63–65, at 63). See also Baker 2005.

17. These two privileges are complemented by the international treaty privilege, which recognizes any person or group in effective control of a country as entitled to undertake binding treaty obligations on behalf of its population, and the international arms privilege, which recognizes such a person or group as entitled to use state funds to import the arms it needs to stay in power.

18. This effect is somewhat mitigated by authoritarian regimes being likewise held responsible for the debts of their democratic predecessors.

19. Economists have known for some time of the negative correlation between countries' resource endowments and their rates of economic growth (the so-called resource curse or Dutch Disease)—exemplified by the relatively low growth rates, over the past 40 years, of resource-rich Nigeria, Kenya, Angola, Mozambique, Zaire, Venezuela, Brazil, Saudi Arabia, Burma (Myanmar), and the Philippines. The causal connections accounting for this correlation, however, have only recently come to be more fully understood. Cf. Lam and Wantchekon 1999, specifically supporting the hypothesis that the causal connection between resource wealth and poor economic growth is mediated through reduced chances for democracy: "all petrostates or resource-dependent countries in Africa fail to initiate meaningful political reforms. . . . besides South Africa, transition to democracy has been successful only in resource-poor countries" (ibid., 31); "a 1 percent increase in the size of the natural resource sector [relative to GDP] generates a decrease by half a percentage point in the probability of survival of democratic regimes" (ibid., 35).

20. This is also suggested by Section 28 of the *Universal Declaration of Human Rights*: "Everyone is entitled to a social and international order in which the rights and freedoms set forth in this Declaration can be fully realized."

## LEGAL PERSPECTIVE

# Universal Declaration of Human Rights

## PREAMBLE

Whereas recognition of the inherent dignity and of the equal and inalienable rights of all members of the human family is the foundation of freedom, justice and peace in the world,

Whereas disregard and contempt for human rights have resulted in barbarous acts which have outraged the conscience of mankind, and the advent of a world in which human beings shall enjoy freedom of speech and belief and freedom from fear and want has been proclaimed as the highest aspiration of the common people,

Whereas it is essential, if man is not to be compelled to have recourse, as a last resort, to rebellion against tyranny and oppression, that human rights should be protected by the rule of law,

Whereas it is essential to promote the development of friendly relations between nations,

Whereas the peoples of the United Nations have in the Charter reaffirmed their faith in fundamental human rights, in the dignity and worth of the human person and in the equal rights of men and women and have determined to promote social progress and better standards of life in larger freedom,

Whereas Member States have pledged themselves to achieve, in co-operation with the United Nations, the promotion of universal respect for and observance of human rights and fundamental freedoms,

Whereas a common understanding of these rights and freedoms is of the greatest importance for the full realization of this pledge,

Now, Therefore THE GENERAL ASSEMBLY proclaims THIS UNIVERSAL DECLARATION OF HUMAN RIGHTS as a common standard of achievement for all peoples and all nations, to the end that every individual and every organ of society, keeping this Declaration constantly in mind, shall strive by teaching and education to promote respect for these rights and freedoms and by progressive measures, national and international, to secure their universal and effective recognition and observance, both among the peoples of Member States themselves and among the peoples of territories under their jurisdiction.

### Article 1.

All human beings are born free and equal in dignity and rights. They are endowed with reason and conscience and should act towards one another in a spirit of brotherhood.

### Article 2.

Everyone is entitled to all the rights and freedoms set forth in this Declaration, without distinction of any kind, such as race, colour, sex, language, religion, political or other opinion, national or social origin, property, birth or other status. Furthermore, no distinction shall be made on the basis of the political, jurisdictional or international status of the country or territory to which a person belongs, whether it be independent, trust, non-self-governing or under any other limitation of sovereignty.

---

*Source:* United Nations Department of Public Information, "Universal Declaration of Human Rights," http://www.unhchr.ch/udhr/lang/eng.htm (accessed March 19, 2003).

*Article 3.*

Everyone has the right to life, liberty and security of person.

*Article 4.*

No one shall be held in slavery or servitude; slavery and the slave trade shall be prohibited in all their forms.

*Article 5.*

No one shall be subjected to torture or to cruel, inhuman or degrading treatment or punishment.

*Article 6.*

Everyone has the right to recognition everywhere as a person before the law.

*Article 7.*

All are equal before the law and are entitled without any discrimination to equal protection of the law. All are entitled to equal protection against any discrimination in violation of this Declaration and against any incitement to such discrimination.

*Article 8.*

Everyone has the right to an effective remedy by the competent national tribunals for acts violating the fundamental rights granted him by the constitution or by law.

*Article 9.*

No one shall be subjected to arbitrary arrest, detention or exile.

*Article 10.*

Everyone is entitled in full equality to a fair and public hearing by an independent and impartial tribunal, in the determination of his rights and obligations and of any criminal charge against him.

*Article 11.*

(1) Everyone charged with a penal offence has the right to be presumed innocent until proved guilty according to law in a public trial at which he has had all the guarantees necessary for his defence.

(2) No one shall be held guilty of any penal offence on account of any act or omission which did not constitute a penal offence, under national or international law, at the time when it was committed. Nor shall a heavier penalty be imposed than the one that was applicable at the time the penal offence was committed.

*Article 12.*

No one shall be subjected to arbitrary interference with his privacy, family, home or correspondence, nor to attacks upon his honour and reputation. Everyone has the right to the protection of the law against such interference or attacks.

*Article 13.*

(1) Everyone has the right to freedom of movement and residence within the borders of each state.

(2) Everyone has the right to leave any country, including his own, and to return to his country.

*Article 14.*

(1) Everyone has the right to seek and to enjoy in other countries asylum from persecution.

(2) This right may not be invoked in the case of prosecutions genuinely arising from non-political crimes or from acts contrary to the purposes and principles of the United Nations.

*Article 15.*

(1) Everyone has the right to a nationality.

(2) No one shall be arbitrarily deprived of his nationality nor denied the right to change his nationality.

*Article 16.*

(1) Men and women of full age, without any limitation due to race, nationality or religion, have the right to marry and to found a family. They are entitled to equal rights as to marriage, during marriage and at its dissolution.

(2) Marriage shall be entered into only with the free and full consent of the intending spouses.

(3) The family is the natural and fundamental group unit of society and is entitled to protection by society and the State.

### Article 17.

(1) Everyone has the right to own property alone as well as in association with others.

(2) No one shall be arbitrarily deprived of his property.

### Article 18.

Everyone has the right to freedom of thought, conscience and religion; this right includes freedom to change his religion or belief, and freedom, either alone or in community with others and in public or private, to manifest his religion or belief in teaching, practice, worship and observance.

### Article 19.

Everyone has the right to freedom of opinion and expression; this right includes freedom to hold opinions without interference and to seek, receive and impart information and ideas through any media and regardless of frontiers.

### Article 20.

(1) Everyone has the right to freedom of peaceful assembly and association.

(2) No one may be compelled to belong to an association.

### Article 21.

(1) Everyone has the right to take part in the government of his country, directly or through freely chosen representatives.

(2) Everyone has the right of equal access to public service in his country.

(3) The will of the people shall be the basis of the authority of government, this will shall be expressed in periodic and genuine elections which shall be by universal and equal suffrage and shall be held by secret vote or by equivalent free voting procedures.

### Article 22.

Everyone, as a member of society, has the right to social security and is entitled to realization, through national effort and international cooperation and in accordance with the organization and resources of each State, of the economic, social and cultural rights indispensable for his dignity and the free development of his personality.

### Article 23.

(1) Everyone has the right to work, to free choice of employment, to just and favourable conditions of work and to protection against unemployment.

(2) Everyone, without any discrimination, has the right to equal pay for equal work.

(3) Everyone who works has the right to just and favorable remuneration ensuring for himself and his family an existence worthy of human dignity, and supplemented, if necessary, by other means of social protection.

(4) Everyone has the right to form and to join trade unions for the protection of his interests.

### Article 24.

Everyone has the right to rest and leisure, including reasonable limitation of working hours and periodic holidays with pay.

### Article 25.

(1) Everyone has the right to a standard of living adequate for the health and well-being of himself and of his family, including food, clothing, housing and medical care and necessary social services, and the right to security in the event of unemployment, sickness, disability, widowhood, old age or other lack of livelihood in circumstances beyond his control.

(2) Motherhood and childhood are entitled to special care and assistance. All children, whether born in or out of wedlock, shall enjoy the same social protection.

### Article 26.

(1) Everyone has the right to education. Education shall be free, at least in the elementary and fundamental stages. Elementary

education shall be compulsory. Technical and professional education shall be made generally available and higher education shall be equally accessible to all on the basis of merit.

(2) Education shall be directed to the full development of the human personality and to the strengthening of respect for human rights and fundamental freedoms. It shall promote understanding, tolerance and friendship among all nations, racial or religious groups, and shall further the activities of the United Nations for the maintenance of peace.

(3) Parents have a prior right to choose the kind of education that shall be given to their children.

### Article 27.

(1) Everyone has the right freely to participate in the cultural life of the community, to enjoy the arts and to share in scientific advancement and its benefits.

(2) Everyone has the right to the protection of the moral and material interests resulting from any scientific, literary or artistic production of which he is the author.

### Article 28.

Everyone is entitled to a social and international order in which the rights and freedoms set forth in this Declaration can be fully realized.

### Article 29.

(1) Everyone has duties to the community in which alone the free and full development of his personality is possible.

(2) In the exercise of his rights and freedoms, everyone shall be subject only to such limitations as are determined by law solely for the purpose of securing due recognition and respect for the rights and freedoms of others and of meeting the just requirements of morality, public order and the general welfare in a democratic society.

(3) These rights and freedoms may in no case be exercised contrary to the purposes and principls of the United Nations.

### Article 30.

Nothing in this Declaration may be interpreted as implying for any State, group or person any right to engage in any activity or to perform any act aimed at the destruction of any of the rights and freedoms set forth herein.

# CASES

# CASE 1.  *Sapora's Patriarchical Society*

Sapora, a large Pacific Rim island, has for years been a leading industrial, commercial, and financial center with a flourishing market and growing trade. GlobeCom, an American telecommunications firm long established in Sapora, has decided to expand its Sapora branch and the volume of business it does with local Saporan companies. Ties with local businesses have flourished quickly, and an extremely profitable business relationship has developed. Sapora has rapidly become a major training ground for GlobeCom managers, and successful tenure in Sapora is viewed as a key step on the way to the top of GlobeCom.

This case was written by Sasha Lyutse. Sapora is fictional, but the case is based in an existing country that is a powerful player in international markets.

Sapora, however, is a traditionally patriarchal society, and its businessmen at the executive level are just that: men. Female executives in the workplace are a rarity, and there is seldom, if ever, a managerial track available to women. Women are often given positions largely designed to make the office more comfortable, such as serving tea and performing basic services. Women are discouraged from aiming at executive positions and are not invited to afterwork social functions that play a vital role in successful employee and corporate bonding—an entrenched aspect of Sapora's business culture. The overwhelmingly male majority of Saporan customers, suppliers, and government officials are also uncomfortable doing business with foreign women, preferring to work with men.

Although GlobeCom abides by strict U.S. gender equality laws in its American branches, its human resource managers who send executives abroad hesitate to violate the unwritten laws and cultural mores of Sapora. They have found over time that female managers working in Sapora tend to be less successful than males; they have a more difficult time dealing with local businesses and are generally offered fewer business opportunities than their male counterparts. Resource managers, who are responsible for the efficacy of the GlobeCom workforce, both domestically and abroad, are sending fewer and fewer woman to fill open posts in Sapora.

The American female's inability to obtain the necessary firsthand experience in dealing with Saporan businesses has become a career handicap. Female employees have found that while in the beginning they move up the company ranks fairly easily in GlobeCom's American branches, they eventually hit a career ceiling because they lack the formative, career-building experience their male counterparts receive in Sapora. It would be difficult, however, to persuade GlobeCom that female managers can succeed in Sapora's culture, which in many subtle and overt ways discourages gender equality.

## Questions

1. Should GlobeCom do business in a country with a patriarchical society? In responding, imagine that GlobeCom could not survive if it stopped doing business in Sapora.
2. Assuming that GlobeCom's female employees are unable to obtain the necessary experience and suffer a career disadvantage because of the situation in Sapora, should the company use some form of handicap (for example, a bonus) to offset the career handicap? Would such a handicap be demeaning?
3. What should U.S. gender equality look like in light of GlobeCom's problem?

## CASE 2.  *Cocaine at the Fortune 500 Level*

Roberto, a pure libertarian in moral and political philosophy, is deeply impressed by his reading of Robert Nozick's account of justice. He lives in Los Angeles and teaches philosophy at a local university. Roberto is also a frequent user of cocaine, which he enjoys immensely and provides to friends at parties. Neither he nor any of his close friends are addicted. Over the years Roberto has become tired of teaching philosophy and now has an opportunity, through old friends who live in Peru, to become a middleman in the cocaine business.

This case was prepared by Tom L. Beauchamp and updated by Jeff Greene and Sasha Lyutse; it relies in part on accounts in the *Wall Street Journal* and the *Economist*.

Although he is disturbed about the effects cocaine has in some persons, he has never witnessed these effects firsthand. He is giving his friends' business offer serious consideration.

Roberto's research has told him the following: Selling cocaine is a $35 billion plus industry. Although he is interested primarily in a Peruvian connection, his research has shown conclusively that the Colombian cartel alone is large enough to place it among the Fortune 500 corporations. Cocaine production in Peru and Bolivia in 1995 represented about 90 percent of the world's cocaine base; the remaining 10 percent was produced in Columbia (*Journal of Inter-American and World Affairs,* 1997). Cocaine is Latin America's second largest export, accounting for 3–4 percent of the GDP of Peru and Bolivia, and up to 8 percent of that of Columbia. The cocaine industry employs close to half a million people in the Andean region alone. Columbian coca cultivation rose 11 percent in 2000.

Former Peruvian President Alan Garcia once described cocaine as Latin America's "only successful multinational." It can be and has been analyzed in traditional business categories, with its own entrepreneurs, chemists, laboratories, employment agencies, small organizations, distribution systems, market giants, growth phases, and so forth. Cocaine's profit margins have narrowed in some markets, while expanding in others. It often seeks new markets in order to expand its product line. For example, in the mid-1980s "crack," a potent form of smoked cocaine, was moved heavily into new markets in Europe. Between the mid-1960s and the late 1990s the demand for cocaine grew dramatically (weathering some up and down markets) because of successful supply and marketing. Middlemen in Miami and Los Angeles were established to increase already abundant profits. Heavy investments were made in airplanes, efficient modes of production, training managers, and regular schedules of distribution. In the late 1980s there was a downturn in cocaine consumption after the deaths of

two prominent athletes. In the early 1990s the market recovered slightly before slipping again in the mid-1990s. However, cocaine remains an enormously powerful industry in many countries.

Roberto sees the cocaine industry as not being subject to taxes, tariffs, or government regulations other than those pertaining to its illegality. It is a pure form of the free market in which supply and demand control transactions. This fact about the business appeals to Roberto, as it seems perfectly suited to his libertarian views. He is well aware that there are severe problems of coercion and violence in some parts of the industry, but he is certain that the wealthy clientele whom he would supply in Los Angeles would neither abuse the drug nor redistribute it to others who might be harmed. Roberto is confident that his Peruvian associates are honorable and that he can escape problems of violence, coercion, and abusive marketing. However, he has just read a newspaper story that cocaine-use emergencies—especially those involving cocaine-induced heart attacks—have tripled in the last 5 years. It is only this fact that has given him pause before deciding to enter the cocaine business. He views these health emergencies as unfortunate but not unfair outcomes of the business. Therefore, it is his humanity and not his theory of justice that gives him pause.

## Questions

1. Would a libertarian—such as Roberto—say that the cocaine business is not unfair so long as no coercion is involved and the system is a pure function of supply and demand?
2. Does justice demand that cocaine be outlawed, or is this not a matter of justice at all? Are questions of justice even meaningful when the activity is beyond the boundaries of law?
3. Is the distinction Roberto draws between what is unfortunate and what is unfair relevant to a decision about whether an activity is just?

# CASE 3.    *CEO Compensation at Qwest*

In April 2002, despite posting a net loss of $4 billion for the previous year and being strained by a $25 billion debt, Qwest Communications awarded its CEO, Joseph Nacchio, a yearly compensation and benefits package of $217.3 million, including pay and potential gains from stock option grants. At the time of this writing, Qwest shares were 83 percent off their 52-week high.

In 2001 Nacchio received a salary of almost $1.2 million, a 27 percent increase over 2000, but his bonus dropped 32 percent to $1.5 million. In addition, he obtained at least $74.5 million from exercising stock options and long-term incentive pay of $24.4 million. Other compensation of $229,705 included a $136,745 allocation for use of corporate aircraft. However, stock options, with a potential future value of $115.6 million, became worthless by September 2002, according to the Investor Responsibility Research Center, since Qwest's share price dropped lower than the $16.81 exercise price of the options. So, as of September 2002, the actual worth of the compensation and benefits package for the year was approximately $101.7 million.

According to the Investor Responsibility Research Center, this was one of the top pay packages for 2001, based on an analysis of CEO pay at 267 companies with revenue of $1 billion or more. A Qwest spokesperson, however, said that Nacchio's pay is on a scale with other firms trying to retain officers and that Qwest has outperformed many competitors. (See *USA TODAY*, April 10, 2002.)

In 2002, despite a 30-month-long stock market slump, there appeared to remain a wide disjuncture between CEO pay and company performance. There was at the time little evidence of substantial CEO-pay-package cuts even in companies that performed poorly. Executive salaries generally rose, despite an economic climate of low stock prices and greater scrutiny of directors and executives as a result of corporate financial and fraud scandals. While average worker salaries were rising just above 3.6 percent, many CEOs were receiving double-digit salary increases, bonuses, stock option grants potentially worth millions, and benefits such as company-owned apartments. (See *USA TODAY*, September 30, 2002.)

## Questions

1. Is Joseph Nacchio's yearly compensation and benefits package of $217.3 million fair, unfair, or neither fair nor unfair?
2. As a matter of fairness, should a CEO's pay be reduced when: (a) other employees are forced to take a reduction or (b) when the company's profit margin is lower than anticipated under the society's economic condition?
3. As a matter of fairness, should the salaries of American CEOs be substantially reduced below their present level? If so, who should be authorized to lower the salary?

---

This case was written by Sasha Lyutse.

# CASE 4.    *Wages of Failure: The Ethics of Executive Compensation*

For the last couple of weeks General Global, a prominent multinational electronics and telecommunications company, was being scolded by editorials in the mainstream press. Its departing CEO, Bill Hogson, had exited with 2 years' pay and bonuses totaling $100 million after working barely a year. Hogson had presided over a tumultuous and lackluster year for which most of General Global executives thought he was to blame. Hogson was finally choosing to step down after a bitter power struggle involving his firing of several top executives, many of whom were now being rehired by the board. The press saw Hogson's generous exit compensation for doing a poor job as a testament to the dauntless greed infecting the highest levels of corporate America.

Hogson's replacement was Janice White, the previous CFO who Hogson had fired only a month earlier. In the face of mounting public outrage over exorbitant executive compensation packages for poor leadership, White has asked the board to base her yearly compensation solely on performance. This was a clear break from General Global's policy of paying the average of industry standard. But White felt this change was necessary to send a strong message to the stakeholders that she too would share the burden should the company have to further tighten its belt. Several hundred employees had already been laid off, and many considered that unfair since those layoffs represented the lion's share of Hogson's stratospheric exit package.

Initially, White's request for a merit-based salary seemed a laudable act of courage and integrity. But when a decision had to be made on whether or not to grant her request, several concerns arose at the meeting:

1. Should all the top executives also be paid accordingly?
2. Should there be a cap on total yearly compensation?
3. Would making such changes put the company at a disadvantage when competing for the best talent?
4. Could such changes make the company less stable?

Some thought it would make little sense to base the CEO's salary on performance without doing the same for all executives. But doing so might prove difficult since it is not always clear how responsible each and everyone is for the company's successes and failures. The CEO, however, sets the agenda and direction of each fiscal year and, thus, seems ultimately most responsible for the consequences. So, paying her according to merit did not necessarily require everyone else to be paid that way as well.

What about a cap on total yearly compensation? Critics in the press argued that no individual should be making $50 million dollars a year, even if deserved. That money could always be better spent elsewhere in year-end bonuses for employees, increasing stock value, etc. But any such cap might make it more difficult to compete for the best talent in the future. It was important to

Case written by Julian Friedland. © 2006 Center for Business and Society, Leeds School of Business, University of Colorado, Boulder, Colorado, USA.

remember that the millions earned in executive compensation were always reinvested into the economy, which in turn benefited everyone.

Perhaps a compromise was reachable between these conflicting concerns. Basing CEO compensation entirely on performance but without caps would keep the company's talent searches competitive by preserving the specter of achieving great wealth. At the same time, it would inspire the CEO to do the best job possible since she would thereby have more to lose by performing poorly.

Furthermore, this solution would promote loyalty across the company since everyone would know that even the CEO's salary would be on the chopping block if profits faltered. Still, there was one last, important concern. Making such a radical change might actually risk long-term stability. If, for example, White underperformed one year, she would likely redouble her efforts in order to compensate for that personal loss of wealth. But what if, despite her efforts, she underperformed the next year as well? Would she be as likely to leave before inflicting further damage on the company? Without a lucrative exit package, she might very well choose to stay on board longer despite her poor track record, to the detriment of the company. High exit compensation packages have the virtue of allowing poor leaders to resign earlier than later, sparing the company any further poor decision making.

It is one thing to inspire the CEO to outdo herself, but quite another to give her hope against hope. No company should seek to motivate an underperforming leader to stay on. Unfortunately, given the political influence of the CEO in the corporation, top executives and shareholders cannot always be relied upon to fire that person. It can often take several years of failure to muster enough courage in the ranks to do so. As General Global's last CEO proved, many executives risked losing their own jobs in the process with no certainty of ever regaining them. Hence there was perhaps an advantage to giving a CEO the luxury of a lucrative exit package in order to increase the chances that, if need be, she might choose to step down, without bringing the company down with her.

Was the answer then to simply deny Janice White's seemingly noble request for performance-based pay? Or would it make sense to accept her request but preserve a relatively high exit package that could double or even triple her compensation for a disappointing performance? Or would that create a disincentive to perform well? This was turning out to be a much more confounding dilemma than it seemed at first. A decision needs to be made nonetheless. What should it be?

### Discussion Questions

1. Do you think executive compensation is generally appropriate or inflated in the United States? Why or why not?

2. Is performance-based pay an attractive solution? Are there any other alternatives to keep from rewarding failure? What are the costs and benefits to these solutions?

3. Are the long-term effects of CEO performance always clear at the end of each fiscal year?

4. Can certain performance-based pay plans make it less likely for CEOs to artificially inflate stock value in the short term? If so, how? If not, why not?

# CASE 5.  *Covering the Costs of Health Care*

Medicare and Medicaid were passed into law in the United States to provide coverage for health-care costs in populations that could not afford adequate coverage, especially the elderly, poor, and disabled. Then, as now, health-care technology produced by major corporations was rapidly being developed and costs were skyrocketing. In 1994, $140 billion was spent in Medicare. Current trends show little letup in this explosion of costs. In 1994 Medicare and Medicaid constituted 16.4 percent of the total federal budget. By 2006 this figure is expected to balloon to approximately 10 percent higher (around 26.4 percent). For U.S. corporations and individuals, health care has become a burdensome expense.

With over 40 million Americans uninsured, health-care costs have been under intense study by many politicians and agencies. In an effort to limit future increases in physician costs, the Omnibus Budget Reconciliation Act of 1989 created a Medicare Fee Schedule that affected 34.7 million U.S. citizens. This schedule attempts to redistribute payments across specialties in medicine and geographic areas of the country. The legislation required that this restructuring be phased in over a 5-year period from 1992 to 1996, but affected very few parties needing coverage. In passing the legislation, members of Congress agreed that Medicare's former payment policies fueled unacceptable increases in expenditure for health-care services. Neither the old legislation nor the new covers the kind of catastrophic illness that can wipe out a family's assets and put a family in lifetime debt.

It has been demonstrated that there is substantial variation across the United States in payment rates for services. Urban, specialist, and in-patient services are typically much higher than rural, generalist, and ambulatory services. Surgeons make more money than those in other specialties. It has been widely agreed that these differentials are independent of quality of services, depending more on urban location, the high costs of specialists, and the like. A large supply of physicians in a single location does not stimulate competition and drive prices down; instead, higher fees for physician services tend to be the norm. Social scientists who have studied the changes made in the Omnibus Budget Reconciliation Act of 1989 and their impact throughout the 1990s predict that large redistributions of Medicare payments among specialties will occur, thus changing longstanding patterns in physicians' salaries.

When President Bill Clinton first came into office, he promised major reforms in the health-care system. The Clinton plan, headed by first lady Hillary Clinton, attempted to steer the nation toward serious health-care reform. The goal was to eliminate waste and inflated prices, and to give health-care access to all—so-called universal access. However, with many of the economic consequences falling on the business community, the Clinton plan met strong criticism. Private interests spent over $300 million, and Republicans fought hard to kill the bill—and they succeeded.

Many believed that the Clinton plan did not adequately handle the primary reason for continued increases in health-care costs, namely advances in technology that push the growth of costs in the health-care industry much higher than costs in the rest of the economy. Consider a typical case, involving

---

This case was prepared by Tom L. Beauchamp and Jeff Greene.

a man named Toney Kincard. For 10 years he was tortured by over 600 seizures a week. Kincard was unable to carry on a conversation, eat dinner with his family, or even shower unsupervised. Despite thousands of dollars spent in drug therapy, he lost both his job and his driver's license. In 1989 he became the second person to try a new product, the Vagus Nerve Stimulator. Since his $50,000 outlay to receive this product, he has been seizure-free and says, "The stimulator was the best thing that happened to my life. It was worth everything it cost."

There is little doubt that such expensive technology is invaluable for improving the lives of many people. However, these products will continue to drive up the price of health care for everyone. Experts believe that advances in molecular biology and genetic therapy, among many other technologies, will continue in the twenty-first century to propel the cost of health care well beyond what government or private insurance can cover.

President George W. Bush continued in his adminstration to take the line—directly opposed to that of Clinton—that government should not increase its commitment to health-care coverage. Bush saw the issues as fundamentally ones of the free market.

## Questions

1. Is a nation obligated to provide quality health care for the elderly or any other person who otherwise could not afford care? Is the obligation unrelated to the ability to pay?
2. Should health care be distributed purely on a free-market basis? Should everyone have access to even the highest priced procedures?
3. Is Medicare justifiable on either utilitarian or egalitarian premises of justice? Could a libertarian possibly support Medicare?

## Suggested Supplementary Readings

*Concepts and Principles of Justice and Social Policy*

ANDERSON, ELIZABETH. 1995. *Value in Ethics and Economics.* Cambridge, MA: Harvard University Press.

ARNESON, RICHARD J. 1992. "Is Socialism Dead? A Comment in Market Socialism and Basic Income Capitalism," *Ethics* 102 (April): 485–511.

BEAUCHAMP, TOM L. 2001. *Philosophical Ethics.* 3rd ed. New York: McGraw-Hill. Chaps. 8–9.

BUCHANAN, ALLEN. 1985. *Ethics, Efficiency and the Market.* Totowa, NJ: Rowman and Allanheld.

FEINBERG, JOEL. 1963. Justice and Personal Desert. In *Nomos 6: Justice,* ed. Carl J. Friedrich and John W. Chapman. New York: Atherton Press.

KIPNIS, KENNETH, and DIANA T. MEYERS. 1985. *Economic Justice.* Totowa, NJ: Rowman and Allanheld.

KYMLICKA, WILL, ed. 1992. *Justice in Political Philosophy: Schools of Thought in Politics,* 2 vols. Brookfield, VT: Ashgate.

MILLER, RICHARD. 1992. *Moral Differences: Truth, Justice, and Conscience in a World of Conflict.* Princeton: Princeton University Press.

SEN, AMARTYA. 1997. "Economics, Business Principles and Moral Sentiments." *Business Ethics Quarterly.* 7:5–15.

SOULE, EDWARD. 2003. *Morality and Markets: The Ethics of Government Regulation.* Lanham, MD: Rowman and Littlefield.

STERBA, JAMES P. 1998. *Justice for Here and Now.* New York: Cambridge University Press.

*Egalitarian Theories*

ARNESON, RICHARD J. 1999. "Egalitarianism and Responsibility." *Journal of Ethics* 3:225–47.

BARRY, BRIAN. 1989. *Theories of Justice.* Berkeley: University of California Press.

CHRISTMAN, JOHN P. 1994. *The Myth of Property: Toward an Egalitarian Theory of Ownership.* New York: Oxford University Press.

COHEN, G. A. 1995. *Self-Ownership, Freedom, and Equality.* Cambridge: Cambridge University Press.

———. 1997. "Where the Action Is: In the Site of Distributive Justice." *Philosophy and Public Affairs* 26:3–30.

DANIELS, NORMAN. 1997. *Justice and Justification: Reflective Equilibrium in Theory and Practice.* New York: Cambridge University Press.

———, ed. 1975. *Reading Rawls: Critical Studies of a Theory of Justice.* New York: Basic Books.

DANIELS, NORMAN, DONALD W. LIGHT, and RONALD L. CAPLAN. 1996. *Benchmarks of Fairness for Health Care Reform.* New York: Oxford University Press.

NAGEL, THOMAS. 1979. Equality. In *Mortal Questions.* Cambridge: Cambridge University Press.

OKIN, SUSAN. 1989. *Justice, Gender, and the Family.* New York: Basic Books.

POGGE, THOMAS W. 1991. *Realizing Rawls.* Ithaca, NY: Cornell University Press.

———. 1994. "An Egalitarian Law of Peoples." *Philosophy and Public Affairs* 23 (Summer): 195–224.

———. 2002. *World Poverty and Human Rights.* Cambridge, UK: Polity Press.

POJMAN, LOUIS, and ROBERT WESTMORELAND, eds. 1997. *Equality: Selected Readings.* New York: Oxford University Press.

POWERS, MADISON, and RUTH FADEN. 2000. "Inequalities in Health, Inequalities in Health Care: Four Generations of Discussion about Justice and Cost-Effectiveness Analysis." *Kennedy Institute of Ethics Journal* 10 (June): 109–27.

RAWLS, JOHN. 1996. *Political Liberalism.* New York: Columbia University Press.

ROEMER, JOHN E. 1996. *Theories of Distributive Justice.* Cambridge, MA: Harvard University Press.

———. 2002. "Egalitarianism against the Veil of Ignorance." *Journal of Philosophy* 99 (April): 167–84.

SEN, AMARTYA. 1997. *Economic Inequality.* Oxford: Clarendon Press.

STARK, ANDREW. 2002. "Beyond Choice: Rethinking the Post-Rawlsian Debate over Egalitarian Justice." *Political Theory: An International Journal of Political Philosophy* 30 (Fall): 36–67.

*Libertarian Theories*

BOAZ, DAVID. 1997. *The Libertarian Reader: Classic and Contemporary Readings.* New York: The Free Press.

ENGELHARDT, H. TRISTRAM JR. 1996. *The Foundations of Bioethics,* 2nd ed. New York: Oxford University Press.

EPSTEIN, RICHARD. 1997. *Mortal Peril: Our Inalienable Right to Health Care?* Reading, MA: Addison-Wesley.

FRIED, BARBARA. 1995. "Wilt Chamberlain Revisited: Nozick's 'Justice in Transfer' and the Problem of Market-Based Distribution." *Philosophy and Public Affairs* 24:226–45.

FRIEDMAN, MILTON. 1962. *Capitalism and Freedom.* Chicago: University of Chicago Press.

HAYEK, FRIEDRICH. 1948. *Individualism and Economic Order.* Chicago: University of Chicago Press.

———. 1960. *The Constitution of Liberty.* Chicago: University of Chicago Press.

———. 1976. *The Mirage of Social Justice.* Vol. 2, *Law, Legislation, and Liberty.* Chicago: University of Chicago Press.

LOMASKY, LOREN. 1987. *Persons, Rights, and the Moral Community.* New York: Oxford University Press.

MACK, ERIC. 1990. "Self-Ownership and the Right of Property." *Monist* (October): 519–43.

———. 1991. "Libertarianism Untamed." *Journal of Social Philosophy* (Winter): 64–72.

MACHAN, TIBOR R., and DOUGLAS B. RASMUSSEN, eds. 1995. *Liberty for the Twenty-First Century: Contemporary Libertarian Thought.* Lanham, MD: Rowman and Littlefield.

PAUL, JEFFREY, ed. 1981. *Reading Nozick.* Totowa, NJ: Rowman and Littlefield.

PERRY, STEPHEN R. 1997. "Libertarianism, Entitlement, and Responsibility." *Philosophy and Public Affairs* 26:351–96.

*Utilitarian Theories*

ALLISON, LINCOLN, ed. 1990. *The Utilitarian Response: Essays in the Contemporary Viability of Utilitarian Political Philosophy.* London: Sage.

FREY, R. G., ed. 1984. *Utility and Rights.* Minneapolis: University of Minnesota Press.

GOLDMAN, ALAN H. 1980. "Business Ethics: Profits, Utilities, and Moral Rights." *Philosophy and Public Affairs* 9:260–86.

GOOLD, SUSAN D. 1996. "Allocating Health Care: Cost-Utility Analysis, Informed Democratic Decision Making, or the Veil of Ignorance?" *Journal of Health Politics, Policy, and Law* 21:69–98.

GRIFFIN, JAMES. 1982. "Modern Utilitarianism." *Revue Internationale de Philosophie,* 36:331–75.

———. 1986. *Well-Being: Its Meaning, Measurement, and Importance.* Oxford: Clarendon Press.

HARDIN, RUSSELL. 1988. *Morality within the Limits of Reason.* Chicago: University of Chicago Press.

HARSANYI, JOHN C. 1985. "Rule Utilitarianism, Equality, and Justice." *Social Philosophy and Policy,* 2:115–27.

———. 1991. "Equality, Responsibility, and Justice as Seen from a Utilitarian Perspective." *Theory and Decision,* 31:141–58.

SEN, AMARTYA, and BERNARD WILLIAMS, eds. 1982. *Utilitarianism and Beyond.* Cambridge: Cambridge University Press.

SINGER, PETER. 1972. "Famine, Affluence and Morality." *Philosophy and Public Affairs* 1:229-43.

*Global Justice*

ARNOLD, DENIS G. 2009. *The Ethics of Global Business.* Malden, MA: Blackwell.

ATTFIELD, ROBIN, and BARRY WILKINS, eds. 1992. *International Justice and the Third World.* New York: Routledge.

BOWIE, NORMAN. 1988. "Fair Markets." *Journal of Business Ethics* 7.

COPP, DAVID. 1992. "The Right to an Adequate Standard of Living: Justice, Autonomy, and the Basic Needs." *Social Philosophy and Policy* 9 (Winter): 231–61.

DEGEORGE, RICHARD T. 1994. "International Business Ethics." *Business Ethics Quarterly* 4:1–9.

HSIEH, NIEN-HE. 2004. "The Obligations of Transnational Corporations: Rawlsian Justice and the Duty of Assistance." *Business Ethics Quarterly* 14:643–61.

JACKSON, KEVIN T. 1993. "Global Distributive Justice and the Corporate Duty to Aid." *Journal of Business Ethics* 12:547–52.

LUPER-FOY, STEVEN. 1988. *Problems of International Justice.* Boulder, CO: Westview Press.

———. 1992. "Justice and Natural Resources." *Environmental Values* 1 (Spring): 47–64.

O'NEILL, ONORA. 2000. "Agents of Justice." *Metaphilosophy* 32:180–95.

POGGE, THOMAS. 2002. *World Poverty and Human Rights.* Cambridge: Polity Press.

RAWLS, JOHN. 1999. *The Law of Peoples.* Cambridge MA: Harvard University Press.

SINGER, PETER. 2004. *One World: The Ethics of Globalization,* 2nd ed. New Haven, CT: Yale University Press.

UNGER, PETER. 1996. *Living High and Letting Die: Our Illusion of Innocence.* Oxford: Oxford University Press.